Chambers School Dictionary

Chambers

CHAMBERS
An imprint of Chambers Harrap Publishers Ltd
7 Hopetoun Crescent, Edinburgh, EH7 4AY
Chambers Harrap is an Hachette Livre UK company

This 3rd edition published by Chambers Harrap Publishers Ltd 2009
First published in 2000
Second edition published 2004

A CIP catalogue record for this book is available from the British Library.

Paperback edition ISBN 978 0550 10451 9

Hardback edition ISBN 978 0550 10534 9

10 9 8 7 6 5 4 3 2 1

Editors
Jennifer Baird
Alison Macaulay
Mary O'Neill
Elspeth Summers

Publishing Manager
Morven Dooner

Data Support
Ruth O'Donovan

Prepress
Nicolas Echallier

www.chambersharrap.co.uk
Typeset in Times New Roman and Frutiger
Printed and bound in Italy by Legoprint

Contents

Preface

The *Chambers School Dictionary* is specially designed for use by students aged 10-14 (Key Stage 3 of the National Curriculum, levels D- E of the Scottish curriculum), and has always been a popular choice among teachers. This new edition contains not only new words but also hundreds of essential terms from curriculum subjects such as mathematics and geography, making this a school dictionary with unrivalled breadth of coverage.

All the features that have made this dictionary a favourite have been retained. Colour is used in the dictionary to highlight entry words and phrases to make them easier to find. Inflected forms which could prove difficult to spell are still given in full, and usage notes help with confusables, spelling and grammar. Interesting word histories (etymologies) are shown at certain entries, and dozens of new ones have been added to this edition.

A series of **Language Workshop** panels appear in this dictionary. These focus on essential language concepts such as nouns and verbs explaining clearly what they are and discussing how they are used. You will find a list of these panels and their page numbers on page vi.

To help make best use of Chambers School titles, teachers can download photocopiable versions of the panels, along with games and exercises, from our website at **www.chamberslearning.com**

Language Workshop panels

Pronunciation

This dictionary gives you help when the pronunciation of a word may not be obvious. Pronunciations are given in brackets, signalled by the word *pronounced*, for example:

obligatory (*pronounced* ob-**lig**-*a*t-*o*-ri)

The way the pronunciations are shown is designed to be easily understandable. The syllables are separated by hyphens, and the stressed syllable (that is, the syllable pronounced with most emphasis) is shown in thick black type. Any vowel (or group of vowels) that is pronounced with an unemphasized 'uh' sound is shown in italic type.

A few sounds are difficult to show in normal English letters. Here is a guide to the letter combinations that are used to show these sounds:

Consonants

'ng' shows the sound as in ri**ng**
'ngg' shows the sound as in fi**ng**er
'th' shows the sound as in **th**in
'dh' shows the sound as in **th**is
'sz' shows the sound as in de**cis**ion, mea**s**ure
'kh' shows the sound as in lo**ch**

Vowels

'uw' shows the sound as in b**oo**k, p**u**t
'oo' shows the sound as in m**oo**n, l**o**se
'ah' shows the sound as in **ar**m, d**a**nce
'aw' shows the sound as in s**aw**, ign**ore**
'er' shows the sound as in f**er**n, b**ir**d, h**ear**d
'ei' shows the sound as in d**ay**, s**a**me
'ai' shows the sound as in m**y**, p**i**ne
'oi' shows the sound as in b**oy**, s**oi**l
'oh' shows the sound as in b**o**ne, n**o**, th**ough**
'ow' shows the sound as in n**ow**, b**ough**

Sound combinations

'eer' shows the sound as in n**ear**, b**eer**, t**ier**
'eir' shows the sound as in h**air**, c**are**, th**ere**
'oor' shows the sound as in p**oor**, s**ure**
'air' shows the sound as in f**ire**, h**igher**

Using your dictionary

The words at the top of the page tell you the first and last entry words on the page

Pronunciations are given for more difficult words

If you do not simply add an *s* to make the plural of a noun, then the plural form is shown

The part of speech (or word class): *noun*, *verb*, etc

If you do not simply add *s*, *ing*, or *ed* to make the different tenses of a verb, then these forms are shown

basketball 59

basketball NOUN a team game in which goals are scored by throwing a ball into a raised horizontal hoop with a net attached

bass[1] (*pronounced* beis) NOUN (*plural* **basses**), *music* the low part in music ▶ADJECTIVE low or deep in tone

bass[2] (*pronounced* bas) NOUN (*plural* **bass** *or* **basses**) a kind of fish of the perch family

bass clef NOUN a musical sign (𝄢) placed on a stave to fix the pitch of the notes

bassoon NOUN a musical wind instrument with low notes

bastard NOUN **1** *old, often offensive* a child born to parents who are not married to each other **2** *slang* a general term of abuse

bat[1] NOUN a shaped piece of wood etc for striking a ball in some games ▶VERB (**batting, batted**) to use the bat in cricket etc

bat[2] NOUN a mouse-like flying animal, active at night

bat[3] VERB (**batting, batted**) to flutter (the eyelids etc)

batch NOUN (*plural* **batches**) a

water in which to wash the body **2** the water in which to wash **3** a washing of the body in water **4** (**baths**) a public swimming pool ▸ VERB to wash (oneself or another person) in a bath

Sometimes examples are given to show how a word is used

bathe VERB **1** to swim in water **2** to wash gently: *bathe your eyes* **3** to take a bath ▸ NOUN the act of bathing: *We went for a bathe in the sea* **bathed in** covered with

bathos (*pronounced* **bei**-thos) NOUN in speech or writing: a sudden change from a very serious or beautiful tone or content to a very ordinary or trivial one **> bathetic** ADJECTIVE

Words which come from the main entry word sometimes appear at the end of an entry

ⓘ From Greek, meaning 'depth'

> Do not confuse with: **pathos**

bathroom NOUN a room containing facilities for washing yourself and usually a lavatory

bat mitzvah (*pronounced* bat **mits**-v*a*) NOUN a Jewish ceremony to mark a girl's coming of age

baton NOUN **1** a small wooden stick **2** a light stick used by a conductor of music

If a word can be confused with another word, a note is given in a box

> Do not confuse with: **batten**

batsman *or* **batswoman** NOUN (*plural* **batsmen** *or* **batswomen**) someone who bats in cricket etc

battalion NOUN a part of a regiment of foot soldiers

batten NOUN **1** a piece of sawn timber **2** a strip of wood used to fasten down a ship's hatches during a storm ▸ VERB: **batten down** to fasten down firmly

Set phrases containing the entry word are given at the end of the entry

Labels used in the dictionary

The list below explains some of the labels which appear in italics beside words or meanings.

The dictionary also has some labels in full (for example *architecture*, *golf* and *music*) which show you the subject area in which a word or meaning is used.

Australian	used in Australian English, rather than in British English
Brit	used generally in British English, but not in US or Australian etc
derogatory	a word that is insulting about the person or thing referred to
euphemistic	used instead of a more direct term to refer to an unpleasant subject
feminine	the female form of a word
formal	used mainly in formal English
informal	often used in spoken or informal English
Irish	used in Irish English
offensive	a word which could offend the person addressed
old	rarely used in English today
S African	used in South African English, rather than in British English
Scottish	used in Scottish English
slang	a very informal word which is less generally acceptable than *informal* words
trademark	a word which is registered as a trademark
US	used in Anerican (and often Canadian) English, rather than in British English

Aa

a *or* **an** ADJECTIVE **1** one: *a knock at the door* **2** any: *an ant has six legs* **3** in, to or for each: *four times a day*

> ⓘ The form **a** is used before words beginning with a consonant sound, eg *a knock*; **an** is used before words beginning with a vowel sound, eg *an ant, an hour.*

aardvark NOUN a nocturnal African mammal with a large snout

aback ADVERB: **taken aback** surprised or slightly shocked

abacus (*pronounced* **ab**-*a*-kus) NOUN (*plural* **abacuses**) a frame with columns of beads for counting

abandon VERB **1** to leave, without intending to return **2** to give up (an idea etc): *abandon hope* ▶NOUN lack of inhibition: *dancing with gay abandon* > **abandoned** ADJECTIVE > **abandonment** NOUN

abase VERB, *formal* to make humble: *abase yourself before God* > **abasement** NOUN

abashed ADJECTIVE embarrassed, confused

abate VERB to make or grow less: *wait for the storm to abate* > **abatement** NOUN

abattoir (*pronounced* **ab**-*a*-twahr) NOUN a slaughterhouse

abbess NOUN the female head of an abbey or a convent

abbey NOUN (*plural* **abbeys**) **1** a monastery or convent run by an abbot or an abbess **2** the church now or formerly attached to such a monastery or convent

abbot NOUN the male head of an abbey

abbreviate VERB to shorten (a word, phrase, etc)
🛈 Comes from Latin *brevis* meaning 'short'

abbreviation NOUN a shortened form of a word or group of words, either with some letters missing, eg *maths* for *mathematics*, or with each word represented by its first letter, eg *BBC* for *British Broadcasting Corporation*

abdicate (*pronounced* **ab**-di-kayt) VERB to give up (a position or responsibility, especially that of king or queen) > **abdication** NOUN

abdomen (*pronounced* **ab**-dom-*en*) NOUN **1** the part of the body between the chest and the hips containing the stomach, bowels and reproductive organs **2** the rear part

A B C D E F G H I J K L M N O P Q R S T U V W X Y Z

of an insect's body > **abdominal** (*pronounced* ab-**dom**-in-*a*l) ADJECTIVE

abduct VERB to take away by force or fraud > **abduction** NOUN > **abductor** NOUN

aberration NOUN an often temporary change from what is normal

abet VERB (**abetting, abetted**) to help or encourage to do wrong, especially to commit a crime: *He was aided and abetted by his partner in crime*

abeyance NOUN: **in abeyance** not being used or dealt with for the time being

abhor VERB (**abhorring, abhorred**) to hate, or regard with horror > **abhorrence** NOUN > **abhorrent** ADJECTIVE

abide VERB to put up with, tolerate **abide by** to keep, act according to: *abide by a decision*

abiding ADJECTIVE lasting

ability NOUN (*plural* **abilities**) **1** power or means to do something **2** talent

🛈 Comes from Latin *habilitas* meaning 'skill'

abject (*pronounced* **ab**-jekt) ADJECTIVE miserable, degraded > **abjectly** ADVERB

ablaze ADJECTIVE & ADVERB gleaming like fire: *a house ablaze with lights*

able ADJECTIVE **1** having the power or means (to do something) **2** clever: *more able students*

able-bodied ADJECTIVE **1** fit and healthy **2** not disabled

ably ADVERB in an efficient or competent way

abnormal ADJECTIVE **1** not normal (in behaviour etc) **2** unusual > **abnormally** ADVERB

abnormality NOUN (*plural* **abnormalities**) **1** something which is abnormal **2** the condition of being abnormal

aboard ADVERB & PREPOSITION on (to) or in(to) (a ship or aeroplane)

abode NOUN a formal word for a dwelling: *of no fixed abode*

abolish VERB to stop or put an end to (eg a custom, law, etc) > **abolition** NOUN

abolitionist NOUN someone who tries to put an end to something, especially slavery or capital punishment

abominable ADJECTIVE **1** hateful **2** very bad, terrible **the Abominable Snowman** a large animal believed to exist in the Himalayas (*also called*: **Yeti**) > **abominably** ADVERB (meaning 2): *behave abominably*

abominate VERB to hate very much

abomination NOUN **1** great hatred **2** anything hateful

Aboriginal (*pronounced* a-b*o*r-**ij**-i-n*a*l) *or* **Aborigine** (*pronounced* a-bor-**ij**-i-nee) NOUN a member of the people who were the original inhabitants of Australia > **Aboriginal** ADJECTIVE

🛈 Comes from Latin *ab* meaning 'from', and *origo* meaning 'beginning'

abort VERB **1** to stop (a plan etc) before its completion **2** to end a pregnancy deliberately by having an abortion

abortion NOUN an operation to end an unwanted or dangerous pregnancy

abortive ADJECTIVE coming to nothing, unsuccessful: *an abortive attempt*

abound VERB to be very plentiful **abounding in** full of, having many

about PREPOSITION **1** around: *look about you* **2** near (in time, size, etc): *about ten o'clock* **3** here and there in: *scattered about the room* ▶ADVERB **1** around: *stood about waiting* **2** in motion or in action: *running about* **3** in the opposite direction: *turned about and walked away* **about to** on the point of (doing something)

above PREPOSITION **1** over, in a higher position than: *above your head* **2** greater than: *above average* **3** too good for: *above criticism* ▶ADVERB **1** at, in or to a higher position, rank, etc **2** earlier on (in a letter etc): *see above for details*

ⓘ Comes from Old English *bufan* meaning 'above'

above board ADJECTIVE open; without fraud or deception ▶ADVERB openly; without fraud or deception

abrasion NOUN **1** the action of rubbing off **2** a graze on the body

abrasive ADJECTIVE **1** rough and scratchy **2** having a harsh and rude manner ▶NOUN something used for rubbing or polishing > **abrasively** ADVERB (meaning 2)

abreast ADVERB side by side **abreast of** up to date with: *keep abreast of current affairs*

abridge VERB to shorten (a book, story, etc) > **abridgement** *or* **abridgment** NOUN

abroad ADVERB **1** in another country **2** *formal* outside: *witches go abroad after dark*

abrupt ADJECTIVE **1** sudden, without warning **2** of speech or behaviour: bad-tempered or snappy > **abruptly** ADVERB > **abruptness** NOUN

abscess (*pronounced* **ab**-ses) NOUN (*plural* **abscesses**) a boil or other swelling filled with pus

abscond VERB to run away secretly: *absconded with the money*

abseil (*pronounced* **ab**-sayl) VERB to let yourself down a rock face using a double rope

ⓘ Comes from German *ab* meaning 'down', and *Seil* meaning 'rope'

absence NOUN the state of being away

absent ADJECTIVE (*pronounced* **ab**-sent) away, not present ▶VERB (*pronounced* ab-**sent**): **absent yourself** to keep away

absentee NOUN someone who is absent > **absenteeism** NOUN

absently ADVERB in a dreamy way: *'I suppose so,' he replied absently*

absent-minded ADJECTIVE forgetful > **absent-mindedly** ADVERB

absolute ADJECTIVE complete, not limited by anything: *absolute power*

absolutely ADVERB **1** completely, certainly **2** (*as an informal enthusiastic reply*) yes, I agree

a b c d e f g h i j k l m n o p q r s t u v w x y z

absolute zero NOUN, *physics* the lowest possible temperature of matter, equal to −273.15°C

absolve VERB, *formal* to pardon: *absolve me of my sins*

absorb VERB **1** to soak up (liquid) **2** to take up the whole attention of: *He was totally absorbed in his book*

absorbent ADJECTIVE able to soak up liquid etc > **absorbency** NOUN (*plural* **absorbencies**)

absorption NOUN **1** the act of absorbing **2** complete mental concentration

abstain VERB **1** to refuse to cast a vote for or against **2** (**abstain from something** *or* **from doing something**) to hold yourself back from it or from doing it

abstention NOUN **1** the act of choosing not to do something, especially not to take food or alcohol **2** a refusal to vote

abstinence (*pronounced* **ab**-stin-ens) NOUN abstaining from alcohol etc > **abstinent** ADJECTIVE

abstract ADJECTIVE **1** existing only as an idea, not as a real thing **2** of art: using shapes and patterns to represent things ▸ NOUN a summary of the main points of a book, speech, etc ▸ VERB to take something out

absurd ADJECTIVE clearly inappropriate, unsuitable or wrong; ridiculous > **absurdity** NOUN (*plural* **absurdities**) > **absurdly** ADVERB

abundance NOUN a plentiful supply

abundant ADJECTIVE plentiful > **abundantly** ADVERB to a great degree, extremely: *abundantly obvious*

abuse VERB (*pronounced a*-**byooz**) **1** to use wrongly **2** to insult or speak unkindly to; treat badly ▸ NOUN (*pronounced a*-**byoos**) **1** wrongful use **2** insulting language or behaviour

abusive ADJECTIVE insulting or rude > **abusively** ADVERB

abut VERB (**abutting, abutted**) to lean on or touch something

abysmal (*pronounced a*-**biz**-m*a*l) ADJECTIVE **1** very bad; terrible **2** bottomless > **abysmally** ADVERB (meaning 1)

abyss (*pronounced a*-**bis**) NOUN (*plural* **abysses**) a bottomless depth

AC ABBREVIATION alternating current (*compare with*: **DC**)

acacia (*pronounced a*-**kay**-sh*a*) NOUN any member of a family of thorny shrubs and trees

academic ADJECTIVE **1** concerned with theoretical education or complicated ideas: *academic qualifications* **2** not practical: *purely of academic interest* **3** of a university etc ▸ NOUN a university or college teacher > **academically** ADVERB (meaning 1): *He's not academically bright*

academy NOUN (*plural* **academies**) **1** a college for special study or training **2** a society for encouraging science or art **3** a senior school

[i] Comes from Greek *Akademeia*, which was Plato's school of philosophy, named after the garden outside Athens where Plato taught

acanthus NOUN (*plural*

A B C D E F G H I J K L M N O P Q R S T U V W X Y Z

acanthuses) a Mediterranean ornamental shrub

a cappella (*pronounced* ah k*a*-**pel**-*a*) ADJECTIVE & ADVERB, *music* sung without accompaniment by musical instruments

accelerate VERB to increase in speed

ⓘ Comes from Latin *celer* meaning 'swift'

acceleration NOUN an increasing of speed; the rate of increase of speed

accelerator NOUN a lever or pedal used to increase the speed of a car

accent NOUN **1** (a mark indicating) stress on a syllable or word **2** a mark used in written French and other languages to show the quality of a vowel **3** emphasis: *The accent must be on hard work* **4** the way in which words are pronounced in a particular area etc: *a Scottish accent* **5** *music* emphasis placed on certain notes or chords

accentuate (*pronounced* *a*k-**sen**-choo-ayt) VERB to make more obvious; emphasize > **accentuation** NOUN

accept VERB **1** to take something offered **2** to agree or submit to

Do not confuse with: **except**

acceptable ADJECTIVE satisfactory; pleasing > **acceptably** ADVERB

acceptance NOUN **1** the act of accepting: *total acceptance of the situation* **2** an official statement that someone or something has been accepted: *an acceptance from Stirling University*

access (*pronounced* **ak**-ses) NOUN **1** a means of approach or entry **2** the right to approach or enter

Do not confuse with: **excess**

accessibility NOUN being accessible

accessible (*pronounced* *a*k-**ses**-i-bl) ADJECTIVE easily approached or reached

accession (*pronounced* *a*k-**sesh**-*o*n) NOUN the act of taking up a new office, or of becoming king or queen: *accession to the throne*

accessory (*pronounced* *a*k-**ses**-*o*r-i) NOUN (*plural* **accessories**) **1** an item chosen to match or complement a piece of clothing or an outfit, eg a piece of jewellery, a handbag, etc **2** a helper, especially in crime

accident NOUN **1** an unexpected event causing injury: *a road accident* **2** a mishap: *I had a little accident with the cream* **3** chance: *I came upon the book by accident*

accidental ADJECTIVE happening by chance > **accidentally** ADVERB

acclaim VERB to praise enthusiastically ▶ NOUN enthusiastic praise: *met with critical acclaim*

acclaimed ADJECTIVE highly praised: *an acclaimed drama*

acclamation NOUN noisy signs of approval

acclimatization *or* **acclimatisation** NOUN becoming accustomed to a new climate or environment

acclimatize *or* **acclimatise** VERB to become accustomed to another climate or situation

accommodate VERB **1** to find room for: *A few families are being accommodated in hotels* **2** to make suitable: *hours which accommodate part-time workers* **3** to be helpful to; supply (with): *We will accommodate any requests from guests on special diets*

accommodating ADJECTIVE making an effort to be helpful

accommodation NOUN a place to live or to stay, lodgings: *student accommodation*

accompaniment NOUN **1** something that accompanies **2** the music played while a singer sings etc

accompanist NOUN someone who plays an accompaniment

accompany VERB (**accompanies, accompanying, accompanied**) **1** to go or be with **2** to play an instrument (eg a piano) while a singer sings etc

accomplice NOUN someone who helps another person, especially to commit a crime

accomplish VERB **1** to complete **2** to manage to do

accomplished ADJECTIVE **1** completed **2** skilled, talented

accomplishment NOUN **1** completion **2** a personal talent or skill

accord VERB **1** to agree (with): *These results do not accord with our previous data* ▶NOUN an official agreement: *an international accord on nuclear disarmament* **of your own accord** of your own free will

accordance NOUN agreement: *in accordance with his wishes*

according ADVERB: **according to** **1** as told by: *according to Tom* **2** in relation to: *paid according to your work*

accordingly ADVERB **1** in a way which suits what has just been said or what is happening: *You know your duty, and I expect you to act accordingly* **2** therefore: *She won her case, and accordingly received full compensation*

accordion NOUN a musical instrument with bellows, a keyboard and metal reeds

accordionist NOUN an accordion player

accost VERB to approach and speak to in a forceful or threatening way

account VERB: **account for** **1** to give a reason (for): *He's had bad news? That would account for his silence* **2** to make up: *Tax accounts for most of the price of a bottle of whisky* ▶NOUN **1** a bill **2** (often **accounts**) a record of finances **3** a description of events etc; an explanation **on account of** because of

accountable ADJECTIVE answerable, responsible: *be accountable for your actions*

accountant NOUN a keeper or inspector of financial accounts > **accountancy** NOUN

accredited ADJECTIVE having official status, or the official power to act: *an accredited member of the diplomatic delegation*

accrue (*pronounced a-***kroo**) VERB to accumulate, collect: *The account*

A B C D E F G H I J K L M N O P Q R S T U V W X Y Z

accrued no interest > **accrued** ADJECTIVE

accumulate VERB **1** to collect: *accumulate a large sum of money* **2** to increase: *Income from investments accumulates rapidly*

accumulation NOUN **1** a collection **2** a mass or pile

accumulator NOUN a type of battery used in a car etc

accuracy NOUN exactness

accurate ADJECTIVE correct, exact > **accurately** ADVERB

accursed ADJECTIVE **1** *formal* under a curse **2** hateful

accusation NOUN **1** the act of accusing **2** a statement accusing someone of something

accuse VERB (**accuse someone of something** *or* **of doing something**) to claim that someone has done something wrong > **the accused** NOUN (*plural* **the accused**) the person charged with a crime etc

accuser NOUN a person who accuses or blames

accustomed ADJECTIVE **1** used to: *accustomed to travel* **2** usual: *his accustomed walk along the path*

ace NOUN **1** the number one in a pack of playing-cards **2** an expert: *a computer ace* **3** *tennis* an unreturned first serve ▸ ADJECTIVE, *informal* excellent

[i] The adjective is a new sense of 'ace', first used in the mid 20th century

acetylene (*pronounced a*-**set**-il-een) NOUN, *chemistry* a colourless, flammable gas used for giving light and heat (*also called*: **ethyne**)

ache NOUN a continuous pain ▸ VERB to be in continuous pain

achieve VERB **1** to get (something) done, accomplish **2** to win

achievement NOUN **1** the gaining of something, usually after working hard for it **2** something that has been done or gained by effort

acid NOUN **1** *chemistry* a substance that dissolves in water to produce hydrogen ions and which can react with bases to form salts (*contrasted with*: **alkali**) **2** *slang* the drug LSD ▸ ADJECTIVE **1** of taste: sharp **2** sarcastic > **acidic** ADJECTIVE

acidify VERB (**acidifies, acidifying, acidified**) to make or become acid

acidity NOUN (*plural* **acidities**) the state of being acid

acid rain NOUN rain containing sulphur and nitrogen compounds and other pollutants

acknowledge VERB **1** to admit the truth of something **2** to admit that you know or are aware of something **3** to (write to) say you have received something **4** to express gratitude or thanks > **acknowledgement** *or* **acknowledgment** NOUN

acme (*pronounced* **ak**-mi) NOUN, *formal* the highest point, perfection

acne (*pronounced* **ak**-ni) NOUN, *medicine* a common skin disease with pimples, caused by overactive sebaceous glands

acorn NOUN the fruit of the oak tree

acoustic (*pronounced a*-**koo**-stik) ADJECTIVE **1** of hearing or sound **2** played without an amplifier: *an acoustic guitar*

a b c d e f g h i j k l m n o p q r s t u v w x y z

A
B
C
D
E
F
G
H
I
J
K
L
M
N
O
P
Q
R
S
T
U
V
W
X
Y
Z

acoustics (*pronounced* a-**koo**-stiks) NOUN **1** *singular* the study of sound **2** *plural* the characteristics of a room etc which affect the way sound is heard in it

acquaint VERB **acquaint with** to make someone familiar with: *Are you acquainted with the facts?*

acquaintance NOUN **1** slight knowledge **2** someone whom you know slightly

acquiesce (*pronounced* ak-wi-**es**) VERB **acquiesce to** *or* **in** to agree to: *acquiesce to their demands/ acquiesce in the terms of this agreement* > **acquiescence** NOUN > **acquiescent** ADJECTIVE

acquire VERB to obtain, get > **acquired** ADJECTIVE gained; not something you were born with or have inherited

acquisition NOUN **1** the act of getting **2** something obtained: *This painting is the art gallery's most recent acquisition*

acquit VERB (**acquitting, acquitted**) to declare (someone) innocent of a crime: *the decision to acquit him of the crime*

acquittal NOUN a legal judgement of 'not guilty'

acre NOUN a land measure of 4840 square yards or about 4000 square metres

acrid (*pronounced* **ak**-rid) ADJECTIVE harsh, bitter

acrimony (*pronounced* **ak**-rim-on-i) NOUN bitterness of feeling or speech > **acrimonious** ADJECTIVE

acrobat NOUN someone who performs gymnastic tricks, tightrope-walking, etc

acrobatic ADJECTIVE able to perform gymnastic tricks; agile

acronym (*pronounced* **ak**-ron-im) NOUN a word formed from the initial letters of other words, eg *radar* for *ra*dio *d*etecting *a*nd *r*anging

ⓘ A word invented in the mid 20th century, and formed from the prefix *acro-*, and Greek *onyma* meaning 'name'

across ADVERB & PREPOSITION to or at the other side (of): *swam across the river/winked at him across the table* **across the board** involving everyone or everything; sweeping

acrylic (*pronounced* a-**kril**-ik) NOUN **1** a synthetically produced fibre **2** paint containing acrylic material ▸ADJECTIVE made with this fibre

act VERB **1** to do something **2** to behave in a particular way: *act tough* **3** to play a dramatic role on stage, film, etc ▸NOUN **1** something done **2** a law passed by a government **3** a section of a play **act up** *informal* to behave or act naughtily or badly

ⓘ Comes from Latin *actum* meaning 'a thing which has been done'

action NOUN **1** a deed, an act **2** a law case **3** dramatic events portrayed in a film, play, etc > **actionable** ADJECTIVE

activate VERB to start (a machine) working

activation energy NOUN, *chemistry* the least amount of energy needed for a chemical reaction to occur

active ADJECTIVE **1** busy; lively **2** able to perform physical tasks **3** *grammar* describing the form of a verb in which the subject performs the action of the verb, eg 'the dog bit the postman' (*compare with:* **passive**) > **actively** ADVERB in a way which involves doing things: *actively involved in nature conservation*

activity NOUN (*plural* **activities**) **1** the state of being active: *The office was a hive of activity* **2** anything that you do, either for pleasure or as part of an organized programme: *outdoor activities/the gang's criminal activities*

actor NOUN someone who acts a part in a play or film

actress NOUN (*plural* **actresses**) a female actor

actual ADJECTIVE real, existing in fact

actuality NOUN fact; reality

actually ADVERB really, in fact, as a matter of fact

actuate VERB to put into action: *a radar detector, actuated by certain frequencies of radio waves*

acumen (*pronounced* **ak**-yuw-men) NOUN quickness of understanding: *He owes his success to his keen business acumen*

acupuncture (*pronounced* **ak**-yuw-pungk-cher) NOUN a method of treating illness by piercing the skin with needles at specific pressure points

ⓘ Comes from Latin *acus* meaning 'needle'

acute ADJECTIVE **1** quick at understanding **2** sudden and severe: *acute back pain/acute difficulties/acute appendicitis* (*compare with*: **chronic**) **3** *maths* of an angle: less than a right angle (*contrasted with*: **obtuse**) **acute accent** a forward-leaning stroke (´) placed over letters in some languages to show their pronunciation > **acutely** ADVERB extremely, painfully: *an acutely embarrassing situation/He was acutely aware that he was being observed* > **acuteness** NOUN the quality of being acute, used especially about mental perception

AD ABBREVIATION in the year of our Lord (from Latin *anno Domini*). Used with a date, eg AD1900, to show that it refers to the time after, and not before, the birth of Christ (*compare with*: **BC**)

ad NOUN, *informal* an advertisement

adage (*pronounced* **a**-dij) NOUN an old saying, a proverb

adagio (*pronounced a*-**dah**-jee-oh) NOUN (*plural* **adagios**), *music* a slow-paced piece of music

ⓘ In Italian *ad agio* means 'at ease'

adamant (*pronounced* **ad**-*a*m-*a*nt) ADJECTIVE not going to change your mind or opinion

Adam's apple NOUN the natural lump which sticks out from a man's throat, a projection of the thyroid cartilage

adapt VERB (**adapt to**) to make suitable for; alter so as to fit

adaptable ADJECTIVE easily altered to suit new conditions

adaptation NOUN a change in the form of something to make

a b c d e f g h i j k l m n o p q r s t u v w x y z

it suitable for another situation or purpose: *a popular television adaptation of this classic novel*

adaptor NOUN a device allowing an electrical plug to be used in a socket for which it was not designed, or several plugs to be used on the same socket

add VERB **1** to make one thing join another to give a sum total or whole **2** to mix in: *add water to the dough* **3** to say further **add up 1** to combine, grow to a large quantity: *add up the different quantities/All these expenses soon add up* **2** to make sense, seem logical: *His story just doesn't add up*

adder NOUN the common name of the viper, a poisonous snake

addict (*pronounced* **a**-dikt) NOUN **1** someone who is dependent on a drug **2** *informal* someone who is extremely fond of a hobby: *a chess addict*

addicted (*pronounced a*-**dik**-tid) ADJECTIVE (**addicted to**) unable to do without

addiction NOUN dependency on a drug etc

addictive (*pronounced a*-**dikt**-iv) ADJECTIVE more and more difficult to do without, the more often it is used

addition NOUN **1** the act of adding **2** something added

additional ADJECTIVE extra; more than usual > **additionally** ADVERB as well as that: *William was not happy at home. Additionally, he was bullied at school*

additive NOUN a chemical etc added to another substance

address VERB **1** to speak to **2** to write the address on (a letter etc) ▸ NOUN (*plural* **addresses**) **1** the name of the house, street and town where someone lives, works, etc **2** *computing* a name and location where you can be contacted by e-mail **3** a formal speech

adept (*pronounced a*-**dept**) ADJECTIVE very skilful

adequacy NOUN being adequate; sufficiency

adequate ADJECTIVE sufficient, enough > **adequately** ADVERB

adhere VERB **1** to stick (to): *adhere to a clean, dry surface* **2** to give support (to), follow: *adhere to a strict dress code*

adherent ADJECTIVE sticking (to) ▸ NOUN a follower or supporter of a cause etc > **adherence** NOUN

adhesion NOUN the act of sticking (to)

adhesive ADJECTIVE sticky, gummed ▸ NOUN something which makes things stick to each other

ad hoc ADJECTIVE set up for a particular purpose only

Adi-Granth (*pronounced* **uh**-dhee grunt) NOUN the Guru Granth Sahib, the holy book of the Sikh religion

ad infinitum (*pronounced* ad in-fi-**nai**-t*u*m) ADVERB for ever

adjacent (*pronounced a*-**jei**-sent) ADJECTIVE (**adjacent to**) lying next to

adjective NOUN a word which tells something about a noun, eg 'the *black* cat,' 'times are *hard*' > **adjectival** ADJECTIVE

adjoin VERB to be joined to: *A large*

LANGUAGE workshop Adjectives

Adjectives act as modifiers of nouns – that is, they tell us something about the noun they relate to. There are different types of adjective that give different types of information:

Descriptive adjectives give information about the qualities of people or things.

The girl was *short* and wore a *blue* jacket.
This woman is *British*.
He is an *excellent* teacher.

Adjectives of quantity inform about the amount of something.

She had a *few* cows, *several* pigs and *some* chickens.
The *four* children drank *ten* bottles of lemonade and ate *half* an apple pie.

Possessive adjectives show ownership of the noun.

John washes *his* car every Sunday.
Don't waste *your* time.

Demonstrative adjectives point to someone or something particular.

Look at *this* letter.
These children read *those* books.

Questioning or interrogative adjectives ask about something.

What coat shall I wear?
Show me *which* dress you like.

? Identify the adjectives in these sentences:

1. You are getting on my nerves.
2. I saw a terrible play at that theatre.
3. The player had numerous chances to score great goals.

a b c d e f g h i j k l m n o p q r s t u v w x y z

A B C D E F G H I J K L M N O P Q R S T U V W X Y Z

shed adjoins the house > **adjoining** ADJECTIVE

adjourn VERB **1** to stop (a meeting etc) with the intention of continuing it at another time or place **2** (**adjourn to**) to go to another place: *adjourn to the lounge* > **adjournment** NOUN

adjudicate VERB **1** to give a judgement on (a dispute etc) **2** to act as a judge at a competition > **adjudication** NOUN

adjudicator NOUN someone who adjudicates

adjunct (*pronounced* **aj**-ungkt) NOUN something joined or added

adjust VERB to rearrange or alter to suit the circumstances > **adjustable** ADJECTIVE > **adjustment** NOUN

ad-lib VERB (**ad-libbing, ad-libbed**) to speak without any plan or preparation ▶ ADJECTIVE without preparation

administer VERB **1** to manage or govern: *South Pacific islands administered by France* **2** to carry out (the law etc) **3** to give (help, medicine, etc): *A qualified doctor must administer the drug to patients*

administrate VERB to manage or govern

administration NOUN **1** management **2** (the body that carries on) the government of a country etc

administrative ADJECTIVE having to do with management or government

administrator NOUN someone involved in the administration of a country etc

admirable ADJECTIVE worthy of being admired > **admirably** ADVERB

admiral NOUN the commander of a navy

Admiralty NOUN (**the Admiralty**) the government office which manages naval affairs

admire VERB **1** to think very highly of **2** to look at with pleasure > **admiration** NOUN > **admirer** NOUN

admissible ADJECTIVE allowable: *admissible evidence*

admission NOUN **1** (the price of) being let in **2** anything admitted

admit VERB (**admitting, admitted**) **1** to let in **2** to acknowledge the truth of, confess **3** (**admit of**) to leave room for, allow: *admits of no other explanation*

admittance NOUN the right or permission to enter

admittedly ADVERB as I must admit: *Admittedly my work could be better*

admonish VERB **1** to warn **2** to rebuke, scold > **admonition** NOUN > **admonitory** ADJECTIVE

ad nauseam (*pronounced* ad **naw**-zi-am) ADVERB to a tiresome degree

adolescent NOUN someone between a child and an adult in age ▶ ADJECTIVE of this age > **adolescence** NOUN

adopt VERB **1** to take as your own (especially a child of other parents) **2** to take (eg precautions), choose formally: *adopt certain new measures in the fight against crime* > **adoption** NOUN

adoptive ADJECTIVE adopted, taken

as your own: *her adoptive country*

adorable ADJECTIVE very loveable

adore VERB **1** to love very much **2** to worship > **adoration** NOUN

adorn VERB to decorate (with ornaments etc): *Her head was adorned with flowers*

adornment NOUN ornament

adrenaline *or* **adrenalin** (*pronounced a*-**dren**-*a*-lin) NOUN a hormone produced in response to fear, anger, etc, which causes an increase in heartbeat and diverts blood towards the muscles

adrift ADVERB drifting, floating

adroit (*pronounced a*-**droit**) ADJECTIVE skilful

ADSL ABBREVIATION, *computing* Asymmetric Digital Subscriber Line, a fast Internet connection over a phone line

adulation (*pronounced* ad-yuw-**lei**-sh*u*n) NOUN great flattery > **adulatory** ADJECTIVE

adult ADJECTIVE grown up ▶ NOUN a grown-up person

adulterate VERB to make impure by adding something else > **adulteration** NOUN

adultery NOUN unfaithfulness to a husband or wife > **adulterer** *or* **adulteress** NOUN

adulthood NOUN the state of being an adult

advance VERB **1** to go forward **2** to put forward (a plan etc): *He advanced a number of proposals* **3** to help the progress of: *research which has advanced our treatment of cancer* **4** to pay before the usual or agreed time: *Could you advance me £50 and take it off my next pay cheque?* ▶ NOUN **1** movement forward **2** improvement **3** a loan of money **in advance** beforehand

advanced ADJECTIVE modern *advanced technology*

advancement NOUN progress

advantage NOUN **1** a better position, superiority **2** gain or benefit ▶ VERB to help, benefit **take advantage of** to make use of (a situation, person, etc) in such a way as to benefit yourself

advantageous ADJECTIVE profitable; helpful

advent (*pronounced* **ad**-vent) NOUN **1** coming, arrival: *before the advent of television* **2** (**Advent**) in the Christian church, the four weeks before Christmas

adventure NOUN a bold or exciting undertaking or experience

adventurer NOUN **1** someone who takes risks, especially in the hope of making a lot of money **2** a mercenary soldier

adventurous ADJECTIVE taking risks, liking adventure

adverb NOUN a word which adds something to the meaning of a verb, adjective or other adverb, eg 'eat *slowly*,' '*extremely* hard,' '*very* carefully' > **adverbial** ADJECTIVE

adversary (*pronounced* **ad**-ver-s*a*r-i) NOUN (*plural* **adversaries**) an enemy; an opponent

adverse (*pronounced* **ad**-vers) ADJECTIVE unfavourable: *adverse criticism*

adversity NOUN (*plural* **adversities**) misfortune

A
B
C
D
E
F
G
H
I
J
K
L
M
N
O
P
Q
R
S
T
U
V
W
X
Y
Z

LANGUAGE workshop Adverbs

Adverbs act as modifiers of verbs – that is, they tell us something about the verb they relate to; for example, how, why, where, when or how often something happens.

The explorers *cautiously* entered the cave.
They went *inside* and *slowly* crept *upstairs*.
The gang of children met at the cinema *yesterday*.

However, an adverb also can modify an adjective:

The woods looked *very* different at night.

An adverb can also modify another adverb:

They swam *remarkably* quickly.

? Identify the adverbs in these sentences:

1. She ran outside, looking rather frightened.
2. You acted very calmly in the circumstances.
3. We are quite excited because we are going to the cinema later.

Forming adverbs

Many adverbs are formed by adding **-ly** to an adjective. If an adjective ends in **-y**, the **y** changes into **i** before adding **-ly**.

quiet - *quietly*
weary - *wearily*

It is important that you do not use the adjective form when you should use the adverb form:

✗ Come quick, and look at this!
✓ Come *quickly*, and look at this!

➲

Adverbs LANGUAGE workshop

Placing adverbs

Some adverbs can be placed at various points in a sentence without changing its meaning:

The explorers *cautiously* entered the cave.
The explorers entered the cave *cautiously*.
Cautiously, the explorers entered the cave.

However, with other adverbs it is important to put them in the correct place in a sentence, otherwise the meaning of the sentence may be confused. Compare the different meanings of these two sentences:

There was a report that the Prime Minister had lost his temper *on the evening news*.
There was a report *on the evening news* that the Prime Minister had lost his temper.

The adverbs *almost*, *also*, *even*, *just*, *mainly* and *only* should always be placed immediately in front of the word they modify. Compare the change in meaning when the adverb *only* is put in front of different words in the following sentence:

Jim gave Jane a kiss.
Only Jim gave Jane a kiss.
Jim *only* gave Jane a kiss.
Jim gave *only* Jane a kiss.
Jim gave Jane *only* a kiss.

A B C D E F G H I J K L M N O P Q R S T U V W X Y Z

advert NOUN, *informal* an advertisement

advertise VERB **1** to make known to the public **2** to stress the good points of (a product for sale)

advertisement NOUN a photograph, short film, etc intended to persuade the public to buy a particular product

advice NOUN **1** something said to help someone trying to make a decision etc **2** a formal notice

> Do not confuse with: **advise**. To help you remember: 'ice' is a noun, 'ise' is not.

advisable ADJECTIVE wise, sensible > **advisability** NOUN

advise VERB **1** to give advice to **2** to recommend (an action etc) > **adviser** *or* **advisor** NOUN

> Do not confuse with: **advice**. To help you remember: 'ice' is a noun, so 'ise' must be the verb.

advisory ADJECTIVE giving advice

advocate NOUN (*pronounced* **ad**-vo-k*a*t) in Scotland, a lawyer who pleads cases in court ▸ VERB (*pronounced* **ad**-vo-keit) to argue for or recommend: *I do not advocate the use of force*

aeon *or* **eon** (*pronounced* **ee**-on) NOUN a very long period of time, an age

aerate (*pronounced* **eir**-eit) VERB to put air or another gas into (a liquid)

aerial ADJECTIVE **1** of, in or from the air: *aerial photography* **2** placed high up or overhead: *aerial railway* ▸ NOUN a wire or rod (or a set of these) by which radio or television signals are received or sent

aero- PREFIX of air or aircraft

> [i] Comes from Greek *aer* meaning 'air'

aerobatics PLURAL NOUN stunts performed by an aircraft

aerobics SINGULAR NOUN a system of physical exercise which aims to strengthen the heart and lungs by increasing the body's oxygen consumption

aerodrome NOUN a landing and maintenance station for aircraft

aerodynamic ADJECTIVE designed to promote more efficient movement through air

aeronautics SINGULAR NOUN the science or art of navigation in the air

aeroplane *or US* **airplane** NOUN a flying machine with fixed wings and an engine (*short form* **plane**)

aerosol NOUN a container of liquid and gas under pressure, from which the liquid is squirted as a mist

aesthetic (*pronounced* ees-**thet**-ik) ADJECTIVE **1** having to do with beauty or its appreciation **2** artistic, pleasing to the eye > **aesthetically** ADVERB

affable ADJECTIVE pleasant, easy to speak to > **affability** NOUN

affair NOUN **1** events etc connected with one person or thing: *the Watergate affair* **2** (**affairs**) personal concerns, transactions, etc: *His affairs seemed to be in order* **3** business, concern: *that's not your affair* **4** a love affair

affect VERB **1** to act upon **2** to have

an effect on; move the feelings of **3** to pretend to feel etc: *affect an air of indifference*

ℹ Meanings 1 and 2 come from Latin *afficere* meaning 'to do something to'; meaning 3 comes from Latin *affectare* meaning 'to strive after'

> Do not confuse with: **effect**. **Affect** is usually a verb. **Effect** is usually a noun. To **affect** means 'to have an **effect** on'.

affectation NOUN pretence

affected ADJECTIVE **1** moved in your feelings **2** not natural, sham

affecting ADJECTIVE moving the feelings

affection NOUN a strong liking

affectionate ADJECTIVE loving

affiliated ADJECTIVE (**affiliated with** *or* **to**) connected with or attached to > **affiliation** NOUN

affinity NOUN (*plural* **affinities**) a close likeness or agreement

affirm VERB to state firmly: *He affirmed that they had an excellent safety record* > **affirmation** NOUN

affirmative ADJECTIVE saying 'yes'

affix VERB to attach to

afflict VERB to cause pain or suffering to: *What sadness afflicts him?*

affliction NOUN great suffering

affluent (*pronounced* **af**-luw-ent) ADJECTIVE wealthy > **affluence** NOUN

afford VERB **1** to be able to pay for **2** *formal* to give, provide with: *I hoped the situation would afford me a chance to speak to him*

affront VERB to insult openly ▸ NOUN an insult

afloat ADVERB & ADJECTIVE floating

afoot ADVERB happening or about to happen: *I could tell something was afoot*

aforesaid (*pronounced a*-**fawr**-sed) ADJECTIVE, *formal* said or named before: *the aforesaid person*

afraid ADJECTIVE **1** frightened **2** *informal* sorry to have to admit that: *I'm afraid there are no tickets left*

afresh ADVERB once again, anew

aft (*pronounced* ahft) ADVERB near or towards the stern of a vessel

after- PREFIX later in time or place: *aftertaste/afterthought*

after PREPOSITION **1** later in time than: *after dinner* **2** following: *arrived one after another/day after day* **3** in memory or honour of: *named after his father* **4** in pursuit of: *run after the bus* **5** about: *asked after her health* **6** despite: *After all my efforts, it still didn't work* **7** in the style of: *after Rubens* ▸ ADVERB later in time or place: *We left soon after* ▸ CONJUNCTION later than the time when: *After she arrived, things improved* **after all** **1** all things considered: *After all, he's still young* **2** despite everything said or done before: *I went after all*

afterbirth NOUN the placenta and membranes expelled from the uterus after giving birth

aftermath NOUN the bad results of something: *the aftermath of the election*

ℹ Originally a second mowing after the main harvest

afternoon NOUN the time between noon and evening ▸ ADJECTIVE

a b c d e f g h i j k l m n o p q r s t u v w x y z

taking place in the afternoon

aftershave NOUN a lotion used on the face after shaving

afterthought NOUN a later thought

afterwards ADVERB later

again ADVERB **1** once more: *Say that again* **2** in or into the original state, place, etc: *there and back again* **3** on the other hand: *Again, I might be wrong* **4** *informal* at another later time: *See you again*

against PREPOSITION **1** in opposition to: *against the law/fight against injustice* **2** in the opposite direction to: *against the wind* **3** on a background of: *clouds against the sky* **4** close to, touching: *lean against the wall* **5** as protection from: *guard against infection*

age NOUN **1** a long period of time **2** the time someone or something has lived or existed ▸ VERB (**ageing** *or* **aging, aged**) to grow or make visibly older: *He has aged ten years* (= seems to have grown ten years older) *in the past six months/That hat ages her* (= makes her look older) **of age** legally an adult

aged ADJECTIVE **1** (*pronounced* **eij**-id) old **2** (*pronounced* eijd) of the age of: *aged five*

ageism NOUN discrimination on grounds of age > **ageist** ADJECTIVE

agency NOUN (*plural* **agencies**) **1** the office or business of an agent **2** action; means by which something is done

agenda NOUN a list of things to be done, especially at a meeting

agent NOUN **1** someone who acts for another **2** someone or something that causes an effect **3** a spy **4** a substance that can cause a chemical reaction (*compare with*: **reagent**)

aggrandize *or* **aggrandise** VERB to make greater

aggravate VERB **1** to make worse **2** *informal* to annoy > **aggravating** ADJECTIVE > **aggravation** NOUN

aggregate (*pronounced* **ag**-ri-g*a*t) NOUN a total

aggressive ADJECTIVE **1** ready to attack first **2** quarrelsome > **aggression** NOUN > **aggressively** ADVERB > **aggressor** NOUN

aggrieved (*pronounced a*-**greevd**) ADJECTIVE hurt, upset

aghast (*pronounced a*-**gahst**) ADJECTIVE struck with horror

agile ADJECTIVE able to move, change direction, etc quickly and easily > **agility** NOUN

agitate VERB **1** to stir up **2** to excite, disturb > **agitated** ADJECTIVE > **agitation** NOUN > **agitator** NOUN

agnostic (*pronounced* ag-**nos**-tik) NOUN someone who believes it is impossible to know whether God exists or not > **agnosticism** NOUN

ago ADVERB in the past, earlier: *That happened five years ago*

agog (*pronounced a*-**gog**) ADJECTIVE eager, excited

agonize *or* **agonise** VERB (to cause) to worry intensely or suffer great anxiety about something

agonized *or* **agonised** ADJECTIVE showing great pain or suffering: *an agonized expression*

agonizing *or* **agonising** ADJECTIVE causing great pain or suffering

agony NOUN (*plural* **agonies**) great pain

agree VERB **1** to be alike in opinions, decisions, etc **2** to say that you will do something: *Toby has agreed to play us a tune* **3** (**agree with**) to suit **4** (**agree with**) to cause no problems in digestion: *The fish didn't agree with me* **5** to be the same or consistent, fit together: *I'd like to believe them both, but their stories don't agree*

agreeable ADJECTIVE **1** pleasant **2** ready to agree > **agreeably** ADVERB

agreement NOUN **1** likeness (especially of opinions) **2** a written statement making a bargain

agri- PREFIX of fields, land use, or farming

🛈 Comes from Latin *ager* meaning 'field'

agriculture NOUN the cultivation of the land, farming > **agricultural** ADJECTIVE

agro- PREFIX of fields, land use or farming: *agrobiology* (= the study of plant nutrition)/*agrochemical* (= a chemical used in farming the land)

🛈 Comes from Greek *agros* meaning 'field'

aground ADJECTIVE & ADVERB stuck on the bottom of the sea or a river: *run aground*

ahead ADVERB in front; in advance: *finishing ahead of time*

-aholic *or* **-oholic** SUFFIX having an addiction to: *workaholic/chocaholic*

🛈 Comes from the ending of the word alc*oholic*

aid VERB to help, assist ▸ NOUN help

AIDS *or* **Aids** ABBREVIATION, *medicine* Acquired Immune Deficiency Syndrome, a disease which destroys the immune system

ail VERB, *old* to be or make ill: *My poor father is ailing/What ails thee?*

ailing ADJECTIVE **1** troubled, in a bad state: *the ailing steel industry* **2** ill

ailment NOUN an illness: *minor ailments*

aim VERB **1** to point (a gun etc) (at) **2** to intend to do: *We were aiming to get there early* **3** to have as your purpose ▸ NOUN **1** the act of, or skill in, aiming **2** the point aimed at, goal, intention

aimless ADJECTIVE without aim or purpose > **aimlessly** ADVERB

air NOUN **1** the mixture of gases (mainly oxygen and nitrogen) which we breathe; the atmosphere **2** a light breeze **3** fresh air **4** space overhead **5** a tune **6** the look or manner (of a person) ▸ VERB **1** to expose to the air **2** to make known (an opinion etc) **on the air** broadcasting

airbag NOUN a bag which automatically inflates inside a car on impact to protect the driver or passenger from injury

airborne ADJECTIVE in the air, flying

air-conditioned ADJECTIVE equipped with a system for filtering and controlling the temperature of the air > **air-conditioner** NOUN > **air-conditioning** NOUN

aircraft NOUN (*plural* **aircraft**) a flying machine

aircraft carrier NOUN a warship that aircraft can take off from and land on

air force NOUN the branch of the armed forces using aircraft

airgun NOUN a gun worked by means of compressed air

airily ADVERB in a light and not very serious way

airing NOUN **1** the act of exposing to the air: *give the room an airing* **2** the act of talking about something openly: *give your views an airing*

airless ADJECTIVE stuffy, with no circulation of fresh air

airline NOUN a company which provides travel by aeroplane

airlock NOUN **1** a bubble in a pipe obstructing the flow of a liquid **2** a compartment with two doors for entering and leaving an airtight spaceship etc

airplane *US* for **aeroplane**

airport NOUN a place where aircraft land and take off, with buildings for customs, waiting-rooms, etc

air raid NOUN an attack by aircraft

airship NOUN a large balloon which can be steered and driven

airstream NOUN a flow of air

airtight ADJECTIVE made so that air cannot pass in or out

airy ADJECTIVE (**airier, airiest**) **1** of or like the air **2** well supplied with fresh air **3** light-hearted

aisle (*pronounced* ail) NOUN **1** the side part of a church **2** a passage between seats in a theatre etc

ajar ADVERB partly open: *leave the door ajar*

aka (*pronounced* ei-kei-**ei**) ABBREVIATION also known as: *Stevens, aka The Fly*

akimbo ADVERB (*placed after the noun*) with hand on hip and elbow bent outward

ⓘ From an Old Norse term meaning 'bowed' or 'curved'

akin ADJECTIVE similar

à la carte ADJECTIVE & ADVERB with each dish chosen and priced separately

alarm NOUN **1** sudden fear **2** something which makes someone take action or warns of danger ▶ VERB to frighten > **alarming** ADJECTIVE

alarmist NOUN someone who frightens others needlessly

alas EXCLAMATION a cry showing grief

albatross NOUN (*plural* **albatrosses**) a type of large seabird

albino (*pronounced* ahl-**been**-oh or *US* ahl-**bain**-oh) NOUN (*plural* **albinos**), *biology* a person or animal with no natural colour in their skin, hair and eye irises

album NOUN **1** a book with blank pages for holding photographs, stamps, etc **2** a record, CD, etc with multiple tracks

albumen (*pronounced* **al**-byuw-men) NOUN the white of eggs

alchemist NOUN someone who practised alchemy

alchemy NOUN an early form of chemistry aimed at changing other metals into gold

alcohol NOUN **1** *chemistry* a compound containing one or more hydroxyl groups and used in dyes, perfumes, etc **2** the compound ethanol, as found in alcoholic drinks **3** drink containing ethanol

alcoholic ADJECTIVE of or containing alcohol ▶NOUN someone addicted to alcohol

alcoholism NOUN physical dependence on or addiction to alcohol

alcove NOUN a recess in a room's wall

ale NOUN a drink made from malt, hops, etc; beer

alert NOUN signal to be ready for action ▶VERB to make alert, warn: *alert them to the dangers of the job* ▶ADJECTIVE **1** watchful **2** quick-thinking **on the alert** on the watch (for)

algae (*pronounced* **al**-gi *or* **al**-ji) NOUN a group of simple plants which includes seaweed

algebra NOUN a part of mathematics in which letters and signs are used to represent numbers

-algia SUFFIX forms nouns relating to pain: *neuralgia/nostalgia*

ⓘ Comes from Greek *algos* meaning 'pain'

alias ADVERB also known as: *Mitchell alias Grassic Gibbon* ▶NOUN (*plural* **aliases**) a false name

alibi NOUN **1** *law* the plea that someone charged with a crime was elsewhere when it was done **2** the state or fact of being elsewhere when a crime was committed

alien ADJECTIVE **1** foreign **2** (**alien to**) not in keeping with: *alien to her nature* ▶NOUN a foreigner

alienate VERB to make someone unfriendly, probably by causing them to feel unwanted or rejected: *We must be careful not to alienate our old supporters*

alight[1] VERB (**alighting, alighted**) **1** to climb etc down: *alight from the train* **2** to settle, land

alight[2] ADJECTIVE & ADVERB on fire, burning

align (*pronounced a*-**lain**) VERB **1** to put in line or bring into line: *Align the text with the margin* **2** to take sides in an argument etc: *align yourself with environmentalists*

alignment NOUN arrangement in a line

alike ADJECTIVE like one another, similar ▶ADVERB in the same way, similarly

alimentary ADJECTIVE of food **alimentary canal** the passage in the body, beginning at the mouth and ending at the anus

alive ADJECTIVE **1** living **2** full of activity **alive to** aware of

alkali NOUN (*plural* **alkalis** *or* **alkalies**), *chemistry* (*compare with*: **acid**) a substance such as soda or potash that dissolves in water to produce hydroxide ions > **alkaline** ADJECTIVE

alkali metal NOUN, *chemistry* a metal, eg sodium or potassium, that forms an alkaline solution in water

alkane NOUN, *chemistry* a hydrocarbon whose carbon atoms form chains linked by single bonds

alkene NOUN, *chemistry* a hydrocarbon whose carbon atoms form chains linked by one or more double bonds

A B C D E F G H I J K L M N O P Q R S T U V W X Y Z

all ADJECTIVE & PRONOUN **1** every one (of): *We are all invited/All letters will be answered* **2** the whole (of): *painted all the house* ▶ ADVERB wholly, completely: *dressed all in red* **all in 1** with everything included: *all-in price* **2** *informal* exhausted: *I felt completely all in* **all over 1** over the whole of **2** everywhere **3** finished, ended **all ready** totally ready

> Do not use this as an alternative spelling for 'already'.

Allah NOUN, *Islam* God

allay VERB **1** to make less, relieve: *tried to allay my fears* **2** to calm

allege VERB to say without proof: *allege that this man was involved in the crime* > **allegation** NOUN

alleged ADJECTIVE claimed to be: *the alleged criminal* > **allegedly** ADVERB

allegiance NOUN loyalty

allegory NOUN (*plural* **allegories**) a story or fable which deals with a subject in a way which is meant to suggest a deeper, more serious subject > **allegorical** ADJECTIVE

allergy NOUN (*plural* **allergies**), *medicine* abnormal sensitiveness of the body to something > **allergic** ADJECTIVE

alleviate VERB to make lighter, lessen: *alleviate their suffering* > **alleviation** NOUN

alley NOUN (*plural* **alleys**) **1** a narrow passage or lane **2** an enclosure for bowls or skittles

alliance NOUN a joining together of two people, nations, etc for a common cause

allied ADJECTIVE joined by an alliance

alligator NOUN a large reptile like a crocodile but with a broader head and blunter snout

alliteration NOUN the repetition of the same sound at the beginning of two or more words close together, eg 'round and round the rugged rock' or 'sing a song of sixpence' > **alliterative** ADJECTIVE

allo- PREFIX other, different, from outside

Comes from Greek *allos* meaning 'other'

allocate VERB to allot, share out, reserve for a particular purpose: *The task of collecting the data has been allocated to you* > **allocation** NOUN

allot VERB (**allotting, allotted**) to give each person a share of: *A ten-minute slot will be allotted to each candidate*

allotment NOUN **1** the act of allotting **2** a small plot of ground for growing vegetables etc

allow VERB **1** to let (someone do something) **2** (**allow for**) to take into consideration (in sums, plans, etc) **3** to admit, confess: *I will allow that we could have handled the situation better* **4** to give, especially at regular intervals: *She allows him £40 a week* > **allowable** ADJECTIVE

allowance NOUN a fixed sum or amount given regularly **make allowances for** to treat differently by taking into consideration special circumstances etc

alloy NOUN a mixture of two or more metals

all right ADJECTIVE in a normal state; not hurt, unhappy or feeling strange

> It is best to avoid the spelling 'alright', since some people say it is incorrect.

all together ADVERB together as a group

> Do not use this as an alternative spelling for 'altogether'.

allude VERB (**allude to**) to refer to indirectly or in passing
Comes from Latin *ad ludere* meaning 'to play at'

> Do not confuse with: **elude**

allure VERB to tempt, draw on by promises etc > **allurement** NOUN > **alluring** ADJECTIVE

allusion NOUN an indirect reference

> Do not confuse with: **delusion** and **illusion**. An **allusion** is a comment which **alludes to** something.

allusive ADJECTIVE referring indirectly, hinting

> Do not confuse with: **elusive** and **illusive**. **Allusive** is related to the verb **allude** and the noun **allusion**.

alluvium NOUN (*plural* **alluvia**) earth, sand, etc brought down and left by flowing rivers > **alluvial** ADJECTIVE

all ways ADVERB in every way possible

> Do not use this as an alternative spelling for 'always'.

ally VERB (**allies, allying, allied**) to join with someone else, especially by an alliance or treaty: *a small organization seeking to ally itself with larger ones* ▸NOUN (*plural* **allies**) someone in alliance with another; a friend

almanac NOUN a calendar for any year, with information about the phases of the moon etc

almighty ADJECTIVE having a lot of power

almond (*pronounced* **ah**-mond) NOUN a flat, tear-shaped nut, the kernel of the fruit of the almond tree

almost ADVERB very nearly but not quite: *almost five years old/almost home*

alms (*pronounced* ahmz) *plural* NOUN gifts to the poor

aloft ADVERB **1** on high **2** upward

alone ADJECTIVE not accompanied by others, solitary: *alone in the house* ▸ADVERB **1** only, without anything else: *That alone is bad enough* **2** not accompanied by others: *Do you live alone?* **leave alone** to leave undisturbed

along PREPOSITION **1** by the side of or near: *Flowers grew along the roadside* **2** over the length of: *walk along the road* ▸ADVERB onward: *Come along!* **along with** together with

alongside PREPOSITION beside ▸ADVERB near a ship's side

aloof ADJECTIVE & ADVERB **1** at

A B C D E F G H I J K L M N O P Q R S T U V W X Y Z

a distance, apart **2** showing no interest in others

aloud ADVERB so as to be heard

alpha NOUN the first letter of the Greek alphabet

alphabet NOUN the letters of a language given in a fixed order
ⓘ From *alpha* and *beta*, the first two letters of the Greek alphabet

alphabetical *or* **alphabetic** ADJECTIVE in the order of the letters of the alphabet

alpha particle NOUN, *physics* a positively charged particle consisting of two protons and two neutrons, identical to a helium nucleus

alpine ADJECTIVE of the Alps or other high mountains

alps PLURAL NOUN high mountains **the Alps** a mountain range in Switzerland and neighbouring countries

already ADVERB **1** before this or that time: *I've already done that* **2** now, before the expected time: *You can't have finished already*

> If you write 'all ready' as two words, it has the very different meaning of 'totally ready': *Are you all ready for the big day?*

Alsatian NOUN a German shepherd dog

also ADVERB in addition, besides, too: *I also need to buy milk*

altar NOUN **1** a raised place for offerings to a god **2** in Christian churches, the communion table

alter VERB to change > **alteration** NOUN

altercation NOUN an argument or quarrel

alter ego NOUN **1** someone's alternative character **2** a trusted friend, a confidant(e)

alternate VERB (*pronounced* **ol**-ter-neit) of two things: to do or happen in turn: *Meetings alternate between my house and hers* ▶ ADJECTIVE (*pronounced* ol-**tern**-at) **1** happening etc in turns **2** every other; one out of two: *on alternate days* > **alternation** NOUN

> Do not confuse: **alternate** and **alternative**. To **alternate** is to move between two things. **Alternate** is the adjective from this verb: *We visit on alternate days*.

alternating current NOUN (*abbrev* **AC**) an electric current that reverses its direction at regular intervals (*compare with*: **direct current**)

alternative ADJECTIVE offering a second possibility: *an alternative solution* ▶ NOUN a second possibility, a different course of action: *I had no alternative but to agree*

> Do not confuse with: **alternate**

alternative energy NOUN energy derived from sources other than nuclear power or the burning of fossil fuels, eg solar energy

alternator NOUN a generator producing alternating current

although CONJUNCTION though, in spite of the fact that

altimeter (*pronounced* al-**tim**-i-ter *or* **al**-ti-mee-ter) NOUN an instrument for measuring height above sea level

altitude NOUN height above sea level

alto NOUN (*plural* **altos**), *music* **1** the male singing voice of the highest pitch **2** the female voice of lowest pitch

> ⓘ An alternative term for the female *alto* voice is **contralto**

altogether ADVERB **1** considering everything, in all: *There were 20 of us altogether* **2** completely: *not altogether satisfied*

> If you write 'all together' as two words, it has the very different meaning of 'together in a group':*It's great to be all together for Christmas*.

altruism NOUN unselfish concern for the good of others > **altruistic** ADJECTIVE

aluminium (*pronounced* al-yuw-**min**-i-*um*) *or US* **aluminum** (*pronounced a*-**loo**-min-*um*) NOUN, *chemistry* an element, a very light metal

always ADVERB **1** for ever: *He'll always remember this day* **2** every time: *She always gets it wrong*

> If you write 'all ways' as two words, it has the very different meaning of 'in every way possible': *I've tried all ways to tell her, but she just won't listen* .

Alzheimer's disease (*pronounced* **alts**-hai-merz) NOUN an illness affecting the brain and causing dementia in middle-aged and elderly people

AM ABBREVIATION amplitude modulation (*compare with*: (**FM**)

am[1] ABBREVIATION before noon (from Latin *ante meridiem*)

am[2] *see* **be**

amalgam NOUN a mixture (especially of metals)

amalgamate VERB **1** to join together, combine: *the company recently amalgamated with a large French firm* **2** to mix > **amalgamation** NOUN

amass VERB to collect in large quantities: *amass a lot of furniture over the years*

amateur NOUN someone who takes part in a sport, activity, etc because they enjoy it and without being paid for doing it (*contrasted with*: **professional**)

amateurish ADJECTIVE not done properly; not skilful

amaze VERB to surprise greatly > **amazed** ADJECTIVE > **amazement** NOUN > **amazing** ADJECTIVE > **amazingly** ADVERB

ambassador NOUN **1** an official sent to another country to look after the interests of their country and government **2** a representative

amber NOUN a hard yellowish fossil resin used in making jewellery ▸ ADJECTIVE **1** made of amber **2** of the colour of amber

ambi- PREFIX **1** both, on both sides **2** round

> ⓘ Comes from Latin *ambo* meaning 'both'

ambidextrous ADJECTIVE able to use both hands with equal skill

a b c d e f g h i j k l m n o p q r s t u v w x y z

ambience NOUN environment, atmosphere

ambient ADJECTIVE: **ambient temperature** the temperature of the air in an enclosed space, eg a room

ambiguity NOUN (*plural* **ambiguities**) uncertainty in meaning

ambiguous ADJECTIVE **1** having two possible meanings **2** not clear

🛈 Comes from Latin *ambiguus* meaning 'changing from one to another'

> Do not confuse with: **ambivalent**

ambition NOUN the desire for success, power, fame, etc > **ambitious** ADJECTIVE > **ambitiously** ADVERB

ambivalent ADJECTIVE having two contrasting feelings or attitudes towards something > **ambivalence** NOUN

🛈 Comes from the prefix *ambi-*, and Latin *valens* meaning 'strong'

> Do not confuse with: **ambiguous**

amble VERB to walk in an unhurried, relaxed way ▸ NOUN an unhurried walk

ambrosia NOUN the mythological food of the Greek gods, which gave eternal youth and beauty

ambulance NOUN a vehicle for carrying people who are ill or injured

ambush NOUN (*plural* **ambushes**) **1** the act of lying hidden in order to make a surprise attack **2** the people hidden in this way **3** the place where they hide ▸ VERB to lie in wait for someone and attack them suddenly

amenable (*pronounced a*-**meen**-*a*-bl) ADJECTIVE open to advice or suggestion > **amenability** NOUN > **amenably** ADVERB

amend VERB **1** to correct; improve (a text or statement) by making small additions **2** to alter (a text or statement) slightly by making small additions **make amends** to make up for having done wrong

amendment NOUN a change, often in something written: *an amendment to the constitution*

amenity (*pronounced a*-**meen**-i-ti *or* a-**men**-i-ti) NOUN (*plural* **amenities**) a pleasant or convenient feature of a place etc

amethyst NOUN a precious stone of a bluish-violet colour

amiable ADJECTIVE likeable; friendly > **amiability** NOUN > **amiably** ADVERB

amicable ADJECTIVE friendly > **amicably** ADVERB

amid *or* **amidst** PREPOSITION in the middle of, surrounded by: *staying calm amidst all the confusion*

🛈 Comes from Old English *on middan* meaning 'in middle'

> Use 'amid' or 'amidst' when the thing or things doing the surrounding cannot be counted: *amidst the confusion/sitting amidst the wild poppies*. Use 'among' or 'amongst' when the thing or things can be counted: *celebrate your birthday among friends*

amino acid NOUN, *chemistry* a compound which contains the $-NH_2$ group, and joins with others to form proteins

amiss ADVERB wrongly; badly

ammeter NOUN a device for measuring electrical current

ammonia NOUN a strong-smelling gas made of hydrogen and nitrogen

ammunition NOUN gunpowder, shot, bullets, bombs, etc

amnesia NOUN loss of memory

amnesiac NOUN & ADJECTIVE (someone) suffering from amnesia

amnesty NOUN (*plural* **amnesties**) a general pardon of wrongdoers

amoeba (*pronounced* *a*-**mee**-b*a*) NOUN (*plural* **amoebas** *or* **amoebae** – *pronounced* *a*-**mee**-bi or *a*-**mee**-bai) a very simple form of animal life found in ponds *etc*

amok *or* **amuck** ADVERB: **run amok** to go mad and do a lot of damage, run riot

[i] From a Malay word meaning 'fighting frenziedly'

among *or* **amongst** PREPOSITION **1** surrounded by or in the middle of: *among friends* **2** giving each a part: *Divide it amongst yourselves* **3** in the group of: *Among all her novels, this is the best*

[i] Comes from Old English *on-gemang* meaning 'in mixture or crowd'

> Use 'among' or 'amongst' when the thing or things doing the surrounding can be counted. Use 'amid' or 'amidst' when the thing or things cannot be counted

amoral (*pronounced* ei-**mo**-r*a*l) ADJECTIVE incapable of distinguishing between right and wrong > **amorality** NOUN

[i] Comes from Greek prefix *a-* meaning 'the opposite of', and Latin *moralis* meaning 'moral'

> Do not confuse with: **immoral**. An **amoral** person behaves badly because they do not understand the difference between right and wrong. An **immoral** person behaves badly in the full knowledge that what they are doing is wrong.

amorous ADJECTIVE loving; ready or inclined to love or make love

amount NOUN **1** total, sum **2** a quantity **amount to** to add up to

amp NOUN **1** an ampere **2** *informal* an amplifier

ampere NOUN (symbol **A**) the standard unit of electric current

ampersand NOUN the character (&) representing *and*

[i] From the phrase *and per se and*, 'and by itself and'

amphi- PREFIX **1** both; on both sides or ends **2** around

[i] Comes from Greek *amphi* meaning 'on both sides' or 'around'

amphibian NOUN **1** an animal, eg a frog, toad or newt, that lives partly on land and returns to water to lay eggs **2** a vehicle for use on land and in water ▸ ADJECTIVE living on land and water > **amphibious** ADJECTIVE

amphitheatre NOUN a theatre with seats surrounding a central arena

ample ADJECTIVE **1** plenty (of) **2** large enough > **amply** ADVERB

amplifier NOUN an electrical device for increasing loudness

amplify VERB (**amplifies, amplifying, amplified**) **1** to make louder **2** to make more pronounced > **amplification** NOUN

amplitude NOUN largeness

amputate VERB to cut off (especially a human limb) > **amputation** NOUN

amputee NOUN someone who has had a limb amputated

amrit NOUN, *Sikhism* **1** a Sikh ceremonial drink **2** the initiation ceremony in which amrit is drunk

amuck *another spelling* of **amok**

amuse VERB **1** to make someone laugh **2** to make someone enjoy himself or herself > **amusement** NOUN

amusing ADJECTIVE **1** funny **2** enjoyable

an *see* **a**

an- *or* **a-** PREFIX without, not, opposite to: *anaerobic/anodyne* (= without pain)

ⓘ Comes from Greek *a-* meaning 'without' or 'not'

ana- *or* **an-** PREFIX up, back, again: *anabolic/aneurism*

ⓘ Comes from Greek prefix *ana-* with the same meaning

anabolic steroids PLURAL NOUN synthetic male sex hormones used to increase the build-up of body tissue, especially muscle

anachronism (*pronounced a-***nak**-r*o*-nizm) NOUN the mistake of referring to, showing, etc something which did not exist or was not yet invented at the time spoken about or depicted > **anachronistic** ADJECTIVE

anaconda NOUN a large South American water snake

anaemia *or US* **anemia** (*both pronounced a-***nee**-mi-*a*) NOUN, *medicine* a shortage of red cells in the blood > **anaemic** *or US* **anemic** (*both pronounced a-***nee**-mik) ADJECTIVE

anaesthesia *or US* **anesthesia** (*both pronounced* an-*e*s-**thee**-zi-*a*) NOUN, *medicine* loss of feeling or sensation > **anaesthetic** *or US* **anesthetic** (*both pronounced* an-*e*s-**thet**-ik) NOUN

anaesthetist (*pronounced a*n-**ees**-th*e*-tist) *or US* **anesthetist** (*pronounced* an-**es**-th*e*-tist) NOUN, *medicine* a doctor trained to administer anaesthetics > **anaesthetize** *or* **anaesthetise** *or US* **anesthetize** VERB

anagram NOUN a word or sentence formed by reordering the letters of another word or sentence, eg *veil* is an anagram of *evil*

anal ADJECTIVE of the anus

analogous ADJECTIVE similar, alike in some way

analogue *or US* **analog** ADJECTIVE (*compare with*: **digital**) of a device: with divisions and pointers on a dial showing information

analogy NOUN (*plural* **analogies**) a likeness; resemblance in certain ways

analyse *or US* **analyze** VERB **1** to break down, separate into parts **2** to examine in detail

analysis NOUN (*plural* **analyses**) **1** a breaking up of a thing into its parts **2** a detailed examination of something

analyst NOUN **1** someone who analyses **2** a psychiatrist or psychologist

anarchic *or* **anarchical** ADJECTIVE **1** refusing to obey any rules **2** in a state of disorder or confusion

anarchist NOUN someone who believes in anarchy (meaning 1)

anarchy NOUN **1** lack or absence of government **2** disorder or confusion

anatomist NOUN a person who specializes in the study of the human body

anatomy NOUN (*plural* **anatomies**) the study of the parts of the body

ancestor NOUN a person from whom someone is descended by birth; a forefather > **ancestral** ADJECTIVE

ancestry NOUN (*plural* **ancestries**) a line of ancestors

anchor NOUN a heavy piece of iron, with hooked ends, for holding a ship fast to the bed of the sea etc ▶VERB **1** to fix by anchor **2** to let down the anchor **weigh anchor** to pull up the anchor

anchorage NOUN a place where a ship can anchor

anchorman *or* **anchorwoman** NOUN the main presenter of a television news programme etc

anchovy NOUN (*plural* **anchovies**) a type of small fish of the herring family with a very strong flavour

ancient ADJECTIVE **1** very old **2** of times long past

ancient monument NOUN a building, grave, etc remaining from ancient times

ancillary ADJECTIVE serving or supporting something more important

and CONJUNCTION **1** used to join two statements, pieces of information, etc: *black and white film/Add milk and stir* **2** in addition to: *2 and 2 make 4*

andro- *or* **andr-** PREFIX having to do with men, male

ⓘ Comes from Greek *aner, andros* meaning 'man' or 'male'

android NOUN a robot in human form

anecdote NOUN a short, interesting or amusing story, usually true > **anecdotal** ADJECTIVE

anemo- PREFIX of the wind

ⓘ Comes from Greek *anemos* meaning 'wind'

anemone (*pronounced a-***nem***-o-*ni) NOUN a type of woodland or garden flower

aneroid barometer NOUN a barometer which measures air pressure without the use of mercury

aneurism (*pronounced* **an***-yoo-*rizm) NOUN **1** *medicine* a swelling in the wall of an artery **2** abnormal enlargement

angel NOUN **1** a messenger or attendant of God or Allah **2** a very good or beautiful person > **angelic** ADJECTIVE as perfectly sweet and good as an angel

anger NOUN a bitter feeling against someone; annoyance, rage ▶VERB to make angry

a b c d e f g h i j k l m n o p q r s t u v w x y z

A B C D E F G H I J K L M N O P Q R S T U V W X Y Z

angina (*pronounced* an-**jai**-n*a*) NOUN, *medicine* a form of heart disease causing acute chest pains

angle NOUN **1** the V-shape made by two lines meeting at a point **2** a corner **3** a point of view ▸ VERB to try to get by hints etc: *angling for a job*

angler NOUN someone who fishes with a rod and line

Anglican ADJECTIVE of the Church of England ▸ NOUN a member of the Church of England

anglicize *or* **anglicise** VERB **1** to turn into the English language **2** to make English in character > **anglicization** NOUN

angling NOUN the sport of fishing with a rod and line

Anglo-Saxon ADJECTIVE & NOUN **1** (of) the people of England before the Norman Conquest **2** (of) their language

angry ADJECTIVE (**angrier, angriest**) feeling or showing anger > **angrily** ADVERB

anguish NOUN very great pain or distress > **anguished** ADJECTIVE

angular ADJECTIVE **1** having angles **2** thin, bony > **angularity** NOUN

animal NOUN **1** a living being which can feel and move of its own accord **2** an animal other than a human ▸ ADJECTIVE of or like an animal

animate VERB (*pronounced* **an**-im-eit) **1** to give life to **2** to make lively ▸ ADJECTIVE (*pronounced* **an**-im-*a*t) living > **animated** ADJECTIVE

animation NOUN **1** liveliness **2** *cinema* a film made from a series of drawings that give the illusion of movement when shown in sequence

animator NOUN, *cinema* an artist who works in animation

animosity NOUN (*plural* **animosities**) bitter hatred, enmity

aniseed NOUN a seed with a flavour like that of liquorice

ankle NOUN the joint connecting the foot and leg

annals PLURAL NOUN yearly historical accounts of events

annex VERB **1** to take possession of (land) **2** to add, attach ▸ NOUN (*also spelled*: **annexe**) a building added to another > **annexation** NOUN

annihilate (*pronounced a*-**nai**-*i*-leit) VERB to destroy completely > **annihilation** NOUN

anniversary NOUN (*plural* **anniversaries**) the day of each year when a particular event is remembered

annotate VERB **1** to make notes upon **2** to add notes or explanation to > **annotation** NOUN

announce VERB to make publicly known > **announcement** NOUN

announcer NOUN someone who announces programmes on TV etc, or reads the news

annoy VERB to make rather angry; irritate > **annoyance** NOUN

annual ADJECTIVE yearly ▸ NOUN **1** a plant that lives for only one year (*compare with*: **biennial**, **perennial**) **2** a book published yearly

annually ADVERB every year

annuity NOUN (*plural* **annuities**) a yearly payment made for a certain period or for life

annul VERB (**annulling, annulled**) **1** to put an end to **2** to declare no longer valid > **annulment** NOUN

anodyne ADJECTIVE **1** soothing, relieving pain **2** bland and harmless: *a fairly anodyne comment*

anoint VERB to smear with ointment or oil

anomaly NOUN (*plural* **anomalies**) something unusual, not according to a rule > **anomalous** ADJECTIVE

anon ABBREVIATION anonymous

anonymous ADJECTIVE without the name of the author, giver, etc being known or given > **anonymously** ADVERB

anorak NOUN a hooded waterproof jacket

anorexia NOUN, *medicine* an emotional illness causing the sufferer to refuse food and become sometimes dangerously thin (*also called*: **anorexia nervosa**) > **anorexic** ADJECTIVE

another ADJECTIVE **1** a different (thing or person): *moving to another job* **2** one more of the same kind: *Have another biscuit* ▶PRONOUN an additional thing of the same kind: *Do you want another?*

answer VERB **1** to speak, write, etc in return or reply **2** to find the result or solution (of a sum, problem, etc) ▶NOUN something said, written, etc in return or reply **answer back** to give a cheeky or aggressive answer to someone in authority **answer for 1** to be responsible for **2** to suffer for, be punished for

answerable ADJECTIVE **1** responsible: *answerable for her actions* **2** able to be answered

ant NOUN a very small insect which lives in organized colonies **have ants in your pants** to be impatient or restless

antagonism NOUN hostility, opposition, enmity > **antagonist** NOUN > **antagonistic** ADJECTIVE

antagonize *or* **antagonise** VERB to make an enemy of, cause dislike

Antarctic ADJECTIVE of the South Pole or regions round it

ante- PREFIX before

ⓘ Comes from Latin *ante* meaning 'before'

anteater NOUN an American animal with a long snout which feeds on ants and termites

antecedent (*pronounced* ant-i-**see**-dent) ADJECTIVE going before in time ▶NOUN **1** someone who lived at an earlier time; an ancestor **2** (**antecedents**) previous conduct, history, etc

antelope NOUN a graceful, swift-running animal like a deer

antenatal ADJECTIVE **1** before birth **2** relating to pregnancy: *antenatal clinic*

antenna NOUN **1** (*plural* **antennae** – *pronounced* an-**ten**-ee) an insect's feeler **2** (*plural* **antennas**) an aerial

anteroom NOUN a room leading into a large room

anthem NOUN **1** a piece of music for a church choir **2** any song of praise

ant-hill NOUN an earth mound built by ants as a nest

antho- PREFIX of or relating to

A B C D E F G H I J K L M N O P Q R S T U V W X Y Z

flowers: *anthology/anthomania* (= a craze for flowers)

ⓘ Comes from Greek *anthos* meaning 'flower'

anthology NOUN (*plural* **anthologies**) a collection of specially chosen poems, stories, etc

ⓘ Comes from Greek *anthos* meaning 'flower', and *logia* meaning 'collection'

anthracite NOUN coal that burns with a hot, smokeless flame

anthrax NOUN, *medicine* an infectious disease of cattle, sheep, etc, sometimes transferred to humans

anthropo- *or* **anthrop-** PREFIX of or relating to humans

ⓘ Comes from Greek *anthropos* meaning 'human being'

anthropoid ADJECTIVE of apes: resembling humans

anthropology NOUN the study of mankind > **anthropological** ADJECTIVE > **anthropologist** NOUN

anti- PREFIX against, opposite: *anti-terrorist*

ⓘ Comes from Greek *anti* meaning 'against'

antibiotic NOUN, *medicine* a medicine taken to kill bacteria that cause disease

antibody NOUN (*plural* **antibodies**) a substance produced in the human body to fight bacteria etc

anticipate VERB **1** to look forward to, expect **2** to see or know in advance **3** to act before (someone or something) > **anticipation** NOUN > **anticipatory** ADJECTIVE

anticlimax NOUN (*plural* **anticlimaxes**) a dull or disappointing ending

anticlockwise ADJECTIVE & ADVERB in the opposite direction to the hands of a clock

antics PLURAL NOUN tricks, odd or amusing actions

antidote NOUN something given to act against the effect of poison

antifreeze NOUN a chemical with a low freezing point, added to a car radiator to prevent freezing

antigen NOUN a substance, eg a bacterium or virus, that stimulates the production of antibodies

antihistamine NOUN, *medicine* a medicine used to treat an allergy

antipathy NOUN (*plural* **antipathies**) extreme dislike

antiperspirant NOUN a substance applied to the body to reduce sweating

antipodes (*pronounced* an-**tip**-*o*d-eez) PLURAL NOUN places on the earth's surface exactly opposite each other, especially Australia and New Zealand in relation to Europe > **antipodean** ADJECTIVE

antiquarian NOUN a dealer in antiques or rare books

antiquated ADJECTIVE grown old, or out of fashion

antique NOUN an old, interesting or valuable object from earlier times ▶ ADJECTIVE **1** old, from earlier times **2** old-fashioned

antiquity NOUN (*plural* **antiquities**) **1** ancient times, especially those of the Greeks and Romans **2** great age **3** (**antiquities**) objects from earlier times

antiseptic ADJECTIVE germ-destroying ▸ NOUN a chemical etc which destroys germs

antisocial ADJECTIVE **1** not fitting in with other people or harmful to them **2** disliking the company of other people

antithesis NOUN (*plural* **antitheses** – *pronounced* an-**ti**-the-seez) the exact opposite: *the antithesis of good taste* > **antithetical** ADJECTIVE

antler NOUN the horn of a deer

antonym NOUN a word which means the opposite of another, eg 'big' and 'small', or 'brave' and 'cowardly'

anus (*pronounced* **ei**-n*u*s) NOUN, *anatomy* the lower opening of the bowel through which faeces pass

anvil NOUN a metal block on which blacksmiths hammer metal into shape

anxiety NOUN (*plural* **anxieties**) worry about what may happen

anxious ADJECTIVE **1** worried **2** full of worry or uncertainty **3** eager, keen: *anxious to please* > **anxiously** ADVERB

any ADJECTIVE **1** some: *Is there any milk?* **2** every, no matter which: *Any day will suit me* ▸ PRONOUN some: *There aren't any left* ▸ ADVERB at all: *I can't work any faster* **at any rate** in any case, whatever happens

anybody PRONOUN any person

anyhow ADVERB **1** in any case: *I think I'll go anyhow* **2** carelessly: *scattered anyhow over the floor*

anyone PRONOUN any person

anything PRONOUN something of any kind

anyway ADVERB at any rate

anywhere ADVERB in any place

apart ADVERB **1** in or into pieces: *came apart in my hands* **2** to or on one side: *set apart for special occasions* **3** in opposite directions **apart from 1** separate, or separately, from **2** except for: *Who else knows apart from us?*

apartheid (*pronounced* a-**paht**-heit *or* a-**paht**-hait) NOUN the political policy of keeping people of different races apart, especially as formerly practised in South Africa

apartment NOUN **1** a room in a house **2** *US* a flat

apathy NOUN lack of feeling or interest > **apathetic** ADJECTIVE

ape NOUN a member of a group of animals related to monkeys, but larger, tailless and walking upright ▸ VERB to imitate

aperitif (*pronounced a*-pe-r*i*-**teef**) NOUN a drink taken before a meal

aperture NOUN an opening, a hole

apex NOUN (*plural* **apexes** *or* **apices** – *pronounced* **ei**-pi-seez) the highest point

aphid (*pronounced* **ei**-fid) NOUN a small insect which feeds on plants

apiarist (*pronounced* **ei**-pi-*a*-rist) NOUN someone who keeps or studies bees

apiary (*pronounced* **ei**-pi-*a*-ri) NOUN (*plural* **apiaries**) a place where bees are kept

apiece ADVERB to or for each one: *three chocolates apiece*

aplomb NOUN self-confidence

a b c d e f g h i j k l m n o p q r s t u v w x y z

A B C D E F G H I J K L M N O P Q R S T U V W X Y Z

apo- *or* **ap-** PREFIX from, off, away, quite
ⓘ Comes from Greek prefix *apo-* with the same meaning

apocalypse NOUN any revelation of the future, especially future destruction > **apocalyptic** ADJECTIVE

apocryphal (*pronounced a-***pok***-rif-al*) ADJECTIVE unlikely to be true

apologetic ADJECTIVE expressing regret > **apologetically** ADVERB

apologize *or* **apologise** VERB to express regret, say you are sorry

apology NOUN (*plural* **apologies**) an expression of regret for having done wrong

apoplexy NOUN sudden loss of ability to feel, move, etc; a stroke > **apoplectic** ADJECTIVE

apostle NOUN a religious preacher, especially one of the disciples of Christ

apostrophe NOUN **1** a mark (') indicating possession: *the minister's cat* **2** the same mark indicating that a letter etc has been missed out, eg *isn't* for *is not*

appal VERB (**appalling, appalled**) to horrify, shock

appalling ADJECTIVE shocking

apparatus NOUN (*plural* **apparatuses** *or* **apparatus**) **1** an instrument or machine **2** instruments, tools or material required for a piece of work

apparel NOUN a formal or literary word for clothing

apparent ADJECTIVE easily seen, evident > **apparently** ADVERB it appears that: *'But I thought they were going out together.' 'Apparently not.'*

apparition NOUN **1** something remarkable which appears suddenly **2** a ghost

appeal VERB **1** to ask earnestly (for help etc): *appeal to the public for information* **2** *law* to take a case that has been lost to a higher court **3** (**appeal to**) to be attractive to someone ▸NOUN **1** a request for help **2** *law* the taking of a case that has been lost to a higher court

appealing ADJECTIVE arousing liking or sympathy

appear VERB **1** to come into view **2** to arrive **3** to seem > **appearance** NOUN

appease VERB to soothe or satisfy, especially by giving what was asked for: *nothing would appease his anger*

appendicitis NOUN, *medicine* inflammation of the appendix

appendix NOUN (*plural* **appendices** *or* **appendixes**) **1** a part added at the end of a book or document containing extra information, notes, etc **2** *anatomy* a small worm-shaped part of the bowels

appertain VERB (**appertain to**), *formal* **1** to belong to **2** to be relevant to

appetite NOUN **1** desire for food **2** taste or enthusiasm (for): *no appetite for violence*

appetizer *or* **appetiser** NOUN a snack taken before a main meal

appetizing *or* **appetising** ADJECTIVE tempting to the appetite

applaud VERB **1** to show that you approve of something by clapping your hands **2** to express strong approval of and admiration for: *I applaud the Prime Minister's decision*

applause NOUN a show of approval by clapping

apple NOUN a round firm fruit, usually red or green **the apple of someone's eye** a person or thing that someone loves very much

appliance NOUN a tool, instrument, machine, etc

applicable (*pronounced* **ap**-li-k*a*-bl *or a*p-**li**-k*a*-bl) ADJECTIVE **1** able to be applied **2** suitable, relevant

applicant NOUN someone who applies or asks

application NOUN **1** the act of applying **2** something applied, eg an ointment **3** a formal request, usually on paper **4** hard work, close attention **5** *computing* (*full form*: **application program**) a computer program which performs a special function, such as word processing, Web browsing, spreadsheet, image editing, etc (*compare with*: **operating system**)

applicator NOUN a tool or device for applying something

applied ADJECTIVE used practically and not just in theory: *applied science*

apply VERB (**applies, applying, applied**) **1** to put on (an ointment etc) **2** to use: *Apply these rules in each case* **3** to ask formally (for): *apply for a job* **4** to be suitable or relevant **apply to** to have an effect on **apply yourself** to work hard

appoint VERB **1** to fix (a date etc) **2** to place in a job: *She was appointed manager* > **appointed** ADJECTIVE (meaning 1): *fail to arrive at the appointed time*

appointment NOUN **1** the act of appointing **2** a job, a post **3** an arrangement to meet someone

apportion VERB to divide in fair shares: *The blame must be apportioned among several different people*

apposite (*pronounced* **ap**-*o*-zit) ADJECTIVE suitable, appropriate

appraise VERB to estimate the value or quality of: *appraise someone's work* > **appraisal** NOUN

appreciable ADJECTIVE noticeable, considerable

appreciate VERB **1** to see or understand the good points, beauties, etc of: *appreciate art* **2** to understand: *I appreciate your point* **3** to rise in value > **appreciation** NOUN

apprehend VERB **1** to arrest: *The escaped prisoner was apprehended early today* **2** *formal* to understand

apprehension NOUN **1** arrest **2** fear or nervousness **3** *formal* understanding

apprehensive ADJECTIVE afraid

apprentice NOUN someone who is learning a trade > **apprenticeship** NOUN

approach VERB **1** to come near **2** to be nearly equal to **3** to speak to in order to ask for something ▶ NOUN (*plural* **approaches**) **1** a coming near to **2** a way leading to a place

approachable ADJECTIVE **1** able

A B C D E F G H I J K L M N O P Q R S T U V W X Y Z

to be reached **2** easy to speak to, friendly

appropriate ADJECTIVE (*pronounced a*-**proh**-pri-*a*t) suitable, fitting ▶ VERB (*pronounced a*-**proh**-pri-eit) **1** to take possession of: *She seems to have appropriated certain items of my clothing* **2** to set (money etc) apart for a purpose: *Funds must be appropriated for this work* > **appropriately** ADVERB: *the appropriately named 'Wall of Death'* > **appropriation** NOUN

> ⓘ 'to appropriate' (meaning 1) is often used as a euphemism for 'to steal'

approval NOUN **1** permission **2** satisfaction, favourable judgement **on approval** on trial, for return to a shop if not bought

approve VERB **1** to agree to, permit **2** to think well (of)

approximate ADJECTIVE (*pronounced a*p-**rok**-sim-*a*t) more or less accurate ▶ VERB (*pronounced a*p-**rok**-sim-eit) **approximate to** to be or come near to > **approximately** ADVERB

approximation NOUN a rough estimate

apricot (*pronounced* **ei**-pri-kot) NOUN an orange-coloured fruit like a small peach

April NOUN the fourth month of the year

🛈 From a Latin word meaning 'open', because spring flowers start to open their buds around April

apron NOUN **1** a garment worn to protect the front of the clothes **2** a hard surface for aircraft to stand on

apron stage NOUN the part of the stage in front of the curtains in a theatre

apropos (*pronounced* a-pro-**poh**) ADVERB: **apropos of** in connection with, concerning

apse NOUN a rounded domed section, especially at the east end of a church

apt ADJECTIVE **1** likely (to): *apt to change his mind* **2** suitable, fitting > **aptly** ADVERB

aptitude NOUN talent, ability

aptness NOUN suitability

aqua- PREFIX of or relating to water

🛈 Comes from Latin *aqua* meaning 'water'

aqualung NOUN a breathing apparatus worn by divers

aquamarine NOUN **1** a type of bluish-green precious stone **2** a bluish-green colour ▶ ADJECTIVE bluish-green

aquarium NOUN (*plural* **aquaria** *or* **aquariums**) a tank or tanks for keeping fish or water animals

aquatic ADJECTIVE living, growing or taking place in water

aqueduct NOUN a bridge for taking a canal etc across a valley

aqueous (*pronounced* **ei**-kwi-*u*s) ADJECTIVE **1** relating to water **2** dissolved in water

aquiline ADJECTIVE **1** like an eagle **2** of a nose: curved or hooked

arable ADJECTIVE of land: used for growing crops

arbiter NOUN **1** a judge, an umpire; someone chosen by opposing parties to decide between them **2** someone who sets a standard or has influence: *arbiter of good taste*

arbitrary ADJECTIVE **1** fixed according to opinion, not objective rules **2** occurring haphazardly > **arbitrarily** ADVERB

arbitrate VERB to act as a judge between people or their claims etc: *arbitrate between the different parties/It falls to me to arbitrate this case* > **arbitration** NOUN > **arbitrator** NOUN

arboreal (*pronounced* ah-**bawr**-ri-*a*l) ADJECTIVE of trees; living in trees

arc NOUN part of a curve or of the circumference of a circle, something that appears curved in shape

arcade NOUN a covered walk, especially one with shops on both sides

arch NOUN (*plural* **arches**) the curved part above people's heads in a gateway or the curved support for a bridge, roof, etc ▶ADJECTIVE mischievous, roguish ▶VERB to raise or curve in the shape of an arch

arch- PREFIX chief, main: *arch-enemy*

[i] Comes from Greek *archos* meaning 'chief'

> ⓘ **Arch-** is usually pronounced *ahch* (as in 'March'), but in *archangel* it is pronounced *ahk* (like 'ark').

-arch (*pronounced* ahrk) SUFFIX chief, ruler: *monarch/matriarch*

[i] Comes from Greek *arche* meaning 'rule'

archaeo- PREFIX of or relating to ancient or primitive things

[i] Comes from Greek *archaios* meaning 'ancient'

archaeology NOUN the study of the people of earlier times from the remains of their buildings etc > **archaeological** ADJECTIVE > **archaeologist** NOUN

archaic (*pronounced* ahrk-**ei**-ik) ADJECTIVE no longer used, old-fashioned

archaism (*pronounced* **ahrk**-ei-izm) NOUN an old-fashioned word etc

archangel NOUN a chief angel

archbishop NOUN a chief bishop

archdeacon NOUN a clergyman next in rank below a bishop

archduke NOUN, *history* the title of the ruling princes of Austria

archer NOUN someone who shoots arrows from a bow

archery NOUN the sport of shooting with a bow and arrows

archetype (*pronounced* **ahrk**-i-taip) NOUN the original pattern or model from which copies are made > **archetypal** ADJECTIVE

archipelago (*pronounced* ahrk-i-**pe**-l*a*-goh) NOUN (*plural* **archipelagoes** *or* **archipelagos**) a group of small islands

[i] From an ancient Greek term meaning 'chief sea', referring to the Aegean Sea, which contains many small islands

architect NOUN someone who plans and designs buildings

architecture NOUN **1** the study or profession of designing and constructing buildings **2** the style of

A B C D E F G H I J K L M N O P Q R S T U V W X Y Z

a building > **architectural** ADJECTIVE

archive NOUN *computing* a place on a computer for storing files that are rarely used

archives PLURAL NOUN **1** historical papers, written records, etc **2** a building etc in which these are kept

archway NOUN a passage or road beneath an arch

-archy SUFFIX forms nouns describing different types of government: *monarchy/oligarchy*

ⓘ Comes from Greek *arche* meaning 'rule'

Arctic *or* **arctic** ADJECTIVE **1** (*usually* **Arctic**) of the district round the North Pole **2** (*usually* **arctic**) very cold

ardent ADJECTIVE eager, passionate > **ardently** ADVERB > **ardour** NOUN

arduous ADJECTIVE difficult, needing a lot of work or effort: *an arduous climb to the top*

are *see* **be**

area NOUN **1** the extent of a surface measured in square metres etc **2** a region, a piece of land or ground

arena NOUN **1** any place for a public contest, show, etc **2** *history* the centre of an amphitheatre etc where gladiators fought

ⓘ From a Latin word meaning 'sand', after the sand-covered arenas in which Roman gladiators fought

arguable ADJECTIVE that can be argued as being true

arguably ADVERB in certain people's opinion (although this opinion could be disagreed with): *This is arguably the best Scottish film of the decade*

argue VERB **1** to quarrel in words **2** to try to prove by giving reasons (that) **3** (**argue for** *or* **against something**) to give reasons for or against something as a way of persuading people

argument NOUN **1** a heated discussion, quarrel **2** reasoning (for or against something)

argumentative ADJECTIVE fond of arguing

aria NOUN a song for a solo voice in an opera

arid ADJECTIVE **1** dry **2** of climate: hot and dry > **aridity** *or* **aridness** NOUN

arise VERB (**arising, arose, arisen**) **1** to rise up **2** to come into being

aristocracy NOUN people of the nobility and upper class

aristocrat NOUN a member of the aristocracy

aristocratic ADJECTIVE of the aristocracy

arithmetic NOUN a way of counting and calculating by using numbers > **arithmetical** ADJECTIVE

ark NOUN (**the Ark**) the covered boat used by Noah in the story of the Flood in the Bible and the Koran

arm NOUN **1** the part of the body between the shoulder and the hand **2** anything jutting out like this **3** (**arms**) weapons ▸ VERB to equip with weapons **chance your arm** to say or do something which, though a bit risky, could possibly get you what you want

armada NOUN a fleet of armed ships

armadillo NOUN (*plural* **armadillos**) a small American

animal whose body is protected by bony plates
[1] From a Spanish word meaning 'armed man', because of the animal's weapon-like plates

armageddon NOUN a final battle or devastation, an apocalypse

armaments PLURAL NOUN equipment for war, especially the guns of a ship, tank, etc

armchair NOUN a comfortable chair with arms at each side

armed ADJECTIVE carrying a weapon, now especially a gun

armistice NOUN a halt in fighting during war, a truce

armour NOUN, *history* a protective suit of metal worn by knights

armoured ADJECTIVE of a vehicle: protected by metal plates

armoury NOUN (*plural* **armouries**) a store for military arms

armpit NOUN the hollow under the arm at the shoulder

army NOUN (*plural* **armies**) **1** a large number of soldiers armed for war **2** a great number of people, etc

aroma NOUN a sweet smell

aromatherapy NOUN a healing therapy involving massage with plant oils

arose *past tense* of **arise**

around PREPOSITION **1** in a circle about **2** on all sides of, surrounding **3** all over, at several places in: *papers scattered around the room* **4** somewhere near in time, place, amount: *I left him around here/ Come back around three o'clock* ▸ ADVERB all about, in various places: *People stood around watching* **get around 1** of a story: to become known to everyone **2** to be active

arouse VERB **1** to awaken **2** to stir, move (a feeling or person) > **arousal** NOUN

arpeggio (*pronounced* ahr-**ped**-jee-oh) NOUN, *music* a chord with the notes played in rapid succession, not at the same time

arrange VERB **1** to put in some order **2** to plan, settle

arrangement NOUN **1** a pattern or particular order **2** an agreed plan

array NOUN **1** order, arrangement **2** clothing **3** *maths* a set of numbers, counters, etc ordered in rows and columns ▸ VERB **1** to put in order: *a collection of insects, arrayed in glass cases* **2** to dress, adorn: *arrayed in fantastic plumage*

arrears PLURAL NOUN: **in arrears** not up to date; behind with payments

arrest VERB **1** to seize, capture, especially by power of the law **2** to stop **3** to catch (the attention etc) ▸ NOUN **1** capture by the police **2** stopping

arrival NOUN **1** the act of arriving **2** someone or something that arrives

arrive VERB to reach a place **arrive at** to reach, come to (a decision etc)

arrogant ADJECTIVE proud, haughty, self-important > **arrogance** NOUN > **arrogantly** ADVERB

arrow NOUN **1** a straight, pointed weapon shot from a bow **2** an arrow shape, eg on a road sign, showing direction

arrowhead NOUN **1** the pointed

A B C D E F G H I J K L M N O P Q R S T U V W X Y Z

LANGUAGE *workshop* Articles

The words **a** and **the** are special words called **articles**.

The is called the definite article, because it refers to one specific example:

> *The* dog from next door ran into *the* butcher's shop and stole some sausages.

A, or **an** if it comes before a vowel, is called the indefinite article, because it refers to a general example of something:

> *A* dog ran into *a* shop and stole some sausages.

metal part at the top of an arrow **2** a concave four-sided figure that has one reflex angle

arsenal NOUN a factory or store for weapons, ammunition, etc

arsenic NOUN, *chemistry* (symbol **As**) an element that, combined with oxygen, makes a strong poison

arson NOUN the crime of setting fire to a house etc on purpose > **arsonist** NOUN

art NOUN **1** drawing, painting, sculpture, etc **2** cleverness, skill; cunning **3** (**arts**) non-scientific school or university subjects

artefact *or* **artifact** NOUN a human-made object

arterial ADJECTIVE of or like arteries

arterial road NOUN a main road carrying traffic

artery NOUN (*plural* **arteries**), *anatomy* a tube which carries blood from the heart all around the body

artful ADJECTIVE wily, cunning > **artfully** ADVERB

arthritis NOUN, *medicine* a condition causing swollen and painful joints > **arthritic** ADJECTIVE

artichoke NOUN a thistle-like plant with an edible flowerhead

article NOUN **1** a thing, object **2** a piece of writing in a newspaper, journal, etc **3** a section of a document **4** *grammar* the name of the words *the, a, an* ▸ VERB to bind (an apprentice etc) by articles of a contract

articulate ADJECTIVE (*pronounced* ah-**tik**-yuw-l*a*t) **1** speaking clearly **2** expressing thoughts clearly ▸ VERB (*pronounced* ah-**tik**-yuw-leit) to express clearly > **articulation** NOUN

articulated lorry NOUN a lorry with a cab which can turn at an angle to the main part of the lorry, making cornering easier

artifact *another spelling of* **artefact**

artificial ADJECTIVE not natural; man-made > **artificiality** NOUN > **artificially** ADVERB

artificial insemination NOUN the insertion of sperm into the uterus by means other than sexual intercourse

artificial intelligence NOUN (*abbrev* **AI**) the ability of computers to perform actions thought to require human intelligence, eg problem solving

artillery NOUN **1** big guns **2** an army division that uses these

artisan NOUN someone who does skilled work with their hands

artist NOUN **1** someone who paints pictures **2** someone skilled in anything **3** an artiste

artiste (*pronounced* ah-**teest**) NOUN a performer in a theatre, circus, etc

artistic ADJECTIVE **1** of artists: *the artistic community* **2** having a talent for art

artistry NOUN skill as an artist

artless ADJECTIVE simple, frank

as CONJUNCTION **1** while, when: *happened as I was walking past* **2** because, since: *We stayed at home as it was raining* **3** in the same way that: *He thinks as I do* ▸ ADVERB for instance: *large books, as this one* **as for** concerning, regarding **as if** *or* **as though** as it would be if **as to** regarding **as well (as)** too, in addition (to)

asbestos NOUN a thread-like mineral which can be woven and will not burn

ascend VERB **1** to climb, go up **2** to rise or slope upwards **ascend the throne** to be crowned king or queen

ascendancy *or* **ascendency** NOUN control (over)

ascendant *or* **ascendent** ADJECTIVE rising

ascent NOUN **1** an upward move or climb **2** a slope upwards; a rise

ascertain VERB **1** to find out **2** to make certain

ascribe VERB (**ascribe to**) to think of as belonging to or due to that person or thing: *ascribing the blame to parents*

asexual reproduction (*pronounced* ei-**seks**-yoo-al) NOUN, *biology* reproduction that does not involve the union of male and female reproductive cells

ash NOUN (*plural* **ashes**) **1** a type of hardwood tree with silvery bark **2** (**ashes**) what is left after anything is burnt **rise from the ashes** to develop and flourish after experiencing ruin or disaster

ashamed ADJECTIVE feeling shame

ashen ADJECTIVE very pale

ashore ADVERB on or on to the shore

ashtray NOUN a small dish for the ash from cigarettes

aside ADVERB on or to one side; apart ▸ NOUN words spoken which those nearby are not supposed to hear

ask VERB **1** to request information about: *asked for my address* **2** to invite: *We've asked over twenty people to come* **ask after someone** to make enquiries about someone's health and wellbeing

askance ADVERB sideways **look askance at** to look at with suspicion or disapproval

askew ADVERB not straight, to one side

asleep ADJECTIVE **1** sleeping **2** of limbs: numbed

asp NOUN a small poisonous snake

asparagus NOUN a plant whose young shoots are eaten as a vegetable

aspect NOUN **1** look, appearance **2** view, point of view **3** the direction in which something, eg the side of a building or a piece of land, faces

asphalt NOUN a tarry mixture used to make pavements, paths, etc

asphyxia (*pronounced a*s-**fik**-si-*a*) NOUN, *medicine* suffocation by smoke or other fumes

asphyxiate VERB to suffocate > **asphyxiation** NOUN

aspiration NOUN a goal which you hope to achieve

aspire VERB (**aspire to** *or* **after**) to try to achieve or reach something difficult, ambitious, etc

aspirin NOUN, *medicine* a pain-killing drug

aspiring ADJECTIVE trying or wishing to be: *an aspiring director*

ass NOUN (*plural* **asses**) **1** a donkey **2** a stupid person

assail VERB to attack

assailant NOUN an attacker

assassin NOUN someone who assassinates, a murderer

[i] Literally 'hashish eater', after an Islamic sect during the Crusades who took the drug

assassinate VERB to murder (especially a politically important person) > **assassination** NOUN

assault NOUN an attack, especially a sudden one ▸ VERB to attack

assault course NOUN a series of physical obstacles to be jumped, climbed, etc

assegai (*pronounced* **as**-*eg*-ai) NOUN a South African spear, tipped with metal

assemblage NOUN a collection, a gathering

assemble VERB **1** to bring (people) together **2** to put together (a machine, piece of furniture, etc) **3** to meet together

assembly NOUN (*plural* **assemblies**) **1** a putting together **2** a gathering of people, especially for a special purpose

assembly line NOUN a series of machines and workers that an article passes along in each stage of its manufacture

assent VERB to agree: *The committee assents to your request* ▸ NOUN agreement

assert VERB **1** to state firmly: *She asserts that she did not take the money* **2** to insist on (a right etc): *women asserting their right to equal pay with men* **assert yourself** to make yourself noticed, heard, etc > **assertion** NOUN

assertive ADJECTIVE forceful, inclined to assert yourself

assess VERB **1** to estimate the value, power, etc of **2** to fix an amount (to be paid in tax etc) > **assessment** NOUN > **assessor** NOUN

asset NOUN **1** an advantage, a help

2 (**assets**) the property of a person, company, etc

assign (*pronounced a*-**sain**) VERB **1** to give to someone as a share or task: *I've assigned these jobs to you* **2** to fix (a time or place): *assign a date for the meeting*

assignation (*pronounced* as-ig-**nei**-sh*u*n) NOUN an appointment to meet

assignment NOUN **1** an act of assigning **2** a task given, especially an essay set for students

assimilate (*pronounced a*-**si**-mi-leit) VERB to take in and understand (facts etc): *assimilate all the information* > **assimilation** NOUN

assist VERB to help > **assistance** NOUN

assistant NOUN **1** a helper, eg to a senior worker **2** someone who serves in a shop etc

associate VERB (*pronounced a*-**soh**-shi-eit) **1** (**associate with**) to keep company with **2** (**associate yourself with**) to join with in partnership or friendship: *associated himself with the radicals* **3** to connect in your mind: *associates gardening with hard work* ▸ ADJECTIVE (*pronounced a*s-**oh**-shi-*a*t) joined or connected (with) ▸ NOUN (*pronounced a*s-**oh**-shi-*a*t) a friend, partner, companion

association NOUN **1** a club, society, union, etc **2** a partnership, friendship **3** a connection made in the mind

assonance NOUN the repetition of the same vowel sound in the same word or in two or more words close together, eg 'my life is fine'

assorted ADJECTIVE various, mixed

assortment NOUN a variety, a mixture

assuage (*pronounced a*-**sweidj**) VERB to soothe, ease (pain, hunger, etc)

assume VERB **1** to take upon yourself: *assume responsibility for the errors* **2** to take as true without further proof, take for granted **3** to put on (a disguise etc)

assumed ADJECTIVE false or pretended: *an assumed air of confidence/an assumed name*

assumption NOUN **1** the act of assuming **2** something taken for granted

assurance NOUN **1** a feeling of certainty; confidence **2** a promise **3** insurance

assure VERB **1** to make (someone) sure: *I assured him of my intention to return to work* **2** to state positively (that)

assured ADJECTIVE certain; confident

asterisk NOUN a star (*) used in printing for various purposes, especially to point out a footnote or insertion

astern ADVERB at or towards the back of a ship

asteroid NOUN one of thousands of small, rocky objects that orbit the sun

asthma (*pronounced* **as**-m*a*) NOUN, *medicine* an illness causing breathing difficulty, coughing, etc > **asthmatic** (*pronounced* as-**mat**-ik) *medicine*, ADJECTIVE

astonish VERB to surprise

A B C D E F G H I J K L M N O P Q R S T U V W X Y Z

greatly > **astonished** ADJECTIVE > **astonishing** ADJECTIVE

astonishment NOUN amazement, wonder

astound VERB to surprise greatly, amaze > **astounding** ADJECTIVE

astral ADJECTIVE of the stars

astray ADVERB out of the right way, straying

astride ADVERB with legs apart ▸ PREPOSITION with legs on each side of

astringent NOUN a lotion etc used for closing up the skin's pores ▸ ADJECTIVE **1** used for closing the pores **2** of manner: sharp, sarcastic

astro- *or* **astr-** PREFIX of or relating to stars or outer space

ⓘ Comes from Greek *astron* meaning 'a star'

astrology NOUN the study of the stars and planets and their supposed influence over people's lives > **astrologer** NOUN

astronaut NOUN someone who travels in space

astronomical ADJECTIVE **1** of astronomy **2** of a number: very large

astronomy NOUN the study of the stars and their movements > **astronomer** NOUN

astute ADJECTIVE cunning, clever > **astutely** ADVERB

asylum NOUN **1** refuge given in a country to someone from a country where they may be in danger **2** *old* a home for the mentally ill

asylum seeker NOUN someone who has fled their native country in search of asylum in another

asymmetrical (*pronounced* ei-si-**met**-rik-*al*) ADJECTIVE displaying asymmetry; lopsided in appearance > **asymmetrically** ADVERB

asymmetry NOUN the inequality in size, shape or position of two halves on either side of a dividing line (*contrasted with*: **symmetry**)

at PREPOSITION **1** showing position, time, etc: *I'll be at home/Come at 7 o'clock* **2** towards: *working at getting fit* **3** with or by: *annoyed at her* **4** occupied with; in a state of: *at play /at liberty* **at all** in any way: *not worried at all*

ate *past tense* of **eat**

atheism NOUN belief that there is no God

atheist NOUN someone who does not believe in God > **atheistic** ADJECTIVE

athlete NOUN someone good at sport, especially running, gymnastics, etc

athletic ADJECTIVE **1** of athletics **2** good at sports; strong, powerful

athletics NOUN running, jumping, etc or competitions in these

-athon *or* **-thon** SUFFIX forms nouns describing events, usually for charity, which are long in terms of time or endurance: *telethon* (= a very long television programme)/*talkathon* (= a long talking-session)

ⓘ Comes from the ending of mara*thon*

atlas NOUN (*plural* **atlases**) a book of maps

ⓘ After a mythological giant called *Atlas*, who was pictured on early books of maps supporting the heavens on his shoulders

ATM ABBREVIATION automatic teller machine

atmosphere NOUN **1** the air round the earth **2** any surrounding feeling or mood: *friendly atmosphere*

atmospheric ADJECTIVE **1** in or of the atmosphere **2** of a place, piece of art, etc: conveying a mood or impression

atmospheric pressure NOUN the pressure exerted by the atmosphere at the earth's surface, due to the weight of the air

atmospherics PLURAL NOUN air disturbances causing crackling noises on the radio etc

atoll NOUN a coral island or reef

atom NOUN **1** *chemistry* the smallest part of an element, consisting of protons and neutrons **2** anything very small

atom bomb *or* **atomic bomb** NOUN a bomb in which the explosion is caused by nuclear energy

atomic ADJECTIVE **1** relating to an atom or atoms **2** using nuclear energy: *atomic bombs*

atomic energy NOUN nuclear energy

atomic number NOUN, *chemistry* (symbol **Z**) the number of protons in the nucleus of an atom

atomizer *or* **atomiser** NOUN an instrument for releasing liquids in a fine spray

atone VERB to make up for wrongdoing: *atone for your sins* > **atonement** NOUN

atrocious ADJECTIVE **1** cruel or wicked **2** *informal* very bad

atrocity NOUN (*plural* **atrocities**) **1** a terrible crime **2** *informal* something very ugly

attach VERB **1** to fasten or join (to) **2** to think of (something) as having: *Don't attach any importance to it*

attaché (*pronounced a*-**tash**-ei) NOUN a junior member of an embassy staff

attaché case NOUN small case for papers etc

attached ADJECTIVE **1** fastened **2** (**attached to**) fond of

attachment NOUN **1** something attached: *a vacuum cleaner attachment* **2** a joining by love or friendship **3** *computing* an electronic file sent with an e-mail message

attack VERB **1** to suddenly or violently try to hurt or damage **2** to speak or write against ▶ NOUN **1** an act of attacking **2** a bout (of an illness etc)

attain VERB to reach; gain

attainable ADJECTIVE able to be attained

attainment NOUN the act of attaining; the thing attained, an achievement or accomplishment

attempt VERB to try ▶ NOUN a try or effort: *a first attempt*

attend VERB **1** to be present at **2** (**attend to**) to pay attention to **3** (**attend to**) to wait on, look after someone **4** to accompany

attendance NOUN **1** the fact of being present: *My attendance was expected* **2** the number of people present: *good attendance at the first night*

attendant NOUN someone employed to look after a public place, shop, etc: *a cloakroom attendant* ▸ADJECTIVE accompanying, related: *stress and its attendant health problems*

attention NOUN **1** careful notice: *pay attention* **2** concentration **3** care **4** *military* a stiffly straight standing position: *stand to attention*

attentive ADJECTIVE **1** giving or showing attention **2** polite
> **attentively** ADVERB

attic NOUN a room just under the roof of a house

ⓘ From *Attica* in ancient Greece, famous for a type of square architectural column used in upper storeys of classical buildings

attire *formal*, VERB to dress ▸NOUN clothing

attitude NOUN **1** a way of thinking or feeling: *a positive attitude* **2** a position of the body

attorney NOUN (*plural* **attorneys**) **1** someone with legal power to act for another **2** *US* a lawyer

attract VERB **1** to draw to or towards **2** to arouse liking or interest

attraction NOUN **1** the power of attracting **2** something which attracts visitors etc: *a tourist attraction*

attractive ADJECTIVE **1** good-looking, likeable **2** pleasing: *attractive price*

attribute VERB (*pronounced* a-**trib**-yoot) **1** to state or consider as the source or cause of: *attribute the accident to human error* **2** to state as the author or originator of: *attributed to Rembrandt* ▸NOUN (*pronounced* **a**-trib-yoot) a quality or characteristic, often with positive connotations: *one of her many attributes/attributes of power*
> **attributable** ADJECTIVE

attributive ADJECTIVE **1** expressing an attribute **2** *grammar* of an adjective: placed immediately before or immediately after the noun it describes, eg 'pretty' ('the pretty girl')

ⓘ Most adjectives can be used in this 'attributive' way. The opposite of attributive (meaning 2) is 'predicative'. An example of an adjective which is only ever used in a predicative way is 'asleep', because you cannot use it to make phrases like 'the asleep girl'.

aubergine (*pronounced* **oh**-ber-szeen) NOUN an oval, dark purple fruit, eaten as a vegetable

auburn ADJECTIVE of hair: reddish-brown in colour

auction NOUN a public sale in which articles are sold to the highest bidder ▸VERB to sell by auction

auctioneer NOUN someone whose job is to sell things by auction

audacious ADJECTIVE daring, bold
> **audacity** NOUN

audible ADJECTIVE able to be heard
> **audibility** NOUN

audience NOUN **1** a number of people gathered to watch or hear a performance etc **2** a formal interview with someone important: *an audience with the Pope*

audio NOUN the reproduction of recorded or radio sound ▸ ADJECTIVE relating to such sound: *an audio tape*

audio- PREFIX of or relating to sounds which can be heard

🛈 Comes from Latin *audio* meaning 'I hear'

audio-typist NOUN a typist able to type from a recording on a tape recorder

audiovisual ADJECTIVE concerned with hearing and seeing at the same time **audiovisual aids** films, recordings, etc used in teaching

audit VERB to examine accounts officially ▸ NOUN an official examination of a company's accounts

audition NOUN a short performance to test whether an actor, singer, etc is suitable for a particular role

auditor NOUN someone who audits accounts

auditorium NOUN (*plural* **auditoria** *or* **auditoriums**) the part of a theatre etc where the audience sits

auditory ADJECTIVE of hearing

augment VERB to increase in size, number or amount > **augmentation** NOUN > **augmentative** ADJECTIVE

August NOUN the eighth month of the year

🛈 Named in honour of the Roman emperor *Augustus* Caesar

august (*pronounced* aw-**gust**) ADJECTIVE full of dignity, stately

aunt NOUN a father's or a mother's sister, or an uncle's wife

au pair NOUN a foreign person, usually a girl, who does domestic work in someone's home in return for board, lodging and pocket money

aural ADJECTIVE relating to the ear

🛈 Comes from Latin *auris* meaning 'ear'

> Do not confuse with: **oral. Oral** means 'relating to the mouth'. It may help to think of the 'O' as looking like an open mouth; and to remember that many words related to listening start with 'au', like 'audition' and 'auditorium'.

aurora borealis NOUN the aurora visible in the northern hemisphere (*also called*: **the northern lights**)

auspices PLURAL NOUN: **under the auspices of** with the support or guidance of

auspicious ADJECTIVE favourable; promising luck

austere ADJECTIVE **1** severe **2** without luxury; simple, sparse > **austerity** NOUN

authentic ADJECTIVE true, real, genuine > **authentically** ADVERB > **authenticity** NOUN

authenticate VERB to show to be true or real > **authentication** NOUN

author NOUN the writer of a book, poem, play, etc

authoritative ADJECTIVE stated by an expert or someone in authority

authority NOUN (*plural* **authorities**) **1** the power or right to control others **2** someone whose

A B C D E F G H I J K L M N O P Q R S T U V W X Y Z

opinion is reliable, an expert **3** someone or a body of people having control (over something) **4** (**the authorities**) people in power

authorize *or* **authorise** VERB **1** to give (a person) the power or the right to do something: *I have authorized him to carry out these tasks* **2** to give permission (for something to be done): *The proposed renovation work has been authorized* > **authorization** NOUN

autism NOUN a disability affecting a person's ability to relate to and communicate with other people > **autistic** ADJECTIVE

auto- *or* **aut-** PREFIX **1** self: *autobiography* **2** self-caused or automatic **3** of or relating to cars
ⓘ Comes from Greek *autos* meaning 'self' or 'same'

autobiography NOUN (*plural* **autobiographies**) the story of someone's life, written or told by themselves > **autobiographical** ADJECTIVE

autocracy NOUN (*plural* **autocracies**) government by an autocrat, or a country ruled by an autocrat

autocrat NOUN a ruler who has complete power

autocratic ADJECTIVE expecting complete obedience

autograph NOUN **1** someone's own signature **2** someone's own handwriting ▶ VERB to write your own name on: *autograph the book*

automate VERB to make automatic by introducing machines etc

automatic ADJECTIVE **1** of a machine etc: working on its own **2** of an action: unconscious, without thinking ▶ NOUN **1** something automatic (eg an automatic washing-machine) **2** a kind of self-loading gun > **automatically** ADVERB: *Second-time offenders will automatically lose their licence*

automatic pilot *or* **autopilot** NOUN a device which can be set to control an aircraft on a course **on automatic pilot** *or* **on autopilot** (doing something) without thinking, as when bored, etc

automation NOUN the use of machines for controlling other machines in factories etc

automaton (*pronounced* aw-**tom**-*a*-ton) NOUN (*plural* **automata**) **1** a mechanical toy or machine made to look and move like a human **2** someone who acts mindlessly, like a machine

automobile NOUN, *US* a car

autonomy NOUN the power or right of a country to govern itself > **autonomous** ADJECTIVE

autopsy NOUN (*plural* **autopsies**) an examination of the internal organs of a body after death

autumn NOUN the season of the year following summer, when leaves change colour and fruits are ripe

autumnal ADJECTIVE **1** relating to autumn **2** like that or those of autumn: *autumnal colours*

auxiliary ADJECTIVE supplementary, additional ▶ NOUN (*plural* **auxiliaries**) a helper, an assistant

auxiliary verb NOUN, *grammar* a short verb, *eg* 'be', 'do', 'have' or 'can', used with other verbs to show tense *etc*, *eg* 'must' in 'I must go'

avail VERB: **avail yourself of** to make use of: *avail yourself of this opportunity* ▸ NOUN: **to no avail** without any effect, of no use

available ADJECTIVE able or ready to be made use of > **availability** NOUN

avalanche NOUN **1** a mass of snow and ice sliding down from a mountain **2** a great amount: *an avalanche of work*

avant-garde ADJECTIVE ahead of fashion, very modern

avarice NOUN greed, especially for riches > **avaricious** ADJECTIVE

avenge VERB to take revenge for (a wrong): *avenge his sister's death/determined to avenge herself*

avenue NOUN **1** a tree-lined street or drive up to a house **2** a means, a way: *avenue of escape*

average NOUN the result obtained by adding several amounts and dividing the total by the number of amounts, eg the average of 3, 7, 9, 13 is 8 (32÷4) ▸ ADJECTIVE **1** ordinary, usual; of medium size etc **2** obtained by working out an average: *The average cost will be £10 each* ▸ VERB **1** to form an average **2** to find the average of

averse ADJECTIVE not fond of, opposed (to)

aversion NOUN **1** extreme dislike or distaste: *an aversion to sprouts* **2** something that is hated

avert VERB **1** to turn away or aside: *avert your eyes* **2** to prevent from happening: *avert the danger*

aviary NOUN (*plural* **aviaries**) a place for keeping birds

aviation NOUN the practice of flying or piloting aircraft

aviator NOUN an aircraft pilot

avid ADJECTIVE eager, greedy: *an avid reader* > **avidity** NOUN

avocado NOUN (*plural* **avocados**) **1** a pear-shaped fruit with a rough peel and rich, creamy flesh **2** a light, yellowish-green colour

avoid VERB to escape, keep clear of > **avoidable** ADJECTIVE > **avoidance** NOUN

avoirdupois (*pronounced* av-wahr-dyoo-**pwah**) NOUN the system of measuring weights in pounds and ounces (*compare with*: **metric system**)

await VERB to wait for

awake VERB **1** to rouse from sleep **2** to stop sleeping ▸ ADJECTIVE not asleep

awaken VERB **1** to awake **2** to arouse (interest etc)

awakening NOUN the act or process of waking up or coming into existence: *the awakening of unfamiliar feelings/a rude awakening* (= an event which brings someone sharply out of a dreamlike state and into the world of harsh reality)

award VERB **1** to give, grant (a prize etc) **2** to grant legally: *awarded custody of the children* ▸ NOUN something that is awarded, a prize etc

a b c d e f g h i j k l m n o p q r s t u v w x y z

aware ADJECTIVE **1** having knowledge (of), conscious (of): *aware of the dangers* **2** alert > **awareness** NOUN

away ADVERB **1** to or at a distance from the speaker or person spoken to: *Throw that ball away* **2** in the proper place: *Put the toys away* **3** in the opposite direction: *He turned away and left* **4** into nothing: *The sound died away* **5** constantly: *working away* **do away with** to abolish, get rid of **get away with** to do (something) without being punished **make away with** to steal and escape with **right** *or* **straight away** immediately

awe NOUN wonder or admiration mixed with fear ▸ VERB to fill with awe: *awed by the occasion*

awesome ADJECTIVE **1** causing awe **2** *informal* remarkable, admirable

awestruck ADJECTIVE full of awe

awful ADJECTIVE **1** *informal* bad: *an awful headache* **2** *informal* very great: *an awful lot* **3** terrible: *I feel awful about this*

awfully ADVERB, *informal* very, extremely: *awfully good of you*

awkward ADJECTIVE **1** clumsy, not graceful **2** difficult to deal with: *awkward customer* > **awkwardly** ADVERB > **awkwardness** NOUN

awning NOUN a covering of canvas etc providing shelter

awry (*pronounced a-***rai**) ADJECTIVE & ADVERB **1** not according to plan, wrong **2** crooked

axe NOUN a tool for chopping ▸ VERB **1** to cancel (a plan etc) **2** to reduce greatly (costs, services, etc) **have an axe to grind** to have a strong point of view or resentful feelings which you tend to express at any opportunity

axiom NOUN **1** a self-evident truth **2** an accepted principle

axis NOUN (*plural* **axes**) **1** the line, real or imaginary, on which a thing turns **2** the axis of the earth, from North to South Pole, around which the earth turns **3** *maths, geography* a fixed line taken as a reference to map points on a graph, *eg* the horizontal x-axis and the vertical y-axis

axle NOUN the rod on which a wheel turns

ayatollah NOUN a religious leader of the Shiah sect of Islam

aye ADVERB yes ▸ NOUN a vote in favour of something

azure (*pronounced* **ei**-*szur*) ADJECTIVE sky-coloured, clear blue

Bb

babble VERB to talk indistinctly or foolishly ▸NOUN indistinct or foolish talk

babe NOUN **1** *old* a baby **2** *informal* a girl or young woman

baboon NOUN a large monkey with a dog-like snout

baby NOUN (*plural* **babies**) a very young child, an infant ▸VERB (**babies, babying, babied**) to treat like a baby

babysit VERB (**babysitting, babysat**) to look after a child while its parents are out > **babysitter** NOUN

bachelor NOUN an unmarried man

bacillus (*pronounced* ba-**sil**-*us*) NOUN (*plural* **bacilli** – *pronounced* ba-**sil**-ai), *biology* a rod-shaped germ found in soil and air

back NOUN **1** the part of the human body from the neck to the base of the spine **2** the upper part of an animal's body **3** the part of anything situated behind: *sitting at the back of the bus* **4** *football etc* a player positioned behind the forwards ▸ADJECTIVE of or at the back ▸ADVERB **1** to or in the place from which someone or something came: *back at the house/walked back home* **2** to or in a former time or condition: *thinking back to their youth* ▸VERB **1** to move backwards **2** to bet on (a horse etc) **3** (often **back up**) to help or support **back down** to change your opinion etc **back out 1** to move out backwards **2** to excuse yourself from keeping to an agreement **back someone up** to support or assist them **back something up** to copy (computer data) onto a disk or tape (*see also*: **backup**) **put your back into** to work hard at **put someone's back up** to irritate someone **with your back to the wall** in desperate difficulties

🛈 Comes from Old English *bæc*

backbone NOUN **1** the spine **2** the main support of something **3** firmness, resolve

backfire VERB **1** of a vehicle: to make an explosive noise in the exhaust pipe **2** of a plan: to go wrong

backgammon NOUN a game similar to draughts, played with dice

background NOUN **1** the space behind the principal figures or objects in a picture **2** details that explain something **3** someone's family, upbringing and education

backhand NOUN, *tennis etc* a stroke played with the back of the hand facing the ball (*compare with*: **forehand**)

backing NOUN **1** support, especially financial support **2** material used on the back of a picture etc **3** a musical accompaniment on a recording

backlash NOUN a violent reaction against something

backstroke NOUN a stroke used in swimming on the back

backward ADJECTIVE **1** to or towards the back: *a backward glance* **2** slow in learning or development

backwards ADVERB **1** towards the back: with your back facing the direction of movement: *walked backwards out of the room* **2** in a reverse direction: *written backwards* **3** towards the past

backwater NOUN **1** a river pool separate from the main stream **2** *derogatory* an isolated place not affected by what is happening in the outside world

bacon NOUN the flesh of a pig, salted and dried and used as food

bacteria (*pronounced* bak-**teer**-i-*a*) PLURAL NOUN (*singular* **bacterium**) a diverse group of microscopic and usually single-celled organisms found in air, water, and living and dead bodies, and responsible for decay, fermentation and a number of diseases
> **bacterial** ADJECTIVE

bad ADJECTIVE (**worse, worst**) **1** not good; wicked **2** not of a good standard: *bad workmanship/bad at maths* **3** (often **bad for**) harmful: *Smoking is bad for you* **4** of food: rotten, decaying **5** severe, serious: *a bad dose of flu*

badge NOUN a mark or sign or brooch-like ornament giving some information about the wearer

badger NOUN a black and white burrowing animal of the weasel family which comes out at night
▸ VERB to pester or annoy

badly ADVERB (**worse, worst**) **1** not well **2** seriously: *badly hurt* **3** very much: *He badly wanted to win*
badly off poor

badminton NOUN a game resembling tennis, played with shuttlecocks

ⓘ The game was first played in its modern form at *Badminton* House in SW England

baffle VERB to be too difficult for; puzzle or confound > **baffling** ADJECTIVE

bag NOUN **1** a holder or container, often of a soft material **2** (*also*: **bagful**) the amount a bag can hold: *a bag of crisps* **3** a quantity of fish or game caught **4** (**bags**): *informal* a large amount: *bags of confidence*
▸ VERB (**bagging, bagged**) **1** to put in a bag **2** to secure possession of, claim: *bag a seat*

bagel *or* **beigel** (*pronounced* **bei**-gel) NOUN a hard, ring-shaped bread roll

ⓘ Comes from Yiddish *beygel*

baggage NOUN luggage

baggy ADJECTIVE (**baggier, baggiest**) of clothes: large and loose

bagpipes PLURAL NOUN a wind instrument made up of a bag and several pipes

baguette NOUN a long narrow French loaf

bail[1] NOUN money given to bail out a prisoner > **bail out** VERB to obtain temporary release of (an untried prisoner) by giving money which will be forfeited if they do not return for trial

Comes from Old French *bail* meaning 'custody'

> Do not confuse with: **bale**

bail[2] VERB: **bail out** to bale out

bail[3] NOUN, *cricket* one of the crosspieces on the top of the wickets

Probably comes from Old French *baillier* meaning 'to enclose', or from Latin *baculum* meaning 'stick'

> Do not confuse with: **bale**

bailiff NOUN **1** an officer who works for a sheriff **2** a landowner's agent

bairn NOUN, *Scottish* a child

Baisakhi (*pronounced* bai-**sak**-ee) *or* **Vaisakhi** NOUN, *Sikhism* a festival commemorating the founding of the Khalsa

From Hindi *Baisakh* meaning 'April'

bait NOUN **1** food put on a hook to make fish bite, or in a trap to attract animals **2** something tempting or alluring ▸ VERB **1** to put bait on a hook etc **2** to worry, annoy

> Do not confuse: **baited** and **bated**, as in the phrase *bated breath*

bake VERB **1** to cook in an oven **2** to dry or harden in the sun or in an oven

baked beans PLURAL NOUN haricot beans baked in tomato sauce and tinned

baker NOUN someone who bakes or sells bread etc

bakery *or* **bakehouse** NOUN (*plural* **bakeries** *or* **bakehouses**) a place used for baking in a shop where baked products are sold

balaclava *or* **balaklava** NOUN a knitted covering for the head and neck

After the battle of *Balaklava* in 1854, during the Crimean War, when such headgear was first worn

balalaika (*pronounced* bal-*a*-**lai**-k*a*) NOUN a Russian musical instrument with a triangular body and normally three strings

balance NOUN **1** physical stability in which the weight of a body is evenly distributed: *I lost my balance and fell over* **2** the money needed to make the two sides of an account equal ▸ VERB **1** to be the same in weight **2** to make both sides of an account the same **3** to make or keep steady: *She balanced it on her head*

balcony NOUN (*plural* **balconies**) **1** a platform built out from the wall of a building **2** an upper floor or gallery in a theatre etc

bald ADJECTIVE **1** without hair **2** plain, frank: *a bald statement* > **baldness** NOUN

a b c d e f g h i j k l m n o p q r s t u v w x y z

A B C D E F G H I J K L M N O P Q R S T U V W X Y Z

balding ADJECTIVE going bald

bale[1] NOUN a large tight bundle of cotton, hay, etc

ⓘ Perhaps comes from Old High German *balla, palla* meaning 'ball'

> Do not confuse with: **bail**

bale[2] VERB: **bale out** *or* **bail out** **1** to escape by parachute from an aircraft in an emergency **2** to scoop water out of a boat

Balfour Declaration NOUN, *history* the statement made in November 1917 by Arthur Balfour, the British Foreign Secretary, that Britain was in favour of establishing a home for the Jewish people in Palestine

balk VERB (**balk at**) to refuse to do something

ball[1] NOUN **1** anything round: *a ball of wool* **2** the round or roundish object used in playing many games **on the ball** *informal* in touch with a situation, alert **play ball** *informal* to play along, cooperate

ball[2] NOUN a formal party at which dancing takes place **have a ball** *informal* to have a great time, enjoy yourself

ballad NOUN a narrative poem with a simple rhyme scheme, usually in verses of four lines

ballast NOUN sand, gravel, etc put into a ship to steady it

ballerina NOUN a female ballet dancer

ballet NOUN a form of stylized dancing which tells a story by mime

ballistic missile NOUN a self-guided missile which falls on to its target

ballistics SINGULAR NOUN the scientific study of the movement of projectiles such as bullets, rockets and missiles > **ballistic** ADJECTIVE

balloon NOUN a bag filled with gas to make it float in the air, especially one made of thin rubber used as a toy etc ▸ VERB to puff or swell out

ballot NOUN a way of voting in secret by marking a paper and putting it into a special box ▸ VERB (**balloting, balloted**) to collect votes from (people) by ballot

ballpark NOUN, *US* a sports field for ball games ▸ ADJECTIVE rough, estimated: *a ballpark figure*

ballpoint NOUN a pen with a tiny ball as the writing point

ballroom NOUN a large room used for public dances etc

balm (*pronounced* bahm) NOUN **1** something soothing **2** a sweet-smelling healing ointment

balmy ADJECTIVE (**balmier, balmiest**) **1** mild, gentle; soothing: *balmy air* **2** sweet-smelling

balsa (*pronounced* **bawl**-*sa*) NOUN a very light wood, from a tropical American tree (*also called*: **balsawood**)

balsam (*pronounced* **bawl**-*sam*) NOUN an oily sweet-smelling substance obtained from certain trees

balustrade (*pronounced* **bal**-*us*-*treid*) NOUN a row of pillars on a balcony etc, joined by a rail

bamboo NOUN the woody, jointed stem of a type of very tall grass

bamboozle VERB to puzzle or confuse

ban NOUN an order forbidding something ▶ VERB (**banning, banned**) to forbid officially (the publication of a book etc)

banal (*pronounced* ba-**nahl**) ADJECTIVE lacking originality or wit; commonplace > **banality** NOUN

banana NOUN the long curved yellow fruit of a type of tropical tree

band NOUN **1** a group of people **2** a group of musicians playing together **3** a strip of some material to put round something **4** a stripe (of colour etc) **5** a group of wavelengths for radio broadcasts ▶ VERB to join together

bandage NOUN a strip of cloth for winding round a wound

bandit NOUN an outlaw or robber, especially a member of a gang of robbers

bandwagon NOUN: **jump** *or* **climb on the bandwagon** to join something because it is successful or popular

bandwidth NOUN **1** the width of a band of radio or television frequencies **2** *computing* the amount of information that can be conveyed in a link between computers

bandy ADJECTIVE (**bandier, bandiest**) of legs: bent outwards at the knee

bane NOUN a cause of ruin or trouble: *the bane of my life*

bang NOUN **1** a sudden, loud noise **2** a heavy blow ▶ VERB **1** to close with a bang, slam **2** to hit, strike: *banged his head*

banger NOUN **1** a type of firework that bangs **2** *informal* a sausage **3** *informal* an old car

bangle NOUN a large ring worn on an arm or leg

banish VERB **1** to order (someone) to leave a country **2** to drive away (doubts, fear, etc) > **banishment** NOUN

banister NOUN the posts and handrail of a staircase

banjo NOUN (*plural* **banjoes** *or* **banjos**) a stringed musical instrument like a guitar, with a long neck and a round body

bank NOUN **1** a mound or ridge of earth etc **2** the edge of a river **3** a place where money is lent, put for safety, etc **4** a place where blood etc is stored till needed **5** a public bin for collecting items for recycling: *a bottle bank* **bank on** to depend on, count on

banker NOUN someone who manages a bank

bank holiday NOUN a day on which all banks and many shops etc are closed

banking NOUN the business conducted by banks

banknote NOUN a piece of paper money issued by a bank

bankrupt NOUN someone who has no money to pay their debts ▶ ADJECTIVE **1** unable to pay debts **2** utterly lacking in: *bankrupt of ideas* > **bankruptcy** NOUN (*plural* **bankruptcies**)

banner NOUN **1** a large flag carried in processions etc, often hung between two poles **2** any flag **3** *computing* an advertisement across the width of a Web page

banns PLURAL NOUN a public announcement of a forthcoming marriage

banquet NOUN a ceremonial dinner

bantam NOUN a small kind of hen

banter VERB to tease in fun ▶NOUN light teasing

Bantu NOUN **1** a group of languages spoken in southern and central Africa **2** the peoples who speak these languages

bap NOUN, *Scottish & N English dialect* a large flat bread roll

Baptist NOUN a member of the Baptist Church, a Christian group which believes that only adult believers should be baptized, by complete immersion in water

baptize *or* **baptise** VERB **1** to dip in, or sprinkle with, water as a sign of admission into the Christian Church **2** to christen, give a name to > **baptism** NOUN > **baptismal** ADJECTIVE

bar NOUN **1** a rod of solid material **2** a broad line or band **3** a piece, a cake: *a bar of soap* **4** a hindrance, a block **5** *geography* a raised area of sand, mud, stones, etc at the mouth of a river or on a beach **6** a room, or counter, where drinks are served in a public house, hotel, etc **7** *law* the rail at which prisoners stand for trial **8** *law* the lawyers who plead in a court **9** *music* a time division ▶PREPOSITION except: *All the runners, bar Ian, finished the race* ▶VERB (**barring, barred**) **1** to fasten with a bar **2** to exclude, shut out: *barred from the competition*

barb NOUN **1** the backward-pointing spike on an arrow, fish-hook, etc **2** *zoology* one of the threadlike structures forming a feather's web

barbarian NOUN an uncivilized person ▶ADJECTIVE uncivilized

barbaric ADJECTIVE **1** uncivilized **2** extremely cruel > **barbarity** NOUN

barbecue NOUN **1** a frame on which to grill food over an open fire **2** an outdoor party providing food from a barbecue ▶VERB to cook (food) on a barbecue

ⓘ From a Haitian creole term for a wooden grid or frame

barbed ADJECTIVE having a barb or barbs

barbed wire NOUN wire with regular clusters of sharp points, used for fencing etc

barbell NOUN a bar with heavy metal weights at each end, used for weightlifting exercises

barber NOUN a men's hairdresser

barbiturate (*pronounced* bahr-**bit**-yuw-r*a*t) NOUN a type of sedative drug

barbule NOUN, *zoology* any of the hairlike filaments on the barb of a bird's feather

bar chart NOUN a chart or graph which uses horizontal or vertical blocks or bars to show amounts

barcode NOUN a series of numbers and parallel lines, used on product labels, which provides information about the product for sales checkouts etc

bard NOUN, *literary* a poet

bare ADJECTIVE **1** uncovered, naked **2** plain, simple **3** empty ▶VERB to uncover, expose > **barely** ADVERB hardly, scarcely

barefaced ADJECTIVE impudent, unashamed: *a barefaced lie*

barefoot *or* **barefooted** ADJECTIVE & ADVERB not wearing shoes or socks

bargain NOUN **1** an agreement, especially about buying or selling **2** something bought cheaply ▸ VERB to argue about a price etc **bargain for** to expect: *more than he bargained for* **into the bargain** in addition, besides

barge NOUN a flat-bottomed boat used on rivers and canals ▸ VERB **1** to rush clumsily **2** to push or bump (into) **3** to push your way (into) rudely

baritone NOUN, *music* **1** a male singing voice between tenor and bass **2** a singer with such a voice

barium NOUN, *chemistry* (symbol **Ba**) a soft, silvery-white, metallic element, soluble compounds of which burn with a green flame

ⓘ Comes from Greek *baris* meaning 'heavy'

bark[1] NOUN the noise made by a dog, fox, etc ▸ VERB **1** to give a bark **2** to speak sharply or angrily

bark[2] NOUN the rough protective outer covering of a tree's trunk and branches

barley NOUN a grain used for food and for making beer and whisky

bar mitzvah (*pronounced* bahr **mits**-v*a*) NOUN a Jewish ceremony to mark a boy's coming of age

barmy ADJECTIVE (**barmier, barmiest**) *informal* crazy; mentally unsound

barn NOUN a building in which grain, hay, etc is stored

barnacle NOUN a type of shellfish which sticks to rocks, ships' hulls, etc

barometer (*pronounced* ba-**rom**-it-*er*) NOUN an instrument which measures the weight or pressure of the air and shows changes in the weather

baron NOUN **1** a nobleman of the lowest rank in the British peerage **2** a powerful person, especially in a business: *drug baron* > **baronial** ADJECTIVE (meaning 1)

baroness NOUN (*plural* **baronesses**) a baron's wife or a female baron

baronet NOUN a man holding the lowest title that can be passed on to an heir > **baronetcy** NOUN the rank of baronet

baroque (*pronounced* ba-**rok**) ADJECTIVE extravagantly ornamented

barracks PLURAL NOUN a place for housing soldiers

barracuda (*pronounced* bar-*a*-**koo**-d*a*) NOUN a large tropical sea fish which feeds on other fish

barrage NOUN **1** heavy gunfire against an enemy **2** an overwhelming number: *a barrage of questions* **3** a bar across a river to make the water deeper

Comes from French, meaning 'bar'

barrel NOUN **1** a wooden cask with curved sides **2** the metal tube of a gun through which the shot is fired

barren ADJECTIVE **1** not able to reproduce, infertile **2** of land or soil:

not able to produce crops or fruit

barricade NOUN a barrier put up to block a street etc ▶ VERB **1** to block or strengthen against attack **2** to shut behind a barrier

barrier NOUN **1** a strong fence etc used for enclosing or keeping out **2** an obstacle

barrister NOUN a lawyer who pleads cases in English or Irish courts

barrow[1] NOUN a small hand-cart

barrow[2] NOUN a mound built over an ancient grave

barter VERB to give one thing in exchange for another ▶ NOUN trading by exchanging goods without using money

basalt (*pronounced* **bas**-alt *or* **bas**-awlt) NOUN a hard, dark-coloured rock thrown up as lava from volcanoes

base[1] NOUN **1** something on which a thing stands or rests **2** the lowest part **3** a place from where an expedition, military action, etc is carried out **4** *chemistry* a compound that contains hydroxyl ions and can neutralize acids **5** *maths* the number of different symbols used in a counting system, eg in the binary number system the base is two, because only the symbols 0 and 1 are used **6** *maths* in logarithms: the number that, when raised to a certain power has a logarithm equal in value to that power **7** *maths* the line or surface on which a geometric figure rests ▶ VERB to use as a foundation: *based on the facts*

base[2] ADJECTIVE worthless, cowardly

baseball NOUN a North American ball game in which players make a circuit of four stations (**bases**) on a field

base jumping the sport of parachuting from low-level objects and structures, *eg* buildings

basement NOUN a storey below ground level in a building

bash *informal*, VERB to hit hard ▶ NOUN (*plural* **bashes**) a heavy blow **have a bash** to make an attempt

bashful ADJECTIVE lacking confidence; shy; self-conscious > **bashfully** ADVERB > **bashfulness** NOUN

basic ADJECTIVE **1** of or forming a base **2** necessary, fundamental > **basically** ADVERB fundamentally, essentially

basil NOUN an aromatic herb used in cooking

basilisk (*pronounced* **bas**-i-lisk) NOUN **1** a mythological reptile with a deadly look and poisonous breath **2** a type of American lizard

basin NOUN **1** a wide, open dish **2** a washhand basin **3** the land drained by a river and its tributaries

basis NOUN (*plural* **bases** – *pronounced* **bei**-seez) **1** something on which a thing rests, a foundation: *the basis of their friendship* **2** the main ingredient

bask VERB **1** to lie in warmth **2** to enjoy, feel great pleasure (in): *basking in glory*

basket NOUN a container made of strips of wood, rushes, etc woven together

basketball NOUN a team game in which goals are scored by throwing a ball into a raised horizontal hoop with a net attached

bass[1] (*pronounced* beis) NOUN (*plural* **basses**), *music* the low part in music ▸ ADJECTIVE low or deep in tone

bass[2] (*pronounced* bas) NOUN (*plural* **bass** *or* **basses**) a kind of fish of the perch family

bass clef NOUN a musical sign (𝄢) placed on a stave to fix the pitch of the notes

bassoon NOUN a musical wind instrument with low notes

bastard NOUN **1** *old, often offensive* a child born to parents who are not married to each other **2** *slang* a general term of abuse

baste VERB to spoon fat over (meat) while roasting to keep (it) from drying out

bastion NOUN **1** a defensive position, a preserve: *the last bastions of male power* **2** a tower on a castle etc

bat[1] NOUN a shaped piece of wood etc for striking a ball in some games ▸ VERB (**batting, batted**) to use the bat in cricket etc

bat[2] NOUN a mouse-like flying animal, active at night

bat[3] VERB (**batting, batted**) to flutter (the eyelids etc)

batch NOUN (*plural* **batches**) a quantity of things made etc at one time

bated ADJECTIVE: **with bated breath** anxiously

bath NOUN **1** a vessel which holds water in which to wash the body **2** the water in which to wash **3** a washing of the body in water **4** (**baths**) a public swimming pool ▸ VERB to wash (oneself or another person) in a bath

bathe VERB **1** to swim in water **2** to wash gently: *bathe your eyes* **3** to take a bath ▸ NOUN the act of bathing: *We went for a bathe in the sea* **bathed in** covered with

bathos (*pronounced* **bei**-thos) NOUN in speech or writing: a sudden change from a very serious or beautiful tone or content to a very ordinary or trivial one > **bathetic** ADJECTIVE

🄸 From Greek, meaning 'depth'

> Do not confuse with: **pathos**

bathroom NOUN a room containing facilities for washing yourself and usually a lavatory

bat mitzvah (*pronounced* bat **mits**-va) NOUN a Jewish ceremony to mark a girl's coming of age

baton NOUN **1** a small wooden stick **2** a light stick used by a conductor of music

> Do not confuse with: **batten**

batsman *or* **batswoman** NOUN (*plural* **batsmen** *or* **batswomen**) someone who bats in cricket etc

battalion NOUN a part of a regiment of foot soldiers

batten NOUN **1** a piece of sawn timber **2** a strip of wood used to fasten down a ship's hatches during a storm ▸ VERB: **batten down** to fasten down firmly

Do not confuse with: **baton**

batter[1] VERB to hit repeatedly > **battered** ADJECTIVE **1** beaten, ill-treated **2** worn out by use

batter[2] NOUN a beaten mixture of flour, milk and eggs, for cooking > **battered** ADJECTIVE dipped in batter and fried

battery NOUN (*plural* **batteries**) **1** a number of large guns **2** a device for storing and transmitting electricity **3** a series of cages etc in which hens are kept for egg-laying

battle NOUN a fight, especially between armies ▸ VERB to fight

battle-axe NOUN **1** *informal* a fierce and domineering older woman **2** *history* a large broad-bladed axe

battlefield NOUN the site of a battle

battlement NOUN a wall on the top of a building, with openings or notches for firing

battleship NOUN a heavily armed and armoured warship

bauble NOUN a brightly coloured ornament of little value

bauxite NOUN a clay-like compound which is the main ore of aluminium

bawdy ADJECTIVE (**bawdier, bawdiest**) of language or writing etc: containing coarsely humorous references to sex > **bawdily** ADVERB > **bawdiness** NOUN

bawl VERB to shout or cry out loudly ▸ NOUN a loud cry

bay[1] NOUN a wide inlet of the sea in a coastline

bay[2] NOUN **1** a space in a room which is set back, a recess **2** a compartment in an aircraft: *the bomb bay*

bay[3] NOUN the laurel tree

bay[4] VERB of dogs: to bark **hold at bay** to fight off **stand at bay** to stand and face attackers etc

bayonet NOUN a steel stabbing blade that can be fixed to the muzzle of a rifle ▸ VERB (**bayoneting, bayoneted**) to stab with this

bay window NOUN a window that forms a recess

bazaar NOUN **1** a sale of goods for charity etc **2** an Eastern marketplace **3** a shop

bazooka (*pronounced* ba-**zoo**-ka) NOUN a portable anti-tank gun which fires small rockets

BBC ABBREVIATION British Broadcasting Corporation

BC ABBREVIATION before Christ: *55BC*

BCC *or* **Bcc** ABBREVIATION blind carbon copy, used to mark a copy of a message sent without the knowledge of the main recipient

BCG ABBREVIATION bacillus Calmette-Guérin, a vaccine that prevents tuberculosis

Be SYMBOL, *chemistry* beryllium

be VERB **1** to live, exist: *There may be some milk left* **2** to have a position, quality, etc: *She wants to be a dentist/If only you could be happy*

ⓘ **be** →*present form* **am, are, is,** *past form* **was, were,** *past participle* **been** The present tense comes from Anglo-Saxon *beon*, to live or exist; the past tense comes from Anglo-Saxon *weran*, to be

[1] Present tense: comes from Anglo-Saxon *beon*, to live or exist; past tense: comes from Anglo-Saxon *weran*, to be

be- PREFIX **1** used **2** to add to words the sense of: around, in all directions, thoroughly: *besiege* **3** to form verbs from adjectives and nouns: *befriend/belittle* **4** to make intransitive verbs (eg *fall*) into transitive verbs (*befall someone*)

beach NOUN (*plural* **beaches**) the shore of the sea etc, especially when sandy or pebbly ▸ VERB to drive or haul (a boat etc) up on the beach

beachcomber NOUN someone who searches beaches for useful articles or things to sell

beach profile NOUN, *geography* a measurement of the height, length and steepness of a beach

beacon NOUN **1** a flashing light or other warning signal **2** *history* a fire on a hill used as a signal of danger

bead NOUN **1** a small pierced ball of glass, plastic, etc, used in needlework or jewellery-making **2** a drop of liquid: *beads of sweat*

beagle NOUN a small hunting hound

beak NOUN **1** the hard, horny part of a bird's mouth with which it gathers food **2** a point, a projection

beaker NOUN a tall cup or glass, usually without a handle, especially one used in laboratory work

beam NOUN **1** a long straight piece of wood or metal **2** a shaft of light **3** a radio signal **4** the greatest breadth of a ship **5** *physics* a directed flow of electromagnetic radiation or particles ▸ VERB **1** to shine **2** to smile broadly

bean NOUN **1** any of various pod-bearing plants **2** the seed of this used as food

bean bag NOUN **1** a small cloth bag filled with dried beans, used like a ball in children's games **2** a very large cushion filled with polystyrene chips etc, kept on the floor as seating

beansprout *or* **beanshoot** NOUN a young shoot of the mung bean plant eaten as a vegetable, especially in Chinese food

bear[1] NOUN a heavy animal with shaggy fur and hooked claws

bear[2] VERB (**bearing, bore, borne**) **1** *formal* to carry **2** to endure, put up with **3** to produce (fruit, children, etc) **bear in mind** to remember, take into account **bear out** to confirm: *This bears out my suspicions* **bear with** to be patient with **bring to bear** to bring into use

ⓘ **Born** is used for the past participle when referring to the birth of a child, idea, etc: *When were you born?* This form is also used in the passive, unless it is followed by the word **by**: *The child was born last week.* Otherwise the form is **borne**: *the baby borne by Ms Smith/I couldn't have borne it any longer.*

a b c d e f g h i j k l m n o p q r s t u v w x y z

bearable ADJECTIVE able to be borne or endured

beard NOUN the hair that grows on a man's chin and cheeks ▶ VERB to face up to, defy

bearer NOUN a carrier or messenger

bearing NOUN **1** behaviour **2** the direction of a line or point from a reference point, expressed as an angle measured in degrees clockwise from the north **3** (**bearings**) *informal* a sense or awareness of your own position or surroundings **4** relevance: *It has no bearing on the issue* **5** part of a machine supporting a moving part

beast NOUN **1** a four-footed animal **2** a brutal person > **beastly** ADJECTIVE (**beastlier, beastliest**) **1** behaving like an animal **2** *informal* horrible **3** *informal* unpleasant

beat VERB (**beating, beat, beaten**) **1** to hit violently and repeatedly **2** to overcome, defeat **3** of a pulse or the heart: to move or throb in the normal way **4** to mark (time) in music **5** to stir (a mixture etc) with quick movements **6** to strike (bushes etc) to rouse birds for shooting ▶ NOUN the regular round of a police officer etc > **beaten** ADJECTIVE **1** of metal: shaped **2** of earth: worn smooth by treading **3** defeated **beat up** *informal* to injure by repeated hitting, kicking, etc

beatific (*pronounced* bee-*a*-**tif**-ik) ADJECTIVE of, or showing, great happiness

beatify (*pronounced* bee-**at**-if-ai) VERB (**beatifies, beatifying, beatified**) **1** *RC Church* to declare someone who has died as holy **2** to make supremely happy > **beatification** NOUN

Beaufort scale (*pronounced* **boh**-fort) NOUN, *meteorology* a system for estimating wind speeds without using instruments

ⓘ Named after Sir Francis *Beaufort* (1774–1857), the British naval officer and scientist who devised it

beautiful ADJECTIVE very attractive or pleasing in appearance, sound, etc > **beautifully** ADVERB

beautify VERB (**beautifies, beautifying, beautified**) to make beautiful

beauty NOUN (*plural* **beauties**) **1** very attractive or pleasing appearance, sound, etc **2** a very attractive person, especially a woman

beaver NOUN **1** an animal that can gnaw through wood and dam streams **2** a member of the most junior branch of the Scout Association

becalmed ADJECTIVE of a sailing ship: unable to move for lack of wind

because CONJUNCTION for the reason that: *We didn't go because it was raining* ▶ ADVERB (**because of**) on account of: *Because of the holiday, the bank will be shut*

beck NOUN: **at someone's beck and call** obeying all their orders or requests

beckon VERB to make a sign (with the finger) to summon someone

become VERB **1** to come to be: *She became angry* **2** to suit: *That tie becomes you* > **becoming** ADJECTIVE

1 suiting someone well **2** of behaviour: appropriate, suitable

bed NOUN **1** a place on which to rest or sleep **2** a plot for flowers etc in a garden **3** the bottom of a river etc ▸VERB (**bedding, bedded**) **1** to plant in soil etc **2** to provide a bed for **3** *informal* to have sexual intercourse with

bed and breakfast (*abbrev* **B and B** *or* **B & B** *or* **b & b**) NOUN **1** at a guesthouse, hotel, etc: overnight accommodation with breakfast included in the price **2** a guesthouse etc that provides accommodation and breakfast

bedclothes PLURAL NOUN sheets, blankets, etc for a bed

bedding NOUN **1** mattress, bedclothes, etc **2** straw etc for cattle to lie on

bedlam NOUN a place full of uproar and confusion

ⓘ After St Mary of *Bethlehem* Hospital, a former mental asylum in London

bed linen NOUN sheets and pillowcases

Bedouin (*pronounced* **bed**-oo-in) NOUN (*plural* **Bedouin** *or* **Bedouins**) a member of a nomadic tent-dwelling Arab tribe that lives in the deserts of the Middle East

ⓘ Comes from French *beduin*, from Arabic *badawi* meaning 'desert-dweller'

bedpan NOUN a wide shallow pan used as a toilet by someone unable to get out of bed

bedraggled ADJECTIVE wet and untidy

bedridden (*pronounced* **bed**-rid-*en*) ADJECTIVE kept in bed by weakness, illness, etc

bedrock NOUN the solid rock under the soil

bedroom NOUN a room for sleeping

bedsore NOUN an ulcer on a person's skin, caused by lying in bed for long periods (*also called*: **pressure sore**)

bedspread NOUN a top cover for a bed

bedstead NOUN a frame supporting a bed

bee NOUN a winged insect that makes honey in wax cells

beech NOUN (*plural* **beeches**) a forest tree with grey, smooth bark

beef NOUN the flesh of an ox or cow, used as food

beefburger NOUN a flattened cake of minced beef, grilled or fried

beefeater NOUN **1** a guardian of the Tower of London **2** a member of the Queen's or King's Guard

beehive NOUN a dome or box in which bees are kept

beeline NOUN: **make a beeline for** to go directly towards

Beelzebub (*pronounced* bi-**el**-zib-ub) NOUN, *old* the Devil, Satan

been *see* **be**

beer NOUN an alcoholic drink flavoured with hops

beet NOUN a plant with a carrot-like root, one type (**sugar beet**) used as a source of sugar, the other (**beetroot**) used as a vegetable

beetle NOUN an insect with four wings, the front pair forming hard covers for the back pair

beetling ADJECTIVE **1** of cliffs etc: overhanging **2** of eyebrows: heavy, frowning

befall VERB (**befalling, befell, befallen**) *formal* to happen to, strike: *A disaster befell them*

before PREPOSITION **1** in front of: *before the entrance to the tunnel* **2** earlier than: *before three o'clock* **3** rather than, in preference to: *I'd die before telling him* ▶ ADVERB **1** in front **2** earlier ▶ CONJUNCTION earlier than the time that: *before he was born*

beforehand ADVERB previously, before the time when something else is done

befriend VERB to become a friend of, help

beg VERB (**begging, begged**) **1** to ask for money etc from others **2** to ask earnestly: *He begged her to stay* **beg the question** to take as being proved the very point that needs to be proved

began *past tense* of **begin**

beggar NOUN someone who begs for money > **beggarly** ADJECTIVE poor; worthless **beggar belief** to be beyond belief, be incredible VERB to make poor

begin VERB (**beginning, began, begun**) to make a start on > **beginner** NOUN > **beginning** NOUN

begrudge VERB to grudge, envy: *He begrudged me my success*

beguile VERB to captivate **beguile into** *or* **out of** to trick (someone) into or out of (something)

begun *past participle* of **begin**

behalf NOUN: **on behalf of 1** as the representative of: *on behalf of my client* **2** in aid of: *collecting on behalf of the homeless*

behave VERB **1** to act (in a certain way): *He always behaves badly at parties* **2** to conduct yourself well: *Can't you behave for just a minute?* > **behaviour** NOUN

behead VERB to cut off the head of

behind PREPOSITION **1** at or towards the back of: *behind the door* **2** after **3** in support of, encouraging: *behind him all the way* ▶ ADVERB **1** at the back **2** not up to date: *behind with his work*

behold VERB, *old* to look (at), see

beige (*pronounced* beisz) NOUN a light brown colour

being NOUN **1** existence **2** a living person or thing

belated ADJECTIVE arriving late > **belatedly** ADVERB

belch VERB **1** to bring up wind from the stomach through the mouth **2** of a fire etc: to send up (smoke) violently

beleaguer (*pronounced* be-**leeg**-*er*) VERB to besiege

belfry (*pronounced* **bel**-fri) NOUN (*plural* **belfries**) the part of a steeple or tower in which the bells are hung

belief NOUN **1** what someone thinks to be true **2** faith

believable ADJECTIVE able to be believed; possible

believe VERB **1** to think of as true or as existing **2** to trust (in) **3** to think or suppose **make believe** to pretend

belittle VERB to make seem small or unimportant

bell NOUN a hollow metal object which gives a ringing sound when struck by the clapper inside

bellicose ADJECTIVE inclined to fight, quarrelsome > **bellicosity** NOUN

belligerent ADJECTIVE quarrelsome, aggressive > **belligerence** *or* **belligerency** NOUN

bellow VERB to roar like a bull ▶ NOUN a deep roar

bellows PLURAL NOUN an instrument for making a blast of air, eg to increase a fire

belly NOUN (*plural* **bellies**) **1** the abdomen **2** the underpart of an animal's body **3** the bulging part of anything ▶ VERB (**bellies, bellying, bellied**) to swell or bulge out

belly button NOUN, *informal* the navel

belong VERB **1** to be someone's property: *This book belongs to me* **2** to be a member of (a club etc) **3** to be born in or live in: *I belong to Glasgow* **4** of an object: to have its place in: *Those glasses belong in the kitchen* > **belongings** PLURAL NOUN what someone possesses

beloved ADJECTIVE much loved, very dear ▶ NOUN someone much loved

below PREPOSITION lower in position, amount, etc than: *Her skirt reached below her knees/40 degrees below zero* ▶ ADVERB **1** in a lower position: *looking down at the street below* **2** further on in a book etc

belt NOUN **1** a strip of leather, cloth, etc worn around the waist **2** a continuous band on a machine for conveying objects in a factory etc **3** a broad strip, eg of land ▶ VERB **1** to put a belt round **2** to beat with a belt **3** *informal* to beat, hit **belt out** *informal* to sing or say very loudly

bemoan VERB to weep about, mourn

bemused ADJECTIVE bewildered; confused

bench NOUN (*plural* **benches**) **1** a long seat **2** a worktable **3** (**the bench**) the judges of a court

benchmark NOUN **1** anything used as a standard or point of reference **2** *surveying* a permanent mark cut on a post, building, etc giving the height above sea level of the land at that spot **3** *computing* a standard program used to compare the performance of different makes of computer

bench test NOUN a test carried out on something, eg computer hardware or software, before it is installed or released

bend VERB (**bending, bent**) **1** to curve **2** to stoop ▶ NOUN **1** a curve **2** a turn in a road

beneath PREPOSITION **1** under, in a lower position than: *sitting beneath the tree reading a book* **2** covered by: *wearing a black dress beneath her coat* **3** considered too low a task etc for: *Sweeping floors was beneath him* ▶ ADVERB below

benediction NOUN, *Christianity* a blessing at the end of worship

benefactor NOUN someone who does good to others

beneficial ADJECTIVE bringing gain or advantage (to)

A B C D E F G H I J K L M N O P Q R S T U V W X Y Z

beneficiary NOUN (*plural* **beneficiaries**) someone who receives a gift, an advantage, etc

benefit NOUN **1** something good to receive or have done to you **2** money received from social security or insurance schemes: *unemployment benefit* ▶ VERB (**benefiting, benefited**) **1** to do good to **2** to gain advantage: *benefited from the cut in interest rates*

benevolence NOUN **1** tendency to do good; kindliness **2** a kind act > **benevolent** ADJECTIVE kindly

benign (*pronounced* bi-**nain**) ADJECTIVE **1** gentle, kindly **2** of disease: not causing death (*contrasted with*: **malignant**)

Benioff zone NOUN, *geography* an earthquake zone generated by collision between plates
ⓘ Named after Hugo *Benioff* (1899–1968), American geophysicist

bent NOUN a natural liking or aptitude (for something) ▶ ADJECTIVE **1** curved, crooked **2** *informal* dishonest **be bent on** to be determined to VERB *past form* of **bend**

benthos NOUN, *biology* the living organisms that are found at the bottom of the sea or a lake > **benthic** ADJECTIVE (*compare with*: **pelagic**)

benzene NOUN, *chemistry* an inflammable colourless liquid hydrocarbon, used as a solvent and in the manufacture of plastics, dyes, drugs, etc

bequeath (*pronounced* bi-**kweedh**) VERB to leave by will

bequest NOUN money, property, etc left in a will

berate VERB to scold severely

bereaved ADJECTIVE suffering from the recent death of a relative or friend > **bereavement** NOUN

bereft ADJECTIVE lacking, deprived (of)

beret (*pronounced* **be**-rei) NOUN a flat, round hat

berkelium NOUN, *chemistry* (symbol **Bk**) an artificially produced radioactive metallic element
ⓘ It was first produced at *Berkeley*, California

Berlin Wall NOUN, *history* a wall separating East Berlin, Germany, from the part of the city occupied by Western powers, built in 1961 to stop emigration from East to West, but mostly taken down when Germany was reunified in 1990

berm NOUN **1** a narrow ledge or path beside an embankment, road, canal, etc **2** *geography* a ridge of sand or stones on a beach, formed by incoming tides

Bermuda shorts *or* **Bermudas** PLURAL NOUN knee-length shorts

berry NOUN (*plural* **berries**) a small juicy fruit enclosing seeds

berserk ADVERB in a frenzy, mad

berth NOUN **1** a room for sleeping in a ship etc **2** the place where a ship is tied up in a dock ▶ VERB to moor (a ship) **give a wide berth to** to keep well away from

beryl NOUN a type of precious stone such as an emerald or aquamarine

beryllium NOUN, *chemistry*

(symbol **Be**) a silvery-grey metallic element, obtained from the mineral beryl

beseech VERB (**beseeching, besought** *or* **beseeched**) to ask earnestly

beset VERB (**besetting, beset**) to attack from all sides; surround

beside PREPOSITION **1** by the side of, near: *the building beside the station* **2** compared with: *Beside her sister she seems quite shy* **be beside yourself** to lose self-control **beside the point** irrelevant

besides PREPOSITION **1** in addition to: *He has other friends, besides me* **2** other than, except: *nothing in the fridge besides some cheese* ▶ ADVERB **1** also, moreover: *Besides, it was your idea* **2** in addition: *plenty more besides*

besiege VERB (**besieging, besieged**) **1** to surround (a town etc) with an army **2** to crowd round; overwhelm: *besieged with letters*

besotted ADJECTIVE (**besotted with**) foolishly fond of

bespoke ADJECTIVE **1** of clothes: ordered to be made **2** *computing* of software: specially created for a specific situation

best ADJECTIVE good in the most excellent way ▶ ADVERB in the most excellent way ▶ VERB to defeat **at best** under the most favourable circumstances **do your best** to try as hard as you can **make the best of** to do as well as possible with

🛈 Comes from Old English *betst/betest*

bestial ADJECTIVE like a beast, beastly

best man NOUN someone who attends a man who is being married

bestow VERB, *formal* to give

best part NOUN the largest or greatest part

bestseller NOUN a book etc which sells exceedingly well

bet NOUN money put down to be lost or kept depending on the outcome of a race etc ▶ VERB (**betting, bet** *or* **betted**) to place a bet

beta test (*pronounced* **bee**-*ta*) NOUN, *computing* a second round of tests run on new software before it is marketed, designed to recreate normal working conditions > **beta testing** NOUN

bête noire (*pronounced* bet **nwahr**) NOUN (*plural* **bêtes noires** – *pronounced* bet **nwahrz**) a particular dislike

betray VERB **1** to give up (secrets, friends, etc) to an enemy **2** to show signs of: *His face betrayed no emotion* > **betrayal** NOUN

betroth (*pronounced* bi-**trohdh**) VERB, *formal* to promise in marriage > **betrothal** NOUN **betrothed to** engaged to be married to

better ADJECTIVE **1** good to a greater degree, of a more excellent kind **2** healthier **3** completely recovered from illness: *Don't go back to work until you're better* ▶ ADVERB in a more excellent way ▶ VERB to improve **get the better of** to defeat, overcome **had better** ought to, must **think better of** to change your mind about

🛈 Comes from Old English *betera*

between PREPOSITION **1** in or

A B C D E F G H I J K L M N O P Q R S T U V W X Y Z

through the space dividing two people or things: *There was an empty seat between us/between 3 o'clock and 6 o'clock* **2** in parts, in shares to: *Divide the chocolates between you* **3** from one thing to another: *the road between Edinburgh and Glasgow* **4** comparing one to the other: *The only difference between them is the price*

> ⓘ Use **between** when individual people or things are named: *Duties are shared between John, James and Catherine.* Use **among** when there is a notion of distrubuting or sharing: *Share the sweets among yourselves.*

bevel NOUN a slanting edge ▶ VERB (**bevelling, bevelled**) to give a slanting edge to > **bevelled** ADJECTIVE

beverage NOUN a drink

Beveridge Report NOUN, *history* a proposal for social reform made in 1942 by William Beveridge, a British economist, that was the basis for the creation of the welfare state

bevy[1] NOUN (*plural* **bevies**) **1** a group of women or girls **2** a flock of quails

bevy[2] *or* **bevvy** NOUN (*plural* **bevies** *or* **bevvies**) *Brit informal* **1** an alcoholic drink **2** a drinking session

bewail VERB to mourn loudly over

beware VERB to watch out for (something dangerous): *Beware of the dog*

bewilder VERB to puzzle, confuse > **bewildering** ADJECTIVE > **bewilderment** NOUN confusion

bewitch VERB to put under a spell; charm > **bewitching** ADJECTIVE charming; very beautiful

beyond PREPOSITION **1** on the far side of: *beyond the next set of traffic lights* **2** later than: *beyond January* **3** more than: *beyond the call of duty* **4** too far gone for: *beyond repair* **5** too difficult or confusing for: *It's beyond me!* ▶ ADVERB on or to the far side, further away

Bh SYMBOL, *chemistry* bohrium

bhajan NOUN, *Hinduism* a devotional hymn

bhakti NOUN, *Hinduism* loving devotion to God

bhangra (*pronounced* **bung**-*ru*) NOUN a style of pop music created from a mix of traditional Punjabi and Western pop

ⓘ Comes from Punjabi, the name of a traditional harvest dance

bhikkhu *or* **bhikshu** NOUN, *Buddhism* a Buddhist monk

bhikkhuni *or* **bhikshuni** NOUN, *Buddhism* a Buddhist nun

Bi SYMBOL, *chemistry* bismuth

bi- PREFIX **1** having two: *biped/bipolar* (= having two poles or extremities)/*bicycle* **2** occurring twice in a certain period, or once in every two periods: *bi-monthly* **3** *chemistry* indicating a salt or compound with twice the amount of the given acid etc: *bicarbonate* **4** *chemistry* indicating a compound with two identical hydrocarbon groups: *biphenyl*

ⓘ Comes from Latin *bis* meaning 'twice' or 'two'

biannual ADJECTIVE happening twice a year

Comes from Latin *bi-* meaning 'two' or 'twice', and *annus* meaning 'year'

> Do not confuse with: **biennial**

bias NOUN **1** the favouring of one person or point of view over any others **2** a tendency to move in a particular direction **3** a weight on or in an object making it move in a particular direction **4** *statistics* an unevenness in a sample due to a systematic error ▶VERB (**biases** *or* **biasses, biasing** *or* **biassing, biased** *or* **biassed**) to give a bias to > **biased** *or* **biassed** ADJECTIVE

bib NOUN **1** a piece of cloth put under a child's chin to protect their clothes from food stains etc **2** a part of an apron, dungarees, etc above the waist, covering the chest

Bible NOUN the holy book of the Christian Church > **Biblical** ADJECTIVE

biblio- PREFIX of or relating to books

Comes from Greek *biblion* meaning 'book'

bibliography NOUN (*plural* **bibliographies**) **1** a list of books (about a subject) **2** the art of classifying books

bicarbonate NOUN, *chemistry* a salt of carbonic acid

bicentenary (*pronounced* bai-sen-**tee**-*na*-ri) NOUN (*plural* **bicentenaries**) the two-hundredth year after an event, eg someone's birth

biceps SINGULAR NOUN, *anatomy* the muscle in front of the upper part of the arm

bicker VERB to quarrel over small matters

biconcave ADJECTIVE, *physics* of a lens: concave on both sides

biconvex ADJECTIVE, *physics* of a lens: convex on both sides

bicycle NOUN a vehicle with two wheels, driven by foot-pedals

bid[1] VERB (**bidding, bade** *or* **bid, bidden** *or* **bid**) **1** to offer a price (for) **2** to make an attempt to achieve something ▶NOUN **1** an offer of a price **2** a bold attempt: *a bid for freedom*

bid[2] VERB (**bidding, bade** *or* **bid, bidden** *or* **bid**) **1** to tell, say: *bidding her farewell* **2** to command **3** to invite

biddable ADJECTIVE compliant; obedient; docile

bidding NOUN **1** a command, request or invitation **2** the offers at an auction **3** *cards* the act of making bids **do someone's bidding** to obey their orders

bide VERB (**biding, bided** *or* **bode**), *Scot or old* **1** to wait or stay **2** to dwell or reside; to stay, especially temporarily **3** to endure or tolerate **bide your time** to wait patiently for the right moment

Comes from Anglo-Saxon *bidan*

bidet (*pronounced* **beed**-ei) NOUN a low wash-basin for washing the genital area and feet

biennial ADJECTIVE happening once every two years ▶NOUN **1** *botany* a plant that takes two years to

a b c d e f g h i j k l m n o p q r s t u v w x y z

A B C D E F G H I J K L M N O P Q R S T U V W X Y Z

complete its life cycle (*compare with:* **annual**, **perennial**) **2** an event taking place or celebrated every two years

[i] Comes from Latin *biennium* meaning 'two years'

> Do not confuse with: **biannual**

bier (*pronounced* beer) NOUN a carriage or frame for carrying a dead body

bifid (*pronounced* **bai**-fid *or* **bi**-fid) ADJECTIVE, *biology* divided into two parts by a deep split

bifocal (*pronounced* bai-**foh**-k*a*l) ADJECTIVE of spectacles or contact lenses: having two separate sections with different focal lengths, one for near vision, and one for viewing distant objects

big ADJECTIVE (**bigger**, **biggest**) **1** large in size, amount, extent, etc **2** important **3** boastful: *big ideas*

bigamy NOUN (*plural* **bigamies**) the crime or fact of having two wives or two husbands at once > **bigamist** NOUN > **bigamous** ADJECTIVE

big game NOUN large animals, such as lions, tigers, and elephants, hunted for sport

bigot NOUN someone with narrow-minded, prejudiced beliefs > **bigoted** ADJECTIVE prejudiced > **bigotry** NOUN

big top NOUN the main tent of a circus

bike NOUN, *informal* a bicycle

bikini NOUN (*plural* **bikinis**) a woman's brief two-piece bathing suit

[i] Named after *Bikini* Atoll atomic test site, because of its supposedly 'explosive' effect on men

bilateral ADJECTIVE **1** having two sides **2** affecting two sides, parties, etc: *bilateral agreement* > **bilaterally** ADVERB

bilberry NOUN (*plural* **bilberries**) a type of plant with an edible dark-blue berry

bile NOUN *biology* a thick alkaline fluid produced by the liver, used in the digestion of fats

bilge NOUN **1** the broadest part of a ship's bottom **2** bilgewater **3** *informal* nonsense

bilgewater NOUN water which lies in the ship's bottom

bilharzia NOUN, *medicine* a tropical disease caused by infestation with parasitic flukes which circulate in the blood

[i] Named after Theodor *Bilharz* (1825–62), the German parisitologist who discovered the flukes

bilingual ADJECTIVE using or fluent in two languages

bilious (*pronounced* **bil**-i-*u*s) ADJECTIVE **1** ill with too much bile; nauseated **2** greenish-yellow in colour

bill[1] NOUN a bird's beak

bill[2] NOUN **1** an account for money **2** an early version of a law before it has been passed by parliament **3** a printed sheet of information

billet NOUN a lodging, especially for soldiers ▸ VERB to lodge (soldiers) in private houses

billiards SINGULAR NOUN a game played with a cue and balls on a table

billion NOUN **1** a million millions (1,000,000,000,000) **2** *US* (now often in Britain) a thousand millions (1,000,000,000)

billionaire *or* **billionairess** NOUN someone who owns money and property worth over a billion pounds, dollars, etc

billow NOUN **1** a great wave **2** a mass of something such as smoke rising on or being swept along by the wind ▸VERB to be filled and swelled with, or moved along by, the wind: *sheets on a washing-line billowing in the wind/a billowing sail/billowing smoke* > **billowy** ADJECTIVE giving the impression of billowing: *billowy clouds*

billy (*plural* **billies**) *or* **billycan** NOUN, *Brit and Australian* a container for cooking, making tea, etc outdoors

billy goat NOUN a male goat

bimbo NOUN (*plural* **bimbos**), *slang* a young woman who is physically attractive but empty-headed

bimodal ADJECTIVE, *statistics* having two modes > **bimodality** NOUN

bin NOUN a container for storing goods or rubbish ▸VERB (**binning, binned**) **1** to put in a bin **2** to throw away

binary (*pronounced* **bai**-*na*-ri) ADJECTIVE **1** made up of two parts or components **2** *computing, maths* denoting a system that consists of two components, especially the numbers 0 and 1

binary digit NOUN, *computing, maths* **1** either of the two digits 0 and 1, used in binary systems **2** (*usually in short form* **bit**) the smallest unit of information

binary number NOUN, *computing, maths* a number represented by a combination of the digits 0 and 1

binary system NOUN, *computing, maths* a mathematical system in which numbers are expressed by two digits only, 1 and 0

bind VERB (**binding, bound**) **1** to tie with a band **2** to fasten together **3** to make to promise **4** to fasten the sections and put a cover on (a book)

binding NOUN **1** anything that binds **2** the cover, stitching, etc which holds a book together

binge VERB (**bingeing** *or* **binging, binged**) to eat and drink too much ▸NOUN a spell of overeating or drinking too much

bingo NOUN a popular gambling game using numbers

bin-liner NOUN a disposable plastic bag used as a lining inside a rubbish bin

binoculars PLURAL NOUN a small double telescope

binomial NOUN **1** *maths* an expression that contains two variables, eg *6x*–3y **2** *biology* a two-part name for an animal or plant, made up of the genus name and then the species name, eg *Homo sapiens* ▸ADJECTIVE **1** *maths* containing two variables **2** consisting of two names or terms

ⓘ Comes from **bi-**+ *nomen* meaning 'name'

bio- PREFIX of or relating to life or living organisms

a b c d e f g h i j k l m n o p q r s t u v w x y z

[i] Comes from Greek *bios* meaning 'life'

bioassay NOUN, *biology* assessing the concentration of a chemical substance by testing its effect on a living organism, eg its effect on plant growth

bioavailability NOUN, *biology* the extent to which, and rate at which, a drug is taken up by the body and reaches the tissues and organs it is intended for

biochemistry NOUN the study of the chemical composition and processes of living matter

biodegradable ADJECTIVE able to be broken down into parts by bacteria

biodiversity NOUN, *biology* the variety of organisms found in a specified geographical region

bioenergetics SINGULAR NOUN, *biology* the scientific study of the use of energy by living organisms, including its conversion from one form to another

bioengineering NOUN **1** *medicine* the application of engineering technology to biology and medicine, especially the manufacture of artificial limbs, heart pacemakers, etc **2** *biology* the application of engineering technology to the synthesis of plant and animal products

bioethics SINGULAR NOUN the study of ethics in biological and medical research and health care

bioflavonoid NOUN, vitamin P, a vitamin important for the capillaries, found in citrus fruit, blackcurrant and rosehips (*also called*: **citrin, flavonoid**)

biogenesis NOUN, *biology* the theory that living matter always arises from other, pre-existing, living matter > **biogenetic** ADJECTIVE

biogeography NOUN the scientific study of the distributions of plants and animals

biographer NOUN someone who writes a biography

biography NOUN (*plural* **biographies**) a written account of someone's life > **biographical** ADJECTIVE

biological ADJECTIVE **1** relating to the way that living organisms grow and behave: *What is the biological explanation for the ageing process?/biological washing powder* (= containing enzymes which break down certain types of dirt) **2** relating to biology

biological control NOUN, *biology* the control of plant or animal pests by the introduction of natural predators or parasites etc, or by interfering with their reproductive behaviour (*short form*: **biocontrol**)

biological warfare NOUN war using as weapons germs which can cause disease

biology NOUN the study of living things > **biologist** NOUN

bioluminescence NOUN, *biology* emission of light by living organisms, eg fireflies and certain fungi

biomass NOUN *biology, geography* all the living things in a given habitat

biome NOUN, *biology* a large community of plants and animals characterized by the main vegetation in the region where they live, eg grassland biome, desert biome

bionics SINGULAR NOUN the use of natural systems as models for artificial systems > **bionic** ADJECTIVE

biophysics SINGULAR NOUN the application of the laws of physics to the study of biological processes > **biophysicist** NOUN

biopsy NOUN (*plural* **biopsies**) the removal of a sample of body tissue for medical examination

biorhythm NOUN, *biology* a periodic change in the behaviour or physiology of many animals and plants (eg hibernation and migration)

BIOS (*pronounced* **bai**-os) ABBREVIATION, *computing* Basic Input-Output System, an essential part of a computer operating system on which more complex functions are based

biosphere NOUN, *biology* the parts of the land, sea and atmosphere in which organisms live

biotechnology NOUN, *biology* the use of living organisms or biological substances to perform an industrial process or manufacture a product

biotin NOUN, *chemistry* vitamin H

biped (*pronounced* **bai**-ped) NOUN an animal with two feet, eg a bird or a human being

biplane NOUN an early type of aeroplane with two sets of wings, one above the other

bipolar ADJECTIVE having two poles or extremes > **bipolarity** NOUN

birch NOUN (*plural* **birches**) **1** a type of hardwood tree **2** a bundle of birch twigs, used for beating ▸ VERB to beat with a birch

bird NOUN a feathered, egg-laying creature **get the bird** *slang* to be booed or hissed at; be dismissed

bird of prey NOUN (*plural* **birds of prey**) a bird (eg a hawk) which kills and eats small animals or birds

birdwatching NOUN the study of birds in their natural surroundings > **birdwatcher** NOUN

birl VERB, *Scottish* to spin round, whirl

Biro NOUN, *trademark* a type of ballpoint pen

ⓘ After László *Bíró* (1899–1985), a Hungarian journalist who invented it

birth NOUN the very beginning of someone's life

birth certificate NOUN an official document that records a person's birth, stating the date and place, the parents, etc

birth control NOUN the prevention of pregnancy, especially by means of contraception

birthday NOUN **1** the day on which someone is born **2** the date of this day each year

birthmark NOUN a mark on the body from birth

birthplace NOUN the place where someone was born: *Shakespeare's birthplace*

birth rate NOUN (sometimes **crude**

birth rate) the number of live births occurring over a period of a year in a given area per thousand inhabitants

birthright NOUN the right which someone may claim because of their parentage

biscuit NOUN dough baked hard in a small cake

bisexual NOUN someone who is sexually attracted to both males and females ▶ ADJECTIVE sexually attracted to both males and females > **bisexuality** NOUN

bishop NOUN a high-ranking member of the clergy (next below an archbishop) in the Roman Catholic Church, the Church of England and some other churches > **bishopric** NOUN the district ruled by a bishop

bismuth NOUN, *chemistry* (symbol **Bi**) a hard, silvery-white, metallic element with a pinkish tinge, used to make alloys and in medicine

bison NOUN (*plural* **bison**) a large wild ox with shaggy hair and a large hump

bistro (*pronounced* **beest**-roh) NOUN (*plural* **bistros**) a small bar or restaurant

bit[1] NOUN a small piece **bit by bit** gradually **do your bit** to do your required share **to bits** apart, in pieces

bit[4] *past tense* of **bite**

bitch NOUN (*plural* **bitches**) **1** a female dog, wolf, etc **2** *slang* an unpleasant woman > **bitchy** ADJECTIVE

bite VERB (**biting, bit, bitten**) to grip, cut or tear with the teeth ▶ NOUN **1** a grip with the teeth **2** the part bitten off **3** a nibble at a fishing bait **4** a wound caused by an animal's or insect's bite

biting ADJECTIVE **1** bitterly and painfully cold **2** of a remark: sharp and hurtful; sarcastic

bits per second NOUN, *computing* (*abbrev* **bps**) a measurement for the rate of transmission of bits

bitten *past participle* of **bite**

bitter ADJECTIVE **1** unpleasant to the taste; sour **2** harsh: *bitter cold* **3** resentful; angry through disappointment

bitterness NOUN **1** the quality of being bitter: *the bitterness of the drink* **2** bitter feelings: *the bitterness I used to feel towards him*

bittersweet ADJECTIVE pleasant and unpleasant at the same time: *a bittersweet love story*

bitty ADJECTIVE (**bittier, bittiest**) piecemeal, scrappy

bivalve *zoology*, ADJECTIVE said of a mollusc: having a shell composed of two valves hinged together by a ligament ▶ NOUN one of many mainly marine species of mollusc with such a shell, eg clam, mussel and scallop

bivariate ADJECTIVE, *maths* involving two variables

bivouac (*pronounced* **biv**-oo-ak) NOUN an overnight camp outdoors without a tent ▶ VERB (**bivouacking, bivouacked**) to sleep outdoors without a tent

bi-weekly ADJECTIVE happening twice a week or once every two weeks

bizarre ADJECTIVE odd, strange

Bk SYMBOL, *chemistry* berkelium

blab VERB (**blabbing, blabbed**) **1** to talk a lot **2** to let out a secret

Black ADJECTIVE of people: dark skinned, especially of African, West Indian or Australian Aboriginal origin belonging or relating to Black people ▸ NOUN a dark-skinned person, especially of African, West Indian or Aboriginal origin

black ADJECTIVE dark and colourless, like coal; without any light; of tea or coffee: without added milk; angry; threatening: *black looks* dirty; soiled; sad or gloomy: *black despair* ▸ NOUN the colour of coal *black clothes worn for mourning* **black out** to become unconscious **in the black** in credit; out of debt

black-and-blue ADJECTIVE *informal* badly bruised

blackball VERB to ostracize, exclude from (a club etc)

black belt NOUN an award for skill in judo, karate, and other martial arts

blackberry NOUN (*plural* **blackberries**) a blackish-purple soft fruit growing on a prickly stem

blackboard NOUN a dark-coloured board for writing on in chalk

black body NOUN, *physics* a hypothetical body that absorbs all the radiation that falls on it, and reflects none

Black Codes PLURAL NOUN, *history* laws passed by Southern states of the USA in 1865–6, which restricted the rights of the slaves freed after the American Civil War

blackcurrant NOUN a widely cultivated shrub or one of the small round black fruits it produces

Black Death NOUN, *history* a deadly epidemic of bubonic plague that swept over Asia and Europe in the 14th century

blacken VERB **1** to make black or dark **2** to dishonour, defame: *blackening his name*

black eye NOUN a bruised area round the eye as the result of a blow

blackguard (*pronounced* **blag-ahrd**) NOUN, *old* a wicked person

blackhead NOUN a small black spot on the skin caused by sweat blocking one of the skin's tiny pores

black hole NOUN a region in space with such a strong gravitational pull that not even light can escape from it

black ice NOUN a thin transparent layer of ice on a road

blacklist NOUN a list of people to be refused credit, jobs, etc ▸ VERB to put on a blacklist

black magic NOUN magic performed for an evil purpose; witchcraft

blackmail NOUN the crime of threatening to reveal secrets unless money is paid ▸ VERB to threaten by blackmail > **blackmailer** NOUN

black market NOUN illegal or dishonest buying and selling

blackout NOUN **1** total darkness caused by putting out or covering all lights **2** a temporary loss of consciousness

black pepper NOUN pepper

produced from the dried fruits of the pepper plant ground without removing their dark outer covering

Black Power NOUN, *history* a militant movement to increase the political influence of black people, especially in the USA

black pudding NOUN sausage made with pig's blood

black sheep NOUN someone who is considered a failure or outsider in a group

Blackshirt NOUN, *history* a member of a Fascist organization, especially in the Nazi SS and in Italy during World War II, named after the colour of the uniform

blacksmith NOUN someone who makes or repairs iron goods, especially horseshoes

black spot NOUN, *chiefly Brit* **1** a dangerous stretch of road where accidents often occur **2** an area where an unfortunate social condition is common: *an unemployment black spot*

black tie NOUN formal evening dress

black widow NOUN a very poisonous American spider, the female of which often eats her mate

bladder NOUN *anatomy* the hollow organ in which urine collects in the body

bladderwrack NOUN a common seaweed with air bladders on its strands

blade NOUN **1** the cutting part of a knife, sword, etc **2** a leaf of grass or wheat

blag VERB (**blagging, blagged**), *slang* **1** to rob or steal **2** to get (something) for nothing: *blagged his way into the club*

blame VERB to find fault with; consider responsible for ▶ NOUN fault; responsibility for something bad > **blameless** ADJECTIVE

blameworthy ADJECTIVE deserving blame

blanch VERB **1** to make white by removing the colour **2** to become pale, especially out of fear **3** *cookery* to prepare (vegetables or meat) by boiling in water for a few seconds **4** *cookery* to remove the skins from (almonds etc) by soaking in boiling water

ⓘ Comes from French *blanc* meaning 'white'

bland ADJECTIVE **1** mild, not strong or irritating: *bland taste* **2** dull, insipid

blank ADJECTIVE **1** clear, unmarked: *a blank sheet of paper* **2** expressionless: *a blank look* ▶ NOUN **1** an empty space **2** a cartridge without a bullet ▶ VERB **1** to ignore (someone) **2** to obscure or hide (something): *I tried to blank the incident from my mind* > **blankly** ADVERB

blank cheque NOUN **1** a cheque which has been signed but on which the amount to be paid has been left blank **2** complete freedom or authority

blanket NOUN **1** a bedcovering of wool etc **2** a widespread, soft covering: *a blanket of snow* ▶ ADJECTIVE covering a group of things: *a blanket agreement* ▶ VERB (**blanketing, blanketed**) to cover widely or thickly

blanket bombing NOUN bombing from the air over a widespread area

blank verse NOUN non-rhyming poetry, especially in a metre of five feet per line

blare VERB to sound loudly ▸NOUN a loud sound, eg on a trumpet

blasé (*pronounced* blah-**zei**) ADJECTIVE indifferent, unconcerned, especially because of being already familiar with something

ⓘ Comes from French *blaser* meaning 'to cloy'

blaspheme VERB **1** to speak irreverently of a god **2** to swear, curse > **blasphemer** NOUN > **blasphemous** ADJECTIVE > **blasphemy** NOUN (*plural* **blasphemies**) **1** the act of speaking irreverently of a god **2** a swear-word: *uttering foul blasphemies*

blast NOUN **1** a blowing or gust of wind **2** a loud note, eg on a trumpet **3** an explosion ▸VERB **1** to break (stones, a bridge, etc) by explosion **2** to produce a loud noise **3** *formal* to wither, destroy ▸INTERJECTION damn! **at full blast** as quickly, strongly, etc as possible

blast-off NOUN the moment of the launching of a rocket

blatant (*pronounced* **bleit**-*a*nt) ADJECTIVE very obvious; shameless: *blatant lie* > **blatantly** ADVERB

blaze NOUN a rush of light or flame ▸VERB **1** to burn with a strong flame **2** to throw out a strong light

blazer NOUN a light jacket often worn as part of a uniform

bleach VERB to whiten, remove the colour from ▸NOUN (*plural* **bleaches**) a substance which bleaches, used for cleaning, whitening clothes, etc

bleak ADJECTIVE dull and cheerless; cold, unsheltered > **bleakly** ADVERB sadly, wistfully > **bleakness** NOUN

bleary ADJECTIVE (**blearier, bleariest**) of eyes: tired and inflamed > **blearily** ADVERB with tired-looking, watery eyes: *He opened his eyes and looked at me blearily*

bleat VERB **1** to cry like a sheep **2** to complain in an irritating or whining way ▸NOUN **1** a sheep's cry **2** an irritating whine

bleed VERB (**bleeding, bled**) **1** to lose blood **2** to draw blood from

bleeding NOUN a flow of blood

bleep NOUN a high-pitched intermittent sound ▸VERB to give out such a sound

bleeper NOUN an electronic device using a bleep as a signal

blemish NOUN (*plural* **blemishes**) a stain; a fault or flaw ▸VERB to stain, spoil

blend VERB to mix together ▸NOUN a mixture

blender NOUN an electric machine which mixes thoroughly and liquidizes food

bless VERB **1** to wish happiness to **2** to make happy **3** to make holy > **blessed** (*pronounced* **bles**-id) *or* (in poetry etc) **blest** ADJECTIVE **1** happy; fortunate **2** made holy, consecrated

blessing NOUN **1** a wish or prayer for happiness **2** a source of happiness or relief: *The extra money was a blessing to them*

a b c d e f g h i j k l m n o p q r s t u v w x y z

A B C D E F G H I J K L M N O P Q R S T U V W X Y Z

blessing in disguise something unexpectedly useful or beneficial

blether VERB, *Scottish* to chatter; talk nonsense

blew *past tense* of **blow**[1]

blight NOUN **1** a disease which makes plants wither **2** a cause of destruction ▶ VERB to destroy

blind ADJECTIVE unable to see ▶ NOUN **1** a window screen **2** a deception, a trick ▶ VERB **1** to make blind **2** to dazzle > **blindness** NOUN

blindfold NOUN a bandage or cover which is put over a person's eyes to prevent them from seeing ▶ ADJECTIVE with the eyes bandaged or covered, so as not to see ▶ VERB to apply a blindfold to

blindly ADVERB without knowledge or direction: *stumbling around blindly*

blink VERB to close the eyes for a moment; shine unsteadily

blinkers PLURAL NOUN pieces of leather over a horse's eyes to prevent it seeing in any direction except in front

bliss NOUN very great happiness > **blissful** ADJECTIVE bringing feelings of great happiness; lovely: *a blissful holiday*

blister NOUN a thin bubble on the skin full of watery matter ▶ VERB to rise up in a blister

blithe (*pronounced* blaidh) ADJECTIVE happy, merry > **blithely** ADVERB: *He blithely imagines he'll pass his exams without studying*

blitz NOUN (*plural* **blitzes**) **1** (also **blitzkreig**) an air attack **2** (**the Blitz**) the series of air-raids on British cities by the German air force in 1940–41 **3** *informal* a burst of intensive activity or work to achieve something

blizzard NOUN a fierce storm of wind and snow

bloated ADJECTIVE swollen, puffed out

blob NOUN **1** a drop of liquid **2** a round spot

block NOUN **1** a lump of wood, stone, etc **2** a connected group of buildings **3** an obstruction: *a road block* **4** an engraved piece of wood or metal for printing **5** *history* the wood on which people were beheaded ▶ VERB to hinder, prevent from progress

blockade VERB to surround (a fort or country) so that food etc cannot reach it ▶ NOUN the surrounding of a place in this way

blog *computing*, *informal*, NOUN short for **weblog** ▶ VERB (**blogged, blogging**) to write a **weblog** > **blogger** NOUN > **blogging** NOUN

blond ADJECTIVE of a man: having fair skin and light-coloured hair

blonde ADJECTIVE of a woman: having fair skin and light-coloured hair ▶ NOUN a woman with this colouring

blood NOUN **1** the red liquid which flows in the bodies of human beings and animals **2** someone's descent or parentage: *royal blood*

blood cell NOUN a cell contained in the blood

blood clot NOUN a clot formed at a bleeding wound or in a blood vessel

bloodcurdling ADJECTIVE causing chilling fear

blood donor NOUN someone who gives blood which is stored and given to others in transfusions etc

blood group NOUN any one of the types into which human blood is classified

bloodhound NOUN a breed of large dog with a good sense of smell

bloodless ADJECTIVE without bloodshed: *bloodless revolution*

blood plasma NOUN the clear, liquid part of blood

bloodshed NOUN violent loss of life, slaughter

bloodshot ADJECTIVE of eyes: inflamed with blood

bloodstream NOUN the flow of blood around the body

bloodthirsty ADJECTIVE (**bloodthirstier, bloodthirstiest**) cruel, eager to kill

blood vessel NOUN, *anatomy* a tube in the body through which blood circulates, eg a vein or artery

bloody ADJECTIVE (**bloodier, bloodiest**) **1** covered with blood **2** extremely violent, gory **3** *slang* terrible, awful > **bloodiness** NOUN

bloom VERB **1** of a plant: to flower **2** to be in good health ▸NOUN **1** a flower **2** rosy colour **3** freshness, perfection **4** a powder on the skin of fresh fruits

bloomers PLURAL NOUN **1** loose underpants with legs gathered above the knee **2** in the past, a woman's outfit of a jacket, skirt and baggy knee-length trousers

ⓘ After Amelia *Bloomer*, 19th-century US feminist who promoted the use of the outfit for women

blossom NOUN **1** a flower **2** the flowers on a fruit tree ▸VERB **1** to produce flowers **2** to open out, develop, flourish

blot NOUN **1** a spot of ink **2** a stain ▸VERB (**blotting, blotted**) **1** to spot, stain **2** to dry (writing) with blotting paper **blot out** to remove from sight or memory

blotch NOUN (*plural* **blotches**) a spot or patch of colour ▸VERB to mark with blotches > **blotched** ADJECTIVE > **blotchy** ADJECTIVE (**blotchier, blotchiest**) with skin or another surface which is temporarily an uneven colour: *Her face was blotchy from crying*

blouse NOUN a woman's loose piece of clothing for the upper body

blow[1] VERB (**blowing, blew, blown**) **1** of wind: to move around **2** to drive air upon or into **3** to sound (a wind instrument) **4** to breathe hard or with difficulty **blow over** to pass and be forgotten **blow up** to destroy or be destroyed by explosion

blow[2] NOUN **1** a hard stroke or knock, eg with the fist **2** *informal* a sudden piece of bad luck

blowtorch *or* **blowlamp** NOUN a tool for aiming a very hot flame at a particular spot, used for paint-stripping etc

blowy ADJECTIVE (**blowier, blowiest**) windy

blubber NOUN the fat of whales and other sea animals

bludgeon NOUN a short stick with a heavy end ▸VERB to hit with a heavy object

blue NOUN the colour of a clear

A B C D E F G H I J K L M N O P Q R S T U V W X Y Z

sky ▸ ADJECTIVE **1** of this colour **2** unhappy, depressed **3** containing sexual material: *blue film*

bluebell NOUN **1** the wild hyacinth **2** in Scotland, the harebell

bluebottle NOUN a large fly with a blue abdomen

blue-chip ADJECTIVE of a business company: reliable for investment; prestigious

Blue Peter NOUN a blue flag with a white centre, raised when a ship is about to sail

blue whale NOUN a rare, bluish whale, which is the largest living animal

bluff[1] VERB to try to deceive by pretending self-confidence ▸ NOUN deception, trickery **call someone's bluff** to challenge someone to prove their claim or promise

bluff[2] ADJECTIVE **1** rough and cheerful in manner **2** frank, outspoken ▸ NOUN a steep bank overlooking the sea or a river

blunder VERB to make a bad mistake ▸ NOUN a bad mistake

blunt ADJECTIVE **1** having an edge or point that is not sharp **2** rough in manner ▸ VERB to make less sharp or less painful > **bluntly** ADVERB frankly, straightforwardly

blur NOUN an indistinct area of something; a smudge, a smear ▸ VERB (**blurring, blurred**) to make indistinct, smudge > **blurred** ADJECTIVE

blurt VERB: **blurt out** to speak suddenly and without thinking

blush NOUN (*plural* **blushes**) **1** a red glow on the face caused by embarrassment etc **2** a reddish glow ▸ VERB to go red in the face

bluster VERB **1** to blow strongly **2** to boast loudly ▸ NOUN **1** a strong wind **2** empty boasting > **blustery** ADJECTIVE very windy

boa NOUN a long scarf of fur or feathers

boa constrictor NOUN a large snake which kills its prey by winding itself round it and crushing it

boar NOUN **1** a male pig **2** a wild pig

board NOUN **1** a sheet of wood **2** a group of people who run a business: *a board of directors* **3** stiff card used to bind books **4** food: *bed and board* ▸ VERB **1** to cover with boards **2** to receive or supply with food and lodging **3** to enter (a ship, aeroplane, etc) > **boarder** NOUN someone who receives food and lodging

boarding house NOUN a house in which people live and take meals as paying guests

boarding school NOUN a school in which food and lodging is given

boast VERB **1** to talk proudly about yourself **2** to have (something worth being proud of): *The hotel boasts magnificent views* ▸ NOUN an act of boasting

boastful ADJECTIVE with a tendency to boast

boat NOUN **1** a vessel for sailing or rowing; a ship **2** a boat-shaped dish: *a sauce boat* ▸ VERB to sail about in a boat

boater NOUN a straw hat with a brim

boatswain *or* **bosun** (*both pronounced* **boh**-*s*un) NOUN an officer who looks after a ship's boats, rigging, etc

bob[1] VERB (**bobbing, bobbed**) to move up and down rapidly

bob[2] VERB (**bobbing, bobbed**) to cut (hair) to about neck level ▸ NOUN a bobbed haircut

bobbin NOUN a reel or spool on which thread is wound

bobble NOUN **1** a woolly ball for decorating hats etc **2** a little ball on the surface of fabric **3** a bobbing action

bobby NOUN (*plural* **bobbies**), *Brit informal* a police officer

🛈 After Sir *Robert* Peel, who introduced the Metropolitan Police Force when Home Secretary in 1828

bobsleigh NOUN a long sledge or two short sledges joined together with one long seat

bode[1] VERB: **bode ill** to be a bad sign **bode well** to be a good sign

bode[2] *past tense* of **bide**

bodice NOUN the close-fitting part of a woman's or a child's dress above the waist

bodily ADJECTIVE of the body

body NOUN (*plural* **bodies**) **1** the whole or main part of a human being or animal **2** a corpse **3** the main part of anything **4** a mass of people **5** a solid object **6** *informal* a bodystocking

bodyguard NOUN someone or a group of people whose job is to protect an important person from harm or attack

body language NOUN communication by means of conscious or unconscious gestures, attitudes, facial expressions, etc

bodywarmer NOUN a padded sleeveless jacket

boffin NOUN, *informal* a research scientist

🛈 Said to come from a scientist who gave his colleagues nicknames from Dickens, Mr Boffin being a character in *Our Mutual Friend*

bog NOUN **1** a marsh **2** *slang* a toilet > **boggy** ADJECTIVE (**boggier, boggiest**) marshy **bog down** to prevent from making progress

bogey NOUN (*plural* **bogeys**) something greatly feared

bogus ADJECTIVE false

bohemian (*pronounced* boh-**hee**-mi-*a*n) NOUN someone who lives outside social conventions, especially an artist or writer ▸ ADJECTIVE of the lifestyle of a bohemian

boil[1] VERB **1** of a liquid: to reach the temperature at which it turns to vapour **2** to bubble up owing to heat **3** *informal* to be hot **4** *informal* to be angry

boil[2] NOUN a kind of inflamed swelling

boiler NOUN a container in which water is heated or steam is produced

boiling point NOUN the temperature at which a liquid turns to vapour (eg, for water, 100°C)

boisterous ADJECTIVE **1** wild, noisy **2** of weather: stormy

bold ADJECTIVE **1** daring, full of

courage **2** cheeky **3** striking, well-marked: *bold colours* **4** of printing type: thick and clear > **boldly** ADVERB (meanings 1, 2 and 3)

bollard NOUN **1** a post to which ropes are fastened on a ship or quay **2** a short post on a street used for traffic control

Bolshevik NOUN **1** *history* a member of the Extreme Socialist Party in revolutionary Russia **2** *derogatory* a communist

ⓘ A Russian word based on *bolshe* 'greater', either because of the majority held by the Bolsheviks in the Social Democratic Congress of 1903, or because of their more extreme programme

bolster NOUN a long cylindrical pillow or cushion **bolster up** to support

bolt NOUN **1** a small metal sliding bar used to fasten a door etc **2** a large screw or pin **3** a roll of cloth ▶ VERB **1** to fasten with a bolt **2** to swallow (food) hurriedly **3** to rush away, escape ▶ ADVERB: **bolt upright** sitting with a very straight back

bomb NOUN **1** a case containing explosive or other harmful material thrown, dropped, timed to go off automatically, etc **2** (**the bomb**) the nuclear bomb ▶ VERB to drop bombs on

bombard VERB **1** to attack with artillery **2** to overwhelm (with): *bombarded with letters* > **bombardment** NOUN

bomber NOUN **1** an aeroplane built for bombing **2** someone who throws or plants bombs

bombshell NOUN **1** a startling piece of news **2** a stunningly attractive woman

bona fide (*pronounced* bohn-*a* **fai**-dei) ADJECTIVE real, genuine: *a bona fide excuse*

ⓘ In Latin, *bona fide* means 'in good faith'

bond NOUN **1** something which binds, eg a rope **2** something which brings people together: *Music was a bond between them* **3** a promise to pay or do something **in bond** in a bonded warehouse

bondage NOUN slavery

bonded warehouse NOUN a warehouse where goods are kept until taxes have been paid on them

bone NOUN **1** a hard material forming the skeleton of animals **2** one of the connected pieces of a skeleton: *the hip bone* ▶ VERB to take the bones out of (meat etc)

bonfire NOUN a large fire in the open air

bonnet NOUN **1** a decorative woman's hat, fastened under the chin **2** the covering over a car engine

bonny (**bonnier, bonniest**) ADJECTIVE good-looking; pretty

bonsai (*pronounced* **bon**-sai) NOUN a miniature or dwarf tree created by special pruning, or the art of growing such trees

bonus NOUN (*plural* **bonuses**) **1** an extra payment in addition to wages **2** something extra

bony ADJECTIVE (**bonier, boniest**) **1** full of bones **2** not fleshy, thin **3** made of bone or a bone-like substance

boo VERB to make a sound of disapproval ▸ NOUN a sound of disapproval

boob[1] NOUN, *informal* a mistake

boob[2] NOUN, *slang* a woman's breast

booby trap NOUN a device hidden or disguised as something harmless, intended to injure the first person to come near it

book NOUN **1** a number of pages bound together **2** a written work which has appeared, or is intended to appear, in the form of a book ▸ VERB to order (places etc) beforehand

book-keeping NOUN the keeping of accounts > **book-keeper** NOUN

booklet NOUN a small paperback book

bookmaker NOUN someone who takes bets and pays winnings

bookmark NOUN **1** something inserted in the pages of a book to mark a place **2** *computing* a record of the location of a favourite Internet site, web page, etc ▸ VERB, *computing* to make an electronic record of (a favourite Internet site etc)

bookworm NOUN **1** *informal* an avid reader **2** a grub which eats holes in books

Boolean operators (*pronounced* **boo**-li-*an*) PLURAL NOUN, *computing* the words 'NOT', 'AND' and 'OR', used to link words in Internet searches (*also called*: **Boolean connectors**)

boom[1] VERB to make a hollow sound or roar ▸ NOUN a loud, hollow sound

boom[2] VERB to increase in prosperity, success, etc ▸ NOUN a rush or increase of trade, prosperity, etc: *oil boom/property boom*

boomerang NOUN a curved piece of wood which when thrown returns to the thrower, a traditional hunting weapon of Australian Aboriginals

boon NOUN something to be grateful for, a blessing

boor NOUN a rough or rude person > **boorish** ADJECTIVE

boost VERB to push up, raise, increase: *boost the sales figures* ▸ NOUN an increase, a rise

booster NOUN **1** a device for increasing the power of a machine etc **2** the first of several stages of a rocket

boot[1] NOUN **1** a heavy shoe covering the foot and lower part of the leg **2** *Brit* a place for stowing luggage in a car **3** *computing* the starting of a computer from its start-up programs **4** a kick ▸ VERB to kick **boot up** *computing* to start (a computer) by running its start-up programs

boot[2] NOUN: **to boot** in addition, as well

bootee NOUN a knitted boot for a baby

booth NOUN **1** a covered stall, eg at a market **2** a small compartment for telephoning, voting, etc

booty NOUN plunder, gains taken in war etc

border NOUN **1** the edge or side of anything **2** the boundary of a country **3** a flowerbed in a garden ▸ VERB: **border on** to be near to: *bordering on the absurd*

A B C D E F G H I J K L M N O P Q R S T U V W X Y Z

borderline NOUN **1** the line dividing two countries etc **2** the line dividing two things: *the borderline between passing and failing* ▸ ADJECTIVE on the borderline between one thing and another: *a borderline pass*

bore[1] VERB to make a hole by piercing ▸ NOUN **1** a pierced hole **2** the size across the tube of a gun

bore[2] VERB to weary, be tiresome to: *This book bores me* ▸ NOUN a tiresome person or thing > **bored** ADJECTIVE

bore[3] *past tense* of **bear**[2]

boredom NOUN lack of interest, weariness

boring ADJECTIVE not at all interesting

born ADJECTIVE by birth, natural: *a born actor* **be born 1** of a baby: to come out of the mother's womb **2** to come into existence

> Do not confuse: **born** and **borne**. **Born** is used for the past participle of **bear** when referring to the birth of a child, idea, etc; otherwise the form is **borne**: *I couldn't have borne it any longer.*

borne *past participle* of **bear**[2]

> Do not confuse: **borne** and **born**

borough NOUN **1** *history* a town with special privileges granted by royal charter **2** a town that elects Members of Parliament

borrow VERB to get on loan > **borrower** NOUN

bosom NOUN **1** the breast **2** midst, centre: *in the bosom of her family* ▸ ADJECTIVE of a friend: close, intimate

boss NOUN (*plural* **bosses**) a manager, a chief ▸ VERB to order about in a high-handed way

bossy ADJECTIVE (**bossier, bossiest**) tending to boss others, domineering

botanist NOUN someone who studies botany

botany NOUN the study of plants > **botanic** *or* **botanical** ADJECTIVE

botch VERB to mend clumsily; do badly ▸ NOUN (*plural* **botches**) a badly done piece of work

both ADJECTIVE & PRONOUN the two, the one and the other: *We're both going to Paris/Both the men are dead* ▸ ADVERB equally, together: *both willing and able*

bother VERB **1** to be a nuisance to: *Stop bothering me!* **2** to take time or trouble over something: *Don't bother with the dishes* ▸ NOUN trouble, inconvenience

bothy NOUN (*plural* **bothies**), *Scot* **1** a hut to give shelter to hillwalkers **2** a simply furnished hut for farm workers

bottle NOUN a hollow narrow-necked vessel for holding liquids ▸ VERB to put in a bottle **bottle up** to keep in, hold back (feelings)

bottle bank NOUN a skip collecting empty glass containers for recycling

bottleneck NOUN **1** a narrow part of a road likely to become crowded with traffic **2** a stage in a process where progress is held up

bottom NOUN **1** the lowest part

or underside of anything **2** the buttocks

bottomless ADJECTIVE extremely deep

boudoir (*pronounced* **bood**-wahr) NOUN, *old* a lady's private room

bough NOUN a branch of a tree

bought *past form of* **buy**

boulder NOUN a large stone

bounce VERB **1** to jump up after striking the ground etc **2** to make (a ball etc) do this ▸ NOUN a jumping back up **bounce back** to recover after a setback or trouble

bouncer NOUN someone employed to force troublemakers to leave a club etc

bouncing ADJECTIVE full of life, lively

bound[1] *past form of* **bind** ADJECTIVE obliged **bound to** certain to NOUN **1** a leap, a jump **2** (**bounds**) borders, limits ▸ VERB **1** to jump, leap **2** to enclose, surround

bound[2] ADJECTIVE: **bound for** on the way to

bound[3] NOUN **1** (**bounds**) borders, limits **2** *maths* a number which shows the upper (the **upper bound**) and lower (the **lower bound**) values in range of possible values

bound[4] VERB to jump, leap ▸ NOUN a leap, a jump

boundary NOUN (*plural* **boundaries**) **1** an edge, a limit **2** a line etc marking an edge

boundless ADJECTIVE having no limit, vast

bountiful *or* **bounteous** ADJECTIVE generous plentiful

bounty NOUN (*plural* **bounties**) **1** a gift generosity **2** a reward

bouquet (*pronounced* boo-**kei**) NOUN **1** a bunch of flowers **2** a scent, eg of wine

bourgeois (*pronounced* **boorsz**-wah) ADJECTIVE of the middle class > **bourgeoisie** NOUN (**the bourgeoisie**) a rather insulting name for middle-class people who have a comfortable but unimaginative lifestyle

bout NOUN **1** a round in a contest **2** a spell, a fit: *a bout of flu*

boutique NOUN a small shop selling fashionable clothes etc

bovine (*pronounced* **boh**-vain) ADJECTIVE **1** of or like cattle **2** *derogatory* stupid

bow[1] (*pronounced* bow) VERB **1** to bend **2** to nod the head or bend the body in greeting **3** to give in: *bow to pressure* ▸ NOUN **1** a bending of the head or body **2** the front part of a ship

bow[2] (*pronounced* boh) NOUN **1** anything in the shape of a curve or arch **2** a weapon for shooting arrows, made of a stick of springy wood bent by a string **3** a looped knot, usually decorative **4** a wooden rod with horsehair stretched along it, by which the strings of a violin etc are played

[i] After Thomas *Bowdler*, who produced a heavily censored edition of Shakespeare in the 19th century

bowels PLURAL NOUN **1** the large and small intestines **2** the innermost or deepest parts of anything: *in the bowels of the earth*

bowl[1] NOUN **1** a basin for holding liquids **2** a basin-shaped hollow

a b c d e f g h i j k l m n o p q r s t u v w x y z

bowl[2] NOUN **1** a heavy wooden ball, used in bowling etc **2** (**bowls**) a game played on a green with specially weighted bowls ▸ VERB **1** to play at bowls **2** to move speedily like a bowl **3** *cricket* to send (the ball) at the wicket **4** *cricket* to put out by knocking the wicket with the ball **bowl over 1** to knock down **2** to surprise greatly

bowler[1] NOUN **1** someone who plays bowls **2** someone who bowls in cricket

bowler[2] NOUN a hat with a rounded top

bowling NOUN **1** the game of bowls **2** the game of tenpin bowling

bow tie NOUN a neck tie with two loops and a knot

box[1] NOUN (*plural* **boxes**) **1** a case for holding anything **2** an enclosure of private seats in a theatre ▸ VERB **1** to put in a box **2** to confine in a small space

box[2] VERB **1** to punch **2** to engage in the sport of boxing

box[3] NOUN **1** a hardwood tree **2** an evergreen shrub

boxer NOUN **1** someone who boxes as a sport **2** a breed of large smooth-haired dog with a head like a bulldog's

boxing NOUN the sport of fighting with the fists wearing padded gloves

Boxing Day NOUN the first weekday after Christmas Day

box office NOUN an office where theatre tickets etc may be bought

boy NOUN a male child

boycott VERB to refuse to do business or trade with ▸ NOUN a refusal to trade or do business

ⓘ After Charles *Boycott*, British estate manager ostracized by the Irish Land League in the 19th century

boyfriend NOUN a male friend, especially in a romantic relationship

boyhood NOUN the time of being a boy

boyish ADJECTIVE **1** of a girl: having an appearance or behaviour which gives an impression of masculinity **2** of a man: having an appearance or behaviour which gives an impression of youthfulness

bra NOUN an article of women's underwear for supporting the breasts

brace NOUN **1** an instrument which draws things together and holds them firmly **2** a piece of wire fitted over teeth to straighten them **3** a pair of pheasant, grouse, etc when shot **4** a carpenter's tool for boring **5** (**braces**) shoulder-straps for holding up trousers ▸ VERB to strengthen, give firmness to

bracelet NOUN **1** a circular ornament placed around the wrist **2** *slang* a handcuff

bracing ADJECTIVE giving strength

bracken NOUN a coarse kind of fern

bracket NOUN **1** a support for something fastened to a wall **2** each of a pair of written or printed marks, eg (), [ ], used to group together several words, figures, etc **3** a grouping, category: *in the same age bracket* ▸ VERB **1** to enclose in brackets **2** to group together

brag VERB (**bragging, bragged**) to boast ▸ NOUN a boast

Brahmin *or* **Brahman** NOUN (*plural* **Brahmins** *or* **Brahmans**) one of the highest-ranking groups of Hindus, from which priests come

braid VERB to plait (the hair) ▸ NOUN **1** a plait of hair **2** decorative ribbon used as trimming

braille NOUN a system of raised marks on paper which blind people can read by feeling

> ⓘ Named after its inventor, French teacher Louis *Braille*

brain NOUN the part of the body inside the skull, the centre of feeling and thinking ▸ VERB to hit hard on the head

brainwash VERB to force (someone) to believe something by using constant pressure
> **brainwashing** NOUN

brainwave NOUN a good idea

brainy ADJECTIVE (**brainier, brainiest**) *informal* clever

brake NOUN a part of a vehicle used for stopping or slowing down ▸ VERB to slow down by using the brake(s)

bramble NOUN **1** the blackberry bush **2** its fruit

bran NOUN the inner husks of wheat etc, separated from flour after grinding

branch NOUN (*plural* **branches**) **1** an arm-like limb of a tree **2** a small shop, bank, etc belonging to a bigger one ▸ VERB to spread out like branches

brand NOUN **1** a make of goods with a special trademark **2** a burning piece of wood **3** a permanent mark made by a red-hot iron ▸ VERB **1** to mark with a brand **2** to mark permanently; impress deeply **3** to mark with disgrace: *branded as a thief*

brandish VERB to wave (a weapon etc) about

brand-new ADJECTIVE absolutely new

brandy NOUN (*plural* **brandies**) an alcoholic spirit made from wine

brass NOUN (*plural* **brasses**) **1** a metal made by mixing copper and zinc **2** *music* brass wind instruments, eg trumpets and horns ▸ ADJECTIVE **1** made of brass **2** playing brass musical instruments: *the brass section*

brass band NOUN a musical band consisting mainly of brass wind instruments

brat NOUN a disapproving name for a child

bravado (*pronounced* bra-**vah**-doh) NOUN a show of bravery; bold pretence

brave ADJECTIVE ready to meet danger, pain, etc without showing fear; courageous, noble ▸ VERB to face or meet boldly and without fear ▸ NOUN a Native American warrior

bravery NOUN the quality of being brave and acting with courage

bravo INTERJECTION well done!

brawl NOUN a noisy quarrel; a fight ▸ VERB to quarrel or fight noisily

brawn NOUN muscle power
> **brawny** ADJECTIVE (**brawnier, brawniest**) big and strong

A B C D E F G H I J K L M N O P Q R S T U V W X Y Z

bray NOUN **1** a cry like that of an ass **2** a pin pressing against a string on a harp to produce a buzzing effect ▸ VERB to cry like an ass

brazen ADJECTIVE **1** impudent, shameless: *brazen hussy* **2** of or like brass > **brazenly** ADVERB **brazen it out** to face a difficult situation with bold impudence

brazier (*pronounced* **breiz**-i-*er*) NOUN an iron basket for holding burning coals

breach NOUN (*plural* **breaches**) **1** a break, a gap **2** a breaking of a law, a promise, etc **3** a quarrel ▸ VERB to make a gap or opening in **breach of the peace** a breaking of the law by noisy, offensive behaviour

bread NOUN food made of flour or meal mixed with water etc and baked

breadth NOUN **1** distance from side to side, width **2** extent: *breadth of knowledge*

breadwinner NOUN someone who earns a living for a family

break VERB (**breaking, broke, broken**) **1** to (cause to) fall to pieces or apart **2** to act against (a law, promise, etc) **3** to interrupt (a silence) **4** to tell (news) **5** to check, soften the effect of (a fall) **6** to cure (a habit) **7** of a boy's voice: to drop to a deep male tone at puberty ▸ NOUN **1** an opening **2** a pause **3** *informal* a lucky chance **break down 1** to divide into parts **2** of an engine: to fail **3** to be overcome with weeping or nervous exhaustion **break in** to tame, train (a wild horse etc) **break into** to enter by force **break out 1** to appear suddenly **2** to escape **break out in something** to become covered (with a rash etc) **break up 1** to (cause to) fall to pieces or apart **2** to separate, leave one another > **breakable** ADJECTIVE

breakage NOUN **1** the act of breaking **2** something broken

breakdown NOUN **1** a division into parts **2** a collapse from nervous exhaustion etc

breaker NOUN a large wave

breakfast NOUN the first meal of the day ▸ VERB to eat this meal

break-in NOUN illegal forced entry of a house etc with intent to steal

breakthrough NOUN a sudden success after some effort

breakwater NOUN a barrier to break the force of waves

breast NOUN **1** either of the milk-producing glands on a woman's body **2** the front part of a human or animal body between neck and belly **3** a part of a jacket or coat which covers the breast **make a clean breast** to make a full confession

breastbone NOUN the bone running down the middle of the breast; the sternum

breath (*pronounced* breth) NOUN **1** the air drawn into and then sent out from the lungs **2** an instance of breathing **3** a very slight breeze

> Do not confuse: **breath** and **breathe**

Breathalyser NOUN, *trademark* a device into which someone breathes to indicate the amount of alcohol in their blood

breathe (*pronounced* breedh) VERB (**breathing, breathed**) **1** to draw in and send out air from the lungs **2** to whisper

> Do not confuse: **breathe** and **breath**

breather NOUN a rest or pause

breathless ADJECTIVE **1** breathing very fast, panting **2** excited

breathtaking ADJECTIVE very surprising or impressive

bred *past form* of **breed**

breech NOUN (*plural* **breeches**) the back part, especially of a gun

breeches (*pronounced* **brich**-iz) PLURAL NOUN trousers reaching to just below the knee

breed VERB (**breeding, bred**) **1** to mate and rear (animals) **2** to cause: *Dirt breeds disease* ▶ NOUN **1** a group of animals etc descended from the same ancestor **2** type, sort: *a new breed of salesmen* > **breeder** NOUN someone who breeds certain animals

breeding NOUN **1** the act of producing or rearing **2** good manners; education and training

breeze NOUN a gentle wind

breeze block NOUN a type of large, grey brick used in building

breezy ADJECTIVE (**breezier, breeziest**) **1** windy, gusty **2** bright, lively > **breezily** ADVERB (meaning 2)

brethren PLURAL NOUN, *old* brothers

breve (*pronounced* breev) NOUN a mark (˘) sometimes put over a vowel to show that it is short or unstressed

brevity (*pronounced* **brev**-i-ti) NOUN shortness, conciseness

brew VERB **1** to make beer **2** to make (tea etc) **3** to be gathering or forming: *There's trouble brewing* **4** to plot, plan: *brewing mischief* > **brewer** NOUN someone who brews beer etc

brewery NOUN (*plural* **breweries**) a place where beer is made

briar *or* **brier** NOUN **1** the wild rose **2** a heather plant whose wood is used for making tobacco pipes

bribe NOUN a gift of money etc given to persuade someone to do something ▶ VERB to offer a bribe to > **bribery** NOUN

bric-à-brac NOUN small odds and ends

brick NOUN **1** a block of baked clay for building **2** a toy building-block of wood etc

bricklayer NOUN someone whose job it is to build with bricks

bridal ADJECTIVE of a bride or a wedding

bride NOUN a woman about to be married, or newly married

bridegroom NOUN a man about to be married, or newly married

bridesmaid NOUN a woman who attends the bride at a wedding

bridge[1] NOUN **1** a structure built to carry a track or road across a river etc **2** the captain's platform on a ship **3** the bony part of the nose **4** a thin piece of wood holding up the strings of a violin etc ▶ VERB **1** to be a bridge over; span **2** to build a bridge over **3** to get over (a difficulty)

A B C D E F G H I J K L M N O P Q R S T U V W X Y Z

bridge[2] NOUN a card game for two pairs of players

bridle NOUN the harness on a horse's head to which the reins are attached ▶ VERB **1** to put on a bridle **2** to toss the head indignantly

bridle path NOUN a path for horse-riders

brief ADJECTIVE short; taking a short time ▶ NOUN a set of notes giving information or instructions, especially to a lawyer about a law case ▶ VERB to instruct or inform **in brief** in a few words > **briefly** ADVERB

briefcase NOUN a flat case for carrying papers

briefs PLURAL NOUN close-fitting underpants

brigade NOUN a body of soldiers, usually two battalions

brigadier (*pronounced* brig-a-**deer**) NOUN a senior army officer

bright ADJECTIVE **1** shining; full of light **2** clever **3** cheerful

brighten VERB to make or grow bright

brilliant ADJECTIVE **1** very clever **2** sparkling **3** *informal* very good, excellent > **brilliance** NOUN > **brilliantly** ADVERB: *brilliantly intelligent/The edges of the diamond gleamed brilliantly/He did brilliantly in his exams*

brim NOUN **1** the edge of a cup etc: *filled to the brim* **2** the protruding lower edge of a hat or cap ▶ VERB (**brimming, brimmed**) to be full

brimstone NOUN, *old* sulphur

brine NOUN salt water > **briny** ADJECTIVE (**brinier, briniest**)

bring VERB (**bringing, brought**) **1** to fetch, lead or carry (to a place) **2** to cause to come: *The medicine brings him relief* **bring about** to cause **bring home to** to make (someone) realize (something) **bring off** to do (something) successfully **bring to** to revive **bring up 1** to rear, feed and educate: *brought up three children single-handed* **2** to mention: *I'll bring it up at the meeting* **3** *informal* to vomit

[i] Comes from Old English *bringan* meaning 'to carry' or 'to bring'

brink NOUN the edge of a cliff etc **on the brink of** almost at the point of, on the verge of: *on the brink of tears*

brisk ADJECTIVE **1** moving quickly: *a brisk walk* **2** lively and efficient: *a brisk manner* > **briskly** ADVERB

bristle NOUN a short, stiff hair on an animal, a brush, etc ▶ VERB **1** of hair etc: to stand on end **2** to show anger and indignation: *He bristled at my remark* > **bristly** ADJECTIVE (**bristlier, bristliest**) having bristles; rough

brittle ADJECTIVE hard but easily broken

broach VERB **1** to begin to talk about: *broached the subject* **2** to open, begin using (eg a cask of wine)

broad ADJECTIVE **1** wide, extensive **2** of an accent etc: strong, obvious > **broadly** ADVERB **1** widely: *smile broadly* **2** generally: *Broadly speaking, we're all afraid of the same things*

broadband ADJECTIVE **1** of telecommunications: operating across a wide range of frequencies (*compare with*: **narrowband**) **2** *computing* accommodating data from a wide range of sources, eg telephone, television, etc

broadcast VERB to transmit (a programme etc) on radio or television ▸ NOUN a programme transmitted on radio or television > **broadcaster** NOUN

broaden VERB to make or grow broader

broad-minded ADJECTIVE tolerant and liberal

broadsheet NOUN a large-format newspaper, usually with in-depth news coverage (*compare with*: **tabloid**)

broadside NOUN **1** a strong attack in an argument etc **2** a shot by all the guns on one side of a ship

brocade NOUN a silk cloth on which fine patterns are sewn

broccoli NOUN a hardy variety of cauliflower with small green or purple flower-heads

brochure (*pronounced* broh-**shoor** *or* **broh**-shur) NOUN a booklet, a pamphlet: *a holiday brochure*

brogue[1] (*pronounced* brohg) NOUN a strong shoe

brogue[2] (*pronounced* brohg) NOUN a broad accent in speaking: *Irish brogue*

broil VERB **1** to make or be very hot **2** *US* to grill

broke *past tense* of **break** ▸ ADJECTIVE, *informal* having no money

broker NOUN someone who buys and sells stocks and shares for others ▸ VERB **1** to act as a broker **2** to negotiate on behalf of others: *broker a deal*

bromide NOUN **1** a chemical compound used as a sedative **2** a monochrome photographic print

bronchus (*pronounced* **brong**-kus) NOUN (*plural* **bronchi** – *pronounced* **brong**-kai) *anatomy* either of the two tubes leading from the windpipe to the lungs

bronco NOUN (*plural* **broncos**) *US* a half-tamed horse

bronze NOUN a golden-brown mixture of copper and tin ▸ ADJECTIVE of this colour > **bronzed** ADJECTIVE suntanned

brooch (*pronounced* brohch) NOUN (*plural* **brooches**) an ornament pinned to the clothing

brood VERB **1** of a hen etc: to sit on eggs **2** to think anxiously for some time ▸ NOUN **1** a number of young birds hatched at one time **2** young animals or children of the same family

broody ADJECTIVE (**broodier, broodiest**) **1** moody, thoughtful **2** *informal* of a woman: eager to have a baby

brook NOUN a small stream

broom NOUN **1** a type of shrub with yellow flowers **2** a brush for sweeping

broomstick NOUN the handle of a broom

brose NOUN, *Scottish* a liquid food of boiling water poured on oatmeal

broth NOUN water in which vegetables and meat, etc have been boiled, used as soup

brothel NOUN a house where

A B C D E F G H I J K L M N O P Q R S T U V W X Y Z

prostitution is practised

brother NOUN **1** a male born of the same parents as yourself **2** a companion, a fellow-worker

brotherhood NOUN **1** comradeship between men **2** a men's association

brother-in-law NOUN (*plural* **brothers-in-law**) **1** the brother of your husband or wife **2** the husband of your sister or sister-in-law

brotherly ADJECTIVE like a brother; affectionate

brought *past form* of **bring**

brow NOUN **1** a forehead **2** an eyebrow **3** the edge of a hill

brown NOUN a dark colour made by mixing red, yellow, black, etc ▸ ADJECTIVE **1** of this colour **2** *informal* suntanned

brownfield site NOUN an area which has been redeveloped for another use (*compare with*: **greenfield site**)

brownie NOUN **1** a helpful fairy or goblin **2** a Brownie Guide

browse VERB **1** to glance through a range of books, shop merchandise, etc **2** of deer etc: to feed on the shoots or leaves of plants **3** *computing* to examine information (in a database etc)

browser NOUN, *computing* a computer program used for searching and managing data from the World Wide Web

bruise NOUN a discoloured area on the skin, the surface of fruit, etc, where it has been struck ▸ VERB to cause bruises (to)

brunette NOUN a woman with dark brown hair

brunt NOUN: **bear** *or* **take the brunt** to take the chief strain

brush NOUN (*plural* **brushes**) **1** an instrument with tufts of bristles, hair, etc for smoothing the hair, cleaning, painting, etc **2** a disagreement, a brief quarrel: *a brush with the law* **3** the tail of a fox **4** undergrowth ▸ VERB **1** to pass a brush over **2** to remove by sweeping **3** to touch lightly in passing

Brussels sprout NOUN a type of vegetable with sprouts like small cabbages on the stem

brutal ADJECTIVE cruel or violent > **brutality** NOUN > **brutally** ADVERB

brute NOUN **1** an animal **2** a cruel person > **brutish** ADJECTIVE

BSE ABBREVIATION bovine spongiform encephalopathy, a brain disease of cattle (*often called*: **mad cow disease**)

Bt ABBREVIATION baronet

bubble NOUN **1** a thin ball of liquid blown out with air **2** a small ball of air in anything ▸ VERB to rise in bubbles

bubbly ADJECTIVE (**bubblier, bubbliest**) **1** full of bubbles **2** lively, vivacious ▸ NOUN, *informal* champagne; sparkling wine

buck[1] NOUN the male of the deer, goat, hare or rabbit ▸ VERB of a horse etc: to attempt to throw (a ride) by rapid jumps into the air

buck[2] NOUN, *US informal* a dollar

bucket NOUN a container for water etc

buckle NOUN a clip for fastening straps or belts ▸ VERB to fasten with a buckle

bud NOUN **1** *biology* in a plant: a knob-like shoot that will eventually develop into a leaf or flower **2** a flower or leaf not fully open ▸ VERB (**budding, budded**) to produce buds

Buddhism NOUN a religion founded in the 6th century BC by Buddha ('the enlightened one'), based on spiritual purity and freedom from human concerns and desires > **Buddhist** NOUN & ADJECTIVE

budding ADJECTIVE showing signs of becoming: *budding author*

budge VERB to move slightly, stir

budgerigar NOUN a kind of small parrot often kept as a pet

budget NOUN **1** a government plan for the year's spending **2** any plan of their future spending ▸ VERB to allow for in a budget: *The project has been budgeted for*

> ⓘ Originally a small bag; the parliamentary sense of *budget* stems from an insult directed at Robert Walpole implying he was a quack or pedlar

budgie NOUN, *informal* a budgerigar

buff NOUN **1** a light yellowish-brown colour **2** an enthusiast, a fan: *a film buff* ▸ VERB to polish
ⓘ The later meaning of 'enthusiast' derives from the *buff*-coloured uniforms once used by volunteer firefighters in New York

buffalo NOUN (*plural* **buffaloes**) **1** a large Asian ox, used to draw loads **2** the North American bison

buffer NOUN something which lessens the force of a blow or collision

buffet[1] (*pronounced* **buf**-it) VERB (**buffeting, buffeted**) to strike, knock about ▸ NOUN a slap or a blow

buffet[2] NOUN (*pronounced* **buwf**-ei) **1** a counter or café serving food and drink **2** a range of dishes set out at a party etc for people to serve themselves

buffoon NOUN a clown, fool > **buffoonery** NOUN silly behaviour, clowning around

bug NOUN **1** a small, especially irritating, insect **2** a disease germ: *a tummy bug* **3** a tiny hidden microphone for recording conversations **4** *computing* a problem in a computer program causing errors in its execution ▸ VERB (**bugging, bugged**) **1** to conceal a microphone in (a room etc) **2** to record with a hidden microphone **3** *informal* to annoy, harass

buggy NOUN (*plural* **buggies**) a child's pushchair

bugle NOUN a small military trumpet > **bugler** NOUN someone who plays the bugle

build VERB (**building, built**) to put together the parts of anything ▸ NOUN physique; physical character: *a man of heavy build* > **builder** NOUN

building NOUN **1** the act or trade of building (houses etc) **2** a house or other built dwelling etc

building society NOUN an institution like a bank which accepts investments and whose main business is to lend people

A
B
C
D
E
F
G
H
I
J
K
L
M
N
O
P
Q
R
S
T
U
V
W
X
Y
Z

money to buy a house

bulb NOUN **1** the rounded part of the stem of an onion, tulip, etc, in which it stores its food **2** a glass globe surrounding the element of an electric light > **bulbous** ADJECTIVE bulb-shaped

bulge NOUN **1** a swelling **2** a noticeable increase ▸ VERB to swell out

bulimia (*pronounced* buw-**lim**-i-*a*) NOUN, *medicine* an eating disorder in which bingeing is followed by self-induced vomiting or purging > **bulimic** ADJECTIVE suffering from bulimia

bulk NOUN **1** large size **2** the greater part: *the bulk of the population*

bulky ADJECTIVE (**bulkier, bulkiest**) taking up a lot of room > **bulkily** ADVERB

bull NOUN the male of animals of the ox family, also of the whale, elephant, etc

bulldog NOUN a breed of strong, fierce-looking dog

bulldoze VERB **1** to use a bulldozer on **2** to force: *bulldozed his way into the room*

bulldozer NOUN a machine for levelling land and clearing away obstacles

bullet NOUN **1** the piece of metal fired from a gun **2** a small shape, such as a circle or square, highlighting each of the various points on a list

bulletin NOUN a report of current news, someone's health, etc

bullet-proof ADJECTIVE not able to be pierced by bullets

bullfight NOUN a public entertainment in Spain etc, in which a bull is baited and usually killed > **bullfighter** NOUN

bullion (*pronounced* **buwl**-yon) NOUN gold or silver in the form of bars etc

bullock NOUN a young bull

bull's-eye NOUN **1** the mark in the middle of a target **2** a striped sweet

bully NOUN (*plural* **bullies**) someone who unfairly uses their size and strength to hurt or frighten others ▸ VERB (**bullies, bullying, bullied**) to act like a bully towards > **bullying** NOUN

bulrush (*pronounced* **buwl**-rush) NOUN (*plural* **bulrushes**) a large strong reed which grows on, in, or near water

bulwark (*pronounced* **buwl**-w*a*rk) NOUN **1** a strong defensive wall **2** a prop, a defence

bum[1] NOUN, *Brit informal* the buttocks

bum[2] *US informal*, NOUN a tramp ▸ ADJECTIVE useless, dud

bumblebee NOUN a type of large bee

bump VERB **1** to strike heavily **2** to knock by accident ▸ NOUN **1** the sound of a heavy blow **2** an accidental knock **3** a raised lump > **bumpy** ADJECTIVE (**bumpier, bumpiest**)

bumper NOUN a bar round the front and back of a car's body to protect it from damage ▸ ADJECTIVE large: *a bumper crop*

bumpkin NOUN, *informal* a clumsy, awkward, country person

bumptious ADJECTIVE self-important

bun NOUN **1** a sweet roll made of egg dough **2** hair wound into a rounded mass

bunch NOUN (*plural* **bunches**) a number of things tied together or growing together ▸ VERB to crowd together

bundle NOUN a number of things loosely bound together ▸ VERB **1** to tie in a bundle **2** to push roughly: *bundled the children into the car*

bung NOUN the stopper of the hole in a barrel, bottle, etc ▸ VERB to stop up with a bung

bungalow NOUN a one-storey detached house

bungee jumping (*pronounced* **bun**-ji) NOUN the sport of jumping from a height with strong rubber ropes attached to the ankles so that the jumper bounces up before reaching the ground

bungle VERB **1** to do badly or clumsily **2** to mishandle, mismanage ▸ NOUN a clumsy or mishandled action

bunion NOUN a lump or swelling on the joint of the big toe

bunk NOUN a narrow bed, eg in a ship's cabin

bunk bed NOUN one of a pair of narrow beds one above the other

bunker NOUN **1** a sandpit on a golf course **2** an underground shelter **3** a large box for keeping coal

bunny NOUN (*plural* **bunnies**) a child's name for a rabbit

Bunsen burner NOUN a gas-burner used in laboratories

bunting NOUN **1** a thin cloth used for making flags **2** flags

buoy (*pronounced* boi) NOUN **1** a floating mark acting as a guide or warning for ships **2** a float, eg a lifebuoy

buoyant ADJECTIVE **1** able to float **2** cheerful, bouncy > **buoyancy** NOUN

burden NOUN **1** a load **2** something difficult to bear, eg poverty or sorrow **3** *old* the chorus of a song > **burdensome** ADJECTIVE

bureau (*pronounced* **byoo**-roh) NOUN (*plural* **bureaux** *or* **bureaus** – *both pronounced* **byoo**-rohz) **1** a writing table **2** an office

ⓘ **Bureau** is a French word, and comes from the name of a type of coarse cloth (*burel*) which was used as a cover for writing tables

bureaucracy (*pronounced* byoo-**rok**-*ra*-si) NOUN government by officials > **bureaucrat** NOUN an administrative official > **bureaucratic** ADJECTIVE **1** involving bureaucracy **2** full of complicated and irritating official procedures

burger NOUN a hamburger

burgh NOUN in Scotland, a borough

burglar NOUN someone who breaks into a house to steal

burglary NOUN (*plural* **burglaries**) a break-in into a house by a person who wants to steal things

burgle VERB to commit burglary

burial NOUN the placing of a body under the ground after death

burlesque NOUN a piece of writing, acting, etc making fun of somebody

burly ADJECTIVE (**burlier, burliest**) broad and strong

A B C D E F G H I J K L M N O P Q R S T U V W X Y Z

burn[1] VERB (**burning, burnt** *or* **burned**) **1** to set fire to **2** to be on fire, or scorching **3** to injure by burning **4** *computing* to record data onto (a compact disc) ▶NOUN an injury or mark caused by fire

burn[2] NOUN, *Scottish* a small stream

burner NOUN **1** the part of a lamp or gas jet from which the flame rises **2** *computing* a CD burner

burnt *past form* of **burn**[1]

burp VERB, *informal* to bring up wind through the mouth from the stomach

burr *or* **bur** NOUN the prickly seedcase or head of certain plants

burrow NOUN a hole or passage in the ground dug by certain animals for shelter ▶VERB to make a passage beneath the ground

burst VERB (**bursting, burst**) **1** to break suddenly (after increased pressure) **2** to move, speak, etc suddenly or violently ▶NOUN **1** an instance of something breaking suddenly **2** a sudden activity: *a burst of gunfire*

bury VERB (**buries, burying, buried**) **1** to place (a dead body etc) under the ground **2** to cover, hide

bus NOUN (*plural* **buses**) a large road vehicle, often used for public transport

busby NOUN (*plural* **busbies**) a tall fur hat worn by soldiers in certain regiments

bush NOUN (*plural* **bushes**) **1** a growing thing between a plant and a tree in size **2** wild, unfarmed country in Africa etc

bushy ADJECTIVE (**bushier, bushiest**) **1** growing thickly: *bushy eyebrows* **2** full of bushes > **bushiness** NOUN

business NOUN (*plural* **businesses**) **1** someone's work or job **2** trade, commerce: *Business is booming* **3** a matter of personal interest or concern: *none of your business*

businesslike ADJECTIVE practical, methodical, alert and prompt

businessman *or* **businesswoman** NOUN (*plural* **businessmen** *or* **businesswomen**) someone who works in commerce

busk VERB to play or sing in the street for money > **busker** NOUN

bus stop NOUN an official stopping place for buses

bust NOUN **1** a woman's breasts **2** a sculpture of someone's head and shoulders

bustle[1] VERB to busy oneself noisily ▶NOUN noisy activity, fuss

bustle[2] NOUN, *history* a stuffed pad worn at the back under a woman's full skirt

busy ADJECTIVE (**busier, busiest**) having a lot to do ▶VERB (**busies, busying, busied**): **busy yourself with** to occupy yourself with > **busily** ADVERB

busybody NOUN (*plural* **busybodies**) someone nosey about others

but CONJUNCTION **1** showing a contrast between two ideas etc: *My brother can swim but I can't* **2** except that, without that: *It never rains but it pours* ▶PREPOSITION except, with the exception of: *No one but Tom had any money/*

Take the next road but one (= the second road) ▸ ADVERB only: *We can but hope* **but for** were it not for; without: *But for your car, we would have been late*

butcher NOUN someone whose work is to carve up meat and sell it ▸ VERB **1** to kill and carve up (an animal) for food **2** to kill cruelly

butchery NOUN great or cruel slaughter

butler NOUN the chief male servant in a household

butt NOUN **1** a large cask, a barrel **2** someone of whom others make fun **3** the thick heavy end of a rifle etc **4** the end of a finished cigarette or cigar **5** a push with the head **6** *US slang* the buttocks ▸ VERB to strike with the head **butt in** to interrupt, interfere

butter NOUN a fatty food made by churning cream ▸ VERB to spread over with butter **butter up** to flatter, soften up

buttercup NOUN a plant with a cup-like yellow flower

butterfly NOUN (*plural* **butterflies**) **1** a kind of insect with large, often patterned wings **2** a swimming stroke where the arms are swung forwards in a circling motion

buttocks PLURAL NOUN the two fleshy parts of the body on which you sit

button NOUN **1** a knob or disc of metal, plastic, etc used to fasten clothing **2** a knob pressed to work an electrical device ▸ VERB to fasten by means of buttons

buttonhole NOUN a hole through which a button is passed ▸ VERB to catch the attention of (someone) and force them to listen

buttress NOUN (*plural* **buttresses**) a support on the outside of a wall ▸ VERB to support, prop up

buxom ADJECTIVE plump and pretty

buy VERB (**buying, bought**) to get in exchange for money ▸ NOUN a purchase: *a good buy*

buyer NOUN **1** a person who buys; a customer **2** a person employed by a large shop or firm to buy goods on its behalf

buzz VERB **1** to make a humming noise like bees **2** *informal* to call, telephone **3** of aircraft: to fly close to ▸ NOUN (*plural* **buzzes**) **1** a humming sound **2** *informal* a phone call

buzzard NOUN a large bird of prey

buzzer NOUN a signalling device which makes a buzzing noise

by ADVERB **1** near: *A crowd stood by, watching* **2** past: *People strolled by* **3** aside: *money put by for an emergency* ▸ PREPOSITION **1** next to, near: *standing by the door* **2** past: *going by the house* **3** through, along, across: *We came by the main road* **4** indicating the person who does something: *written by Burns/played by a young actor* **5** of time: not after: *It'll be ready by four o'clock* **6** during the time of: *working by night* **7** by means of: *by train* **8** to the extent of: *taller by a head* **9** used to express measurements, compass directions, etc: *6 metres by 4 metres/north by northwest* **10** in the quantity of: *sold by the pound/paid by the week*

A B C D E F G H I J K L M N O P Q R S T U V W X Y Z

bye[1] *or* **bye-bye** INTERJECTION, *informal* goodbye

bye[2] NOUN, *cricket* **1** a ball bowled past the wicket **2** a run made from this

by-election NOUN an election for parliament during a parliamentary session

bygone ADJECTIVE past ▶ NOUN (**bygones**) old grievances or events that have been, or should be, forgotten

by-law *or* **bye-law** NOUN a local (not a national) law

bypass NOUN a road built round a town etc so that traffic need not pass through it

by-product NOUN something useful obtained during the manufacture of something else

byroad *or* **byway** NOUN a secondary or side road

bystander NOUN someone who stands watching an event or accident

byte (*pronounced* bait) NOUN, *computing* a unit of eight bits, used to measure data or memory

byword NOUN someone or something well known for a particular quality

Cc

°C ABBREVIATION degree(s) Celsius or centigrade

cab NOUN **1** a taxi **2** in the past, a hired carriage

cabaret (*pronounced* **kab**-*a*-rei) NOUN **1** an entertainment consisting of variety acts **2** a restaurant with a cabaret

cabbage NOUN a type of vegetable with tightly packed edible green leaves

caber (*pronounced* **kei**-ber) NOUN a heavy pole tossed in competition at Scottish Highland games

cabin NOUN **1** a wooden hut **2** a small room used for living quarters in a ship **3** the part of a commercial aircraft containing passenger seating

cabin crew NOUN the flight attendants on a commercial airline

cabinet NOUN **1** a cupboard which has shelves and doors **2** a similar container for storage or display **3** a wooden case with drawers **4** a selected number of government ministers who decide on policy

cabinet-maker NOUN a maker of fine furniture

cable NOUN **1** a strong rope or thick metal line **2** a line of covered telegraph wires laid under the sea or underground **3** a telegram sent by such a line **4** an underground wire **5** *informal* cable television ▶ VERB to telegraph by cable

cable car NOUN a small carriage suspended from a moving cable

cable television NOUN a service transmitting television programmes to individual subscribers by underground cable

cacao NOUN a tree from whose seeds cocoa and chocolate are made

cache (*pronounced* kash) NOUN **1** a store or hiding place for ammunition, treasure, etc **2** things hidden

[i] Comes from French *cacher* meaning 'to hide'

cachet (*pronounced* ka-**shei**) NOUN **1** prestige, credit **2** an official stamp or seal

cackle NOUN **1** the sound made by a hen or goose **2** a laugh which sounds like this

caco- PREFIX bad, incorrect

[i] Comes from Greek *kakos* meaning 'bad'

cacophony NOUN (*plural* **cacophonies**) an unpleasant noise
> **cacophonous** ADJECTIVE

cactus NOUN (*plural* **cactuses** *or*

cacti – *pronounced* **kak**-tai) a type of prickly plant

CAD ABBREVIATION, *technology* computer-aided design

cad NOUN, *old* a mean, despicable person

cadaver (*pronounced* ka-**dav**-er) NOUN a human corpse > **cadaverous** ADJECTIVE

caddie NOUN an assistant who carries a golfer's clubs

caddy NOUN (*plural* **caddies**) a box for keeping tea fresh

cadence NOUN **1** a fall of the voice, eg at the end of a sentence **2** *music* a group of chords ending a piece of music

cadenza NOUN, *music* a musical passage at the end of a movement, concerto, etc

cadet (*pronounced* ka-**det**) NOUN **1** an officer trainee in the armed forces or police service **2** a school pupil who takes military training

cadge VERB (**cadging, cadged**) to beg > **cadger** NOUN

Caesarean (*pronounced* se-**zeir**-i-an) *medicine*, ADJECTIVE of a birth: involving delivery by cutting through the walls of the mother's abdomen ▸ NOUN (*also called*: **Caesarean section**) a Caesarean birth or operation

ⓘ After Julius *Caesar*, who was supposed to be the first child delivered by this method

café NOUN a small restaurant serving coffee, tea, snacks, etc

cafeteria NOUN a self-service restaurant

caffeine NOUN a stimulating drug found in coffee and tea

caftan *or* **kaftan** NOUN a long-sleeved, ankle-length Middle-Eastern garment

cage NOUN **1** a barred enclosure for birds or animals **2** a lift used by miners ▸ VERB (**caging, caged**) to close up in a cage

cagey *or* **cagy** ADJECTIVE (**cagier, cagiest**) unwilling to speak freely; wary > **caginess** NOUN

cagoule NOUN a lightweight anorak

cahoots PLURAL NOUN: **in cahoots with** in collusion with

cairn NOUN **1** a heap of stones marking a grave, or on top of a mountain **2** a breed of small terrier

cairngorm NOUN a brown or yellow variety of quartz, used for brooches etc

cajole VERB to coax by flattery > **cajolery** NOUN

cake NOUN **1** a baked piece of dough made from flour, eggs, sugar, etc **2** something pressed into a lump: *a cake of soap* ▸ VERB to become dry and hard: *boots caked with mud*
have your cake and eat it to enjoy both of two alternative things

calamine lotion NOUN a pink lotion containing a zinc salt, used to soothe the skin

calamitous ADJECTIVE extremely unfortunate, disastrous

calamity NOUN (*plural* **calamities**) a great disaster, a misfortune

calcium NOUN, *chemistry* (symbol **Ca**) a silvery-white metallic element which forms the chief part of lime and is a basic component of teeth and bones

calculable ADJECTIVE able to be counted or measured

calculate VERB **1** to count, work out by mathematics **2** to think out in an exact way

ⓘ Based on a Latin word meaning 'stone', from the use of stones in the past as an aid to counting

calculating ADJECTIVE thinking selfishly

calculation NOUN a mathematical reckoning, a sum

calculator NOUN a machine which makes mathematical calculations

calculus NOUN a mathematical system of calculation concerned with **differentiation** and **integration**

calendar NOUN a table or list showing the year divided into months, weeks and days

calf[1] NOUN (*plural* **calves**) **1** the young of a cow or ox **2** the young of certain other mammals, eg an elephant or whale **3** calf's skin cured as leather

calf[2] NOUN (*plural* **calves**) the back of the lower part of the leg

calibrate VERB **1** to mark the scale on (a measuring instrument) **2** to check or adjust the scale of (a measuring instrument)

calibre *or US* **caliber** NOUN **1** the measurement across the opening of a tube or gun **2** of a person: quality of character, ability

> ⓘ This is one of a large number of words which are spelled with an **-re** ending in British English, but with an **-er** in American English, eg *centre/center, metre/meter, lustre/luster*.

call VERB **1** to cry aloud **2** to name: *What is your cat called?* **3** to summon: *call the doctor/call for help* **4** to make a short visit: *I'll call on my way home* **5** to telephone ▶ NOUN **1** a loud cry **2** a short visit **3** a telephone conversation **call off** to cancel

call centre NOUN a building where workers provide services to a company's customers by telephone

calligram NOUN a poem or word written or printed so that its appearance on the page represents its meaning or subject, eg a poem about growth where the size of the letters gets bigger

calligraphy NOUN the art of handwriting

calling NOUN a vocation

callipers *or* **calipers** PLURAL NOUN **1** an instrument like compasses, used to measure thickness **2** (**calliper**) a splint to support the leg, made of two metal rods

callous ADJECTIVE cruel, hardhearted > **callously** ADVERB > **callousness** NOUN

ⓘ Comes from Latin *callosus* meaning 'thick-skinned'

> Do not confuse with: **callus**

callus NOUN (*plural* **calluses**) an area of thickened or hardened skin

ⓘ Comes from Latin *callus* meaning 'hardened skin'

> Do not confuse with: **callous**

calm ADJECTIVE **1** still or quiet **2** not anxious or flustered ▶ NOUN **1** absence of wind **2** quietness, peacefulness ▸VERB to make peaceful > **calmly** ADVERB

calorie NOUN **1** a measure of heat **2** a measure of the energy-giving value of food

calve VERB to give birth to a calf

calypso NOUN (*plural* **calypsos**) a West Indian improvised song

calyx (*pronounced* **keil**-iks *or* **kal**-iks) NOUN (*plural* **calyces** – *pronounced* **keil**-i-seez *or* **kal**-i-seez – *or* **calyxes**) the outer covering or cup of a flower, enclosing the petals, stamens and carpels

CAM ABBREVIATION, *technology* computer-aided manufacturing or manufacture

camaraderie NOUN comradeship, fellowship

camber NOUN a slight curve on a road etc making the middle higher than the sides

camcorder NOUN a hand-held device combining a video camera and video recorder

came *past tense* of **come**

camel NOUN an animal native to Asia and Africa, with a humped back, used for transport

cameo NOUN (*plural* **cameos**) a gem or stone with a figure carved in relief

camera[1] NOUN an instrument for taking photographs

camera[2] NOUN: **in camera** in private

ⓘ A Latin phrase meaning 'in a room'

camera phone NOUN a mobile phone with which you can take photographs to display on the phone's screen

camisole (*pronounced* **kam**-i-sohl) NOUN a woman's undervest with thin shoulder straps

camomile NOUN a plant with pale yellow flowers, used as a medicinal herb

camouflage (*pronounced* **kam**-*o*-flahsz) NOUN **1** the disguising of the appearance of something to blend in with its background **2** natural protective colouring in animals ▸VERB to disguise by camouflage

camp NOUN **1** a group of tents, caravans, etc forming a temporary settlement **2** fixed military quarters ▸VERB **1** to pitch tents **2** to set up a temporary home > **camper** NOUN

campaign NOUN **1** organized action in support of a cause or movement **2** a planned series of battles or movements during a war ▸VERB **1** to organize support: *campaigning against the poll tax* **2** to serve in a military campaign > **campaigner** NOUN

camp bed NOUN a small portable folding bed

camphor NOUN a pungent solid oil obtained from a cinnamon tree, or a synthetic substitute for it, used to repel insects etc

campion NOUN a plant with pink or white star-shaped flowers

campsite NOUN an area set aside for pitching tents

campus NOUN (*plural* **campuses**) the grounds and buildings of a university or college

can[1] VERB (**can, could**) **1** to be able to (do something): *Can anybody here play the piano?* **2** to have permission to (do something): *asked if I could have the day off* **can but** can only: *We can but hope*

🛈 Comes from Old English *cunnan* meaning 'to know how to' or 'to be able'

can[2] NOUN a sealed tin container for preserving food or liquids ▸ VERB (**canning, canned**) to put into a sealed tin to preserve

canal NOUN an artificial waterway for boats

canary NOUN (*plural* **canaries**) a songbird with yellow plumage, kept as a pet

cancan NOUN a high-kicking dance performed by women

cancel VERB (**cancelling, cancelled**) **1** to put off permanently, call off: *cancel all engagements for the week* **2** to mark for deletion by crossing with lines > **cancellation** NOUN **cancel out** to make ineffective by balancing each other

cancer NOUN a serious disease in which cells in the body grow rapidly into lumps which can spread and may cause death > **cancerous** ADJECTIVE

candid ADJECTIVE frank, open, honest > **candidly** ADVERB

candidacy *or* **candidature** NOUN the state of being a candidate for something

candidate NOUN **1** an entrant for an examination, or competitor for a job, prize, etc **2** an entrant in a political election

🛈 From a Latin word meaning 'dressed in white', because of the white togas worn by electoral candidates in ancient Rome

candle NOUN a stick of wax containing a wick, used for giving light **not worth the candle** not worth the effort or expense needed

candlestick NOUN a holder for a candle

candy NOUN **1** sugar crystallized by boiling **2** *US* (*plural* **candies**) sweets, chocolate

candy floss NOUN a fluffy mass of spun sugar served on a stick

cane NOUN **1** the woody stem of bamboo, sugar cane, etc **2** a walking stick ▸ VERB to beat with a cane

canine (*pronounced* **kei**-nain) ADJECTIVE of dogs

canine tooth NOUN a sharp-pointed tooth found on each side of the upper and lower jaw

canister NOUN a tin or other container for tea etc

cannabis NOUN a narcotic drug obtained from the hemp plant

cannibal NOUN **1** someone who eats human flesh **2** an animal that eats its own kind > **cannibalism** NOUN > **cannibalistic** ADJECTIVE

cannon NOUN a large gun mounted on a wheel-carriage

🛈 Comes from Italian *canna* meaning 'reed' or 'tube'

> Do not confuse with: **canon**

cannonball NOUN a solid metal ball shot from a cannon

cannot VERB **1** used with another verb to express inability to do something: *I cannot understand this* **2** used to refuse permission: *He cannot see me today*

A B C D E F G H I J K L M N O P Q R S T U V W X Y Z

canny ADJECTIVE (**cannier, canniest**) wise, shrewd, cautious > **cannily** ADVERB

canoe NOUN a light narrow boat moved along by paddles

canon NOUN **1** a rule used as a standard to judge by **2** a list of saints **3** an accepted or established list: *not in the literary canon* **4** *music* a piece of music in which parts follow each other repeating the melody

Comes from Greek *kanon* meaning 'a straight rod'

> Do not confuse with: **cannon**

canonical ADJECTIVE part of an accepted canon: *the canonical text*

canonize *or* **canonise** VERB make (someone) a saint > **canonization** NOUN

canopy NOUN (*plural* **canopies**) a canvas or cloth covering suspended over a bed etc

can't *short form of* **cannot**

cant[1] NOUN **1** the slang or vocabulary of a particular group: *thieves' cant* **2** insincere talk

cant[2] NOUN a slope, an incline ▸ VERB to tilt from a level position

cantankerous ADJECTIVE crotchety, bad-tempered, quarrelsome

cantata NOUN a short piece of music for a choir

canteen NOUN **1** a place serving food and drink in a workplace etc **2** a water-flask **3** *Brit* a case for storing cutlery

canter VERB to move at an easy gallop ▸ NOUN an easy gallop

Originally *Canterbury gallop*, referring to the pace at which pilgrims rode to the town

cantilever NOUN a large projecting bracket used to support a balcony or staircase

cantilever bridge NOUN a bridge consisting of upright piers with cantilevers extending to meet one another

canvas NOUN (*plural* **canvases**) **1** coarse, strong cloth used for sails, tents, etc **2** a piece of this stretched and used for painting on

canvass VERB to go round asking for votes, money, etc > **canvasser** NOUN

canyon NOUN a deep, steep-sided river valley

cap NOUN **1** a peaked soft hat **2** a lid, a top **3** a contraceptive diaphragm ▸ VERB (**capping, capped**) **1** to put a cap on **2** to set a limit to (a budget etc) **3** to do better than, improve on: *No-one can cap this story* **4** to select for a national sports team **5** to confer a university degree on

capability NOUN (*plural* **capabilities**) the ability, potential or skill to do something: *He has the capability to do it, but does he have the commitment?*

capable ADJECTIVE able to cope with difficulties without help

capable of able or likely to achieve, produce, etc: *capable of a better performance*

capably ADVERB in an efficient and confident way

capacity NOUN (*plural* **capacities**) **1** power of understanding **2** ability to do something: *capacity for* *growth* **3** the amount that something can hold **4** post, position: *in her capacity as leader* **to capacity** to the greatest extent possible: *filled to capacity*

cape[1] NOUN a thick shawl or covering for the shoulders

cape[2] NOUN, *geography* a point of land running into the sea

caper[1] VERB to leap, dance about ▶ NOUN **1** a leap **2** *informal* a prank, an adventure

caper[2] NOUN the flower-bud of a shrub, pickled or salted for eating

capillary NOUN (*plural* **capillaries**) **1** a type of narrow blood vessel that forms a network connecting arteries with veins **2** a very fine tube ▶ ADJECTIVE very fine, like a hair

capital ADJECTIVE **1** chief, most important **2** punishable by death: *a capital offence* **3** *informal, old* excellent **4** of a letter: written or printed in upper case, eg A, B or C ▶ NOUN **1** the chief city of a country: *Paris is the capital of France* **2** an upper-case letter **3** money for running a business **4** money invested; accumulated wealth **make capital out of** to turn to your advantage

capitalism NOUN a system in which a country's wealth is owned by individuals, not by the State

capitalist NOUN someone who supports or practises capitalism > **capitalistic** ADJECTIVE

capitalize *or* **capitalise** VERB **1** to write in capital letters **2** (**capitalize on**) to turn to your advantage > **capitalization** NOUN

capital punishment NOUN punishment by death

capitulate VERB to give in to an enemy or to persuasion > **capitulation** NOUN

cappuccino (*pronounced* kap-*u*-**chee**-no-h) NOUN (*plural* **cappuccinos**) coffee made with frothy milk

> ⓘ Originally meaning 'horror', from an Italian word which translates as 'hedgehog head'

capricious ADJECTIVE full of caprice; impulsive, fickle > **capriciously** ADVERB in a way which is characterized by mood swings or unpredictable behaviour: *The car has been behaving a bit capriciously*

capsize VERB of a boat: to upset, overturn

capsule NOUN **1** a small gelatine case containing a dose of medicine etc **2** a self-contained, detachable part of a spacecraft **3** *biology* a dry seed-pod on a plant

captain NOUN **1** the commander of a company of soldiers, a ship or an aircraft **2** the leader of a sports team, club, etc ▶ VERB to lead

captaincy NOUN (*plural* **captaincies**) the rank of captain

caption NOUN a piece of text below a newspaper article, photograph, cartoon, etc, explaining it

captivate VERB to charm, fascinate

captive NOUN a prisoner ▶ ADJECTIVE **1** taken or kept prisoner **2** not able to get away: *a captive audience*

captivity NOUN **1** the state of being

A B C D E F G H I J K L M N O P Q R S T U V W X Y Z

a prisoner **2** the enclosure of an animal in a zoo etc, not in the wild

captor NOUN someone who takes a prisoner

capture VERB **1** to take by force **2** to get hold of; seize: *capture the imagination* ▶NOUN **1** the act of capturing **2** something captured

car NOUN **1** a small enclosed motor vehicle **2** *US* a train carriage

carafe (*pronounced* ka-**raf**) NOUN a bottle for serving wine, water, etc

caramel NOUN **1** sugar melted and browned **2** a sweet made with sugar and butter

carat NOUN **1** a measure of purity for gold **2** a measure of weight for gemstones

ⓘ Perhaps from Greek *keration* meaning 'a carob-seed, used as a weight'

> Do not confuse with: **carrot**

caravan NOUN **1** a covered vehicle with living accommodation drawn behind a car **2** a number of travellers etc crossing the desert together

carbohydrate NOUN, *biology, chemistry* a compound of carbon, hydrogen and oxygen, *eg* sugar or starch

carbon NOUN, *chemistry* (symbol **C**) an element of which charcoal is one form

carbonate NOUN, *chemistry* a compound which contains the group CO_3 ▶VERB to add carbon dioxide to something eg to make a fizzy drink > **carbonated** ADJECTIVE

carbon cycle NOUN, *biology* the continuous process by which carbon is exchanged between organisms and the environment

carbon dating NOUN a technique for measuring the age of organic remains based on the amount of carbon-14 they contain (*also called*: **radiocarbon dating**)

carbon dioxide NOUN, *chemistry* a gas present in the air and breathed out by humans and animals

carbon fixation NOUN, *biology* the process by which carbon is converted into carbon compounds by plants and algae

carboniferous ADJECTIVE producing or containing coal or carbon

carbon monoxide NOUN, *chemistry* a poisonous gas with no smell

carbuncle NOUN **1** a fiery-red precious stone **2** an inflamed swelling under the skin

carburettor *or* **carburetter** *or* *US* **carburetor** NOUN the part of a car engine which changes the petrol into vapour

carcass *or* **carcase** NOUN (*plural* **carcasses** *or* **carcases**) the dead body (of an animal)

card NOUN **1** pasteboard or very thick paper **2** an illustrated, folded square of paper sent in greeting etc **3** a tool for combing wool etc **4** (**cards**) any of the many types of games played with a pack of special cards **5** a small rectangular piece of stiff plastic issued by a bank, shop, etc to a customer, used when making payments, as a guarantee for a cheque, for operating a cash machine, etc (*see also*: **cash card**, **credit card**, **debit card**) ▸ VERB to comb (wool etc)

cardboard NOUN stiff material made from pulped paper

cardiac ADJECTIVE of the heart: *cardiac failure*

ⓘ Comes from Greek *kardia* meaning 'heart'

cardigan NOUN a knitted woollen jacket

ⓘ Named after the 7th Earl of *Cardigan*, who advocated the use of buttonable woollen jackets

cardinal ADJECTIVE **1** principal, important **2** of a sin: very bad (*compare with*: **venial**) ▸ NOUN the highest rank of priest in the Roman Catholic Church, from which the Pope is selected

cardinal number NOUN a number which expresses quantity, eg 1, 2, 3 (*contrasted with*: **ordinal number**)

cardiovascular ADJECTIVE relating to the heart and blood vessels

care NOUN **1** close attention **2** worry, anxiety **3** protection, keeping: *in my care* ▸ VERB to be concerned or worried: *I don't care what happens now* **care for 1** to look after **2** to feel affection or liking for **care of** at the house of (often written as **c/o**) **take care** to be careful; watch out

career NOUN **1** life work; trade, profession **2** course, progress through life **3** a headlong rush ▸ VERB to run rapidly and wildly: *careering along the road*

carefree ADJECTIVE having no worries

careful ADJECTIVE attentive, taking care > **carefully** ADVERB

careless ADJECTIVE paying little attention; not taking care > **carelessly** ADVERB

carer NOUN a person who looks after someone who cannot look after themselves

caress VERB to touch or stroke gently and lovingly ▸ NOUN (*plural* **caresses**) a gentle touch

caretaker NOUN someone who looks after a building ▸ ADJECTIVE in charge temporarily; interim: *a caretaker government*

carfuffle *another spelling of* **kerfuffle** NOUN commotion, fuss

cargo NOUN (*plural* **cargoes**) a ship's load

caribou NOUN (*plural* **caribou** *or* **caribous**) the North American reindeer

caricature NOUN a picture of someone which exaggerates certain of their features ▸ VERB to draw a caricature of > **caricaturist** NOUN

carnage NOUN slaughter, killing

carnation NOUN a type of garden flower, often pink, red or white

carni- *or* **carn-** PREFIX of or relating to meat or flesh: *carnivore/ carnage*

carnival NOUN a celebration with festivities, processions, etc

carnivore NOUN a flesh-eating animal

carnivorous ADJECTIVE eating meat or flesh

carol NOUN a hymn or song sung at Christmas

carousel (*pronounced* kar-*u*-**sel**) NOUN **1** *US* a merry-go-round **2** a

a b c d e f g h i j k l m n o p q r s t u v w x y z

A B C D E F G H I J K L M N O P Q R S T U V W X Y Z

rotating conveyor belt for luggage at an airport etc

carp[1] NOUN a freshwater fish found in ponds

carp[2] VERB to find fault with small errors; complain about nothing

car park NOUN a place where cars etc may be left for a time

carpe diem INTERJECTION a Latin phrase meaning 'seize the day' (ie make the most of the present)

carpel NOUN, *botany* the female part of a flower, consisting of a stigma, style and ovary

carpenter NOUN a worker in wood, eg for building

carpentry NOUN the trade of a carpenter

carpet NOUN the woven covering of floors, stairs, etc ▶ VERB to cover with a carpet

car pool NOUN **1** a number of cars owned by a business for use by employees **2** an arrangement between car owners to take turns at driving each other to work etc

carriage NOUN **1** a vehicle for carrying people **2** the act or cost of carrying **3** a way of walking; bearing

carrier NOUN **1** someone who carries goods **2** a machine or container for carrying **3** someone who passes on a disease

carrier pigeon NOUN a pigeon used to carry messages

carrion NOUN rotting animal flesh

carrot NOUN a vegetable with an edible orange-coloured root

ⓘ Comes from French *carotte*

Do not confuse with: **carat**

carry VERB (**carries, carrying, carried**) **1** to pick up and take to another place **2** to contain and take to a destination: *cables carrying electricity* **3** to bear, have as a mark: *carry a scar* **4** of a voice: to be able to be heard at a distance **5** to win, succeed: *carry the day* **6** to keep for sale: *We don't carry cigarettes* **carried away** overcome by emotion; overexcited **carry on** to continue (doing) **carry out** to accomplish; succeed in doing **carry the can** to accept responsibility for an error **carry weight** to have force or authority

carry-on NOUN a fuss, a to-do

carry-out NOUN a takeaway meal

cart NOUN **1** a horse-drawn vehicle used for carrying loads **2** a small, wheeled vehicle pushed by hand ▶ VERB **1** to carry by cart **2** to drag, haul: *carted off the stage*

carte blanche (*pronounced* kahrt **blonsh**) NOUN freedom of action; a free hand

ⓘ In French, **carte blanche** means 'white card', and the expression refers to a blank piece of paper which a person has signed and given to you, thus giving you their official advance permission for whatever you wish to write on the paper

carthorse NOUN a large, heavy working horse

cartilage NOUN a strong, elastic material that surrounds the joints of humans and animals; gristle

cartography NOUN the science of map-making > **cartographer** NOUN

carton NOUN a small container

made of cardboard, plastic, etc

cartoon NOUN **1** a comic drawing, or strip of drawings, often with a caption **2** an animated film **3** a drawing used as the basis for a large painting etc

cartoonist NOUN someone who draws cartoons

cartridge NOUN **1** a case holding the powder and bullet fired by a gun **2** a spool of film or tape enclosed in a case **3** a tube of ink for loading a pen **4** the part of a record-player which holds the stylus **5** a container of ink for a printer

cartwheel NOUN **1** the wheel of a cart **2** a sideways somersault with hands touching the ground

carve VERB **1** to make or shape by cutting **2** to cut up (meat) into slices

cascade NOUN **1** a waterfall **2** an abundant hanging display: *a cascade of curls* ▶ VERB to fall like or in a waterfall

case¹ NOUN a container or outer covering

ⓘ Comes from Latin *capsa* meaning 'a holder' or 'a box'

case² NOUN **1** that which happens, an occurrence **2** a statement of facts; a set of arguments **3** a matter requiring investigation **4** a trial in a law-court: *a murder case*

ⓘ Comes from Latin *casus* meaning 'a falling'

casement NOUN **1** a window-frame **2** a window that swings on hinges

cash NOUN money in the form of coins and notes ▶ VERB to turn into, or change for, money **cash in on** to profit from

cashback NOUN a facility whereby a person paying for goods by debit card may also withdraw cash

cash card NOUN a card issued by a bank etc that allows the holder to use a cash dispenser

cash dispenser NOUN a cash machine

cashew NOUN a kidney-shaped nut produced by a tropical tree

cashier NOUN someone who looks after the receiving and paying of money ▶ VERB, *military* to dismiss (an officer) in disgrace

cash machine NOUN an electronic machine, often in the outside wall of a bank, from which one can obtain cash using a cash card

cashmere NOUN fine soft goat's wool from the Kashmir goat

cash register NOUN a machine for holding money that records the amount put in

casino (*pronounced* ka-**see**-noh) NOUN (*plural* **casinos**) a building in which gambling takes place

cask NOUN a barrel for wine etc

casket NOUN **1** a small box for holding jewels etc **2** *US* a coffin

casserole NOUN **1** a covered dish for cooking and serving food **2** food cooked in a casserole

cassette NOUN **1** a small case for film, magnetic recording tape, etc **2** the magnetic tape itself

cassock NOUN a long robe worn by priests

cast VERB (**casting, cast**) **1** to throw, fling **2** to throw off; drop, shed: *The snake cast its skin* **3** to shape in a mould **4** to choose (actors) for

A B C D E F G H I J K L M N O P Q R S T U V W X Y Z

a play or film **5** to give a part to (an actor etc) ▸NOUN **1** something shaped in a mould **2** plaster encasing a broken limb **3** the actors in a play **4** a small heap of earth thrown up by a worm **5** a type: *cast of mind* **6** an eye squint > **cast down** ADJECTIVE depressed > **cast off** ADJECTIVE used by someone else, second-hand

castanets PLURAL NOUN hollow shells of ivory or hard wood, clicked together to accompany a dance

ⓘ From a Spanish word for 'chestnuts', because of their shape

castaway NOUN a deserted or shipwrecked person

caste NOUN a class or rank of people, especially in the Indian subcontinent

castigate VERB to scold, punish > **castigation** NOUN

castle NOUN a fortified house or fortress

castor *or* **caster** NOUN a small wheel, eg on the legs or bottom of furniture

castor oil *or* **caster oil** NOUN a kind of palm oil used medicinally

castor sugar *or* **caster sugar** NOUN very fine granulated sugar

castrate VERB to remove the testicles of

casual ADJECTIVE **1** happening by chance: *a casual encounter* **2** not regular, temporary: *casual labour* **3** informal: *casual clothes* **4** not careful, unconcerned: *a casual attitude to work* > **casually** ADVERB

casualty NOUN (*plural* **casualties**) **1** someone who is killed or wounded **2** a casualty department

casualty department NOUN a hospital department for treating accidental injuries, emergencies, etc

cat NOUN **1** a sharp-clawed, furry animal kept as a pet **2** an animal of a family which includes lions, tigers, etc

cata- *or* **cath-** PREFIX down: *catastrophe* (= a turning down)/ *cathode* (= a going down)

ⓘ Comes from Greek *kata* meaning 'down'

cataclysm NOUN **1** a violent change; an upheaval **2** a great flood of water

catacombs PLURAL NOUN an underground burial place

catalogue NOUN an ordered list of names, books, objects for sale, etc ▸VERB **1** to list in order **2** to compile details of (a book) for a library catalogue

catalytic converter NOUN a device containing catalysts, attached to car engines to reduce the polluting gases produced

catamaran NOUN a boat with two parallel hulls

catapult NOUN **1** a small forked stick with a piece of elastic attached, used for firing small stones **2** *history* a weapon for throwing heavy stones in warfare

cataract NOUN **1** a waterfall **2** *medicine* a disease of the outer eye

catarrh NOUN inflammation of the lining of the nose and throat causing a discharge

catastrophe (*pronounced* ka-**tas**-tro-fi) NOUN a sudden disaster

catastrophic (*pronounced* kat-*a*s-**trof**-ik) ADJECTIVE disastrous, absolutely terrible

catch VERB (**catching, caught**) **1** to take hold of, capture **2** to become infected with (a disease): *catch a cold* **3** to be in time for: *catch the last train* **4** to surprise (in an act): *caught him stealing* ▶NOUN **1** a haul of fish etc **2** something you are lucky to have got or won **3** a hidden flaw or disadvantage: *Where's the catch?* **4** a fastening: *a window catch* > **catchy** ADJECTIVE (**catchier, catchiest**) of a tune: easily remembered **catch on** to become popular **catch-22** an absurd situation with no way out **catch up on 1** to draw level with, overtake **2** to get up-to-date with (work etc)

catching ADJECTIVE infectious

catchment NOUN **1** the area served by a particular school, hospital, etc **2** the area from which a river or reservoir draws its water supply

catchphrase NOUN a phrase which is popular for a while

catchword NOUN a word which is popular for a while

catechize *or* **catechise** (*pronounced* **kat**-*e*-kaiz) VERB to question someone very thoroughly

categorical ADJECTIVE allowing no doubt or argument: *a categorical denial* > **categorically** ADVERB

categorize *or* **categorise** VERB to divide into categories

category NOUN (*plural* **categories**) a class or group of similar people or things

cater VERB **1** to provide food **2** to supply what is required: *cater for all tastes*

caterer NOUN someone whose job is to provide ready-prepared food and drinks for people

caterpillar NOUN an insect larva that feeds on plant leaves ▶ADJECTIVE moving on rotating metal belts: *a caterpillar tractor*

[i] Based on an Old French phrase which translates as 'hairy cat'

caterwaul VERB to howl or yell like a cat

cathedral NOUN **1** the church of a bishop **2** the chief church in a bishop's district

Catherine wheel NOUN a firework which spins as it burns

cathode NOUN the negative electrode in a battery or other electronic device (*contrasted with*: **anode**)

cathode ray tube NOUN a device in a television set etc, which causes a narrow beam of electrons to strike against a screen

catholic ADJECTIVE **1** wide, comprehensive: *a catholic taste in literature* **2** (**Catholic**) of the Roman Catholic Church

catkin NOUN a tuft of small flowers adapted for wind pollination on certain trees, eg the willow and hazel

cat's cradle NOUN a children's game of creating patterns by winding string around the fingers

Cat's-eye NOUN, *trademark* a small

mirror fixed in a road surface to reflect light from vehicles at night

cattle PLURAL NOUN oxen, bulls and cows, and other grass-eating animals of this family

caucus (*pronounced* **kaw**-kus) NOUN (*plural* **caucuses**), *US* a meeting of members of a political party to nominate candidates for election etc

caught *past form* of **catch**

cauldron NOUN a large pan

cauliflower NOUN a kind of cabbage with an edible white flower-head

cause NOUN **1** something that makes something happen **2** a reason for action: *cause for complaint* **3** an aim for which a group or person works: *the cause of peace* ▶ VERB to make happen

causeway NOUN a raised road over wet ground or shallow water

caustic ADJECTIVE **1** burning, corroding **2** sarcastic, bitter, severe: *caustic wit*

cauterize *or* **cauterise** VERB to burn away flesh with a hot iron etc in order to make a wound heal cleanly

caution NOUN **1** carefulness because of potential danger: *approach with caution* **2** a warning ▶ VERB to warn

cautionary ADJECTIVE giving a warning

cautious ADJECTIVE careful, showing caution

cavalcade NOUN a procession on horseback, in cars, etc

cavalier NOUN, *history* (**Cavalier**) a supporter of the king in the English Civil War of the 17th century (*compare with*: **Roundhead**) ▶ ADJECTIVE offhand, careless: *in a cavalier fashion*

cavalry NOUN soldiers mounted on horses

cave NOUN a hollow place in the earth or in rock **cave in** to fall or collapse inwards

caveat (*pronounced* **kav**-i-at) NOUN a warning

caveman *or* **cavewoman** NOUN (*plural* **cavemen** *or* **cavewomen**) a prehistoric cave-dweller

cavern NOUN a deep hollow place in the earth

cavernous ADJECTIVE **1** huge and hollow **2** full of caverns

caviar *or* **caviare** NOUN the pickled eggs of the sturgeon, eaten as a delicacy

cavity NOUN (*plural* **cavities**) **1** a hollow place, a hole **2** a decayed hollow in a tooth

cavort VERB to dance or leap around

caw VERB to call like a crow ▶ NOUN a crow's call

cc ABBREVIATION cubic centimetre(s)

CCTV ABBREVIATION closed-circuit television

CD ABBREVIATION compact disc

CD burner *or* **CD recorder** NOUN a device used to record data onto compact discs

CDI *or* **CD-i** ABBREVIATION compact disc interactive, a type of CD-ROM that responds intelligently to a user's instructions

CD-R ABBREVIATION compact disc

recordable, a CD that can be written to

CD-ROM ABBREVIATION compact disc read-only memory, a CD that lets you look at but not alter text

CD-RW ABBREVIATION compact disc rewritable, a CD that can be recorded on many times

cease VERB to come or bring to an end

ceasefire NOUN **1** an order to stop firing weapons **2** an agreed, although maybe temporary, end to active hostilities

ceaseless ADJECTIVE without stopping

cedar NOUN a large evergreen tree with a hard, sweet-smelling wood

cede VERB to yield, give up

ceilidh *or Irish* **ceilí** (*pronounced* **kei**-li) NOUN an event involving traditional Scottish or Irish dancing, sometimes combined with musical performances

ceiling NOUN **1** the inner roof of a room **2** an upper limit

celebrate VERB to commemorate an event (eg a birthday or marriage) by going out, having a party, etc
> **celebrated** ADJECTIVE famous
> **celebration** NOUN

celebrity NOUN (*plural* **celebrities**) **1** a famous person, a star **2** fame

celery NOUN a type of vegetable with edible fibrous stalks

celestial ADJECTIVE **1** of the sky: *celestial bodies* (= stars and planets) **2** heavenly

celibacy NOUN a lifestyle without sexual intercourse > **celibate** ADJECTIVE abstaining from sexual intercourse

cell NOUN **1** a small room in a prison, monastery, etc **2** *biology* the smallest, fundamental part of living things **3** *electronics* the part of an electric battery containing electrodes

cellar NOUN an underground room used for storing coal, wine, etc

cellist (*pronounced* **chel**-ist) NOUN someone who plays the cello

cello (*pronounced* **chel**-oh) NOUN (*short for*: **violoncello**) a stringed musical instrument, similar in shape to a violin but much larger

cellophane NOUN, *trademark* a thin transparent wrapping material

cellphone NOUN a mobile phone

cellular ADJECTIVE made of or having cells

celluloid NOUN, *trademark* a very hard, elastic substance used for making photographic film etc

cellulose NOUN a complex carbohydrate found in plants and wood, used to make paper, textiles, etc

cell wall NOUN the outermost layer of cells in plants, bacteria, etc

Celsius (*pronounced* **sel**-si-*us*) ADJECTIVE **1** of a temperature scale: consisting of a hundred degrees, on which water freezes at 0° and boils at 100° **2** of a degree: measured on this scale: *10° Celsius*

Celtic ADJECTIVE & NOUN **1** of the Celts, a group of ancient peoples of Europe, or their descendants in Wales, Scotland and Ireland **2** (of) their languages

cement NOUN **1** the mixture of clay and lime used to secure bricks in

A B C D E F G H I J K L M N O P Q R S T U V W X Y Z

a wall **2** something used to make two things stick together ▸ VERB **1** to put together with cement **2** to join firmly, fix: *cemented their friendship*

cemetery NOUN (*plural* **cemeteries**) a place where the dead are buried

cenotaph NOUN a monument to someone or a group buried elsewhere

censor NOUN someone whose job is to examine books, films, etc with the power to delete any of the contents or forbid them to be shown or released ▸ VERB to examine (books etc) in this way

Comes from Latin *censor*

> Do not confuse: **censor** and **censure**

censorious ADJECTIVE fault-finding; judgemental

censure NOUN blame; expression of disapproval ▸ VERB to blame, criticize

Comes from Latin *censura* meaning 'censorship'

> Do not confuse: **censure** and **censor**

census NOUN (*plural* **censuses**) a periodical official count of the people who live in a country

Comes from Latin *census* meaning 'a register'

> Do not confuse with: **consensus**

cent NOUN a coin which is the hundredth part of a larger coin, eg of a euro or a US dollar

Comes from Latin *centum* meaning 'a hundred'

centaur NOUN a mythological creature, half man and half horse

centenarian NOUN someone a hundred or more years old

centenary NOUN (*plural* **centenaries**) a hundredth anniversary; the hundredth year since an event took place

centennial ADJECTIVE **1** having lasted a hundred years **2** happening every hundred years ▸ NOUN a centenary

centi- *or* **cent-** PREFIX hundred; a hundredth part of

Comes from Latin *centum* meaning 'a hundred'

centigrade ADJECTIVE **1** of a temperature scale: consisting of a hundred degrees **2** measured on this scale: *5° centigrade* **3** Celsius

centigram *or* **centigramme** NOUN (*abbrev* **cg**) a hundredth part of a gram

centilitre NOUN (*abbrev* **cl**) a hundredth part of a litre

centimetre NOUN (*abbrev* **cm**) a hundredth part of a metre

centipede NOUN a small crawling insect with many legs

central ADJECTIVE **1** belonging to the centre **2** chief, main: *the central point of the argument*

central government NOUN administration of the affairs of a whole country (*compare with*: **local government**)

central heating NOUN heating of a building by water, steam or air from a central point

centralize *or* **centralise** VERB **1** to group in a single place **2** to bring (eg a government department, an industry, etc) under one central control > **centralization** NOUN

central nervous system NOUN the brain and spinal cord

centre *or US* **center** NOUN **1** the middle point or part **2** a building used for some special activity: *sports centre/shopping centre* ▶ VERB (**centring, centred**) to put in the centre

> ⓘ This is one of a large number of words which are spelled with an **-re** ending in British English, but with an **-er** in American English eg *metre/meter, calibre/caliber, lustre/luster.*

centrifugal (*pronounced* sen-tri-**fyoo**-g*a*l *or* sen-**trif**-yoo-g*a*l) ADJECTIVE moving away from a centre or an axis of rotation (*contrasted with*: **centripetal**

centripetal (*pronounced* sen-**trip**-i-t*a*l *or* sen-tri-**peet**-*a*l) ADJECTIVE moving towards a centre or an axis of rotation (*contrasted with*: **centrifugal**

centurion NOUN, *history* a commander of 100 Roman soldiers

century NOUN (*plural* **centuries**) **1** a hundred years **2** *cricket* a hundred runs

ceramic ADJECTIVE **1** made of pottery **2** of pottery-making ▶ NOUN **1** something made of pottery **2** (**ceramics**) the art of pottery

cereal NOUN **1** grain used as food **2** a breakfast food prepared from grain

cerebral ADJECTIVE of the brain

cerebral palsy NOUN a disorder caused by brain injury at birth, causing poor muscle control

ceremonial ADJECTIVE with or of ceremony > **ceremonially** ADVERB

ceremonious ADJECTIVE full of ceremony, formal > **ceremoniously** ADVERB

ceremony NOUN (*plural* **ceremonies**) the formal acts that accompany an important event: *the marriage ceremony*

certain ADJECTIVE **1** sure; not to be doubted **2** fixed, settled **3** particular but unnamed: *stopping at certain places/a certain look*

certainly ADVERB **1** definitely, without any doubt **2** of course

certainty NOUN (*plural* **certainties**) **1** a sure thing: *It's almost a certainty that he will be re-elected* **2** the quality of being certain: *I can tell you this with absolute certainty*

certificate NOUN a written or printed statement giving details of a birth, passed examination, etc

certify VERB (**certifies, certifying, certified**) to put down in writing as an official promise or statement etc

cervical (*pronounced* ser-**vai**-k*a*l *or* **ser**-vi-k*a*l) ADJECTIVE of the cervix

cervix NOUN (*plural* **cervixes** *or* **cervices** – *pronounced* **ser**-vi-seez *or* ser-**vai**-seez) the neck of the womb

cessation NOUN a ceasing or stopping; an ending

cf ABBREVIATION compare (from Latin *confer*)

CFC ABBREVIATION chlorofluorocarbon

cg ABBREVIATION centigram(s)

CGI NOUN computer-generated imagery, often used in animated films

chador (*pronounced* **chud**-er) NOUN a thick veil worn by Muslim women

chafe VERB **1** to make hot or sore by rubbing **2** to wear away by rubbing **3** to become annoyed

chaff NOUN **1** husks of corn left after threshing **2** something of little value **3** good-natured teasing ▶ VERB to tease jokingly

chaffinch NOUN (*plural* **chaffinches**) a small songbird of the finch family

chagrin (*pronounced* **sha**-grin *or* sha-**green**) NOUN annoyance, irritation

chain NOUN **1** a number of metal links or rings passing through one another **2** (**chains**) these links used to tie a prisoner's limbs; fetters **3** a number of connected things: *a mountain chain* **4** a group of shops owned by one person or company **5** *chemistry* a number of atoms of an element joined together ▶ VERB to fasten or imprison with a chain

chain mail NOUN armour made of iron links

chain reaction NOUN *chemistry* a chemical process in which each reaction in turn causes a similar reaction

chainsaw NOUN a power-driven saw with teeth on a rotating chain

chain store NOUN one of several shops under the same ownership

chair NOUN **1** a seat for one person with a back to it **2** a university professorship: *the chair of French literature* **3** a chairman or chairwoman

chairlift NOUN a row of chairs on a rotating cable for carrying people up mountains etc

chairman, **chairperson** *or* **chairwoman** NOUN (*plural* **chairmen**, **chairpersons** *or* **chairwomen**) someone who presides at or is in charge of a meeting

chalet (*pronounced* **shal**-ei) NOUN **1** a small wooden house used by holidaymakers **2** a summer hut used by Swiss herdsmen in the Alps

chalice NOUN a cup for wine, used eg in church services

chalk NOUN **1** a type of limestone **2** a compressed stick of coloured powder used for writing or drawing ▶ VERB to mark with chalk

chalky ADJECTIVE (**chalkier, chalkiest**) **1** of chalk **2** white, pale

challenge VERB **1** to question another's right to do something **2** to ask (someone) to take part in a contest, eg to settle a quarrel ▶ NOUN **1** a questioning of another's right **2** a call to a contest **3** a problem or task that is stimulating and interesting

challenger NOUN someone who challenges a person such as a champion or holder of an important position to a competition for their status

challenging ADJECTIVE interesting but difficult

chamber (*pronounced* **cheim**-ber)

NOUN **1** a room **2** a place where a parliament meets **3** a room where legal cases are heard by a judge **4** an enclosed space or cavity **5** the part of a gun that holds the cartridges

chamberlain NOUN an officer appointed by the crown or a local authority to carry out certain duties

chamber music NOUN music for a small group of players, suitable for performance in a room rather than a large hall

chamberpot NOUN a receptacle for urine etc, used in the bedroom

chameleon (*pronounced* ka-**meel**-yon) NOUN a small lizard able to change its colour to match its surroundings

chamois NOUN **1** (*pronounced* **sham**-wah) a goat-like deer living in mountainous country **2** (*pronounced* **sham**-i) a soft leather formerly made from chamois skin, now from the skins of sheep and goats (*also spelled*: **shammy**)

champ VERB to chew noisily **champing at the bit** impatient to act

champagne (*pronounced* sham-**pein**) NOUN a type of white sparkling wine

champion NOUN **1** someone who has beaten all others in a competition **2** a strong supporter of a cause: *a champion of free speech* ▶VERB to support the cause of

championship NOUN **1** the act of championing **2** a contest to find a champion

chance NOUN **1** a risk, a possibility **2** something unexpected or unplanned **3** an opportunity ▶VERB **1** to risk **2** to happen by accident ▶ADJECTIVE happening by accident **by chance** not by arrangement, unexpectedly **chance upon** to meet or find unexpectedly

chancel NOUN the part of a church near the altar

chancellor NOUN **1** a high-ranking government minister **2** the head of a university **Chancellor of the Exchequer** the minister in the British cabinet in charge of government spending

chancy ADJECTIVE (**chancier, chanciest**) risky

chandelier (*pronounced* shan-de-**leer**) NOUN a fixture hanging from the ceiling with branches for holding lights

change VERB **1** to make or become different **2** to give up or leave (a job, house, etc) for another **3** to put on different clothes **4** to give (money of one kind) in exchange for (money of another kind) ▶NOUN **1** the act of making or becoming different **2** another set of clothing **3** money in the form of coins **4** money returned when a buyer gives more than the price of an article **the change of life** the menopause

changeable ADJECTIVE likely to change; often changing

changeling NOUN in stories: a fairy child secretly left in place of a human one

channel NOUN **1** a watercourse; the bed of a stream, canal or river **2** a passage for ships through an area of water **3** a narrow sea **4** a groove; a gutter **5** a band of frequencies for a radio or television signal ▶VERB (**channelling, channelled**) to direct into a particular course

chant VERB to recite in a singing manner ▶ NOUN a singing recitation

Chanukkah *see* **Hanukkah**

chaos (*pronounced* **kei**-os) NOUN disorder, confusion

chaotic ADJECTIVE disordered, confused > **chaotically** ADVERB

chap NOUN, *informal* a man

chapati *or* **chapatti** (*pronounced* cha-**paht**-ee) NOUN a round of unleavened Indian bread

chapel NOUN **1** a small church **2** a small part of a larger church

chaperon *or* **chaperone** (*pronounced* **shap**-*e*-rohn) NOUN a woman who accompanies a younger one when she goes out in public ▶ VERB to act as a chaperon to

chaplain NOUN a member of the clergy accompanying an army, navy, etc

chapped ADJECTIVE of skin: cracked by cold or wet weather

chapter NOUN **1** a division of a book **2** a branch of a society or organization **chapter of accidents** a series of accidents

char[1] VERB (**charring, charred**) to burn until black

char[2] VERB to do odd jobs of housework, cleaning, etc ▶ NOUN, *informal* a charwoman

character NOUN **1** the nature and qualities of someone **2** the good and bad points which make up a person's nature **3** self-control, firmness **4** someone noted for eccentric behaviour **5** someone in a play, story or film

characteristic NOUN a typical and noticeable feature of someone or something ▶ ADJECTIVE typical

characteristically ADVERB typically, as always: *His suggestions were characteristically tactful*

characterization *or* **characterisation** NOUN the creation and development of the different characters in a book, story or piece of drama: *Jane Austen's power of characterization*

characterize *or* **characterise** VERB **1** to be typical of **2** to describe (as)

charade (*pronounced* sh*a*-**rahd** *or* sh*a*-**reid**) NOUN **1** a ridiculous pretence **2** (**charades**) a game in which players have to guess a word from gestures representing its sound or meaning

charcoal NOUN wood burnt black, used for fuel or sketching

charge VERB **1** to accuse: *charged with murder* **2** to ask (a price) **3** to ask to do; give responsibility for **4** to load (a gun) **5** to attack in a rush ▶ NOUN **1** accusation for a crime **2** a price, a fee **3** an attack **4** the gunpowder in a shell or bullet **5** care, responsibility **6** someone looked after by another person **in charge** in command or control **take charge of** to take command of

charger NOUN a horse used in battle

chariot NOUN, *history* a wheeled carriage used in battle

charioteer NOUN a chariot-driver

charisma (*pronounced* k*a*-**riz**-m*a*) NOUN a personal quality that impresses others

charismatic ADJECTIVE full of charisma or charm

charitable ADJECTIVE **1** giving to the poor; kindly **2** of a charity: *charitable status* > **charitably** ADVERB (meaning 1)

charity NOUN (*plural* **charities**) **1** donation of money to the poor etc **2** an organization which collects money and gives it to those in need **3** kindness, humanity

charlatan (*pronounced* **shahr**-l*at*-*an*) NOUN someone who claims greater powers or abilities than they really have

charm NOUN **1** something thought to have magical powers **2** a magical spell **3** personal power to attract ▸VERB **1** to please greatly, delight **2** to put under a spell

charming ADJECTIVE lovely, delightful

chart NOUN **1** a table or diagram giving particular information: *a temperature chart* **2** a geographical map of the sea **3** a rough map ▸VERB to make into a chart; plot

charter NOUN a written paper showing the official granting of rights, lands, etc ▸VERB to hire (a boat, aeroplane, etc) ▸ADJECTIVE hired for a special purpose: *a charter flight* > **chartered** ADJECTIVE

chase VERB **1** to run after, pursue **2** to hunt ▸NOUN a pursuit, a hunt

chasm (*pronounced* **ka**-zm) NOUN **1** a steep drop between high rocks etc **2** a wide difference; a gulf

chassis (*pronounced* **shas**-i) NOUN (*plural* **chassis** – *pronounced* **shas**-iz) **1** the frame, wheels and machinery of a car **2** an aeroplane's landing carriage

chaste ADJECTIVE **1** pure, virtuous **2** modest, decent

chastely ADVERB in a pure, virtuous way

chasten VERB **1** to make humble **2** to scold

chastened ADJECTIVE humble or sorry, as a result of receiving a scolding

chastise VERB to punish, especially by beating > **chastisement** NOUN

chastity NOUN sexual purity and virtue

chat VERB (**chatting, chatted**) to talk in an easy, friendly way ▸NOUN a friendly conversation

chateau (*pronounced* **shat**-oh) NOUN (*plural* **chateaux** – *pronounced* **shat**-ohz) a French castle or country house

chat room NOUN, *computing* a place on the Internet where people can exchange messages

chat show NOUN a radio or TV programme in which personalities talk informally with their host

chatter VERB **1** to talk idly or rapidly; gossip **2** of teeth: to rattle together because of cold

chatterbox NOUN (*plural* **chatterboxes**) someone who talks a great deal

chatty ADJECTIVE (**chattier, chattiest**) willing to talk, talkative > **chattily** ADVERB

chauffeur (*pronounced* **shoh**-fer) NOUN someone employed to drive a car

chauvinism (*pronounced*

A B C D E F G H I J K L M N O P Q R S T U V W X Y Z

shoh-vin-izm) NOUN **1** extreme nationalism or patriotism **2** sexism towards women > **chauvinist** NOUN > **chauvinistic** ADJECTIVE

ⓘ After Nicholas *Chauvin*, Napoleonic French soldier and keen patriot

cheap ADJECTIVE **1** low in price, inexpensive **2** of little value, worthless

cheapen VERB to make cheap

cheaply ADVERB for a low price: *You can see that this skirt was cheaply made*

cheat VERB **1** to deceive **2** to act dishonestly to gain an advantage ▶ NOUN **1** someone who cheats **2** a dishonest trick

check VERB **1** to bring to a stop **2** to hold back, restrain **3** to see if (a total etc) is correct or accurate **4** to see if (a machine etc) is in good condition or working properly ▶ NOUN **1** a sudden stop **2** a restraint **3** a test of correctness or accuracy **4** a square, eg on a draughtboard **5** a pattern of squares **check in** *or* **check out** to record your arrival at or departure from (a hotel etc)

Do not confuse with: **cheque**

checked ADJECTIVE patterned with squares

checkered *another spelling of* **chequered**

checkers *another spelling of* **chequers**

checkmate NOUN, *chess* a position from which the king cannot escape

checkout NOUN a place where payment is made in a supermarket

cheek NOUN **1** the side of the face below the eye **2** a buttock **3** insolence, disrespectful behaviour

cheeky ADJECTIVE (**cheekier, cheekiest**) impudent, insolent > **cheekily** ADVERB

cheep VERB to make a faint sound like a small bird ▶ NOUN the sound of a small bird

cheer NOUN a shout of approval or welcome ▶ VERB **1** to shout approval **2** to encourage, urge on **3** to comfort, gladden **cheer up** to make or become less gloomy

cheerful ADJECTIVE happy, in good spirits > **cheerfully** ADVERB > **cheerfulness** NOUN

cheerio INTERJECTION goodbye!

cheerless ADJECTIVE sad, gloomy

cheers INTERJECTION **1** good health! **2** regards, best wishes

cheery ADJECTIVE (**cheerier, cheeriest**) lively and merry > **cheerily** ADVERB

cheese NOUN a solid food made from milk

cheesecake NOUN a cake with a biscuit base topped with sweet cream cheese

cheesecloth NOUN loosely woven thin cotton cloth

cheesy ADJECTIVE (**cheesier, cheesiest**) **1** tasting of cheese **2** of a smile: broad **3** *informal* inferior, cheap

cheetah NOUN a member of the cat family with a spotted coat, the fastest land mammal

chef NOUN a cook in a restaurant

chemical ADJECTIVE relating to the reactions between elements etc

▶ NOUN a substance formed by or used in a chemical process

chemist NOUN **1** someone who studies chemistry **2** someone who makes up and sells medicines; a pharmacist **3** a shop selling medicines, toiletries, cosmetics, etc

chemistry NOUN the study of the elements and the ways they combine or react with each other

chemotherapy (*pronounced* keem-oh-**the**-r*a*p-i) NOUN treatment of infectious diseases or cancer using chemical compounds

cheque *or US* **check** NOUN a written order to a banker to pay money from a bank account to another person

> Do not confuse with: **check**

cheque book NOUN a book containing cheques

chequered *or* **checkered** ADJECTIVE **1** marked like a chessboard **2** partly good, partly bad: *a chequered career*

cherish VERB **1** to protect and treat with fondness or kindness **2** to keep in your mind or heart: *cherish a hope*

cherry NOUN (*plural* **cherries**) **1** a small bright-red fruit with a stone **2** the tree that produces this fruit

cherub NOUN (*plural* **cherubs** *or* **cherubim** *pronounced* **cher**-*u*-bim *or* **cher**-yoo-bim) **1** an angel with a plump, childish face and body **2** a beautiful child

chess NOUN a game for two players in which pieces are moved in turn on a board marked in alternate black and white squares

chessboard NOUN the board on which you play chess

chessman *or* **chesspiece** NOUN (*plural* **chessmen** *or* **chesspieces**) any of the little figures which you move on a chessboard when playing chess

chest NOUN **1** a large strong box **2** the part of the body between the neck and the stomach **chest of drawers** a piece of furniture fitted with a set of drawers

chestnut NOUN **1** a reddish-brown edible nut (**sweet chestnut**), or the tree that produces it **2** a reddish-brown inedible nut (**horse chestnut**), or the tree that produces it **3** a reddish-brown horse **4** an old joke

chew VERB **1** to break up (food) with the teeth before swallowing **2** to reflect or ponder (on)

chic (*pronounced* sheek) ADJECTIVE smart and fashionable ▶ NOUN style; fashionable elegance

chick NOUN **1** a chicken **2** *slang* a girl, a young woman

chicken NOUN **1** the young of birds, especially of domestic poultry **2** *informal* a coward ▶ ADJECTIVE, *informal* cowardly

chickenpox NOUN an infectious disease which causes red, itchy spots

chickpea NOUN a plant of the pea family with a yellow-brown edible seed

chicory NOUN **1** a plant with sharp-tasting leaves eaten in salads **2** its root, roasted and ground to mix with coffee

A B C D E F G H I J K L M N O P Q R S T U V W X Y Z

chide VERB to scold with words

chief ADJECTIVE **1** main, most important **2** largest ▶ NOUN **1** a leader or ruler **2** the head of a department, organization, etc

chiefly ADVERB mainly, for the most part

chieftain NOUN the head of a clan or tribe

chiffon (*pronounced* **shif**-*on*) NOUN a thin, flimsy material made of silk or nylon

chihuahua (*pronounced* chi-**wah**-wah) NOUN a breed of very small dog, originally from Mexico

chilblain NOUN a painful swelling on hands and feet, caused by constricted blood vessels in cold weather

child NOUN (*plural* **children**) **1** a young human being **2** a son or daughter: *She has two children*

ⓘ Comes from Old English *cild*

childhood NOUN the time of being a child

childish ADJECTIVE **1** of or like a child **2** silly, immature > **childishly** ADVERB

childlike ADJECTIVE innocent

childminder NOUN a person who is paid to look after other people's children in his or her home

chill NOUN **1** coldness **2** an illness that causes fever and shivering **3** lack of warmth or enthusiasm ▶ ADJECTIVE cold ▶ VERB **1** to make cold **2** to refrigerate

chilli *or* **chili** NOUN (*plural* **chillis** *or* **chillies**) **1** the hot-tasting pod of a kind of pepper, sometimes dried for cooking **2** a dish or sauce made with this

chilly ADJECTIVE (**chillier, chilliest**) cold

chime NOUN **1** the sound of bells ringing **2** **chimes** a set of bells, eg in a clock ▶ VERB **1** to ring **2** of a clock: to strike

chimney NOUN (*plural* **chimneys**) a passage allowing smoke or heated air to escape from a fire

chimneypot NOUN a metal or earthenware pipe placed at the top of a chimney

chimneystack NOUN **1** a tall chimney, eg in a factory **2** a number of chimneys built in a brick or stone structure on a roof

chimney sweep NOUN someone employed to clean chimneys

chimpanzee NOUN a type of African ape

chin NOUN the part of the face below the mouth

china NOUN **1** fine kind of earthenware; porcelain **2** articles made of this

chink NOUN **1** a narrow opening **2** the sound of coins etc striking together

chintz NOUN (*plural* **chintzes**) a cotton cloth with brightly coloured patterning

ⓘ From a Hindi word for painted or multicoloured cotton

chip VERB (**chipping, chipped**) to break or cut small pieces (from or off) ▶ NOUN **1** a small piece chipped off **2** a part damaged by chipping **3** a long thin piece of fried potato **4** *US* a potato or corn crisp **5** *see* **integrated circuit**

chip and PIN NOUN a system

where the user of a credit or debit card types in a secret number on a device in a shop

chipmunk NOUN a kind of small N American squirrel

chiropodist (*pronounced* ki-**rop**-*o*-dist) NOUN someone who treats minor disorders and diseases of the feet

chiropody (*pronounced* ki-**rop**-*o*-di) NOUN the profession of caring for people's feet and treating minor foot problems such as corns

chirp *or* **chirrup** VERB of a bird: to make a sharp, shrill sound

chirpy ADJECTIVE merry, cheerful

chisel NOUN a metal tool to cut or hollow out wood, stone, etc ▸ VERB (**chiselling, chiselled**) to cut with a chisel

chit NOUN **1** a short note **2** a child, a young woman: *chit of a girl*

chit-chat NOUN gossip, talk ▸ VERB to gossip, talk

chivalrous (*pronounced* **shiv**-*a*l-r*u*s) ADJECTIVE gallant, showing traditional good manners especially to women

chivalry (*pronounced* **shiv**-*a*l-ri) NOUN **1** kindness, especially towards women or the weak **2** *history* the standard of behaviour expected of knights in medieval times

chive NOUN an onion-like herb used in cooking

chloride NOUN, *chemistry* a compound which contains chlorine and another element

chlorinate VERB to add chlorine to

chlorinated ADJECTIVE mixed with chlorine or containing chlorine

chlorine (*pronounced* **kloh**-reen) NOUN, *chemistry* (symbol **Cl**) a yellowish-green gas with a sharp smell, used as a bleach and disinfectant

chlorofluorocarbon NOUN, *chemistry* (*abbrev* **CFC**) a compound of chlorine, fluorine and carbon, formerly used as an aerosol propellant and refrigerant, but now banned by many countries as a result of its damaging effects on the ozone layer

chloroform NOUN, *chemistry* a colourless liquid whose vapour causes unconsciousness if inhaled

chlorophyll NOUN a green pigment in some plants and algae that traps light energy to use in photosynthesis

chloroplast NOUN a tiny structure in the cells of green algae and green plants that contains chlorophyll

chock-a-block ADJECTIVE completely full or congested

chock-full ADJECTIVE completely full

chocolate NOUN **1** a sweet made from the seeds of the cacao tree **2** a drink made from these seeds ▸ ADJECTIVE dark brown in colour

chocolatey ADJECTIVE tasting of chocolate

choice NOUN **1** the act or power of choosing **2** something chosen ▸ ADJECTIVE of a high quality: *choice vegetables*

choir NOUN **1** a group or society of singers **2** a part of a church where a choir sits

[i] Comes from Latin *chorus*

meaning 'a band of singers and dancers'

choke VERB **1** to stop or partly stop the breathing of **2** to block or clog (a pipe etc) **3** to have your breathing stopped or interrupted, eg by smoke ▶ NOUN a valve in a petrol engine which controls the inflow of air

cholera (*pronounced* **kol**-*e*-ra) NOUN an infectious intestinal disease, causing severe vomiting and diarrhoea

cholesterol (*pronounced* ko-**lest**-*er*-ol) NOUN a substance found in body cells which carries fats through the bloodstream

chomp VERB, *informal* to munch noisily

choose VERB (**choosing, chose, chosen**) **1** to select and take from two or several things: *Choose whichever book you like* **2** to decide, prefer to: *We chose to leave before the film began*

chop VERB (**chopping, chopped**) **1** to cut into small pieces **2** to cut with a sudden blow ▶ NOUN **1** a chopping blow **2** a slice of meat containing a bone: *a mutton chop* **chop and change** to keep changing

chopper NOUN **1** a knife or axe for chopping **2** *informal* a helicopter

choppy ADJECTIVE (**choppier, choppiest**) of the sea: not calm, having small waves

chopsticks PLURAL NOUN a pair of small sticks of wood, ivory, etc used for eating Chinese food

ⓘ Literally 'quick sticks', from Pidgin English *chop* for 'quick'

choral ADJECTIVE sung by or written for a choir

chord NOUN **1** a musical sound made by playing several notes together **2** *maths* a straight line joining any two points on a curve

ⓘ Meaning 1 of **chord** comes from the word 'accord', while meaning 2 comes from the Greek *chorde* meaning 'a string'. From this you might expect meaning 1 to be spelt without an 'h', but through the influence of meaning 2 their spellings have become identical.

> Do not confuse with: **cord**

chore NOUN **1** a dull, boring job **2** (**chores**) housework

choreographer (*pronounced* kor-ei-**og**-r*a*-fer) NOUN a person who designs dances and dance steps, usually for a team of dancers eg in a ballet or a musical

choreography (*pronounced* kor-ei-**og**-r*a*-fi) NOUN the arrangement of dancing and dance steps

chorister NOUN a member of a choir

chortle VERB to laugh, chuckle

chorus NOUN (*plural* **choruses**) **1** a band of singers and dancers **2** a choir or choral group **3** a part of a song repeated after each verse

chose *past tense* of **choose**

chosen *past participle* of **choose**

christen VERB **1** to baptize in the name of Christ **2** to give a name to

christening NOUN, *Christianity* the ceremony of baptism

Christian NOUN a believer in Christianity ▶ ADJECTIVE of Christianity

Christianity NOUN the religion which follows the teachings of Christ

Christian name NOUN a first or personal name

Christmas NOUN an annual Christian holiday or festival, in memory of the birth of Christ, held on 25 December

Christmas Eve NOUN 24 December

Christmassy ADJECTIVE typical of, or suitable for, Christmas

Christmas tree NOUN an evergreen tree hung with lights, decorations and gifts at Christmas

chromatic ADJECTIVE **1** of colours **2** coloured **3** *music* of or written in a scale in which each note is separated from the next by a semitone

chromatography NOUN, *chemistry* a technique for separating the substances in a mixture

chromium NOUN, *chemistry* (symbol **Cr**) a hard metallic element which does not rust and is used to plate other metals

chromosome NOUN, *biology* a rod-like part of a body cell that determines the characteristics of an individual

chronic ADJECTIVE **1** of a disease: long-term and progressing slowly (*compare with*: **acute**) **2** *informal* very bad > **chronically** ADVERB

chronicle NOUN a record of events in the order they happened ▸ VERB to write down events in order > **chronicler** NOUN

chrono- *or* **chron-** PREFIX of or relating to time: *chronological*

ⓘ Comes from Greek *chronos* meaning 'time'

chronological ADJECTIVE arranged in the order of the time of happening > **chronologically** ADVERB

chronology NOUN the arrangement of events in the order they occurred

chrysalis (*pronounced* **kri**-sa-lis) NOUN (*plural* **chrysalises**) an insect (especially a butterfly or moth) in its early stage of life, with no wings and encased in a soft cocoon

chrysanthemum (*pronounced* kri-**san**-the-m*u*m *or* kri-**zan**-the-m*u*m) NOUN a type of colourful garden flower with a large bushy head

chubby ADJECTIVE (**chubbier, chubbiest**) plump

chuck VERB **1** to throw, toss **2** to pat gently under the chin **chuck out** *informal* **1** to throw away, get rid of **2** to expel

chuckle NOUN a quiet laugh ▸ VERB to laugh quietly

chuffed ADJECTIVE, *informal* very pleased

chug VERB (**chugging, chugged**) of a vehicle: to move along making a thudding noise

chum NOUN, *informal* a close friend

chummy ADJECTIVE (**chummier, chummiest**) very friendly

chump NOUN **1** *informal* an idiot **2** a piece of lamb or mutton cut from the loin **off your chump** *informal* off your head; mad

chunk NOUN a thick piece

chunky ADJECTIVE (**chunkier,**

A B C D E F G H I J K L M N O P Q R S T U V W X Y Z

chunkiest) heavy, thick

church NOUN (*plural* **churches**) **1** a building for public, especially Christian, worship **2** any group of people who meet together for worship

churchyard NOUN a burial ground next to a church

churn NOUN a machine for making butter from milk ▸ VERB **1** to make (butter) in a churn **2** to shake or stir about violently: *My stomach was churning*

chute (*pronounced* shoot) NOUN **1** a sloping trough for sending water, parcels, etc to a lower level **2** a sloping structure for children to slide down, with steps for climbing back up

chutney NOUN (*plural* **chutneys**) a pickle made with vegetables or fruit and vinegar

CIA ABBREVIATION Central Intelligence Agency, a US government organization that collects secret political, military, etc information about other countries

CID ABBREVIATION Criminal Investigation Department, the police department in the UK that is responsible for solving serious crimes

-cide SUFFIX forms words describing murder or killing, or a person or thing that murders or kills: *suicide/ homicide/insecticide*

ⓘ Comes from Latin *caedere* meaning 'to kill'

cider NOUN an alcoholic drink made from fermented apple juice

cigar NOUN a roll of tobacco leaves for smoking

cigarette NOUN a tube of fine tobacco enclosed in thin paper

cilium NOUN (*plural* **cilia**) a hair-like growth found in certain cells and micro-organisms, used eg for movement or the removal of foreign bodies

cinder NOUN a burnt-out piece of coal

cinema NOUN **1** a place where films are shown **2** films as an art form or industry

cinnamon NOUN a yellowish-brown spice obtained from tree bark

cipher (*pronounced* **sai**-fer) NOUN **1** a secret writing, a code **2** nought, zero **3** someone of no importance

ⓘ Originally meaning 'zero' and later 'number', because of the early use of numbers in encoded documents

circa PREPOSITION about (in dates): *circa 1900*

circle NOUN **1** a figure formed from an endless curved line **2** something in the form of a circle; a ring **3** a society or group of people **4** a tier of seats in a theatre etc ▸ VERB **1** to enclose in a circle **2** to move round in a circle

circuit NOUN **1** a movement in a circle **2** a connected group of places, events, etc: *the American tennis circuit* **3** the path of an electric current

circular ADJECTIVE round, like a circle ▸ NOUN a letter sent round to a number of people

circulate VERB **1** to move round **2** to send round: *circulate a memo*

circulation NOUN **1** the act of

circulating **2** the movement of the blood through the body **3** the total sales of a newspaper or magazine

circulatory system NOUN the system that circulates blood through the body; the heart and blood vessels

circum- *or* **circu-** PREFIX round: *circumnavigate/circuit*

ⓘ Comes from Latin *circum* meaning 'all around'

circumcentre NOUN, *maths* the centre of a circle circumscribing another figure

circumcircle NOUN, *maths* a circle drawn round another figure, especially round a triangle and touching all its points

circumcise VERB **1** to cut away the foreskin of the penis, for medical or religious reasons **2** to cut away the clitoris, especially as a religious rite
> **circumcision** NOUN

circumference NOUN, *maths* **1** the outside line of a circle or closed curve **2** the length of this line

circumnavigate VERB to sail or fly right round something
> **circumnavigator** NOUN

circumspection NOUN caution

circumstance NOUN **1** a condition of time, place, etc which affects a person, an action or an event **2** (**circumstances**) the state of someone's financial affairs

circumstantial ADJECTIVE of evidence: pointing to a conclusion without giving absolute proof

circumstantiate VERB to prove by giving details

circumvent VERB **1** to get round (a difficulty) **2** to outwit
> **circumvention** NOUN

circus NOUN (*plural* **circuses**) **1** a travelling company of clowns, acrobats, etc **2** a large sports arena

cirrus (*pronounced* **si**-rus) NOUN (*plural* **cirri** – *pronounced* **si**-rai), a fleecy kind of cloud

cissy NOUN (*plural* **cissies**), *informal* an effeminate person

cistern NOUN a tank for storing water

citadel NOUN a fortress within a city

citation NOUN **1** something quoted **2** a summons to appear in court **3** official recognition of an achievement or action

cite VERB **1** to quote as an example or as proof **2** to summon to appear in court

ⓘ Comes from Latin *citare* meaning 'to call'

> Do not confuse with: **sight** and **site**

citizen NOUN someone who lives in a city or town

citizenship NOUN the rights or state of being a citizen

citric acid NOUN, *chemistry* a sharp-tasting organic acid found in citrus fruits

citron NOUN a fruit similar to a lemon

citrus fruit NOUN any of a group of fruits including the orange, lemon and lime

city NOUN (*plural* **cities**) **1** a large town **2** a town with a cathedral **3** (**the City**) the part of London

a b c d e f g h i j k l m n o p q r s t u v w x y z

regarded as the centre of British financial affairs

civic ADJECTIVE relating to a city or citizens

civics SINGULAR NOUN the study of people's duties as citizens

civil ADJECTIVE **1** relating to a community **2** non-military, civilian **3** polite

civil engineer NOUN an engineer who plans bridges, roads, etc

civilian NOUN someone who is not in the armed forces ▶ ADJECTIVE non-military

civility NOUN politeness, good manners

civilization *or* **civilisation** NOUN **1** making or becoming civilized **2** life under a civilized system **3** a particular culture: *a prehistoric civilization*

civilize *or* **civilise** VERB to bring (a people) under a regular system of laws, education, etc

civilized *or* **civilised** ADJECTIVE living under a system of laws, education, etc; not savage

civil law NOUN law concerned with citizens' rights, not criminal acts (*compare with*: **criminal law**)

civil marriage NOUN a marriage which does not take place in church

civil rights NOUN the rights of a citizen to freedom and equality, regardless of race, religion, sex or sexuality

civil servant NOUN someone who works in the civil service

civil service NOUN the paid administrative officials of the country, excluding the armed forces

civil war NOUN war between citizens of the same country

CJD ABBREVIATION, *medicine* Creutzfeldt-Jakob disease, a rare degenerative brain disease, characterized by dementia, wasting of muscle tissue and various neurological abnormalities

cl ABBREVIATION centilitre(s)

clad ADJECTIVE, *literary* clothed: *clad in leather from head to toe*

claim VERB **1** to demand as a right **2** to state as a truth; assert (that) ▶ NOUN an act of claiming

claimant NOUN someone who makes a claim

clairvoyant ADJECTIVE able to see into the future, or to contact the spirit world ▶ NOUN someone with clairvoyant powers > **clairvoyance** NOUN

clam NOUN a large shellfish with two shells hinged together

clamber VERB to climb awkwardly or with difficulty

clammy ADJECTIVE (**clammier, clammiest**) moist and sticky

clamour NOUN a loud, continuous noise or outcry ▶ VERB **1** to cry aloud **2** to make a loud demand (for)

clamp NOUN a piece of metal, wood, etc used to fasten things together ▶ VERB to bind with a clamp **clamp down on** to suppress firmly

clan NOUN **1** a number of families with the same surname, traditionally under a single chieftain **2** a sect, a clique

ⓘ From Scottish Gaelic *clann* meaning 'children'

clandestine (*pronounced* klan-

des-tin) ADJECTIVE hidden, secret, underhand

clang VERB to make a loud, deep ringing sound ▸ NOUN a loud, deep ring

clank NOUN a sound like that made by metal hitting metal ▸ VERB to make this sound

clansman *or* **clanswoman** NOUN (*plural* **clansmen** *or* **clanswomen**), a member of a clan

clap NOUN **1** the noise made by striking together two things, especially the hands **2** a burst of sound, especially thunder ▸ VERB (**clapping, clapped**) **1** to strike noisily together **2** to strike the hands together to show approval **3** *informal* to put suddenly, throw: *clap in jail*

claptrap NOUN meaningless words, nonsense

claret NOUN a type of red wine

clarify VERB (**clarifies, clarifying, clarified**) to make clear and understandable

clarinet NOUN a musical wind instrument, usually made of wood

clarion NOUN, *old* **1** a kind of trumpet **2** a shrill, rousing noise

clarity NOUN clearness

clash NOUN (*plural* **clashes**) **1** a loud noise made by striking swords etc **2** a disagreement, a fight ▸ VERB **1** to bang noisily together **2** to disagree **3** of events: to take place at the same time **4** of two colours etc: not to look well together

clasp NOUN **1** a hook or pin for fastening: *a hair clasp* **2** a handshake **3** an embrace ▸ VERB **1** to hold closely; grasp **2** to fasten

class NOUN (*plural* **classes**) **1** a rank or order of people or things **2** a group of schoolchildren or students taught together **3** *biology* a group of plants or animals with something in common ▸ VERB **1** to place in a class **2** to arrange in some order

classic NOUN **1** a great book or other work of art **2** something typical and influential of its kind **3** (**classics**) the study of ancient Greek and Latin literature ▸ ADJECTIVE **1** excellent **2** standard, typical of its kind: *a classic example* **3** simple and elegant in style: *a classic black dress*

classical ADJECTIVE **1** of a classic or the classics **2** of music: serious, not light

classification NOUN **1** the activity of arranging things into classes or categories **2** the label or name that you give something in order to indicate its class or category

classify VERB (**classifies, classifying, classified**) **1** to arrange in classes **2** to put into a class or category **3** to declare (information) to be secret > **classified** ADJECTIVE

classmate NOUN a fellow pupil or student in your class

classroom NOUN a room in a school or college where lessons take place

classy ADJECTIVE (**classier, classiest**) elegant, stylish

clatter NOUN a noise of plates etc banged together

clause NOUN **1** *grammar* a group of words that contains a subject and its related verb **2** a part of a will, act of parliament, etc

claustrophobia (*pronounced* klos-tr*o*-**foh**-bi-*a*) NOUN an abnormal fear of enclosed spaces

claustrophobic ADJECTIVE **1** suffering from or affected by claustrophobia: *She can't go in because she'll get claustrophobic* **2** causing feelings of anxiety related to being in an enclosed space or to feeling trapped or enclosed in some other way: *a claustrophobic little room*

claw NOUN **1** an animal's or bird's foot with hooked nails **2** a hooked nail on one of these feet ▸ VERB to scratch or tear

clay NOUN soft, sticky earth, often used to make pottery, bricks, etc > **clayey** ADJECTIVE

clean ADJECTIVE **1** free from dirt; pure **2** neat, complete: *a clean break* ▸ ADVERB completely: *got clean away* ▸ VERB to make clean; free from dirt > **cleanly** ADVERB (meaning 2)

cleaner NOUN **1** someone employed to clean a building etc **2** a substance which cleans

cleanliness (*pronounced* **klen**-li-n*e*s) NOUN the quality of being free from dirt

cleanse (*pronounced* klenz) VERB to make clean

cleanser NOUN a substance that cleanses, especially the skin

clear ADJECTIVE **1** bright, undimmed **2** free from mist or cloud: *clear sky* **3** transparent **4** free from difficulty or obstructions **5** easy to see, hear or understand **6** after deductions and charges have been made: *clear profit* **7** without a stain **8** without touching: *clear of the rocks* ▸ VERB **1** to make clear **2** to empty **3** to free from blame **4** to leap over without touching **5** of the sky: to become bright **clear out** *or* **clear off** to go away > **clearness** NOUN (adjective, meanings 1, 2, 3, 4 and 5)

clearance NOUN **1** the activity of getting rid of all the things which are in a certain place so that a new start can be made: *a clearance sale* (= a cut-price sale in a shop to get rid of all the old stock)/*the Highland Clearances* (= the removal of tenant farmers from the Scottish Highlands by landowners in the 19th century) **2** (**the Clearances**) *see* **Highland Clearances** **3** permission to do something: *receive official clearance for the project*

clear-cut ADJECTIVE distinct, obvious

clearing NOUN land free of trees

clearly ADVERB **1** obviously **2** in a clear way

cleavage NOUN **1** splitting **2** the way in which two things are split or divided **3** the hollow between a woman's breasts

cleaver NOUN a heavy knife for splitting meat carcasses etc

clef NOUN a musical sign, 𝄞 (**treble clef**) or 𝄢 (**bass clef**), placed on a stave to fix the pitch of the notes

cleft NOUN an opening made by splitting; a crack ▸ VERB *past form* of **cleave**

clement ADJECTIVE mild; merciful

clench VERB to press firmly together: *clenching his teeth*

clergy PLURAL NOUN the ministers of the Christian church

clergyman *or* **clergywoman** NOUN (*plural* **clergymen** *or* **clergywomen**) a Christian minister

cleric NOUN a member of the clergy

clerical ADJECTIVE **1** relating to office work **2** of the clergy

clerk NOUN an office worker who writes letters, keeps accounts, etc ▸ VERB to act as clerk

clever ADJECTIVE **1** quick in learning and understanding **2** intelligent, skilful: *a clever answer* > **cleverly** ADVERB

cliché (*pronounced* **klee**-shei) NOUN an idea, phrase, etc that has been used too much and has little meaning

ⓘ From a French word for 'stereotype', in the sense of a fixed printing plate

click NOUN a short sharp sound like a clock's tick ▸ VERB **1** to make this sound **2** *computing* to press and release a button on a mouse to select an option on the screen

client NOUN **1** a customer of a shop etc **2** someone who goes to a lawyer etc for advice **3** *computing* a program used to contact and download data from a server

clientele (*pronounced* klee-*en*-**tel** *or* klai-*en*-**tel**) NOUN the customers of a lawyer, shopkeeper, etc

cliff NOUN a very steep, rocky slope, especially by the sea

cliffhanger NOUN a story that keeps you in suspense until the end

climactic ADJECTIVE most important or intense, of the climax: *the climactic moment of the play*

climate NOUN **1** the weather conditions of a particular area **2** general condition or situation: *in the present cultural climate* > **climatic** ADJECTIVE (meaning 1)

climate change NOUN change in the Earth's climate, especially global warming caused by the greenhouse effect

climax NOUN (*plural* **climaxes**) the point of greatest interest or importance in a situation

climb VERB **1** to go to the top of **2** to go up using hands and feet **3** to slope upward ▸ NOUN an act of climbing

climber NOUN **1** someone who climbs **2** a plant which climbs up walls etc

clinch VERB **1** to grasp tightly **2** to settle (an argument, bargain, etc) ▸ NOUN (*plural* **clinches**) **1** *boxing* a position in which the boxers hold each other with their arms **2** a passionate embrace

cling VERB (**clinging, clung**) to stick or hang on (to) > **clingy** ADJECTIVE (**clingier, clingiest**)

clingfilm NOUN thin transparent plastic material used to wrap food

clinic NOUN a place or part of a hospital where a particular kind of treatment is given

clinical ADJECTIVE **1** of a clinic **2** based on observation: *clinical medicine* **3** objective, cool and unemotional: *a clinical approach*

clinically ADVERB **1** according

a b c d e f g h i j k l m n o p q r s t u v w x y z

A B C D E F G H I J K L M N O P Q R S T U V W X Y Z

to medical diagnosis: *clinically depressed* **2** as an object of medical observation: *His skin condition is clinically interesting*

clink NOUN a ringing sound of knocked glasses etc

clip VERB (**clipping, clipped**) **1** to cut (off) **2** to fasten with a clip ▶ NOUN **1** something clipped off **2** a small fastener **3** *informal* a smart blow

clipper NOUN **1** a fast-sailing ship **2** (**clippers**) large scissors for clipping

clique (*pronounced* kleek) NOUN a small group of people who help each other but keep others at a distance

clitoris (*pronounced* **klit**-or-is) NOUN (*plural* **clitorises**), *anatomy* a small highly sensitive structure at the front of the external female sex organs > **clitoral** ADJECTIVE

cloak NOUN **1** a loose outer garment with no sleeves **2** something which hides: *under the cloak of darkness* ▶ VERB **1** to cover as with a cloak **2** to hide

cloakroom NOUN a place where coats, hats, etc may be left for a time

clock NOUN a machine for measuring time **clock in** *or* **clock out** to record your time of arrival at, or departure from, work

clockwise ADJECTIVE turning or moving in the same direction as the hands of a clock

clockwork ADJECTIVE worked by machinery such as that of a clock **like clockwork** smoothly, without difficulties

clod NOUN **1** a thick lump of turf **2** a stupid man

clodhopper NOUN a stupid, clumsy person > **clodhopping** ADJECTIVE

clog NOUN a shoe with a wooden sole ▶ VERB (**clogging, clogged**) to block (pipes etc)

cloister NOUN **1** a covered-in walk in a monastery or convent **2** a monastery or convent > **cloistered** ADJECTIVE **1** shut up in a monastery etc **2** sheltered

clone NOUN **1** *biology* a cell or organism from a single ancestor **2** *genetics* a genetically-engineered copy of a sequence of DNA ▶ VERB **1** *biology* to grow a new cell or organism from a single cell **2** *genetics* to make copies of a DNA sequence

close[1] (*pronounced* klohs) ADJECTIVE **1** near in time, place, etc **2** shut up, with no opening **3** without fresh air, stuffy **4** narrow, confined **5** mean **6** secretive **7** beloved, very dear: *a close friend* **8** decided by a small amount: *a close contest* ▶ NOUN **1** a narrow passage off a street **2** the gardens, walks, etc near a cathedral

close[2] (*pronounced* klohz) VERB **1** to shut **2** to finish **3** to come closer to and fight (with) ▶ NOUN the end

closed ADJECTIVE, *maths* **1** of a curve: having no end points, as in a circle **2** of a set: having as members the results of an operation (eg addition) on other members of the set

closed-circuit television NOUN (*abbrev* **CCTV**) a system of television cameras and receivers for use in shops etc

closely ADVERB **1** carefully: *observe*

something closely/listen closely **2** strongly, intimately: *He was closely involved in these activities* **3** in a way that brings things close together: *objects packed closely together in a box*

closet NOUN, *US* a cupboard ▸ VERB to take into a room for a private conference **closeted with** in private conference with

closure NOUN the act of closing

clot NOUN **1** a lump that forms in blood, cream, etc **2** *informal* an idiot ▸ VERB (**clotting, clotted**) to form into clots

cloth NOUN **1** woven material of cotton, wool, silk, etc **2** a piece of this **3** a table-cover

clothe VERB **1** to put clothes on **2** to provide with clothes **3** to cover

clothes PLURAL NOUN **1** things worn to cover the body and limbs, eg shirt, trousers, skirt **2** sheets and coverings for a bed

clothing NOUN clothes

cloud NOUN **1** a mass of tiny drops of water or ice floating in the sky **2** a mass of anything: *a cloud of bees* ▸ VERB to become dim or blurred > **clouded** ADJECTIVE > **cloudless** ADJECTIVE (noun, meaning 1)

cloudy ADJECTIVE (**cloudier, cloudiest**) **1** darkened with clouds **2** not clear or transparent

clout NOUN, *informal* **1** a blow **2** influence, power ▸ VERB, *informal* to hit

clove[1] NOUN **1** a flower bud of the clove tree, used as a spice **2** a small section of a bulb of garlic

ⓘ The spice gets its name from French *clou* meaning 'nail' because of its shape

clove[2] *past tense* of **cleave**

cloven-hoofed ADJECTIVE having a divided hoof like an ox, sheep, etc

clover NOUN a field plant with leaves usually in three parts **in clover** in luxury

clown NOUN **1** a comedian with a painted face and comical clothes in a circus **2** a fool

clowning NOUN silly or comical behaviour

clownish ADJECTIVE like a clown; awkward

cloying ADJECTIVE over-sweet, sickly

club NOUN **1** a heavy stick **2** a stick used to hit the ball in golf **3** a group of people who meet for social events etc **4** the place where these people meet **5** (**clubs**) one of the four suits in playing cards ▸ VERB (**clubbing, clubbed**) to beat with a club **club together** to put money into a joint fund for some purpose

cluck NOUN a sound like that made by a hen ▸ VERB to make this sound

clue NOUN a sign or piece of evidence that helps to solve a mystery

clump NOUN a cluster of trees or shrubs ▸ VERB to walk heavily

clumsy ADJECTIVE (**clumsier, clumsiest**) **1** awkward in movement or actions **2** tactless, thoughtless: *a clumsy apology* > **clumsily** ADVERB

clung *past form* of **cling**

cluster NOUN **1** a bunch of fruit etc **2** a crowd ▸ VERB to group together in clusters

a b c d e f g h i j k l m n o p q r s t u v w x y z

A B C D E F G H I J K L M N O P Q R S T U V W X Y Z

clutch VERB **1** to hold firmly **2** to seize, grasp ▶ NOUN (*plural* **clutches**) **1** a grasp **2** part of a car engine used for changing gears **3** a brood of chickens

clutter NOUN **1** a muddled or disordered collection of things **2** disorder, confusion, untidiness ▶ VERB **1** to crowd together untidily **2** (often **clutter up**) to fill or cover in an untidy, disordered way

cm ABBREVIATION centimetre(s)

CND ABBREVIATION Campaign for Nuclear Disarmament, a British organization whose aim is to persuade countries to get rid of nuclear weapons

CO ABBREVIATION **1** carbon monoxide **2** Commanding Officer

Co ABBREVIATION **1** Company **2** County

c/o ABBREVIATION care of

co- also **col-**, **com-**, **con-**, **cor-** PREFIX **1** joint, working with, together with: *co-author/co-driver/connect/compound/collision/correspond* **2** sometimes just gives extra emphasis to a word: *corroborate/commemorate*

ⓘ Comes from Latin *cum* meaning 'with'

coach NOUN (*plural* **coaches**) **1** a bus for long-distance travel **2** a closed, four-wheeled horse carriage **3** a railway carriage **4** trainer or instructor ▶ VERB to train or help to prepare for an examination, sports contest, etc

coagulate (*pronounced* koh-**ag**-yuw-leit) VERB to thicken; clot

coal NOUN a black substance dug out of the earth and used for burning, making gas, etc

coalfield NOUN an area where there is coal to be mined

coal gas NOUN the mixture of gases obtained from coal, used for lighting and heating

coalition (*pronounced* koh-*a*-**li**-sh*u*n) NOUN a joining together of different parts or groups

coalmine NOUN a mine from which coal is dug

coarse ADJECTIVE **1** not fine in texture; rough, harsh **2** vulgar

coarsen VERB to make coarse

coast NOUN the border of land next to the sea ▶ VERB **1** to sail along or near a coast **2** to move without the use of power on a bike, in a car, etc

coastal ADJECTIVE of or on the coast

coastguard NOUN someone who acts as a guard along the coast to help those in danger in boats etc

coat NOUN **1** an outer garment with sleeves **2** an animal's covering of hair or wool **3** a layer of paint ▶ VERB to cover with a coat or layer **coat of arms** the badge or crest of a family

coating NOUN a covering

coax VERB to persuade to do what is wanted without using force

cob NOUN **1** a head of corn **2** a male swan

cobalt (*pronounced* **koh**-bawlt) NOUN **1** *chemistry* a silvery metal **2** a blue colouring obtained from this

cobble NOUN (*also called*: **cobblestone**) a rounded stone used in paving roads ▶ VERB **1** to mend (shoes) **2** to repair roughly or hurriedly

cobbled ADJECTIVE of streets: paved with cobbles

cobbler NOUN someone who mends shoes

cobra (*pronounced* **koh**-br*a* *or* **ko**-br*a*) NOUN a poisonous snake found in India and Africa

cobweb NOUN a spider's web

cocaine NOUN, *medicine* an addictive narcotic drug, used medicinally as a local anaesthetic and illegally as a stimulant

cock NOUN **1** the male of most kinds of bird, especially of the farmyard hen **2** a tap or valve for controlling the flow of liquid **3** a hammer-like part of a gun which fires the shot **4** a small heap of hay ▸ VERB **1** to draw back the cock of a gun **2** to set (the ears) upright to listen **3** to tilt (the head) to one side

cockatoo NOUN a kind of parrot

cockerel NOUN a young cock

cocker spaniel NOUN a breed of small spaniel

cockle NOUN a type of shellfish
warm the cockles of the heart to make someone feel happy and contented

cockleshell NOUN the shell of a cockle

cockney NOUN (*plural* **cockneys**) **1** someone born in the East End of London **2** the speech characteristic of this area
ⓘ Literally 'cock's egg', an old word for a misshapen egg, which was later applied to an effeminate person, and so to a soft-living city-dweller

cockpit NOUN **1** the space for the pilot or driver in an aeroplane or small boat **2** a pit where game cocks fight

cockroach NOUN (*plural* **cockroaches**) a type of large insect that infests houses etc

cocksure ADJECTIVE very confident, often without cause

cocktail NOUN a mixed alcoholic drink

cocky ADJECTIVE (**cockier, cockiest**) conceited, self-confident

cocoa NOUN a drink made from the ground seeds of the cacao tree

coconut NOUN the large, hard-shelled nut of a type of palm tree
ⓘ Based on a Portuguese word meaning 'grimace', because of the resemblance of the three marks on the base of the fruit to a human face

cocoon NOUN a protective covering of silk spun by the larva of a butterfly, moth, etc

cod NOUN (*plural* **cod**) a fish often eaten as food, found in the northern seas

code NOUN **1** a way of signalling or sending secret messages, using letters etc agreed beforehand **2** a book or collection of laws, rules, etc

codify VERB (**codifies, codifying, codified**) to arrange in an orderly way, classify

coed (*pronounced* koh-**ed**) ADJECTIVE, *informal* coeducational

coeducation NOUN the education of boys and girls together
> **coeducational** ADJECTIVE

coefficient NOUN *maths* a number appearing before a variable, eg 5 in *5x*, showing the variable is to be multiplied by that number

coerce VERB to force, compel > **coercion** NOUN > **coercive** ADJECTIVE

coexist VERB to exist at the same time > **coexistence** NOUN > **coexistent** ADJECTIVE

coffee NOUN **1** a drink made from the roasted, ground beans of the coffee shrub **2** a pale brown colour

coffer NOUN a chest for holding money, gold, etc

coffin NOUN a box in which a dead body is buried or cremated

cog NOUN a tooth on a wheel

cogent (*pronounced* **koh**-jent) ADJECTIVE convincing, believable > **cogency** NOUN

cognac (*pronounced* **kon**-yak) NOUN a kind of French brandy

cognition NOUN the mental processes enabling humans to experience things, process knowledge, etc

cogwheel NOUN a toothed wheel

cohere VERB to stick together

coherence NOUN connection between thoughts, ideas, etc

coherent ADJECTIVE **1** sticking together **2** clear and logical in thought or speech

cohesion NOUN the act of sticking together

cohesive ADJECTIVE of a group: consisting of members who are closely linked together or associated with each other

cohort NOUN **1** *history* a tenth part of a Roman legion **2** a group of people who share a belief **3** a follower or companion

coil VERB to wind in rings; twist ▸ NOUN **1** a wound arrangement of hair, rope, etc **2** a contraceptive device fitted in the uterus

coin NOUN a piece of stamped metal used as money ▸ VERB **1** to make metal into money **2** to make up (a new word etc)

coinage NOUN **1** the system of coins used in a country **2** a newly made word

coincide VERB (often **coincide with**) **1** to be the same as: *Their interests coincide/His story coincides with mine* **2** to happen at the same time as: *coincided with his departure*

coincidence NOUN the occurrence of two things simultaneously without planning

coincidental ADJECTIVE happening by chance, the result of a coincidence: *Any resemblance to real people is purely coincidental* > **coincidentally** ADVERB

coke NOUN **1** a type of fuel made by heating coal till the gas is driven out **2** *informal* cocaine

col- *see* **co-**

cola NOUN a soft drink made with flavouring from the nuts of a tropical tree

colander (*pronounced* **kol**-*a*n-der) NOUN a bowl with small holes in it for straining vegetables, pasta, etc

cold ADJECTIVE **1** low in temperature **2** lower in temperature than is comfortable **3** unfriendly ▸ NOUN **1** the state of being cold **2** an infectious disease causing shivering, running nose, etc > **coldly** ADVERB (adjective, meanings

2 and 3) > **coldness** NOUN

cold-blooded ADJECTIVE **1** of fishes *etc*: having cold blood **2** cruel; lacking in feelings

cold feet PLURAL NOUN lack of courage

cold sore NOUN a blister on or near the mouth, caused by a contagious virus

cold war NOUN a power struggle between nations without open warfare

coleslaw NOUN a salad made from finely sliced raw cabbage, onion and carrot, mixed together in mayonnaise

colic NOUN a severe stomach pain

collaborate VERB **1** to work together (with) **2** to work with (an enemy) to betray your country > **collaboration** NOUN > **collaborator** NOUN

ⓘ Comes from Latin *col-* meaning 'together with', and *laborare* meaning 'to work'

> Do not confuse with: **corroborate**

collage (*pronounced* ko-**lahsz**) NOUN a design made of scraps of paper, cloth, etc pasted on wood, card, etc

collapse VERB **1** to fall or break down **2** to cave or fall in **3** to become unable to continue ▶NOUN a falling down or caving in

collapsible ADJECTIVE of a chair etc: able to be folded up

collar NOUN **1** a band, strip, etc worn round the neck **2** part of a garment that fits round the neck ▶VERB, *informal* to seize

collarbone NOUN either of two bones joining the breast bone and shoulderblade

collate VERB **1** to examine and compare **2** to gather together and arrange in order: *collate the pages for the book*

collateral NOUN assets offered as additional security for repayment of a debt

colleague NOUN someone who works in the same company etc as yourself

collect VERB **1** to bring together **2** to gather together: *collect stamps*

collected ADJECTIVE **1** gathered together **2** calm, composed

collection NOUN **1** the act of collecting **2** a number of objects or people **3** money gathered from a group of people, eg for a present or at a church service

collective ADJECTIVE **1** acting together **2** of several things or people, not of one: *a collective decision* ▶NOUN a business etc owned and managed by the workers

collector NOUN someone who collects a particular group of things: *stamp collector*

college NOUN **1** a building housing students, forming part of a university **2** a higher-education institute: (*see also*: **sixth-form college**): *art college*

collegiate ADJECTIVE (*pronounced* ko-**lee**-ji-*at*) of a university: divided into colleges

collide VERB to come together with great force; clash

collie NOUN a breed of long-haired dog with a pointed nose

collier NOUN **1** a coalminer **2** a ship that carries coal

colliery NOUN (*plural* **collieries**) a coalmine

collision NOUN **1** a crash between two moving vehicles etc **2** a disagreement, clash of interests, etc

colloquial ADJECTIVE used in everyday speech but not in formal writing or speaking > **colloquially** ADVERB

colloquialism NOUN an example of colloquial speech

collude VERB to plot secretly with someone

collusion NOUN a secret or clandestine agreement

cologne (*pronounced* ko-**lohn**) NOUN light perfume made with plant oils and alcohol

colon[1] NOUN a punctuation mark (:) used eg to introduce a list of examples

colon[2] NOUN, *anatomy* a part of the bowel

colonel (*pronounced* **ker**-nel) NOUN a senior army officer in charge of a regiment

colonial ADJECTIVE of colonies abroad

colonialism NOUN the policy of setting up colonies abroad

colonialist NOUN someone who supports the policy of setting up and maintaining colonies abroad ▶ ADJECTIVE related to colonialism

colonist NOUN a settler

colonize *or* **colonise** VERB **1** to set up a colony in **2** to settle (people) in a colony > **colonization** NOUN

colonnade NOUN a row of columns or pillars

colony NOUN (*plural* **colonies**) **1** a group of settlers or the settlement they make in another country **2** a group of people, animals, etc of the same type living together

colossal ADJECTIVE huge, enormous

colossus NOUN (*plural* **colossuses** *or* **colossi** – *pronounced* ko-**los**-ai), an enormous statue

colour *or US* **color** NOUN **1** a quality that an object shows in the light, eg redness, blueness, etc **2** a shade or tint **3** vividness, brightness **4** (**colours**) a flag or standard ▶ VERB **1** to put colour on **2** to blush **3** to influence: *coloured my attitude to life* **off colour** unwell

colour-blind ADJECTIVE unable to distinguish between certain colours, eg red and green

coloured ADJECTIVE **1** having colour **2** an old-fashioned and offensive word meaning 'not white-skinned'

> ⓘ It is generally considered more correct to say 'black' for meaning 2.

colourful ADJECTIVE **1** brightly coloured **2** vivid, interesting

colouring NOUN **1** shade or combination of colours **2** complexion

colourless ADJECTIVE **1** without colour **2** dull, bland

colt NOUN a young horse

column NOUN **1** an upright stone or

wooden pillar **2** something of a long or tall, narrow shape **3** a vertical line of print, figures, etc on a page **4** a regular feature in a newspaper **5** an arrangement of troops etc one behind the other

columnist (*pronounced* **ko**-lum-nist *or* **ko**-lum-ist) NOUN someone who writes a regular newspaper column

com- *see* **co-**

coma (*pronounced* **koh**-ma) NOUN unconsciousness lasting a long time

comatose ADJECTIVE **1** in or of a coma **2** drowsy, sluggish

comb NOUN **1** a toothed instrument for separating or smoothing hair, wool, etc **2** the fleshy crest of certain birds **3** a collection of cells for honey ▸ VERB **1** to arrange or smooth with a comb **2** to search through thoroughly

combat VERB to fight or struggle against ▸ NOUN a fight or struggle

combatant NOUN someone who is fighting ▸ ADJECTIVE fighting

combative ADJECTIVE quarrelsome; fighting

combination NOUN **1** a joining together of things or people **2** a set of things or people combined **3** a series of letters or figures dialled to open a safe, lock, etc

combine VERB to join together ▸ NOUN a number of traders etc who join together

combine harvester NOUN a machine that both cuts and threshes crops

combustible ADJECTIVE liable to catch fire and burn ▸ NOUN anything that will catch fire

combustion NOUN catching fire and burning

come VERB (**coming, came, come**) **1** to move towards this place: *Come here!* **2** to draw near: *Christmas is coming* **3** to arrive: *We'll have tea when she comes* **4** to happen, occur: *The index comes at the end* **come about** to happen **come across** *or* **come upon** to meet or find accidentally **come by** to obtain **come into** to inherit **come of age** to reach the age at which you become an adult for legal purposes **come round** *or* **come to** to recover from a faint etc **come upon** *see* **come across** **to come** in the future: *in years to come*

[1] Comes from Old English *cuman*

comedian NOUN a performer who tells jokes, acts in comedy, etc

comedy NOUN (*plural* **comedies**) **1** a light-hearted or amusing play or film **2** such plays as a genre (*contrasted with*: **tragedy**)

comely ADJECTIVE (**comelier, comeliest**) good-looking, pleasing
> **comeliness** NOUN

comet NOUN a rock-like body which orbits the sun and has a tail of light

comfort VERB to help, soothe (someone in pain or distress) ▸ NOUN **1** ease; quiet enjoyment **2** something or someone that brings ease and happiness

comfortable ADJECTIVE **1** at ease; free from trouble, pain, etc **2** giving comfort **3** having enough money for a pleasant lifestyle

a b c d e f g h i j k l m n o p q r s t u v w x y z

comfortably ADVERB **1** easily, happily, or without any problems: *At this rate, he'll win comfortably* **2** in a way which involves no pain or physical irritation: *Are you sitting comfortably?* **3** financially well: *comfortably off*

comfy ADJECTIVE (**comfier, comfiest**), *informal* comfortable

comic ADJECTIVE **1** of or to do with comedy **2** amusing, funny ▸ NOUN **1** a professional comedian **2** a magazine with illustrated stories, strip cartoons, etc

comical ADJECTIVE funny, amusing
> **comically** ADVERB

comic strip NOUN a strip of small pictures outlining a story

comma NOUN a punctuation mark (,) indicating a pause in a sentence

command VERB **1** to give an order **2** to be in charge of **3** to look over or down upon: *commanding a view* ▸ NOUN **1** an order **2** control: *in command of the situation*

commandeer VERB to seize (something) especially for the use of an army

commander NOUN **1** someone who commands **2** a naval officer next in rank below captain

commandment NOUN an order or command

commando NOUN (*plural* **commandoes**) a soldier in an army unit trained for special tasks

commemorate VERB to honour the memory of (a person or event) with a ceremony etc
> **commemoration** NOUN

commence VERB to begin

commencement NOUN the start or beginning

commend VERB **1** to praise **2** to give into the care of

commendable ADJECTIVE praiseworthy

commendation NOUN praise

comment NOUN **1** a remark **2** a criticism ▸ VERB to remark on; criticize

commentary NOUN (*plural* **commentaries**) **1** a description of an event etc by someone who is watching it **2** a set of explanatory notes for a book etc

commentator NOUN someone who gives or writes a commentary

commerce NOUN the buying and selling of goods between people or nations; trade, dealings

commercial ADJECTIVE **1** of or to do with commerce **2** paid for by advertisements: *commercial radio* ▸ NOUN an advertisement on radio, TV, etc

commercially ADVERB **1** in a way which can make money: *a commercially attractive proposal* **2** as a large-scale industrial process: *A home-made gift is more personal than a commercially produced one* **3** on the open market: *It will be a while before these gadgets are commercially available*

commiserate VERB to sympathize (with)

commiseration NOUN pity
> **commiserations** PLURAL NOUN an expression of sympathy when someone has failed to do or achieve something

commission NOUN **1** the act of committing **2** a document giving authority to an officer in the armed forces **3** an order for a work of art **4** a fee or percentage for doing business on another's behalf **5** a group of people appointed to investigate something ▸ VERB to give a commission or power to **in** *or* **out of commission** in or not in use

commissionaire (*pronounced* k*o*-mi-sh*o*n-**eir**) NOUN a uniformed doorkeeper

commissioner NOUN **1** someone with high authority in a district **2** a member of a commission

commit VERB (**committing, committed**) **1** to give or hand over; entrust **2** to make a promise to do: *committed to finishing this book* **3** to do, bring about: *commit a crime*

commitment NOUN **1** a promise **2** a task that must be done

committal NOUN the act of committing

committed ADJECTIVE strong in belief or support: *a committed socialist*

committee NOUN a number of people chosen from a larger body, eg a club, to perform certain tasks on its behalf

commodity NOUN (*plural* **commodities**) **1** an article to be bought or sold **2** (**commodities**) goods, produce

commodore NOUN an officer next above a captain in the navy

common ADJECTIVE **1** shared by all or many: *common belief* **2** seen or happening often: *a common occurrence* **3** ordinary, normal: *the common cold* ▸ NOUN **1** land belonging to the people of a town, parish, etc **2** (**the Commons**) the House of Commons

commoner NOUN someone who is not a noble

common factor NOUN, *maths* a factor shared by two or more numbers, eg 5 is a common factor of 15 and 20

common fraction another term for **vulgar fraction**

common law NOUN unwritten law based on custom or previous court judgements

common noun NOUN, *grammar* a name for any one of a class of things (*contrasted with*: **proper noun**)

commonplace ADJECTIVE ordinary

common room NOUN a sitting room for the students or staff in a school, university, etc

common sense NOUN practical good sense

commonwealth NOUN an association of self-governing states

commotion NOUN a disturbance among several people

communal ADJECTIVE common, shared > **communally** ADVERB

commune NOUN a group of people living together, sharing work, etc ▸ VERB to talk together

communicable ADJECTIVE able to be passed on to others: *a communicable disease*

communicate VERB **1** to make known, tell **2** to pass on **3** to get in touch (with) **4** to have a connecting door

A B C D E F G H I J K L M N O P Q R S T U V W X Y Z

communication NOUN **1** a means of conveying information **2** a message **3** a way of passing from place to place

communicative ADJECTIVE willing to give information, talkative

communion NOUN **1** the act of sharing thoughts, feelings, etc; fellowship **2** (**Communion**) in the Christian Church, the celebration of the Lord's supper

communiqué (*pronounced* kom-**yoon**-ik-ei) NOUN an official announcement

communism NOUN a form of socialism in which industry is controlled by the state

communist ADJECTIVE of communism ▶NOUN someone who believes in communism

community NOUN (*plural* **communities**) **1** a group of people living in one place **2** the public in general

commute VERB **1** to travel regularly between two places, eg between home and work **2** to change (a punishment) for one less severe: *commute a sentence*

commuter NOUN someone who travels regularly some distance from their home to work

compact ADJECTIVE fitted or packed closely together ▶NOUN a bargain or agreement

compact disc *or* **compact disk** NOUN, *computing* a small disc on which digitally recorded sound, graphics or text can be read by a laser beam

companion NOUN someone or something that accompanies; a friend

companionable ADJECTIVE friendly

companionship NOUN friendship; the act of accompanying someone

company NOUN (*plural* **companies**) **1** a gathering of people **2** a business firm **3** a part of a regiment **4** a ship's crew **5** companionship

ⓘ Comes from French *compagnie* meaning 'company' or 'a gathering of people'

comparable (*pronounced* **kom**-pa-ra-bl *or* kom-**pa**-ra-bl) ADJECTIVE roughly similar or equal in some way: *The two films are comparable in terms of quality*

comparative ADJECTIVE **1** judged by comparing with something else; relative: *comparative improvement* **2** near to being: *a comparative stranger* **3** *grammar* the degree of an adjective or adverb between positive and superlative, eg *blacker*, *better*, *more courageous*

> **comparatively** ADVERB in comparison to others: *The test was comparatively easy*

compare VERB **1** to look at things together to see how similar or different they are **2** to liken **beyond compare** much better than all rivals

comparison NOUN the act of comparing

compartment NOUN a separate part or division, eg of a railway carriage

compass NOUN (*plural* **compasses**)

1 an instrument with a magnetized needle for showing direction **2** (**compasses**) an instrument with one fixed and one movable leg for drawing circles

compassion NOUN pity for another's suffering; mercy

compassionate ADJECTIVE pitying, merciful > **compassionately** ADVERB

compatibility NOUN the natural tendency for two or more people or groups to get on well together

compatible ADJECTIVE **1** able to live with, agree with, etc **2** of pieces of electronic equipment, computer software, etc: able to be used together > **compatibly** ADVERB

compatriot NOUN (*pronounced* kom-**pat**-ri-*o*t *or* kom-**peit**-ri-*o*t) a fellow-countryman or -countrywoman

compel VERB (**compelling, compelled**) to force to do something

compelling ADJECTIVE **1** convincing: *compelling arguments* **2** fascinating: *a compelling TV series*

compendium NOUN (*plural* **compendiums** *or* **compendia**) **1** a concise summary **2** a collection of board games, puzzles, etc

compensate VERB to make up for wrong or damage done, especially by giving money > **compensation** NOUN

compère NOUN someone who introduces acts as part of an entertainment ▸ VERB to act as compère

compete VERB to try to beat others in a race, contest, etc

competent ADJECTIVE **1** capable, efficient **2** skilled; properly trained or qualified > **competence** NOUN > **competently** ADVERB

competition NOUN **1** a contest between rivals **2** rivalry

competitive ADJECTIVE **1** of sport: based on competitions **2** wanting to win or be more successful than others

competitor NOUN someone who competes; a rival

compilation NOUN **1** a collection of several short, related pieces of writing, music or information **2** the activity of compiling something

compile VERB to make (a book etc) from information that has been collected

compiler NOUN a person whose job consists of compiling

complacency *or* **complacence** NOUN a lazy attitude resulting from an exaggerated belief in your own security

complacent ADJECTIVE self-satisfied and with a tendency to be lazy > **complacently** ADVERB

complain VERB **1** to express dissatisfaction about something **2** to grumble

complaint NOUN **1** a statement of dissatisfaction **2** an illness

complement NOUN **1** something which completes or fills up **2** the full number or quantity needed to fill something **3** *maths* the angle that must be added to a given angle to make up a right angle

> Do not confuse with: **compliment**. Remember **COMPLEment** and **COMPLEte** are related in meaning, and the first six letters of both words are the same.

complementary ADJECTIVE **1** together making up a whole **2** *maths* of angles: making up a right angle

> Do not confuse with: **complimentary**. **Complementary** is related to the noun **complement**.

complete ADJECTIVE **1** having nothing missing; whole **2** finished ▸VERB **1** to finish **2** to make whole > **completion** NOUN

completely ADVERB totally, absolutely

complex ADJECTIVE **1** made up of many parts **2** complicated, difficult ▸NOUN (*plural* **complexes**) **1** a set of repressed emotions and ideas which affect someone's behaviour **2** an exaggerated reaction, an obsession: *She has a complex about her height/ an inferiority complex* **3** a group of related buildings: *sports complex*

complexion NOUN **1** the colour or look of the skin of the face **2** appearance

complexity NOUN (*plural* **complexities**) the quality of being complicated or difficult: *the complexity of this problem*

compliance NOUN the act of complying; agreement with another's wishes

compliant ADJECTIVE yielding, giving agreement

complicate VERB to make difficult

complicated ADJECTIVE difficult to understand; detailed

complication NOUN **1** a difficulty **2** a development in an illness which makes things worse

complicity NOUN (*plural* **complicities**) a shared involvement in a crime or other misdeed

compliment NOUN **1** an expression of praise or flattery **2** (**compliments**) good wishes ▸VERB to praise, congratulate: *complimented me on my cooking*

> Do not confuse with: **complement**. Remember, if you make a **complIment**, you are being **polIte**, and an 'I' comes after the 'L' in both words.

complimentary ADJECTIVE **1** flattering, praising **2** given free: *complimentary ticket*

> Do not confuse with: **complementary**. **Complimentary** is related to the noun **compliment**.

comply VERB (**complies, complying, complied**) to agree to do something that someone else orders or wishes; obey a rule or law

component ADJECTIVE forming one of the parts of a whole ▸NOUN one of several parts, eg of a machine

compose VERB **1** to put together or in order; arrange **2** to create (a piece of music, a poem, etc)

composed ADJECTIVE quiet, calm

composer NOUN someone who writes music

composite ADJECTIVE made up of parts

composition NOUN **1** the act of composing **2** a created piece of writing or music **3** a mixture of things

compos mentis ADJECTIVE sane, rational

compost NOUN a mixture of rotted organic material used to enrich soil and nourish plants

composure NOUN calmness, self-possession

compound ADJECTIVE (*pronounced* **kom**-pownd) **1** made up of a number of different parts **2** not simple ▶ NOUN (*pronounced* **kom**-pownd) **1** *chemistry* a substance formed from two or more elements in fixed proportions **2** an enclosure round a building **3** a word made up of two or more words, eg: *tablecloth*

compound sentence NOUN, *grammar* (*also called*: **co-ordinate sentence**) a sentence made up of two or more simple sentences joined by a co-ordinating conjunction (*compare with*: **complex sentence**, **simple sentence**)

comprehend VERB **1** to understand **2** to include > **comprehension** NOUN (meaning 1)

comprehensible ADJECTIVE able to be understood

comprehensive ADJECTIVE taking in or including much or all

comprehensive school NOUN a state-funded school providing all types of secondary education

compress VERB (*pronounced* kom-**pres**) **1** to press together **2** to force into a narrower or smaller space ▶ NOUN (*pronounced* **kom**-pres) a pad used to create pressure on a part of the body or to reduce inflammation > **compression** NOUN

comprise VERB **1** to include, contain **2** to consist of

> Do not confuse with: **consist**

> ⓘ Remember, you do not need the word 'of' after **comprise**. You say *the exam* comprises *three parts*, but *the exam* consists of *three parts*.

compromise NOUN an agreement reached by both sides giving up something ▶ VERB **1** to make a compromise **2** to put in a difficult or embarrassing position by being indiscreet

compulsion NOUN an irresistible urge driving someone to do something

compulsive ADJECTIVE unable to stop yourself, obsessional: *a compulsive liar*

> Do not confuse: **compulsive** and **compulsory**

compulsory ADJECTIVE **1** requiring to be done **2** forced upon someone

> Do not confuse: **compulsory** and **compulsive**

compunction NOUN regret

computation NOUN counting, calculation

compute VERB to count, calculate

A B C D E F G H I J K L M N O P Q R S T U V W X Y Z

computer NOUN an electronic machine that stores information of various kinds and sorts it very quickly

computerize *or* **computerise** VERB **1** to transfer (a system or procedure) to computer control **2** to install computers in (a place) > **computerization** NOUN

computer science NOUN the study of the design and operation of computers

comrade NOUN a companion, a friend

con- *see* **co-**

con VERB (**conning, conned**) to trick, play a confidence trick on ▸NOUN a trick, a deceit (*see also*: **pros and cons**)

concave ADJECTIVE hollow or curved inwards (*contrasted with*: **convex**) > **concavity** NOUN (*plural* **concavities**)

conceal VERB to hide, keep secret > **concealment** NOUN

concede VERB **1** to give up, yield **2** to admit the truth of something: *I concede that you may be right*

conceit NOUN a too high opinion of yourself; vanity

conceited ADJECTIVE full of conceit; vain

conceivable ADJECTIVE able to be imagined > **conceivably** ADVERB

conceive VERB **1** to form in the mind, imagine **2** to become pregnant

concentrate VERB **1** to direct all your attention or effort towards something **2** to bring together to one place

concentrated ADJECTIVE made stronger or less dilute

concentration NOUN **1** intense mental effort **2** the act of concentrating or the state of being concentrated

concentration camp NOUN a prison camp for civilians, especially in the Nazi regime

concentric ADJECTIVE, *maths* of circles: placed one inside the other with the same centre point (*contrasted with*: **eccentric**)

concept NOUN a general idea about something

conception NOUN **1** the act of conceiving **2** an idea

concern VERB **1** to have to do with **2** to make uneasy **3** to interest, affect ▸NOUN **1** anxiety **2** a cause of anxiety, a worry **3** a business **concern yourself with** to be worried about

concerning PREPOSITION about: *concerning your application*

concert NOUN a musical performance **in concert** together

Do not confuse with: **consort**

concerted ADJECTIVE planned or performed together

concertina NOUN a type of musical wind instrument, with bellows and keys

concerto (*pronounced* kon-**cher**-toh) NOUN (*plural* **concertos**) a long piece of music for a solo instrument with orchestral accompaniment

concession NOUN **1** a granting or allowing of something: *a concession for oil exploration*

LANGUAGE workshop — Conditionals

Conditionals express the possibility of an action, or an imaginary situation. A conditional uses the forms **would**, **could**, **might** or **may** in front of the verb.

I *would like* a cup of cocoa.
I *could come* tomorrow.
We *might go* to the park if the sun comes out.

Sometimes the word **of** is used mistakenly instead of the word **have** in conditionals, and you should be careful not to do this:

✗ I would of gone, but I was too busy.
✓ I *would have* gone, but I was too busy.

? How would you make these sentences conditional? What effect does it have on the tone of the sentence?
1. I will come to visit you soon.
2. Hannah can visit next week.

2 something granted or allowed **3** a reduction in the price of something for children, the unemployed, senior citizens, etc

conciliate VERB to win over (someone previously unfriendly or angry)

conciliation NOUN the act or process of making peace with a person or group

conciliatory ADJECTIVE having the aim of making peace: *a conciliatory gesture*

concise ADJECTIVE brief, using few words

[1] Comes from Latin *concisus* meaning 'cut up'

Do not confuse with: **precise**

conclude VERB **1** to end **2** to reach a decision or judgement; settle

concluding ADJECTIVE last, final

conclusion NOUN **1** an end **2** a decision, judgement

conclusive ADJECTIVE of evidence etc: convincing, leaving no room for doubt: *conclusive proof*

conclusively ADVERB in a way which leaves no doubt: *prove conclusively that there is no other*

a b c d e f g h i j k l m n o p q r s t u v w x y z

life in the solar system

concoct VERB **1** to mix together (a dish or drink) **2** to make up, invent: *concoct a story* > **concoction** NOUN

concord NOUN agreement

concourse NOUN **1** a crowd **2** a large open space in a building etc

concrete ADJECTIVE **1** solid, real **2** made of concrete ▸ NOUN a mixture of gravel, cement, etc used in building

concur VERB (**concurring, concurred**) to agree

concurrence NOUN agreement

concurrent ADJECTIVE **1** happening together **2** agreeing > **concurrently** ADVERB (meaning 1)

concussion NOUN temporary harm done to the brain from a knock on the head

condemn VERB **1** to blame **2** to sentence to (a certain punishment) **3** to declare (a building) unfit for use > **condemnation** NOUN (meaning 1)

condensation NOUN **1** the act of condensing **2** drops of liquid formed from vapour

condense VERB **1** to make (a substance) go into a smaller space **2** of steam: to turn to liquid

condescend VERB to act towards someone as if you are better than them > **condescending** ADJECTIVE > **condescension** NOUN

condiment NOUN a seasoning for food, especially salt or pepper

condition NOUN **1** the state in which anything is: *in poor condition* **2** something that must happen before some other thing happens **3** a point in a bargain, treaty, etc

conditional ADJECTIVE depending on certain things happening > **conditionally** ADVERB

condolence NOUN **1** sharing in another's sorrow; sympathy **2 condolences** an expression of sympathy: *offer my condolences*

condom NOUN a contraceptive rubber sheath

condone VERB to allow (an offence) to pass unchecked

conducive ADJECTIVE helping, favourable (to): *conducive to peace*

conduct VERB (*pronounced* kon-**dukt**) **1** to lead, guide **2** to control, be in charge of **3** *music* to direct (an orchestra or choir) **4** to transmit (electricity etc) **5** to behave: *conducted himself correctly* ▸ NOUN (*pronounced* **kon**-dukt) behaviour

conduction NOUN transmission of heat, electricity, etc

conductor NOUN **1** someone who directs an orchestra or choir **2** someone who collects fares on a bus etc **3** something that transmits heat, electricity, etc

conduit (*pronounced* **kon**-dit *or* **kon**-dyuw-it) NOUN a channel or pipe to carry water, electric wires, etc

cone NOUN **1** a shape that is circular at the bottom and comes to a point **2** the fruit of a pine or fir tree etc **3** an ice-cream cornet

confectioner NOUN someone who makes or sells sweets, cakes, etc

confectionery NOUN **1** sweets, cakes, etc **2** the shop or business of a confectioner

confederacy NOUN (*plural* **confederacies**) **1** a league, an alliance **2** (**the Confederacy**) *US history* the union of Southern states in the American Civil War

confederate ADJECTIVE **1** joined together by treaty **2** *US history* supporting the Confederacy ▶ NOUN someone acting in an alliance with others

confederation NOUN a union, a league

confer VERB (**conferring, conferred**) **1** to talk together **2** to give, grant: *confer a degree*

conference NOUN an organized meeting for discussion of matters of common interest

confess VERB to own up, admit to (wrong)

confessed ADJECTIVE admitted, not secret

confession NOUN an admission of wrongdoing

confetti PLURAL NOUN small pieces of coloured paper thrown at weddings or other celebrations

confidant *or feminine* **confidante** (*pronounced* con-fi-**dont**) NOUN someone trusted with a secret

> Do not confuse with: **confident**

confide VERB: **confide in 1** to tell secrets to **2** *formal* to hand over to someone's care

confidence NOUN **1** trust, belief **2** self-assurance, boldness **3** something told privately

confidence trick NOUN a trick to get money etc from someone by first gaining their trust

confident ADJECTIVE **1** very self-assured **2** certain of an outcome: *confident that they would win* > **confidently** ADVERB

> Do not confuse with: **confidant** and **confidante**

confidential ADJECTIVE **1** to be kept as a secret: *confidential information* **2** entrusted with secrets > **confidentially** ADVERB

confiding ADJECTIVE trusting

confine VERB **1** to shut up, imprison **2** to keep within limits

confinement NOUN **1** the state of being confined **2** imprisonment **3** the time of a woman's labour and childbirth

confines (*pronounced* **kon**-fainz) PLURAL NOUN limits

confirm VERB **1** to make firm, strengthen: *confirm a booking* **2** to make sure **3** to show to be true **4** to admit into full membership of a church

confirmation NOUN **1** a making sure **2** proof **3** the ceremony by which someone is made a full member of a church

confirmed ADJECTIVE settled in a habit etc: *a confirmed bachelor*

confiscate VERB to take away, as a punishment > **confiscation** NOUN

conflagration NOUN a large, widespread fire

conflict NOUN (*pronounced* **kon**-flikt) **1** a struggle, a contest **2** a battle **3** disagreement ▶ VERB (*pronounced* kon-**flikt**) of

LANGUAGE workshop — Conjunctions

Conjunctions have the function of joining words, phrases or clauses in a sentence. There are different kinds of conjunctions.

Co-ordinating conjunctions

Co-ordinating conjunctions join two elements of equal importance.

Jack *and* Jill
You can wash the car *or* the windows.

When only co-ordinating conjunctions are used in a sentence to join two or more clauses, a compound sentence (also called a co-ordinate sentence) is formed:

I went for the shopping *but* Asif cooked the dinner.

Many people say that co-ordinating conjunctions should not come at the start of sentence. Therefore it is best to avoid doing this, although you may see it done for effect:

You are silly. But I like you.

Subordinating conjunctions

Subordinating conjunctions join two clauses so that one becomes the main clause (which carries the main meaning of the sentence), and one becomes a subordinate clause (which gives additional information).

⊃

statements etc: to contradict each other > **conflicting** ADJECTIVE

confluence (*pronounced* **kon**-fluw-*ens*) NOUN, *geography* a place where rivers, streams, etc join and flow together

conform VERB to follow the example of most people in behaviour, dress, etc

conformation NOUN the way something is made up from different parts; structure

Conjunctions LANGUAGE workshop

When subordinating conjunctions are used in a sentence to join two or more of its clauses, a complex sentence is formed:

I am going to bed *because* I am tired.

Subordinating conjunctions can come at the start of a sentence:

Although she was worried about his teeth, Mum gave Bernard money for sweets.

Correlative conjunctions

Correlative conjunctions always work in pairs.

both . . . and is used to link two things.
I play *both* football *and* tennis.

not only . . . but also is a more emphatic way to link two things.
I play *not only* football *but also* tennis.

whether . . . or is used to link alternatives.
They can't decide *whether* to play football *or* tennis.

either . . . or is also used to link alternatives.
We play *either* football *or* tennis.

neither . . . nor is used to link negative alternatives.
He can play *neither* football *nor* tennis.

conformity NOUN (*plural* **conformities**) **1** likeness **2** the act of conforming

confound VERB to puzzle, confuse

confront VERB **1** to face, meet: *confronted the difficulty* **2** to bring face to face (with): *confronted with the evidence*

confrontation NOUN a situation in which two people or groups are challenging each other openly

confuse VERB **1** to mix up, disorder

A B C D E F G H I J K L M N O P Q R S T U V W X Y Z

2 to puzzle, bewilder > **confusion** NOUN

confusing ADJECTIVE puzzling, bewildering

congeal VERB **1** to become solid, especially by cooling: *congealed blood* **2** to freeze

congenial ADJECTIVE agreeable, pleasant > **congenially** ADVERB

congenital ADJECTIVE of a disease: present in someone from birth

congested ADJECTIVE **1** overcrowded, especially with traffic **2** clogged **3** of part of the body: too full of blood > **congestion** NOUN

congratulate VERB to express joy to (someone) at their success

congratulations PLURAL NOUN an expression of joy at someone's success

congratulatory ADJECTIVE expressing congratulations

congregate VERB to come together in a crowd

congregation NOUN a gathering, especially of people in a church

congress NOUN (*plural* **congresses**) **1** a large meeting of people from different countries etc for discussion **2** (**Congress**) the parliament of the United States, consisting of the Senate and the House of Representatives

congruent ADJECTIVE *maths* of figures: identical in size and shape > **congruence** NOUN

conic *or* **conical** ADJECTIVE cone-shaped

conifer (*pronounced* **kon**-i-fer *or* **kohn**-i-fer) NOUN a cone-bearing tree > **coniferous** ADJECTIVE

conjecture NOUN a guess ▸ VERB to guess > **conjectural** ADJECTIVE

conjugal ADJECTIVE of marriage

conjugate VERB *grammar* to give the different grammatical parts of (a verb), indicating number, person, tense, mood and voice > **conjugation** NOUN

conjunction NOUN **1** *grammar* a word that joins sentences or phrases, eg *and, but* **2** a union, a combination **in conjunction with** together with, acting with

conjure VERB to perform tricks that seem magical

conjuror *or* **conjurer** NOUN someone who performs conjuring tricks

conker NOUN **1** a horse chestnut **2** (**conkers**) a game in which conkers are tied on strings and players try to hit and break each other's

con man NOUN someone who regularly plays confidence tricks on people in order to cheat them out of money

connect VERB to join or fasten together

connection NOUN **1** something that connects **2** a state of being connected **3** a train, aeroplane, etc which takes you on the next part of a journey **4** an acquaintance, a friend **in connection with** concerning

connive **connive at** to disregard (a misdeed) > **connivance** NOUN

connoisseur (*pronounced* kon-o-**ser**) NOUN someone with an expert knowledge of a subject: *a wine connoisseur*

connotation NOUN **1** a meaning **2** what is suggested by a word in addition to its simple meaning

conquer VERB **1** to gain by force **2** to overcome: *conquered his fear of heights* > **conqueror** NOUN

conquest NOUN **1** something won by force **2** an act of conquering

conscience NOUN an inner sense of what is right and wrong

conscientious ADJECTIVE careful and diligent in work etc > **conscientiously** ADVERB

conscious ADJECTIVE **1** aware of yourself and your surroundings; awake **2** aware, knowing: *I was conscious that someone was watching me* **3** deliberate, intentional: *a conscious effort* > **consciously** ADVERB > **consciousness** NOUN: *lose consciousness*

conscript NOUN (*pronounced* **kon**-skript) someone obliged by law to serve in the armed forces ▸VERB (*pronounced* kon-**skript**) to compel to serve in the armed forces > **conscription** NOUN

consecrate VERB to set apart for sacred use > **consecration** NOUN

consecutive ADJECTIVE coming in order, one after the other

consensus NOUN an agreement of opinion

[1] Comes from Latin *consensus* meaning 'agreement'

> Do not confuse with: **census**

consent VERB to agree (to) ▸NOUN **1** agreement **2** permission **age of consent** the age at which someone is legally able to consent to sexual intercourse

consequence NOUN **1** something that follows as a result **2** importance

consequent ADJECTIVE following as a result > **consequently** ADVERB

consequential ADJECTIVE **1** following as a result **2** important

conservation NOUN the maintaining of old buildings, the countryside, etc in an undamaged state

conservationist NOUN someone who encourages and practises conservation

conservative ADJECTIVE **1** resistant to change **2** moderate, not extreme: *conservative estimate* ▸NOUN **1** someone of conservative views **2** (**Conservative**) a supporter of the Conservative Party

Conservative Party NOUN a right-wing political party in the UK

conservatory (*pronounced* kon-**ser**-va-tri) NOUN (*plural* **conservatories**) a glasshouse for plants, or a similar room used as a lounge, attached to and entered from the house

conserve VERB to keep from being wasted or lost; preserve

consider VERB **1** to think about carefully **2** to think of as, regard as: *I consider her a friend* **3** to pay attention to the wishes of (someone)

considerable ADJECTIVE fairly large, substantial

considerably ADVERB substantially, quite a lot: *He got considerably more votes than I did*

considerate ADJECTIVE taking

A B C D E F G H I J K L M N O P Q R S T U V W X Y Z

others' wishes into account; thoughtful

consideration NOUN **1** serious thought **2** thoughtfulness for others **3** a small payment

considering PREPOSITION taking into account: *considering your age*

consign (*pronounced* kon-**sain**) VERB to give into the care of

consignment (*pronounced* kon-**sain**-ment) NOUN a load, eg of goods

consist VERB to be made up (of)

> Do not confuse with: **comprise**

> ⓘ You need the word 'of' after **consist**, but not after **comprise**. You say *the exam* consists of *three parts*, but *the exam* comprises *three parts*.

consistency NOUN (*plural* **consistencies**) **1** thickness, firmness: *the consistency of double cream* **2** the quality of always being the same

consistent ADJECTIVE **1** not changing, regular **2** of statements etc: not contradicting each other > **consistently** ADVERB

consolation NOUN something that makes trouble etc more easy to bear

consolation prize NOUN a prize sometimes given to someone coming second in a competition

console VERB to comfort, cheer up

consolidate VERB **1** to make or become strong **2** to unite > **consolidation** NOUN

consonant NOUN a letter of the alphabet that is not a vowel, eg b, c, d

consort NOUN (*pronounced* **kon**-sawrt) **1** a husband or wife **2** a companion ▶ VERB (*pronounced* kon-**sawrt**): **consort with** to keep company with

> Do not confuse with: **concert**

conspicuous ADJECTIVE clearly seen, noticeable > **conspicuously** ADVERB

conspiracy NOUN (*plural* **conspiracies**) a plot by a group of people

conspirator NOUN someone who takes part in a conspiracy

conspire VERB to plan or plot together

constable (*pronounced* **kun**-sta-bl *or* **kon**-sta-bl) NOUN **1** a police officer **2** *history* a high officer of state

constabulary NOUN the police force

constant ADJECTIVE **1** never stopping **2** never changing **3** faithful ▶ NOUN, *maths* a symbol representing a value that does not vary > **constancy** NOUN

constantly ADVERB always

constellation NOUN a group of stars

constipated ADJECTIVE suffering from constipation

constipation NOUN, *medical* sluggish working of the bowels

constituency NOUN (*plural* **constituencies**) **1** a district which has a member of parliament **2** the voters in such a district

constituent ADJECTIVE making or forming: *constituent parts of the* *brain* ▶ NOUN **1** a necessary part **2** a voter in a constituency

constitute VERB **1** to set up, establish **2** to form, make up **3** to be the equivalent of: *This action constitutes a crime*

constitution NOUN **1** the way in which something is made up **2** the natural condition of a body in terms of health etc: *a weak constitution* **3** a set of laws or rules governing a country or organization

constitutional ADJECTIVE of a constitution ▶ NOUN a short walk for the sake of your health

constrain VERB to force to act in a certain way

constraint NOUN **1** compulsion, force **2** restraint, repression

constrict VERB **1** to press together tightly **2** to surround and squeeze

construct VERB to build, make

construction NOUN **1** the act of constructing **2** something built **3** *grammar* the arrangement of words in a sentence **4** meaning

constructive ADJECTIVE **1** of construction **2** helping to improve: *constructive criticism* > **constructively** ADVERB (meaning 2)

consul NOUN **1** someone who looks after their country's affairs in a foreign country **2** *history* a chief ruler in ancient Rome > **consular** ADJECTIVE > **consulate** NOUN **1** the official residence of a consul **2** the duties and authority of a consul

consult VERB to seek advice or information from: *consult your doctor/consult a dictionary*

consultant NOUN **1** someone who gives professional or expert advice **2** the senior grade of hospital doctor

consultation NOUN **1** the activity of looking in eg reference books for information **2** a meeting with someone to exchange ideas and opinions **3** discussion

consume VERB **1** to eat up **2** to use or use up **3** to destroy

consumer NOUN someone who buys, eats or uses goods, energy, resources, etc

consummate VERB (*pronounced* **kon**-*sum*-eit or **kon**-syoo-meit) **1** to complete **2** to make (marriage) legally complete by sexual intercourse ▶ ADJECTIVE (*pronounced* **kon**-syoo-m*a*t *or* kon-**sum**-*a*t) complete, perfect: *a consummate dancer*

consumption NOUN **1** the act of consuming **2** an amount consumed **3** *old* tuberculosis

cont *or* **contd** ABBREVIATION continued

contact NOUN **1** touch **2** meeting, communication **3** an acquaintance; someone who can be of help: *business contacts* **4** someone who has been with someone suffering from an infectious disease ▶ VERB to get into contact with

contact lens NOUN a plastic lens worn in contact with the eyeball

contagious ADJECTIVE of a disease: spreading easily from person to person by ordinary contact

contain VERB **1** to hold or have inside **2** to hold back: *couldn't contain her anger*

container NOUN a box, tin, jar, etc

for holding anything

contaminate VERB to make impure or dirty > **contaminated** ADJECTIVE > **contamination** NOUN

contemplate (*pronounced* **kon**-temp-leit) VERB **1** to look at or think about attentively **2** to consider as a possibility: *contemplating suicide* > **contemplation** NOUN

contemplative (*pronounced* kon-**temp**-lat-iv *or* **kon**-temp-leit-iv) ADJECTIVE quiet and absorbed in thought: *in contemplative mood*

contemporary ADJECTIVE belonging to the same time ▸ NOUN (*plural* **contemporaries**) someone of roughly the same age as yourself

contempt NOUN complete lack of respect; scorn **contempt of court** deliberate disobedience to and disrespect for the law and those who carry it out

contemptible ADJECTIVE deserving scorn, worthless

> Do not confuse: **contemptible** and **contemptuous**. **Contemptible** is formed from **contempt** + **-ible** meaning 'able to be scorned, worthy of scorn'. It is used in phrases like *a contemptible little tell-tale*.

contemptuous ADJECTIVE scornful

> Do not confuse: **contemptuous** and **contemptible**. **Contemptuous** means 'full of contempt' (for something or someone). Use it in phrases like *a contemptuous laugh* or *He was contemptuous of my achievement*.

contend VERB **1** to struggle against **2** to hold firmly to a belief; maintain (that) > **contender** NOUN someone taking part in a contest

content[1] (*pronounced* kon-**tent**) ADJECTIVE happy, satisfied ▸ NOUN happiness, satisfaction ▸ VERB to make happy, satisfy

content[2] (*pronounced* **kon**-tent) NOUN **1** (often **contents**) what is contained in something **2** the subject matter of a book, speech, etc **3** the proportion in which an ingredient is present: *a diet with a high starch content* **4** (**contents**) (a list of) the chapters in a book

contented ADJECTIVE happy, content

contention NOUN **1** an opinion strongly held **2** a quarrel, a dispute

contentious ADJECTIVE quarrelsome

contentment NOUN happiness, content

contest VERB (*pronounced* kon-**test**) to fight for, argue against ▸ NOUN (*pronounced* **kon**-test) a fight, a competition

contestant NOUN someone who takes part in a contest

context NOUN **1** the place in a book etc to which a certain part belongs **2** the background of an event, remark, etc

contiguous ADJECTIVE touching, close > **contiguity** NOUN

continent NOUN any of the seven large divisions of the earth's land surface (Europe, Asia, Africa, Antarctica, Australia, North America, South America) (**the**

A B C D E F G H I J K L M N O P Q R S T U V W X Y Z

Continent) *Brit* the mainland of Europe

continental ADJECTIVE **1** of a continent **2** *Brit* European **3** *geography* of climate: with low rainfall and warm in summer and cool in winter, because of being inland

contingency NOUN (*plural* **contingencies**) a chance happening

contingency plan NOUN a plan of action in case something does not happen as expected

contingent ADJECTIVE depending (on) ▶ NOUN a group, especially of soldiers

continual ADJECTIVE happening again and again at close intervals

> Do not confuse with: **continuous**. Something which is **continual** happens often, but there are short breaks when it is not happening. Something which is **continuous** happens all the time without stopping. So you could talk about, for example, ***continual*** *interruptions*, but *the* ***continuous*** *lapping of waves on a beach.*

continually ADVERB all the time, repeatedly

continuation NOUN **1** the act of continuing **2** a part that continues, an extension

continue VERB to keep on, go on (doing something)

continuity NOUN the state of having no gaps or breaks

continuous ADJECTIVE coming in a steady stream without any gap or break > **continuously** ADVERB

> Do not confuse with: **continual**

contort VERB to twist or turn violently > **contorted** ADJECTIVE > **contortion** NOUN

contortionist NOUN someone who can twist their body into strange shapes

contour NOUN (often **contours**) outline, shape

contour line NOUN, *geography* a line drawn on a map through points all at the same height above sea level

contra- *see* **counter-**

contraband NOUN **1** goods legally forbidden to be brought into a country **2** smuggled goods

contraception NOUN the deliberate prevention of pregnancy using natural or artificial methods

contraceptive ADJECTIVE used to prevent the conceiving of children ▶ NOUN a contraceptive device or drug

contract VERB (*pronounced* kon-**trakt**) **1** to become or make smaller **2** to bargain for **3** to promise in writing ▶ NOUN (*pronounced* **kon**-trakt) a written agreement

contraction NOUN **1** a shortening **2** a shortened form of a word **3** a muscle spasm, eg during childbirth

contractor NOUN someone who promises to do work, or supply goods, at an arranged price

contradict VERB to say the opposite of; deny > **contradiction** NOUN

contradictory ADJECTIVE **1** contradicting something **2** of two pieces of information: contradicting each other

contraflow NOUN two lines of traffic going in opposite directions on the same side of a main road

contralto NOUN (*plural* **contraltos**), *music* the lowest singing voice in women

contraption NOUN a machine, a device

contrary[1] (*pronounced* **kon**-tr*a*-ri) ADJECTIVE opposite ▶ NOUN (*plural* **contraries**) the opposite **on the contrary** just the opposite

contrary[2] (*pronounced* kon-**treir**-ri) ADJECTIVE always doing or saying the opposite, perverse

contrast VERB (*pronounced* kon-**trast**) **1** to compare so as to show differences **2** to show a marked difference from ▶ NOUN (*pronounced* **kon**-trast) a difference between (two) things

contravene VERB to break (a law etc) > **contravention** NOUN

contretemps (*pronounced* **kon**-tr*e*-tom) NOUN a mishap at an awkward moment

contribute VERB **1** to give (money, help, etc) along with others **2** to supply (articles etc) for a publication **3** to help to cause: *contributed to a nervous breakdown*

contribution NOUN something given or supplied **make a contribution** to give or supply something, play a part

contributor NOUN a person or thing that contributes

contributory ADJECTIVE contributing to, or playing a part in some result: *a contributory factor*

con-trick NOUN *short for* **confidence trick**

contrite ADJECTIVE very sorry for having done wrong > **contrition** NOUN

contrivance NOUN an act of contriving; an invention

contrive VERB **1** to plan **2** to bring about, manage: *contrived to be out of the office*

contrived ADJECTIVE unconvincingly artificial: *The plot seemed contrived*

contro- *see* **counter-**

control NOUN **1** authority to rule, manage, guide, etc **2** (often **controls**) means by which a driver keeps a machine powered or guided ▶ VERB **1** to exercise control over **2** to have power over > **controlled** ADJECTIVE > **controller** NOUN

controversial ADJECTIVE likely to cause argument

controversy (*pronounced* **kon**-tr*o*-ver-si *or* kon-**trov**-*er*-si) NOUN (*plural* **controversies**) an argument, a disagreement

conundrum NOUN a riddle, a question

conurbation NOUN a group of towns forming a single built-up area

convalesce VERB to recover health gradually after being ill > **convalescence** NOUN

convalescent NOUN someone convalescing from illness

convection NOUN the spreading of heat by movement of heated air or water

convector NOUN a heater which works by convection

convene VERB to call or come together

convener NOUN **1** someone who calls a meeting **2** the chairman or chairwoman of a committee

convenience NOUN **1** suitableness, handiness **2** a means of giving ease or comfort **3** *informal* a public lavatory **at your convenience** when it suits you best

convenient ADJECTIVE easy to reach or use, handy > **conveniently** ADVERB

convent NOUN a building accommodating an order of nuns

convention NOUN **1** a way of behaving that has become usual, a custom **2** a large meeting, an assembly: *a Star Trek convention* **3** a treaty or agreement

conventional ADJECTIVE **1** done by habit or custom **2** having traditional attitudes and behaviour > **conventionally** ADVERB

converge VERB to come together, meet at a point > **convergence** NOUN > **convergent** ADJECTIVE

conversation NOUN talk, exchange of ideas, news, etc

conversational ADJECTIVE **1** to do with conversation **2** talkative

converse[1] VERB (*pronounced* kon-**vers**) to talk ▸NOUN (*pronounced* **kon**-vers), *formal* conversation

converse[2] (*pronounced* **kon**-vers) NOUN the opposite ▸ADJECTIVE opposite

convert VERB (*pronounced* kon-**vert**) **1** to change (from one thing into another) **2** to turn from one religion to another ▸NOUN (*pronounced* **kon**-vert) someone who has been converted > **conversion** NOUN

convertible ADJECTIVE able to be changed from one thing to another ▸NOUN a car with a folding roof

convex ADJECTIVE curving outwards (*contrasted with*: **concave**) > **convexity** NOUN (*plural* **convexities**)

convey VERB **1** to carry, transport **2** to send **3** *law* to hand over: *convey property*

conveyance NOUN **1** the act of conveying **2** a vehicle

conveyancing NOUN, *law* the process of handing over from one party to another the legal ownership of property

conveyor *or* **conveyor belt** NOUN an endless moving mechanism for conveying articles, especially in a factory

convict *law*, VERB (*pronounced* kon-**vikt**) to declare or prove that someone is guilty ▸NOUN (*pronounced* **kon**-vikt) someone found guilty of a crime and sent to prison

conviction NOUN **1** *law* the passing of a guilty sentence on someone in court **2** a strong belief

convince VERB **1** to make (someone) believe that something is true **2** to persuade (someone) by showing > **convinced** ADJECTIVE

convivial ADJECTIVE jolly, festive > **conviviality** NOUN

convoy VERB to go along with and

protect ▸ NOUN **1** merchant ships protected by warships **2** a line of army lorries with armed guard

convulse VERB to cause to shake violently: *convulsed with laughter*

convulsion NOUN **1** a sudden stiffening or jerking of the muscles **2** a violent disturbance > **convulsive** ADJECTIVE

coo NOUN a sound like that of a dove ▸ VERB to make this sound

cook VERB **1** to prepare (food) by heating **2** *informal* to alter (accounts etc) dishonestly ▸ NOUN someone who cooks and prepares food

cooker NOUN a stove for cooking

cookery NOUN the art of cooking

cookie NOUN a biscuit

cool ADJECTIVE **1** slightly cold **2** calm, not excited **3** *informal* acceptable **4** *informal* good, fashionable ▸ VERB to make or grow cool; to calm > **coolness** NOUN (adjective, meanings 1 and 2)

coolly ADVERB **1** in a calm way **2** in a slightly unfriendly way

co-op *see* **co-operative society**

coop NOUN a box or cage for hens etc ▸ VERB to shut (up) as in a coop

cooper NOUN someone who makes barrels

co-operate VERB to work or act together > **co-operation** NOUN

co-operative NOUN a business or farm etc owned by the workers

co-opt VERB to choose (someone) to join a committee or other body

co-ordinate VERB (*pronounced* koh-**awrd**-in-eit) to make things fit in or work smoothly together ▸ NOUN (*pronounced* koh-**awrd**-in-at), *maths* one of a set of numbers used to indicate the position of a point, line or surface in relation to a system of axes

co-ordination NOUN **1** the activity or skill of co-ordinating things **2** the ability to move and use the different parts of your body smoothly together: *You must have good co-ordination if you want to be a dancer* **3** *grammar* the linking of words, phrases or clauses in a sentence by using conjunctions

coot NOUN a water bird with a white forehead

cop NOUN, *slang* a police officer ▸ VERB (**copping, copped**) to catch, seize **cop it** to land in trouble **cop out** to avoid responsibility

cope VERB to struggle or deal successfully (with), manage

coping NOUN the top layer of stone in a wall

copious ADJECTIVE plentiful > **copiously** ADVERB

copper NOUN **1** *chemistry* a hard reddish-brown metal **2** a reddish-brown colour **3** a coin made from copper **4** a large vessel made of copper, for boiling water

copperplate NOUN a style of very fine and regular handwriting

coppice *or* **copse** NOUN a group of low-growing trees

copy NOUN (*plural* **copies**) **1** an imitation **2** a print or reproduction of a picture etc **3** an individual example of a certain book etc ▸ VERB (**copies, copying, copied**) **1** to make a copy of **2** to imitate

copy and paste VERB, *computing*

to copy text or data from one document or program to another

copyright NOUN the right of one person or body to publish a book, perform a play, print music, etc ▸ ADJECTIVE of or protected by the law of copyright

coquettish ADJECTIVE flirtatious

cor- *see* **co-**

coral NOUN a hard substance made from the skeletons of tiny animals, used to make jewellery

coral reef NOUN a rock-like mass of coral built up gradually from the seabed

cord NOUN **1** thin rope or strong string **2** a thick strand of anything

ⓘ Comes from French *corde* meaning 'a rope'

> Do not confuse with: **chord**

cordial ADJECTIVE cheery, friendly ▸ NOUN a concentrated fruit drink that is usually diluted before it is drunk > **cordiality** NOUN

cordon NOUN a line of guards, police, etc to keep people back

cordon bleu (*pronounced* kawr-dong **bler**) ADJECTIVE of a cook or cooking: first-class, excellent

ⓘ Literally 'blue ribbon' in French, after the ribbon worn by the Knights of the Holy Ghost

corduroy NOUN a ribbed cotton cloth resembling velvet

core NOUN the inner part of anything, especially fruit ▸ VERB to take out the core of (fruit)

corgi NOUN a breed of short-legged dog

cork NOUN **1** the outer bark of a type of oak found in southern Europe etc **2** a stopper for a bottle etc made of cork or other material ▸ ADJECTIVE made of cork ▸ VERB to plug or stop up with a cork

corkscrew NOUN a tool with a screw-like spike for taking out corks ▸ ADJECTIVE shaped like a corkscrew

corm NOUN the bulb-like underground stem of certain plants, eg the crocus

cormorant NOUN a type of big seabird with black or dark brown plumage and a long neck

corn NOUN **1** wheat, oats or maize **2** a small lump of hard skin, especially on a toe

cornea (*pronounced* **kawr**-ni-*a*) NOUN the transparent covering of the eyeball

corned beef NOUN salted tinned beef

corner NOUN **1** the point where two walls, roads, etc meet **2** a small secluded place **3** *informal* a difficult situation ▸ VERB to force into a position from which there is no escape

cornerstone NOUN **1** the stone at the corner of a building's foundations **2** something upon which a lot depends

cornet NOUN **1** a musical instrument like a small trumpet **2** an ice-cream in a cone-shaped wafer

cornflour NOUN finely ground maize flour

cornflower NOUN a type of plant with a blue flower

cornice NOUN an ornamental border round a ceiling

A B C D E F G H I J K L M N O P Q R S T U V W X Y Z

corny ADJECTIVE (**cornier, corniest**) of a joke: old and stale

corona NOUN a halo of luminous gases around the sun

coronary NOUN (*plural* **coronaries**) (*short for* **coronary thrombosis**) a heart disease caused by blockage of one of the arteries supplying the heart

coronation NOUN the crowning of a king or queen

coroner NOUN a government officer who holds inquiries into the causes of sudden or accidental deaths

coronet NOUN **1** a small crown **2** a crown-like headdress

corporal[1] NOUN the rank next below sergeant in the British army

corporal[2] ADJECTIVE of the body

corporal punishment NOUN physical punishment by beating

corporate ADJECTIVE of or forming a whole; united

corporation NOUN a body of people acting as one for administrative or business purposes

corps (*pronounced* kawr) NOUN (*plural* **corps** – *pronounced* kawrz) **1** a division of an army **2** an organized group

> Do not confuse: **corps** and **corpse**

corpse NOUN a dead body

corpulence NOUN obesity, fatness

corpulent ADJECTIVE fat

corpus NOUN (*plural* **corpora**) a collection of writing etc

corpuscle NOUN, *anatomy* **1** a very small particle **2** a red or white blood cell > **corpuscular** ADJECTIVE

corral NOUN, *US* a fenced enclosure for animals ▶ VERB (**corralling, corralled**) to enclose, pen

correct VERB **1** to remove errors from **2** to set right **3** to punish ▶ ADJECTIVE **1** having no errors **2** true **3** suitable and acceptable

correction NOUN **1** the putting right of a mistake **2** punishment

corrective ADJECTIVE with the purpose of putting right some fault or of punishing someone

correlate VERB **1** of two or more things: to have a connection: *Your prediction does not correlate with the result* **2** to combine or compare (information, reports, etc) ▶ NOUN either of two related things > **correlation** NOUN

correspond VERB **1** to write letters to **2** to be similar (to), match

correspondence NOUN **1** letters **2** likeness, similarity

correspondent NOUN **1** someone who writes letters **2** someone who contributes reports to a newspaper etc

ⓘ Comes from Latin *cor* meaning 'with' and *respondere* meaning 'to answer'

corridor NOUN a passageway

corrie NOUN, *geography* a deep semicircular hollow on a mountain slope

corroborate VERB to give evidence which strengthens evidence already given
> **corroboration** NOUN
> **corroborative** ADJECTIVE

ⓘ Comes from Latin *cor-* giving

emphasis, and *roborare* meaning 'to make strong'

> Do not confuse with: **collaborate**

corrode VERB **1** *chemistry* of a metal or alloy: to gradually wear away through corrosion, to rust **2** to eat away at, erode > **corrosion** NOUN

corrosive ADJECTIVE **1** able to destroy or wear away materials such as metal by reacting chemically with them: *Nitric acid is highly corrosive* **2** having the effect of gradually wearing down or destroying something

corrugated (*pronounced* **kor**-*u*-gei-tid *or* **kor**-juw-gei-tid) ADJECTIVE folded or shaped into ridges: *corrugated iron*

corrupt VERB **1** to make evil or rotten **2** to make dishonest, bribe ▶ ADJECTIVE **1** dishonest, taking bribes **2** bad, rotten

corruptible ADJECTIVE able to be corrupted, usually because of being innocent or naive

corruption NOUN **1** dishonesty, often involving the taking of bribes **2** the process of taking away someone's innocence or goodness: *corruption of the mind* **3** the unconscious changing of a word in speech or text, or a word which has changed in this way: *'Yeah' is a corruption of the word 'yes'*

corset NOUN a tight-fitting undergarment worn to support the body

cortège (*pronounced* kawr-**tesz**) NOUN a funeral procession

cosh NOUN (*plural* **coshes**) a short heavy stick ▶ VERB to hit with a cosh

cosmetic NOUN something designed to improve the appearance, especially of the face ▶ ADJECTIVE **1** applied as a cosmetic **2** superficial, for appearances only

cosmic ADJECTIVE **1** of the universe or outer space **2** *informal* excellent

cosmology NOUN astronomy that deals with the evolution of the universe

cosmonaut NOUN an astronaut of the former USSR

cosmopolitan ADJECTIVE **1** including people from many countries **2** familiar with, or comfortable in, many different countries

cosmos NOUN the universe

cosset VERB to treat with too much kindness, pamper

cost VERB (**costing, cost**) **1** to be priced at **2** to cause the loss of: *The war cost many lives* ▶ NOUN what must be spent or suffered in order to get something

costly ADJECTIVE (**costlier, costliest**) high-priced, valuable > **costliness** NOUN

costume NOUN **1** a set of clothes **2** clothes to wear in a play **3** fancy dress **4** a swimsuit

costume jewellery NOUN inexpensive, imitation jewellery

cosy ADJECTIVE (**cosier, cosiest**) warm and comfortable ▶ NOUN (*plural* **cosies**) a covering to keep a teapot etc warm

cot NOUN **1** a small high-sided bed for children **2** *US* a small collapsible bed; a camp bed

a b c d e f g h i j k l m n o p q r s t u v w x y z

cot death NOUN the sudden unexplained death in sleep of an apparently healthy baby (*see also*: **sudden infant death syndrome**)

cottage NOUN a small house, especially in the countryside or a village

cotton NOUN **1** a soft fluffy substance obtained from the seeds of the cotton plant **2** cloth made of cotton ▸ ADJECTIVE made of cotton

cotton wool NOUN cotton in a fluffy state, used for wiping or absorbing

couch NOUN (*plural* **couches**) a sofa ▸ VERB to express verbally: *couched in archaic language*

couch potato NOUN (*plural* **couch potatoes**) someone who spends their free time watching TV, playing computer games, etc

cougar NOUN, *US* the puma

cough NOUN a noisy effort of the lungs to throw out air, mucus, etc from the throat ▸ VERB to make this effort

could VERB **1** the form of the verb **can**[1] used to express a condition: *He could afford it if he tried/I could understand a small mistake, but this is ridiculous* **2** *past form* of the verb **can**[1]

ⓘ Comes from Old English *cuthe* meaning 'was able'

council NOUN a group of people elected to discuss or give advice about policy, government, etc

ⓘ Comes from Latin *concilium* meaning 'a calling together'

> Do not confuse with: **counsel**

councillor NOUN a member of a council

counsel NOUN **1** advice **2** *US* someone who gives legal advice; a lawyer ▸ VERB (**counselling, counselled**) to give advice to

ⓘ Comes from Latin *consilium* meaning 'advice'

> Do not confuse with: **council**

counsellor NOUN someone who gives advice

count[1] VERB **1** to find the total number of, add up **2** to say numbers in order (1, 2, 3, etc) **3** to think, consider: *Count yourself lucky!* ▸ NOUN **1** the act of counting **2** the number counted, eg of votes at an election **3** a charge, an accusation **4** a point being considered **count on** to rely on, depend on

count[2] NOUN a nobleman in certain countries

countdown NOUN a count backwards to zero, the point where the action takes place

countenance NOUN **1** the face **2** the expression on someone's face ▸ VERB to tolerate, encourage

counter- also **contra-**, **contro-** PREFIX **1** against, opposing: *counter-argument* **2** opposite

ⓘ Comes from Latin *contra* meaning 'against'

counter[1] VERB to answer or oppose (a move, act, etc) by another ▸ ADVERB in the opposite direction ▸ ADJECTIVE opposed; opposite

counter[2] NOUN **1** a token used in counting or gambling instead of a coin **2** a small plastic disc used in games such as ludo etc **3** a table across which payments are made in a shop

counteract VERB to block or defeat (an action) by doing the opposite

counterattack NOUN an attack made by the defenders upon an attacking enemy ▶ VERB to launch a counterattack

counterfeit ADJECTIVE **1** not genuine, not real **2** made in imitation for criminal purposes: *counterfeit money* ▶ VERB to make a copy of

counterfoil NOUN a part of a cheque, postal order, etc kept by the payer or sender

counterpane NOUN a top cover for a bed

counterpart NOUN someone or something which is just like or which corresponds to another person or thing

counterpoint NOUN the combining of two or more melodies to make a piece of music

counterpoise NOUN a weight which balances another weight

countersign VERB to sign your name after someone else's signature to show that a document is genuine

countess NOUN (*plural* **countesses**) **1** a woman of the same rank as a count or earl **2** the wife or widow of a count or earl

countless ADJECTIVE too many to be counted, very many

country NOUN (*plural* **countries**) **1** a nation **2** a land under one government **3** the land in which someone lives **4** a district which is not in a town or city **5** an area or stretch of land ▶ ADJECTIVE belonging to the country

🛈 Comes from Old French *contrée* meaning 'a stretch of land'

countryman *or* **countrywoman** NOUN (*plural* **countrymen** *or* **countrywomen**) **1** someone who lives in a rural area **2** someone who belongs to the same country as you

countryside NOUN the parts of a country other than towns and cities

county NOUN (*plural* **counties**) a division of a country

coup (*pronounced* koo) NOUN **1** a sudden outstandingly successful move or act **2** a coup d'état

coup d'état (*pronounced* koo dei-**tah**) NOUN (*plural* **coups d'état** – *pronounced* koo dei-**tah**) a sudden and violent change in government

couple NOUN **1** a pair, two of a kind together **2** a husband and wife ▶ VERB to join together

couplet NOUN two lines of rhyming verse

coupon NOUN a piece of paper which may be exchanged for goods or money

courage NOUN bravery, lack of fear

courageous ADJECTIVE brave, fearless

courgette NOUN (*pronounced* koor-**szet**) a type of small marrow

courier NOUN **1** someone who acts as a guide for tourists **2** a messenger

course NOUN **1** a path in which anything moves **2** movement from point to point **3** a track along which athletes etc run **4** a direction to be followed: *The ship held its course* **5** line of action: *the best course to follow* **6** a part of a meal **7** a number of things following each other: *a course of twelve lectures/a course of treatment* **8** one of the rows of bricks in a wall ▶ VERB **1** to move quickly **2** to hunt **in due course** after a while, in its proper time **in the course of** during

ⓘ Comes from French *cours* meaning 'course', 'lesson' or 'currency'

court NOUN **1** an open space surrounded by houses **2** an area marked out for playing tennis etc **3** the people who attend a monarch etc **4** a royal residence **5** *law* a room or building where legal cases are heard or tried ▶ VERB **1** to try to win someone's love **2** to try to gain: *courting her affections* **3** to come near to achieving: *courting disaster*

courteous ADJECTIVE polite; obliging > **courteously** ADVERB

courtesy NOUN (*plural* **courtesies**) politeness

courtier NOUN a member of a royal court

courtly ADJECTIVE having fine manners

court-martial NOUN (*plural* **courts-martial** *or* **court-martials**) a court held within the armed forces to try those who break military laws ▶ VERB to try in a court-martial

courtship NOUN the act or time of courting or wooing

courtyard NOUN a court or enclosed space beside a house

cousin NOUN the son or daughter of an uncle or aunt

cove NOUN a small inlet on the sea coast; a bay

coven (*pronounced* **kuv**-en) NOUN a gathering of witches

covenant NOUN an important agreement between people to do or not to do something

cover VERB **1** to put or spread something on or over **2** to hide **3** to stretch over: *The hills were covered with heather/My diary covers three years* **4** to include, deal with: *covering the news story* **5** to be enough for: *Five pounds should cover the cost* **6** to travel over: *covering 3 kilometres a day* **7** to point a weapon at: *had the gangster covered* ▶ NOUN something that covers, hides or protects **cover up 1** to cover completely **2** to conceal deliberately

coverage NOUN **1** an area covered: *a mobile phone network with good coverage* **2** the extent of news covered by a newspaper etc **3** the amount of protection given by an insurance policy

covert (*pronounced* **kuv**-ert *or* **koh**-vert) ADJECTIVE secret, not done openly ▶ NOUN (*pronounced* **kuv**-ert) a hiding place for animals or birds when hunted

cover-up NOUN a deliberate concealment, especially by people in authority

covet (*pronounced* **kuv**-it) VERB to long to have, especially something belonging to another person

covetous ADJECTIVE having a tendency to want things, especially things which belong to other people > **covetously** ADVERB > **covetousness** NOUN

cow¹ NOUN **1** the female of various types of ox, bred by humans for giving milk **2** the female of an elephant, whale, etc

cow² VERB to frighten, subdue

coward NOUN someone who has no courage and shows fear easily > **cowardly** ADJECTIVE

cowardice NOUN lack of courage

cowboy NOUN a man who works with cattle on a ranch

cowed ADJECTIVE frightened, subdued

cower VERB to crouch down or shrink back through fear

cowgirl NOUN a woman who works with cattle on a ranch

cowherd NOUN someone who looks after cows

cowl NOUN **1** a hood, especially that of a monk **2** a cover for a chimney

cowslip NOUN a yellow wild flower

coxcomb NOUN **1** in the past, a head-covering notched like a cock's comb, worn by a jester **2** a vain or conceited person

coy ADJECTIVE too modest or shy

coyote (*pronounced* koi-**oh**-ti *or* kai-**oh**-ti) NOUN (*plural* **coyote** *or* **coyotes**) a type of small North American wolf

CPU ABBREVIATION, *computing* central processing unit

crab NOUN **1** a sea creature with a shell and five pairs of legs, the first pair of which have large claws **2** (**crabs**) pubic lice

crab apple NOUN a type of small, bitter apple

crabbed (*pronounced* **krab**-id) ADJECTIVE bad-tempered

crack VERB **1** to (cause to) make a sharp, sudden sound **2** to break partly without falling to pieces **3** to break into (a safe) **4** to decipher (a code) **5** to break open (a nut) **6** to make (a joke) ▶NOUN **1** a sharp sound **2** a split, a break **3** a narrow opening **4** *informal* a sharp, witty remark **5** *informal* a pure form of cocaine ▶ADJECTIVE excellent: *a crack tennis player* **crack up** to collapse with laughter

cracked ADJECTIVE **1** split, damaged **2** *informal* mad, crazy

cracker NOUN **1** a hollow paper tube containing a small gift, which breaks with a bang when the ends are pulled **2** a thin, crisp biscuit **3** *informal* something excellent: *a cracker of a story*

crackle VERB to make a continuous cracking noise

crackling NOUN **1** a cracking sound **2** the rind or outer skin of roast pork

-cracy SUFFIX forms nouns describing different types of government, or the members of a ruling group: *democracy/ aristocracy*

ⓘ Comes from Greek *kratos* meaning 'power'

cradle NOUN **1** a baby's bed, especially one which can be rocked **2** a frame under a ship that is being built

craft NOUN **1** a trade, a skill **2** a boat, a small ship **3** slyness, cunning

craftsman *or* **craftswoman** NOUN (*plural* **craftsmen** *or*

A B C D E F G H I J K L M N O P Q R S T U V W X Y Z

craftswomen) someone who works at a trade, especially with their hands

crafty ADJECTIVE (**craftier, craftiest**) cunning, sly > **craftily** ADVERB

crag NOUN a rough steep rock

craggy ADJECTIVE (**craggier, craggiest**) 1 rocky 2 of a face: well-marked, lined

cram VERB (**cramming, crammed**) 1 to fill full, stuff 2 to learn up facts for an examination in a short time

cramp NOUN 1 a painful stiffening of the muscles 2 (**cramps**) an acute stomach pain ▸ VERB 1 to confine in too small a space 2 to hinder, restrict

cramped ADJECTIVE 1 overcrowded, without enough room 2 of handwriting: small and closely written

cranberry NOUN (*plural* **cranberries**) a type of red, sour berry

crane NOUN 1 a large wading bird with long legs, neck and bill 2 a machine for lifting and moving heavy weights ▸ VERB to stretch out (the neck) to see round or over something

cranefly NOUN (*plural* **craneflies**) a long-legged, two-winged insect (*also called*: **daddy-long-legs**)

cranium (*pronounced* **krei**-ni-*um*) NOUN, *anatomy* (*plural* **crania** *or* **craniums**) the skull

crank NOUN 1 a handle for turning an axle 2 a lever which converts a horizontal movement into a rotating one 3 an eccentric ▸ VERB to start (an engine) with a crank

cranky ADJECTIVE (**crankier, crankiest**) 1 odd, eccentric 2 cross, irritable

cranny NOUN (*plural* **crannies**) a small opening or crack

crape *another spelling* of **crêpe**

crash NOUN (*plural* **crashes**) 1 a noise of heavy things breaking or banging together 2 a collision causing damage, eg between vehicles 3 the failure of a business ▸ ADJECTIVE short but intensive: *a crash course in French* ▸ VERB 1 to be involved in a crash 2 of a business: to fail 3 of a computer program: to break down, fail 4 (*also*: **gatecrash**) *informal* to attend (a party) uninvited

crass ADJECTIVE stupid > **crassly** ADVERB

crate NOUN a container for carrying goods, often made of wooden slats

crater NOUN 1 the bowl-shaped mouth of a volcano 2 a hole made by an explosion

cravat (*pronounced* kra-**vat**) NOUN a scarf worn in place of a tie

ⓘ From a French word for 'Croat', because of the linen neck-bands worn by 17th-century Croatian soldiers

crave VERB to long for (something) > **craving** NOUN

craven ADJECTIVE, *old* cowardly

crawl VERB 1 to move on hands and knees 2 to move slowly: *The traffic was crawling* 3 to be covered (with): *crawling with wasps* 4 to be obsequious; fawn ▸ NOUN 1 the act of crawling 2 a swimming stroke of kicking the legs and alternating the arms

crawler NOUN *informal* an obsequious, fawning person

crayon NOUN a coloured pencil or stick of wax for drawing

craze NOUN a temporary fashion or enthusiasm

crazy ADJECTIVE (**crazier, craziest**) mad, unreasonable > **crazily** ADVERB > **craziness** NOUN

creak VERB to make a sharp, grating sound like a hinge in need of oiling > **creaky** ADJECTIVE

cream NOUN **1** the fatty substance which forms on milk **2** something like this in texture: *cleansing cream/shaving cream* **3** the best part: *the cream of society* ▸ VERB **1** to take the cream from **2** to take away (the best part)

creamy ADJECTIVE (**creamier, creamiest**) full of or like cream

crease NOUN **1** a mark made by folding **2** *cricket* a line showing the position of a batsman and bowler ▸ VERB **1** to make creases in **2** to become creased

create VERB **1** to bring into being; make **2** *informal* to make a fuss

creation NOUN **1** the act of creating **2** something created

creative ADJECTIVE having the ability to create, artistic > **creativity** NOUN

creator NOUN the person who has created something (**the Creator**) God

creature NOUN an animal or person

crèche (*pronounced* kresh) NOUN a nursery for children

credentials PLURAL NOUN documents carried as proof of identity, character, etc

credible ADJECTIVE able to be believed > **credibility** NOUN

> Do not confuse with: **credulous**

credit NOUN **1** recognition of good qualities, achievements, etc: *Give him credit for some common sense* **2** good qualities **3** a source of honour: *a credit to the family* **4** trustworthiness in ability to pay for goods **5** the sale of goods to be paid for later **6** the side of an account on which payments received are entered **7** a sum of money in a bank account **8** belief, trust **9** (**credits**) the naming of people who have helped in a film etc ▸ VERB **1** to believe **2** to enter on the credit side of an account **credit someone with** to believe them to have: *I credited him with more sense*

creditable ADJECTIVE bringing honour or good reputation to

creditably ADVERB in a way which can be approved of or admired

credit card NOUN a card allowing the holder to pay for purchased articles at a later date

creditor NOUN someone to whom money is owed

credulity NOUN willingness to believe things which may be untrue

credulous ADJECTIVE believing too easily

> Do not confuse with: **credible**

creed NOUN a summary of belief, especially religious belief

creek NOUN **1** a small inlet or bay on the sea coast **2** a short river

A B C D E F G H I J K L M N O P Q R S T U V W X Y Z

creep VERB (**creeping, crept**) **1** to move slowly and silently **2** to move with the body close to the ground **3** to shiver with fear or disgust: *makes your flesh creep* **4** of a plant: to grow along the ground or up a wall etc ▸ NOUN **1** a move in a creeping way **2** *informal* an unpleasant person (**the creeps**) *informal* a feeling of disgust or fear **creep up on** to approach silently from behind

creeper NOUN a plant growing along the ground or up a wall etc

creepy ADJECTIVE (**creepier, creepiest**) unsettlingly sinister

cremate VERB to burn (a dead body) > **cremation** NOUN

crematorium NOUN (*plural* **crematoria** *or* **crematoriums**) a place where dead bodies are burnt

crêpe (*pronounced* kreip *or* krep) NOUN **1** a type of fine, crinkly material **2** a thin pancake

crêpe paper NOUN paper with a crinkled appearance

crept *past form* of **creep**

crescendo (*pronounced* kri-**shen**-doh) NOUN (*plural* **crescendos**) **1** *music* a musical passage that becomes increasingly loud **2** a climax

crescent ADJECTIVE shaped like the new or old moon; curved ▸ NOUN **1** something in a curved shape **2** a curved road or street

cress NOUN a plant with small, slightly bitter-tasting leaves, used in salads

crest NOUN **1** a tuft on the head of a cock or other bird **2** the top of a hill, wave, etc **3** feathers on top of a helmet **4** a badge

crestfallen ADJECTIVE downhearted, discouraged

cretin NOUN, *informal* an idiot, a fool

crevasse (*pronounced* kre-**vas**) NOUN a deep split in snow or ice

> Do not confuse: **crevasse** and **crevice**

crevice (*pronounced* **krev**-is) NOUN a crack, a narrow opening

crew[1] NOUN **1** the people who man a ship, aircraft, etc **2** a gang, a mob ▸ VERB to act as a member of a crew

crew[2] *past form* of **crow** (meaning 1)

crewcut NOUN an extremely short hairstyle

crib NOUN **1** a manger **2** a child's bed **3** a ready-made translation of a school text etc ▸ VERB (**cribbing, cribbed**) to copy someone else's work

crick NOUN a sharp pain, especially in the neck ▸ VERB to produce a crick in

cricket[1] NOUN a game played with bats, ball and wickets, between two sides of eleven players each

cricket[2] NOUN an insect similar to a grasshopper

cricketer NOUN someone who plays cricket

cried *past form of* **cry**

crime NOUN an act or deed which is against the law

criminal ADJECTIVE **1** forbidden by law **2** very wrong ▸ NOUN someone guilty of a crime

crimp VERB to press into small ridges: *Crimp the edges of the pastry*

crimson NOUN a deep red colour ▶ ADJECTIVE of this colour

cringe VERB **1** to crouch or shrink back in fear or embarrassment **2** to behave in too humble a way

crinkle VERB **1** to wrinkle, crease **2** to make a crackling sound

crinkly ADJECTIVE wrinkled

cripple NOUN, *offensive* a disabled person ▶ VERB **1** to make lame **2** to make less strong, less efficient, etc: *Their policies crippled the economy* > **crippled** ADJECTIVE

crisis NOUN (*plural* **crises**) **1** a deciding moment, a turning point **2** a time of great danger or suspense

crisp ADJECTIVE **1** stiff and dry; brittle **2** cool and fresh: *crisp air* **3** firm and fresh: *crisp lettuce* **4** sharp ▶ NOUN a thin, crisp piece of fried potato eaten cold > **crispness** NOUN > **crispy** ADJECTIVE

criss-cross ADJECTIVE having a pattern of crossing lines ▶ VERB to move across and back: *Railway lines criss-cross the landscape*
ⓘ Based on the phrase *Christ's cross*

criterion (*pronounced* krai-**tee**-ri-on) NOUN (*plural* **criteria**) a means or rule by which something can be judged; a standard

> ⓘ **Criteria** is a plural form. *A criteria* is wrong.

critic NOUN **1** someone who judges the merits or faults of a book, film, etc **2** someone who finds faults in a thing or person

critical ADJECTIVE **1** fault-finding **2** using analysis and assessment: *a critical commentary/critical thinking* **3** to do with or at a crisis **4** very ill **5** serious, very important

criticism NOUN **1** finding faults **2** reasoned analysis and assessment, especially of art, literature, music, etc **3** the act of criticizing

criticize *or* **criticise** VERB **1** to find fault with **2** to give an opinion or judgement on

croak VERB to make a low, hoarse sound like a frog ▶ NOUN a low, hoarse sound > **croaky** ADJECTIVE (**croakier, croakiest**)

crochet (*pronounced* **kroh**-shei) NOUN a form of knitting done with one hooked needle ▶ VERB to work in crochet

crock NOUN **1** an earthenware pot or jar **2** an old and decrepit person or thing

crockery NOUN china or earthenware dishes

crocodile NOUN **1** a large reptile found in rivers in Asia, Africa, etc **2** a procession of children walking two by two

crocus NOUN (*plural* **crocuses**) a yellow, purple or white flower which grows from a corm

croft NOUN a small farm with a cottage, especially in the Scottish Highlands

crofter NOUN someone who farms on a croft

crofting NOUN farming on a croft

croissant (*pronounced* **krwah**-song) NOUN a curved flaky roll of rich bread dough

crone NOUN an ugly old woman

crony NOUN (*plural* **cronies**)

A B C D E F G H I J K L M N O P Q R S T U V W X Y Z

informal a close friend

crook NOUN **1** a shepherd's or bishop's stick bent at the end **2** a criminal ▸ VERB to bend or form into a hook

crooked (*pronounced* **kruwk**-id) ADJECTIVE **1** bent, hooked **2** dishonest, criminal

croon VERB to sing or hum in a low voice > **crooning** NOUN

crop NOUN **1** natural produce gathered for food from fields, trees or bushes **2** a part of a bird's stomach **3** a riding whip **4** the hair on the head **5** a short haircut ▸ VERB (**cropping, cropped**) **1** to cut short **2** to gather a crop (of wheat etc) **crop up** to happen unexpectedly

cropper NOUN: **come a cropper** **1** to fail badly **2** to have a bad fall

croquet (*pronounced* **kroh**-kei) NOUN a game in which players use long-handled mallets to drive wooden balls through hoops in the ground

cross NOUN (*plural* **crosses**) **1** a shape (×) or (+) formed of two lines intersecting in the middle **2** *Christianity* a monument, symbol, etc in the shape (†) that represents the cross on which Christ was executed; a crucifix **3** the result of breeding an animal or plant with one of another kind: *a cross between a horse and a donkey* **4** a trouble that must be endured ▸ VERB **1** to mark with a cross **2** to go to the other side of (a room, road, etc) **3** to lie or pass across **4** to meet and pass **5** to go against the wishes of **6** to draw two lines across to validate (a cheque) **7** to breed (one kind) with (another) ▸ ADJECTIVE bad-tempered, angry **cross out** to delete (something) by drawing a line through it

crossbow NOUN a bow fixed to a wooden stand with a device for pulling back the string

cross-country ADJECTIVE of a race: across fields etc, not on roads

cross-examine VERB to question closely in court to test the accuracy of a statement etc > **cross-examination** NOUN

cross-eyed ADJECTIVE having a squint

crossfire NOUN gunfire coming from different directions

crosshatching NOUN shading consisting of sets of lines drawn across each other

crossing NOUN **1** a place where a street, river, etc may be crossed **2** a journey over the sea

crossly ADVERB angrily

cross-pollination NOUN, *botany* the transfer of pollen from one plant to another

cross-reference NOUN a statement in a reference book directing the reader to further information in another section

crossroads SINGULAR NOUN a place where roads cross each other

cross-section NOUN **1** a section made by cutting across something **2** a sample taken as representative of the whole: *a cross-section of voters*

crossword NOUN a puzzle in which letters are written into blank squares to form words in answer to numbered clues

crotch NOUN (*plural* **crotches**) the area between the tops of the legs

crotchet NOUN a musical note (♩) equivalent to a quarter of a whole note or semibreve

crotchety ADJECTIVE bad-tempered

crouch VERB **1** to stand with the knees well bent **2** of an animal: to lie close to the ground

croup (*pronounced* kroop) NOUN a children's disease causing difficulty in breathing and a harsh cough

crow NOUN **1** a large bird, generally black **2** the cry of a cock **3** the happy sounds made by a baby ▸VERB (**crowing, crew** *or* **crowed**) **1** (*past tense* **crew**[1]) to cry like a cock **2** to boast **3** of a baby: to make happy noises **as the crow flies** in a straight line

crowbar NOUN a large iron bar used as a lever

crowd NOUN a number of people or things together ▸VERB **1** to gather into a crowd **2** to fill too full **3** to keep too close to, impede: *Don't crowd me!*

crown NOUN **1** a jewelled headdress worn by monarchs on ceremonial occasions **2** the top of the head **3** the highest part of something **4** *Brit* an old coin worth five shillings ▸VERB **1** to put a crown on **2** to make a monarch **3** *informal* to hit on the head **4** to reward, finish happily: *crowned with success*

crow's-nest NOUN a sheltered and enclosed platform near the masthead of a ship from which a lookout is kept

crucial ADJECTIVE extremely important, critical: *crucial question* > **crucially** ADVERB

crucible NOUN a small container for melting metals etc

crucifix NOUN (*plural* **crucifixes**) a figure or picture of Christ fixed to the cross

crucifixion NOUN **1** the act of crucifying **2** death on the cross, especially that of Christ

crucify VERB (**crucifies, crucifying, crucified**) to put to death by fixing the hands and feet to a cross

crude ADJECTIVE **1** not purified or refined: *crude oil* **2** roughly made or done **3** vulgar, blunt, tactless: *a crude joke* > **crudely** ADVERB > **crudity** NOUN

cruel ADJECTIVE (**crueller, cruellest**) **1** deliberately causing pain or distress **2** having no pity for others' sufferings > **cruelly** ADVERB > **cruelty** NOUN (*plural* **cruelties**)

cruet (*pronounced* **kroo**-it) NOUN **1** a small jar for salt, pepper, mustard, etc **2** two or more such jars on a stand

cruise VERB to travel by car, ship, etc at a steady speed ▸NOUN a journey by ship made for pleasure

cruiser NOUN a middle-sized warship

crumb NOUN a small bit of anything, especially bread: *a crumb of comfort*

crumble VERB **1** to break into crumbs or small pieces **2** to fall to pieces ▸NOUN a dish of stewed fruit etc topped with crumbs

crumbly ADJECTIVE (**crumblier, crumbliest**) having a tendency to fall to pieces

A B C D E F G H I J K L M N O P Q R S T U V W X Y Z

crumpet NOUN a soft, flat cake, baked on a griddle

crumple VERB **1** to crush into creases or wrinkles **2** to become creased **3** to collapse

crunch VERB **1** to chew hard so as to make a noise **2** to crush ▸ NOUN (*plural* **crunches**) **1** a noise of crunching **2** (**the crunch**) *informal* a testing moment, a turning-point > **crunchy** ADJECTIVE (**crunchier, crunchiest**)

crusade NOUN **1** a movement undertaken for some good cause **2** *history* a Christian expedition to regain the Holy Land from the Turks

crusader NOUN someone who goes on a crusade

crush VERB **1** to squeeze together **2** to beat down, overcome: *crush the opposition to the bill* **3** to crease, crumple ▸ NOUN (*plural* **crushes**) **1** a violent squeezing **2** a pressing crowd of people **3** a drink made by squeezing fruit

crushed ADJECTIVE **1** squeezed, squashed **2** completely defeated or miserable

crust NOUN a hard outside coating, *eg* on bread, a pie, a planet

crustacean (*pronounced* krus-**tei**-sh*u*n) NOUN one of a large group of animals with a hard shell, including crabs, lobsters, shrimps *etc*

crusty ADJECTIVE (**crustier, crustiest**) **1** having a crust **2** cross, irritable

crutch NOUN (*plural* **crutches**) **1** a stick held under the armpit or elbow, used for support in walking **2** a support, a prop

crux NOUN (*plural* **cruxes**) the most important or difficult part of a problem

cry VERB (**cries, crying, cried**) **1** to make a loud sound in pain or sorrow **2** to weep **3** to call loudly ▸ NOUN (*plural* **cries**) a loud call **cry off** to cancel **cry over spilt milk** to be worried about a misfortune that is past

crying ADJECTIVE **1** weeping **2** calling loudly **3** requiring notice or attention: *a crying need*

crypt NOUN an underground cell or chapel, especially one used for burial

cryptic ADJECTIVE mysterious, difficult to understand: *a cryptic remark* > **cryptically** ADVERB

crypto- *or* **crypt-** PREFIX hidden: *cryptic*

[i] Comes from Greek *kryptos* meaning 'hidden'

crystal NOUN **1** very clear glass often used for making drinking glasses etc **2** the regular shape taken by each small part of certain substances, eg salt or sugar

crystalline ADJECTIVE made up of crystals

crystallize *or* **crystallise** VERB **1** *chemistry* to form into crystals **2** to take a form or shape, become clear > **crystallization** NOUN

cub NOUN **1** the young of certain animals, eg foxes **2** a Cub Scout

cube NOUN **1** a solid body having six equal square sides **2** *maths* the answer to a sum in which a number is multiplied by itself twice: *8 is the cube of 2*

cube root NOUN, *maths* the number which, multiplied by itself and then by itself again, gives a certain other number (eg 2 is the cube root of 8)

cubic ADJECTIVE **1** of cubes **2** in the shape of a cube **3** in volume: *a cubic metre*

cubicle NOUN a small room closed off in some way from a larger one

cuboid NOUN, *maths* a solid body having six rectangular faces, the opposite faces of which are equal

Cub Scout NOUN a junior Scout

cuckoo NOUN a bird which visits Britain in summer and lays its eggs in the nests of other birds

cucumber NOUN a creeping plant with a long green fruit used in salads

cud NOUN food regurgitated by certain animals, eg sheep and cows

cuddle VERB to put your arms round, hug ▸NOUN a hug, an embrace > **cuddly** ADJECTIVE (**cuddlier, cuddliest**) pleasant to cuddle: *cuddly kittens*

cue[1] NOUN **1** a sign to tell an actor when to speak etc **2** a hint, an indication

cue[2] NOUN the stick used to hit a ball in pool, billiards and snooker

cuff NOUN **1** the end of a sleeve near the wrist **2** *US* the turned-back hem of a trouser leg **3** a blow with the open hand ▸VERB to hit with the hand **off the cuff** without planning or rehearsal

cufflinks PLURAL NOUN a pair of ornamental buttons etc used to fasten a shirt cuff

cuisine (*pronounced* kwi-**zeen**) NOUN **1** the art of cookery **2** a style of cooking: *Mexican cuisine*

cul-de-sac (*pronounced* **kul**-de-sak) NOUN (*plural* **cul-de-sacs** *or* **culs-de-sac**) a street closed at one end

culinary ADJECTIVE of or used for cookery

cull VERB **1** to gather **2** to choose from a group **3** to pick out (seals, deer, etc) from a herd and kill for the good of the herd ▸NOUN such a killing

culminate VERB **1** to reach the highest point **2** to reach the most important or greatest point, end (in): *an investigation culminating in several arrests* > **culmination** NOUN

culpable ADJECTIVE guilty, blameworthy

culprit NOUN **1** someone who is to blame for something **2** *English law, US law* a prisoner accused but not yet tried

cult NOUN **1** a religious sect **2** a general strong enthusiasm for something: *the cult of physical fitness*

cultivate VERB **1** to grow (vegetables etc) **2** to plough, sow: *cultivate the land* **3** to try to develop and improve: *cultivated my friendship* > **cultivation** NOUN

cultivated ADJECTIVE **1** farmed, ploughed **2** educated, informed

cultural ADJECTIVE **1** to do with a culture: *cultural differences* **2** to do with the arts: *a cultural visit to the gallery*

culture NOUN **1** a type of civilization with its associated customs: *ancient Greek culture* **2** development of the mind by education **3** educated tastes in art, music, etc **4** cultivation of plants

cultured ADJECTIVE well-educated in literature, art, etc

cum PREPOSITION used for both of two stated purposes: *a newsagent-cum-grocer*

cumbersome ADJECTIVE awkward to handle

cumulative ADJECTIVE increasing with additions: *cumulative effect*

cunning ADJECTIVE **1** sly, clever in a deceitful way **2** skilful, clever ▸ NOUN **1** slyness **2** skill, knowledge

cup NOUN **1** a hollow container holding liquid for drinking **2** an ornamental vessel given as a prize in sports events ▸ VERB (**cupping, cupped**) to make (hands etc) into the shape of a cup

cupboard NOUN a shelved recess, or a box with drawers, used for storage

cupful NOUN (*plural* **cupfuls**) as much as fills a cup

Cupid (*pronounced* **kyoop**-id) NOUN the Roman god of sexual love

cupola (*pronounced* **kyoop**-ol-*a*) NOUN a curved ceiling or dome on the top of a building

cup-tie NOUN a game in a sports competition for which the prize is a cup

curable ADJECTIVE able to be treated and cured

curate NOUN a member of the Church of England clergy assisting a rector or vicar

curator NOUN someone who has charge of a museum, art gallery, etc

curb VERB to hold back, restrain ▸ NOUN a restraint

> Do not confuse with: **kerb**

curd NOUN **1** milk thickened by acid **2** the cheese part of milk (*compare with*: **whey**)

curdle VERB to turn into curd

cure NOUN **1** freeing from disease, healing **2** something which frees from disease ▸ VERB **1** to heal **2** to get rid of (a bad habit etc) **3** to preserve by drying, salting, etc

curfew NOUN an order forbidding people to be out of their houses after a certain time

curio NOUN (*plural* **curios**) an article valued for its oddness or rarity

curiosity NOUN (*plural* **curiosities**) **1** strong desire to find something out **2** something unusual, an oddity

curious ADJECTIVE **1** anxious to find out **2** unusual, odd > **curiously** ADVERB

curl VERB **1** to twist (hair) into small coils **2** of hair: to grow naturally in small coils **3** of smoke: to move in a spiral **4** to twist, form a curved shape **5** to play at the game of curling ▸ NOUN a small coil or roll, eg of hair

curler NOUN **1** something used to make curls **2** someone who plays the game of curling

curlew NOUN a wading bird with very long slender bill and legs

curling NOUN a game played by throwing round, flat stones along a sheet of ice

curly ADJECTIVE having curls

curmudgeon NOUN a bad-tempered or mean person

currant NOUN **1** a small black raisin **2** a berry of various kinds of soft fruit: *redcurrant*

> Do not confuse: **currant** and **current**

currency NOUN (*plural* **currencies**) **1** the money used in a particular country **2** the state of being generally known: *The story gained currency*

current ADJECTIVE belonging to the present time: *the current year/ current affairs* ▶ NOUN a stream of water, air or electrical power moving in one direction

> Do not confuse: **current** and **currant**

current account NOUN a bank account from which money may be withdrawn by cheque

curriculum NOUN (*plural* **curriculums** *or* **curricula**) the course of study at a university, school, etc

curriculum vitae (*pronounced* k*u*-**rik**-yuw-l*u*m **vee**-tai) NOUN (*plural* **curricula vitae**) (*abbrev* **CV**) a brief account of a person's education and career, used for job applications

curry NOUN (*plural* **curries**) a dish containing a mixture of spices with a strong, peppery flavour ▶ VERB (**curries, currying, curried**) to make into a curry by adding spices

curse VERB **1** to use swear-words **2** to wish evil towards ▶ NOUN **1** a wish for evil or a magic spell **2** an evil or a great misfortune or the cause of this

cursed ADJECTIVE (*pronounced* kerst) under a curse

cursor NOUN a flashing symbol that appears on a VDU screen to show the position for entering data

cursorily ADVERB briefly, hurriedly, without taking a lot of care

cursory ADJECTIVE hurried

curt ADJECTIVE of someone's way of speaking: clipped and unfriendly
> **curtly** ADVERB

curtail VERB to make less, reduce
> **curtailment** NOUN

curtain NOUN a piece of material hung to cover a window, stage, etc

curtsy *or* **curtsey** NOUN (*plural* **curtsies** *or* **curtseys**) a bow made by bending the knees

curvature NOUN **1** a curving or bending **2** a curved piece **3** *medicine* an abnormal curving of the spine

curve NOUN **1** a rounded line, like part of the edge of a circle **2** a bend: *a curve in the road*

cushion NOUN **1** a fabric casing stuffed with feathers, foam, etc, for resting on **2** a soft pad

cushy ADJECTIVE, *informal* (**cushier, cushiest**) easy and comfortable: *a cushy job*

cusp NOUN **1** a point **2** *astrology* a division between signs of the zodiac

custard NOUN a sweet sauce made from eggs, milk and sugar

custodian NOUN **1** a keeper **2** a caretaker, eg of a museum

custody NOUN **1** care, guardianship **2** arrest or imprisonment: *taken into custody*

A B C D E F G H I J K L M N O P Q R S T U V W X Y Z

custom NOUN **1** something done by habit **2** the regular or frequent doing of something; habit **3** the buying of goods at a shop **4** (**customs**) taxes on goods coming into a country **5** (**customs**) the government department that collects these

customary ADJECTIVE usual

custom-built ADJECTIVE built to suit a particular purpose

customer NOUN **1** someone who buys from a shop **2** *informal* a person: *an awkward customer*

customize *or* **customise** VERB to make changes to (something) to suit particular needs or tastes

cut VERB (**cutting, cut**) **1** to make a slit in, remove or divide, with a blade: *cut a hole/cut a slice of bread* **2** to wound **3** to trim with a blade etc: *cut the grass/My hair needs cutting* **4** to reduce in amount **5** to shorten (a play, book, etc) by removing parts **6** to refuse to acknowledge (someone you know) **7** to divide (a pack of cards) in two **8** to stop filming **9** *informal* to play truant from (school) ▶NOUN **1** a slit made by cutting **2** a wound made with something sharp **3** a stroke, a blow **4** a thrust with a sword **5** the way something is cut **6** the shape and style of clothes **7** a piece of meat **cut down 1** to take down by cutting **2** to reduce **cut down on** to reduce the intake of **cut in** to interrupt **cut off 1** to separate, isolate: *cut off from the mainland* **2** to stop: *cut off supplies* **cut out 1** to shape (a dress etc) by cutting **2** *informal* to stop: *Cut it out* **3** of an engine: to fail

cut-and-dried ADJECTIVE settled beforehand; decided

cut and paste VERB, *computing* to take a graphic or text out of one document and put it into another

cute ADJECTIVE **1** smart, clever **2** pretty and pleasing

cuticle NOUN the hard skin around the bottom and side edges of finger and toe nails

cutlass NOUN (*plural* **cutlasses**) a short, broad sword

cutlery NOUN knives, forks, spoons, etc

cutlet NOUN a slice of meat with the bone attached

cut-throat ADJECTIVE fiercely competitive: *cut-throat business* ▶NOUN a ruffian

cutting NOUN **1** a piece cut from a newspaper **2** a trench cut in the earth or rock for a road etc **3** a shoot of a tree or plant ▶ADJECTIVE wounding, hurtful: *a cutting remark*

cut-up ADJECTIVE distressed

cyanide NOUN a kind of poison

cyber- (*pronounced* **saib**-*er*) PREFIX relating to computers or electronic media: *cyberspace/cyber-selling*
ⓘ This prefix was taken from the word **cyber***netics*, meaning 'the study of communication or control systems'. Its origin is the Greek word *kybernetes*, meaning 'the person who steers a boat or ship'

cyberspace NOUN the three-dimensional artificial environment of virtual reality

cycle NOUN **1** a bicycle **2** a round of events following on from one another repeatedly: *the cycle of the* *seasons* **3** a series of poems, stories, etc written about a single person or event ▸ VERB **1** to ride a bicycle **2** to move in a cycle; rotate

cycle lane NOUN a section of road marked off for cyclists to use

cyclist NOUN someone who rides a bicycle

cyclone NOUN **1** a whirling windstorm **2** a system of winds blowing in a spiral > **cyclonic** ADJECTIVE

cygnet (*pronounced* **sig**-net) NOUN a young swan

🛈 Comes from Latin *cygnus* meaning 'swan'

> Do not confuse with: **signet**

cylinder NOUN a solid or hollow tube-shaped object

cylindrical ADJECTIVE shaped like a cylinder

cymbals (*pronounced* **sim**-balz) PLURAL NOUN brass, plate-like musical instruments, beaten together in pairs

cynic (*pronounced* **sin**-ik) NOUN someone who believes the worst about people > **cynicism** NOUN

cynical (*pronounced* **sin**-i-kal) ADJECTIVE sneering; believing the worst of people > **cynically** ADVERB

cypress NOUN a type of evergreen tree

cyst (*pronounced* sist) NOUN *medicine* an abnormal liquid-filled blister within the body or just under the skin

cystic fibrosis NOUN, *medicine* a hereditary disease which is present at birth or appears in early childhood, and causes breathing problems

cystitis NOUN, *medicine* inflammation of the bladder, often caused by infection

-cyte (*pronounced* sait) SUFFIX forms nouns describing different types of cell in the body: *leucocyte/ phagocyte*

🛈 Comes from Latin *kytos* meaning 'container' or 'hollow vessel'

cytoplasm NOUN the jelly-like material that makes up most of a cell

czar *another spelling* of **tsar**

czarina *another spelling* of **tsarina**

a b c d e f g h i j k l m n o p q r s t u v w x y z

Dd

dab VERB to touch gently with a pad *etc* to soak up moisture ▶ NOUN **1** the act of dabbing **2** a small lump of something soft **3** a gentle blow, a pat **4** a small kind of flounder

dabble VERB **1** to play in water with hands or feet **2** to do in a half-serious way or as a hobby: *He dabbles in computers*

dachshund (*pronounced* **daks**-huwnt *or* **daks**-huwnd) NOUN a breed of dog with short legs and a long body

ⓘ Comes from German *Dachs* meaning 'badger', and *Hund* meaning 'dog'

dad *or* **daddy** NOUN (*plural* **dads** *or* **daddies**) *informal* a father

daffodil NOUN a yellow trumpet-shaped flower which grows from a bulb

daft ADJECTIVE, *informal* silly

dagger NOUN a short sword for stabbing

daily ADJECTIVE & ADVERB every day ▶ NOUN (*plural* **dailies**) **1** a paper published every day **2** *informal* someone employed to clean a house regularly

dainty ADJECTIVE (**daintier, daintiest**) **1** small and neat **2** pleasant-tasting ▶ NOUN (*plural* **dainties**) a tasty morsel of food > **daintily** ADVERB (adjective, meaning 1)

dairy NOUN (*plural* **dairies**) **1** a building for storing milk and making butter and cheese **2** a shop which sells milk, butter, cheese, etc

dairy products PLURAL NOUN food made of milk, butter, or cheese

daisy NOUN (*plural* **daisies**) a small common flower with white petals

ⓘ From an Old English name meaning 'day's eye', so called because of its opening during the day

daisy chain NOUN a string of daisies threaded through each other's stems

dalai lama (*pronounced* **dal**-ai **lah**-m*a*) NOUN the spiritual leader of Tibetan Buddhism

dale NOUN low ground between hills

dally VERB (**dallies, dallying, dallied**) **1** to waste time idling or playing **2** to play (with) > **dalliance** NOUN

Dalmatian NOUN a breed of large spotted dog

dam NOUN **1** a wall of earth, concrete, etc to keep back water

2 water kept in like this ▶ VERB (**damming, dammed**) 1 to keep back by a dam 2 to hold back, restrain (tears etc)

damage NOUN 1 hurt, injury 2 (**damages**) money paid by one person to another to make up for injury, insults, etc ▶ VERB to spoil, make less effective or unusable

dame NOUN 1 a comic woman in a pantomime, played by a man in drag 2 (**Dame**) the title of a woman of the same rank as a knight

damn VERB 1 to sentence to unending punishment in hell 2 to condemn as wrong, bad, etc ▶ INTERJECTION an expression of annoyance

damnation NOUN 1 unending punishment in hell 2 condemnation

damning ADJECTIVE leading to conviction or ruin: *damning evidence*

damp NOUN 1 moist air 2 wetness, moistness ▶ VERB 1 to wet slightly 2 to make (emotions, interest, etc) less fierce or intense ▶ ADJECTIVE moist, slightly wet

damp-course NOUN a layer of damp-proof material inside a wall or under a floor

dampen VERB 1 to make or become damp; moisten 2 to lessen (enthusiasm etc)

damper NOUN, *music* a pad which touches the strings inside a piano, silencing each note after it has been played **put a damper on something** to make it less cheerful

dampness NOUN the quality of being damp

damsel NOUN, *old* a young girl or unmarried woman

damson NOUN a type of small dark-red plum

dance VERB to move in time to music ▶ NOUN 1 a sequence of steps in time to music 2 a social event with dancing > **dancer** NOUN > **dancing** NOUN & ADJECTIVE

dandelion NOUN a type of common plant with a yellow flower

ℹ From the French phrase *dent de lion*, meaning 'lion's tooth'

dandruff NOUN dead skin which collects under the hair and falls off in flakes

danger NOUN 1 something potentially harmful: *The canal is a danger to children* 2 potential harm: *unaware of the danger*

dangerous ADJECTIVE 1 unsafe, likely to cause harm 2 full of risks > **dangerously** ADVERB

dangle VERB to hang loosely

dank ADJECTIVE moist, wet, and cold

dappled ADJECTIVE marked with spots or splashes of colour

dare VERB 1 to be brave or bold enough (to): *I didn't dare tell him* 2 to lay yourself open to, risk: *daring his wrath* 3 to challenge: *dared him to cross the railway line* **I dare say** I suppose: *I dare say you're right*

daredevil NOUN a rash person fond of taking risks ▶ ADJECTIVE rash, risky

daring ADJECTIVE bold, fearless ▶ NOUN boldness > **daringly** ADVERB

dark ADJECTIVE 1 without light 2 black or near to black 3 gloomy

4 evil: *dark deeds* ▸ NOUN absence of light, nightfall > **darkness** NOUN **in the dark** knowing nothing about something **keep dark** to keep (something) secret

darken VERB to make or grow dark or darker

dark horse NOUN someone about whom little is known

darling NOUN **1** a word showing affection **2** someone dearly loved; a favourite

darn VERB to mend (clothes) with crossing rows of stitches ▸ NOUN a patch mended in this way

dart NOUN **1** a pointed weapon for throwing or shooting **2** something which pierces ▸ VERB to move quickly and suddenly

dartboard NOUN the board used in playing the game of darts

darts SINGULAR NOUN a game in which small darts are thrown at a board marked off in circles and numbered sections

dash VERB **1** to throw or knock violently, especially so as to break **2** to ruin (hopes) **3** to depress, sadden (spirits) **4** to rush with speed or violence ▸ NOUN (*plural* **dashes**) **1** a rush **2** a short race **3** a small amount of a drink etc **4** liveliness **5** a short line (–) to show a break in a sentence etc

dashboard NOUN a panel with dials, switches, etc in front of the driver's seat in a vehicle

dashing ADJECTIVE **1** hasty **2** smart, elegant

dastardly ADJECTIVE, *formal* cowardly

data (*pronounced* **dei**-*ta or* **dah**-*ta*) PLURAL NOUN (*singular* **datum**) **1** available facts from which conclusions may be drawn **2** facts stored in a computer

database NOUN, *computing* a collection of systematically stored files that are often connected with each other

date[1] NOUN **1** a statement of time in terms of the day, month and year, eg 23 December 1995 **2** the time at which an event occurs **3** the period of time to which something belongs **4** *informal* an appointment ▸ VERB **1** to give a date to **2** to belong to a certain time: *dates from the 12th century* **3** to become old-fashioned: *That dress will date quickly*

date[2] NOUN **1** a type of palm tree **2** its blackish, shiny fruit with a hard stone

datum *singular* of **data**

daub VERB **1** to smear **2** to paint roughly

daughter NOUN a female child, considered in relation to her parents

daughter-in-law NOUN (*plural* **daughters-in-law**) a son's wife

daunt VERB **1** to frighten **2** to be discouraging

dauntless ADJECTIVE unable to be frightened

dawn NOUN **1** daybreak **2** a beginning: *the dawn of a new era* ▸ VERB **1** to become day **2** to begin to appear **dawn on** to become suddenly clear to (someone)

dawning NOUN a rather poetic way of saying 'dawn'

day NOUN **1** the time of light, from sunrise to sunset **2** twenty-four hours, from one midnight to the next **3** the time or hours spent at work **4** (often **days**) a particular time or period: *in the days of steam* **day in, day out** on and on, continuously **the other day** recently: *I saw her just the other day*

daydream NOUN an imagining of pleasant events while awake ▸ VERB to imagine in this way

dayglo NOUN, *trademark* a luminously bright colour

daylight NOUN **1** the light of day, sunlight **2** a clear space

day-release NOUN time off from work for training or education

daze VERB **1** to stun with a blow **2** to confuse, bewilder

dazzle VERB **1** to shine on so as to prevent from seeing clearly **2** to shine brilliantly **3** to fascinate, impress deeply

DC ABBREVIATION **1** District of Columbia (US) **2** detective constable **3** direct current (*compare with*: **AC**)

DDT NOUN dichlorodiphenyltrichloroethane, an insecticide that is also poisonous to humans and animals

deacon NOUN **1** the lowest rank of clergy in the Church of England **2** a church official in other churches

deaconess NOUN (*plural* **deaconesses**) a woman deacon

dead ADJECTIVE **1** not living, without life **2** cold and cheerless **3** numb **4** not working; no longer in use **5** complete, utter: *dead silence* **6** exact: *the dead centre* **7** certain: *a dead shot* ▸ ADVERB **1** completely: *dead certain* **2** suddenly and completely: *stop dead* ▸ NOUN **1** those who have died: *speak well of the dead* **2** the time of greatest stillness etc: *the dead of night*

dead-beat ADJECTIVE having no strength left

deaden VERB to lessen (pain etc)

dead end NOUN **1** a road etc closed at one end **2** a job etc not leading to promotion

dead heat NOUN a race in which two or more runners finish equal

deadline NOUN a date by which something must be done

[i] Originally a line in a military prison. The penalty for crossing it was death

deadlock NOUN a standstill resulting from a complete failure to agree

deadly (**deadlier, deadliest**) ADJECTIVE **1** likely to cause death, fatal **2** intense, very great: *a deadly hush* ▸ ADVERB intensely, extremely: *deadly dull* > **deadliness** NOUN

deadpan ADJECTIVE & ADVERB without expression on the face

dead ringer NOUN, *informal* someone looking exactly like someone else

deaf ADJECTIVE **1** unable to hear **2** refusing to listen: *deaf to her pleas*

deafen VERB **1** to make deaf **2** to be unpleasantly loud **3** to make (walls etc) soundproof

deafening ADJECTIVE extremely loud

deaf-mute *often considered offensive*, NOUN someone who can neither hear nor speak

deal NOUN **1** an agreement, especially in business **2** an amount or quantity: *a good deal of paper* **3** the dividing out of playing-cards in a game ▸ VERB (**dealing, dealt** – *pronounced* delt) **1** to divide, give out **2** to trade (in) **3** to do business (with) **deal with** to take action concerning, cope with

dealer NOUN **1** someone who deals out cards at a game **2** a trader **3** a stockbroker

dean NOUN **1** the chief religious officer in a cathedral church **2** the head of a faculty in a university

dear ADJECTIVE **1** high in price **2** highly valued; much loved ▸ NOUN **1** someone who is loved **2** someone who is lovable or charming ▸ ADVERB at a high price: *It cost them dear*

dearly ADVERB **1** very much, sincerely: *love someone dearly* **2** involving a great cost, either financially or in some other way: *His freedom was dearly bought*

death NOUN **1** the state of being dead, the end of life **2** the end of something: *the death of steam railways*

deathly ADJECTIVE **1** very pale or ill-looking **2** deadly

debar VERB (**debarring, debarred**) to keep from, prevent

debase VERB **1** to lessen in value **2** to make bad, wicked, etc > **debased** ADJECTIVE > **debasement** NOUN

debatable ADJECTIVE arguable, doubtful: *a debatable point* > **debatably** ADVERB

debate NOUN **1** a discussion, especially a formal one before an audience **2** an argument ▸ VERB to engage in debate, discuss

debauched ADJECTIVE inclined to debauchery

debilitate VERB to make weak

debit NOUN an amount owed, spent, or deducted from a bank account ▸ VERB (**debiting, debited**) to mark down as a debit

debit card NOUN a plastic card which transfers money directly from a purchaser's account to a retailer's

debonair (*pronounced* deb-*o*-**neir**) ADJECTIVE especially of a man: of pleasant and cheerful appearance and behaviour

debrief VERB to gather information from an astronaut, spy, etc after a mission > **debriefing** NOUN

debris (*pronounced* **deb**-ree) NOUN **1** the remains of something broken, destroyed, etc **2** rubbish

debt (*pronounced* det) NOUN something that is owed, usually money **in debt** owing money

debtor (*pronounced* **det**-*o*r) NOUN someone who owes a debt

debut *or* **début** (*pronounced* **dei**-byoo) NOUN the first public appearance, eg of an actor ▸ ADJECTIVE first before the public: *debut concert*

deca- *or* **dec-** PREFIX ten, multiplied by ten: *decathlon*

[i] Comes from Greek *deka* meaning 'ten'

decade NOUN **1** a period of ten years **2** a set or series of ten

decadence (*pronounced* **dek**-*a*-

dens) NOUN a falling from high to low standards in morals, etc

decadent (*pronounced* **dek**-*a*-dent) ADJECTIVE wicked, throwing away moral standards for the sake of pleasure

decaff (*pronounced* **dee**-kaf) *informal*, ADJECTIVE decaffeinated

decaffeinated (*pronounced* dee-**kaf**-i-neit-id) ADJECTIVE with the caffeine removed

decagon NOUN a figure with ten sides

decamp VERB to run away

decant VERB to pour (wine etc) from a bottle into a decanter

decanter NOUN an ornamental bottle with a glass stopper for wine, whisky, etc

decapitate VERB to cut the head from > **decapitation** NOUN

decathlon NOUN an athletics competition comprising contests in ten separate disciplines

decay VERB to become bad, worse or rotten ▸ NOUN the process of rotting or worsening > **decayed** ADJECTIVE

decease NOUN, *formal* death

deceased *formal*, ADJECTIVE dead ▸ NOUN (**the deceased**) a dead person

deceit NOUN the act of deceiving

deceitful ADJECTIVE inclined to deceive; lying > **deceitfully** ADVERB

deceive VERB to tell lies so as to mislead > **deceiver** NOUN

decelerate VERB to slow down > **deceleration** NOUN

December NOUN the twelfth month of the year

ⓘ From a Latin word meaning 'tenth', because December was originally the tenth month of the year, before January and February were added

decent ADJECTIVE **1** respectable **2** good enough, adequate: *decent salary* **3** kind: *decent of you to help* > **decency** NOUN (meanings 1 and 3) > **decently** ADVERB

deception NOUN **1** the act of deceiving **2** something that deceives or is intended to deceive

deceptive ADJECTIVE misleading: *Appearances may be deceptive* > **deceptively** ADVERB

deci- PREFIX one-tenth: *decimal/ decimate*

ⓘ Comes from Latin *decimus* meaning 'tenth'

decibel (*pronounced* **des**-i-bel) NOUN (ABBREV **dB**) a unit of loudness of sound

decide VERB **1** to make up your mind to do something: *I've decided to take your advice* **2** to settle (an argument etc)

decided ADJECTIVE **1** clear: *a decided difference* **2** with your mind made up: *He was decided on the issue*

decidedly ADVERB definitely

deciduous (di-**sid**-yuw-*us*) ADJECTIVE of a tree: having leaves that fall in autumn

decimal ADJECTIVE **1** numbered by tens **2** of ten parts or the number 10 ▸ NOUN, *maths* a decimal fraction

decimal currency NOUN a system of money in which each coin or note is either a tenth of another or

a b c d e f g h i j k l m n o p q r s t u v w x y z

ten times another in value

decimal fraction NOUN, *maths* a fraction expressed in tenths, hundredths, thousandths, etc, separated by a decimal point

decimalize *or* **decimalise** VERB to convert (figures or currency) to decimal form > **decimalization** NOUN

decimal place NOUN, *maths* a digit to the right of a decimal point, eg in 0.26, 2 is in the first decimal place

decimal point NOUN, *maths* a dot used to separate units from decimal fractions, eg 0.1=1/10, 2.33=233/100

decimate VERB to make much smaller in numbers by destruction

[i] Literally 'reduce by a tenth'; from Latin *decem* meaning ten

decipher (*pronounced* di-**sai**-fer) VERB **1** to translate (a code) into ordinary, understandable language **2** to make out the meaning of: *can't decipher his handwriting*

decision NOUN **1** the act of deciding **2** clear judgement, firmness: *acting with decision*

decisive ADJECTIVE **1** final, putting an end to a contest etc: *a decisive defeat* **2** showing decision and firmness: *a decisive manner* > **decisively** ADVERB

deck[1] NOUN **1** a platform forming the floor of a ship, bus, etc **2** a pack of playing-cards **3** the turntable of a record-player **clear the decks** to get rid of old papers, work, etc before starting something fresh

deck[2] VERB to decorate, adorn

deckchair NOUN a collapsible chair of wood and canvas etc

declaim VERB **1** to make a speech in impressive, dramatic language **2** to speak violently (against) > **declamation** NOUN

declamatory ADJECTIVE of a speech or announcement: impressive and dramatic

declare VERB **1** to make known (goods or income on which tax is payable) **2** to announce formally or publicly: *declare war* **3** to say firmly **4** *cricket* to end an innings before ten wickets have fallen > **declaration** NOUN

decline VERB **1** to say 'no' to, refuse: *I had to decline his offer* **2** to weaken, become worse **3** to slope down ▶ NOUN **1** a downward slope **2** a gradual worsening of health etc

decode VERB to translate (a coded message) into ordinary, understandable language

decommission VERB to take out of operation (eg a warship, atomic reactor, or weapons used in a war)

decompose VERB **1** to rot, decay **2** to separate in parts or elements > **decomposition** NOUN

décor (*pronounced* **dei**-kawr) NOUN the decoration of, and arrangement of objects in, a room etc

decorate VERB **1** to add ornament to **2** to paint or paper the walls of (a room etc) **3** to pin a badge or medal on (someone) as a mark of honour > **decoration** NOUN > **decorative** ADJECTIVE

decorator NOUN someone who decorates houses, rooms, etc

A B C D E F G H I J K L M N O P Q R S T U V W X Y Z

decorum (*pronounced* di-**kaw**-*rum*) NOUN good behaviour

decoy VERB to lead into a trap or into evil ▶ NOUN something or someone intended to lead another into a trap

decrease VERB (*pronounced* di-**krees**) to make or become less in number ▶ NOUN (*pronounced* **dee**-krees) a growing less

decree NOUN **1** an order, a law **2** *law* a judge's decision ▶ VERB (**decreeing, decreed**) to give an order

decrepit ADJECTIVE **1** weak and infirm because of old age **2** in ruins or disrepair > **decrepitude** NOUN

dedicate VERB **1** to devote yourself (to): *dedicated himself to music* **2** to set apart for a special or sacred purpose **3** to inscribe or publish (a book etc) in tribute to someone or something: *I dedicate this book to my father* > **dedicated** ADJECTIVE > **dedication** NOUN

deduce VERB to find out by putting together all that is known

> Do not confuse: **deduce** and **deduct**

deduct VERB to subtract, take away (from)

deduction NOUN **1** a subtraction **2** finding something out using logic, or a thing which has been found out in this way

deed NOUN **1** something done, an act **2** *law* a signed statement or bargain

deem VERB, *formal* to judge or consider: *deemed unsuitable for children*

deep ADJECTIVE **1** being or going far down **2** hard to understand; cunning **3** involved to a great extent: *deep in debt/deep in thought* **4** intense, strong: *a deep red colour/deep affection* **5** low in pitch ▶ NOUN (**the deep**) the sea **in deep water** in serious trouble

deepen VERB to make or become deep or deeper

deep-freeze NOUN a low-temperature refrigerator that can freeze food and preserve it frozen for a long time

deep-seated ADJECTIVE firmly fixed, not easily removed

deer NOUN (*plural* **deer**) an animal with antlers in the male, eg the reindeer

deface VERB to spoil the appearance of, disfigure > **defacement** NOUN

defamatory (*pronounced* di-**fam**-*a*-to-ri) ADJECTIVE intended to harm, or having the effect of harming, someone's reputation

defame VERB to try to harm the reputation of > **defamation** NOUN

default VERB to fail to do something you ought to do, eg to pay a debt ▶ NOUN **1** failure to do something you ought to do **2** *computing* a preset action taken by a computer system unless a user's instruction overrides it > **defaulter** NOUN **by default** because of a failure to do something

defeat VERB to beat, win a victory over ▶ NOUN a win, a beating

defecate (*pronounced* **def**-*e*-keit) VERB to empty waste matter from

A B C D E F G H I J K L M N O P Q R S T U V W X Y Z

the bowels > **defecation** NOUN

defect NOUN (*pronounced* **dee**-fekt) a lack of something needed for completeness or perfection; a flaw ▶ VERB (*pronounced* di-**fekt**) to desert a country, political party, etc to join or go to another

defective ADJECTIVE **1** faulty; incomplete **2** not having normal mental or physical ability

> Do not confuse with: **deficient**

defence *or US* **defense** NOUN **1** the act of defending against attack **2** a means or method of protection **3** *law* the argument defending the accused person in a case (*contrasted with*: **prosecution**) **4** *law* the lawyer(s) putting forward this argument

defenceless ADJECTIVE without defence

defend VERB **1** to guard or protect against attack **2** *law* to conduct the defence of **3** to support against criticism

defendant NOUN **1** someone who resists attack **2** *law* the accused person in a law case

defensible ADJECTIVE able to be defended

defensive ADJECTIVE **1** used for defence **2** expecting criticism, ready to justify actions **on the defensive** prepared to defend yourself against attack or criticism

defer VERB (**deferring, deferred**) **1** to put off to another time **2** to give way (to): *He deferred to my wishes*

deference NOUN **1** willingness to consider the wishes etc of others **2** the act of giving way to another

defiance NOUN open disobedience or opposition > **defiant** ADJECTIVE > **defiantly** ADVERB

deficiency NOUN (*plural* **deficiencies**) **1** lack, need **2** an amount lacking

deficient ADJECTIVE lacking in what is needed

> Do not confuse with: **defective**

deficit (*pronounced* **def**-i-sit) NOUN an amount by which a sum of money etc is too little

define VERB **1** to fix the bounds or limits of **2** to outline or show clearly **3** to state the exact meaning of

definite ADJECTIVE **1** having clear limits, fixed **2** exact **3** certain, sure

definite article NOUN, *grammar* the name given to the word *the*

definitely ADVERB certainly, without doubt

definition NOUN **1** an explanation of the exact meaning of a word or phrase **2** sharpness or clearness of outline

definitive ADJECTIVE **1** fixed, final **2** not able to be bettered: *the definitive biography* > **definitively** ADVERB (meaning 1)

deflate VERB **1** to let the air out of (a tyre etc) **2** to reduce in self-importance or self-confidence

deflation NOUN **1** *economics* a reduction of the amount of money in circulation in a country, resulting in a lower level of industrial activity, industrial output, and employment, and a lower rate of increase in wages and prices **2** the letting out of air (from eg a tyre) **3** the feeling of sadness or disappointment which you get eg when your hopes have been dashed

deflect VERB to turn aside (from a fixed course) > **deflection** NOUN

deforestation NOUN the removal of all or most of the trees in a forested area

deform VERB **1** to spoil the shape of **2** to make ugly

deformed ADJECTIVE badly or abnormally formed

deformity NOUN (*plural* **deformities**) **1** something abnormal in shape **2** the fact of being badly shaped

defraud VERB **1** to cheat **2** (**defraud someone of something**) to take or keep it from them by cheating or fraud

defrost VERB to remove frost or ice from; thaw

deft ADJECTIVE clever with the hands, handy > **deftly** ADVERB

defunct ADJECTIVE no longer active or in use

defy VERB (**defies, defying, defied**) **1** to dare to do something, challenge **2** to resist openly **3** to make impossible: *Its beauty defies description*

degenerate ADJECTIVE (*pronounced* di-**jen**-e-r*a*t) having become immoral or very bad ▸ VERB (*pronounced* di-**jen**-e-reit) to become or grow bad or worse > **degeneration** NOUN

degradation NOUN humiliation, loss of dignity

degrade VERB **1** to lower in grade or rank **2** to disgrace

degrading ADJECTIVE humiliating and embarrassing

degree NOUN **1** a step or stage in a process **2** rank or grade **3** amount, extent: *a degree of certainty* **4** a unit of temperature used eg in the Celsius, Fahrenheit and Kelvin scales **5** a unit by which angles are measured, one 360th part of the circumference of a circle **6** a certificate given by a university, gained by examination or given as an honour

dehydrate VERB **1** to remove water from (food etc) **2** to lose excessive water from the body > **dehydrated** ADJECTIVE > **dehydration** NOUN

deign (*pronounced* dein) VERB to act as if doing a favour: *She deigned to answer us*

deity (*pronounced* **dei**-it-i) NOUN (*plural* **deities**) a god or goddess

déjà vu (*pronounced* dei-szah **voo**) NOUN the feeling of having experienced something before

dejected ADJECTIVE gloomy, dispirited > **dejection** NOUN

delay VERB **1** to put off, postpone **2** to keep back, hinder ▸ NOUN **1** a postponement **2** a hindrance

delectable ADJECTIVE delightful, pleasing > **delectably** ADVERB

delectation NOUN, *formal* delight, enjoyment

delegate VERB (*pronounced* **del**-ig-eit) to give (a task) to someone else to do ▸ NOUN (*pronounced* **del**-ig-*a*t) someone acting on behalf of another; a representative

delegation NOUN a group of delegates

a b c d e f g h i j k l m n o p q r s t u v w x y z

A B C D E F G H I J K L M N O P Q R S T U V W X Y Z

delete VERB to rub or strike out (eg a piece of writing) > **deletion** NOUN

deli (*pronounced* **del**-i) NOUN, *informal* a **delicatessen**

deliberate VERB (*pronounced* di-**lib**-*e*-reit) to think carefully or seriously (about) ▸ADJECTIVE (*pronounced* di-**lib**-*e*-r*a*t) **1** intentional, not accidental **2** slow in deciding **3** not hurried > **deliberately** ADVERB

deliberation NOUN **1** careful thought **2** calmness, coolness **3** (**deliberations**) *formal* discussions

delicacy NOUN (*plural* **delicacies**) **1** tact **2** something delicious to eat

delicate ADJECTIVE **1** not strong, frail **2** easily damaged **3** fine, dainty: *delicate features* **4** pleasant to taste **5** tactful **6** requiring skill or care: *a delicate operation*

delicatessen (*pronounced* del-i-ka-**tes**-*e*n) NOUN a shop selling eg cheeses, cooked meats, and unusual or imported foods

delicious ADJECTIVE **1** very pleasant to taste **2** giving pleasure > **deliciously** ADVERB

delight VERB **1** to please greatly **2** to take great pleasure (in) ▸NOUN great pleasure

delighted ADJECTIVE very pleased

delightful ADJECTIVE very pleasing > **delightfully** ADVERB

delinquency NOUN **1** wrongdoing, misdeeds **2** failure in duty

delinquent ADJECTIVE **1** guilty of an offence or misdeed **2** not carrying out your duties ▸NOUN **1** someone, especially a young person, guilty of an offence **2** someone who fails in their duty

delirious (*pronounced* di-**lir**-i-*u*s) ADJECTIVE **1** raving, wandering in the mind **2** wildly excited > **deliriously** ADVERB

delirium (*pronounced* di-**lir**-i-*u*m) NOUN **1** a delirious state, especially caused by fever **2** wild excitement

deliver VERB **1** to hand over **2** to give out (eg a speech, a blow) **3** to set free, rescue **4** to assist at the birth of (a child) > **deliverance** NOUN (meaning 3)

delivery NOUN (*plural* **deliveries**) **1** a handing over, eg of letters **2** the birth of a child **3** a style of speaking

delta NOUN, *geography* the flat, triangular stretch of land at the mouth of a river, where it splits into branches

ⓘ From the fourth letter of the Greek alphabet, which was triangular in shape

delude VERB to deceive

ⓘ Comes from Latin *deludere* meaning 'to play false'

deluge (*pronounced* **del**-yooj) NOUN **1** a great flood of water **2** an overwhelming amount: *a deluge of work* ▸VERB **1** to flood, drench **2** to overwhelm

delusion NOUN a false belief, especially as a symptom of mental illness

> Do not confuse with: **allusion** and **illusion**. **Delusion** comes from the verb **delude**

delve VERB **1** to dig **2** to rummage, search through: *delved in her bag for her keys*

demand VERB **1** to ask, or ask for, firmly **2** to insist: *I demand that you listen* **3** to require, call for: *demanding attention* ▶ NOUN **1** a forceful request **2** an urgent claim: *many demands on his time* **3** a need for certain goods etc

demean VERB to lower, degrade

demeanour NOUN behaviour, conduct

demented ADJECTIVE mad, insane

demise NOUN, *formal* death

demobilize *or* **demobilise** VERB **1** to break up an army after a war is over **2** to free (a soldier) from army service > **demobilization** NOUN

democracy NOUN a form of government in which the people govern themselves or elect representatives to govern them

democrat NOUN **1** someone who believes in democracy **2** (**Democrat**) *US* a supporter of the Democratic Party

democratic ADJECTIVE **1** of or governed by democracy **2** (**Democratic**) *US* belonging to the Democratic Party > **democratically** ADVERB

Democratic Party NOUN one of the two chief political parties in the USA, generally inclining to left of centre (*compare with*: **Republican Party**)

demolish VERB **1** to destroy completely **2** to pull down (a building etc) > **demolition** NOUN

demon NOUN an evil spirit, a devil > **demonic** ADJECTIVE

demonstrable (*pronounced* **dem**-*on*-stra-bl *or* dem-**on**-stra-bl) ADJECTIVE able to be shown clearly > **demonstrably** ADVERB

demonstrate VERB **1** to show clearly; prove **2** to show (a machine etc) in action **3** to express an opinion by marching, showing placards, etc in public

demonstration NOUN **1** a showing, a display **2** a public expression of opinion by a procession, mass meeting, etc

demonstrative (*pronounced* di-**mon**-stra-tiv) ADJECTIVE **1** pointing out; proving **2** inclined to show feelings openly

demonstrator NOUN **1** a person who takes part in a public demonstration to express their opinion about something **2** a person who explains how something works, or shows you how to do something

demoralize *or* **demoralise** VERB to take away the confidence of > **demoralization** NOUN

demote VERB to reduce to a lower rank or grade > **demotion** NOUN

den NOUN **1** the lair of a wild animal **2** a small private room for working etc

denial NOUN the act of denying **in denial** doggedly refusing to accept something

denim NOUN a hard-wearing cotton cloth used for jeans, overalls, etc
ⓘ **Denim** was first manufactured in the town of Nîmes in the south of France, and this is how it got its name (*de Nîmes* means 'from Nîmes')

denomination NOUN **1** name, title

A
B
C
D
E
F
G
H
I
J
K
L
M
N
O
P
Q
R
S
T
U
V
W
X
Y
Z

2 a value of a coin, stamp, etc **3** a religious sect > **denominational** ADJECTIVE

denominator NOUN, *maths* the lower number in a vulgar fraction by which the upper number is divided, eg the 3 in 2/3 (*compare with*: **numerator**)

denote VERB to mean, signify

dénouement (*pronounced* dei-**noo**-mong) NOUN the ending of a story where mysteries etc are explained

ⓘ Literally 'untying' or 'unravelling', from French

denounce VERB **1** to accuse publicly of a crime **2** to inform against: *denounced him to the enemy*

dense ADJECTIVE **1** closely packed together; thick **2** very stupid > **densely** ADVERB (meaning 1)

density NOUN (*plural* **densities**) **1** thickness **2** weight in proportion to volume **3** *computing* the extent to which data can be held on a floppy disk

dent NOUN a hollow made by a blow or pressure ▸ VERB to make a dent in

dental ADJECTIVE of or for a tooth or teeth

dentist NOUN a doctor who examines teeth and treats dental problems

dentistry NOUN the work of a dentist

dentures PLURAL NOUN a set of false teeth

denunciation NOUN a strongly expressed public criticism or condemnation

deny VERB (**denies, denying, denied**) **1** to declare to be untrue: *He denied that he did it* **2** to refuse, forbid: *He was denied the right to appeal* **deny yourself** to do without things you want or need

deodorant NOUN something that hides unpleasant smells, especially body smells such as perspiration

depart VERB **1** to go away **2** to turn aside (from): *departing from the plan*

department NOUN a self-contained section within a shop, university, government, etc

departure NOUN **1** the act of leaving or going away **2** a break with something expected or traditional **a new departure** a new course of action

depend VERB (**depend on**) **1** to rely on **2** to receive necessary financial support from **3** to be controlled or decided by: *It all depends on the weather*

dependable ADJECTIVE able to be trusted

dependant NOUN someone who is kept or supported by another

> Do not confuse: **dependant** and **dependent**

dependence *or* **dependency** NOUN the state of being dependent

dependent ADJECTIVE relying or depending (on)

> Do not confuse: **dependent** and **dependant**

depict VERB **1** to draw, paint, etc **2** to describe

deplete VERB to make smaller in amount or number > **depletion** NOUN

deplorable ADJECTIVE regrettable; very bad

deplore VERB to disapprove of, regret: *deplored his use of language*

deploy VERB to place in position ready for action

deport VERB to send (someone) out of a country > **deportation** NOUN

depose VERB to remove from a high position, especially a monarch from a throne > **deposition** NOUN

deposit VERB (**depositing, deposited**) **1** to put or set down **2** to put in for safe keeping, eg money in a bank ▶ NOUN **1** money paid in part payment of something **2** money put in a bank account **3** a solid that has settled at the bottom of a liquid **4** a layer of coal, iron, etc occurring naturally in rock

depository NOUN (*plural* **depositories**) a place where anything is deposited

depot (*pronounced* **dep**-oh) NOUN **1** a storehouse **2** a building where railway engines, buses, etc are kept and repaired

deprave VERB to make wicked

depraved ADJECTIVE wicked

depravity (*pronounced* di-**prav**-i-ti) NOUN wickedness

deprecate (*pronounced* **dep**-ri-keit) VERB to show disapproval of, condemn

[i] Comes from Latin *de* meaning 'away', and *precari* meaning 'to pray'

> Do not confuse: **deprecate** and **depreciate**

deprecating *or* **deprecatory** ADJECTIVE disapproving, extremely critical

deprecation NOUN the act or process of disapproving of, devaluing or condemning something: *self-deprecation* (= bringing yourself down, being too self-critical)

depreciate (*pronounced* dip-**ree**-shi-eit) VERB **1** to lessen the value of **2** to fall in value > **depreciation** NOUN

[i] Comes from Latin *de* meaning 'down', and *pretium* meaning 'price'

> Be careful. **Depreciate** is most frequently used to refer to a fall or a bringing down in financial value. Don't use it when you really mean **deprecate**.

depress VERB **1** to make gloomy or unhappy **2** to press down **3** to make lower in value or intensity

depressed ADJECTIVE gloomy, in low spirits

depressing ADJECTIVE having the effect of making you gloomy or unhappy

depression NOUN **1** low spirits, gloominess **2** a hollow **3** a lowering in value **4** a low period in a country's economy with unemployment, lack of trade, etc **5** (**the Depression**) *another term for* **the Great Depression** **6** a region of low atmospheric pressure that is associated with unsettled weather

a b c d e f g h i j k l m n o p q r s t u v w x y z

A B C D E F G H I J K L M N O P Q R S T U V W X Y Z

deprivation NOUN great hardship caused by being deprived of necessities, rights, etc

deprive VERB (**deprive of**) to take away from

deprived ADJECTIVE suffering from hardship; disadvantaged

Dept ABBREVIATION department

depth NOUN **1** deepness **2** a deep place **3** the deepest part: *from the depth of her soul* **4** the middle: *the depth of winter* **5** intensity, strength: *depth of colour* **in depth** thoroughly, carefully **out of your depth** concerned in problems too difficult to understand

deputation NOUN a group of people chosen and sent as representatives

deputize *or* **deputise** VERB to take another's place, act as substitute

deputy NOUN (*plural* **deputies**) **1** a delegate, a representative **2** a person appointed to act for another person in their absence

derail VERB to cause (a train etc) to leave the rails > **derailment** NOUN

deranged ADJECTIVE mad, insane

derby (*pronounced* **dahr**-bi) NOUN (*plural* **derbies**) a sports event between two teams from the same area

derelict (*pronounced* **de**-re-likt) ADJECTIVE broken-down, abandoned

dereliction NOUN neglect of what should be attended to: *dereliction of duty*

deride VERB to laugh at, mock

derision NOUN mockery

derisive (*pronounced* di-**rai**-siv) ADJECTIVE mocking

derisory (*pronounced* di-**rai**-so-ri) ADJECTIVE so small or inadequate as to be not worth taking seriously, laughable: *He offered me a derisory* (= ridiculously small) *sum for the work I'd done*

derivative (*pronounced* di-**riv**-a-tiv) ADJECTIVE not original ▶ NOUN **1** a word formed on the base of another word, eg *fabulous* from *fable* **2** stock market trading in futures and options

derive VERB **1** to be descended or formed (from) **2** to trace (a word) back to the beginning of its existence **3** to receive, obtain: *derive satisfaction* > **derivation** NOUN

dermatitis NOUN inflammation of the skin

dermato- also **dermat-**, **-derm-** PREFIX & WORD PARTICLE of or relating to the skin: *dermatology/ dermatitis/hypodermic/pachyderm/ taxidermist*

derogatory ADJECTIVE **1** harmful to reputation, dignity, etc **2** scornful, belittling, disparaging

derring-do (*pronounced* de-ring-**doo**) NOUN *old* daring action, boldness

[i] Based on a misprint of a medieval English phrase *dorring do*, meaning 'daring to do'

descant (*pronounced* **des**-kant) NOUN, *music* a tune played or sung above the main tune

descend VERB **1** to go or climb down **2** to slope downwards **3** to go from a better to a worse state **descend from** to have as an ancestor: *claims he's descended from Napoleon*

descendant NOUN someone descended from another

descent NOUN **1** an act of descending **2** a downward slope

describe VERB **1** to give an account of in words **2** to draw the outline of, trace

description NOUN **1** the act of describing **2** an account of something in words **3** sort, kind: *people of all descriptions*
> **descriptive** ADJECTIVE (meaning 1)

desecrate (*pronounced* **des**-i-kreit) VERB **1** to spoil (something sacred) **2** to treat without respect
> **desecration** NOUN

> Do not confuse with: **desiccate**. Remember that **desecRate** and **sacRed** are related, and they both contain an **R**.

desert[1] (*pronounced* di-**zert**) VERB **1** to run away from (the army) **2** to leave, abandon: *deserted his wife/His courage deserted him*
> **deserter** NOUN (meaning 1)
> **desertion** NOUN

desert[2] (*pronounced* **dez**-ert) NOUN a stretch of barren country with very little rainfall

ℹ Comes from Latin *desertum* meaning 'deserted'

> Do not confuse with: **dessert**

desert island NOUN an uninhabited island in a tropical area

deserve VERB to have earned as a right, be worthy of: *You deserve a holiday*

deservedly (*pronounced* di-**zer**-vid-li) ADVERB justly

deserving ADJECTIVE worthy of being rewarded or helped

desiccate (*pronounced* **des**-i-keit) VERB **1** to dry up **2** to preserve by drying: *desiccated coconut*

ℹ Comes from Latin *desiccare* meaning 'to dry up'

> Do not confuse with: **desecrate**. Remember that **desecRate** and **sacRed** are related, and they both contain an **R**.

design VERB **1** to make a plan of (eg a building or an article of clothing) before it is made **2** to intend ▶ NOUN **1** a plan, a sketch **2** a painted picture, pattern, etc **3** an intention **have designs on** to plan to get for yourself

designation (*pronounced* dez-ig-**nei**-shon) NOUN a name, a title

designing ADJECTIVE crafty, cunning

desirable ADJECTIVE pleasing; worth having > **desirability** NOUN

desire VERB to wish for greatly ▶ NOUN **1** a longing for **2** a wish

desist VERB, *formal* to stop (doing something)

desk NOUN a table for writing, reading, etc

desolate ADJECTIVE **1** deeply unhappy **2** empty of people, deserted **3** barren

desolation NOUN **1** deep sorrow **2** barren land **3** ruin

despair VERB to give up hope ▶ NOUN **1** lack of hope **2** a cause of despair: *She was the despair of her mother*

A B C D E F G H I J K L M N O P Q R S T U V W X Y Z

despairing ADJECTIVE in despair

despatch *another spelling of* **dispatch**

desperate ADJECTIVE **1** without hope, despairing **2** very bad, awful **3** reckless; violent

desperately ADVERB very much, very intensely: *desperately proud of his baby daughter/missing you desperately*

desperation NOUN the feeling you have when your situation is so bad that you are prepared to do anything to get out of it

despicable ADJECTIVE contemptible, hateful

despise VERB to look on with contempt

despite PREPOSITION in spite of: *We had a picnic despite the weather*

despoil VERB to rob, plunder
> **despoliation** NOUN

despondent ADJECTIVE downhearted, dejected
> **despondency** NOUN

dessert (*pronounced* de-**zert**) NOUN fruits, sweets, etc served at the end of a meal

[i] Comes from Old French *dessert* meaning 'the clearing of the table'

> Do not confuse with: **desert**

destination NOUN the place to which someone or something is going

destine VERB to set apart for a certain use

destined ADJECTIVE **1** bound (for) **2** intended (for) by fate: *destined to succeed*

destiny NOUN (*plural* **destinies**) what is destined to happen; fate

destitute ADJECTIVE in need of food, shelter, etc (**destitute of**) completely lacking in: *destitute of wit*

destitution NOUN the state of having nothing, not even food and shelter

destroy VERB **1** to pull down, knock to pieces **2** to ruin **3** to kill

destroyer NOUN **1** someone who destroys **2** a type of fast warship

destructible ADJECTIVE able to be destroyed

destruction NOUN **1** the act of destroying or being destroyed **2** ruin **3** death

destructive ADJECTIVE **1** doing great damage **2** of criticism: pointing out faults without suggesting improvements

desultory (*pronounced* **dez**-*ul*-*to*-ri) ADJECTIVE **1** moving from one thing to another without a fixed plan **2** changing from subject to subject, rambling

detach VERB to unfasten, remove (from)

detachable ADJECTIVE able to be taken off: *a detachable lining*

detached ADJECTIVE **1** standing apart, by itself: *a detached house* **2** not personally involved, showing no emotion

detachment NOUN **1** the state of being detached **2** a body or group (eg of troops on special service)

detail NOUN a small part, fact, item, etc ▸ VERB **1** to describe fully, give particulars of **2** to set to do a special job or task: *detailed to keep watch*

in detail giving attention to details, item by item
detailed ADJECTIVE with nothing left out
detain VERB **1** to hold back **2** to keep late **3** to keep under guard
detect VERB **1** to discover **2** to notice > **detection** NOUN
detective NOUN someone who tries to find criminals or watches suspects
detention NOUN **1** imprisonment **2** a forced stay after school as a punishment
deter VERB (**deterring, deterred**) to discourage or prevent through fear
detergent NOUN a soapless substance used with water for washing dishes etc
deteriorate VERB to grow worse: *Her health is deteriorating rapidly* > **deterioration** NOUN
determination NOUN **1** the fact of being determined **2** stubbornness, firmness of purpose
determine VERB **1** to decide (on) **2** to fix, settle: *determined his course of action*
determined ADJECTIVE **1** firmly decided; having a strong intention: *determined to succeed* **2** fixed, settled
deterrent NOUN something, especially a threat of some kind, which deters or discourages people from a particular course of action
detest VERB to hate greatly
detestable ADJECTIVE very hateful
detonate VERB to (cause to) explode
detonation NOUN an explosion
detonator NOUN something which sets off an explosive
detour NOUN a circuitous route
detract VERB to take away (from), lessen > **detraction** NOUN
detriment NOUN harm, damage, disadvantage
detrimental ADJECTIVE disadvantageous (to), causing harm or damage
deuce (*pronounced* dyoos) NOUN *tennis* a score of forty points each
devastate VERB **1** to lay in ruins **2** to overwhelm with grief etc > **devastation** NOUN
develop VERB (**developing, developed**) **1** to (cause to) grow bigger or more advanced **2** to acquire gradually: *developed a taste for opera* **3** to become active or visible **4** to unfold gradually **5** to use chemicals to make (a photograph) appear
developer NOUN a chemical mixture used to make an image appear from a photograph
Developing World NOUN a name for the underdeveloped countries in Africa, Asia and Latin America (*also called*: **the Third World**)
development NOUN **1** growth in size or sophistication **2** work done on studying and improving on previous or basic models, designs, or techniques **3** improvement of land so as to make it more fertile, useful or profitable **4** an area of housing built by a developer **5** an occurrence that affects or influences a situation **6** the gradual unfolding of something, eg a story **7** the

a b c d e f g h i j k l m n o p q r s t u v w x y z

A B C D E F G H I J K L M N O P Q R S T U V W X Y Z

process of using chemicals to make a photograph appear

deviate VERB to turn aside, especially from a standard course

deviation NOUN **1** something which is different, or which departs from the normal course **2** *statistics* the amount of difference between the average of a group of numbers and one of the numbers in that group

device NOUN **1** a tool, an instrument **2** a plan **3** a design on a coat of arms

> Do not confuse with: **devise**. To help you remember: 'ice' is a noun, 'ise' is not!

devil NOUN **1** an evil spirit **2** Satan **3** a wicked person

devilish ADJECTIVE very wicked

devil's advocate NOUN someone who argues against a proposal in order to test it

devious ADJECTIVE **1** not direct, roundabout **2** not straightforward

devise VERB **1** to make up, put together **2** to plan, plot

> Do not confuse with: **device**. To help you remember: 'ice' is a noun ... so 'ise' must be the verb!

devoid ADJECTIVE (**devoid of**) empty of, free from: *devoid of curiosity*

devolution NOUN the act of devolving, especially of giving certain powers to a regional government by a central government

devolutionist NOUN a supporter of devolution

devolve VERB **1** to fall as a duty (on) **2** to delegate (power) to a regional or national assembly

devote VERB to give up wholly (to)

devoted ADJECTIVE **1** loving and loyal **2** given up (to): *devoted to her work*

devotee (*pronounced* dev-oh-**tee**) NOUN a keen follower

devotion NOUN great love

devour VERB **1** to eat up greedily **2** to destroy

devout ADJECTIVE **1** earnest, sincere **2** religious > **devoutly** ADVERB

dew NOUN tiny drops of water which form from the air as it cools at night > **dewy** ADJECTIVE

dexterity NOUN skill, quickness > **dexterous** *or* **dextrous** ADJECTIVE

dhoti (*pronounced* **doh**-ti) NOUN (*plural* **dhotis**) a piece of cloth worn around the hips by some Hindu men

di- PREFIX two, twice or double: *carbon dioxide* (= having molecules containing two oxygen atoms)

ⓘ Comes from Greek *dis* meaning 'two', 'twice' or 'double'

diabetes (*pronounced* dai-*a*-**bee**-teez) NOUN a disease in which there is too much sugar in the blood

diabetic NOUN & ADJECTIVE (someone) suffering from diabetes

diabolical *or* **diabolic** ADJECTIVE devilish, very wicked > **diabolically** ADVERB

diadem NOUN a kind of crown

diagnose VERB to identify (a cause of illness) after making an examination

diagnosis NOUN (*plural*

diagnoses) the identification (of the cause of illness in a patient) by examination > **diagnostic** ADJECTIVE

diagonal ADJECTIVE going from one corner to the opposite corner ▸ NOUN a line from one corner to the opposite corner > **diagonally** ADVERB

diagram NOUN a drawing to explain something

dial NOUN **1** the face of a clock or watch **2** a rotating disc over the numbers on some telephones ▸ VERB (**dialling, dialled**) to call (a number) on a telephone using a dial or buttons

dialect NOUN a way of speaking found only in a certain area or among a certain group of people

dialogue NOUN a talk between two or more people

dialysis (*pronounced* dai-**al**-i-sis) NOUN *medicine* removal of impurities from the blood by a kidney machine

diameter (*pronounced* dai-**am**-i-ter) NOUN *maths* a line which dissects a circle, passing through its centre, and which is equal to twice its radius

diamond NOUN **1** a very hard, precious stone **2** an elongated, four-cornered shape (♦) **3** a playing-card with red diamond pips

diaper NOUN, *US* a baby's nappy

ⓘ Originally a kind of decorated white silk. The current US meaning was used in British English in the 16th century

diaphragm (*pronounced* **dai**-*a*-fram) NOUN **1** *anatomy* a layer of muscle separating the lower part of the body from the chest **2** a thin dividing layer

diarrhoea (*pronounced* dai-*a*-**ree**-*a*) NOUN frequent emptying of the bowels, with too much liquid in the faeces

diary NOUN (*plural* **diaries**) **1** a record of daily happenings **2** a book detailing these

dice NOUN (*plural* **dice**) (*also called*: **die**) a small cube with numbered sides or faces, used in certain games ▸ VERB to cut (food) into small cubes

dictate VERB (*pronounced* dik-**teit**) **1** to speak the text of (a letter etc) for someone else to write down **2** to give firm commands ▸ NOUN (*pronounced* **dik**-teit) an order, a command

dictation NOUN the act of dictating

dictator NOUN an all-powerful ruler

dictatorial ADJECTIVE like a dictator; domineering

diction NOUN **1** manner of speaking **2** choice of words

dictionary NOUN (*plural* **dictionaries**) **1** a book giving the words of a language in alphabetical order, together with their meanings **2** any alphabetically ordered reference book: *a medical dictionary*

did *see* **do**[1]

die[1] VERB (**dying, died**) **1** to lose life **2** to wither **die down** to become less intense

die[2] NOUN **1** a stamp or punch for making raised designs on money etc **2** another word for **dice**

A B C D E F G H I J K L M N O P Q R S T U V W X Y Z

diehard NOUN an obstinate or determined person

diesel (*pronounced* **dee**-zel) NOUN an internal combustion engine in which heavy oil is ignited by heat generated by compression

diet[1] NOUN **1** food **2** a course of recommended foods, eg to lose weight ▶ VERB (**dieting, dieted**) to eat certain kinds of food only, especially to lose weight > **dietetic** ADJECTIVE

diet[2] NOUN a council, an assembly

differ VERB (**differing, differed**) to disagree **differ from** to be unlike

difference NOUN **1** a point in which things differ **2** the amount by which one number is greater than another **3** a disagreement

different ADJECTIVE **1** varying, not the same **2** unusual **3** (**different from**) unlike

differentiate VERB to make a difference or distinction between

differentiation NOUN **1** making a distinction **2** *biology* the way cells, body parts or plant parts change so as to serve a specific function

difficult ADJECTIVE **1** not easy, hard to do, understand or deal with **2** hard to please

difficulty NOUN (*plural* **difficulties**) **1** lack of easiness, hardness **2** anything difficult **3** anything which makes something difficult; an obstacle, hindrance, etc **4** (**difficulties**) troubles

diffident ADJECTIVE shy, not confident > **diffidence** NOUN

diffraction NOUN, *physics* the spreading of a light wave when it encounters an obstacle

diffuse VERB (*pronounced* dif-**yooz**) to spread in all directions ▶ ADJECTIVE (*pronounced* dif-**yoos**) widely spread

dig VERB (**digging, dug**) **1** to turn up (earth) with a spade etc **2** to make (a hole) by this means **3** to poke or push (something) into ▶ NOUN **1** a poke, a thrust **2** an archaeological excavation

digest[1] (*pronounced* dai-**jest**) VERB **1** to break down (food) in the stomach into a form that the body can make use of **2** to think over **3** *chemistry* to soften or disintegrate in heat or moisture

digest[2] (*pronounced* **dai**-jest) NOUN **1** a summing-up **2** a collection of written material

digestible ADJECTIVE able to be digested

digestion NOUN the act or power of digesting

digestive ADJECTIVE aiding digestion

digger NOUN a machine for digging

digit NOUN **1** a finger or toe **2** any of the numbers 0–9

digital ADJECTIVE (*compare with*: **analogue**) **1** of a device: showing information in the form of digits rather than with pointers on a dial **2** using information supplied and stored as binary digits

digital audio tape NOUN (*abbrev* **DAT**) a magnetic audio tape on which sound has been recorded digitally

digital camera NOUN a camera which records photographic images in digital form to be viewed on a computer

digital recording NOUN the recording of sound by storing electrical pulses representing the audio signal on compact disc, digital audio tape, etc

digital television *or* **digital TV** NOUN a method of TV broadcasting, using digital rather than traditional analogue signals

dignified ADJECTIVE stately, serious

dignitary NOUN (*plural* **dignitaries**) someone of high rank or office

dignity NOUN **1** manner showing a sense of your own worth or the seriousness of the occasion **2** high rank

digress VERB to wander from the point in speaking or writing > **digression** NOUN

dike *or* **dyke** NOUN **1** a wall; an embankment **2** a ditch

dilapidated ADJECTIVE falling to pieces, needing repair

dilate VERB to make or grow larger, swell out > **dilatation** *or* **dilation** NOUN

dilemma NOUN a situation offering a difficult choice between two options

diligent ADJECTIVE hard-working, industrious > **diligence** NOUN > **diligently** ADVERB

dilly-dally VERB (**dilly-dallies, dilly-dallying, dilly-dallied**) to loiter, waste time

dilute (*pronounced* dai-**loot** *or* di-**loot**) VERB to lessen the concentration of (a liquid etc), especially by adding water ▶ ADJECTIVE > **diluted** ADJECTIVE > **dilution** NOUN

dim ADJECTIVE (**dimmer, dimmest**) **1** not bright or clear **2** not understanding clearly, stupid ▶ VERB (**dimming, dimmed**) to make or become dim

dime NOUN a tenth of a US or Canadian dollar, ten cents

dimension NOUN **1** a measurement of length, width or thickness **2** (**dimensions**) size, measurements

diminish VERB to make or grow less

diminuendo NOUN (*plural* **diminuendoes** *or* **diminuendos**), *music* a fading or falling sound

dimly ADVERB vaguely, not brightly or clearly

dimness NOUN haziness, half-light, lack of clarity

dimple NOUN a small hollow, especially on the cheek or chin

din NOUN a loud, lasting noise ▶ VERB (**dinning, dinned**) to put (into) someone's mind by constant repetition

dine VERB to eat dinner

diner NOUN **1** someone who dines **2** a restaurant car on a train **3** *US* a small, cheap restaurant

dinghy (*pronounced* **ding**-i *or* **ding**-gi) NOUN (*plural* **dinghies**) a small rowing boat

dingy (*pronounced* **din**-ji) ADJECTIVE (**dingier, dingiest**) dull, faded or dirty-looking > **dinginess** NOUN

dinner NOUN **1** a main evening meal **2** a midday meal, lunch

A B C D E F G H I J K L M N O P Q R S T U V W X Y Z

dinosaur NOUN any of various types of extinct giant reptile
ⓘ Coined in the 19th century, from Greek words which translate as 'terrible lizard'

dint NOUN a hollow made by a blow, a dent **by dint of** by means of

dip VERB (**dipping, dipped**) **1** to plunge into a liquid quickly **2** to lower (eg a flag) and raise again **3** to slope down **4** to look briefly (into a book etc) ▶ NOUN **1** a liquid in which anything is dipped **2** a creamy sauce into which biscuits etc are dipped **3** a downward slope **4** a hollow **5** a short bathe or swim

diploid (*pronounced* **dip**-loid) *biology*, ADJECTIVE of a cell: having two sets of chromosomes, one from each parent (*compare with*: **haploid**)

diploma NOUN a document certifying that you have passed a certain examination or completed a course of study
ⓘ From a Greek word meaning a letter folded double

diplomacy NOUN **1** the business of making agreements, treaties, etc between countries **2** skill in making people agree, tact

diplomat NOUN someone engaged in diplomacy

diplomatic ADJECTIVE **1** of diplomacy **2** tactful

dire ADJECTIVE dreadful: *in dire need*

direct ADJECTIVE **1** straight, not roundabout **2** frank, outspoken ▶ VERB **1** to point or aim at **2** to show the way **3** to order, instruct **4** to control, organize **5** to put a name and address on (a letter)

direct current NOUN (*abbrev*: **DC**) an electric current flowing in one direction (*compare with*: **alternating current**

direction NOUN **1** the act of directing **2** the place or point to which someone moves, looks, etc **3** an order **4** guidance **5** (**directions**) instructions on how to get somewhere

directly ADVERB **1** straight away, immediately: *I shall do it directly* **2** straight: *I looked directly at him* **3** just, exactly: *directly opposite*

directness NOUN frankness, with no effort to be tactful

director NOUN **1** a manager of a business etc **2** the person who controls the shooting of a film etc

directory NOUN (*plural* **directories**) **1** a book of names and addresses etc **2** *computing* a named group of files on a computer disk

direct speech NOUN speech reported in the speaker's exact words (*contrasted with*: **indirect speech**)

dirge NOUN a lament; a funeral hymn

dirt NOUN any unclean substance, such as mud, dust, dung, etc

dirt track NOUN an earth track for motorcycle racing

dirty ADJECTIVE (**dirtier, dirtiest**) **1** not clean, soiled **2** obscene, lewd ▶ VERB (**dirties, dirtying, dirtied**) to soil with dirt > **dirtily** ADVERB

dis- also **dif-**, **di-** PREFIX **1** apart: *disjointed/divide* **2** not: *dislike*
ⓘ Comes from Latin prefix *dis-*, *di-* with the same meaning

disability NOUN (*plural* **disabilities**) something which disables

disable VERB to take away power or strength from

disabled ADJECTIVE having a severely restricted lifestyle as the result of an injury, or a physical or mental illness or handicap

disadvantage NOUN an unfavourable circumstance, a drawback

disadvantaged ADJECTIVE suffering a disadvantage, especially poverty or homelessness

disadvantageous ADJECTIVE not advantageous

disagree VERB **1** (often **disagree with**) to hold different opinions (from) **2** to quarrel **3** (**disagree with**) of food: to make (someone) feel ill

disagreeable ADJECTIVE unpleasant

disagreement NOUN a difference of opinion or quarrel

disallow VERB to not allow

disappear VERB to go out of sight, vanish > **disappearance** NOUN

disappoint VERB **1** to fail to come up to the hopes or expectations (of) **2** to fail to fulfil

disappointed ADJECTIVE sad because your hopes or expectations have not been fulfilled

disappointment NOUN something which disappoints you

disapprove VERB to have an unfavourable opinion (of) > **disapproval** NOUN

disarm VERB **1** to take a weapon away from **2** to get rid of war weapons **3** to make less angry, charm

disarmament NOUN the removal or disabling of war weapons

disarray NOUN disorder

disaster NOUN an extremely unfortunate happening, often causing great damage or loss > **disastrous** ADJECTIVE > **disastrously** ADVERB

disband VERB to break up, separate: *The gang disbanded* > **disbandment** NOUN

disbelief NOUN inability to believe something

disc NOUN **1** a flat, round shape **2** *anatomy* a pad of cartilage between vertebrae **3** a gramophone record or compact disc **4** *computing see* **disk**

discard VERB to throw away as useless

discern VERB to see, realize

discernible ADJECTIVE noticeable: *no discernible difference*

discerning ADJECTIVE quick at noticing; discriminating: *a discerning eye*

discernment NOUN good taste, ability to judge between good and bad things

discharge VERB (*pronounced* dis-**chahrj**) **1** to unload (cargo) **2** to set free **3** to dismiss **4** to fire (a gun) **5** to perform (duties) **6** to pay (a debt) **7** to give off (eg smoke) **8** to let out (pus) ▸ NOUN (*pronounced* **dis**-chahrj) **1** a discharging **2** dismissal **3** pus etc discharged from the body **4** performance (of duties) **5** payment

a b c d e f g h i j k l m n o p q r s t u v w x y z

disciple (*pronounced* di-**sai**-pl) NOUN **1** someone who believes in another's teaching **2** one of the followers of Christ

disciplinary ADJECTIVE relating to the enforcement of rules and discipline, and the punishment of disobedience and other offences

discipline NOUN **1** training in an orderly way of life **2** order kept by means of control **3** punishment **4** a subject of study or training ▸ VERB **1** to bring to order **2** to punish

disc jockey NOUN someone who introduces and plays recorded music on the radio, at a club, etc

disclaim VERB to refuse to have anything to do with, deny

disclaimer NOUN a denial

disclose VERB to uncover, reveal, make known

disclosure NOUN **1** the act of disclosing **2** something disclosed

disco NOUN (*plural* **discos**) an event or place where recorded music is played for dancing

discolour *or US* **discolor** VERB to spoil the colour of; stain > **discoloration** NOUN

discomfort NOUN lack of comfort, uneasiness

disconcert VERB to upset, confuse

disconnect VERB to separate, break the connection between

disconnected ADJECTIVE **1** separated, no longer connected **2** of thoughts etc: not following logically, rambling

discontent NOUN dissatisfaction

discontented ADJECTIVE dissatisfied, cross

discontinue VERB to stop, cease to continue

discord NOUN **1** disagreement, quarrelling **2** *music* a jarring of notes

discordant ADJECTIVE **1** *music* made up of notes which do not make pleasant harmonies, creating a strange or unpleasant effect **2** strange or unpleasant because not made up of parts which fit well together

discount NOUN (*pronounced* **dis**-kownt) a small sum taken off the price of something: *10% discount* ▸ VERB (*pronounced* dis-**kownt**) **1** to leave out, not consider: *completely discounted my ideas* **2** to allow for exaggeration in (eg a story)

discourage VERB **1** to take away the confidence, hope, etc of **2** to try to prevent by showing dislike or disapproval: *discouraged his plan* > **discouragement** NOUN

discouraging ADJECTIVE giving little hope or encouragement

discourteous ADJECTIVE not polite; rude > **discourteously** ADVERB > **discourtesy** NOUN (*plural* **discourtesies**)

discover VERB **1** to find out **2** to find by chance, especially for the first time > **discoverer** NOUN

discovery NOUN (*plural* **discoveries**) **1** the act of finding or finding out **2** something discovered

discredit VERB (**discrediting, discredited**) **1** to refuse to believe **2** to cause to doubt **3** to disgrace ▸ NOUN **1** disgrace **2** disbelief

discreditable ADJECTIVE disgraceful

discreet ADJECTIVE wisely cautious, tactful > **discreetly** ADVERB

> Do not confuse with: **discrete**

discrepancy NOUN (*plural* **discrepancies**) a difference or disagreement between two things: *some discrepancy in the figures*

discrete ADJECTIVE separate, distinct

> Do not confuse with: **discreet**. It may help you to think of **Crete**, which is an island separate from the rest of Greece.

discretion NOUN wise caution, tact **at someone's discretion** according to that person's own judgement

discriminate VERB **1** to make differences (between), distinguish **2** to treat (people) differently because of their gender, race, etc

discriminating ADJECTIVE showing good judgement

discrimination NOUN **1** ability to discriminate **2** unfair treatment on grounds of gender, race, etc

discursive ADJECTIVE involving discussion: *a discursive essay*

discus NOUN (*plural* **discuses**) a heavy disc thrown in an athletic competition

discuss VERB to talk about > **discussion** NOUN

disdain VERB **1** to look down on, scorn **2** to be too proud to do ▸ NOUN scorn > **disdainful** ADJECTIVE

disease NOUN illness

diseased ADJECTIVE affected by disease

disembark VERB to put or go ashore > **disembarkation** NOUN

disembodied ADJECTIVE of a soul etc: separated from the body

disengage VERB to separate, free > **disengaged** ADJECTIVE

disentangle VERB to free from entanglement, unravel

disfigure VERB to spoil the beauty or appearance of > **disfigurement** NOUN

disgrace NOUN the state of being out of favour; shame ▸ VERB to bring shame on

disgraceful ADJECTIVE shameful; very bad > **disgracefully** ADVERB

disgruntled ADJECTIVE discontented, sulky

disguise VERB **1** to change the appearance of **2** to hide (feelings etc) ▸ NOUN **1** a disguised state **2** a costume etc which disguises

disgust NOUN **1** strong dislike, loathing **2** indignation ▸ VERB **1** to cause loathing, revolt **2** to make indignant > **disgusted** ADJECTIVE

disgusting ADJECTIVE sickening; causing disgust

dish NOUN (*plural* **dishes**) **1** a plate or bowl for food **2** food prepared for eating **3** a saucer-shaped aerial for receiving information from a satellite ▸ VERB **1** to serve (food) **2** to deal (out), distribute

dishearten VERB to take away courage or hope from > **disheartened** ADJECTIVE > **disheartening** ADJECTIVE

dishevelled (*pronounced* di-**shev**-eld) ADJECTIVE untidy, with hair etc disordered

dishonest ADJECTIVE not honest,

a b c d e f g h i j k l m n o p q r s t u v w x y z

deceitful > **dishonesty** NOUN

dishonour *or US* **dishonor** NOUN disgrace, shame ▶ VERB to cause shame to > **dishonourable** ADJECTIVE

disillusion VERB to take away a false belief from

disillusioned ADJECTIVE unhappy and disappointed after your happy impressions of something have been destroyed > **disillusionment** NOUN

disinfect VERB to destroy disease-causing germs in

disinfectant NOUN a substance that kills germs

disintegrate VERB to fall into pieces; break down

disintegration NOUN **1** the act of breaking down into pieces **2** the state of being broken down

disinterested ADJECTIVE unbiased, not influenced by personal feelings

> Do not confuse with: **uninterested**. It is generally a positive thing to be **disinterested** (= fair), especially if you are trying to make an unbiased decision. It is generally a negative thing to be **uninterested** (= bored).

disjointed ADJECTIVE of speech etc: not well connected together

disk NOUN **1** *US spelling* of **disc** **2** *computing* a flat round magnetic plate used for storing data

disk drive NOUN, *computing* the part of a computer that records data on to and retrieves data from disks

dislike VERB to not like, disapprove of ▶ NOUN disapproval

dislocate VERB **1** to put (a bone) out of joint **2** to upset, disorder > **dislocation** NOUN

dislodge VERB **1** to drive from a place of rest, hiding, or defence **2** to knock out of place accidentally

disloyal ADJECTIVE not loyal, unfaithful > **disloyalty** NOUN

dismal ADJECTIVE gloomy; sorrowful, sad

ⓘ Based on a Latin phrase *dies mali* 'evil days', referring to two days each month which were believed to be unusually unlucky

dismantle VERB **1** to remove fittings, furniture, etc from **2** to take to pieces

dismay VERB to make to feel hopeless, upset ▶ NOUN hopelessness or discouragement: *watching in dismay*

dismember VERB **1** to tear to pieces **2** to cut the limbs from

dismiss VERB **1** to send or put away **2** to remove (someone) from a job, sack **3** to close (a law case) > **dismissal** NOUN

dismount VERB to come down off a horse, bicycle, etc

disobedient ADJECTIVE refusing or failing to obey

disobey VERB to neglect or refuse to do what is commanded > **disobedience** NOUN

disorder NOUN **1** lack of order, confusion **2** a disease or illness ▶ VERB to throw out of order

disorderly ADJECTIVE **1** out of order **2** behaving in a lawless and noisy manner > **disorderliness** NOUN

disown VERB to deny having any

relationship to, or connection with

disparage VERB to speak of as being of little worth or importance; belittle > **disparagement** NOUN > **disparaging** ADJECTIVE

disparity NOUN (*plural* **disparities**) great difference, inequality

dispatch *or* **despatch** VERB 1 to send off (a letter etc) 2 to kill, finish off 3 to do or deal with quickly ▸NOUN (*plural* **dispatches** *or* **despatches**) 1 the act of sending off 2 a report to a newspaper 3 speed in doing something 4 killing 5 (**dispatches**) official papers (especially military or diplomatic)

dispel VERB (**dispelling, dispelled**) to drive away, make disappear

dispensable ADJECTIVE able to be done without

dispensary NOUN (*plural* **dispensaries**) a place where medicines are given out

dispensation NOUN special leave to break a rule etc

dispense VERB 1 to give out 2 to prepare (medicines) for giving out **dispense with something** to do without it

dispenser NOUN 1 a machine that issues something to you 2 a holder or container from which you can get something one at a time or in measured quantities

dispersal NOUN a scattering

disperse VERB 1 to scatter; spread 2 to (cause to) vanish

dispersion NOUN a scattering

dispirited ADJECTIVE sad, discouraged

displace VERB 1 to put out of place 2 to disorder, disarrange 3 to put (someone) out of office > **displacement** NOUN

displaced person NOUN someone forced to leave his or her own country because of war, political reasons, etc

display VERB to set out for show ▸NOUN a show, exhibition

displease VERB to offend, annoy

displeasure NOUN annoyance, disapproval

disposable ADJECTIVE intended to be thrown away

disposal NOUN the act or process of getting rid of something **at your disposal** available for your use

dispose VERB 1 to arrange, settle 2 to get rid (of): *They disposed of the body*

disposed ADJECTIVE inclined, willing **be well disposed towards someone** to favour them and be inclined to treat them well

disposition NOUN 1 arrangement 2 nature, personality 3 *law* the handing over of property etc to another

disproportionate ADJECTIVE too big or too little in comparison to something else

disprove VERB to prove to be false

dispute VERB to argue about ▸NOUN an argument, quarrel

disqualification NOUN the act of disqualifying someone or the state of being disqualified

disqualify VERB (**disqualifies, disqualifying, disqualified**) 1 to put out of a competition for breaking rules 2 to take away a qualification or right

A B C D E F G H I J K L M N O P Q R S T U V W X Y Z

disquiet NOUN uneasiness, anxiety

disregard VERB to pay no attention to, ignore ▶ NOUN neglect

disrepair NOUN a state of bad repair

disrepute NOUN bad reputation

disrespect NOUN rudeness, lack of politeness > **disrespectful** ADJECTIVE

disrupt VERB **1** to break up **2** to throw (a meeting etc) into disorder

disruption NOUN an obstacle or disturbance

disruptive ADJECTIVE causing disorder

dissatisfaction NOUN displeasure, annoyance

dissect (*pronounced* dai-**sekt**) VERB **1** to divide into parts **2** to study and criticize > **dissection** NOUN

dissemble VERB to hide, disguise intentions etc

dissent VERB **1** to have a different opinion **2** to break away, especially from an established church ▶ NOUN **1** disagreement **2** separation, especially from an established church

dissertation NOUN a long piece of writing or talk on a particular (often academic) subject

disservice NOUN harm, a bad turn

dissident NOUN someone who disagrees, especially with a political regime

dissimilar ADJECTIVE not the same > **dissimilarity** NOUN (*plural* **dissimilarities**)

dissipate VERB **1** to (cause to) disappear **2** to waste, squander > **dissipation** NOUN overindulgence in extravagant living

dissipated ADJECTIVE worn out by indulging in pleasures; dissolute

dissociate VERB to separate **dissociate yourself from** to refuse to be associated with

dissolve VERB **1** to melt **2** to break up **3** to put an end to

dissonance NOUN **1** *music* discord, especially used deliberately for musical effect **2** disagreement > **dissonant** ADJECTIVE

dissuade VERB to persuade not to do something: *We dissuaded her from leaving school* > **dissuasion** NOUN

distance NOUN **1** the space between things **2** a far-off place or point: *in the distance* **3** coldness of manner

distant ADJECTIVE **1** far off or far apart in place or time: *distant era/ distant land* **2** not close: *distant cousin* **3** cold in manner

distantly ADVERB **1** with a dreamy or cold manner **2** not closely: *distantly related*

distaste NOUN dislike

distasteful ADJECTIVE disagreeable, unpleasant

distemper NOUN **1** a kind of paint used chiefly for walls **2** a viral disease of dogs, foxes, etc ▶ VERB to paint with distemper

distend VERB to swell; stretch outwards > **distension** NOUN

distil VERB (**distilling, distilled**) **1** to purify (liquid) by heating it to a vapour and condensing it **2** to extract the spirit or essence from **3** to (cause to) fall in drops > **distillation** NOUN > **distiller** NOUN

distillery NOUN (*plural* **distilleries**)

a place where whisky, brandy, etc is distilled

distinct ADJECTIVE **1** clear; easily seen or noticed: *a distinct improvement* **2** different: *The two languages are quite distinct*

> Do not confuse: **distinct** and **distinctive**

distinction NOUN **1** a difference **2** outstanding worth or merit

distinctive ADJECTIVE different, special, easily recognizable: *That singer has a very distinctive voice* > **distinctively** ADVERB

> Do not confuse: **distinctive** and **distinct**

distinguish VERB **1** to recognize a difference (between) **2** to mark off as different **3** to recognize **4** to give distinction to

distinguished ADJECTIVE **1** outstanding, famous **2** dignified

distort VERB **1** to twist out of shape **2** to turn or twist (a statement etc) from its true meaning **3** to make (a sound) unclear and harsh > **distortion** NOUN

distract VERB **1** to divert (the attention) **2** to trouble, confuse **3** to make mad

distracted ADJECTIVE mad with pain, grief, etc

distraction NOUN **1** something which diverts your attention **2** anxiety, confusion **3** amusement **4** madness

distraught ADJECTIVE extremely agitated or anxious

distress NOUN **1** pain, trouble, sorrow **2** a cause of suffering ▸ VERB to cause pain or sorrow to > **distressed** ADJECTIVE > **distressing** ADJECTIVE

distribute VERB **1** to divide among several **2** to spread out widely

distribution NOUN **1** the process of distributing or being distributed **2** the pattern of things spread out

district NOUN a region of a country or town

distrust NOUN lack of trust, suspicion ▸ VERB to have no trust in > **distrustful** ADJECTIVE

disturb VERB **1** to confuse, worry, upset **2** to interrupt

disturbance NOUN **1** an outbreak of violent behaviour, especially in public **2** an act of disturbing, agitating or disorganizing **3** psychological damage or illness

disturbed ADJECTIVE **1** mentally or emotionally ill or damaged **2** full of trouble and anxiety

disuse NOUN the state of being no longer used

disused ADJECTIVE no longer used

ditch NOUN (*plural* **ditches**) a long, narrow, hollow trench dug in the ground, especially to carry water

dither VERB **1** to hesitate, be undecided **2** to act in a nervous, uncertain manner ▸ NOUN a state of indecision

ditto NOUN (often written as **do**) the same as already written or said

ditto marks a character (") written below a word in a text, meaning it is to be repeated

ditty NOUN (*plural* **ditties**) a simple, short song

A B C D E F G H I J K L M N O P Q R S T U V W X Y Z

dive VERB (**diving, dived** *or US* **dove**) **1** to plunge headfirst into water **2** to swoop through the air **3** to go down steeply and quickly ▸ NOUN an act of diving

diver NOUN **1** someone who works under water using special breathing equipment **2** a type of diving bird

diverge VERB to separate and go in different directions; differ > **divergence** NOUN > **divergent** ADJECTIVE

diverse ADJECTIVE different, various

diversify VERB (**diversifies, diversifying, diversified**) to make or become different or varied

diversion NOUN **1** turning aside **2** an alteration to a traffic route **3** an amusement

diversity NOUN difference; variety

divert VERB **1** to turn aside, change the direction of **2** to entertain, amuse

diverting ADJECTIVE entertaining, amusing

divide VERB **1** to separate into parts **2** to share (among) **3** to (cause to) go into separate groups **4** *maths* to find out how many times one number contains another

dividend NOUN **1** *maths* an amount to be divided (*compare with:* **divisor**) **2** a share of profits from a business

dividers PLURAL NOUN measuring compasses, used in geometry to measure lengths

divine ADJECTIVE **1** of a god; holy **2** *informal* splendid, wonderful ▸ VERB **1** to guess **2** to foretell, predict

divinity NOUN (*plural* **divinities**) **1** a god **2** the nature of a god **3** religious studies

division NOUN **1** the act of dividing **2** a barrier, a separator **3** a section, especially of an army **4** separation **5** disagreement

divisional ADJECTIVE of a division

divisor (*pronounced* di-**vai**-sor) NOUN, *maths* the number by which another number (the **dividend**) is divided

divorce NOUN **1** the legal ending of a marriage **2** a complete separation ▸ VERB **1** to end a marriage with **2** to separate (from)

divulge (*pronounced* dai-**vulj** *or* di-**vulj**) VERB to let out, make known (a secret etc)

Diwali (*pronounced* dee-**wah**-lee), **Dewali** *or* **Divali** (*pronounced* dee-**vah**-lee) NOUN the Hindu and Sikh festival of lamps, celebrated in October or November

DIY ABBREVIATION do-it-yourself

dizzy ADJECTIVE (**dizzier, dizziest**) **1** experiencing or causing a spinning sensation in the head **2** *informal* silly; not reliable or responsible **3** *informal* bewildered > **dizzily** ADVERB

DJ ABBREVIATION disc jockey

DNA ABBREVIATION deoxyribonucleic acid, a compound of which the chromosomes and genes of almost all living things are composed, carrying genetic instructions for passing on hereditary characteristics

do VERB (**does, doing, did, done**) **1** to carry out, perform (a job etc) **2** to perform an action on, eg clean (dishes), arrange (hair), etc **3** *slang* to swindle **4** to act: *Do as you please* **5** to get on: *I hear she's doing very well/How are you doing?* **6** to be enough: *A pound will do* **7** used to avoid repeating a verb: *I seldom see him now, and when I do, he ignores me* **8** used with a more important verb in questions: *Do you see what I mean?* **9** used with a more important verb in sentences with **not**: *I don't know* **10** used with a more important verb for emphasis: *I do hope she'll be there* ▸ NOUN (*plural* **dos**) *informal* a social event, a party **do away with** *informal* to put an end to, destroy **do down** to get the better of **do in** *informal* **1** to exhaust, wear out **2** to murder **done to death** too often repeated **do or die** a desperate final attempt at something whatever the consequences **do out of** to swindle out of **do someone proud** *see* **proud** **do up** **1** to fasten **2** to renovate

[i] Comes from Old English *don*

docile (*pronounced* **doh**-sail) ADJECTIVE tame, easy to manage > **docilely** ADVERB > **docility** NOUN

dock[1] NOUN (often **docks**) a deepened part of a harbour where ships go for loading, repair, etc ▸ VERB **1** to put in or enter a dock **2** of a spacecraft: to join on to another craft in space

dock[2] VERB to clip or cut short (an animal's tail)

dock[3] NOUN a weed with large leaves

dock[4] NOUN the box in a law court where the accused person stands

dockyard NOUN a naval harbour with docks, stores, etc

doctor NOUN **1** someone trained in and licensed to practise medicine **2** someone with the highest university degree in any subject ▸ VERB **1** to treat as a patient **2** to tamper with, alter

doctrine (*pronounced* **dok**-trin) NOUN a belief that is taught > **doctrinal** (*pronounced* dok-**trai**-n*a*l) ADJECTIVE

document NOUN a written statement giving proof, information, etc

documentary NOUN (*plural* **documentaries**) a film giving information about real people or events ▸ ADJECTIVE **1** of or in documents: *documentary evidence* **2** of a documentary

doddle NOUN, *informal* an easy task

dodecagon (*pronounced* doh-**dek**-*a*-gon) NOUN, *maths* a flat figure with twelve sides

dodge VERB to avoid by a sudden or clever movement ▸ NOUN a trick

dodo NOUN (*plural* **dodoes** *or* **dodos**) a type of large, extinct bird

doe NOUN the female of certain animals, eg a deer, rabbit or hare

doer NOUN an active person who does a lot of things

dog NOUN **1** a four-footed animal often kept as a pet **2** a member of the dog family which includes wolves, foxes, etc ▸ ADJECTIVE of certain animals: male ▸ VERB (**dogging, dogged**) **1** to follow and watch constantly **2** to hamper, plague: *dogged by ill health* **dog in**

A B C D E F G H I J K L M N O P Q R S T U V W X Y Z

the manger someone who stands in the way of a plan or proposal **go to the dogs** *informal* to be ruined

dog collar NOUN **1** a collar for dogs **2** the stiff white collar worn by certain members of the clergy

dog-eared ADJECTIVE of a page: turned down at the corner

dogfight NOUN a fight between aeroplanes at close quarters

dogfish NOUN a kind of small shark

dogged (*pronounced* **dog**-id) ADJECTIVE determined, stubborn: *dogged refusal* > **doggedly** ADVERB

doggy-paddle *or* **dog-paddle** NOUN a simple style of swimming

dogma NOUN an opinion, especially religious, accepted or fixed by an authority

dogmatic ADJECTIVE **1** of dogma **2** stubbornly forcing your opinions on others > **dogmatically** ADVERB

do-gooder NOUN someone who tries to help others in a self-righteous way

dog-paddle *see* **doggy-paddle**

dogsbody NOUN (*plural* **dogsbodies**), *informal* someone who is given unpleasant or dreary tasks to do

dog's breakfast *or* **dog's dinner** NOUN a complete mess

dog's life NOUN a life of misery

dog-tag NOUN **1** a dog's identity disc **2** an identity disc worn by soldiers etc

dog-tired ADJECTIVE, *informal* completely worn out

doily *or* **doyley** NOUN (*plural* **doilies** *or* **doyleys**) a perforated paper napkin

ⓘ Originally a light summer fabric, named after *Doily*'s drapery shop in 17th-century London

doings PLURAL NOUN actions

Dolby NOUN, *trademark* a system for reducing background noise, used in recording music or soundtracks

doldrums PLURAL NOUN low spirits: *in the doldrums*

ⓘ The *doldrums* take their name from an area of the ocean about the equator famous for calms and variable winds

dole VERB to deal (out) in small amounts ▸ NOUN, *informal* a payment made by the state to unemployed people

doleful ADJECTIVE sad, unhappy > **dolefully** ADVERB

doll NOUN a toy in the shape of a small human being

dollar NOUN the main unit of currency in several countries, eg the USA, Canada, Australia and New Zealand

ⓘ From a shortened form of *Joachimsthaler*, the name of a silver coin produced at Joachimsthal in what is now the Czech Republic

dolphin NOUN a type of sea animal like a porpoise

dolt NOUN a stupid person > **doltish** ADJECTIVE

domain NOUN **1** a kingdom **2** a country estate **3** an area of interest or knowledge

domain name NOUN, *computing* in e-mail and website addresses: the name and location of the server

dome NOUN **1** the shape of a

half sphere or ball 2 the roof of a building etc in this shape > **domed** ADJECTIVE

domestic ADJECTIVE 1 of the home or house 2 of an animal: tame, domesticated 3 not foreign, of your own country: *domestic products* ▶NOUN a live-in maid etc

domesticated ADJECTIVE 1 of an animal: tame, used for farming etc 2 fond of doing housework, cooking, etc

domesticity NOUN home life

domestic science NOUN, *old* cookery, needlework, etc, taught as a subject (now called **home economics**)

domicile (*pronounced* **dom**-i-sail) NOUN the country etc in which someone lives permanently

dominant ADJECTIVE ruling; most powerful or important > **dominance** NOUN

dominate VERB 1 to have command or influence over 2 to be most strong, or most noticeable 3 to tower above, overlook: *The castle dominates the skyline* > **domination** NOUN

domineering ADJECTIVE overbearing, like a tyrant

dominion NOUN 1 rule, authority 2 an area with one ruler or government

domino NOUN (*plural* **dominoes**) a piece used in the game of dominoes

dominoes SINGULAR NOUN a game played on a table with pieces marked with dots, each side of which must match a piece placed next to it

don NOUN a college or university lecturer ▶VERB (**donning, donned**) to put on (a coat etc)

donate VERB to present a gift

donation NOUN a gift of money or goods

done *past participle* of **do**[1] ADJECTIVE finished

donkey NOUN (*plural* **donkeys**) a type of animal with long ears, related to the horse (*also called*: **ass**)

donor NOUN 1 a giver of a gift 2 someone who agrees to let their body organs be used for transplant operations

don't *short for* **do not**

doom NOUN 1 judgement; fate 2 ruin

doomed ADJECTIVE 1 destined, condemned 2 bound to fail or be destroyed

door NOUN 1 a hinged barrier which closes the entrance to a room or building 2 the entrance itself

doorstep NOUN the step in front of the door of a house

doorway NOUN the space filled by a door, the entrance

dope NOUN, *informal* 1 the drug cannabis 2 an idiot ▶VERB to drug (someone or something), especially illegally

dormant ADJECTIVE sleeping, inactive: *a dormant volcano*

dormitory NOUN (*plural* **dormitories**) a room with beds for several people

dormouse NOUN (*plural* **dormice**) a small, mouse-like, furry-tailed rodent which hibernates

a b c d e f g h i j k l m n o p q r s t u v w x y z

A B C D E F G H I J K L M N O P Q R S T U V W X Y Z

ⓘ Probably from Latin *dormire* meaning 'to sleep', and English *mouse*

dorsal ADJECTIVE of the back: *a dorsal fin* (*compare with* **ventral**)

DOS (*pronounced* dos) ABBREVIATION, *computing* disk operating system

dosage NOUN the proper size of dose: *The dosage for adults is 1-2 tablets*

dose NOUN **1** a quantity of medicine to be taken at one time **2** a bout of something unpleasant: *a dose of flu* ▸ VERB to give medicine to

doss VERB, *informal* to lie down to sleep somewhere temporary

dossier (*pronounced* **dos**-i-ei) NOUN a set of papers containing information about a certain person or subject

dot NOUN a small, round mark ▸ VERB (**dotting, dotted**) **1** to mark with a dot **2** to scatter **on the dot** exactly on time

dotage (*pronounced* **doh**-tij) NOUN the foolishness and childishness of old age

dotcom ADJECTIVE of a company: trading on the Internet ▸ NOUN a dotcom company

dote VERB (**dote on**) to be foolishly fond of

double VERB **1** to multiply by two **2** to fold ▸ NOUN **1** twice as much: *Whatever he is offering, I'll pay you double* **2** someone so like another as to be mistaken for them ▸ ADJECTIVE **1** containing twice as much: *a double dose/double the amount* **2** made up of two of the same sort **3** folded over **4** deceitful **at the double** very quickly **double back** to turn sharply and go back the way you have come **double up 1** to writhe in pain **2** to share accommodation (with)

double agent NOUN a spy paid by two rival countries, but loyal to only one

double bass NOUN a type of large stringed musical instrument played by plucking the strings

double-breasted ADJECTIVE of a coat: with one half of the front overlapping the other

double-cross VERB to cheat

double-dealer NOUN a deceitful, cheating person > **double-dealing** NOUN

double-decker NOUN a bus with two floors

double-Dutch NOUN incomprehensible talk, gibberish

double glazing NOUN two sheets of glass in a window to keep in the heat or keep out noise

doublet NOUN in the past, a man's close-fitting jacket

double-take NOUN a second look at something surprising or confusing

doubly ADVERB **1** extra, especially: *Check the door to make doubly sure you have locked it* **2** in two ways: *He's doubly responsible for the mess we're in*

doubt (*pronounced* dowt) VERB **1** to be unsure or undecided about **2** to think unlikely: *I doubt that we'll be able to go* ▸ NOUN a lack of certainty or trust; suspicion **no doubt** probably, surely

doubtful ADJECTIVE **1** unlikely, uncertain or unreliable **2** strange, raising suspicion **doubtful about something** unsure about it

doubtless ADVERB probably

dough NOUN **1** a mass of flour, moistened and kneaded **2** *informal* money

doughnut NOUN a ring-shaped cake fried in fat

dour (*pronounced* door) ADJECTIVE dull, humourless

dove[1] (*pronounced* duv) NOUN a type of pigeon

dove[2] (*pronounced* dohv) *US past form* of **dive**

dovecote NOUN a small building for housing pigeons

dovetail VERB to fit one thing exactly into another

dowdy ADJECTIVE (**dowdier, dowdiest**) not smart, badly dressed

down[1] ADVERB **1** towards or in a lower position: *fell down/sitting down* **2** to a smaller size: *grind down* **3** to a later generation: *handed down from mother to daughter* **4** on the spot, in cash: *£10 down* ▶PREPOSITION **1** towards or in the lower part of: *rolled back down the hill* **2** along: *strolling down the road* ▶ADJECTIVE going downwards: *the down escalator* **go down with** *or* **be down with** to become or be ill with

down[2] NOUN light, soft feathers

down-at-heel ADJECTIVE worn down, shabby

downcast ADJECTIVE sad

downfall NOUN ruin, defeat

downhearted ADJECTIVE discouraged

download *computing*, VERB (*pronounced* down-**lohd**) to transfer (information from the Internet) from one computer to another ▶NOUN (*pronounced* **down**-lohd) **1** an act of downloading **2** something downloaded

downpour NOUN a heavy fall of rain

downs PLURAL NOUN low, grassy hills

downstairs ADJECTIVE on a lower floor of a building ▶ADVERB to a lower floor

downstream ADVERB further down a river, in the direction of its flow

downtrodden ADJECTIVE kept in a lowly, inferior position

downwards *or* **downward** ADVERB moving or leading down

downy ADJECTIVE (**downier, downiest**) soft, feathery

dowry NOUN (*plural* **dowries**) money and property brought by a woman to her husband on their marriage

-dox SUFFIX forms words related to opinions or beliefs: *orthodox/heterodox*

[i] Comes from Greek *doxa* meaning 'opinion'

doze VERB to sleep lightly ▶NOUN a light, short sleep

dozen NOUN twelve

dpi *or* **DPI** ABBREVIATION, *computing* dots per inch

drab ADJECTIVE (**drabber, drabbest**) dull, monotonous

draft NOUN **1** a rough outline, a sketch **2** a group of people selected for a special purpose **3** *US* conscription into the army **4** an order for payment of money **5** US spelling of **draught** ▶ VERB **1** to make a rough plan **2** to select for a purpose **3** *US* to conscript

> Do not confuse with: **draught**

drag VERB (**dragging, dragged**) **1** to pull roughly **2** to move slowly and heavily **3** to trail along the ground **4** to search (a riverbed etc) with a net or hook ▶ NOUN **1** a dreary task **2** *informal* a tedious person **3** *informal* clothes for one sex worn by the other **4** *physics* a force that slows down movement through a liquid or gas **drag your feet** *or* **drag your heels** to be slow to do something

dragon NOUN **1** an imaginary fire-breathing, winged reptile **2** a fierce, intimidating person, especially a woman

dragonfly NOUN (*plural* **dragonflies**) a winged insect with a long body and double wings

dragoon NOUN a heavily armed horse soldier ▶ VERB to force or bully (into)

drain VERB **1** to clear (land) of water by trenches or pipes **2** to drink the contents of (a glass etc) **3** to use up completely ▶ NOUN a channel or pipe used to carry off water etc

drainage NOUN the drawing-off of water by rivers, pipes, etc

drained ADJECTIVE **1** emptied of liquid **2** sapped of strength

drake NOUN a male duck

drama NOUN **1** a play for acting in the theatre **2** exciting or tense action

dramatic ADJECTIVE **1** relating to plays **2** exciting, thrilling **3** unexpected, sudden
> **dramatically** ADVERB

dramatist NOUN a playwright

dramatize *or* **dramatise** VERB **1** to turn into a play for the theatre **2** to make vivid or sensational
> **dramatization** NOUN

drank *past tense* of **drink**

drape VERB to arrange (cloth) to hang gracefully ▶ NOUN (**drapes**) *US* curtains

draper NOUN a dealer in cloth

drapery NOUN (*plural* **draperies**) **1** cloth goods **2** a draper's shop

drastic ADJECTIVE severe, extreme
> **drastically** ADVERB

draught (*pronounced* drahft) *or US* **draft** NOUN **1** a current of air **2** the act of drawing or pulling **3** something drawn out **4** a drink taken all at once **5** (**draughts**) a game for two, played by moving pieces on a board marked with squares (a **draughtboard**)

> Do not confuse with: **draft**

draughtsman *or* **draughtswoman** NOUN (*plural* **draughtsmen** *or* **draughtswomen**) **1** someone employed to draw plans **2** someone skilled in drawing

draughty ADJECTIVE (**draughtier, draughtiest**) full of air currents, chilly

draw VERB (**drawing, drew, drawn**) **1** to make a picture with pencil, crayons, etc **2** to pull after or along **3** to attract: *drew a large crowd* **4** to obtain money from a fund:

drawing a pension **5** to require (a depth) for floating: *This ship draws 20 feet* **6** to approach, come: *Night is drawing near* **7** to score equal points in a game ▸ NOUN **1** an equal score **2** a lottery **draw a blank** to get no result **draw a conclusion** to form an opinion from evidence heard **draw on 1** to approach **2** to use as a resource: *drawing on experience* **draw out 1** to lengthen **2** to persuade (someone) to talk and be at ease **draw the line at** to refuse to allow or accept **draw up 1** to come to a stop **2** to move closer **3** to plan, write out (a contract etc)

drawback NOUN a disadvantage

drawbridge NOUN a bridge at the entrance to a castle which can be drawn up or let down

drawer NOUN **1** someone who draws **2** (*pronounced* drawr) a sliding box fitting into a chest, table, etc

drawing NOUN a picture made by pencil, crayon, etc

drawing pin NOUN a pin with a large flat head for fastening paper on a board etc

drawing room NOUN a sitting room

drawl VERB to speak in a slow, lazy manner ▸ NOUN a drawling voice

drawn *past participle* of **draw** **drawn and quartered** *history* disembowelled and cut in pieces after being hanged

dread NOUN great fear ▸ VERB to be greatly afraid of > **dreaded** ADJECTIVE ADJECTIVE terrifying

dreadful ADJECTIVE **1** terrible **2** *informal* very bad > **dreadfully** ADVERB

dreadlocks NOUN thick, twisted strands of hair

dream NOUN **1** a series of images and sounds in the mind during sleep **2** something imagined, not real **3** something very beautiful **4** a hope, an ambition: *Her dream was to go to Mexico* ▸ VERB (**dreaming, dreamt** – *pronounced* dremt – *or* **dreamed** – *pronounced* dremt *or* dreemd) to have a dream **dream up** to invent

dreamy ADJECTIVE (**dreamier, dreamiest**) **1** sleepy, half-awake **2** vague, dim **3** *informal* beautiful or handsome > **dreamily** ADVERB

dreary ADJECTIVE (**drearier, dreariest**) gloomy, cheerless > **drearily** ADVERB

dredge[1] VERB to drag a net or bucket along a river bed or seabed to bring up fish, mud, etc ▸ NOUN an instrument for dredging a river etc

dredge[2] VERB to sprinkle (with sugar or flour)

dregs PLURAL NOUN **1** sediment on the bottom of a liquid: *dregs of wine* **2** last remnants **3** a worthless or useless part: *the dregs of society*

drench VERB to soak

dress VERB **1** to put on clothes or a covering **2** to prepare (food etc) for use **3** to arrange (hair) **4** to treat and bandage (wounds) ▸ NOUN (*plural* **dresses**) **1** clothes **2** a one-piece woman's garment combining skirt and top **3** a style of clothing: *formal dress* ▸ ADJECTIVE of clothes: for formal use: *a dress shirt*

A B C D E F G H I J K L M N O P Q R S T U V W X Y Z

dresser NOUN a kitchen sideboard for dishes

dressing NOUN **1** a covering **2** a seasoned sauce poured over salads etc **3** a bandage

dressing-gown NOUN a loose, light coat worn indoors over pyjamas etc

dressmaking NOUN making women's clothes > **dressmaker** NOUN

dress rehearsal NOUN the final rehearsal of a play etc, in which the actors wear their costumes

dressy ADJECTIVE (**dressier, dressiest**) stylish, smart

drew *past tense* of **draw**

dribble VERB **1** to (cause to) fall in small drops **2** to let saliva run down the chin **3** *football, hockey, etc* to move the ball forward little by little

dried *see* **dry**

drift NOUN **1** a pile of snow, sand, etc driven by the wind **2** the direction in which something is driven **3** the general meaning of someone's words ▸ VERB **1** to go with the tide or current **2** to be driven into heaps by the wind **3** to wander about **4** to live aimlessly

drifter NOUN **1** someone who drifts **2** a fishing boat that uses drift nets

drill VERB **1** to make a hole in **2** to make with a drill **3** to exercise (soldiers) **4** to sow (seeds) in rows ▸ NOUN **1** a tool for making holes in wood etc **2** military exercise **3** a row of seeds or plants

drily *another spelling* of **dryly**

drink VERB (**drinking, drank, drunk**) **1** to swallow (a liquid) **2** to take alcoholic drink, especially excessively ▸ NOUN **1** liquid to be drunk **2** alcoholic liquids **drink in** to listen to eagerly **drink to** to drink a toast to **drink up** to finish a drink

drip VERB (**dripping, dripped**) **1** to fall in drops **2** to let (water etc) fall in drops ▸ NOUN **1** a drop **2** a continual dropping, eg of water **3** a device for adding liquid slowly to a vein etc

drip-dry VERB to dry (a garment) by hanging it up to dry without wringing it first

dripping NOUN fat from roasting meat

drive VERB (**driving, drove, driven**) **1** to control or guide (a car etc) **2** to go in a vehicle: *driving to work* **3** to force or urge along **4** to hurry on **5** to hit (a ball, nail, etc) hard **6** to bring about: *drive a bargain* ▸ NOUN **1** a journey in a car **2** a private road to a house **3** an avenue or road **4** energy, enthusiasm **5** a campaign: *a drive to save the local school* **6** a games tournament: *a whist drive* **7** a hard stroke with a club or bat **what are you driving at?** what are you suggesting or implying?

drive-in NOUN, *US* a cinema where the audience watches the screen while staying in their cars

drivel *informal*, NOUN nonsense ▸ VERB (**drivelling, drivelled**) to talk nonsense

driven *past participle* of **drive**

driver NOUN **1** someone who drives a car etc **2** a wooden-headed golf club

drizzle NOUN light rain ▸ VERB to rain lightly > **drizzly** ADJECTIVE

droll ADJECTIVE **1** funny, amusing **2** odd

drone VERB **1** to make a low humming sound **2** to speak in a dull, boring voice ▸ NOUN **1** a low humming sound **2** a dull, boring voice **3** the low-sounding pipe of a bagpipe **4** a male bee **5** a lazy, idle person

drool VERB **1** to produce saliva **2** to show uncontrolled admiration for

droop VERB **1** to hang down: *Your hem is drooping* **2** to grow weak or discouraged

drop NOUN **1** a small round or pear-shaped blob of liquid **2** a small quantity: *a drop of whisky* **3** a fall from a height: *a drop of six feet* **4** a small, flavoured sweet: *a pear drop* ▸ VERB (**dropping, dropped**) **1** to fall suddenly **2** to let fall **3** to fall in drops **4** to set down from a car etc: *Drop me at the corner* **5** to give up, abandon (a friend, habit, etc) **drop back** to fall behind others in a group **drop in** to pay a brief visit **drop off** to fall asleep **drop out** to withdraw from a class, from society, etc

drop-down menu NOUN, *computing* a menu on a computer screen viewed by making a single click on a button on the toolbar (*compare with:* **pull-down menu**)

droplet NOUN a tiny drop

droppings PLURAL NOUN animal or bird faeces

dross NOUN **1** scum produced by melting metal **2** waste material, impurities **3** coal dust **4** anything worthless

drought NOUN a prolonged period of time when no rain falls

drove NOUN **1** a number of moving cattle or other animals **2** (**droves**) a great number of people ▸ *past tense of* **drive** ▸ *past form of* **drive**

drover NOUN someone who drives cattle

drown VERB **1** to die by suffocating in water **2** to kill in this way **3** to flood or soak completely **4** to block out (a sound) with a louder one

drowsy ADJECTIVE (**drowsier, drowsiest**) sleepy > **drowsily** ADVERB

drudge VERB to do very humble or boring work ▸ NOUN someone who does such work

drudgery NOUN hard, uninteresting work

drug NOUN **1** a substance used in medicine to treat illness, kill pain, etc **2** a stimulant or narcotic substance taken habitually for its effects ▸ VERB (**drugging, drugged**) to administer drugs to

drum NOUN **1** a musical instrument of skin etc stretched on a round frame and beaten with sticks **2** a cylindrical container: *an oil drum/ biscuit drum* ▸ VERB (**drumming, drummed**) **1** to beat a drum **2** to tap continuously with the fingers > **drummer** NOUN

drumstick NOUN **1** a stick for beating a drum **2** the lower part of the leg of a cooked chicken etc

drunk ADJECTIVE showing the effects (giddiness, unsteadiness, etc) of drinking too much alcohol ▸ NOUN someone who is drunk, or habitually drunk ▸ PAST PARTICIPLE of **drink**

A B C D E F G H I J K L M N O P Q R S T U V W X Y Z

drunkard NOUN a drunk

drunken ADJECTIVE **1** habitually drunk **2** caused by too much alcohol: *a drunken stupor* **3** involving much alcohol: *a drunken spree* > **drunkenness** NOUN

dry ADJECTIVE (**drier, driest**) **1** not moist or wet **2** thirsty **3** uninteresting: *makes very dry reading* **4** reserved, matter-of-fact **5** of wine: not sweet **6** of a sense of humour: funny in a quiet, subtle way ▶ VERB (**dries, drying, dried**) to make or become dry

dry-clean VERB to clean (clothes etc) with chemicals, not with water

dryly *or* **drily** ADVERB **1** in a reserved, matter-of-fact, emotionless way **2** with quiet, subtle humour

dryness NOUN the quality of being dry

dry rot NOUN a disease caused by fungus, which reduces wood to a dry and crumbly mass

dry-stone ADJECTIVE of a wall: built of stone without cement or mortar

DTI ABBREVIATION Department of Trade and Industry

DTP ABBREVIATION desktop publishing

dual ADJECTIVE double; made up of two

> Do not confuse with: **duel**

dual carriageway NOUN a road divided by a central barrier or boundary, with each side used by traffic moving in one direction

dual-purpose ADJECTIVE able to be used for two purposes

dub[1] VERB (**dubbing, dubbed**) **1** to declare (a man) a knight by touching each shoulder with a sword **2** to name or nickname

dub[2] VERB (**dubbing, dubbed**) **1** to add sound to (a film) **2** to give (a film) a new soundtrack in a different language

dubiety (*pronounced* juw-**bai**-i-ti) NOUN doubt

dubious (*pronounced* **dyoo**-bi-*us*) ADJECTIVE **1** doubtful, uncertain **2** probably dishonest: *dubious dealings*

duchess NOUN (*plural* **duchesses**) **1** a woman of the same rank as a duke **2** the wife or widow of a duke

duchy NOUN (*plural* **duchies**) the land owned by a duke or duchess

duck[1] NOUN **1** a web-footed bird, with a broad, flat beak **2** *cricket* a score of no runs

ⓘ The meaning in cricket comes from the use of 'duck's egg' to mean a nought on a scoring sheet

duck[2] VERB **1** to lower the head quickly as if to avoid a blow **2** to push (someone's head) under water **duck out (of)** to avoid responsibility (for)

duck-billed platypus *see* **platypus**

duckling NOUN a baby duck

duct NOUN a pipe for carrying liquids, electric cables, etc

dud ADJECTIVE, *informal* useless, broken

dudgeon NOUN: **in high dudgeon** very angry, indignant

due ADJECTIVE **1** owed, needing to be paid: *The rent is due next week* **2** expected to arrive etc: *They're due here at six* **3** proper, appropriate: *due care* ▸ADVERB directly: *due south* ▸NOUN **1** something you have a right to: *Give him his due, he did own up in the end* **2** (**dues**) the amount of money charged for belonging to a club etc **due to** brought about by, caused by

duel NOUN a formalized fight with pistols or swords between two people ▸VERB (**duelling, duelled**) to fight in a duel

> Do not confuse with: **dual**

duellist NOUN someone who fights in a duel

duet (*pronounced* dyoo-**et**) NOUN a piece of music for two singers or players

duff ADJECTIVE, *informal* useless, broken

duffel bag NOUN a cylindrical canvas bag tied with a drawstring

duffel coat NOUN a heavy woollen coat, fastened with toggles

[i] After *Duffel*, a town in Belgium where the fabric was first made

duffer NOUN, *informal* a stupid or incompetent person

dug *past form* of **dig**

dugout NOUN **1** a boat made by hollowing out the trunk of a tree **2** a rough shelter dug out of a slope or bank or in a trench **3** *football* a bench beside the pitch for team managers, trainers and substitutes

duke NOUN a nobleman next in rank below a prince

dukedom NOUN the title, rank or lands of a duke

dulcet (*pronounced* **dul**-sit) ADJECTIVE pleasant-sounding, melodious

dull ADJECTIVE **1** not lively **2** slow to understand or learn **3** not exciting or interesting **4** of weather: cloudy, not bright or clear **5** not bright in colour **6** of sounds: not clear or ringing **7** blunt, not sharp **8** of pain: present in the background, but not acute ▸VERB to make dull > **dullness** NOUN > **dully** ADVERB (adjective, meanings 1, 5, 6 and 8)

duly ADVERB at the proper or expected time; as expected: *He duly arrived*

dumb ADJECTIVE **1** without the power of speech **2** silent **3** *informal* stupid

dumbfounded ADJECTIVE astonished

dumbly ADVERB in silence

dumb show NOUN acting without words

dummy NOUN (*plural* **dummies**) **1** a mock-up of something used for display **2** a model used for displaying clothes etc **3** an artificial teat used to comfort a baby **4** *slang* a stupid person

dummy run NOUN a try-out, a practice

dump VERB **1** to throw down heavily **2** to unload and leave (rubbish etc) **3** to sell at a low price ▸NOUN a place for leaving rubbish **in the dumps** *informal* feeling low or depressed

dumpling NOUN a cooked ball of dough

A B C D E F G H I J K L M N O P Q R S T U V W X Y Z

dumpy ADJECTIVE (**dumpier, dumpiest**) short and thick or fat

dun[1] ADJECTIVE greyish-brown, mouse-coloured

dun[2] VERB (**dunning, dunned**) to press for payment

dunce NOUN a stupid or slow-learning person

ⓘ Originally a term of abuse applied to followers of the medieval Scottish philosopher, John *Duns Scotus*

dunderhead NOUN, *informal* a stupid person

dune NOUN a low hill of sand caused by drifting

dung NOUN animal faeces, manure

dungarees PLURAL NOUN trousers made of coarse, hard-wearing material with a bib

dungeon NOUN a dark underground prison

duo NOUN (*plural* **duos**) **1** a pair of musicians or performers **2** people considered a pair

dupe NOUN someone easily cheated ▶ VERB to deceive, trick

duplicate ADJECTIVE (*pronounced* **joo**-pli-k*a*t) exactly the same ▶ NOUN (*pronounced* **joo**-pli-k*a*t) an exact copy ▶ VERB (*pronounced* **joo**-pli-keit) to make a copy or copies of > **duplication** NOUN

duplicity NOUN deceit, double-dealing > **duplicitous** ADJECTIVE

durable ADJECTIVE lasting, able to last; wearing well > **durability** NOUN

duration NOUN the time a thing lasts **for the duration** for a long time, for ages

duress (*pronounced* dyoo-**res**) NOUN illegal force used to make someone do something **under duress** under the influence of force, threats, etc

during PREPOSITION **1** throughout all or part of: *We lived here during the war* **2** at a particular point within: *She died during the night*

dusk NOUN twilight, partial dark

dusky ADJECTIVE (**duskier, duskiest**) dark-coloured > **duskiness** NOUN

dust NOUN **1** fine grains or specks of earth, sand, etc **2** fine powder ▶ VERB **1** to remove dust from: *dusted the table* **2** to sprinkle lightly with powder

dustbin NOUN, *geography* a container for household rubbish

duster NOUN a cloth for removing dust

dustman NOUN (*plural* **dustmen**) someone employed to collect household rubbish

dusty ADJECTIVE (**dustier, dustiest**) covered with dust

dutiful ADJECTIVE obedient > **dutifully** ADVERB

duty NOUN (*plural* **duties**) **1** something a person ought to do **2** an action required to be done **3** a tax **4** (**duties**) the various tasks involved in a job

duty-free ADJECTIVE not taxed

duvet (*pronounced* **doo**-vei) NOUN a quilt stuffed with feathers or synthetic material, used instead of blankets

DVD ABBREVIATION digital versatile disc or digital video disc, a CD that can store large amounts of audio and visual content

DVD-ROM ABBREVIATION digital versatile disc read only memory, a type of disk capable of holding a greater amount of video or audio data than a conventional CD

dwarf NOUN (*plural* **dwarfs** *or* **dwarves**) an undersized person, animal or plant ▶ VERB to make to appear small by comparison ▶ ADJECTIVE not growing to full or usual height: *a dwarf cherry tree*

dwell VERB to live, inhabit, stay **dwell on** to think habitually about something: *dwelling on the past*

dwindle VERB to grow less, waste away

dye VERB (**dyeing, dyed**) to give a colour to (fabric etc) ▶ NOUN a powder or liquid for colouring > **dyeing** NOUN

dying *present participle* of **die**[1]

dyke *another spelling* of **dike**

dynamic ADJECTIVE forceful, energetic > **dynamically** ADVERB

dynamics SINGULAR NOUN the scientific study of movement and force (also called: **kinetics**)

dynamite NOUN a type of powerful explosive

dynamo NOUN (*plural* **dynamos**) a device for turning mechanical energy into electricity

dynasty (*pronounced* **din**-*as*-ti) NOUN (*plural* **dynasties**) a succession of monarchs, leaders, etc of the same family > **dynastic** ADJECTIVE

dys- (*pronounced* dis) PREFIX forms words which describe disorders of some part of the body or of the mind: *dyslexia/dyspepsia/dysentery*

[i] Comes from Greek prefix *dys-* meaning 'badly'

dysentery (*pronounced* **dis**-en-te-ri) NOUN a severe infectious disease of the intestine causing fever, pain and diarrhoea

dyslexia NOUN difficulty in learning to read and write and in spelling

dyslexic NOUN & ADJECTIVE (someone) suffering from dyslexia

A B C D E F G H I J K L M N O P Q R S T U V W X Y Z

Ee

E[1] ABBREVIATION **1** east; eastern **2** the drug Ecstasy

E[2] NOUN **1** *music* the third note in the scale of C major **2** *informal* a tablet of the drug Ecstasy

each ADJECTIVE of two or more things: every one taken individually: *There is a postbox on each side of the road/She was late on each occasion* ▸ PRONOUN every one individually: *Each of them won a prize* **each other** used when an action takes place between two people: *We don't see each other very often*

eager ADJECTIVE keen, anxious to do or get (something) > **eagerly** ADVERB

eagle NOUN a kind of large bird of prey

eaglet NOUN a young eagle

ear NOUN **1** the part of the body through which you hear sounds **2** a head (of corn etc) **lend an ear** to listen

eardrum NOUN the membrane in the middle of the ear (*also called*: **tympanic membrane**)

earl NOUN a member of the British aristocracy between a marquis and a viscount

earlobe NOUN the soft fleshy part at the bottom of the human ear

early ADJECTIVE (**earlier, earliest**) **1** in good time **2** at or near the beginning: *in an earlier chapter* **3** sooner than expected: *You're early!* ▸ ADVERB: *The bus left early* > **earliness** NOUN

earmark VERB to mark or set aside for a special purpose

earmuffs PLURAL NOUN two pads of warm material joined by a band across the head, which you use to cover your ears to stop them getting cold

earn VERB **1** to receive (money) for work **2** to deserve

earnest ADJECTIVE serious, serious-minded ▸ NOUN seriousness **in earnest** meaning what you say or do > **earnestly** ADVERB

earnings PLURAL NOUN pay for work done

earphones PLURAL NOUN a pair of tiny speakers fitting in or against the ear for listening to a radio etc

ear-piercing ADJECTIVE very loud or shrill

earplugs PLURAL NOUN a pair of plugs placed in the ears to block off outside noise

earring NOUN a piece of jewellery worn on the ear

earshot NOUN the distance at which a sound can be heard

earth NOUN **1** the third planet from the sun; our world **2** its surface **3** soil **4** the hole of a fox, badger, etc **5** an electrical connection with the ground ▸ VERB to connect electrically with the ground

earthenware NOUN pottery, dishes made of clay

earthiness NOUN coarseness, naturalness, lack of refinement

earthly ADJECTIVE of the earth as opposed to heaven

earthquake NOUN a movement of the earth's crust, causing the surface to shake

earthshattering ADJECTIVE of great importance

earthworm NOUN the common worm

earthy ADJECTIVE (**earthier, earthiest**) **1** like soil **2** covered in soil **3** coarse and natural, not refined

earwig NOUN a type of insect with pincers at its tail

ease NOUN **1** freedom from difficulty: *finished the race with ease* **2** freedom from pain, worry or embarrassment **3** rest from work ▸ VERB **1** to make or become less painful or difficult **2** to move carefully and gradually: *Ease the stone into position* **at ease** comfortable, relaxed **stand at ease** to stand with your legs apart and arms behind your back

easel NOUN a stand for an artist's canvas while painting etc

easily ADVERB **1** without difficulty **2** without pain, worry or discomfort **3** obviously, clearly, beyond doubt or by a long way: *He's easily the most accomplished actor in Britain today* **4** very possibly: *He could easily be out*

easiness NOUN the quality of being or feeling easy

east NOUN the direction from which the sun rises, one of the four main points of the compass ▸ ADJECTIVE in or to the east

Easter NOUN **1** the Christian celebration of Christ's rising from the dead **2** the weekend when this is celebrated each year, sometime in spring

easterly ADJECTIVE of the wind: coming from or facing the east

eastern ADJECTIVE of the east

eastward *or* **eastwards** ADJECTIVE & ADVERB towards the east

easy ADJECTIVE (**easier, easiest**) **1** not hard to do **2** free from pain, worry or discomfort

eat VERB (**eating, ate, eaten**) **1** to chew and swallow (food) **2** to destroy gradually, waste away

eatable ADJECTIVE fit to eat, edible

eaves PLURAL NOUN the edge of a roof overhanging the walls

eavesdrop VERB (**eavesdropping, eavesdropped**) to listen secretly to a private conversation
> **eavesdropper** NOUN

ebb NOUN **1** the flowing away of the tide after high tide **2** a lessening, a worsening ▸ VERB **1** to flow away **2** to grow less or worse

ebony NOUN a type of black, hard wood ▶ ADJECTIVE **1** made of ebony **2** black

eccentric ADJECTIVE **1** odd, acting strangely **2** of circles: not having the same centre (*contrasted with*: **concentric**)

eccentricity NOUN (*plural* **eccentricities**) oddness of manner or conduct

echo NOUN (*plural* **echoes**) **1** the repetition of a sound caused by its striking a surface and coming back **2** something that evokes a memory: *echoes of the past* ▶ VERB **1** to send back sound **2** to repeat (a thing said)

eclipse NOUN **1** the covering of the whole or part of the sun (**solar eclipse**) or moon (**lunar eclipse**), eg when the moon comes between the sun and the earth **2** loss of position or prestige ▶ VERB **1** to throw into the shade **2** to blot out (someone's achievement) by doing better

eco- PREFIX relating to the environment: *ecofriendly/eco-summit*

eco-friendly ADJECTIVE not harmful to or threatening the environment

ecological ADJECTIVE **1** having to do with plants, animals, etc and their natural surroundings **2** concerned with protecting and preserving plants, animals and the natural environment > **ecologically** ADVERB

ecologist NOUN someone who studies, or is an expert in, ecology

ecology NOUN the study of plants, animals, etc in relation to their natural surroundings

🄸 Comes from Greek *oikos* meaning 'house', and *logos* meaning 'discourse'

e-commerce NOUN, *computing* the buying and selling of goods on the Internet

economic ADJECTIVE **1** concerning economy **2** making a profit

> Do not confuse: **economic** and **economical**

economical ADJECTIVE thrifty, not wasteful

economics SINGULAR NOUN the study of how money is created and spent

economist NOUN someone who studies or is an expert on economics

economize *or* **economise** VERB to be careful in spending or using

economy NOUN (*plural* **economies**) **1** the management of a country's finances **2** the careful use of something, especially money

ecosystem NOUN a community of living things and their relationship with their environment

Ecstasy NOUN a powerful hallucinatory drug

ecstasy NOUN (*plural* **ecstasies**) very great joy or pleasure > **ecstatic** ADJECTIVE > **ecstatically** ADVERB

-ectomy *see* **-tomy**

eczema (*pronounced* **ek**-sim-*a*) NOUN a skin disease causing itching red patches on the skin

eddy NOUN (*plural* **eddies**) a circling current of water or air running against the main stream ▶ VERB to flow in circles

edge NOUN **1** the border of

anything, farthest from the middle **2** a line joining two vertices in a figure **3** sharpness: *put an edge on my appetite* **4** advantage: *Brazil had the edge at half-time* ▸ VERB **1** to put a border on **2** to move little by little: *edging forward* **on edge** nervous, edgy **set someone's teeth on edge** to grate on their nerves, make them wince

edgeways ADVERB sideways

edging NOUN a border, a fringe

edgy ADJECTIVE (**edgier, edgiest**) unable to relax, irritable

edible ADJECTIVE fit to be eaten

edict NOUN an order, a command

edifice NOUN a large building

edify VERB (**edifies, edifying, edified**) to improve the mind, enlighten > **edifying** ADJECTIVE

edit VERB to prepare (a text, film, etc) for publication or broadcasting

edition NOUN **1** the form in which a book etc is published after being edited **2** the copies of a book, newspaper, etc printed at one time **3** a special issue of a newspaper, eg for a local area

editor NOUN **1** someone who edits a book, film, etc **2** the chief journalist of a newspaper or section of a newspaper: *the sports editor*

editorial ADJECTIVE of editing ▸ NOUN a newspaper column written by or on behalf of the chief editor, giving an opinion on a topic

educate VERB to teach (people), especially in a school or college

educated ADJECTIVE knowledgeable and cultured, as a result of receiving a good education

educated guess NOUN a guess based on knowledge of the subject involved

education NOUN **1** the process or system of teaching in schools and other establishments **2** the development of a person's knowledge

educational ADJECTIVE **1** concerned with formal teaching **2** concerned with giving information, rather than simply entertaining or amusing

eel NOUN a long, ribbon-shaped fish

eerie ADJECTIVE causing fear of the unknown > **eerily** ADVERB

ⓘ Originally a Scots word meaning 'afraid' or 'cowardly'

efface VERB to rub out **efface yourself** to avoid drawing attention to yourself

effect NOUN **1** the result of an action **2** strength, power: *The pills had little effect* **3** an impression produced: *the effect of the sunset* **4** general meaning **5** use, operation: *That law is not yet in effect* ▸ VERB to bring about

ⓘ Comes from Latin *effectus* meaning 'finished'

> Do not confuse with: **affect**. **Effect** is usually a noun. **Affect** is usually a verb. To **affect** means 'to have an **effect** on'.

effective ADJECTIVE **1** producing the desired effect **2** actual

effectual ADJECTIVE able to do what is required

effeminate ADJECTIVE unmanly, womanish

a b c d e f g h i j k l m n o p q r s t u v w x y z

A B C D E F G H I J K L M N O P Q R S T U V W X Y Z

effervesce VERB to froth up > **effervescence** NOUN > **effervescent** ADJECTIVE

efficient ADJECTIVE able to do things well; capable > **efficiency** NOUN > **efficiently** ADVERB

effigy NOUN (*plural* **effigies**) a likeness of a person carved in stone, wood, etc

effluent NOUN **1** a stream flowing from another stream or lake **2** liquid industrial waste; sewage

effort NOUN **1** an attempt using a lot of strength or ability **2** hard work

effrontery NOUN impudence

effusive ADJECTIVE speaking freely, gushing > **effusively** ADVERB

EFL ABBREVIATION English as a foreign language

eg ABBREVIATION for example (from Latin *exempli gratia*)

egg NOUN **1** an oval shell containing the embryo of a bird, insect or reptile **2** (*also called*: **ovum**) a human reproductive cell **3** a hen's egg used for eating **egg on** to urge, encourage

eggplant NOUN, *US* an aubergine

ego NOUN (*plural* **egos**) **1** the conscious self **2** self-conceit, egotism

egoism *or* **egotism** NOUN the habit of considering only your own interests, selfishness > **egoist** *or* **egotist** NOUN > **egoistic** *or* **egotistic** ADJECTIVE

Eid *or* **Eid-ul-Fitr** *see* **Id-ul-Fitr** NOUN a Muslim festival celebrating the end of Ramadan

eiderdown NOUN **1** soft feathers from the eider, a type of northern sea-duck **2** a feather quilt

eight NOUN the number 8 ▸ ADJECTIVE 8 in number

eighteen NOUN the number 18 ▸ ADJECTIVE 18 in number

eighteenth ADJECTIVE the last of a series of eighteen ▸ NOUN one of eighteen equal parts

eighth ADJECTIVE the last of a series of eight ▸ NOUN one of eight equal parts

eightieth ADJECTIVE the last of a series of eighty ▸ NOUN one of eighty equal parts

eighty NOUN the number 80 ▸ ADJECTIVE 80 in number

either ADJECTIVE & PRONOUN **1** one or other of two: *Either bus will go there/Either of the dates would suit me* **2** each of two, both: *There is a crossing on either side of the road* ▸ CONJUNCTION used with **or** to show alternatives: *Either he goes or I do* ▸ ADVERB any more than another: *That won't work either*

ejaculate VERB **1** to emit semen **2** to shout out, exclaim > **ejaculation** NOUN

eject VERB **1** to throw out **2** to force to leave a house, job, etc > **ejection** NOUN

elaborate VERB (*pronounced* **i-lab-**o-reit) **1** to work out in detail: *You must elaborate your escape plan* **2** (often **elaborate on**) to explain fully ▸ ADJECTIVE (*pronounced* **i-lab-**o-rat) highly detailed or decorated > **elaboration** NOUN

elapse VERB of time: to pass

elastic ADJECTIVE able to stretch and spring back again, springy ▸ NOUN a piece of cotton etc interwoven with rubber to make it springy > **elasticity** NOUN

elated ADJECTIVE in high spirits, very pleased > **elation** NOUN

elbow NOUN the joint where the arm bends ▶ VERB to push with the elbow, jostle

elbow-grease NOUN, *informal* **1** vigorous rubbing **2** hard work, effort

elbow-room NOUN plenty of room to move

elder[1] ADJECTIVE older ▶ NOUN someone who is older

elder[2] NOUN a type of tree with purple-black berries

elderberry NOUN (*plural* **elderberries**) a berry from the elder tree

elderly ADJECTIVE nearing old age

eldest ADJECTIVE oldest

elect VERB **1** to choose by voting **2** to choose (to) ▶ ADJECTIVE **1** chosen **2** (*placed after the noun*) chosen for a post but not yet in it: *president elect*

election NOUN the choosing by vote of people to sit in parliament, hold an official position, etc

electorate NOUN all those who have the right to vote

electric *or* **electrical** ADJECTIVE produced or worked by electricity

electrician NOUN someone skilled in working with electricity

electricity NOUN a form of energy used to give light, heat and power

electric shock NOUN a violent jerking of the body caused by an electric current passing through it

electrify VERB (**electrifies, electrifying, electrified**) **1** to supply with electricity **2** to excite greatly

electro- PREFIX electric, of or by electricity

[i] Comes from Greek *elektro-*, a form of *elektron* meaning 'amber'

electrocute VERB to kill by an electric current > **electrocution** NOUN

electrode NOUN a conductor through which an electric current enters or leaves a battery etc

electromagnet NOUN a piece of soft metal magnetized by an electric current > **electromagnetic** ADJECTIVE

electron NOUN a very light particle with the smallest possible charge of electricity, which orbits the nucleus of an atom (*see also*: **neutron**, **proton**)

electronic ADJECTIVE of or using electrical circuits

electronics SINGULAR NOUN a branch of physics dealing with electrical circuits and their use in machines etc

electroplating NOUN using an electric current to coat an object with metal

elegant ADJECTIVE **1** graceful, well-dressed, fashionable **2** of clothes etc: well-made and tasteful > **elegance** NOUN > **elegantly** ADVERB

elegy NOUN (*plural* **elegies**) a poem written on someone's death

element NOUN **1** a part of anything **2** a substance that cannot be split chemically into simpler substances, eg oxygen, iron, etc **3** a heating wire carrying the current in an electric heater or kettle **4** (**elements**) basic

A B C D E F G H I J K L M N O P Q R S T U V W X Y Z

facts or skills **5** (**elements**) the powers of nature, the weather **in your element** in the surroundings you find enjoyable or natural

elemental ADJECTIVE of the elements

elementary ADJECTIVE **1** at the first stage **2** simple

elephant NOUN a very large animal with a thick skin, a trunk and two ivory tusks

elevate VERB to raise to a higher position

elevation NOUN **1** the act of raising up **2** rising ground **3** height **4** a drawing of a building as seen from the side **5** *maths* an angle measuring height: *the sun's elevation*

elevator NOUN, *US* a lift in a building

eleven NOUN **1** the number 11 **2** a team of eleven players, eg for cricket ▶ ADJECTIVE 11 in number

elevenses PLURAL NOUN coffee, biscuits, etc taken around eleven o'clock in the morning

eleventh ADJECTIVE the last of a series of eleven ▶ NOUN one of eleven equal parts

elf NOUN (*plural* **elves**) a tiny, mischievous supernatural creature that looks like a little human being

elicit VERB to draw out (information etc)

🛈 Comes from Latin *elicit-*, a form of *elicere* meaning 'to lure out'

> Do not confuse with: **illicit**

eligible ADJECTIVE fit or worthy to be chosen, especially for marriage > **eligibility** NOUN

eliminate VERB **1** to get rid of **2** to exclude, omit > **elimination** NOUN

élite *or* **elite** (*pronounced* ei-**leet**) NOUN a part of a group selected as, or believed to be, the best

elixir (*pronounced* e-**liks**-eer) NOUN a liquid believed to give eternal life, or to be able to turn iron etc into gold

elk NOUN a very large deer found in N Europe and Asia, related to the moose

ellipse NOUN (*plural* **ellipses**) an oval shape

elliptic *or* **elliptical** ADJECTIVE **1** oval **2** having part of the words or meaning left out

elm NOUN a tree with a rough bark and leaves with saw-like edges

elocution NOUN **1** the art of what is thought to be correct speech **2** style of speaking

elongate VERB to stretch out lengthwise, make longer > **elongation** NOUN

elope VERB to run away from home to get married > **elopement** NOUN

eloquent ADJECTIVE **1** good at expressing thoughts in words **2** persuasive > **eloquence** NOUN

else ADVERB otherwise: *Come inside or else you will catch cold* ▶ ADJECTIVE other than the person or thing mentioned: *Someone else has taken her place*

elsewhere ADVERB in or to another place

elude VERB **1** to escape by a trick **2** to be too difficult to remember or understand

🛈 Comes from Latin *eludere* meaning 'to outplay'

> Do not confuse with: **allude**

elusive ADJECTIVE hard to catch

> Do not confuse with: **allusive** and **illusive**. **Elusive** comes from the verb **elude**.

em- *see* **in-**

emaciated ADJECTIVE very thin, like a skeleton

e-mail *or* **email** NOUN electronic mail, messages exchanged across a network of computers

emanate VERB to flow, come out from > **emanation** NOUN

emancipate VERB to set free, eg from slavery or repressive social conditions > **emancipation** NOUN

embalm VERB to preserve (a dead body) from decay by treating it with spices or drugs

embankment NOUN a bank of earth or stone to keep back water, or carry a railway over low-lying places

embargo NOUN (*plural* **embargoes**) an official order forbidding something, especially trade with another country

embark VERB to go on board ship **embark on** to start (a new career etc)

embarrass VERB to make (someone) feel uncomfortable and self-conscious > **embarrassed** ADJECTIVE > **embarrassing** ADJECTIVE > **embarrassment** NOUN

embassy NOUN (*plural* **embassies**) the offices and staff of an ambassador in a foreign country

embellish VERB **1** to decorate **2** to add details to (a story etc) > **embellishment** NOUN

ember NOUN a piece of wood or coal glowing in a fire

embezzle VERB to use for yourself money entrusted to you > **embezzlement** NOUN

emblem NOUN an image which represents something: *The dove is the emblem of peace*

embodiment NOUN a person or thing that perfectly symbolizes some idea or quality

embody VERB (**embodies, embodying, embodied**) **1** to include **2** to express, give form to: *embodying the spirit of the age*

emboss VERB to make a pattern in leather, metal, etc, which stands out from a flat surface > **embossed** ADJECTIVE

embrace VERB **1** to throw your arms round in affection **2** to include **3** to accept, adopt eagerly ▶ NOUN an affectionate hug

embroider VERB **1** to decorate with designs in needlework **2** to add false details to (a story)

embroidery NOUN **1** the art or practice of sewing designs on to cloth **2** the designs sewn on to cloth

embroil VERB **1** to get (someone) into a quarrel, or into a difficult situation **2** to throw into confusion

embryo NOUN (*plural* **embryos**), *biology* the beginning of anything

embryonic ADJECTIVE in an early stage of development

emerald NOUN a bright green precious stone

emerge VERB **1** to come out **2** to become known or clear > **emergence** NOUN

A B C D E F G H I J K L M N O P Q R S T U V W X Y Z

emergency NOUN (*plural* **emergencies**) an unexpected event requiring very quick action

emergency exit NOUN a way out of a building for use in an emergency

emetic ADJECTIVE causing vomiting ▶NOUN an emetic medicine

emigrant NOUN someone who emigrates

emigrate VERB to leave your country to settle in another > **emigration** NOUN

Comes from Latin *emigrare*, from *e* meaning 'from', and *migrare* meaning 'to remove'

> Do not confuse with: **immigrate**. You are **emigrating** when you leave your home country (the E comes from the Latin meaning 'from'). You **immigrate** to the country where you plan to start living (the IM comes from the Latin meaning 'into').

émigré (*pronounced* ei-mee-**grei**) NOUN someone who is forced to emigrate for political reasons

eminence NOUN **1** distinction, fame **2** a title of honour **3** a hill

eminent ADJECTIVE famous, notable

Comes from Latin *eminens* meaning 'standing out'

> Do not confuse with: **imminent**

eminently ADVERB very, obviously: *eminently suitable*

emit VERB (**emitting, emitted**) to send or give out (light, sound, etc) > **emission** NOUN

emotion NOUN a feeling that disturbs or excites the mind, eg fear, love, hatred

emotional ADJECTIVE **1** moving the feelings **2** of a person: tending to show feelings easily or excessively > **emotionally** ADVERB

emotive ADJECTIVE causing emotion rather than thought

empathize *or* **empathise** VERB to share another person's feelings

empathy NOUN the ability to share another person's feelings etc

emperor NOUN the ruler of an empire

emphasis NOUN **1** stress placed on a word or part of a word in speaking **2** greater attention or importance: *The emphasis is on playing, not winning*

emphasize *or* **emphasise** VERB to put emphasis on; call attention to

emphatic ADJECTIVE spoken strongly: *an emphatic 'no'* > **emphatically** ADVERB

empire NOUN **1** a group of nations etc under the same ruling power **2** a large business organization including several companies

empirical ADJECTIVE based on experiment and experience, not on theory alone > **empiricism** NOUN

employ VERB **1** to give work to **2** to use **3** to occupy the time of ▶NOUN employment

employee NOUN someone who works for someone else in return for payment

employer NOUN someone who gives work to employees

employment NOUN work, occupation

emporium NOUN (*plural* **emporia** *or* **emporiums**) a large shop; a market

empower VERB **1** to authorize **2** to give self-confidence to

empress NOUN the female ruler of an empire

empty ADJECTIVE (**emptier, emptiest**) **1** containing nothing or no one **2** unlikely to result in anything: *empty threats* ▶ VERB (**empties, emptying, emptied**) to make or become empty ▶ NOUN (*plural* **empties**) an empty bottle etc > **emptiness** NOUN

emu NOUN a type of Australian bird which cannot fly

emulate VERB to try to do as well as, or better than > **emulation** NOUN

emulsion NOUN a milky liquid, especially that made by mixing oil and water

en- *see* **in-**

enable VERB to make it possible for, allow: *The money enabled him to retire*

enact VERB to act, perform

enamel NOUN **1** a glassy coating fired on to metal **2** a paint with a glossy finish **3** the smooth white coating of the teeth ▶ VERB (**enamelling, enamelled**) to coat or paint with enamel

enamoured ADJECTIVE (**enamoured of**) fond of

encampment NOUN a military camp

encapsulate VERB to capture the essence of; describe briefly and accurately

enchant VERB **1** to delight, please greatly **2** to put a spell or charm on > **enchanter, enchantress** NOUN (meaning 2)

enchanting ADJECTIVE delightful, charming

enchantment NOUN **1** a feeling of delight and wonder **2** a spell or charm

enclave NOUN an area enclosed within foreign territory

enclose VERB **1** to put inside an envelope with a letter etc **2** to put (eg a wall) around

enclosure NOUN **1** the act of enclosing **2** something enclosed eg with a letter **3** a small field with a high fence or wall round it

encompass VERB to surround; to include

encore (*pronounced* **ong**-kawr) NOUN **1** an extra performance of a song etc in reply to audience applause **2** a call for an encore

encounter VERB **1** to meet by chance **2** to come up against (a difficulty, enemy, etc) ▶ NOUN a meeting, a fight

encourage VERB **1** to give hope or confidence to **2** to urge (to do) > **encouragement** NOUN > **encouraging** ADJECTIVE (meaning 1)

encumber VERB to burden, load down

encumbrance NOUN a heavy burden, a hindrance

encyclopedia *or* **encyclopaedia** NOUN a reference book containing information on

A B C D E F G H I J K L M N O P Q R S T U V W X Y Z

many subjects, or on a particular subject

encyclopedic *or* **encyclopaedic** ADJECTIVE giving complete information

end NOUN **1** the last point or part **2** death **3** the farthest point of the length of something: *at the end of the road* **4** a result aimed at **5** a small piece left over ▶ VERB to bring or come to an end **on end 1** standing on one end **2** in a series, without a stop: *go for days on end without eating*

ⓘ Comes from Old English *ende*

endanger VERB to put in danger or at risk

endangered species NOUN a plant or animal in danger of becoming extinct

endear VERB to make dear or more dear

endearing ADJECTIVE appealing

endearment NOUN an expression of love

endeavour VERB to try hard (to) ▶ NOUN a determined attempt

ending NOUN the last part

endorse VERB **1** to give your support to something said or written **2** to indicate on a motor licence that the owner has broken a driving law > **endorsement** NOUN

endurance NOUN the ability to withstand long periods of pressure, hardship, etc

endure VERB to bear without giving way; last

enema (*pronounced* **en**-im-*a*) NOUN the injection of fluid into the bowels

enemy NOUN (*plural* **enemies**) **1** someone hostile to another; a foe **2** someone armed to fight against another **3** someone who is against something: *an enemy of socialism*

energetic ADJECTIVE active, lively > **energetically** ADVERB

energy NOUN (*plural* **energies**) **1** strength to act, vigour **2** a form of power, eg electricity, heat, etc

enfold VERB to enclose, embrace

enforce VERB to cause (a law etc) to be carried out

enfranchise VERB **1** to set free **2** to give the right to vote to

engage VERB **1** to begin to employ (workers etc) **2** to book in advance **3** to take or keep hold of (someone's attention etc) **4** to be busy with, be occupied (in) **5** to begin fighting

engaged ADJECTIVE **1** bound by a promise of marriage **2** busy with something **3** of a telephone, room: in use

engagement NOUN **1** a promise of marriage **2** an appointment to meet **3** a fight: *naval engagement*

engaging ADJECTIVE pleasant, charming

engine NOUN **1** a machine which converts heat or other energy into motion **2** the part of a train which pulls the coaches

engineer NOUN **1** someone who works with, or designs, engines or machines **2** someone who designs or makes bridges, roads, etc ▶ VERB to bring about by clever planning

engineering NOUN the science of designing machines, roadmaking, etc

engrave VERB **1** to draw with a special tool on glass, metal, etc **2** to make a deep impression on: *engraved on his memory*

engraving NOUN a print made from a cut-out drawing in metal or wood

engross VERB to take up the whole interest or attention

engulf VERB to swallow up wholly

enhance VERB to improve, make greater or better

enigma NOUN something or someone difficult to understand, a mystery > **enigmatic** ADJECTIVE

enjoy VERB **1** to take pleasure in **2** to experience, have (something beneficial): *enjoying good health*

enjoyable ADJECTIVE pleasant and satisfying

enjoyment NOUN **1** pleasure and satisfaction **2** the experiencing or having (of something beneficial)

enlarge VERB **1** to make larger **2 enlarge on** to say much or more about something

enlargement NOUN **1** an increase in size **2** a larger photograph made from a smaller one **3** *maths* a transformation that produces a larger figure with its dimensions in the same ratio (*compare with*: **reflection**, **rotation**, **translation**)

enlighten VERB **1** to give more knowledge or information to **2** to correct the false beliefs of

enlightenment NOUN **1** new understanding or awareness **2** (**The Enlightenment**) a European philosophical movement of the 18th century, which believed in human progress and questioned tradition and authority

enlist VERB **1** to join an army etc **2** to obtain the support and help of

enliven VERB to make more active or cheerful

en masse (*pronounced* on **mas**) ADVERB all together, in a body

enmity NOUN hostility

enormity NOUN **1** hugeness **2** extreme wickedness

enormous ADJECTIVE very large

enormously ADVERB **1** very greatly, a great deal: *enjoy yourself enormously* **2** extremely: *enormously confident*

enough ADJECTIVE & PRONOUN (in) the number or amount wanted or needed: *I have enough coins/Do you have enough money?* ▶ ADVERB as much as is wanted or necessary: *She's been there often enough to know the way*

enquire *see* **inquire**

enquiring *see* **inquiring**

enquiry *see* **inquiry**

enrage VERB to make angry

enrich VERB **1** to make something richer in quality or value **2** to make more wealthy > **enriched** ADJECTIVE

enrol *or* **enroll** VERB (**enrolling, enrolled**) to enter (a name) in a register or list, eg as a member or student > **enrolment** NOUN

en route (*pronounced* on **root**) ADVERB on the way

ensconce VERB: **ensconce yourself** to settle yourself comfortably

ensemble NOUN **1** the parts of a thing taken together **2** an outfit of clothes **3** a group of musicians

a b c d e f g h i j k l m n o p q r s t u v w x y z

A B C D E F G H I J K L M N O P Q R S T U V W X Y Z

enslave VERB to make a slave of
ensue VERB **1** to follow, come after **2** to result (from)
ensure VERB to make sure

> Do not confuse with: **insure**

entail VERB to bring as a result, involve: *The job entailed extra work*
entangle VERB **1** to make tangled or complicated **2** to involve (in difficulties)
entente (*pronounced* on-**tont**) NOUN a friendly agreement or relationship between countries
enter VERB **1** to go or come in or into **2** to put (a name etc) on to a list **3** to take part (in) **4** to begin (on)
enterprise NOUN **1** an undertaking, especially if risky or difficult **2** boldness in trying new things **3** a business concern
enterprising ADJECTIVE inventive, clever, original, go-ahead
entertain VERB **1** to amuse **2** to receive as a guest **3** to give a party **4** to consider (eg a suggestion)
entertainer NOUN someone who entertains professionally
entertaining ADJECTIVE amusing
entertainment NOUN **1** performances and activities that amuse and interest people **2** a performance or activity organized for the public
enthral VERB (**enthralling, enthralled**) to hold the attention or give great delight to
enthuse VERB to be enthusiastic (about)
enthusiasm NOUN great interest and keenness
enthusiast NOUN someone who is very keen on a certain activity
enthusiastic ADJECTIVE greatly interested, very keen > **enthusiastically** ADVERB
entice VERB to attract with promises, rewards, etc
enticing ADJECTIVE very attractive and tempting
entire ADJECTIVE whole, complete
entirely ADVERB utterly, wholly, fully, absolutely
entirety NOUN whole and complete state
entitle VERB **1** to give a name to (a book etc) **2** to give (someone) a right to > **entitlement** NOUN
entity NOUN (*plural* **entities**) something which exists; a being
entomology NOUN the study of insects > **entomologist** NOUN
entrails PLURAL NOUN the inner parts of an animal's body, the bowels
entrance[1] (*pronounced* **en**-trans) NOUN **1** a place for entering, eg a door **2** the act of coming in **3** the right to enter
entrance[2] (*pronounced* in-**trahns**) VERB **1** to delight, charm **2** to bewitch > **entrancing** ADJECTIVE
entrant NOUN someone who goes in for a race, competition, etc
entrepreneur (*pronounced* on-tr*e*-pr*e*-**ner**) NOUN someone who undertakes an enterprise, often involving financial risk
entrepreneurial (*pronounced* ong-tr*e*-pr*e*-**ner**-i-*a*l *or* ong-tr*e*-pr*e*-**nyoo**-ri-*a*l) ADJECTIVE of an entrepreneur

entrust *or* **intrust** VERB to place in someone else's care

entry NOUN (*plural* **entries**) **1** the act of entering **2** a place for entering, a doorway **3** a name or item in a record book

E-number NOUN an identification code for food additives, eg E102 for tartrazine

enumerate VERB **1** to count **2** to mention individually > **enumeration** NOUN

enunciate VERB to pronounce distinctly > **enunciation** NOUN

envelop (*pronounced* in-**vel**-op) VERB **1** to cover by wrapping **2** to surround entirely: *enveloped in mist*

envelope NOUN **1** a sealable paper cover, especially for a letter **2** any wrapper or cover

enviable ADJECTIVE worth envying, worth having

envious ADJECTIVE feeling envy > **enviously** ADVERB

environment NOUN the particular surroundings, circumstances, etc in which a person or an animal lives > **environmental** ADJECTIVE

environs (*pronounced* in-**vai**-ronz) PLURAL NOUN surrounding area, neighbourhood

envisage VERB to visualize, picture in the mind

envoy (*pronounced* **en**-voi) NOUN a messenger, especially one sent to deal with a foreign government

envy NOUN (*plural* **envies**) greedy desire for someone else's property, qualities, etc ▸ VERB (**envies, envying, envied**) to feel envy for

enzyme NOUN, *biology, chemistry* a substance produced in a living body which affects the speed of chemical changes

eon *another spelling* of **aeon**

epaulet *or* **epaulette** NOUN a shoulder ornament on a uniform

ephemeral ADJECTIVE very short-lived, fleeting > **ephemerality** NOUN

epi- *or* **ep-** PREFIX upon or over: *epidermis*

ℹ Comes from Greek *epi* meaning 'on' or 'over'

epic NOUN a long poem, story, film, etc about heroic deeds ▸ ADJECTIVE **1** of an epic; heroic **2** large-scale, impressive

epicentre *or US* **epicenter** NOUN the centre of an earthquake

epicure NOUN a person who appreciates fine food and drink > **epicurean** ADJECTIVE

epidemic NOUN a widespread outbreak of a disease etc

epidermis NOUN the top covering of the skin > **epidermal** *or* **epidermic** ADJECTIVE

epiglottis NOUN, *anatomy* the flap of cartilage at the back of the tongue which closes the windpipe during swallowing

epigram NOUN a short, witty saying > **epigrammatic** ADJECTIVE

epilepsy NOUN, *medicine* an illness causing attacks of unconsciousness and convulsions

epileptic ADJECTIVE **1** suffering from epilepsy **2** of epilepsy: *an epileptic fit* ▸ NOUN someone suffering from epilepsy

epilogue *or US* **epilog** NOUN **1** the very end part of a book, programme, etc **2** a speech at the end of a play

epiphany NOUN **1** (**Epiphany**) a Christian festival celebrated on 6 January commemorating the showing of Christ to the three wise men **2** a sudden revelation or insight

episode NOUN **1** one of several parts of a story etc **2** an interesting event

episodic ADJECTIVE happening at irregular intervals

epistle NOUN a formal letter, especially one from an apostle of Christ in the Bible

epitaph NOUN words on a gravestone about a dead person

epithet NOUN a word used to describe someone; an adjective

epitome (*pronounced* i-**pit**-*o*m-i) NOUN a perfect example or representative of something: *the epitome of good taste*

epitomize *or* **epitomise** VERB to be the epitome of something

epoch (*pronounced* **eep**-ok) NOUN an extended period of time, often marked by a series of important events > **epochal** (*pronounced* **ep**-ok-*a*l) ADJECTIVE

equ- PREFIX of or relating to horses: *equine/equestrian*

ⓘ Comes from Latin *equus* meaning 'horse'

equal ADJECTIVE **1** of the same size, value, quantity, etc **2** evenly balanced ▸NOUN someone of the same rank, cleverness, etc as another ▸VERB (**equalling, equalled**) **1** to be or make equal to **2** to be the same as > **equally** ADVERB

equality NOUN equal treatment for all the people in a group or society

equalize *or* **equalise** VERB to make equal

equalizer *or* **equaliser** NOUN a goal etc which draws the score in a game

equanimity NOUN evenness of temper, calmness

equate VERB **1** to regard or treat as the same **2** to state as being equal

equation NOUN *maths* a statement, especially in mathematics, that two things are equal

equator NOUN an imaginary line around the earth, halfway between the North and South Poles

ⓘ From a Latin word meaning literally 'something that makes equal', because night and day are of equal length there

equatorial ADJECTIVE on or near the equator

equestrian ADJECTIVE **1** of horse-riding **2** on horseback ▸NOUN a horse-rider

equi- PREFIX equal

ⓘ Comes from Latin *aequus* meaning 'equal'

equilateral ADJECTIVE, *maths* of a triangle or other polygon: with all sides equal (*compare with*: **isosceles**)

equilibrium NOUN **1** *physics* equal balance between weights, forces, etc, so there is no tendency to move **2** a balanced state of mind or feelings

equine ADJECTIVE of or like a horse

equinox NOUN either of the times (about 21 March and 23 September) when the sun crosses the equator, making night and day equal in length > **equinoctial** ADJECTIVE

equip VERB (**equipping, equipped**) to supply with everything needed for a task

equipment NOUN a set of tools etc needed for a task; an outfit

equity NOUN **1** fairness, just dealing **2** (**Equity**) the trade union for the British acting profession **negative equity** *see* **negative equity**

equivalent ADJECTIVE equal in value, power, meaning, etc ▸ NOUN something that is the equal of another

equivocal ADJECTIVE having more than one meaning; ambiguous, uncertain > **equivocally** ADVERB

era NOUN a period in history: *the Jacobean era/the era of steam*

eradicate VERB to get rid of completely > **eradication** NOUN

erase VERB **1** to rub out **2** to remove

eraser NOUN something which erases, a rubber

erasure NOUN **1** a letter or word that has been rubbed out **2** the complete removal or destruction of something

erect VERB **1** to build **2** to set upright ▸ ADJECTIVE standing straight up

erection NOUN **1** the act of erecting **2** something erected or erect

ermine (*pronounced* **er**-min) NOUN **1** a stoat **2** its white fur

[i] From *Armenia*, because the ermine was known to the Romans as the 'Armenian mouse'

erode VERB to wear away, destroy gradually

erosion NOUN **1** a gradual destruction: *the erosion of my confidence* **2** *geography* the gradual wearing away of the land by water, wind *etc*

erotic ADJECTIVE of or arousing sexual desire

erotica PLURAL NOUN erotic art or literature

err VERB **1** to make a mistake **2** to sin

errand NOUN a short journey to carry a message, buy something, etc

errant ADJECTIVE **1** doing wrong **2** *old* wandering in search of adventure: *knight errant*

erratic ADJECTIVE **1** irregular, not following a fixed course **2** not steady or reliable in behaviour > **erratically** ADVERB

erroneous ADJECTIVE wrong, mistaken > **erroneously** ADVERB

error NOUN **1** a mistake **2** wrongdoing

erudite ADJECTIVE well-educated or well-read, learned > **erudition** NOUN

erupt VERB to break out or through

eruption NOUN **1** an outburst from a volcano **2** a rash or spot on the skin

escalate VERB to increase in amount, intensity, etc > **escalation** NOUN

escalator NOUN a moving stairway

escapade NOUN an adventure

escape VERB **1** to get away safe or free **2** of gas etc: to leak **3** to slip from memory: *His name escapes me* ▸ NOUN the act of escaping

escapism NOUN the tendency to escape from reality by daydreaming etc > **escapist** NOUN & ADJECTIVE

a b c d e f g h i j k l m n o p q r s t u v w x y z

A B C D E F G H I J K L M N O P Q R S T U V W X Y Z

escarpment NOUN a steep side of a hill or rock (*also called*: **scarp**)

escort NOUN someone who accompanies others for protection, courtesy, etc ▶ VERB to act as escort to

Eskimo NOUN (*plural* **Eskimos**) Inuit

ⓘ Based on a Native American name meaning 'eaters of raw flesh'

ESP ABBREVIATION extrasensory perception, the supposed ability to perceive things without the normal senses, eg what someone is thinking or what will happen in the future

especially ADVERB particularly

> Do not confuse with: **specially**. **Especially** means 'particularly, above all': *I like making cakes, especially for birthdays* . **Specially** means 'for a special purpose': *I made this cake specially for your birthday* .

Esperanto NOUN an international language created in the 19th century

espionage NOUN spying, especially by one country to find out the secrets of another

esplanade NOUN a level roadway, especially along a seafront

espresso NOUN strong coffee made by extraction under high pressure

Esq *abbreviation or* **Esquire** NOUN a courtesy title written after a man's name: *Robert Brown, Esq*

essay NOUN (*pronounced* **es**-ei) **1** a written composition **2** an attempt ▶ VERB (*pronounced* es-**ei**) to try

essence NOUN **1** the most important part or quality of something **2** a concentrated extract from a plant etc: *vanilla essence*

essential ADJECTIVE absolutely necessary ▶ NOUN an absolute requirement

essentially ADVERB **1** basically **2** necessarily

establish VERB **1** to settle in position **2** to found, set up **3** to show to be true, prove (that)

established ADJECTIVE **1** firmly set up **2** accepted, recognized **3** of a church: officially recognized as national

establishment NOUN **1** a place of business, residence, etc **2** (**The Establishment**) the people holding influential positions in a community

estate NOUN **1** a large piece of private land **2** someone's total possessions **3** land built on with houses, factories, etc: *housing estate/industrial estate*

estate agent NOUN someone who sells and leases property for clients

estate car NOUN a car with an inside luggage compartment and a rear door

esteem VERB to think highly of; value ▶ NOUN high value or opinion

esteemed ADJECTIVE respected, valued

estimate VERB (*pronounced* **es**-tim-eit) to judge roughly the size, amount or value of something ▶ NOUN (*pronounced* **es**-tim-*a*t) a rough judgement of size etc

estimation NOUN opinion, judgement

estranged ADJECTIVE no longer friendly; separated

estuary NOUN (*plural* **estuaries**) the wide lower part of a river, up which the tide travels

etc *or* **&c** ABBREVIATION and other things of the same sort

[i] from Latin *et cetera*

etch VERB to draw on metal or glass by eating out the lines with acid

etching NOUN a picture printed from an etched metal plate

eternal ADJECTIVE **1** lasting for ever **2** seemingly endless

eternally ADVERB for ever

eternity NOUN **1** time without end **2** the time or state after death

ether NOUN a colourless liquid used as an anaesthetic, or to dissolve fats

ethereal (*pronounced* i-**theer**-ri-*a*l) ADJECTIVE delicate, airy, spirit-like > **ethereality** NOUN > **ethereally** ADVERB

ethical ADJECTIVE having to do with right behaviour, justice, duty; right, just, honourable > **ethically** ADVERB

ethics SINGULAR NOUN **1** the study of right and wrong **2** (belief in) standards leading to right, ethical behaviour

ethnic ADJECTIVE **1** of race or culture **2** of the culture of a particular race or group > **ethnically** ADVERB

ethnic cleansing NOUN the removal of the members of less powerful ethnic groups by the most powerful ethnic group living in an area

ethnicity NOUN racial or cultural character

ethnic minority NOUN a section of a society belonging to a different racial group than the majority

ethnocentric ADJECTIVE believing in the superiority of your own culture > **ethnocentrism** NOUN

ethnology NOUN the study of human cultures and civilizations > **ethnological** ADJECTIVE > **ethnologist** NOUN

etiolated ADJECTIVE of a plant: yellow through lack of sunlight > **etiolation** NOUN

etiquette NOUN rules governing correct social behaviour

etymology NOUN (*plural* **etymologies**) **1** the study of the history of words **2** the history of a word > **etymological** ADJECTIVE

EU ABBREVIATION European Union

eucalyptus NOUN (*plural* **eucalyptuses** *or* **eucalypti**) a large Australian evergreen tree whose leaves produce a pungent oil

Eucharist NOUN **1** the Christian sacrament of the Lord's Supper **2** bread and wine etc taken as a sacrament

eulogize *or* **eulogise** VERB to praise greatly

eulogy NOUN (*plural* **eulogies**) a speech, poem, etc in praise of someone

eunuch (*pronounced* **yoo**-*nuk*) NOUN a castrated man

euphemism (*pronounced* **yoof**-*e*-mizm) NOUN a vague word or phrase used to refer to an unpleasant subject, eg 'passed on' for 'died' > **euphemistic** ADJECTIVE

euphoria NOUN a feeling of great happiness, joy > **euphoric** ADJECTIVE

Euro- PREFIX of Europe or the

A B C D E F G H I J K L M N O P Q R S T U V W X Y Z

European community: *Euro-budget/Eurocrat*

euro NOUN the unit of currency of some members of the European Union, made up of 100 cents

European Union NOUN (*abbrev* **EU**) an economic and political association of European states

Eurosceptic NOUN & ADJECTIVE, *Brit* (someone) opposed to strengthening the powers of the European Union

euthanasia NOUN the killing of someone painlessly, especially to end suffering

evacuate VERB **1** to (cause to) leave, especially because of danger **2** to empty (the bowels) > **evacuation** NOUN

evacuee NOUN someone who has been evacuated (from danger)

evade VERB to avoid or escape, especially by cleverness or trickery

evaluate VERB to find or state the value or worth of > **evaluation** NOUN

evangelical ADJECTIVE **1** spreading Christian teaching **2** strongly supporting and speaking for some cause

evangelist NOUN **1** a person who spreads Christian teaching **2** (**Evangelist**) an author of a Gospel, especially Matthew, Mark, Luke or John > **evangelistic** ADJECTIVE

evaporate VERB **1** of water: to change into vapour **2** to vanish > **evaporation** NOUN

evasion NOUN **1** the act of evading **2** an attempt to avoid the point of an argument or accusation

evasive ADJECTIVE with the purpose of evading; not straightforward: *an evasive answer*

eve NOUN **1** the evening or day before a festival: *New Year's Eve* **2** the time just before an event: *the eve of the revolution*

even ADJECTIVE **1** level, smooth **2** equal **3** of a number: able to be divided by 2 without a remainder (*contrasted with*: **odd**) **4** calm ▸ ADVERB **1** used to emphasize another word: *even harder than before/even a child would understand* **2** exactly, just ▸ VERB to make even or smooth **even out** to become equal **get even with** to get revenge on

even-handed ADVERB fair, unbiased

evening NOUN the last part of the day and early part of the night

evenly ADVERB **1** levelly, smoothly **2** equally **3** calmly

evenness NOUN the quality of being even

evensong NOUN an evening service in the Anglican church

event NOUN **1** an important or memorable happening **2** an item in a programme of sports etc

eventful ADJECTIVE exciting

eventual ADJECTIVE **1** final **2** happening as a result

eventuality NOUN (*plural* **eventualities**) a possible happening

eventually ADVERB at last, finally

ever ADVERB **1** always, for ever **2** at any time, at all: *I won't ever see her again* **3** that has existed, on record: *the best ever*

evergreen NOUN a tree with green leaves all the year round
everlasting ADJECTIVE lasting for ever, eternal
evermore ADVERB, *old* forever
every ADJECTIVE each of several things without exception **every other** one out of every two, alternate
everybody *or* **everyone** PRONOUN each person without exception
everyday ADJECTIVE **1** daily **2** common, usual
everything PRONOUN all things
everywhere ADVERB in every place
evict VERB to force (someone) out of their house, especially by law > **eviction** NOUN
evidence NOUN **1** a clear sign; proof **2** information given in a law case
evident ADJECTIVE easily seen or understood
evidently ADVERB seemingly, obviously
evil ADJECTIVE wicked, very bad; malicious ▸ NOUN wickedness > **evilly** ADVERB
evocative ADJECTIVE evoking memories or atmosphere
evoke VERB to draw out, produce: *evoking memories of their childhood*
evolution NOUN **1** gradual development **2** *biology* the belief that the higher forms of life have gradually developed out of the lower > **evolutionary** ADJECTIVE
evolve VERB **1** to develop gradually **2** to work out (a plan etc)
ewe NOUN a female sheep
ex NOUN, *informal* a former husband, wife or lover
ex- PREFIX **1** no longer, former: *ex-husband/ex-president* **2** outside, not in: *ex-directory number*

ⓘ Comes from Latin *ex* meaning 'out of' or 'from'

exacerbate VERB to make worse or more severe

ⓘ Comes from Latin *acerbare* meaning 'to embitter'

> Do not confuse with: **exasperate**

exact ADJECTIVE **1** accurate, precise **2** careful ▸ VERB to compel to pay, give, etc: *exacting revenge*
exacting ADJECTIVE **1** asking too much **2** wearying, tiring
exactly ADVERB **1** precisely **2** as a reply to something someone has said: 'that's right' or 'I agree'
exactness NOUN accuracy, correctness
exaggerate VERB to make (something) seem larger or greater than it really is > **exaggeration** NOUN
exalt VERB **1** to raise in rank **2** to praise **3** to make joyful
exaltation NOUN **1** joy **2** the act of praising and glorifying someone or something
exam NOUN an examination
examination NOUN **1** a formal test of knowledge or skill: *driving examination* **2** a close inspection or inquiry **3** formal questioning
examine VERB **1** to put questions

A B C D E F G H I J K L M N O P Q R S T U V W X Y Z

to (pupils etc) to test knowledge **2** to question (a witness) **3** to look at closely, inquire into **4** to look over (someone's body) for signs of illness > **examiner** NOUN (meaning 1)

example NOUN **1** something taken as a representative of its kind: *an example of an early computer game* **2** a warning: *make an example of someone*

exasperate VERB to make very angry > **exasperation** NOUN

ⓘ Comes from Latin *asperare* meaning 'to make rough'

> Do not confuse with: **exacerbate**

excavate VERB **1** to dig, scoop out **2** to uncover by digging

excavation NOUN **1** the act of digging out **2** a hollow made by digging

excavator NOUN a machine used for excavating

exceed VERB to go beyond, be greater than

ⓘ Comes from Latin *ex-* meaning 'beyond', and *cedere* meaning 'to go'

exceedingly ADVERB very

excel VERB (**excelling, excelled**) **1** to do very well **2** to be better than

excellence NOUN the fact of being excellent, very high quality

Excellency NOUN (*plural* **Excellencies**) a title of ambassadors etc

excellent ADJECTIVE unusually or extremely good

except PREPOSITION leaving out, not counting ▸ CONJUNCTION with the exception (that) ▸ VERB to leave out, not to count **except for** with the exception of

excepting PREPOSITION except

exception NOUN **1** something left out **2** something unlike the rest: *an exception to the rule* **take exception to** to object to, be offended by

ⓘ Comes from Latin *exceptio* meaning 'an exception, restriction or objection'

exceptional ADJECTIVE standing out from the rest

exceptionally ADVERB very, extremely

excerpt (*pronounced* **ek**-sert) NOUN a part chosen from a whole work: *excerpt from a play*

ⓘ Comes from Latin *excerptum* meaning 'picked out'

> Do not confuse with: **exert**

excess NOUN (*pronounced* ik-**ses**) **1** a going beyond what is usual or proper **2** the amount by which one thing is greater than another **3** (**excesses**) very bad behaviour ▸ ADJECTIVE (*pronounced* **ek**-ses) beyond the amount allowed

ⓘ For origin, see **exceed**

> Do not confuse with: **access**

excessive ADJECTIVE too much, too great, etc > **excessively** ADVERB

exchange VERB to give (one thing) and get another in return ▸ NOUN **1** the act of exchanging **2** exchanging money of one country for that of another **3** the difference between the value of money in different places: *rate of exchange* **4** a central office or building: *telephone exchange* **5** a place where business shares are bought and sold

exchequer NOUN a government office concerned with a country's finances **Chancellor of the Exchequer** *see* **chancellor**

ℹ From the chequered cloth formerly used on the tables of tax offices, and on which accounts were recorded

excise[1] VERB to cut off or out
> **excision** NOUN

excise[2] NOUN tax on goods etc made and sold within a country and on certain licences etc

excitable ADJECTIVE easily excited

excite VERB **1** to rouse the feelings of **2** to move to action

excited ADJECTIVE unable to be calm because of extreme feelings of happiness, impatience or arousal

excitement NOUN the state of being excited

exciting ADJECTIVE creating feelings of excitement

exclaim VERB to cry or shout out

exclamation NOUN a sudden shout

exclamation mark NOUN a punctuation mark (!) used for emphasis, or to indicate surprise etc

exclude VERB **1** to shut out **2** to prevent from sharing or taking part: *He was excluded from school* **3** to leave out of consideration
> **exclusion** NOUN

exclusive ADJECTIVE **1** only open to certain people, select: *an exclusive club* **2** not obtainable elsewhere: *exclusive offer* **3** (**exclusive of**) not including

excommunicate VERB to expel from membership of a church
> **excommunication** NOUN

excrement NOUN the waste matter passed out of the body by humans or animals

excreta PLURAL NOUN discharged waste products

excrete VERB to discharge (waste matter) from the body > **excretion** NOUN

excruciating ADJECTIVE **1** of pain etc: very severe **2** painfully bad: *an excruciating performance*

excursion NOUN an outing for pleasure, eg a picnic

excusable ADJECTIVE pardonable

excuse VERB (*pronounced* eks-**kyooz**) **1** to forgive, pardon **2** to set free from a duty or task ▶ NOUN (*pronounced* eks-**kyoos**) an explanation for having done something wrong

execute VERB **1** to perform: *execute a dance step* **2** to carry out: *execute instructions* **3** to put to death legally

execution NOUN **1** a doing or performing: *execution of a duty* **2** killing by order of the law

executioner NOUN someone with the job of putting condemned prisoners to death

executive ADJECTIVE having power to act or carry out laws ▶ NOUN **1** the part of a government with such power **2** a business manager

executor NOUN someone who sees that the requests stated in a will are carried out

A B C D E F G H I J K L M N O P Q R S T U V W X Y Z

exemplary ADJECTIVE **1** worth following as an example: *exemplary conduct* **2** acting as a warning: *exemplary punishment*

exemplify VERB (**exemplifies, exemplifying, exemplified**) **1** to be an example of **2** to demonstrate by example

exempt VERB to grant freedom from an unwelcome task, payment, etc ▸ ADJECTIVE free (from), not liable for payment, etc > **exemption** NOUN

exercise NOUN **1** a task for practice **2** a physical routine for training muscles etc ▸ VERB **1** to give exercise to **2** to use: *exercise great care*

Comes from Latin *exercere* meaning 'to make thoroughly effective'

Do not confuse with: **exorcize**

exert VERB to bring into action, use: *exerting great influence* **exert yourself** to make a great effort

Comes from Latin *exsert-*, a form of *exserere* meaning 'to thrust out'

Do not confuse with: **excerpt**

exertion NOUNor **exertions** PLURAL NOUN effort(s); hard work

exeunt VERB of more than one person: leave the stage (a direction printed in the script of a play): *exeunt Rosencrantz and Guildenstern*

exhale VERB to breathe out > **exhalation** NOUN

exhaust VERB **1** to tire out **2** to use up completely: *We've exhausted our supplies* **3** to say all that can be said about (a subject etc) ▸ NOUN a device for expelling waste fumes from internal combustion engines

exhausted ADJECTIVE **1** tired out **2** emptied; used up > **exhaustion** NOUN

exhaustive ADJECTIVE extremely thorough: *exhaustive research* > **exhaustively** ADVERB

exhibit VERB to show; put on public display ▸ NOUN something on display in a gallery etc

exhibition NOUN a public show, an open display

exhibitionism NOUN a tendency to try to attract people's attention

exhibitionist NOUN someone who tries to get people's attention all the time, a show-off

exhibitor NOUN a person who has presented something belonging to them for display at an exhibition

exhilarate VERB to make joyful or lively, refresh > **exhilarating** ADJECTIVE > **exhilaration** NOUN

exhort VERB to urge (to do) > **exhortation** NOUN

exhume VERB to dig out (a buried body) > **exhumation** NOUN

exile NOUN **1** someone who lives outside their own country, by choice or unwillingly **2** a period of living in a foreign country ▸ VERB to drive (someone) away from their own country; banish

exist VERB to be, have life; live

existence NOUN life, being

existent ADJECTIVE existing at the moment

exit NOUN **1** a way out **2** the act of going out: *a hasty exit*

exodus NOUN a going away of many people (especially those leaving a country for ever)

exonerate VERB to free from blame > **exoneration** NOUN

exorbitant ADJECTIVE going beyond what is usual or reasonable: *exorbitant price*

exorcism NOUN the act of driving away evil spirits

exorcist NOUN a person who drives evil spirits away

exorcize *or* **exorcise** VERB **1** to drive out (an evil spirit) **2** to free (a place, person) from possession by an evil spirit

Comes from Greek *ex* meaning 'out', and *horkos* meaning 'an oath'

> Do not confuse with: **exercise**

exoskeleton NOUN in some invertebrates: an external skeleton that forms a rigid covering

exothermic ADJECTIVE, *chemistry* of a process, especially a reaction: involving the release of heat (*contrasted with*: **endothermic**)

exotic ADJECTIVE **1** coming from a foreign country **2** unusual, colourful

expand VERB **1** to grow wider or bigger **2** to open out

expanse NOUN a wide stretch of land etc

expansion NOUN a growing, stretching or spreading

expansive ADJECTIVE **1** spreading out **2** talkative; open and eager to talk > **expansively** ADVERB

expat NOUN, *informal* an expatriate

expatriate ADJECTIVE living outside your native country ▶ NOUN someone living abroad

expect VERB **1** to think of as likely to happen or arrive soon: *What did you expect her to say?* **2** to think, assume: *I expect he's too busy*

expectancy NOUN the feeling of excitement that you get when you know something good is about to happen

expectant ADJECTIVE **1** hopeful, expecting **2** waiting to become: *expectant mother*

expectation NOUN a firm belief or hope that something will happen

expecting ADJECTIVE, *informal* pregnant

expedience *or* **expediency** NOUN speed or convenience in a particular situation, rather than fairness or truth

expedient ADJECTIVE done for speed or convenience rather than fairness or truth ▶ NOUN something done to get round a difficulty

expedition NOUN **1** a journey with a purpose, often for exploration **2** people making such a journey

expeditionary ADJECTIVE of or forming an expedition

expel VERB (**expelling, expelled**) **1** to drive or force out **2** to send away in disgrace, eg from a school

expend VERB to spend, use up

expenditure NOUN an amount spent or used up, especially money

expense NOUN **1** cost **2** something money is spent on: *The house was a continual expense* **3** (**expenses**) money spent in carrying out a job etc

A B C D E F G H I J K L M N O P Q R S T U V W X Y Z

expensive ADJECTIVE costing a lot of money > **expensively** ADVERB

experience NOUN **1** an event in which you are involved: *a horrific experience* **2** knowledge gained from events, practice, etc ▸ VERB to go through, undergo

experienced ADJECTIVE skilled, knowledgeable

experiment NOUN a trial, a test (of an idea, machine, etc) ▸ VERB to carry out experiments

experimental ADJECTIVE of something new: being done for the first time, to see how successful it will be > **experimentally** ADVERB

expert ADJECTIVE highly skilful or knowledgeable (in a particular subject) ▸ NOUN someone who is highly skilled or knowledgeable > **expertly** ADVERB

expertise (*pronounced* eks-per-**teez**) NOUN skill

expire VERB **1** to come to an end, become invalid: *Your visa has expired* **2** to die

expiry NOUN the end or finish

explain VERB **1** to make clear **2** to give reasons for: *Please explain your behaviour*

explanation NOUN a statement which makes clear something difficult or puzzling; a reason (eg for your behaviour)

explanatory (*pronounced* eks-**plan**-*a*t-ri) ADJECTIVE intended to make clear

expletive NOUN an exclamation, especially a swear word

explicable ADJECTIVE able to be explained

explicit ADJECTIVE plainly stated or shown; outspoken, frank > **explicitly** ADVERB

explode VERB **1** to blow up like a bomb with loud noise **2** to prove to be wrong or unfounded: *That explodes your theory*

exploit NOUN (*pronounced* **eks**-ploit) a daring deed; a feat ▸ VERB (*pronounced* eks-**ploit**) **1** to make use of selfishly **2** to make good use of (resources etc) > **exploitation** NOUN

exploration NOUN **1** travel for the sake of discovery **2** the act of searching or searching for something thoroughly

exploratory (*pronounced* eks-**plo**-r*a*t-ri) ADJECTIVE of surgery: aiming to establish the nature of a complaint rather than to treat it

explore VERB **1** to make a journey of discovery **2** to think about very carefully, research > **explorer** NOUN (meaning 1)

explosion NOUN **1** a sudden violent increase in pressure, which generates heat and shock waves **2** a sudden outburst or surge

explosive ADJECTIVE **1** liable to explode **2** hot-tempered ▸ NOUN something that will explode, eg gunpowder

exponent NOUN **1** someone who shows skill in a particular art or craft: *an exponent of karate* **2** *maths* an index

exponential ADJECTIVE **1** *maths* relating to exponents **2** having an increasingly steep rate of increase

export VERB (*pronounced* eks-

pawt) 1 to sell goods etc in a foreign country 2 *computing* to send data from one computer, program, etc to another ▸ NOUN (*pronounced* **eks**-pawt) 1 an act of exporting 2 something exported
> **exportation** NOUN

expose VERB 1 to place in full view 2 to show up (a hidden crime etc) 3 to lay open to the sun or wind 4 to allow light to reach and act on (a film)

exposure NOUN 1 the state of being allowed to experience something or be affected by something 2 appearance or mention in public, eg on television or in newspapers 3 the extremely harmful effects of severe cold on a person's body 4 the fact of revealing something about someone, usually something unpleasant, that has been kept secret 5 a single photograph or frame on a film

express VERB 1 to show by action 2 to put into words 3 to press or squeeze out ▸ ADJECTIVE 1 clearly stated: *express instructions* 2 sent in haste: *express messenger* ▸ NOUN a fast train, bus, etc

expression NOUN 1 the look on someone's face: *expression of horror* 2 showing meaning or emotion through language, art, etc 3 a show of emotion in an artistic performance etc 4 a word or phrase: *idiomatic expression* 5 *maths* a symbol or combination of symbols 6 pressing or squeezing out

expressive ADJECTIVE expressing meaning or feeling clearly

expulsion NOUN 1 the act of driving or forcing a person or thing out 2 the sending away of someone in disgrace, eg from a school

exquisite (*pronounced* **eks**-kwiz-it *or* iks-**kwiz**-it) ADJECTIVE 1 extremely beautiful 2 excellent 3 very great, utter: *exquisite pleasure*

extemporize *or* **extemporise** (*pronounced* iks-**tem**-po-raiz) VERB to make up on the spot, improvise

extend VERB 1 to stretch, make longer 2 to hold out: *extended a hand* 3 to last, carry over: *My holiday extends into next week*

extension NOUN 1 a part added, eg to a building 2 an additional amount of time on a schedule, holiday, etc 3 an additional telephone connected with a main one

extensive ADJECTIVE 1 wide; covering a large space 2 happening in many places 3 wide-ranging, sweeping: *extensive changes*
> **extensively** ADVERB

extent NOUN 1 the space something covers 2 degree: *to a great extent*

extenuate VERB 1 to lessen 2 to make (something) seem less bad: *extenuating circumstances*

exterior ADJECTIVE on the outside; outer: *exterior wall* ▸ NOUN the outside of a building etc

exterminate VERB to kill off completely (a race, a type of animal, etc), wipe out > **extermination** NOUN

external ADJECTIVE 1 outside; on the outside 2 not central: *external considerations*

extinct ADJECTIVE 1 of an old volcano: no longer erupting 2 no longer in existence

A B C D E F G H I J K L M N O P Q R S T U V W X Y Z

extinction NOUN making or becoming extinct

extinguish VERB **1** to put out (fire etc) **2** to put an end to

extinguisher NOUN a spray containing chemicals for putting out fires

extol VERB (**extolling, extolled**) to praise greatly

extort VERB to take by force or threats > **extortion** NOUN

extortionate ADJECTIVE of a price: much too high

extra ADJECTIVE more than is usual or necessary; additional ▶ ADVERB unusually; more than is average: *extra large* ▶ NOUN **1** something extra **2** someone employed to be one of a crowd in a film

extra- PREFIX outside, beyond

ⓘ Comes from Latin *extra* meaning 'outside'

extract VERB (*pronounced* eks-**trakt**) **1** to draw or pull out, especially by force: *extract a tooth* **2** to remove selected parts of a book etc **3** to draw out from a mixture by pressure or chemical action ▶ NOUN (*pronounced* **eks**-trakt) **1** an excerpt from a book etc **2** a substance obtained by extracting: *vanilla extract*

extraction NOUN **1** the act of extracting **2** someone's descent or lineage: *of Irish extraction*

extracurricular ADJECTIVE done outside school or college hours

extradite VERB to hand over (someone wanted for trial) to the police of another country > **extradition** NOUN

extramarital ADJECTIVE happening outside a marriage: *extramarital affair*

extramural ADJECTIVE of a university department: teaching courses which are not part of the regular degree courses

extraneous ADJECTIVE having nothing to do with the subject: *extraneous information*

extraordinary ADJECTIVE **1** not usual, exceptional **2** very surprising **3** specially employed: *ambassador extraordinary* > **extraordinarily** ADVERB (meanings 1 and 2)

extrasensory ADJECTIVE beyond the range of the ordinary senses: *extrasensory perception*

extraterrestrial ADJECTIVE from outside the earth ▶ NOUN a being from another planet

extravagant ADJECTIVE **1** spending too freely; wasteful **2** too great, overblown: *extravagant praise* > **extravagance** NOUN > **extravagantly** ADVERB

extravaganza NOUN an extravagant creation or production

extreme ADJECTIVE **1** far from the centre **2** far from the ordinary or usual **3** very great: *extreme sadness* ▶ NOUN an extreme point

extremely ADVERB very, exceptionally

extremist NOUN someone who carries ideas foolishly far > **extremism** NOUN

extremity (*pronounced* eks-**trem**-it-i) NOUN (*plural* **extremities**) **1** a part or place furthest from the centre **2** the quality of being extreme **3** (**extremities**) the hands and feet

extricate VERB to free from (difficulties etc); to disentangle

ⓘ Comes from Latin *extricare* meaning 'to disentangle'

extrovert NOUN an outgoing, sociable person (*contrasted with*: **introvert**)

exuberant ADJECTIVE in very high spirits > **exuberance** NOUN > **exuberantly** ADVERB

exude VERB to give off in large amounts: *exuding sweat/exuded happiness*

exult VERB to be very glad, rejoice greatly: *exulting in their victory* > **exultant** ADJECTIVE > **exultation** NOUN

eye NOUN **1** the part of the body with which you see **2** the ability to notice: *an eye for detail* **3** sight **4** something the shape of an eye, eg the hole in a needle ▸ VERB (**eyeing, eyed**) to look at with interest: *eyeing the last slice of cake*

eyeball NOUN the round part of the eye; the eye itself (the part between the eyelids)

eyebrow NOUN the hairy ridge above the eye

eye-catching ADJECTIVE drawing attention; striking

eyelash NOUN one of the hairs on the edge of the eyelid

eyelet NOUN a small hole for a shoelace etc

eyelid NOUN the skin covering of the eye

eye-opener NOUN an unexpected or revealing sight, experience, etc

eyesight NOUN the ability to see

eyesore NOUN anything that is ugly (especially a building)

eye tooth NOUN a canine tooth

eyewash NOUN a liquid for soothing the eyes

eyewitness NOUN someone who sees a thing done (eg a crime committed)

eyrie (*pronounced* **ee**-*e*-ri) NOUN the nest of an eagle or other bird of prey

Ff

°F ABBREVIATION degree(s) Fahrenheit

FA ABBREVIATION, *Brit* Football Association

fable NOUN a story about animals etc, including a lesson or moral

fabric NOUN **1** cloth **2** framework; the external parts of a building *etc*

fabricate VERB to make up (lies) > **fabrication** NOUN

fabulous ADJECTIVE **1** *informal* very good, excellent **2** imaginary, mythological

fabulously ADVERB extremely, unbelievably: *fabulously rich*

façade (*pronounced* fa-**sahd**) NOUN **1** the front of a building **2** a deceptive appearance or act; a mask

face NOUN **1** the front part of the head **2** the front of anything **3** appearance **4** one of the flat surfaces of a solid figure ▸ VERB **1** to turn or stand in the direction of **2** to stand opposite to **3** to put an additional surface on **face up to** to meet or accept boldly: *facing up to responsibilities*

facelift NOUN **1** a surgical operation to smooth and firm the tissues of the face **2** any procedure for improving the external appearance of something

face pack NOUN a cosmetic paste applied to the face and left to dry before being peeled or washed off

facet (*pronounced* **fas**-it) NOUN **1** a side of a many-sided object, eg a cut gem **2** an aspect; a characteristic

facetious (*pronounced* fa-**see**-sh*us*) ADJECTIVE not meant seriously; joking > **facetiously** ADVERB

facial ADJECTIVE of the face

facile (*pronounced* **fas**-ail) ADJECTIVE **1** not deep or thorough; superficial, glib **2** fluent

facilitate VERB to make easy

facility NOUN (*plural* **facilities**) **1** ease **2** skill, ability **3** (**facilities**) buildings, equipment, etc provided for a purpose: *sports facilities*

facsimile (*pronounced* fak-**sim**-i-li) NOUN an exact copy

fact NOUN **1** something known or held to be true **2** reality **3** *law* a deed **in fact** actually, really

Comes from Latin *factum* meaning 'something done or accomplished'

faction NOUN a group that is part of a larger group: *rival factions*

factor NOUN **1** something affecting the course of events **2** someone who does business for another **3** *maths* a number which exactly divides into another (eg 3 is a factor of 6)

factorize *or* **factorise** VERB, *maths* to find the factors of (a number or expression)

factory NOUN (*plural* **factories**) a workshop producing goods in large quantities

factual ADJECTIVE consisting of facts; real, not fictional: *factual account*

faculty NOUN (*plural* **faculties**) **1** power of the mind, eg reason **2** a natural power of the body, eg hearing **3** a department of study in a university: *Faculty of Arts*

fad NOUN **1** an odd like or dislike **2** a temporary fashion > **faddy** ADJECTIVE

fade VERB **1** to lose colour or strength or cause to lose colour or strength **2** to disappear gradually, eg from sight or hearing

faeces *or US* **feces** (*pronounced* **fees**-eez) PLURAL NOUN solid excrement

faff VERB, *informal* to dither, fumble: *Don't faff about*

fag NOUN **1** tiring work **2** *slang* a cigarette

fag end NOUN, *informal* **1** a cigarette butt **2** the very end, the tail end

faggot *or US* **fagot** NOUN **1** a bundle of sticks **2** a meatball

Fahrenheit NOUN a temperature scale on which water freezes at 32° and boils at 212° ▸ ADJECTIVE measured on this scale: *70° Fahrenheit*

fail VERB **1** to (declare to) be unsuccessful **2** to break down, stop **3** to lose strength **4** to be lacking or insufficient **5** to disappoint **without fail** certainly, for sure

failing NOUN a fault; a weakness

fail-safe ADJECTIVE made to correct automatically, or be safe, if a fault occurs

failure NOUN **1** the act of failing **2** someone or something that fails

faint ADJECTIVE **1** lacking in strength, brightness, etc **2** about to lose consciousness: *feel faint* ▸ VERB to fall down unconscious ▸ NOUN a loss of consciousness

> Do not confuse with: **feint**

faint-hearted ADJECTIVE cowardly, timid

faintly ADVERB dimly, not clearly

faintness NOUN **1** lack of strength, brightness, etc **2** a feeling of weakness, as if you were about to lose consciousness

fair[1] ADJECTIVE **1** of a light colour: *fair hair* **2** of weather: clear and dry **3** unbiased, just: *fair assessment* **4** good enough but not excellent **5** *old* beautiful

fair[2] NOUN **1** a large market held at fixed times **2** an exhibition of goods from different producers etc: *craft fair* **3** a travelling collection of merry-go-rounds, stalls, etc

ⓘ Comes from Late Latin *feria* meaning 'market'

> Do not confuse with: **fare**

fair-haired ADJECTIVE having light-coloured hair; blond

a b c d e f g h i j k l m n o p q r s t u v w x y z

A B C D E F G H I J K L M N O P Q R S T U V W X Y Z

fairly ADVERB **1** in a just and reasonable way **2** rather, reasonably **3** only moderately, to a limited extent

fairness NOUN the quality of being reasonable or just in your treatment of people

fair trade NOUN a system of trade in which fair prices are paid for goods, especially those produced in developing countries

fairway NOUN *golf* the mown part on a golf course, between the tee and the green

fair-weather friend NOUN someone who is a friend only when things are going well

fairy NOUN (*plural* **fairies**) a small imaginary creature, human in shape, with magical powers

fairy light NOUN a small coloured or white light for decorating Christmas trees etc

fairy story *or* **fairy tale** NOUN **1** a traditional story of fairies, giants, etc **2** *informal* a lie

faith NOUN **1** trust **2** belief in a religion or creed **3** loyalty to a promise: *kept faith with them*

faithful ADJECTIVE **1** loyal; keeping your promises **2** true, accurate: *faithful account of events* **3** believing in a particular religion or creed > **faithfully** ADVERB (meanings 1 and 2)

faithless ADJECTIVE **1** untrustworthy, inconstant **2** without faith or belief, especially in God or Christianity

fake ADJECTIVE not genuine, forged ▸NOUN **1** someone who is not what they pretend to be **2** a forgery ▸VERB to make an imitation or forgery of

falcon NOUN a kind of bird of prey

falconry NOUN the training of falcons for hunting > **falconer** NOUN

fall VERB (**falling, fell, fallen**) **1** to drop down **2** to become less **3** of a fortress etc: to be captured **4** to die in battle **5** to happen, occur: *Christmas falls on a Monday this year* ▸NOUN **1** a dropping down **2** something that falls: *a fall of snow* **3** lowering in value etc **4** *US* autumn **5** an accident involving falling **6** ruin, downfall, surrender **7** (**falls**) a waterfall **fall out with** to quarrel with **fall through** of a plan: to fail, come to nothing **fall flat** to fail to have the intended effect

fallacy NOUN (*plural* **fallacies**) a false belief; something believed to be true but really false

fall guy NOUN *informal* a scapegoat

fallible ADJECTIVE liable to make a mistake or to be wrong > **fallibility** NOUN

Fallopian tubes PLURAL NOUN two tubes along which egg cells pass from a woman's ovaries to her uterus

fallout NOUN radioactive dust resulting from the explosion of an atomic bomb etc

fallow ADJECTIVE of land: left unsown for a time after being ploughed

fallow deer NOUN a type of yellowish-brown deer

false ADJECTIVE **1** untrue **2** not real, fake **3** not natural: *false teeth*

falsehood NOUN a lie, an untruth

falseness *or* **falsity** NOUN quality of being false

falsetto NOUN a singing voice forced higher than its natural range

falsify VERB (**falsifies, falsifying, falsified**) to make false, alter for a dishonest purpose: *falsified his tax forms*

falsity *see* **falseness**

falter VERB to stumble or hesitate

fame NOUN the quality of being well-known, renown

famed ADJECTIVE famous

familiar ADJECTIVE **1** well-known **2** seen, known, etc before **3** well-acquainted (with) **4** over-friendly, cheeky > **familiarity** NOUN

familiarize *or* **familiarise** VERB to make quite accustomed or acquainted (with)

family NOUN (*plural* **families**) **1** a couple and their children **2** the children alone **3** a group of people related to one another **4** *biology* a group of animals, languages *etc* with common characteristics

ⓘ Comes from Latin *familia* meaning 'the slaves in a household'

famine NOUN a great shortage of food, usually caused by an increase in population or failure of food crops

famished ADJECTIVE, *informal* very hungry

famous ADJECTIVE well-known, having fame

famously ADVERB, *informal* very well: *get along famously*

fan[1] NOUN **1** a device or appliance for making a rush of air **2** a small hand-held device for cooling the face ▸VERB (**fanning, fanned**) **1** to cause a rush of air with a fan **2** to increase the strength of: *fanning her anger* **fan out** to spread out in the shape of a fan

fan[2] NOUN an admirer, a devoted follower: *a fan of traditional music*

fanatic NOUN someone who is over-enthusiastic about something ▸ADJECTIVE fanatical

fanatical ADJECTIVE wildly or excessively enthusiastic > **fanatically** ADVERB

fanciful ADJECTIVE **1** inclined to have fancies **2** imaginary, not real > **fancifully** ADVERB

fancy NOUN (*plural* **fancies**) **1** a sudden liking or desire: *He had a fancy for ice-cream* **2** imagination **3** something imagined ▸ADJECTIVE (**fancier, fanciest**) not plain, elaborate ▸VERB (**fancies, fancying, fancied**) **1** to picture, imagine **2** to have a liking or a sudden wish for **3** to think without being sure

fancy dress NOUN an elaborate costume worn eg for a party, often representing a famous character

fanfare NOUN a loud flourish from a trumpet or bugle

fang NOUN **1** a long tooth of a wild animal **2** the poison-tooth of a snake

fantastic ADJECTIVE **1** very unusual, strange **2** *informal* very great **3** *informal* excellent

fantasy NOUN (*plural* **fantasies**) **1** an imaginary scene, story, etc **2** an idea not based on reality

fanzine (*pronounced* **fan**-zeen) NOUN, *informal* **1** a magazine for a particular group of fans **2** a small-circulation magazine

FAO ABBREVIATION for the attention of

FAQ *or* **faq** (*pronounced* fak) ABBREVIATION, *computing* frequently asked question(s), a question or list of common questions relating to a particular topic

far (**farther, farthest**) ADVERB **1** at or to a long way: *far off* **2** very much: *far better* ▸ ADJECTIVE **1** a long way off, distant: *a far country* **2** more distant: *the far side* (*see also* **further**)

farce NOUN **1** a play with far-fetched characters and plot **2** a ridiculous situation

ⓘ Based on a French word meaning 'stuffing', after humorous scenes that were performed in between the acts of a play

farcical ADJECTIVE absurd, ridiculous

fare VERB, *formal* to get on (either well or badly): *They fared well in the competition* ▸ NOUN **1** the price of a journey **2** a paying passenger in a taxi etc **3** food

ⓘ Comes from Old English *faran*

> Do not confuse with: **fair**

farewell EXCLAMATION & NOUN goodbye

far-fetched ADJECTIVE very unlikely: *a far-fetched story*

far-flung ADJECTIVE extending over a great distance

farm NOUN **1** an area of land for growing crops, breeding and feeding animals, etc **2** a place where certain animals, fish, etc are reared: *a salmon farm* ▸ VERB to work on a farm **farm out** to give (work) to others to do for payment

farmer NOUN the owner or tenant of a farm

farmhouse NOUN the house attached to a farm

farmstead NOUN a farm and farmhouse

farmyard NOUN the yard surrounded by farm buildings

far-sighted ADJECTIVE foreseeing what is likely to happen and preparing for it

farther and **farthest** *see* **far**

farthing NOUN an old coin, worth ½ of an old penny

fascinate VERB **1** to charm, attract irresistibly **2** to hypnotize

fascinating ADJECTIVE extremely interesting

fascination NOUN an intense and deep interest

fascism (*pronounced* **fash**-iz-em) NOUN a form of authoritarian government characterized by extreme nationalism and suppression of individual freedom

ⓘ From the *fasces*, a bundle of rods with an axe in the middle, carried before magistrates in ancient Rome to symbolize their power to inflict punishment

fascist (*pronounced* **fash**-ist) NOUN **1** a supporter of fascism **2** a right-wing extremist

fashion NOUN **1** the style in which something is made, especially clothes **2** a way of behaving or dressing which is popular for a time **3** a manner, a way: *acting in a strange fashion* ▸ VERB to shape, form **after a fashion** to some extent, in a way **in fashion** fashionable

fashionable ADJECTIVE up-to-date, agreeing with the latest style

fast[1] ADJECTIVE **1** quick-moving **2** of a clock: showing a time in advance of the correct time **3** of dyed colour: fixed, not likely to wash out ▸ ADVERB **1** quickly **2** firmly: *stand fast* **3** soundly, completely: *fast asleep*

fast[2] VERB to go without food voluntarily, eg for religious reasons or as a protest ▸ NOUN a period of fasting

fasten VERB to fix; make firm by tying, nailing, etc > **fastener** *or* **fastening** NOUN

fastidious ADJECTIVE difficult to please, liking things properly done in every detail

fastidiously ADVERB extremely thoroughly, taking much care

fast-track ADJECTIVE of a career: liable for quick promotion

fat NOUN an oily substance made by the bodies of animals and by plants ▸ ADJECTIVE **1** having a lot of fat; plump **2** thick, wide

fatal ADJECTIVE causing death or disaster

fatality NOUN (*plural* **fatalities**) a death, especially caused by accident or disaster

fate NOUN **1** what the future holds; fortune, luck **2** end, death: *met his fate bravely*

fated ADJECTIVE doomed

fateful ADJECTIVE with important consequences; crucial, significant

father NOUN **1** a male parent **2** a priest **3** the creator or inventor of something: *Poe is the father of crime fiction*

fatherhood NOUN the state of being a father

father-in-law NOUN (*plural* **fathers-in-law**) the father of someone's husband or wife

fatherland NOUN someone's native country

fatherly ADJECTIVE kind and protective

fathom NOUN a measure of depth of water (6 feet, 1.83 metres) ▸ VERB to understand, get to the bottom of

fatigue (*pronounced* fa-**teeg**) NOUN **1** great tiredness after physical or mental effort **2** weakness or strain caused by use: *metal fatigue* ▸ VERB to tire out

fatten VERB to make or become fat

fatty ADJECTIVE (**fattier, fattiest**) containing a lot of fat

fatty acid NOUN one of a group of acids found in animal and vegetable fats

fatuous (*pronounced* **fat**-yoo-*us*) ADJECTIVE very foolish > **fatuously** ADVERB

faucet (*pronounced* **faw**-set) NOUN, *US* a water tap

fault NOUN **1** a mistake **2** a flaw, something bad or wrong, eg with a machine **3** a long crack in the earth's surface where a section of the rock layer has slipped

faultless ADJECTIVE perfect > **faultlessly** ADVERB

faulty ADJECTIVE (**faultier, faultiest**) having a fault or faults

faun NOUN a mythological creature, half human and half animal

Do not confuse with: **fawn**

A B C D E F G H I J K L M N O P Q R S T U V W X Y Z

fauna NOUN the animals of a district or country as a whole

faux pas (*pronounced* foh **pah**) NOUN (*plural* **faux pas**) an embarrassing mistake, a blunder

favour *or US* **favor** NOUN **1** a kind action **2** goodwill, approval **3** a gift, a token ▸ VERB **1** to show preference for **2** to be an advantage to: *The darkness favoured our escape* **in favour of 1** in support of **2** for the benefit of

favourable ADJECTIVE **1** showing approval **2** advantageous, helpful (to)

favourably ADVERB in a positive or advantageous way **compare favourably with** to be better than, or at least as good as (the other thing or things mentioned)

favourite ADJECTIVE best liked ▸ NOUN **1** a liked or best-loved person or thing **2** a competitor, horse, etc expected to win a race

favouritism NOUN showing favour towards one person etc more than another

fawn[1] NOUN **1** a young deer **2** a light yellowish-brown colour ▸ ADJECTIVE of this colour

fawn[2] VERB **1** to show affection as a dog does **2** **fawn on** to flatter in a grovelling fashion

> Do not confuse with: **faun**

fax NOUN (*plural* **faxes**) **1** a machine that scans a document electronically and transfers the information by a telephone line to a receiving machine that produces a corresponding copy **2** a document copied and sent in this way ▸ VERB to send by fax

FBI ABBREVIATION, *US* Federal Bureau of Investigation

FE ABBREVIATION Further Education

fear NOUN an unpleasant feeling caused by danger, evil, etc

fearful ADJECTIVE **1** timid, afraid **2** terrible

fearfully ADVERB **1** timidly, showing fear **2** extremely, dreadfully

fearless ADJECTIVE brave, daring > **fearlessly** ADVERB

feasible ADJECTIVE able to be done, likely > **feasibility** NOUN > **feasibly** ADVERB

feast NOUN **1** a rich and plentiful meal **2** a festival day commemorating some event ▸ VERB to eat or hold a feast

feat NOUN a deed requiring some effort

feather NOUN one of the growths which form the outer covering of a bird

feathery ADJECTIVE **1** covered in feathers **2** soft **3** light

feature NOUN **1** an identifying mark, a characteristic **2** a special article in a newspaper etc **3** the main film in a cinema programme **4** a special attraction **5** (**features**) the various parts of someone's face, eg eyes, nose, etc ▸ VERB **1** to have as a feature **2** to take part (in) **3** to be prominent in

February NOUN the second month of the year

From a Latin name for a feast of purification

fed *past form* of **feed**

federal ADJECTIVE joined by treaty or agreement

federation NOUN a group of states etc joined together for a common purpose, a league

fed up ADJECTIVE tired, bored and disgusted

fee NOUN a price paid for work done, or for a special service

feeble ADJECTIVE weak > **feebly** ADVERB

feed VERB (**feeding, fed**) **1** to give food to **2** to eat food **3** to supply with necessary materials ▸ NOUN food for animals: *cattle feed*

feedback NOUN **1** responses and reactions (to something) **2** *computing* the process in which part of the output of a system is returned to the input, in order to regulate the following output **3** in a public-address system: the return of some of the output sound to the microphone, producing a whistle

feel VERB (**feeling, felt**) **1** to explore by touch **2** to experience, be aware of: *He felt no pain* **3** to believe, consider **4** to think (yourself) to be: *I feel ill* **5** to be sorry (for): *We felt for her in her grief* ▸ NOUN an act of touching **feel like** to want, have an inclination for: *Do you feel like going out tonight?*

feeler NOUN one of two thread-like parts on an insect's head for sensing danger etc

feelgood ADJECTIVE *informal* causing a feeling of comfort or security: *feelgood movie*

feeling NOUN **1** sense of touch **2** emotion: *spoken with great feeling* **3** affection **4** an impression, belief

feelings PLURAL NOUN what someone feels inside; emotions

feet *plural* of **foot**

feign (*pronounced* fein) VERB to pretend to feel or be: *feigning illness*

feint[1] (*pronounced* feint) NOUN **1** a pretence **2** a move to put an enemy off guard ▸ VERB to make a feint

> Do not confuse with: **faint**

feint[2] ADJECTIVE of paper: ruled with faint lines: *narrow feint* (= having lines which are close together)

feisty (*pronounced* **fai**-sti) ADJECTIVE (**feistier, feistiest**) *informal* **1** spirited **2** irritable, touchy

felicity NOUN happiness

feline (*pronounced* **fee**-lain) ADJECTIVE **1** of or relating to cats **2** like a cat

fell[1] NOUN a barren hill

fell[2] VERB to cut down (a tree)

fell[3] *past tense* of **fall**

fellow NOUN **2** one of a pair **3** a member of an academic society, college, etc **4** a man, a boy

fellowship NOUN **1** comradeship, friendship **2** an award to a university graduate

felon (*pronounced* **fel**-on) NOUN someone who commits a serious crime

felony (*pronounced* **fel**-o-ni) NOUN (*plural* **felonies**) a serious crime

felt[1] NOUN a type of rough cloth made of rolled and pressed wool

felt[2] *past form* of **feel**

female ADJECTIVE of the sex which

produces children ▸ NOUN a human or animal of this sex

feminine ADJECTIVE **1** of or relating to women **2** characteristic of women

femininity NOUN **1** the circumstance of being a woman **2** the quality of being feminine, or of having physical and mental characteristics traditionally thought suitable and essential for women

feminism NOUN a social and cultural movement aiming to win equal rights for women > **feminist** NOUN & ADJECTIVE

femur (*pronounced* **fee**-mer) NOUN the thigh bone

fen NOUN low marshy land, often covered with water

fence NOUN a railing, hedge, etc for closing in animals or land ▸ VERB **1** to close in with a fence **2** to fight with swords

fencing NOUN **1** material for fences **2** the sport of fighting with swords, using blunted weapons

fend VERB: **fend for yourself** to look after and provide for yourself

fender NOUN **1** a low guard round a fireplace to keep in coal etc **2** a piece of matting over a ship's side acting as a buffer against the quay **3** *US* the bumper of a car

feng shui (*pronounced* fung **shwei**) NOUN positioning furniture, buildings, etc in a way thought to bring good fortune or happiness

ferment VERB (*pronounced* fe-**ment**) **1** to change by fermentation **2** to stir up (trouble etc) ▸ NOUN (*pronounced* **fer**-ment) **1** a state of agitation or excitement **2** a substance that causes fermentation

🛈 Comes from Latin *fermentum* meaning 'yeast'

fermentation NOUN a reaction caused by bringing certain substances together, eg by adding yeast to dough in bread-making

fern NOUN a plant with no flowers and feather-like leaves

ferocious ADJECTIVE fierce, savage > **ferociously** ADVERB > **ferocity** NOUN

-ferous SUFFIX forms adjectives related to the idea of carrying or containing: *coniferous* (= producing cones)

🛈 Comes from Latin *ferre* meaning 'to carry'

ferret NOUN a small weasel-like animal used to chase rabbits out of their warrens ▸ VERB to search busily and persistently

ferry VERB (**ferries, ferrying, ferried**) to carry over water by boat, or overland by aeroplane ▸ NOUN (*plural* **ferries**) a boat which carries passengers and cars etc across a channel

fertile ADJECTIVE **1** able to produce children or young **2** full of ideas, creative, productive > **fertility** NOUN

fertilize *or* **fertilise** VERB **1** to make (soil etc) fertile **2** to start the process of reproduction in (an egg or plant) by combining them with sperm or pollen > **fertilization** NOUN

fertilizer *or* **fertiliser** NOUN manure or chemicals used to make soil more fertile

fervent ADJECTIVE very eager; intense > **fervently** ADVERB

fervour *or US* **fervor** NOUN ardour, zeal

fest *or* **-fest** NOUN & SUFFIX a gathering or festival around some subject: *news-fest/trade fest*

ⓘ Comes from German *Fest* meaning 'a festival'

fester VERB of a wound: to produce pus because of infection

festival NOUN **1** a celebration; a feast **2** a season of musical, theatrical, or other performances

festive ADJECTIVE **1** of a feast **2** in a happy, celebrating mood

festivity NOUN (*plural* **festivities**) a celebration, a feast

festoon VERB to decorate with chains of ribbons, flowers, etc

fetal *or* **feotus** ADJECTIVE relating to the fetus

fetch VERB **1** to go and get **2** to bring in (a price): *fetched £100 at auction*

fete *or* **fête** NOUN a public event with stalls, competitions, etc to raise money ▶ VERB to entertain lavishly, make much of

fetish NOUN (*plural* **fetishes**) **1** a sacred object believed to carry supernatural power **2** an object of excessive fixation or (especially sexual) obsession > **fetishist** NOUN > **fetishistic** ADJECTIVE

fetlock NOUN the part of a horse's leg just above the foot

fetters PLURAL NOUN, *formal* chains for imprisonment

fettle NOUN: **in fine fettle** in good health or condition

fetus *or* **foetus** NOUN (*plural* **fetuses** *or* **foetuses**) **1** the embryo of some mammals during the later stages of development in the uterus **2** a young human being in the womb, from the end of the eighth week after conception until birth (*compare with*: **embryo**)

feud (*pronounced* fyood) NOUN a private, drawn-out war between families, clans, etc

feudal (*pronounced* **fyood**-*al*) ADJECTIVE, *history* of a social system under which tenants were bound to give certain services to the overlord in return for their tenancies > **feudalism** NOUN > **feudalist** ADJECTIVE

fever NOUN an above-normal body temperature and quickened pulse

fevered ADJECTIVE **1** having a fever **2** very excited

feverish ADJECTIVE **1** having a slight fever **2** excited **3** too eager, frantic: *feverish pace*

few ADJECTIVE (**fewer, fewest**) not many: *only a few tickets left* **a good few** *or* **quite a few** several, a considerable number

fiancé (*pronounced* fi-**on**-sei) NOUN the man a woman is engaged to marry

fiancée (*pronounced* fi-**on**-sei) NOUN the woman a man is engaged to marry

fiasco NOUN (*plural* **fiascos**) a complete failure

ⓘ Based on an Italian phrase *far fiasco* 'make a bottle', meaning forget your lines on stage

fib VERB (**fibbing, fibbed**) to lie about something unimportant

▸ NOUN an unimportant lie > **fibber** NOUN

fibre *or US* **fiber** NOUN **1** a single thread or string of a substance **2** the indigestible parts of plants or seeds, that help food move through the body

fibreglass NOUN a lightweight material made of very fine threads of glass, used for building boats etc

fibre-optic ADJECTIVE of a cable: made of glass or plastic filaments which transmit light signals

fibrous ADJECTIVE thread-like, stringy

fickle ADJECTIVE changeable; not stable or loyal

fiction NOUN **1** stories about imaginary characters and events **2** a lie

ⓘ Comes from Latin *fictio* meaning 'a forming'

fictional ADJECTIVE imagined, created for a story: *fictional character*

ⓘ For origin, see **fiction**

> Do not confuse: **fictional** and **fictitious**

fictitious ADJECTIVE **1** not real, imaginary **2** untrue

ⓘ Comes from Latin *ficticius* meaning 'counterfeit'

fiddle NOUN **1** a violin **2** a tricky or delicate operation **3** *informal* a cheat, a swindle ▸ VERB **1** to play the violin **2** to play aimlessly (with) **3** to interfere, tamper (with) **4** *informal* to falsify (accounts etc) with the intention of cheating

fiddly ADJECTIVE (**fiddlier, fiddliest**) needing delicate or careful handling

fidelity NOUN **1** faithfulness **2** truth, accuracy

fidget VERB (**fidgeting, fidgeted**) to move about restlessly

field NOUN **1** a piece of enclosed ground for pasture, crops, sports, etc **2** an area of land containing a natural resource: *goldfield/coalfield* **3** a branch of interest or knowledge **4** those taking part in a race ▸ VERB, *cricket, rounders, etc* to catch the ball and return it

fielder NOUN someone whose role is to catch and return the ball in cricket, rounders, etc

field marshal NOUN the highest ranking army officer

fieldwork NOUN practical work done outside the classroom or home

fiend NOUN **1** an evil spirit **2** *informal* a wicked person **3** *informal* an extreme enthusiast: *a crossword fiend*

fiendish ADJECTIVE **1** evil or wicked **2** extremely bad **3** very complicated or clever

fierce ADJECTIVE **1** very angry-looking, hostile, likely to attack **2** intense, strong: *fierce competition* > **fiercely** ADVERB

fiery ADJECTIVE (**fierier, fieriest**) **1** like fire **2** quick-tempered, volatile > **fieriness** NOUN

fiesta NOUN a religious festival or carnival

fifteen NOUN the number 15 ▸ ADJECTIVE 15 in number

fifteenth ADJECTIVE the last of a series of fifteen ▸ NOUN one of fifteen equal parts

fifth ADJECTIVE the last of a series of five ▶NOUN one of five equal parts

fiftieth ADJECTIVE the last of a series of fifty ▶NOUN one of fifty equal parts

fifty NOUN the number 50 ▶ADJECTIVE 50 in number

fig NOUN **1** a soft roundish fruit with thin, dark skin and red pulp containing many seeds **2** the tree which bears it

fight VERB (**fighting, fought**) **1** to struggle with fists, weapons, etc **2** to quarrel **3** to go to war with ▶NOUN a struggle; a battle

fighter NOUN **1** someone who fights **2** a fast military aircraft that attacks other aircraft

figment NOUN an imaginary story or idea

figurative ADJECTIVE of a word: used not in its ordinary meaning but to show likenesses, eg 'she was a tiger' for 'she was as ferocious as a tiger'; metaphorical (*contrasted with*: **literal**) > **figuratively** ADVERB

figure NOUN **1** outward form or shape **2** a number **3** a geometrical shape **4** an unidentified person: *A shadowy figure approached* **5** a diagram or drawing on a page ▶VERB to appear, take part: *He figures in the story* **figure out** to work out, understand

figurehead NOUN **1** a carved wooden figure fixed to the prow of a ship **2** a leader who has little real power

filament (*pronounced* **fil**-*a*-ment) NOUN **1** a slender thread or fibre **2** a fine wire that emits heat and light when an electric current passes through it, eg in a light bulb

file[1] NOUN **1** a loose-leaf book etc to hold papers **2** *computing* an amount of computer data held under a single name **3** a line of soldiers etc walking one behind another ▶VERB **1** to put (papers etc) in a file **2** to walk in a file

file[2] NOUN a steel tool with a roughened surface for smoothing wood, metal, etc ▶VERB to rub with a file

file extension NOUN, *computing* the 2- or 3-letter suffix, *eg* doc, bmp, xls, *etc*, at the end of a computer file name, separated from the rest of the name by a full stop and showing the file format

filename NOUN, *computing* a name or reference used to specify a file stored in a computer

filibuster NOUN a long speech given in parliament to delay the passing of a law

fill VERB **1** to put (something) into until there is no room for more: *Fill the bucket with water* **2** to become full: *Her eyes filled with tears* **3** to satisfy, fulfil (a requirement etc) **4** to occupy: *fill a post* **5** to appoint someone to (a job etc): *Have you filled the vacancy?* **6** to put something in (a hole) to stop it up ▶NOUN as much as is needed to fill: *We ate our fill* **fill in 1** to fill (a hole) **2** to complete (a form etc) **3** to do another person's job while they are absent: *I'm filling in for Anne* **fill up** to fill completely

fillet NOUN a piece of meat or fish with bones removed ▶VERB (**filleting, filleted**) to remove the bones from

filling NOUN something used to fill a hole or gap ▸ ADJECTIVE of food: satisfying

filling-station NOUN a garage which sells petrol

filly NOUN (*plural* **fillies**) a young female horse

film NOUN **1** a thin skin or coating **2** a strip of celluloid coated with chemicals, on which photographs are taken **3** a narrative photographed on celluloid and shown in a cinema, on television, etc ▸ VERB **1** to photograph on celluloid **2** to develop a thin coating: *His eyes filmed over*

film star NOUN a famous actor or actress in films

filter NOUN **1** a substance that allows liquid and gas through but traps solid matter **2** a green arrow on a traffic light signalling one lane of traffic to move while the main stream is held up ▸ VERB (**filtering, filtered**) **1** to strain through a filter **2** to move or arrive gradually: *The news filtered through* **3** of cars etc: to join a stream of traffic gradually **4** of a lane of traffic: to move in the direction shown by a filter

filth NOUN **1** dirt **2** obscene words or pictures

filthily ADVERB dirtily or obscenely

filthiness NOUN extreme dirtiness or obscenity

filthy ADJECTIVE (**filthier, filthiest**) **1** very dirty **2** obscene, lewd

filtration NOUN filtering

fin NOUN a flexible projecting part of a fish's body used for balance and swimming

final ADJECTIVE **1** last **2** allowing of no argument: *The judge's decision is final* ▸ NOUN the last contest in a competition: *World Cup final*

finale (*pronounced* fi-**nah**-li) NOUN the last part of anything (eg a concert)

finality NOUN the quality of being final and decisive

finalize *or* **finalise** VERB to put (eg plans) in a final or finished form

finally ADVERB in the end, at last, eventually, lastly

finance NOUN **1** money affairs **2** the study or management of these **3** (**finances**) the money someone has to spend ▸ VERB to supply with sums of money > **financial** ADJECTIVE (noun, meaning 1) > **financially** ADVERB (noun, meaning 1)

financier NOUN someone who manages (public) money

finch NOUN (*plural* **finches**) a small bird

find VERB (**finding, found**) **1** to come upon accidentally or after searching: *I found an earring in the street* **2** to discover **3** to judge to be: *finds it hard to live on her pension* ▸ NOUN something found, especially something of interest or value **find out** to discover, detect

[i] Comes from Old English *findan*

fine[1] ADJECTIVE **1** made up of very small pieces, drops, etc **2** not coarse: *fine linen* **3** thin, delicate **4** slight: *a fine distinction* **5** beautiful, handsome **6** of good quality; pure **7** bright, not rainy **8** well, healthy

fine² NOUN money to be paid as a punishment ▸ VERB to compel to pay (money) as punishment

finesse (*pronounced* fi-**nes**) NOUN cleverness and subtlety in handling situations etc

finger NOUN one of the five branching parts of the hand ▸ VERB to touch with the fingers

fingering NOUN **1** the positioning of the fingers in playing a musical instrument **2** the showing of this by numbers

fingerprint NOUN the mark made by the tip of a finger, used by the police as a means of identification

finish VERB **1** to end or complete the making of **2** to stop: *When do you finish work today?* ▸ NOUN (*plural* **finishes**) **1** the end (eg of a race) **2** the last coating of paint, polish, etc

finished ADJECTIVE **1** ended, complete **2** of a person: ruined, not likely to achieve further success etc

finite ADJECTIVE having an end or limit

fiord *or* **fjord** (*pronounced* **fee-awd**) NOUN a long narrow sea inlet between steep hills, especially in Norway

fir NOUN a kind of cone-bearing tree

fir cone NOUN one of the small, woody cones which grow on a fir tree and hold its seeds

fire NOUN **1** the heat and light given off by something burning **2** a mass of burning material, objects, etc **3** a heating device: *electric fire* **4** eagerness, keenness ▸ VERB (**firing, fired**) **1** to set on fire **2** to make (a gun) explode, shoot

fire alarm NOUN a device to sound a bell etc as a warning of fire

firearm NOUN a gun, eg a pistol

fire brigade NOUN a company of firefighters

fire engine NOUN a vehicle carrying firefighters and their equipment

fire escape NOUN a means of escape from a building in case of fire

firefighter NOUN someone whose job it is to put out fires

firefly NOUN (*plural* **fireflies**) a type of insect which glows in the dark

fireguard NOUN a framework of iron placed in front of a fireplace for safety

fireman *or* **firewoman** NOUN (*plural* **firemen** *or* **firewomen**) a firefighter

fireplace NOUN a recess in a room below a chimney for a fire

firewall NOUN, *computing* a piece of software that stops unauthorized access to a computer network

fireworks PLURAL NOUN **1** devices which, when lit, produce coloured sparks, flares, etc, often with accompanying loud bangs **2** *informal* angry behaviour

firm ADJECTIVE **1** not easily moved or shaken **2** with mind made up ▸ NOUN a business company

firmament NOUN, *formal* the heavens, the sky

first ADJECTIVE & ADVERB before all others in place, time, or rank ▸ ADVERB before doing anything else

first-aid NOUN treatment of a wounded or sick person before the doctor's arrival

A B C D E F G H I J K L M N O P Q R S T U V W X Y Z

first-class ADJECTIVE of the highest standard, best kind, etc

first-hand ADJECTIVE direct

First Minister NOUN the leader of the parliament in Scotland or the assembly in Northern Ireland or Wales

first name NOUN a person's name that is not their surname

first-rate ADJECTIVE first-class

firth NOUN especially in Scotland, a narrow arm of the sea, especially at a river mouth

fiscal ADJECTIVE **1** of the public revenue **2** of financial matters

fish NOUN (*plural* **fish** *or* **fishes**) a kind of animal that lives in water, and breathes through gills ▸ VERB **1** to try to catch fish with rod, nets, etc **2** to search (for): *fishing for a handkerchief in her bag* **3** to try to obtain: *fish for compliments*

fisherman NOUN (*plural* **fishermen**) a man who fishes, especially for a living

fishmonger (*pronounced* **fish**-mung-ger) NOUN someone who sells fish for eating

fishy ADJECTIVE (**fishier, fishiest**) **1** like a fish **2** doubtful, arousing suspicion

fission NOUN splitting into pieces

fissure NOUN a crack

fist NOUN a tightly shut hand

fit[1] ADJECTIVE (**fitter, fittest**) **1** suited to a purpose; proper **2** in good training or health ▸ VERB (**fitting, fitted**) **1** to be of the right size or shape for **2** to be suitable for

fit[2] NOUN a sudden attack or spasm of laughter, illness, etc

fitful ADJECTIVE coming or doing in bursts or spasms > **fitfully** ADVERB

fitness NOUN good physical health and strength

fitting ADJECTIVE suitable ▸ NOUN something fixed or fitted in a room, house, etc

five NOUN the number 5 ▸ ADJECTIVE 5 in number

[i] Comes from Old English *fif*

fix VERB **1** to make firm; fasten **2** to mend, repair

fixed ADJECTIVE settled; set in position

fixedly (*pronounced* **fik**-sid-li) ADVERB steadily, intently: *staring fixedly*

fixture NOUN **1** a piece of furniture etc fixed in position **2** an arranged sports match or race

fizz VERB to make a hissing sound ▸ NOUN (*plural* **fizzes**) a hissing sound

fizzle VERB **fizzle out** to fail, coming to nothing

fizzy ADJECTIVE (**fizzier, fizziest**) of a drink: forming bubbles on the surface

fjord *another spelling* of **fiord**

flabbergasted ADJECTIVE, *informal* very surprised

flabby ADJECTIVE (**flabbier, flabbiest**) not firm, soft, limp; weak, feeble > **flabbily** ADVERB

flaccid (*pronounced* **flak**-sid) ADJECTIVE **1** hanging loosely **2** limp, not firm

flag[1] NOUN a banner, standard, or ensign

flag[2] VERB (**flagging, flagged**) to become tired or weak

flag[3] NOUN a flat paving-stone (*also called*: **flagstone**)
flagon NOUN a large container for liquid
flagrant ADJECTIVE **1** conspicuous **2** openly wicked > **flagrancy** NOUN > **flagrantly** ADVERB
flagstone *see* **flag**[3]
flail VERB to wave or swing in the air
flair NOUN talent, skill: *a flair for languages*
flak NOUN **1** anti-aircraft fire **2** *informal* strong criticism
flake NOUN **1** a thin slice or chip of anything **2** a very small piece of snow etc ▸ VERB to form into flakes **flake off** to break off in flakes
flaky ADJECTIVE (**flakier, flakiest**) **1** forming flakes, crumbly: *flaky pastry* **2** *US informal* eccentric
flamboyant ADJECTIVE **1** splendidly coloured **2** too showy, gaudy
flame NOUN the bright leaping light of a fire ▸ VERB **1** to burn brightly **2** *computing slang* to send abusive electronic mail to
flaming ADJECTIVE **1** burning **2** red **3** *informal* violent: *a flaming temper*
flamingo NOUN (*plural* **flamingos** *or* **flamingoes**) a type of long-legged bird with pink or white plumage
flammable ADJECTIVE easily set on fire

> ⓘ **Flammable** and **inflammable** mean the same thing.

flan NOUN a flat, open tart
flank NOUN the side of an animal's body, of an army, etc ▸ VERB **1** to go by the side of **2** to be situated at the side of
flannel NOUN **1** loosely woven woollen fabric **2** a small towel or face cloth
flap NOUN **1** anything broad and loose-hanging: *tent flap* **2** the sound of a wing etc moving through air **3** *informal* a panic: *getting in a flap over nothing* ▸ VERB (**flapping, flapped**) **1** to hang down loosely **2** to move with a flapping noise **3** *informal* to get into a panic
flapjack NOUN **1** *Brit* a biscuit made with rolled oats, butter, and sugar **2** *US* a pancake
flare VERB (**flaring, flared**) **1** to blaze up **2** to widen towards the edge ▸ NOUN a bright light, especially one used at night as a signal, to show the position of a boat in distress etc > **flared** ADJECTIVE
flash NOUN (*plural* **flashes**) **1** a quick burst of light **2** a moment, an instant ▸ VERB **1** to shine out suddenly **2** to pass quickly **in a flash** very quickly or suddenly
flashlight NOUN **1** a burst of light in which a photograph is taken **2** *US* an electric torch
flashy ADJECTIVE (**flashier, flashiest**) showy, gaudy
flask NOUN **1** a narrow-necked bottle **2** a small flat bottle **3** an insulated bottle or vacuum flask
flat[1] ADJECTIVE (**flatter, flattest**) **1** level: *a flat surface* **2** of a drink: no longer fizzy **3** leaving no doubt, downright: *a flat denial* **4** *music* a semitone below the right musical

a b c d e f g h i j k l m n o p q r s t u v w x y z

A B C D E F G H I J K L M N O P Q R S T U V W X Y Z

pitch **5** of a tyre: punctured **6** dull, uninteresting ▸ ADVERB stretched out: *lying flat on her back* ▸ NOUN **1** *music* a sign (♭) which lowers a note by a semitone **2** a punctured tyre **flat out** *informal* as fast as possible, with as much effort as possible

flat[2] NOUN an apartment on one storey of a building

flatfish NOUN a flat-bodied fish with its eyes on the upper surface, eg a sole

flatly ADVERB in a definite or emphatic way: *He flatly refused to help*

flatness NOUN the quality of being flat

flat rate NOUN a rate which is the same in all cases

flatten VERB to make or become flat

flatter VERB to praise insincerely > **flattery** NOUN

flatulence NOUN wind in the stomach > **flatulent** ADJECTIVE

flaunt (*pronounced* flawnt) VERB to display in an obvious way: *flaunted his wealth*

> Do not confuse with: **flout**. Remember that the use of **flaunt** is perfectly illustrated in the well-known phrase 'if you've got it, **flaunt** it'. On the other hand, when you **flout** something, you treat it with contempt instead of showing it off, eg you might '*flout* the rules' or '*flout* tradition'.

flautist (*pronounced* **flawt**-ist) NOUN a flute player

flavour *or US* **flavor** NOUN **1** taste: *lemon flavour* **2** quality or atmosphere: *an exotic flavour* ▸ VERB to give a taste to

flavouring NOUN an ingredient used to give a particular taste: *chocolate flavouring*

flaw NOUN a fault, an imperfection

flawless ADJECTIVE with no faults or blemishes > **flawlessly** ADVERB

flax NOUN a plant whose fibres are woven into linen cloth

flaxen ADJECTIVE **1** made of or looking like flax **2** of hair: fair

flay VERB to strip the skin off

flea NOUN a small, wingless, blood-sucking insect with great jumping power

fleck NOUN a spot, a speck

flecked ADJECTIVE marked with spots or patches

fled *past form* of **flee**

fledgling NOUN a young bird with fully grown feathers

flee VERB (**fleeing, fled**) to run away from danger etc

fleece NOUN **1** a sheep's coat of wool **2** a garment for the upper body which is made of fluffy, warm fabric ▸ VERB **1** to clip wool from **2** *slang* to rob by cheating

fleecy ADJECTIVE (**fleecier, fleeciest**) soft and fluffy like wool

fleet[1] NOUN **1** a number of ships **2** a number of cars or taxis

fleet[2] ADJECTIVE, *poetic* swift; nimble, quick in movement

fleeting ADJECTIVE passing quickly: *fleeting glimpse* > **fleetingly** ADVERB

flesh NOUN **1** the soft tissue which covers the bones of humans and animals **2** meat **3** the body as distinct from the soul or spirit **4** the soft eatable part of fruit **flesh and blood 1** relations, family **2** human, mortal

fleshy ADJECTIVE (**fleshier, fleshiest**) fat, plump

flew *past tense* of **fly**[2]

flex[1] VERB to bend

flex[2] NOUN (*plural* **flexes**) a length of covered wire attached to electrical devices

flexible ADJECTIVE **1** easily bending **2** willing to adapt to new or different conditions > **flexibility** NOUN

flexitime NOUN a system in which an agreed number of hours' work is done at times chosen by the worker

flick VERB to strike lightly with a quick movement ▶NOUN a quick, sharp movement: *a flick of the wrist*

flicker VERB **1** to flutter **2** to burn unsteadily ▶NOUN **1** a brief or unsteady light **2** a fleeting appearance or occurrence: *a flicker of hope*

flight[1] NOUN **1** the act of flying **2** a journey by plane **3** a flock (of birds) **4** a number (of steps)

flight[2] NOUN the act of fleeing or escaping

flighty ADJECTIVE (**flightier, flightiest**) changeable, impulsive

flimsy ADJECTIVE (**flimsier, flimsiest**) **1** thin; easily torn or broken etc **2** weak: *a flimsy excuse*

flinch VERB to move or shrink back in fear, pain, etc

fling VERB (**flinging, flung**) to throw ▶NOUN **1** a throw **2** a casual attempt **3** *informal* a brief romantic affair

flint NOUN a kind of hard stone ▶ADJECTIVE made of flint

flip VERB (**flipping, flipped**) to toss lightly ▶NOUN a light toss or stroke

flippant ADJECTIVE joking, not serious > **flippancy** NOUN > **flippantly** ADVERB

flipper NOUN **1** a limb of a seal, walrus, etc **2** a webbed rubber shoe worn by divers

flip side NOUN, *informal* **1** the converse of anything **2** the reverse side of a record *etc*

flirt VERB to behave in a playful sexual manner ▶NOUN someone who flirts **flirt with** to take an interest in (something) without committing yourself seriously to it **flirt with danger** to take unnecessary risks > **flirtation** NOUN

flirtatious ADJECTIVE fond of flirting

flit VERB (**flitting, flitted**) **1** to move quickly and lightly from place to place **2** *Scottish* to move house

float VERB **1** to keep on the surface of a liquid without sinking **2** to set going: *float a fund* ▶NOUN **1** a cork etc on a fishing line **2** a van delivering milk etc **3** a platform on wheels, used in processions **4** a sum of money set aside for giving change

flock NOUN **1** a number of animals or birds together **2** a large number of people ▶VERB to go (to) in large numbers or in a large crowd **flock together** to gather in a crowd

floe (*pronounced* floh) NOUN a sheet of floating ice

A B C D E F G H I J K L M N O P Q R S T U V W X Y Z

flog VERB (**flogging, flogged**) **1** to beat, lash **2** *slang* to sell > **flogging** NOUN (meaning 1)

flood NOUN **1** a great flow, especially of water **2** the rise or flow of the tide **3** a great quantity: *a flood of letters* ▸ VERB **1** to (cause to) overflow **2** to cover or fill with water

floodlight VERB (**floodlighting, floodlit**) to illuminate with floodlighting ▸ NOUN a light used to floodlight

floodlighting NOUN strong artificial lighting to illuminate an exterior or stage

floor NOUN **1** the base level of a room on which people walk **2** a storey of a building: *a flat on the third floor* ▸ VERB **1** to make a floor **2** *informal* to knock flat **3** *informal* to puzzle: *floored by the question*

flop VERB (**flopping, flopped**) **1** to sway or swing about loosely **2** to fall or sit down suddenly and heavily **3** to move about clumsily **4** *informal* to fail badly ▸ NOUN **1** an act of flopping **2** *informal* a complete failure

floppy ADJECTIVE (**floppier, floppiest**) flopping, soft, and flexible

floppy disk NOUN, *computing* a flexible computer disk, often in a harder case, used to store data

flora NOUN the plants of a district or country as a whole

floral ADJECTIVE (made) of flowers

florist NOUN a seller or grower of flowers

floss NOUN **1** fine silk thread **2** thin, often waxed thread for passing between the teeth to clean them ▸ VERB to clean (teeth) with dental floss

flotilla NOUN a fleet of small ships

flotsam NOUN floating objects washed from a ship or wreck

flounce[1] VERB to walk away suddenly and impatiently, eg in anger

flounce[2] NOUN a gathered decorative strip sewn on to the hem of a dress

flounder[1] VERB **1** to struggle to move your legs and arms in water, mud, etc **2** to have difficulty in speaking or thinking clearly, or in acting efficiently

> ⓘ **Flounder** was probably formed by a gradual blending of 'blunder' and 'founder'

> Do not confuse with: **founder**

flounder[2] NOUN a small flatfish

flour NOUN **1** finely ground wheat **2** any grain crushed to powder: *rice flour*

flourish VERB **1** to be successful, especially financially **2** to grow well, thrive **3** to be healthy **4** to wave or brandish as a show or threat ▸ NOUN (*plural* **flourishes**) **1** a fancy stroke in writing **2** a sweeping movement with the hand, a sword, etc

floury ADJECTIVE **1** covered with flour **2** powdery

> Do not confuse with: **flowery**

flout VERB to treat with contempt,

defy openly: *flouted the speed limit*
[i] Probably comes from *floute*, a form found in Middle English meaning 'to play the flute'

> Do not confuse with: **flaunt**

flow VERB **1** to run, as water **2** to move or come out in an unbroken run **3** of the tide: to rise ▶NOUN a smooth or unbroken run: *flow of ideas* > **flowing** ADJECTIVE

flow chart NOUN a diagram showing a sequence of operations

flower NOUN **1** the part of a plant or tree from which fruit or seeds grow **2** the best of anything ▶VERB **1** of plants etc: to produce a flower **2** to be at your best, flourish

flowering NOUN of plants: producing flowers

flowery ADJECTIVE **1** full of or decorated with flowers **2** using fine-sounding, fancy language: *flowery prose style*

> Do not confuse with: **floury**

flown *past participle* of **fly**[2]

flu NOUN, *informal* influenza

fluctuate VERB **1** to vary in number, price, etc **2** to be always changing > **fluctuation** NOUN

flue NOUN a passage for air and smoke in a stove or chimney

fluent ADJECTIVE finding words easily in speaking or writing without any awkward pauses > **fluency** NOUN

fluff NOUN soft, downy material ▶VERB **1** to spoil something by doing it badly or making a mistake **2** to shake or arrange into a soft mass: *She fluffed up her hair* > **fluffy** ADJECTIVE

fluid NOUN a substance whose particles can move about freely, a liquid or gas ▶ADJECTIVE **1** flowing **2** not settled or fixed: *My plans for the weekend are fluid*

fluke NOUN an accidental or unplanned success

flume NOUN a water chute at a leisure pool

flummox VERB *informal* to bewilder, confuse totally

flung *past form* of **fling**

flunk VERB, *slang* to fail

fluorescence NOUN the emission of light by an object when exposed to ultraviolet light or X-rays > **fluorescent** ADJECTIVE

fluoride NOUN a chemical added to water or toothpaste to prevent tooth decay

flurry NOUN (*plural* **flurries**) a sudden rush of wind etc

flush[1] NOUN (*plural* **flushes**) **1** a reddening of the face **2** freshness, glow ▶VERB **1** to become red in the face **2** to clean by a rush of water

flush[2] ADJECTIVE **1** having the surface level with the surface around **2** *informal* well supplied with money

fluster NOUN excitement caused by hurry ▶VERB to harass, confuse

flute NOUN a high-pitched musical wind instrument

fluted ADJECTIVE decorated with grooves

flutter VERB to move (eyelids, wings, etc) back and forth quickly ▶NOUN **1** a quick beating of the

A B C D E F G H I J K L M N O P Q R S T U V W X Y Z

pulse etc **2** nervous excitement: *in a flutter*

flux NOUN **1** a flow **2** constant change: *in a state of flux*

fly[1] NOUN (*plural* **flies**) **1** a small winged insect **2** a fish-hook made to look like a fly to catch fish

fly[2] VERB (**flies, flying, flew, flown**) **1** to move through the air on wings or in an aircraft **2** *informal* to run away ▸ NOUN (usually **flies**) a flap of material with buttons or a zip, especially at the front of trousers

flyer NOUN a small poster or advertising sheet

flying saucer NOUN a disc-shaped object believed to be an alien spacecraft

flyover NOUN a road built on pillars to cross over another

flysheet NOUN the outer covering of a tent

FM ABBREVIATION frequency modulation (*compare with*: **AM**)

foal NOUN a young horse ▸ VERB to give birth to a foal

foam NOUN a mass of small bubbles on liquids ▸ VERB to produce foam

foam rubber NOUN a sponge-like form of rubber for stuffing chairs, mattresses, etc

fob[1] NOUN **1** *history* a small watch pocket **2** an ornamental chain hanging from such a pocket

fob[2] VERB (**fobbing, fobbed**) to force to accept (something worthless): *I won't be fobbed off with a silly excuse*

focal ADJECTIVE central, pivotal: *focal point*

focus NOUN (*plural* **focuses** *or* **foci** – *pronounced* **foh**-sai) **1** the meeting point for rays of light **2** the point to which light, a look, or someone's attention is directed ▸ VERB (**focusing, focused**) **1** to adjust (the lens of the eye or an optical instrument) to get the clearest possible image **2** to direct (one's attention etc) to one point

fodder NOUN dried food, eg hay or oats, for farm animals

foe NOUN, *formal* an enemy

foetal *another spelling of* **fetal**

foetus *another spelling of* **fetus**

fog NOUN thick mist ▸ VERB (**fogging, fogged**) **1** to cover in fog **2** to bewilder, confuse > **foggy** ADJECTIVE

foghorn NOUN a horn used as a warning to or by ships in fog

fogy *or* **fogey** NOUN (*plural* **fogies** *or* **fogeys**) someone with old-fashioned views

foil[1] VERB to defeat, disappoint

foil[2] NOUN metal in the form of paper-thin sheets

foil[3] NOUN a blunt sword with a button at the end, used in fencing practice

foist VERB **1** to pass off as genuine **2** to palm off (something undesirable) on someone

fold NOUN **1** a part laid on top of another **2** an enclosure for sheep etc ▸ VERB to lay one part on top of another

folder NOUN a cover to hold papers

foliage NOUN leaves

folk PLURAL NOUN **1** people **2** a nation, race **3** (*also*: **folks**) family or relations

folklore NOUN the study of the customs, beliefs, stories, etc of a people

folk music NOUN traditional music of a particular culture

folk song NOUN a traditional song passed on orally

follicle NOUN, *anatomy* a small cavity or sac in a body part, eg the pit surrounding a root of hair

follow VERB **1** to go or come after **2** to happen as a result **3** to act according to: *Follow your instincts* **4** to understand: *I don't follow you*

follower NOUN **1** someone who follows **2** a supporter, disciple: *a follower of Jung*

following NOUN supporters: *The team has a large following* ▶ ADJECTIVE next in time: *We left the following day* ▶ PREPOSITION after, as a result of: *Following the fire, the house collapsed*

folly NOUN (*plural* **follies**) **1** foolishness **2** a purposeless building

fond ADJECTIVE **1** loving; tender **2** *old* foolish **fond of** having a liking for

fondle VERB to caress

fondly ADVERB with fondness

fondness NOUN **1** affection, love, tenderness **2** liking

font[1] NOUN **1** a basin holding water for baptism **2** a main source: *a font of knowledge*

font[2] *or* **fount** NOUN a particular style of letters and characters

food NOUN substances which living beings eat

food chain NOUN the sequence in which food is transferred from one living thing to another in an ecosystem, eg plants are eaten by herbivores, which may then be eaten by carnivores

food processor NOUN an electrical appliance for chopping, blending, etc food

foodstuff NOUN something used for food

food web NOUN a group of interrelated food chains

fool NOUN **1** a silly person **2** *history* a court jester **3** a dessert made of fruit, sugar, and whipped cream ▶ VERB to deceive **fool about** to behave in a playful or silly manner

foolery NOUN silliness, foolish behaviour

foolhardy ADJECTIVE rash, taking foolish risks

foolish ADJECTIVE unwise, ill-considered > **foolishly** ADVERB

foolproof ADJECTIVE unable to go wrong

foolscap NOUN paper for writing or printing, 43×34 cm (17×13 inches) [i] Referring to the original watermark used on this size of paper, showing a jester's cap and bells

foot NOUN (*plural* **feet**) **1** the part of the leg below the ankle **2** the lower part of anything **3** (*plural* **feet** *or* **foot**) twelve inches, 30 cm **foot the bill** to pay up **not put a foot wrong** to make no mistakes, behave well

football NOUN **1** a game played by two teams of 11 on a field with a round ball **2** *US* a game played with an oval ball which can be handled or kicked **3** a ball used in football

foothill NOUN a smaller hill at the foot of a mountain

A B C D E F G H I J K L M N O P Q R S T U V W X Y Z

foothold NOUN **1** a place to put the foot in climbing **2** a firm position from which to begin something

footing NOUN balance; degree of friendship, seniority, etc

footlight NOUN a light at the front of a stage, which shines on the actors

footloose ADJECTIVE unattached, with no responsibilities

footnote NOUN a note at the bottom of a page

footpath NOUN **1** a path or track for walkers **2** a pavement

footprint NOUN a mark of a foot

footstep NOUN the sound of someone's foot when walking

footwear NOUN shoes, boots, etc

for PREPOSITION **1** sent to or to be given to: *There is a letter for you* **2** towards: *headed for home* **3** during (an amount of time): *waited for three hours* **4** on behalf of: *for me* **5** because of: *for no good reason* **6** as the price of: *£5 for a ticket* **7** in order to obtain: *only doing it for the money*

for- PREFIX forms words containing a notion of 'loss' or of 'not having or not doing something': *forbid/ forget*

Comes from Latin *foris* meaning 'outside'

> Note that **for-** has a different meaning from the prefix **fore-** (which is connected with 'be**fore**', 'in front of' or 'be**fore**hand'). There are a few words which do not fit this general rule of thumb: note the spelling of 'foreclose' and 'forward'. See also the note at 'forgo'

forage (*pronounced* **for**-ij) NOUN food for horses and cattle ▸ VERB to search for food, fuel, etc

foray (*pronounced* **for**-ei) NOUN **1** a raid **2** a brief journey

forbade *past tense* of **forbid**

forbearance NOUN control of temper

forbid VERB (**forbidding, forbade, forbidden**) to order not to

forbidden ADJECTIVE not allowed

forbidding ADJECTIVE rather frightening

force NOUN **1** strength, power **2** compulsion, especially with threats or violence **3** a group of workers, soldiers, etc **4** (**the forces**) those in the army, navy, and air force **5** (**the force**) the police ▸ VERB **1** to make, compel: *forced him to go* **2** to get by violence: *force an entry* **3** to break open

forced ADJECTIVE done unwillingly, with effort: *a forced laugh*

forceful ADJECTIVE **1** acting with power **2** persuasive, convincing, powerful > **forcefully** ADVERB > **forcefulness** NOUN

forceps (*pronounced* **faw**-seps) NOUN (*plural* **forceps**) surgical pincers for holding or lifting

forcible ADJECTIVE **1** done by force **2** strong and effective **3** powerful > **forcibly** ADVERB

ford NOUN a shallow crossing-place in a river ▸ VERB to cross (water) on foot

fore- PREFIX **1** before **2** beforehand **3** in front

Comes from the Old English prefix *fore-*

> Note that **fore-** has a different meaning from the prefix **for-** (which usually indicates some notion of 'loss' or 'not having or not doing something'). There are a few words which do not fit this general rule of thumb: note the spelling of 'foreclose' and 'forward'. See also the note at 'forgo'

forearm (*pronounced* **faw**-rahm) NOUN the part of the arm between elbow and wrist

foreboding NOUN a feeling of coming evil

forecast VERB (**forecasting, forecast**) to tell about beforehand, predict ▸ NOUN a prediction

forefather NOUN, *formal* an ancestor

forefinger NOUN the finger next to the thumb (*also called*: **index finger**)

forefront NOUN the very front

foregone ADJECTIVE: **a foregone conclusion** a result that can be guessed rightly in advance (*see also*: **forgo**)

foreground NOUN the part of a view or picture nearest the person looking at it

forehead NOUN the part of the face above the eyebrows

foreign ADJECTIVE **1** belonging to another country **2** not belonging naturally in a place etc: *a foreign body in an eye* **3** not familiar

foreigner NOUN **1** someone from another country **2** someone unfamiliar

foreleg NOUN an animal's front leg

forelock NOUN the lock of hair next to the forehead

foreman NOUN (*plural* **foremen**) **1** an overseer of a group of workers **2** the leader of a jury

foremost ADJECTIVE the most famous or important

forensic ADJECTIVE relating to courts of law or criminal investigation

forensic medicine NOUN the branch of medicine concerned with finding causes of injury and death

forerunner NOUN an earlier example or sign of what is to follow: *the forerunner of cinema*

foresee VERB (**foreseeing, foresaw, foreseen**) to see or know beforehand

foresight NOUN **1** ability to see what will happen later **2** a fitting on the front of the barrel of a gun to help the aim

forest NOUN a large piece of land covered with trees

forestall VERB to upset someone's plan by acting earlier than they expect

forester NOUN a worker in a forest

forestry NOUN the science of forest-growing

foretaste NOUN a sample of what is to come

foretell VERB (**foretelling, foretold**) to tell in advance, prophesy

forethought NOUN thought or care for the future

foretold *past form* of **foretell**

forever *or* **for ever** ADVERB

1 for all time 2 continually: *forever complaining* ▸ NOUN 1 an endless period of time 2 *informal* a very long time

foreword (*pronounced* **faw-**werd) NOUN a piece of writing at the beginning of a book

> Do not confuse with: **forward**. It is helpful to remember that the foreWORD in a book is made up of WORDs

forfeit VERB to lose (a right) as a result of doing something: *forfeit the right to appeal* ▸ NOUN something given in compensation or punishment for an action, eg a fine

forge[1] NOUN 1 a blacksmith's workshop 2 a furnace in which metal is heated ▸ VERB (**forging, forged**) 1 to hammer (metal) into shape 2 to imitate (a signature, banknote, etc) for criminal purposes > **forger** NOUN (verb, meaning 2)

forge[2] VERB to move steadily on: *forged ahead with the plan*

forgery NOUN (*plural* **forgeries**) 1 something imitated for criminal purposes 2 the act of criminal forging

forget VERB (**forgetting, forgot, forgotten**) to lose or put away from the memory

forgetful ADJECTIVE likely to forget, having a tendency to forget things > **forgetfully** ADVERB

forgive VERB (**forgiving, forgave, forgiven**) 1 to be no longer angry with 2 to overlook (a fault, debt, etc)

forgiveness NOUN pardon

forgiving ADJECTIVE merciful, willing to forgive other people for their faults

forgo VERB (**forgoes, forgoing, forwent, forgone**) to give up, do without

> It is possible to spell **forgo** and many of its forms with an 'e' – 'forego', 'forewent', etc. However, it is probably less confusing to stick to the basic spellings shown above when you are writing, and to keep the 'e' spelling for **forego** meaning 'to go before' (most commonly used in the expression 'a foregone conclusion'). See also prefix entries **for-** and **fore-**

forgot and **forgotten** *see* **forget**

fork NOUN 1 a pronged tool for piercing and lifting things 2 the point where a road, tree, etc divides into two branches ▸ VERB to divide into two branches etc

fork-lift truck NOUN a small vehicle with two horizontal prongs that can be raised and lowered to move or stack goods

forlorn ADJECTIVE pitiful, unhappy

form NOUN 1 shape or appearance 2 kind, type 3 a paper with printed questions and space for answers 4 a long seat 5 a school class 6 the nest of a hare ▸ VERB 1 to give shape to 2 to make

formal ADJECTIVE 1 done according to custom or convention: *formal dress* 2 stiffly polite > **formally** ADVERB

formality NOUN (*plural* **formalities**) 1 something which

A B C D E F G H I J K L M N O P Q R S T U V W X Y Z

must be done but has little meaning: *the nomination was only a formality* **2** cold correctness of manner

format NOUN **1** the size, shape, etc of a printed book **2** the design or arrangement of an event, eg a television programme **3** *computing* the description of the way data is arranged on a disk ▶VERB (**formatting, formatted**) **1** to arrange into a specific format **2** *computing* to arrange (data) for use on a disk **3** *computing* to prepare (a disk) for use by dividing it into sectors

formation NOUN **1** the act of forming **2** arrangement, eg of aeroplanes in flight

former ADJECTIVE **1** of an earlier time **2** of the first-mentioned of two (*contrasted with*: **latter**)

formerly ADVERB in earlier times; previously

formica (*pronounced* for-**mai**-ka) NOUN, *trademark* a tough, heat-resistant material used for covering work surfaces

formic acid NOUN, *chemistry* an acid found in ants

formidable ADJECTIVE **1** fearsome, frightening **2** difficult to overcome

formula NOUN (*plural* **formulas** *or* **formulae** – *pronounced* **faw**-myuw-lee) **1** a set of rules to be followed **2** *chemistry* an arrangement of signs or letters used in chemistry, arithmetic *etc* to express an idea briefly, *eg* H_2O = water

formulate VERB **1** to set down clearly: *formulate the rules* **2** to make into a formula

forsake VERB (**forsaking, forsook, forsaken**) to desert

forsaken ADJECTIVE deserted; miserable

fort NOUN a place of defence against an enemy

forte (*pronounced* **for**-tei) NOUN someone's particular talent or speciality

forth ADVERB forward, onward

forthcoming ADJECTIVE **1** happening soon **2** willing to share knowledge; friendly and open

forthright ADJECTIVE outspoken, straightforward

forthwith ADVERB immediately

fortieth ADJECTIVE the last of a series of forty ▶NOUN one of forty equal parts

fortifications PLURAL NOUN walls etc built to strengthen a position

fortify VERB (**fortifies, fortifying, fortified**) to strengthen against attack

fortitude NOUN courage in meeting danger or bearing pain

fortnight NOUN two weeks

fortnightly ADJECTIVE & ADVERB once a fortnight

FORTRAN (*pronounced* **faw**-tran) NOUN a computer language

fortress NOUN (*plural* **fortresses**) a fortified place

fortuitous ADJECTIVE happening by chance > **fortuitously** ADVERB

fortunate ADJECTIVE lucky > **fortunately** ADVERB

fortune NOUN **1** luck (good or bad) **2** large sum of money

forty NOUN the number 40 ▶ADJECTIVE 40 in number

A B C D E F G H I J K L M N O P Q R S T U V W X Y Z

forum NOUN (*plural* **fora**) **1** a public place where speeches are made **2** a meeting to talk about a particular subject **3** **4** *history* a market-place in ancient Rome

forward ADJECTIVE **1** advancing: *a forward movement* **2** near or at the front **3** *derogatory* too quick to speak or act, pert ▶ VERB **1** to help towards success: *forwarded his plans* **2** to send on (letters) ▶ ADVERB forwards

> Do not confuse with: **foreword**. It is helpful to remember that **forWARD** is an indication of direction, similar to backWARDs and homeWARDs.

forwards ADVERB onward, towards the front

forwent *past tense* of **forgo**

fossil NOUN the hardened remains of the shape of a plant or animal found in rock

fossil fuel NOUN a fuel derived from the remains of ancient plants and animals, eg coal and natural gas

fossilize *or* **fossilise** VERB to change into a fossil

foster VERB **1** to bring up or nurse (a child not your own) **2** to help on, encourage

foster-child NOUN a child fostered by a family

foster-parent NOUN someone who brings up a fostered child

fought *past form* of **fight**

foul ADJECTIVE **1** very dirty **2** smelling or tasting bad **3** stormy: *foul weather/in a foul temper* ▶ VERB **1** to become entangled with **2** to dirty **3** to play unfairly ▶ NOUN a breaking of the rules of a game

foul play NOUN a criminal act

found[1] VERB to establish, set up

found[2] *past form* of **find**

foundation NOUN **1** the basis on which anything rests **2** (**foundations**) the underground structure supporting a building **3** a sum of money left or set aside for a special purpose **4** an organization etc supported in this way

founder VERB **1** of a ship: to sink **2** of a horse: to stumble, go lame

[i] Comes from Old French *fondrer* meaning 'to fall in'

> Do not confuse with: **flounder**

foundling NOUN a child abandoned by its parents

foundry NOUN (*plural* **foundries**) a workshop where metal founding is done

fount *see* **font**[2]

fountain NOUN **1** a rising jet of water **2** the pipe or structure from which it comes

fountain pen NOUN a pen with a metal nib and a cartridge of ink

four NOUN the number 4 ▶ ADJECTIVE 4 in number

[i] Comes from Old English *feower*

fourteen NOUN the number 14 ▶ ADJECTIVE 14 in number

fourteenth ADJECTIVE the last of a series of fourteen ▶ NOUN one of fourteen equal parts

fourth ADJECTIVE the last of a series of four ▶ NOUN **1** one of four equal parts **2** *music* an interval of four notes

fowl NOUN (*plural* **fowls** *or* **fowl**) a bird, especially a domestic cock or hen

fox NOUN (*plural* **foxes**) a wild animal related to the dog, with reddish-brown fur and a long bushy tail ▶ VERB **1** to trick by cleverness **2** to puzzle, baffle

foxglove NOUN a tall wild flower

foxhound NOUN a breed of dog trained to chase foxes

foxtrot NOUN a ballroom dance made up of walking steps and turns

foxy ADJECTIVE (**foxier, foxiest**) cunning

foyer (*pronounced* **foi**-ei) NOUN an entrance hall to a theatre, hotel, etc

fraction NOUN **1** a part, not a whole number, eg 4⁄5 **2** a small part

fracture NOUN a break in something hard, especially in a bone of the body

fragile ADJECTIVE easily broken > **fragility** NOUN

fragment NOUN (*pronounced* **frag**-ment) a part broken off; something not complete ▶ VERB (*pronounced* frag-**ment**) to break into pieces

fragmentary ADJECTIVE consisting of small pieces, not amounting to a connected whole

fragmentation NOUN breaking up, division into fragments

fragrance NOUN sweet scent

fragrant ADJECTIVE sweet-smelling

frail ADJECTIVE physically weak

frailty NOUN (*plural* **frailties**) weakness

frame VERB (**framing, framed**) **1** to put a frame round **2** to put together, construct **3** *slang* to make (someone) appear to be guilty of a crime ▶ NOUN **1** a case or border round anything **2** build of human body **3** state (of mind)

framework NOUN the outline or skeleton of something

franc NOUN **1** the standard unit of money in Switzerland, Liechtenstein, etc **2** the former standard unit of money in France, Belgium, and Luxembourg, replaced in 2002 by the euro

franchise NOUN **1** the right to vote in a general election **2** a right to sell the goods of a particular company ▶ VERB to give a business franchise to

Franco- PREFIX of France, French: *Francophile*

frank ADJECTIVE open, speaking your mind

frankincense NOUN a sweet-smelling resin used as incense

frankly ADVERB **1** openly **2** to be honest, I tell you

frankness NOUN the quality of being frank

frantic ADJECTIVE wildly excited or anxious > **frantically** ADVERB

frater- *or* **fratri-** PREFIX brother: *fraternize with someone* (= to behave towards them with brotherly friendliness)/*fratricide*

[i] Comes from Latin *frater* meaning 'brother'

fraternal ADJECTIVE brotherly; of a brother > **fraternally** ADVERB

fraternity NOUN (*plural* **fraternities**) **1** a society, a brotherhood **2** a North American

A B C D E F G H I J K L M N O P Q R S T U V W X Y Z

male college society (*compare with*: **sorority**)

fraternize *or* **fraternise** VERB to make friends (with)

fraud NOUN **1** deceit, dishonesty **2** an impostor; a fake

fraudulent ADJECTIVE deceitful, dishonest > **fraudulently** ADVERB

fraught ADJECTIVE anxious, tense **fraught with** filled with: *fraught with danger*

fray[1] VERB to wear away

fray[2] NOUN a fight, a brawl

freak NOUN **1** an unusual event **2** an odd or eccentric person

freckle NOUN a small brown spot on the skin

free ADJECTIVE (**freer, freest**) **1** not bound or shut in **2** costing nothing **3** open or available to all ▶ VERB (**freeing, freed**) to make or set free **free someone from something** *or* **free someone of something** to get rid of it for them

ⓘ Comes from Old English *freo*

-free ADJECTIVE (added to another word) not containing or involving: *additive-free/cruelty-free*

freebie NOUN, *informal* a free event, performance, etc

freedom NOUN the state of being free; liberty

freehand ADJECTIVE of drawing: done without the help of rulers, tracing, etc

freehold ADJECTIVE of an estate: belonging to the holder or their heirs for all time

freelance *or* **freelancer** NOUN someone working independently (such as a writer who is not employed by any one newspaper)

ⓘ Originally referring to a medieval knight who would fight for anyone who paid him

Freemason NOUN a member of a certain men's society, sworn to secrecy

free-range ADJECTIVE **1** of poultry: allowed to move about freely and feed out of doors **2** of eggs: laid by free-range poultry

free speech NOUN the right to express opinions of any kind

freestyle ADJECTIVE of swimming, skating, etc: in which any style may be used

freeware NOUN, *computing* software programs offered to the public at no cost

freeway NOUN, *US* a road for high-speed traffic

freewheel VERB to travel on a bicycle or car, especially downhill, without using mechanical power

freeze VERB (**freezing, froze, frozen**) **1** to turn into ice **2** to make (food) very cold in order to preserve **3** to go stiff with cold, fear, etc **4** to fix (prices or wages) at a certain level

freezer NOUN a refrigerated cabinet in which food is made, or kept, frozen

freezing point NOUN the point at which liquid becomes a solid (of water, 0°C)

freight NOUN **1** load, cargo **2** a charge for carrying a load

freighter NOUN a ship or aircraft that carries cargo

freight train NOUN a goods train

French fries PLURAL NOUN *US* fried potatoes
French polish NOUN a kind of varnish for furniture
French toast NOUN bread dipped in egg and fried
French window NOUN a long window also used as a door
frenetic ADJECTIVE frantic
frenzied ADJECTIVE mad
> **frenziedly** ADVERB
frenzy NOUN **1** a fit of madness **2** wild excitement
frequency NOUN (*plural* **frequencies**) **1** the rate at which something happens **2** *physics* the number of times a wave is repeated per unit time
frequent ADJECTIVE (*pronounced* **free**-kw*e*nt) happening often ▸ VERB (*pronounced* fri-**kwent**) to visit often
fresco NOUN (*plural* **frescoes** *or* **frescos**) a picture painted on a wall while the plaster is still damp
fresh ADJECTIVE **1** new, unused: *fresh sheet of paper* **2** newly made or picked; not preserved: *fresh fruit* **3** cool, refreshing: *fresh breeze* **4** not tired **5** *informal* cheeky, impertinent ▸ ADVERB newly: *fresh-laid eggs*
freshen VERB to make fresh
freshly ADVERB newly, recently
freshwater ADJECTIVE of inland rivers, lakes, etc, not of the sea
fret[1] VERB (**fretting, fretted**) to worry or show discontent
fret[2] NOUN one of the ridges on the fingerboard of a guitar
fretful ADJECTIVE showing feelings of worry or discontent
fretwork NOUN decorative cut-out work in wood
friar NOUN a member of one of the Roman Catholic brotherhoods, especially someone who has vowed to live in poverty
friary NOUN (*plural* **friaries**) a building where friars live
friction NOUN **1** rubbing of two things together **2** quarrelling, bad feeling
Friday NOUN the sixth day of the week
ⓘ After *Freya*, the Norse goddess of love
fridge NOUN, *informal* refrigerator
fried *see* **fry**[1]
friend NOUN **1** someone who knows another person well and likes them **2** sympathizer, helper
ⓘ Comes from Old English *freon* meaning 'to love'
friendly ADJECTIVE (**friendlier, friendliest**) **1** kind **2** on good terms (with) ▸ NOUN (*plural* **friendlies**) a sports match that is not part of a competition > **friendliness** NOUN
-friendly ADJECTIVE (added to another word) **1** not harmful towards: *dolphin-friendly* **2** compatible with or easy to use for: *child-friendly*
friendship NOUN the state of being friends; mutual affection
frieze NOUN **1** a part of a wall below the ceiling, often ornamented with designs **2** a picture on a long strip of paper etc, often displayed on a wall
frigate (*pronounced* **frig**-*a*t) NOUN a small warship

fright NOUN sudden fear: *gave me a fright/took fright and ran away*

frighten VERB to make afraid > **frightening** ADJECTIVE

frightful ADJECTIVE **1** causing terror **2** *informal* very bad

frightfully ADVERB **1** very badly **2** *informal* extremely

frigid (*pronounced* **frij**-id) ADJECTIVE **1** frozen, cold **2** cold in manner **3** sexually unresponsive > **frigidity** NOUN > **frigidly** ADVERB

frill NOUN **1** an ornamental edging **2** an unnecessary ornament > **frilly** ADJECTIVE

fringe NOUN **1** a border of loose threads **2** hair cut to hang over the forehead **3** a border of soft material, paper, etc ▸ VERB to edge round

Frisbee NOUN, *trademark* a plastic plate-like object skimmed through the air as a game

ⓘ Based on the name of the *Frisbie* bakery in Connecticut, whose lightweight pie tins inspired the invention

frisk VERB **1** to skip about playfully **2** *informal* to search (someone) closely for concealed weapons etc

frisky ADJECTIVE (**friskier, friskiest**) lively, playful, and keen to have fun > **friskily** ADVERB

fritter NOUN a piece of fried batter containing fruit etc

fritter away VERB to waste, squander

frivolity NOUN (*plural* **frivolities**) levity, lack of seriousness

frivolous ADJECTIVE playful, not serious > **frivolously** ADVERB

frizzy ADJECTIVE (**frizzier, frizziest**) of hair: massed in small curls

fro ADVERB: **to and fro** forwards and backwards

frock NOUN **1** a woman's or girl's dress **2** a monk's wide-sleeved garment

frock-coat NOUN a man's double-breasted coat that reaches down to the knees

frog NOUN a small greenish jumping animal living on land and in water

frogman NOUN (*plural* **frogmen**) *informal* an underwater diver with flippers and breathing apparatus

frogmarch VERB to seize (someone) from behind and push them forward while holding their arms tight behind their back

frolic NOUN a merry, light-hearted playing ▸ VERB (**frolicking, frolicked**) to play light-heartedly

from PREPOSITION **1** used before the place, person, etc that is the starting point of an action etc: *sailing from England to France/The office is closed from Friday to Monday* **2** used to show separation: *Warn them to keep away from there*

frond NOUN, *botany* a leaf-like growth, especially a branch of a fern or palm

front NOUN **1** the part of anything nearest the person who sees it **2** the part which faces the direction in which something moves **3** the fighting line in a war **4** the boundary between two air masses that have different temperatures ▸ ADJECTIVE at or in the front **in front of** at the head of, before

frontage NOUN the front part of a building

frontier NOUN a boundary between countries

frontispiece NOUN a picture at the very beginning of a book

frost NOUN **1** frozen dew **2** the coldness of weather needed to form ice ▶VERB **1** to cover with frost **2** *US* to ice (a cake)

frosted ADJECTIVE having an appearance as if covered in frost, eg glass with a specially roughened surface

frosting NOUN, *US* icing on a cake etc

frosty ADJECTIVE (**frostier, frostiest**) **1** of weather: cold enough for frost to form **2** cold, unwelcoming: *gave me a frosty look*

froth NOUN foam on liquids ▶VERB to throw up foam > **frothy** ADJECTIVE

frown VERB to wrinkle the brows in deep thought, disapproval, etc ▶NOUN **1** a wrinkling of the brows **2** a disapproving look **frown on** to look upon with disapproval

froze and **frozen** *see* **freeze**

fructose NOUN a natural sugar found in honey and fruit

frugal ADJECTIVE **1** careful in spending, thrifty **2** costing little, small: *a frugal meal* > **frugality** NOUN

frugally ADVERB in a way which reduces spending to a minimum

fruit NOUN **1** the part of a plant containing the seed **2** result: *All their hard work bore fruit*

fruiterer NOUN someone who sells fruit

fruitful ADJECTIVE **1** producing plenty of fruit **2** producing good results: *a fruitful meeting*

fruition (*pronounced* froo-**ish**-*on*) NOUN **1** ripeness **2** a good result

fruitless ADJECTIVE useless, done in vain

fruit machine NOUN a gambling machine into which coins are put

frump NOUN a plain, badly or unfashionably dressed woman > **frumpish** ADJECTIVE

frustrate VERB **1** to make to feel powerless **2** to bring to nothing: *frustrated his wishes*

frustration NOUN **1** a feeling of irritation and annoyance as a result of being powerless or unable to do something **2** the bringing to nothing or spoiling of something

fry[1] VERB (**fries, frying, fried**) to cook in hot fat ▶NOUN (*plural* **fries**) food cooked in hot fat

fry[2] PLURAL NOUN a young fish **small fry** unimportant people or things

fuchsia (*pronounced* **fyoo**-sh*a*) NOUN a plant with long hanging flowers

fudge[1] NOUN a soft, sugary sweet

fudge[2] VERB to cheat ▶NOUN a cheat

fuel NOUN a substance such as coal, gas, or petrol, used to keep a fire or engine going

fuel cell NOUN a device that produces electricity by oxidizing a fuel

fugitive ADJECTIVE running away, on the run ▶NOUN someone who is running away from the police etc: *a fugitive from justice*

fugue (*pronounced* fyoog) NOUN

A B C D E F G H I J K L M N O P Q R S T U V W X Y Z

a piece of music in which a theme is introduced in one part and developed as other parts take it up

-ful SUFFIX **1** full of: *joyful* **2** causing: *wonderful/stressful* **3** forming nouns referring to the amount a container will hold: *spoonful*

fulcrum (*pronounced* **fuwl**-krum) NOUN (*plural* **fulcrums** *or* **fulcra**) the point on which a lever turns, or a balanced object rests

fulfil *or US* **fulfill** VERB (**fulfilling, fulfilled**) to carry out (a task, promise, etc)

fulfilment NOUN **1** successful completion, accomplishment **2** satisfaction with things achieved

full ADJECTIVE **1** holding as much as can be held **2** plump: *a full face* ▶ ADVERB (used with *adjectives*) fully: *full-grown* **full of** having a great deal or plenty of

fullback NOUN a defensive player in football etc, the nearest to their team's goal-line

full moon NOUN the moon when it appears at its largest

full stop NOUN a punctuation mark (.) placed at the end of a sentence

full-time ADJECTIVE for the whole of the working week: *a full-time job* (*compare with*: **part-time**)

fully ADVERB **1** entirely, completely **2** at least

fulmar (*pronounced* **fuwl**-mar) NOUN a white sea bird

fulsome ADJECTIVE, *formal* overdone: *fulsome praise*

fumble VERB **1** to use the hands awkwardly **2** to drop (a thrown ball etc)

fume VERB **1** to give off smoke or vapour **2** to be in a silent rage

fumes PLURAL NOUN smoke, vapour

fumigate VERB to kill the germs in (a place) by means of strong fumes > **fumigation** NOUN

fun NOUN enjoyment, a good time: *Are you having fun?* **make fun of** to tease, make others laugh at

function NOUN **1** a special job, use, or duty of a machine, person, part of the body, etc **2** an organized event such as a party, reception, etc **3** *maths* the relation of every element in a set (the **domain**) to a single element of another set (the **codomain**) ▶ VERB **1** to work, operate: *The engine isn't functioning properly* **2** to carry out usual duties: *I can't function at this time in the morning*

functional ADJECTIVE **1** designed to be efficient rather than decorative; plain **2** in working order

fund NOUN **1** a sum of money for a special purpose: *charity fund* **2** a store or supply

fundamental ADJECTIVE **1** of great or far-reaching importance **2** basic, essential: *fundamental to her happiness* ▶ NOUN **1** a necessary part **2** (**fundamentals**) the groundwork, the first stages

funeral NOUN the ceremony of burial or cremation

funereal (*pronounced* fyoo-**neer**-i-*a*l) ADJECTIVE mournful

funfair NOUN an amusement park

fungus NOUN (*plural* **fungi** – *pronounced* **fung**-gee) **1** a soft, spongy plant growth, *eg* a mushroom **2** disease-growth on animals and plants > **fungoid** ADJECTIVE like a fungus

funk[1] NOUN, *informal* funky music

funk[2] NOUN, *informal* fear, panic

funky ADJECTIVE (**funkier, funkiest**), *informal* **1** of jazz and pop music: unsophisticated, earthy and soulful, like early blues **2** fashionable, trendy **3** odd, eccentric

funnel NOUN **1** a cone ending in a tube, for pouring liquids into bottles **2** a tube or passage for escape of smoke, air, etc ▸ VERB (**funnelling, funnelled**) to pass through a funnel; channel

funny ADJECTIVE (**funnier, funniest**) **1** amusing **2** odd > **funnily** ADVERB

funny bone NOUN part of the elbow which gives a prickly feeling when knocked

fur NOUN **1** the short fine hair of certain animals **2** their skins covered with fur **3** a coating on the tongue, on the inside of kettles, etc ▸ VERB (**furring, furred**) to line or cover with fur

furious ADJECTIVE **1** extremely angry **2** stormy **3** fast, energetic and rather disorganized > **furiously** ADVERB

furlong NOUN one-eighth of a mile (220 yards, 201.17 metres)

furnace NOUN a very hot oven for melting iron ore, making steam for heating etc

furnish VERB **1** to fit up (a room or house) completely **2** to supply: *furnished with enough food for a week*

furnishings PLURAL NOUN fittings, furniture

furniture NOUN movable articles in a house, eg tables, chairs

furore (*pronounced* fyoo-**raw**-ri) NOUN uproar; excitement

furrier (*pronounced* **fu**-ri-*er*) NOUN someone who trades in or works with furs

furrow NOUN **1** a groove made by a plough **2** a deep groove **3** a deep wrinkle ▸ VERB **1** to cut deep grooves in **2** to wrinkle: *furrowed brow*

furry ADJECTIVE (**furrier, furriest**) covered with fur

further ADVERB & ADJECTIVE to a greater distance or degree; in addition ▸ VERB to help on or forward

furthermore ADVERB in addition to what has been said

furthest ADVERB to the greatest distance or degree

furtive ADJECTIVE stealthy, sly: *furtive glance* > **furtively** ADVERB

fury NOUN violent anger

fuse VERB (**fusing, fused**) **1** to melt **2** to join together **3** to put a fuse in (a plug etc) **4** of a circuit etc: to stop working because of the melting of a fuse ▸ NOUN **1** a wire which melts when an electric current exceeds a certain value, put in an electric circuit for safety **2** any device for causing an explosion to take place automatically

fuselage (*pronounced* **fyoo**-ze-lahsz) NOUN the body of an aeroplane

fusion NOUN **1** *chemistry* melting,

A B C D E F G H I J K L M N O P Q R S T U V W X Y Z

changing from a solid to a liquid **2** a merging, a joining together: *a fusion of musical traditions*

fuss NOUN **1** unnecessary activity, excitement or attention, often about something unimportant: *making a fuss about nothing* **2** strong complaint ▸VERB **1** to be unnecessarily concerned about details **2** to worry too much

fussy ADJECTIVE (**fussier, fussiest**) **1** over-elaborate **2** choosy, finicky **3** partial, in favour of one thing over another: *Either will do; I'm not fussy* > **fussily** ADVERB (meanings 1 and 2) > **fussiness** NOUN (meanings 1 and 2)

fusty ADJECTIVE (**fustier, fustiest**) mouldy; stale-smelling

futile ADJECTIVE useless; having no effect

futility NOUN uselessness

futon (*pronounced* **foo**-ton) NOUN a sofa bed with a low frame and detachable mattress

future ADJECTIVE happening later in time ▸NOUN **1** the time to come: *foretell the future* **2** the part of your life still to come: *planning for their future* **3** *grammar* the future tense in verbs

fuzz NOUN **1** fine, light hair or feathers **2** *Brit slang* the police

fuzzy ADJECTIVE (**fuzzier, fuzziest**) **1** covered with fuzz, fluffy **2** tightly curled: *fuzzy hairdo*

Gg

g ABBREVIATION gram(s)
gabble VERB to talk fast, chatter ▶ NOUN fast talk
gaberdine NOUN **1** a heavy overcoat **2** a heavy wool or cotton fabric
gable NOUN the triangular area of wall at the end of a building with a ridged roof
gadget NOUN a small simple machine or tool: *a gadget to unlock your mobile phone*
Gaelic NOUN **1** (*pronounced* **ga**-lik) the language of the Scottish Highlands **2** (*pronounced* **gei**-lik) the Irish language ▶ ADJECTIVE written or spoken in Gaelic
gag VERB (**gagging, gagged**) to silence someone by putting something over their mouth ▶ NOUN **1** a piece of cloth etc put in or over someone's mouth to silence them **2** *informal* a joke
gaggle NOUN a flock of geese
gaiety and **gaily** *see* **gay**
gain VERB **1** to win; earn **2** to reach **3** to get closer, especially in a race: *gaining on the leader* **4** to take on (eg weight) ▶ NOUN **1** something gained **2** profit
gait NOUN way or manner of walking

> Do not confuse with: **gate**

gaiter NOUN a cloth ankle-covering, fitting over the shoe, sometimes reaching to the knee
gala NOUN **1** a public festival **2** a sports meeting: *swimming gala*
galaxy NOUN (*plural* **galaxies**) **1** a system of stars **2** an impressive gathering **3** (**the Galaxy**) the Milky Way
gale NOUN a strong wind
gall (*pronounced* gawl) NOUN **1** a growth caused by insects on trees and plants **2** bitterness of feeling
gallant ADJECTIVE **1** brave; noble **2** polite or attentive towards women ▶ NOUN a gallant man
gallantry NOUN gallant behaviour
galleon NOUN, *history* a large Spanish sailing ship
gallery NOUN (*plural* **galleries**) **1** a long passage **2** the top floor of seats in a theatre **3** a room or building for showing artworks
galley NOUN (*plural* **galleys**) **1** *history* a long, low-built ship driven by oars **2** a ship's kitchen
galling ADJECTIVE annoying, frustrating: *it was galling to lose by only one point*

A B C D E F G H I J K L M N O P Q R S T U V W X Y Z

gallivant VERB to travel or go out for pleasure

gallon NOUN a measure for liquids (8 pints, 4.546 litres)

gallop VERB **1** to move by leaps **2** to (cause to) move very fast ▸ NOUN a fast pace

gallows SINGULAR NOUN a wooden framework on which criminals were hanged

galore ADVERB (*placed after the noun*) in plenty: *whisky galore*
🛈 Based on an Irish Gaelic phrase *go leor*, meaning 'sufficient'

galoshes *or* **goloshes** PLURAL NOUN waterproof shoes worn over other shoes

galvanize *or* **galvanise** VERB **1** to stir into activity **2** to stimulate by electricity **3** to coat (iron etc) with zinc

gambit NOUN **1** *chess* a first move involving sacrificing a piece to make the player's position stronger **2** an opening move in a transaction, or an opening remark in a conversation

gamble VERB **1** to play games for money **2** to risk money on the result of a game, race, etc **3** to take a wild chance ▸ NOUN a risk; a bet on a result

gambol VERB (**gambolling, gambolled**) to leap playfully

game NOUN **1** a contest played according to rules **2** (**games**) athletic competition **3** wild animals and birds hunted for sport ▸ ADJECTIVE **1** plucky **2** of a limb: lame

gamekeeper NOUN someone who looks after game birds, animals, fish, etc

gamete NOUN in sexually reproducing organisms: a specialized sex cell, especially an **ovum** or **sperm**, which fuses with another gamete of the opposite type during fertilization (*also called*: **germ cell**)

gaming NOUN & ADJECTIVE gambling

gamma ray NOUN an electromagnetic ray that is stronger than an X-ray

gammon NOUN leg of a pig, salted and smoked

gamut NOUN the whole range or extent of anything

gander NOUN a male goose

gang NOUN **1** a group of people who meet regularly: *I'm going out for a drink with the gang tonight* **2** a team of criminals

gangrene NOUN, *medicine* the rotting of some part of the body
> **gangrenous** ADJECTIVE

gangster NOUN a member of a gang of criminals

gangway NOUN **1** a passage between rows of seats, eg on a plane or in a theatre **2** a movable bridge leading from a quay to a ship

gannet NOUN a large white sea bird

gaol *another spelling of* **jail**

gaoler *another spelling of* **jailer**

gap NOUN an opening or space between things

gape VERB **1** to open the mouth wide (as in surprise) **2** to be wide open

gap year NOUN a year spent by

a student between school and university doing non-academic activities

garage NOUN **1** a building for storing a car or cars **2** a shop which carries out car repairs and sells petrol, oil, etc

garb *formal*, NOUN dress ▶ VERB to clothe

garbage NOUN rubbish

garble VERB to mix up, muddle: *garbled account of events*

🛈 Originally meaning 'sift', which gradually developed into the sense of confusing by leaving out too much

garden NOUN a piece of ground on which flowers or vegetables are grown ▶ VERB to work in a garden

gardener NOUN someone who tends a garden

gargantuan ADJECTIVE extremely large, huge

🛈 Named after *Gargantua*, a giant with an enormous appetite in a 16th-century French novel by Rabelais

gargle VERB to rinse the throat with a liquid, without swallowing

gargoyle NOUN a grotesque carving of a human or animal head, jutting out from a roof

garish ADJECTIVE tastelessly over-bright: *garish book cover*

garland NOUN flowers or leaves tied or woven into a circle

garlic NOUN an onion-like plant with a strong smell and taste, used in cooking

garment NOUN an article of clothing

garnet NOUN a semi-precious stone, usually red in colour

garnish VERB to decorate (a dish of food) ▶ NOUN (*plural* **garnishes**) a decoration on food > **garnishing** NOUN

garret NOUN an attic room

garrison NOUN a group of troops for guarding a fortress

garrulous ADJECTIVE fond of talking > **garrulity** NOUN

garter NOUN a broad elastic band to keep a stocking up

gas NOUN (*plural* **gases**) **1** a substance like air (though you can smell some gases) **2** a natural or manufactured form of this which will burn and is used as a fuel **3** *US* petrol ▶ VERB (**gassing, gassed**) to poison with gas

gaseous ADJECTIVE in gas form

gash NOUN (*plural* **gashes**) a deep, open cut ▶ VERB to cut deeply into

gasket NOUN a layer of padding used to make airtight or gas-tight joints

gas mask NOUN a covering for the face to prevent breathing in poisonous gas

gasoline NOUN, *US* petrol

gasometer NOUN a tank for storing gas

gasp NOUN the sound made by a sudden intake of breath ▶ VERB **1** to breathe with difficulty **2** to say breathlessly **3** *informal* to want badly: *gasping for a cup of tea*

gastric ADJECTIVE relating to the stomach: *gastric ulcer*

gasworks NOUN place where gas is made

A B C D E F G H I J K L M N O P Q R S T U V W X Y Z

gate NOUN **1** a door across an opening in a wall, fence, etc **2** the number of people at a football match **3** the total entrance money paid by the people at a football match

> Do not confuse with: **gait**

gateau (*pronounced* **gat**-oh) NOUN (*plural* **gateaus** *or* **gateaux**) a rich cake, usually layered and filled with cream

gatecrash VERB to go to a party uninvited > **gatecrasher** NOUN

gateway NOUN **1** an opening containing a gate **2** an entrance **3** *computing* a connection between networks

gather VERB **1** to bring together, or meet, in one place **2** to pick (flowers etc) **3** to increase in: *gather speed* **4** to learn, come to the conclusion (that): *I gather you don't want to go*

gathering NOUN a crowd

gauche (*pronounced* gohsh) ADJECTIVE awkward and clumsy in people's company

ⓘ Taken from the French word for 'left', because of the supposed awkwardness of using the left hand

gaudy ADJECTIVE showy; vulgarly bright in colour > **gaudily** ADVERB

gauge (*pronounced* geij) VERB **1** to measure **2** to make a guess ▸ NOUN a measuring device: *a rain gauge*

gaunt ADJECTIVE thin, haggard

gauntlet[1] NOUN **1** a long glove (often of leather) with a guard for the wrist, used for some sports etc: *the falcon landed on his leather gauntlet* **2** *history* an iron glove worn with armour **take up the gauntlet** to accept a challenge **throw down the gauntlet** to offer a challenge

gauntlet[2] NOUN: **run the gauntlet** to expose yourself to criticism, hostility, etc

ⓘ The *gauntlet* was an old military punishment of being made to run past a line of soldiers armed with sticks; the word is of Swedish origin and unrelated to **gauntlet**[1].

gauze NOUN thin cloth that you can see through

gawky ADJECTIVE (**gawkier, gawkiest**) awkward

gay ADJECTIVE **1** homosexual **2** lively; merry, full of fun **3** brightly coloured ▸ NOUN a homosexual > **gaiety** NOUN (meaning 2) > **gaily** ADVERB (meanings 2 and 3)

gaze VERB to look steadily ▸ NOUN a fixed look

gazelle NOUN a small deer

GB, Gb *or* **Gbyte** ABBREVIATION, *computing* gigabyte(s)

GBH *or* **gbh** ABBREVIATION, *law* grievous bodily harm, the crime of deliberately causing someone a serious physical injury

GDP ABBREVIATION gross domestic product

gear NOUN **1** clothing and equipment needed for a particular job, sport, etc **2** a connection by means of a set of toothed wheels between a car engine and the wheels ▸ VERB: **gear to** to adapt to, design for what is needed

geese *plural* of **goose**

gel (*pronounced* jel) NOUN a jelly-like substance, especially one used for styling the hair

gelatine NOUN a jelly-like substance made from hooves, animal bones, etc, and used to make food set

gelatinous (*pronounced* jel-**at**-in-*us*) ADJECTIVE jelly-like

gelding NOUN a castrated horse

gem NOUN **1** (*also called*: **gemstone**) a precious stone, especially when cut **2** someone or something greatly valued

gender NOUN *grammar* (in grammar, especially in languages other than English) any of three types of noun, masculine, feminine or neuter

gene NOUN the basic unit of heredity responsible for passing on specific characteristics from parents to offspring

genealogical ADJECTIVE relating to genealogy

genealogy NOUN (*plural* **genealogies**) **1** the history of families from generation to generation **2** a personal family history

general ADJECTIVE **1** not detailed, broad: *a general idea of the person's interests* **2** involving everyone: *a general election* **3** to do with several different things: *general knowledge* **4** of most people: *the general opinion* **5** (**in general**) generally ▶ NOUN a high-ranking army officer

generalize *or* **generalise** VERB to make a broad general statement, meant to cover all individual cases > **generalization** NOUN

generally ADVERB **1** usually, in most cases **2** by most people: *generally known*

general practitioner NOUN a doctor who treats most ordinary illnesses

generate VERB to produce, bring into being: *generate electricity/ generate good will*

generation NOUN **1** creation, making **2** a step in family descent **3** people born at about the same time: *the generation who were teenagers in the 90s*

generator NOUN a machine for making electricity *etc*

generic ADJECTIVE general, applicable to any member of a group or class

generous ADJECTIVE giving plentifully; kind > **generosity** NOUN > **generously** ADVERB

genesis NOUN beginning, origin

genetic ADJECTIVE **1** relating to genes **2** inherited through genes: *genetic disease* > **genetically** ADVERB

genetically modified ADJECTIVE (*abbrev* **GM**) of an organism: having had its genes artificially altered so it has fewer defects

genetic engineering *or* **genetic manipulation** NOUN the science of altering the genetic structure of an organism to change its characteristics

genetics SINGULAR NOUN the study of the way characteristics are passed from one generation to the next

A B C D E F G H I J K L M N O P Q R S T U V W X Y Z

genial ADJECTIVE good-natured > **geniality** NOUN > **genially** ADVERB

genie NOUN (*plural* **genii** – *pronounced* **jeen**-i-ai) a guardian spirit

genitals NOUN *plural* the organs of sexual reproduction

genius NOUN (*plural* **geniuses**) **1** unusual cleverness **2** someone who is unusually clever

genocide NOUN the deliberate extermination of a race of people > **genocidal** ADJECTIVE

genome NOUN the full set of chromosomes of an organism, or the total number of genes in the set

gent NOUN, *informal* a man

genteel ADJECTIVE good-mannered, especially excessively

gentile (*pronounced* **jen**-tail) NOUN a non-Jew

gentility NOUN **1** aristocracy **2** good manners, refinement, often in excess

gentle ADJECTIVE **1** mild-mannered, not brutal **2** mild, not extreme: *gentle breeze* **3** having a pleasant light or soft quality, not harsh or forceful > **gentleness** NOUN > **gently** ADVERB

gentleman NOUN (*plural* **gentlemen**) **1** a man, especially one of noble birth **2** a well-mannered man

gentry NOUN a wealthy, land-owning class of people

gents SINGULAR NOUN (**the gents**) *informal* a men's public toilet

genuine ADJECTIVE **1** real, not fake or pretended: *genuine antique/ She may have been lying, but her distress was genuine* **2** honest and straightforward > **genuinely** ADVERB (meaning 1) > **genuineness** NOUN

genus (*pronounced* **jee**-nus) NOUN (*plural* **genera**: *pronounced* **jen**-*e*-ra) a category of organisms into which a family is divided, and which in turn is subdivided into species

geo- PREFIX of or relating to the earth: *geography/geometry* (= a branch of mathematics originally concerned with measuring the earth)

ⓘ Comes from Greek *ge* meaning 'earth'

geographer NOUN someone who studies geography

geography NOUN the study of the surface of the earth and its inhabitants > **geographic** *or* **geographical** ADJECTIVE

geologist NOUN someone who studies geology

geology NOUN the study of the earth's history as shown in its rocks and soils > **geological** ADJECTIVE

geometric *or* **geometrical** ADJECTIVE **1** relating to geometry **2** of a shape or pattern: made up of angles and straight lines

geometry NOUN the branch of mathematics which deals with the study of lines, angles, and figures

geranium NOUN a plant with thick leaves and bright red or pink flowers

gerbil (*pronounced* **jerb**-il) NOUN a small, rat-like desert animal, often kept as a pet

geriatric ADJECTIVE **1** dealing with

old people **2** *informal* very old

geriatrics SINGULAR NOUN the health and care of the elderly

germ NOUN **1** a small living organism which can cause disease **2** the earliest or initial form of something, eg a fertilized egg **3** that from which anything grows: *germ of an idea*

German shepherd NOUN a breed of large wolf-like dog (*also called*: **alsatian**)

germinate VERB *biology* of a seed or spore: to show the first signs of development > **germination** NOUN

gerund NOUN an action noun with the ending *-ing*, eg watch*ing*, wait*ing*

gestation NOUN in mammals: the period of time when a young animal develops in the uterus

gesticulate VERB to wave the hands and arms about in excitement etc > **gesticulation** NOUN

gesture NOUN **1** a meaningful action with the hands, head, etc **2** an action expressing your feelings or intent: *gesture of good will*

get VERB (**getting, got** *US* **getting, got, gotten**) **1** to go and find, take hold of, obtain: *get a carton of milk on the way home/I'll get you, you rascal!/I'm at the station. Can you come and get me?* **2** to go or move **3** to cause to be done: *get your hair cut* **4** to receive: *get a letter* **5** to cause to be in some condition: *get the car started* **6** to arrive: *what time did you get home?* **7** to catch or have (a disease): *I think I've got flu* **8** to become: *get rich* **get at 1** to reach **2** to hint at: *what are you getting at?* **3** to criticize continually: *stop getting at me* **get away with** to escape punishment for **get on with** to be on friendly terms with **get over** to recover from **get up 1** to stand up **2** to get out of bed

ⓘ Comes from Old Norse *geta*

> **Get** is one of the most overused words in the English language. Make sure you don't use it too much!

geyser (*pronounced* **geez**-*er*) NOUN a natural hot spring

ghastly ADJECTIVE **ghastlier, ghastliest 1** *informal* very ill: *feeling ghastly* **2** horrible, ugly **3** very pale, death-like **4** *informal* very bad > **ghastliness** NOUN

gherkin NOUN a small pickled cucumber

ghetto NOUN (*plural* **ghettos** *or* **ghettoes**) a poor residential part of a city in which a certain group (especially of immigrants) lives

ghost NOUN the spirit of a dead person

ghostly ADJECTIVE like a ghost

ghoul (*pronounced* gool) NOUN **1** an evil spirit which robs dead bodies **2** someone unnaturally interested in death and disaster > **ghoulish** ADJECTIVE

giant NOUN **1** an imaginary being, like a human but enormous **2** a very tall or large person ▸ ADJECTIVE huge

giantess NOUN a female giant

gibber VERB **1** to speak nonsense **2** to make meaningless noises; babble

gibberish NOUN words without meaning; rubbish

A B C D E F G H I J K L M N O P Q R S T U V W X Y Z

gibbet NOUN, *history* a gallows where criminals were executed, or hung up after execution

gibbon NOUN a large, tailless ape

gibe *another spelling* of **jibe**

giblets (*pronounced* **jib**-lets) PLURAL NOUN organs from the inside of a chicken or other fowl

giddy ADJECTIVE **giddier, giddiest** **1** unsteady, dizzy **2** causing dizziness: *from a giddy height* > **giddiness** NOUN (meaning 1)

gift NOUN **1** something freely given, eg a present **2** a natural talent: *a gift for music* **look a gift horse in the mouth** to find fault with a gift

gifted ADJECTIVE having special natural power or ability

gigabyte NOUN (*abbrev* **GB, Gb** *or* **Gbyte**) a measure of computer data or memory, equal to 1024 megabytes

gigantic ADJECTIVE huge, of giant size

giggle VERB to laugh in a nervous or silly manner ▸NOUN a nervous or silly laugh

gild (*pronounced* gild) VERB **1** to cover with beaten gold **2** to make bright **gild the lily** to try to improve something already beautiful enough

ⓘ Comes from Old English *gyldan* which is related to *gold*

> Do not confuse with: **guild**

gill (*pronounced* gil) NOUN one of the openings on the side of a fish's head through which it breathes

gilt (*pronounced* gilt) NOUN beaten gold used for gilding ▸ADJECTIVE **1** covered with thin gold **2** gold in colour

> Do not confuse with: **guilt**.
> **Gilt** is a past participle of the verb 'gild'.

gimmick NOUN something meant to attract attention

gin[1] NOUN an alcoholic drink made from grain, flavoured with juniper berries

gin[2] NOUN a trap or snare

ginger NOUN a hot-tasting root, used as a seasoning in food ▸ADJECTIVE **1** flavoured with ginger: *ginger biscuits* **2** reddish-brown in colour: *ginger hair*

gingerbread NOUN cake flavoured with ginger

gingerly ADVERB very carefully and gently: *opened the door gingerly*

gipsy *another spelling* of **Gypsy**

giraffe NOUN an African animal with very long legs and neck

> ⓘ Called a *camelopard* until the 17th century

girder NOUN a beam of iron, steel or wood used in building

girdle NOUN **1** a belt for the waist **2** a tight-fitting piece of underwear to slim the waist

girl NOUN a female child or young woman

girlfriend NOUN a female friend, especially in a romantic relationship

girlhood NOUN the state or time of being a girl

girlie ADJECTIVE girlish

girlish ADJECTIVE of a woman's

appearance or behaviour: attractively youthful, like that of a girl

girth NOUN **1** measurement round the middle **2** a strap tying a saddle on a horse

gist (*pronounced* jist) NOUN the main points or ideas of a story, argument, etc: *give me the gist of what happened*

give VERB (**giving, gave, given**) **1** to hand over freely or in exchange **2** to utter (a shout or cry) **3** to break, crack: *the bridge gave under the weight of the train* **4** to produce: *this lamp gives a good light* > **giver** NOUN (meaning 1) **give away 1** to hand over (something) to someone without payment **2** to betray: *his guilty behaviour gave him away* **give in** to yield **give rise to** to cause **give up 1** to hand over **2** to yield **3** to stop, abandon (a habit etc) **give way 1** to yield **2** to collapse **3** to let traffic crossing your path go before you

[i] Comes from Old English *gefan*

giveaway NOUN (*plural* **giveaways**) something that you say or do which reveals a secret to other people

given ADJECTIVE **1** stated or specified: *on a given day* **2** assumed to be true ▶ NOUN something accepted as true: *that he is wrong is a given*

glacé (*pronounced* glah-**sei**) ADJECTIVE iced or sugared: *glacé cherries*

glacial ADJECTIVE **1** of ice or glaciers **2** icy, cold: *glacial expression*

glacier NOUN, *geography* a slow-moving river of ice in valleys between high mountains

glad ADJECTIVE **1** pleased: *I'm glad you were able to come* **2** giving pleasure: *glad tidings* **3** (**glad to**) perfectly willing and happy to
> **gladly** ADVERB (meanings 1 and 3)
> **gladness** NOUN (meanings 1 and 2)

gladden VERB to make glad

glade NOUN an open space in a wood

gladiator NOUN, *history* in ancient Rome, a man trained to fight with other men or with animals for the amusement of spectators
> **gladiatorial** ADJECTIVE

glam ADJECTIVE, *slang* glamorous

glamorous ADJECTIVE **1** dressing and behaving in a way which people find fascinating and attractive **2** fashionable and extravagant

glamour NOUN fascination, charm, beauty, especially artificial

glance NOUN a quick look ▶ VERB to take a quick look at **glance off** to hit and fly off sideways

gland NOUN an organ that produces a specific chemical substance (eg a hormone) for use inside the body

glandular ADJECTIVE of, or affecting, the glands

glandular fever NOUN an infectious disease with symptoms including a slight fever and an enlargement of the glands

glare NOUN **1** an unpleasantly bright light **2** an angry or fierce look ▶ VERB **1** to shine with an unpleasantly bright light **2** to look angrily

glaring ADJECTIVE **1** dazzling **2** very clear, obvious: *glaring mistake*

A B C D E F G H I J K L M N O P Q R S T U V W X Y Z

glaringly ADVERB extremely, in a way that cannot be missed: *glaringly obvious*

glass NOUN (*plural* **glasses**) **1** a hard transparent substance made from metal and other oxides **2** (**glasses**) spectacles **3** a drinking vessel made of glass **4** *old* a mirror ▸ ADJECTIVE made of glass

glass ceiling NOUN a barrier to promotion at work experienced by some women

glasshouse NOUN a greenhouse

glassy ADJECTIVE **1** of eyes: without expression **2** of surfaces, especially water: smooth and shiny with no ripples

glaze VERB **1** to cover with a thin coating of glass or other shiny stuff **2** to ice (a cake etc) **3** to put panes of glass in a window **4** of eyes: to become glassy ▸ NOUN **1** a shiny surface **2** sugar icing

glazier NOUN someone who sets glass in window frames

gleam VERB **1** to glow **2** to flash ▸ NOUN **1** a beam of light **2** brightness

glean VERB to collect, gather

glee NOUN **1** joy **2** a song in parts

gleeful ADJECTIVE merry, usually in a mischievous way > **gleefully** ADVERB

glen NOUN in Scotland, a long narrow valley

glib ADJECTIVE **1** speaking smoothly and fluently (often insincerely and superficially) **2** quick and ready, but showing little thought: *glib reply* > **glibly** ADVERB

glide VERB **1** to move smoothly and easily: *she glided effortlessly across the ice* **2** to travel by glider ▸ NOUN the act of gliding

glider NOUN an aeroplane without an engine

glimmer NOUN **1** a faint light **2** a faint indication: *a glimmer of hope* ▸ VERB to burn or shine faintly

glimpse NOUN a brief view ▸ VERB to get a brief look at

glint VERB to sparkle, gleam ▸ NOUN a sparkle, a gleam

glisten VERB to sparkle

glitter VERB to sparkle ▸ NOUN **1** sparkling **2** shiny granules used for decorating paper etc

glittery ADJECTIVE shiny, sparkly

glitz NOUN showiness, garishness > **glitzy** ADJECTIVE

ⓘ Originally a Yiddish word meaning 'glitter'

gloat VERB to look at or think about with malicious joy: *gloating over their rivals' defeat*

global ADJECTIVE **1** of or affecting the whole world: *global warming* **2** applying generally: *global increase in earnings*

globalization *or* **globalisation** NOUN expansion of a company or an industry all over the world

global warming NOUN an increase in the temperature of the earth's atmosphere, great enough to cause changes in the earth's climate

globe NOUN **1** the earth **2** a ball with a map of the world drawn on it **3** a ball, a sphere

globular ADJECTIVE ball-shaped

globule NOUN **1** a droplet **2** a small ball-shaped piece

glockenspiel NOUN a musical instrument consisting of a series of graded metal bars that are struck with hammers

gloom NOUN dullness, darkness: sadness

gloomy ADJECTIVE **1** sad, depressed **2** miserable, depressing **3** dimly lighted > **gloomily** ADVERB > **gloominess** NOUN

glorify VERB (**glorifies, glorifying, glorified**) **1** to make glorious **2** to praise highly

glorious ADJECTIVE **1** splendid **2** deserving great praise **3** delightful > **gloriously** ADVERB

glory NOUN (*plural* **glories**) **1** fame, honour **2** great show, splendour ▸ VERB to rejoice, take great pleasure (in)

gloss[1] NOUN brightness on the surface ▸ VERB to make bright **gloss over** to try to hide (a fault etc) by treating it quickly or superficially

gloss[2] VERB to add an explanatory note of (something)

glossary NOUN (*plural* **glossaries**) a list of words with their meanings

glossy ADJECTIVE shiny, highly polished

glove NOUN **1** a covering for the hand with a separate covering for each finger **2** a boxing glove

glow VERB **1** to burn without a flame **2** to give out a steady light **3** to be flushed from heat, cold, etc **4** to be radiant with emotion: *glow with pride* ▸ NOUN **1** a glowing state **2** great heat **3** bright light

glower (*pronounced* **glow**-er) VERB to stare (at) with a frown

glowing ADJECTIVE **1** giving out a steady light **2** flushed **3** radiant **4** full of praise: *glowing report*

glow-worm NOUN a kind of beetle which glows in the dark

glucose NOUN, *biology, chemistry* a sugar found in fruits *etc*

glue NOUN a substance for sticking things together ▸ VERB to join with glue > **gluey** ADJECTIVE

glum ADJECTIVE (**glummer, glummest**) sad, gloomy > **glumly** ADVERB

glut VERB (**glutting, glutted**) **1** to feed greedily till full **2** to supply too much to (a market) ▸ NOUN an oversupply: *a glut of fish on the market*

gluten NOUN a sticky protein found in wheat and certain other cereals, which is responsible for coeliac disease

glutinous ADJECTIVE sticky, gluey

glutton NOUN **1** someone who eats too much **2** someone who is eager for anything: *a glutton for punishment*

gluttonous ADJECTIVE **1** fond of overeating **2** eating greedily

gluttony NOUN greediness in eating

glycerine (*pronounced* **gli**-se-reen) NOUN a colourless, sticky, sweet-tasting liquid

GM ABBREVIATION genetically modified, used to describe a plant or animal in which some of the genes have been changed using genetic engineering: *GM crops*

GMT ABBREVIATION Greenwich Mean Time

A B C D E F G H I J K L M N O P Q R S T U V W X Y Z

gnarled (*pronounced* narld) ADJECTIVE knotty, twisted

gnash (*pronounced* nash) VERB to grind (the teeth)

gnat (*pronounced* nat) NOUN a small blood-sucking fly, a midge

gnaw (*pronounced* naw) VERB to bite at with a scraping action

gnome (*pronounced* nohm) NOUN a small, imaginary, human-like creature who lives underground, often guarding treasure

GNP ABBREVIATION gross national product

gnu (*pronounced* noo *or* nyoo) NOUN a type of African antelope, with a large head, horns and a long mane (*also called*: **wildebeest**)

GNVQ ABBREVIATION General National Vocational Qualification

go VERB (**going, went, gone**) **1** to move: *I want to go home/when are you going to Paris?* **2** to leave: *time to go* **3** to lead: *that road goes north* **4** to become: *go mad* **5** to work: *the car is going at last* **6** to intend (to do): *I'm going to have a bath* **7** to be removed or taken: *the best seats have all gone now* **8** to be given, awarded, etc: *the first prize went to Janet* ▸ NOUN **1** *informal* an attempt, a try: *have a go* **2** fashion, style: *all the go* **3** the act or process of going **4** energy, spirit **from the word go** from the start **go about** to try, set about **go ahead** to proceed (with), begin on **go along with** to agree with **go back on** to fail to keep (a promise etc) **go for 1** to aim to get **2** to attack **go off 1** to explode **2** to become rotten **3** to come to dislike **go on 1** to continue **2** to talk too much **go round** to be enough for everyone: *will the trifle go round?* **go under** to be ruined: *the restaurant finally went under last winter* **on the go** very active

ⓘ Comes from Old English *gan* meaning 'to go'

goad NOUN something used to urge action ▸ VERB to urge on by annoying

go-ahead ADJECTIVE eager to succeed ▸ NOUN permission to act

goal NOUN **1** the upright posts between which the ball is to be driven in football and other games **2** a score in football and other games **3** anything aimed at or wished for: *my goal is to pass this exam*

goat NOUN an animal of the sheep family with horns and a long-haired coat

gob NOUN, *slang* the mouth

gobble VERB **1** to eat quickly **2** to make a noise like a turkey

go-between NOUN someone who helps two people to communicate with each other

goblet NOUN **1** a large cup without handles **2** a drinking glass with a stem

goblin NOUN a mischievous, ugly spirit in folklore

gobsmacked ADJECTIVE, *slang* shocked, astonished

gobstopper NOUN a hard round sweet for sucking

god NOUN **1** a male supernatural being who is worshipped **2** (**God**) the creator and ruler of the world in the Christian, Jewish, etc religions

goddaughter NOUN a girl for

whom a godmother or godfather is responsible

goddess NOUN a female supernatural being who is worshipped

godfather NOUN a man who agrees to see that a child is brought up according to the beliefs of the Christian Church

godly ADJECTIVE (**godlier, godliest**) holy, pious

godmother NOUN a woman who agrees to see that a child is brought up according to the beliefs of the Christian Church

godsend NOUN a very welcome piece of unexpected good fortune

godson NOUN a boy for whom a godmother or godfather is responsible

goggles PLURAL NOUN spectacles for protecting the eyes from dust, sparks, etc

go-kart NOUN a small low-powered racing car

gold NOUN **1** *chemistry* a precious yellow metal **2** riches ▶ ADJECTIVE **1** made of gold **2** having the colour of gold

golden ADJECTIVE **1** of or like gold **2** very fine

golden rule NOUN a guiding principle

golden wedding NOUN the 50th anniversary of a wedding

goldfinch NOUN a small colourful bird

goldfish NOUN a golden-yellow Chinese carp, often kept as a pet

gold-leaf NOUN gold beaten to a thin sheet

gold medal NOUN a medal given to a competitor who comes first

goldsmith NOUN a maker of gold articles

golf NOUN a game in which a ball is struck with a club and aimed at a series of holes on a large open course

golf club NOUN **1** a club used in golf **2** a society of golf players **3** the place where they meet

golfer NOUN someone who plays golf

goloshes *another spelling of* **galoshes**

gondola NOUN **1** a canal boat used in Venice **2** a car suspended from an airship, cable railway, etc

gondolier NOUN a boatman who rows a gondola

gone *past participle of* **go**

gong NOUN a metal plate which makes a booming sound when struck, used to summon people to meals etc

good ADJECTIVE **1** having desired or positive qualities: *a good butcher will bone it for you/a good restaurant* **2** having a positive effect: *fruit is good for you* **3** virtuous: *a good person* **4** kind: *she was good to me* **5** pleasant, enjoyable: *a good time* **6** substantial, sufficiently large: *a good income*

ⓘ Comes from Old English *god*

good afternoon INTERJECTION a common formal greeting used when meeting or leaving people in the afternoon

goodbye NOUN (*plural* **goodbyes**) what you say when leaving people

good-day INTERJECTION an old-fashioned greeting used when meeting or leaving people

good-evening INTERJECTION a common formal greeting used when meeting or leaving people in the evening

good-for-nothing ADJECTIVE useless, lazy

good morning EXCLAMATION a common formal greeting used when meeting or leaving people in the morning

good name NOUN good reputation

good-natured ADJECTIVE kind, cheerful

goodness NOUN the quality of being good ▶ INTERJECTION an exclamation of surprise

goodnight EXCLAMATION a phrase used when leaving people at night

goods PLURAL NOUN **1** personal belongings **2** things to be bought and sold

good taste NOUN good judgement for what is aesthetically pleasing or socially acceptable

goodwill NOUN **1** kind wishes **2** a good reputation in business

goofy ADJECTIVE, *US* stupid, silly

goose NOUN (*plural* **geese**) a web-footed bird larger than a duck

gooseberry NOUN a sour-tasting, pale green berry

goosebumps *or* **goosepimples** PLURAL NOUN small bumps on the skin caused by cold or fear

gopher NOUN **1** a small, burrowing rodent **2** *computing* a piece of software used to search for or index services on the Internet

gore[1] NOUN a mass of blood ▶ VERB to pierce with horns, tusks, etc: *gored by an elephant*

gore[2] NOUN a triangular-shaped piece of cloth in a garment etc

gorge NOUN a narrow valley between hills ▶ VERB (**gorging, gorged**) to eat greedily till full: *gorging himself on chocolate biscuits*

gorgeous ADJECTIVE **1** beautiful, very attractive **2** showy, splendid **3** *informal* excellent, very enjoyable

gorilla NOUN the largest kind of ape

Do not confuse with: **guerrilla**

[i] The *Gorillai* were a tribe of hairy people in ancient times

gormless ADJECTIVE, *Brit* stupid, senseless

gorse *or* **furze** NOUN a prickly bush with yellow flowers

gory ADJECTIVE full of gore; bloody: *a very gory film*

gosling NOUN a young goose

go-slow NOUN a slowing of speed at work as a form of protest

gospel NOUN **1** the teaching of Christ **2** *informal* the absolute truth

gossamer NOUN **1** fine spider-threads floating in the air or lying on bushes **2** a very thin material

gossip NOUN **1** talk, not necessarily true, about other people's personal affairs etc **2** someone who listens to and passes on gossip ▶ VERB (**gossiping, gossiped**) **1** to engage in gossip **2** to chatter

[i] Originally *godsibb*, meaning 'godparent'

got *past form* of **get**

gouge (*pronounced* gowj) NOUN a chisel with a hollow blade for cutting grooves ▶ VERB (**gouging**, **gouged**) to scoop (out)

goulash NOUN (*plural* **goulashes**) a stew of meat and vegetables, flavoured with paprika

gourd (*pronounced* goord) NOUN a large fleshy fruit

gourmand (*pronounced* goor-**mond**) NOUN a glutton

gourmet (*pronounced* **goor**-mei) NOUN someone who loves good wines or food

gout NOUN, *medicine* a painful swelling of the smaller joints, especially of the big toe

govern VERB **1** to rule, control **2** to put into action the laws etc of a country

ⓘ Comes from Latin *gubernare* meaning 'to steer a ship'

governess NOUN especially in the past, a woman employed to teach young children at their home

government NOUN **1** rule; control **2** the people who rule and administer the laws of a country

governor NOUN someone who rules a state or country etc

gown NOUN **1** a woman's formal dress **2** a loose robe worn by members of the clergy, lawyers, etc

GP ABBREVIATION General Practitioner, a doctor who treats most ordinary illnesses

grab VERB (**grabbing**, **grabbed**) **1** to seize or grasp suddenly: *grabbed me by the arm* **2** to secure possession of quickly: *grab a seat* **3** to get in a hurry: *grab a bite to eat* ▶ NOUN a sudden grasp or catch

grace NOUN **1** beauty of form or movement **2** a short prayer at a meal **3** (**Grace**) a title used in addressing or referring to a duke or archbishop: *Your Grace* **with bad grace** unwillingly **with good grace** willingly

graceful ADJECTIVE **1** beautiful in appearance or movement **2** done in a neat way **3** polite > **gracefully** ADVERB

gracious ADJECTIVE kind, polite ▶ INTERJECTION expressing surprise or shock > **graciously** ADVERB

gradation NOUN arrangement in order of rank, difficulty, etc

grade NOUN a step or placing according to quality or rank; class ▶ VERB to arrange in order, eg from easy to difficult **make the grade** to reach the necessary standard

gradient NOUN **1** a slope on a road, railway, etc **2** the amount of a slope, worked out by dividing the vertical distance by the horizontal distance

gradual ADJECTIVE step by step; going slowly but steadily > **gradually** ADVERB

graduate VERB (*pronounced* **grad**-yoo-eit) **1** to divide into regular spaces **2** to pass university examinations and receive a degree ▶ NOUN (*pronounced* **grad**-yoo-at) someone who has passed university examinations and received a degree

graduation NOUN the act of getting a degree from a university, or the ceremony to celebrate this

graffiti PLURAL NOUN, *sometimes*

A B C D E F G H I J K L M N O P Q R S T U V W X Y Z

used as singular words or drawings scratched or painted on a wall etc

graft VERB **1** to fix a shoot or twig of one plant on to another for growing **2** *medicine* to fix (skin) from one part of the body on to another part **3** *medicine* to transfer (a part of the body) from one person to another ▸NOUN **1** living tissue (eg skin) which is grafted **2** a shoot grafted **3** hard work

Grail NOUN the plate or cup believed to have been used by Christ at the Last Supper

grain NOUN **1** a seed eg of wheat, oats **2** corn in general **3** a very small quantity **4** the run of the lines of fibre in wood, leather, etc **against the grain** against your natural feelings or instincts

-gram *or* **-gramme** SUFFIX forms words for things which are written, printed or drawn: *telegram/anagram*

ⓘ Comes from Greek *gramma* meaning 'letter'

gram *or* **gramme** NOUN (*abbrev* **g**) the basic unit of weight in the metric system

grammar NOUN **1** the correct use of words in speaking or writing: *his grammar is very bad* **2** the rules applying to a particular language: *French grammar*

grammar school NOUN a kind of secondary school

grammatical ADJECTIVE correct according to rules of grammar > **grammatically** ADVERB

gramme *another spelling* of **gram**

gramophone NOUN, *trademark*, *old* a record-player

gran NOUN, *informal* a grandmother

granary NOUN (*plural* **granaries**) a storehouse for grain

grand ADJECTIVE great; noble; fine

ⓘ Comes from French *grand* meaning 'big'

grandchild NOUN a son's or daughter's child

granddaughter NOUN a son's or daughter's daughter

grandeur (*pronounced* **grand**-yer) NOUN greatness

grandfather NOUN a father's or mother's father

grandiose ADJECTIVE planned on a large scale

grandmaster NOUN a chess-player of the greatest ability

grandmother NOUN a father's or mother's mother

grandparent NOUN a grandmother or grandfather

grand piano NOUN a piano with a large flat top

grandson NOUN a son's or daughter's son

grandstand NOUN rows of raised seats at a sports ground giving a good view

granite NOUN a hard rock of greyish or reddish colour

granny NOUN (*plural* **grannies**) *informal* a grandmother

grant VERB **1** to give, allow (something asked for) **2** to admit as true ▸NOUN money awarded for a special purpose: *a research grant*

granted *or* **granting** CONJUNCTION (often with **that**) even if, assuming: *granted that you are right* **take for granted**

1 to assume that something will happen without checking 2 to treat (someone) casually, without respect or kindness

granular ADJECTIVE made up of grains

granulated ADJECTIVE broken into grains: *granulated sugar*

granule NOUN a tiny grain or part

grape NOUN the green or black smooth-skinned berry from which wine is made

grapefruit NOUN a sharp-tasting fruit like a large yellow orange

grapevine NOUN 1 a climbing plant that produces grapes 2 (**the grapevine**) the spreading of information through casual conversation

-graph *or* **-graphy** SUFFIX 1 of or relating to writing: *biography/ autograph* 2 used to form words describing printed images or pictures: *photograph(y)*

graph NOUN lines drawn on squared paper to show changes in quantity, eg in temperature or money spent > **graphical** ADJECTIVE

graphic ADJECTIVE 1 relating to writing, drawing or painting 2 vivid, well told 3 explicit: *graphic violence* ▶NOUN a visual image, eg a painting, print, illustration or diagram > **graphically** ADVERB

graphics SINGULAR NOUN the art of drawing according to mathematical principles ▶PLURAL NOUN 1 the pictures in a magazine 2 the use of computers to display data in a pictorial form 3 pictures produced by computer

graphite NOUN a form of carbon used in making pencils

grapple VERB: **grapple with** 1 to struggle with 2 to try to deal with (a problem etc)

grasp VERB 1 to clasp and grip with the fingers or arms 2 to understand ▶NOUN 1 a grip with the hand or arms 2 someone's power of understanding

grasping ADJECTIVE greedy, mean

grass NOUN (*plural* **grasses**) 1 the plant covering fields of pasture 2 a kind of plant with long narrow leaves, eg wheat, reeds, bamboo 3 *slang* the drug marijuana

grasshopper NOUN a type of jumping insect

grassland NOUN an area of grass or grass-like plants

grass snake NOUN a type of harmless snake

grassy ADJECTIVE covered with grass

grate[1] VERB 1 to rub food, eg cheese, against a rough surface in order to break it down into small pieces 2 to make a harsh, grinding sound 3 to irritate

grate[2] NOUN a framework of iron bars for holding a fire

grateful ADJECTIVE 1 feeling thankful 2 showing or giving thanks > **gratefully** ADVERB

grater NOUN an instrument with a rough surface for rubbing cheese or other food into small pieces

gratification NOUN pleasure; satisfaction

gratify VERB (**gratifying, gratified**) to please; satisfy

grating NOUN a frame of iron bars

gratitude NOUN thankfulness; desire to repay kindness

gratuitous ADJECTIVE uncalled-for, done without good reason: *gratuitous violence* > **gratuitously** ADVERB

gratuity NOUN (*plural* **gratuities**) a money gift in return for a service; a tip

grave NOUN a pit in which a dead person is buried ▶ ADJECTIVE **1** serious, important: *grave error* **2** not cheerful, solemn > **gravely** ADVERB > **gravity** NOUN

grave accent (*pronounced* grahv) NOUN a backward-leaning stroke (`) placed over letters in some languages to show their pronunciation

gravel NOUN small stones or pebbles

gravestone NOUN a stone placed to mark a grave

graveyard NOUN a place where the dead are buried, a cemetery

gravitate VERB to move towards as if strongly attracted (to)

gravity NOUN **1** the force of attraction between the earth and any object in its gravitational field, which pulls the object towards the ground **2** seriousness, importance: *gravity of the situation*

gravy NOUN (*plural* **gravies**) a sauce made from the juices of meat that is cooking

gray *US spelling of* **grey**

graze VERB **1** to feed on (growing grass) **2** to scrape the skin of **3** to touch lightly in passing ▶ NOUN **1** a scraping of the skin **2** a light touch

grazing NOUN grass land for animals to graze on

grease NOUN **1** thick animal fat **2** an oily substance ▶ VERB to smear with grease, apply grease to

greasy ADJECTIVE **1** full of, or covered in, grease **2** of skin: having a slightly moist appearance because the body releases a lot of natural oils into it **3** wet and slippery

great ADJECTIVE **1** very large **2** powerful **3** very important, distinguished **4** very talented: *a great singer* **5** of high rank, noble **6** *informal* excellent, very good > **greatness** NOUN (meanings 1, 2, 3, 4 and 5)

ⓘ Comes from Old English

great-grandchild NOUN the son or daughter of a grandson or grand-daughter

great-grandfather NOUN the father of a grandfather or grandmother

great-grandmother NOUN the mother of a grandfather or grandmother

greatly ADVERB very much

greed NOUN great and selfish desire for food, money, etc

greedy ADJECTIVE full of greed > **greedily** ADVERB

green ADJECTIVE **1** of the colour of growing grass etc **2** inexperienced, naive **3** concerned with care of the environment: *the green movement* ▶ NOUN **1** the colour of growing grass **2** a piece of ground covered with grass **3** (**Green**) a member of the Green Party; an environmentalist **4** (**greens**) green vegetables for food

green belt NOUN open land or parkland surrounding a town or city

greenery NOUN green plants

greenfield site NOUN a newly developed commercial or industrial site (*compare with*: **brownfield site**)

green fingers NOUN: **have green fingers** to be a skilful gardener

greenfly NOUN (*plural* **greenfly**) a bright green, small insect which attacks plants

greengrocer NOUN someone who sells fresh vegetables

greenhouse NOUN a building with large glass panes in which plants are grown

greenhouse effect NOUN (**the greenhouse effect**) the warming-up of the earth's surface due to the sun's heat being trapped in the atmosphere by carbon dioxide and other gases (**greenhouse gases**), the increased output of which causes the earth to warm more quickly (**the enhanced greenhouse effect**)

green light NOUN (**the green light**) permission to go ahead with a plan

Green Party NOUN a political party concerned with conserving natural resources and decentralizing political and economic power

greet VERB **1** to meet someone with kind words **2** to say hello etc to **3** to react to, respond to: *greeted the news with relief*

greeting NOUN **1** words of welcome or kindness **2** reaction, response

gregarious ADJECTIVE sociable, liking the company of others

grenade NOUN a small bomb thrown by hand

ⓘ From a French word for 'pomegranate', because of its shape

grew *past tense* of **grow**

grey *or US* **gray** ADJECTIVE **1** of a colour between black and white **2** grey-haired, old ▶ NOUN **1** grey colour **2** a grey horse

greyhound NOUN a breed of fast-running dog

grid NOUN **1** a grating of bars **2** a network of lines, eg for helping to find a place on a map **3** a network of wires carrying electricity over a wide area

grid reference NOUN a set of numbers or letters used to indicate a place on a grid

grief NOUN deep sorrow, especially after bereavement **come to grief** to meet with misfortune

grievance NOUN a cause for complaining

grieve VERB to feel grief or sorrow

grievous ADJECTIVE **1** painful; serious **2** causing grief

griffin *or* **griffon** NOUN a mythological animal with the body and legs of a lion and the beak and wings of an eagle

grill VERB **1** to cook directly under heat (provided by an electric or gas cooker) **2** to question closely ▶ NOUN **1** a frame of bars for grilling food on **2** grilled food **3** the part of a cooker used for grilling

grille NOUN a metal grating over a door, window, etc

A B C D E F G H I J K L M N O P Q R S T U V W X Y Z

grim ADJECTIVE **1** stern, fierce-looking **2** terrible; very unpleasant: *a grim sight* **3** unyielding, stubborn: *grim determination* > **grimly** ADVERB

grimace NOUN a twisting of the face in fun or pain ▸ VERB to make a grimace

grime NOUN dirt

grimy ADJECTIVE covered with a layer of ground-in dirt

grin VERB (**grinning, grinned**) to smile broadly ▸ NOUN a broad smile **grin and bear it** to suffer something without complaining

grind VERB (**grinding, ground**) **1** to crush to powder **2** to sharpen by rubbing **3** to rub together: *grinding his teeth* ▸ NOUN hard or unpleasant work

grinder NOUN someone or something that grinds

grindstone NOUN a revolving stone for grinding or sharpening tools **back to the grindstone** back to work **keep your nose to the grindstone** to work hard without stopping

grip NOUN **1** a firm hold, a grasp: *these shoes have a good grip* **2** a way of holding or grasping; control: *a loose grip* **3** a handle or part for holding **4** a travelling bag, a holdall ▸ VERB (**gripping, gripped**) to take a firm hold of

gripe NOUN **1** a sharp stomach pain **2** *informal* a complaint ▸ VERB to complain

gripping ADJECTIVE commanding attention, compelling: *a gripping thriller*

grisly ADJECTIVE (**grislier, grisliest**) frightful, hideous

ⓘ Comes from Old English *grislic* which is related to *agrisan* meaning 'to terrify'

gristle NOUN a tough elastic substance in meat > **gristly** ADJECTIVE

grit NOUN **1** a mixture of rough sand and gravel, spread on icy surfaces **2** courage ▸ VERB (**gritting, gritted**) **1** to apply grit to (an icy surface): *has the road been gritted?* **2** to clench: *grit your teeth*

gritty ADJECTIVE (**grittier, grittiest**)**1** covered in grit or having a texture like grit **2** honest in the portrayal of harsh realities: *a gritty drama* > **grittiness** NOUN

grizzly bear NOUN a type of large bear of North America

groan VERB **1** to moan in pain, disapproval, etc **2** to be full or loaded: *a table groaning with food*

grocer NOUN a dealer in certain kinds of food and household supplies

groceries PLURAL NOUN food etc sold by grocers

groggy ADJECTIVE (**groggier, groggiest**) weak and light-headed after being ill or beaten

ⓘ Originally meaning 'drunk', from *grog*, a mixture of rum and water

groin NOUN the part of the body where the inner thigh joins the torso

groom NOUN **1** a bridegroom **2** someone in charge of horses ▸ VERB **1** to look after (a horse) **2** to make smart and tidy

groove NOUN a furrow, a long hollow ▸ VERB to cut a groove (in)

grope VERB to search (for) by feeling around as if blind: *groping for his socks in the dark*

gross ADJECTIVE **1** coarse **2** very fat **3** great, obvious: *gross error* **4** of money: total, before any deductions for tax etc: *gross profit* **5** *US informal* disgusting, revolting ▸ NOUN **1** the whole taken together **2** twelve dozen

grossly ADVERB extremely

grotesque ADJECTIVE very odd or unnatural-looking

grotto NOUN (*plural* **grottoes** *or* **grottos**) a cave

grotty ADJECTIVE (**grottier, grottiest**) dirty or shabby

ground[1] NOUN **1** the surface of the earth **2** (*also*: **grounds**) a good reason: *ground for complaint* **3** (**grounds**) lands surrounding a large house etc **4** (**grounds**) dregs: *coffee grounds* ▸ VERB **1** of a ship: to strike the seabed and become stuck **2** to prevent (aeroplanes) from flying **3** to prevent (someone in your charge) from going out: *that's it! You're grounded*

ground[2] *past form* of **grind**

ground floor NOUN the storey of a building at street level

grounding NOUN the first steps in learning something

groundless ADJECTIVE without reason

groundnut *same as* **peanut**

groundwork NOUN the first stages of a task

group NOUN a number of people or things together ▸ VERB **1** to form or gather into a group **2** to classify

ⓘ Comes from French *groupe* meaning 'group'

grouse NOUN (*plural* **grouse**) a game bird hunted on moors and hills

grove NOUN a small group of trees

grovel VERB (**grovelling, grovelled**) to be overly humble

grow VERB (**growing, grew, grown**) **1** to become bigger or stronger: *the local population is growing* **2** to become: *grow old* **3** to rear, cause to grow (plants, trees, etc): *grow from seed*

growl VERB to utter a deep sound like a dog ▸ NOUN an angry dog's deep sound

grown *past participle* of **grow**

growth NOUN **1** growing **2** increase: *growth in market shares* **3** something that grows **4** something abnormal that grows on the body

grub NOUN **1** the form of an insect after being hatched from the egg, eg a caterpillar **2** *informal* food

grubby ADJECTIVE (**grubbier, grubbiest**) dirty > **grubbily** ADVERB > **grubbiness** NOUN

grudge VERB to be unwilling to accept or allow: *I don't grudge him his success* ▸ NOUN a feeling of resentment: *she bears a grudge against me*

gruel NOUN a thin mixture of oatmeal boiled in water

gruelling ADJECTIVE straining, exhausting

gruesome ADJECTIVE horrible

ⓘ Originally a Scots word, derived

A B C D E F G H I J K L M N O P Q R S T U V W X Y Z

from *grue* meaning 'to be terrified'

gruff ADJECTIVE **1** rough in manner **2** of a voice: deep and harsh

grumble VERB to complain in a bad-tempered, discontented way ▶ NOUN a complaint

grumpy ADJECTIVE (**grumpier, grumpiest**) cross, bad-tempered > **grumpily** ADVERB

grunge NOUN, *informal* **1** grime, dirt **2** a style of rock music > **grungy** ADJECTIVE

grunt VERB to make a sound like that of a pig ▶ NOUN a pig-like snort

guarantee NOUN **1** a promise to do something **2** a statement by the maker that something will work well **3** money put down which will be forfeited if a promise is broken ▶ VERB to give a guarantee

guard VERB to keep safe from danger or attack ▶ NOUN **1** someone or a group whose duty it is to protect **2** a screen etc which protects from danger **3** someone in charge of a railway train or coach

guarded ADJECTIVE careful, not revealing much: *guarded comments*

guardian NOUN **1** someone with the legal right to take care of an orphan **2** someone who protects or guards

guerrilla NOUN one of a small band which makes sudden attacks on a larger army but does not fight openly ▶ ADJECTIVE of fighting: in which many small bands acting independently make sudden raids on an enemy: *guerrilla tactics*

Comes from Spanish *guerrilla* meaning 'little war'

> Do not confuse with: **gorilla**

guess VERB **1** to say without sure knowledge: *I can only guess the price* **2** *US* to suppose: *I guess I'll go* ▶ NOUN (*plural* **guesses**) an estimate

guest NOUN a visitor received and entertained in another's house or in a hotel etc

guffaw VERB to laugh loudly ▶ NOUN a loud laugh

guidance NOUN help or advice towards doing something

guide VERB **1** to show the way to, lead, direct **2** to influence ▶ NOUN **1** someone who shows tourists around **2** someone who leads travellers on a route unfamiliar to them **3** a guidebook **4** (**Guide**) a girl belonging to the Guides organization

guidebook NOUN a book with information for tourists about a place

guided missile NOUN an explosive rocket which after being fired can be guided to its target by radio waves

guide dog NOUN a dog trained to guide a blind person safely

guild NOUN **1** an association for those working in a particular trade or profession **2** a society, a social club

Comes from Old English *gield* meaning 'payment' or 'idol'

> Do not confuse with: **gild**

guile NOUN cunning, deceit

guillotine NOUN **1** *history* an

instrument with a falling blade used for executing by beheading **2** a machine with a blade for cutting paper ▶ VERB **1** to behead with the guillotine **2** to cut (paper) with a guillotine

ⓘ Named after Joseph *Guillotin*, a French doctor who recommended its use for executions during the French Revolution

guilt NOUN **1** a sense of shame **2** blame for wrongdoing, eg breaking the law

> Do not confuse with: **gilt**

guilty ADJECTIVE **1** ashamed about something bad you have done **2** having done something wrong **3** officially judged to have committed a crime > **guiltily** ADVERB (meaning 1)

guinea fowl NOUN a bird resembling a pheasant, with white-spotted feathers

guinea pig NOUN **1** a rodent about the size of a rabbit **2** someone used as the subject of an experiment

guise NOUN appearance, dress, especially in disguise: *in the guise of a priest*

guitar NOUN a stringed musical instrument with frets and a waisted body

gulf NOUN a large inlet of the sea

gull NOUN a seagull

gullet NOUN a passage by which food goes down into the stomach

gullible ADJECTIVE easily tricked

gully NOUN (*plural* **gullies**) a channel worn by water

gulp VERB to swallow quickly and in large mouthfuls ▶ NOUN a sudden fast swallowing

gum NOUN **1** the firm flesh in which the teeth grow **2** sticky juice got from some trees and plants **3** a sticky substance used as glue **4** a flavoured gummy sweet, chewing gum ▶ VERB (**gumming, gummed**) to stick with gum > **gummy** ADJECTIVE

gumption NOUN good sense

gum tree NOUN a tree that gives gum or gum resin, especially the eucalyptus

gun NOUN any weapon firing bullets or shells

gunboat NOUN a small warship with heavy guns

gunfire NOUN the firing of guns

gung-ho ADJECTIVE boisterously enthusiastic

ⓘ Based on a Chinese phrase meaning 'work together'

gunpowder NOUN an explosive in powder form

gurgle VERB **1** of water: to make a bubbling sound **2** to make such a sound, eg in pleasure ▶ NOUN: *the baby's gurgles*

guru (*pronounced* **goo**-roo) NOUN **1** a Hindu spiritual teacher **2** a revered instructor, a mentor

gush VERB **1** to flow out in a strong stream **2** to talk at length with exaggerated emotions: *gushing on about the wedding* ▶ NOUN (*plural* **gushes**) a strong or sudden flow: *gush of tears*

gusset NOUN a piece of material sewn into a seam join to strengthen or widen part of a garment

A B C D E F G H I J K L M N O P Q R S T U V W X Y Z

gust NOUN a sudden blast of wind

gusto NOUN enthusiasm **with gusto** enthusiastically

gusty ADJECTIVE (**gustier, gustiest**) windy

gut NOUN **1** the alimentary canal **2** animal intestines used as strings for musical instruments **3** (**guts**) spirit, courage ▶ VERB (**gutting, gutted**) **1** to take out the inner parts of: *gut a fish* **2** to destroy completely, especially by fire: *gutted the building*

gutter NOUN a water channel on a roof, at the edge of a roadside, etc

gutter press NOUN that part of the press that specializes in sensational journalism

guttersnipe NOUN, *old* a poor child living in the streets

guttural ADJECTIVE harsh in sound, as if formed in the throat

guy[1] NOUN **1** *Brit* an effigy of Guy Fawkes, traditionally burned on 5 November **2** *informal* a man

guy[2] NOUN a steadying rope for a tent etc

guzzle VERB to eat or drink greedily

gym NOUN, *informal* **1** a gymnasium **2** gymnastics

gymkhana NOUN a meeting for horse-riding competitions

gymnasium NOUN (*plural* **gymnasiums** *or* **gymnasia**) a building or room equipped for physical exercises

gymnast NOUN someone who does gymnastics

gymnastic ADJECTIVE relating to gymnastics

gymnastics PLURAL NOUN exercises to strengthen the body

gynaecology NOUN the treatment of disorders of the female reproductive system

Gypsy *or* **Gipsy** NOUN (*plural* **Gypsies** *or* **Gipsies**) a member of a wandering people; a Romany
[i] Based on *Egyptian*, because of the belief that the Romanies came originally from Egypt

gyrate VERB to whirl round > **gyration** NOUN > **gyratory** ADJECTIVE

Hh

a b c d e f g h i j k l m n o p q r s t u v w x y z

haberdashery NOUN materials for sewing, mending, etc

habit NOUN **1** something you are used to doing: *nasty habits* **2** someone's usual behaviour **3** the dress of a monk or nun **make a habit of** to do regularly or frequently

habitable ADJECTIVE fit to live in

habitat NOUN the natural home of an animal or plant

habitation NOUN a dwelling place

habitual ADJECTIVE usual, formed by habit

habitually ADVERB usually, as a matter of habit

habituate VERB to make accustomed

hack[1] VERB **1** to cut or chop up roughly **2** *informal* to use a computer to get unauthorized access to files or other systems ▶NOUN **1** a rough cut, a gash **2** a short, dry cough

hack[2] NOUN **1** a writer who does hard work for low pay **2** a riding horse kept for hire ▶VERB to ride on horseback, especially along ordinary roads

hacker NOUN, *informal* **1** a skilled computer operator **2** someone who breaks into government or commercial computer systems

hackles PLURAL NOUN the hair on a dog's neck **make someone's hackles rise** to make them angry

hackneyed ADJECTIVE overused, not fresh or original: *hackneyed phrase*

hacksaw NOUN a saw for cutting metal

haddock NOUN (*plural* **haddock** *or* **haddocks**) a small edible N Atlantic fish

Hadith (*pronounced* **had**-ith) NOUN the collection of traditions about Muhammad

haemo- *or US* **hemo-** PREFIX of or relating to blood

🄸 Comes from Greek *haima* meaning 'blood'

haemoglobin *or US* **hemoglobin** (*both pronounced* heem-*o*-**glohb**-in) NOUN the oxygen-carrying substance in red blood cells

haemophilia *or US* **hemophilia** (*both pronounced* heem-*o*-**fil**-i-*a*) NOUN a hereditary disease causing extreme bleeding when cut

haemophiliac *or US*

A B C D E F G H I J K L M N O P Q R S T U V W X Y Z

hemophiliac (*both pronounced* heem-*o*-**fil**-i-ak) NOUN someone suffering from haemophilia

haemorrhage *or US* **hemorrhage** (*both pronounced* **hem**-o-r*i*j) NOUN a large amount of bleeding

hag NOUN **1** *offensive* an ugly old woman **2** a witch

haggard ADJECTIVE gaunt and hollow-eyed, from tiredness
🛈 Originally a falconer's term for an untamed hawk

haggis NOUN (*plural* **haggises**) a Scottish dish made from chopped sheep's offal and oatmeal, seasoned and boiled in a bag traditionally made from the animal's stomach

haggle VERB to argue determinedly over a price

haiku NOUN a Japanese form of poem written in three lines of 5, 7, and 5 syllables

hail[1] VERB **1** to greet, welcome **2** to call to, attract the attention of ▶ NOUN **1** a call from a distance **2** greeting, welcome **hail from** to come from, belong to

hail[2] NOUN **1** frozen raindrops **2** a falling mass: *a hail of bullets* ▶ VERB **1** to shower with hail **2** to descend in a mass

hailstone NOUN a piece of hail

hair NOUN a thread-like growth on the skin of an animal; the whole mass of these (as on the head) **split hairs** to worry about unimportant details; nitpick

hair-breadth *or* **hair's-breadth** NOUN a very small distance

hairdresser NOUN someone who cuts, washes, styles, and colours hair

hairdryer *or* **hairdrier** NOUN an electrical device which blows hot air to dry hair

hair-raising ADJECTIVE terrifying

hairspray NOUN a fine spray to fix a hairstyle

hairstyle NOUN a way of cutting or wearing the hair

hairy ADJECTIVE (**hairier, hairiest**) **1** covered with hair **2** *informal* risky, dangerous > **hairiness** NOUN

hajj *or* **hadj** (*pronounced* haj) NOUN (*plural* **hajjes** *or* **hadjes**) the annual Muslim pilgrimage to Mecca

halal (*pronounced* **hal**-al) NOUN meat from animals that have been slaughtered according to Islamic law ▶ ADJECTIVE from animals slaughtered in this way

halcyon (*pronounced* **hal**-si-*o*n) ADJECTIVE: **halcyon days** a time of peace and happiness
🛈 From the Greek word for 'kingfisher' in the phrase 'kingfisher days', a period of calm weather in mid-winter

hale ADJECTIVE: **hale and hearty** healthy

half NOUN (*plural* **halves**) one of two equal parts ▶ ADJECTIVE **1** being one of two equal parts: *a half bottle of wine* **2** not full or complete: *a half smile* ▶ ADVERB partly, to some extent

half-baked ADJECTIVE *informal* not properly thought out, incomplete

half-board NOUN a hotel charge for bed, breakfast, and another meal

half-brother NOUN a brother sharing only one parent

half day NOUN a day in which someone attends school or work only in the morning or afternoon

half-hearted ADJECTIVE not eager

half-mast ADVERB of a flag: hoisted halfway up the mast to show that someone important has died

half moon NOUN the moon when half is visible

half-sister NOUN a sister sharing only one parent

half-term NOUN a short holiday halfway through a school or college term

half-time NOUN an interval halfway through a sports game

halfway ADVERB & ADJECTIVE at or to a point equally far from the beginning and the end

halibut NOUN (*plural* **halibut** *or* **halibuts**) a large edible flatfish

hall NOUN **1** (*also called*: **hallway**) a passage at the entrance to a house **2** a large public room **3** a large country house

hallelujah *or* **halleluia** INTERJECTION expressing praise to God (*also*: **alleluia**)

hallmark NOUN **1** a mark put on gold and silver articles to show quality **2** a characteristic sign: *the hallmark of a good editor*

hallo *another spelling* of **hello**

hallowed ADJECTIVE, *old* holy, sacred

Hallowe'en NOUN the evening of 31 October, traditionally a time when spirits are believed to be around

hallucinate (*pronounced* ha-**loo**-si-neit) VERB to see something that is not actually there > **hallucination** NOUN

hallucinatory ADJECTIVE causing hallucinations, or like a hallucination

hallway *see* **hall**

halo NOUN (*plural* **haloes** *or* **halos**) **1** a circle of light surrounding eg the sun or moon **2** in paintings etc: a ring of light around the head of a saint, angel, etc as a sign of holiness

halogen (*pronounced* **hal**-*o*-jen) NOUN, *chemistry* one of a group of elements that includes chlorine, bromine and iodine

halt VERB to come or bring to a stop ▸ NOUN **1** a stop, a standstill: *call a halt* **2** a stopping place

halter NOUN a head-rope for holding and leading a horse

halting ADJECTIVE hesitant, uncertain

halve VERB to divide in two

ham[1] NOUN the meat from a pig's thigh salted and dried

ham[2] NOUN, *informal* **1** an actor who overacts **2** an amateur radio operator

hamburger NOUN a round cake of minced beef, cooked by frying or grilling

hamlet NOUN a small village

hammer NOUN **1** a tool with a heavy metal head for beating metal, driving nails, etc **2** a striking piece in a clock, piano, pistol, etc ▸ VERB **1** to drive or shape with a hammer **2** *informal* to defeat overwhelmingly **hammer**

A B C D E F G H I J K L M N O P Q R S T U V W X Y Z

and tongs *informal* determinedly, violently

hammock NOUN a length of netting, canvas, etc hung up by the corners, and used as a bed

hamper[1] VERB to hinder, impede

hamper[2] NOUN a large basket with a lid

hamster NOUN a small rodent with large cheek pouches, often kept as a pet

hamstring NOUN a tendon at the back of the knee

hand NOUN **1** the part of the human body at the end of the arm **2** a pointer, eg on a clock **3** help, aid: *Can you give me a hand?* **4** a measure (four inches, 10.16 centimetres) for the height of horses **5** a worker, a labourer **6** a style of handwriting **7** side, direction: *left-hand side* **8** *cards* a group of playing-cards dealt to someone **9** *informal* clapping, applause: *a big hand* ▸ VERB to pass (something) with the hand **at hand** near by **change hands** to pass to another owner **hand over fist** *informal* progressing quickly and steadily: *making money hand over fist* **in hand 1** in your possession: *cash in hand* **2** in preparation, under control **out of hand 1** out of control **2** at once: *to dismiss it out of hand* **take in hand** to take charge of **try your hand at** to have a go at, attempt **at first hand** directly from the source **wash your hands of** to give up all responsibility for

handbag NOUN a small bag for personal belongings

handbook NOUN a small book giving information or directions

handcuffs PLURAL NOUN steel bands joined by a short chain, put round the wrists of prisoners

handful NOUN (*plural* **handfuls**) **1** as much as can be held in one hand **2** a small amount **3** *informal* a difficult and demanding child, pet, etc

handicap NOUN **1** something that makes an action more difficult **2** a disadvantage, such as having to run a greater distance, given to the best competitors in a race **3** a race in which handicaps are given **4** a physical or mental disability ▸ VERB **1** to give a handicap to **2** to burden, impede

ⓘ Originally a gambling game in which wagers were drawn by *hand* from a *cap*

handicapped ADJECTIVE **1** having or given a handicap **2** physically or mentally disabled

handicraft NOUN skilled work done by hand, not machine

hand-in-hand ADJECTIVE **1** holding hands **2** in partnership

handiwork NOUN **1** thing(s) made by hand **2** something done by a particular person etc: *the handiwork of a sick mind*

handkerchief NOUN (*plural* **handkerchiefs**) a small cloth for wiping the nose etc

handle VERB **1** to touch, hold or use with the hand **2** to manage, cope with ▸ NOUN **1** the part of anything meant to be held in the hand **2** a way of understanding something: *trying to get a handle on something*

handlebars PLURAL NOUN a steering bar at the front of a bicycle with a handle at each end

handler NOUN **1** someone who trains and works with an animal, eg a police dog **2** someone who handles something: *baggage handler*

hand-me-down NOUN *informal* a second-hand piece of clothing, especially one that used to belong to another member of the family

handout NOUN a sheet or bundle of information given out at a lecture etc

hand-picked ADJECTIVE chosen carefully

handrail NOUN a narrow rail running alongside a stairway for support

handsome ADJECTIVE **1** good-looking **2** generous: *a handsome gift*

hands-on ADJECTIVE involving practical experience

handstand NOUN an act of balancing on the hands with the legs in the air

hand-to-mouth ADJECTIVE with barely enough to live on and nothing to spare

handwriting NOUN writing with pen or pencil > **handwritten** ADJECTIVE

handy ADJECTIVE (**handier, handiest**) **1** useful or convenient to use **2** easily reached, near **3** clever with the hands > **handily** ADVERB (meanings 1 and 2)

handyman NOUN (*plural* **handymen**) a man who does odd jobs around the house

hang VERB (**hanging, hung** *or* **hanged**) **1** to fix or be fixed to a point off the ground **2** to be suspended in the air **3** to attach (wallpaper) to a wall **4** (*past form* **hanged**) to put (a prisoner) to death by putting a rope round their neck and letting them fall **get the hang of** *informal* to understand, learn how to use **hang about** *or* **hang around** to remain near, loiter **hang back** to hesitate **hang down** to droop or fall downwards **hang fire** to delay **hang on 1** to depend on **2** *informal* to wait, linger

ⓘ Comes from Old English *hangian*

hangar (*pronounced* **hang**-*ar*) NOUN a shed for aeroplanes

ⓘ Comes from French *hangar* meaning 'a shed'

> Do not confuse: **hangar** and **hanger**

hangdog ADJECTIVE guilty-looking

hanger NOUN a frame on which a coat etc is hung

ⓘ For origin, see **hang**

hanger-on NOUN (*plural* **hangers-on**) someone who stays near someone in the hope of gaining some advantage

hang-gliding NOUN a form of gliding by hanging in a harness under a large kite

hanging NOUN an execution in which the prisoner is hanged

hangman NOUN (*plural* **hangmen**) an executioner who hangs people

hangnail NOUN a torn shred of skin beside a fingernail

a b c d e f g h i j k l m n o p q r s t u v w x y z

A B C D E F G H I J K L M N O P Q R S T U V W X Y Z

hangover NOUN **1** uncomfortable after-effects of being drunk **2** something remaining: *a hangover from the 1960s*

hank NOUN a coil or loop of string, rope, wool, etc

hanker VERB to long for something: *hankering after a chocolate biscuit*

hankie *or* **hanky** NOUN (*plural* **hankies**) *informal* a handkerchief

Hanukkah (*pronounced* **hah**-*nuw*-ka) *or* **Chanukkah** NOUN the Jewish festival of lights held in mid-December

haphazard ADJECTIVE depending on chance, without planning or system > **haphazardly** ADVERB

hapless ADJECTIVE unlucky

happen VERB **1** to take place **2** to occur by chance **3** to chance to do: *Did you happen to see the news?*

happening NOUN an event

happy ADJECTIVE (**happier, happiest**) **1** joyful **2** contented **3** fortunate, lucky: *a happy coincidence* **4** willing: *happy to help* > **happily** ADVERB > **happiness** NOUN

happy-go-lucky ADJECTIVE easy-going, taking things as they come

harangue (*pronounced* ha-**rang**) NOUN a loud aggressive speech ▸ VERB to deliver a harangue

harass (*pronounced* **har**-as) VERB to annoy persistently, pester > **harassment** NOUN

harbour *or US* **harbor** NOUN **1** a place of shelter for ships **2** a shelter, a place of safety ▸ VERB to give shelter or refuge to

hard ADJECTIVE **1** solid, firm **2** not easily broken or put out of shape **3** not easy to do, understand, etc **4** not easy to please **5** not easy to bear **6** having no kind or gentle feelings **7** of water: containing many minerals and so not forming a good lather **8** of drugs: habit-forming ▸ ADVERB **1** with great effort or energy: *She works hard* **2** strongly, violently > **hardness** NOUN **hard of hearing** rather deaf

hard-and-fast ADJECTIVE strict, rigid

hardback NOUN a book bound in a hard cover (*compare with*: **paperback**)

hardboard NOUN light strong board made from compressed wood pulp

hard disk NOUN, *computing* a rigid magnetic disk, normally sealed within a hard drive, used to store large amounts of data

hard drive NOUN, *computing* a disk drive that holds, reads data stored on and writes to a hard disk

harden VERB to make hard

hard-hearted ADJECTIVE having no kind feelings

hard-hit ADJECTIVE badly affected

hard labour NOUN tiring work given to prisoners as part of their punishment

hardline ADJECTIVE refusing to change or compromise: *a hardline socialist*

hardly ADVERB scarcely; only just; with difficulty

hardship NOUN something difficult to bear

hard shoulder NOUN the surfaced

strip on the outer edges of a motorway, used when stopping in an emergency

hard up ADJECTIVE, *informal* short of money

hardware NOUN **1** ironmongery **2** *computing* the casing, processor, disk drives, etc of a computer, not the programs which it runs (*contrasted with*: **software**)

hardwood NOUN the wood of certain trees including oak, ash, elm, etc

hardy ADJECTIVE (**hardier, hardiest**) strong, robust, tough > **hardiness** NOUN

hare NOUN a fast-running animal, like a large rabbit

hare-lip NOUN a split in the upper lip at birth, often occurring with a cleft palate

harem (*pronounced* **hei**-rem *or* hah-**reem**) NOUN **1** the women's rooms in an Islamic house **2** a set of wives and concubines

harlequin (*pronounced* **hah**-li-kwin) NOUN a comic pantomime character wearing a multicoloured costume

harm NOUN hurt, damage ▸ VERB **1** to wound, damage **2** to do wrong to

harmful ADJECTIVE having a bad or damaging effect on people or things

harmless ADJECTIVE **1** safe, eg to eat, use, or touch **2** causing no annoyance or disturbance to anyone

harmonic ADJECTIVE, *music* relating to harmony or harmonics ▸ NOUN a ringing sound produced by lightly touching a string being played

harmonica NOUN a mouth organ

harmonious ADJECTIVE **1** pleasant-sounding **2** peaceful, without disagreement

harmonize *or* **harmonise** VERB **1** to bring into harmony **2** to agree, go well (with) **3** *music* to add the different parts to a melody > **harmonization** NOUN

harmony NOUN (*plural* **harmonies**) **1** agreement of one part, colour, or sound with another **2** agreement between people: *living in harmony* **3** *music* a part intended to agree in sound with the melody

harness NOUN (*plural* **harnesses**) **1** the leather and other fittings for a workhorse **2** an arrangement of straps etc attaching something to the body: *parachute harness* ▸ VERB **1** to put a harness on a horse **2** to use as a resource: *harnessing the power of the wind*

harp NOUN a triangular, stringed musical instrument played upright by plucking with the fingers ▸ VERB to play the harp **harp on about** to talk too much about > **harpist** NOUN

harpoon NOUN a spear tied to rope, used for killing whales ▸ VERB to strike with a harpoon

harpsichord NOUN an early musical instrument with keys, played like a piano

harrowing ADJECTIVE very distressing

harry VERB (**harries, harrying, harried**) **1** to plunder, lay waste **2** to harass, worry

harsh ADJECTIVE rough, bitter; cruel > **harshly** ADVERB

a b c d e f g **h** i j k l m n o p q r s t u v w x y z

A B C D E F G **H** I J K L M N O P Q R S T U V W X Y Z

harvest NOUN **1** the time of the year when ripened crops are gathered in **2** the crops gathered at this time ▶ VERB to gather in (a crop)

has *see* **have**

has-been NOUN, *informal* someone no longer important or popular

hash NOUN a dish of chopped meat etc **make a hash of** *informal* to spoil completely

hashish NOUN the strongest form of the drug made from hemp (*see also* **cannabis**)

hassle *informal*, VERB to cause problems for ▶ NOUN difficulty, trouble

haste NOUN speed, hurry **make haste** to hurry

hasten VERB **1** to hurry (on) **2** to drive forward

hasty ADJECTIVE (**hastier, hastiest**) hurried; done without thinking > **hastily** ADVERB

hat NOUN a covering for the head **keep something under your hat** to keep it secret

hatch¹ NOUN (*plural* **hatches**) a door or cover over an opening in a floor, wall, etc

hatch² VERB **1** to produce (young) from eggs **2** to form and set working: *They hatched a plan*

hatchback NOUN a car with a sloping rear door which opens upwards

hatchet NOUN a small axe **bury the hatchet** to put an end to a quarrel

hate VERB to dislike very much ▶ NOUN great dislike

hateful ADJECTIVE horrible, causing hatred

hatred NOUN extreme dislike

hat-trick NOUN **1** *cricket* the putting out of three batsmen by three balls in a row **2** *football* three goals scored by the same player **3** any action performed three times in a row

haughty ADJECTIVE (**haughtier, haughtiest**) proud, looking on others with scorn > **haughtily** ADVERB

haul VERB to drag, pull with force ▶ NOUN **1** a strong pull **2** *informal* a difficult or tiring job: *a long haul* **3** an amount gathered at one time: *a haul of fish* **4** a rich find, booty

haulage NOUN **1** the carrying of goods **2** money charged for this

haunch NOUN (*plural* **haunches**) **1** the fleshy part of the hip **2** a leg and loin of meat, especially venison

haunt VERB **1** to visit often **2** of a ghost: to inhabit, linger in (a place) ▶ NOUN a place often visited

haunted ADJECTIVE inhabited by ghosts

have VERB (**has, having, had**) **1** used with another verb to show that an action is in the past and completed: *We have decided to move house* **2** to own, possess: *Do you have a cat?* **3** to hold, contain: *The hotel has a swimming pool* **4** to give birth to: *have a baby* **5** to suffer from: *have a cold* **6** to cause to be done: *have your hair cut* **7** to put up with: *I won't have him being so rude* **have done with** to finish **have it out** to settle by argument

[i] Comes from Old English *habban*

haven NOUN a place of safety

haversack NOUN a bag made of canvas etc with shoulder-straps, for carrying on the back

havoc NOUN great destruction

hawk[1] NOUN a bird of prey like a falcon

hawk[2] VERB to carry (goods) round, usually from door to door, trying to sell them > **hawker** NOUN

hawthorn NOUN a prickly tree with white flowers and small red berries

hay NOUN cut and dried grass, used as cattle food

hay fever NOUN an illness with effects like a bad cold, caused by pollen etc

haystack *or* **hayrick** NOUN hay built up into a mound

haywire ADJECTIVE, *informal* of things: out of order; not working properly

hazard NOUN **1** chance **2** risk of harm or danger ▸VERB **1** to risk **2** to put forward (a guess) at the risk of being wrong

hazardous ADJECTIVE dangerous, risky

haze NOUN a thin mist

hazel NOUN a nut-producing tree of the birch family ▸ADJECTIVE light greenish-brown in colour

hazelnut NOUN a light brown nut produced by the hazel tree

hazy ADJECTIVE (**hazier, haziest**) **1** misty **2** not clear, vague > **hazily** ADVERB > **haziness** NOUN

H-bomb NOUN a hydrogen bomb

he PRONOUN a male person or animal already spoken about (used only as the subject of a verb): *he ate a banana*

head NOUN **1** the uppermost part of the body, containing the brain, skull, etc **2** someone's mind: *can't get that tune out of my head* **3** a person in charge, a chief **4** (**heads**) the side of a coin showing the head of a monarch or leader ▸VERB **1** to lead **2** to go in front of **3** to go in the direction of: *heading for home* **4** to hit (a ball) with the head **head off** to turn aside, deflect: *head off an attack* **head over heels** completely, thoroughly: *head over heels in love* **off your head** *informal* mad, crazy **per head** per person

headache NOUN **1** a pain in the head **2** *informal* a worrying problem

headband NOUN a band worn round the head

headboard NOUN a board across the top end of a bed

headdress NOUN (*plural* **headdresses**) a covering for the head, especially a highly decorative one used in ceremonies

header NOUN *football* a shot at goal striking the ball with the head

headfirst ADVERB **1** with the head first: *fall headfirst down the stairs* **2** rashly, without thinking

heading NOUN words at the head of a chapter, paragraph, etc

headland NOUN a point of land running out into the sea, a cape

headlight NOUN a strong light on the front of a car etc

headline NOUN a line in large letters at the top of a newspaper page

A B C D E F G H I J K L M N O P Q R S T U V W X Y Z

headlong ADJECTIVE & ADVERB headfirst

headmaster NOUN a **head teacher**

headmistress NOUN a **head teacher**

head-on ADJECTIVE & ADVERB with the head or front first

headphones PLURAL NOUN a listening device that fits over the ears

headquarters SINGULAR NOUN & PLURAL NOUN place from which the chief officers of an army etc control their operations; the chief office (of a business etc)

headrest NOUN a support for the head in a vehicle etc

head start NOUN a boost or advantage at the beginning of something

headstone NOUN a gravestone

headstrong ADJECTIVE determined, stubborn

head teacher NOUN (sometimes **headmaster** or **headmistress**) the principal teacher of a school

headway NOUN progress: *making headway with the backlog*

heady ADJECTIVE (**headier, headiest**) exciting

heal VERB to make or become healthy or sound; cure > **healer** NOUN

health NOUN **1** someone's physical condition: *How's your health?* **2** good or natural physical condition **your health!** (as a toast) a wish that someone may have good health

health centre NOUN a building where nurses and doctors hold clinics

health visitor NOUN a trained nurse who visits people in their homes

healthy ADJECTIVE (**healthier, healthiest**) **1** in good health or condition **2** encouraging good health > **healthily** ADVERB

heap NOUN **1** a pile of things thrown one on top of another **2** (*usually* **heaps**) *informal* a great many (of) ▸ VERB to throw in a pile

hear VERB (**hearing, heard**) **1** to receive (sounds) by the ear **2** to listen to **3** to be told, understand: *I hear you want to speak to me* EXCLAMATION a cry to show agreement with a speaker

hearing NOUN **1** the act or power of listening **2** an investigation and listening to evidence

hearing aid NOUN a small electronic device worn on or in the ear to help hearing

hearsay NOUN gossip, rumour

hearse NOUN a car for carrying a dead body to the grave etc

heart NOUN **1** the part of the body which acts as a blood pump **2** the inner or chief part of anything: *the heart of the problem* **3** courage: *take heart* **4** will, enthusiasm: *His heart isn't in it* **5** love, affection: *with all my heart* **6** a sign (♥) representing a heart, or often love **7** this sign used in one of the suits of playing-cards

heartache NOUN sorrow, grief

heart attack NOUN a sudden and painful interruption in the functioning of the heart

heartbeat NOUN **1** the pulsing of the heart **2** a single pulsing action of the heart

heartbreak NOUN great sorrow or grief > **heartbreaking** ADJECTIVE

heartbroken ADJECTIVE very upset, very sad

heartburn NOUN a burning feeling in the chest after eating, indigestion

hearten VERB to cheer on, encourage

heartfelt ADJECTIVE felt deeply, sincere: *heartfelt thanks*

hearth NOUN a fireplace

heartily ADVERB **1** cheerfully and with great enthusiasm **2** thoroughly, absolutely: *I'm heartily sick of his moaning*

heartless ADJECTIVE cruel

heart-rending ADJECTIVE very moving, very upsetting

heart-throb NOUN *informal* someone, especially a male, that many people find very attractive

heart-to-heart NOUN a frank, intimate discussion

hearty ADJECTIVE (**heartier, heartiest**) **1** strong, healthy **2** of a meal: large, satisfying **3** eager, over-cheerful

heat NOUN **1** high temperature **2** anger **3** *sport* a round in a competition, race, etc ▶ VERB to make or become hot **in heat** of a female animal: ready for mating in the breeding season

heath NOUN **1** barren, open country **2** heather

heathen NOUN someone who does not believe in an established religion, especially someone who worships idols ▶ ADJECTIVE of heathens, pagan

heather NOUN a plant with small purple, white, or pink flowers growing on moorland ▶ ADJECTIVE of the colour of purple heather

heat wave NOUN a period of hot weather

heave VERB **1** to lift by force **2** to throw **3** to rise and fall **4** to produce, let out (especially a sigh)

heaven NOUN **1** (often **the heavens**) the sky **2** (often **Heaven**) the dwelling place of God; paradise **3** any place of great happiness

heavenly ADJECTIVE **1** living in heaven **2** *informal* delightful

heavily ADVERB **1** with great force, in great amount: *It was raining heavily* **2** to a serious or great extent, intensely: *heavily in debt* **3** loudly and deeply: *He sighed heavily/breathing heavily* **4** in a thick, solid-looking way: *He was short, but heavily built* **5** in a slow, sleepy, or sad way: *'I can't help you,' he said heavily*

heavy ADJECTIVE (**heavier, heaviest**) **1** of great weight **2** great in amount, force, etc: *heavy rainfall* **3** not easy to bear **4** slow; sleepy **5** loud and deep: *heavy breathing* **6** having a thick, solid appearance: *heavy eyebrows/a heavy oak table* > **heaviness** NOUN

heavy-duty ADJECTIVE designed to withstand very hard wear

heavy-handed ADJECTIVE clumsy, awkward

heavy industry NOUN industries such as coalmining, steel-making, shipbuilding, etc using heavy equipment (*compare with*: **light industry**)

A B C D E F G H I J K L M N O P Q R S T U V W X Y Z

heavy metal NOUN a very loud repetitive form of rock music

heavyweight NOUN **1** a boxer in the highest weight category **2** *informal* someone very important or powerful

Hebrew NOUN an ancient language spoken in its modern form by Jews in Israel

heckle VERB to shout insults at or ask awkward questions of (a public speaker) > **heckler** NOUN

hectare NOUN 10 000 square metres

hectic ADJECTIVE rushed; feverish

hecto- *or* **hect-** PREFIX forms words of measurement equal to one hundred times the basic unit: *hectare* (= 100 ares, each equivalent to 100 square metres)

ⓘ Comes from Greek *hekaton* meaning 'one hundred'

hedge NOUN a fence of bushes, shrubs, etc ▸VERB **1** to make a hedge **2** to shut in with a hedge **3** to avoid giving a straight answer **hedge your bets** to keep open two or more possible courses of action

hedgehog NOUN a small animal with prickly spines on its back

hedgerow NOUN a row of bushes forming a hedge

heed VERB to give attention to, listen to **pay heed to** to take notice of

heedless ADJECTIVE careless

heel NOUN the back part of the foot ▸VERB **1** to hit (especially a ball) with the heel **2** to put a heel on (a shoe) **take to your heels** *or* **show a clean pair of heels** to run away

hefty ADJECTIVE (**heftier, heftiest**) *informal* **1** powerful, muscular **2** heavy

Hegira *or* **Hejira** (*pronounced* **hej**-i-r*a*) NOUN the Islamic era, dating from AD 622

heifer (*pronounced* **hef**-*er*) NOUN a young cow

height NOUN **1** the state of being high **2** distance from bottom to top **3** the highest point **4** (often **heights**) a high place

heighten VERB to make higher, greater, stronger, etc

heinous (*pronounced* **hei**-n*us*) ADJECTIVE extremely bad, atrocious: *heinous crime*

heir NOUN the legal inheritor of a title or property on the death of the owner

heiress NOUN (*plural* **heiresses**) a woman or girl who is the legal inheritor of a large amount of property or money

heirloom NOUN something that has been handed down in a family from generation to generation

hejab *another spelling* of **hijab**

held *past form* of **hold**[1]

helicopter NOUN a flying machine kept in the air by propellers rotating on a vertical axis

ⓘ A coinage based on Greek words meaning 'spiral wing'

helio- PREFIX of or relating to the sun: *heliograph*/*heliotrope* (= a plant that turns its flowers towards the sun) /*helium* (= a gas first discovered in the atmosphere of the sun)

ⓘ Comes from Greek *helios* meaning 'the sun'

helium NOUN, *chemistry* (symbol **He**) a very light gas

helix (*pronounced* **hee**-liks) NOUN (*plural* **helices** – *pronounced* **hee-li-seez** – *or* **helixes**) a screw-shaped coil

hell NOUN **1** a place of punishment of the wicked after death **2** (often **Hell**) the dwelling place of the Devil **3** any place of great misery or pain

hellbent on ADJECTIVE, *informal* determined to

hellish ADJECTIVE, *informal* very bad, unpleasant, horrible, or difficult > **hellishly** ADVERB

hello *or* **hallo** *or* **hullo** NOUN (*plural* **hellos** *or* **helloes** etc) a greeting used between people

helm NOUN the wheel or handle by which a ship is steered

helmet NOUN an armoured or protective covering for the head

helmsman NOUN (*plural* **helmsmen**) the person who steers a ship

help VERB **1** to aid, do something useful for **2** to give the means for doing something to **3** to stop yourself from (doing): *I can't help liking him* ▶ NOUN **1** aid, assistance **2** someone who assists > **helper** NOUN **help yourself** serve yourself, take what you want

🛈 Comes from Old English *helpan*

helpful ADJECTIVE useful, giving help > **helpfully** ADVERB

helping NOUN a share, especially of food

helpless ADJECTIVE useless; powerless > **helplessly** ADVERB

helter-skelter ADVERB in a great hurry, in confusion ▶ NOUN a spiral slide in a fairground etc

hem NOUN the border of a garment doubled down and stitched ▶ VERB (**hemming, hemmed**) to put or form a hem on **hem in** to surround

hemi- PREFIX half

🛈 Comes from Greek *hemi* meaning 'half'

hemisphere NOUN **1** a half of a sphere or ball-shape **2** half of the earth: *western hemisphere/southern hemisphere* > **hemispherical** ADJECTIVE

hemline NOUN the height of a hem on a dress or skirt

hemlock NOUN a poisonous plant with spotted leaves

hemo- *US spelling* of **haemo-**

hemp NOUN a plant used for making ropes, bags, sails, etc and the drug cannabis

hen NOUN **1** a female bird **2** a female domestic fowl

hence ADVERB **1** from this place or time: *ten years hence* **2** for this reason: *hence, I am unable to go*

henceforth *or* **henceforward** ADVERB from now on

henna NOUN a reddish plant dye used for colouring the hair and decorating the skin

henpecked ADJECTIVE of a husband: dominated by his wife

hepatitis NOUN inflammation of the liver caused by one of several viruses

hepta- PREFIX seven

🛈 Comes from Greek *hepta* meaning 'seven'

heptagon NOUN a seven-sided figure > **heptagonal** ADJECTIVE

A B C D E F G H I J K L M N O P Q R S T U V W X Y Z

her PRONOUN a female person already spoken about (used only as the object in a sentence): *Have you seen her?* ▶ ADJECTIVE belonging to such a person: *her house*

herald NOUN **1** something that is a sign of future things **2** *history* someone who carried and read important notices ▶ VERB **1** to announce loudly **2** to be a sign of

heraldic (*pronounced* hi-**ral**-dik) ADJECTIVE of heraldry

heraldry NOUN the study of coats of arms, crests, etc

herb NOUN a plant used in the making of medicines or in cooking

ⓘ Comes from French *herbe* meaning 'grass'

herbaceous ADJECTIVE **1** of a plant: with a stem which dies every year **2** of a flower-bed: filled with such plants

herbal ADJECTIVE of or using herbs: *herbal remedy*

herbalism NOUN the study and use of plants in medicine

herbicide NOUN a chemical used to kill weeds

herbivore NOUN an animal which feeds on plants > **herbivorous** ADJECTIVE

Herculean ADJECTIVE requiring tremendous strength or effort: *a Herculean task*

ⓘ After the Greek hero, *Hercules*, who was given twelve seemingly impossible tasks to do by the gods

herd NOUN **1** a group of animals of one kind **2** (**the herd**) most people ▶ VERB to group together like a herd of animals

here ADVERB at, in, or to this place: *He's here already/Come here!*

hereby ADVERB, *formal* by this means

hereditary ADJECTIVE passed on from parents to children

heredity NOUN the passing on of physical qualities from parents to children

heresy (*pronounced* **he**-re-si) NOUN (*plural* **heresies**) an opinion which goes against the official (especially religious) view > **heretic** (*pronounced* **he**-re-tik) NOUN > **heretical** (*pronounced* he-**ret**-i-kal) ADJECTIVE

heritage NOUN something passed on by or inherited from an earlier generation

hermaphrodite (*pronounced* her-**maf**-ro-dait) NOUN an animal which has the qualities of both male and female sexes

hermit NOUN someone who lives alone, often for religious reasons

hermitage NOUN the dwelling of a hermit

hermit crab NOUN a kind of crab which lives in the abandoned shell of a shellfish

hernia NOUN the bursting out of part of an internal organ through a weak spot in surrounding body tissue

hero NOUN (*plural* **heroes**) **1** someone much admired for their bravery **2** the chief male character in a story, film, etc

heroic ADJECTIVE **1** brave as a hero **2** of heroes > **heroically** ADVERB

heroin (*pronounced* **he**-roh-in)

NOUN a very addictive drug derived from morphine

heroine (*pronounced* **he**-roh-in) NOUN **1** a woman much admired for her bravery **2** the chief female character in a story, film, etc

heroism (*pronounced* **he**-roh-izm) NOUN bravery

heron NOUN a large water bird, with long legs and neck

herpes (*pronounced* **her**-peez) NOUN a name for various types of a skin disease caused by a virus

herring NOUN (*plural* **herring** *or* **herrings**) an edible sea fish with silvery colouring, which moves in large shoals

hers PRONOUN something belonging to a female person already spoken about: *The idea was hers*

herself PRONOUN **1** used reflexively: *She washed herself* **2** used for emphasis: *She herself won't be there but her brother will*

hertz NOUN (*plural* **hertz**; symbol **Hz**) the standard unit of frequency for radio waves etc

hesitant ADJECTIVE undecided about whether to do something or not, because of anxiety or worry about the possible results > **hesitancy** NOUN

hesitate VERB **1** to pause because of uncertainty **2** to be unwilling (to do something): *I hesitate to ask* > **hesitation** NOUN

hessian NOUN a type of coarse cloth

hetero- PREFIX forms words containing the idea of 'other' or 'different'

ⓘ Comes from Greek *heteros* meaning 'other'

heterogeneous (*pronounced* het-e-r*o*-**jeen**-i-*us*) ADJECTIVE composed of many different kinds (*contrasted with*: **homogeneous**)

heterosexual NOUN someone who is sexually attracted to the opposite sex ▶ADJECTIVE sexually attracted to the opposite sex (*contrasted with*: **homosexual**) > **heterosexuality** NOUN

hex NOUN a spell to bring bad luck; a curse

hexa- PREFIX six

ⓘ Comes from Greek *hex* meaning 'six'

hexagon NOUN a six-sided figure > **hexagonal** ADJECTIVE

hey EXCLAMATION expressing surprise or dismay or to attract someone's attention

heyday NOUN the time of greatest strength, the prime

ⓘ From an old English expression *heyda*, meaning 'hurrah'.

HGV ABBREVIATION heavy goods vehicle (now called **large goods vehicle**)

hi INTERJECTION, *informal* **1** hello **2** hey

hiatus (*pronounced* hai-**ei**-t*us*) NOUN (*plural* **hiatus** *or* **hiatuses**) a gap, a rift

hibernate VERB of an animal: to pass the winter in a sleep-like state > **hibernation** NOUN > **hibernator** NOUN

hiccup NOUN **1** a sharp gasp, caused by laughing, eating, drinking, etc **2** (**hiccups**) a fit of such gasping

A B C D E F G H I J K L M N O P Q R S T U V W X Y Z

3 *informal* a minor setback or difficulty ▶ VERB to make a hiccuping sound

hidden ADJECTIVE **1** concealed, out of sight **2** unknown: *hidden meaning*

hide[1] VERB (**hiding, hid, hidden**) to put or keep out of sight ▶ NOUN a concealed place from which to watch birds etc

hide[2] NOUN the skin of an animal

hideous ADJECTIVE **1** horrible, ghastly **2** very ugly

hideout NOUN a place where someone goes to hide or to get away from others

hiding NOUN *informal* a beating

hierarchy (*pronounced* **hai**-*e*-rah-ki) NOUN (*plural* **hierarchies**) a number of people or things arranged in graded order > **hierarchical** ADJECTIVE

hieroglyphics (*pronounced* hai-*e*-ro-**glif**-iks) PLURAL NOUN ancient Egyptian writing, in which pictures are used as letters

hi-fi ADJECTIVE *short for* **high-fidelity** ▶ NOUN, *informal* high-quality equipment for reproducing recorded sound

higgledy-piggledy ADVERB & ADJECTIVE, *informal* in a complete muddle

high ADJECTIVE **1** raised far above **2** extending far upwards, tall **3** well up on any scale of measurement, rank, etc **4** great, large: *high hopes/ high prices* **5** of sound: shrill, acute in pitch **6** of meat: beginning to go bad ▶ ADVERB **1** far above in the air **2** well up on any scale **3** to a high degree **on your high horse** *informal* behaving with exaggerated pride or superiority

[1] Comes from Old English *heah*

highbrow ADJECTIVE, *often derogatory* intellectual, very literary (*contrasted with*: **lowbrow**)

highchair NOUN a tall chair with a small detachable table, for young children

high court NOUN **1** a supreme court **2** (**the High Court**) the supreme court for civil cases in England and Wales

Higher NOUN an examination in Scottish secondary schools, usually taken at the end of the 5th year

high-fidelity ADJECTIVE reproducing sound very clearly

high-five NOUN a greeting made by slapping together one another's raised palms

high-flier NOUN a highly ambitious and successful person

high-handed ADJECTIVE thoughtless, overbearing

high jump NOUN an athletics contest in which competitors jump over a high bar which is raised after every jump **for the high jump** *informal* expecting trouble or punishment

Highlands NOUN (**the Highlands**) a mountainous region, especially the north of Scotland

highlight NOUN **1** a bright spot or area in a picture **2** a lighter patch in the hair, often bleached or dyed **3** the most memorable part or experience: *the highlight of the week* ▶ VERB to emphasize, make the focus of attention

highlighter NOUN a coloured felt-tip pen used to mark but not obscure lines of text

highly ADVERB **1** very: *highly delighted* **2** to or at a high level **3** in an approving way: *I've always thought highly of him*

highly-strung ADJECTIVE nervous, easily excited

high-minded ADJECTIVE having strong principles and high moral standards

Highness NOUN (*plural* **Highnesses**) a title of a monarch

high-rise ADJECTIVE of a building: having many storeys ▸ NOUN a building with many storeys

high road NOUN a main road

high school NOUN a secondary school

high seas PLURAL NOUN: (**the high seas**) the open seas

high-spirited ADJECTIVE bold, lively

high-tech *or* **hi-tech** ADJECTIVE (*short for* **high-technology**) using advanced, especially electronic, equipment and devices

high tide *or* **high water** NOUN the time when the tide is farthest up the shore

highway NOUN the public road

Highway Code NOUN a set of official rules for road users in Britain

highwayman NOUN (*plural* **highwaymen**), *history* a robber who attacked people on the public road

hijab *or* **hejab** NOUN a covering for a Muslim woman's head and face
[1] Arabic

hijack VERB to steal (a car, aeroplane, etc) while it is moving, forcing the driver or pilot to take a new route ▸ NOUN the action of hijacking a vehicle etc > **hijacker** NOUN

hike VERB to travel on foot through countryside ▸ NOUN a country walk > **hiker** NOUN

hilarious ADJECTIVE extremely funny

hilarity NOUN great amusement and laughter

hill NOUN a mound of high land, less high than a mountain

hillock NOUN a small hill

hilly ADJECTIVE (**hillier, hilliest**) covered with hills

hilt NOUN the handle of a sword **up to the hilt** thoroughly, completely

him PRONOUN a male person already spoken about (used only as the object in a sentence): *I saw him yesterday/What did you say to him?*

himself PRONOUN **1** used reflexively: *He cut himself shaving* **2** used for emphasis: *He wrote it himself*

hind[1] ADJECTIVE at the back: *hind legs*

hind[2] NOUN a female deer

hinder VERB to keep back, delay, prevent

hindrance NOUN something that hinders

hindsight NOUN realizing what should have been done after an event: *With hindsight, I shouldn't have said that*

Hinduism NOUN a religion whose followers believe people who die are born again in different bodies > **Hindu** NOUN & ADJECTIVE

hinge NOUN a joint on which a door, lid, etc turns ▸ VERB **1** to move on a hinge **2** to depend (on): *Everything hinges on the weather*

hint NOUN **1** a remark which suggests a meaning without stating it clearly: *I'll give you a hint* **2** a slight impression, a suggestion: *a hint of panic in her voice* ▸ VERB to suggest without stating clearly: *He hinted that he might be there*

hinterland NOUN an area lying inland from the coast

hip[1] NOUN the part of the side of the body just below the waist

hip[2] NOUN the fruit of the wild rose

hip[3] ADJECTIVE (**hipper, hippest**) *informal* very fashionable, trendy

hip flask NOUN a small pocket flask for alcohol

hip-hop NOUN a popular culture movement which started in the US in the early 1980s and is associated with rap music, graffiti art, and baggy sports clothes

hippie NOUN, *informal* a member of a youth movement, which originated in the 1960s, rebelling against conventional society, dress codes, etc

hippo *short for* **hippopotamus**

Hippocratic oath (*pronounced* hip-*o*-**krat**-ik) NOUN an oath taken by a doctor agreeing to observe a code of medical ethics

hippopotamus NOUN (*plural* **hippopotami** – *pronounced* hip-*o*-**pot**-*a*-mai – *or* **hippopotamuses**) a large African mammal living in and near rivers (often shortened to **hippo**)

ⓘ Based on a Greek word which translates as 'river horse'

hire NOUN money paid for work done, or for the use of something belonging to another person ▸ VERB to give or get the use of by paying money

hire-purchase NOUN a way of buying an article by paying for it in instalments

his PRONOUN something belonging to such a person: *That jacket is his*

Hispanic ADJECTIVE **1** Spanish **2** Spanish-American

hiss VERB to make a sound like a snake ▸ NOUN (*plural* **hisses**) such a sound, made to show anger or displeasure

histamine (*pronounced* **his**-*ta*-meen) NOUN *biochemistry* a chemical present in pollen etc which can cause an allergic reaction

historian NOUN someone who studies or writes history

historic ADJECTIVE important, likely to be remembered

historical ADJECTIVE **1** of history **2** true of something in the past

history NOUN (*plural* **histories**) **1** the study of the past **2** a description of past events, society, etc

histrionics PLURAL NOUN an exaggerated show of strong feeling

hit VERB (**hitting, hit**) **1** to strike with a blow **2** to occur suddenly to: *It finally hit me* ▸ NOUN **1** a blow, a stroke **2** a shot which hits a target **3** a success **4** a successful song, recording, etc **5** *slang* a murder by criminals **6** *computing* an instance of a computer file, especially a website, being contacted: *50 hits to our website today* **hit on** *or* **hit upon** to come upon, discover **hit the ceiling** *or* **hit the roof** to explode with anger **hit the ground running** to react immediately and efficiently **hit the nail on the head** to identify the important point, be exactly right

hit-and-miss ADJECTIVE, *informal* haphazard, sometimes working and sometimes not

hit-and-run ADJECTIVE of a driver: driving away after causing injury without reporting the accident

hitch VERB **1** to fasten with a hook etc **2** to lift with a jerk **3** *informal* to hitch-hike ▶ NOUN (*plural* **hitches**) **1** a jerk **2** an unexpected stop or delay

hitch-hike VERB to travel by getting free lifts from passing vehicles > **hitch-hiker** NOUN

hi-tech *another spelling* of **high-tech**

hither ADVERB, *old* to this place **hither and thither** back and forwards

hitman NOUN (*plural* **hitmen**) *slang* someone employed to kill or attack others

HIV ABBREVIATION human immuno-deficiency virus, the virus which can cause AIDS

hive NOUN **1** a box or basket where bees live **2** a busy place: *hive of industry*

HIV-positive ADJECTIVE carrying HIV

HM ABBREVIATION Her or His Majesty

HMS ABBREVIATION **1** Her or His Majesty's Service **2** Her or His Majesty's Ship

hoard NOUN a hidden store of treasure, food, etc ▶ VERB to store up secretly

ⓘ Comes from Old English *hord* meaning 'treasure' or 'secret place'

> Do not confuse with: **horde**

hoarding NOUN a fence of boards

hoarse ADJECTIVE (**hoarser, hoarsest**) having a harsh voice, eg from a cold or cough

hoax NOUN (*plural* **hoaxes**) a trick played to deceive ▶ VERB to play a hoax on

hob NOUN **1** the top of a cooker, with rings for heating etc **2** a small shelf next to a fireplace for keeping pans etc hot

hobble VERB **1** to walk with short unsteady steps **2** to tie the legs of (a horse etc) loosely **3** to impede, hamper

hobby NOUN (*plural* **hobbies**) a favourite way of passing your spare time

ⓘ Originally *hobby-horse*, a horse used in morris dances and therefore for amusement or pleasure

hobby-horse NOUN **1** a toy wooden horse **2** a favourite subject of discussion

hobgoblin NOUN a mischievous fairy

hobnob VERB (**hobnobbing, hobnobbed**) to be on friendly terms (with); socialize (with)

a b c d e f g h i j k l m n o p q r s t u v w x y z

A B C D E F G H I J K L M N O P Q R S T U V W X Y Z

hockey NOUN an eleven-a-side ballgame played with clubs curved at one end

hoe NOUN a tool used for weeding, loosening earth, etc ▶ VERB (**hoeing, hoed**) to use a hoe

hog NOUN, *US* a pig ▶ VERB (**hogging, hogged**) *informal* to take or use selfishly **go the whole hog** to do something thoroughly

Hogmanay (*pronounced* hog-ma-**nei**) NOUN the name in Scotland for 31 December and the celebrations held that night

ⓘ From an old French word *aguillanneuf*, a gift given at New Year

hoi polloi PLURAL NOUN the masses, the rabble

ⓘ Taken from a Greek phrase for 'the people'

hoist VERB to lift, raise ▶ NOUN a lift, an elevator for goods

hoity-toity ADJECTIVE haughty, superior

hold[1] VERB (**holding, held**) **1** to keep in your possession or power; have **2** to contain **3** to occupy (a position etc) **4** to think, believe **5** to put on, organize: *hold a meeting* **6** to apply: *That rule doesn't hold any longer* **7** to stop (shooting etc): *hold fire* **8** to wait on a telephone without hanging up for the person on the other end to return ▶ NOUN **1** grip, grasp **2** influence: *a hold over the others* **hold forth** to speak at length **hold good** to be true **hold off** to delay or refrain from doing something **hold on** *informal* to wait **hold out** to refuse to give in **hold over** to keep till later **hold up 1** to support **2** to hinder **3** to attack and demand money from

ⓘ Comes from Old English *haldan*

hold[2] NOUN a large space for carrying a ship's cargo

holdall NOUN a large carrying bag with a zip

holder NOUN **1** a container **2** someone who holds (a position etc)

hold-up NOUN **1** an armed attempt at robbery **2** a delay, or something that causes it

hole NOUN **1** an opening in something solid **2** a pit, a burrow **3** *informal* a miserable place

holiday NOUN **1** a day when businesses etc are closed **2** a period away from work for rest

holier-than-thou ADJECTIVE superior and smug

holiness NOUN **1** the quality of being holy or sacred **2** (**Holiness**) a title used in addressing or referring to religious leaders such as the Pope

hollow ADJECTIVE **1** having empty space inside, not solid **2** false, unreal: *hollow victory/hollow smile* ▶ NOUN **1** a sunken place **2** a dip in the land ▶ VERB to scoop (out)

holly NOUN (*plural* **hollies**) an evergreen shrub with scarlet berries and prickly leaves

holocaust NOUN **1** a great destruction (by fire) **2** *history* (**the Holocaust**) the mass killing of Jews by the Nazis in World War II

hologram NOUN a 3-D image created by laser beams

holograph NOUN a document written entirely by one person

holster NOUN a case for a pistol

holy ADJECTIVE (**holier, holiest**) **1** of or like God **2** religious, righteous **3** for religious use; sacred

homage NOUN a show of respect; an acknowledgement of debt: *paying homage to the pioneers of cinema*

home NOUN **1** the place where someone lives **2** the house of someone's family **3** a centre or place of origin: *Nashville is the home of country music* **4** a place where children, the elderly, etc live and are looked after ▸ADJECTIVE **1** of someone's house or family: *home comforts* **2** domestic, not foreign: *home affairs* ▸ADVERB **1** towards home **2** to the full length: *drive the nail home* **bring home to** to make (someone) realize

ⓘ Comes from Old English *ham*

home economics SINGULAR NOUN the study of how to run a home

homeless ADJECTIVE without a home and living, sleeping, etc in public places or in hostels > **homelessness** NOUN

homely ADJECTIVE (**homelier, homeliest**) **1** plain but pleasant **2** *US* plain, not attractive

home-made ADJECTIVE made at home

homeo- *or* **homoeo-** (*both pronounced* hom-i-o *or* hoh-mi-o) PREFIX like, similar: *homeostasis/homoeopathy*

ⓘ Comes from Greek *homoios* meaning 'similar'

homeopath *or* **homoeopath** (*pronounced* **hom**-i-*o*-path) NOUN a practitioner of homeopathy

homeopathic *or* **homoeopathic** (*pronounced* hom-i-*o*-**path**-ik) ADJECTIVE of or using homeopathy (*contrasted with*: **allopathic**)

homeopathy *or* **homoeopathy** (*pronounced* hom-i-**op**-*a*-thi) NOUN the treatment of illness by small quantities of substances that produce symptoms similar to those of the illness

home page NOUN, *computing* the first page that appears on a computer screen after a connection is made to the Internet, or the access page of a Web site

home rule NOUN government of a country etc by its own parliament

Home Secretary NOUN, *Brit* the government minister who deals with domestic issues, eg law and order, immigration, etc

homesick ADJECTIVE longing for home

home truth NOUN a frank statement of something true but unpleasant

homewards ADVERB towards home

homework NOUN work for school etc done at home

homi- PREFIX of or relating to men or people: *homicide*

ⓘ Comes from Latin *homo* meaning 'man'

homicidal ADJECTIVE likely to commit murder

homicide NOUN **1** the killing of a human being **2** someone who kills a person

homo- PREFIX **1** same: *homosexual/*

A B C D E F G H I J K L M N O P Q R S T U V W X Y Z

homonym **2** of or relating to homosexuality: *homoerotic*
ⓘ Comes from Greek *homos* meaning 'same'

homoeopathy *another spelling* of **homeopathy**

homogeneous (*pronounced* hom-oh-**jee**-ni-*us*) ADJECTIVE of the same kind, or composed of parts of the same kind (*contrasted with*: **heterogeneous**) > **homogeneity** *or* (meaning 2) **homogeny** NOUN

homo sapiens (*pronounced* hoh-moh **sap**-i-enz) NOUN the name for modern man as a species

homosexual NOUN someone who is sexually attracted to the same sex ▶ ADJECTIVE sexually attracted to the same sex (*contrasted with*: **heterosexual**) > **homosexuality** NOUN

hone VERB to sharpen (a knife etc)

honest ADJECTIVE truthful; not inclined to steal, cheat, etc

honestly ADVERB **1** truthfully **2** without cheating or stealing etc **3** when you are trying to convince someone of something: really **4** an expression of annoyance: *Honestly, I don't know why I bother!*

honesty NOUN the quality of being honest, truthful, or trustworthy

honey NOUN **1** a sweet, thick fluid made by bees from the nectar of flowers **2** *informal* sweetheart, dear

honeycomb NOUN a network of wax cells in which bees store honey

honeymoon NOUN a holiday spent immediately after marriage ▶ VERB to spend a honeymoon

honeysuckle NOUN a climbing shrub with sweet-smelling flowers

honk NOUN a noise like the cry of the wild goose or the sound of a motor horn ▶ VERB to make this sound

honorary ADJECTIVE **1** done to give honour **2** without payment

honour *or US* **honor** NOUN **1** respect for truth, honesty, etc **2** fame, glory **3** reputation, good name **4** a title of respect, especially to a judge: *Your Honour* **5** a privilege **6** (**honours**) recognition given for exceptional achievements ▶ VERB **1** to give respect to **2** to give high rank to **3** to pay when due: *honour a debt* **do the honours** *informal* to perform a ceremonial task

honourable ADJECTIVE worthy of honour > **honourably** ADVERB

-hood SUFFIX meaning 'the state of being': *childhood, likelihood*

hood[1] NOUN **1** a covering for the head **2** a protective cover for anything **3** *US* the bonnet of a car

hoodwink VERB to deceive

hoof NOUN (*plural* **hoofs** *or* **hooves**) the horny part on the feet of certain animals (eg horses) **on the hoof** *informal* on the move, while moving

hook NOUN **1** a bent piece of metal etc for hanging things on **2** a piece of metal on the end of a line for catching fish ▶ VERB to hang or catch with a hook **by hook or by crook** by one means or another, whatever the cost

hooked ADJECTIVE **1** curved, bent **2** caught by a hook **3** *informal* addicted (to), fascinated (by): *hooked on heroin*

hooligan NOUN a wild, unruly person

hooliganism NOUN unruly behaviour

hoop NOUN a thin ring of wood or metal

hooray *another spelling* of **hurrah**

hoot VERB **1** to sound (a siren, car horn, etc) **2** of an owl: to call, cry **3** to laugh loudly ▶ NOUN **1** the sound made by a car horn, siren, or owl **2** a shout of scorn or disgust **3** *informal* someone or something extremely funny

hooter NOUN **1** a siren or horn which makes a hooting sound **2** *slang* a large nose

Hoover NOUN, *trademark* a vacuum cleaner ▶ VERB (**hoover**) to vacuum (a floor etc)

hop[1] VERB (**hopping, hopped**) to leap on one leg ▶ NOUN a short jump on one leg

hop[2] NOUN a climbing plant with bitter-tasting fruits used in brewing beer

hope NOUN **1** the state of expecting or wishing something good to happen **2** something desired ▶ VERB to expect or wish good to happen

hopeful ADJECTIVE **1** confident or optimistic about something **2** promising, encouraging

hopefully ADVERB **1** with hope **2** used when expressing hopes: 'I hope that … '

hopeless ADJECTIVE **1** without hope **2** *informal* very bad: *He is hopeless at maths* > **hopelessly** ADVERB

hopscotch NOUN a hopping game over lines drawn on the ground

horde NOUN a large crowd or group

ⓘ Comes from Turkish *ordu* meaning 'camp'

> Do not confuse with: **hoard**

horizon NOUN **1** the imaginary line formed where the earth meets the sky **2** the limit of someone's experience or understanding

horizontal ADJECTIVE lying level or flat > **horizontally** ADVERB

hormone NOUN a substance produced by certain glands of the body, which acts on a particular organ > **hormonal** ADJECTIVE

horn NOUN **1** a hard growth on the heads of certain animals, eg deer, sheep **2** something curved or sticking out like an animal's horn **3** part of a car which gives a warning sound **4** a brass wind instrument (originally made of horn)

horned ADJECTIVE having horns

hornpipe NOUN a lively sailor's dance

horoscope NOUN a prediction of someone's future based on the position of the stars at their birth

horrendous ADJECTIVE, *informal* awful, terrible

horrible ADJECTIVE **1** causing horror, dread, or fear **2** *informal* unpleasant, detestable, or foul > **horribly** ADVERB

horrid ADJECTIVE hateful; very unpleasant

horrific ADJECTIVE **1** terrifying **2** *informal* awful, very bad > **horrifically** ADVERB

A B C D E F G H I J K L M N O P Q R S T U V W X Y Z

horrify VERB (**horrifies, horrifying, horrified**) to frighten greatly, shock: *We were horrified by his behaviour* > **horrifying** ADJECTIVE

horror NOUN **1** great fear, terror **2** something which causes fear

horse NOUN **1** a four-footed animal with hooves and a mane **2** a wooden frame for drying clothes on **3** a piece of gymnastic equipment for vaulting **from the horse's mouth** directly from the source, first-hand **horses for courses** people will do best in situations which suit them individually

horse chestnut NOUN a tree which produces a shiny, inedible nut (a conker)

horsefly NOUN (*plural* **horseflies**) a large fly which bites

horseplay NOUN rough play, fooling around

horsepower NOUN (*abbrev* **hp**) a unit of mechanical power for car engines

horseradish NOUN (*plural* **horseradishes**) a plant with a sharp-tasting root which is used in sauces

horseshoe NOUN **1** a shoe for horses, made of a curved piece of iron **2** anything shaped like a horseshoe, especially as a symbol of good luck

horticulture NOUN the study and art of gardening > **horticultural** ADJECTIVE

hosanna NOUN an exclamation of praise to God

hose NOUN **1** (*plural* **hose**) an old-fashioned word meaning 'a covering for the legs or feet', eg stockings **2** (*plural* **hoses**) a rubber tube for carrying water

hosiery NOUN stockings, tights, etc

hospice NOUN a home providing special nursing care for incurable invalids

hospitable ADJECTIVE showing kindness to guests or strangers > **hospitably** ADVERB

hospital NOUN a building for the treatment of the sick and injured

hospitality NOUN the quality of being hospitable, or of being friendly and welcoming to guests and strangers, entertaining them with food or drink, or providing them with accommodation

host[1] NOUN **1** someone who welcomes and entertains guests **2** the person on a television or radio show who introduces guests and performers to the audience, or interviews them **3** *biology* the person or animal on which an insect or other organism is living or feeding as a parasite

host[2] NOUN a very large number

hostage NOUN someone held prisoner by an enemy to make sure that an agreement will be kept to

hostel NOUN a building providing rooms for students etc

hostelry NOUN (*plural* **hostelries**) *old* an inn

hostess NOUN (*plural* **hostesses**) **1** a woman who welcomes and entertains guests **2** *old* an air hostess

hostile ADJECTIVE **1** of an enemy **2** not friendly **3** showing dislike or opposition (to)

hostility NOUN **1** unfriendliness,

dislike **2** (*plural* **hostilities**) acts of warfare

hot ADJECTIVE (**hotter, hottest**) **1** very warm **2** spicy **3** *slang* sexually attractive or excited **4** *slang* radioactive **5** *slang* stolen **6** *slang* not safe

hot air NOUN, *informal* meaningless talk

hotbed NOUN a centre or breeding ground for anything: *a hotbed of rebellion*

hot-blooded ADJECTIVE passionate, easily angered

hot dog NOUN a hot sausage in a long roll

hotel NOUN a building with several rooms which people can pay to stay in for a number of nights

hotfoot ADVERB, *informal* in great haste

hotheaded ADJECTIVE inclined to act rashly without thinking

hothouse NOUN a heated glasshouse for plants ▸ VERB to give (a child) intensive schooling at an early age

hotline NOUN a direct telephone line between heads of government

hot potato NOUN a touchy subject

hot seat NOUN, *informal* an uncomfortable or difficult position

hound NOUN a dog used in hunting ▸ VERB to hunt, pursue

hour NOUN **1** sixty minutes, the 24th part of a day **2** a time or occasion: *the hour of reckoning*

hourglass NOUN (*plural* **hourglasses**) an instrument which measures the hours by the running of sand from one glass into another

hourly ADJECTIVE happening or done every hour ▸ ADVERB every hour

house NOUN (*pronounced* hows) **1** a building in which people live **2** a household **3** a business firm **4** a building where school boarders stay ▸ VERB (*pronounced* howz) to provide a house for; accommodate **like a house on fire** *informal* very successfully, extremely well **on the house** free, complimentary

[i] Comes from Old English *hus*

house arrest NOUN confinement under guard in a private house, hospital, etc

houseboat NOUN a river barge with a cabin for living in

household NOUN the people who live together in a house

householder NOUN someone who owns or pays the rent of a house

household name *or* **household word** NOUN someone or something that is well known and often mentioned by people

housekeeper NOUN someone employed to look after the running of a house

house-proud ADJECTIVE proud of keeping your house clean and tidy

house-trained ADJECTIVE of a pet: trained to go outdoors to pass urine and faeces

house-warming NOUN a party held when someone moves into a new house

housewife NOUN (*plural* **housewives**) a woman who looks after a house and her family

housework NOUN the work

a b c d e f g h i j k l m n o p q r s t u v w x y z

A B C D E F G H I J K L M N O P Q R S T U V W X Y Z

involved in keeping a house clean and tidy

housing NOUN **1** accommodation, eg houses, flats, etc **2** a casing for a machine etc

hovel NOUN a small squalid dwelling

hover VERB **1** to stay in the air in the same spot **2** to stay near, linger (about) **3** to be undecided or uncertain

hovercraft NOUN a craft able to travel over land or sea supported on a cushion of air

how ADVERB **1** in what manner: *How are they getting there?* **2** to what extent: *How old are you?/ How cold is it outside?* **3** to a great extent: *How young he seems/How well you play* **4** by what means: *How do you switch this on?* **5** in what condition: *How is she?*

however ADVERB **1** no matter how **2** in spite of that

howl VERB **1** to make a long, loud sound like that of a dog or wolf **2** to yell in pain, anger, etc **3** to laugh loudly ▸NOUN a howling sound

howler NOUN, *informal* a ridiculous mistake

HP *or* **hp** ABBREVIATION **1** hire-purchase **2** horsepower

HQ ABBREVIATION headquarters

HRT ABBREVIATION hormone replacement therapy, a treatment to restore the balance of hormones in older women

HTML ABBREVIATION, *computing* hypertext markup language, the language used to create World Wide Web documents

http ABBREVIATION, *computing* hypertext transfer protocol, by which documents are transferred over the Internet

hub NOUN **1** the centre part of a wheel through which the axle passes **2** a thriving centre of anything: *the hub of the entertainment industry*

hubbub NOUN a confused sound of many voices

ⓘ Originally meaning 'battle' or 'war cry', based on an Irish Gaelic word

huddle VERB to crowd together ▸NOUN a close group

hue NOUN colour, shade

hue and cry NOUN a commotion, a fuss

huff NOUN a fit of bad temper and sulking

hug VERB (**hugging, hugged**) **1** to hold tightly with the arms **2** to keep close to: *hugging the kerb* ▸NOUN a tight embrace

huge ADJECTIVE (**huger, hugest**) extremely big

hula hoop NOUN a light hoop for spinning round the waist

hulk NOUN **1** an old ship unfit for use **2** something big and clumsy

hulking ADJECTIVE, *informal* big and clumsy

hull NOUN the body or framework of a ship

hullabaloo NOUN, *informal* a noisy disturbance

hullo *another spelling of* **hello**

hum VERB (**humming, hummed**) **1** to make a buzzing sound like that of bees **2** to sing with the lips shut

3 *informal* of a place: to be noisily busy ▸ NOUN **1** the noise of bees **2** any buzzing, droning sound

human ADJECTIVE **1** relating to people as opposed to animals or gods **2** having natural qualities, feelings, etc ▸ NOUN a man, woman, or child

human being NOUN a member of the human race

humane ADJECTIVE kind, showing mercy, gentle > **humanely** ADVERB

humanism NOUN a set of ideas about or interest in ethics and mankind, not including religious belief > **humanist** NOUN

humanitarian ADJECTIVE kind to fellow human beings

humanity NOUN **1** people in general **2** kindness, gentleness

human rights PLURAL NOUN the rights every person has to justice, freedom, etc

humble ADJECTIVE (**humbler, humblest**) **1** modest, meek **2** not of high rank, unimportant ▸ VERB to make (someone) feel low and unimportant

humbug NOUN **1** nonsense, rubbish **2** a kind of hard minty sweet

humdrum ADJECTIVE dull, not exciting

humid ADJECTIVE of air etc: moist, damp

humidifier NOUN a device which controls the amount of humidity in the air

humidity NOUN dampness

humiliate VERB to make (someone) feel humble or ashamed, hurt someone's pride > **humiliating** ADJECTIVE > **humiliation** NOUN

humility NOUN humble state of mind, meekness

hummingbird NOUN a small brightly coloured bird which beats its wings rapidly making a humming noise

humorist NOUN a comedian, a comic writer

humorous ADJECTIVE funny, amusing

humour *or US* **humor** NOUN **1** the ability to see things as amusing or ridiculous **2** funniness; the amusing side of anything: *failed to see the humour of the situation* **3** state of mind; temper, mood: *He is in good humour today* ▸ VERB to please or gratify (someone) by doing what they wish

hump NOUN **1** a lump, a mound **2** a lump on the back

humpback NOUN **1** a back with a hump **2** someone with a hump on their back ▸ ADJECTIVE of a bridge: rising and falling so as to form a hump shape

humus (*pronounced* **hyoom**-*us*) NOUN soil made of rotted leaves etc

hunch NOUN (*plural* **hunches**) a suspicion that something is untrue or is going to happen etc ▸ VERB to draw (your shoulders) up towards your ears and forward towards your chest, giving your body a rounded, stooping appearance

hunchback NOUN a humpback

hunchbacked ADJECTIVE humpbacked

hundred NOUN the number 100 ▸ ADJECTIVE 100 in number

A B C D E F G H I J K L M N O P Q R S T U V W X Y Z

hundredth ADJECTIVE the last of a series of one hundred ▶ NOUN one of a hundred equal parts

hundredweight NOUN 112 pounds, 50.8 kilograms (*often written*: **cwt**)

hunger NOUN **1** a desire for food **2** a strong desire for anything ▶ VERB **1** to long (for) **2** to go without food

hunger strike NOUN a refusal to eat as a protest

hungover ADJECTIVE suffering from a hangover

hungry ADJECTIVE (**hungrier, hungriest**) wanting or needing food > **hungrily** ADVERB

hunk NOUN, *informal* a muscular, sexually attractive man

hunker VERB: **hunker down** to squat

hunt VERB **1** to chase (animals or birds) for food or sport **2** to search (for) ▶ NOUN **1** chasing wild animals **2** a search > **hunter** NOUN

huntsman *or* **huntswoman** NOUN (*plural* **huntsmen** *or* **huntswomen**) someone who hunts

hurdle NOUN **1** a light frame to be jumped over in a race **2** a difficulty which must be overcome

hurl VERB to throw with force

hurly-burly NOUN a great stir, uproar

hurrah *or* **hurray** INTERJECTION a shout of joy, approval, etc

hurricane NOUN a violent tropical windstorm originating in the Atlantic, with wind blowing at a speed of over 75 miles (120 kilometres) per hour (*see also*: **cyclone, typhoon**)

hurried ADJECTIVE done in a hurry > **hurriedly** ADVERB

hurry VERB (**hurries, hurrying, hurried**) **1** to act or move quickly **2** to make (someone) act quickly ▶ NOUN eagerness to act quickly, haste: *in a hurry*

hurt VERB (**hurting, hurt**) **1** to cause pain or distress to **2** to injure physically, wound **3** to damage, spoil ▶ NOUN **1** pain, distress **2** damage

hurtful ADJECTIVE causing pain, distress, or damage

hurtle VERB to rush at great speed

husband NOUN a married man (the partner of a **wife**) ▶ VERB to spend or use (eg money, strength) carefully

hush INTERJECTION be quiet! ▶ NOUN, *informal* silence, quiet ▶ VERB to make quiet **hush up** to stop (a scandal etc) becoming public

hush-hush ADJECTIVE, *informal* top-secret

husk NOUN the dry thin covering of certain fruits and seeds

husky[1] ADJECTIVE (**huskier, huskiest**) of a voice: deep and rough > **huskily** ADVERB

husky[2] NOUN (*plural* **huskies**) a Canadian sledge-dog

hussar (*pronounced* hu-**zah**) NOUN a light-armed horse soldier

hussy NOUN (*plural* **hussies**) a forward, cheeky girl

hustle VERB **1** to push rudely **2** to hurry

hut NOUN a small wooden building

hutch NOUN (*plural* **hutches**) a box in which pet rabbits are housed

hyacinth NOUN a sweet-smelling

flower which grows from a bulb

hyaena *another spelling of* **hyena**

hybrid NOUN an animal or plant bred from two different kinds, eg a mule, which is a hybrid from a horse and an ass

hydrant NOUN a connection to which a hose can be attached to draw water off the main water supply

hydraulic ADJECTIVE **1** carrying water **2** worked by water or other fluid

hydro- *or* **hydr-** PREFIX water: *hydroelectricity/hydraulic*

🛈 Comes from Greek *hydor* meaning 'water'

hydro NOUN (*plural* **hydros**) a hotel with a swimming pool and gymnasium etc

hydrocarbon NOUN a compound containing only carbon and hydrogen

hydroelectricity NOUN electricity obtained from water-power
> **hydroelectric** ADJECTIVE

hydrofoil NOUN a boat with a device which raises it out of the water as it speeds up

hydrogen NOUN, *chemistry* (symbol **H**) the lightest gas, which with oxygen makes up water

hydrogen bomb NOUN an extremely powerful bomb using hydrogen

hydrophobia NOUN **1** a fear of water, a symptom of rabies **2** rabies
> **hydrophobic** ADJECTIVE

hyena *or* **hyaena** NOUN a dog-like wild animal with a howl sounding like laughter

hygiene (*pronounced* **hai**-jeen) NOUN the maintaining of cleanliness as a means to health > **hygienic** ADJECTIVE

hymn NOUN a religious song of praise

hype *informal*, NOUN extravagant advertisement or publicity ▶ VERB to promote extravagantly

hyper- PREFIX to a greater extent than usual, excessive: *hypersensitive*

🛈 Comes from Greek *hyper* meaning 'over'

hyperactive ADJECTIVE of a child: abnormally active

hyperbole (*pronounced* hai-**per**-bo-li) NOUN exaggeration
> **hyperbolic** *or* **hyperbolical** ADJECTIVE

hyperlink NOUN, *computing* a piece of text a user can click on to take them to another file (*also called*: **link**)

hypermarket NOUN a large self-service store stocking a wide range of goods

hypertext NOUN, *computing* electronic text containing cross-references which can be accessed by keystrokes etc

hyphen NOUN a short stroke (-) used to link or separate parts of a word or phrase: *touch-and-go/re-elect*

hyphenate VERB to join (two or more words) with a hyphen
> **hyphenated** ADJECTIVE
> **hyphenation** NOUN

hypnosis NOUN **1** a sleep-like state in which suggestions are obeyed

2 hypnotism

hypnotic ADJECTIVE **1** of hypnosis or hypnotism **2** causing a sleep-like state

hypnotism NOUN the putting of someone into hypnosis > **hypnotist** NOUN

hypnotize *or* **hypnotise** VERB to put someone into hypnosis

hypo- PREFIX below, under: *hypodermic/hypothermia*

ⓘ Comes from Greek *hypo* meaning 'under'

hypoallergenic ADJECTIVE specially formulated to reduce the risk of allergy

hypochondria NOUN over-anxiety about your own health

hypochondriac NOUN someone who is over-anxious about their health, and who is inclined to think they are ill when they are perfectly healthy ▸ ADJECTIVE relating to or affected with hypochondria

hypocrite (*pronounced* **hip**-*o*-krit) NOUN someone who pretends to be something they are not, or to believe something they do not > **hypocrisy** NOUN > **hypocritical** ADJECTIVE

hypodermic ADJECTIVE used for injecting drugs just below the skin ▸ NOUN a hypodermic syringe

hypotenuse (*pronounced* hai-**pot**-*e*-nyooz) NOUN, *maths* (*abbrev* **hyp.**) the longest side of a right-angled triangle

hypothermia NOUN an abnormally low body temperature caused by exposure to cold

hypothesis (*pronounced* hai-**poth**-*e*-sis) NOUN (*plural* **hypotheses**) something taken as true for the sake of argument

hypothetical ADJECTIVE supposed, based on an idea or a possibility rather than on facts

hysterectomy NOUN (*plural* **hysterectomies**) surgical removal of the womb

hysteria NOUN a nervous excitement causing uncontrollable laughter, crying, etc

ⓘ Based on a Greek word for 'womb', because hysteria was originally thought to be caused by a disorder of the womb

hysterical ADJECTIVE **1** suffering from a severe emotional disturbance, often as a result of shock **2** wild with panic, excitement, or anger **3** very funny > **hysterically** ADVERB

hysterics PLURAL NOUN a fit of hysteria **in hysterics** *informal* laughing uncontrollably

I

I[1] PRONOUN the word used by a speaker or writer in mentioning themselves (as the subject of a verb): *you and I/I, myself*

I[2] PRONOUN the word used by a speaker or writer in mentioning themselves (as the subject of a verb): *you and I/I, myself*

> ⓘ After a preposition, **me** should always be used: ✓ *between you and me* ✓ *between John and me*

ice NOUN **1** frozen water **2** ice-cream ▶ VERB **1** to cover with icing **2** to freeze

ice age NOUN a long period when the earth was mostly covered with ice

iceberg NOUN a huge mass of floating ice

icebox NOUN, *US* refrigerator

icecap NOUN, *geography* a permanent covering of ice, as found at the North and South Poles

ice-cream NOUN a sweet creamy mixture, flavoured and frozen

ice floe NOUN a piece of floating ice

ice hockey NOUN hockey played with a rubber disc (called a **puck**) on an ice rink

ice lolly NOUN a portion of frozen, flavoured water or ice-cream on a stick

ice-skate NOUN a skate for moving on ice

ice-skating NOUN the sport of moving about on ice wearing ice-skates

icicle NOUN a hanging, pointed piece of ice formed by the freezing of dropping water

icing NOUN powdered sugar, mixed with water or egg-white, spread on cakes or biscuits **icing on the cake** an agreeable extra detail, added to something which is already satisfactory

icon NOUN **1** (*also*: **ikon**) a painted or mosaic image of Christ or a saint **2** *computing* a small graphic image which is clicked to access a particular program or file

ICT ABBREVIATION information and communication technology

icy ADJECTIVE (**icier, iciest**) **1** covered with ice **2** very cold **3** unfriendly
> **icily** ADVERB

ID ABBREVIATION identification ▶ NOUN a means of identification, eg a driving licence: *show some ID*

I'd *short for* I would, I should *or* I

A B C D E F G H I J K L M N O P Q R S T U V W X Y Z

had: *I'd sooner go than stay*

id NOUN, *psychoanalysis* the unconscious part of the personality, the source of instincts and dreams

idea NOUN **1** a thought, a notion **2** a plan

ideal ADJECTIVE **1** perfect **2** existing in imagination only (*contrasted with*: **real**) ▶NOUN the highest and best; a standard of perfection

idealism NOUN the belief that perfection can be reached

idealist NOUN someone who thinks that perfection can be reached > **idealistic** ADJECTIVE

idealize *or* **idealise** VERB to think of as perfect > **idealization** NOUN

ideally ADVERB in ideal circumstances: *Ideally all children should have a place in nursery school*

identical ADJECTIVE the same in all details > **identically** ADVERB

identification NOUN **1** an official document, such as a passport or driving licence, that proves who you are **2** the process of finding out who someone is or what something is

identify VERB (**identifies, identifying, identified**) to claim to recognize, prove to be the same: *He identified the man as his attacker* **identify with 1** to feel close to or involved with **2** to think of as the same, equate: *identifying money with happiness*

Identikit (picture) NOUN *trademark* a rough picture of a wanted person which police put together from descriptions

identity NOUN (*plural* **identities**) **1** who or what someone or something is **2** the state of being the same **3** *maths* an equation that is true for all possible values of the unknown variables

ideological ADJECTIVE **1** of or relating to an ideology **2** resulting from a clash between different ideologies

ideology NOUN (*plural* **ideologies**) a set of ideas, often political or philosophical

idiocy NOUN feeble-mindedness, foolishness

idiom NOUN a common expression whose meaning cannot be guessed from the individual words, eg 'I'm feeling *under the weather*' > **idiomatic** ADJECTIVE > **idiomatically** ADVERB

idiosyncrasy NOUN (*plural* **idiosyncrasies**) a personal oddness of behaviour > **idiosyncratic** ADJECTIVE

idiot NOUN a stupid person; a fool

idiotic ADJECTIVE extremely foolish, ridiculous > **idiotically** ADVERB

idle ADJECTIVE **1** not working: *machines lying idle* **2** lazy **3** meaningless, without a useful purpose: *idle chatter* ▶VERB **1** to spend time in doing nothing **2** of an engine: to run without doing any work > **idly** ADVERB

idol NOUN **1** an image worshipped as a god **2** someone much loved or honoured: *pop idols*

idolize *or* **idolise** VERB to adore, worship

Id-ul-Fitr *or* **Eid-ul-Fitr** NOUN (also **Eid**) a Muslim festival celebrating the end of Ramadan

idyll NOUN **1** a poem on a pastoral theme **2** a time of pleasure and contentment

idyllic ADJECTIVE very happy and content, blissful

ie ABBREVIATION that is, that means (from Latin *id est*)

if CONJUNCTION **1** on condition that, supposing that: *If you go, I'll go* **2** whether: *Do you know if she'll be there?*

ig- *see* **in-**

igloo NOUN an Inuit snow hut

igneous ADJECTIVE **1** relating to fire **2** of rocks: formed by the cooling and hardening of magma or molten lava

ignite VERB **1** to set on fire **2** to catch fire

ignition NOUN **1** the act of setting on fire or catching fire **2** the sparking part of a motor engine

ignoble ADJECTIVE dishonourable; of low birth

ignominious ADJECTIVE bringing disgrace or dishonour

ignoramus (*pronounced* ig-n*o*-**rei**-m*u*s) NOUN an ignorant person

ignorant ADJECTIVE **1** knowing little **2** (**ignorant of**) unaware of > **ignorance** NOUN

ignore VERB to take no notice of

iguana (*pronounced* ig-**wah**-n*a*) NOUN a type of large lizard

ikon *another spelling* of **icon**

il- *see* **in-**

I'll *short for* I shall, I will

ill ADJECTIVE **1** unwell, sick **2** evil, bad **3** unlucky ▶ ADVERB badly ▶ NOUN **1** evil **2** (**ills**) misfortunes, troubles

ill-at-ease ADJECTIVE uncomfortable

illegal ADJECTIVE against the law > **illegality** NOUN (*plural* **illegalities**)

illegal immigrant NOUN an immigrant who has not been authorized to enter a country

illegible ADJECTIVE impossible to read > **illegibility** NOUN > **illegibly** ADVERB

illegitimate ADJECTIVE born of parents not married to each other

ill-feeling NOUN dislike, resentment

ill-gotten ADJECTIVE obtained in a dishonest or unethical way

illicit ADJECTIVE unlawful, forbidden

ⓘ Comes from Latin *il-* meaning 'not', and *licitus* meaning 'allowed'

> Do not confuse with: **elicit**

illiterate ADJECTIVE not able to read or write > **illiteracy** NOUN

ill-natured ADJECTIVE bad-tempered

illness NOUN disease, sickness

illogical ADJECTIVE not logical, not showing sound reasoning > **illogicality** NOUN > **illogically** ADVERB

illuminate VERB **1** to light up **2** to make more clear

illuminated ADJECTIVE of a manuscript: decorated with ornamental lettering

illusion NOUN **1** something which deceives the mind or eye **2** a mistaken belief

🄸 Comes from Latin *illudere* meaning 'to make sport of'

> Do not confuse with: **allusion** and **delusion**

illusory ADJECTIVE mistaken or untrue, despite seeming believable

illustrate VERB **1** to draw pictures for (a book etc) **2** to explain, show by example > **illustrative** ADJECTIVE

illustration NOUN **1** a picture in a book etc **2** an example which illustrates

illustrator NOUN someone who illustrates books etc

illustrious ADJECTIVE famous, distinguished

ill-will NOUN dislike, resentment

I'm *short for* I am

im- *see* **in-**

image NOUN **1** a likeness made of someone or something **2** a striking likeness: *She is the image of her mother* **3** a picture in the mind **4** public reputation

imagery NOUN words that suggest images, used to make a piece of writing more vivid

imaginary ADJECTIVE existing only in the imagination, not real

🄸 Comes from Latin prefix *imagin-*, a form of the word for 'image', and Latin suffix *-arius* meaning 'connected with'

> Do not confuse with: **imaginative**

imagination NOUN the power of forming pictures in the mind of things not present or experienced

imaginative ADJECTIVE **1** having a lively imagination **2** done with imagination: *an imaginative piece of writing*

🄸 Comes from Latin prefix *imaginat-*, a form of a verb meaning 'to imagine', and French suffix *-ive* meaning 'tending to'

> Do not confuse with: **imaginary**

imagine VERB **1** to form a picture in the mind, especially of something that does not exist **2** to think, suppose

imam NOUN **1** the person who leads the prayers in a mosque **2** (**Imam**) an Islamic leader

imbecile NOUN a feeble-minded person; a fool > **imbecility** NOUN

imbue VERB to fill or affect (with): *imbued her staff with enthusiasm*

imitate VERB to try to be the same as, copy

imitation NOUN a copy ▶ ADJECTIVE made to look like: *imitation leather*

imitator NOUN someone who copies, or tries to do the same things as, someone else

immaculate ADJECTIVE spotless; very clean and neat > **immaculately** ADVERB

immaterial ADJECTIVE of little importance

immature ADJECTIVE not mature > **immaturity** NOUN

immediacy NOUN of paintings, photographs, writing, etc: a striking quality, giving the observer a strong sense of involvement

immediate ADJECTIVE **1** happening straight away: *immediate reaction*

2 close: *immediate family* **3** direct: *my immediate successor*

immediately ADVERB without delay

immemorial ADJECTIVE going further back in time than can be remembered

immense ADJECTIVE very large > **immensity** NOUN

immensely ADVERB greatly

immerse VERB to plunge something into liquid so that it is completely covered **immerse yourself in** to give your whole attention to

immersion NOUN **1** the plunging of something into liquid so that it is completely covered **2** deep involvement in a certain subject or situation

immigrant NOUN someone who immigrates or has immigrated

immigrate VERB to come into a country and settle there > **immigration** NOUN

Comes from Latin *immigrare*, from *in* meaning 'into', and *migrare* meaning 'to remove'

> Do not confuse with: **emigrate**. You **immigrate** to a new country where you plan to start living (the IM comes from the Latin meaning 'into'). You are **emigrating** when you leave your original or home country (the E comes from the Latin meaning 'from').

imminent ADJECTIVE about to happen: *imminent danger*

Comes from Latin *imminens* meaning 'overhanging'

> Do not confuse with: **eminent**

immobile ADJECTIVE **1** without moving **2** not easily moved > **immobility** NOUN

immobilize *or* **immobilise** VERB to put out of action

immoral ADJECTIVE **1** wrong, unscrupulous **2** sexually improper > **immorality** NOUN > **immorally** ADVERB

> Do not confuse with: **amoral**. An **immoral** person behaves badly in the full knowledge that what they are doing is wrong. An **amoral** person behaves badly because they do not understand the difference between right and wrong.

immortal ADJECTIVE **1** living forever **2** famous forever

immortality NOUN unending life or fame

immortalize *or* **immortalise** VERB to make immortal or famous forever

immovable ADJECTIVE not able to be moved or changed > **immovably** ADVERB

immune ADJECTIVE **1** not likely to catch a particular disease: *immune to measles* **2** not able to be affected by: *She is immune to his charm* > **immunity** NOUN

immune system NOUN the natural defensive system of an organism that identifies and neutralizes harmful matter within itself

immunize *or* **immunise** VERB to make someone immune to (a disease), especially by inoculation **> immunization** NOUN

immunology NOUN the study of the human immune system

imp NOUN **1** a small malignant spirit **2** a mischievous child **> impish** ADJECTIVE

impact NOUN (*pronounced* **im**-pakt) **1** the blow of one thing striking another; a collision **2** strong effect: *made an impact on the audience* ▶ VERB (*pronounced* **im**-pakt or im-**pakt**) to press firmly together **impact on** to affect strongly

impair VERB to damage, weaken **> impairment** NOUN

impala NOUN a large African antelope

impale VERB to pierce through with a spear etc

impart VERB to tell (information, news, etc) to others

impartial ADJECTIVE not favouring one side over another; unbiased **> impartiality** NOUN **> impartially** ADVERB

impassable ADJECTIVE of a road, path, etc: not able to be travelled along

impasse (*pronounced* **am**-pas) NOUN a situation from which there seems to be no way out

impassioned ADJECTIVE moved by strong feeling

impassive ADJECTIVE not easily moved by strong feeling **> impassively** ADVERB

impatient ADJECTIVE **1** restlessly eager **2** irritable, short-tempered **> impatience** NOUN **> impatiently** ADVERB

impeach VERB to accuse publicly of, or charge with, misconduct **> impeachment** NOUN

impeccable ADJECTIVE faultless, perfect **> impeccably** ADVERB

impede VERB to hinder, keep back

impediment NOUN **1** a hindrance **2** a speech defect, eg a stutter or stammer

impel VERB (**impelling, impelled**) **1** to urge **2** to drive on

impending ADJECTIVE about to happen: *a feeling of impending doom*

impenetrable ADJECTIVE **1** not allowing light etc through **2** incomprehensible, inscrutable

imperative ADJECTIVE **1** necessary, urgent **2** *grammar* of the mood of a verb: indicating a command, eg *look!* or *read this*

imperceptible ADJECTIVE so small as not to be noticed

imperfect ADJECTIVE having a fault or flaw, not perfect ▶ NOUN, *grammar* (**the imperfect**) the tense used to describe continuing or incomplete actions or states in the past, eg: *The sun **was shining** and the birds **were singing***

imperfection NOUN a fault or a flaw

imperfectly ADVERB not perfectly or thoroughly

imperial ADJECTIVE **1** of an emperor or empire **2** commanding, superior

imperialism NOUN the policy of annexing the territory of, and ruling, other nations and people **> imperialist** ADJECTIVE: *imperialist policies*

imperial system NOUN the system of weights and measures using inches and feet, ounces and pounds, etc

imperious ADJECTIVE having an air of authority, haughty

impermeable ADJECTIVE not able to be passed through: *impermeable by water*

impersonal ADJECTIVE **1** not influenced by personal feelings **2** not connected with any person > **impersonally** ADVERB

impersonate VERB to dress up as, or act the part of, someone > **impersonation** NOUN

impersonator NOUN someone who impersonates others

impertinent ADJECTIVE **1** cheeky, impudent **2** *old* not pertinent, irrelevant > **impertinence** NOUN (meaning 1) > **impertinently** ADVERB (meaning 1)

impervious ADJECTIVE (**impervious to**) not able to be affected by: *impervious to criticism*

impetuous ADJECTIVE rushing into action, rash > **impetuosity** NOUN

impetus (*pronounced* **im**-pet-us) NOUN **1** moving force, motivation **2** impulse

impinge VERB: **impinge on** *or* **impinge upon 1** to come in contact with **2** to trespass on, interfere with

implacable ADJECTIVE not able to be soothed or calmed > **implacably** ADVERB

implant VERB (*pronounced* im-**plant**) to fix in, plant firmly ▶ NOUN (*pronounced* **im**-plant) an artificial organ, graft, etc inserted into the body: *breast implants*

implement NOUN a tool ▶ VERB to carry out, fulfil (eg a promise) > **implementation** NOUN

implicate VERB to bring in, involve: *The statement implicates you in the crime*

implication NOUN something meant though not actually said

implicit ADJECTIVE **1** understood, meant though not actually said **2** unquestioning: *implicit obedience*

implicitly ADVERB without questioning or doubting: *trust someone implicitly*

implode VERB to collapse inwards suddenly > **implosion** NOUN

implore VERB to beg, entreat

imply VERB to suggest: *Her silence implies disapproval*

Comes from Latin *implicare* meaning 'to involve'

> Do not confuse with: **infer. Implying** is an action of expression – you **imply** something by dropping subtle hints about it. **Inferring** is an action of understanding – you **infer** something by drawing conclusions from what you have seen or heard.

impolite ADJECTIVE not polite, rude

import VERB (*pronounced* im-**pawt** *or* **im**-pawt) **1** to bring in (goods) from abroad for sale **2** to load a file, data, etc into a program ▶ NOUN (*pronounced* **im**-pawt) **1** the act of importing **2** something imported from abroad for sale **3** meaning, significance > **importation** NOUN

a b c d e f g h i j k l m n o p q r s t u v w x y z

A B C D E F G H I J K L M N O P Q R S T U V W X Y Z

important ADJECTIVE worthy of attention; special > **importance** NOUN > **importantly** ADVERB

🛈 Comes from Latin *importare* meaning 'to bring in'

impose VERB to place (a tax etc) on **impose on** to take advantage of, inconvenience

imposing ADJECTIVE impressive, commanding attention

imposition NOUN a burden, an inconvenience

impossible ADJECTIVE **1** not able to be done or to happen **2** extremely difficult to deal with, intolerable > **impossibility** NOUN (meaning 1) > **impossibly** ADVERB

impostor *or* **imposter** NOUN someone who pretends to be someone else in order to deceive

impotent (*pronounced* **im**-pot-ent) ADJECTIVE without power or effectiveness > **impotence** NOUN > **impotently** ADVERB

impound VERB to seize possession of (something) by law: *goods impounded by Customs*

impoverish VERB **1** to make financially poor **2** to lessen in quality: *an impoverished culture* > **impoverishment** NOUN

impracticable ADJECTIVE not able to be done > **impracticability** NOUN

🛈 Comes from prefix *im-* meaning 'not', and *practicable*

> Do not confuse: **impracticable** and **impractical**

impractical ADJECTIVE lacking common sense > **impracticality** NOUN

🛈 Comes from prefix *im-* meaning 'not', and *practical*

imprecise ADJECTIVE not precise, vague

impregnable ADJECTIVE too strong to be taken by attack: *an impregnable fortress*

impregnate VERB **1** to make pregnant **2** to saturate: *a tissue impregnated with perfume*

impress VERB **1** to arouse the interest or admiration of **2** to mark by pressing upon **3** to fix deeply in the mind

impression NOUN **1** someone's thoughts or feelings about something: *My impression is that it's likely to rain* **2** a deep or strong effect: *The film left a lasting impression on me* **3** a mark made by impressing

impressionable ADJECTIVE easily influenced or affected

impressionism NOUN an artistic or literary style aiming to reproduce personal impressions of things or events

impressionist NOUN **1** a follower of impressionism **2** an entertainer who impersonates people

impressive ADJECTIVE having a strong effect on the mind

imprint VERB (*pronounced* im-**print**) **1** to stamp, press **2** to fix in the mind ▸ NOUN (*pronounced* **im**-print) **1** the printer's or publisher's name etc on a book **2** a common title for a series of related books from one publisher

imprison VERB to shut up as in a prison > **imprisonment** NOUN

improbable ADJECTIVE not likely to happen > **improbability** NOUN

impromptu ADJECTIVE & ADVERB without preparation or rehearsal

improper ADJECTIVE **1** not suitable; wrong **2** indecent

improper fraction NOUN a fraction greater than 1 (as 5⁄4, 11⁄8)

impropriety NOUN (*plural* **improprieties**) something improper

improve VERB to make or become better > **improvement** NOUN

improvise VERB **1** to put together from available materials: *We improvised a stretcher* **2** to create (a tune, script, etc) spontaneously: *The actors had to improvise their lines* > **improvisation** NOUN

impudent ADJECTIVE cheeky, insolent > **impudence** NOUN > **impudently** ADVERB

impulse NOUN **1** a sudden force or push **2** a sudden urge resulting in sudden action

impulsive ADJECTIVE acting on impulse, without taking time to consider > **impulsively** ADVERB

impunity NOUN freedom from punishment, injury or loss

impure ADJECTIVE mixed with other substances; not clean

impurity NOUN (*plural* **impurities**) **1** a small amount of something which is present in, and spoils the quality of, another substance **2** the state of being impure

in- PREFIX **1** (also **il-**, **im-**, **ir-**, **em-**, **en-**) into, on, towards: *inshore/illusion/impulse/embrace* (= to take in the arms)/*endure* **2** (also **ig-**, **il-**, **im-**, **ir-**) not: *inaccurate/ignoble* (= not noble)/*illiterate/improper/irregular* (= not regular)

in PREPOSITION **1** showing position in space or time: *sitting in the garden/born in the 60s* **2** showing state, manner, etc: *in part/in cold blood* ▶ ADVERB **1** towards the inside, not out **2** in power **3** *informal* in fashion ▶ ADJECTIVE **1** that is in, inside or coming in **2** *informal* fashionable **be in for 1** to be trying to get (a prize etc) **2** to be about to receive (trouble, punishment)

inability NOUN (*plural* **inabilities**) lack of power, means, etc (to do something)

inaccessible ADJECTIVE not able to be easily reached or obtained

inaccurate ADJECTIVE **1** not correct **2** not exact > **inaccuracy** NOUN (*plural* **inaccuracies**)

inaction NOUN lack of action

inactive ADJECTIVE **1** not active **2** not working, doing nothing

inactivity NOUN idleness; rest

inadequate ADJECTIVE **1** not enough **2** unable to cope with a situation > **inadequacy** NOUN

inadmissible ADJECTIVE not allowable: *inadmissible evidence*

inadvertent ADJECTIVE unintentional

inadvisable ADJECTIVE not advisable, unwise

inalienable ADJECTIVE not able to be removed or transferred: *inalienable rights*

inane ADJECTIVE silly, foolish, mindless

inanimate ADJECTIVE without life

inapplicable ADJECTIVE not applicable

inappropriate ADJECTIVE not suitable

inarticulate ADJECTIVE **1** unable to express yourself clearly **2** said indistinctly

inattentive ADJECTIVE not paying attention > **inattention** NOUN

inaudible ADJECTIVE not loud enough to be heard

inaugural ADJECTIVE relating to, or performed at, an inauguration

inaugurate VERB to mark the beginning of (eg a presidency) with a ceremony > **inauguration** NOUN

inauspicious ADJECTIVE unlucky, unlikely to end in success

inborn ADJECTIVE innate, natural: *inborn talent*

in-box NOUN, *computing* a file for storing incoming e-mail

inbred ADJECTIVE **1** inborn **2** resulting from inbreeding

inbreeding NOUN repeated mating and producing of offspring within the same family, or closely related individuals of a species

inc ABBREVIATION **1** incorporated **2** inclusive **3** including

Inca NOUN, *history* a member of a complex pre-Columbian civilization in Peru > **Incan** ADJECTIVE

incalculable ADJECTIVE not able to be counted or estimated

incandescent ADJECTIVE **1** white-hot **2** *informal* extremely angry

incantation NOUN a spell

incapable ADJECTIVE **1** unable (to do what is expected) **2** helpless (through drink etc)

incapacitate VERB **1** to take away power, strength or rights **2** to disable

incapacity NOUN **1** inability **2** disability

incarcerate VERB to imprison > **incarceration** NOUN

incarnate ADJECTIVE having human form: *the devil incarnate*

incarnation NOUN **1** a person whose appearance or behaviour are the perfect example of a particular quality, eg beauty or honour **2** of a spirit: appearance in a physical form

incendiary ADJECTIVE meant for setting (buildings etc) on fire: *an incendiary bomb*

incense VERB (*pronounced* in-**sens**) to make angry ▶ NOUN (*pronounced* **in**-sens) a mixture of resins, gums, etc burned to give off fumes, especially in religious ceremonies

incentive NOUN something which encourages someone to do something

inception NOUN beginning

incessant ADJECTIVE going on without pause

incest NOUN illegal sexual intercourse between close relatives

incestuous ADJECTIVE **1** involving incest **2** done within a close-knit group

inch NOUN (*plural* **inches**) one twelfth of a foot (about 2.5 centimetres) ▶ VERB to move very gradually

incidence NOUN **1** the frequency of

something occurring **2** a falling of a ray of light etc

incident NOUN a happening

incidental ADJECTIVE **1** happening in connection with something: *an incidental expense* **2** casual

incidentally ADVERB by the way

incinerate VERB to burn to ashes > **incineration** NOUN

incinerator NOUN an apparatus for burning rubbish etc

incise VERB to cut into, engrave

incision NOUN **1** cutting into something **2** a cut, a gash

incisive ADJECTIVE sharp, clear, firm

incisor NOUN a front tooth

incite VERB to move to action; urge on > **incitement** NOUN

inclement ADJECTIVE of weather: stormy > **inclemency** NOUN

inclination NOUN **1** liking, tendency **2** a slope

incline VERB (*pronounced* in-**klain**) **1** to lean, slope (towards) **2** to bend, bow **3** to have a liking for ▸NOUN (*pronounced* **in**-klain) a slope

inclined ADJECTIVE **1** talented or gifted **2** (**inclined to**) having a tendency, or a hesitant desire to

include VERB to count in, along with others

inclusion NOUN the act of including something, or the fact that it is included

inclusive ADJECTIVE including everything mentioned: *From Tuesday to Thursday inclusive is 3 days*

incognito (*pronounced* in-cog-**neet**-oh) ADJECTIVE & ADVERB in disguise, with identity concealed ▸NOUN (*plural* **incognitos**) a disguise

incoherent ADJECTIVE **1** unconnected, rambling **2** speaking in an unconnected, rambling way > **incoherence** NOUN

income NOUN **1** personal earnings **2** gain, profit

incoming ADJECTIVE approaching, next

incomparable ADJECTIVE without equal

incompatible ADJECTIVE **1** of statements: contradicting each other **2** of people: not suited, bound to disagree > **incompatibility** NOUN

incompetent ADJECTIVE not good enough at doing a job > **incompetence** NOUN

incomplete ADJECTIVE not finished

incomprehensible ADJECTIVE not able to be understood, puzzling

incomprehension NOUN the state of not understanding something

inconceivable ADJECTIVE not able to be imagined or believed

inconclusive ADJECTIVE not leading to a definite decision or conclusion

incongruous ADJECTIVE **1** not matching well **2** out of place, unsuitable > **incongruity** (*plural* **incongruities**)

inconsequential ADJECTIVE unimportant > **inconsequence** NOUN

inconsiderable ADJECTIVE slight, unimportant

inconsiderate ADJECTIVE not thinking of others

inconsistent ADJECTIVE not consistent, contradicting:

a b c d e f g h i j k l m n o p q r s t u v w x y z

inconsistent statements
> **inconsistency** NOUN

inconsolable ADJECTIVE not able to be comforted

inconspicuous ADJECTIVE not noticeable

inconstant ADJECTIVE often changing > **inconstancy** NOUN

incontinent ADJECTIVE **1** unable to control the bladder or bowels **2** uncontrolled, unrestrained
> **incontinence** NOUN

inconvenience NOUN minor trouble or difficulty: *I don't want you to go to any inconvenience on my behalf*

inconvenient ADJECTIVE causing awkwardness or difficulty

incorporate VERB **1** to contain as parts of a whole: *The new complex incorporates a theatre, cinema and restaurant* **2** to include, take account of: *The new text incorporates the author's changes*

incorporated ADJECTIVE (*abbrev* **inc**) formed into a company or society

incorrect ADJECTIVE wrong

incorrigible ADJECTIVE too bad to be put right or reformed

increase VERB (*pronounced* in-**krees**) to grow, make greater or more numerous ▶ NOUN (*pronounced* **in**-krees) **1** growth **2** the amount added by growth

increasingly ADVERB more and more

incredible ADJECTIVE impossible to believe > **incredibility** NOUN
ⓘ Comes from Latin *incredibilis* meaning 'beyond belief'

Do not confuse: **incredible** and **incredulous**. **Incredible** means unbelievable. **Incredulous** means unbelieving. You might, for example, be **incredulous** at (= unable to believe) another person's **incredible** (= unbelievable) stupidity.

incredibly ADVERB extremely, unbelievably

incredulity (*pronounced* in-kred-**yool**-it-i) NOUN disbelief

incredulous (*pronounced* in-**kred**-yul-*us*) ADJECTIVE not believing what is said > **incredulously** ADVERB
ⓘ Comes from Latin *incredulus* meaning 'unbelieving'

increment NOUN an annual increase in a salary

incriminate VERB to show that (someone) has taken part in a crime

incubate VERB of birds: to brood, hatch (eggs)

incubation period NOUN the time that it takes for a disease to develop from infection to the first symptoms

incubator NOUN **1** a large heated box for hatching eggs **2** a hospital crib for rearing premature babies

incumbent ADJECTIVE resting on (someone) as a duty: *it is incumbent upon me to warn you* ▶ NOUN someone who holds an official position

incur VERB (**incurring, incurred**) to bring (blame, debt, etc) upon yourself

incurable ADJECTIVE unable to be cured

incursion NOUN an invasion, a raid:

incursions across the border

indebted ADJECTIVE having reason to be grateful: *We are indebted to you for your kindness*

indecent ADJECTIVE offending against normal or usual standards of (especially sexual) behaviour > **indecency** NOUN

indecent assault NOUN an assault involving indecency but not rape

indecipherable ADJECTIVE **1** illegible **2** incomprehensible

indecision NOUN slowness in making up your mind, hesitation

indecisive ADJECTIVE **1** not coming to a definite result **2** unable to make up your mind

indeed ADVERB **1** in fact: *She is indeed a splendid cook* **2** (used for emphasis) really: *Did he indeed?* ▶ INTERJECTION expressing surprise, disbelief, irony, etc

indefensible ADJECTIVE **1** unable to be defended **2** inexcusable

indefinable ADJECTIVE not able to be stated or described clearly

indefinite ADJECTIVE **1** not fixed, uncertain: *indefinite about her plans* **2** without definite limits: *an indefinite period of leave*

indefinite article NOUN, *grammar* the name given to the adjectives *a* and *an*

indefinitely ADVERB for an indefinite period of time

indelible ADJECTIVE unable to be rubbed out or removed > **indelibly** ADVERB

indent VERB to begin a new paragraph by going in from the margin

indentation NOUN **1** a hollow, a dent **2** an inward curve in an outline, coastline, etc

independent ADJECTIVE **1** free to think or act for yourself **2** not relying on someone else for support, guidance, etc **3** of a country: self-governing > **independence** NOUN

indescribable ADJECTIVE not able to be described

indestructible ADJECTIVE not able to be destroyed

indeterminate ADJECTIVE not fixed, indefinite

index NOUN (*plural* **indexes**) **1** an alphabetical list giving the page number of subjects mentioned in a book **2** an indication **3** (*plural* **indices**) *maths another word for* **exponent**(meaning 2) **4** a numerical scale showing changes in the cost of living, wages, etc

index finger NOUN the forefinger

Indian ink NOUN a very black ink used by artists

Indian summer NOUN a period of sun and warm weather in autumn

indicate VERB to point out, show

indication NOUN a sign

indicative ADJECTIVE pointing out, being a sign of: *indicative of his attitude*

indicator NOUN **1** something which indicates; a pointer **2** a flashing light on either side of a vehicle for signalling to other drivers

indices *plural* of **index** (meaning 3)

indict (*pronounced* in-**dait**) VERB to accuse formally of a crime

A B C D E F G H I J K L M N O P Q R S T U V W X Y Z

indictment (*pronounced* in-**dait**-ment) NOUN something which shows or proves how bad something else is

indie (*pronounced* **in**-di) *informal*, NOUN an independent record, film or television company ▶ ADJECTIVE of a band: using an independent company to record their music

indifferent ADJECTIVE **1** neither very good nor very bad **2** (**indifferent to**) showing no interest in > **indifference** NOUN (meaning 2)

indigenous ADJECTIVE native to a country or area: *the indigenous population/indigenous flora and fauna*

indigestible ADJECTIVE difficult to digest

indigestion NOUN discomfort or pain in the abdomen or lower part of the chest caused by difficulty in digesting food

indignant ADJECTIVE angry, especially because of wrong done to yourself or others > **indignation** NOUN

indignity NOUN (*plural* **indignities**) **1** loss of dignity **2** insult

indigo NOUN a purplish-blue colour ▶ ADJECTIVE purplish-blue

indirect ADJECTIVE **1** not straight or direct **2** not affecting or affected directly

indirect speech *or* **reported speech** NOUN speech reported not in the speaker's actual words, eg *They said that they'd leave the next day* rather than *They said, 'We'll leave tomorrow'* (*contrasted with*: **direct speech**)

indirect tax NOUN a tax on particular goods, paid by the customer in the form of a higher price

indiscreet ADJECTIVE **1** rash, not cautious **2** giving away too much information

indiscretion NOUN a rash or unwise remark or act, rash or unwise behaviour

indiscriminate ADJECTIVE making no distinction between one person (or thing) and another: *indiscriminate killing*

indispensable ADJECTIVE not able to be done without, necessary

indisputable ADJECTIVE not able to be denied

indistinct ADJECTIVE not clear to someone's eye, ear or mind

indistinguishable ADJECTIVE **1** difficult to make out **2** too alike to tell apart

individual ADJECTIVE **1** relating to a single person or thing **2** distinctive, unusual: *a very individual style of writing* ▶ NOUN a single person or thing

individualist NOUN someone with an independent or distinctive lifestyle > **individualism** NOUN > **individualistic** ADJECTIVE

individuality NOUN **1** separate existence **2** the quality of standing out from others

indivisible ADJECTIVE not able to be divided

indoctrinate VERB to teach (a person or group) to accept and believe a particular set of ideas or beliefs without criticizing them

> **indoctrination** NOUN

indolent ADJECTIVE lazy
> **indolence** NOUN

indomitable ADJECTIVE unconquerable, unyielding

indoor ADJECTIVE done, happening, belonging, etc inside a building

indoors ADVERB in or into a building etc

indubitable ADJECTIVE not to be doubted

induce VERB **1** to persuade: *Nothing could induce her to stay* **2** to bring on, cause

inducement NOUN something which encourages or persuades: *Money is an inducement to work*

induction NOUN **1** the formal installation of someone in a new post **2** the production of electricity in something by placing it near an electric source **3** the drawing of conclusions from particular cases

indulge VERB **1** to be inclined to give in to the wishes of; spoil: *She indulges that child too much* **2** to give way to, not restrain: *indulging his sweet tooth*

indulgence NOUN **1** the act of indulging **2** a pardon for a sin

indulgent ADJECTIVE not strict, kind

industrial ADJECTIVE **1** related to or used in trade or manufacture **2** of a country: having highly developed industry

industrialist NOUN someone who owns a large industrial organization or is involved in its management at a senior level

industrialize *or* **industrialise** VERB to introduce industry to (a country, region, etc)
> **industrialization** NOUN

industrious ADJECTIVE hard-working

industry NOUN (*plural* **industries**) **1** the business of producing goods: *He works in industry* **2** a branch of trade or manufacture: *the clothing industry* **3** steady attention to work

inebriated ADJECTIVE drunk

inedible ADJECTIVE not eatable

ineffective ADJECTIVE useless, having no effect

ineffectual ADJECTIVE achieving nothing

inefficient ADJECTIVE **1** not efficient, not capable **2** wasting time, energy, etc > **inefficiency** NOUN (*plural* **inefficiencies**)

ineligible ADJECTIVE not qualified or not suitable to be chosen

inept ADJECTIVE clumsy, badly done
> **ineptitude** NOUN

[i] Comes from Latin *ineptus* meaning 'useless'

inequality NOUN (*plural* **inequalities**) **1** lack of equality, unfairness **2** unevenness

inert ADJECTIVE **1** not moving or able to move **2** disinclined to move or act; indolent **3** not lively **4** chemically inactive

inert gas *see* **noble gas**

inertia NOUN **1** lack of energy or the will to move or act; indolence **2** *physics* the resistance of an object to a change in its state of motion eg when you try to stop a moving object, or to set a stationary object in motion **3** *see* **industrial inertia**

A B C D E F G H I J K L M N O P Q R S T U V W X Y Z

inescapable ADJECTIVE unable to be avoided

inessential ADJECTIVE not essential, unnecessary

inestimable ADJECTIVE too great to be estimated

inevitable ADJECTIVE not able to be avoided; certain to happen > **inevitability** NOUN

inexact ADJECTIVE not exact, approximate

inexcusable ADJECTIVE too bad to be excused or justified

inexhaustible ADJECTIVE very plentiful; not likely to be used up

inexorable ADJECTIVE not able to be persuaded; relentless

inexpensive ADJECTIVE cheap in price

inexperience NOUN lack of (skilled) knowledge or experience > **inexperienced** ADJECTIVE

inexplicable ADJECTIVE not able to be explained

inexpressible ADJECTIVE not able to be described in words

inextricable ADJECTIVE not able to be disentangled

infallible ADJECTIVE **1** never making an error **2** certain to produce the desired result: *infallible cure* > **infallibility** NOUN

infamous ADJECTIVE having a very bad reputation; notorious, disgraceful

infamy NOUN public disgrace, notoriety

infancy NOUN **1** early childhood, babyhood **2** the beginning of anything: *when psychiatry was in its infancy*

infant NOUN a baby

infanticide NOUN **1** the murder of a child **2** a child murderer

infantile ADJECTIVE **1** of babies **2** childish

infantry NOUN foot-soldiers

infatuated ADJECTIVE filled with foolish, intense love > **infatuation** NOUN

infect VERB **1** to contaminate (water, food, etc) with disease-causing pollutants **2** to pass on disease-causing micro-organisms to (a living organism) **3** to pass on, spread (eg enthusiasm)

infection NOUN **1** the invasion of a living organism by disease-causing micro-organisms **2** a disease caused by such a micro-organism, which can be spread to others **3** something that spreads widely and affects many people

infectious ADJECTIVE **1** of a disease: caused by micro-organisms, and able to be transmitted by air, water, bodily fluids, etc (*compare with*: **contagious**) **2** likely to spread from person to person: *Her laugh is so infectious*

infer VERB (**inferring, inferred**) to reach a conclusion from facts or reasoning: *Am I to infer from what you say that you wish to resign?*
[i] Comes from Latin *inferre* meaning 'to bring in'

> **Infer** is sometimes used to mean 'imply' or 'suggest': *'Are you inferring that I'm a liar?'*, but this use is considered incorrect by some people.

inference NOUN a conclusion that you reach, based on information which you have been given

inferior ADJECTIVE **1** lower in any way **2** not of best quality ▸NOUN someone lower in rank etc > **inferiority** NOUN

inferiority complex NOUN a constant feeling that you are less good in some way than other people

infernal ADJECTIVE **1** belonging or relating to hell **2** *informal* annoying, blasted

inferno NOUN **1** hell **2** (*plural* **infernos**) a raging fire

infertile ADJECTIVE **1** of soil: not producing much **2** not able to bear children or young > **infertility** NOUN

infest VERB to swarm over: *infested with lice*

infidel NOUN someone who does not believe in a particular religion (especially Christianity or Islam)

infidelity NOUN unfaithfulness, disloyalty

infighting NOUN rivalry or quarrelling between members of the same group

infiltrate VERB to enter (an organization etc) secretly to spy or cause damage > **infiltration** NOUN

infinite ADJECTIVE without end or limit

infinitely ADVERB very much: *Your work is infinitely better now*

infinitive NOUN, *grammar* the form of a verb which expresses the action but not person, place or time, often written as *to* + the base form, eg: *I hate* ***to lose***

infinity NOUN space or time without end

infirm ADJECTIVE feeble, weak

infirmary NOUN (*plural* **infirmaries**) a hospital

infirmity NOUN (*plural* **infirmities**) a physical weakness

inflame VERB **1** to make hot or red **2** to arouse passion in > **inflamed** ADJECTIVE

inflammable ADJECTIVE **1** easily set on fire **2** easily excited

inflammation NOUN heat in a part of the body, with pain, redness and swelling

inflammatory ADJECTIVE arousing passion (especially anger)

inflatable ADJECTIVE able to be inflated for use

inflate VERB **1** to blow up (a balloon, tyre, etc) **2** to puff up (with pride), exaggerate: *an inflated sense of her own importance* **3** to increase to a great extent

inflation NOUN **1** the act of inflating **2** an economic situation in which prices and wages keep forcing each other to increase

inflect VERB **1** to change the tone of (your voice) **2** to vary the endings of (a word) to show tense, number, gender, etc

inflection NOUN **1** change in the tone of your voice **2** a change in the basic form of a word to show tense, number, etc **3** the new form of a word which has been changed in this way: *The inflections of the verb 'find' are: 'finds', 'finding' and 'found'* > **inflectional** ADJECTIVE

inflexible ADJECTIVE not yielding,

A B C D E F G H I J K L M N O P Q R S T U V W X Y Z

unbending > **inflexibility** NOUN

inflict VERB to bring down (blows, punishment, etc) on > **infliction** NOUN

influence NOUN the power to affect other people or things ▸ VERB to have power over > **influential** ADJECTIVE

influenza NOUN an infectious illness with fever, headache, muscle pains, etc

influx NOUN **1** a flowing in **2** the arrival of large numbers of people

info NOUN, *informal* information

inform VERB **1** to give knowledge to **2** (**inform on** *or* **against**) to give incriminating evidence about someone to the authorities

informal ADJECTIVE not formal; relaxed, friendly > **informality** NOUN

informant NOUN someone who informs

information NOUN knowledge, news

information technology NOUN (*abbrev* **IT**) the development and use of computer systems and applications

informative ADJECTIVE giving information

informer NOUN someone who gives information to the police or authorities

infra- PREFIX below, beneath: *infrasound*

ⓘ Comes from Latin *infra* meaning 'below' or 'underneath'

infra-red ADJECTIVE of rays of heat: with wavelengths longer than visible light

infrastructure NOUN inner structure, framework

infrequent ADJECTIVE rare, happening seldom

infringe VERB to break (a rule or law) > **infringement** NOUN

infuriate VERB to drive into a rage

infuriating ADJECTIVE extremely annoying

infuse VERB of herbs, tea: to soak or be soaked in hot water to release flavour **infuse someone with** to inspire or fill someone with (a positive feeling, desire, etc)

infusion NOUN **1** the act of infusing **2** a tea formed by steeping a herb etc in water

ingenious (*pronounced* in-**jeen**-i-*us*) ADJECTIVE **1** skilful in inventing **2** cleverly thought out

ingenuity *from* **ingenious** NOUN cleverness; quickness of ideas

ingot NOUN a block of metal (especially gold or silver) cast in a mould

ingrained ADJECTIVE deeply fixed: *ingrained laziness/ingrained dirt*

ingratiate VERB to work your way into someone's favour by flattery etc > **ingratiating** ADJECTIVE

ingratitude NOUN lack of gratitude or thankfulness

ingredient NOUN one of the things of which a mixture is made

ingrown ADJECTIVE of a nail: growing into the flesh

inhabit VERB to live in

inhabitant NOUN someone who lives permanently in a place

inhalation NOUN **1** the act of inhaling **2** a medicine which is inhaled

inhale VERB to breathe in

inhaler NOUN a small, portable device for breathing in medicine, steam, etc

inherent ADJECTIVE inborn, being a natural, essential or permanent part

inherit VERB **1** to receive property, a title, etc as an heir **2** to get (a characteristic) from your parents etc: *She inherits her sense of humour from her father* > **inheritance** NOUN

inheritor NOUN an heir

inhibit VERB to hold back, prevent

inhibited ADJECTIVE unable to express your feelings

inhibition NOUN a holding back of natural impulses etc, restraint

inhospitable ADJECTIVE unwelcoming, unfriendly

inhuman ADJECTIVE not human; brutal > **inhumanity** NOUN

inhumane ADJECTIVE cruel

inimitable ADJECTIVE impossible to imitate

initial ADJECTIVE of or at the beginning: *initial difficulties* ▶NOUN the letter beginning a word, especially someone's name ▶VERB (**initialling, initialled**) to sign with the initials of your name

initially ADVERB at first: *Initially, I did not like her*

initiate VERB **1** to begin, start: *initiate the reforms* **2** to give first lessons to **3** to make someone formally a member of a society etc > **initiation** NOUN (meanings 1 and 3)

initiative NOUN **1** the right to take the first step **2** readiness to take a lead

inject VERB **1** to force (a fluid etc) into the veins or muscles with a syringe **2** to put (eg enthusiasm) into > **injection** NOUN

in-joke NOUN a joke only understood by a particular group

injunction NOUN an official order or command

injure VERB to harm, damage, wrong

injured ADJECTIVE hurt; offended

injury NOUN (*plural* **injuries**) **1** hurt, damage, harm **2** a wrong

injustice NOUN **1** unfairness **2** a wrong

ink NOUN a coloured liquid used in writing, printing, etc ▶VERB to mark with ink

inkling NOUN a hint or slight sign

inky ADJECTIVE (**inkier, inkiest**) **1** of or covered in ink **2** very dark

inlaid *past form* of **inlay**

inland ADJECTIVE **1** not beside the sea **2** happening inside a country ▶ADVERB towards the inner part of a country

inland revenue NOUN taxes etc collected within a country

in-laws PLURAL NOUN, *informal* relatives by marriage

inlay NOUN decoration made by fitting pieces of different shapes and colours into a background ▶VERB (**inlaying, inlaid**) to fit into a background as decoration > **inlaid** ADJECTIVE

inlet NOUN a small bay

inmate NOUN a resident, an occupant (especially of an institution): *the inmates of the prison*

A B C D E F G H I J K L M N O P Q R S T U V W X Y Z

inmost ADJECTIVE the most inward, the farthest in

inn NOUN a public house or small hotel in the country

innards PLURAL NOUN **1** internal parts **2** entrails

innate ADJECTIVE inborn, natural

inner ADJECTIVE **1** farther in **2** of feelings etc: hidden

innermost ADJECTIVE farthest in; most secret

innings SINGULAR NOUN **1** a team's turn for batting in cricket **2** a turn, a go at something

innkeeper NOUN someone who keeps an inn

innocent ADJECTIVE **1** not guilty, blameless **2** having no experience of how unpleasant people, and life in general, can be, and therefore tending to trust everyone **3** harmless **4** (**innocent of**) lacking, without > **innocence** NOUN (meanings 1 and 2)

innocuous ADJECTIVE not harmful or offensive

innovation NOUN something new

innuendo NOUN (*plural* **innuendoes**) an indirectly unpleasant or critical reference, eg about someone's character

innumerable ADJECTIVE too many to be counted

innumerate ADJECTIVE not understanding arithmetic or mathematics > **innumeracy** NOUN

inoculate VERB, *medicine* to produce a mild form of a disease (in a person or animal) so they produce antibodies against it > **inoculation** NOUN

inoffensive ADJECTIVE harmless, giving no offence

inoperative ADJECTIVE not active, not working

inopportune ADJECTIVE at a bad or inconvenient time

inordinate ADJECTIVE going beyond the limit, unreasonably great

inorganic ADJECTIVE **1** not of animal or vegetable origin **2** of a chemical compound: not containing carbon

in-patient NOUN a patient who stays in a hospital during their treatment (*contrasted with*: **out-patient**)

input NOUN **1** an amount (of energy, labour, etc) put into something **2** *computing* data fed into a computer (*contrasted with*: **output**) ▶ VERB to enter (data) into a computer

inquest NOUN a legal inquiry into a case of sudden death

inquire *or* **enquire** VERB to ask

inquiring *or* **enquiring** ADJECTIVE questioning, curious: *inquiring mind*

inquiry *or* **enquiry** NOUN (*plural* **inquiries** *or* **enquiries**) **1** a question; a search for information **2** an official investigation

inquisition NOUN a careful questioning or investigation

inquisitive ADJECTIVE **1** very curious **2** fond of prying, nosy > **inquisitively** ADVERB

inroad NOUN a raid, an advance **make inroads into** to use up large amounts of: *The holiday made inroads into their savings*

insane ADJECTIVE mad, not sane > **insanity** NOUN

insanitary ADJECTIVE not sanitary; encouraging the spread of disease

insatiable ADJECTIVE not able to be satisfied: *insatiable appetite*

inscribe VERB to write or engrave (eg a name) on a book, monument, etc

inscribed ADJECTIVE, *maths* of a figure: enclosed by another figure

inscription NOUN the writing on a book, monument, etc

inscrutable ADJECTIVE not able to be understood, mysterious

insect NOUN a small six-legged creature with wings and a body divided into sections

insecticide NOUN powder or liquid for killing insects

insectivore NOUN an animal or plant which feeds on insects > **insectivorous** ADJECTIVE

insecure ADJECTIVE **1** not safe; not firm **2** lacking confidence, not feeling settled > **insecurity** NOUN

inseminate VERB **1** to plant, introduce (into) **2** to impregnate, especially artificially > **insemination** NOUN

insensible ADJECTIVE **1** unconscious, unaware (of) **2** not having feeling

insensitive ADJECTIVE **1** (**insensitive to**) not feeling: *insensitive to cold* **2** unsympathetic (to): *insensitive to her grief* **3** unappreciative, crass > **insensitivity** NOUN

inseparable ADJECTIVE not able to be separated or kept apart > **inseparably** ADVERB

insert VERB (*pronounced* in-**sert**) to put in or among ▶ NOUN (*pronounced* **in**-sert) **1** a special feature added to a television programme etc **2** a separate leaflet or pull-out section in a magazine etc > **insertion** NOUN

inset NOUN **1** an insert **2** a small picture, map, etc in a corner of a larger one

inshore ADJECTIVE & ADVERB in or on the water but near or towards the shore

inside NOUN **1** the inner side, space or part **2** indoors ▶ ADJECTIVE **1** being on or in the inside **2** indoor **3** coming from or done by someone within an organization: *inside information* ▶ ADVERB to, in or on the inside ▶ PREPOSITION to the inside of; within

insidious ADJECTIVE **1** likely to trap those who are not careful, treacherous **2** of a disease: coming on gradually and unnoticed

insight NOUN the ability to gain a relatively rapid, clear understanding of a complex situation, problem, etc

insignia PLURAL NOUN signs or badges showing that someone holds an office, award, etc

insignificant ADJECTIVE of little importance > **insignificance** NOUN

insincere ADJECTIVE not sincere > **insincerity** NOUN

insinuate VERB **1** to hint (at a fault) indirectly **2** to put in gradually and secretly **3** to work yourself into (someone's favour etc)

insinuation NOUN a sly hint

insipid ADJECTIVE **1** dull, without liveliness **2** tasteless, bland

insist VERB **1** to urge something strongly: *insist on punctuality* **2** to refuse to give way, hold firmly to your intentions: *He insists on walking there* **3** to go on saying (that): *She insists that she saw a UFO*

insistent ADJECTIVE **1** insisting on having or doing something **2** forcing you to pay attention > **insistence** NOUN (meaning 1) > **insistently** ADVERB (meaning 1)

in situ ADVERB & ADJECTIVE in position, in place

insolent ADJECTIVE rude, impertinent, insulting > **insolence** NOUN

insoluble ADJECTIVE **1** not able to be dissolved **2** of a problem: not able to be solved > **insolubility** NOUN

insolvent ADJECTIVE not able to pay your debts, impoverished > **insolvency** NOUN

insomnia NOUN sleeplessness

insomniac NOUN someone who suffers from insomnia

inspect VERB **1** to look carefully into, examine **2** to look over (troops etc) ceremonially

inspection NOUN careful examination

inspector NOUN **1** an official who inspects **2** a police officer below a superintendent and above a sergeant in rank

inspiration NOUN **1** something or someone that influences or encourages others **2** a brilliant idea

inspirational ADJECTIVE inspiring, brilliant

inspire VERB **1** to encourage, rouse **2** to be the source of creative ideas **3** to breathe in

inspired ADJECTIVE **1** seeming to be aided by higher powers **2** brilliantly good

instability NOUN lack of steadiness or stability

install *or* **instal** VERB (**installs** *or* **instals, installing, installed**) **1** to place in position, ready for use: *Has the telephone been installed?* **2** to introduce formally to a new job etc > **installation** NOUN

instalment NOUN **1** a part of a sum of money paid at fixed times until the whole amount is paid **2** one part of a serial story

instance NOUN an example, a particular case ▶ VERB to mention as an example **at the instance of** at the request of **for instance** for example

instant ADJECTIVE **1** immediate, urgent **2** able to be prepared almost immediately: *instant coffee* ▶ NOUN **1** a very short time, a moment **2** point or moment of time: *I need it this instant*

instantaneous ADJECTIVE done or happening very quickly

instantly ADVERB immediately

instead ADVERB in place of someone or something: *You can go instead* **instead of** in place of

instep NOUN the arching, upper part of the foot

instigate VERB to stir up, encourage

instigation NOUN: **at someone's instigation** following that person's instructions or wishes

instil *or* **instill** VERB (**instils** *or* **instills, instilling, instilled**) to put in little by little (especially ideas into the mind)

instinct NOUN a natural feeling or knowledge which someone has without thinking and without being taught

instinctive ADJECTIVE due to instinct

institute VERB to set up, establish, start ▶ NOUN a society, organization, etc or the building it uses

institution NOUN **1** an organization, building, etc established for a particular purpose (especially care or education) **2** an established custom > **institutional** ADJECTIVE

institutionalize *or* **institutionalise** VERB **1** to confine in an institution **2** to make an established custom of

instruct VERB **1** to teach **2** to direct, command > **instructor** NOUN

instruction NOUN **1** teaching **2** a command **3** (**instructions**) rules showing how something is to be used

instructive ADJECTIVE containing or giving information or knowledge

instrument NOUN **1** something used for a particular purpose, a tool **2** a device for producing musical sounds, eg a piano, a harp

instrumental ADJECTIVE **1** helpful in bringing (something) about **2** written for or played by musical instruments, without voice accompaniment

instrumentalist NOUN someone who plays on a musical instrument

insubordinate ADJECTIVE rebellious, disobedient > **insubordination** NOUN

insufferable ADJECTIVE too annoying, unpleasant, etc to be endured

insufficient ADJECTIVE not enough > **insufficiency** NOUN

insular ADJECTIVE **1** of an island or islands **2** narrow-minded, prejudiced > **insularity** NOUN

insulate VERB **1** to cover with a material that will not let through electrical currents, heat, frost, etc **2** to cut off, isolate > **insulation** NOUN

insulator NOUN a material that will not let through electrical currents, heat, etc

insulin NOUN, *medicine* a substance used in the treatment of diabetes

ⓘ Based on the Latin word for 'island', because insulin is secreted by the *islets* of Langerhans

insult VERB to treat with scorn or rudeness ▶ NOUN a rude or scornful remark

insulting ADJECTIVE scornful, rude

insure VERB to arrange for payment of a sum of money on (something) if it should be lost, damaged, stolen, etc

> Do not confuse with: **ensure**

> **insurance** NOUN

insurgent ADJECTIVE rising up in rebellion ▶ NOUN a rebel > **insurgency** NOUN

insurmountable ADJECTIVE not able to be got over or dealt with

intact ADJECTIVE whole, unbroken

intake NOUN an amount of people or things taken in: *this year's intake of students*

intangible ADJECTIVE **1** not able to be felt by touch **2** difficult to define or describe, not clear

integer NOUN, *maths* any positive or negative whole number or zero, as opposed to a fraction

integral ADJECTIVE **1** of or essential to a whole: *an integral part of the machine* **2** made up of parts forming a whole

integrate VERB **1** to fit parts together to form a whole **2** to enable (racial groups) to mix freely and live on equal terms > **integration** NOUN

integrated circuit NOUN interconnected electronic components etched on to a tiny piece of a semiconductor such as silicon (*also called*: **chip**)

integrity NOUN **1** honesty **2** wholeness, completeness

intellect NOUN the thinking power of the mind

intellectual ADJECTIVE **1** involving or requiring intellect **2** having a highly developed ability to think, reason and understand ▶ NOUN someone of natural ability or with academic interests

intelligence NOUN **1** mental ability **2** information sent, news

intelligent ADJECTIVE clever, quick at understanding

intelligentsia NOUN the intellectuals within a particular society

intelligible ADJECTIVE able to be understood

intend VERB to mean or plan (to do something)

intense ADJECTIVE **1** very great **2** tending to feel emotions deeply > **intensely** ADVERB

intensifier NOUN, *grammar* a word that adds emphasis to another word, eg *very* good, *extremely* difficult

intensify VERB (**intensifies, intensifying, intensified**) to increase, make more concentrated

intensity NOUN (*plural* **intensities**) strength, eg of feeling, colour, energy, etc

intensive ADJECTIVE very thorough, concentrated

intensive care NOUN a unit in a hospital where the condition of a patient who is critically ill is carefully monitored

intent NOUN purpose ▶ ADJECTIVE **1** with all your concentration (on), attentive **2** determined (to)

intention NOUN **1** what someone means to do, an aim **2** meaning

intentional ADJECTIVE done on purpose > **intentionally** ADVERB

inter- PREFIX between, among, together: *intermingle/ interplanetary*

ⓘ Comes from Latin *inter* meaning 'between', 'among' or 'mutually'

interact VERB to act on one another

interactive ADJECTIVE allowing two-way communication, eg between a computer or television and its user

interactive whiteboard NOUN a display board which responds to input and on which computer output can be projected

intercept VERB **1** to stop or catch (a person, missile, etc) on their way from one place to another **2** to cut off, interrupt (a view, the light, etc) **3** *maths* to cut a line, plane, etc with another line, plane, etc that crosses it

interchange VERB **1** to put each in the place of the other **2** to alternate ▶NOUN **1** the act of interchanging **2** a junction of two or more major roads on separate levels

interchangeable ADJECTIVE able to be used one for the other

intercom NOUN a telephone system within a building, aeroplane, etc

intercourse NOUN **1** communication **2** dealings between people etc **3** sexual intercourse

interest NOUN **1** special attention, curiosity **2** someone's personal concern or field of study **3** advantage, benefit **4** a sum paid for the loan of money ▶VERB to catch or hold the attention of

interested ADJECTIVE having or taking an interest

interesting ADJECTIVE holding the attention

interest rate NOUN a charge made for borrowing money, usually shown as a percentage of the amount borrowed

interface NOUN, *computing* a connection between two parts of the same system

interfere VERB **1** (**interfere in**) to take part in what is not your business, meddle in **2** (**interfere with**) to get in the way of, hinder, have a harmful effect on: *interfering with her work*

interference NOUN **1** the act of interfering **2** the spoiling of radio or television reception by another station or disturbance from traffic etc

interim NOUN time between; the meantime ▶ADJECTIVE temporary

interior ADJECTIVE **1** inner **2** inside a building **3** inland ▶NOUN **1** the inside of anything **2** the inland part of a country

interject VERB **1** to make a sudden remark in a conversation **2** to exclaim

interjection NOUN a word or phrase of exclamation, eg *Ah!* or *Oh dear!*

interlock VERB **1** to lock or clasp together **2** to fit into each other

interloper NOUN someone who enters without permission, an intruder

interlude NOUN **1** an interval **2** a short piece of music played between the parts of a play, film, etc

intermediary NOUN (*plural* **intermediaries**) someone who mediates between two people, for example in trying to settle a quarrel

intermediate ADJECTIVE in the middle; coming between two points, stages or extremes

interminable ADJECTIVE never-ending, boringly long

intermission NOUN an interval, a pause

intermittent ADJECTIVE stopping every now and then and starting again

a b c d e f g h i j k l m n o p q r s t u v w x y z

A B C D E F G H I J K L M N O P Q R S T U V W X Y Z

intern VERB (*pronounced* in-**tern**) to keep (someone from an enemy country) prisoner during a war

internal ADJECTIVE **1** of the inner part, especially of the body **2** inside, within a country, organization, etc: *internal affairs*

international ADJECTIVE **1** happening between nations **2** concerning more than one nation **3** worldwide ▸ NOUN a sports match between teams of two countries

internee NOUN someone from an enemy country who is confined as a prisoner during a war

Internet NOUN an international computer network linking users through telephone lines

Internet service provider NOUN (*abbrev* **ISP**) a company or organization that provides access to the Internet

internment NOUN confinement within a country or prison, especially during a war
[i] Comes from French *interne* meaning 'internal'

interplanetary ADJECTIVE between planets

interplay NOUN the action and influence of two or more things on each other

interpret VERB **1** to explain the meaning of something **2** to translate **3** to bring out the meaning of (music, a part in a play, etc) in performance **4** to take the meaning of something to be > **interpretation** NOUN

interpreter NOUN someone who translates (on the spot) the words of a speaker into another language

interrogate VERB to examine by asking questions > **interrogation** NOUN > **interrogator** NOUN

interrogative NOUN a word used in asking a question, eg who? where? ▸ ADJECTIVE questioning

interrupt VERB **1** to stop (someone) while they are saying or doing something **2** to stop doing (something) **3** to get in the way of, cut off (a view etc) > **interruption** NOUN

intersect VERB of lines: to meet and cross

intersection NOUN **1** the point where two lines cross **2** a crossroads

intersperse VERB to scatter here and there in > **interspersion** NOUN

intertwine VERB to twine or twist together

interval NOUN **1** a time or space between two things **2** a short pause in a programme etc

intervene VERB **1** to come or be between, or in the way **2** to join in (in order to stop) a fight or quarrel between other persons or nations > **intervention** NOUN

interview NOUN a formal meeting of one person with others to apply for a job, give information to the media etc ▸ VERB **1** to ask questions etc of in an interview **2** to conduct an interview

intestines PLURAL NOUN the inside parts of the body, especially the bowels and passages leading to them > **intestinal** ADJECTIVE

intimacy NOUN (*plural* **intimacies**) **1** close friendship **2** familiarity **3** sexual intercourse

intimate ADJECTIVE (*pronounced* **in**-tim-*at*) **1** knowing a lot about, familiar (with) **2** of friends: very close **3** private, personal: *intimate details* **4** having a sexual relationship (with) ▸NOUN (*pronounced* **in**-tim-*at*) a close friend ▸VERB (*pronounced* **in**-tim-eit) **1** to hint **2** to announce > **intimately** ADVERB

intimation NOUN **1** a hint **2** announcement

intimidate VERB to frighten or threaten into submission > **intimidating** ADJECTIVE > **intimidation** NOUN

into PREPOSITION **1** to the inside: *into the room* **2** towards: *into the millennium* **3** to a different state: *a tadpole changes into a frog* **4** *maths* expressing the idea of division: *2 into 4 goes twice*

intolerable ADJECTIVE too bad, painful, etc to be endured

intolerant ADJECTIVE not willing to put up with (people of different ideas, religion, etc) > **intolerance** NOUN

intonation NOUN the rise and fall of the voice

intoxicate VERB to make drunk

ⓘ Literally, to affect with arrow-poison

intoxication NOUN drunkenness

intra- PREFIX within: *intramural*

ⓘ Comes from Latin *intra* meaning 'within'

intractable ADJECTIVE difficult, stubborn > **intractability** NOUN

intranet NOUN, *computing* a restricted network of computers, eg in a company

intransigent ADJECTIVE refusing to change or come to an agreement > **intransigence** NOUN

intransitive ADJECTIVE, *grammar* of a verb: not needing an object, eg to *go*, to *fall*

in-tray NOUN an office tray for letters and work still to be dealt with (*contrasted with*: **out-tray**)

intrepid ADJECTIVE without fear, brave > **intrepidity** NOUN

intricate ADJECTIVE complicated, having many twists and turns > **intricacy** NOUN (*plural* **intricacies**)

intrigue NOUN (*pronounced* **in**-treeg) **1** secret plotting or a secret plot **2** a secret love affair ▸VERB (*pronounced* in-**treeg**) (**intriguing, intrigued**) **1** to plot, scheme **2** to rouse the curiosity of, fascinate > **intriguing** ADJECTIVE

intrinsic ADJECTIVE belonging to something as part of its nature

introduce VERB **1** to bring in or put in **2** to present (someone) to another person by name

introduction NOUN **1** the introducing of someone or something **2** an essay at the beginning of a book etc briefly explaining its contents

introductory ADJECTIVE coming at the beginning

introspective ADJECTIVE inward-looking, fond of examining your own thoughts and feelings > **introspection** NOUN

introvert NOUN a person who tends to be uncommunicative and unsociable (*contrasted with*: **extrovert**)

A B C D E F G H I J K L M N O P Q R S T U V W X Y Z

intrude VERB to thrust yourself into somewhere uninvited > **intrusion** NOUN > **intrusive** ADJECTIVE

intruder NOUN someone who breaks in or intrudes

intuition NOUN **1** ability to understand something without thinking it out **2** an instinctive feeling or belief

Inuit NOUN **1** the Eskimo people, especially those in Greenland, Canada and N Alaska **2** their language

inundate VERB **1** to flood **2** to overwhelm: *inundated with work* > **inundation** NOUN

invade VERB **1** to enter (a country etc) as an enemy to take possession **2** to interfere with (someone's rights, privacy, etc) > **invader** NOUN > **invasion** NOUN

invalid[1] (*pronounced* in-**val**-id) ADJECTIVE **1** not legally effective **2** mistaken, incorrect or unacceptable: *invalid data* > **invalidity** NOUN

invalid[2] (*pronounced* **in**-val-id) NOUN someone who is ill or disabled ▶ ADJECTIVE **1** ill or disabled **2** suitable for people who are ill or disabled ▶ VERB to make an invalid of **invalid out** to discharge from the army as an invalid **invalidity** NOUN

invalidate VERB to prove to be wrong, or make legally ineffective

invaluable ADJECTIVE priceless, essential

invariable ADJECTIVE unchanging

invariably ADVERB always

invasion *see* **invade**

invective NOUN abusive words; scorn

inveigle VERB (**inveigle into**) to coax, trick or persuade someone into doing something

invent VERB **1** to make or think up for the first time **2** to make up (a story, an excuse) > **inventor** NOUN

invention NOUN something invented

inventive ADJECTIVE good at inventing, resourceful

inventory NOUN (*plural* **inventories**) a detailed list of contents

inverse ADJECTIVE opposite, reverse ▶ NOUN **1** the opposite **2** *maths* one of two numbers that cancel each other out in a mathematical operation, eg the inverse of 3 in addition is -3, because 3+-3= 0 > **inversely** ADVERB

inversion NOUN **1** a turning upside-down **2** a reversal

invert VERB **1** to turn upside down **2** to reverse the order of

invertebrate ADJECTIVE of an animal: not having a backbone ▶ NOUN an animal with no backbone, eg a worm or insect

inverted commas PLURAL NOUN punctuation marks, which look like commas or commas upside down (' ' or " "), showing where direct speech begins and ends

invest VERB **1** to put money in a firm, property, etc to make a profit **2** to give a particular quality to

investigate VERB to search into with care > **investigator** NOUN

investigation NOUN a careful search

investiture NOUN a ceremony before taking on an important office

investment NOUN **1** money invested **2** something in which money is invested **3** *old* a siege

investor NOUN someone who invests

inveterate ADJECTIVE **1** firmly fixed in a habit: *an inveterate gambler* **2** deep-rooted

invigilate VERB to supervise (an examination etc) > **invigilator** NOUN

invigorate VERB to strengthen, refresh > **invigorating** ADJECTIVE

invincible ADJECTIVE not able to be defeated or overcome > **invincibility** NOUN

invisible ADJECTIVE not able to be seen > **invisibility** NOUN

invitation NOUN a request to do something

invite VERB **1** to ask (someone) to do something, especially to come for a meal etc **2** to seem to ask for: *inviting punishment*

inviting ADJECTIVE tempting, attractive

in vitro ADVERB & ADJECTIVE taking place in an artificial environment such as a test tube

invoice NOUN a letter sent with goods with details of price and quantity ▶ VERB to send an invoice to (a customer)

invoke VERB **1** to call upon in prayer **2** to ask for (eg help) > **invocation** NOUN

involuntary ADJECTIVE not done willingly or intentionally > **involuntarily** ADVERB

involve VERB **1** to have as a consequence, require **2** to take part (in), be concerned (in): *involved in publishing/involved in the scandal* > **involvement** NOUN

involved ADJECTIVE complicated

invulnerable ADJECTIVE not vulnerable, not able to be hurt > **invulnerability** NOUN

inward ADJECTIVE **1** placed within **2** situated in the mind or soul ▶ ADVERB (*also* **inwards**) towards the inside

inwardly ADVERB **1** within **2** in your heart, privately

iodine NOUN, *chemistry* (symbol **I**) a liquid chemical used to kill germs

ion NOUN an electrically charged atom or group of atoms > **ionic** ADJECTIVE

ionizer *or* **ioniser** NOUN a device which sends out negative ions to improve the quality of the air

iota NOUN a little bit, a jot

🛈 After the smallest letter in the Greek alphabet

IOU NOUN *short for* I owe you, a note given as a receipt for money borrowed

IQ ABBREVIATION intelligence quotient, a measure of a person's intellectual ability

ir- *see* **in-**

irascible ADJECTIVE easily made angry > **irascibility** NOUN

irate ADJECTIVE angry

ire NOUN, *formal* anger

iridescent ADJECTIVE **1** coloured like a rainbow **2** shimmering with changing colours > **iridescence** NOUN

iris NOUN (*plural* **irises**) **1** the

coloured part of the eye around the pupil **2** a lily-like flower which grows from a bulb

irk VERB to weary, annoy

irksome ADJECTIVE tiresome

iron (*pronounced* **ai**-*on or Scottish* **ai**-r*on*) NOUN **1** a common metal, widely used to make tools etc **2** an iron instrument: *a branding iron* **3** a golf club (originally with an iron head) **4** an appliance for pressing clothes **5** (**irons**) a prisoner's chains ▸ ADJECTIVE **1** made of iron **2** stern, resolute: *iron will* **3** of a rule: not to be broken ▸ VERB to press (clothes) with an iron **iron out** to smooth out (difficulties)

Iron Age NOUN human culture at the stage of using iron for tools etc

Iron Curtain NOUN, *history* a notional barrier between the West and the countries of the former Soviet bloc

ironic *or* **ironical** ADJECTIVE **1** containing or expressing irony **2** of a person: frequently using irony > **ironically** ADVERB

ironmonger NOUN a shopkeeper selling household tools, gardening equipment, etc

ironmongery NOUN goods sold by an ironmonger

irony NOUN (*plural* **ironies**) **1** a form of humour in which someone says the opposite of what is obviously true **2** an absurd contradiction or paradox: *The irony of it was that she would have given him the money if he hadn't stolen it*

irrational ADJECTIVE **1** against logic or common sense **2** *maths* of a number: unable to be expressed as an integer or common fraction > **irrationality** NOUN

irregular ADJECTIVE **1** uneven, variable **2** against the rules > **irregularity** NOUN (*plural* **irregularities**)

irrelevant ADJECTIVE not having to do with what is being spoken about > **irrelevance** *or* **irrelevancy** NOUN (*plural* **irrelevancies**)

irreparable ADJECTIVE not able to be repaired

irreplaceable ADJECTIVE too good or rare to be replaced

irrepressible ADJECTIVE not restrainable or controllable

irresistible ADJECTIVE too strong or too charming to be resisted

irrespective ADJECTIVE taking no account of: *irrespective of the weather*

irresponsible ADJECTIVE having no sense of responsibility, thoughtless

irreverent ADJECTIVE having no respect, eg for holy things > **irreverence** NOUN

irreversible ADJECTIVE not able to be changed back to a previous state > **irreversibly** ADVERB

irrevocable (*pronounced* i-**rev**-*ok*-*a*-bl) ADJECTIVE not to be changed

irrigate VERB to supply (land) with water by canals *etc* > **irrigation** NOUN

irritable ADJECTIVE cross, easily annoyed > **irritability** NOUN

irritant NOUN someone or something that causes annoyance or discomfort

irritate VERB **1** to annoy **2** to cause discomfort to (the skin, eyes, etc) > **irritation** NOUN

ISDN ABBREVIATION, *computing* integrated services digital network, an advanced telecommunications network

-ish SUFFIX **1** from that place: *English* **2** like: *girlish* **3** a little: *quietish*

Islam NOUN **1** the Muslim religion, based on the teachings of the prophet Muhammad **2** the followers of this religion as a group > **Islamic** ADJECTIVE

island NOUN **1** an area of land surrounded by water **2** an isolated place, a haven

islander NOUN an inhabitant of an island

isle NOUN, *formal* an island

-ism SUFFIX **1** indicating a system, set of beliefs, etc: *socialism/ Catholicism* **2** indicating prejudice against a particular group: *racism/ sexism*

ⓘ Comes from Greek suffix *-ismos*, used to form nouns of action from verbs

iso- PREFIX equal: *isobar/isotherm*

ⓘ Comes from Greek *isos* meaning 'equal'

isobar NOUN a line on the map connecting places where atmospheric pressure is the same

isolate VERB **1** to place or keep separate from other people or things **2** to consider (something) by itself: *isolate the problem* > **isolated** ADJECTIVE > **isolation** NOUN

isolationism NOUN the political policy of avoiding as much as possible any dealings with other countries > **isolationist** ADJECTIVE

isomer NOUN a chemical substance with the same molecular weight as another, but with its atoms in a different arrangement > **isomeric** ADJECTIVE

isosceles ADJECTIVE of a triangle: with two sides equal (*compare with*: **equilateral**)

isotherm NOUN a line on the map connecting places which have the same temperature

isotope NOUN an atom with the same atomic number as, but different mass number from, another

ISP ABBREVIATION, *computing* Internet service provider

issue VERB **1** to go or come out **2** to give out (orders etc) **3** to publish ▶ NOUN **1** a flowing out **2** something published **3** one number in a series of magazines etc **4** result, consequence **5** a matter being discussed **6** *formal* children: *He died without issue* **take issue with** to disagree with

IT ABBREVIATION information technology, the development and use of computer systems and applications

it PRONOUN **1** the thing spoken of: *I meant to bring the book, but I left it at home* **2** used in sentences with no definite subject: *It snowed today* **3** used in phrases as a kind of object: *go it alone*

italicize *or* **italicise** VERB to print in italics

a b c d e f g h i j k l m n o p q r s t u v w x y z

A B C D E F G H I J K L M N O P Q R S T U V W X Y Z

italics PLURAL NOUN a kind of type which *slopes to the right*

itch NOUN **1** an irritating feeling in the skin, made better by scratching **2** a strong desire ▶ VERB **1** to have an itch **2** to be impatient (to do), long (to): *itching to open his presents*
> **itchy** ADJECTIVE (**itchier, itchiest**)

item NOUN a separate article in a list

itemize *or* **itemise** VERB to list in items

itinerant ADJECTIVE travelling from place to place, especially on business ▶ NOUN someone who travels around, especially a tramp, pedlar, etc

itinerary NOUN (*plural* **itineraries**) a route or plan of a journey

-itis SUFFIX used to describe diseases which involve inflammation: *tonsillitis* (= inflammation of the tonsils)/*bronchitis* (= inflammation of the windpipe)

[i] Comes from Greek suffix *-itis* meaning 'belonging to'

it's *short for* it is *or* it has

its ADJECTIVE belonging to it: *Keep the hat in its box*

> Do not confuse: **its** and **it's**. **Its**, meaning 'belonging to it', is spelt with no apostrophe ('). **It's** means 'it is' or 'it has'.

itself PRONOUN **1** used reflexively: *The cat licked itself* **2** used for emphasis or contrast: *After I've read the introduction, I'll begin the book itself*

ITV ABBREVIATION Independent Television, a group of British television companies that broadcast programmes paid for by advertising

ivory NOUN (*plural* **ivories**) the hard white substance which forms the tusks of the elephant, walrus, etc

ivy NOUN (*plural* **ivies**) a creeping evergreen plant

Jj

jab VERB (**jabbing, jabbed**) **1** to prod (someone) **2** to strike with a quick punch ▶ NOUN **1** a prod **2** *informal* an injection: *flu jab*

jabber VERB to talk rapidly and indistinctly

jack NOUN **1** a device with a lever for raising heavy weights **2** (*also called*: **knave**) the playing-card between ten and queen **jack up 1** to raise with a jack **2** to raise (prices etc) steeply

jackal NOUN a dog-like wild animal

jackass NOUN **1** a male ass **2** *informal* an idiot

jackboots PLURAL NOUN large boots reaching above the knee

jackdaw NOUN a type of small crow

jacket NOUN **1** a short coat **2** a loose paper cover for a book

jacket potato NOUN a baked potato

jack-in-the-box NOUN a doll fixed to a spring inside a box that leaps out when the lid is opened

jack-knife NOUN **1** a large folding knife **2** a dive forming a sharp angle and then straightening ▶ VERB of a vehicle and its trailer: to swing together to form a sharp angle

jackpot NOUN a fund of prize money which increases until someone wins it

Jacobean ADJECTIVE, *history* relating to the period when James VI of Scotland and I of England reigned (1603--1625)

Jacobite NOUN, *history* a supporter of James VII of Scotland and II of England and his descendants

Jacuzzi (*pronounced* ja-**koo**-zi) NOUN, *trademark* a bath fitted with underwater jets that massage and invigorate the body

jade NOUN a hard green mineral substance used for ornaments

jaded ADJECTIVE tired or bored

jagged ADJECTIVE rough-edged, uneven

jaguar NOUN a S American animal similar to a leopard

jail NOUN a prison

jailer NOUN someone in charge of a jail or prisoners

jam NOUN **1** fruit boiled with sugar till it is set **2** a crush **3** a blockage caused by crowding **4** *informal* a difficult situation ▶ VERB (**jamming, jammed**) **1** to press or squeeze tight **2** to crowd full **3** to stick and so be unable to move: *The back wheel* *has jammed* **4** to cause interference with another radio station's broadcast **5** *music* to play with other musicians in an improvised style

jamb NOUN the side post of a door

jamboree NOUN **1** a large, lively gathering **2** a rally of Scouts

jammy ADJECTIVE (**jammier, jammiest**) **1** covered or filled with jam **2** *informal* lucky

jam-packed ADJECTIVE packed tightly

jangle VERB **1** to make a harsh ringing noise **2** to irritate

janitor NOUN **1** a caretaker **2** a doorkeeper

ⓘ Comes from Latin *janua* meaning 'a door'

January NOUN the first month of the year

ⓘ After *Janus*, a Roman god who had two faces, one looking into the new year, the other looking back to the old year

jape NOUN, *informal* a trick, a practical joke

jar NOUN a glass or earthenware bottle with a wide mouth ▶ VERB (**jarring, jarred**) **1** to have a harsh, startling effect **2** to be discordant, not agree: *His ideas jarred with my attitude*

jargon NOUN special words used within a particular trade, profession, etc

jarring ADJECTIVE harsh, startling

jasmine NOUN a shrub with white or yellow sweet-smelling flowers

jaundice NOUN a disease which causes the skin and eyes to turn yellow, caused by an excess of a bile pigment in the blood

jaundiced ADJECTIVE **1** having jaundice **2** discontented, bitter

jaunt NOUN a short journey for pleasure

jaunty ADJECTIVE cheerful
> jauntily ADVERB

javelin NOUN a long spear for throwing

jaw NOUN **1** the lower part of the face, including the mouth and chin **2** (**jaws**) an animal's mouth

jay NOUN a brightly coloured bird like a crow

jaywalker NOUN someone who walks carelessly among traffic

jaywalking NOUN walking carelessly among traffic
> jaywalker NOUN

jazz NOUN a style of music with a strong rhythm, based on African-American folk music **jazz up** to make (something) more lively or colourful

jazzy ADJECTIVE (**jazzier, jazziest**) **1** resembling or containing certain elements of jazz **2** colourful, flamboyant

JCB NOUN *trademark* a type of mobile digger used in the construction industry

ⓘ **JCB** is an abbreviation of *J C Bamford*, the manufacturer's name

jealous ADJECTIVE **1** wanting to have what someone else has; envious **2** guarding closely (your possessions etc) **> jealousy** NOUN

jeans PLURAL NOUN denim trousers

Jeep NOUN, *trademark* a light four-wheel-drive, usually military, vehicle that can travel over rough country

jeer VERB to make fun of, scoff ▶ NOUN a scoff

Jehovah NOUN the Hebrew God of the Old Testament

jelly NOUN (*plural* **jellies**) **1** fruit juice boiled with sugar till it becomes firm **2** a transparent wobbly food, often fruit-flavoured

jellyfish NOUN a sea animal with a jelly-like body

jeopardize *or* **jeopardise** VERB to put in danger or at risk

jeopardy NOUN danger of harm or loss: *His job was in jeopardy after the takeover*

ⓘ Originally a gambling term, based on French *jeu parti* meaning 'even chance'

jerk VERB to give a sudden sharp movement ▶ NOUN a sudden sharp movement

jerky ADJECTIVE (**jerkier**, **jerkiest**) moving or coming in jerks > **jerkily** ADVERB

jerry-built ADJECTIVE hastily and badly built

jersey NOUN (*plural* **jerseys**) a sweater, pullover

jest NOUN a joke ▶ VERB to joke

jester NOUN, *history* a fool employed to amuse a royal court etc

jet NOUN **1** a hard black mineral, used for ornaments and jewellery **2** a spout of flame, air or liquid **3** a jet plane

jet-black ADJECTIVE very black

jet lag NOUN tiredness caused by the body's inability to cope with being in a new time zone

jet plane NOUN an aeroplane driven by jet propulsion

jet propulsion NOUN high-speed forward motion produced by sucking in air or liquid and forcing it out from behind

jetsam NOUN goods thrown overboard and washed ashore

jet set NOUN (**the jet set**) rich people who enjoy frequent expensive holidays

jet stream NOUN **1** *meteorology* a band of high-speed winds far above the earth **2** the exhaust of a jet engine

jettison VERB **1** to throw overboard **2** to abandon

jetty NOUN (*plural* **jetties**) a small pier

Jew NOUN a member of the Hebrew race

jewel NOUN **1** a precious stone **2** someone or something highly valued

jewelled *or US* **jeweled** ADJECTIVE set with jewels

jeweller *or US* **jeweler** NOUN someone who makes or sells articles made of precious jewels and metals

jewellery *or US* **jewelry** NOUN articles made of precious jewels and metals

Jewish ADJECTIVE of the Jews

Jew's harp NOUN a small harp-shaped musical instrument played between the teeth

Jezebel NOUN a wicked, scheming woman

ⓘ After the wicked Queen *Jezebel*, the wife of King Ahab in the Bible

jib NOUN **1** a three-cornered sail in front of a ship's foremast **2** the

A B C D E F G H I J K L M N O P Q R S T U V W X Y Z

jutting-out arm of a crane **jib at** to refuse to do, object to

jibe *or* **gibe** VERB to jeer, scoff ▸NOUN a jeer

jiffy NOUN, *informal* a moment

Jiffy bag NOUN, *trademark* a padded envelope

jig NOUN a lively dance or tune for this dance ▸VERB (**jigging, jigged**) to jump or jerk up and down

jigsaw *or* **jigsaw puzzle** NOUN a puzzle consisting of many different-shaped pieces that fit together to form a picture

jihad (*pronounced* jee-**had**) NOUN a holy war for the Muslim faith

jilt VERB to cast aside (a lover)

jingle NOUN **1** a clinking sound like that of coins **2** a simple rhyme or tune, especially one used in an advertisement

jingoism (*pronounced* **jing**-goh-i-zm) NOUN chauvinism, narrow-minded nationalism > **jingoistic** ADJECTIVE

jinx NOUN someone or something thought to bring bad luck

[i] Probably from the *Jynx* bird which was once invoked in spells and charms

jitterbug NOUN an energetic dance popular in the 1940s

jitters PLURAL NOUN: **have the jitters** *informal* to be very nervous

jittery ADJECTIVE very nervous, shaking with nerves

jive NOUN a style of fast dancing to jazz or rock-and-roll music

job NOUN **1** someone's regular paid work **2** a piece of work

job centre NOUN a government office where information about available jobs is shown

job lot NOUN a mixed collection of objects sold as one item at an auction, etc

job-share NOUN the division of one job between two people, each working part-time

jockey NOUN (*plural* **jockeys**) someone who rides in horse races, especially as a profession ▸VERB to push your way into a good position

jockstrap NOUN a genital support for men while playing sports

jocular ADJECTIVE joking, merry > **jocularity** NOUN > **jocularly** ADVERB

jocund ADJECTIVE merry, cheerful

jodhpurs PLURAL NOUN riding breeches, fitting tightly from knee to ankle

joey NOUN (*plural* **joeys**) *Aust, informal* a young kangaroo

jog VERB (**jogging, jogged**) **1** to nudge, push slightly **2** to run at a gentle pace, especially for exercise ▸NOUN a gentle run > **jogging** NOUN (meaning 2)

jogger NOUN someone who runs gently to keep fit

joggle VERB to shake slightly

joie de vivre (*pronounced* szwah d*e* **vee**-vr*e*) NOUN enthusiasm for life; sparkle, spirit

join VERB **1** to connect, fasten **2** to become a member of: *joined the swimming club* **3** to meet ▸NOUN the place where two or more things join **join battle** to begin fighting in battle

joiner NOUN someone who makes wooden fittings, furniture, etc

joint NOUN **1** the place where two

or more things join **2** the place where two bones are joined, eg an elbow or knee **3** meat containing a bone **4** *slang* a cannabis cigarette ▸ ADJECTIVE **1** united: *a joint effort* **2** shared among more than one: *joint bank account*

jointly ADVERB together

joist NOUN the beam to which the boards of a floor or the beams of a ceiling are nailed

joke NOUN something said or done to cause laughter ▸ VERB to make a joke, tease

joker NOUN **1** someone who jokes **2** an extra playing-card in a pack, with a picture of a jester on it

jolliness *or* **jollity** NOUN merriment

jolly ADJECTIVE merry

jolt VERB **1** to shake suddenly **2** to go forward with sudden jerks ▸ NOUN a sudden jerk

joss-stick NOUN a stick of gum which gives off a sweet smell when burned

jostle VERB to push or knock against

jot NOUN a very small amount ▸ VERB (**jotting, jotted**) (usually **jot down**) to write down hurriedly or briefly

jotter NOUN a book for taking notes

joule NOUN (symbol **J**) the standard unit of measurement of work, energy and heat

journal NOUN **1** a personal account of each day's events; a diary **2** a newspaper, a magazine

journalism NOUN the business of recording events for the media > **journalist** NOUN > **journalistic** ADJECTIVE

journey NOUN (*plural* **journeys**) a distance travelled ▸ VERB to travel

journeyman NOUN a craftsman qualified in a particular trade

joust NOUN, *history* the armed contest between two knights on horseback at a tournament ▸ VERB to fight on horseback at a tournament

jovial ADJECTIVE cheerful, good-humoured > **joviality** NOUN

jowl NOUN the lower part of the jaw or cheek

joy NOUN gladness

joyful *or* **joyous** ADJECTIVE full of joy

joyless ADJECTIVE dismal

joyride NOUN a reckless trip for amusement in a stolen car > **joyrider** NOUN

joystick NOUN a control lever for eg an aeroplane or a video game

JP ABBREVIATION Justice of the Peace

JPEG (*pronounced* **jei**-peg) ABBREVIATION, *computing* Joint Photographic Experts Group, a standard format for image files

Jr ABBREVIATION Junior: *John Brown Jr*

jubilant ADJECTIVE triumphant, full of rejoicing > **jubilation** NOUN

jubilee NOUN celebrations arranged for the anniversary of a coronation *etc*

[i] From a Hebrew word for 'ram's horn', which was blown to announce the start of a celebratory Jewish year

Judaism NOUN the Jewish religion or way of life > **Judaic** ADJECTIVE

judder NOUN a strong vibration or jerky movement

A B C D E F G H I J K L M N O P Q R S T U V W X Y Z

judge VERB **1** to make a decision on (a law case) after hearing all the evidence **2** to form an opinion **3** to decide the winners in a competition etc ▶ NOUN **1** an official who hears cases in the law-courts and decides on them according to the country's or state's laws **2** someone skilled in evaluating anything: *a good judge of character*

judgement *or* **judgment** NOUN **1** a decision in a law case **2** an opinion **3** good sense in forming opinions

judicial ADJECTIVE of a judge or court of justice > **judicially** ADVERB

judiciary NOUN the judges of a country or state

judicious ADJECTIVE wise, sensible > **judiciously** ADVERB

judo NOUN a Japanese form of wrestling for self-defence

jug NOUN a dish for liquids with a handle and a shaped lip for pouring

juggernaut NOUN a large articulated lorry

ⓘ From a Hindi word for a large wagon used to carry the image of the god Krishna in religious processions

juggle VERB **1** to toss a number of things (balls, clubs, etc) into the air and catch them in order **2** to handle or present in a deceitful way > **juggler** NOUN (meaning 1)

jugular vein NOUN the large vein at the side of the neck that carries blood from the head to the heart

juice NOUN the liquid in fruits, vegetables, etc

juicy ADJECTIVE **1** full of juice **2** *informal* sensational, scandalous: *juicy gossip*

jujitsu NOUN a Japanese martial art similar to judo

jukebox NOUN a coin-operated machine which plays records and CDs you select

July NOUN the seventh month of the year

ⓘ Named in honour of the Roman general *Julius* Caesar

jumble VERB to throw together without order, muddle ▶ NOUN **1** a confused mixture **2** second-hand goods to be sold in a jumble sale

jumble sale NOUN a sale of odds and ends, cast-off clothing, etc

jumbo NOUN (*plural* **jumbos**) **1** a child's name for an elephant **2** a jumbo jet ▶ ADJECTIVE very large

jumbo jet NOUN a large jet aircraft

jump VERB **1** to spring off the ground **2** to make a sudden startled movement **3** to pass over without spending time on: *He jumped a few chapters* ▶ NOUN **1** a leap **2** a sudden start

jumper NOUN a sweater, a jersey

jumpsuit NOUN a one-piece garment combining trousers and top

jumpy ADJECTIVE (**jumpier, jumpiest**) easily startled

junction NOUN a place or point of joining, especially of roads or railway lines

juncture NOUN point: *It's too early to decide at this juncture*

June NOUN the sixth month of the year

ⓘ After *Juno*, the queen of the Roman gods

jungle NOUN a dense growth of trees and plants in tropical areas

junior ADJECTIVE **1** younger **2** in a lower class or rank ▸NOUN a person younger than the one in question: *She's three years his junior*

juniper NOUN an evergreen shrub with berries and prickly leaves

junk[1] NOUN worthless articles, rubbish

junk[2] NOUN a Chinese flat-bottomed sailing ship, high in the bow and stern

junket NOUN **1** a dish made of curdled milk sweetened and flavoured **2** a trip made by a government official and paid for out of public funds

junk food NOUN convenience food with little nutritional value

junkie *or* **junky** NOUN (*plural* **junkies**) *slang* a drug addict

junk mail NOUN unsolicited mail, especially advertising material

jurisdiction NOUN **1** a legal authority or power **2** the district over which a judge, court, etc has power

jurisprudence NOUN the study or knowledge of law

juror NOUN someone who serves on a jury

jury NOUN (*plural* **juries**) **1** a group of people selected to reach a decision on whether an accused person appearing in court is guilty or not **2** a group of judges for a competition, etc

juryman, jurywoman NOUN someone who serves on a jury

just[1] ADJECTIVE **1** fair in judgement: *a just ruler* **2** correct, right: *a just result* > **justly** ADVERB

just[2] ADVERB **1** exactly: *just right* **2** not long since: *only just arrived* **3** merely, only: *just a brief visit* **4** really, absolutely: *just beautiful*

justice NOUN **1** fairness in making judgements **2** what is right or rightly deserved **3** a judge

Justice of the Peace NOUN (*abbrev* **JP**) a citizen who acts as a judge for certain matters

justifiable ADJECTIVE able to be justified or defended, having good grounds: *justifiable anger* > **justifiably** ADVERB

justification NOUN **1** good reason **2** the arrangement of text so that it forms an even margin down the page

justify VERB (**justifies, justifying, justified**) **1** to prove or show to be right or desirable **2** to make (text) form an even margin down the page

jut VERB (**jutting, jutted**) to stand or stick out

jute NOUN fibre from certain plants for making sacking, canvas, etc

juvenile ADJECTIVE **1** young; of young people **2** childish ▸NOUN a young person

juxtapose VERB to place side by side > **juxtaposition** NOUN

Kk

kaftan *another spelling of* **caftan**

kaiser (*pronounced* **kaiz**-er) NOUN, *history* a German emperor

kale NOUN a cabbage with open curled leaves

kaleidoscope NOUN a tube held to the eye and turned, so that loose, coloured shapes reflected in two mirrors change patterns

kaleidoscopic ADJECTIVE **1** with changing colours **2** changing quickly

kamikaze NOUN, *history* a Japanese pilot trained to make a suicidal attack ▸ ADJECTIVE suicidal, self-destructive

kangaroo NOUN a large Australian animal with long hindlegs and great jumping power, the female carrying its young in a pouch on the front of her body

kaolin (*pronounced* **kei**-oh-lin) NOUN a soft white clay used for making fine porcelain, bricks and cement, and in some medicines (*also called*: **china clay**)

kaput (*pronounced* ka-**poot**) ADJECTIVE, *slang* broken, not working

karaoke (*pronounced* kar-i-**oh**-kei) NOUN an entertainment of singing well-known songs against pre-recorded backing music

karate (*pronounced* ka-**ra**-ti) NOUN a Japanese form of unarmed fighting using blows and kicks

karma NOUN, *Buddhism, Hinduism* someone's destiny as determined by their actions in a previous life

karyotype NOUN, *biology* the number and shape of chromosomes in a cell nucleus

kayak NOUN **1** an Inuit sealskin canoe **2** a lightweight canoe for one person, manoeuvred with a single paddle

KB, **Kb** *or* **Kbit** ABBREVIATION, *computing* kilobyte(s)

kebab NOUN small pieces of meat or vegetables cooked on a skewer

kedgeree NOUN a dish made with rice, fish and hard-boiled eggs

keek VERB, *Scottish* to look, peep

keel NOUN the piece of a ship's frame that lies lengthways along the bottom **keel over** to overturn, fall over

keen[1] ADJECTIVE **1** eager, enthusiastic **2** very sharp; bitingly cold > **keenness** NOUN

keen[2] VERB to wail in grief; lament > **keening** NOUN

keenly ADVERB intensely, passionately, alertly

keep VERB (**keeping, kept**) **1** to hold on to, not give or throw away **2** to look after, support **3** to store: *Keep everything in one place* **4** to fulfil (a promise) **5** to remain in a position or state: *keep to the left/ keep warm* **6** (also **keep on**) to continue (doing something): *Keep taking the tablets* **7** of food: to stay in good condition **8** to celebrate: *keep Christmas* ▸ NOUN **1** food, board: *earn your keep* **2** a castle stronghold **keep out 1** to exclude **2** to stay outside **keep up** to go on with, continue **keep up with** to go as fast etc as

ⓘ Comes from Old English *cepan*

keeper NOUN someone who looks after something: *zookeeper*

keeping NOUN care, charge **in keeping with** suitable for or fitting in with

keepsake NOUN a gift in memory of an occasion etc

keg NOUN a small cask or barrel

kelp NOUN a type of large brown seaweed

kelvin NOUN, *physics* a measure of temperature

ken NOUN knowledge or understanding: *beyond the ken of the average person*

kendo NOUN a Japanese martial art using bamboo staves

kennel NOUN **1** a hut for a dog **2** (**kennels**) a place where dogs can be looked after

kenning NOUN a phrase used in Old English poetry to refer to something without saying its name, eg, 'mouse chaser' meaning 'cat'

kept *past form* of **keep**

kerb NOUN the edge of a pavement

> Do not confuse with: **curb**

kerchief NOUN a square of cloth used as a headscarf

kernel NOUN **1** a soft substance in the shell of a nut, or inside the stone of a fruit **2** the important part of anything

kerosene *or* **kerosine** NOUN paraffin oil obtained from shale or the distillation of petroleum

kestrel NOUN a type of small falcon which hovers

ketchup NOUN a flavouring sauce made from tomatoes etc

ⓘ Originally spelt *catsup*, as it still is in US English; based on a Chinese word for 'fish brine'

kettle NOUN a container with a spout for boiling water

kettledrum NOUN a drum made of a metal bowl covered with stretched skin etc

key NOUN **1** a device which is turned in a corresponding hole to lock or unlock, tighten, tune, etc **2** a lever pressed on a piano etc to produce a note **3** a button on a typewriter or computer keyboard which is pressed to type letters **4** the chief note of a piece of music **5** something which explains a mystery or deciphers a code **6** a book containing answers to exercises ▸ VERB to type on a typewriter or computer ▸ ADJECTIVE important, essential

A B C D E F G H I J K L M N O P Q R S T U V W X Y Z

keyboard NOUN **1** the keys in a piano or organ arranged along a flat board **2** the keys of a typewriter or computer **3** an electronic musical instrument with keys arranged as on a piano etc

keyed-up ADJECTIVE excited

keyhole NOUN the hole in which a key of a door is placed **keyhole surgery** surgery using miniature instruments, performed through tiny holes instead of large openings in the patient's flesh

keynote NOUN **1** the chief note of a piece of music **2** the chief point about anything

keypad NOUN a device with buttons that can be pushed to operate a television, telephone, etc

keystone NOUN the stone at the highest point of an arch holding the rest in position

kg ABBREVIATION kilogram(s)

KGB ABBREVIATION, *history* Committee of State Security (in Russian, *Komitet Gosudarstvennoi Bezopasnosti*), the former Soviet secret police

khaki ADJECTIVE greenish-brown in colour ▸NOUN **1** greenish-brown **2** cloth of this colour used for military uniforms

ⓘ From an Urdu word meaning 'dusty'

kibbutz (*pronounced* ki-**bootz**) NOUN (*plural* **kibbutzim**) a farming settlement in Israel in which all share the work

kick VERB **1** to hit or strike out with the foot **2** of a gun: to spring back violently when fired ▸NOUN **1** a blow with the foot **2** the springing-back of a gun when fired **for kicks** *informal* for fun

kick-off NOUN the start (of a football game)

kid NOUN **1** *informal* a child **2** a young goat **3** the skin of a young goat ▸ADJECTIVE made of kid leather **with kid gloves** very carefully or tactfully

kidnap VERB (**kidnapping, kidnapped**) to carry (someone) off by force, often demanding money for their return > **kidnapper** NOUN > **kidnapping** NOUN

kidney NOUN (*plural* **kidneys**), *anatomy* either of a pair of organs in the lower back which filter waste from the blood and produce urine

kidney bean NOUN a bean with a curved shape like a kidney

kill VERB **1** to cause death to **2** to put an end to: *kill the rumours* ▸NOUN **1** the act of killing **2** the animals killed by a hunter **be in at the kill** to be there at the most exciting moment > **killer** NOUN

killing **make a killing** to make a lot of money quickly

kiln NOUN a large oven or furnace for baking pottery, bricks, etc or for drying grain, hops, etc

kilo- PREFIX a thousand: *kilogram/ kilometre*

ⓘ Comes from Greek *chilioi* meaning 'a thousand'

> In computing terminology **kilo-** does not mean exactly 1000, but 1024 (= 2^{10})

kilobyte NOUN (*abbrev* **KB, Kb** *or*

Kbyte) a measure of computer data or memory, equal to 1024 bytes

> See note at entry for prefix 'kilo-'

kilocalorie NOUN a measure of energy equal to 1000 calories

kilogram *or* **kilogramme** NOUN (*abbrev* **kg**) the standard measure of weight, equal to 1000 grams

kilolitre NOUN (*abbrev* **kl**) a measure of volume equal to 1000 litres

kilometre NOUN (*abbrev* **km**) a measure of length equal to 1000 metres

kilowatt NOUN (*abbrev* **kW**) a measure of electrical power equal to 1000 watts

kilt NOUN a pleated tartan skirt reaching to the knee, part of traditional Scottish dress

kilter NOUN: **out of kilter** out of sequence, off balance

kimono NOUN (*plural* **kimonos**) a loose Japanese robe, fastened with a sash

kin NOUN members of the same family, relations **kith and kin** *see* **kith** **next of kin** your nearest relative

kind[1] NOUN a sort, type **in kind** in goods, not money: *paid in kind*

kind[2] ADJECTIVE having good feelings towards others; generous, gentle > **kindness** NOUN

kindergarten NOUN a nursery school

kind-hearted ADJECTIVE kind

kindle VERB **1** to light a fire **2** to catch fire **3** to stir up (feelings)

kindling NOUN material for starting a fire

kindly ADVERB in a kind way
▶ ADJECTIVE kind, warm-hearted
> **kindliness** NOUN

kindred NOUN relatives, relations
▶ ADJECTIVE of the same sort; related: *a kindred spirit*

kinetic ADJECTIVE of or expressing motion: *kinetic energy/kinetic sculpture* (= sculpture which moves)

kinetic energy NOUN the energy a body has as a result of being in motion (*compare with*: **potential energy**)

king NOUN **1** the male ruler of a nation, especially one who has inherited the title **2** a playing-card with a picture of a king **3** the most important chess piece, which must be protected from checkmate

kingcup NOUN the marsh marigold

kingdom NOUN **1** the area ruled by a king **2** any of the major divisions of the natural world, ie animal, plant or mineral

kingfisher NOUN a type of fish-eating bird with brightly coloured feathers

kingly ADJECTIVE like a king; royal

kingpin NOUN the most important person in an organization

king-size ADJECTIVE of a larger than usual size

kink NOUN **1** a bend or curl in a rope, hair, etc **2** a peculiarity of the mind

kinky ADJECTIVE (**kinkier, kinkiest**) twisted, contorted

kinsfolk PLURAL NOUN relations, relatives

a b c d e f g h i j k l m n o p q r s t u v w x y z

A B C D E F G H I J K L M N O P Q R S T U V W X Y Z

kinsman, **kinswoman** NOUN a close relation

kiosk NOUN **1** a small stall for the sale of papers, sweets, etc **2** a telephone box

kip NOUN, *slang* a bed ▶ VERB (**kipping, kipped**) to go to bed, sleep

kipper NOUN a smoked and dried herring

kirk NOUN, *Scottish* a church

kiss VERB **1** to touch lovingly with the lips **2** to touch gently **kiss of life** a mouth-to-mouth method of restoring breathing

kit NOUN an outfit of clothes, tools, etc necessary for a particular job

kitchen NOUN a room where food is cooked

kitchenette NOUN a small kitchen

kitchen garden NOUN a vegetable garden

kite NOUN **1** a light frame, covered with paper or other material, for flying in the air **2** a four-sided figure, with two pairs of equal sides that are not parallel **3** a kind of hawk

kith NOUN: **kith and kin** friends and relatives

kitsch NOUN sentimental or vulgar tastelessness in art, design, etc

kitten NOUN a young cat **have kittens** *informal* to make a great fuss

kittenish ADJECTIVE behaving like a kitten, playful

kitty[1] NOUN (*plural* **kitties**) a sum of money set aside for a purpose

kitty[2] NOUN (*plural* **kitties**) *informal* a cat or kitten

kiwi NOUN **1** a fast-running almost wingless bird of New Zealand **2** a kiwi fruit

kiwi fruit NOUN an edible fruit with a thin hairy skin and bright green flesh

kl ABBREVIATION kilolitre(s)

kleptomania NOUN an uncontrollable desire to steal
> **kleptomaniac** NOUN & ADJECTIVE

km ABBREVIATION kilometre(s)

knack (*pronounced* nak) NOUN a special talent or ability: *a knack for saying the right thing*

knacker (*pronounced* **nak**-er) NOUN a buyer of old horses for slaughter ▶ VERB, *informal* to exhaust, tire out

knapsack (*pronounced* **nap**-sak) NOUN a bag for food, clothes, etc slung on the back

knave (*pronounced* neiv) NOUN **1** a cheating rogue **2** in playing-cards, the jack

knavery (*pronounced* **neiv**-*e*-ri) NOUN dishonesty

knavish (*pronounced* **neiv**-ish) ADJECTIVE cheating, wicked

knead (*pronounced* need) VERB **1** to work (dough etc) by pressing with the fingers **2** to massage

knee (*pronounced* nee) NOUN the joint at the bend of the leg

kneecap (*pronounced* **nee**-kap) NOUN the flat round bone on the front of the knee joint ▶ VERB to cause to suffer

kneel (*pronounced* neel) VERB (**kneeling, knelt**) to go down on one or both knees

knell (*pronounced* nel) NOUN **1** the tolling of a bell for a death or funeral **2** a warning of a sad end or failure

knickerbockers (*pronounced* **nik**-*e*-bok-*ez*) PLURAL NOUN loose breeches tucked in at the knee

[i] Named after Diedrich *Knickerbocker*, a fictional Dutchman invented by US author Washington Irving in the 19th century

knickers (*pronounced* **nik**-*ez*) PLURAL NOUN women's or girls' underpants

knick-knack (*pronounced* **nik**-nak) NOUN a small, ornamental article

knife (*pronounced* naif) NOUN (*plural* **knives**) a tool for cutting ▶ VERB to stab **at knife point** under threat of injury

knight (*pronounced* nait) NOUN **1** *Brit* a rank, with the title *Sir*, awarded by the monarch or the government **2** a piece used in chess, shaped like a horse's head ▶ VERB to raise to the rank of knight

knighthood (*pronounced* **nait**-huwd) NOUN the rank of a knight

knightly (*pronounced* **nait**-li) ADJECTIVE **1** to do with knights **2** gallant, courageous

knit (*pronounced* nit) VERB (**knitting, knitted**) **1** to form a garment from yarn by making a series of knots using knitting needles **2** to join closely

knitting (*pronounced* **nit**-ing) NOUN the art of producing something knitted

knitting needles PLURAL NOUN a pair of thin pointed rods used in knitting

knob (*pronounced* nob) NOUN **1** a small rounded projection **2** a round door-handle

knock (*pronounced* nok) VERB **1** to tap on something, especially a door, to have it opened **2** to strike, hit ▶ NOUN **1** a sudden stroke **2** a tap (on a door) **knock back** *informal* to eat or drink greedily **knock down 1** to demolish **2** *informal* to reduce in price **knock off** *informal* **1** to stop work for the day **2** to plagiarize, copy illegally **knock out** to hit (someone) hard enough to make them unconscious **knock up 1** to put together hastily **2** to knock on someone's door to wake them up

knocker (*pronounced* **nok**-er) NOUN a hinged weight on a door for knocking with

knock-kneed (*pronounced* nok-**need**) ADJECTIVE having knees that touch in walking

knoll (*pronounced* nohl) NOUN a small rounded hill

knot (*pronounced* not) NOUN **1** a hard lump, eg one made by tying string, or found in wood at the join between trunk and branch **2** a tangle **3** a small gathering, a cluster of people **4** a measure of speed for ships (about 1.85 kilometre per hour) ▶ VERB (**knotting, knotted**) to tie in a knot

knotted (*pronounced* **not**-id) ADJECTIVE full of knots

knotty (*pronounced* **not**-i) ADJECTIVE (**knottier, knottiest**) **1** having knots **2** difficult, complicated: *knotty problem*

know (*pronounced* noh) VERB (**knowing, known, knew**) **1** to be

A B C D E F G H I J K L M N O P Q R S T U V W X Y Z

aware or sure of **2** to identify or recognize: *I don't know this song* [i] Comes from Old English *cnawan*

knowing (*pronounced* **noh**-ing) ADJECTIVE clever; cunning

knowingly (*pronounced* **noh**-ing-li) ADVERB **1** intentionally **2** in a way which shows you understand something which is secret or which has not been directly expressed

knowledge (*pronounced* **nol**-ij) NOUN **1** that which is known **2** information **3** ability, skill

knowledgeable (*pronounced* **nol**-ij-*a*-bl) ADJECTIVE showing or having knowledge

knuckle (*pronounced* **nu**-kl) NOUN a joint of the fingers **knuckle under** to give in, yield

knuckleduster NOUN a metal covering worn on the knuckles as a weapon

knucklehead NOUN, *informal* an idiot

koala NOUN an Australian tree-climbing animal resembling a small bear

kohl NOUN a black powder used as an eyeliner

kookaburra *another word* for **laughing jackass**

Koran, **Qoran, Quran** *or* **Qur'an** NOUN (*pronounced* kaw-**ran** *or* ko-**ran**) the sacred book of Islam

kosher (*pronounced* **ko**-sher) ADJECTIVE **1** *Judaism* pure and clean according to Jewish law **2** *informal* acceptable, all right

kowtow VERB (usually **kowtow to**) to treat with too much respect [i] Based on a Chinese phrase meaning to prostrate yourself before the emperor

krill NOUN a small shrimplike creature eaten by whales etc

krypton NOUN, *chemistry* (symbol **Kr**) an inert gas present in the air, used in fluorescent lighting

kudos (*pronounced* **kyood**-os) NOUN fame, glory

kung-fu NOUN a Chinese form of self-defence

kW ABBREVIATION kilowatt(s)

kyrie (*pronounced* **kee**-ri-ei) NOUN **1** a prayer in the Roman Catholic mass following the opening anthem **2** a musical setting for this

Ll

l ABBREVIATION litre(s)
lab NOUN, *informal* a laboratory
label NOUN a small written note fixed onto something listing its contents, price, etc ▶ VERB (**labels, labelling, labelled**) **1** to fix a label to **2** to call by a certain name: *The media labelled him a 'love rat'*
laboratory NOUN (*plural* **laboratories**) a scientist's workroom
laborious ADJECTIVE requiring hard work; wearisome
labour *or US* **labor** NOUN **1** hard work **2** workers on a job **3** the process of childbirth ▶ VERB **1** to work hard **2** to move slowly or with difficulty
laboured ADJECTIVE showing signs of effort
labourer NOUN someone who does heavy unskilled work
Labour Party NOUN one of the chief political parties of the UK, supporting greater social equality
labrador NOUN a large black or fawn-coloured dog
labyrinth (*pronounced* **lab**-ir-inth) NOUN a maze
lace NOUN **1** a cord for fastening shoes etc **2** decorative fabric made with fine thread ▶ VERB **1** to fasten with a lace **2** to add alcohol to (a drink)
lacerate (*pronounced* **las**-*e*-reit) VERB **1** to tear, rip **2** to wound > **laceration** NOUN
lack VERB **1** to be missing: *What's lacking is a sense of adventure* **2** to be without: *She lacks intelligence* ▶ NOUN want, need
lackey NOUN (*plural* **lackeys**) **1** a manservant **2** someone who acts like a slave
lacklustre *or US* **lackluster** ADJECTIVE dull, insipid
laconic ADJECTIVE using few words to express meaning > **laconically** ADVERB
lacquer NOUN a varnish ▶ VERB to varnish
lacrosse NOUN a twelve-a-side ball game played with sticks having a shallow net at the end
lactate VERB to produce or secrete milk
lactic ADJECTIVE of milk
lactose NOUN a sugar obtained by evaporating whey (*also called*: **milk sugar**)

A B C D E F G H I J K L M N O P Q R S T U V W X Y Z

lad NOUN a boy, a youth

ladder NOUN **1** a set of rungs or steps between two supports, for climbing up or down **2** a run from a broken stitch, in a stocking etc

laden ADJECTIVE loaded, burdened

ladle NOUN a large spoon for lifting liquid out of a container ▸ VERB to lift with a ladle

lady NOUN (*plural* **ladies**) **1** a woman of good manners **2** a title for the wife of a knight, lord or baronet, or a daughter of a member of the aristocracy **3** (**the ladies**) a public lavatory for women

ladybird NOUN a small beetle, usually red with black spots

ladyship NOUN used in talking to or about a titled lady: *your ladyship*

lag VERB (**lagging, lagged**) **1** to move slowly and fall behind **2** to cover (a boiler or pipes) with a warm covering for insulation ▸ NOUN a delay

lager NOUN a light beer

lagging NOUN material for covering pipes etc for insulation

lagoon NOUN a shallow stretch of water separated from the sea by low sandbanks, rocks, etc

laid *past form* of **lay**[1]

laid-back ADJECTIVE, *informal* relaxed, easy-going

laid-up ADJECTIVE ill in bed

lain *past participle* of **lie**[2]

lair (*pronounced* leir) NOUN the den of a wild beast

ⓘ Comes from Old English *leger* meaning 'a couch'

> Do not confuse with: **layer**

laird NOUN in Scotland, a landowner

laissez-faire (*pronounced* les-ei-**feir**) NOUN a general principle of not interfering

lake NOUN a large stretch of water surrounded by land

lamb NOUN **1** a young sheep **2** the meat of this animal **3** a gentle person

lame ADJECTIVE **1** unable to walk, disabled **2** not good enough, not very convincing or impressive: *a lame excuse* ▸ VERB to make lame > **lamely** ADVERB (adjective, meaning 2)

lament (*pronounced* la-**ment**) VERB **1** to mourn, feel or express grief for **2** to regret ▸ NOUN **1** a show of grief **2** a mournful poem or piece of music > **lamentation** NOUN

lamentable (*pronounced* **lam**-*en*-t*a*b-l) ADJECTIVE **1** pitiful: *a lamentable waste of young lives* **2** very bad: *a lamentable performance*

laminated ADJECTIVE made by putting layers together: *laminated glass*

lamp NOUN a device which gives out light, containing an electric bulb, candle, etc

lampoon NOUN a piece of ridicule or satire directed at someone ▸ VERB to ridicule, satirize

lamppost NOUN a pillar supporting a street lamp

lance NOUN a long shaft of wood, with a spearhead ▸ VERB to cut open (a boil etc) with a knife

lance-corporal NOUN a soldier with rank just below a corporal

land NOUN **1** the solid portion of the earth's surface **2** ground **3** soil **4** a part of a country ▶ VERB **1** to arrive on land or on shore **2** to set (an aircraft, ship, etc) on land or on shore

landing NOUN **1** a coming ashore or to ground **2** a place for getting on shore **3** the level part of a staircase between the flights of steps

landlocked ADJECTIVE almost or completely shut in by land

landlord *or* **landlady** NOUN (*plural* **landlords** *or* **landladies**) **1** the owner of land or accommodation for rent **2** the owner or manager of an inn etc

landmark NOUN **1** an object on land that serves as a guide **2** an important event

land mine NOUN a bomb laid on or near the surface of the ground which explodes when someone passes over it

landscape NOUN **1** an area of land and the features it contains **2** a painting, photograph, etc of inland scenery

landscape gardening NOUN the art of laying out grounds so as to produce the effect of a picturesque landscape

landslide NOUN a mass of land that slips down from the side of a hill

landslide victory NOUN a win in an election in which a great mass of votes goes to one side

lane NOUN **1** a narrow street or passage **2** a part of the road, sea or air to which cars, ships, aircraft, etc must keep

language NOUN **1** human speech **2** the speech of a particular people or nation

languid ADJECTIVE lacking liveliness

languish VERB **1** to grow weak, droop **2** to pine: *The dog was languishing for its master*
> **languishing** ADJECTIVE

languor (*pronounced* **lang**-gor) NOUN a languid state, listlessness

laniard *another spelling of* **lanyard**

lank ADJECTIVE **1** tall and thin **2** of hair: straight and limp

lanky ADJECTIVE (**lankier, lankiest**)tall and thin

lanolin NOUN a fat extracted from sheep's wool

lantern NOUN a lamp or light contained in a transparent case, usually of glass

lanyard *or* **laniard** NOUN **1** a short rope used for fastening rigging etc on a ship **2** a cord for hanging a whistle etc round the neck

lap VERB (**lapping, lapped**) **1** to lick up with the tongue **2** to wash or flow against **3** to wrap round, surround **4** to get a lap ahead of other competitors in a race ▶ NOUN **1** the front part, from waist to knees, of someone seated **2** a fold **3** one round of a racetrack or competition course **lap up** to accept (praise etc) greedily

lapel NOUN the part of a coat joined to the collar and folded back on the chest

lapse VERB **1** to fall into bad habits **2** to cease, be no longer valid ▶ NOUN **1** a mistake, a failure **2** a period of time passing

laptop NOUN a compact portable computer combining screen, keyboard, and processor in one unit (*also called*: **laptop computer**)

lapwing NOUN a type of bird of the plover family (*also called*: **peewit**)

larceny NOUN stealing, theft

larch NOUN (*plural* **larches**) a cone-bearing deciduous tree

lard NOUN the melted fat of a pig ▸ VERB **1** to put strips of bacon in meat before cooking **2** to smear, lay on thickly

larder NOUN **1** a room or place where food is kept **2** a stock of food

large ADJECTIVE great in size, amount, etc **at large 1** at liberty, free **2** in general: *the public at large*

ⓘ Comes from French *large* meaning 'broad' or 'wide'

largely ADVERB mainly, to a great extent

lark NOUN **1** a general name for several kinds of singing bird **2** a piece of fun or mischief ▸ VERB to fool about, behave mischievously

larva NOUN (*plural* **larvae** – *pronounced* **lah**-vee) an insect in its first stage after coming out of the egg, a grub

laryngitis (*pronounced* lar-in-**jai**-tis) NOUN inflammation of the larynx

larynx (*pronounced* **lar**-ingks) NOUN (*plural* **larynxes** *or* **larynges** – *pronounced* la-**rin**-jeez) the upper part of the windpipe containing the vocal cords

lasagne (*pronounced* la-**zan**-*ya*) PLURAL NOUN flat sheets of pasta ▸ SINGULAR NOUN (also **lasagna**) a baked dish made with this

laser NOUN **1** a very narrow powerful beam of light, used for eg printing, optical scanning, surgical operations, etc **2** an instrument that concentrates light into such a beam

ⓘ An acronym of '*l*ight *a*mplification by *s*timulated *e*mission of *r*adiation'

lash NOUN (*plural* **lashes**) **1** a thong or cord of a whip **2** a stroke with a whip **3** an eyelash ▸ VERB **1** to strike with a whip **2** to fasten tightly with a rope etc **3** to attack with bitter words **lash out 1** to kick or swing out without thinking **2** to speak angrily **3** to spend extravagantly

lass NOUN (*plural* **lasses**) a girl

lasso (*pronounced* la-**soo**) NOUN (*plural* **lassoes** *or* **lassos**) a long rope with a loop that tightens when the rope is pulled, used for catching wild horses etc ▸ VERB (**lassos** *or* **lassoes, lassoing, lassoed**) to catch with a lasso

last ADJECTIVE **1** coming after all the others: *last person to arrive* **2** the final one remaining: *last ticket* **3** most recent: *my last employer* ▸ ADVERB **1** after all others **2** most recently **3** lastly ▸ VERB **1** to continue, go on **2** to remain in good condition ▸ NOUN a foot-shaped tool on which shoes are made or repaired **at last** in the end **on your last legs** completely worn out, about to collapse **to the last** to the end

lastly ADVERB finally

last rites PLURAL NOUN religious ceremonies performed for a person who is dying

last straw NOUN the last in a series

of unpleasant events, which makes a situation unbearable

last word NOUN the final comment or decision about something

latch NOUN (*plural* **latches**) **1** a wooden or metal catch used to fasten a door **2** a light door-lock ▸VERB to fasten with a latch

latchkey NOUN a key to raise the latch of a door

late ADJECTIVE & ADVERB **1** coming after the expected time: *His train was late* **2** far on in time: *It's getting late* **3** recent: *our late disagreement* **4** recently dead: *the late author* **5** recently, but no longer, holding an office or position: *the late chairman* **of late** recently > **lateness** NOUN (meanings 1 and 2)

lately ADVERB recently

latent ADJECTIVE hidden, undeveloped as yet: *latent ability/ latent hostility*

lateral ADJECTIVE of, at, to or from the side

lateral thinking NOUN thinking which seeks new ways of looking at a problem and does not merely proceed in logical stages

latex (*pronounced* **lei**-teks) NOUN the milky juice of plants, especially of the rubber tree

lathe (*pronounced* leidh) NOUN a machine for turning and shaping articles of wood, metal, etc

[i] Probably comes from Old Danish *lad* meaning 'a supporting framework'

lather NOUN **1** a foam or froth, eg from soap and water **2** *informal* a state of agitation: *She was in a lather about the broken window* ▸VERB to cover with lather

Latin NOUN the language of ancient Rome

latitude NOUN *geography* the distance, measured in degrees, of a place north or south of the equator

latrine (*pronounced* la-**treen**) NOUN a toilet in a camp, barracks, etc

latter ADJECTIVE **1** (*contrasted with*: **former**) the last of two things mentioned: *Between working and sleeping, I prefer the latter* **2** recent

latterly ADVERB recently

lattice NOUN **1** a network of crossed wooden etc strips **2** a window constructed this way

laud VERB, *formal* to praise

laudable ADJECTIVE worthy of being praised > **laudably** ADVERB

laugh VERB to make sounds with the voice in showing amusement, scorn, etc ▸NOUN the sound of laughing

laughable ADJECTIVE comical, ridiculous

laughing stock NOUN an object of scornful laughter

laughter NOUN the act or noise of laughing

launch VERB **1** to slide (a boat or ship) into water, especially on its first voyage **2** to fire off (a rocket etc) **3** to start off on a course **4** to put (a product) on the market with publicity **5** to throw, hurl ▸NOUN (*plural* **launches**) **1** the act of launching **2** a large motor boat

launch pad NOUN the area for launching a spacecraft or missile

A B C D E F G H I J K L M N O P Q R S T U V W X Y Z

launder VERB to wash and iron clothes etc

launderette NOUN a shop where customers may wash clothes etc in washing machines

laundry NOUN (*plural* **laundries**) **1** a place where clothes are washed **2** clothes to be washed

laurel NOUN **1** the bay tree, from which ceremonial wreaths were made in ancient times **2** (**laurels**) honours or victories gained **rest on your laurels** to be content with past successes and not try for any more

lava NOUN molten rock etc thrown out by a volcano, becoming solid as it cools

lavatory NOUN (*plural* **lavatories**) a toilet

lavender NOUN **1** a sweet-smelling plant with small pale-purple flowers **2** a pale purple colour

lavish VERB to spend or give very freely ▸ ADJECTIVE very generous

law NOUN **1** the official rules that apply in a country or state **2** one such rule **3** a scientific rule stating the conditions under which certain things always happen

law-abiding ADJECTIVE obeying the law

law court NOUN a place where people accused of crimes are tried

lawful ADJECTIVE allowed by law > **lawfully** ADVERB

lawless ADJECTIVE paying no attention to, and not observing, the laws

lawn NOUN an area of smooth grass, eg as part of a garden

lawnmower NOUN a machine for cutting grass

lawn tennis NOUN tennis played on a hard or grass court

lawsuit NOUN a quarrel or dispute to be settled by a court of law

lawyer NOUN someone whose work it is to give advice in matters of law

lax ADJECTIVE **1** not strict **2** careless, negligent > **laxity** NOUN

laxative NOUN a medicine which loosens the bowels

lay[1] VERB (**laying, laid**) **1** to place or set down: *lay the book on the table* **2** to put (eg a burden, duty) on (someone): *new laws laying a heavy burden of responsibility on teachers/try to lay the blame on someone else* **3** to beat down: *All the barley in the field had been laid flat by the storm* **4** to make to leave or subside: *lay a ghost* **5** to set in order, arrange: *lay a trap/ lay the table* **6** of a hen: to produce eggs: *Young hens quite often lay double-yolkers* **7** to bet, wager: *He's sure to be late. I'd lay money on it* **lay down 1** to assert: *laying down the law* **2** to store (eg wine) **lay off 1** to dismiss (workers) temporarily **2** *informal* to stop: *lay off arguing* **lay waste** to ruin, destroy

> Do not confuse with: **lie**. It may help to remember that the verb **lay** always takes an object, while an object is not used with the verb **lie**.

lay[2] *past tense* of **lie**[2] ADJECTIVE **1** not of the clergy **2** without special training in a particular subject

lay[3] NOUN, *old* a short poem or song

layabout NOUN a lazy idle person

lay-by NOUN (*plural* **lay-bys**) a parking area at the side of a road

layer NOUN a thickness forming a covering or level

> Do not confuse with: **lair**. Layer comes from the verb 'to lay'

layered ADJECTIVE having a number of distinct layers: *layered cake*

layman NOUN (*plural* **laymen**)a man without special training in a subject

layout NOUN the way something, eg a printed page, is arranged

laze VERB to be lazy; idle

lazy ADJECTIVE (**lazier, laziest**) not inclined to work; idle > **lazily** ADVERB

lazybones NOUN, *informal* an idler

lb ABBREVIATION pound(s) (in weight)

LCD *or* **lcd** ABBREVIATION liquid crystal display, used in digital devices to display figures

leach VERB to allow liquid to seep slowly through or out of something

[i] Comes from Old English *leccan* meaning 'to water' or 'to moisten'

> Do not confuse with: **leech**

lead[1] (*pronounced* leed) VERB (**leads, leading, led**) **1** to show the way by going first **2** to direct, guide **3** to persuade **4** to live (a busy, quiet, etc life) **5** of a road: to go (to) ▶ NOUN **1** the first or front place **2** guidance, direction **3** a leash for a dog etc

lead[2] (*pronounced* led) NOUN **1** *chemistry* (symbol **Pb**) a soft bluish-grey metal **2** the part of a pencil that writes, which is actually made of graphite

leaden ADJECTIVE **1** made of lead **2** lead-coloured **3** dull, heavy

leader NOUN **1** someone who leads or goes first; a chief **2** a column in a newspaper expressing the editor's opinions

leadership NOUN **1** the state of being a leader **2** the ability to lead

leading question NOUN one asked in such a way as to suggest the desired answer

leaf NOUN (*plural* **leaves**) **1** a part of a plant growing from the side of a stem **2** a page of a book **3** a hinged flap on a table etc **turn over a new leaf** to begin again and do better

leaflet NOUN a small printed sheet

leafy ADJECTIVE (**leafier, leafiest**) **1** of a plant or tree: having a lot of leaves **2** of a place: having a lot of trees and plants

league NOUN **1** a union of people, nations, etc for the benefit of each other **2** an association of clubs for games **3** *old* a measure of distance, approximately 3 miles (about 4.8 kilometres) **in league with** allied with

leak NOUN **1** a hole through which liquid passes **2** an escape of gas or liquid **3** a release of secret information ▶ VERB **1** to escape, pass out **2** to give (secret information) to the media etc

leakage NOUN a leaking

lean VERB (**leaning, leaned** *or* **leant** – *pronounced* lent) **1** to slope over to one side **2** to rest (against) **3** to rely (on) ▸ ADJECTIVE **1** thin **2** poor, scanty **3** of meat: not fat

leaning NOUN a liking for, or interest in, something

leap VERB (**leaps, leaping, leaped** *or* **leapt** – *pronounced* lept) **1** to move with jumps **2** to jump (over) ▸ NOUN a jump

leapfrog NOUN a game in which one player leaps over another's bent back

leap year NOUN a year which has 366 days (February having 29), occurring every fourth year

learn VERB (**learns, learning, learnt** *or* **learned**) **1** to get to know (something) **2** to gain skill

learned (*pronounced* **ler**-nid) ADJECTIVE having or showing great knowledge

learner NOUN someone who is learning something

learning NOUN knowledge

lease NOUN **1** an agreement giving the use of a house etc in return for payment of rent **2** the period of this agreement ▸ VERB to let or rent

leasehold NOUN property or land held by lease

leash NOUN (*plural* **leashes**) a lead by which a dog etc is held ▸ VERB to put (a dog etc) on a leash

least ADJECTIVE the smallest amount of anything: *He had the least money* ▸ ADVERB (often **the least**) the smallest or lowest degree: *I like her least* **at least** at any rate, anyway **not in the least** not at all

leather NOUN the skin of an animal, prepared by tanning for use

leathering NOUN a thrashing

leathery ADJECTIVE like leather; tough

leave[1] VERB (**leaving, left**) **1** to allow to remain **2** to abandon, forsake **3** to depart (from) **4** to hand down to someone in a will **5** to give over to someone's responsibility, care, etc: *Leave the choice to her*

leave[2] NOUN **1** permission to do something (eg to be absent) **2** a holiday **take your leave of 1** to part from **2** to say goodbye to

leavened ADJECTIVE raised with yeast

lecherous ADJECTIVE lustful in a sexual way > **lechery** NOUN

lectern NOUN a stand for a book to be read from

lecture NOUN **1** a formal talk on a certain subject given to an audience **2** a scolding ▸ VERB **1** to deliver a lecture **2** to scold

lecturer NOUN someone who lectures, especially to students

LED ABBREVIATION light-emitting diode, a semiconductor that lights up when an electric current passes through it

led *past form* of **lead**[1]

ledge NOUN a shelf or projecting rim: *window-ledge*

ledger NOUN the accounts book of an office or shop

lee NOUN the side away from the wind, the sheltered side: *in the lee of the mountain*

leech NOUN (*plural* **leeches**) a kind of blood-sucking worm

ⓘ Comes from Old English *læce*

A B C D E F G H I J K L M N O P Q R S T U V W X Y Z

> Do not confuse with: **leach**

leek NOUN a long green and white vegetable of the onion family

leer NOUN a sly, sidelong or lustful look ▶ VERB to look sideways or lustfully (at)

leeward ADJECTIVE & ADVERB in the direction towards which the wind blows

leeway NOUN room to manoeuvre, latitude

left[1] ADJECTIVE on or of the side of the body that in most people has the less skilful hand (*contrasted with* **right**) ▶ ADVERB on or towards the left side ▶ NOUN **1** the left side **2** a political grouping with left-wing ideas etc

left[2] *past form* of **leave**[1]

left-click VERB, *computing* to press and release the left-hand button on a computer mouse

left-field ADJECTIVE, *informal* odd, eccentric

left-handed ADJECTIVE **1** using the left hand rather than the right **2** awkward

left wing NOUN the more radical or socialist members of a group or political party ▶ ADJECTIVE (**left-wing**) belonging or relating to the left wing

leg NOUN **1** one of the limbs by which humans and animals walk **2** a long slender support for a table etc **3** one stage in a journey, contest, etc

legacy NOUN (*plural* **legacies**) **1** something which is left by will **2** something left behind by the previous occupant of a house, job, etc

legal ADJECTIVE **1** allowed by law, lawful **2** of law

legality NOUN (*plural* **legalities**) the state of being legal

legalize *or* **legalise** VERB to make lawful

legend NOUN **1** a traditional story handed down, a myth **2** a caption

legendary ADJECTIVE **1** of legend; famous **2** not to be believed

leggings PLURAL NOUN close-fitting trousers for women

legible ADJECTIVE able to be read easily > **legibility** NOUN

legion NOUN **1** *history* a body of from three to six thousand Roman soldiers **2** a very great number

legionary NOUN (*plural* **legionaries**) a soldier of a legion

Legionnaires' disease NOUN a serious disease similar to pneumonia caused by a bacterium

legislate VERB to make laws > **legislation** NOUN

legislative ADJECTIVE law-making

legislature NOUN the part of the government which has the powers of making laws

legitimate ADJECTIVE **1** lawful **2** of a child: born of parents married to each other **3** correct, reasonable > **legitimacy** NOUN

legless ADJECTIVE, *informal* drunk

legroom NOUN room to move the legs

leisure NOUN time free from work, spare time

leisurely ADJECTIVE unhurried: *leisurely pace*

lemming NOUN **1** a small rat-like animal of the arctic regions, reputed

A B C D E F G H I J K L M N O P Q R S T U V W X Y Z

to follow others of its kind over sea cliffs when migrating **2** someone who follows others unquestioningly

lemon NOUN **1** an oval fruit with pale yellow rind and sour juice **2** the tree that bears this fruit

lemonade NOUN a soft drink flavoured with lemons

lemur (*pronounced* **lee**-mer) NOUN a long-tailed animal related to the monkey but with a pointed nose

ℹ From a Latin word meaning 'ghost', because the animal has a thin, pale face and appears at night

lend VERB (**lending, lent**) **1** to give use of for a time **2** to give, add (a quality) to someone or something: *His presence lent an air of respectability to the occasion* **lend itself to** to be suitable for, adapt easily to

length NOUN **1** extent from end to end in space or time **2** the quality of being long **3** a great extent **4** a piece of cloth etc **at length 1** in detail **2** at last

lengthen VERB to make or grow longer

lengthways *or* **lengthwise** ADVERB in the direction of the length: *Measure the picture lengthways*

lengthy (**lengthier, lengthiest**) ADJECTIVE **1** long **2** tiresomely long

lenient (*pronounced* **lee**-ni-ent) ADJECTIVE merciful, punishing only lightly > **lenience** *or* **leniency** NOUN

lens NOUN (*plural* **lenses**) **1** a piece of glass curved on one or both sides, used in spectacles, cameras, etc **2** a part of the eye

Lent NOUN in the Christian church, a period of fasting before Easter lasting forty days

lent *past form* of **lend**

lentil NOUN the seed of a pod-bearing plant, used in soups etc

leopard NOUN an animal of the cat family with a spotted skin

leopardess NOUN (*plural* **leopardesses**) a female leopard

leotard NOUN a tight-fitting, stretchy garment worn for dancing, gymnastics, etc

ℹ After Jules *Léotard*, a French trapeze artist who popularized it

leper NOUN **1** someone with leprosy **2** an outcast

leprechaun NOUN a creature in Irish folklore

leprosy NOUN a contagious skin disease causing thickening or numbness in the skin

lesbian NOUN a female homosexual ▸ ADJECTIVE of a woman: homosexual

less ADJECTIVE **1** not as much: *take less time* **2** smaller: *Think of a number less than 40* ▸ ADVERB not as much, to a smaller extent: *He goes less often than he should* ▸ NOUN a smaller amount: *He has less than I have* ▸ PREPOSITION minus: *5 less 2 equals 3*

lessen VERB to make smaller

lesser ADJECTIVE smaller

lesson NOUN **1** something which is learned or taught **2** a part of the Bible read in church **3** a period of teaching

lest CONJUNCTION for fear that, in case

let VERB (**letting, let**) **1** to allow **2** to grant use of (eg a house, shop, farm) in return for payment **let down** to fail to act as expected, disappoint **let off** to excuse, not punish **let up** to become less

lethal (*pronounced* **lee**-th*a*l) ADJECTIVE causing death

lethargy (*pronounced* **leth**-*a*r-ji) NOUN a lack of energy or interest; sleepiness > **lethargic** ADJECTIVE

let's *short for* let us: *Let's go home*

letter NOUN **1** a mark expressing a sound **2** a written message **3** (**letters**) learning: *a woman of letters* **to the letter** according to the exact meaning of the words: *following instructions to the letter*

lettering NOUN letters which have been drawn or painted, usually in a particular style

lettuce NOUN a kind of green plant whose leaves are used in a salad

leukaemia *or US* **leukemia** (*pronounced* loo-**kee**-mi-*a*) NOUN a cancerous disease of the white blood cells in the body

level NOUN **1** a flat, smooth surface **2** a height, position, etc in comparison with some standard: *water level* **3** an instrument for showing whether a surface is level: *spirit level* **4** personal rank or degree of understanding: *a bit above my level* ▶ ADJECTIVE **1** flat, even, smooth **2** horizontal ▶ VERB (**levelling, levelled**) **1** to make flat, smooth or horizontal **2** to make equal **3** to aim (a gun etc) **4** to pull down (a building etc)

level crossing NOUN a place where a road crosses a railway track

level-headed ADJECTIVE having good sense

level playing-field NOUN a position of equality from which to compete fairly

lever NOUN **1** a bar of metal, wood, etc used to raise or shift something heavy **2** a handle for operating a machine **3** a method of gaining advantage

leveret (*pronounced* **lev**-*e*-rit) NOUN a young hare

levitate VERB to float in the air

levitation NOUN the illusion of raising a heavy body in the air without support

levity NOUN lack of seriousness, frivolity

levy VERB (**levies, levying, levied**) to collect (eg a tax, army conscripts) by order ▶ NOUN (*plural* **levies**) money, troops, etc collected by order

lewd ADJECTIVE taking delight in indecent thoughts or acts

lexical ADJECTIVE of words

lexicon NOUN **1** a dictionary **2** a glossary of terms

liability NOUN (*plural* **liabilities**) **1** legal responsibility **2** a debt **3** a disadvantage

liable ADJECTIVE **1** legally responsible (for) **2** likely or apt (to do something or happen)

liaise (*pronounced* lee-**eiz**) VERB to make a connection (with), be in touch (with)

liaison (*pronounced* lee-**eiz**-on) NOUN **1** contact, communication **2** a sexual affair

liar NOUN someone who tells lies

A B C D E F G H I J K L M N O P Q R S T U V W X Y Z

Lib Dem *short for* Liberal Democrat

libel NOUN something written to hurt another's reputation ▸ VERB (**libelling, libelled**) to write something libellous about

libellous ADJECTIVE containing a written false statement which hurts a person's reputation

liberal ADJECTIVE generous; broad-minded, tolerant ▸ NOUN (**Liberal**) a member of the former Liberal Party, which supported social and political reform > **liberality** NOUN

Liberal Democrats PLURAL NOUN one of the chief political parties of Great Britain, formed in 1988 from the Liberal Party and the Social Democratic Party, supporting democratic reform

liberate VERB to set free > **liberation** NOUN

liberty NOUN (*plural* **liberties**) **1** freedom, especially of speech or action **2** (**liberties**) rights, privileges **take liberties** to behave rudely or impertinently

libido (*pronounced* li-**bee**-doh) NOUN sexual drive or urge

librarian NOUN a person employed in or in charge of a library

library NOUN (*plural* **libraries**) **1** a collection of books, records, etc **2** a building or room housing these

libretto NOUN (*plural* **libretti** *or* **librettos**) *music* the words of an opera, musical show, etc

lice *plural* of **louse**

licence NOUN **1** a document giving permission to do something, eg to keep a television set, drive a car, etc **2** too great freedom of action

> Do not confuse: **licence** and **license**. **Licence/license** and **practice/practise** follow the same pattern: you spell the verbs with an S (**licenSe, practiSe**), and the nouns with a C (**licenCe, practiCe.**)

license VERB to permit

licensee NOUN someone to whom a licence is given

lichen (*pronounced* **laik**-en) NOUN a large group of moss-like plants that grow on rocks etc

lick VERB **1** to pass the tongue over **2** of flames: to reach up, touch ▸ NOUN **1** the act of licking **2** a tiny amount **lick into shape** to make vigorous improvements on

licorice *another spelling* of **liquorice**

lid NOUN **1** a cover for a box, pot, etc **2** the cover of the eye

lido (*pronounced* **lee**-doh) NOUN **1** a bathing beach **2** an open-air swimming pool

lie[1] NOUN a false statement meant to deceive ▸ VERB (**lying, lied**) to tell a lie

lie[2] VERB (**lying, lay, lain**) **1** to rest in a flat position: *Lie flat on your back* **2** to be or remain in a state or position: *lie dormant* ▸ NOUN the position or situation in which something lies **lie low** to keep quiet or hidden **the lie of the land** the present state of affairs

> Do not confuse with: **lay**. It may help to remember that an object is not used with the verb **lie**, while the verb **lay** always takes an object.

lie in wait to keep hidden in order to surprise someone

lieu (*pronounced* lyoo *or* loo) NOUN: **in lieu of** instead of

lieutenant (*pronounced* lef-**ten**-*a*nt *or US* loo-**ten**-*a*nt) NOUN **1** an army officer below a captain **2** in the navy, an officer below a lieutenant-commander **3** a rank below a higher officer: *lieutenant-colonel*
ⓘ From a French word meaning literally 'holding a place'

life NOUN (*plural* **lives**) **1** the period between birth and death **2** the state of being alive **3** liveliness **4** manner of living **5** the story of someone's life **6** living things: *animal life*
ⓘ Comes from Old English *lif*

lifebelt NOUN a ring made of cork or filled with air for keeping someone afloat

lifeboat NOUN a boat for rescuing people in difficulties at sea

lifebuoy NOUN a float to support someone awaiting rescue at sea

lifecycle NOUN the various stages through which a living thing passes

life drawing NOUN drawing from a live human model

lifeguard NOUN an expert swimmer employed to save people in danger of drowning

life jacket NOUN a buoyant jacket for keeping someone afloat in water

lifeless ADJECTIVE **1** dead **2** not lively, spiritless

lifelike ADJECTIVE like a living person

lifeline NOUN a vital means of communication

lifelong ADJECTIVE lasting the length of a life

life-size ADJECTIVE full size, as in life

lifespan NOUN the length of someone's life

lifestyle NOUN the way in which someone lives

life-support machine NOUN a device for keeping a person alive during severe illness, space travel, etc

lifetime NOUN the period during which someone is alive

lift VERB **1** to raise, take up **2** *informal* to steal **3** of fog: to disappear, disperse ▶NOUN **1** a moving platform carrying goods or people between floors in a large building **2** a ride in someone's car etc **3** a boost

lift-off NOUN the take-off of a rocket, spacecraft, etc

ligament NOUN a tough tissue that connects the bones of the body

light[1] NOUN **1** the brightness given by the sun, moon, lamps, etc that makes things visible **2** a source of light, eg a lamp **3** a flame on a cigarette lighter **4** a hint, clue, or help towards understanding: *shed a little light on the subject* ▶ADJECTIVE **1** bright **2** of a colour: pale **3** having light, not dark ▶VERB (**lighting, lit** *or* **lighted**) **1** to give light to **2** to set fire to **bring to light** to reveal, cause to be noticed **come to light** to be revealed or discovered **in the light of** taking into consideration (information etc)

light[2] ADJECTIVE **1** not heavy **2** easy

to bear or do: *light work* **3** easy to digest **4** nimble **5** lively **6** not grave, cheerful **7** not serious: *light reading* **8** of rain etc: little in quantity

lighten VERB **1** to make less heavy **2** to make or become brighter **3** of lightning: to flash

lightening (*pronounced* **lait**-en-ing) NOUN a making or becoming lighter or brighter

> Do not confuse with: **lightning**

lighter NOUN **1** a device with a flame etc for lighting **2** a large open boat used in unloading and loading ships

light-fingered ADJECTIVE apt to steal

light-headed ADJECTIVE dizzy

light-hearted ADJECTIVE cheerful

lighthouse NOUN a tower-like building with a flashing light to warn or guide ships

light industry NOUN the production of smaller goods, eg knitwear, glass, electronics components, etc (*compare with*: **heavy industry**)

lighting NOUN **1** a means of providing light **2** the combination of lights used eg in a theatre or a nightclub

lightly ADVERB **1** gently **2** not seriously

lightning NOUN an electric flash in the clouds

> Do not confuse with: **lightening**

lightning conductor NOUN a metal rod on a building etc which conducts electricity down to earth

lightweight NOUN a weight category in boxing ▶ ADJECTIVE not serious enough to demand much concentration

light-year NOUN the distance light travels in a year (6 billion miles)

like[1] ADJECTIVE the same as or similar to ▶ ADVERB in the same way as: *He sings like an angel* ▶ NOUN something or someone that is the equal of another: *You won't see her like again*

like[2] VERB **1** to be pleased with **2** to be fond of

ⓘ Comes from Old English *lician* meaning 'to please' or 'to be suitable'

likeable *or* **likable** ADJECTIVE attractive, lovable

likelihood NOUN probability

likely ADJECTIVE **1** probable **2** liable (to do something) ▶ ADVERB probably

liken VERB to think of as similar, compare: *She likened the experience to a nightmare*

likeness (*plural* **likenesses**) NOUN **1** similarity, resemblance **2** a portrait, photograph, etc of someone

likewise ADVERB **1** in the same way **2** also

liking NOUN **1** fondness **2** satisfaction: *to my liking*

lilac NOUN a small tree with hanging clusters of pale purple or white flowers ▶ ADJECTIVE of pale purple colour

lilt NOUN a striking rhythm or swing ▶ VERB to have this rhythm

lily NOUN (*plural* **lilies**) a tall plant

grown from a bulb with large white or coloured flowers

lily-of-the-valley NOUN (*plural* **lilies-of-the-valley**) a plant with small white bell-shaped flowers

limb NOUN **1** a leg or arm **2** a branch

limber ADJECTIVE easily bent, supple **limber up** to exercise so as to become supple

limbo[1] NOUN, *Christianity* the land bordering Hell, reserved for those unbaptized before death **in limbo** forgotten, neglected

limbo[2] NOUN a W Indian dance in which the dancer passes under a low bar

lime[1] NOUN a white, lumpy powder of calcium oxide, used in making glass and cement (*also called*: **quicklime**)

lime[2] NOUN **1** a tree related to the lemon **2** the greenish-yellow fruit of this tree **3** the greenish-yellow colour of this fruit

lime[3] NOUN a deciduous tree or shrub with clusters of sweet-smelling flowers (*also called*: **linden**)

limelight NOUN the glare of publicity **in the limelight** attracting publicity or attention

limerick NOUN a type of humorous poetry in five-line verses

ⓘ After *Limerick* in Ireland, the name of which was repeated in nonsense songs in an old Victorian parlour game

limestone NOUN white, grey, or black rock consisting mainly of calcium carbonate

limit NOUN **1** the farthest point or place **2** a boundary **3** the largest (or smallest) extent, degree, etc **4** a restriction ▸ VERB to set or keep to a limit

limitation NOUN **1** something which limits **2** a weak point, a flaw

limo NOUN, *informal* a limousine

limousine NOUN a large, luxurious car, especially one with a separate compartment for the driver

ⓘ Named after a type of cloak worn in *Limousin* in France, because the car's roof was supposedly similar in shape

limp ADJECTIVE **1** not stiff, floppy **2** weak ▸ VERB **1** to walk with an awkward or uneven step, often because one leg is weak or injured **2** of a damaged ship etc: to move with difficulty ▸ NOUN **1** the act of limping **2** a limping walk

limpet NOUN **1** a small cone-shaped shellfish which clings to rocks **2** someone who is difficult to get rid of

limpid ADJECTIVE clear, transparent

linden *see* **lime**[3]

line[1] NOUN **1** a cord, rope, etc **2** a long thin stroke or mark **3** a wrinkle **4** a row of people, printed words, etc **5** a service of ships or aircraft **6** a railway **7** a telephone connection **8** a short letter **9** a family from generation to generation **10** course, direction **11** a subject of interest, activity, etc **12** (**lines**) army trenches **13** (**lines**) a written school punishment exercise ▸ VERB **1** to mark out with lines **2** (often **line up**) to place in a row or alongside of **3** to form lines along (a street)

a b c d e f g h i j k l m n o p q r s t u v w x y z

line[2] VERB to cover on the inside: *line a dress*

lineage (*pronounced* **lin**-i-ij) NOUN descent, traced back to your ancestors

linear (*pronounced* **lin**-i-*a*r) ADJECTIVE **1** made of lines **2** in one dimension (length, breadth or height) only

line graph NOUN a chart or graph which uses horizontal or vertical lines to show amounts

linen NOUN **1** cloth made of flax **2** articles made of linen: *tablelinen/ bedlinen*

liner NOUN a ship or aeroplane working on a regular service

linger VERB **1** to stay for a long time or for longer than expected **2** to loiter, delay

linguist NOUN **1** someone skilled in languages **2** someone who studies language

linguistic ADJECTIVE to do with language

linguistics SINGULAR NOUN the scientific study of languages and of language in general

lining NOUN a covering on the inside

link NOUN **1** a ring of a chain **2** a single part of a series **3** anything connecting two things **4** *computing* a hyperlink ▶ VERB **1** to connect with a link **2** to join closely **3** to be connected

links PLURAL NOUN **1** a stretch of flat or slightly hilly ground near the seashore **2** a golf course by the sea

linnet NOUN a small songbird of the finch family

lino NOUN, *informal* linoleum

linoleum NOUN, *dated* a type of smooth, hard-wearing covering for floors

linseed NOUN flax seed

linseed oil NOUN oil from flax seed

lint NOUN **1** a soft woolly material for putting over wounds **2** fine pieces of fluff

lintel NOUN a timber or stone over a doorway or window

lion NOUN a powerful animal of the cat family, the male of which has a shaggy mane **the lion's share** the largest share

lioness NOUN (*plural* **lionesses**) a female lion

lip NOUN **1** either of the two fleshy flaps in front of the teeth forming the rim of the mouth **2** the edge of a jug etc

liposuction (*pronounced* **lip**-oh-suk-sh*o*n) NOUN a surgical operation to remove unwanted body fat by sucking it out through an incision in the skin

lip-reading NOUN reading what someone says from the movement of their lips

lip-service NOUN saying one thing but believing another: *paying lip-service to the rules*

lipstick NOUN a stick of red, pink, etc colouring for the lips

liquefy VERB (**liquefies, liquefying, liquefied**) to make or become liquid > **liquefaction** NOUN

liqueur (*pronounced* lik-**yoor**) NOUN a strong alcoholic drink, strongly flavoured and sweet

> Do not confuse with: **liquor**

liquid NOUN a flowing, water-like substance ▸ ADJECTIVE **1** flowing **2** looking like water **3** soft and clear

liquidate VERB **1** to close down, wind up the affairs of (a bankrupt business company) **2** *slang* to kill, murder > **liquidation** NOUN > **liquidator** NOUN

liquidize *or* **liquidise** VERB **1** to make liquid **2** to make into a purée

liquidizer *or* **liquidiser** NOUN a machine for liquidizing

liquor (*pronounced* **lik**-er) NOUN an alcoholic drink, especially a spirit (eg whisky)

> Do not confuse with: **liqueur**

liquorice *or* **licorice** NOUN **1** a plant with a sweet-tasting root **2** a black, sticky sweet flavoured with this root

lisp VERB **1** to say *th* for *s* or *z* because of being unable to pronounce these letters correctly **2** to speak imperfectly, like a child ▸ NOUN a speech disorder of this kind

list[1] NOUN a series of names, numbers, prices, etc written down one after the other ▸ VERB to write down in this way: *List your chosen subjects*

list[2] VERB of a ship: to lean over to one side ▸ NOUN a slope to one side

listen VERB to hear, pay attention to > **listener** NOUN

listeria NOUN a bacterium found in certain foods which can damage the nervous system if not killed during cooking

listless ADJECTIVE weary, without energy or interest

lit *past form* of **light**[1] and **light**[3]

liter *US spelling* of **litre**

literacy NOUN ability to read and write

literal ADJECTIVE of a word or phrase: following the exact or most obvious meaning (*contrasted with*: **figurative**)

literally ADVERB exactly as stated, not just as a figure of speech: *He was literally blinded by the flash*

> ⓘ It is generally considered wrong to use the word **literally** when something did not actually happen, as in *I literally laughed my head off.*

literary ADJECTIVE **1** relating to books, authors, etc **2** knowledgeable about books

literate ADJECTIVE able to read and write

literature NOUN **1** the books etc that are written in any language **2** anything in written form on a subject

lithe (*pronounced* laidh) ADJECTIVE bending easily, supple, flexible

lithium (*pronounced* **lith**-i-*u*m) NOUN, *chemistry* (symbol **Li**) a light metallic element used in batteries and alloys

litigation NOUN a law case

litmus paper NOUN treated paper which changes colour when dipped in an acid or alkaline solution

litmus test NOUN anything which indicates underlying attitudes etc

litre *or US* **liter** NOUN (*abbrev* **l**)

A B C D E F G H I J K L M N O P Q R S T U V W X Y Z

the basic unit for measuring liquids in the metric system

litter NOUN **1** an untidy mess of paper, rubbish, etc **2** a heap of straw as bedding for animals **3** a number of animals born at one birth **4** a bed for carrying the sick and injured ▶ VERB **1** to scatter rubbish carelessly about **2** to produce a litter of young

little ADJECTIVE small in quantity or size ▶ ADVERB **1** (**a little**) to a small extent or degree **2** not much **3** not at all: *Little does she know* ▶ PRONOUN a small amount, distance, etc: *Have a little more/Move a little to the right*

Comes from Old English *lytel*

live[1] (*pronounced* liv) VERB **1** to have life **2** to dwell **3** to pass your life in a certain way: *to live well* **4** to continue to be alive **5** to survive **6** to be lifelike or vivid **live down** to live until (an embarrassment etc) is forgotten by others **live on 1** to continue to live **2** to be supported by: *to live on benefits* **live up to** to be as good as expected from

Comes from Old English *lifian*

live[2] (*pronounced* laiv) ADJECTIVE **1** having life, not dead **2** full of energy **3** of a television broadcast etc: seen as the event takes place, not recorded **4** charged with electricity and apt to give an electric shock

livelihood (*pronounced* **laiv**-li-huwd) NOUN someone's means of living, eg their daily work

lively ADJECTIVE full of life, high spirits > **liveliness** NOUN

liven VERB to make lively

liver NOUN a large gland in the body that carries out several important functions including purifying the blood

livery NOUN (*plural* **liveries**) the uniform of a manservant etc

livestock (*pronounced* **laiv**-stok) NOUN farm animals

livewire (*pronounced* **laiv**-wair) NOUN a very lively, energetic person

livid ADJECTIVE very angry

living ADJECTIVE **1** having life **2** active, lively **3** of a likeness: exact ▶ NOUN means of living

living room NOUN an informal sitting room

lizard NOUN a four-footed reptile

llama NOUN a S American animal of the camel family without a hump

lo INTERJECTION, *old* look

load VERB **1** to put (what is to be carried) on or in a vehicle etc: *Load the furniture into the van* **2** to put the ammunition in (a gun) **3** to put a film in (a camera) **4** to weight for some purpose: *loaded dice* ▶ NOUN **1** as much as can be carried at once **2** cargo **3** a heavy weight or task **4** the power carried by an electric circuit

loaded question NOUN one meant to trap someone into making a damaging admission

loaf NOUN (*plural* **loaves**) a shaped mass of bread ▶ VERB to pass time idly or lazily

loafer NOUN **1** an idler **2** (**loafers**) casual shoes

loam NOUN a rich soil > **loamy** ADJECTIVE

loan NOUN something lent,

especially a sum of money ▸ VERB to lend

loath *or* **loth** (*pronounced* lohth) ADJECTIVE unwilling (to)

> Do not confuse: **loath** and **loathe**. Remember that **loaTHE** has an ending common to a few other verbs, eg cloTHE and baTHE.

loathe (*pronounced* lohdh) VERB to dislike greatly

loathing (*pronounced* **lohdh**-ing) NOUN great hate or disgust

loathsome (*pronounced* **lohdh**-som) ADJECTIVE causing loathing or disgust, horrible

loaves *plural* of **loaf**

lob NOUN **1** *cricket* a slow, high ball bowled underhand **2** *tennis* a ball high overhead dropping near the back of the court ▸ VERB (**lobbing, lobbed**) **1** to send (a ball) in such a movement **2** *informal* to throw

lobby NOUN (*plural* **lobbies**) **1** a small entrance hall **2** a passage off which rooms open **3** a group of people who try to influence the government or another authority ▸ VERB (**lobbies, lobbying, lobbied**) **1** to try to influence (public officials) **2** to conduct a campaign to influence public officials

lobe NOUN **1** the hanging-down part of an ear **2** a division of the brain, lungs, etc

lobotomy (*plural* **lobotomies**) NOUN **1** the surgical operation of cutting into a lobe or gland **2** a surgical operation on the front lobes of the brain which has the effect of changing the patient's character

lobster NOUN a kind of shellfish with large claws, used for food

lobster pot NOUN a basket in which lobsters are caught

local ADJECTIVE of or confined to a certain place ▸ NOUN, *informal* **1** the public house nearest someone's home **2** **locals** the people living in a particular place or area

Comes from Latin *locus* meaning 'a place'

local colour NOUN details in a story which make it more interesting and realistic

locale NOUN scene, location

local government NOUN administration of the local affairs of a district by an elected council (*compare with*: **central government**)

locality NOUN (*plural* **localities**) a particular place and the area round about

localize *or* **localise** VERB to confine to one area, keep from spreading

locate VERB **1** to find **2** to set in a particular place: *a house located in the Highlands*

location NOUN **1** the act of locating **2** position, situation **on location** of filming etc: in natural surroundings, not in a studio

loch NOUN, *Scottish* **1** a lake **2** an arm of the sea

lock[1] NOUN **1** a fastening for doors etc needing a key to open it **2** a part of a canal for raising or lowering boats **3** the part of a gun which explodes the charge **4** a tight hold ▸ VERB **1** to fasten with a lock **2** to become fastened **lock, stock and barrel** completely **lock up** to shut in with a lock

lock² NOUN **1** a section of hair **2** (**locks**) hair

locker NOUN a small cupboard

locker-room NOUN a room for changing clothes and storing personal belongings

locket NOUN a little ornamental case hung round the neck

lockjaw NOUN a form of tetanus which stiffens the jaw muscles

locksmith NOUN a person who makes locks

lock-up NOUN a lockable garage

locomotion NOUN movement from place to place

locomotive NOUN a railway engine ▸ ADJECTIVE of or capable of locomotion

locum NOUN (*plural* **locums**) a doctor, dentist, etc taking another's place for a time

locust NOUN a large insect of the grasshopper family which destroys growing plants

lodge NOUN **1** a small house, often at the entrance to a larger building **2** a beaver's dwelling **3** a house occupied during the shooting or hunting season **4** a branch of a society ▸ VERB **1** to live in rented rooms **2** to become fixed (in) **3** to put in a safe place **4** to make (a complaint, appeal, etc) officially

lodger NOUN someone who stays in rented rooms

lodging NOUN **1** a place to stay, sleep, etc **2** (**lodgings**) a room or rooms rented in someone else's house

loft NOUN **1** a room just under a roof **2** a gallery in a hall, church, etc

lofty (**loftier, loftiest**) ADJECTIVE **1** of great height **2** noble, proud
> **loftily** ADVERB (meaning 2)

log NOUN **1** a thick, rough piece of wood, part of a felled tree **2** a device for measuring a ship's speed **3** a logbook ▸ VERB (**logging, logged**) to write down (events) in a logbook **log in** *or* **on** *computing* to start a session on a computer, usually by typing in a password **log out** *or* **off** *computing* to end a session on a computer, using a closing command

logbook NOUN **1** an official record of a ship's or aeroplane's progress **2** a record of progress, attendance, etc **3** the registration documents of a motor vehicle

loggerhead NOUN: **at loggerheads** quarrelling

logic NOUN **1** the study of reasoning correctly **2** correctness of reasoning

logical ADJECTIVE according to the rules of logic or sound reasoning
> **logically** ADVERB

logo NOUN (*plural* **logos**) a symbol of a business firm etc consisting of a simple picture or lettering

-logy *or* **-ology** SUFFIX **1** forms words describing the scientific or serious study of something: *biology/psychology* **2** forms terms related to words or discourse: *eulogy*

ⓘ Comes from Greek *logos* meaning 'word' or 'reason'

loin NOUN **1** the back of an animal cut for food **2** (**loins**) the lower part of the body from the bottom rib to the pelvis

loincloth NOUN a piece of cloth worn round the hips, especially in India and south-east Asia

loiter VERB **1** to proceed, move slowly **2** to linger **3** to stand around

loll VERB **1** to lie lazily about **2** of the tongue: to hang down or out

lollipop NOUN a large boiled sweet on a stick

lollop VERB (**lolloping, lolloped**) **1** to bound clumsily **2** to lounge, idle

lolly NOUN (*plural* **lollies**) **1** *informal* a lollipop **2** *slang* money

lone ADJECTIVE alone; standing by itself

lonely (**lonelier, loneliest**) ADJECTIVE **1** lone **2** lacking or needing companionship **3** of a place: having few people
> **loneliness** NOUN

lonesome ADJECTIVE **1** lone **2** feeling lonely

long ADJECTIVE **1** not short, measuring a lot from end to end **2** measuring a certain amount: *cut a strip 2cm long/the film is 3 hours long* **3** far-reaching **4** slow to do something ▸ADVERB **1** for a great time **2** through the whole time: *all day long* ▸VERB to wish very much (for): *longing to see him again* **before long** soon **in the long run** in the end **so long** *informal* goodbye

🛈 Adjective: comes from Old English *lang/long*; adverb: comes from Old English *lange/longe*; verb: comes from Old English *langian*

longevity (*pronounced* lon-**jev**-i-ti) NOUN great length of life

longhand NOUN writing in full (*contrasted with*: **shorthand**)

longing NOUN a strong desire

longitude (*pronounced* **lon**-ji-tyood *or* **long**-gi-tyood) NOUN *geography* the distance, measured in degrees, of a place east or west of the Greenwich meridian

long johns PLURAL NOUN, *informal* men's long underpants reaching to the ankles

long jump NOUN an athletics contest in which competitors jump as far as possible along the ground from a running start

long-range ADJECTIVE **1** able to reach a great distance **2** looking a long way into the future

longship NOUN a narrow Viking sailing ship

long-sighted ADJECTIVE able to see things at a distance but not those close at hand

long-standing ADJECTIVE begun a long time ago, having lasted a long time

long-suffering ADJECTIVE putting up with troubles without complaining

long-term ADJECTIVE **1** extending over a long time **2** taking the future, not just the present, into account

long-wave ADJECTIVE of radio: using wavelengths over 1000 metres (*compare with*: **short-wave**)

long-winded ADJECTIVE using too many words

loo NOUN, *informal* a toilet

loofah NOUN the dried inner part of the fibrous fruit of a tropical plant, used as a rough sponge

look VERB **1** to turn the eyes towards

so as to see **2** to appear, seem: *You look tired/It looks as if I can go after all* **3** to face: *His room looks south* ▸NOUN **1** the act of looking **2** the expression on someone's face **3** appearance **4** (**looks**) personal appearance **look after** to take care of, take responsibility for **look down on** to think of as being inferior **look for** to search for **look forward to** to anticipate with pleasure **look into** to investigate **look on 1** to stand by and watch **2** to think of (as): *He looks on her as his mother* **look out!** be careful! **look over** to examine briefly

ⓘ Comes from Old English *locian* meaning 'to look'

look-alike NOUN someone who looks physically like someone else

looking-glass NOUN, *old* a mirror

lookout NOUN **1** (someone who keeps) a careful watch **2** a high place for watching from **3** concern, responsibility: *That's your lookout*

loom NOUN a machine for weaving cloth ▸VERB to appear indistinctly, often threateningly

loony *informal*, NOUN (*plural* **loonies**) a lunatic, an insane person ▸ADJECTIVE (**loonier, looniest**) mad, insane

loop NOUN **1** a doubled-over part in a piece of string etc **2** a U-shaped bend **loop the loop** to fly (an aircraft) upwards, back and down as if going round in a circle

loophole NOUN **1** a narrow slit in a wall **2** a way of avoiding a difficulty

loose (*pronounced* loos) ADJECTIVE **1** not tight, slack **2** not tied, free **3** not closely packed **4** vague, not exact **5** careless ▸VERB **1** to make loose, slacken **2** to untie **break loose** to escape **on the loose** free > **loosely** ADVERB (adjective, meanings 1, 3, 4 and 5)

> Do not confuse with: **lose**

loose-leaf ADJECTIVE having a cover that allows pages to be inserted or removed

loosen VERB to make loose or looser

loot NOUN goods stolen or plundered ▸VERB to plunder, ransack

lop VERB (**lopping, lopped**) to cut off the top or ends of

lope VERB to run with a long stride

lopsided ADJECTIVE leaning to one side, not symmetrical

loquacious (*pronounced* lok-**wei**-sh*us*) ADJECTIVE talkative > **loquacity** (*pronounced* lok-**was**-*it*-i) NOUN

lord NOUN **1** the owner of an estate **2** a title for a male member of the aristocracy, bishop, judge, etc **3** *old* a master, a ruler **4** (**the Lord**) God or Christ **lord it over someone** to act in a domineering manner towards them **drunk as a lord** extremely drunk **House of Lords** the upper (non-elected) house of the British parliament

Lord Chancellor NOUN the head of the English legal system

lordly ADJECTIVE (**lordlier, lordliest**) **1** relating to a lord **2** noble, proud

lordship NOUN **1** power, rule **2** used in talking to or about a lord: *his lordship*

lore NOUN knowledge, beliefs, etc handed down through generations

lorgnette (*pronounced* lawn-**yet**) NOUN eyeglasses with a handle

lorry NOUN (*plural* **lorries**) a motor vehicle for carrying heavy loads

lose (*pronounced* looz) VERB (**losing, lost**) **1** to cease to have, have no longer **2** to have (something) taken away from you **3** to put (something) where it cannot be found **4** to waste (time) **5** to miss (a train, a chance, etc) **6** to not win (a game)

> Do not confuse with: **loose**

loser NOUN **1** someone unlikely to succeed at anything **2** someone who loses a game or contest

loss NOUN (*plural* **losses**) **1** the act of losing **2** something which is lost **3** waste, harm, destruction **at a loss** uncertain what to do or say

lost ADJECTIVE **1** not able to be found **2** no longer possessed; thrown away **3** not won **4** ruined **lost in** completely taken up by, engrossed in: *lost in thought*

lot NOUN **1** a large number or quantity **2** someone's fortune or fate **3** a separate portion **draw lots** to decide who is to do something by drawing names out of a hat etc

loth *another spelling of* **loath**

lotion NOUN a liquid for treating or cleaning the skin or hair

lottery NOUN (*plural* **lotteries**) an event in which money or prizes are won through drawing lots

lotus NOUN (*plural* **lotuses**) **1** a kind of water-lily **2** a mythical tree whose fruit caused forgetfulness

louche (*pronounced* loosh) ADJECTIVE shady, disreputable

[i] A French word, literally meaning 'squinting'

loud ADJECTIVE **1** making a great sound; noisy **2** showy, over-bright ▶ADVERB in a way that makes a great sound; noisily > **loudly** ADVERB (adjective, meaning 1) > **loudness** NOUN (adjective, meaning 1)

loudhailer NOUN a megaphone with microphone and amplifier

loudmouth NOUN, *informal* someone who talks offensively and too much

loudspeaker NOUN a device for converting electrical signals into sound

lounge VERB **1** to lie back in a relaxed way **2** to move about lazily ▶NOUN a sitting room

lounge lizard someone who spends a lot of time aimlessly at social events

lounger NOUN **1** a lazy person **2** an extending chair or light couch for relaxing on

louse (*pronounced* lows) NOUN (*plural* **lice**) a small blood-sucking insect sometimes found on the bodies of animals and people

lousy (*pronounced* **low**-zi) ADJECTIVE (**lousier, lousiest**) **1** swarming with lice **2** *informal* inferior, of poor quality

lout NOUN a clumsy or boorish man

louvre *or US* **louver** (*pronounced* **loo**-ver) NOUN a slat set at an angle

louvre door NOUN a slatted door

A B C D E F G H I J K L M N O P Q R S T U V W X Y Z

allowing air and light to pass through

louvre window NOUN **1** a window covered with sloping slats **2** a window with narrow panes that can be set open at an angle

lovable *or* **loveable** ADJECTIVE worthy of love

love NOUN **1** a great liking or affection **2** a loved person **3** *tennis* no score, zero ▸ VERB to be very fond of; like very much **in love (with) 1** feeling love and desire (for) **2** having a great liking (for): *in love with his own voice* **make love to 1** to have sexual intercourse with **2** *old* to make sexual advances to, court

love affair NOUN a relationship between people in love but not married

lovebite NOUN a mark on the skin caused by the sucking bites of a lover

love-child NOUN (*plural* **love-children**), *old* an illegitimate child

lovely ADJECTIVE (**lovelier, loveliest**) beautiful; delightful > **loveliness** NOUN

lovemaking NOUN **1** *old* courtship **2** sexual play and intercourse

lover NOUN **1** someone who loves another **2** an admirer, an enthusiast: *an art lover* **3** someone who is having a love affair

lovesick ADJECTIVE languishing with love

loving ADJECTIVE full of love > **lovingly** ADVERB

low¹ ADJECTIVE **1** not high; not lying or reaching far up **2** of a voice: not loud **3** cheap: *low air fares* **4** feeling sad, depressed **5** humble **6** mean, unworthy ▸ ADVERB **1** in or to a low position **2** not loudly **3** cheaply **keep a low profile** to not make your feelings or presence known

low² VERB to make the noise of cattle; bellow, moo

lowbrow ADJECTIVE designed to be popular, not intellectual (*contrasted with*: **highbrow**)

lowdown *informal*, NOUN (**the lowdown**) information

lower (*pronounced* **loh**-er) ADJECTIVE less high ▸ VERB **1** to make less high: *lower the price* **2** to let or come down: *lower the blinds*

lower-case ADJECTIVE of a letter: not a capital, eg *a not A* (*contrasted with*: **upper-case**)

low-key ADJECTIVE not elaborate, unpretentious

lowland NOUN land which is comparatively low-lying and flat (*also*: **lowlands**)

lowly ADJECTIVE (**lowlier, lowliest**) low in rank, humble > **lowliness** NOUN

loyal ADJECTIVE faithful, true > **loyally** ADVERB

loyalist NOUN someone loyal to their sovereign or country

loyalty NOUN (*plural* **loyalties**) **1** faithful support of eg your friends **2** (**loyalties**) feelings of faithful friendship and support, especially for a particular person or thing

lozenge NOUN **1** a diamond-shaped figure **2** a small sweet for sucking

LP NOUN, *old* a long-playing record

LSD ABBREVIATION lysergic acid

diethylamide, a hallucinogenic drug

Ltd ABBREVIATION limited liability

lubricant NOUN something which lubricates; an oil

lubricate VERB **1** to apply oil etc to (something) to overcome friction and make movement easier **2** to ply with alcohol > **lubrication** NOUN

lucid ADJECTIVE **1** easily understood **2** clear in mind; not confused > **lucidity** NOUN > **lucidly** ADVERB

Lucifer NOUN Satan, the Devil

luck NOUN **1** fortune, either good or bad **2** chance: *as luck would have it* **3** good fortune: *Have any luck?*

lucky ADJECTIVE (**luckier, luckiest**) **1** fortunate, having good luck **2** bringing good luck: *lucky charm* **3** happening as a result of good luck: *a lucky coincidence* > **luckily** ADVERB

lucrative ADJECTIVE profitable

ludicrous ADJECTIVE ridiculous > **ludicrously** ADVERB > **ludicrousness** NOUN

ludo NOUN a game played with counters on a board

lug[1] VERB (**lugging, lugged**) to pull or drag with effort

lug[2] NOUN, *informal* the ear

luggage NOUN suitcases and other travelling baggage

lugubrious (*pronounced* lu-**goo**-bri-*us*) ADJECTIVE mournful, dismal > **lugubriously** ADVERB

lukewarm ADJECTIVE **1** neither hot nor cold **2** not very keen, unenthusiastic

lull VERB to soothe or calm ▶ NOUN a period of calm

lullaby (*pronounced* **lul**-*a*-bai) NOUN (*plural* **lullabies**) a song to lull children to sleep

lumbago (*pronounced* lum-**bei**-goh) NOUN a pain in the lower part of the back

lumbar ADJECTIVE of or in the lower part of the back

lumber NOUN sawn-up timber ▶ VERB to move about clumsily

lumberjack NOUN someone who fells, saws and shifts trees

luminescent ADJECTIVE giving out light > **luminescence** NOUN

luminous ADJECTIVE **1** giving light **2** shining; clear > **luminosity** NOUN

lump NOUN **1** a small, solid mass of indefinite shape **2** a swelling **3** the whole taken together: *considered in a lump* ▶ VERB **1** to form into lumps **2** to treat as being alike: *lumped all of us together*

lump sum NOUN an amount of money given all at once

lumpy ADJECTIVE (**lumpier, lumpiest**) full of lumps

lunacy NOUN madness, insanity

lunar ADJECTIVE of the moon: *lunar eclipse*

lunatic (*pronounced* **loo**-*na*-tik) NOUN someone who is insane or crazy ▶ ADJECTIVE insane, mad

lunch NOUN (*plural* **lunches**) a midday meal ▶ VERB to eat lunch

luncheon NOUN, *formal* lunch

lung NOUN either of the two bag-like organs which fill with and expel air in the course of breathing

lunge NOUN a sudden thrust or push ▶ VERB to thrust or plunge forward suddenly

lupin (*pronounced* **loo**-pin) NOUN a type of garden plant with flowers on long spikes

lurch VERB to roll or pitch suddenly to one side; stagger ▶NOUN (*plural* **lurches**) a pitch to one side **leave in the lurch** to leave in a difficult position without help

lure NOUN something which entices; a bait ▶VERB to attract, entice away

lurid ADJECTIVE **1** glaring, garish: *lurid book cover* **2** horrifying, sensational: *lurid story*

lurk VERB **1** to keep out of sight; be hidden **2** to move or act secretly and slyly > **lurker** NOUN

lurking ADJECTIVE vague, hidden

luscious ADJECTIVE sweet, delicious, juicy

lush ADJECTIVE of grass etc: thick and plentiful

lust NOUN **1** a greedy desire for power, riches, etc **2** a strong sexual desire ▶VERB to have a strong desire (for)

luster *US spelling of* **lustre**

lustful ADJECTIVE full of, or showing, strong sexual desire

lustre *or US* **luster** NOUN brightness, shine, gloss

> ⓘ This is one of a large number of words which is spelled with an **-re** ending in British English, but with an **-er** in American English, eg *centre/center, calibre/caliber, metre/meter*.

lustrous ADJECTIVE bright, shining

lusty ADJECTIVE (**lustier, lustiest**) lively, strong > **lustily** ADVERB

lute NOUN a stringed musical instrument with a pear-shaped, round-backed body and fretted fingerboard

luxuriant ADJECTIVE **1** thick with leaves, flowers, etc: *ornamental gardens full of luxuriant plants* **2** richly ornamented

> Do not confuse with: **luxurious**

luxuriate VERB **1** to be luxuriant **2** to enjoy; take delight (in)

luxurious ADJECTIVE full of luxuries; very comfortable: *a luxurious new home* > **luxuriously** ADVERB

> Do not confuse with: **luxuriant**

luxury NOUN (*plural* **luxuries**) **1** something very pleasant or expensive but not necessary: *Having a car is a luxury* **2** the use or enjoyment of such things

LW ABBREVIATION long-wave

Lycra NOUN, *trademark* a lightweight synthetic elastic fabric

lying *see* **lie**[1] , **lie**[2]

lymph NOUN a colourless fluid in the body, containing mostly white blood cells

lymph node *or* **lymph gland** NOUN in the lymphatic system: one of many small rounded structures, found in large clusters in the neck, armpit, and groin, that produce antibodies in immune responses

lynch VERB to condemn and put to death without legal trial

ⓘ Named after William *Lynch*, 19th-century Virginian planter who organized unofficial trials of suspected criminals

lynch mob NOUN a group of people who go out to lynch someone

lynx NOUN (*plural* **lynxes**) a wild animal of the cat family, noted for its keen sight

lyre NOUN an ancient stringed musical instrument, played like a harp

lyric NOUN **1** a short poem, often expressing the poet's feelings **2** (**lyrics**) the words of a song
▶ADJECTIVE **1** of a lyric **2** full of joy

lyrical ADJECTIVE **1** lyric **2** song-like **3** full of enthusiastic praise
> **lyrically** ADVERB

lyricism NOUN a song-like quality

lyricist NOUN someone who writes the words for songs

-lysis SUFFIX forms words containing the idea of splitting-up or breaking-down into smaller or simpler parts: *analysis*
[i] Comes from Greek *lysis* meaning 'a loosening'

Mm

m[1] ABBREVIATION **1** metre(s) **2** mile(s) **3** million(s)

m[2] SYMBOL metre

MA ABBREVIATION Master of Arts, a degree in a non-scientific subject such as a language

mac short for **mackintosh**

macabre (*pronounced* ma-**kah**-ber) ADJECTIVE gruesome, horrible

macaroni NOUN pasta shaped into short, hollow tubes

macaroon NOUN a sweet cake or biscuit made with ground almonds and sugar

macaw NOUN a long-tailed, brightly coloured parrot

mace[1] NOUN a heavy staff with an ornamental head, carried as a sign of office

mace[2] NOUN a spice made from the covering of a nutmeg

macerate (*pronounced* **mas**-*e*-reit) VERB **1** to make into pulp by steeping **2** to emaciate

machete (*pronounced* ma-**shet**-i) NOUN a heavy knife used to cut through foliage etc

machine NOUN **1** a working arrangement of wheels, levers, etc **2** a (motor) bicycle **3** a political party organization ▸ VERB to make, shape or sew with a machine

machine code NOUN, *computing* a system of symbols that can be understood by a computer

machine gun NOUN an automatic, rapid-firing gun

machinery NOUN **1** machines in general **2** the working parts of a machine **3** organization: *the machinery of local government*

machine tool NOUN a stationary, power-driven machine used for cutting and shaping metal, wood or plastic

machinist NOUN someone who operates, makes or repairs a machine

machismo (*pronounced* ma-**kiz**-moh *or* ma-**chiz**-moh) NOUN overt or aggressive masculinity

Mach number (*pronounced* mahk *or* mak *or* mahkh) NOUN the ratio of the speed of an aircraft to the speed of sound (eg Mach 5 = 5 times the speed of sound)

macho (*pronounced* **mach**-oh) ADJECTIVE overtly or aggressively masculine

mackerel NOUN an edible sea fish with wavy markings

mackintosh NOUN (*plural* **mackintoshes**) a waterproof overcoat

macro NOUN, *computing* a single instruction that prompts a computer to carry out a series of short instructions embedded in it

macro- PREFIX forms words for things which are long, large or great: *macromolecule/macrobiotic*
ⓘ Comes from Greek *makros* meaning 'long' or 'great'

macrobiotic ADJECTIVE of diet: consisting of organic unprocessed food, especially vegetables, and originally intended to prolong life

mad ADJECTIVE (**madder, maddest**) **1** mentally disturbed, insane **2** wildly foolish **3** furious with anger **like mad** very quickly or energetically: *We had to work like mad to finish* > **madness** NOUN (meanings 1 and 2)

madam NOUN a polite form of address to a woman

madcap NOUN a rash, hot-headed person ▸ADJECTIVE foolishly rash: *a madcap scheme*

mad cow disease *see* **BSE**

madden VERB to make angry or mad

maddening ADJECTIVE extremely annoying

made *past form* of **make**

madhouse NOUN **1** a place of confusion and noise **2** *old* an insane asylum

madly ADVERB **1** insanely **2** extremely: *madly in love*

madman *or* **madwoman** NOUN (*plural* **madmen** *or* **madwomen**) someone who is mad

Madonna NOUN the Virgin Mary as depicted in art

maestro (*pronounced* **mais**-troh) NOUN (*plural* **maestros**) someone highly skilled in an art, especially music

magazine NOUN **1** a paperback periodical publication containing articles, stories and pictures **2** a storage place for military equipment **3** a place for extra cartridges in a rifle
ⓘ The meaning of *magazine* as a periodical developed from the military use, being intended as a storehouse or treasury of information

magenta NOUN a reddish-purple colour ▸ADJECTIVE of this colour

maggot NOUN a small worm-like creature, the grub of a bluebottle etc

magic NOUN **1** a process which supposedly uses supernatural forces, spells, etc to produce results which cannot be explained or which are remarkable **2** conjuring tricks ▸ADJECTIVE **1** using magic: *magic tricks* **2** used in magic: *a magic wand* **3** wonderful or mysterious

magical ADJECTIVE **1** of or produced by magic **2** very wonderful or mysterious > **magically** ADVERB

magician NOUN someone skilled in magic

magistrate NOUN someone with the power to enforce the law, eg a justice of the peace

magma NOUN molten rock

magnanimous (*pronounced* mag-**nan**-im-*us*) ADJECTIVE very generous > **magnanimously** ADVERB

magnate NOUN someone with great power or wealth

magnesium NOUN, *chemistry* (symbol **Mg**) a white metal which burns with an intense white light

magnet NOUN **1** a piece of iron, steel, etc which has the power to attract other pieces of metal **2** someone or something that attracts strongly

magnetic ADJECTIVE **1** having the powers of a magnet **2** strongly attractive: *a magnetic personality*

magnetic field NOUN the area which is affected by a magnet

magnetic north NOUN the direction in which the magnetized needle of a compass points, slightly east or west of true north

magnetic pole NOUN **1** either of two areas on a magnet where the magnetic field is strongest **2** *geography* the two points on the earth's surface (**North Pole** and **South Pole**) at either end of its axis

magnetism NOUN **1** the properties of attraction possessed by a magnet **2** attraction, great charm

magnetize *or* **magnetise** VERB **1** to make magnetic **2** to attract, influence

magnification NOUN **1** the process of making objects appear larger or closer, or the power that instruments such as microscopes and binoculars have to do this **2** a measure of how much larger or closer an object is made to appear than it is in reality

magnificent ADJECTIVE **1** splendid in appearance or action **2** excellent, very fine > **magnificence** NOUN > **magnificently** ADVERB

magnify VERB (**magnifies, magnifying, magnified**) **1** to make (something) appear larger by using special lenses **2** to exaggerate

magnifying glass NOUN a lens through which things appear larger

magnitude NOUN **1** size or extent **2** importance

magnolia NOUN a tree which produces large, white or purplish, sweet-scented flowers

magnum NOUN a bottle of wine or champagne equal to two ordinary bottles

magnum opus NOUN a great work, a masterpiece

magpie NOUN a black-and-white bird of the crow family, known for its habit of collecting objects

maharaja *or* **maharajah** NOUN an important Indian prince, especially the ruler of a state

mah-jong NOUN a Chinese table game played with small painted bricks

mahogany NOUN (*plural* **mahoganies**)**1** a tropical American hardwood tree **2** its hard reddish-brown wood, often used for furniture

maid NOUN **1** a female servant **2** *old* an unmarried woman; a young girl

maiden NOUN, *old* an unmarried girl; a virgin ▶ ADJECTIVE **1** unmarried: *a maiden aunt* **2** first, initial: *a maiden voyage*

maiden name NOUN the surname

of a married woman before her marriage

mail[1] NOUN letters, parcels, etc carried by post ▸VERB to post

mail[2] NOUN body armour of steel rings or plates

mailbox NOUN **1** *esp N Am* a public or private letter box **2** *computing* a part of a computer's memory in which e-mail messages are stored

mail order NOUN **1** a system of buying and selling goods by post **2** an order for goods to be sent by post

mail shot NOUN unsolicited advertising material sent by post

maim VERB to cripple, disable

main ADJECTIVE chief, most important ▸NOUN, *old* the ocean **in the main** for the most part **the mains** a supply of gas, water or electricity through a branching system of pipes or conductors

main clause NOUN, *grammar* a clause in a sentence that can make sense on its own, eg *'I liked the book* that you gave me for my birthday' (*compare with*: **subordinate clause**)

mainframe NOUN, *computing* a large, powerful computer to which several smaller computers can be linked ▸ADJECTIVE of a computer: of the large, powerful type rather than the small-scale kind

mainland NOUN a large piece of land off whose coast lie smaller islands

mainly ADVERB chiefly, mostly

mainstay NOUN the chief support

maintain VERB **1** to keep (something) as it is **2** to continue to keep in good working order **3** to support (a family etc) **4** to state (an opinion) firmly

maintenance NOUN **1** the act of maintaining; upkeep, repair **2** means of support, especially money for food, clothing, etc

maize NOUN a type of corn widely grown for food

majestic ADJECTIVE stately, regal

majesty NOUN (*plural* **majesties**) **1** greatness of rank or manner **2** (**Majesty**) a title used in addressing or referring to a king or queen: *Your Majesty/a royal visit from Their Majesties*

major ADJECTIVE great in size, importance, etc (*contrasted with*: **minor**) ▸NOUN a senior army officer

majority NOUN (*plural* **majorities**) **1** the greater number or quantity **2** the difference in amount between the greater and the lesser number **3** the age when someone becomes legally an adult (18 in the UK)

make VERB (**making, made**) **1** to form, construct **2** to cause to be: *He makes me mad at times* **3** to bring about: *make trouble* **4** to amount to: *2 and 2 make 4* **5** to earn: *She made £300 last week* **6** to force: *I made him do it* **7** to undergo (a journey etc) **8** to prepare (a meal etc): *I'll make some tea* ▸NOUN **1** kind, shape, form **2** brand **make believe** to pretend **make good 1** to do well **2** to carry out (a promise) **3** to make up for (a loss) **make light of** to treat as unimportant **make much of** to fuss over, treat as important **make nothing of 1** to be unable to understand, do, etc **2** to make light

A B C D E F G H I J K L M N O P Q R S T U V W X Y Z

of **make off** to run away **make out** **1** to see in the distance or indistinctly **2** to declare, prove **3** to write out (a bill, cheque, etc) **make up 1** to form a whole: *Eleven players make up the side* **2** to put together, invent (a false story) **3** to put make-up on the face **4** to be friendly again after a quarrel **make up for** to give or do something in return for damage done **on the make** *informal* looking for personal gain

🄸 Comes from Old English *macian*

make-believe NOUN fantasy

maker NOUN the person or organization that has made something **meet your maker** to die

makeshift ADJECTIVE used for a time as a substitute for something better

make-up NOUN cosmetics

maladjusted ADJECTIVE of a person: unable to deal with everyday situations and relationships

malady NOUN (*plural* **maladies**) illness, disease

malaise (*pronounced* ma-**leiz**) NOUN a feeling or general air of unease, depression or despondency

malaria NOUN a fever caused by the bite of a particular type of mosquito > **malarial** ADJECTIVE

🄸 From an Italian phrase meaning 'bad air', malarial fever being originally thought to be caused by poisonous marsh gases

male ADJECTIVE of the sex that is able to father children or young; masculine ▸NOUN a member of this sex

malevolent ADJECTIVE wishing ill to others; spiteful > **malevolence** NOUN > **malevolently** ADVERB

malformation NOUN faulty or wrong shape > **malformed** ADJECTIVE

malfunction VERB to fail to work or operate properly ▸NOUN failure to operate

malice NOUN ill will; spite

malicious ADJECTIVE intending harm; spiteful > **maliciously** ADVERB

malign (*pronounced* ma-**lain**) VERB to say or write unpleasant things about someone, especially falsely or spitefully

malignant (*pronounced* ma-**lig**-nant) ADJECTIVE **1** wishing harm to someone, spiteful **2** of a disease: likely to cause death (*contrasted with*: **benign**) > **malignantly** ADVERB

malinger (*pronounced* ma-**ling**-ger) VERB to pretend to be ill to avoid work etc > **malingerer** NOUN

mall (*pronounced* mawl) NOUN, *originally US* a shopping centre

malleable (*pronounced* **mal**-i-a-bl) ADJECTIVE **1** of metal: able to be beaten out by hammering **2** of people: easy to influence > **malleability** NOUN

mallet NOUN a heavy wooden hammer

malnutrition NOUN lack of sufficient or proper food; undernourishment

malpractice NOUN **1** wrongdoing **2** professional misconduct

malt NOUN **1** barley or other grain prepared for making beer or whisky **2** a malt whisky

maltreat VERB to treat roughly or unkindly > **maltreatment** NOUN

mammal NOUN a member of the class of animals of which the female parent feeds the young with her own milk > **mammalian** ADJECTIVE

mammogram NOUN an X-ray taken of a woman's breast to detect early signs of cancer

mammoth NOUN a very large elephant, now extinct ▸ ADJECTIVE enormous, huge: *mammoth savings*

man NOUN (*plural* **men**) **1** a grown-up human male **2** a human being **3** the human race **4** *informal* a husband **5** a piece in chess or draughts ▸ VERB (**manning, manned**) to supply with workers, crew, etc: *man the boats* **the man in the street** the ordinary person **to a man** every single one

🛈 Comes from Old English *mann*

manacle NOUN, *formal* a handcuff ▸ VERB to handcuff

manage VERB **1** to have control or charge of **2** to deal with, cope: *can't manage on his own* **3** to succeed: *managed to finish on time*

manageable ADJECTIVE easily managed or controlled

management NOUN **1** those in charge of a business etc **2** the art of managing a business etc

manager NOUN someone in charge of a business etc

manageress NOUN a female manager of a shop etc

Mancunian (*pronounced* man-**kyoo**-ni-*a*n) NOUN someone born or living in Manchester

mandarin NOUN **1** a small orange-like citrus fruit **2** *history* a senior Chinese official

mandate NOUN **1** a right or power to act on someone else's behalf **2** a command, especially one given from a superior to a subordinate

mandatory ADJECTIVE compulsory

mandolin *or* **mandoline** NOUN a round-backed stringed instrument similar to a lute

mane NOUN **1** long hair on the head and neck of a horse or male lion **2** a long or thick head of hair

maneuver *US spelling* of **manoeuvre**

manful ADJECTIVE courageous and noble-minded > **manfully** ADVERB

manganese NOUN, *chemistry* (symbol **Mn**) a hard, easily broken metal of a greyish-white colour

mangle NOUN a machine for squeezing water out of clothes or for smoothing them ▸ VERB **1** to squeeze (clothes) through a mangle **2** to crush, tear, damage badly

mango NOUN (*plural* **mangoes**) **1** the fruit of a tropical Indian tree, with juicy orange flesh **2** the tree which produces mangoes

mangrove NOUN a type of tree which grows in swamps in hot countries

mangy (*pronounced* **meinj**-ee) ADJECTIVE (**mangier, mangiest**) **1** shabby, squalid **2** of an animal: suffering from mange

manhandle VERB to handle roughly

manhole NOUN a hole (into a drain,

sewer, etc) large enough to let a person through

manhood NOUN the state of being a man

mania (*pronounced* **mei**-ni-*a*) NOUN **1** a form of mental illness in which the sufferer is over-active, over-excited and unreasonably happy **2** extreme fondness or enthusiasm: *a mania for computer games*

maniac NOUN **1** a mad person **2** a very rash or over-enthusiastic person

manic (*pronounced* **man**-ik) ADJECTIVE **1** suffering from mania **2** very energetic or excited

manicure NOUN **1** the care of hands and nails **2** professional treatment for the hands and nails ▶ VERB to perform a manicure on

manicurist NOUN someone who performs manicures

manifest ADJECTIVE easily seen or understood ▶ VERB to show plainly

manifestation NOUN behaviour, actions or events which reveal or display something

manifestly ADVERB obviously, clearly

manifesto NOUN (*plural* **manifestoes** *or* **manifestos**) a public announcement of intentions, eg by a political party

manifold ADJECTIVE many and various

manioc NOUN tapioca

manipulate VERB **1** to handle something, especially in a skilful way **2** to control or influence someone cleverly and unscrupulously, to your own advantage

mankind NOUN the human race

manly ADJECTIVE brave, strong
> **manliness** NOUN

mannequin NOUN **1** someone who models clothes for prospective buyers **2** a display dummy

manner NOUN **1** the way in which something is done **2** the way in which someone behaves **3** (**manners**) polite behaviour towards others **all manner of** all kinds of

mannerism NOUN an odd and obvious habit or characteristic

mannerly ADJECTIVE polite

manoeuvre *or US* **maneuver** NOUN **1** a planned movement of troops, ships or aircraft **2** a trick, a cunning plan ▶ VERB **1** to perform a manoeuvre **2** to manipulate

manor NOUN **1** a large house, usually attached to a country estate **2** *history* the land belonging to a lord or squire > **manorial** ADJECTIVE

manpower NOUN the number of people available for work

manse NOUN the house of a minister in certain Christian churches, eg the Church of Scotland

mansion NOUN a large house

manslaughter NOUN killing someone without deliberate intent

mantelpiece NOUN a shelf over a fireplace

mantle NOUN **1** a cloak or loose outer garment **2** a covering: *a mantle of snow* **3** a thin, transparent shade around the flame of a gas or paraffin lamp

mantra NOUN, *Hinduism, Buddhism* a word or phrase,

chanted or repeated inwardly in meditation

manual ADJECTIVE **1** of the hand or hands **2** worked by hand **3** working with the hands: *a manual worker* ▸NOUN a handbook giving instructions on how to use something: *a car manual* > **manually** ADVERB (adjective, meaning 2)

manufacture VERB to make (articles or materials) in large quantities, usually by machine ▸NOUN **1** the process of manufacturing **2** a manufactured article > **manufacturer** NOUN

manure NOUN a substance, especially animal dung, spread on soil to make it more fertile ▸VERB to treat with manure

manuscript NOUN **1** the prepared material for a book etc before it is printed **2** a book or paper written by hand

Manx ADJECTIVE of or relating to the Isle of Man

many ADJECTIVE a large number of: *Many people were present* ▸NOUN a large number: *Many survived* **many a** a large number of: *Many a voice was raised*

Maori NOUN a member of a race of people who were first to arrive in New Zealand

map NOUN a flat drawing of all or part of the earth's surface, showing geographical features ▸VERB (**mapping, mapped**) **1** to make a map of **2** *maths* to correspond single members of a set (the **domain**) with single members of another set (the **codomain**) **map something out** to plan something

maple NOUN **1** a tree related to the sycamore, one variety of which produces sugar **2** its hard, light-coloured wood, used for furniture etc

mapping NOUN, *maths* a diagram showing the correspondence of single members of one set with those of another

mar VERB (**marring, marred**) to spoil, deface

maracas PLURAL NOUN a pair of filled gourds shaken as a percussion instrument

marathon NOUN a long-distance foot-race, usually covering 26 miles 385 yards

ⓘ After the distance run by a Greek soldier from *Marathon* to Athens with news of the victory over the Persians in 490 BC

marauding ADJECTIVE roaming about with the intention of plundering or killing

marble NOUN **1** limestone that takes a high polish, used for sculpture, decorating buildings, etc **2** a small glass ball used in a children's game

March NOUN the third month of the year

ⓘ After *Mars*, the Roman god of war

march VERB **1** to (cause to) walk in time with regular steps **2** to go on steadily ▸NOUN (*plural* **marches**) **1** a marching movement **2** a piece of music for marching to **3** the distance covered by marching **4** a steady progression of events: *the march of time*

Mardi Gras (*pronounced* mahr-di **grah**) NOUN a carnival held on

Shrove Tuesday in certain countries

mare NOUN a female horse

margarine (*pronounced* **mahr**-*ja*-reen) NOUN an edible spread similar to butter, made mainly of vegetable fats

margin NOUN **1** an edge, a border **2** the blank edge on the page of a book **3** additional space or room; allowance: *a margin for error*

marginal ADJECTIVE **1** of or in a margin **2** borderline, close to a limit **3** of a political constituency: without a clear majority for any one candidate or party **4** of little effect or importance: *a marginal improvement* ▸ NOUN a marginal political constituency

marginalize *or* **marginalise** VERB to make less important or central

marginally ADVERB very slightly, to a very small degree

marigold NOUN a kind of plant with a yellow or orange flower

marijuana NOUN an illegal drug made from the plant hemp

marina NOUN a place with moorings for yachts, dinghies, etc

marinade NOUN a mixture of oil, wine, herbs, spices, etc in which food is soaked for flavour before it is cooked ▸ VERB to marinate

marinate VERB to steep in a marinade

marine ADJECTIVE of the sea ▸ NOUN a soldier trained to serve on land or at sea

mariner (*pronounced* **ma**-rin-*er*) NOUN, *old* a sailor

marionette NOUN a puppet moved by strings

marital ADJECTIVE of marriage

maritime ADJECTIVE **1** of the sea or ships **2** lying near the sea **3** *geography* of climate: cool in summer and mild in winter, because of the nearness of the sea

marjoram NOUN a sweet-smelling herb used in cooking

mark NOUN **1** a sign that can be seen **2** a stain, spot, etc **3** a target aimed at **4** a trace **5** a point used to assess the merit of a piece of schoolwork etc **6** the starting-line in a race: *On your marks!* ▸ VERB **1** to make a mark on; stain **2** to observe, watch **3** to stay close to (an opponent in football etc) **4** to award marks to (a piece of schoolwork etc) **mark off** to separate, distinguish **mark time** **1** to move the feet up and down, as if marching, but without going forward **2** to keep things going without progressing **up to the mark** coming up to the required standard

marked ADJECTIVE easily noticed: *a marked improvement*

markedly ADVERB noticeably

marker NOUN **1** a pen with a thick point, used for writing signs etc **2** something used to show a position

market NOUN **1** a public place for buying and selling **2** (a country, place, etc where there is) a need or demand (for certain types of goods): *the teenage market* ▸ VERB to put on sale **on the market** for sale

market forces PLURAL NOUN, *business* the effect of supply and demand on the price and quantity of a product being traded

market garden NOUN an area of land in which fruit and vegetables are grown to be sold

marketing NOUN the act or practice of advertising and selling

marksman *or* **markswoman** NOUN (*plural* **marksmen** *or* **markswomen**) someone who shoots well

marmalade NOUN a jam made from citrus fruit, especially oranges

marmoset NOUN a type of small monkey found in America

maroon[1] NOUN **1** a brownish-red colour **2** a firework used as a distress signal ▸ ADJECTIVE brownish-red

maroon[2] VERB **1** to abandon on an island etc without means of escape **2** to leave in a helpless or uncomfortable position

marquee (*pronounced* mahr-**kee**) NOUN a large tent used for large gatherings, eg a wedding reception or circus

marquess *or* **marquis** (*both pronounced* **mahr**-kwis) NOUN (*plural* **marquesses** *or* **marquises**) a nobleman below a duke in rank

marriage NOUN **1** the ceremony by which two people become husband and wife **2** a joining together: *a marriage of minds*

marrow NOUN **1** the soft substance in the hollow part of bones **2** a long vegetable with a thick green or striped skin and soft white flesh

marry VERB (**marries, marrying, married**) to join, or be joined, together in marriage

marsh NOUN (*plural* **marshes**) a piece of low-lying wet ground

marshal NOUN **1** a high-ranking officer in the army or air force **2** someone who directs processions etc **3** *US* a law-court official **4** *US* the head of a police force ▸ VERB (**marshalling, marshalled**) **1** to arrange (troops, facts, arguments, etc) in order **2** to show the way, conduct, lead

marshmallow NOUN **1** a spongy, jelly-like sweet made from sugar and egg-whites **2** a marsh plant with pink flowers, similar to the hollyhock

marshy ADJECTIVE (**marshier, marshiest**) wet underfoot; boggy

marsupial NOUN an animal which carries its young in a pouch, eg the kangaroo

marten NOUN an animal related to the weasel

martial ADJECTIVE **1** of war or battle **2** warlike

martial art NOUN a combative sport or method of self-defence

martial law NOUN the government of a country by its army

Martian NOUN a potential or imaginary being from the planet Mars

martyr NOUN someone who suffers death or hardship for their beliefs ▸ VERB to execute or make suffer for beliefs

martyrdom NOUN the death or suffering of a martyr

marvel NOUN something astonishing or wonderful ▸ VERB (**marvelling, marvelled**) to feel amazement (at)

A B C D E F G H I J K L M N O P Q R S T U V W X Y Z

marvellous ADJECTIVE 1 astonishing, extraordinary 2 *informal* excellent, very good

Marxist NOUN a follower of the theories of Karl Marx; a communist > **Marxism** NOUN

marzipan NOUN a mixture of ground almonds, sugar, etc, used in cake-making and confectionery

mascara NOUN a cosmetic used to colour the eyelashes

mascot NOUN a person, animal or thing believed to bring good luck

masculine ADJECTIVE 1 of the male sex 2 manly > **masculinity** NOUN

mash VERB to beat or crush into a pulp ▸NOUN (*plural* **mashes**) 1 mashed potato 2 a mixture of bran, meal, etc, used as animal food

mask NOUN 1 a cover for the face for disguise or protection: *an oxygen mask/a surgical mask/a Hallowe'en mask* 2 a pretence, a disguise ▸VERB 1 to hide, disguise 2 to cover the face with a mask

mason NOUN 1 someone who carves stone 2 a Freemason

masonry NOUN stonework

masquerade (*pronounced* mas-ke-**reid** *or* mahs-ke-**reid**) NOUN 1 a dance at which masks are worn 2 pretence ▸VERB to pretend to be someone else: *masquerading as a journalist*

Mass NOUN (*plural* **Masses**) 1 (in some Christian churches) the celebration commemorating Christ's last meal with his disciples 2 music for a Mass

mass NOUN (*plural* **masses**) 1 *physics* the amount of matter that an object contains 2 a lump or quantity gathered together 3 a large quantity 4 the main part or body 5 a measure of quantity of matter in an object ▸ADJECTIVE 1 of a mass 2 of or consisting of large numbers or quantities ▸VERB to form into a mass **the masses** ordinary people

massacre NOUN the merciless killing of a large number of people ▸VERB to kill (a large number) in a cruel way

massage (*pronounced* **mas**-ahsz) NOUN the rubbing of parts of the body to remove pain or tension ▸VERB to perform massage on

masseur (*pronounced* mas-**er**) NOUN someone who performs massage

masseuse (*pronounced* mas-**erz**) NOUN a female masseur

massif (*pronounced* mas-**eef**) NOUN, *geography* a mountainous plateau surrounded by lowland

massive ADJECTIVE bulky, heavy, huge

massively ADVERB enormously, heavily

mass media PLURAL NOUN means of communicating information to a large number of people, eg television, radio and the press

mass production NOUN production in large quantities of articles all exactly the same

mast NOUN a long upright pole holding up the sails etc in a ship, or holding an aerial, flag, etc

mastectomy (*plural* **mastectomies**) NOUN the surgical removal of a woman's breast or breasts

master NOUN **1** someone who controls or commands **2** an owner of a dog etc **3** an employer **4** a male teacher **5** the commander of a merchant ship **6** someone who is very skilled in something, an expert **7** a degree at the level above a bachelor: *Master of Arts* ▶ADJECTIVE chief, controlling: *a master switch* ▶VERB **1** to overcome, defeat **2** to become able to do or use properly: *I've finally mastered this computer program*

masterful ADJECTIVE strong-willed and expecting to be obeyed

masterkey NOUN a key which is so made that it opens a number of different locks

masterly ADJECTIVE showing the skill of an expert or master, clever

mastermind VERB to plan, work out the details of (a scheme etc)

master of ceremonies NOUN someone who directs the form and order of events at a public occasion; a compère

masterpiece NOUN the best example of someone's work, especially a very fine picture, book, piece of music, etc

mastery NOUN **1** victory (over) **2** control (of) **3** great skill (in)

masticate VERB, *formal* to chew > **mastication** NOUN

mastiff NOUN a breed of large, powerful dog

masturbate VERB to rub or stroke the sexual organs to a state of orgasm > **masturbation** NOUN

mat NOUN **1** a piece of material (coarse plaited plant fibre, carpet, etc) for wiping shoes on, covering the floor, etc **2** a piece of material, wood, etc put under dishes on a table to protect the surface ▶ADJECTIVE another spelling of **matt**

matador NOUN the person who kills the bull in bullfights

match[1] NOUN (*plural* **matches**) a small stick of wood etc tipped with a substance which catches fire when rubbed against an abrasive surface

match[2] NOUN (*plural* **matches**) **1** a person or thing similar to or the same as another **2** a person or thing agreeing with or suiting another **3** an equal **4** someone suitable for marriage **5** a contest or game ▶VERB **1** to be of the same make, size, colour, etc **2** to set (two things, teams, etc) against each other **3** to hold your own with, be equal to

matchbox NOUN (*plural* **matchboxes**) a box for holding matches

matchless ADJECTIVE having no equal

matchmaker NOUN someone who tries to arrange marriages or partnerships

matchstick NOUN a single match

mate NOUN **1** a friend, a companion **2** an assistant worker: *a plumber's mate* **3** a husband or wife **4** the sexual partner of an animal, bird, etc **5** a merchant ship's officer, next in rank to the captain ▶VERB **1** to marry **2** to bring or come together to breed

material ADJECTIVE **1** made of matter, able to be seen and felt **2** not spiritual, concerned with physical

A B C D E F G H I J K L M N O P Q R S T U V W X Y Z

comfort, money, etc: *a material outlook on life* **3** important, essential: *no material difference* ▸NOUN **1** something out of which anything is, or may be, made **2** cloth, fabric

materialism NOUN **1** a tendency to attach too much importance to material things (eg physical comfort, money) **2** the belief that only things we can see or feel really exist or are important > **materialist** NOUN > **materialistic** ADJECTIVE

materialize *or* **materialise** VERB **1** to appear in bodily form **2** to happen, come about

materially ADVERB **1** to a large extent, greatly **2** relating to objects, possessions or physical comfort, rather than to emotional or spiritual wellbeing

maternal ADJECTIVE **1** of a mother **2** like a mother, motherly **3** related through your mother: *her maternal grandmother* > **maternally** ADVERB

maternity NOUN the state of being a mother, motherhood ▸ADJECTIVE of or for a woman having or about to have a baby: *maternity clothes*

math NOUN, *US informal* mathematics

mathematical ADJECTIVE **1** of or done by mathematics **2** very exact

mathematician NOUN an expert in mathematics

mathematics SINGULAR NOUN the study of measurements, numbers and quantities

maths SINGULAR NOUN, *informal* mathematics

matinée (*pronounced* **mat**-in-ei) NOUN an afternoon performance in a theatre or cinema

matriarch (*pronounced* **meit**-ri-ahrk) NOUN a woman who controls a family or community

matriarchal (*pronounced* meit-ri-**ahrk**-*a*l) ADJECTIVE of a family, community or social system: controlled by women

matrices *plural* of **matrix**

matriculate VERB to admit, or be admitted, to a university > **matriculation** NOUN

matrimonial ADJECTIVE relating to marriage

matrimony NOUN, *formal* marriage

matrix (*pronounced* **mei**-triks) NOUN (*plural* **matrices** – *pronounced* **mei**-tri-seez– *or* **matrixes**) **1** *maths* a rectangular table of data in rows and columns, used to show relationships between quantities etc **2** a mould in which metals etc are shaped **3** a mass of rock in which gems etc are found

matron (*pronounced* **meit**-ron) NOUN **1** a married woman **2** a senior nurse in charge of a hospital **3** *old* a woman in charge of housekeeping or nursing in a school, hostel, etc

matronly (*pronounced* **meit**-ron-li) ADJECTIVE **1** of a woman: dignified, staid **2** rather plump

matt *or* **mat** ADJECTIVE having a dull surface; not shiny or glossy

matted ADJECTIVE thickly tangled

matter NOUN **1** anything that takes up space, can be seen, felt, etc; material, substance **2** a subject written or spoken about

3 (**matters**) affairs, business **4** trouble, difficulty: *What is the matter?* **5** importance: *of no great matter* **6** *medicine* pus ▸VERB **1** to be of importance: *It doesn't matter* **2** *medicine* to give out pus **a matter of course** something that is to be expected **a matter of opinion** a subject on which different opinions are held **as a matter of fact** in fact

matter-of-fact ADJECTIVE keeping to the actual facts; unimaginative, uninteresting

matting NOUN material from which mats are made

mattress NOUN (*plural* **mattresses**) a thick layer of padding covered in cloth, usually as part of a bed

mature ADJECTIVE **1** fully grown or developed **2** ripe, ready for use ▸VERB **1** to (cause to) become mature **2** of an insurance policy etc: to be due to be paid out > **maturely** ADVERB

maturity NOUN ripeness

maudlin ADJECTIVE silly, sentimental

ⓘ From Mary *Magdalene* in the New Testament of the Bible, who was frequently depicted crying in paintings

maul VERB to hurt badly by rough or savage treatment: *mauled by a lion*

Maundy Thursday NOUN the day before Good Friday in the Christian calendar

mausoleum NOUN a large or elaborate tomb

mauve NOUN a light bluish-purple colour ▸ADJECTIVE of this colour

maverick NOUN someone who refuses to conform; a determined individualist

ⓘ After Samuel *Maverick*, a Texas rancher who never branded his cattle

mawkish ADJECTIVE weak and sentimental

maxi- PREFIX very large or long: *maxi-skirt*

maxim NOUN a general truth or rule about behaviour etc

maximum ADJECTIVE greatest, most ▸NOUN (*plural* **maximums** *or* **maxima**) **1** the greatest number or quantity **2** the highest point or degree

May NOUN the fifth month of the year

ⓘ After *Maia*, the Roman earth goddess

may VERB (**may, might**) **1** used with another verb to express permission or possibility: *You may watch the film/I thought I might find him there* **2** used to express a wish: *May your wishes come true*

maybe ADVERB perhaps

Mayday NOUN the first day of May

mayday NOUN an international distress signal

mayfly NOUN (*plural* **mayflies**) a short-lived insect that appears in May

mayhem NOUN widespread chaos or confusion

mayonnaise (*pronounced* mei-o-**neiz**) NOUN a sauce made of eggs, oil and vinegar or lemon juice

mayor NOUN the chief elected public official of a city or town

A B C D E F G H I J K L M N O P Q R S T U V W X Y Z

ⓘ Note: *mayor* is used for a woman mayor, never *mayoress*.

maypole NOUN a decorated pole traditionally danced around on Mayday

maze NOUN **1** a series of winding paths in a park etc, planned to make exit difficult **2** something complicated and confusing: *a maze of regulations*

MB *or* **Mb** ABBREVIATION, *computing* megabyte(s)

MBE ABBREVIATION Member of the Order of the British Empire, a special honour in the UK, given for achievement

MC ABBREVIATION **1** master of ceremonies **2** Military Cross, an honour given to officers in the British Army who have shown exceptional bravery

MD ABBREVIATION **1** Doctor of Medicine (from Latin *Medicinae Doctor*) **2** Managing Director

ME ABBREVIATION myalgic encephalomyelitis, a condition of chronic fatigue and muscle pain following a viral infection

me PRONOUN the word used by a speaker or writer in mentioning themselves: *she kissed me/give it to me*

ⓘ **Me** should always be used after a preposition, not **I**: ✓*between you and me* ✓*between John and me*

mead NOUN an alcoholic drink made with honey

meadow NOUN a field of grass

meadowsweet NOUN a wild flower with sweet-smelling, cream-coloured flowers

meagre *or US* **meager** ADJECTIVE **1** thin **2** poor in quality **3** scanty, not enough

meal¹ NOUN the food eaten at one time, eg breakfast or dinner

meal² NOUN grain ground to a coarse powder

mean¹ ADJECTIVE **1** not generous with money etc **2** unkind, selfish **3** lowly, humble > **meanness** NOUN

mean² NOUN, *maths* average

mean³ VERB (**meaning, meant**) **1** to intend to express; indicate: *What do you mean?/When I say no, I mean no* **2** to intend: *How do you mean to do that?* **mean well** to have good intentions

meander (*pronounced* mee-**and**-er) VERB **1** of a river: to flow in a winding course **2** to wander about slowly and aimlessly

ⓘ After *Maeander*, the ancient Roman name for the winding river Menderes in Turkey

meaning NOUN **1** what is intended to be expressed or conveyed **2** purpose, intention

meaningful ADJECTIVE full of significance; expressive

meaningless ADJECTIVE **1** pointless **2** having no meaning

means NOUN **1** *singular* an action or instrument by which something is brought about: *a means of transport* **2** *plural* money, property, etc: *a woman of means* **by all means** **1** certainly, of course **2** in every way possible **by no means** certainly not; not at all

meantime NOUN: **in the meantime** meanwhile

meanwhile ADVERB in the time between two things happening

measles NOUN an infectious disease causing red spots

measly ADJECTIVE (**measlier, measliest**), *informal* mean, stingy

measure NOUN **1** size or amount (found by measuring) **2** an instrument or container for measuring **3** musical time **4** (**measures**) a plan of action: *measures to prevent crime* **5** a law brought before parliament to be considered ▸ VERB **1** to find out size, quantity, etc by using some form of measure **2** to be of a certain length, amount, etc **3** to indicate the measurement of **4** to mark (off) or weigh (out) in portions **for good measure** as a bonus

measured ADJECTIVE steady, unhurried

measurement NOUN **1** the act of measuring **2** the size, amount, etc found by measuring

meat NOUN animal flesh used as food

meaty ADJECTIVE (**meatier, meatiest**) **1** full of meat; tasting of meat **2** of a book etc: full of information

Mecca NOUN **1** the birthplace of Muhammad **2** (*usually* **mecca**) a place of pilgrimage

mechanic NOUN a skilled worker with tools or machines

mechanical ADJECTIVE **1** of machinery: *mechanical engineering* **2** worked by machinery **3** of an action etc: done without thinking > **mechanically** ADVERB

mechanics NOUN **1** *singular* the study and art of constructing machinery **2** *plural* the actual details of how something works: *The mechanics of the plan are beyond me*

mechanism NOUN **1** a piece of machinery **2** the way a piece of machinery works **3** an action by which a result is produced

mechanize *or* **mechanise** VERB **1** to change (the manufacture of something, a procedure, etc) from a manual to a mechanical process **2** to supply (troops) with armoured vehicles > **mechanization** NOUN

medal NOUN a metal disc stamped with a design, inscription, etc, made to commemorate an event or given as a prize

medallion NOUN a large medal or piece of jewellery like one

medallist NOUN someone who has gained a medal

meddle VERB **1** to concern yourself with things that are not your business **2** to interfere or tamper (with) > **meddler** NOUN

meddlesome ADJECTIVE fond of meddling

media PLURAL NOUN (**the media**) television, newspapers, etc as a form of communication

mediaeval *another spelling* of **medieval**

median NOUN, *maths* **1** a straight line from an angle of a triangle to the centre of the opposite side **2** the middle value or point of a series of numbers, eg the median of 1, 5, 11 is 5 (*compare with*: **mean**[2], **mode**) ▶ADJECTIVE mid, middle

mediate VERB to act as a peacemaker (between) > **mediation** NOUN

mediator NOUN someone who tries to make peace between people who are quarrelling

medic NOUN, *informal* a medical worker or student

medical ADJECTIVE of doctors or their work ▶NOUN a health check, a physical examination

medicate VERB to give medicine to

medicated ADJECTIVE including medicine or disinfectant

medication NOUN **1** medical treatment **2** a medicine

medicinal ADJECTIVE **1** used in medicine **2** used as a medicine > **medicinally** ADVERB

medicine NOUN **1** something given to a sick person to make them better **2** the science or practice of treating or preventing illnesses

medicine man NOUN a tribal healer or shaman

medieval *or* **mediaeval** ADJECTIVE of or in the Middle Ages

mediocre ADJECTIVE not very good, ordinary > **mediocrity** NOUN

meditate VERB **1** to think deeply and in quietness **2** to contemplate religious or spiritual matters **3** to consider, think about

meditation NOUN **1** deep, quiet thought **2** contemplation on a religious or spiritual theme

Mediterranean ADJECTIVE **1** relating to the area of the Mediterranean Sea **2** *geography* of climate: with mild winters and hot, dry summers

medium NOUN (*plural* **media** *or* **mediums**) **1** a means or substance through which an effect is produced **2** (*plural* **mediums**) someone through whom spirits (of dead people) are said to speak ▶ADJECTIVE middle or average in size, quality, etc **the media** *see* **media**

medley NOUN (*plural* **medleys**) **1** a mixture **2** a piece of music put together from a number of other pieces

meek ADJECTIVE gentle, uncomplaining > **meekly** ADVERB

meet[1] VERB (**meeting, met**) **1** to come face to face (with) **2** to come together, join **3** to make the acquaintance of **4** to pay (bills etc) fully **5** to be suitable for, satisfy: *able to meet the demand* ▶NOUN a gathering for a sports event

meet[2] ADJECTIVE, *old* proper, suitable

meeting NOUN a gathering of people for a particular purpose

mega- PREFIX **1** great, huge: *megaphone* **2** a million: *megaton*
ⓘ Comes from Greek *megas* meaning 'big'

megabyte NOUN (*abbrev* **MB** or **Mb**) a measure of computer data or memory, roughly equivalent to a million bytes

megalith NOUN a huge stone erected in prehistoric times

megalomania NOUN an exaggerated idea of your own importance or abilities

megalomaniac NOUN someone suffering from megalomania

megaphone NOUN a portable cone-shaped device with microphone and amplifier to increase sound

megaton ADJECTIVE of a bomb: having an explosive force equal to a million tons of TNT

melancholy (*pronounced* **mel**-*a*n-ko-li) NOUN lowness of spirits, sadness ▶ ADJECTIVE sad, depressed > **melancholic** ADJECTIVE

melanin NOUN the dark pigment in human skin or hair

mêlée (*pronounced* **mel**-ei) NOUN a confused fight between two groups of people

mellifluous ADJECTIVE sweet-sounding

mellow ADJECTIVE **1** of fruit: ripe, juicy, sweet **2** having become pleasant or agreeable with age **3** of light, colour, etc: soft, not harsh ▶ VERB to make or become mellow

melodic ADJECTIVE of or relating to melody

melodious ADJECTIVE pleasant sounding; tuneful

melodramatic ADJECTIVE exaggerated, sensational, over-dramatic

melody NOUN (*plural* **melodies**) **1** a tune **2** pleasant music

melon NOUN a large, round fruit with soft, juicy flesh

melt VERB **1** to make or become liquid, eg by heating **2** to disappear gradually: *The crowd melted away* **3** to make or become emotionally tender: *His heart melted at the sight*

meltdown NOUN the process in which the radioactive fuel in a nuclear reactor overheats and melts through the insulation into the environment

melting point NOUN the temperature at which a solid turns to liquid

member NOUN **1** someone who belongs to a group or society **2** a limb or organ of the body

Member of Parliament NOUN someone elected to the House of Commons (*short form* **MP**)

membership NOUN **1** the group of people who are members, or the number of members, of a club etc **2** the state of being a member

membrane NOUN a thin skin or covering, especially as part of a human or animal body, plant, etc

memento NOUN (*plural* **mementos**) something by which an event is remembered

memento mori (*pronounced* mi-**men**-toh **mawr**-ai *or* **mawr**-ee) NOUN (*plural* **memento mori**) an object used as a reminder of human mortality

memo NOUN (*plural* **memos**) *short for* **memorandum**

memoirs (*pronounced* **mem**-wahrz) PLURAL NOUN a personal account of someone's life; an autobiography

memorable ADJECTIVE worthy of being remembered; famous > **memorably** ADVERB

memorandum NOUN (*plural* **memoranda**) (*short form* **memo**) **1** a note which acts as a reminder

A B C D E F G H I J K L M N O P Q R S T U V W X Y Z

2 a written statement of something under discussion **3** a brief note sent to colleagues in an office etc

memorial NOUN a monument commemorating a historical event or person ▶ADJECTIVE commemorating an event or person

memorize *or* **memorise** VERB to learn by heart

memory NOUN (*plural* **memories**) **1** the power to remember **2** the mind's store of remembered things **3** something remembered: *childhood memories* **4** *computing* a store of information **5** what is remembered about someone: *Her memory lives on* **in memory of** in remembrance of, as a memorial of

menace NOUN **1** potential harm or danger **2** someone persistently threatening or annoying ▶VERB to be a danger to; threaten

menacing ADJECTIVE looking evil or threatening

menagerie (*pronounced* me-**naj**-*e*-ri) NOUN **1** a collection of wild animals **2** a place where these are kept

mend VERB to repair; make or grow better ▶NOUN a repaired part **on the mend** getting better, recovering

mendacious ADJECTIVE not true; lying > **mendaciously** ADVERB > **mendacity** NOUN

menial (*pronounced* **meen**-i-*a*l) ADJECTIVE of work: unskilled, unchallenging

meningitis NOUN, *medicine* an illness caused by inflammation of the covering of the brain

menopause NOUN the ending of menstruation in middle age

menstrual ADJECTIVE of menstruation

menstrual cycle NOUN in some primates including humans: a repeating cycle of reproductive changes happening about once in every 28 days in humans

menstruate VERB to experience menstruation

menstruation NOUN the monthly discharge of blood from a woman's womb

mental ADJECTIVE **1** of the mind **2** done, made, happening, etc in the mind: *mental arithmetic* **3** of illness: affecting the mind > **mentally** ADVERB

mentality NOUN (*plural* **mentalities**) **1** mental power **2** type of mind; way of thinking

menthol NOUN a sharp-smelling substance obtained from peppermint oil

mention VERB **1** to speak of briefly **2** to remark (that) ▶NOUN a mentioning, a remark

mentor NOUN someone who gives advice as a tutor or supervisor

[i] After *Mentor*, who guided Telemachus in his search for his father in Homer's poem *The Odyssey*

menu NOUN (*plural* **menus**) **1** (a card with) a list of dishes to be served at a meal **2** *computing* a list of options

menu bar NOUN, *computing* a bar in a window giving a list of options

MEP ABBREVIATION Member of the European Parliament, a politician who represents a constituency in one of the member countries at the European Parliament

mercantile ADJECTIVE of buying and selling; trading

mercenary ADJECTIVE **1** working for money **2** influenced by the desire for money ▸NOUN (*plural* **mercenaries**) a soldier paid by a foreign country to fight in its army

merchandise NOUN goods to be bought and sold

merchant NOUN someone who carries on a business in the buying and selling of goods, a trader ▸ADJECTIVE of trade

merchant bank NOUN a bank providing banking services for trade and business

merchant navy NOUN ships and crews employed in trading

merciful ADJECTIVE **1** willing to forgive or be lenient **2** easing or relieving pain, trouble or difficulty

mercifully ADVERB fortunately, to one's great relief

merciless ADJECTIVE showing no mercy; cruel > **mercilessly** ADVERB

mercurial ADJECTIVE of someone's personality: changeable, unpredictable

mercury NOUN, *chemistry* (symbol **Hg**) a heavy, silvery, liquid metallic element (*also called*: **quicksilver**)

mercy NOUN (*plural* **mercies**) lenience or forgiveness towards an enemy etc; pity **at someone's mercy** in their power

mere ADJECTIVE nothing more than: *mere nonsense*

merely ADVERB only, simply

meretricious ADJECTIVE, *formal* superficially attractive, flashy

[i] Comes from Latin *meretrix* meaning 'a prostitute'

merge VERB **1** to combine or join together **2** to blend, come together gradually

merger NOUN a joining together, eg of business companies

meridian (*pronounced* me-**rid**-i-*an*) NOUN **1** an imaginary line around a sphere passing through its poles, eg the prime meridian around the earth **2** the highest point of the sun's path **3** in Chinese medicine: a main energy channel in the body

meringue (*pronounced* me-**rang**) NOUN a baked cake or shell made of sugar and egg-white

merino NOUN (*plural* **merinos**) **1** a sheep with very fine soft wool **2** its wool, or a soft fabric made from it

merit NOUN **1** positive worth or value **2** a commendable quality ▸VERB to deserve

mermaid NOUN an imaginary sea creature with a woman's upper body and a fish's tail

merry ADJECTIVE (**merrier**, **merriest**) **1** full of fun; cheerful and lively **2** slightly drunk > **merrily** ADVERB (meaning 1)

merry-go-round NOUN, *Brit* a fairground roundabout with wooden horses etc for riding on

mesh NOUN (*plural* **meshes**) **1** network, netting **2** the opening between the threads of a net ▸VERB of gears etc: to interconnect, engage

mesmeric ADJECTIVE **1** hypnotic

2 commanding complete attention, fascinating

mesmerize *or* **mesmerise** VERB 1 to hypnotize 2 to hold the attention of completely; fascinate

ℹ An earlier term than *hypnotize*, the word comes from the name of the 18th-century Austrian doctor, Franz Anton *Mesmer*, who claimed to be able to cure disease through the influence of his will on patients

mess NOUN (*plural* **messes**) 1 an untidy or disgusting sight 2 disorder, confusion 3 a group of soldiers etc who take their meals together, or the place where they eat **mess up** to make untidy, dirty or muddled **mess with** *US informal* to interfere with, fool with

message NOUN 1 a piece of news or information sent from one person to another 2 a lesson, a moral: *a children's story with a message* **get the message** *informal* to understand, get the point

messaging NOUN the sending of text or picture messages by mobile phone

messenger NOUN someone who carries a message

Messiah NOUN 1 *Christianity* Jesus Christ 2 *Judaism* the saviour expected by the Jews 3 (**messiah**) a saviour, a deliverer

messy ADJECTIVE (**messier, messiest**) 1 dirty 2 untidy, disordered > **messily** ADVERB

metabolic ADJECTIVE of metabolism

metabolism NOUN, *biology* 1 the combined chemical changes in the cells of a living organism that provide energy for living processes and activity 2 the conversion of nourishment into energy

metal NOUN any of a group of substances (eg gold, silver, iron, etc) able to conduct heat and electricity

metallic ADJECTIVE 1 relating to or made of metal 2 shining like metal: *metallic thread*

metallic bond NOUN, *chemistry* a chemical bond that holds the atoms of a metal together

metallurgy NOUN the study of metals > **metallurgic** *or* **metallurgical** ADJECTIVE > **metallurgist** NOUN

metamorphic ADJECTIVE 1 to do with metamorphosis 2 of rocks: formed when other rocks undergo a change through heat and pressure

metamorphose (*pronounced* met-*a*-**mawr**-fohz) VERB to change completely in appearance or character

metamorphosis (*pronounced* met-*a*-**mawr**-fos-is) NOUN (*plural* **metamorphoses**) 1 a complete change in appearance or character; a transformation 2 *biology* a change of physical form that occurs during the growth of some creatures, eg from a tadpole into a frog

metaphor NOUN a way of describing something by suggesting that it is, or has the qualities of, something else, eg: *The camel is the ship of the desert* See also **Language Study** panel

metaphorical ADJECTIVE using a metaphor or metaphors

metaphorically ADVERB not in real terms, but as an imaginative way of describing something

metaphysics NOUN **1** the study of being and knowledge **2** any abstruse or abstract philosophy
> **metaphysical** ADJECTIVE
> **metaphysician** NOUN

mete VERB: **mete out** to deal out (punishment etc)

meteor NOUN a small piece of matter moving rapidly through space, becoming bright as it enters the earth's atmosphere

meteoric ADJECTIVE **1** of a meteor **2** extremely rapid: *her meteoric rise to fame*

meteorite NOUN a meteor which falls to the earth as a piece of rock

meteorologist NOUN someone who studies or forecasts the weather

meteorology NOUN the study of weather and climate
> **meteorological** ADJECTIVE

-meter SUFFIX forms words for measuring devices: *speedometer/ barometer*

ⓘ Comes from Greek *metron* meaning 'measure'

meter[1] NOUN an instrument for measuring the amount of gas, electricity, etc used ▶ VERB to measure with a meter

meter[2] *US spelling of* **metre**

meth NOUN, *slang* the drug methadone

methadone NOUN a synthetic drug similar to morphine, used as a painkiller and as a heroin substitute when treating addiction

methane NOUN a colourless gas produced by rotting vegetable matter

methanol NOUN a colourless, flammable, toxic liquid used as a solvent and antifreeze (*also called*: **wood spirit**)

method NOUN **1** a planned or regular way of doing something **2** orderly arrangement

methodical ADJECTIVE orderly, done or acting according to some plan

meths SINGULAR NOUN, *informal* methylated spirits

methylated spirits NOUN an alcohol with added violet dye, used as a solvent or fuel

meticulous ADJECTIVE careful and accurate about small details
> **meticulously** ADVERB

métier (*pronounced* **mei**-ti-ei) NOUN, *formal* occupation, profession

metre *or US* **meter** NOUN the arrangement of syllables in poetry, or of musical notes, in a regular rhythm

ⓘ Comes from Greek *metron* meaning 'measure'

> ⓘ This is one of a large number of words which is spelled with an **-re** ending in British English, but with an **-er** in American English, eg *centre/center*, *calibre/caliber*, *lustre/luster*.

metric ADJECTIVE **1** of the metric system **2** metrical

metrical ADJECTIVE **1** of poetry: of or in metre **2** arranged in the form of verse

metrication NOUN the change-over of a country's units of measurements to the metric system

metric system NOUN the system of weights and measures based on tens, eg 1 metre = 10 decimetres = 100 centimetres etc (*compare with*: **avoirdupois**)

metronome NOUN, *music* an instrument that keeps a regular beat, used for music practice

metropolis NOUN (*plural* **metropolises**) a large city, usually the capital city of a country

> **metropolitan** ADJECTIVE

mezzanine NOUN **1** a low storey between two main storeys **2** *US* a balcony in a theatre

mg ABBREVIATION milligram(s)

MI5 NOUN, *informal* a British government agency which works to prevent other countries from getting information about the UK

MI6 NOUN, *informal* a British espionage and intelligence agency which sends people to other countries to get secret political and military information about them

miaow NOUN the sound made by a cat ▸VERB to make the sound of a cat

miasma (*pronounced* mai-**az**-ma) NOUN an unhealthy or depressing atmosphere

mica NOUN a mineral which glitters and divides easily into thin transparent layers

mice *plural* of **mouse**

mickey NOUN: **take the mickey** *informal* to tease, make fun of someone

micro NOUN, *informal* (*plural* **micros**) **1** a microwave oven **2** a microcomputer

micro- PREFIX **1** very small: *microchip/microphone* (= an instrument which picks up and can amplify small sounds) **2** using a microscope: *microsurgery*

ⓘ Comes from Greek *mikros* meaning 'small'

microbe NOUN a tiny living organism

microbiology NOUN the study of micro-organisms

microchip NOUN a tiny piece of silicon designed to act as a complex electronic circuit

microclimate NOUN the climate of a small place within a larger area

microcomputer NOUN a small desktop computer containing a microprocessor

microcosm NOUN a version on a small scale: *a microcosm of society*

microfiche (*pronounced* **maik**-roh-feesh) NOUN a sheet of microfilm suitable for filing

microfilm NOUN narrow photographic film on which books, newspapers, etc are recorded in miniaturized form ▸VERB to record on microfilm

micro-organism NOUN an organism that can only be seen through a microscope

microphone NOUN an instrument which picks up sound waves for broadcasting, recording or amplifying

microprocessor NOUN a computer processor consisting of one or more microchips

microscope NOUN a scientific instrument which magnifies very small objects placed under its lens

microscopic ADJECTIVE tiny, minuscule

microsecond NOUN a millionth of a second

microsurgeon NOUN a surgeon who performs microsurgery

microsurgery NOUN delicate surgery carried out under a microscope

microwave NOUN **1** a microwave oven **2** a very short radio wave **3** a short electromagnetic wave used for cooking food and transmitting data

microwave oven NOUN an oven which cooks food by passing microwaves through it

mid- PREFIX placed or occurring in the middle: *mid-morning*

ⓘ Comes from Old English *midd*

midday NOUN noon

midden NOUN a rubbish or dung heap

middle NOUN the point or part of anything equally distant from its ends or edges; the centre ▶ADJECTIVE **1** occurring in the middle or centre **2** coming between extreme positions etc: *trying to find a middle way* **in the middle of** in the midst of doing, busy doing

middle-aged ADJECTIVE between youth and old age

Middle Ages NOUN (**the Middle Ages**) the time roughly between AD500 and AD1500

middle class NOUN the class of people between the working and upper classes, usually thought of as being made up of educated people with professional or business careers

middle-of-the-road ADJECTIVE bland, unadventurous

middle school NOUN a school for children from 8 or 9 to 12 or 13 years old

middling ADJECTIVE **1** of middle size or quality **2** neither good nor bad; mediocre

midge NOUN a small biting insect

midget NOUN an abnormally small person or thing ▶ADJECTIVE very small

midland NOUN the central, inland part of a country

midnight NOUN twelve o'clock at night ▶ADJECTIVE occurring at midnight

midriff NOUN the middle of the body, just below the ribs

midst NOUN the middle **in our midst** among us

midsummer NOUN the time around 21 June, which is the summer solstice and the longest day in the year

midway ADVERB halfway

midwife NOUN (*plural* **midwives**) a nurse trained to assist women during childbirth

> ⓘ Meaning literally 'with woman'

midwifery (*pronounced* **mid**-wif-*e*-ri *or* mid-**waif**-ri) NOUN the practice or occupation of being a midwife

midwinter NOUN the time around

21 December, the winter solstice and shortest day in the year

might[1] NOUN power, strength

might[2] *past tense* of **may**

🛈 Comes from Old English *mihte*

mighty ADJECTIVE (**mightier, mightiest**) very great or powerful ▸ADVERB, *US informal* very

> **mightiness** NOUN

migraine (*pronounced* **mee**-grein *or* **mai**-grein) NOUN a severe form of headache

migrant NOUN **1** someone migrating, or recently migrated, from another country **2** a bird that migrates annually

migrate VERB **1** to change your home or move to another area or country **2** of birds: to fly to a warmer region for the winter

> **migration** NOUN

migratory ADJECTIVE **1** migrating **2** wandering

mike NOUN, *informal* a microphone

mild ADJECTIVE **1** not harsh or severe; gentle **2** of flavour: not sharp or bitter **3** of weather: not cold **4** of an illness: not serious

≠ (meaning 4) acute

mildew NOUN whitish patches on plants, fabric, etc caused by fungus

mildly ADVERB **1** in a mild or calm manner **2** slightly **to put it mildly** expressing oneself much less strongly than one could, in a particular situation: *She was quite annoyed, to put it mildly*

mile NOUN a measure of length (1.61 kilometres or 1760 yards)

mileage NOUN **1** distance in miles **2** travel expenses (counted by the mile) **3** the amount of use or benefit you can get out of something: *He got a lot of mileage out of that story*

mileometer *or* **milometer** NOUN an instrument in a motor vehicle for recording the number of miles travelled

milestone NOUN **1** a stone beside the road showing the number of miles to a certain place **2** something which marks an important event

milieu (*pronounced* meel-**yer**) NOUN (*plural* **milieux** – *pronounced* meel-**yer** *or* meel-**yerz** – *or* **milieus**) surroundings

militant ADJECTIVE **1** fighting, warlike **2** aggressive, favouring or taking part in forceful action ▸NOUN someone who is militant

military ADJECTIVE of soldiers or warfare ▸NOUN (**the military**) the army

militia NOUN a group of fighters, not regular soldiers, trained for emergencies

milk NOUN **1** a white liquid produced by female mammals as food for their young **2** this liquid, especially from cows, used as a drink ▸VERB **1** to draw milk from **2** to obtain (money, information, etc) from, especially dishonestly

milk float NOUN a vehicle that makes deliveries of milk to homes

milkman NOUN a man who sells or delivers milk

milkshake NOUN a drink of milk and a flavouring whipped together

milk tooth NOUN a tooth from the first set of teeth in humans and other mammals

milky ADJECTIVE (**milkier, milkiest**) **1** like milk, creamy **2** white

Milky Way NOUN (**the Milky Way**) a bright band of stars seen in the night sky

mill NOUN **1** a machine for grinding or crushing grain, coffee, etc **2** a building where grain is ground **3** a factory ▸VERB **1** to grind **2** to cut grooves round the edge of (a coin) **3** to move round aimlessly in a crowd

millennium NOUN (*plural* **millennia**) a period of a thousand years

miller NOUN someone who grinds grain

millet NOUN a type of grain used for food

milli- *or* **mill-** PREFIX thousand; a thousandth part of: *millimetre/ millennium/millipede* (= an insect with many although not actually a thousand legs)

ⓘ Comes from Latin *mille* meaning 'thousand'

milligram *or* **milligramme** NOUN (*abbrev* **mg**) a thousandth of a gram

millilitre NOUN (*abbrev* **ml**) a thousandth of a litre

millimetre NOUN (*abbrev* **mm**) a thousandth of a metre

milliner NOUN someone who makes and sells women's hats

millinery NOUN the goods sold by a milliner

million NOUN a thousand thousands (1,000,000)

millionaire *or* **millionairess** NOUN someone who owns money and property worth over a million pounds, dollars, etc

millipede NOUN a small crawling insect with a long body and many pairs of legs

millisecond NOUN (*abbrev* **ms**) a thousandth of a second

millstone NOUN **1** one of two heavy stones used to grind grain **2** something felt as a burden or hindrance

mime NOUN **1** a theatrical art using body movements and facial expressions in place of speech **2** a play performed through mime ▸VERB **1** to perform a mime **2** to express through mime

mimic VERB (**mimicking, mimicked**) to imitate, especially in a mocking way ▸NOUN someone who mimics
> **mimicry** NOUN

min ABBREVIATION minute

minaret NOUN a slender tower on a mosque

mince VERB **1** to cut or chop into small pieces **2** to walk primly with short steps ▸NOUN meat chopped finely **not mince matters** to not try to soften an unpleasant fact or statement

mincemeat NOUN a chopped-up mixture of dried fruit, suet, etc **make mincemeat of** to pulverize, destroy

mince pie NOUN a pie filled with mince or mincemeat

mincer NOUN a machine for mincing food

mind NOUN **1** consciousness, intelligence, understanding **2** intention: *I've a good mind to tell him so* ▸VERB **1** to see to, look

A B C D E F G H I J K L M N O P Q R S T U V W X Y Z

after: *mind the children* **2** to watch out for, be careful of: *Mind the step* **3** to object to: *Do you mind if I open the window?* **change your mind** to change your opinion or intention **in two minds** undecided **make up your mind** to decide **out of your mind** mad, crazy **presence of mind** ability to act calmly and sensibly **speak your mind** to speak frankly

minder NOUN **1** someone who looks after a child etc **2** an aide or bodyguard to a public figure

mindful ADJECTIVE (**mindful of**) paying attention to

mindless ADJECTIVE foolish, unthinking; pointless

mine[1] NOUN **1** an underground pit or system of tunnels from which metals, coal, etc are dug **2** a heavy charge of explosive material ▶ VERB **1** to dig or work a mine **2** to lay explosive mines in

mine[2] PRONOUN a thing or things belonging to me: *That drink is mine*

minefield NOUN an area covered with explosive mines

miner NOUN someone who works in a mine

mineral NOUN a natural substance mined from the earth, eg coal, metals, gems, etc ▶ ADJECTIVE of or containing minerals

mineralogy NOUN the study of minerals > **mineralogist** NOUN

mineral water NOUN **1** water containing small amounts of minerals **2** *informal* carbonated water

minestrone (*pronounced* min-is-**troh**-ni) NOUN a thick Italian vegetable soup containing rice or pasta

minesweeper NOUN a ship which removes explosive mines

mingle VERB to mix

mini- PREFIX smaller than average; compact: *minibus/minicab*

[i] The prefix **mini-** is an abbreviation of '**mini**ature'

miniature NOUN **1** a small-scale painting **2** a small bottle of spirits ▶ ADJECTIVE on a small scale

minibus NOUN (*plural* **minibuses**) a type of small bus

minimal ADJECTIVE very little indeed: *minimal fuss*

minimize *or* **minimise** VERB **1** to make something seem small or unimportant **2** to make as small as possible

minimum NOUN (*plural* **minimums** *or* **minima**) the smallest possible quantity ▶ ADJECTIVE the least possible

minimum wage NOUN the lowest wage per hour which can legally be paid for a particular type of work

minion NOUN a slave-like follower

miniscule *another spelling* of **minuscule**

> ⓘ The **miniscule** spelling is not yet standard.

minister NOUN **1** the head of a government department: *the minister of trade* **2** a member of the clergy **3** an agent, a representative ▶ VERB (**minister to**) to help, supply the needs of

ministerial ADJECTIVE of a minister

ministry NOUN (*plural* **ministries**)

1 a government department or its headquarters **2** the work of a member of the clergy

mink NOUN a small, weasel-like animal or its fur

minnow NOUN a type of very small river or pond fish

minor ADJECTIVE **1** of less importance, size, etc **2** small, unimportant (*contrasted with*: **major**) ▶ NOUN someone not yet legally an adult (ie in the UK, under 18)

minority NOUN (*plural* **minorities**) **1** the smaller number or part **2** the state of being a minor

Minotaur NOUN (**the Minotaur**) a mythological creature with a bull's head

minster NOUN a large church or cathedral

minstrel NOUN **1** *history* a medieval travelling musician **2** a singer, an entertainer

mint[1] NOUN a plant with strong-smelling leaves, used as flavouring

mint[2] NOUN **1** a place where coins are made **2** *informal* a large sum of money: *cost a mint* ▶ VERB to make coins **in mint condition** in perfect condition

minuet NOUN **1** a kind of slow, graceful dance, popular in the 17th and 18th centuries **2** the music for this

minus PREPOSITION **1** used to show subtraction, represented by the sign (−), eg *five minus two equals three* or *5−2=3* **2** *informal* without: *I'm minus my car today* ▶ ADJECTIVE of a quantity less than zero

minuscule (*pronounced* **min**-is-kyool) NOUN a small cursive script originally used by monks for manuscripts ▶ ADJECTIVE **1** written in minuscule **2** tiny, minute

minute[1] (*pronounced* **min**-it) NOUN **1** a sixtieth part of an hour **2** *maths* in measuring an angle, the sixtieth part of a degree **3** a very short time **4** (**minutes**) notes taken of what is said at a meeting

minute[2] (*pronounced* mai-**nyoot**) ADJECTIVE **1** very small **2** very exact

miracle NOUN **1** a wonderful act beyond normal human powers **2** a fortunate happening with no natural cause or explanation > **miraculous** ADJECTIVE > **miraculously** ADVERB

mirage (*pronounced* mi-**rahsz** *or* **mi**-rahsz) NOUN an optical illusion, usually resembling a pool of water on the horizon in deserts, caused by the refraction of light by very hot air near the ground

mire NOUN deep mud > **miry** ADJECTIVE

mirror NOUN a reflective piece of glass which shows the image of someone looking into it ▶ VERB **1** to reflect like a mirror **2** to copy exactly

mirth NOUN merriment, laughter > **mirthful** ADJECTIVE

mirthless ADJECTIVE of a laugh or smile: not showing genuine amusement

mis- PREFIX wrong(ly), bad(ly): *mispronounce/misapply*

ⓘ Comes from Old English prefix *mis-* with the same meaning

misadventure NOUN an unlucky happening

A B C D E F G H I J K L M N O P Q R S T U V W X Y Z

misanthropist NOUN someone who hates humanity > **misanthropic** ADJECTIVE > **misanthropy** NOUN

misappropriate (*pronounced* mis-*a*p-**roh**-pri-eit) VERB to put to a wrong use, eg use (someone else's money) for yourself

misbehave VERB to behave badly > **misbehaviour** NOUN

miscarriage NOUN **1** a going wrong, failure: *a miscarriage of justice* **2** the accidental loss of a foetus during pregnancy

miscarry VERB (**miscarries, miscarrying, miscarried**) **1** to go wrong or astray **2** to be unsuccessful **3** to have a miscarriage in pregnancy

miscellaneous ADJECTIVE assorted, made up of several kinds

miscellany NOUN (*plural* **miscellanies**) a mixture or collection of things, eg pieces of writing

mischief NOUN **1** naughtiness **2** *old* harm, damage

mischievous ADJECTIVE naughty, teasing; causing trouble > **mischievously** ADVERB

misconceive VERB to misunderstand

misconception NOUN a wrong idea, a misunderstanding

misconduct NOUN bad or immoral behaviour

misconstruction NOUN a wrong interpretation

misconstrue VERB to misunderstand

miscreant NOUN a wicked person

misdeed NOUN a bad deed; a crime

misdemeanour NOUN a minor offence

miser NOUN someone who hoards money and spends very little

miserable ADJECTIVE **1** very unhappy; wretched **2** having a tendency to be bad-tempered and grumpy **3** depressing

miserly ADJECTIVE stingy, mean

misery NOUN (*plural* **miseries**) **1** great unhappiness, pain, poverty, etc **2** a person who is always sad or bad-tempered

misfire VERB **1** of a gun: to fail to go off **2** of a plan: to go wrong

misfit NOUN **1** someone who cannot fit in happily in society etc **2** something that fits badly

misfortune NOUN **1** bad luck **2** an unlucky accident

misgiving NOUN fear or doubt, eg about the result of an action

misguided ADJECTIVE acting from or showing mistaken ideas or bad judgement

mishandle VERB to treat badly or roughly

mishap NOUN an unlucky accident, especially a minor one

misinform VERB to give someone incorrect or misleading information

misinterpret VERB to interpret wrongly

misjudge VERB to judge unfairly or wrongly

mislay VERB (**mislaying, mislaid**) to put (something) aside and forget where it is; lose

mislead VERB (**misleading, misled**) to give a false idea (to); deceive > **misleading** ADJECTIVE

misogyny (*pronounced* mi-so-jin-i) NOUN hatred of women > **misogynist** NOUN

misplace VERB to put in the wrong place; mislay

misprint NOUN a mistake in printing

misquote VERB to make a mistake in repeating something written or said

misrepresent VERB to give a wrong idea of (someone's words, actions, etc)

Miss NOUN (*plural* **Misses**) **1** a form of address used before the surname of an unmarried woman **2** (**miss**) a young woman or girl

miss VERB **1** to fail to hit, see, hear, understand, etc **2** to discover the loss or absence of **3** to feel the lack of: *missing old friends* ▸ NOUN (*plural* **misses**) **1** the act of missing **2** a failure to hit a target **3** a loss **miss out 1** to leave out **2** to be left out of something worthwhile or advantageous

misshapen ADJECTIVE abnormally or badly shaped

missile NOUN a weapon or other object that is thrown or fired

missing ADJECTIVE lost

mission NOUN **1** a task that someone is sent to do **2** a group of representatives sent to another country **3** a group sent to spread a religion **4** the headquarters of such groups **5** someone's chosen task or purpose: *His only mission is to make money*

missionary NOUN (*plural* **missionaries**) someone sent abroad etc to spread a religion

misspell VERB (**misspelling, misspelled** *or* **misspelt**) to spell wrongly > **misspelling** NOUN

misspent ADJECTIVE spent unwisely, wasted: *a misspent youth*

mist NOUN a cloud of moisture in the air; thin fog or drizzle **mist up** *or* **mist over** to cover or become covered with condensation > **misty** ADJECTIVE (**mistier, mistiest**)

mistake VERB (**mistaking, mistook, mistaken**) **1** to misunderstand, be wrong or make an error about **2** to take (one thing or person) for another: *He mistook the house in the dark* ▸ NOUN a wrong action or statement; an error

mistaken ADJECTIVE making an error, unwise: *a mistaken belief*

Mister *full form* of **Mr**

mistletoe NOUN a plant with white berries, used as a Christmas decoration

mistreat VERB to treat badly; abuse

mistress NOUN (*plural* **mistresses**) **1** a female teacher **2** a female owner of a dog etc **3** a woman skilled in an art **4** a woman who is the lover though not the legal wife of a man **5** *full form* of **Mrs**

mistrust NOUN a lack of trust or confidence in ▸ VERB to have no trust or confidence in

misunderstand VERB to fail to understand someone or something properly

misunderstanding NOUN **1** a mistake about a meaning **2** a slight disagreement

misuse (*pronounced* mis-

A B C D E F G H I J K L M N O P Q R S T U V W X Y Z

yoos) NOUN bad or wrong use ▸(*pronounced* mis-**yooz**) VERB **1** to use wrongly **2** to treat badly

mite NOUN **1** something very small, eg a tiny child **2** a very small spider **3** *history* a very small coin

mitigate VERB to make (punishment, anger, etc) less great or severe: *Reasonable efforts must be made to mitigate the risks to society* > **mitigation** NOUN

ⓘ Comes from Latin *mitigare* meaning 'to make mild or soft'

mitre NOUN **1** the pointed headdress worn by archbishops and bishops **2** a slanting joint between two pieces of wood

mitt *or* **mitten** NOUN a glove without separate divisions for the four fingers

mix VERB **1** to unite or blend two or more things together **2** to have social contact with other people ▸NOUN (*plural* **mixes**) a mixture, a blending **mix up** to confuse, muddle

mixed ADJECTIVE **1** jumbled together **2** confused, muddled **3** consisting of different kinds **4** for both sexes: *mixed doubles*

mixed number NOUN, *maths* a number consisting of an integer and a vulgar fraction, eg 2¾

mixed-up ADJECTIVE confused, bewildered, emotionally unstable

mixer NOUN **1** a machine that mixes food **2** someone who mixes socially **3** a soft drink added to alcohol

mixture NOUN **1** a number of things mixed together **2** a medicine

ml ABBREVIATION millilitre(s)

mm ABBREVIATION millimetre(s)

MMR ABBREVIATION, *medicine* measles, mumps and rubella, a vaccine given to protect children against these diseases

mnemonic (*pronounced* ni-**mon**-ik) NOUN a rhyme etc which helps you to remember something

moan NOUN a low sound of grief or pain ▸VERB to make this sound

moat NOUN a deep trench round a castle etc, often filled with water

mob NOUN a noisy crowd ▸VERB (**mobbing, mobbed**) to crowd round, or attack, in disorder: *mobbed by fans*

mobbed ADJECTIVE, *informal* very busy, crowded

mobile ADJECTIVE **1** able to move or be moved easily **2** not fixed, changing quickly ▸NOUN **1** a decoration or toy hung so that it moves slightly in the air **2** *informal* a mobile phone

mobile phone NOUN a small portable telephone, powered by a battery, that operates by means of a cellular radio system

mobility NOUN freedom or ease of movement, either in physical or career terms

mobilize *or* **mobilise** VERB to gather (troops etc) together ready for active service > **mobilization** NOUN

moccasin NOUN a soft leather shoe of the type originally worn by Native Americans

mocha (*pronounced* **mok**-*a or* **mohk**-*a*) NOUN **1** a fine coffee **2** coffee and chocolate mixed together **3** a deep brown colour

mock VERB to laugh at, make fun of ▸ADJECTIVE false, pretended, imitation: *mock battle*

mockery NOUN **1** the act of mocking **2** a ridiculous imitation

MOD ABBREVIATION Ministry of Defence

modal verb NOUN, *grammar* a verb which modifies the sense of a main verb', eg *can*, *may*, *must*, etc

mode NOUN **1** a manner of doing or acting **2** kind, sort; fashion **3** *maths* the most frequent value in a set of numbers (*compare with*: **mean**^{2}, **median**)

model NOUN **1** a design or pattern to be copied **2** a small-scale copy of something: *a model railway* **3** a living person who poses for an artist **4** someone employed to wear and display new clothes ▸ADJECTIVE **1** acting as a model **2** fit to be copied, perfect: *model behaviour* ▸VERB (**modelling, modelled**) **1** to make a model of **2** to plan, build or create something according to a particular pattern **3** to wear and display (clothes)

modem NOUN, *computing* a device that allows data to be transferred from one computer to another via telephone lines

moderate VERB (*pronounced* **mod**-*e*-reit) to make or become less great or severe ▸ADJECTIVE (*pronounced* **mod**-*e*-r*a*t) **1** keeping within reason, not going to extremes **2** of medium or average quality, ability, etc

moderately ADVERB slightly, quite, fairly

moderation NOUN **1** a lessening or calming down **2** the practice of not going to extremes

modern ADJECTIVE belonging to the present or to recent times; not old > **modernity** NOUN

modernize *or* **modernise** VERB to bring up to date > **modernization** NOUN

modest ADJECTIVE **1** not exaggerating achievements; not boastful **2** not very large: *modest salary* **3** behaving decently; not shocking > **modesty** NOUN

modicum NOUN (*plural* **modicums**) a small amount

modify VERB (**modifies, modifying, modified**) **1** to make a slight change in: *modified my design* **2** to make less extreme: *modified his demands* > **modification** NOUN

modular ADJECTIVE of or composed of modules

modulate VERB **1** to vary or soften in tone or pitch **2** *music* to change key > **modulation** NOUN

module NOUN **1** a set course forming a unit in an educational scheme **2** a separate, self-contained section of a spacecraft

mogul NOUN a powerful or influential person, especially in a business or industry

mohair NOUN **1** the long silky hair of an Angora goat **2** fabric made from this

moist ADJECTIVE damp, very slightly wet

moisten VERB to make slightly wet or damp

moisture NOUN slight wetness; water or other liquid in tiny drops in the atmosphere or on a surface

moisturizer *or* **moisturiser** NOUN a cosmetic cream that restores moisture to the skin

molar NOUN a back tooth used for grinding food

molasses SINGULAR NOUN a thick dark syrup left when sugar is refined

mole[1] NOUN **1** a small burrowing animal, with tiny eyes and soft fur **2** a spy who successfully infiltrates a rival organization

mole[2] NOUN a small dark spot on the skin, often raised

molecular ADJECTIVE to do with a molecule or molecules: *molecular formula/molecular weight*

molecule NOUN a group of two or more atoms linked together

molehill NOUN a small heap of earth created by a burrowing mole

molest VERB **1** to annoy or torment **2** to injure or abuse sexually

mollify VERB (**mollifies, mollifying, mollified**) to calm down; lessen the anger of

mollusc NOUN any of a group of boneless animals, usually with hard shells, eg shellfish and snails

mollycoddle VERB to pamper, overprotect

molten ADJECTIVE of metal etc: melted

moment NOUN **1** a very short space of time; an instant **2** importance, consequence

momentary ADJECTIVE lasting for a moment > **momentarily** ADVERB

momentous ADJECTIVE of great importance: *a momentous discovery*

momentum NOUN (*plural* **momenta**) the force that an object gains as it moves

mon- *see* **mono-**

monarch NOUN a king, queen, emperor or empress

monarchist NOUN someone who believes in government by a monarch

monarchy NOUN (*plural* **monarchies**) **1** government by a monarch **2** an area governed by a monarch **3** the royal family

monastery NOUN (*plural* **monasteries**) a building housing a group of monks

Monday NOUN the second day of the week

ⓘ From an Old English word meaning 'day of the moon'

monetarism (*pronounced* **mun**-it-*ar*-izm) NOUN an economic policy based on control of a country's money supply

monetary (*pronounced* **mun**-i-*tar*-i) ADJECTIVE of money or coinage

money NOUN **1** coins and banknotes used for payment **2** wealth

ⓘ The Roman goddess Juno was known in ancient times as Juno *Moneta*, and it was in her temple in Rome that money was coined. This resulted in the word *moneta* being used first to mean 'a mint', and then the money which was made there

mongoose NOUN (*plural* **mongooses**) a small weasel-like animal which kills snakes

mongrel NOUN an animal of mixed breed

monitor NOUN **1** an instrument used to check the operation of a system or apparatus **2** a screen in a television studio showing the picture being transmitted **3** a computer screen **4** a school pupil given certain responsibilities ▸VERB **1** to keep a check on **2** to listen to and report on foreign broadcasts etc

monk NOUN a member of a male religious group living secluded in a monastery

monkey NOUN (*plural* **monkeys**) **1** a long-tailed primate mammal **2** a mischievous child **monkey about** to fool about

monkey nut NOUN a peanut

monkey puzzle NOUN a pine tree with prickly spines along its branches

monkey wrench NOUN an adjustable spanner

monkfish NOUN (*plural* **monkfish** *or* **monkfishes**) a type of sea fish used as food

mono- *or* **mon-** PREFIX one, single: *monarch* (= a person who is the sole ruler of a country)/*carbon monoxide* (= a gas with only one oxygen atom in its molecule)

[i] Comes from Greek *monos* meaning 'single' or 'alone'

monochrome ADJECTIVE **1** in one colour **2** black and white

monocle NOUN a single eyeglass

monogamy NOUN having only one spouse or mate at a time
> **monogamous** ADJECTIVE

monogram NOUN two or more letters, usually initials, made into a single design

monolith NOUN **1** an upright block of stone **2** something unmovable or intractable

monologue NOUN a long speech by one person

monopolize *or* **monopolise** VERB **1** to have exclusive rights to provide a particular service or product **2** to dominate, while excluding all others: *monopolizing the conversation*

monopoly NOUN (*plural* **monopolies**) **1** an exclusive right to make or sell something **2** complete unshared possession, control, etc

monorail NOUN a railway on which the trains run along a single rail

monotone NOUN a single, unchanging tone

monotonous ADJECTIVE **1** in a single tone **2** unchanging, dull
> **monotonously** ADVERB

monotony NOUN lack of variety

monsoon NOUN a wind that blows around the area of the Indian Ocean and S Asia, from the north-east in winter (the **dry monsoon**) and from the south-west in summer (the **wet monsoon**)

monster NOUN **1** something of unusual size or appearance **2** a huge terrifying creature **3** an evil person ▸ADJECTIVE huge

monstrosity NOUN (*plural* **monstrosities**) **1** something unnatural **2** something very ugly

monstrous ADJECTIVE huge, horrible

montage (*pronounced* **mon-tahsz**) NOUN **1** a composite picture

2 a film made up of parts of other films

month NOUN a twelfth part of a year, approximately four weeks

monthly ADJECTIVE & ADVERB happening once a month ▶ NOUN (*plural* **monthlies**) a magazine etc published once a month

monument NOUN a building, pillar, tomb, etc built in memory of someone or an event

monumental ADJECTIVE **1** of or relating to a monument **2** huge, enormous > **monumentally** ADVERB (meaning 2)

moo NOUN the sound made by a cow

mood NOUN the state of a person's feelings or temper

moody ADJECTIVE (**moodier, moodiest**) **1** often changing in mood **2** ill-tempered, cross > **moodily** ADVERB (meaning 2)

moon NOUN the heavenly body which travels round the earth once each month and reflects light from the sun ▶ VERB **1** to wander (about) or spend time idly **2** to gaze dreamily (at)

moonbeam NOUN a beam of light from the moon

moonlight NOUN the light of the moon ▶ VERB to work secretly at a second job, usually avoiding paying tax on the money earned

moonshine NOUN **1** the shining of the moon **2** rubbish; foolish ideas or talk **3** alcoholic spirits which have been illegally distilled or smuggled

moor[1] NOUN a large stretch of open ground, often covered with heather

moor[2] VERB to tie up or anchor (a ship etc)

moorhen NOUN a kind of water bird

moorings PLURAL NOUN **1** the place where a ship is moored **2** the anchor, rope, etc holding a moored ship

moorland NOUN a stretch of moor

moose NOUN (*plural* **moose**) a large deer-like animal, found in N America

moot point NOUN a debatable point; a question with no obvious solution

mop NOUN **1** a pad of sponge or a bunch of short pieces of coarse yarn, fabric, etc on a handle for washing or cleaning **2** a thick head of hair ▶ VERB (**mopping, mopped**) **1** to clean with a mop **2** to clean or wipe: *mopped his brow* **mop up** to clean up

mope VERB to be unhappy and gloomy

moped (*pronounced* **moh**-ped) NOUN a pedal bicycle with a motor

moraine NOUN, *geography* a ridge of rocks and gravel left by a glacier

moral ADJECTIVE **1** relating to the principles of right and wrong **2** considered by society to be good or proper: *moral behaviour* ▶ NOUN **1** the lesson of a story **2** (**morals**) principles and standards of (especially sexual) behaviour

morale (*pronounced* mo-**rahl**) NOUN spirit and confidence

morality NOUN a system of moral standards based on principles of right and wrong

moralize *or* **moralise** VERB **1** to write or speak, often critically, about moral standards **2** to draw a lesson from a story or event

moral support NOUN encouragement without active help

moral victory NOUN a failure that can really be seen as a success

moratorium NOUN (*plural* **moratoriums** *or* **moratoria**) an official suspension or temporary ban

morbid ADJECTIVE **1** too concerned with gloomy, unpleasant things, especially death **2** diseased, unhealthy > **morbidity** NOUN > **morbidly** ADVERB

more ADJECTIVE a greater number or amount of: *more money* ▶ ADVERB to a greater extent: *more beautiful/ more than I can say* ▶ NOUN **1** a greater proportion or amount **2** a further or additional number: *There are more where this came from*

moreish ADJECTIVE of food etc: enjoyable, making you want more

moreover ADVERB besides

morgue (*pronounced* mawrg) NOUN a place where dead bodies are laid, awaiting identification etc

MORI ABBREVIATION Market and Opinion Research Institute, a British organization that carries out and publishes opinion polls

moribund ADJECTIVE **1** dying **2** stagnant

morn NOUN, *poetic* morning

morning NOUN the part of the day before noon ▶ ADJECTIVE of or in the morning

morning star NOUN Venus when it rises before the sun

moron NOUN *informal* an idiot > **moronic** ADJECTIVE

morose ADJECTIVE bad-tempered, gloomy > **morosely** ADVERB > **morosity** NOUN

morphine NOUN a drug which causes sleep or deadens pain

morphology NOUN *linguistics* the study of forms and structures of words

morse NOUN a signalling code in which each letter is represented by a particular set of dots and dashes (*also called*: **morse code**)

morsel NOUN a small piece, eg of food

mortal ADJECTIVE **1** liable to die **2** causing death; deadly: *mortal injury* ▶ NOUN a human being

mortality NOUN (*plural* **mortalities**) **1** the state of being mortal **2** death **3** frequency of death; death-rate: *infant mortality*

mortally ADVERB **1** fatally: *mortally wounded* **2** very much, dreadfully: *mortally offended*

mortar NOUN **1** a heavy bowl for crushing and grinding substances with a pestle **2** a short gun for throwing shells **3** a mixture of lime, sand and water, used for fixing stones etc

mortarboard NOUN a university or college cap with a square flat top

mortgage (*pronounced* **mawr-gij**) NOUN a sum of money lent through a legal agreement for buying buildings, land, etc ▶ VERB to offer (buildings etc) as security for money borrowed

A B C D E F G H I J K L M N O P Q R S T U V W X Y Z

mortice *another spelling of* **mortise**

mortician NOUN, *US* an undertaker

mortify VERB (**mortifies, mortifying, mortified**) to make someone feel ashamed or humble: *I was mortified by her behaviour* > **mortification** NOUN > **mortifying** ADJECTIVE

mortise lock *or* **mortice lock** NOUN a lock whose mechanism is sunk into the edge of a door

mortuary NOUN (*plural* **mortuaries**) a place where dead bodies are kept before burial or cremation

mosaic NOUN a picture or design made up of many small pieces of coloured glass, stone, etc

Moses basket NOUN a soft portable cot for babies

Moslem *another spelling of* **Muslim**

mosque NOUN an Islamic place of worship

mosquito NOUN (*plural* **mosquitoes** *or* **mosquitos**) a biting or blood-sucking insect, often carrying disease

moss NOUN (*plural* **mosses**) a very small flowerless plant, found in moist places

mossy ADJECTIVE (**mossier, mossiest**) covered with moss

most ADJECTIVE the greatest number or amount of: *Most children attend school regularly* ▸ADVERB **1** very, extremely: *most grateful* **2** to the greatest extent: *the most severely injured/the most difficult* ▸NOUN the greatest number or amount: *Most of the choir are here* **at most** not more than **for the most part** mostly

mostly ADVERB mainly, chiefly

MOT NOUN a compulsory annual check on behalf of the *M*inistry *o*f *T*ransport on vehicles over three years old

motel NOUN a hotel built to accommodate motorists

moth NOUN **1** a flying insect that resembles a butterfly, seen mostly at night **2** the cloth-eating grub of the clothes-moth

mothball NOUN a small ball of chemical used to protect clothes from moths ▸VERB (*also* **put in mothballs**) to put aside for later use etc

moth-eaten ADJECTIVE **1** full of holes made by moths **2** tatty, shabby

mother NOUN **1** a female parent **2** (*also called*: **mother superior**) the female head of a convent ▸VERB **1** to be the mother of **2** to care for like a mother

motherboard NOUN, *computing* a printed circuit board into which other boards can be slotted

motherhood NOUN the state of being a mother

mother-in-law NOUN (*plural* **mothers-in-law**) the mother of your husband or wife

motherland NOUN the country of your birth

motherly ADJECTIVE of or like a mother

mother-of-pearl NOUN a hard, shiny substance which forms a layer on the inside of certain shells, eg oysters (*also called*: **nacre**)

mother tongue NOUN a native language

motif (*pronounced* moh-**teef**) NOUN a distinctive feature or idea in a piece of music, a play, etc

Do not confuse with: **motive**

motion NOUN **1** the act or state of moving **2** a single movement **3** a suggestion put before a meeting for discussion ▸VERB **1** to make a signal by a movement or gesture **2** to direct (someone) in this way: *The policeman motioned us forward*

motionless ADJECTIVE not moving

motivate VERB to cause (someone) to act in a certain way > **motivation** NOUN a motivating force

motive NOUN the cause of someone's actions; a reason

Do not confuse with: **motif**

motley ADJECTIVE made up of different colours or kinds

motocross NOUN the sport of motorcycle racing across rough terrain

motor NOUN **1** an engine which causes motion **2** a car ▸VERB to travel by motor vehicle

motorcade NOUN a procession of cars carrying a head of state etc

motorcycle *or* **motorbike** NOUN a bicycle with a petrol-driven engine > **motorcyclist** *or* **motorbiker** NOUN

motorist NOUN someone who drives a car

motorize *or* **motorise** VERB to supply with an engine

motorway NOUN a road for fast-moving traffic, with separate carriageways for vehicles travelling in opposite directions

mottled ADJECTIVE marked with spots or blotches

motto NOUN (*plural* **mottoes**) a phrase which acts as a guiding principle or rule

mould[1] *or N Am* **mold** NOUN a shape into which a liquid is poured to take on that shape when it cools or sets: *a jelly mould* ▸VERB **1** to form in a mould **2** to shape

mould[2] *or N Am* **mold** NOUN **1** a fluffy growth on stale food etc **2** soil containing rotted leaves etc

moulding NOUN a decorated border of moulded plaster round a ceiling etc

mouldy *or N Am* **moldy** ADJECTIVE (**mouldier, mouldiest**) affected by mould; stale

moult VERB of an animal: to shed its feathers, hair or skin

mound NOUN **1** a bank of earth or stones **2** a hill; a heap

mount VERB **1** to go up, ascend **2** to climb on to (a horse, bicycle, etc) **3** to fix (a picture etc) on to a backing or support **4** to fix (a gemstone) in a casing **5** to organize (an exhibition) ▸NOUN **1** a support or backing for display **2** a horse, bicycle, etc to ride on **3** in place names: a mountain: *Mount Everest*

mountain NOUN **1** a large hill **2** a large quantity

mountain bike NOUN a sturdy bike with thick, deep-tread tyres and straight handlebars, designed for riding over hilly terrain

mountaineer NOUN a mountain climber

mountainous ADJECTIVE **1** having many mountains **2** huge

mounted ADJECTIVE on horseback: *mounted police*

Mounties PLURAL NOUN, *informal* (**the Mounties**) the Canadian mounted police

mourn VERB **1** to grieve for **2** to be sorrowful > **mourner** NOUN

mournful ADJECTIVE sad

mourning NOUN **1** grief felt or shown over a death **2** the period during which someone grieves **3** dark-coloured clothes traditionally worn by mourners

mouse NOUN (*plural* **mice**) **1** a small gnawing animal, found in houses and fields **2** a shy, timid, uninteresting person **3** *computing* a device moved by hand on a flat surface, causing corresponding cursor movements on a screen

mousse (*pronounced* moos) NOUN a frothy set dish made from eggs, cream, etc, that can be either sweet or savoury: *chocolate mousse/ salmon mousse*

moustache *or US* **mustache** NOUN unshaved hair above a man's upper lip

mousy ADJECTIVE (**mousier, mousiest**) **1** of a light-brown colour **2** shy, timid, uninteresting

mouth NOUN (*pronounced* mowth) **1** the opening in the head through which an animal or person eats and makes sounds **2** the point of a river where it flows into the sea **3** an opening, an entrance ▶ VERB (*pronounced* mowdh) **1** to shape (words) without actually speaking **2** to speak pompously or insincerely

mouthful NOUN (*plural* **mouthfuls**) as much as fills the mouth

mouth organ NOUN a small wind instrument, moved across the lips

mouthpiece NOUN **1** the part of a musical instrument, tobacco-pipe, etc held in the mouth **2** someone who speaks for others

movable *or* **moveable** ADJECTIVE able to be moved, changed, etc

move VERB **1** to (cause to) change place or position **2** to change where you live, work, etc **3** to rouse or affect the feelings of **4** to rouse into action **5** *formal* to propose, suggest ▶ NOUN **1** an act of moving **2** an act of changing homes or premises **3** a step, an action **4** a shifting of a piece in a game of chess etc

movement NOUN **1** the act or manner of moving **2** a change of position **3** *music* a division of a piece of music **4** a group of people united in a common aim: *the peace movement* **5** an organized attempt to achieve an aim: *the movement to reform the divorce laws*

movie NOUN a cinema film **the movies** the cinema

moving ADJECTIVE **1** in motion **2** having an affect on the emotions > **movingly** ADVERB (meaning 2) ≠ (meaning 1) immobile

mow VERB (**mowing, mowed, mown**) to cut (grass, hay, etc) with a scythe or machine **mow someone down** *or* **mow something down** to destroy them in great numbers

mower NOUN a machine for mowing

MP ABBREVIATION **1** Member of Parliament **2** Military Police

MP3 ABBREVIATION, *computing* MPEG-1 Layer 3, a compressed file format that allows fast downloading of audio data from the Internet

MPhil ABBREVIATION Master of Philosophy, an advanced degree in philosophy or other subjects

Mr NOUN (*short for* **Mister**) the form of address used before a man's surname

Mrs NOUN the form of address used before a married woman's surname

MS ABBREVIATION **1** multiple sclerosis, a progressive disease of the central nervous system, resulting in paralysis **2** manuscript

Ms NOUN a form of address used before the surname of a married or unmarried woman

MSc ABBREVIATION Master of Science, an advanced degree in a subject such as biology or physics

MSG ABBREVIATION monosodium glutamate

MSP ABBREVIATION Member of the Scottish Parliament

Mt ABBREVIATION Mount(ain): *Mt Etna*

much ADJECTIVE a great amount of ▶ADVERB to or by a great extent: *much loved/much faster* ▶PRONOUN **1** a great amount **2** something important: *made much of it* **much the same** nearly the same

muck NOUN dung, dirt, filth

mucus NOUN slimy fluid secreted from the nose etc

mud NOUN wet, soft earth

muddle VERB **1** to confuse, bewilder **2** to mix up **3** to make a mess of ▶NOUN **1** a mess **2** a state of confusion

muddy ADJECTIVE (**muddier, muddiest**) **1** covered with mud **2** unclear, confused ▶VERB to make or become muddy

mudguard NOUN a shield or guard over wheels to catch mud splashes

muesli NOUN a mixture of grains, nuts and fruit eaten with milk

muff[1] NOUN a tube of warm fabric to cover and keep the hands warm

muff[2] VERB to fail in an opportunity, eg to catch a ball

muffin NOUN **1** a round, flat, spongy cake, toasted and eaten hot with butter **2** a small, sweet cake made of flour or corn meal with fruit, nuts, chocolate, etc

muffle VERB **1** to wrap up for warmth etc **2** to deaden (a sound)

mug[1] NOUN **1** a large, straight-sided cup **2** *informal* someone who is easily fooled **3** *informal* the face

mug[2] VERB (**mugging, mugged**) to attack and rob (someone) in the street > **mugger** NOUN

mug[3] VERB: **mug up** *informal* to study hard; swot up

muggy ADJECTIVE (**muggier, muggiest**) of weather: warm and damp > **mugginess** NOUN

mulberry NOUN (*plural* **mulberries**) **1** a tree on whose leaves silkworms are fed **2** its purple berry

mulch NOUN (*plural* **mulches**) loose

straw etc laid down to protect plant roots ▸ VERB to cover with mulch

mule[1] NOUN an animal bred from a female horse and a male donkey

mule[2] NOUN a backless slipper

mulish ADJECTIVE stubborn

mulled ADJECTIVE of wine etc: mixed with spices and served warm

mullet NOUN a small, edible sea fish

mull over VERB to think over, ponder over

multi- PREFIX many

ⓘ Comes from Latin *multus* meaning 'many'

multi-access *see* **multi-user**

multicellular ADJECTIVE consisting of many cells: *multicellular organisms*

multicoloured ADJECTIVE having many colours

multicultural ADJECTIVE of a society, community, etc: made up of or involving several distinct racial or religious groups

multifarious ADJECTIVE of many kinds

multimedia ADJECTIVE of a computer: able to run various sound and visual applications

multimillionaire NOUN someone who has property worth several million pounds (or dollars)

multinational company NOUN a large business that has operations in several countries (*also called*: **transnational corporation**)

multiple ADJECTIVE **1** affecting many parts: *multiple injuries* **2** involving many things of the same sort: *vehicles in a multiple crash* ▸ NOUN, MATHS a number or quantity which contains another number an exact number of times

multiple sclerosis NOUN (*abbrev* **MS**) a progressive nerve disease resulting in paralysis

multiplex ADJECTIVE of a cinema: including several screens and theatres in one building

multiplication NOUN the act of multiplying > **multiplicative** ADJECTIVE

multiplicity NOUN: **a multiplicity of** a great number of

multiplier NOUN *maths* the number by which another (the **multiplicand**) is to be multiplied

multiply VERB (**multiplies, multiplying, multiplied**) **1** to increase **2** to increase a number by adding it to itself a certain number of times: *2 multiplied by 3 is 6*

multiracial ADJECTIVE consisting of or taking in many races

multitasking NOUN **1** *computing* the action of running several processes simultaneously **2** of a person: doing several things at the same time

multitude NOUN a great number; a crowd

multitudinous ADJECTIVE very many

multi-user ADJECTIVE, *computing* of a system: consisting of several terminals linked to a main computer (*also*: **multi-access**)

mum NOUN, *informal* mother

mumble VERB to speak indistinctly

mummify VERB (**mummifies, mummifying, mummified**) to make into a mummy (meaning 2)

mummy[1] NOUN (*plural* **mummies**), *informal* mother

mummy[2] NOUN (*plural* **mummies**) a dead body preserved by wrapping in bandages and treating with wax, spices, etc

mumps SINGULAR NOUN an infectious disease affecting glands at the side of the neck, causing swelling

munch VERB to chew noisily

mundane ADJECTIVE dull, ordinary

municipal ADJECTIVE of or owned by a city or town

municipality NOUN (*plural* **municipalities**) a city or town; an area covered by local government

munitions PLURAL NOUN weapons and ammunition used in war

mural ADJECTIVE of or on a wall ▶NOUN a painting or design on a wall

murder VERB to kill someone unlawfully and on purpose ▶NOUN the act of murdering

murderer NOUN someone who commits murder

murderous ADJECTIVE capable or guilty of murder; wicked

murky ADJECTIVE (**murkier, murkiest**) dark, gloomy
> **murkiness** NOUN

murmur NOUN **1** a low, indistinct, continuous sound **2** a hushed speech or tone ▶VERB **1** to make a murmur **2** to complain, grumble

muscle NOUN **1** fleshy tissue which contracts and stretches to cause body movements **2** an area of this in the body **3** physical strength or power

muscular ADJECTIVE **1** of or relating to muscles **2** strong

muscular dystrophy NOUN, *medicine* a hereditary disease in which the muscles gradually deteriorate

Muse NOUN any of the nine goddesses of poetry, music, dancing, etc in classical mythology

muse VERB to think (over) in a quiet, leisurely way

museum NOUN a building for housing and displaying objects of artistic, scientific or historic interest

mush NOUN (*plural* **mushes**) **1** something soft and pulpy **2** an overly sentimental film, song, etc

mushroom NOUN a fungus, usually umbrella-shaped, with some edible varieties ▶VERB to grow very quickly: *Buildings mushroomed all over town*

mushy ADJECTIVE (**mushier, mushiest**) **1** soft and pulpy **2** overly sentimental

music NOUN **1** the art of arranging, combining, etc certain sounds able to be produced by the voice, or by instruments **2** an arrangement of such sounds or its written form **3** a sweet or pleasant sound

musical ADJECTIVE **1** of music **2** sounding sweet or pleasant **3** having a talent for music ▶NOUN a light play or film with a lot of songs and dancing in it > **musically** ADVERB

musician NOUN **1** a specialist in music **2** someone who plays a musical instrument

musk NOUN a strong perfume, obtained from the male musk deer or artificially

musket NOUN an early rifle-like gun that was loaded through the barrel, once used by soldiers

musketeer NOUN a soldier armed with a musket

Muslim *or* **Moslem** NOUN a follower of the Islamic religion ▸ADJECTIVE Islamic

muslin NOUN a fine, soft cotton cloth

mussel NOUN an edible shellfish with two separate halves to its blue-black shell

must VERB **1** used with another verb to express necessity: *I must finish this today* **2** expressing compulsion: *You must do as you're told* **3** expressing certainty or probability: *That must be the right answer* ▸NOUN something that must be done; a necessity

[i] Comes from Old English *moste*

mustache *US spelling of* **moustache**

mustang NOUN a North American wild horse

mustard NOUN **1** a plant with sharp-tasting seeds **2** a hot yellow paste made from its seeds, used as a condiment or seasoning

muster VERB to gather up or together (eg troops, courage) **pass muster** to be accepted as satisfactory

musty ADJECTIVE (**mustier, mustiest**) smelling old and stale > **mustiness** NOUN

mutable ADJECTIVE changeable

mutate VERB **1** *biology* to undergo mutation **2** to change

mutation NOUN **1** *biology* a change in the genes or chromosomes of an organism which may result in a change in the appearance or behaviour of the organism **2** any change

mute ADJECTIVE **1** not able to speak; dumb **2** silent **3** of a letter in a word: not pronounced ▸NOUN a mute person

muted ADJECTIVE **1** of a sound: made quieter, hushed: *muted criticism* **2** of a colour: not bright

mutilate VERB **1** to inflict great physical damage on; maim **2** to damage greatly > **mutilation** NOUN

mutineer NOUN someone who takes part in a mutiny

mutinous ADJECTIVE rebellious; refusing to obey orders

mutiny VERB (**mutinies, mutinying, mutinied**) **1** to rise against those in power **2** to refuse to obey the commands of military officers ▸NOUN (*plural* **mutinies**) refusal to obey commands; rebellion

mutt NOUN, *slang* **1** a dog **2** an idiot

mutter VERB to speak in a low voice; mumble

mutton NOUN meat from a sheep, used as food

mutual ADJECTIVE **1** given by each to the other(s); reciprocal: *mutual help* **2** shared by two or more: *a mutual friend*

mutually ADVERB of a relationship between two people or things: each to the other, in both directions

Muzak NOUN, *trademark* recorded music played in shops etc

muzzle NOUN **1** an animal's nose

and mouth **2** an arrangement of straps fastened over an animal's mouth to prevent it biting **3** the open end of a gun ▶VERB **1** to put a muzzle on (a dog etc) **2** to prevent from speaking freely

muzzy ADJECTIVE (**muzzier, muzziest**) cloudy, confused

MW ABBREVIATION medium-wave

my ADJECTIVE belonging to me: *This is my book*

myna *or* **mynah** NOUN a bird which can imitate human speech

myopic ADJECTIVE short-sighted

myriad (*pronounced* **mi**-ri-*a*d) NOUN a very great number ▶ADJECTIVE very many, countless

myrrh NOUN a bitter-tasting resin used in medicines, perfumes, etc

myrtle NOUN a type of evergreen shrub

myself PRONOUN **1** used reflexively: *I can see myself in the mirror* **2** used for emphasis: *I wrote this myself*

mysterious ADJECTIVE **1** puzzling, difficult to understand **2** secret, hidden, intriguing > **mysteriously** ADVERB

mystery NOUN (*plural* **mysteries**) **1** something that cannot be or has not been explained; something puzzling **2** a deep secret

mystic NOUN someone who seeks knowledge of sacred or mystical things by going into a state of spiritual ecstasy

mystical ADJECTIVE having a secret or sacred meaning beyond ordinary human understanding

mystify VERB (**mystifies, mystifying, mystified**) **1** to puzzle greatly **2** to confuse, bewilder

mystique (*pronounced* mis-**teek**) NOUN a compelling atmosphere of mystery about someone or something

myth NOUN **1** a story about gods, heroes, etc of ancient times; a fable **2** something imagined or untrue: *a popular myth*

mythical ADJECTIVE **1** of or relating to a myth **2** invented, imagined

mythological ADJECTIVE of myth or mythology; mythical

mythology NOUN **1** the study of myths **2** a collection of myths

A B C D E F G H I J K L M N O P Q R S T U V W X Y Z

Nn

nab VERB (**nabbing, nabbed**) *informal* **1** to snatch, seize **2** to arrest

nadir (*pronounced* **nei**-deer *or* **na**-deer) NOUN **1** the point of the heavens opposite the zenith **2** the lowest point of anything

naff ADJECTIVE, *slang* inferior, crass, tasteless

nail NOUN **1** a horny covering protecting the tips of the fingers and toes **2** a thin, pointed piece of metal for fastening wood etc ▸VERB **1** to fasten with nails **2** *informal* to catch, trap **hit the nail on the head** **1** to identify a problem exactly **2** to state something precisely

naive *or* **naïve** (*both pronounced* nai-**eev**) ADJECTIVE **1** simple in thought, manner or speech **2** inexperienced and lacking knowledge of the world > **naiveté** *or* **näïveté** (*both pronounced* nai-**eev**-i-tei) NOUN

naked ADJECTIVE **1** without clothes **2** having no covering **3** not hidden nor controlled > **nakedly** ADVERB (meaning 3)

namby-pamby ADJECTIVE childish, feeble

ⓘ Originally a nickname of the 18th-century sentimental English poet, *Ambrose* Philips

name NOUN **1** a word by which a person, place or thing is known **2** fame, reputation: *making a name for himself* **3** an offensive description: *Don't call people names* **4** authority: *I arrest you in the name of the king* ▸VERB **1** to give a name to **2** to speak of by name, mention **3** to appoint: *She was named as the new head teacher*

nameless ADJECTIVE without a name, not named

namely ADVERB that is to say

namesake NOUN someone with the same name as another person

nanny NOUN (*plural* **nannies**) a children's nurse

nanny goat NOUN a female goat

nano- PREFIX **1** a thousand millionth: *nanosecond* **2** microscopic in size: *nanoplankton*

ⓘ Comes from Greek *nanos* meaning 'a dwarf'

napalm (*pronounced* **nei**-pahm) NOUN petroleum jelly, used to make bombs

nape NOUN the back of the neck

napkin NOUN a small piece of cloth

or paper for wiping the lips at meals

nappy NOUN (*plural* **nappies**) a piece of cloth, or thick pad, put between a baby's legs to absorb urine and faeces

narcissism NOUN excessive admiration of yourself > **narcissistic** ADJECTIVE

narcissus NOUN (*plural* **narcissi** – *pronounced* nahr-**sis**-ai– *or* **narcissuses**) a plant like a daffodil with a white, star-shaped flower

narcotic NOUN, *medicine* a type of drug that brings on sleep or stops pain

narky ADJECTIVE (**narkier, narkiest**), *informal* irritable, complaining

narrate VERB to tell a story > **narration** NOUN > **narrator** NOUN

narrative NOUN a story ▶ ADJECTIVE telling a story

narrow ADJECTIVE **1** of small extent from side to side; not wide: *a narrow road* **2** with little to spare: *a narrow escape* **3** lacking wide interests or experience: *narrow views* ▶ VERB to make or become narrow

narrow-gauge ADJECTIVE of a railway: having the distance between rails less than the standard gauge of 4 feet 8 inches or 1.435 metres (*compare with*: **broad-gauge**)

narrowly ADVERB closely; barely

narrow-minded ADJECTIVE unwilling to accept or tolerate new ideas

narrows PLURAL NOUN a narrow sea passage, a strait

NASA ABBREVIATION in the USA: National Aeronautics and Space Administration

nasal ADJECTIVE **1** of the nose **2** sounded through the nose

nascent (*pronounced* **nei**-sent) ADJECTIVE beginning to develop, in an early stage > **nascency** NOUN

nasturtium NOUN a climbing plant with brightly coloured flowers

nasty ADJECTIVE (**nastier, nastiest**) **1** very disagreeable or unpleasant **2** of a problem etc: difficult to deal with **3** of an injury: serious > **nastily** ADVERB (meaning 1)

natal (*pronounced* **nei**-tal) ADJECTIVE of birth

nation NOUN **1** the people living in the same country, or under the same government **2** a race of people: *the Jewish nation*

national ADJECTIVE of, relating to or belonging to a nation or race ▶ NOUN someone belonging to a nation: *a British national* > **nationally** ADVERB

national anthem NOUN a nation's official song or hymn

national call NOUN a long-distance, but not international, telephone call

nationalism NOUN the desire to bring the people of a nation together under their own government > **nationalist** NOUN & ADJECTIVE > **nationalistic** ADJECTIVE

nationality NOUN (*plural* **nationalities**) membership of a particular nation

nationalize *or* **nationalise** VERB to place (industries etc) under

the control of the government
> **nationalization** NOUN

national park NOUN an area of countryside owned by the nation and preserved

nationwide ADJECTIVE & ADVERB over the whole of a nation

native ADJECTIVE **1** born in a person: *native intelligence* **2** of someone's birth: *my native land* ▶NOUN **1** someone born in a certain place: *a native of Scotland* **2** an inhabitant of a country from earliest times before the discovery by explorers, settlers, etc

Native American NOUN a member of one of the peoples originating in America

Nativity NOUN: (**the Nativity**) the birth of Christ

NATO ABBREVIATION North Atlantic Treaty Organization, an alliance of countries providing mutual military protection

natural ADJECTIVE **1** of nature **2** produced by nature; not artificial **3** of a quality etc: present at birth, not learned afterwards **4** unpretentious, simple **5** of a result etc: expected, normal ▶NOUN **1** someone with a natural ability **2** *music* a note which is neither a sharp nor a flat, shown by the sign (♮)

natural gas NOUN gas suitable for burning, found in the earth or under the sea

natural history NOUN the study of animals and plants

naturalist NOUN someone who studies animal and plant life

naturalize *or* **naturalise** VERB to give the rights of a citizen to (someone born in another country)

naturally ADVERB **1** by nature **2** simply **3** of course

natural number NOUN, *maths* the numbers 1, 2, 3, and so on, and sometimes including 0; a positive integer

natural resources PLURAL NOUN the natural wealth of a country in its forests, minerals, water, etc

natural selection NOUN, *biology* evolution by survival of the fittest, who pass their characteristics on to the next generation

nature NOUN **1** the things which make up the physical world, eg animals, trees, rivers, mountains, etc **2** the qualities which characterize someone or something: *a kindly nature*

-natured ADJECTIVE (added to another word) having a certain temper or personality: *good-natured*

nature reserve NOUN an area of land kept to preserve the animals and plants in it

nature trail NOUN a path through the countryside with signposts showing natural features

naturism NOUN the belief in nudity practised openly > **naturist** NOUN

naught NOUN nothing: *plans came to naught*

> Do not confuse with: **nought**

naughty ADJECTIVE (**naughtier, naughtiest**) bad, misbehaving
> **naughtily** ADVERB

nausea NOUN a feeling of sickness

A B C D E F G H I J K L M N O P Q R S T U V W X Y Z

nauseate VERB to make sick, fill with disgust > **nauseating** ADJECTIVE sickening

nauseous ADJECTIVE sickening; disgusting feeling sick

nautical ADJECTIVE of ships or sailors

ⓘ Comes from Greek *nautes* meaning 'a sailor'

nautical mile NOUN a measure of distance traditionally used at sea, approximately 1.85 kilometres (6080 feet)

nautilus NOUN (*plural* **nautiluses** *or* **nautili** – *pronounced* **naw**-ti-lai) a small sea creature related to the octopus

naval ADJECTIVE of the navy

nave NOUN the middle or main part of a church

navel NOUN the small hollow in the centre of the front of the belly

navigable ADJECTIVE able to be used by ships

navigate VERB **1** to steer or pilot a ship, aircraft, etc on its course **2** to sail on, over or through **3** to move around the different parts of a website

navigation NOUN the art of navigating > **navigational** ADJECTIVE of or used in navigation

navigator NOUN someone who steers or sails a ship etc

navvy NOUN (*plural* **navvies**) a labourer working on roads etc

navy NOUN (*plural* **navies**) **1** a nation's fighting ships **2** the men and women serving on these

navy blue NOUN & ADJECTIVE dark blue

nay ADVERB, *old* no

Nazi (*pronounced* **naht**-si) NOUN, *history* a member of the German National Socialist Workers' Party, a fascist party ruling Germany in 1933--45 under Adolf Hitler > **Nazism** NOUN

NB *or* **nb** ABBREVIATION note well

ⓘ Comes from Latin *nota bene*

NCO ABBREVIATION non-commissioned officer

NE ABBREVIATION north-east; north-eastern

Neanderthal (*pronounced* ni-**an**-der-*tal*) ADJECTIVE **1** of a primitive type of human living during the Stone Age **2** *informal* primitive or old-fashioned

neap tide NOUN a tidal pattern that occurs at the first and last quarters of the Moon, when there is least variation between high and low tides (*compare with*: **spring tide**)

near ADJECTIVE **1** not far away in place or time **2** close in relationship, friendship, etc **3** barely avoiding or almost reaching (something): *a near disaster* ▶ADVERB at or to a place or time not far away ▶PREPOSITION close to ▶VERB to approach or come close to: *The building is nearing completion*

nearby ADVERB to or at a short distance: *Do you live nearby?*

nearly ADVERB **1** almost: *nearly four o'clock* **2** closely: *nearly related*

nearside ADJECTIVE of the side of a vehicle: furthest from the centre of the road (*contrasted with*: **offside**)

near-sighted ADJECTIVE short-sighted

A B C D E F G H I J K L M N O P Q R S T U V W X Y Z

neat ADJECTIVE **1** trim, tidy **2** skilfully done **3** of an alcoholic drink: not diluted with water etc

nebula NOUN (*plural* **nebulae** – *pronounced* **neb**-yuw-lee) a shining cloud-like appearance in the night sky, produced by very distant stars or by a mass of gas and dust

nebulizer *or* **nebuliser** NOUN a device with a mouthpiece, used for administering a drug as a fine mist

nebulous ADJECTIVE hazy, vague

necessarily (*pronounced* **nes**-*e*-s*a*-ri-li *or* nes-*e*-**se**-ri-li) ADVERB for certain, definitely, inevitably

necessary ADJECTIVE not able to be done without ▸ NOUN (*plural* **necessaries**) something that cannot be done without, such as food, clothing, etc

necessitate VERB to make necessary; force > **necessity** NOUN (*plural* **necessities**) **1** something necessary **2** great need; want, poverty

neck NOUN **1** the part between the head and body **2** a narrow passage or area: *neck of a bottle/neck of land* **neck and neck** running side by side, staying exactly equal

necklace NOUN a string of beads or precious stones etc worn round the neck

necktie NOUN, *US* a man's tie

nectar NOUN **1** the sweet liquid collected from flowers by bees to make honey **2** the drink of the ancient Greek gods **3** a delicious drink

nectarine NOUN a kind of peach with a smooth skin

née (*pronounced* nei) ADJECTIVE born (in stating a woman's surname before her marriage): *Mrs Janet Brown, née Phillips*

need VERB **1** to be without, be in want of **2** to require ▸ NOUN **1** necessity, needfulness **2** difficulty, want, poverty

ⓘ Comes from Old English *ned, nied, nyd*

needful ADJECTIVE necessary

needle NOUN **1** a small, sharp piece of steel used in sewing, with a small hole (**eye**) at the top for thread **2** a long, thin piece of metal, wood, etc used eg in knitting **3** a thin tube of steel attached to a hypodermic syringe etc **4** the moving pointer in a compass **5** the long, sharp-pointed leaf of a pine, fir, etc **6** a stylus on a record-player

needless ADJECTIVE unnecessary

needy ADJECTIVE (**needier, neediest**) poor

ne'er ADJECTIVE, *formal* never

ne'er-do-well NOUN a lazy, worthless person

nefarious (*pronounced* ni-**feir**-i-*us*) ADJECTIVE very wicked; villainous, shady

neg- PREFIX forms words containing the meaning 'not': *neglect* (= not to trouble oneself about)

ⓘ Comes from Latin word-beginning *neg-* meaning 'not'

negate VERB **1** to prove the opposite **2** to refuse to accept, reject (a proposal etc)

negative ADJECTIVE **1** meaning or saying 'no', as an answer **2** of a person, attitude, etc: timid, lacking spirit or ideas **3** *maths* of a number: less than zero **4** *biology* in a direction away from a stimulus (*contrasted with*: **positive**) ▸NOUN **1** a word or statement by which something is denied **2** the photographic film from which prints are made, in which light objects appear dark and dark objects appear light

negative equity NOUN a situation where the value of a property falls below the value of the mortgage held on it

neglect VERB **1** to treat carelessly **2** to fail to give proper attention to **3** to fail to do ▸NOUN lack of care and attention

neglectful ADJECTIVE careless, having a habit of not bothering to do things

negligée NOUN a women's loose dressing-gown made of thin material

negligent ADJECTIVE careless, not paying enough attention > **negligence** NOUN > **negligently** ADVERB

🛈 Comes from Latin *negligens* meaning 'neglecting'

> Do not confuse: **negligent** and **negligible**

negligible ADJECTIVE not worth thinking about, very small: *a negligible amount*

🛈 Comes from an old spelling of French *négligeable* meaning 'able to be neglected'

negotiable ADJECTIVE able to be negotiated

negotiate VERB **1** to discuss a subject (with) in order to reach agreement **2** to arrange (a treaty, payment, etc) **3** to get past (an obstacle or difficulty) > **negotiation** NOUN > **negotiator** NOUN (meanings 1 and 2)

Negro NOUN (*plural* **Negroes**), *offensive* a Black African, or Black person of African descent

neigh VERB to cry like a horse ▸NOUN a horse's cry

neighbour *or US* **neighbor** NOUN someone who lives near another

neighbourhood NOUN **1** a district: *a poor neighbourhood* **2** the surrounding district or area: *in the neighbourhood of Paris* **in the neighbourhood of** approximately, nearly

neighbouring ADJECTIVE near or next in position

neighbourly ADJECTIVE friendly and helpful

neither ADJECTIVE & PRONOUN not either: *Neither bus goes that way/ Neither can afford it* ▸CONJUNCTION (*sometimes with* **nor**) used to show alternatives in the negative: *Neither Bill nor David knew the answer/She is neither eating nor sleeping*

nemesis NOUN (*plural* **nemeses**) fate, punishment that is bound to follow wrongdoing

🛈 After *Nemesis*, who was the goddess of revenge in Greek mythology

neo- PREFIX new, recently, or a new or recent form of: *neo-Nazi/ neonatal*

🛈 Comes from Greek *neos* meaning 'new'

Neolithic ADJECTIVE relating to the later Stone Age

neologism (*pronounced* nee-**ol**-*o*-jism) NOUN a new word or expression > **neologistic** ADJECTIVE

neon NOUN, *chemistry* (symbol **Ne**) an element in the form of a gas that glows red when electricity is passed through it

neonate NOUN a newborn child > **neonatal** ADJECTIVE

neon lighting NOUN a form of lighting in which an electric current is passed through a small quantity of neon

nephew NOUN the son of a brother or sister, or of a brother-in-law or sister-in-law

nerd NOUN, *informal* a socially inept, irritating person

nerve NOUN **1** *anatomy* one of the fibres which carry feeling from all parts of the body to the brain **2** courage, coolness **3** *informal* impudence, cheek ▶VERB to strengthen the nerve or will of

nerve cell NOUN, *anatomy* any of the cells in the nervous system (*also called*: **neurone** or **neuron**)

nerve-racking *or* **nerve-wracking** ADJECTIVE causing nervousness or stress

nerves PLURAL NOUN, *informal* nervousness or stress

nervous ADJECTIVE **1** of the nerves: *the nervous system* **2** easily excited or frightened; timid **3** worried, frightened or uneasy > **nervously** ADVERB (meaning 3) > **nervousness** NOUN (meanings 2 and 3)

nervous system NOUN, *anatomy* the brain, spinal cord and nerves of an animal or human being

nervy ADJECTIVE (**nervier, nerviest**) excitable, jumpy

nest NOUN **1** a structure in which birds (and some animals and insects) live and rear their young **2** a shelter, a den ▶VERB to build a nest and live in it

nestle (*pronounced* **ne**-sl) VERB **1** to lie close together as in a nest **2** to settle comfortably

nestling (*pronounced* **nest**-ling) NOUN a newly hatched bird

Net NOUN, *informal* (**the Net**) the Internet

net[1] NOUN **1** a loose arrangement of crossed and knotted cord, string or thread **2** a piece of this, used for catching fish, weaving over the hair, etc, or fitted to a frame to form a goal in some sports **3** fine meshed material, used to make curtains, petticoats, etc **4** *maths* a flat figure made up of polygons which fold and join to form a polyhedron ▶VERB (**netting, netted**) **1** to catch or cover with a net **2** to put (a ball) into a net

net[2] *or* **nett** ADJECTIVE **1** of profit etc: remaining after expenses and taxes have been paid **2** of weight: not including packaging ▶VERB (**netting, netted**) to make by way of profit

netball NOUN a team game in which a ball is thrown into a high net

nether ADJECTIVE lower

nethermost ADJECTIVE lowest

netiquette NOUN, *computing* etiquette on the Internet, especially in e-mail

A B C D E F G H I J K L M N O P Q R S T U V W X Y Z

nett *another spelling of* **net**[2]

netting NOUN fabric of netted string, wire, etc

nettle NOUN a plant covered with hairs which sting sharply ▶VERB to make angry, provoke

nettle rash *a non-technical name for* **urticaria**

network NOUN **1** an arrangement of lines crossing one another **2** a widespread organization **3** a system of linked computers, radio stations, etc

neur- *or* **neuro-** PREFIX of the nerves: *neuralgia*

ⓘ Comes from Greek *neuron* meaning 'nerve'

neuralgia NOUN a pain in the nerves, especially in those of the head and face

neurone *or* **neuron** *see* **nerve cell**

neurosis NOUN (*plural* **neuroses**) a type of mental illness in which the patient suffers from extreme anxiety

neurotic ADJECTIVE **1** suffering from neurosis **2** in a bad nervous state ▶NOUN someone suffering from neurosis > **neurotically** ADVERB

neuter ADJECTIVE **1** *grammar* neither masculine nor feminine **2** of an animal: neither male nor female **3** of an animal: infertile, sterile ▶VERB to sterilize (an animal)

neutral ADJECTIVE **1** taking no side in a quarrel or war **2** of a colour: not strong or definite **3** of a chemical substance: neither acid nor alkaline ▶NOUN **1** a person or a nation that takes no side in a war etc **2** the gear position used when a vehicle is not moving > **neutrality** NOUN (adjective, meaning 1)

neutralize *or* **neutralise** VERB **1** to make neutral **2** to make useless or harmless

neutron NOUN, *physics* an uncharged particle which forms part of the nucleus of an atom (*see also* **electron, proton**)

neutron bomb NOUN a nuclear bomb that kills people by intense radiation but leaves buildings intact

never ADVERB **1** not ever; at no time **2** under no circumstances

nevertheless ADVERB in spite of that: *I hate opera, but I shall come with you nevertheless*

nevus *US spelling of* **naevus**

new ADJECTIVE **1** recent; not seen or known before **2** not used or worn; fresh

ⓘ Comes from Old English *niwe, neowe*

newcomer NOUN someone lately arrived

newfangled ADJECTIVE new and not thought very good

newly ADVERB (*used before past participles*) only recently: *a newly published book*

new moon NOUN **1** the moment when the moon is directly in line between the earth and sun and becomes invisible **2** the moon when it becomes visible again as a narrow crescent

news SINGULAR NOUN **1** report of a recent event or recent events **2** new information: *Is there any news on Tom's health?*

newsagent NOUN a shopkeeper who sells newspapers

newsgroup NOUN, *computing* on the Internet, a group of individuals who share information, often on a particular subject

newspaper NOUN a paper printed daily or weekly containing news

newt NOUN a small lizard-like animal, living on land and in water

newton NOUN, *physics* (symbol **N**) the standard unit used to measure force

new town NOUN a town specially built to relieve overcrowding in nearby cities

next ADJECTIVE nearest, closest in place, time, etc: *the next page* ▶ADVERB in the nearest place or at the nearest time: *Do that sum next*

ⓘ Comes from Old English *nehst* meaning 'nearest'

NHS ABBREVIATION, *Brit* National Health Service

nib NOUN a pen point

nibble VERB to take little bites (of) ▶NOUN a little bite

nice ADJECTIVE **1** agreeable, pleasant **2** careful, precise, exact: *a nice distinction*

nicely ADVERB pleasantly; very well

nicety (*pronounced* **nais**-*e*-ti) NOUN (*plural* **niceties**) a small fine detail **to a nicety** with great exactness

niche (*pronounced* neesh) NOUN **1** a hollow in a wall for a statue, vase, etc **2** a suitable place in life: *She hasn't yet found her niche* **3** *business* a gap in a market for a type of product

nick NOUN **1** a little cut, a notch **2** *slang* prison, jail ▶VERB **1** to cut notches in **2** *slang* to steal

nickel NOUN **1** *chemistry* (symbol **Ni**) a greyish-white metallic element used for mixing with other metals and for plating **2** *US* a 5-cent coin

nickname NOUN an informal name used instead of someone's real name, eg for fun or as an insult

nicotine NOUN a poisonous substance contained in tobacco

ⓘ Named after Jean *Nicot*, 16th-century French ambassador who sent tobacco samples back from Portugal

niece NOUN the daughter of a brother or sister, or of a brother-in-law or sister-in-law

niff NOUN, *slang* a bad smell

nifty ADJECTIVE (**niftier, niftiest**), *slang* **1** fine, smart, neat **2** speedy, agile

niggardly ADJECTIVE mean, stingy

niggle VERB to irritate, rankle ▶NOUN **1** an irritation **2** a minor criticism

niggling ADJECTIVE **1** unimportant, trivial, fussy **2** of a worry or fear: small but always present

nigh ADJECTIVE, *old* near

night NOUN the period of darkness between sunset and sunrise ▶ADJECTIVE **1** of or for night: *the night hours* **2** happening, active, etc at night: *the night shift*

ⓘ Comes from Old English *niht*

nightdress (*plural* **nightdresses**)

or **nightgown** NOUN a garment worn in bed

nightfall NOUN the beginning of night

nightingale NOUN a small bird, the male of which sings beautifully by night and day

nightly ADJECTIVE & ADVERB **1** by night **2** every night

nightmare NOUN a frightening dream

ⓘ The *-mare* ending comes from an old English word meaning 'evil spirit', nightmares being thought to be caused by an evil spirit pressing on the body

nightshirt NOUN a garment like a long shirt worn in bed

nihilism (*pronounced* **nai**-hil-izm *or* **ni**-hil-izm) NOUN belief in nothing, extreme scepticism > **nihilist** NOUN > **nihilistic** ADJECTIVE

nil NOUN nothing

nimble ADJECTIVE quick and neat, agile > **nimbly** ADVERB

nimbus NOUN (*plural* **nimbuses** *or* **nimbi** – *pronounced* **nim**-bai) a rain cloud

nincompoop NOUN a weak, foolish person

nine NOUN the number 9 ▸ADJECTIVE 9 in number

nineteen NOUN the number 19 ▸ADJECTIVE 19 in number

nineteenth ADJECTIVE the last of a series of nineteen ▸NOUN one of nineteen equal parts

ninetieth ADJECTIVE the last of a series of ninety ▸NOUN one of ninety equal parts

ninety NOUN the number 90 ▸ADJECTIVE 90 in number

ninny NOUN (*plural* **ninnies**) a fool

ninth ADJECTIVE the last of a series of nine ▸NOUN one of nine equal parts

nip VERB (**nipping, nipped**) **1** to pinch, squeeze tightly **2** to be stingingly painful **3** to bite, cut (off) **4** to halt the growth of, damage (plants etc) **5** *informal* to go nimbly or quickly ▸NOUN **1** a pinch **2** a sharp coldness in the weather: *a nip in the air* **3** a small amount: *a nip of whisky*

nipper NOUN, *informal* **1** a child, a youngster **2** (**nippers**) pincers, pliers

nipple NOUN the pointed part of the breast from which a baby sucks milk

nippy ADJECTIVE (**nippier, nippiest**), *informal* **1** speedy, nimble **2** frosty, very cold

Nirvana NOUN **1** the state to which a Buddhist or Hindu aspires as the best attainable **2** (**nirvana**) a blissful state

nit NOUN **1** the egg of a louse or other small insect **2** *informal* an idiot, a nitwit

nitrate NOUN, *chemistry* a substance formed from nitric acid

nitric acid NOUN, *chemistry* a strong acid containing nitrogen

nitrogen NOUN, *chemistry* (*symbol* **N**) a gas forming nearly four-fifths of ordinary air

nitrogen cycle NOUN, *chemistry* a continuous exchange of nitrogen between organisms and the environment

A B C D E F G H I J K L M **N** O P Q R S T U V W X Y Z

nitroglycerine NOUN, *chemistry* a powerful kind of explosive

nitwit NOUN a very stupid person

No[1], **No.** *or* **no** ABBREVIATION number

No[2] SYMBOL, *chemistry* nobelium

no ADJECTIVE **1** not any: *They have no money* **2** not a ▶ADVERB not at all: *The patient is no better* ▶INTERJECTION expressing a negative: *Are you feeling better today? No* ▶NOUN (*plural* **noes**) **1** a refusal **2** a vote against **no way** *informal* under no circumstances, absolutely not **no dice** no answer, no success **no doubt** surely **no go** not possible, futile **no joke** not something to laugh about or dismiss

no-ball NOUN, *cricket* a bowled ball disallowed by the rules

Nobel prize NOUN an annual international prize awarded for achievements in arts, science, politics, etc

noble ADJECTIVE **1** great and good, fine **2** of aristocratic birth ▶NOUN an aristocrat > **nobility** NOUN **1** the aristocracy **2** goodness, greatness of mind or character > **nobleman, noblewoman** NOUN > **nobly** ADVERB

nobody PRONOUN not any person ▶NOUN (*plural* **nobodies**) someone of no importance: *just a nobody*

nocturnal ADJECTIVE happening or active at night

nocturne NOUN a piece of music intended to have an atmosphere of night-time

nod VERB (**nodding, nodded**) **1** to bend the head forward quickly, often as a sign of agreement **2** to let the head drop in weariness ▶NOUN an action of nodding **a nodding acquaintance with** a slight knowledge of **nod off** to fall asleep

nodule NOUN a small rounded lump or swelling

Noel *or* **Noël** (*pronounced* noh-**el**) NOUN Christmas

noise NOUN a sound, often one which is loud or harsh ▶VERB, *old* to spread (a rumour etc) > **noiseless** ADJECTIVE > **noisy** ADJECTIVE (**noisier, noisiest**) making a loud sound

nomad NOUN **1** one of a group of people without a fixed home who wander with their animals in search of pasture **2** someone who wanders from place to place > **nomadic** ADJECTIVE

no-man's-land NOUN land owned by no one, especially that lying between two opposing armies

nom de plume NOUN (*plural* **noms de plume**) a pen name

nomenclature (*pronounced* no-**men**-kl*a*-cher) NOUN **1** a system of naming **2** names

nominal ADJECTIVE **1** in name only **2** very small: *a nominal fee*

nominate VERB to propose (someone) for a post or for election; appoint > **nomination** NOUN

nominee NOUN someone whose name is put forward for a post

-nomy SUFFIX forms words relating to different systems of regulation, or to the science and study of how these work: *astronomy/autonomy* (= the power or right of a country or person to regulate themselves)

ⓘ Comes from Greek *nomos* meaning 'law'

non- PREFIX not (used with many words to change their meaning to the opposite): *non-aggression/non-event/non-smoking*

ⓘ Comes from Latin *non* meaning 'not'

nonagenarian NOUN someone from ninety to ninety-nine years old

nonagon NOUN a nine-sided figure

nonchalant (*pronounced* **non**-sha-lant) ADJECTIVE not easily roused or upset, cool > **nonchalance** NOUN > **nonchalantly** ADVERB

non-committal ADJECTIVE unwilling to express, or not expressing, an opinion

nonconformist NOUN someone who does not agree with accepted attitudes, modes of behaviour, etc ▸ADJECTIVE not agreeing with accepted attitudes or behaviour > **nonconformity** NOUN

nondescript ADJECTIVE lacking anything noticeable or interesting

none ADVERB not at all: *none the worse* ▸PRONOUN not one, not any

nonentity NOUN (*plural* **nonentities**) someone of no importance

non-existent ADJECTIVE not existing, not real

nonplussed ADJECTIVE taken aback, confused

nonsense NOUN **1** words that have no sense or meaning **2** foolishness > **nonsensical** ADJECTIVE

non sequitur (*pronounced* non **sek**-wi-tur) NOUN a remark unconnected with what has gone before

ⓘ A Latin phrase meaning literally 'it does not follow'

non-stop ADJECTIVE going on without a stop

noodle NOUN a long thin strip of pasta, eaten in soup or served with a sauce

nook NOUN **1** a corner **2** a small recess **every nook and cranny** *informal* everywhere

noon NOUN twelve o'clock midday

no one *or* **no-one** PRONOUN not any person, nobody

noose NOUN a loop in a rope etc that tightens when pulled

nor CONJUNCTION (*often with* **neither**) used to show alternatives in the negative: *Neither James nor I can speak French*

Nordic ADJECTIVE **1** relating to Finland or Scandinavia **2** of skiing: involving cross-country and jumping events

norm NOUN a pattern or standard to judge other things from

normal ADJECTIVE ordinary, usual according to a standard > **normality** NOUN > **normally** ADVERB

north NOUN one of the four chief directions, that to the left of someone facing the rising sun ▸ADJECTIVE **1** in or to the north **2** of the wind: from the north ▸ADVERB in, to or towards the north: *We headed north* ▸ADJECTIVE & ADVERB in or to the north > **northerner** NOUN someone living in a northern region or country

north-east NOUN the point of the compass midway between north and east

A B C D E F G H I J K L M N O P Q R S T U V W X Y Z

northerly ADJECTIVE **1** of the wind: coming from the north **2** in or towards the north

northern lights PLURAL NOUN (**the northern lights**) the **aurora borealis**

North Pole NOUN the point on the Earth's surface that represents the northern end of its axis

northward *or* **northwards** ADJECTIVE & ADVERB towards the north

north-west NOUN the point of the compass midway between north and west

nose NOUN **1** the part of the face by which people and animals smell and breathe **2** a jutting-out part, eg the front of an aeroplane ▸VERB **1** to track by smelling **2** *informal* to interfere in other people's affairs, pry (into) **3** to push a way through: *The ship nosed through the ice*

nosedive NOUN a headfirst dive, especially by an aeroplane ▸VERB to dive headfirst

nosey *or* **nosy** ADJECTIVE (**nosier, nosiest**) inquisitive, fond of prying

no-show NOUN someone expected who does not arrive

nostalgia NOUN **1** a longing for past times **2** a longing for home > **nostalgic** ADJECTIVE > **nostalgically** ADVERB

nostril NOUN either of the two openings of the nose

not ADVERB expressing a negative, refusal or denial: *I am not going/ Give it to me, not to him/I did not break the window*

notability NOUN (*plural* **notabilities**) a well-known person

notable ADJECTIVE worth taking notice of; important, remarkable ▸NOUN an important person > **notably** ADVERB

notary NOUN (*plural* **notaries**) an official who sees that written documents are drawn up in a way required by law

notation NOUN **1** the showing of numbers, musical sounds, etc by signs: *sol-fa notation/mathematical notation* **2** a set of such signs

notch NOUN (*plural* **notches**) a small V-shaped cut ▸VERB to make a notch > **notched** ADJECTIVE

note NOUN **1** a short explanation **2** a short letter **3** a piece of paper used as money: *£5 note* **4** a single sound or the sign standing for it in music **5** a key on the piano etc ▸VERB **1** to make a note of **2** to notice **of note** well-known, distinguished **take note of** to notice particularly

notebook NOUN **1** a small book for taking notes **2** a small laptop computer

noted ADJECTIVE well-known

notepaper NOUN writing paper

noteworthy ADJECTIVE notable, remarkable

nothing NOUN **1** no thing, not anything **2** nought, zero **3** something of no importance ▸ADVERB not at all: *He's nothing like his father*

nothingness NOUN **1** non-existence **2** space, emptiness

notice NOUN **1** a public announcement **2** attention: *The colour attracted my notice* **3** a

LANGUAGE workshop Nouns

Nouns are words that name things. Nouns can be classified in many different ways.

Concrete and abstract nouns

Concrete nouns refer to physical things you can touch:

house, *book*, *door*, *pig*, *tree*

Abstract nouns refer to things you cannot touch, such as qualities or actions:

anger, *sunshine*, *thought*, *kick*, *leap*

Count and noncount/mass nouns

Count nouns name things that can be counted one by one, for example:

one *book*, two *bells*, three *flowers*, five hundred *apples*

Noncount nouns (also called mass nouns) name things that cannot be counted, for example:

help, *excitement*, *luck*, *oxygen*, *milk*, *furniture*

Some nouns can be count or noncount depending on what they mean.

Your kindness is much appreciated.
I appreciate all your little *kindnesses*.

? Is *dream* a count or noncount noun?
What about the word *life*?

Singular and plural nouns

Count nouns can be either singular or plural. A singular noun refers to one thing or person and takes a singular verb, for example:

The *boy runs*.
The *biceps is* an important muscle.

Nouns

LANGUAGE workshop

A plural noun refers to more than one thing or person and takes a plural verb, for example:

The *boys run*.
These *scissors are* sharp.

Some nouns can be treated as both singular and plural:

The family is on holiday.
The family are on holiday.

? Is *trousers* a singular or a plural noun? What about the word *bacteria*?

Proper and common nouns

Proper nouns name particular people, groups, places, events and occasions, and they usually begin with a capital letter, for example:

Mr Green, *Manchester United*, *The Louvre*, *Atlantic Ocean*, *Lake Geneva*, *Tuesday*, *April*

Common nouns refer to any of a class of things, but do not specifically name them, for example:

my *teacher*, the *team*, a *museum*, an *ocean*, this *month*

? Is *brother* a proper or a common noun?

Collective nouns

Collective nouns refer to a group of similar people or things that make up a larger whole, for example:

a *flock* (of sheep), a *team* (of players), a *pile* (of coins, papers), a *bunch* (of flowers)

period of warning given before leaving, or before dismissing someone from, a job ▶VERB to see, observe, take note of

noticeable ADJECTIVE easily noticed, standing out > **noticeably** ADVERB

notifiable ADJECTIVE that must be reported: *a notifiable disease*

notify VERB (**notifies, notifying, notified**) **1** to inform **2** to give notice of > **notification** NOUN

notion NOUN **1** an idea **2** a vague belief or opinion

notorious ADJECTIVE well known because of badness: *a notorious criminal* > **notoriety** NOUN

notwithstanding PREPOSITION in spite of: *Notwithstanding his poverty, he refused all help*

nougat (*pronounced* **noo**-gah *or* **nug**-et) NOUN a sticky kind of sweet containing nuts etc

nought NOUN the figure 0, zero

> Do not confuse with: **naught**

noun NOUN, *grammar* the word used as the name of someone or something, eg *John* and *tickets* in the sentence *John bought the tickets* →*See also* **Language Workshop panel**

nourish VERB **1** to feed **2** to encourage the growth of

nourishing ADJECTIVE giving the body what is necessary for health and growth

nourishment NOUN **1** food **2** an act of nourishing

novel (*pronounced* **nov**-el) ADJECTIVE new and strange ▶NOUN a book telling a long story

novelist (*pronounced* **nov**-el-ist) NOUN a writer of novels

novelty (*pronounced* **nov**-el-ti) NOUN (*plural* **novelties**) **1** something new and strange **2** newness **3** a small, cheap souvenir or toy

November NOUN the eleventh month of the year

ⓘ From a Latin word meaning 'ninth', because November was originally the ninth month of the year, before January and February were added

novice NOUN a beginner

now ADVERB **1** at the present time: *I can see him now* **2** immediately before the present time: *I thought of her just now* **3** in the present circumstances: *I can't go now because my mother is ill* ▶CONJUNCTION (often **now that**) because, since: *You can't go out now that it's raining* **now and then** *or* **now and again** sometimes, from time to time

nowadays ADVERB in present times, these days

nowhere ADVERB not in, or to, any place

no-win ADJECTIVE of a situation: in which you are bound to lose or fail

noxious ADJECTIVE harmful: *noxious fumes*

ⓘ Comes from Latin *noxius* meaning 'hurtful'

> Do not confuse with: **obnoxious**

nozzle NOUN a spout fitted to the

end of a pipe, tube, etc

NSPCC ABBREVIATION National Society for the Prevention of Cruelty to Children

nuance (*pronounced* **nyoo**-ons) NOUN a slight difference in meaning or colour etc

nubile ADJECTIVE of a young woman: attractive, and old enough to be sexually mature > **nubility** NOUN

nuclear ADJECTIVE **1** of a nucleus, especially that of an atom **2** produced by the splitting of the nuclei of atoms

nuclear energy NOUN energy released or absorbed during reactions taking place in atomic nuclei

nuclear family NOUN a family unit made up of mother, father and children

nuclear fission NOUN, *physics* the spontaneous or induced disintegration of a heavy atomic nucleus into two or more lighter fragments, with a release of nuclear energy

nuclear fusion NOUN, *physics* the process in which a new, heavy atomic nucleus is produced when two lighter nuclei combine with each other, with a release of nuclear energy

nuclear missile NOUN a missile whose warhead is an atomic bomb

nuclear reactor NOUN, *physics* apparatus for producing nuclear energy

nucleus NOUN (*plural* **nuclei** – *pronounced* **nyoo**-klee-ai) **1** *physics* the positively charged central part of an atom **2** *biology* the part of a plant or animal cell that controls its development **3** the central part round which something collects or from which it grows: *the nucleus of my book collection*

nude ADJECTIVE without clothes, naked ▸ NOUN **1** an unclothed human figure **2** a painting or statue of such a figure **in the nude** naked

nudge NOUN a gentle push, eg with the elbow or shoulder ▸ VERB: *I nudged him*

nudist NOUN someone who is in favour of going without clothes in public > **nudism** NOUN

nudity NOUN the state of being nude

nugget NOUN a lump, especially of gold

nuisance NOUN someone or something annoying or troublesome

null **null and void** having no legal force

nullify VERB (**nullifies, nullifying, nullified**) **1** to make useless or of no effect **2** to declare to be null and void

numb ADJECTIVE having lost the power to feel or move ▸ VERB to make numb

number NOUN **1** a word or figure showing how many, or showing a position in a series **2** a collection of people or things **3** a single issue of a newspaper or magazine **4** a popular song or piece of music ▸ VERB **1** to count **2** to give numbers to **3** to amount to in number

🛈 Comes from French *nombre* meaning 'number'

numeral NOUN a figure (eg 1, 2, etc) used to express a number

numerate (*pronounced* **nyom-***e*-*rat*) ADJECTIVE able to do arithmetic

numerator NOUN, *maths* the number above the line in vulgar fractions, eg 2 in 2/3 (*compare with*: **denominator**)

numerical *or* **numeric** ADJECTIVE of, in, using or consisting of numbers

numerous ADJECTIVE many

nun NOUN a member of a female religious group living in a convent

nuptial ADJECTIVE of marriage

nuptials PLURAL NOUN, *formal* a wedding ceremony

nurse NOUN someone who looks after sick or injured people, especially in a hospital ▸ VERB **1** to look after sick people etc **2** to give (a baby) milk from the breast **3** to hold or look after with care: *He nurses his tomato plants* **4** to encourage (feelings) in yourself: *nursing her wrath*

nursery NOUN (*plural* **nurseries**) **1** a room for young children **2** a place where young plants are reared **3** a nursery school

nursery school NOUN a school for very young children

nursing home NOUN a small private hospital, especially one for old people

nurture VERB to bring up, rear; to nourish: *nurture tenderness* ▸ NOUN care, upbringing; food, nourishment

NUT ABBREVIATION National Union of Teachers

nut NOUN **1** a fruit with a hard shell which contains a kernel **2** a small metal block with a hole in it for screwing on the end of a bolt

nutcrackers PLURAL NOUN an instrument for cracking nuts open

nutmeg NOUN a hard, aromatic seed used as a spice in cooking

nutrient NOUN a substance which provides nourishment

nutriment NOUN nourishment, food

nutrition NOUN nourishment, food

nutritious ADJECTIVE valuable as food, nourishing

nutshell NOUN the case containing the kernel of a nut **in a nutshell** expressed very briefly

nutty ADJECTIVE (**nuttier, nuttiest**) **1** containing, or having, the flavour of nuts **2** *informal* mad, insane

nuzzle VERB **1** to press, rub or caress with the nose **2** to lie close to, snuggle, nestle

NVQ ABBREVIATION, *Brit* National Vocational Qualification

NW ABBREVIATION north-west; north-western

nylon NOUN **1** a synthetic material used to make fibres **2** (**nylons**) stockings made of nylon

nymph NOUN **1** a mythological female river or tree spirit **2** a beautiful girl **3** *biology* an insect not yet fully developed

NZ ABBREVIATION New Zealand

Oo

A B C D E F G H I J K L M N **O** P Q R S T U V W X Y Z

o *or* **oh** INTERJECTION expressing surprise, admiration, pain, etc

oak NOUN **1** a tree which produces acorns as fruit **2** its hard wood > **oak** *or* **oaken** ADJECTIVE made of oak

OAP ABBREVIATION **1** Old Age Pension, money paid by the government to people who have retired **2** Old Age Pensioner, an elderly, retired person

oar NOUN a pole for rowing, with a flat blade at one end ▸ VERB to row **put your oar in** to interfere in

oasis NOUN (*plural* **oases** – *pronounced* oh-**ei**-seez) a place in a desert where water is found and trees etc grow

oat NOUN **1** a type of grassy plant **2** (**oats**) the grains of this plant, used as food

oatcake NOUN a thin, flat biscuit made of oatmeal

oath NOUN (*plural* **oaths** – *pronounced* ohdhz) **1** a solemn promise to speak the truth, keep your word, be loyal, etc **2** a swear-word

oatmeal NOUN meal made by grinding oat grains

OBE ABBREVIATION Officer of the Order of the British Empire, a special honour in the UK, given for work that has helped the country

obedience NOUN **1** the act of obeying **2** willingness to obey

obedient ADJECTIVE obeying, ready to obey > **obediently** ADVERB

obelisk NOUN a tall four-sided pillar with a pointed top

obese ADJECTIVE very overweight > **obesity** NOUN

obey VERB to do what you are told to do

obituary NOUN (*plural* **obituaries**) a notice in a newspaper etc of someone's death, sometimes with a brief biography

object NOUN (*pronounced* **ob**-jekt) **1** something that can be seen or felt **2** an aim, a purpose: *The object of the exercise is to make Internet access available to everyone* **3** *grammar* the word in a sentence which stands for the person or thing on which the action of the verb is done, eg *me* in the sentence *He hit me* ▸ VERB (*pronounced* *ob*-**jekt**) (**object to**) to feel or show disapproval of something

objection NOUN **1** the act of objecting **2** a reason for objecting

objectionable ADJECTIVE nasty, disagreeable

objective ADJECTIVE not influenced by personal interests, fair (*contrasted with*: **subjective**) ▸NOUN aim, purpose, goal > **objectively** ADVERB > **objectivity** NOUN

objector NOUN someone who objects to something

obligation NOUN **1** a promise or duty by which someone is bound: *under an obligation to help* **2** a debt of gratitude for a favour received

obligatory (*pronounced* ob-**lig**-*a*t-*o*-ri) ADJECTIVE required to be done with no exceptions by law, rule or custom

oblige VERB **1** to force, compel: *We were obliged to go home* **2** to do a favour or service to: *Oblige me by shutting the door*

obliged ADJECTIVE owing or feeling gratitude for a favour or service done

obliging ADJECTIVE ready to help others

oblique ADJECTIVE **1** slanting **2** indirect, not straight or straightforward: *an oblique reference* > **obliquely** ADVERB

obliterate VERB **1** to blot out (writing etc), efface **2** to destroy completely > **obliteration** NOUN

oblivion NOUN **1** forgetfulness, unconsciousness **2** the state of being forgotten

oblivious ADJECTIVE unaware, unconscious, forgetful

oblong NOUN a rectangle which is longer than it is wide, eg ▯ ▸ADJECTIVE of this shape

obnoxious ADJECTIVE offensive, causing dislike > **obnoxiously** ADVERB

ⓘ Comes from Latin *obnoxius* meaning 'liable to punishment' or 'guilty of'

> Do not confuse with: **noxious**

oboe NOUN (*plural* **oboes**) a high-pitched woodwind instrument

ⓘ From a French word meaning literally 'high wood'

oboist NOUN someone who plays the oboe

obscene ADJECTIVE **1** sexually indecent, lewd **2** disgusting, repellent

obscenity NOUN (*plural* **obscenities**) **1** the state or quality of being obscene: *the obscenity of war* **2** an obscene act or word: *The youths shouted obscenities at the police*

obscure ADJECTIVE **1** dark **2** not clear or easily understood **3** unknown, not famous: *an obscure poet* ▸VERB **1** to darken **2** to make less clear

obscurity NOUN **1** the state of being difficult to see or understand **2** the state of being unknown or forgotten

obsequious ADJECTIVE submissive and fawning

observance NOUN the act of obeying or keeping (a law, tradition, etc)

observant ADJECTIVE good at noticing

observation NOUN **1** the act of seeing and noting; attention **2** a remark

observatory NOUN (*plural*

observatories) a place for making observations of the stars, weather, etc

observe VERB **1** to notice **2** to watch with attention **3** to remark (that) **4** to obey (a law etc) **5** to keep, preserve: *observe a tradition* > **observer** NOUN

obsess VERB to fill the mind completely

obsession NOUN **1** a feeling or idea which someone cannot stop thinking about **2** the state of being obsessed

obsessive ADJECTIVE **1** forming an obsession **2** having or likely to have an obsession

obsolescence NOUN being obsolescent

obsolescent ADJECTIVE going out of date

ⓘ Comes from Latin *obsolescere* meaning 'to go out of use, wear out'

obsolete ADJECTIVE gone out of use

ⓘ Comes from Latin *obsoletus* meaning 'grown old, worn out, gone out of use'

> Do not confuse: **obsolete** and **obsolescent**

obstacle NOUN something which stands in the way and hinders

obstacle race NOUN a race in which obstacles have to be passed, climbed, etc

obstetrician NOUN a doctor trained in obstetrics

obstetrics SINGULAR NOUN the branch of medicine and surgery dealing with pregnancy and childbirth

obstinate ADJECTIVE **1** of a person: rigidly sticking to decisions or opinions and unwilling to be influenced by persuasion **2** difficult to deal with, defeat or remove: *obstinate stains*

obstruct VERB **1** to block or close **2** to hold back or hinder > **obstruction** NOUN

obstructive ADJECTIVE causing or meant to cause an obstruction

obtain VERB **1** to get, gain **2** to be in use, be valid: *That rule still obtains* > **obtainable** ADJECTIVE (meaning 1)

obtrusive ADJECTIVE **1** too noticeable **2** pushy, impudent

obtuse ADJECTIVE **1** *maths* of an angle: greater than a right angle (*contrasted with*: **acute**) **2** blunt, not pointed **3** stupid, slow to understand

obvious ADJECTIVE easily seen or understood; plain, evident

obviously ADVERB in an obvious way; as is obvious, clearly

occasion NOUN **1** a particular time: *on that occasion* **2** a special event: *a great occasion* **3** a cause, a reason: *You had no occasion to get cross* **4** opportunity ▶VERB to cause

occasional ADJECTIVE happening or used now and then > **occasionally** ADVERB

Occident NOUN (**the Occident**) the West

occidental ADJECTIVE from or relating to the Occident; western

occult ADJECTIVE **1** secret, mysterious **2** supernatural

occupancy NOUN (*plural* **occupancies**) the act, fact or period of occupying (a house, flat, etc)

occupant NOUN a person who occupies, has, or takes possession of something, not always the owner

occupation NOUN **1** the act of occupying or state of being occupied: *the students' occupation of the building* **2** an activity that occupies someone's attention or free time **3** someone's trade or job

occupational therapy NOUN the treatment of a mental or physical disease or injury by a course of suitable activities

occupier NOUN someone who lives in a building, as a tenant or owner

occupy VERB (**occupies, occupying, occupied**) **1** to live in **2** to keep busy **3** to take up, fill (space, time, etc) **4** to seize, capture (a town, country, etc)

occur VERB (**occurring, occurred**) **1** to happen **2** to appear, be found **occur to someone** to come into their mind: *That never occurred to me* > **occurrence** NOUN

ocean NOUN **1** the expanse of salt water surrounding all the land masses of the earth **2** one of five main divisions of this, ie the Atlantic, Pacific, Indian, Arctic or Antarctic

ocelot NOUN a wild American cat like a small leopard

ochre *or US* **ocher** (*pronounced* **oh**-ker) NOUN a fine pale-yellow or red clay, used for colouring

o'clock ADVERB used after a number from one to twelve: specifying the time, indicating the number of hours after midday or midnight

OCR ABBREVIATION, *computing* optical character recognition, a computer's ability to read written or printed letters or numbers

octa- also **octo-**, **oct-** PREFIX eight: *octave/octopus/October* (which was the eighth month in the Roman calendar)

ⓘ Comes from Latin and Greek *octo* meaning 'eight'

octagon NOUN an eight-sided figure

octagonal ADJECTIVE having eight sides

octane NOUN a colourless liquid found in petroleum and used in petrol

octave NOUN, *music* a range of eight notes, eg from one C to the next C above or below it

octo- *see* **octa-**

October NOUN the tenth month of the year

ⓘ From a Latin word meaning 'eighth', because October was originally the eighth month of the year, before January and February were added

octogenarian NOUN someone from eighty to eighty-nine years old

octopus NOUN (*plural* **octopuses**) a sea creature with eight arms

ocular ADJECTIVE of or relating to the eye

odd ADJECTIVE **1** of a number: leaving a remainder of one when divided by two, eg the numbers 3, 17, 31 (*contrasted with*: **even**) **2** unusual, strange **3** not one of a matching pair or group, left over: *an odd glove/wearing odd socks*

oddity NOUN (*plural* **oddities**)

A B C D E F G H I J K L M N O P Q R S T U V W X Y Z

1 queerness, strangeness **2** a strange person or thing

odd jobs PLURAL NOUN jobs of different kinds, done occasionally and not part of regular employment

odds PLURAL NOUN **1** the chances of something happening: *The odds are he will win* **2** difference: *It makes no odds* **at odds** quarrelling **odds and ends** small objects of different kinds and with little value

ode NOUN a type of poem, often written to someone or something: *ode to autumn*

odious ADJECTIVE hateful
> **odiously** ADVERB

odour NOUN smell, either pleasant or unpleasant

odourless ADJECTIVE without smell

odyssey NOUN (*plural* **odysseys**) a long, adventurous journey

oesophagus (*pronounced* ee-**sof**-*ag*-*us*) *or US* **esophagus** (*pronounced* i-**sof**-*ag*-*us*) NOUN the narrow muscular tube through which food passes from the mouth to the stomach

oestrogen (*pronounced* **ees**-tr*o*-jen) *or US* **estrogen** (*pronounced* **es**-tr*o*-jen) NOUN a female sex hormone which regulates the menstrual cycle, prepares the body for pregnancy, etc

of PREPOSITION **1** belonging to: *the house of my parents* **2** from (a place, person, etc): *within two miles of his home* **3** from among: *one of my pupils* **4** made from, made up of: *a house of bricks* **5** indicating an amount, a measurement, etc: *a gallon of petrol* **6** about, concerning: *talk of old friends* **7** with, containing: *a class of twenty children/a cup of coffee* **8** as a result of: *die of hunger* **9** indicating removal or taking away: *robbed her of her jewels* **10** indicating a connection between an action and its object: *the joining of the pieces* **11** indicating character, qualities, etc: *a man of good taste/It was good of you to come* **12** *US* (in telling the time) before, to: *ten of eight*

off ADVERB **1** away from a place, or from a particular state, position, etc: *He walked off muttering/Switch the light off* **2** entirely, completely: *Finish off your work* ▸ADJECTIVE **1** cancelled: *The holiday is off* **2** rotten, bad: *The meat is off* **3** not working, not on: *The control is in the off position* **4** not quite pure in colour: *off-white* ▸PREPOSITION **1** not on, away from: *fell off the table* **2** taken away: *10% off the usual price* **3** below the normal standard: *off his game* **be off** to go away, leave quickly **off and on** occasionally **off the cuff** *see* **cuff** **off the wall** *see* **wall**

offal NOUN some internal organs of an animal (heart, liver, etc), used as food

off-beat ADJECTIVE not standard, eccentric

off-chance NOUN a slight chance **on the off-chance** just in case

off-colour ADJECTIVE not feeling well

offence *or US* **offense** NOUN **1** displeasure, hurt feelings **2** a crime, a sin **take offence at** to be angry or feel hurt at

offend VERB **1** to hurt the feelings of; insult, displease **2** to do wrong

offender NOUN a person who has committed an offence

offensive NOUN **1** the position of someone who attacks: *go on the offensive* **2** an attack ▸ ADJECTIVE **1** insulting, disgusting **2** used for attack or assault: *an offensive weapon*

offer VERB **1** to put forward (a gift, payment, etc) for acceptance or refusal **2** to lay (a choice, chance, etc) before **3** to say that you are willing to do something ▸ NOUN **1** an act of offering **2** a bid of money **3** something proposed

offering NOUN **1** a gift **2** a collection of money in church

offhand ADJECTIVE **1** said or done without thinking or preparing **2** rude, curt ▸ ADVERB without preparation; impromptu: *I can't remember his name offhand*

office NOUN **1** a place where business is carried on **2** the people working in such a place **3** a duty, a job **4** a position of authority, especially in the government **5** (**offices**) services, helpful acts

officer NOUN **1** someone who carries out a public duty **2** someone holding a commission in the armed forces

official ADJECTIVE **1** done or given out by those in power: *an official announcement/official action* **2** forming part of the tasks of a job or office: *official duties* **3** having full and proper authority ▸ NOUN someone who holds an office in the service of the government etc

> Do not confuse with: **officious**. **Official** is a neutral adjective showing neither approval nor disapproval, and it is used most often with reference to position or authority rather than people's characters.

officially ADVERB **1** as an official, formally **2** as announced or said in public (though not necessarily truthfully)

officiate VERB to perform a duty or service, especially as a clergyman at a wedding etc

officious ADJECTIVE fond of interfering, especially in a pompous way > **officiously** ADVERB

> Do not confuse with: **official**. **Officious** is a negative adjective showing disapproval, and it is used to describe people and their characters.

offing NOUN: **in the offing** expected to happen soon, forthcoming

off-licence NOUN a shop selling alcohol which must not be drunk on the premises

off-line *or* **offline** ADJECTIVE & ADVERB, *computing* **1** not under the control of the central processing unit **2** not switched on or connected (*compare with*: **on-line**)

offload VERB to unload

offpeak ADJECTIVE not at the time of highest use or demand: *an offpeak travel card*

off-putting ADJECTIVE unpleasant, distracting

offset VERB to weigh against, make

up for: *The cost was partly offset by a grant*

offshoot NOUN **1** a shoot growing out of the main stem **2** a small business, project, etc created out of a larger one: *an offshoot of an international firm*

offshore ADJECTIVE & ADVERB **1** in or on the sea close to the coast **2** at a distance from the shore **3** from the shore: *offshore winds*

offside ADJECTIVE & ADVERB **1** (*pronounced* of-**said**) *sport* illegally ahead of the ball, eg in football, in an illegal position between the ball and the opponent's goal (*contrasted with*: **onside**) **2** (*pronounced* **of**-said) of the side of a vehicle: nearest to the centre of the road: (*contrasted with*: **nearside**): *the offside wing mirror*

offspring NOUN **1** someone's child or children **2** the young of animals etc

often ADVERB many times

ogle VERB to look at (someone or something) in an admiring or amorous way

ohm NOUN (symbol Ω) the standard unit of electrical resistance

-oholic *see* **-aholic**

-oid SUFFIX forms technical terms containing the meaning 'like': *anthropoid/android* (= a humanlike robot)/*tabloid* (= originally a trademark for a medicine in tablet form)

ⓘ Comes from Greek *eidos* meaning 'form'

oil NOUN **1** a greasy liquid obtained from plants (eg olive oil), from animals (eg whale oil), and from minerals (eg petroleum) **2** (**oils**) oil paints ▸ VERB to smear with oil, put oil on or in

oilfield NOUN an area where mineral oil is found

oil paint NOUN paint made by mixing a colouring substance with oil

oil painting NOUN a picture painted in oil paints

oil rig NOUN a structure set up for drilling an oil well

oilskin NOUN **1** cloth made waterproof with oil **2** a heavy coat made of this

oil well NOUN a hole drilled into the earth's surface or into the seabed to extract petroleum

oily ADJECTIVE (**oilier, oiliest**) **1** of or like oil **2** obsequious, too friendly or flattering

oink NOUN the noise of a pig ▸ VERB to make this noise

ointment NOUN a greasy substance rubbed on the skin to soothe, heal, etc

OK *or* **okay** INTERJECTION, ADJECTIVE & ADVERB all right > **okay** VERB (**okaying, okayed**) to mark or pass as being acceptable

ⓘ The origin of this word is uncertain, but it probably comes from the initial letters of the phrase *oll korrect*, used as a playful way of spelling 'all correct'

old ADJECTIVE **1** advanced in age, aged **2** having a certain age: *ten years old* **3** not new, having existed a long time: *an old joke* **4** belonging to the past **5** worn, worn-out

6 out-of-date, old-fashioned
7 of a person's past, replaced by something different in the present: *I preferred my old school to the one I'm at now* **of old** from the past, from history

ⓘ Comes from Old English *ald*

old age NOUN the later part of life

olden ADJECTIVE: **the olden days** past times

old-fashioned ADJECTIVE in a style from the past, out-of-date

old guard NOUN the conservative element in an organization etc

old hand NOUN someone with long experience in a job etc

old maid NOUN **1** *derogatory* a spinster **2** a game played by passing and matching playing-cards

olfactory ADJECTIVE of or used for smelling: *olfactory glands*

oligarchy (*pronounced* **ol**-ig-ahrk-i) NOUN government by a small exclusive group > **oligarchic** *or* **oligarchical** ADJECTIVE

olive NOUN **1** a small, oval fruit with a hard stone, which is pressed to produce a cooking oil **2** the Mediterranean tree that bears this fruit ▶ ADJECTIVE of a yellowish-green colour

olive branch NOUN a sign of a wish for peace

-ology *see* **-logy**

Olympic Games PLURAL NOUN an international athletics competition held every four years (*also called*: **Olympics**)

ombudsman NOUN an official appointed to look into complaints against government departments

ⓘ From a Swedish word meaning 'administration man', introduced into English in the 1960s

omega (*pronounced* **oh**-mi-g*a*) NOUN the last letter of the Greek alphabet

omelette *or* **omelet** NOUN beaten eggs fried in a single layer in a pan

omen NOUN a sign of future events

ominous ADJECTIVE suggesting future trouble > **ominously** ADVERB

omission NOUN **1** something omitted **2** the act of omitting

omit VERB (**omitting, omitted**) **1** to leave out **2** to fail to do

omni- PREFIX all: *omniscient* (= all-knowing)/*omnipotent* (= all-powerful)

ⓘ Comes from Latin *omnis* meaning 'all'

omnibus NOUN (*plural* **omnibuses**) **1** *old* a bus **2** a book containing several connected items

ⓘ A Latin word meaning 'for all', because it originally referred to a vehicle which could seat a large number of people

omnibus edition NOUN a radio or TV programme made up of material from preceding editions of a series

omnipotence NOUN unlimited power

omnipotent (*pronounced* om-**ni**-p*o*-tent) ADJECTIVE **1** of God or a deity: having absolute, unlimited power **2** with very great power or influence > **omnipotence** NOUN

omnipresent ADJECTIVE especially of God or a deity: present everywhere at the same time > **omnipresence** NOUN

A B C D E F G H I J K L M N O P Q R S T U V W X Y Z

omnivore NOUN an organism that feeds on both plants and animals > **omnivorous** ADJECTIVE

on PREPOSITION **1** touching or fixed to the outer or upper side: *on the table* **2** supported by: *standing on one foot* **3** receiving, taking, etc: *suspended on half-pay/on antibiotics* **4** occurring in the course of a specified time: *on the following day* **5** about: *a book on Scottish history* **6** with: *Do you have your cheque book on you?* **7** next to, near: *a city on the Rhine* **8** indicating membership of: *on the committee* **9** in the process or state of: *on sale/on show* **10** by means of: *Can you play that on the piano?* **11** followed by: *disaster on disaster* ▶ ADVERB **1** so as to be touching or fixed to the outer or upper side: *Put your coat on* **2** onwards, further: *They carried on towards home* **3** at a further point: *later on* ▶ ADJECTIVE **1** working, performing: *The television is on* **2** arranged, planned: *Do you have anything on this afternoon?* **from now on** after this time, henceforth **on and off** occasionally, intermittently **on and on** continually **you're on!** I agree, accept the challenge, etc

once ADVERB **1** at an earlier time in the past: *People once lived in caves* **2** for one time only: *I've been to Paris once in the last two years* ▶ NOUN one time only: *Do it just this once* ▶ CONJUNCTION when: *Once you've finished, you can go* **all at once** suddenly **at once** **1** immediately: *Come here at once!* **2** (sometimes **all at once**) at the same time, together: *trying to do several things all at once* **for once** on this one occasion: *For once, will you do the washing-up?* **once and for all** for the last time **once upon a time** at some time in the past

oncology NOUN the diagnosis and treatment of cancer > **oncologist** NOUN

oncoming ADJECTIVE approaching from the front: *oncoming traffic*

one NOUN **1** the number 1 **2** a particular member of a group: *She's the one I want to meet* ▶ PRONOUN **1** a single person or thing: *one of my cats* **2** in formal or pompous English used instead of **you**, meaning anyone: *One must do what one can* ▶ ADJECTIVE **1** 1 in number, a single: *We had only one reply* **2** identical, the same: *We are all of one mind* **3** some, an unnamed (time etc): *one day soon* **one another** used when an action takes place between two or more people: *They looked at one another*

[i] Comes from Old English *an*

onerous ADJECTIVE heavy, hard to bear or do: *onerous task*

oneself PRONOUN **1** used reflexively: *wash oneself* **2** used for emphasis: *One prefers to feed the dogs oneself*

one-sided ADJECTIVE with one person, side, etc having a great advantage over the other: *a one-sided match*

one-way ADJECTIVE for traffic moving in one direction only

ongoing ADJECTIVE continuing: *ongoing talks*

onion NOUN a bulb vegetable with

a strong taste and smell **know your onions** *informal* to know your subject or job well

on-line *or* **online** ADJECTIVE & ADVERB, *computing* **1** under the control of a central processing unit **2** switched on or connected (*compare with*: **off-line**)

onlooker NOUN someone who watches an event, but does not take part in it

only ADVERB **1** not more than: *only two weeks left* **2** alone, solely: *Only you are invited* **3** not longer ago than: *I saw her only yesterday* **4** indicating an unavoidable result: *He'll only be offended if you ask* ▸ ADJECTIVE single, solitary: *an only child* ▸ CONJUNCTION, *informal* but, except that: *I'd like to go, only I have to work* **only too** extremely: *I'm only too pleased to help*

onomatopoeia (*pronounced* on-oh-mat-oh-**pee**-*a*) NOUN the forming of a word which sounds like the thing it refers to, eg *moo, swish* > **onomatopoeic** ADJECTIVE

onset NOUN **1** beginning **2** an attack

onside *see* **offside**

onslaught NOUN a fierce attack

onus NOUN burden; responsibility

onward ADJECTIVE going forward in place or time: *the onward march of science* > **onward** *or* **onwards** ADVERB: *We stumbled onward, close to exhaustion/from four o'clock onwards*

-onym (*pronounced* on-im) *or* **-nym** SUFFIX forms terms containing the idea of 'word' or 'name': *synonym/pseudonym*
ⓘ Comes from Greek *onyma* meaning 'a name'

onyx NOUN a precious stone with layers of different colours

oodles PLURAL NOUN, *informal* lots (of), many

ooze VERB **1** to flow gently or slowly: *The mud oozed between her toes* **2** to exude: *He oozed charm* ▸ NOUN **1** soft mud **2** a gentle flow

opacity NOUN opaqueness

opal NOUN a bluish-white precious stone, with flecks of various colours

opalescent NOUN milky and iridescent

opaque ADJECTIVE not able to be seen through > **opaqueness** NOUN

OPEC ABBREVIATION Organization of the Petroleum-Exporting Countries, an association that negotiates with oil companies on production, prices, etc

open ADJECTIVE **1** not shut, allowing entry or exit **2** not enclosed or fenced **3** showing the inside or inner part; uncovered **4** not blocked **5** free for all to enter **6** honest, frank **7** of land: without many trees ▸ VERB **1** to make open; unlock **2** to begin **in the open 1** out-of-doors, in the open air **2** widely known, not secret **open to** likely or willing to receive: *open to attack/open to suggestions* **with open arms** warmly, enthusiastically: *She was welcomed with open arms*

open-air ADJECTIVE outside; in the open air: *an open-air swimming pool*

open air NOUN (**the open air**) any place not indoors or underground

open book NOUN someone or

A B C D E F G H I J K L M N O P Q R S T U V W X Y Z

something that has no secrets and can be easily understood

open-cast ADJECTIVE of a mine: excavating from the surface downwards

open-ended ADJECTIVE without definite limits: *an open-ended agreement*

opener NOUN something that opens: *a tin opener*

open-heart ADJECTIVE of surgery: performed on a heart which has been temporarily stopped, with blood being circulated by a heart-lung machine

opening NOUN **1** a hole, a gap **2** an opportunity **3** a vacant job

openly ADVERB without trying to hide or conceal anything

open-minded ADJECTIVE ready to consider or take up new ideas

open-plan ADJECTIVE with large rooms, undivided by walls or partitions: *an open-plan office/an open-plan school*

opera[1] NOUN a play in which the characters sing accompanied by an orchestra

opera[2] *plural* of **opus**

operable ADJECTIVE of a disease or injury: able to be treated by surgery

operate VERB **1** to act, work **2** to bring about an effect **3** to perform an operation

operatic ADJECTIVE of or for opera: *an operatic voice*

operating ADJECTIVE of or for surgical operations

operating system (*abbrev* **OS**) NOUN, *computing* a program which manages all other software programs on a computer and the hardware devices linked to that computer, eg printer, scanner, disk drives, etc (*compare with*: **application**)

operation NOUN **1** action **2** method or way of working **3** the cutting of a part of the human body to treat disease or repair damage **4** (**operations**) movements of armies, troops

operational ADJECTIVE working

operative ADJECTIVE **1** working, in action **2** of a rule etc: in force, having effect ▶NOUN a worker in a factory etc

operator NOUN **1** someone who works a machine **2** someone who connects telephone calls **3** a mathematical symbol showing which operation is to be carried out, eg + for addition

operetta NOUN a play with light music, singing and often dancing

ophthalmologist NOUN, *medicine* a doctor who specializes in eye diseases, defects and injuries

opiate NOUN **1** a drug containing opium used to make someone sleep **2** anything that calms or dulls the mind or feelings

opinion NOUN **1** what someone thinks or believes **2** professional judgement or point of view: *He wanted another opinion on his son's condition* **3** judgement of the value of someone or something: *I have a low opinion of her*

opinionated ADJECTIVE having and expressing strong opinions

opinion poll NOUN a survey of what people think of something

opium NOUN a drug made from the dried juice of a type of poppy

opponent NOUN someone who opposes; an enemy, a rival

opportune ADJECTIVE coming at the right or a convenient time: *I waited for an opportune moment to speak to her*

opportunist NOUN someone who takes advantage of a favourable situation > **opportunism** NOUN > **opportunistic** ADJECTIVE

opportunity NOUN (*plural* **opportunities**) a chance (to do something)

opposable ADJECTIVE of the thumb: able to face and touch the fingers on the same hand

oppose VERB **1** to struggle against, resist **2** to stand against, compete against

opposite ADJECTIVE **1** facing, across from **2** lying on the other side (of) **3** as different as possible: *I was trying to cheer her up but had the opposite effect* ▸ PREPOSITION **1** facing, across from: *He lives opposite the post office* **2** acting a role in a play, opera, etc in relation to another: *She played Ophelia opposite his Hamlet* ▸ NOUN something as different as possible (from something else): *Black is the opposite of white*

opposition NOUN **1** resistance **2** those who resist **3** (**the opposition**) the main political party that is against the governing party

oppress VERB **1** to govern harshly like a tyrant **2** to treat cruelly **3** to distress, worry greatly > **oppression** NOUN

oppressive ADJECTIVE **1** oppressing **2** cruel, harsh **3** of weather: close, tiring

opt VERB to choose; to decide between several options: *She opted to take the job/I opted for the red dress* **opt out** to decide not to take part in something

optic *or* **optical** ADJECTIVE relating to the eyes or sight

optical fibre NOUN a thin, flexible strand of glass or plastic used to convey information, eg in the cables for telephones, cable television, etc

optical illusion NOUN an impression that something seen is different from what it is

optician NOUN someone who makes and sells spectacles

optics SINGULAR NOUN the study of light and its practical application in devices and systems

optimal ADJECTIVE very best, optimum

optimism NOUN the habit of taking a positive, hopeful view of things (*contrasted with*: **pessimism**) > **optimist** NOUN > **optimistic** ADJECTIVE > **optimistically** ADVERB

optimize *or* **optimise** VERB to make the most of (a situation)

optimum ADJECTIVE best, most favourable: *optimum conditions*

option NOUN **1** choice; the right or power to choose **2** something that is or may be chosen

optional ADJECTIVE left to choice, not compulsory: *alloy wheels and other optional extras*

opulence NOUN wealth and luxury > **opulent** ADJECTIVE

A B C D E F G H I J K L M N O P Q R S T U V W X Y Z

or CONJUNCTION **1** used (often with **either**) to show alternatives: *Would you prefer tea or coffee?* **2** (often **or else**) because if not: *You'd better go or you'll miss your bus*

oral ADJECTIVE **1** spoken, not written: *oral literature* **2** relating to the mouth: *oral hygiene* ▶ NOUN an oral examination or test

ⓘ Comes from Latin *or-*, a form of *os* meaning 'mouth'

> Do not confuse with: **aural**. Aural means 'relating to the ear'. It may help to think of the 'O' of 'oral' as looking like an open mouth.

orange NOUN **1** a juicy citrus fruit, with a thick reddish-yellow skin **2** the colour of this fruit ▶ ADJECTIVE of this colour

orang-utan NOUN a large man-like ape, with long arms and long reddish hair

ⓘ Based on a Malay phrase which translates as 'wild man'

orator NOUN a public speaker

oratorio NOUN (*plural* **oratorios**), *music* a sacred story set to music, performed by soloists, choir and often orchestra

orb NOUN anything in the shape of a ball, a sphere

orbit NOUN range or area of influence: *within his orbit* ▶ VERB to go round the earth etc in space

orchard NOUN a large garden of fruit trees

orchestra NOUN a group of musicians playing together under a conductor

orchestrate VERB **1** to arrange (a piece of music) for an orchestra **2** to organize (a situation, the elements of a plan, etc) so as to produce the best effect

orchid (*pronounced* **awr**-kid) NOUN a plant with unusually shaped, often brightly coloured, flowers

ordain VERB **1** to declare something to be law **2** to admit (someone) as a member of the clergy: *He was ordained a priest in 1976*

ordeal NOUN **1** a hard trial or test **2** suffering, painful experience

order NOUN **1** an instruction to act made by someone in authority **2** a request or list of requests: *put an order in with the grocer* **3** an arrangement according to a system **4** an accepted way of doing things **5** a tidy or efficient state **6** peaceful conditions: *law and order* **7** rank, position, class **8** a society or brotherhood, eg of monks **9** any of the groups of animals or plants into which a class is divided and which in turn is subdivided into one or more families ▶ VERB **1** to give an order to, tell to do **2** to put in an order for: *I've ordered another copy of the book* **3** to arrange **in order 1** correct according to what is regularly done: *Is your passport in order?* **2** in a tidy arrangement **in order to** for the purpose of: *In order to live you must eat* **out of order 1** not working **2** not the correct way of doing things: *He shouldn't have said that. It was out of order* **3** not in a tidy arrangement: *The papers on his desk were all out of order*

orderly ADJECTIVE **1** in proper

order 2 well-behaved, quiet ▶NOUN (*plural* **orderlies**) 1 a soldier who carries the orders and messages of an officer 2 a hospital attendant who does routine jobs

ordinal number NOUN a number which shows order in a series, eg first, second, third (*compare with*: **cardinal number**)

ordinance NOUN a command; a law

ordinarily ADVERB usually, normally

ordinariness NOUN being ordinary

ordinary ADJECTIVE 1 common, usual 2 normal; not exceptional **out of the ordinary** unusual

Ordnance Survey NOUN a government office which produces official detailed maps

ore NOUN a mineral from which a metal is obtained: *iron ore*

oregano (*pronounced* o-ri-**gah**-noh *or US* o-**reg**-*a*n-oh) NOUN a Mediterranean herb used in cooking

organ NOUN 1 an internal part of the body, eg the liver 2 a large musical wind instrument with a keyboard 3 a means of spreading information, eg a newspaper: *an organ of conservatism*

organic ADJECTIVE 1 of or produced by the bodily organs 2 of, or with the characteristics of, a living organism 3 made up of parts each with its separate function 4 (grown) without the use of artificial fertilizers etc 5 of a chemical compound: containing carbon atoms arranged in chains or rings > **organically** ADVERB

organism NOUN any living thing

organist NOUN someone who plays the organ

organization *or* **organisation** NOUN 1 the act of organizing 2 a group of people working together for a purpose > **organizational** *or* **organisational** ADJECTIVE

organize *or* **organise** VERB 1 to arrange, set up (an event etc) 2 to form into a whole > **organizer** *or* **organiser** NOUN

orgasm NOUN the climax of sexual excitement > **orgasmic** ADJECTIVE

orgy NOUN (*plural* **orgies**) a drunken or other unrestrained celebration

Orient NOUN, *old* (**the Orient**) the countries of the East

oriental ADJECTIVE eastern; from the East

orientate VERB (also **orient**) 1 to find your position and sense of direction 2 to set or put facing a particular direction

orientation NOUN 1 the act or an instance of orientating or being orientated 2 a position relative to a fixed point

orienteering NOUN the sport of finding your way across country with the help of map and compass

orifice NOUN, *formal* an opening

origami NOUN the Japanese art of folding paper to make figures shaped like animals, birds, etc

origin NOUN 1 the starting point 2 the place from which someone or something comes 3 cause

original ADJECTIVE 1 first in time 2 not copied: *an original painting* 3 able to think or do something new: *an original mind* ▸ NOUN **1** the earliest version **2** a model from which other things are made: *Send a copy and keep the original*

originally ADVERB **1** in or from the beginning: *His family is from Ireland originally* **2** in a new and different way: *She dresses very originally*

originate VERB **1** to bring or come into being **2** to produce

ornament (*pronounced* **awr**-na-ment) NOUN something added to give or enhance beauty ▸ VERB (*pronounced* **awr**-na-ment) to adorn, decorate

ornamental ADJECTIVE used for ornament; decorative

ornate ADJECTIVE richly decorated
> **ornately** ADVERB

ornithologist NOUN someone who studies or is an expert on birds

orphan NOUN a child who has lost both parents

orphanage NOUN a home for orphans

orthodox ADJECTIVE **1** agreeing with the prevailing or established religious, political, etc views (*contrasted with*: **heterodox**) **2** normal, generally practised and accepted

orthopaedics *or US* **orthopedics** SINGULAR NOUN the branch of medicine which deals with bone diseases and injuries

oscillate VERB **1** to swing to and fro like the pendulum of a clock **2** to keep changing your mind
> **oscillation** NOUN

🛈 From Latin *oscillum*, literally 'small face', referring to a mask of the god Bacchus which hung in Roman vineyards and swung to and fro in the wind

-osis SUFFIX **1** *medicine* forms terms for diseased conditions: *neurosis/thrombosis* **2** forms words describing different processes: *metamorphosis* (= the process of changing appearance or character)/*osmosis* (= a gradual process of absorption or assimilation)

🛈 Comes from Greek suffix *-osis*, used to form nouns from verbs

osmosis NOUN **1** diffusion of liquids through a membrane **2** gradual absorption or assimilation

osprey NOUN (*plural* **ospreys**) a type of eagle which eats fish

ostensible ADJECTIVE of a reason etc: apparent, but not always real or true

ostentatious ADJECTIVE showy, meant to catch the eye

osteopathy (*pronounced* ost-ee-**op**-ath-i) NOUN a system of healing or treatment of bone and joint disorders, mainly involving manipulation and massage

ostracize *or* **ostracise** VERB to banish (someone) from the company of a group of people

ostrich NOUN (*plural* **ostriches**) a large African bird with showy plumage, which cannot fly but runs very fast

other ADJECTIVE **1** the second of two: *Where is the other sock?* **2** remaining, not previously mentioned: *These are for the other* *children* **3** different, additional: *There must be some other reason* **4** (**every other**) every second: *I visit Gran every other day* **5** recently past: *the other day* ▶ PRONOUN **1** the second of two **2** those remaining, those not previously mentioned: *The others arrived the next day* **3** the previous one: *one after the other* **other than** except: *no hope other than to retreat* **someone or other** *or* **something or other** someone or something not named or specified: *There's always someone or other here*

otherwise CONJUNCTION or else: *Be quiet; otherwise leave* ▶ ADVERB **1** in a different way **2** in different circumstances: *I took the bus, otherwise I'd have been late*

-otomy *see* **-tomy**

OTT ABBREVIATION, *informal* over-the-top, extravagant

otter NOUN a type of river animal living on fish

ought VERB **1** used with other verbs to indicate duty or need: *We ought to set an example/I ought to practise more* **2** to indicate what can be reasonably expected: *It's August; the weather ought to be fine*

ounce NOUN (*abbrev* **oz**) a unit of weight, equal to one-sixteenth of a pound (about 28.35 grams)

our ADJECTIVE belonging to us: *our house*

ours PRONOUN something belonging to us: *The green car is ours*

ourselves PRONOUN **1** used reflexively: *We exhausted ourselves swimming* **2** used for emphasis: *We ourselves don't like it, but other people may*

oust VERB **1** to drive out (from) **2** to drive out and take the place of: *She ousted him as leader of the party*

out ADVERB **1** into or towards the open air: *go out for a walk* **2** from inside: *take out a handkerchief* **3** not inside: *out of prison* **4** far from here: *out in the Far East* **5** not at home, not in the office, etc: *She's out at the moment* **6** aloud: *shouted out* **7** to or at an end: *Hear me out* **8** inaccurate: *The total was five pounds out* **9** *informal* on strike **10** published, released (for viewing, hire or purchase): *The video is out next week* **11** no longer hidden: *The secret is out* **12** openly admitting to being homosexual **13** dismissed from a game of cricket, baseball, etc **14** finished, having won at cards, etc **15** no longer in power or office **16** determined: *out to win*

out-and-out ADJECTIVE complete, total, thorough: *an out-and-out liar*

outback NOUN the wild interior parts of Australia

outbid VERB to offer a higher price than (somebody else)

outboard ADJECTIVE on the outside of a ship or boat: *an outboard motor*

outbreak NOUN a beginning, a breaking out, eg of war or disease: *an outbreak of salmonella*

outbuilding NOUN a building that is separate from the main building

outburst NOUN a bursting out, especially of angry feelings

outcast NOUN someone driven away from friends and home

A B C D E F G H I J K L M N O P Q R S T U V W X Y Z

outcome NOUN result

outcry NOUN (*plural* **outcries**) a widespread show of anger, disapproval, etc

outdo VERB (**outdoing, outdid, outdone**) to do better than

outdoor ADJECTIVE of, for or in the open air

outdoors ADVERB **1** outside the house **2** in or into the open air

outer ADJECTIVE nearer the edge, surface, etc; further away

outermost ADJECTIVE nearest the edge; furthest away

outfit NOUN a set of clothes worn together, often for a special occasion etc

outfitter NOUN a seller of outfits, especially men's clothes

outgoings PLURAL NOUN money spent or being spent

outgrow VERB (**outgrowing, outgrew, outgrown**) to get too big or old for (clothes, toys, etc)

outhouse NOUN a shed

outing NOUN a trip, excursion

outlandish ADJECTIVE looking or sounding very strange

outlaw NOUN someone put outside the protection of the law; a robber or bandit ▸VERB **1** to place beyond the protection of the law **2** to ban, forbid by law

outlay NOUN money paid out

outlet NOUN **1** a passage to the outside, eg for a water pipe **2** a means of expressing or getting rid of (a feeling, energy, etc) **3** a market for goods

outline NOUN **1** the outer line of a figure in a drawing etc **2** a sketch showing only the main lines **3** the main points etc, without the details: *an outline of the plot* **4** the most important features of something ▸VERB to draw an outline of

outlive VERB to live longer than

outlook NOUN **1** a view from a window etc **2** what is thought likely to happen: *the weather outlook*

outlying ADJECTIVE far from the centre, distant

outnumber VERB to be greater in number than: *Their team outnumbered ours*

out-of-date *or* **out of date** ADJECTIVE **1** old-fashioned **2** no longer valid: *This voucher is out of date/an out-of-date ticket*

out-patient NOUN a patient who does not stay in a hospital while receiving treatment (*contrasted with*: **in-patient**)

output NOUN **1** the goods produced by a machine, factory, etc; the amount of work done by a person **2** data transferred from a computer to a disk, tape or output device such as a VDU or printer (*contrasted with*: **input**)

outrage NOUN **1** an act of great violence **2** an act which shocks or causes offence ▸VERB **1** to injure, hurt by violence **2** to insult, shock

outrageous ADJECTIVE **1** violent, very wrong **2** not moderate, extravagant

outright ADVERB completely ▸ADJECTIVE complete, thorough

outset NOUN start, beginning

outside NOUN the outer surface or place: *the outside of the box*

▶ADJECTIVE **1** in, on or of the outer surface or place: *the outside seat* **2** relating to leisure rather than your full-time job: *outside interests* **3** slight, remote: *an outside chance of winning* ▶ADVERB out of doors; in or into the open air: *Let's eat outside* ▶PREPOSITION beyond the range of, not within: *outside the building/outside working hours* **at the outside** at the most: *ten miles at the outside*

outsider NOUN **1** someone not included in a particular social group **2** a runner etc whom no one expects to win

outskirts PLURAL NOUN the outer areas of a city etc

outspoken ADJECTIVE bold and frank in speech

outstanding ADJECTIVE **1** well-known **2** excellent **3** of a debt: unpaid

outstretched ADJECTIVE reaching out

out-tray NOUN an office tray for letters and work already dealt with (*contrasted with*: **in-tray**)

outward ADJECTIVE **1** towards or on the outside **2** of a journey: away from home, not towards it

outwardly ADVERB on the outside, in appearance: *He was outwardly confident*

outweigh VERB to be more important than: *The advantages outweigh the disadvantages*

outwit VERB (**outwitting, outwitted**) to defeat or get the better of (someone) by being clever or cunning

outwith PREPOSITION, *Scottish* outside of, beyond

oval ADJECTIVE having the shape of an egg, or, roughly, an ellipse ▶NOUN an egg or elliptical shape

ovary NOUN (*plural* **ovaries**) **1** *biology* one of two organs in the female body in which eggs are formed **2** *botany* the part of the flower that contains the ovules

ovation NOUN an outburst of cheering, hand-clapping, etc

oven NOUN a covered place for baking; a small furnace

over- PREFIX too much, to too great an extent: *overcook/over-excited*

over PREPOSITION **1** higher than, above: *The number is over the door/She won over £200/We've lived here for over thirty years* **2** across: *going over the bridge* **3** on the other side of: *the house over the road* **4** on top of: *threw his coat over the body* **5** here and there on: *paper scattered over the carpet* **6** about: *They quarrelled over their money* **7** by means of: *over the telephone* **8** during, throughout: *over the years* **9** while doing, having, etc: *fell asleep over his dinner* ▶ADVERB **1** above, higher up: *Two birds flew over* **2** across a distance: *He walked over and spoke* **3** downwards: *Did you fall over?* **4** above in number etc: *aged four and over* **5** as a remainder: *three left over* **6** through: *Read the passage over* ▶ADJECTIVE finished: *The sale is over* ▶NOUN, *cricket* a fixed number of balls bowled from one end of the wicket **over again** once more

overall NOUN **1** a garment worn

over ordinary clothes to protect them against dirt **2** (**overalls**) hard-wearing trousers with a bib worn as work clothes ▶ ADJECTIVE **1** from one end to the other: *overall length* **2** including everything: *overall cost* **over all** altogether: *His work's quite good, over all*

overarm ADJECTIVE of bowling etc: with the arm above the shoulder (*compare with*: **underarm**)

overawe VERB to frighten or astonish into silence

overbalance VERB to lose your balance and fall

overbearing ADJECTIVE over-confident, domineering

overboard ADVERB out of a ship into the water: *Man overboard!*

overcast ADJECTIVE of the sky: cloudy

overcoat NOUN an outdoor coat worn over all other clothes

overcome VERB to get the better of, defeat ▶ ADJECTIVE helpless from exhaustion, emotion, etc

overdo VERB **1** to do too much **2** to exaggerate: *They rather overdid the righteous indignation* **3** to cook (food) too long

overdose NOUN too great an amount (of medicine, a drug, etc) ▶ VERB to give or take too much medicine etc

overdraft NOUN the amount of money overdrawn from a bank

overdraw VERB to draw more money from the bank than you have in your account: *He's £500 overdrawn*

overdue ADJECTIVE **1** later than the stated or anticipated time: *Her baby is overdue* **2** of a bill etc: still unpaid although the time for payment has passed

overflow VERB **1** to flow or spill over: *The river overflowed its banks/The crowd overflowed into the next room* **2** to be so full as to flow over ▶ NOUN **1** something that overflows **2** a pipe or channel for getting rid of excess water etc

overgrown ADJECTIVE **1** covered with plant growth **2** grown too large or beyond normal size: *Boston is just an overgrown farm town*

overhaul VERB to examine carefully and carry out repairs ▶ NOUN a thorough examination and repair

overhead ADVERB directly above: *The aeroplane flew overhead* ▶ ADJECTIVE placed high above the ground: *overhead cables* ▶ NOUN (**overheads**) the regular expenses of a business etc, eg rent, rates, electricity

overhear VERB to hear what you were not meant to hear

overjoyed ADJECTIVE filled with great joy

overlap VERB **1** to extend over and partly cover: *The two pieces of cloth overlapped* **2** to cover a part of the same area or subject as another; partly coincide ▶ NOUN the amount by which something overlaps

overleaf ADJECTIVE on the other side of a leaf of a book

overload VERB to load or fill too much

overlook VERB **1** to look down on from a higher point; have or give

A B C D E F G H I J K L M N O P Q R S T U V W X Y Z

a view of: *The house overlooked the village* **2** to fail to see, miss **3** to pardon, not punish

overlord NOUN, *history* a lord with power over other lords

overly ADVERB too, excessively

overnight ADVERB **1** during the night: *staying overnight with a friend* **2** in a very short time: *His hair turned grey overnight* ▶ ADJECTIVE **1** for the night or for a night: *an overnight bag/an overnight stop* **2** got or made in a very short time: *an overnight success*

overpass NOUN a road going over above another road, railway, canal, etc

overpower VERB **1** to defeat through greater strength **2** to overwhelm, make helpless > **overpowering** ADJECTIVE **1** unable to be resisted **2** overwhelming, very strong: *an overpowering smell*

overrate VERB to value more highly than is deserved: *Her books are overrated* > **overrated** ADJECTIVE

overreach VERB: **overreach yourself** to try to do or get more than you can and so fail

override VERB **1** to ignore, set aside: *overriding the committee's decisions* **2** to take over control from: *override the automatic alarm signal*

overrule VERB to go against or cancel an earlier judgement or request

overrun VERB **1** to grow or spread over: *overrun with weeds* **2** to take possession of (a country)

overseas ADJECTIVE & ADVERB abroad; beyond the sea

oversee VERB to watch over, supervise

overshadow VERB to lessen the importance of (someone or something) by doing better than them

oversight NOUN **1** something left out or forgotten by mistake **2** failure to notice

overstep VERB to go further than (a set limit, rules, etc)

overt ADJECTIVE not hidden or secret; openly done

overtake VERB to catch up with and pass

overthrow VERB to defeat

overtime NOUN **1** time spent working beyond the agreed normal hours **2** payment for this, usually at a higher rate

overtone NOUN an additional meaning or association, not directly stated

overture NOUN **1** a piece of music played as an introduction to an opera **2** a proposal intended to open discussions: *overtures of peace*

overweight ADJECTIVE above an acceptable or healthy weight

overwhelm VERB **1** to defeat completely **2** to load with too great an amount: *overwhelmed with work* **3** to overcome, make helpless: *overwhelmed with grief*

overwhelming ADJECTIVE physically or mentally crushing; intensely powerful

overwork VERB to work more than is good for you

A
B
C
D
E
F
G
H
I
J
K
L
M
N
O
P
Q
R
S
T
U
V
W
X
Y
Z

overwrought ADJECTIVE excessively nervous or excited, agitated

ovulate VERB to release an egg cell from the ovary > **ovulation** NOUN

ovum NOUN (*plural* **ova**), *biology* the egg from which the young of animals and people develop

owe VERB **1** to be in debt to: *I owe Peter three pounds* **2** to have (a person or thing) to thank for: *He owes his success to his family* **owing to** because of

owl NOUN a bird of prey which comes out at night

owlet NOUN a young owl

own VERB **1** to have as a possession **2** to admit, confess to be true ▶ ADJECTIVE belonging to the person mentioned: *Is this all your own work?* **hold your own** to keep your place or position, not weaken **on your own 1** by your own efforts **2** alone

owner NOUN someone who possesses anything > **ownership** NOUN

own goal NOUN a goal scored by mistake against your own side

ox NOUN (*plural* **oxen**) a male cow, usually castrated, used for pulling loads etc

oxidation NOUN, *chemistry* a chemical reaction that involves the addition of oxygen to, or the removal of hydrogen from, a substance which loses electrons

oxide NOUN a compound of oxygen and another element

oxidize *or* **oxidise** VERB **1** to combine with oxygen **2** to become rusty

oxygen NOUN, *chemistry* (symbol **O**) a gas with no taste, colour or smell, forming part of the air and of water

ⓘ Based on two Greek words, meaning 'producing acid'

oxymoron (*pronounced* ok-si-**maw**-ron) NOUN a figure of speech in which contradictory terms are used together, eg *cruel kindness*, *falsely true*, etc

oyster NOUN a type of shellfish, often eaten raw

oz ABBREVIATION ounce(s)

ozone NOUN a form of oxygen, O_3

ozone layer NOUN a layer of the upper atmosphere where ozone is formed, which protects the earth from the sun's ultraviolet rays

Pp

p ABBREVIATION **1** page **2** pence

pace NOUN **1** a step **2** rate of walking, running, etc ▸VERB **1** to measure by steps **2** to walk backwards and forwards

pacemaker NOUN **1** someone who sets the pace in a race **2** an electronic device used to correct weak or irregular heart rhythms

pacifist NOUN someone who is against war

pacify VERB (**pacifies, pacifying, pacified**) **1** to make peaceful **2** to calm, soothe

pack NOUN **1** a bundle, especially one carried on the back **2** a set of playing-cards **3** a group of animals, especially dogs or wolves ▸VERB **1** to place (clothes etc) in a case or trunk for a journey **2** to press or crowd together closely **pack in** to cram in tightly **send someone packing** to send them away forcefully

package NOUN a bundle, a parcel ▸VERB **1** to put into a container **2** to wrap

package holiday *or* **package tour** NOUN a holiday or tour arranged by an organizer with all travel and accommodation included in the price

packaging NOUN the wrappers or containers in which goods are packed

packet NOUN **1** a small parcel **2** a container made of paper, cardboard, etc

pack ice NOUN a mass of pieces of floating ice driven together by currents etc

packing NOUN **1** the act of putting things in cases, parcels, etc **2** material for wrapping goods to pack **3** something used to fill an empty space

pact NOUN **1** an agreement **2** a treaty, a contract

pad[1] NOUN **1** a soft cushion-like object to prevent jarring, rubbing etc **2** a bundle of sheets of paper fixed together **3** the paw of certain animals **4** a rocket-launching platform ▸VERB (**padding, padded**) **1** to stuff or protect with a soft material **2** (often **pad out**) to fill (something) up with unnecessary material

pad[2] VERB (**padding, padded**) to walk making a dull, soft noise

padding NOUN **1** stuffing material **2** words included in a speech, book, etc just to fill space or time

A B C D E F G H I J K L M N O P Q R S T U V W X Y Z

paddle[1] VERB to wade in shallow water

paddle[2] NOUN a short, broad, spoon-shaped oar ▸ VERB to move forward by the use of paddles; row

paddle steamer NOUN a steamer driven by two large wheels made up of paddles

paddock NOUN a small, closed-in field used for pasture

paddy field NOUN a muddy field in which rice is grown

padlock NOUN a removable lock with a hinged, U-shaped bar

paediatrician *or US* **pediatrician** NOUN a doctor who specializes in studying and treating children's illnesses

paediatrics *or US* **pediatrics** SINGULAR NOUN the treatment of children's diseases

paedo- (*pronounced* pee-doh)also **paed-** (*pronounced* peed), *also* **pedo-**, **ped-** PREFIX of or relating to children: *paedophile/ pedagogical* (relating to the education of children)

ⓘ Comes from Greek *paidos* meaning 'of a boy'

paedophile *or US* **pedophile** NOUN an adult who has sexual desire for children

pagan NOUN someone who does not believe in any religion; a heathen ▸ ADJECTIVE to do with pagans or paganism > **paganism** NOUN

page[1] NOUN one side of a blank, written, or printed sheet of paper

page[2] NOUN **1** a boy servant **2** a boy who carries the train of the bride's dress in a marriage service ▸ VERB to contact someone using a pager

pageant (*pronounced* **paj**-*a*nt) NOUN **1** a show or procession made up of scenes from history **2** an elaborate parade or display > **pageantry** NOUN (meaning 2)

pager NOUN a small radio device that can be used to receive a signal, usually a beeping noise, from elsewhere

pagoda NOUN an Eastern temple, especially in China or India

paid *past form* of **pay**

pail NOUN an open vessel of tin, zinc, plastic, etc for carrying liquids; a bucket

pain NOUN **1** feeling caused by hurt to mind or body **2** threat of punishment: *under pain of death* **3** (**pains**) care: *takes great pains with his work* ▸ VERB to cause suffering to, distress

pained ADJECTIVE showing pain or distress: *a pained expression*

painful ADJECTIVE **1** causing pain: *a painful injury* **2** affected by something which causes pain: *a painful finger* **3** causing distress: *a painful duty* **4** laborious: *painful progress* > **painfully** ADVERB

painkiller NOUN a medicine taken to lessen pain

painless ADJECTIVE without pain > **painlessly** ADVERB

painstaking ADJECTIVE very careful > **painstakingly** ADVERB

paint VERB **1** to apply colour to in the form of liquid or paste **2** to describe in words ▸ NOUN a liquid substance used for colouring and applied with a brush, a spray, etc

painter NOUN **1** someone whose trade is painting **2** an artist who works in paint

painting NOUN **1** the act or art of creating pictures with paint **2** a painted picture

pair NOUN **1** two of the same kind **2** a set of two ▸ VERB **1** to join to form a pair **2** to go in twos **3** to mate

pajamas *US* for **pyjamas**

pal NOUN, *informal* a friend

palace NOUN the house of a king, queen, archbishop or aristocrat

ⓘ From the *Palatine* Hill in Rome, where the Roman emperors lived

palaeontology NOUN the study of extinct life forms by examining their fossilized remains > **palaeontologist** NOUN

palatable ADJECTIVE **1** pleasant to the taste **2** acceptable, pleasing

palate (*pronounced* **pal**-*a*t) NOUN **1** the roof of the mouth **2** the sense of taste

ⓘ Comes from Latin *palatum* meaning 'the roof of the mouth'

> Do not confuse with: **palette** and **pallet**

palatial (*pronounced* pa-**lei**-sh*a*l) ADJECTIVE like a palace, magnificent

pale[1] NOUN a wooden stake used in making a fence to enclose ground

pale[2] ADJECTIVE **1** light or whitish in colour **2** not bright ▸ VERB to make or turn pale

palette (*pronounced* **pal**-*e*t) NOUN a board or plate on which an artist mixes paints

ⓘ Comes from Italian *paletta* meaning 'a small shovel'

> Do not confuse with: **pallet** and **palate**

palindrome NOUN a word or phrase that reads the same backwards as forwards, eg 'level'

ⓘ From Greek *palindromos*, meaning 'running back'

paling NOUN a row of wooden stakes forming a fence

palisade NOUN a fence of pointed wooden stakes

pall[1] (*pronounced* pawl) NOUN **1** the cloth over a coffin at a funeral **2** a dark covering or cloud: *a pall of smoke*

pall[2] (*pronounced* pawl) VERB to become dull or uninteresting

pallbearer NOUN one of those carrying or walking beside the coffin at a funeral

pallet[1] (*pronounced* **pal**-*e*t) NOUN a straw bed or mattress

ⓘ Comes from French *paille* meaning 'straw'

pallet[2] (*pronounced* **pal**-*e*t) NOUN a platform that can be lifted by a fork-lift truck for stacking goods

ⓘ Shares the same origin as 'palette'

> Do not confuse with: **palette** and **palate**

palliative (*pronounced* **pal**-i-*a*-tiv) ADJECTIVE making less severe or harsh ▸ NOUN something which lessens pain, eg a drug

pallid ADJECTIVE pale

pallor NOUN paleness

palm[1] NOUN the inner surface of the hand between the wrist and the base of the fingers **palm off** to give with the intention of cheating: *That shopkeeper palmed off a foreign coin on me*

palm[2] NOUN a tall tree with broad fan-shaped leaves, which grows in hot countries

palpable ADJECTIVE **1** *medicine* able to be touched or felt **2** easily noticed, obvious

palpitations PLURAL NOUN uncomfortable rapid beating of the heart

palsy (*pronounced* **pawl**-zi) NOUN a loss of power and feeling in the muscles

paltry (*pronounced* **pawl**-tri) ADJECTIVE (**paltrier, paltriest**) of little value

pampas PLURAL NOUN (*pronounced* **pam**-p*a*z) *or* SINGULAR NOUN (*pronounced* **pam**-p*a*s) (**the pampas**) the vast, treeless plains of South America

pampas grass NOUN a type of very tall, feathery grass

pamper VERB to spoil (a child etc) by giving too much attention to

pamphlet NOUN a small book, stitched or stapled, often with a light paper cover

pan- PREFIX all, whole: *pandemonium/panoply*

ⓘ Comes from Greek *pan*, a form of *pas* meaning 'all'

pan[1] NOUN **1** a broad, shallow pot used in cooking, a saucepan **2** a shallow dent in the ground **3** the bowl of a toilet

pan[2] VERB (**panning, panned**) to move a television or film camera so as to follow an object or give a wide view **pan out 1** to turn out (well or badly) **2** to come to an end

panacea (*pronounced* pan-*a*-**see**-*a*) NOUN a cure for all things

panache (*pronounced* p*a*-**nash**) NOUN a sense of style, swagger

ⓘ Literally meaning 'a plume', from the use of feathers in flamboyant headgear

Pan-American ADJECTIVE including all America or Americans, North and South

pancake NOUN a thin cake of flour, eggs, sugar and milk, fried in a pan or on a griddle

pancreas (*pronounced* **pang**-kri-*a*s) NOUN, *anatomy* a gland behind the stomach producing fluids that aid digestion

panda NOUN **1** a large black-and-white bear-like animal found in Tibet etc **2** a raccoon-like animal found in the Himalayas

pandemic ADJECTIVE of a disease etc: occurring over a wide area and affecting a large number of people

pandemonium NOUN a state of confusion and uproar

ⓘ The name of the capital of Hell in Milton's *Paradise Lost* (1667)

pander NOUN a pimp ▶ VERB (**pander to**) to indulge, easily comply with

ⓘ After *Pandarus*, who acts as a go-between in the story of Troilus and Cressida

pane NOUN a sheet of glass

panel NOUN **1** a flat rectangular piece of wood such as is set into a door or wall **2** a group of people chosen to judge a contest, take part in a television quiz, etc

pang NOUN a sudden sharp pain; a twinge

panic NOUN **1** a sudden and great fright **2** fear that spreads from person to person ▶VERB (**panicking, panicked**) **1** to throw into panic **2** to act wildly through fear

ⓘ From a Greek word meaning 'fear of the god Pan'. Pan was said to roam about the woodland and scare people and animals

pannier NOUN **1** a basket slung over a horse's back **2** a light container attached to a bicycle etc

panoply (*pronounced* **pan**-*o*-pli) NOUN (*plural* **panoplies**) **1** the ceremonial dress, equipment, etc associated with a particular event: *the panoply of a military funeral* **2** *history* a full suit of armour

panorama NOUN a wide view of a landscape, scene, etc

pansy NOUN (*plural* **pansies**) a flower like the violet but larger

pant VERB **1** to gasp for breath **2** to say breathlessly **3** to wish eagerly (for)

panther NOUN **1** a large leopard **2** *US* a puma

panties PLURAL NOUN thin, light knickers worn by women and children

pantomime NOUN a Christmas play, with songs, jokes, etc, based on a popular fairy tale, eg Cinderella

pantry NOUN (*plural* **pantries**) a room for storing food

pants PLURAL NOUN **1** underpants **2** women's short-legged knickers **3** *US* trousers

papacy (*pronounced* **pei**-p*a*-si) NOUN the position or power of the Pope

papal (*pronounced* **pei**-p*a*l) ADJECTIVE of, or relating to, the pope or the papacy

paparazzo (*pronounced* pa-p*a*-**rat**-soh) NOUN (*plural* **paparazzi** – *pronounced* pa-p*a*-**rat**-see) a press photographer who hounds celebrities etc

ⓘ After the name of a photographer in Federico Fellini's film *La Dolce Vita*

papaya (*pronounced* p*a*-**pai**-*a*) NOUN a green-skinned edible fruit from S America (*also called*: **pawpaw**)

paper NOUN **1** a material made from rags, wood, etc used for writing or wrapping **2** a single sheet of this **3** a newspaper **4** an essay on a learned subject **5** a set of examination questions **6** (**papers**) documents proving someone's identity, nationality, etc ▶VERB to cover up (especially walls) with paper

paperback NOUN a book bound in a flexible paper cover (*compare with*: **hardback**)

paperchase NOUN a game in which one runner leaves a trail of paper so that others may track them

paperweight NOUN a heavy glass, metal, etc object used to keep papers in place

papier-mâché (*pronounced* pap-yei-**mash**-ei) NOUN a substance consisting of paper pulp and some sticky liquid or glue, shaped into models, bowls, etc

A B C D E F G H I J K L M N O P Q R S T U V W X Y Z

paprika (*pronounced* **pa**-pri-k*a or* p*a*-**pree**-k*a*) NOUN a type of ground red pepper

papyrus (*pronounced* p*a*-**pai**-r*u*s) NOUN (*plural* **papyri** – *pronounced* p*a*-**pai**-rai– *or* **papyruses**) a reed used by the ancient Egyptians etc to make paper

par NOUN **1** an accepted standard, value, etc **2** *golf* the number of strokes allowed for each hole if the play is perfect **below par 1** not up to standard **2** not feeling very well **on a par with** equal to or comparable with

parable NOUN a story (eg in the Bible) which teaches a moral lesson

parabola (*pronounced* p*a*-**rab**-*o*-l*a*) NOUN **1** a curve **2** *maths* the intersection of a cone by a plane parallel to its sloping side

paracetamol (*pronounced* pa-r*a*-**set**-*a*-mol) NOUN a pain-relieving drug

parachute NOUN an umbrella-shaped device made of light material and rope which supports someone or something dropping slowly to the ground from an aeroplane ▶ VERB to drop by parachute

parachutist NOUN someone dropped by parachute from an aeroplane

parade NOUN **1** an orderly arrangement of troops for inspection or exercise **2** a procession of people, vehicles, etc in celebration of some event ▶ VERB **1** to arrange (troops) in order **2** to march in a procession **3** to display in an obvious way

paradise NOUN **1** heaven **2** a place or state of great happiness

paradox NOUN (*plural* **paradoxes**) a saying which seems to contradict itself but which may be true

paradoxical ADJECTIVE combining two apparently contradictory elements: *It is paradoxical that many people are homeless when there are many empty houses*
> **paradoxically** ADVERB

paraffin NOUN, *Brit* a liquid obtained from petroleum or coal which is used as a fuel in aeroplanes, heaters, etc (*N Am & Aust name*: **kerosene**)

paragliding NOUN the sport of gliding supported by a modified type of parachute

paragon NOUN a model of perfection or excellence: *a paragon of good manners*

paragraph NOUN **1** a division of a piece of writing shown by beginning the first sentence on a new line **2** a short item in a newspaper

parakeet NOUN a small, brightly coloured parrot

parallel ADJECTIVE **1** of lines: going in the same direction and never meeting, always remaining equidistant **2** similar or alike in some way: *parallel cases* ▶ NOUN **1** *maths* a line or plane parallel with something else **2** something comparable in some way with something else **3** *geography* a line to mark latitude, drawn east and west across a map or round a globe at a set distance from the equator

parallelogram NOUN, *maths* a four-sided figure, the opposite sides of which are parallel and equal in length

parallel port NOUN, *computing* a socket or plug for connecting a device such as a printer to a computer

paralyse *or US* **paralyze** VERB **1** to affect with paralysis **2** to make helpless or ineffective **3** to bring to a halt

paralysis NOUN (*plural* **paralyses**) loss of the power to move and feel in part of the body

paralytic ADJECTIVE **1** suffering from paralysis **2** *informal* helplessly drunk ▸NOUN a paralysed person

paramedic NOUN someone helping doctors and nurses, eg a member of an ambulance crew

paramedical ADJECTIVE denoting personnel or services that are supplementary to and support the work of the medical profession

parameter (*pronounced* pa-**ram**-i-*ter*) NOUN (often **parameters**) the limiting factors which affect the way in which something can be done

ⓘ Comes from Greek *para* meaning 'beside' or 'beyond', and *metron* meaning 'measure'

> Do not confuse with: **perimeter**. Notice that words starting with **peri-** often relate to the idea of 'going around' and the **perimeter** of a figure or shape is the line that goes around it.

paramilitary ADJECTIVE **1** on military lines and intended to supplement the military **2** organized illegally as a military force ▸NOUN (*plural* **paramilitaries**) **1** a group organized in this way **2** a member of a such a group

paramount ADJECTIVE very greatest, supreme: *of paramount importance*

paranoia NOUN **1** a form of mental disorder characterized by delusions of grandeur, persecution, etc **2** intense, irrational fear or suspicion

paranoid ADJECTIVE suffering from paranoia

paranormal ADJECTIVE beyond what is normal in nature or scientific explanation

parapet NOUN a low wall on a bridge or balcony to prevent people falling over the side

paraphernalia PLURAL NOUN belongings; gear, equipment

ⓘ Originally a woman's property which was not part of her dowry, and which therefore remained her own after marriage

paraphrase VERB to express (a piece of writing) in other words ▸NOUN an expression in different words

paraplegia (*pronounced* par-*a*-**plee**-ji-*a*) NOUN, *medicine* paralysis of the lower part of the body and legs

paraplegic *medicine*, ADJECTIVE of paraplegia ▸NOUN someone who suffers from paraplegia

parasite NOUN an animal, plant or person living on another without being any use in return > **parasitic** ADJECTIVE

parasol NOUN a light umbrella used as a sunshade

A B C D E F G H I J K L M N O P Q R S T U V W X Y Z

paratrooper NOUN a soldier who is specially trained to drop from an aeroplane using a parachute

paratroops PLURAL NOUN soldiers carried by air to be dropped by parachute into enemy country

parboil VERB to partly cook (food) by boiling for a short time

parcel NOUN a wrapped and tied package to be sent by post ▸ VERB (**parcelling, parcelled**): **parcel something out** to divide it into portions **parcel something up** to wrap it up as a package **part and parcel** an absolutely necessary part

parch VERB **1** to make hot and very dry **2** to make thirsty

parched ADJECTIVE **1** very dry **2** very thirsty

parchment NOUN **1** the dried skin of a goat or sheep used for writing on **2** paper resembling this

pardon VERB **1** to forgive **2** to free from punishment **3** to allow to go unpunished ▸ NOUN **1** forgiveness **2** the act of pardoning

pardonable ADJECTIVE able to be forgiven

pare VERB **1** to peel or cut off the edge or outer surface of **2** to make smaller gradually

parent NOUN a father or mother

parentage NOUN descent from parents or ancestors: *of Italian parentage*

parental ADJECTIVE **1** of parents **2** with the manner or attitude of a parent

parenthesis (*pronounced* pa-**ren**-the-sis) NOUN (*plural* **parentheses** – *pronounced* pa-**ren**-the-seez) **1** a word or group of words in a sentence forming an explanation or comment, often separated by brackets or dashes, eg he and his wife (*so he said*) were separated **2** (**parentheses**) brackets

parenthetical ADJECTIVE **1** of the nature of a parenthesis **2** using parenthesis

parenthood NOUN the state of being a parent

pariah (*pronounced* pa-**rai**-*a*) NOUN someone driven out from a community or group; an outcast
ⓘ Originally a member of a low caste in southern India

parish NOUN (*plural* **parishes**) a district with its own church and minister or priest

parishioner (*pronounced* pa-**rish**-*on-er*) NOUN a member of a parish

parity NOUN equality

park NOUN **1** a public place for walking, with grass and trees **2** an enclosed piece of land surrounding a country house ▸ VERB to stop and leave (a car etc) in a place

parka NOUN a type of thick jacket with a hood

Parkinson's disease NOUN a disease causing trembling in the hands etc and rigid muscles

parliament NOUN **1** the chief law-making council of a nation **2** (**Parliament**) *Brit* the House of Commons and the House of Lords

parliamentary ADJECTIVE **1** of, for or concerned with parliament: *a parliamentary candidate* **2** used in or suitable for parliament: *parliamentary procedures*

parlour *or US* **parlor** NOUN a sitting room in a house

parlourmaid *or US* **parlormaid** NOUN a woman or girl whose job is to wait at table

parochial (*pronounced* pa-**roh**-ki-*a*l) ADJECTIVE **1** relating to a parish **2** interested only in local affairs; narrow-minded > **parochially** ADVERB

parody NOUN (*plural* **parodies**) an amusing imitation of someone's writing style, subject matter, etc ▶ VERB (**parodies, parodying, parodied**) to make a parody of

parole (*pronounced* pa-**rohl**) NOUN the release of a prisoner before the end of a sentence on condition that they will have to return if they break the law ▶ VERB to release on parole

From French *parole* meaning 'word' because prisoners are released on their word of honour

paroxysm NOUN a fit of pain, rage, laughter, etc > **paroxysmal** ADJECTIVE

parquet (*pronounced* **pahr**-kei) NOUN a floor covering of wooden blocks arranged in a pattern

parrot NOUN a bird with a hooked bill and often brightly coloured feathers

Parsee *or* **Parsi** NOUN a member of an Indian religious sect descended from the Persian Zoroastrians

parsimonious ADJECTIVE too careful in spending money; stingy

parsimony (*pronounced* **pahr**-si-mo-ni) NOUN great care in spending money, meanness

parsley NOUN a bright-green, leafy herb, used in cookery

parsnip NOUN a plant with an edible, yellowish root shaped like a carrot

parson NOUN a member of the clergy, especially one in charge of a parish of the Church of England

parsonage NOUN a parson's house

part NOUN **1** a portion, a share **2** a piece forming part of a whole: *the various parts of a car engine* **3** a character taken by an actor in a play **4** a role in an action or event: *played a vital part in the campaign* **5** *music* the notes to be played or sung by a particular instrument or voice **6** (**parts**) talents: *a man of many parts* ▶ VERB **1** to divide **2** to separate, send or go in different ways **3** to put or keep apart **in good part** without being hurt or taking offence **part with** to let go, be separated from

Comes from Latin *pars* meaning 'a part', 'a section' or 'a share'

partake **partake of 1** to eat or drink some of **2** to take a part in

partial ADJECTIVE **1** in part only, not total or complete: *partial payment* **2** having a liking for (someone or something): *partial to cheese*

partiality NOUN (*plural* **partialities**) **1** the favouring of one thing more than another, bias **2** a particular liking (for something)

partially ADVERB not completely or wholly; not yet to the point of completion: *The house is only partially built*

participant *or* **participator** NOUN someone who takes part in anything

participate VERB **1** to take

A B C D E F G H I J K L M N O P Q R S T U V W X Y Z

part (in) **2** to have a share (in)
> **participation** NOUN

participatory ADJECTIVE capable of being participated in or shared

participle NOUN, *grammar* **1** a form of a verb which can be used with other verbs to form tenses, eg 'he was *eating*' or 'she has *arrived*' **2** a form of verb used as an adjective, eg '*stolen* jewels' **3** a form of a verb used as a noun, *eg* '*running* makes me tired'

particle NOUN a very small piece: *a particle of sand*

particular ADJECTIVE **1** relating to a single definite person, thing, etc considered separately from others: *I want this particular colour* **2** special: *Take particular care of the china* **3** fussy, difficult to please: *particular about her food* ▸NOUN (**particulars**) the facts or details about someone or something
> **particularly** ADVERB

parting NOUN **1** the act of separating or dividing **2** a place of separation **3** a going away (from each other), a leave-taking **4** a line dividing hair on the head brushed in opposite directions

partisan (*pronounced* pahr-ti-**zan** *or* **pahr**-ti-zan) ADJECTIVE giving strong support or loyalty to a particular cause, theory, etc, often without considering other points of view ▸NOUN someone with partisan views

partition NOUN **1** a division **2** something which divides, eg a wall between rooms ▸VERB **1** to divide into parts **2** to divide by making a wall etc **3** *maths* to split (a number) into component parts, eg 24 into 12+12 or 14+10

partly ADVERB in part, or in some parts; not wholly or completely: *The house is built partly of stone and partly of wood*

partner NOUN **1** someone who shares the ownership of a business etc with another or others **2** one of a pair in games, dancing, etc **3** a husband, wife, or lover ▸VERB to act as someone's partner

partnership NOUN **1** a relationship in which two or more people or groups operate together as partners **2** the status of a partner: *She was offered a partnership at the age of 30* **3** a business or other enterprise jointly owned or run by two or more people etc

part of speech NOUN (*plural* **parts of speech**) *grammar* any of the grammatical groups into which words are divided, eg noun, verb, adjective, preposition

partridge NOUN (*plural* **partridge** *or* **partridges**) a bird with brown or grey feathers which is shot as game

part-time ADJECTIVE for only part of the working week: *I went part-time in my job* (*compare with*: **full-time**)

party NOUN (*plural* **parties**) **1** a gathering of guests: *a birthday party/dinner party* **2** a group of people travelling together: *a party of tourists* **3** a number of people with the same plans or ideas: *a political party* **4** someone taking part in, or approving, an action

party line NOUN **1** a shared telephone line **2** the official policy laid down by the leaders of a political party

pass VERB **1** to go, move, travel, etc: *He passed out of sight over the hill* **2** to move on or along: *Pass the salt* **3** to go by: *I saw the bus pass our house* **4** to overtake **5** of parliament: to put (a law) into force **6** to be successful in (an examination) **7** to be declared healthy or in good condition after (an inspection) **8** to come to an end: *The feeling of dizziness passed* **9** to hand on, give: *He passed the story on to his son* **10** to spend (time): *passing a pleasant hour by the river* **11** to make, utter (eg a remark) ▶NOUN **1** a narrow passage over or through a range of mountains **2** a ticket or card allowing someone to go somewhere **3** success in an examination **4** a sexual advance **pass away** to die **pass off** to present (a forgery etc) as genuine **pass on 1** to go forward, proceed **2** to hand on **3** to die **pass out** to faint **pass up** to fail to take up (an opportunity)

passable ADJECTIVE **1** fairly good **2** of a river etc: able to be crossed > **passably** ADVERB (meaning 1)

passage NOUN **1** the act of passing: *the passage of time* **2** a journey in a ship **3** a corridor **4** a way through **5** a part of the text of a book

passageway NOUN a passage, a way through

passenger NOUN a traveller, not a member of the crew, in a train, ship, aeroplane, etc

passer-by NOUN (*plural* **passers-by**) someone who happens to pass by when something happens

passing ADJECTIVE **1** going by: *a passing car* **2** not lasting long: *passing interest* **3** casual: *a passing remark* ▶NOUN **1** the act of someone or something which passes **2** a going away, a coming to an end **3** death

passion NOUN **1** strong feeling, especially anger or love **2** (**the Passion**) the sufferings and death of Christ

passionate ADJECTIVE **1** easily moved to passion **2** full of passion > **passionately** ADVERB

passionfruit NOUN the edible, oblong fruit of a tropical plant

passive ADJECTIVE **1** making no resistance **2** acted upon, not acting **3** *grammar* describing the form of a verb in which the subject undergoes, rather than performs, the action of the verb, eg: *'The postman was bitten by the dog'* (*compare with*: **active**) > **passively** ADVERB > **passivity** NOUN

passive smoking NOUN the involuntary inhaling of smoke from tobacco smoked by others

Passover NOUN a Jewish festival celebrating the exodus of the Israelites from Egypt (*also*: **Pesach**)

passport NOUN a card or booklet which gives someone's name and description, needed to travel in another country

password NOUN **1** a secret word which allows those who know it to pass **2** *computing* a word typed into a computer to allow access to restricted data

past NOUN **1** (**the past**) the time gone by **2** someone's previous life or career **3** *grammar* the past tense ▸ADJECTIVE **1** of an earlier time: *past kindnesses* **2** just over, recently ended: *the past year* **3** gone, finished: *The time for argument is past* ▸PREPOSITION **1** after: *It's past midday* **2** up to and beyond, further than: *Go past the traffic lights* ▸ADVERB by: *She walked past, looking at no one*

pasta NOUN **1** a dough used in making spaghetti, macaroni, etc **2** the prepared shapes of this, eg spaghetti

paste NOUN **1** pastry dough **2** a gluey liquid for sticking paper etc together **3** any soft, kneadable mixture: *almond paste* **4** fine glass used to make imitation gems ▸VERB **1** to stick something with paste **2** *computing* to insert (text that has been cut or copied from another document etc)

pastel ADJECTIVE of a colour: soft, pale ▸NOUN **1** a chalk-like crayon used for drawing **2** a drawing made with this

pasteurize *or* **pasteurise** VERB to heat food (especially milk) in order to kill harmful germs in it > **pasteurization** NOUN

ⓘ Named after Louis *Pasteur*, the 19th-century French chemist who invented the process

pastiche (*pronounced* pas-**teesh**) NOUN a humorous imitation, a parody

pastime NOUN a hobby, a spare-time interest

pastor NOUN a member of the clergy

pastoral ADJECTIVE **1** relating to country life **2** of a pastor or the work of the clergy

past participle NOUN, *grammar* the form of a verb used after an auxiliary verb to indicate that something took place in the past, for instance *gone* in 'he has *gone*'

pastry NOUN (*plural* **pastries**) **1** a flour paste used to make the bases and crusts of pies, tarts, etc **2** a small cake

past tense NOUN, *grammar* the tense of a verb which indicates that something took place in the past

pasture NOUN ground covered with grass on which cattle graze

pasty[1] (*pronounced* **peis**-ti) ADJECTIVE (**pastier, pastiest**) **1** like paste **2** pale

pasty[2] (*pronounced* **pas**-ti) NOUN (*plural* **pasties**) a pie containing meat and vegetables in a covering of pastry

pat NOUN **1** a light, quick blow or tap with the hand **2** a small lump of butter etc **3** a cake of animal dung ▸VERB (**patting, patted**) to strike gently, tap **off pat** memorized thoroughly, ready to be said when necessary

patch VERB to mend (clothes) by putting in a new piece of material to cover a hole ▸NOUN (*plural* **patches**) **1** a piece of material sewn on to mend a hole **2** a small piece of ground **patch up 1** to mend, especially hastily or clumsily **2** to settle (a quarrel)

patchwork NOUN fabric formed of small patches or pieces of material sewn together

patchy ADJECTIVE (**patchier,**

patchiest) uneven, mixed in quality
> **patchily** ADVERB

pate (*pronounced* peit) NOUN, *formal* the head: *a bald pate*

pâté *or* **paté** (*pronounced* **pa**-tei) NOUN a paste made of finely minced meat, fish or vegetables, flavoured with herbs, spices, etc

patent (*pronounced* **pei**-tent) NOUN an official written statement granting someone the sole right to make or sell something that they have invented ▶ADJECTIVE **1** protected from copying by a patent **2** open, easily seen ▶VERB to obtain a patent for

patent leather NOUN leather with a very glossy surface

patently ADVERB openly, clearly: *patently obvious*

pater- *or* **patri-** PREFIX father: *paternal*

🄸 Comes from Latin *pater* meaning 'father'

paternal ADJECTIVE **1** of a father **2** like a father, fatherly **3** on the father's side of the family: *my paternal grandfather*

paternity NOUN the state or fact of being a father

paternity leave NOUN leave of absence from work for a father after the birth of a child

-path SUFFIX **1** forms words describing people who are suffering from particular disorders **2** forms words describing people who provide therapy for particular disorders: *osteopath* (= someone who provides therapy for bone and muscle injuries)

🄸 Comes from Greek *patheia* meaning 'suffering'

path NOUN **1** a way made by people or animals walking on it, a track **2** the route to be taken by a person or vehicle: *in the lorry's path* **3** a course of action, a way of life

pathetic ADJECTIVE **1** causing pity **2** causing contempt; feeble, inadequate: *a pathetic attempt*
> **pathetically** ADVERB

pathname NOUN, *computing* a name that specifies the location of a particular file within a directory

patho- (*pronounced* path-oh) PREFIX of or relating to diseases or other disorders: *pathology*

🄸 Comes from Greek *patheia* meaning 'suffering'

pathogen NOUN a micro-organism, eg a bacterium or virus, that causes infection or disease

pathological ADJECTIVE **1** relating to disease **2** *informal* compulsive, obsessive: *a pathological liar*

pathologist NOUN **1** a doctor who studies the causes and effects of disease **2** a doctor who makes post-mortem examinations

pathology NOUN the study of diseases

pathos (*pronounced* **pei**-thos) NOUN a quality that arouses pity

pathway NOUN a path

-pathy SUFFIX forms words describing disorders and therapies: *osteopathy*

🄸 Comes from Greek *patheia* meaning 'suffering'

patience NOUN **1** the ability or willingness to be patient **2** (*also* *called*: **solitaire**) a card game played by one person

patient ADJECTIVE suffering delay, discomfort, etc without complaint or anger ▸ NOUN someone under the care of a doctor etc > **patiently** ADVERB

patio (*pronounced* **pat**-i-oh) NOUN (*plural* **patios**) a paved open yard attached to a house

patri- PREFIX father: *patricide*

patriarch (*pronounced* **pei**-tri-ahrk) NOUN **1** the male head of a family or tribe **2** a high-ranking bishop of the Orthodox Church

patriarchal (*pronounced* pei-tri-**ahrk**-k*a*l) ADJECTIVE ruled or controlled by men or patriarchs

patriarchy (*pronounced* **pei**-tri-ahr-ki) NOUN (*plural* **patriarchies**) a society in which a man is head of the family and descent is traced through the male line

patriot (*pronounced* **pat**-ri-*o*t *or* **peit**-ri-*o*t) NOUN someone who loves and is loyal to their country

patriotic ADJECTIVE loyal or devoted to your country > **patriotically** ADVERB

patriotism NOUN love of and loyalty to your country

patrol VERB (**patrolling, patrolled**) to keep guard or watch by moving regularly around (an area etc) ▸ NOUN **1** the act of keeping guard in this way **2** the people keeping watch **3** a small group of Scouts or Guides

patrol car NOUN a police car used to patrol an area

patron (*pronounced* **pei**-tron) NOUN **1** someone who protects or supports (an artist, a form of art, etc) **2** a customer of a shop etc

patronage (*pronounced* **pat**-ro-nij) NOUN the support given by a patron

patronize *or* **patronise** (*pronounced* **pat**-ro-naiz) VERB **1** to be a patron towards: *Patronize your local shops* **2** to treat (someone) as an inferior, look down on: *Don't patronize me*

patron saint NOUN a saint chosen as the protector of a country etc

patter[1] VERB of rain, footsteps, etc: to make a quick tapping sound ▸ NOUN the sound of falling rain, of footsteps, etc

patter[2] NOUN **1** chatter; rapid talk, especially that used by salesmen to encourage people to buy their goods **2** the jargon of a particular group

pattern NOUN **1** an example suitable to be copied **2** a model or guide for making something **3** a decorative design **4** a sample: *a book of tweed patterns* **5** *maths* a systematic arrangement of numbers, shapes, etc

patterned ADJECTIVE having a design, not self-coloured

patty NOUN (*plural* **patties**) a small, flat cake of chopped meat etc

paucity NOUN, *formal* smallness of number or quantity

paunch NOUN (*plural* **paunches**) a fat stomach

pauper NOUN a very poor person

pause NOUN **1** a short stop, an interval **2** a break or hesitation in speaking or writing **3** *music* a symbol (𝄐) showing the holding

A B C D E F G H I J K L M N O P Q R S T U V W X Y Z

of a note or rest ▶ VERB to stop for a short time

pave VERB to lay (a street) with stone or concrete to form a level surface for walking on **pave the way for** to prepare or make the way easy for

pavement NOUN a paved footway at the side of a road for pedestrians

pavilion NOUN **1** a building in a sports ground with facilities for changing clothes **2** a large ornamental building **3** a large tent

paw NOUN the foot of an animal ▶ VERB **1** of an animal: to scrape with one of the front feet **2** to handle or touch roughly or rudely **3** to strike out wildly with the hand: *paw the air*

pawn VERB to put (an article of some value) in someone's keeping in exchange for a sum of money which, when repaid, buys back the article ▶ NOUN **1** *chess* a small piece of the lowest rank **2** someone who lets themselves be used by another for some purpose **in pawn** having been pawned

pawnbroker NOUN someone who lends money in exchange for pawned articles

pawnshop NOUN a pawnbroker's place of business

pawpaw *another word for* **papaya**

pay VERB (**paying, paid**) **1** to give (money) in exchange for (goods etc): *I paid £30 for it* **2** to suffer the punishment (for) **3** to be advantageous or profitable: *It pays to be prepared* **4** to give (eg attention) ▶ NOUN money given or received for work; wages **pay off 1** to pay in full and discharge (workers) owing to lack of work **2** to have good results: *His hard work paid off* **pay out 1** to spend **2** to give out (a length of rope etc)

(verb, meaning 1) remit, discharge, remunerate, recompense, reimburse; (verb, meaning 2) atone, compensate, answer

payable ADJECTIVE requiring to be paid

PAYE ABBREVIATION pay as you earn, a system by which income tax is deducted from a salary before it is given to the worker

payee NOUN someone to whom money is paid

payment NOUN **1** the act of paying **2** money paid for goods etc

payphone NOUN a coin- or card-operated public telephone

payroll NOUN a register of employees that lists the wage or salary due to each

PC ABBREVIATION **1** police constable **2** personal computer **3** privy councillor **4** political correctness

pc ABBREVIATION **1** postcard **2** per cent

PE ABBREVIATION physical education

pea NOUN **1** a climbing plant which produces round, green seeds in pods **2** the seed itself, eaten as a vegetable

peace NOUN **1** quietness, calm **2** freedom from war or disturbance **3** a treaty bringing this about

peaceable ADJECTIVE of a quiet nature, fond of peace

peaceful ADJECTIVE quiet; calm
> **peacefully** ADVERB

a b c d e f g h i j k l m n o p q r s t u v w x y z

A B C D E F G H I J K L M N O P Q R S T U V W X Y Z

peach NOUN (*plural* **peaches**) **1** a juicy, velvety-skinned fruit **2** the tree that bears it **3** an orangey-pink colour

peacock NOUN a large bird, the male of which has brightly coloured, patterned tail feathers

peak NOUN **1** the pointed top of a mountain or hill **2** the highest point **3** the jutting-out part of the brim of a cap ▶VERB **1** to rise to a peak **2** to reach the highest point: *Prices peaked in July*

peaked ADJECTIVE **1** pointed **2** of a cap: having a peak

peaky ADJECTIVE (**peakier, peakiest**) looking pale and unhealthy

peal NOUN **1** a set of bells tuned to each other **2** the changes rung on such bells **3** a succession of loud sounds: *peals of laughter* ▶VERB to sound loudly

> Do not confuse with: **peel**

peanut NOUN a type of nut similar to a pea in shape (*also called*: **groundnut, monkey nut**)

peanut butter NOUN a paste of ground roasted peanuts, spread on bread etc

pear NOUN a tree-growing fruit that is narrow at the top and widens at the bottom

pearl NOUN **1** a gem formed in the shell of the oyster and several other shellfish **2** a valuable remark etc: *pearls of wisdom*

pear-shaped ADJECTIVE narrow at the top and wider at the bottom

peasant NOUN someone who works and lives on the land, especially in an underdeveloped area

peat NOUN turf cut out of boggy places, dried and used as fuel

pebble NOUN a small, roundish stone

pebble dash NOUN a coating for outside walls with small stones set into the mortar

peck VERB **1** to strike with the beak **2** to pick up with the beak **3** to eat little, nibble (at) **4** to kiss quickly and briefly ▶NOUN **1** a sharp blow with the beak **2** a brief kiss

peckish ADJECTIVE slightly hungry

pectoral ADJECTIVE of the breast or chest: *pectoral muscles*

peculiar ADJECTIVE strange, odd: *He is a very peculiar person*
peculiar to belonging to one person or thing only: *a custom peculiar to England*

peculiarity NOUN (*plural* **peculiarities**) that which marks someone or something off from others in some way; something odd

pedagogic (*pronounced* ped-*a*-**gog**-ik *or* ped-*a*-**goj**-ik) *or* **pedagogical** ADJECTIVE, *old* of a teacher or of education

pedal NOUN **1** a lever worked by the foot on a bicycle, piano, harp, etc **2** a key worked by the foot on an organ ▶VERB (**pedalling, pedalled**) **1** to work the pedals of **2** to ride on a bicycle

pedant NOUN **1** someone who makes a great show of their knowledge **2** someone overly fussy about minor details

pedantic ADJECTIVE over-concerned with correctness

pedantry NOUN **1** fussiness about unimportant details **2** a display of knowledge

peddle VERB to travel from door to door selling goods

pedestal NOUN the foot or support of a pillar, statue, etc

pedestrian ADJECTIVE **1** going on foot **2** for those on foot **3** unexciting, dull: *a pedestrian account* ▶NOUN someone who goes or travels on foot

pedestrian crossing NOUN a place where pedestrians may cross the road when the traffic stops

pediatrics, **pediatrician** *US spelling* of **paediatrics**, **paediatrician**

pedicure NOUN a treatment for the feet, including treating corns, cutting nails, etc

pedigree NOUN **1** a list of someone's ancestors **2** the ancestry of a pure-bred animal **3** a distinguished descent or ancestry ▶ADJECTIVE of an animal: pure-bred, from a long line of ancestors of the same breed

ⓘ Literally 'crane's foot', because the lines of a family tree were thought to resemble the forked feet of the bird

pedlar NOUN someone who peddles, a hawker

pedo- *see* **paedo-**

pee *informal*, VERB (**peeing, peed**) to urinate ▶NOUN **1** the act of urinating **2** urine

peek VERB to peep, glance, especially secretively ▶NOUN a secret look

peel VERB **1** to strip off the outer covering or skin of: *peel an apple* **2** of skin, paint, etc: to come off in small pieces **3** to lose skin in small flakes, eg as a result of sunburn ▶NOUN skin, rind

ⓘ Comes from Latin *pelare* meaning 'to deprive of hair'

> Do not confuse with: **peal**

peep[1] VERB **1** to look through a narrow opening, round a corner, etc **2** to look slyly or quickly (at) **3** to begin to appear: *The sun peeped out* ▶NOUN a quick look, a glimpse, often from hiding

peep[2] NOUN a high, small sound ▶VERB to make such a sound

peer[1] NOUN **1** someone's equal in rank, merit, or age **2** a nobleman of the rank of baron upwards **3** a member of the House of Lords

peer[2] VERB to look at with half-closed eyes, as if with difficulty

peerage NOUN **1** a peer's title **2** the peers as a group

peerless ADJECTIVE without any equal, better than all others

peeve VERB, *informal* to irritate

peeved ADJECTIVE, *informal* annoyed

peewit NOUN the lapwing

peg NOUN **1** a pin or stake of wood, metal, etc **2** a hook fixed to a wall for hanging clothes etc ▶VERB (**pegging, pegged**) **1** to fasten with a peg **2** to fix (prices etc) at a certain level

pejorative (*pronounced* pe-**jor**-a-tiv) ADJECTIVE showing disapproval, scorn, etc: *a pejorative remark*

Pekinese *or* **Pekingese** NOUN a breed of small dog with a long coat and flat face

pelican NOUN a large water bird with a pouched bill for storing fish

pelican crossing NOUN a street-crossing where the lights are operated by pedestrians

ℹ Taken from the phrase '*pe*destrian *li*ght *con*trolled crossing'

pellet NOUN **1** a small ball of shot etc **2** a small pill

pell-mell ADVERB in great confusion; headlong

pelmet NOUN a strip of fabric or a narrow board at the top of a window to hide a curtain rail

pelt[1] VERB **1** to throw (things) at **2** to run fast **3** of rain: to fall heavily ▶ NOUN: **at full pelt** at top speed

pelt[2] NOUN the untreated skin of an animal

pelvis NOUN (*plural* **pelvises** *or* **pelves** – *pronounced* **pel**-veez) the frame of two hip-bones which is attached to the spine and the bones of the legs

pen[1] NOUN an instrument with a nib for writing in ink ▶ VERB (**penning, penned**) to write (eg a letter)

pen[2] NOUN a small enclosure for sheep, cattle, etc ▶ VERB (**penning, penned**) to enclose in a pen

pen[3] NOUN a female swan

penalize *or* **penalise** (*pronounced* **pee**-n*a*-laiz) VERB **1** to punish **2** to put under a disadvantage

penal servitude NOUN imprisonment with hard labour as an added punishment

penalty NOUN (*plural* **penalties**) **1** punishment **2** a disadvantage put on a player or team for having broken a rule of a game

penance NOUN punishment willingly suffered by someone to make up for a wrong

pence *a plural* of **penny**

penchant (*pronounced* **pon**-shon) NOUN an inclination (for), a bias

pencil NOUN an instrument containing a length of graphite or other substance for writing, drawing, etc ▶ VERB (**pencilling, pencilled**) to draw, mark, etc with a pencil

pendant NOUN **1** an ornament hung from a necklace etc **2** a necklace with such an ornament

pendent ADJECTIVE hanging

pending ADJECTIVE awaiting a decision or attention: *This matter is pending* ▶ PREPOSITION awaiting, until the coming of: *pending confirmation*

pendulous ADJECTIVE hanging down, drooping

pendulum NOUN a swinging weight which drives the mechanism of a clock

penetrate VERB **1** to pierce or pass into or through **2** to enter by force
> **penetration** NOUN

penetrating ADJECTIVE **1** of a sound: piercing **2** keen, probing: *a penetrating question*

pen friend *or* **pen pal** NOUN someone you have never seen (usually living abroad) with whom you exchange letters

penguin NOUN a large sea bird of Antarctic regions, which cannot fly

penicillin NOUN a medicine obtained from mould, which kills many bacteria

peninsula (*pronounced* pe-**nin**-sjuw-l*a*) NOUN a piece of land almost surrounded by water > **peninsular** ADJECTIVE

penis NOUN (*plural* **penises** *or* **penes** – *pronounced* **pee**-neez) the part of the body which a male human or animal uses in sexual intercourse and for urinating

penitent ADJECTIVE sorry for your sins ▶ NOUN a penitent person

penitentiary NOUN (*plural* **penitentiaries**), *US* a prison

penknife NOUN (*plural* **penknives**) a pocket knife with folding blades

pen name NOUN a name adopted by a writer instead of their own name

pennant NOUN a long flag coming to a point at the end

penniless ADJECTIVE having no money

penny NOUN (*plural* **pence** *or* **pennies**) **1** a coin worth 1/100 of £1 **2** (*plural* **pence**) used to show an amount in pennies: *The newspaper costs forty-two pence* **3** (*plural* **pennies**) used for a number of coins: *I need five pennies for the coffee machine*

penny-pinching ADJECTIVE, *derogatory* mean, stingy

pension NOUN a sum of money paid regularly to a retired person, a widow, someone wounded in war, etc ▶ VERB: **pension off** to dismiss or allow to retire with a pension

pensionable ADJECTIVE having or giving the right to a pension: *pensionable age*

pensioner NOUN someone who receives a pension

pensive ADJECTIVE thoughtful > **pensively** ADVERB

pent *or* **pent-up** ADJECTIVE **1** shut up, not allowed to go free **2** of emotions: not freely expressed

penta- PREFIX five

ⓘ Comes from Greek *pente* meaning 'five'

pentagon NOUN a flat figure with five sides > **pentagonal** ADJECTIVE

pentathlon (*pronounced* pen-**tath**-l*o*n) NOUN an athletic contest comprising five events > **pentathlete** NOUN

pentatonic ADJECTIVE, *music* of a scale: consisting of five notes, ie a major scale omitting the fourth and seventh

Pentecost NOUN **1** a Jewish festival held fifty days after Passover **2** a Christian festival held seven weeks after Easter

penthouse NOUN a luxurious flat at the top of a building

Pentium NOUN, *trademark* a type of fast microprocessor used in personal computers

penultimate ADJECTIVE last but one

penury NOUN poverty, want

peony (*pronounced* **pee**-*o*-ni) NOUN (*plural* **peonies**) a type of garden plant with large red, white or pink flowers

A B C D E F G H I J K L M N O P Q R S T U V W X Y Z

people PLURAL NOUN **1** the men, women and children of a country or nation **2** persons generally ▸VERB **1** to fill with people **2** to inhabit, make up the population of

ⓘ Comes from Latin *populus* meaning 'a people' or 'a nation'

pep *informal*, NOUN spirit, verve

pepper NOUN **1** a plant whose berries are dried, powdered and used as seasoning **2** the spicy powder it produces **3** a hot-tasting hollow fruit containing many seeds, eaten raw, cooked or pickled ▸VERB to sprinkle with pepper **pepper with** to throw at or hit: *peppered with bullets*

peppercorn NOUN the dried berry of the pepper plant

pepper mill NOUN a device for grinding peppercorns over food

peppermint NOUN **1** a type of plant with a powerful taste and smell **2** a flavouring taken from this and used in sweets etc

peppery ADJECTIVE **1** containing much pepper **2** inclined to be hot-tempered

pep pill NOUN a pill containing a stimulating drug

pep talk NOUN a talk meant to encourage or arouse enthusiasm

per PREPOSITION **1** in, out of **2** for each: *£2 per dozen* **3** in each: *six times per week*

per annum ADVERB in each year

per capita *or* **per head** ADVERB for each person

perceive VERB **1** to become aware of through the senses **2** to see **3** to understand

per cent *or* **percent** ADVERB (symbol **%**) out of every hundred: *five per cent* (= 5 out of every hundred)

percentage NOUN the number of parts per hundred, eg **½** expressed as a percentage = 50%

perceptible ADJECTIVE able to be seen or understood > **perceptibly** ADVERB

perception NOUN the ability to perceive; understanding

perceptive ADJECTIVE able or quick to perceive or understand

perch[1] NOUN (*plural* **perches**) **1** a rod on which birds roost **2** a high seat or position ▸VERB to roost

perch[2] NOUN (*plural* **perches**) a type of freshwater fish

perchance ADVERB, *old* by chance; perhaps

percolate VERB **1** of a liquid: to drip or drain through small holes in a porous material **2** to cause (a liquid) to do this **3** of news etc: to pass slowly down or through

percolator NOUN a device for percolating: *a coffee percolator*

percussion NOUN **1** a striking of one object against another **2** musical instruments played by striking, eg drums, cymbals, etc

percussive ADJECTIVE making the noise of percussion; loud, striking

perdition NOUN **1** utter loss or ruin **2** everlasting punishment

peregrine (*pronounced* **pe**-ri-grin) NOUN a type of falcon

peremptory (*pronounced* pi-**remp**-*to*-ri) ADJECTIVE **1** urgent **2** of a command: to be obeyed at once

3 domineering, dictatorial

perennial ADJECTIVE **1** lasting through the year **2** everlasting, perpetual **3** of a plant: growing from year to year ▶NOUN a perennial plant (*compare with*: **annual, biennial**

perestroika (*pronounced* pe-ri-**stroi**-k*a*) NOUN reconstruction, restructuring of the state (originally in the former Soviet Union)

perfect ADJECTIVE (*pronounced* **per**-fikt) **1** complete, finished **2** faultless **3** exact ▶VERB (*pronounced* per-**fekt**) **1** to make perfect **2** to finish ▶NOUN, *grammar* the perfect tense, formed by *have* and the past participle, *eg He has failed* (**present perfect**), *He had failed* (**past perfect**), *He will have failed* (**future perfect**)

perfection NOUN **1** the state of being perfect **2** the highest state or degree

perfectionist NOUN someone who is satisfied only by perfection

perforate VERB to make a hole or holes through

perforated ADJECTIVE pierced with holes

perform VERB **1** to do, act **2** to act (a part) on the stage **3** to provide entertainment for an audience **4** to play (a piece of music)

performance NOUN **1** an entertainment in a theatre etc **2** the act of doing something **3** the level of success of a machine, car, etc

performance poetry NOUN poetry written to be read out in public

performer NOUN someone who acts or performs

perfume NOUN (*pronounced* **per**-fyoom) **1** smell, fragrance **2** a fragrant liquid put on the skin; scent ▶VERB (*pronounced* per-**fyoom** *or* **per**-fyoom) **1** to put scent on or in **2** to give a sweet smell to

perfumery NOUN (*plural* **perfumeries**) a shop or factory where perfume is sold or made

perfunctory ADJECTIVE done carelessly or half-heartedly: *a perfunctory inspection*
> **perfunctorily** ADVERB

perhaps ADVERB it may be (that); possibly: *Perhaps she'll resign*

peri- PREFIX around: *perimeter* (= the outside line around a figure or shape)/*perinatal* (= around the time of birth)

🄸 Comes from Greek *peri* meaning 'around'

peril NOUN a great danger **at your peril** at your own risk

perilous ADJECTIVE very dangerous
> **perilously** ADVERB

perimeter (*pronounced* pe-**rim**-i-t*e*r) NOUN **1** the outside line enclosing a figure or shape **2** the outer edge of any area

🄸 Comes from Greek *peri* meaning 'around', and *metron* meaning 'measure'

> Do not confuse with: **parameter**. Notice that words starting with **peri-** often relate to the idea of 'going around' and the **perimeter** of a figure or shape is the line that goes around it.

perinatal (*pronounced* pe-ri-**nei**-t*a*l) ADJECTIVE, *medicine* relating

A B C D E F G H I J K L M N O P Q R S T U V W X Y Z

to the period between the seventh month of pregnancy and the first week of the baby's life

perineum (*pronounced* pe-ri-**nee**-*u*m) NOUN (*plural* **perinea**), *anatomy* the part of the body between the genitals and the anus

period NOUN **1** a stretch of time **2** a stage in the earth's development or in history **3** a full stop after a sentence **4** a time of menstruation

periodic ADJECTIVE **1** of a period **2** happening at regular intervals, eg every month or year **3** happening every now and then: *a periodic clearing out of rubbish*

periodical ADJECTIVE issued or done at regular intervals; periodic ▸NOUN a magazine which appears at regular intervals > **periodically** ADVERB

periodic table NOUN, *chemistry* a table in which chemical elements are arranged by atomic number and in groups with similar properties

peripatetic (*pronounced* pe-ri-p*a*-**tet**-ik) ADJECTIVE moving from place to place; travelling

peripheral (*pronounced* pe-**rif**-*e*-r*a*l) ADJECTIVE **1** of or on a periphery; away from the centre **2** not essential, of little importance ▸NOUN, *computing* a device in a computer system connected to and controlled by the central processing unit

periphery (*pronounced* pe-**rif**-*e*-ri) NOUN (*plural* **peripheries**) **1** the line surrounding something **2** an outer boundary or edge

periscope NOUN a tube with mirrors by which a viewer in a submarine etc is able to see objects on the surface

perish VERB **1** to be destroyed, pass away completely; die **2** to decay, rot

perishable ADJECTIVE liable to go bad quickly

periwinkle[1] NOUN a small shellfish, shaped like a small snail, eaten as food when boiled

periwinkle[2] NOUN a creeping evergreen plant with a small blue flower

perjure **perjure yourself** to tell a lie when you have sworn to tell the truth, especially in a court of law

perjury NOUN (*plural* **perjuries**) the crime of lying while under oath in a court of law

perk[1] NOUN, *informal* something of value allowed in addition to payment for work

perk[2] VERB: **perk up** to recover energy or spirits

perky ADJECTIVE (**perkier, perkiest**) jaunty, in good spirits > **perkily** ADVERB

perm NOUN *short for* **permanent wave**▸ VERB to give a permanent wave to (hair)

permaculture NOUN farming without using artificial fertilizers and with minimal weeding

permafrost NOUN, *geology* permanently frozen subsoil

permanence *or* **permanency** NOUN the state of continuing or remaining for a long time or for ever

permanent ADJECTIVE lasting, not temporary > **permanently** ADVERB

permanent wave NOUN a wave

or curl put into the hair by a special process and usually lasting for some months

permeable ADJECTIVE able to be permeated by liquids, gases, etc

permeate VERB **1** to pass into through small holes, soak into **2** to fill every part of

permissible ADJECTIVE allowable

permission NOUN agreement or authorization to do something

permissive ADJECTIVE **1** allowing something to be done **2** too tolerant > **permissiveness** NOUN

permit VERB (*pronounced* per-**mit**) (**permitting, permitted**) **1** to agree to an action, allow **2** to make possible ▸ NOUN (*pronounced* **per**-mit) a written order, allowing someone to do something: *a fishing permit*

permutation NOUN **1** any of several different ways in which things can be ordered or arranged **2** the act of changing the order of things

pernicious ADJECTIVE destructive

pernickety ADJECTIVE fussy about small details

peroxide NOUN, *chemistry* a chemical (hydrogen peroxide) used for bleaching hair etc

perpendicular ADJECTIVE **1** standing upright, vertical **2** at right angles (to) ▸ NOUN, *maths* a line or plane at right angles to another line or plane

perpetrate VERB to commit (a sin, error, etc) > **perpetration** NOUN

🛈 Comes from Latin *perpetrare* meaning 'to achieve'

Do not confuse with: **perpetuate**

perpetrator NOUN a person who perpetrates; the one who is guilty

perpetual ADJECTIVE everlasting, unending > **perpetually** ADVERB

perpetuate VERB to make last for ever or for a long time

🛈 Comes from Latin *perpetuare* meaning 'to cause to continue uninterruptedly'

Do not confuse with: **perpetrate**

perpetuity NOUN: **in perpetuity** **1** for ever **2** for the length of someone's life

perplex VERB **1** to puzzle, bewilder **2** to make more complicated

perplexity NOUN (*plural* **perplexities**) **1** a puzzled state of mind **2** something which puzzles

per se (*pronounced* per **sei**) ADVERB in itself, essentially

persecute VERB **1** to harass over a period of time **2** to cause to suffer, especially because of religious beliefs > **persecution** NOUN > **persecutor** NOUN

🛈 Comes from Latin *persequi* meaning 'to follow persistently'

Do not confuse with: **prosecute**

perseverance NOUN the act of persevering

persevere VERB to keep trying to do a thing (in spite of difficulties)

persist VERB **1** to hold fast to (eg an idea) **2** to continue to do something in spite of difficulties **3** to survive, last

persistence NOUN **1** persisting **2** being persistent

persistent ADJECTIVE **1** obstinate, refusing to be discouraged **2** lasting, not dying out > **persistently** ADVERB

person NOUN **1** a human being **2** someone's body: *jewels hidden on his person* **3** form, shape: *Trouble arrived in the person of Gordon* **in person** personally, not represented by someone else

persona NOUN (*plural* **personas** *or* **personae** – *pronounced* per-**soh**-nee) the outward part of the personality presented to others

personable ADJECTIVE good-looking

personage NOUN a well-known person

personal ADJECTIVE **1** your own; private: *personal belongings* **2** of a remark: insulting, offensive to the person it is aimed at

ⓘ Comes from Latin *persona* meaning 'an actor's mask'

> Do not confuse with: **personnel**

personal computer NOUN (*abbrev* **PC**) a microcomputer designed for personal use

personality NOUN (*plural* **personalities**) **1** all of a person's characteristics as seen by others **2** a well-known person

personally ADVERB **1** speaking from your own point of view **2** by your own action, not using an agent or representative: *He thanked me personally*

personal organizer NOUN a small loose-leaf filing system containing a diary and an address book, maps, indexes, etc

personal stereo NOUN a small portable cassette player with earphones

personification NOUN **1** giving human qualities to things or ideas **2** in art or literature, representing an idea or quality as a person **3** a person or thing that is seen as a perfect example of a quality: *the personification of patience*

personify VERB (**personifies, personifying, personified**) **1** to talk about things, ideas, etc as if they were living persons (eg 'Time marches on') **2** to typify, be a perfect example of

personnel (*pronounced* per-so-**nel**) NOUN the people employed in a firm etc

> Do not confuse with: **personal**. **Personnel** is a noun coming from French company terminology, used to describe the 'person-assets' of a company (= the people who work for it) in contrast to its 'material-assets' (= all its non-human items of value).

perspective NOUN **1** a point of view **2** the giving of a sense of depth, distance, etc in a painting like that in real life **in perspective** **1** of an object in a painting etc: of a size in relation to other things that it would have in real life **2** of an event: in its true degree of importance when considered in relation to other events: *Keep things in perspective*

Perspex NOUN, *trademark* a transparent plastic which looks like glass

perspicacious ADJECTIVE of clear or sharp understanding > **perspicacity** NOUN

perspicuity NOUN clearness in expressing thoughts

perspiration NOUN sweat

perspire VERB to sweat

persuade VERB to bring someone to do or think something, by arguing with them or advising them

persuasion NOUN **1** the act of persuading **2** a firm belief, especially a religious belief

persuasive ADJECTIVE having the power to convince

pert ADJECTIVE saucy, cheeky

pertain VERB: **pertain to** to belong to, have to do with: *duties pertaining to the job*

pertinent ADJECTIVE connected with the subject spoken about, to the point

perturb VERB to disturb greatly; to make anxious or uneasy > **perturbation** NOUN

perusal NOUN perusing; careful reading

peruse VERB to read (with care)

pervade VERB to spread through: *Silence pervaded the room*

perverse ADJECTIVE obstinate in holding to the wrong point of view; unreasonable

perverseness *or* **perversity** NOUN stubbornness

perversion NOUN **1** the act of perverting **2** an unnatural or perverted act

pervert VERB (*pronounced* per-**vert**) **1** to turn away from what is normal or right: *pervert the course of justice* **2** to turn (someone) to crime or evil; corrupt ▸NOUN (*pronounced* **per**-vert) someone who commits unnatural or perverted acts

pessimism NOUN the habit of thinking that things will always turn out badly (*contrasted with*: **optimism**) > **pessimist** NOUN > **pessimistic** ADJECTIVE > **pessimistically** ADVERB

pest NOUN **1** a troublesome person or thing **2** a creature that is harmful or destructive, eg a mosquito

pester VERB to annoy continually

pesticide NOUN any substance which kills insect pests

pestle NOUN a tool for pounding things to powder in a **mortar**

pet[1] NOUN **1** a tame animal kept in the home, such as a cat **2** a favourite ▸ADJECTIVE **1** kept as a pet **2** favourite **3** chief: *my pet hate* ▸VERB (**petting, petted**) **1** to pat or stroke (an animal etc) **2** to fondle

pet[2] NOUN a fit of sulks

petal NOUN one of the leaf-like parts of a flower, often scented and brightly coloured

peter VERB: **peter out** to fade or dwindle away to nothing

petite (*pronounced* pe-**teet**) ADJECTIVE small and neat in appearance

petition NOUN a request or note of

A B C D E F G H I J K L M N O P Q R S T U V W X Y Z

protest signed by many people and sent to a government or authority ▸ VERB to send a petition to

petrel NOUN a small, long-winged sea bird

Petri dish (*pronounced* **peet**-ri *or* **pet**-ri) NOUN a shallow, circular container used for growing bacteria etc

petrify VERB (**petrifies, petrifying, petrified**) **1** to turn into stone **2** to turn (someone) stiff with fear

petrochemical NOUN a chemical made from petroleum or natural gas

petrol NOUN petroleum when refined as fuel for use in cars etc

petroleum NOUN oil in its raw, unrefined form, extracted from natural wells below the earth's surface

petticoat NOUN an underskirt worn by women

pettish ADJECTIVE sulky

petty ADJECTIVE (**pettier, pettiest**) **1** of little importance, trivial **2** small-minded; spiteful > **pettiness** NOUN

petty cash NOUN money paid or received in small sums

petulance NOUN being petulant

petulant ADJECTIVE **1** cross, irritable **2** unreasonably impatient

petunia NOUN a S American flowering plant related to tobacco

pew NOUN a seat or bench in a church

pewter NOUN a mixture of tin and lead

PG ABBREVIATION parental guidance (denoting a film that is possibly not suitable for young children)

pH NOUN, *chemistry* a measure of the acidity or alkalinity of a solution

phallic ADJECTIVE relating to or resembling a phallus

phallus NOUN (*plural* **phalluses** *or* **phalli** – *pronounced* **fal**-ai) (a representation of) a penis

phantom NOUN a ghost

Pharaoh (*pronounced* **fei**-roh) NOUN, *history* a ruler of ancient Egypt

pharmaceutical (*pronounced* fahr-m*a*-**syoo**-ti-k*a*l) ADJECTIVE relating to the making up of medicines and drugs

pharmacist NOUN someone who prepares and sells medicines

pharmacological ADJECTIVE relating to or involving pharmacology

pharmacologist NOUN an expert in pharmacology

pharmacology NOUN the scientific study of drugs and their effects

pharmacy NOUN (*plural* **pharmacies**) **1** the art of preparing medicines **2** a chemist's shop

phase NOUN **1** one in a series of changes in the shape or appearance of something (eg the moon) **2** a stage in the development of something (eg a war, a scheme, etc) ▸ VERB (**phase in** *or* **out**) to introduce or end something in stages

PhD ABBREVIATION Doctor of Philosophy, a higher university degree

pheasant NOUN a bird with brightly coloured feathers which is shot as game

phenomenal ADJECTIVE very unusual, remarkable
> **phenomenally** ADVERB

phenomenon NOUN (*plural* **phenomena**) **1** an event (especially in nature) that is observed by the senses: *the phenomenon of lightning* **2** something remarkable or very unusual, a wonder

phil- *see* **philo-**

philander (*pronounced* fi-**lan**-der) VERB to flirt, or have casual love affairs, with women

philanderer NOUN a womanizer

philanthropist NOUN someone who does good to others

philanthropy (*pronounced* fi-**lan**-thr*o*-pi) NOUN love of mankind, often shown by giving money for the benefit of others

philharmonic (*pronounced* fil-ahr-**mon**-ik) ADJECTIVE (in names of orchestras etc) music-loving

philistine (*pronounced* **fil**-is-tain) NOUN someone ignorant of, or hostile to, culture and the arts

ⓘ After a people of ancient Palestine, enemies of the Israelites

philo- *or* **phil-** PREFIX forms words related to the love of a particular thing: *philharmonic/philosopher* (= a friend or lover of wisdom)

ⓘ Comes from Greek *philos* meaning 'friend', and *phileein* meaning 'to love'

philology NOUN the study of words and their history

philosopher NOUN someone who studies philosophy

philosophical *or* **philosophic** ADJECTIVE **1** of philosophy **2** calm, not easily upset

philosophy NOUN (*plural* **philosophies**) **1** the study of the nature of the universe, or of human behaviour **2** someone's personal view of life

phlegm (*pronounced* flem) NOUN **1** thick slimy matter that lines the air passages, brought up by coughing **2** coolness of temper, calmness

phlegmatic (*pronounced* fleg-**mat**-ik) ADJECTIVE not easily excited

-phobe SUFFIX forms words describing people who suffer from particular phobias

ⓘ Comes from Greek *phobos* meaning 'fear'

phobia NOUN an intense, often irrational, fear or dislike

ⓘ Comes from Greek *phobos* meaning 'fear'

phoenix (*pronounced* **fee**-niks) NOUN (*plural* **phoenixes**) a mythological bird believed to burn itself and to rise again from its ashes

phon- PREFIX forms words relating to sound or speech: *phonetics*

ⓘ Comes from Greek *phone* meaning 'sound' or 'voice'

phone NOUN *short for* **telephone**

phonecard NOUN a card that can be used instead of cash to operate certain public telephones

phonetic ADJECTIVE **1** relating to the sounds of language **2** of a word: spelt according to sound, eg *flem* for 'phlegm'

phonetics SINGULAR NOUN **1** the study of the production and perception of speech sounds **2** a

A B C D E F G H I J K L M N O P Q R S T U V W X Y Z

system of writing according to sound

phoney *or* **phony** *informal*, ADJECTIVE (**phonier, phoniest**) fake, not genuine

phosphate NOUN, *chemistry* a soil fertilizer containing phosphorus

phosphorescent ADJECTIVE glowing in the dark

phosphorus NOUN, *chemistry* (symbol **P**) a wax-like, poisonous substance that gives out light in the dark

photo- PREFIX **1** of or relating to light: *photosensitive/photograph* **2** forms words relating to photography: *photocopy/photogenic* ⓘ Comes from Greek *photos* meaning 'of light'

photo NOUN (*plural* **photos**) *informal* a photograph

photocopier NOUN a machine that makes photocopies

photocopy NOUN (*plural* **photocopies**) a copy of a document made by a device which photographs and develops images ▸ VERB (**photocopies, photocopying, photocopied**) to make a photocopy of

photofit NOUN, *trademark* a method of making identification pictures by combining photographs of individual features

photogenic (*pronounced* foh-*toh*-**jen**-ik) ADJECTIVE looking attractive in photographs

photograph NOUN a picture taken with a camera ▸ VERB to take a picture with a camera

photographer NOUN a person who takes photographs, especially professionally

photography NOUN the art of taking pictures with a camera

photon NOUN the smallest unit of light

photosensitive ADJECTIVE affected by light

photosynthesis NOUN the conversion of light into complex compounds by plants

phrasal verb NOUN, *grammar* a phrase made up of a verb and an adverb or preposition, the meaning of which cannot be worked out from its separate parts, eg 'put up with'

phrase NOUN **1** *grammar* a group of words smaller than a clause, expressing a single idea, eg 'after dinner', 'on the water' **2** a short saying or expression **3** *music* a short group of bars forming a distinct unit ▸ VERB to express in words: *He could have phrased it more tactfully*

physical ADJECTIVE **1** relating to the body: *physical strength/physical exercises* **2** relating to things that can be seen or felt > **physically** ADVERB: *She is physically fit*

physical education NOUN instruction in sports, games and keeping fit (*short form*: **PE**)

physician NOUN a doctor specializing in medical rather than surgical treatment

physicist NOUN someone who specializes in physics

physics SINGULAR NOUN the science which includes the study of heat, light, sound, electricity, magnetism, etc

physio- PREFIX **1** of or relating to the body or the natural processes of life: *physiology* **2** forms words describing the treatment of disease by physical rather than medicinal means: *physiotherapy*

🛈 Comes from Greek *physis* meaning 'nature'

physiological ADJECTIVE relating to or involving physiology

physiology NOUN the study of the way in which living bodies work, including blood circulation, food digestion, etc

physiotherapist NOUN a person skilled in treatment by physiotherapy

physiotherapy NOUN the treatment of disease by bodily exercise, massage, etc rather than by drugs

physique (*pronounced* fi-**zeek**) NOUN **1** the build of someone's body **2** bodily strength

pi (*pronounced* pai) NOUN, *maths* a number that is equal to the circumference of any circle divided by its diameter, approximately 3.142

pianist NOUN someone who plays the piano

piano NOUN (*plural* **pianos**) a large musical instrument played by striking keys

🛈 A shortened form of *pianoforte*, which was formed from the Italian words for 'soft' and 'loud'

piazza (*pronounced* pee-**at**-sa) NOUN a market-place or town square surrounded by buildings

piccolo NOUN (*plural* **piccolos**) a small, high-pitched flute

pick[1] VERB **1** to choose **2** to pluck, gather (flowers, fruit, etc) **3** to peck, bite, nibble (at) **4** to poke, probe (teeth etc) **5** to open (a lock) with a tool other than a key ▸NOUN **1** choice: *take your pick* **2** the best or best part **pick a quarrel** to start a quarrel deliberately **pick on 1** to single out for criticism etc **2** to nag at **pick up 1** to lift up **2** to learn (a language, habit, etc) **3** to give (someone) a lift in a car **4** to find or get by chance **5** to improve, gain strength

pick[2] NOUN **1** a pickaxe **2** an instrument for picking, eg a toothpick

pickaxe NOUN a heavy tool for breaking ground, pointed at one end or both ends

picket NOUN **1** a pointed stake **2** a small sentry-post or guard **3** a number of workers on strike who prevent others from going into work ▸VERB (**picketing, picketed**) **1** to fasten (a horse etc) to a stake **2** to place a guard or a group of strikers at (a place)

pickle NOUN **1** a liquid in which food is preserved **2** vegetables preserved in vinegar **3** *informal* an awkward, unpleasant situation ▸VERB to preserve with salt, vinegar, etc

pickpocket NOUN someone who robs people's pockets or handbags

picky ADJECTIVE (**pickier, pickiest**) choosy, fussy

picnic NOUN a meal eaten outdoors, often during an outing etc ▸VERB (**picnicking, picnicked**) to have a picnic > **picnicker** NOUN

pictorial ADJECTIVE **1** having

pictures **2** consisting of pictures **3** calling up pictures in the mind

picture NOUN **1** a painting or drawing **2** a portrait **3** a photograph **4** a film **5** a vivid description ▸ VERB **1** to make a picture of **2** to see in the mind, imagine **the pictures** the cinema

picturesque ADJECTIVE such as would make a good or striking picture; pretty, colourful

pie NOUN meat, fruit, or other food baked in a casing or covering of pastry

piece NOUN **1** a part or portion of anything **2** a single article or example: *a piece of paper* **3** an artistic work: *a piece of popular music* **4** a coin **5** a man in chess, draughts, etc ▸ VERB to put (together)

piecemeal ADVERB by pieces, little by little

piecework NOUN work paid according to how much is done, not to the time spent on it

pie chart NOUN a circular diagram split into sections showing the different percentages into which a whole amount is divided

pier NOUN **1** a platform stretching from the shore into the sea as a landing place for ships **2** a pillar supporting an arch, bridge, etc

pierce VERB to make a hole through

piercing ADJECTIVE shrill, loud; sharp

piffle NOUN, *informal* nonsense

pig NOUN a farm animal, from whose flesh ham and bacon are made

pigeon NOUN a bird of the dove family

Comes from Latin *pipire* meaning 'to cheep'

pigeonhole NOUN a small division in a case or desk for papers etc ▸ VERB **1** to lay aside **2** to classify, put into a category

piggyback NOUN a ride on someone's back with your arms round their neck

piggy bank NOUN a china pig with a slit along its back to insert coins for saving

pigheaded ADJECTIVE stubborn

piglet NOUN a young pig

pigment NOUN **1** paint or other substance used for colouring **2** a substance in animals and plants that gives colour to the skin etc
> **pigmentation** NOUN (meaning 2)

pigmy *another spelling* of **pygmy**

pigsty *or* **piggery** NOUN (*plural* **pigsties** *or* **piggeries**) a place where pigs are kept

pigtail NOUN hair formed into a plait

pike[1] NOUN (*plural* **pike** *or* **pikes**) a freshwater fish

pike[2] NOUN a weapon like a spear, with a long shaft and a sharp head

pilchard NOUN a small sea fish like a herring, often tinned

pile[1] NOUN **1** a number of things lying one on top of another, a heap **2** a great quantity **3** a large building ▸ VERB (often **pile up** *or* **pile something up**) to make or form a pile or heap

pile[2] NOUN a large stake or pillar driven into the earth as a foundation for a building, bridge, etc

pile[3] NOUN the thick, soft surface on carpets and on cloth such as velvet

A B C D E F G H I J K L M N O P Q R S T U V W X Y Z

piles PLURAL NOUN haemorrhoids

pilfer VERB to steal small things

pilgrim NOUN a traveller to a holy place

pilgrimage NOUN a journey to a holy place

pill NOUN **1** a tablet of medicine **2** (often **the pill**) a contraceptive in the form of a small tablet taken by mouth

pillar NOUN **1** an upright support for roofs, arches, etc **2** someone or something that gives support: *a pillar of the community*

pillarbox NOUN (*plural* **pillarboxes**) a tall box with a slot through which letters etc are posted

pillion NOUN **1** a seat for a passenger on a motorcycle **2** *old* a light saddle for a passenger on horseback, behind the main saddle

pillow NOUN a soft cushion for the head ▸ VERB to rest or support on a pillow

pillowcase *or* **pillowslip** NOUN a cover for a pillow

pilot NOUN **1** someone who steers a ship in or out of a harbour **2** someone who flies an aeroplane **3** a guide, a leader ▸ ADJECTIVE of a scheme, programme, etc: as a test which may be modified before the final version: *a pilot project* ▸ VERB (**piloting, piloted**) to steer, guide

pilot light NOUN **1** a small gas-light from which larger jets are lit **2** an electric light showing that a current is switched on

pimple NOUN a small round infected swelling on the skin

PIN (*pronounced* pin) ABBREVIATION personal identification number (for automatic teller machines etc)

pin NOUN **1** a short, pointed piece of metal with a small round head, used for fastening fabric **2** a wooden or metal peg **3** a skittle ▸ VERB (**pinning, pinned**) **1** to fasten with a pin **2** to hold fast, pressed against something: *The bloodhound pinned him to the ground*

pinafore NOUN **1** an apron to protect the front of a dress **2** a sleeveless dress worn over a jersey, blouse, etc

pinball NOUN a game played on a slot-machine in which a ball runs down a sloping board between obstacles

pincers PLURAL NOUN **1** a tool like pliers, but with sharp points for gripping, pulling out nails, etc **2** the claw of a crab or lobster

pinch VERB **1** to squeeze (especially flesh) between the thumb and forefinger; nip **2** to grip tightly, hurt by tightness **3** *informal* to steal ▸ NOUN (*plural* **pinches**) **1** a squeeze, a nip **2** a small amount (eg of salt) **at a pinch** if really necessary or urgent **feel the pinch** to suffer from lack of money

pinched ADJECTIVE of a face: looking cold, pale or thin

pine[1] NOUN **1** an evergreen tree with needle-like leaves which produces cones **2** the soft wood of such a tree used for furniture etc

pine[2] VERB **1** to waste away, lose strength **2** to long (for something)

pineapple NOUN a large tropical fruit with tough spiny skin, shaped like a pine cone

ping NOUN a whistling sound such

as that of a bullet ▸VERB to make a brief high-pitched sound

ping-pong NOUN, *trademark* table tennis

pink NOUN **1** a pale red colour **2** a sweet-scented garden flower like a carnation **3** a healthy or good state: *feeling in the pink*

pinkie NOUN, *Scot & N Amer informal* the little finger

pinnacle NOUN **1** a slender spire or turret **2** a high pointed rock or mountain **3** the highest point

pint NOUN a liquid measure equal to just over ½ litre

pioneer NOUN **1** an explorer **2** an inventor, or an early exponent of something: *pioneers of the cinema* ▸VERB to act as a pioneer

pious ADJECTIVE respectful in religious matters

pip[1] NOUN a seed of a fruit

pip[2] NOUN a short beep as part of a time signal etc on the radio or telephone

pip[3] NOUN **1** a spot or symbol on dice or cards **2** a star on an army officer's tunic

pipe NOUN **1** a tube for carrying water, gas, etc **2** a tube with a bowl at the end, for smoking tobacco **3** (**pipes**) a musical instrument made of several small pipes joined together **4** (**pipes**) bagpipes ▸VERB **1** to play (notes, a tune) on a pipe or pipes **2** to whistle, chirp **3** to speak in a shrill, high voice **4** to convey (eg water) by pipe **pipe down** *informal* to become silent, stop talking **pipe up** to speak up, express an opinion

pipeline NOUN a long line of pipes, eg to carry oil from an oilfield **in the pipeline** in preparation, soon to become available

piper NOUN someone who plays a pipe, especially the bagpipes

pipette (*pronounced* pi-**pet**) NOUN a small glass tube used in laboratories

piping ADJECTIVE high-pitched, shrill ▸NOUN **1** a length of tubing **2** a system of pipes **3** a narrow ornamental cord for trimming clothes **4** a strip of decorative icing round a cake **piping hot** very hot

piquant (*pronounced* **peek**-*a*nt) ADJECTIVE **1** sharp-tasting, spicy **2** arousing interest > **piquancy** NOUN

pique (*pronounced* peek) NOUN anger caused by wounded pride, spite, resentment, etc ▸VERB **1** to wound the pride of **2** to arouse (curiosity)

piracy NOUN **1** the activity of pirates **2** unauthorized publication or reproduction of copyright material

piranha (*pronounced* pi-**rah**-n*a*) NOUN a S American river-fish, some types of which eat flesh

pirate NOUN **1** someone who robs ships at sea **2** someone who steals or plagiarizes another's work

pirouette NOUN a rapid whirling on the toes in dancing ▸VERB to twirl in a pirouette

pistachio (*pronounced* pi-**stash**-i-oh) NOUN (*plural* **pistachios**) a greenish nut, often used as a flavouring

pistol NOUN a small gun held in the hand

piston NOUN a round piece of metal

that moves up and down inside a cylinder, eg in an engine

pit NOUN **1** a hole in the ground **2** a place from which coal and other minerals are dug **3** the ground floor of a theatre behind the stalls **4** (often **pits**) a place beside the racetrack for repairing and refuelling racing cars etc ▸VERB (**pitting, pitted**) to set one thing or person against another: *pitting my wits against his*

pitch[1] VERB **1** to fix a tent etc to the ground **2** to throw **3** to fall heavily; lurch: *pitch forward* **4** to set the level or key of a tune ▸NOUN (*plural* **pitches**) **1** a throw **2** an attempt at selling or persuading: *a sales pitch* **3** the height or depth of a note **4** a peak, an extreme point: *reach fever pitch* **5** the field for certain sports **6** *cricket* the ground between wickets **7** the slope of a roof etc **8** the spot reserved for a street seller or street entertainer

pitch[2] NOUN a thick, dark substance obtained by boiling down tar

pitch-dark ADJECTIVE very dark

pitcher NOUN a kind of large jug

pitchfork NOUN a fork for lifting and throwing hay

piteous *or* **pitiable** ADJECTIVE deserving pity; wretched

pitfall NOUN a trap, a possible danger

pith NOUN **1** the soft substance in the centre of plant stems **2** the white substance under the rind of an orange, lemon, etc **3** the important part of anything

pithy ADJECTIVE (**pithier, pithiest**) **1** full of pith **2** full of meaning, to the point: *a pithy saying*

pitiable *see* **piteous**

pitiful ADJECTIVE poor, wretched

pittance NOUN a very small wage or allowance

pitted ADJECTIVE marked with small holes

pituitary gland NOUN, *physiology* a gland in the brain affecting growth

pity NOUN (*plural* **pities**) **1** feeling for the sufferings of others, sympathy **2** a cause of grief **3** a regrettable fact ▸VERB (**pities, pitying, pitied**) to feel sorry for

pivot NOUN **1** the pin or centre on which anything turns **2** something or someone greatly depended on ▸VERB (**pivoting, pivoted**) **1** to turn on a pivot **2** to depend (on)

pivotal ADJECTIVE **1** acting as a pivot **2** crucially important; critical

pixel NOUN, *electronics* the smallest element in an image on a TV or computer screen, consisting of a tiny dot

pixellated ADJECTIVE, *electronics* of a picture: broken down into a number of small squares
> **pixellation** NOUN

pixie *or* **pixy** NOUN (*plural* **pixies**) a kind of fairy

pizza NOUN a flat piece of dough spread with tomato, cheese, etc and baked

placard NOUN a printed notice (as an advertisement etc) placed on a wall etc

placate VERB to calm, make less angry, etc

place NOUN **1** a physical location; any area or building **2** a particular spot **3** an open space in a town: *a market place* **4** a seat in a theatre,

A B C D E F G H I J K L M N O P Q R S T U V W X Y Z

train, at a table, etc **5** a position on a course, in a job, etc **6** rank ▸ VERB **1** to put in a particular place **2** to find a place for **3** to give (an order for goods etc) **4** to remember who someone is: *I can't place him at all* **in place 1** in the proper position **2** suitable **in place of** instead of **out of place 1** not in the proper position **2** unsuitable

ⓘ Comes from Latin *platea* meaning 'a street'

placebo (*pronounced* pl*a*-**see**-boh) NOUN (*plural* **placebos**), *medicine* a substance resembling a drug but with no medicinal ingredients

placed ADJECTIVE **1** having a place **2** among the first three in a competition

placenta (*pronounced* pl*a*-**sen**-t*a*) NOUN, *biology* a part of the womb that connects an unborn mammal to its mother, shed at birth

placid ADJECTIVE calm, not easily disturbed

plagiarism (*pronounced* **plei**-j*a*-rizm) NOUN plagiarizing

plagiarize *or* **plagiarise** (*pronounced* **plei**-j*a*-raiz) VERB to steal or borrow from the writings or ideas of someone else without permission

plague NOUN **1** *medicine* a fatal infectious disease carried by rat fleas **2** a great and troublesome quantity: *a plague of flies* ▸ VERB to pester or annoy continually

plaice NOUN (*plural* **plaice**) a type of edible flatfish

plaid (*pronounced* plad) NOUN a long piece of cloth (especially tartan) worn over the shoulder

plain ADJECTIVE **1** flat, level **2** simple, ordinary **3** without ornament or decoration **4** clear, easy to see or understand **5** not good-looking, not attractive ▸ NOUN a level stretch of land

plain-clothes ADJECTIVE of a police officer: wearing ordinary clothes, not uniform

plain text NOUN, *computing* the format of most e-mail messages, using simple upper-case and lower-case letters

plaintiff NOUN, *law* someone who takes action against another in the law courts

plaintive ADJECTIVE sad, sorrowful

plait (*pronounced* plat) NOUN **1** a length of hair arranged by intertwining three or more separate pieces **2** threads etc intertwined in this way ▸ VERB to form into a plait

plan NOUN **1** a diagram of a building, town, etc as if seen from above **2** a scheme or arrangement to do something ▸ VERB (**planning, planned**) **1** to make a sketch or plan of **2** to decide or arrange to do

plane[1] *short for* **aeroplane**

plane[2] NOUN **1** *maths* a flat surface on which a line joining two points lies **2** a level surface **3** a standard (of achievement etc) ▸ ADJECTIVE flat, level ▸ VERB **1** to smooth with a plane **2** to glide over water etc

plane[3] NOUN a carpentry tool for smoothing wood

planet NOUN any of the bodies (eg the earth, Venus) which move round the sun or round another fixed star

plank NOUN a long, flat piece of timber

plankton NOUN microscopic creatures floating in seas, lakes, etc

plant NOUN **1** a living growth, usually from the ground, and usually with a stem, a root and leaves **2** a factory or machinery ▶ VERB **1** to put (something) into the ground so that it will grow **2** to put (an idea) into the mind **3** to put in position: *plant a bomb* **4** to set down firmly: *plant your feet on the floor* **5** *informal* to place (something) as false evidence

plantation NOUN **1** an area planted with trees **2** an estate for growing cotton, sugar, rubber, tobacco, etc

plaque NOUN **1** a decorative plate of metal, china, etc for fixing to a wall **2** *dentistry* a film of saliva and bacteria which forms on the teeth

plasma NOUN *biology* the liquid part of blood and certain other fluids

plaster NOUN **1** a mixture of lime, water and sand which sets hard, for covering walls etc **2** (*also called*: **plaster of Paris**) a fine mixture containing gypsum used for moulding, making casts for broken limbs, etc **3** a small dressing which can be stuck over a wound ▶ ADJECTIVE made of plaster ▶ VERB **1** to apply plaster to **2** to cover too thickly (with)

plasterer NOUN someone whose trade is plastering walls

plastic ADJECTIVE **1** easily moulded or shaped **2** made of plastic ▶ NOUN a chemically manufactured substance that can be moulded when soft, formed into fibres, etc

Plasticine NOUN, *trademark* a soft clay-like substance used for modelling

plastic surgery NOUN an operation to repair or replace damaged areas of skin, or to improve the appearance of a facial or other body feature

plate NOUN **1** a shallow dish for holding food **2** a flat piece of metal, glass, china, etc **3** gold and silver articles **4** a sheet of metal used in printing **5** a book illustration **6** the part of false teeth that fits to the mouth **7** *same as* **tectonic plate** ▶ VERB to cover with a coating of metal

plateau (*pronounced* **plat**-oh) NOUN (*plural* **plateaus** *or* **plateaux** – *pronounced* **plat**-oh *or* **plat**-ohz) **1** a broad level stretch of high land **2** a steady, unchanging state: *Prices have now reached a plateau*

platelet NOUN, *physiology* a cell fragment in blood that is responsible for clotting around bleeding

platform NOUN **1** a raised level surface for passengers at a railway station **2** a raised floor for speakers, entertainers, etc **3** *computing* the hardware and software used by a computer system

plating NOUN a thin covering of metal

platinum NOUN, *chemistry* (symbol **Pt**) a heavy and very valuable steel-grey metal

platitude NOUN a dull, ordinary remark made as if it were important

platonic ADJECTIVE of a relationship: not sexual

ⓘ After the Greek philosopher *Plato*, whose teachings were

A B C D E F G H I J K L M N O P Q R S T U V W X Y Z

interpreted in the Middle Ages as advocating this sort of relationship

platoon NOUN a section of a company of soldiers

platter NOUN a large, flat plate

platypus NOUN (*plural* **platypuses**) a small water animal of Australia that has webbed feet and a duck-like bill and lays eggs (*also called*: **duck-billed platypus**)

plausible ADJECTIVE **1** seeming to be truthful or honest **2** seeming probable or reasonable

play VERB **1** to amuse yourself **2** to take part in a game **3** to gamble **4** to act (on a stage etc) **5** to perform on (a musical instrument) **6** to carry out (a trick) **7** to trifle or fiddle (with): *Don't play with your food* **8** to move over lightly: *The firelight played on his face* ▶NOUN **1** amusement, recreation **2** gambling **3** a story for acting, a drama **4** a way of behaving: *foul play* **5** freedom of movement **play at** to treat in a light-hearted, not serious way: *He only plays at being a businessman* **play off** to set off (one person) against another to gain some advantage for yourself **play on** to make use of (someone's feelings) to turn to your own advantage **play the game** to act fairly and honestly

ⓘ Comes from Old English verb *plegian* and noun *plega*

player NOUN **1** an actor **2** someone who plays a game, musical instrument, etc: *a lute player*

playful ADJECTIVE **1** wanting to play: *a playful kitten* **2** fond of joking, not serious > **playfully** ADVERB

playground NOUN an open area for playing at school, in a park, etc

playgroup NOUN a group of young children who play together supervised by adults

playing-card NOUN one of a pack of cards used in playing card games

playmate NOUN a friend with whom you play

play-off NOUN **1** a game to decide a tie **2** a game between the winners of other competitions

playwright NOUN a writer of plays

PLC ABBREVIATION public limited company

plea NOUN **1** an excuse **2** *law* an accused person's answer to a charge in a law court **3** an urgent request

plead VERB **1** *law* to state your case in a law court **2** to give as an excuse **plead guilty** *or* **not guilty** *law* to admit or deny guilt in a law court **plead with** to beg earnestly

pleasant ADJECTIVE giving pleasure; agreeable

please VERB **1** to give pleasure or delight to **2** to satisfy **3** to choose, like (to do): *Do as you please* ▶INTERJECTION added for politeness to a command or request: *Please keep off the grass* **if you please** please

pleasurable ADJECTIVE delightful, pleasant

pleasure NOUN **1** enjoyment, joy, delight **2** what you wish: *What is your pleasure?* **at your pleasure** when or if you please

pleat NOUN a fold in cloth, which has been pressed or stitched down ▶VERB to put pleats in

pleated ADJECTIVE having pleats

plectrum NOUN (*plural* **plectrums** *or* **plectra**) a small piece of horn, metal, etc used for plucking the strings of a guitar

pledge NOUN **1** something handed over as security for a loan **2** a solemn promise ▸ VERB **1** to give as security, pawn **2** to promise solemnly: *pledged himself to carry out the plan* **3** to drink to the health of, toast

plentiful *or* **plenteous** ADJECTIVE not scarce, abundant

plenty NOUN **1** a full supply, as much as is needed **2** a large number or quantity (of)

plethora (*pronounced* **pleth**-*o*-r*a*) NOUN too large a quantity of anything: *a plethora of politicians*

pliable ADJECTIVE **1** easily bent or folded **2** easily persuaded

pliers PLURAL NOUN a tool used for gripping, bending, and cutting wire etc

plight NOUN a bad state or situation

plinth NOUN **1** the square slab at the foot of a column **2** the base or pedestal of a statue, vase, etc

plod VERB (**plodding, plodded**) **1** to travel slowly and steadily **2** to work on steadily

plonk[1] *informal*, NOUN a sound made by something dropping heavily ▸ VERB to drop (something) heavily: *plonked his bag on the floor*

plonk[2] NOUN, *informal* cheap wine

plop NOUN the sound made by a small object falling into water ▸ VERB (**plopping, plopped**) to make this sound

plot[1] NOUN **1** a plan for an illegal or malicious action **2** the story of a play, novel, etc ▸ VERB (**plotting, plotted**) **1** to plan secretly **2** to make a chart, graph, etc of **3** to mark points on a graph using co-ordinates

plot[2] NOUN a small piece of ground

plough *or US* **plow** (*both pronounced* plow) NOUN a farm tool for turning over the soil ▸ VERB **1** to turn up the ground in furrows **2** *informal* to work through slowly: *ploughing through the ironing*

plover (*pronounced* **pluv**-*er*) NOUN any of several kinds of bird of shores and open country that nest on the ground

ploy NOUN a stratagem, dodge or manoeuvre to gain an advantage

pluck VERB **1** to pull out or off **2** to pick (flowers, fruit, etc) **3** to strip off the feathers of (a bird) before cooking it ▸ NOUN courage, spirit

pluck up courage to prepare yourself to face a danger or difficulty

plucky ADJECTIVE (**pluckier, pluckiest**) *informal* brave, determined

plug NOUN **1** an object fitted into a hole to stop it up **2** a fitting on an appliance put into a socket to connect with an electric current **3** *informal* a brief advertisement ▸ VERB (**plugging, plugged**) **1** to stop up with a plug **2** *informal* to advertise, publicize

plum NOUN **1** a soft fruit, often dark red or purple, with a stone in the centre **2** the tree that produces this fruit ▸ ADJECTIVE very good, very profitable etc: *a plum job*

plumage (*pronounced* **ploo**-mij)

A B C D E F G H I J K L M N O P Q R S T U V W X Y Z

NOUN the feathers of a bird
ⓘ Comes from French *plume* meaning 'feather'

plumb NOUN a lead weight hung on a string (**plumbline**), used to test if a wall has been built straight up, wallpaper hung straight, etc ▶ADJECTIVE & ADVERB standing straight up, vertical ▶VERB to test the depth of (the sea etc)

plumber NOUN someone who fits and mends water, gas, and sewage pipes

plumbing NOUN **1** the work of a plumber **2** the drainage and water systems of a building etc

plume NOUN **1** a feather, especially an ornamental one **2** something looking like a feather: *a plume of smoke*

plummet NOUN a weight of lead hung on a line, for taking depths at sea ▶VERB (**plummeting, plummeted**) to plunge

plump[1] ADJECTIVE fat, rounded, well filled out ▶VERB **1** (often **plump up** or **plump out**) to grow fat, swell **2** to beat or shake (cushions etc) back into shape

plump[2] VERB to sit or sink down heavily **plump for something** to choose, vote for it

plum pudding NOUN a rich pudding containing dried fruit

plunder VERB to carry off goods by force, loot, rob ▶NOUN goods seized by force

plunge VERB **1** to dive (into water etc) **2** to rush or lurch forward **3** to thrust suddenly (into): *He plunged the knife into its neck* ▶NOUN a thrust; a dive

plural ADJECTIVE more than one ▶NOUN, *grammar* the form which shows more than one, eg *mice* is the plural of *mouse* (*compare with*: **singular**)

plus PREPOSITION used to show addition and represented by the sign (+): *Five plus two equals seven* ▶ADJECTIVE of a quantity more than zero ▶ADVERB, *informal* and a bit extra: *She earns £20,000 plus*

plush NOUN cloth with a soft velvety surface on one side ▶ADJECTIVE, *informal* luxurious

ply[1] VERB (**plies, plying, plied**) **1** to work at steadily **2** to make regular journeys: *The ferry plies between Oban and Mull* **3** to use (a tool) energetically **4** to keep supplying with (food, questions to answer, etc)

ply[2] NOUN: **two-ply, three-ply, etc** having two, three, etc layers or strands

plywood NOUN a board made up of thin sheets of wood glued together

PM ABBREVIATION prime minister

pm ABBREVIATION after noon (from Latin *post meridiem*)

pneumatic (*pronounced* nyoo-**mat**-ik) ADJECTIVE **1** filled with air **2** worked by air: *a pneumatic drill*
ⓘ Comes from Greek *pneuma* meaning 'breath'

pneumonia (*pronounced* nyoo-**moh**-ni-*a*) NOUN a disease in which the lungs become inflamed
ⓘ Comes from Greek *pneumon* meaning 'lung'

PO ABBREVIATION **1** post office **2** postal order

poach[1] VERB to cook gently in boiling water or stock

poach[2] VERB to catch fish or hunt game illegally

poacher NOUN someone who hunts or fishes illegally

pocket NOUN **1** a small pouch or bag, especially as part of a garment **2** a personal supply of money: *well beyond my pocket* **3** a small isolated area: *a pocket of unemployment* ▶VERB (**pocketing, pocketed**) **1** to put in a pocket **2** *informal* to steal **in** *or* **out of pocket** having gained or lost money on a deal etc

pocket money NOUN an allowance of money for personal spending

pockmark NOUN a scar or small hole in the skin left by disease

pod NOUN a long seedcase of the pea, bean, etc ▶VERB (**podding, podded**) **1** to remove from a pod **2** to form pods

podcasting NOUN a method of publishing sound files on the Internet, enabling people to create broadcasts without sophisticated equipment > **podcast** NOUN > **podcaster** NOUN

podgy ADJECTIVE (**podgier, podgiest**) short and fat

podium NOUN (*plural* **podiums** *or* **podia**) a low pedestal, a platform

poem NOUN a piece of imaginative writing set out in lines which often have a regular rhythm or rhyme

poet NOUN someone who writes poetry

poetic ADJECTIVE of or like poetry > **poetically** ADVERB

poetic justice NOUN a fitting reward or punishment

poetic licence NOUN a departure from truth, logic, etc for the sake of effect

poetry NOUN **1** the art of writing poems **2** poems

po-faced ADJECTIVE stupidly solemn, humourless

poignancy (*pronounced* **poi**-ny*a*n-si) NOUN a poignant quality

poignant (*pronounced* **poi**-ny*a*nt) ADJECTIVE **1** sharp, keen **2** very painful or moving; pathetic

point NOUN **1** a sharp end of anything **2** a headland **3** a dot: *decimal point* **4** a full stop in punctuation **5** an exact place or spot **6** an exact moment of time **7** the chief matter of an argument **8** the meaning of a joke **9** a mark in a competition **10** a purpose, an advantage: *There is no point in going* **11** a movable rail to direct a railway engine from one line to another **12** an electrical wall socket **13** a mark of character: *He has many good points* ▶VERB **1** to make pointed: *point your toes* **2** to direct, aim **3** to indicate with a gesture: *pointing to the building* **4** to fill (wall joints) with mortar

[i] Comes from French *point* meaning 'dot' or 'stitch', and *pointe* meaning 'sharp point'

point-blank ADJECTIVE **1** of a shot: fired from very close range **2** of a question: direct

pointed ADJECTIVE **1** having a point, sharp **2** of a remark: obviously aimed at someone

pointer NOUN **1** a rod for pointing

2 a type of dog used to show where game has fallen after it has been shot

pointless ADJECTIVE having no meaning or purpose

point of view NOUN (*plural* **points of view**) someone's attitude towards something

poise VERB 1 to balance, keep steady 2 to hover in the air ▶ NOUN 1 a state of balance 2 dignity, self-confidence

poised ADJECTIVE 1 balanced, having poise 2 prepared, ready: *poised for action*

poison NOUN 1 a substance which, when taken into the body, kills or harms 2 anything harmful ▶ VERB 1 to kill or harm with poison 2 to add poison to 3 to make bitter or bad: *poisoned her mind*

poisonous ADJECTIVE 1 harmful because of containing poison 2 *informal* of a person, remark, etc: malicious

poke VERB 1 to push (eg a finger or stick) into something 2 to prod, thrust at 3 to search about inquisitively ▶ NOUN 1 a nudge, a prod 2 a prying search

poker[1] NOUN a rod for stirring up a fire

poker[2] NOUN a card game in which players bet on their chance of winning

poky ADJECTIVE (**pokier, pokiest**) cramped and shabby

polar ADJECTIVE 1 of the regions round the North or South Poles 2 of climate: very cold and dry

polar bear NOUN a type of large, white bear found in the Arctic

polarity NOUN (*plural* **polarities**) the state of having two opposite poles

polarize *or* **polarise** VERB 1 to give polarity to 2 to split into opposing sides

Polaroid NOUN, *trademark* 1 a plastic through which light is seen less brightly, used in sunglasses 2 a camera that develops individual pictures in a few seconds

pole[1] NOUN 1 the north or south end of the earth's axis (**the North** or **South Pole**) 2 either of the opposing points of a magnet or electric battery

pole[2] NOUN a long, rounded rod or post

polecat NOUN 1 a large kind of weasel 2 *US* a skunk

Pole Star NOUN (**the Pole Star**) the star most directly above the North Pole

pole vault NOUN a sport in which an athlete jumps over a bar with the aid of a flexible pole

police NOUN the body of men and women whose work it is to see that laws are obeyed etc ▶ VERB to keep law and order in (a place) by use of police

policeman NOUN (*plural* **policemen**) a male police officer

police officer NOUN a member of a police force

police station NOUN the headquarters of the police in a district

policewoman NOUN (*plural* **policewomen**) a female police officer

policy[1] NOUN (*plural* **policies**) an agreed course of action

policy[2] NOUN (*plural* **policies**)

a written agreement with an insurance company

polio *short for* **poliomyelitis**

poliomyelitis (*pronounced* poh-li-oh-mai-*e*-**lai**-tis) NOUN a disease of the spinal cord, causing weakness or paralysis of the muscles

polish VERB **1** to make smooth and shiny by rubbing **2** to improve (a piece of writing etc) **3** to make more polite ▶ NOUN (*plural* **polishes**) **1** a gloss on a surface **2** a substance used for polishing **3** fine manners, style, etc

polite ADJECTIVE having good manners, courteous > **politely** ADVERB

political ADJECTIVE of government, politicians, or politics

politician NOUN someone involved in politics, especially a member of parliament

politics SINGULAR NOUN the art or study of government

polka (*pronounced* **pol**-k*a or* **pohl**-k*a*) NOUN a lively dance or the music for it

poll (*pronounced* pohl) NOUN **1** a counting of voters at an election **2** total number of votes **3** (*also called*: **opinion poll**) a test of public opinion by asking what people think of something ▶ VERB **1** to cut or clip off (hair, branches, etc) **2** to receive (votes): *They polled 5000 votes*

pollen NOUN the fertilizing powder of flowers

pollination NOUN the transfer of pollen to achieve fertilization

polling station NOUN the building where people go to vote during an election

pollute VERB **1** to make dirty or impure **2** to make (the environment) harmful to life

pollution NOUN **1** the act of polluting **2** dirt

polo NOUN a game like hockey played on horseback

polo neck NOUN **1** a close-fitting neck with a part turned over at the top **2** a jumper with a neck like this

poltergeist (*pronounced* **pohl**-ter-gaist) NOUN a kind of ghost believed to move furniture and throw objects around a room

poly- PREFIX **1** many, much: *polyglot/polygon* **2** *chemistry* a polymer of: *polystyrene* (= a polymer of styrene)/*polythene* (= the name of a number of polymers of ethylene)

ⓘ Comes from Greek *polys* meaning 'much'

polyester NOUN a synthetic material often used in clothing

polygamy (*pronounced* po-**lig**-*a*-mi) NOUN the fact of having more than one wife or husband at the same time (*compare with*: **bigamy**, **monogamy**) > **polygamist** NOUN > **polygamous** ADJECTIVE

polyglot ADJECTIVE speaking, or written in, many languages ▶ NOUN someone fluent in many languages

polygon NOUN, *maths* a figure with many angles and sides > **polygonal** ADJECTIVE

polygraph NOUN an instrument which measures pulse rate etc, used as a lie-detector

polymer NOUN, *chemistry* a chemical compound made up

A B C D E F G H I J K L M N O P Q R S T U V W X Y Z

of linked smaller molecules (**monomers**)

polyphonic (*pronounced* pol-i-**fon**-ik) ADJECTIVE relating to polyphony

polyphony (*pronounced* po-**lif**-*o*n-i) NOUN musical composition in parts, each with a separate melody (*compare with*: **homophony**)

polystyrene NOUN a tough thermoplastic material which resists moisture, used for packing, disposable cups, etc

polytechnic NOUN formerly, a college which taught technical and vocational subjects

polythene NOUN a type of plastic that can be moulded when hot

polyunsaturated ADJECTIVE, *chemistry* of oil: containing no cholesterol

polyurethane (*pronounced* pol-i-**yoo**-ri-thein) NOUN, *chemistry* a resin used to produce foam materials

pomegranate (*pronounced* **pom**-i-gran-it) NOUN a fruit with a thick skin, many seeds and pulpy edible flesh

ⓘ Comes from Old French *pome grenate* meaning 'grainy apple'

pomp NOUN solemn and splendid ceremony, magnificence

pompous ADJECTIVE self-important, excessively dignified

> **pomposity** NOUN

poncho NOUN (*plural* **ponchos**) a S American cloak made of a blanket with a hole for the head

pond NOUN a small lake or pool

ponder VERB to think over, consider

pontiff NOUN **1** a Roman Catholic bishop **2** the Pope

pontificate VERB to speak in a pompous manner

pontoon[1] NOUN a flat-bottomed boat used to support a temporary bridge (a **pontoon bridge**)

pontoon[2] NOUN a card game in which players try to collect 21 points

pony NOUN (*plural* **ponies**) a small horse

ponytail NOUN a hairstyle in which the hair is drawn back and gathered by a band

pony-trekking NOUN riding cross-country in small parties

poodle NOUN a breed of dog with curly hair often clipped in a fancy way

pool[1] NOUN **1** a small area of still water **2** a deep part of a river

pool[2] NOUN **1** a joint fund or stock (of money, typists, etc) **2** the money played for in a gambling game ▸ VERB to put (money etc) into a joint fund

pools PLURAL NOUN (**the pools**) organized betting on football match results (*also called*: **football pools**)

poor ADJECTIVE **1** having little money or property **2** not good: *This work is poor* **3** lacking (in): *poor in sports facilities* **4** deserving pity: *Poor Tom has broken his leg* ▸ PLURAL NOUN (**the poor**) poor people in general

poorly ADJECTIVE, *informal* in bad health, ill

pop[1] NOUN **1** a sharp quick noise, eg that made by a cork coming out of a bottle **2** *informal* a fizzy soft drink ▸ VERB (**popping, popped**) **1** to make a pop **2** to move quickly, dash: *pop in/pop along the road*

pop[2] NOUN popular music ▸ADJECTIVE of music: popular

popadom *or* **popadum** NOUN a thin circle of dough fried in oil until crisp

popcorn NOUN maize grains that puff up and burst open when heated

Pope *or* **pope** NOUN the bishop of Rome, head of the Roman Catholic Church

poplar NOUN a tall, narrow, quick-growing tree

poplin NOUN strong cotton cloth

poppy NOUN (*plural* **poppies**) a scarlet flower growing wild in fields etc, or any of various related species

populace NOUN the people of a country or area

popular ADJECTIVE **1** of the people: *the popular vote* **2** liked by most people **3** widely held or believed: *popular belief*

popularity NOUN the state of being generally liked

popularize *or* **popularise** VERB to make popular or widely known

populate VERB to fill (an area) with people **>** **populated** ADJECTIVE

population NOUN the number of people living in a place

populous ADJECTIVE full of people

pop-up ADJECTIVE *computing* of a utility: appearing on the screen when an option is selected: *a pop-up menu*

porcelain NOUN a kind of fine china

porch NOUN (*plural* **porches**) a covered entrance to a building

porcupine NOUN a large rodent covered with sharp quills

pore[1] NOUN **1** a tiny hole **2** the hole of a sweat gland in the skin

[i] Comes from Greek *poros* meaning 'a passage'

pore[2] VERB: **pore over** to study closely or eagerly

> Do not confuse with: **pour**

pork NOUN the flesh of the pig, prepared for eating

porn NOUN, *informal* pornography

pornography NOUN literature or art that is sexually explicit and often offensive

porous ADJECTIVE **1** having pores **2** allowing fluid to pass through

porpoise NOUN a blunt-nosed sea animal of the dolphin family

porridge NOUN a food made from oatmeal boiled in water or milk

port[1] NOUN **1** a harbour **2** a town with a harbour

port[2] NOUN the left side of a ship as you face the front

port[3] NOUN, *computing* a socket or plug for connecting a hardware device to a computer

port[4] NOUN a strong, dark-red, sweet wine

portability NOUN the quality of being portable

portable ADJECTIVE able to be lifted and carried ▸NOUN a computer, telephone, etc that can be carried around

portal NOUN, *formal* a grand entrance or doorway

portcullis NOUN (*plural* **portcullises**), *history* a grating which is let down quickly to close a gateway

portentous (*pronounced* pawr-**ten**-*tus*) ADJECTIVE **1** strange, wonderful **2** important, weighty

a b c d e f g h i j k l m n o p q r s t u v w x y z

porter[1] NOUN a doorkeeper

porter[2] NOUN **1** someone employed to carry luggage, push hospital trolleys, etc **2** a kind of dark-brown beer

portfolio NOUN (*plural* **portfolios**) **1** a flat case for carrying papers, drawings, etc **2** *politics* the job of a government minister

porthole NOUN a small, round window in a ship's side

portion NOUN **1** a part **2** a share, a helping ▶ VERB to divide into parts

portly ADJECTIVE (**portlier, portliest**) stout and dignified

portrait NOUN **1** a drawing, painting or photograph of a person **2** a description of a person, place, etc

portray VERB **1** to make a painting or drawing of **2** to describe in words **3** to act the part of > **portrayal** NOUN

pose NOUN **1** a position of the body: *a relaxed pose* **2** behaviour put on to impress others, a pretence ▶ VERB **1** to position yourself for a photograph etc **2** to put forward (a problem, question, etc) (**pose as**) to pretend or claim to be

poser[1] NOUN a difficult question

poser[2] NOUN, *derogatory* someone who poses to impress others

posh ADJECTIVE, *informal* high-class; smart

ⓘ The word probably comes from a Romany word meaning 'a smart person', although many people think it stands for *Port Out, Starboard Home*, which represented the most desirable position of cabins for European passengers on ships travelling to Asia and back

position NOUN **1** place, situation **2** manner of standing, sitting, etc; posture: *in a crouching position* **3** a rank or job: *a high position in a bank* ▶ VERB to place

positive ADJECTIVE **1** meaning or saying 'yes': *a positive answer* (*contrasted with*: **negative**) **2** not able to be doubted: *positive proof* **3** certain, convinced: *I am positive that she did it* **4** definite: *a positive improvement* **5** *maths* of a number: greater than zero **6** *grammar* of an adjective or adverb: of the first degree of comparison, not comparative or superlative, eg *big*, not *bigger* or *biggest*

positron NOUN, *physics* a particle with a positive electrical charge

posse (*pronounced* **pos**-i) NOUN, *US* a body of men enlisted by a sheriff to assist him

possess VERB **1** to own, have **2** to take hold of your mind: *Anger possessed her*

possessed ADJECTIVE **1** in the power of an evil spirit **2** obsessed

possession NOUN **1** the state of possessing or of being possessed **2** (**possessions**) someone's property or belongings

possessive ADJECTIVE **1** *grammar* of an adjective or pronoun: showing possession, for example *my, mine, your, their*, etc **2** over-protective and jealous in attitude

possibility NOUN (*plural* **possibilities**) something that may happen or that may be done

possible ADJECTIVE **1** able to happen or to be done **2** not unlikely

🛈 Comes from Latin *possibilis* meaning 'which may exist' or 'which may be done'

possibly ADVERB perhaps

post- PREFIX after: *postgraduate/ post-mortem*

🛈 Comes from Latin *post* meaning 'after' or 'behind'

post[1] NOUN an upright pole or stake ▸VERB **1** to put up, stick up (a notice etc) **2** to put (information etc) on an Internet site

post[2] NOUN **1** a job: *a teaching post* **2** a place of duty: *The soldier remained at his post* **3** a settlement, a camp: *a military post/trading post* ▸VERB to send or station somewhere: *posted abroad*

post[3] NOUN the service which delivers letters and other mail ▸VERB to put (a letter) in a postbox for collection

postage NOUN money paid for sending a letter etc by post

postage stamp NOUN a small printed label to show that postage has been paid

postal ADJECTIVE of or by post

postal order NOUN a document bought at a post office which can be exchanged for a stated amount of money

postbox NOUN (*plural* **postboxes**) a box with an opening in which to post letters etc

postcard NOUN a card for sending a message by post

postcode NOUN a short series of letters and numbers, used for sorting mail by machine

poster NOUN **1** a large notice or placard **2** a large printed picture

posterior ADJECTIVE **1** coming after in time **2** at or nearer the back ▸NOUN the buttocks

posterity NOUN **1** all future generations **2** someone's descendants

postgraduate ADJECTIVE of study etc: following on from a first university degree ▸NOUN someone continuing to study after a first degree

posthumous (*pronounced* **pos-tyuw-m*us***) ADJECTIVE **1** of a book: published after the author's death **2** of a child: born after the father's death

Post-it NOUN, *trademark* a small sticky label for writing messages on

postman *or* **postwoman** NOUN (*plural* **postmen** *or* **postwomen**) someone who delivers letters

postmark NOUN a date stamp put on a letter at a post office

postmaster *or* **postmistress** NOUN a person in charge of a post office

post-mortem NOUN an examination of a dead body to find out the cause of death

post office NOUN an office for receiving and sending off letters by post etc

postpone VERB to put off to a future time > **postponement** NOUN

postscript NOUN an added remark at the end of a letter, after the sender's name

postulate VERB to assume or take for granted (that)

posture NOUN **1** the manner in which someone holds themselves in standing or walking **2** a position, a pose

A B C D E F G H I J K L M N O P Q R S T U V W X Y Z

postwar ADJECTIVE relating to the time after a war

posy NOUN (*plural* **posies**) a small bunch of flowers

pot[1] NOUN **1** a deep vessel used in cooking, as a container or for growing plants **2** (**pots**) *informal* a great deal: *pots of money* ▶ VERB (**potting, potted**) **1** to plant in a pot **2** to make articles of baked clay

pot[2] NOUN *slang* the drug marijuana

potash NOUN potassium carbonate, obtained from the ashes of wood

potassium NOUN, *chemistry* (symbol **K**) a soft, silvery-white, metallic element

potato NOUN (*plural* **potatoes**) **1** a plant with round, starchy roots which are eaten as a vegetable **2** the vegetable itself

potboiler NOUN, *derogatory* a book etc of little artistic value, produced simply to make money

potency NOUN (*plural* **potencies**) power, strength

potent ADJECTIVE powerful, strong

potential ADJECTIVE that may develop, possible ▶ NOUN the possibility of further development

potential energy NOUN, *physics* the energy a body has as a result of its position or condition (*compare with*: **kinetic energy**)

potentiality NOUN (*plural* **potentialities**) a possibility

pothole NOUN **1** a deep cave **2** a hole worn in a road surface

potholer NOUN someone who explores caves > **potholing** NOUN

potion NOUN a drink, often containing medicine or poison

pot luck NOUN: **take pot luck** to take whatever is available or offered

pot plant NOUN a household plant kept in a pot

potpourri (*pronounced* poh-**poo**-ri) NOUN **1** a scented mixture of dried petals etc **2** a mixture or medley

pot shot NOUN a casual or random shot

potted ADJECTIVE **1** of meat: pressed down and preserved in a jar **2** condensed and simplified: *potted history*

potter[1] NOUN someone who makes articles of baked clay

potter[2] VERB **1** to do small odd jobs **2** to dawdle

pottery NOUN (*plural* **potteries**) **1** articles made of baked clay **2** a place where such things are made **3** the art of making them

potty[1] ADJECTIVE (**pottier, pottiest**) *informal* mad, eccentric

potty[2] NOUN (*plural* **potties**) *informal* a child's chamberpot

pouch NOUN (*plural* **pouches**) **1** a pocket or small bag **2** a bag-like fold on the front of a kangaroo, for carrying its young

pouffe (*pronounced* poof) NOUN a low, stuffed seat without back or arms

poultice (*pronounced* **pohl**-tis) NOUN a wet dressing spread on a bandage and put on inflamed skin

poultry NOUN farmyard fowls, eg hens, ducks, geese, turkeys

pounce VERB: **pounce on something** *or* **someone** to seize or attack them NOUN a sudden attack

pound[1] NOUN **1** the standard unit of money in Britain, shown by the sign

(£), equal to 100 new pence **2** (*abbrev* **lb**) a measure of weight, equal to 16 ounces (about ½ kilogram)

pound² NOUN an enclosure for animals

pound³ VERB **1** to beat into powder **2** to beat heavily **3** to walk or run with heavy steps

pour VERB **1** to flow in a stream: *The blood poured out* **2** to make flow: *pour the tea* **3** to rain heavily

🛈 Comes from Middle English *pouren*

> Do not confuse with: **pore**

pout VERB to push out the lips sulkily to show displeasure ▶NOUN a sulky look

poverty NOUN **1** the state of being poor **2** lack, want: *poverty of ideas*

POW ABBREVIATION prisoner of war

powder NOUN **1** a substance made up of very fine particles **2** gunpowder **3** cosmetic face powder ▶VERB **1** to sprinkle or dab with powder **2** to grind down to powder

powdered ADJECTIVE **1** in fine particles **2** covered with powder

powdery ADJECTIVE **1** covered with powder **2** like powder: *powdery snow*

power NOUN **1** strength, force **2** ability to do things **3** authority or legal right **4** a strong nation **5** someone in authority **6** the force used for driving machines: *electric power/steam power* **7** *maths* the product obtained by multiplying a number by itself a given number of times (eg 2×2×2 or 2^3 is the third power of 2)

power-driven *or* **powered** ADJECTIVE worked by electricity, not by hand

powerful ADJECTIVE having great power, strength, vigour, authority, influence, force or effectiveness

powerless ADJECTIVE without power or ability

power station NOUN a building where electricity is produced

power tool NOUN a hand-held tool worked by electrical power

pp ABBREVIATION pages

practicable ADJECTIVE able to be used or done: *a plan that is practicable in reality*

🛈 Comes from an old spelling of French *praticable* meaning 'able to be put into practice'

practical ADJECTIVE **1** preferring action to thought **2** efficient **3** learned by practice, rather than from books: *practical knowledge*

🛈 Comes from an old spelling of French *pratique* meaning 'handy', + suffix *-al*

practical joke NOUN a joke consisting of action, not words; a trick played on someone

practically ADVERB **1** in a practical way **2** in effect, in reality **3** almost: *practically empty*

practice NOUN **1** habit: *It is my practice to get up early* **2** the actual doing of something: *I always intend to get up early but in practice I stay in bed* **3** repeated performance to improve skill: *piano practice/in practice for the race* **4** the business of a doctor, lawyer, etc

> Do not confuse: **practice** and **practise**. To help you remember 'ice' is a noun, 'ise' is not!

practise *or US* **practice** VERB **1** to perform or exercise repeatedly to improve a skill: *She practises judo nightly* **2** to make a habit of: *practise self-control* **3** to follow (a profession): *practise dentistry*

practitioner NOUN someone engaged in a profession: *a medical practitioner*

pragmatic *or* **pragmatical** ADJECTIVE practical; matter-of-fact; realistic

prairie NOUN a stretch of level grassland in N America

praise VERB **1** to speak highly of **2** to glorify (God) by singing hymns etc ▸ NOUN an expression of approval

praiseworthy ADJECTIVE deserving to be praised

pram NOUN a small wheeled carriage for a baby, pushed by hand (*short for* **perambulator**)

prance VERB **1** to strut or swagger about **2** to dance about **3** of a horse: to spring from the hind legs

prank NOUN a trick played for mischief

prat NOUN, *informal* an idiot

prattle VERB to talk or chatter meaninglessly ▸ NOUN meaningless talk

prawn NOUN a type of shellfish like the shrimp

pray VERB **1** to speak to God **2** to ask earnestly, beg

ⓘ Comes from French *prier*, from Latin *precarius* meaning 'obtained by prayer'

> Do not confuse with: **prey**

prayer NOUN **1** a request, thanks, etc given to God **2** an earnest request for something

praying mantis *see* **mantis**

pre- PREFIX **1** before: *prehistoric* **2** to the highest degree: *pre-eminent*

ⓘ Comes from Latin *prae* meaning 'in front of' or 'before'

preach VERB **1** to give a sermon **2** to teach, speak in favour of: *preach caution*

preacher NOUN a religious teacher

preamble NOUN something said as an introduction

prearrange VERB to arrange beforehand

precarious ADJECTIVE uncertain, risky, dangerous

precaution NOUN care taken beforehand to avoid an accident etc
> **precautionary** ADJECTIVE

precede VERB to go before in time, rank, or importance

ⓘ Comes from Latin *praecedere* meaning 'to go before'

> Do not confuse with: **proceed**

precedence NOUN the right to go before; priority

precedent NOUN a past action which serves as an example or rule for the future

preceding ADJECTIVE going before; previous

precept NOUN a guiding rule, a commandment

precinct NOUN **1** an area enclosed

by the boundary walls of a building **2** (**precincts**) the area closely surrounding any place **3** *US* an administrative district

precious ADJECTIVE **1** highly valued or valuable **2** over-fussy or precise

precipice NOUN a steep cliff

precipitate VERB (*pronounced* pri-**sip**-it-eit) **1** to throw head foremost **2** to force into (hasty action etc) **3** to hasten (death, illness etc) ▶ ADJECTIVE (*pronounced* pri-**sip**-it-it) **1** headlong **2** hasty, rash ▶ NOUN (*pronounced* pri-**sip**-it-it) *chemistry* a suspension of small solid particles in a solution

precipitation NOUN **1** great hurry **2** *meteorology* rainfall

precipitous ADJECTIVE very steep

précis (*pronounced* **prei**-see) NOUN (*plural* **précis** – *pronounced* **prei**-seez) a summary of a piece of writing

precise ADJECTIVE **1** definite **2** exact, accurate > **precisely** ADVERB

[i] Comes from Latin *praecisus* meaning 'cut short'

> Do not confuse with: **concise**

precision NOUN **1** preciseness **2** exactness, accuracy

preclude VERB to prevent, make impossible

precocious ADJECTIVE of a child: unusually advanced or well-developed > **precocity** NOUN

precognitive ADJECTIVE knowing beforehand, foretelling

preconceive VERB to form (ideas etc) before having actual knowledge or experience

preconception NOUN an idea formed without actual knowledge

precursor NOUN a person or thing which goes before; an early form of something: *the precursor of jazz*

predate VERB to happen before in time

predator NOUN a bird or animal that kills others for food > **predation** NOUN

predatory (*pronounced* **pred**-*a*-to-ri) ADJECTIVE **1** of a predator **2** using other people for your own advantage

predecessor NOUN the previous holder of a job or office

predetermine VERB to settle beforehand

predicament NOUN an unfortunate or difficult situation

predict VERB to foretell, forecast

predictable ADJECTIVE able to be foretold

prediction NOUN an act of predicting; something predicted

predilection (*pronounced* pree-di-**lek**-shon) NOUN a preference, a liking for something

predispose VERB **1** to make (someone) in favour of something beforehand: *We were predisposed to believe her* **2** to make liable (to): *predisposed to colds* > **predisposition** NOUN

predominance NOUN being predominant

predominant ADJECTIVE **1** ruling **2** most noticeable or outstanding

predominantly ADVERB mostly, mainly: *Her books are predominantly about life in Africa*

predominate VERB **1** to be the strongest or most numerous **2** to have control (over)

pre-eminence NOUN a pre-eminent quality or state: *His pre-eminence in the field of family law*

pre-eminent ADJECTIVE outstanding, excelling all others > **pre-eminently** ADVERB

pre-empt VERB to block or stop by making a first move > **pre-emptive** ADJECTIVE

preen VERB **1** of a bird: to arrange its feathers **2** to smarten your appearance in a conceited way **preen yourself** to show obvious pride in your achievements

prefabricated ADJECTIVE made of parts made beforehand, ready to be fitted together

preface (*pronounced* **pref**-is) NOUN an introduction to a book etc ▸VERB to precede or introduce (with)

prefect NOUN **1** the head of an administrative district in France etc **2** a senior pupil in some schools with certain powers

prefer VERB (**preferring, preferred**) **1** to like better: *I prefer tea to coffee* **2** to put forward (a claim or request)

preferable (*pronounced* **pref**-*ra*-bl) ADJECTIVE more desirable

preference NOUN **1** greater liking **2** something preferred: *What is your preference?*

preferential ADJECTIVE giving preference

prefix NOUN (*plural* **prefixes**) a syllable or element at the beginning of a word which adds to or alters its meaning, eg *dis-*, *un-*, *re-*, in *dis*like, *un*happy, *re*gain

pregnancy NOUN (*plural* **pregnancies**) the state of being pregnant or the time during which a female is pregnant

pregnant ADJECTIVE **1** carrying a developing embryo in the womb **2** full of meaning: *a pregnant pause*

prehistoric ADJECTIVE relating to the time before history was written down

prehistory NOUN the period before historical records

prejudice NOUN **1** an unfair feeling for or against anything **2** an opinion formed without careful thought **3** harm, injury ▸VERB **1** to fill with prejudice **2** to do harm to, damage: *His late arrival prejudiced his chances of success*

prejudiced ADJECTIVE showing prejudice

prejudicial ADJECTIVE damaging, harmful

preliminary ADJECTIVE going before, preparatory: *preliminary investigation* ▸NOUN (*plural* **preliminaries**) something that goes or is done before

prelude (*pronounced* **prel**-yood) NOUN **1** a piece of music played as an introduction to the main piece **2** a preceding event: *a prelude to war*

premature ADJECTIVE coming, born, etc before the right, proper or expected time

premeditate VERB to think out beforehand, plan: *premeditated murder* > **premeditation** NOUN

premenstrual ADJECTIVE before menstruation

premier (*pronounced* **prem**-i-*er*) ADJECTIVE first, leading, foremost ▸NOUN a prime minister

> Do not confuse: **premier** and **première**

première (*pronounced* **prem**-i-eir) NOUN a first performance of a play, film, etc

premise *or* **premiss** NOUN (*plural* **premises** *or* **premisses**) something assumed from which a conclusion is drawn

premises PLURAL NOUN a building and its grounds

premium (*pronounced* **pree**-mi-*u*m) NOUN (*plural* **premiums**) **1** a reward **2** a payment on an insurance policy **at a premium** very desirable and therefore difficult to obtain

premonition NOUN a feeling that something is going to happen; a forewarning

prenatal ADJECTIVE before birth, or before giving birth

preoccupation NOUN **1** being preoccupied **2** something that preoccupies: *She has a preoccupation with death*

preoccupied ADJECTIVE deep in thought

preoccupy VERB (**preoccupies, preoccupying, preoccupied**) to completely engross the attention of (someone)

preordain VERB to determine beforehand

prep NOUN, *informal* preparation

prepaid *past form* of **prepay**

preparation NOUN **1** an act of preparing **2** study for a lesson **3** something prepared for use, eg a medicine

preparatory ADJECTIVE acting as an introduction to or preparation for

preparatory school NOUN a private school educating children of primary-school age

prepare VERB **1** to make or get ready **2** to train, equip

prepared ADJECTIVE **1** ready **2** willing

prepay VERB (**prepaying, prepaid**) to pay beforehand

prepayment NOUN payment in advance

preposition NOUN, *grammar* a word placed before a noun, pronoun, etc to show its relation to another word, eg '*through* the door', '*in* the town', 'written *by* me'

> Do not confuse with: **proposition**

prepossessing ADJECTIVE pleasant, making a good impression

preposterous ADJECTIVE very foolish, absurd

prep school NOUN a preparatory school

pre-Raphaelite NOUN any of a group of 19th-century British artists who painted in a truthful, natural style

prerequisite NOUN something necessary before another thing can happen

prerogative NOUN a right enjoyed by someone because of their rank or position

presbyter (*pronounced* **prez**-bi-*ter*) NOUN, *Christianity* a minister or elder in a Presbyterian church

Presbyterian ADJECTIVE **1** of a church: managed by ministers and elders **2** belonging to such a church

A B C D E F G H I J K L M N O P Q R S T U V W X Y Z

▸NOUN a member of a Presbyterian church

presbytery NOUN (*plural* **presbyteries**) **1** a body of presbyters **2** the house of a Roman Catholic priest

prescribe VERB **1** to lay down as a rule **2** to order the use of (a medicine)

ⓘ Comes from Latin *praescribere* meaning 'to write before'

> Do not confuse with: **proscribe**. It may help to remember that the **pre-** in **prescribe** means 'before', and that the whole verb refers to the process by which a doctor has to write down an order for medication before it can be obtained by a patient.

prescription NOUN **1** a doctor's written instructions for preparing a medicine **2** something prescribed

> Do not confuse with: **proscription**. **Prescription** is related to the verb **prescribe**.

prescriptive ADJECTIVE laying down rules

presence NOUN **1** the state of being present **2** someone's personal appearance, manner, etc **in your presence** while you are present

presence of mind NOUN calmness; ability to act sensibly in an emergency, difficulty, etc

present[1] (*pronounced* **prez**-ent) ADJECTIVE **1** here, in this place **2** happening or existing now: *present rates of pay/the present situation* ▸NOUN **1** the time now **2** *grammar* the present tense

present[2] NOUN (*pronounced* **prez**-ent) a gift ▸VERB (*pronounced* pri-**zent**) **1** to hand over (a gift) formally **2** to offer, put forward **3** to introduce (someone) to another **present yourself 1** to introduce yourself **2** to arrive

presentation NOUN **1** the giving of a present **2** something presented **3** a formal talk or demonstration **4** a showing of a play etc

presently ADVERB soon

present participle NOUN, *grammar* the form of a verb used after an auxiliary verb to indicate that something is taking place in the present, for instance *going* in 'I am *going*'

present tense NOUN, *grammar* the tense describing events happening now, eg 'we *are* on holiday'

preservation NOUN preserving or being preserved

preservative NOUN a substance added to food to prevent it from going bad

preserve VERB **1** to keep safe from harm **2** to keep in existence, maintain **3** to treat (food) so that it will not go bad ▸NOUN **1** a place where game animals, birds, etc are protected **2** jam

preside VERB to be in charge at a meeting etc

presidency NOUN (*plural* **presidencies**) the position of president or time of being president

president NOUN **1** the leading member of a society etc **2** the head of a republic

press VERB **1** to push on, against or down **2** to urge, force **3** to iron (clothes etc) ▸NOUN (*plural* **presses**)

1 a crowd **2** a printing machine **3** (**the press**) the news media, journalists

pressing ADJECTIVE requiring immediate action, insistent

press-up NOUN an exercise performed by raising and lowering the body on the arms while face down

pressure NOUN **1** *physics* a measure of the force on or against a surface **2** strong persuasion, compulsion **3** stress, strain **4** urgency

pressure cooker NOUN a pan in which food is cooked quickly by steam under pressure

pressure group NOUN a group of people who try to influence public opinion and government policy on a particular issue

pressurize *or* **pressurise** VERB **1** to fit (an aeroplane etc) with a device that maintains normal air pressure **2** to force (someone) to do something

prestige (*pronounced* pre-**steesz**) NOUN reputation, influence due to rank, success, etc

prestigious (*pronounced* pre-**stij**-*us*) ADJECTIVE having or giving prestige

presumably ADVERB I suppose

presume VERB to take for granted, assume (that) (**presume on**) to take advantage of (someone's kindness etc)

presumption NOUN **1** something presumed, a strong likelihood **2** arrogant or impertinent behaviour

presumptuous ADJECTIVE insolent or arrogant

presuppose VERB to take for granted

pretence *or US* **pretense** NOUN **1** the act of pretending **2** a false claim

pretend VERB **1** to make believe, fantasize **2** to make a false claim: *pretending to be ill*

pretender NOUN someone who lays claim to something (especially to the crown)

pretension NOUN **1** a claim (whether true or not) **2** self-importance

pretentious ADJECTIVE self-important; showy, ostentatious

pretext NOUN an excuse

pretty ADJECTIVE (**prettier, prettiest**) pleasing or attractive to see, listen to, etc ▶ADVERB fairly, quite: *pretty good* > **prettiness** NOUN

prevail VERB **1** to win, succeed **2** to be most usual or common (**prevail against** *or* **over**) to gain control over (**prevail on**) to persuade (someone): *She prevailed on me to stay*

prevailing ADJECTIVE **1** controlling **2** most common: *the prevailing mood*

prevalent (*pronounced* **prev**-*a*-lent) ADJECTIVE common, widespread > **prevalence** NOUN

prevaricate VERB to avoid telling the truth > **prevarication** NOUN > **prevaricator** NOUN

prevent VERB to hinder, stop happening > **preventible** ADJECTIVE > **prevention** NOUN the act of preventing

preventive *or* **preventative** ADJECTIVE of medicine: helping to prevent illness

preview NOUN a view of a performance, exhibition, etc before its official opening

previous ADJECTIVE earlier; former; prior > **previously** ADVERB

prey NOUN **1** an animal killed by others for food **2** a victim ▶ VERB: **prey on someone** *or* **something** **1** to seize and eat them: *preying on smaller birds* **2** to stalk and harass them

Comes from Latin *praeda* meaning 'booty'

Do not confuse with: **pray**

price NOUN **1** the money for which something is bought or sold, the cost **2** something that must be given up in order to gain something: *the price of fame*

priceless ADJECTIVE **1** very valuable **2** *informal* very funny

pricey *or* **pricy** ADJECTIVE (**pricier, priciest**) *informal* expensive

prick VERB **1** to pierce slightly **2** to give a sharp pain to **3** to stick up (the ears) ▶ NOUN a pricking feeling on the skin

prickle NOUN a sharp point on a plant or animal ▶ VERB **1** to be prickly **2** to feel prickly

prickly ADJECTIVE (**pricklier, prickliest**) **1** full of prickles **2** stinging, pricking

pride NOUN **1** too great an opinion of yourself **2** pleasure in having done something well **3** dignity **4** a group of lions ▶ VERB: **pride yourself on** to feel or show pride in

priest NOUN **1** a member of the clergy in the Roman Catholic, Orthodox and Anglican churches **2** an official in a non-Christian religion

priestess NOUN (*plural* **priestesses**) a female non-Christian priest

priesthood NOUN those who are priests

prig NOUN a smug, self-righteous person > **priggish** ADJECTIVE

prim ADJECTIVE (**primmer, primmest**) unnecessarily formal and correct

prima ballerina NOUN the leading female dancer of a ballet company

prima donna NOUN **1** a leading female opera singer **2** a woman who is over-sensitive and temperamental

primaeval *another spelling of* **primeval**

primary ADJECTIVE **1** first **2** most important, chief

primary colour NOUN one of the colours from which all others can be made, that is red, blue, and yellow

primary school NOUN a school for the early stages of education

primate NOUN **1** a member of the highest order of mammals, including humans, monkeys and apes, which has hands and grasping thumbs **2** an archbishop

prime ADJECTIVE **1** first in time or importance **2** best quality, excellent **3** of a number: having only two factors, itself and 1, eg 3 (which has the factors 1 and 3 but no others) ▶ NOUN the time of greatest health and strength: *the prime of life* ▶ VERB **1** to prepare the surface of for painting: *prime a canvas* **2** to prepare by supplying detailed information: *She was well primed before the meeting*

prime minister NOUN the head of a government

primeval *or* **primaeval** ADJECTIVE **1** relating to the beginning of the world **2** primitive, instinctive

primitive ADJECTIVE **1** belonging to very early times or the earliest stages of development **2** old-fashioned **3** not skilfully made, rough

primrose NOUN a pale-yellow spring flower common in woods and hedges

prince NOUN **1** the son of a king or queen **2** a ruler of certain states

princess NOUN (*plural* **princesses**) the daughter of a king or queen

principal ADJECTIVE most important, chief ▶NOUN **1** the head of a school or university **2** a leading part in a play etc **3** money in a bank on which interest is paid

ⓘ Comes from Latin *principalis* meaning 'first'

> Do not confuse: **principal** and **principle.** It may help to remember that the adjective **principAl** means 'first or most important', and it contains an A, the first letter of the alphabet.

principality NOUN (*plural* **principalities**) a state ruled by a prince

principally ADVERB chiefly, mostly

principle NOUN **1** a general truth or law **2** the theory on which the working of a machine is based **3** (**principles**) someone's personal rules of behaviour, sense of right and wrong, etc

ⓘ Comes from Latin *principium* meaning 'beginning'

print VERB **1** to mark letters on paper with type **2** to write in capital letters **3** to publish in printed form **4** to stamp patterns on (cloth etc) **5** to make a finished photograph ▶NOUN **1** a mark made by pressure: *a footprint* **2** printed lettering **3** a photograph made from a negative **4** a printed reproduction of a painting etc **5** cloth printed with a design **in print** of a book: published and available to buy

printed circuit NOUN a wiring circuit, formed by printing a design on copper foil bonded to a flat base

printer NOUN **1** someone who prints books, newspapers, etc **2** *computing* a machine that prints, attached to a computer system

printout NOUN, *computing* the printed information produced by a computer

prior ADJECTIVE **1** earlier **2** previous (to)

prioritize *or* **prioritise** VERB **1** to decide what must be done first **2** to make (something) a priority

priority NOUN (*plural* **priorities**) **1** first position **2** the right to be first: *Ambulances must have priority in traffic* **3** something that must be done first: *Our priority is to get him into hospital*

priory NOUN (*plural* **priories**) a building where a community of monks or nuns live

prise VERB to force open or off with a lever: *prised off the lid*

> Do not confuse with: **prize**

prism NOUN **1** a triangular glass tube that breaks light into different colours **2** *maths* a solid with two congruent, parallel polygons at either end (the **bases**) and with parallelograms as its other faces

prison NOUN **1** a building for holding criminals **2** a place where someone is confined against their will

prisoner NOUN someone held under arrest or locked up

prisoner of war NOUN (*plural* **prisoners of war**) someone captured by the enemy forces during war

pristine ADJECTIVE in the original or unspoilt state

privacy (*pronounced* **pri**-*va*-si *or* **prai**-*va*-si) NOUN freedom from intrusion or observation; secrecy

private ADJECTIVE **1** relating to an individual, not to the general public; personal **2** not open to the public **3** secret, not generally known ▸ NOUN the lowest rank of ordinary soldier (not an officer)

private eye NOUN, *informal* a private detective

privately ADVERB in a private way

privation NOUN **1** want, poverty, hardship **2** taking away, loss

privatize *or* **privatise** VERB to transfer from state to private ownership, denationalize
> **privatization** NOUN

privet (*pronounced* **pri**-vit) NOUN a type of shrub used for hedges

privilege NOUN a right available to one person or to only a few people

privileged ADJECTIVE having privileges

privy ADJECTIVE: **privy to** knowing about (something secret)

prize NOUN **1** a reward **2** something won in a competition **3** something captured **4** something highly valued ▸ ADJECTIVE very fine, worthy of a prize ▸ VERB to value highly

> Do not confuse with: **prise**

pro- PREFIX **1** before, forward, front: *proactive, progenitor* **2** in favour of: *pro-devolution*

[i] Comes from Latin and Greek *pro* meaning 'before' or 'for'

pro *short for* **professional**

probability NOUN (*plural* **probabilities**) **1** likelihood **2** something likely to happen

probable ADJECTIVE **1** likely to happen **2** likely to be true

probably ADVERB very likely

probation NOUN **1** a trial period in a new job etc **2** a system of releasing prisoners on condition that they commit no more offences and report regularly to the authorities

probe NOUN **1** a long, thin instrument used to examine a wound **2** a thorough investigation **3** a spacecraft for exploring space ▸ VERB **1** to examine very carefully **2** to investigate thoroughly to find out information

problem NOUN a question to be solved; a matter which is difficult to deal with

problematic *or* **problematical** ADJECTIVE doubtful, uncertain

procedure NOUN **1** a method of

doing business **2** a course of action

proceed VERB **1** to go on with, continue **2** to begin (to do something) **3** to take legal action (against)

Comes from Latin *procedere* meaning 'to go forward'

Do not confuse with: **precede**

proceeding NOUN **1** a step forward **2** (**proceedings**) a record of the meetings of a society, lectures at a conference, etc **3** a law action

proceeds (*pronounced* **proh**-seedz) PLURAL NOUN profit made from a sale etc

process NOUN (*plural* **processes**) **1** a series of operations in manufacturing goods **2** a series of events producing change or development **3** a lawcourt case **in the process of** in the course of

procession NOUN a line of people or vehicles moving forward in order

processor NOUN *computing* a central processing unit or microprocessor

proclaim VERB to announce publicly, declare openly

proclamation NOUN an official announcement made to the public

procrastinate VERB to put things off, delay doing something till a later time > **procrastination** NOUN

procure VERB to obtain; to bring about

prod VERB (**prodding, prodded**) to poke; urge on

prodigious ADJECTIVE **1** strange, astonishing **2** enormous

prodigy NOUN (*plural* **prodigies**) **1** a wonder **2** someone astonishingly clever: *a child prodigy*

produce VERB (*pronounced* proh-**dyoos**) **1** to bring into being **2** to bring about, cause **3** to prepare (a programme) for broadcasting on radio or television **4** to prepare (a play etc) for the stage **5** to make, manufacture ▸NOUN (*pronounced* **prod**-yoos) food grown or produced on a farm or in a garden

producer NOUN someone who produces a play, television programme, etc

product NOUN **1** something produced **2** a result **3** *maths* the number that results from the multiplication of two or more numbers

production NOUN **1** the act of producing; the process of producing or being produced: *The new model goes into production next year* **2** the quantity produced or rate of producing it: *an increase in oil production* **3** a particular presentation of a play, opera, ballet, etc: *a new production of 'The Marriage of Figaro'*

productive ADJECTIVE fruitful, producing results

productivity NOUN the rate of work done

Prof ABBREVIATION Professor

profane ADJECTIVE **1** not sacred **2** treating holy things without respect

profanity (*pronounced* pro-**fan**-it-i) NOUN (*plural* **profanities**) **1** swearing **2** lack of respect for sacred things

profess VERB **1** to declare (a belief etc) openly **2** to pretend, claim: *He professes to be an expert on football*

professed ADJECTIVE **1** declared **2** pretended

profession NOUN **1** an occupation requiring special training, eg that of a doctor, lawyer, teacher, etc **2** an open declaration

professional ADJECTIVE **1** of a profession **2** earning a living from a game or an art (*contrasted with*: **amateur**) **3** skilful, competent ▶NOUN **1** someone who works in a profession **2** someone who earns money from a game or art

professionalism NOUN **1** a professional status **2** professional expertise or competence

professionally ADVERB in a professional way; in terms of your profession: *professionally qualified*

professor NOUN **1** a teacher of the highest rank in a university **2** *US* a university teacher

proficiency NOUN skill

proficient ADJECTIVE skilled, expert

profile NOUN **1** an outline **2** a side view of a face, head, etc **3** a short description of someone's life, achievements, etc

profit NOUN **1** gain, benefit **2** money got by selling an article for a higher price than was paid for it ▶VERB (**profiting, profited**) to gain (from), benefit

profitable ADJECTIVE bringing profit or gain

profiteer NOUN someone who makes large profits unfairly ▶VERB to make large profits unfairly

profligate (*pronounced* **prof**-li-git) ADJECTIVE **1** living an immoral life **2** very extravagant ▶NOUN a profligate person > **profligacy** NOUN

profound ADJECTIVE **1** very deep **2** deeply felt **3** showing great knowledge or understanding: *a profound comment*

profundity NOUN **1** being profound **2** depth

profuse ADJECTIVE abundant, lavish, extravagant > **profusion** NOUN

prognosis NOUN (*plural* **prognoses** – *pronounced* prog-**noh**-seez) a prediction of the course of a disease

program *computing*, NOUN a set of instructions telling a computer to carry out certain actions ▶VERB (**programming, programmed**) **1** to give instructions to **2** to prepare instructions to be carried out by a computer > **programmer** NOUN

programme *or US* **program** NOUN **1** a booklet with details of an entertainment, ceremony, etc **2** a scheme, a plan **3** a TV or radio broadcast

progress NOUN (*pronounced* **proh**-gres) **1** advance, forward movement **2** improvement ▶VERB (*pronounced* pr*o*-**gres**) **1** to go forward **2** to improve

progression NOUN **1** the process of moving forwards or advancing in stages **2** *music* a succession of chords, the advance from one to the next being determined on a fixed pattern **3** *maths* a sequence of numbers, each of which bears a specific relationship to the preceding one, eg an arithmetic progression or a geometric progression

progressive ADJECTIVE **1** going forward **2** favouring reforms

prohibit VERB **1** to forbid **2** to prevent

prohibition NOUN the act of forbidding, especially the forbidding by law of making and selling alcoholic drinks

prohibitive ADJECTIVE **1** prohibiting **2** of price: too expensive, discouraging

project NOUN (*pronounced* **proj**-ekt) **1** a plan, a scheme **2** a task **3** a piece of study or research ▸ VERB (*pronounced* pr*oh*-**jekt**) **1** to throw out or up **2** to jut out **3** to cast (an image, a light, etc) on to a surface **4** to plan, propose

projectile NOUN a missile

projection NOUN **1** an act of projecting **2** something projected **3** something which juts out **4** a mapping of points of a three-dimensional figure onto a plane

projectionist NOUN someone who operates a film projector

projector NOUN a machine for projecting pictures on a screen

proletariat (*pronounced* proh-l*e*-**teir**-i-*a*t) NOUN the ordinary working people

proliferate VERB to grow or increase in number rapidly

prolific ADJECTIVE producing a lot, fruitful

prologue NOUN a preface or introduction to a play etc

prolong VERB to make longer

prom NOUN, *informal* short for **1** promenade **2** promenade concert

promenade (*pronounced* prom-*e*-**nahd**) NOUN **1** a level roadway or walk, especially by the seaside **2** a walk, a stroll ▸ VERB to walk for pleasure

prominent ADJECTIVE **1** standing out, easily seen **2** famous, distinguished > **prominence** NOUN

promiscuity NOUN indulgence in many casual sexual relationships

promiscuous ADJECTIVE **1** having many casual sexual relationships **2** mixed in kind **3** not making distinctions between people or things

promise VERB **1** to give your word (to do or not do something) **2** to show signs for the future: *The weather promises to improve* ▸ NOUN **1** a statement of something promised **2** a sign of something to come **3** a sign of future success: *Her painting shows great promise*

promising ADJECTIVE showing signs of being successful

promontory NOUN (*plural* **promontories**) a headland jutting out into the sea

promote VERB **1** to raise to a higher rank **2** to help onwards, encourage **3** to advertise, encourage the sales of

promotion NOUN **1** advancement in rank or honour **2** encouragement **3** advertising, or an effort to publicize and increase sales of a particular brand

promotional ADJECTIVE relating to or involving promotion

prompt ADJECTIVE **1** quick, immediate **2** punctual ▸ NOUN

LANGUAGE workshop Pronouns

Pronouns are essentially words that stand for nouns. There are many different types of pronoun.

Personal pronouns

Personal pronouns refer to specific people, places or things.

We saw *him*.
They went to see *it*.

Personal pronouns can have different forms depending on whether they are the subject or the object in a sentence. It is a common mistake to use the wrong one, so you should be careful with them when using Standard English:

✗ Him and me went to the shops.
✓ *He* and *I* went to the shops.

Some people wrongly use the subject form **I** when they should use the object form **me**, because they think it sounds better.

✗ Dad gave sweets to John and I.
✓ Dad gave sweets to John and *me*.

Reflexive pronouns

Reflexive pronouns are sometimes called compound pronouns. These are forms that end in **-self** or **-selves**.

I hurt *myself*.
I hope you enjoy *yourselves*.

Some people wrongly use reflexive pronouns when they should use simple personal pronouns, because they think it sounds better.

✗ He handed over two pens, one for you and one for myself.
✓ He handed over two pens, one for you and one for *me*.

➲

Pronouns

LANGUAGE workshop

Possessive pronouns

Possessive pronouns indicate ownership.

The cakes are *his*, the sweets are *mine*, and the biscuits are *theirs*.

Remember: possessive pronouns never have apostrophes.

Indefinite pronouns

Indefinite pronouns refer to non-specific people or things.

Nobody knows *anything* about what happened.
Many are called, *some* are chosen, but *few* succeed.

Interrogative pronouns

Interrogative pronouns begin questions.

Whose is this?
Who are you?
Which shirt should I wear?

Demonstrative pronouns

Demonstrative pronouns 'point to' the nouns they replace.

These (books) are good books.
That (habit) is an annoying habit.

It is a common mistake to use a personal pronoun rather than the correct demonstrative pronoun in some cases, so you should be careful not to do this when using Standard English:

✗ Give me them books.
✗ Give me they books.
✓ Give me *those* books.

LANGUAGE workshop — Pronouns

Relative pronouns

Relative pronouns are special pronouns that begin relative clauses:

Can we see a film *that* I like, for a change?
The boy *who* was climbing the trees had an accident.

? What type of pronoun are the following?

I	someone
them	several
its	why
yours	those

Sometimes when you use pronouns, a sentence is confusing. Try to be clear what you mean!

✗ If the cat does not like raw fish, cook it.
✓ Cook the fish if your cat does not like raw fish.

computing a question, statement, etc which appears on a computer screen, indicating that it is ready for a command ▸ VERB **1** to move to action **2** to supply words to (an actor who has forgotten their lines) > **promptness** NOUN

prompter NOUN a person positioned offstage to prompt actors when they forget their lines

promptly ADVERB **1** without delay **2** punctually

prone ADJECTIVE lying face downward **prone to** inclined to: *prone to laziness*

prong NOUN the spike of a fork

pronged ADJECTIVE having prongs

pronoun NOUN, *grammar* a word used instead of a noun, eg *I*, *you*, *who*

pronounce VERB **1** to speak (words, sounds) **2** to announce (an opinion), declare

pronounced ADJECTIVE noticeable, marked

pronouncement NOUN a statement, an announcement

pronto ADVERB, *informal* quickly

pronunciation NOUN the way a word is said

-proof SUFFIX protected against: *waterproof*

proof NOUN **1** evidence that makes

something clear beyond doubt **2** the standard strength of whisky etc **3** *printing* a copy of a printed sheet for correction before publication **4** *maths* a step-by-step process that proves the truth of a mathematical proposition ▶ ADJECTIVE able to keep out or withstand: *proof against attack*

proofread VERB to read and correct printed page proofs of a text > **proofreader** NOUN

prop[1] NOUN a support ▶ VERB (**propping, propped**) to hold up, support

prop[2] *informal* short for **propeller**

prop[3] *informal* short for **stage property** (= an item needed on stage for a play)

propaganda NOUN **1** the spreading of ideas to influence public opinion **2** material used for this, eg posters, leaflets

propagandist NOUN someone who spreads propaganda

propagate VERB **1** to spread (ideas etc) **2** to produce (new plants)

propagator NOUN **1** a person or thing that propagates **2** a heated box with a cover in which plants may be grown from cuttings or seeds

propane NOUN a gas used as fuel

propel VERB (**propelling, propelled**) to drive forward

propellant NOUN **1** an explosive for firing a rocket **2** the gas in an aerosol used to release the contents as a fine spray

propeller NOUN a shaft with revolving blades which drives forward a ship, aircraft, etc

propensity NOUN (*plural* **propensities**) a natural inclination: *a propensity for bumping into things*

proper ADJECTIVE **1** right, correct: *the proper way to do it* **2** full, thorough: *a proper search* **3** prim, well-behaved

properly ADVERB **1** in the right way **2** thoroughly

proper noun *or* **proper name** NOUN, *grammar* a name for a particular person, place, or thing, eg *Shakespeare*, *the Parthenon* (*contrasted with*: **common noun**)

property NOUN (*plural* **properties**) **1** something that is owned: *That book is my property* **2** land or buildings **3** a quality: *the property of dissolving easily* **4** (**properties**) the furniture etc required by actors in a play

prophecy (*pronounced* **prof**-*e*-si) NOUN (*plural* **prophecies**) **1** foretelling the future **2** something prophesied

> Do not confuse: **prophecy** and **prophesy**. The spelling with the 'c' is the noun, the spelling with the 's' the verb. It may help to remember that this is a common pattern, seen also in such pairs as *practice/practise*, *licence/license*, *and advice/advise*.

prophesy (*pronounced* **prof**-*e*-sai) VERB (**prophesies, prophesying, prophesied**) to foretell the future, predict

prophet NOUN **1** someone who claims to foretell events **2** someone who tells what they believe to be the will of God

A B C D E F G H I J K L M N O P Q R S T U V W X Y Z

proponent NOUN someone in favour of a thing

proportion NOUN **1** a part of a total amount: *A large proportion of income is taxed* **2** relation in size, number, etc compared with something else: *The proportion of girls to boys is small* **in** or **out of proportion** appropriate or inappropriate in size or degree when compared with other things

proportional or **proportionate** ADJECTIVE **1** matching in number, size, etc **2** in proportion

proportional representation NOUN a voting system in which parties are represented in proportion to their voting strength

proposal NOUN **1** an act of proposing **2** anything proposed **3** an offer of marriage

propose VERB **1** to put forward for consideration, suggest **2** to intend **3** to make an offer of marriage (to)

proposition NOUN **1** a proposal, a suggestion **2** a statement **3** a situation that must be dealt with: *a tough proposition*

> Do not confuse with: **preposition**

proprietor or **proprietress** NOUN (*plural* **proprietors** or **proprietresses**) an owner, especially of a hotel

propriety NOUN (*plural* **proprieties**) **1** fitness, suitability **2** correct behaviour, decency

propulsion NOUN an act of driving forward

prosaic (*pronounced* proh-**zei**-ik) ADJECTIVE dull, not interesting

pros and cons PLURAL NOUN the arguments for and against anything

proscribe VERB to ban, prohibit

[i] Comes from Latin *proscribere* meaning 'to publish in writing'.

> Do not confuse with: **prescribe**. It may help to remember that **PROscribe** and **PROhibit** share the same three first letters.

proscription NOUN proscribing or being proscribed

> Do not confuse with: **prescription**. **Proscription** is related to the verb **proscribe**.

proscriptive ADJECTIVE tending to proscribe

prose NOUN **1** writing which is not in verse **2** ordinary written or spoken language

prosecute VERB **1** to bring a case against someone in a court **2** *formal* to carry on (studies, an investigation, etc)

[i] Comes from Latin *prosequi* meaning 'to accompany someone on their way forth'

> Do not confuse with: **persecute**

prosecution NOUN **1** an act of prosecuting **2** *law* those bringing the case in a trial (*contrasted with*: **defence**)

prosody (*pronounced* **pros**-o-di) NOUN the study of the rhythms and construction of poetry

prospect NOUN (*pronounced* **pros**-pekt) **1** a view, a scene **2** a future outlook or expectation: *the prospect of a free weekend/a job with good prospects* ▸VERB (*pronounced* pros-**pekt**) to search for gold or other minerals

prospective ADJECTIVE soon to be, likely to be: *the prospective election*

prospector NOUN someone who prospects for minerals

prospectus NOUN (*plural* **prospectuses**) a booklet giving information about a school, organization, etc

prosper VERB to get on well, succeed

prosperity NOUN success, good fortune

prosperous ADJECTIVE successful, wealthy

prostate NOUN, *anatomy* a gland around the base of a man's bladder which releases a fluid used in semen

prostitute NOUN someone who offers sexual intercourse for payment > **prostitution** NOUN

prostrate ADJECTIVE (*pronounced* **pros**-treit) **1** lying flat face downwards **2** worn out, exhausted ▸VERB (*pronounced* pros-**treit**) **1** to lie on the ground as a sign of respect: *prostrated themselves before the emperor* **2** to exhaust, tire out completely

prostrated ADJECTIVE worn out by grief, tiredness, etc

protagonist NOUN a chief character in a play etc

protect VERB to shield from danger, keep safe > **protection** NOUN

protectionism NOUN the policy of protecting home industry from foreign competition, especially by charging high import duties > **protectionist** NOUN & ADJECTIVE

protective ADJECTIVE giving protection; intended to protect

protector NOUN a guardian, a defender

protectorate NOUN a country which is partly governed and defended by another country

protégé *or feminine* **protégée** (*both pronounced* **proh**-te-szei) NOUN a pupil or employee who is taught or helped in their career by someone important or powerful

protein NOUN a substance present in milk, eggs, meat, etc, which is a necessary part of a human or animal diet

protest VERB (*pronounced* proh-**test**) **1** to object strongly **2** to declare solemnly: *protesting his innocence* ▸NOUN (*pronounced* **proh**-test) a strong objection

Protestant NOUN a member of one of the Christian churches that broke away from the Roman Catholic Church at the time of the Reformation

protestation NOUN **1** a solemn declaration **2** a protest

protocol NOUN correct formal or diplomatic procedures

proton NOUN, *physics* a particle with a positive electrical charge, forming part of the nucleus of an atom (*see also* **electron**, **neutron**)

prototype NOUN the original model from which something is copied

protract VERB to lengthen in time

protractor NOUN, *maths* an instrument for drawing and measuring angles on paper

protrude VERB to stick out, thrust forward > **protrusion** NOUN

protuberance NOUN a swelling, a bulge > **protuberant** ADJECTIVE

proud ADJECTIVE **1** thinking too highly of yourself, conceited **2** feeling pleased at an achievement etc **3** dignified, self-respecting: *too proud to accept the money* **do someone proud** to treat them grandly

prove VERB **1** to show to be true or correct **2** to try out, test **3** to turn out (to be): *His prediction proved correct*

provenance (*pronounced* **prov**-*e*-n*a*ns) NOUN source, origin

proverb NOUN a well-known wise saying, eg 'nothing ventured, nothing gained'

proverbial ADJECTIVE well-known, widely spoken of

provide VERB to supply

provided *or* **providing** CONJUNCTION on condition that

providence NOUN **1** foresight; thrift **2** (**Providence**) God

provident ADJECTIVE thinking of the future; thrifty

province NOUN **1** a division of a country **2** the extent of someone's duties or knowledge **3** (**the provinces**) all parts of a country outside the capital

provincial ADJECTIVE **1** of a province or provinces **2** *derogatory* narrow-minded, parochial

provision NOUN **1** an agreed arrangement **2** a rule or condition **3** (**provisions**) a supply of food

provisional ADJECTIVE used for the time being; temporary

proviso (*pronounced* pro-**vai**-zoh) NOUN (*plural* **provisos**) a condition laid down beforehand

provocative (*pronounced* pro-**vok**-*a*-tiv) ADJECTIVE **1** tending to rouse anger **2** likely to arouse sexual interest

provoke VERB **1** to cause, result in **2** to rouse to anger or action: *Don't let him provoke you* > **provocation** NOUN (meaning 2)

provoking ADJECTIVE annoying

provost NOUN the mayor of a burgh in Scotland

prow NOUN the front part of a ship

prowess NOUN skill, ability

prowl VERB to go about stealthily

proximity NOUN nearness

proxy NOUN (*plural* **proxies**) someone who acts or votes on behalf of another

prude NOUN an over-modest, priggish person > **prudery** NOUN > **prudish** ADJECTIVE

prudent ADJECTIVE wise and cautious > **prudence** NOUN > **prudently** ADVERB

prune[1] VERB **1** to trim (a tree) by cutting off unneeded twigs **2** to shorten, reduce

prune[2] NOUN a dried plum

pry VERB (**pries, prying, pried**) to look closely into things that are not your business > **prying** ADJECTIVE

PS ABBREVIATION postscript

psalm (*pronounced* sahm) NOUN a sacred song

pseud- (*pronounced* syood *or* sood) *or* **pseudo-** PREFIX false: *pseudonym*
ⓘ Comes from Greek *pseudes* meaning 'false'

pseudo (*pronounced* **syood**-oh *or* **sood**-oh) ADJECTIVE, *informal* false, fake, pretended: *His Spanish accent is pseudo*

pseudonym (*pronounced* **syoo**-d*o*-nim *or* **soo**-d*o*-nim) NOUN a false name used by eg an author

psych- *see* **psycho-**

psychedelic (*pronounced* sai-k*e*-**del**-ik) ADJECTIVE bright and multi-coloured

psychiatrist (*pronounced* sai-**kai**-*a*-trist) NOUN someone who treats mental illness

psychiatry (*pronounced* sai-**kai**-*a*-tri) NOUN the treatment of mental illness > **psychiatric** (*pronounced* sai-ki-**at**-rik) ADJECTIVE

psychic (*pronounced* **sai**-kik) *or* **psychical** ADJECTIVE **1** relating to the mind **2** able to read other people's minds, or tell the future

psycho- (*pronounced* **sai**-koh) *or* **psych-** PREFIX relating to the mind: *psychology/psychoanalysis*

[i] Comes from Greek *psyche* meaning 'soul'

psychoanalyse *or US* **psychoanalyze** VERB to treat by psychoanalysis

psychoanalysis NOUN a method of treating mental illness by discussing with the patient its possible causes in their past > **psychoanalyst** NOUN

psychological ADJECTIVE of psychology or the mind

psychology NOUN the science which studies the human mind > **psychologist** NOUN

psychosis NOUN (*plural* **psychoses** – *pronounced* sai-**koh**-seez) a mental illness

psychosomatic ADJECTIVE of an illness: having a psychological cause

psychotherapy NOUN treatment of mental illness by psychoanalysis etc > **psychotherapist** NOUN

psychotic ADJECTIVE affected by mental illness, mad

PT ABBREVIATION, *old* physical training

PTA ABBREVIATION parent teacher association

ptarmigan (*pronounced* **tahr**-mi-g*a*n) NOUN a mountain-dwelling bird of the grouse family, which turns white in winter

pterodactyl (*pronounced* ter-*oh*-**dak**-til) NOUN an extinct flying reptile

PTO ABBREVIATION please turn over

pub short for **public house**

puberty (*pronounced* **pyoo**-bert-i) NOUN the time when the body becomes sexually mature and the reproductive organs become functional

pubic (*pronounced* **pyoo**-bik) ADJECTIVE of the lowest part of the abdomen: *pubic hair*

public ADJECTIVE **1** relating to or shared by the people of a community or nation in general: *public opinion/public library* **2** generally or widely known: *a public figure* ▸ NOUN (**the public**) people in general **in public** in front of or among other people

public address system NOUN a system of microphones, amplifiers and loudspeakers used to enable an audience to hear voices, music, etc

a b c d e f g h i j k l m n o p q r s t u v w x y z

A B C D E F G H I J K L M N O **P** Q R S T U V W X Y Z

publican NOUN the keeper of an inn or public house

publication NOUN **1** the act of making news etc public **2** the act of publishing a book, newspaper, etc **3** a published book, magazine, etc

public house NOUN a building where alcoholic drinks are sold and consumed; a pub

publicity NOUN advertising; bringing to public notice or attention

publicize *or* **publicise** VERB to make public, advertise

public relations PLURAL NOUN the relations between a business etc and the public ▶SINGULAR NOUN a department of a business etc dealing with this

publish VERB **1** to make generally known **2** to prepare and put out (a book etc) for sale

publisher NOUN someone who publishes books

puce ADJECTIVE of a brownish-purple colour

puck NOUN a thick disc of rubber that is struck in ice hockey

pucker VERB to wrinkle ▶NOUN a wrinkle, a fold

pudding NOUN **1** the sweet course of a meal **2** a sweet dish made with eggs, flour, milk, etc **3** a type of sausage: *mealy pudding*

puddle NOUN a small, often muddy, pool

puerile (*pronounced* **pyoor**-ail) ADJECTIVE childish, silly > **puerility** NOUN

ⓘ Comes from Latin *puerilis* meaning 'childish'

puff VERB **1** to blow out in small gusts **2** to breathe heavily, eg after running **3** to blow up, inflate **4** to swell (up or out) ▶NOUN **1** a short, sudden gust of wind, breath, etc **2** a powder puff **3** a piece of advertising

puffin NOUN a type of sea bird, with a short, thick, brightly coloured beak

puff pastry NOUN a light, flaky kind of pastry

puffy ADJECTIVE (**puffier, puffiest**) **1** swollen, flabby **2** breathing heavily

pug NOUN a breed of small dog with a snub nose

pugilism (*pronounced* **pyoo**-ji-lizm) NOUN boxing > **pugilist** NOUN

ⓘ Comes from Latin *pugil* meaning 'a boxer'

pugnacious ADJECTIVE quarrelsome, fond of fighting > **pugnacity** NOUN

ⓘ Comes from Latin *pugnax* meaning 'warlike'

puke NOUN & VERB, *slang* (to) vomit

pull VERB **1** to move or try to move (something) towards yourself by force **2** to drag, tug **3** to stretch, strain: *pull a muscle* **4** to tear: *pull to pieces* ▶NOUN **1** the act of pulling **2** a pulling force, eg of a magnet **3** a handle for pulling **4** *informal* advantage, influence **pull out 1** to withdraw from a competition etc **2** of a driver or vehicle: to move into the centre of the road **pull through** to get safely to the end of a difficult or dangerous experience **pull yourself together** to regain self-control or self-possession **pull up** to stop, halt

pull-down menu NOUN, *computing* a menu on a computer screen viewed by clicking on a button on the toolbar and keeping the mouse pressed down (*compare with:* **drop-down menu**)

pulley NOUN (*plural* **pulleys**) a grooved wheel fitted with a cord and set in a block, used for lifting weights etc

pull-out NOUN a complete section that can be taken out of a newspaper etc

pullover NOUN a knitted garment for the top half of the body, a jersey

pulmonary (*pronounced* **pul**-mo-na-ri *or* **puwl**-mo-na-ri) ADJECTIVE relating to the lungs

pulp NOUN **1** the soft fleshy part of a fruit **2** a soft mass of wood etc which is made into paper **3** any soft mass ▶ VERB to reduce to pulp

pulpit NOUN an enclosed platform in a church for the minister or priest

pulsate VERB to beat, throb

pulse NOUN the regular beating or throbbing of the heart and arteries as blood flows through them ▶ VERB to throb, pulsate

pulses PLURAL NOUN beans, peas, lentils and other edible seeds of this family

pulverize *or* **pulverise** VERB to make or crush into powder

puma NOUN an American wild animal like a large cat

pumice (*pronounced* **pum**-is) *or* **pumice stone** NOUN a piece of light solidified lava used for smoothing skin and for rubbing away stains

pummel VERB (**pummelling, pummelled**) to beat with the fists

pump[1] NOUN **1** a machine used for making water rise from beneath the ground to the surface **2** a machine for drawing out or forcing in air, gas, etc: *a bicycle pump* ▶ VERB **1** to raise or force with a pump **2** *informal* to draw out information from by clever questioning

pump[2] NOUN a kind of thin- or soft-soled shoe for dancing, gymnastics, etc

pumpkin NOUN a large, roundish, thick-skinned, orange fruit, with stringy, edible flesh

pun NOUN a play upon words which sound similar but have different meanings, eg 'two *pears* make a *pair*' ▶ VERB (**punning, punned**) to make a pun

punch[1] VERB to hit with the fist ▶ NOUN (*plural* **punches**) a blow with the fist

punch[2] NOUN (*plural* **punches**) a tool for punching holes ▶ VERB to make a hole in with a tool: *punch a ticket*

punch[3] NOUN a drink made of spirits or wine, water, sugar, etc

punch-drunk ADJECTIVE dizzy from being hit

punchline NOUN the words that give the main point to a joke

punctilious ADJECTIVE paying attention to details, especially in behaviour; fastidious

punctual ADJECTIVE **1** on time, not late **2** strict in keeping the time of appointments > **punctuality** NOUN

punctuate VERB **1** to divide up sentences by commas, full stops, etc **2** to interrupt at intervals: *The silence was punctuated by occasional coughing*

A B C D E F G H I J K L M N O P Q R S T U V W X Y Z

punctuation NOUN the use of punctuation marks

punctuation mark NOUN any of the symbols used in punctuating sentences, eg full stop, comma, colon, question mark, etc

puncture NOUN **1** an act of pricking or piercing **2** a small hole made with a sharp point **3** a hole in a tyre

pundit NOUN an expert

pungent ADJECTIVE **1** sharp-tasting or sharp-smelling **2** of a remark: strongly sarcastic

punish VERB **1** to make (someone) suffer for a fault or crime **2** to inflict suffering on **3** to treat roughly or harshly

punishable ADJECTIVE likely to bring punishment

punishment NOUN pain or constraints inflicted for a fault or crime

punitive (*pronounced* **pyoo**-ni-tiv) ADJECTIVE inflicting punishment or suffering

punk NOUN **1** a type of loud and aggressive rock music **2** a young person who dresses in a shocking way and listens to punk music **3** *US* a useless person

punnet NOUN a small basket or container for soft fruit

punt NOUN a flat-bottomed boat with square ends ▸VERB to move (a punt) by pushing a pole against the bottom of a river

punter NOUN **1** a professional gambler **2** *informal* a customer, a client **3** *informal* an ordinary person

puny ADJECTIVE (**punier, puniest**) little and weak

pup NOUN **1** a young dog **2** the young of certain other animals, eg a seal

pupa (*pronounced* **pyoo**-pa) NOUN (*plural* **pupae** – *pronounced* **pyoo**-pee), *zoology* the stage in the growth of an insect in which it changes from a larva to its mature form, eg from a caterpillar into a butterfly

pupil[1] NOUN someone who is being taught by a teacher

pupil[2] NOUN, *anatomy* the dark round opening in the middle of the eye which varies in size to allow more or less light in

puppet NOUN **1** a doll which is moved by strings or wires **2** a doll that fits over the hand and is moved by the fingers **3** someone who acts exactly as they are told to

puppeteer NOUN someone who operates puppets

puppy NOUN (*plural* **puppies**) a young dog

puppy fat NOUN temporary fat in childhood or adolescence

puppy love NOUN immature love when very young

purchase VERB to buy ▸NOUN **1** the act of buying **2** something which is bought **3** the power to lift by using a lever etc **4** firm grip or hold

purchaser NOUN someone who buys

purdah NOUN the seclusion of Hindu or Islamic women from strangers, behind a screen or under a veil

pure ADJECTIVE **1** clean, spotless **2** free from dust, dirt, etc **3** not mixed with other substances **4** free from faults or sin, innocent

5 utter, absolute, nothing but: *pure nonsense*

purée (*pronounced* **pyoor**-ei) NOUN food made into a pulp by being put through a sieve or liquidizing machine ▸ VERB (**puréeing, puréed**) to make into a purée, pulp

purely ADVERB **1** in a pure way **2** wholly, entirely: *purely on merit* **3** merely, only: *purely for the sake of appearance*

purge VERB **1** to make clean, purify **2** to clear (something) of anything unwanted ▸ NOUN **1** a removal of impurities **2** a removal of something unwanted

purify VERB (**purifies, purifying, purified**) to make pure > **purification** NOUN

purist NOUN someone who insists on correctness

puritan NOUN **1** someone of strict, often narrow-minded, morals **2** (**Puritan**) *history* one of a group believing in strict simplicity in worship and daily life > **puritanical** ADJECTIVE > **puritanism** NOUN

purity NOUN the state of being pure

purl VERB to knit in stitches made with the wool in front of the work

purloin VERB to steal

purple NOUN a dark colour formed by the mixture of blue and red

purpose (*pronounced* **per**-pohs) NOUN **1** aim, intention **2** use, function (of a tool etc) ▸ VERB to intend **on purpose** intentionally **to the purpose** to the point

purposeful ADJECTIVE determined > **purposefully** ADVERB

purposely ADVERB intentionally

purr NOUN the low, murmuring sound made by a cat when pleased ▸ VERB of a cat: to make this sound

purse NOUN **1** a small bag for carrying money **2** *US* a handbag ▸ VERB to close (the lips) tightly

purser NOUN the officer who looks after a ship's money

pursue VERB **1** to follow after (in order to overtake or capture), chase **2** to be engaged in, carry on (studies, an enquiry, etc) **3** to follow (a route, path, etc)

pursuer NOUN someone who pursues

pursuit NOUN **1** the act of pursuing **2** an occupation or hobby

pus NOUN a thick, yellowish liquid produced from infected wounds

push VERB **1** to press hard against **2** to thrust (something) away with force, shove **3** to urge on **4** to make a big effort ▸ NOUN (*plural* **pushes**) **1** a thrust **2** effort **3** *informal* energy and determination

pushchair NOUN a folding chair on wheels for a young child

pushy ADJECTIVE (**pushier, pushiest**) aggressively assertive

pussy *or* **puss** NOUN (*plural* **pussies** *or* **pusses**) *informal* a cat, a kitten

pussy-willow NOUN an American willow tree with silky catkins

put VERB (**putting, put**) **1** to place, lay, set: *put the book on the table* **2** to bring to a certain position or state: *put the light on/put it out of your mind* **3** to express: *put the question more clearly* **put about 1** to change course at sea **2** to spread (news) **put by** to set aside, save up

put down to defeat **put in for** to make a claim for, apply for **put off** **1** to delay **2** to turn (someone) away from their plan or intention **put out** **1** to extinguish (a fire, light, etc) **2** to annoy, embarrass **put up** **1** to build **2** to propose, suggest (a plan, candidate, etc) **3** to let (someone) stay in your house etc **4** to stay as a guest (in someone's house) **put up with** to bear patiently, tolerate

ⓘ Comes from Late Old English *putian*

putative (*pronounced* **pyoo**-*ta*-tiv) ADJECTIVE supposed, commonly accepted

ⓘ Comes from Latin *putare* meaning 'to suppose'

putrid (*pronounced* **pyoo**-trid) ADJECTIVE rotten; stinking

putsch (*pronounced* puwch) NOUN (*plural* **putsches**) a sudden move to seize political power; a coup d'état

putt VERB, *golf* to send (a ball) gently forward

putter NOUN a golf club used for putting

putty NOUN a cement made from ground chalk, used in putting glass in windows etc

puzzle VERB **1** to present with a difficult problem, situation, etc **2** to be difficult (for someone) to understand: *Her moods puzzled him* ▶NOUN **1** a difficulty which needs a lot of thought **2** a toy or riddle to test knowledge or skill: *a crossword puzzle/jigsaw puzzle* **puzzle something out** to consider long and carefully in order to solve (a problem)

PVC ABBREVIATION polyvinyl chloride

pygmy *or* **pigmy** NOUN (*plural* **pygmies** *or* **pigmies**) a member of one of the unusually short peoples of equatorial Africa

pyjamas *or US* **pajamas** PLURAL NOUN a sleeping suit consisting of trousers and a top

pylon NOUN **1** a high steel tower supporting electric power cables **2** a guiding mark at an airfield

pyramid NOUN **1** *maths* a solid shape figure with a square or triangular base, with sloping sides which come to a point at the top **2** *history* a building of this shape, built on a square base, used as a tomb in ancient Egypt

pyre NOUN a pile of wood on which a dead body is burned

Pyrex NOUN, *trademark* a type of glassware that will withstand heat

pyro- (*pronounced* pai-roh) PREFIX relating to fire, heat or fever

ⓘ Comes from Greek *pyr* meaning 'fire'

pyromaniac NOUN someone who gets pleasure from starting fires

pyrotechnics PLURAL NOUN a display of fireworks

python NOUN a large, non-poisonous snake which crushes its victims

A B C D E F G H I J K L M N O P Q R S T U V W X Y Z

Qq

QC ABBREVIATION Queen's Counsel

QED *or* **qed** (*pronounced* kyoo ee **dee**) ABBREVIATION *quod erat demonstrandum* (Latin), which was to be demonstrated (used to signify a statement or theory that has at that point been shown to be true or proved)

quack[1] NOUN the cry of a duck ▶VERB to make the noise of a duck

quack[2] NOUN someone who falsely claims to have medical knowledge or training

quad *short for* **1** quadruplet **2** quadrangle

quadrangle NOUN **1** *maths* a figure with four equal sides and angles **2** a four-sided courtyard surrounded by buildings in a school, college, etc (*short form*: **quad**)

quadrangular ADJECTIVE having the shape of a quadrangle

quadrant NOUN **1** *maths* one quarter of the circumference or area of a circle **2** *maths* one of the four areas into which a plane is divided by axes **3** an instrument used in astronomy, navigation, etc for measuring heights

quadratic equation *maths* an equation that involves the square of a variable or unknown quantity

quadri- *or* **quadru-** PREFIX four: *quadrilateral/quadruped*

[1] Comes from Latin *quattuor* meaning 'four'

quadriceps SINGULAR NOUN (*plural* **quadricepses** *or* **quadriceps**) the large four-part muscle that runs down the front of the thigh

quadrilateral NOUN a four-sided figure or area ▶ADJECTIVE four-sided

quadrille (*pronounced* kw*a*-**dril**) NOUN a dance for four couples arranged to form a square

quadriplegia (*pronounced* kwod-ri-**plee**-ji-*a*) NOUN, *medicine* paralysis of both arms and both legs

quadriplegic NOUN someone suffering from quadriplegia

quadruped NOUN a four-footed animal

quadruple ADJECTIVE **1** four times as much or many **2** made up of four parts ▶VERB to make or become four times greater: *quadrupled the price*

quadruplet NOUN one of four children born to the same mother at one birth (*short form*: **quad**)

quaff (*pronounced* kwahf *or* kwof) VERB to drink up eagerly

A B C D E F G H I J K L M N O P Q R S T U V W X Y Z

quagmire NOUN wet, boggy ground

quail[1] NOUN a type of small bird like a partridge

quail[2] VERB to shrink back in fear

quaint ADJECTIVE pleasantly odd or old-fashioned

quake VERB to shake, tremble with fear ▸ NOUN, *informal* an earthquake

Quaker NOUN a member of a Christian religious group opposed to violence and war, founded in the 17th century

ⓘ Originally a nickname given to the group because their founder, George Fox, told them to *quake* at the word of God

qualification NOUN a skill that makes someone suitable for a job a qualifying statement

qualified ADJECTIVE having the necessary qualifications for a job

qualify VERB (**qualifies, qualifying, qualified**) **1** to be suitable for a job or position **2** to pass a test **3** to lessen the force of (a statement) by adding or changing words

qualitative ADJECTIVE relating to quality rather than quantity (*contrasted with*: **quantitative**)

quality NOUN (*plural* **qualities**) **1** an outstanding feature of someone or thing: *Kindness is a quality admired by all* **2** degree of worth: *cloth of poor quality*

qualm (*pronounced* kwahm) NOUN doubt about whether something is right

quandary NOUN (*plural* **quandaries**) **1** a state of uncertainty **2** a situation in which it is difficult to decide what to do

quango (*pronounced* **kwang**-goh) NOUN (*plural* **quangos**) an official body, funded and appointed by the government, that supervises some national activity etc

quantifiable ADJECTIVE capable of being quantified

quantify VERB (**quantifies, quantifying, quantified**) to measure or state the quantity of

quantitative ADJECTIVE relating to quantity rather than quality (*contrasted with*: **qualitative**)

quantity NOUN (*plural* **quantities**) **1** amount: *a large quantity of paper* **2** a symbol which represents an amount: *X is the unknown quantity*

quantum NOUN (*plural* **quanta**), *physics* the smallest amount of energy, charge *etc* that can exist on its own

quantum leap NOUN a huge, dramatic jump

quarantine NOUN the isolation of people or animals who might be carrying an infectious disease ▸ VERB to put in quarantine

quark (*pronounced* kwahrk) NOUN, *physics* a sub-atomic particle

ⓘ A word invented by James Joyce in *Finnegans Wake* (1939)

quarrel NOUN an angry disagreement or argument ▸ VERB (**quarrelling, quarrelled**) **1** to disagree violently or argue angrily (with) **2** to find fault (with)

quarrelsome ADJECTIVE fond of quarrelling, inclined to quarrel

quarry[1] NOUN (*plural* **quarries**) a pit from which stone is taken for building ▸ VERB (**quarries,**

quarrying, quarried) to dig (stone etc) from a quarry

quarry[2] NOUN (*plural* **quarries**) **1** a hunted animal **2** someone or something eagerly looked for

quart NOUN an imperial measure of liquids, equal to 2 pints (1.136 litres)

quarter NOUN **1** one of four equal parts of something **2** a fourth part of a year, three months **3** a district of a town, city, etc: *the Spanish quarter* **4** a section of the public or society, certain people or a certain person: *No help came from any quarter* **5** (**quarters**) lodgings, accommodation **6** mercy shown to an enemy: *No quarter was given by either side* ▸VERB **1** to divide into four equal parts **2** to accommodate

quarterdeck NOUN the upper deck of a ship between the stern and the mast nearest it

quarter-final NOUN a match in a competition immediately before a semi-final

quarterly ADJECTIVE happening every three months ▸ADVERB every three months ▸NOUN (*plural* **quarterlies**) a magazine etc published every three months

quartet NOUN **1** a group of four players or singers **2** a piece of music written for such a group

quartz NOUN a hard substance often in crystal form, found in rocks

quasar (*pronounced* **kwei**-zar) NOUN an extremely distant, star-like object in the sky

quash (*pronounced* kwosh) VERB **1** to crush, put down (eg a rebellion) **2** to wipe out, annul (eg a judge's decision)

quasi- (*pronounced* **kwei**-zai) PREFIX to some extent, but not completely: *quasi-historical*

[i] Comes from Latin *quasi* meaning 'as if'

quaver VERB **1** to shake, tremble **2** to speak in a shaking voice ▸NOUN **1** a trembling of the voice **2** *music* a note (♪) equal to half a crotchet in length

quay (*pronounced* kee) NOUN a solid landing place for loading and unloading boats

queasy ADJECTIVE (**queasier, queasiest**) **1** feeling nauseous **2** easily shocked or disgusted
> **queasiness** NOUN

queen NOUN **1** a female monarch **2** the wife of a king **3** a playing-card with a picture of a queen **4** the most powerful piece in chess **5** an egg-laying female bee, ant or wasp

queen bee NOUN **1** an egg-laying female bee **2** a woman who is the centre of attention

queenly ADJECTIVE of or like a queen

queen mother NOUN the mother of the reigning king or queen who was once herself queen

queer ADJECTIVE **1** odd, strange **2** *informal* (sometimes *derogatory*) homosexual ▸NOUN, *informal* (sometimes *derogatory*) a homosexual

quell VERB **1** to crush (a rebellion etc) **2** to remove (fears, suspicions, etc)

quench VERB **1** to drink and so satisfy (thirst) **2** to put out (eg a fire)

a b c d e f g h i j k l m n o p q r s t u v w x y z

A B C D E F G H I J K L M N O P Q R S T U V W X Y Z

querulous ADJECTIVE complaining

query NOUN (*plural* **queries**) a question ▸ VERB (**queries, querying, queried**) to question (eg a statement)

quest NOUN a search

question NOUN **1** a sentence requiring an answer, eg 'where do you live?' **2** a subject, matter, etc: *the energy question/a question of ability* **3** a matter for dispute or doubt: *There's no question of him leaving* ▸ VERB **1** to ask questions of (someone) **2** to express doubt about, query: *questioning my authority* **out of the question** not even to be considered, unthinkable

questionable ADJECTIVE doubtful

question mark NOUN a symbol (?) put after a question in writing

questionnaire NOUN a written list of questions to be answered by several people to provide information for a survey

queue NOUN a line of people, vehicles, etc, especially when waiting for something ▸ VERB to stand in, or form, a queue

quibble VERB to avoid an important part of an argument by quarrelling over details ▸ NOUN a petty argument or complaint

quiche (*pronounced* keesh) NOUN an open pastry case filled with beaten eggs, cheese, etc and baked

quick ADJECTIVE **1** done or happening in a short time **2** acting without delay, fast-moving: *a quick brain* ▸ NOUN a tender area of skin under the nails ▸ ADVERB, *informal* quickly **the quick** *old* the living

quicken VERB to speed up, become or make faster

quicklime *see* **lime**[1]

quickly ADVERB without delay, rapidly

quicksand NOUN sand that sucks in anyone who stands on it

quicksilver NOUN mercury

quickstep NOUN a ballroom dance like a fast foxtrot

quick-tempered ADJECTIVE easily made angry

quid NOUN, *slang* a pound (£1)

quiescent (*pronounced* kwi-**es**-*ent*) ADJECTIVE not active
> **quiescence** NOUN

quiet ADJECTIVE **1** making little or no noise **2** calm: *a quiet life/quiet seas* ▸ NOUN **1** the state of being quiet **2** lack of noise, peace ▸ VERB to make or become quiet
> **quietness** NOUN

Do not confuse with: **quite**

quieten VERB to make or become quiet

quietly ADVERB in a quiet way; with little or no sound

quiff NOUN a tuft of hair brushed up and back from the forehead

quill NOUN **1** a large feather of a goose or other bird made into a pen **2** one of the sharp spines of a porcupine

quilt NOUN a bed cover filled with down, feathers, etc

quilted ADJECTIVE made of two layers of material with padding between them

quin *short for* **quintuplet**

quince NOUN a pear-like fruit with a

sharp taste, used to make jams etc

quinine NOUN a bitter drug from the bark of a S American tree, used to treat malaria

quint- PREFIX fifth

ⓘ Comes from Latin *quintus* meaning 'fifth'

quintessence NOUN **1** the most important part of anything **2** the purest part or form of something

ⓘ Literally 'fifth essence', sought after by medieval alchemists as the highest essence

quintessential ADJECTIVE central, essential

quintet NOUN **1** a group of five players or singers **2** a piece of music written for such a group

quintuplet NOUN one of five children born to a mother at the same time (*short form*: **quin**)

quip NOUN a witty remark or reply ▶VERB (**quipping, quipped**) to make a witty remark

quirk NOUN **1** an odd feature of someone's behaviour **2** a trick, a sudden turn: *a quirk of fate* > **quirky** ADJECTIVE (**quirkier, quirkiest**)

quit VERB (**quitting, quit** *or* **quitted**) **1** to give up, stop: *I'm going to quit smoking* **2** to leave, resign from (a job)

quite ADVERB **1** fairly, moderately: *quite good* **2** completely, entirely: *quite empty*

> Do not confuse with: **quiet**

quits ADJECTIVE, *informal* even, especially in relation to money borrowed and lent

quiver[1] NOUN a tremble, a shake ▶VERB to tremble, shake

quiver[2] NOUN a carrying case for arrows

quixotic (*pronounced* kwik-**sot**-ik) ADJECTIVE having noble but foolish and unrealistic aims

ⓘ After Don *Quixote*, the knight in Cervantes's 16th-century Spanish romance > **quixotically** ADVERB

quiz VERB (**quizzing, quizzed**) to question ▶NOUN (*plural* **quizzes**) a competition to test knowledge

quizzical ADJECTIVE of a look: as if asking a question, especially mockingly

quoits (*pronounced* koits) SINGULAR NOUN a game in which heavy flat rings (**quoits**) are thrown on to small rods

quorum NOUN the least number of people who must be present at a meeting before any business can be done

quota NOUN a part or share to be given or received by each member of a group

quotation NOUN **1** the act of repeating something said or written **2** the words repeated **3** a price stated

quotation marks PLURAL NOUN marks (" " or ' ') used in writing to show that someone's words are being repeated exactly, eg: *He said, 'I'm going out'* (*also called*: **inverted commas, speech marks**)

quote VERB **1** to repeat the words of (someone) exactly as said or written **2** to give or state (a price for something)

Rr

rabbi (*pronounced* **rab**-ai) NOUN (*plural* **rabbis**) a Jewish priest or teacher of the law

rabbit NOUN a small, burrowing, long-eared animal

rabble NOUN a disorderly, noisy crowd

rabies (*pronounced* **rei**-beez) NOUN a disease transmitted by the bite of an infected animal, causing fear of water and madness (*also called*: **hydrophobia**)

raccoon *or* **racoon** NOUN a small, furry animal of N America with black eye patches

race[1] NOUN **1** a group of people with the same ancestors and physical characteristics, eg skin colour and height **2** descent: *of noble race*

race[2] NOUN a competition to find the fastest person, animal, vehicle, etc ▶VERB **1** to run fast **2** to take part in a race

racecourse *or* **racetrack** NOUN a course over which races are run

racehorse NOUN a horse bred and used for racing

racial ADJECTIVE of or according to race

racism *or* **racialism** NOUN **1** the belief that some races of people are superior to others **2** prejudice on the grounds of race > **racist** *or* **racialist** NOUN & ADJECTIVE

racket[1] *or* **racquet** NOUN a bat made up of a strong frame strung with gut or nylon for playing tennis, badminton, etc

racket[2] NOUN, *informal* **1** a great noise, a din **2** a dishonest way of making a profit

racketeer NOUN someone who makes money dishonestly

racoon *another spelling* of **raccoon**

racquet *another spelling* of **racket**[1]

racy ADJECTIVE (**racier, raciest**) of a story: full of action, and often involving sexual exploits

radar NOUN a method of detecting solid objects using radio waves which bounce back off the object and indicate its position on a screen

radiance NOUN brightness, splendour

radiant ADJECTIVE **1** sending out rays of light, heat, etc **2** showing joy and happiness: *a radiant smile*

radiate VERB **1** to send out rays of light, heat, etc **2** to spread or send out from a centre

radiation NOUN **1** energy in the form of electromagnetic waves or photons, eg heat and light **2** emissions of particles that arise from radioactive decay

radiator NOUN **1** a device (especially a series of connected hot-water pipes) which sends out heat **2** the part of a car which cools the engine

radical ADJECTIVE **1** thorough: *a radical change* **2** basic, deep-seated: *radical differences* **3** proposing dramatic changes in the method of government ▸ NOUN someone who has radical political views

radio NOUN (*plural* **radios**) a device for sending and receiving signals by means of electromagnetic waves ▸ VERB (**radioing, radioed**) to send a message to (someone) by radio

radioactive ADJECTIVE giving off particles or rays which are often dangerous but which can be used in medicine

radioactivity NOUN, *physics* (*also called*: **radioactive decay**) the spontaneous disintegration of the nuclei of certain heavy elements, eg radium and uranium, resulting in the emission of particles or radiation

radiographer (*pronounced* rei-di-**og**-ra-fer) NOUN, *medicine* a technician involved in radiology, eg in taking X-rays or giving radiotherapy

radiography (*pronounced* rei-di-**og**-ra-fi) NOUN, *medicine* photography of the interior of the body by X-rays

radiotherapy NOUN the treatment of certain diseases by X-rays or radioactive substances

radish NOUN (*plural* **radishes**) a plant with a sharp-tasting root, eaten raw in salads

radium NOUN, *chemistry* (symbol **Ra**) a radioactive metal used in radiotherapy

radius NOUN (*plural* **radii** – *pronounced* **rei**-di-ai) **1** *maths* a straight line from the centre to the circumference of a circle **2** an area within a certain distance from a central point: *houses within a radius of 10km*

RAF ABBREVIATION Royal Air Force

raffle NOUN a way of raising money by selling numbered tickets, one or more of which wins a prize ▸ VERB to give as a prize in a raffle

raft NOUN a number of logs etc fastened together and used as a boat

rafter NOUN one of the sloping beams supporting a roof

rag[1] NOUN **1** a torn or worn piece of cloth **2** (**rags**) worn-out, shabby clothes **3** *informal* a newspaper ▸ ADJECTIVE made of rags: *a rag doll*

rag[2] VERB (**ragged, ragging**) to tease, play tricks on

rag doll NOUN a floppy doll made of scrap material

rage NOUN great anger, fury ▸ VERB **1** to be violently angry **2** of a storm, battle, etc: to be violent **all the rage** *informal* very fashionable or popular

ragged (*pronounced* **rag**-id) ADJECTIVE **1** in torn, shabby clothes **2** torn and tattered

ragtime NOUN a style of jazz music with a highly syncopated melody

raid NOUN **1** a short, sudden attack

2 an unexpected visit by the police to catch a criminal, recover stolen goods, etc ▶VERB to make a raid on
> **raider** NOUN

rail[1] NOUN **1** a bar of metal used in fences **2** (**rails**) strips of steel which form the track on which trains and trams run **3** the railway: *I came here by rail*

rail[2] VERB: **rail against** *or* **at something** *or* **someone** to complain about or criticize them angrily or bitterly

railing NOUN a fence or barrier of rails

railway *or US* **railroad** NOUN a track laid with steel rails on which trains run

rain NOUN **1** water falling from the clouds in drops **2** a great number of things falling: *a rain of bullets* ▶VERB to pour or fall in drops: *It's raining today*

rainbow NOUN **1** the brilliant coloured bow or arch sometimes to be seen in the sky opposite the sun when rain is falling **2** (**Rainbow**) a member of the most junior branch of the Guides

raincoat NOUN a waterproof coat to keep out the rain

rainfall NOUN the amount of rain that falls in a certain time

rainforest NOUN a tropical forest with very heavy rainfall

rainy ADJECTIVE (**rainier, rainiest**) **1** full of rain: *rainy skies* **2** showery, wet: *a rainy day*

raise VERB **1** to lift up: *raise the flag* **2** to make higher: *raise the price* **3** to bring up (a subject) for consideration **4** to bring up (a child, family, etc) **5** to breed or grow (eg pigs, crops) **6** to collect, get together (a sum of money)
Comes from Old Norse *reisa* meaning 'to cause to rise'

> Do not confuse with: **raze**

raisin NOUN a dried grape

Raj NOUN, *history* (**the Raj**) the time of British rule in India, 1858–1947

raja *or* **rajah** NOUN, *history* an Indian prince

rake[1] NOUN a tool, like a large comb with a long handle, for smoothing earth, gathering hay, etc ▶VERB **1** to draw a rake over **2** to scrape (together) **3** to aim gunfire at (eg a ship) from one end to the other

rake[2] NOUN, *old* someone who lives an immoral life

rakish ADJECTIVE at a slanting, jaunty angle

rally VERB (**rallies, rallying, rallied**) **1** to gather again: *rally troops* **2** to come together for a joint action or effort: *The club's supporters rallied to save it* **3** to recover from an illness ▶NOUN (*plural* **rallies**) **1** a gathering **2** a political mass meeting **3** an improvement in health after an illness **4** *tennis* a long series of shots before a point is won or lost **5** a competition to test driving skills over an unknown route

RAM ABBREVIATION, *computing* random access memory

ram NOUN **1** a male sheep **2** something heavy, especially as part of a machine, for ramming ▶VERB (**ramming, rammed**) **1** to press or push down hard **2** of a ship, car, etc: to run into and cause damage to

Ramadan NOUN **1** the ninth month of the Islamic calendar, a period of fasting by day **2** the fast itself

ramble VERB **1** to walk about for pleasure, especially in the countryside **2** to speak in an aimless or confused way ▶NOUN a country walk for pleasure

rambler NOUN **1** someone who goes walking in the country for pleasure **2** a climbing rose or other plant

ramification NOUN **1** a branch or part of a subject, plot, etc **2** a consequence, usually indirect and one of several

ramp NOUN a sloping surface (eg of a road)

rampage VERB to rush about angrily or violently **on the rampage** rampaging

rampant ADJECTIVE **1** widespread and uncontrolled **2** *heraldry* standing on the left hind leg: *a lion rampant*

rampart NOUN a mound or wall built as a defence

ramshackle ADJECTIVE badly made, falling to pieces

ran *past tense of* **run**

ranch NOUN (*plural* **ranches**) a large farm in North America for rearing cattle or horses

rancid ADJECTIVE of butter: smelling or tasting off or bad

rancour *or US* **rancor** NOUN ill-will, hatred

random ADJECTIVE done without any aim or plan; chance: *a random sample* **at random** without any plan or purpose

random access memory NOUN, *computing* (*abbrev* **RAM**) a computer memory in which data can be directly located

rang *past tense of* **ring**[1] and [2]

range NOUN **1** a line or row: *a range of mountains* **2** extent, number: *a wide range of goods* **3** a piece of ground with targets for shooting or archery practice **4** the distance which an object can be thrown, or across which a sound can be heard **5** the distance between the top and bottom notes of a singing voice **6** a large kitchen stove with a flat top ▶VERB **1** to set in a row or in order **2** to wander (over) **3** to stretch, extend

ranger NOUN a keeper who looks after a forest or park

Ranger Guide NOUN an older member of the Guide movement

rank[1] NOUN **1** a row or line (eg of soldiers) **2** class, order: *the upper ranks of society/the rank of captain* **3** (**the ranks**) ordinary soldiers, not officers ▶VERB **1** to place in order of importance, merit, etc **2** to have a place in an order: *Apes rank above dogs in intelligence* **the rank and file 1** soldiers of the rank of private **2** ordinary people, the majority

rank[2] ADJECTIVE **1** of a plant: growing too plentifully **2** having a strong, unpleasant taste or smell **3** absolute: *rank nonsense*

rankle VERB to cause lasting annoyance, bitterness, etc

ransack VERB to search thoroughly; plunder

ransom NOUN the price paid for the freeing of a captive ▶VERB to pay money to free (a captive)

A B C D E F G H I J K L M N O P Q R S T U V W X Y Z

rant VERB to talk foolishly and angrily for a long time

rap VERB (**rapping, rapped**) **1** (often **rap on**) to strike with a quick, sharp blow **2** to perform a rhythmic monologue to music with a pronounced beat **3** to criticize sharply **rap out** to say (something) sharply

rape[1] VERB to have sexual intercourse with (someone) against their will, usually by force ▶ NOUN **1** the act of raping **2** the act of seizing and carrying off by force

rape[2] NOUN a type of plant like the turnip whose seeds give oil

rapid ADJECTIVE quick, fast: *a rapid rise to fame* > **rapidity** NOUN > **rapidness** NOUN

rapids PLURAL NOUN a part in a river where the current flows swiftly

rapport (*pronounced* ra-**pawr**) NOUN a good relationship, sympathy

rapt ADJECTIVE having the mind fully occupied, engrossed: *rapt attention*

rapture NOUN great delight

rapturous ADJECTIVE experiencing or demonstrating rapture

rare[1] ADJECTIVE seldom found, uncommon

> Do not confuse with: **unique**. You can talk about something being **rare**, quite **rare**, very **rare** *etc*. It would be incorrect, however, to describe something as very **unique**, since things either are or are not **unique** – there are no levels of this quality

rare[2] ADJECTIVE of meat: lightly cooked

rarefy (*pronounced* **reir**-i-fai) VERB (**rarefies, rarefying, rarefied**) to make thin or less dense

raring ADJECTIVE: **raring to go** *informal* very keen to go, start, etc

rarity NOUN (*plural* **rarities**) **1** something uncommon **2** uncommonness

rascal NOUN a naughty or wicked person

rash[1] ADJECTIVE acting, or done, without thought > **rashness** NOUN

rash[2] NOUN (*plural* **rashes**) redness or outbreak of spots on the skin

rasher NOUN a thin slice (of bacon or ham)

rasp NOUN **1** a coarse file **2** a rough, grating sound ▶ VERB **1** to rub with a file **2** to make a rough, grating noise **3** to say in a rough voice

raspberry NOUN (*plural* **raspberries**) **1** a type of soft red berry **2** the bush which bears this fruit

rasping ADJECTIVE of a sound: rough and unpleasant

rat NOUN a gnawing animal, larger than a mouse ▶ VERB (**ratting, ratted**) to hunt or kill rats **rat on** *informal* to inform against

rate NOUN **1** the frequency with which something happens or is done: *a high rate of road accidents* **2** speed: *speak at a tremendous rate* **3** level of cost, price, etc: *paid at a higher rate* **4** (**rates**) the sum of money to be paid by the owner of a shop etc to pay for local public services ▶ VERB **1** to work out the value of for taxation etc **2** to value: *I don't rate his work very highly*

rather ADVERB **1** somewhat, fairly: *It's rather cold today* **2** more willingly: *I'd rather talk about it now than later* **3** more correctly speaking: *He agreed, or rather he didn't say no*

ratification NOUN ratifying or being ratified

ratify VERB (**ratifies, ratifying, ratified**) to approve officially and formally: *ratified the treaty*

rating NOUN a sailor below the rank of an officer

ratio NOUN (*plural* **ratios**) the proportion of one thing to another: *a ratio of two parts flour to one of sugar*

ration NOUN **1** a measured amount of food given out at intervals **2** an allowance ▶VERB **1** to deal out (eg food) in measured amounts **2** to allow only a certain amount to (someone)

rational ADJECTIVE **1** able to reason **2** sensible; based on reason: *rational arguments* **3** *maths* denoting a number that can be expressed as a fraction whose denominator is not zero, eg 1 or ⅓ > **rationality** NOUN > **rationally** ADVERB

rationalize *or* **rationalise** VERB **1** to think up a good reason for (an action or feeling) so as not to feel guilty about it **2** to make (an industry or organization) more efficient and profitable by reorganizing it to get rid of unnecessary costs and labour > **rationalization** NOUN

rat race NOUN, *informal* a fierce, unending competition for success or wealth

rattle VERB **1** to give out short, sharp, repeated sounds: *The coins rattled in the tin* **2** *informal* to fluster or irritate ▶NOUN **1** a sharp noise, quickly repeated several times **2** a toy or instrument which makes such a sound **rattle off** to go through (a list of names etc) quickly

rattlesnake NOUN a poisonous snake with bony rings on its tail which rattle when shaken

ratty ADJECTIVE (**rattier, rattiest**) irritable

raucous ADJECTIVE hoarse, harsh: *a raucous voice*

raunchy ADJECTIVE (**raunchier, raunchiest**) sexually suggestive, lewd

ravage VERB to cause destruction or damage to; plunder ▶PLURAL NOUN damaging effects: *the ravages of time*

rave VERB **1** to talk wildly, as if mad **2** *informal* to talk very enthusiastically (about) ▶NOUN a large party held in a warehouse etc with electronic music

raven NOUN a type of large, black bird of the crow family ▶ADJECTIVE of hair: black and glossy

ravenous (*pronounced* **rav**-en-*us*) ADJECTIVE very hungry

ravine (*pronounced* *ra*-**veen**) NOUN a deep, narrow valley between hills

raving ADJECTIVE mad, crazy

ravish VERB **1** to plunder **2** to rape **3** to delight

ravishing ADJECTIVE lovely; very attractive

raw ADJECTIVE **1** not cooked **2** not prepared, refined, or processed: *raw* *cotton/raw data* **3** of weather: cold **4** sore **get a raw deal** *informal* to be treated unjustly

raw materials PLURAL NOUN substances in their natural state, used in manufacturing

ray[1] NOUN **1** a line of light, heat, etc **2** a small degree or amount: *a ray of hope* **3** any of several lines going outwards from a centre

ray[2] NOUN a kind of flat-bodied fish

rayon NOUN a type of artificial silk

raze VERB to destroy, knock flat (a town, house, etc)

Comes from French *raser* meaning 'to shave'

> Do not confuse with: **raise**

razor NOUN a sharp-edged instrument for shaving

razzmatazz NOUN showiness, glamorous or extravagant show

RC ABBREVIATION Roman Catholic

re- PREFIX **1** again, once more: *recreate/redo* **2** back: *reclaim/refund*

Comes from Latin prefix *re-* with the same meaning

re PREPOSITION concerning, about

reach VERB **1** to arrive at: *reach the summit/Your message never reached me* **2** to stretch out (the hand) so as to touch: *I couldn't reach the top shelf* **3** to extend ▸ NOUN (*plural* **reaches**) **1** a distance that can be travelled easily: *within reach of home* **2** the distance someone can stretch their arm **3** a straight part of a stream or river between bends

react VERB **1** to act or behave in response to something done or said **2** *chemistry* to undergo a chemical change: *Metals react with sulphuric acid*

reaction NOUN **1** behaviour as a result of action **2** a movement against a situation or belief: *a reaction against Victorian morality* **3** *chemistry* chemical change

reactionary ADJECTIVE favouring a return to old ways, laws, etc ▸ NOUN (*plural* **reactionaries**) someone who holds reactionary views

read (*pronounced* reed) VERB (**reading, read** – *pronounced* red) **1** to look at and understand, or say aloud written or printed words **2** to study a subject in a university or college: *reading law*

readable ADJECTIVE quite interesting to read

reader NOUN **1** someone who reads books etc **2** someone who reads manuscripts for a publisher **3** a senior university lecturer **4** a reading book for children

readily ADVERB easily; willingly

readiness NOUN **1** the state of being ready and prepared **2** willingness: *the readiness of the troops to fight*

read-only memory NOUN, *computing* (*abbrev* **ROM**) memory with data that can be read, but not written to

read-out NOUN **1** *computing* data from a computer; output **2** data from a radio transmitter

ready ADJECTIVE (**readier, readiest**) **1** prepared: *packed and ready to go* **2** willing: *always ready to help* **3** quick: *too ready to find fault*

4 available for use: *Your coat is ready for collection*

ready-made ADJECTIVE of clothes: made for general sale, not made specially for one person

real ADJECTIVE **1** actually existing, not imagined **2** not imitation, genuine: *real leather* **3** sincere: *a real love of music* **the real Mackay** *or* **the real McCoy** the genuine article, the real thing

realism NOUN the showing or viewing of things as they really are

realist NOUN someone who claims to see life as it really is

realistic ADJECTIVE **1** lifelike **2** viewing things as they really are > **realistically** ADVERB

reality NOUN (*plural* **realities**) that which is real and not imaginary; truth

reality TV NOUN a genre of television programme which presents members of the public as subjects

realize *or* **realise** VERB **1** to come to understand, know: *I never realized you could sing* **2** to make real, accomplish: *realize an ambition* **3** to get (money) for: *realized £16,000 on the sale of the house* > **realization** NOUN

really ADVERB **1** in fact **2** very: *really dark hair*

realm (*pronounced* relm) NOUN **1** a kingdom, a country **2** an area of activity or interest

ream NOUN **1** a measure for paper, 20 quires **2** (**reams**) *informal* a large quantity, especially of paper: *She wrote reams in her English exam*

reap VERB **1** to cut and gather (corn etc) **2** to gain: *reap the benefits of hard work*

reaper NOUN **1** someone who reaps **2** a machine for reaping

rear[1] NOUN **1** the back part of anything **2** the last part of an army or fleet **3** *informal* the buttocks **bring up the rear** to come or be last in a series

rear[2] VERB **1** to bring up (children) **2** to breed (animals) **3** of an animal: to stand on its hindlegs

reason NOUN **1** cause, excuse: *What is the reason for this noise?* **2** purpose: *What is your reason for visiting America?* **3** the power of the mind to form opinions, judge right and truth, etc **4** common sense ▶ VERB to think out (opinions etc) **reason with** to try to persuade by arguing

reasonable ADJECTIVE **1** sensible **2** fair

reassurance NOUN something which reassures, or the feeling of being reassured

reassure VERB to take away (someone's) doubts or fears

reassuring ADJECTIVE that reassures

rebate NOUN a part of a payment or tax which is given back to the payer

rebel NOUN (*pronounced* **reb**-el) someone who opposes or fights against those in power ▶ VERB (*pronounced* ri-**bel**) (**rebelling, rebelled**) to take up arms against or oppose those in power

rebellion NOUN **1** an open or armed

a b c d e f g h i j k l m n o p q r s t u v w x y z

fight against those in power **2** a refusal to obey

rebellious ADJECTIVE rebelling or likely to rebel > **rebelliousness** NOUN

reboot VERB, *computing* to restart (a computer) using its start-up programs

rebound VERB (*pronounced* ri-**bownd**) to bounce back: *The ball rebounded off the wall* ▶NOUN (*pronounced* **ree**-bownd) **1** the act of rebounding **2** *informal* a reaction following an emotional situation or crisis: *on the rebound*

rebuff NOUN a blunt refusal or rejection ▶VERB to reject bluntly

rebuke VERB to scold, blame ▶NOUN a scolding

rebut VERB (**rebutting, rebutted**) to deny (what has been said)

rebuttal NOUN a rejection or contradiction

recall (*pronounced* ri-**kawl**) VERB **1** to call back: *recalled to headquarters* **2** to remember ▶NOUN (*pronounced* **ree**-kawl) **1** a signal or message to return **2** the act of recalling or remembering

recant VERB **1** to take back what you have said **2** to reject publicly your beliefs > **recantation** NOUN

recap 1 recapitulation **2** recapitulate

recapitulate VERB to go over again quickly the chief points of anything (eg a discussion)

recapitulation NOUN an act or instance of recapitulating or summing up

recapture VERB to capture (what has escaped or been lost)

recast VERB (**recasting, recast**) to shape in a new form

recede VERB **1** to go back **2** to become more distant **3** to slope backwards

receding ADJECTIVE **1** going or sloping backwards **2** becoming more distant

receipt (*pronounced* ri-**seet**) NOUN **1** the act of receiving (especially money or goods) **2** a written note saying that money has been received

receive VERB **1** to have something given or brought to you: *receive a gift/receive a letter* **2** to meet and welcome: *receiving visitors* **3** to take (goods), knowing them to be stolen

receiver NOUN **1** someone who receives stolen goods **2** the part of a telephone through which words are heard and into which they are spoken **3** an apparatus through which television or radio broadcasts are received

recent ADJECTIVE happening, done or made only a short time ago

recently ADVERB a short time ago

receptacle NOUN an object to receive or hold things, a container

reception NOUN **1** a welcome: *a warm reception* **2** the quality of radio or television signals

receptionist NOUN someone employed in an office or hotel to answer the telephone etc

receptive ADJECTIVE quick to take in or accept ideas etc

recess NOUN (*plural* **recesses**) **1** part of a room set back from the rest, an alcove **2** the time during which parliament or the law courts do not work **3** (**recesses**) remote parts: *in the recesses of my memory*

recession NOUN **1** the act of moving back **2** a temporary fall in a country's or world business activities

recipe (*pronounced* **re**-si-pi) NOUN instructions on how to prepare or cook a certain kind of food

recipient NOUN someone who receives something

reciprocal (*pronounced* ri-**sip**-*ro*-k*a*l) ADJECTIVE both given and received: *reciprocal affection* ▸NOUN, *maths* one of a pair of numbers whose product is 1, eg 4 is the reciprocal of ¼

reciprocate VERB to feel or do the same in return: *I reciprocate his dislike of me*

recital (*pronounced* ri-**sai**-t*a*l) NOUN **1** the act of reciting **2** a musical performance **3** the facts of a story told one after the other

recite VERB to repeat aloud from memory

reckless ADJECTIVE rash, careless > **recklessly** ADVERB

reckon VERB **1** to count **2** to consider, believe

reckoning NOUN **1** the settling of debts, grievances, etc **2** payment for sins **3** a bill **4** a sum, calculation

reclaim VERB **1** to claim back **2** to win back (land from the sea) by draining, building banks, etc **3** to make (waste land) fit for use

reclamation NOUN reclaiming or being reclaimed

recline VERB to lean or lie on your back or side

recluse NOUN someone who lives alone and avoids other people

reclusive ADJECTIVE solitary

recognition NOUN the act of recognizing someone or something

recognizable *or* **recognisable** ADJECTIVE capable of being recognized

recognize *or* **recognise** VERB **1** to know from a previous meeting etc **2** to admit, acknowledge: *Everyone recognized his talent* **3** to show appreciation of: *They recognized her courage by giving her a medal*

recoil VERB (*pronounced* ri-**koil**) **1** to shrink back in horror or fear **2** of a gun: to jump back after a shot is fired ▸NOUN (*pronounced* **ree**-koil) a shrinking back

recollect VERB to remember

recollection NOUN **1** the act or power of remembering **2** a memory, something remembered

recommend VERB **1** to urge, advise: *I recommend that you take a long holiday* **2** to speak highly of

recommendation NOUN **1** the act of recommending **2** a point in favour of someone or something

recompense VERB to pay money to or reward (a person) to make up for loss, inconvenience, etc ▸NOUN payment in compensation

reconcile VERB **1** to bring together in friendship, after a quarrel **2** to show that two statements, facts, etc do not contradict each other **be reconciled to** *or* **reconcile yourself**

A B C D E F G H I J K L M N O P Q R S T U V W X Y Z

to to agree to accept (an unwelcome fact or situation) patiently: *I became reconciled to her absence*

reconciliation NOUN the fact of being friendly with someone again, after an argument, dispute or conflict: *There seems little hope of reconciliation*

reconnaissance (*pronounced* ri-**kon**-is-*a*ns) NOUN a survey to obtain information, especially before a battle

reconstitute VERB **1** to put back into its original form: *reconstitute the milk* **2** to make up or form in a different way

reconstruct VERB **1** to rebuild **2** to create an impression of (a past event etc) using what is known **3** to re-enact (a crime) > **reconstruction** NOUN

record VERB (*pronounced* ri-**kawd**) **1** to write down for future reference **2** to put (music, speech, etc) on tape or disc so that it can be listened to later **3** to show in writing (eg a vote) **4** to show, register: *The thermometer recorded 30°C yesterday* ▶ NOUN (*pronounced* **rek**-awd) **1** a written report of facts **2** a round, flat piece of plastic on which sounds are recorded for playing on a record player **3** the best known performance: *John holds the school record for the mile* **break** *or* **beat the record** to do better than any previous performance **off the record** of a remark etc: not to be made public

recorder NOUN **1** someone who records **2** a type of simple musical wind instrument **3** a judge in certain courts

recording NOUN **1** the act of recording **2** recorded music, speech, etc

record player NOUN a machine for playing records

recount VERB **1** (*pronounced* ree-**kownt**) to count again **2** (*pronounced* ri-**kownt**) to tell (the story of) ▶ NOUN (*pronounced* **ree**-kownt) a second count, especially of votes in an election

recoup (*pronounced* ri-**koop**) VERB to make good, recover (expenses, losses, etc)

ⓘ Comes from French *recouper* meaning 'to cut back'

> Do not confuse with: **recuperate**

recover VERB **1** to get possession of again **2** to become well again after an illness

recoverable ADJECTIVE able to be recovered

recovery NOUN (*plural* **recoveries**) **1** a return to health **2** the regaining of something lost etc

recreation (*pronounced* rek-ree-**ei**-sh*o*n) NOUN a sport, hobby, etc done in your spare time

recriminate VERB to accuse your accuser in return

recrimination NOUN (usually **recriminations**) an accusation made by someone who is himself or herself accused of something

recruit NOUN a newly enlisted soldier, member, etc ▶ VERB to enlist (someone) in an army, political party, etc > **recruitment** NOUN

rectangle NOUN a four-sided figure

with all its angles right angles and its opposite sides equal in length; an oblong

rectangular ADJECTIVE of or like a rectangle

recti- *or* **rect-** PREFIX forms words containing the meaning 'straight' or 'correct': *rectilineal/rectangle*

ⓘ Comes from Latin *rectus* meaning 'straight' or 'right'

rectify VERB (**rectifies, rectifying, rectified**) to put right

rector NOUN **1** a member of the Anglican clergy in charge of a parish **2** the head teacher of some Scottish secondary schools **3** a Scottish university official elected by the students

rectory NOUN (*plural* **rectories**) the house of an Anglican rector

rectum NOUN (*plural* **recta** *or* **rectums**), *anatomy* the lower part of the alimentary canal

recuperate VERB to recover strength or health

ⓘ Comes from Latin *recuperare* meaning 'to recover'

> Do not confuse with: **recoup**

recuperation NOUN recovery

recur VERB (**recurring, recurred**) to happen again

recurrent ADJECTIVE happening often or regularly > **recurrence** NOUN

recycle VERB **1** to remake into something different **2** to treat (material) by some process in order to use it again

red ADJECTIVE (**redder, reddest**) **1** of the colour of blood **2** of hair: of a reddish-brown colour ▶NOUN either of these colours **see red** to become very angry

red deer NOUN a type of reddish-brown deer

redeem VERB **1** to buy back (eg articles from a pawnbroker) **2** to save from sin or condemnation **3** to free (yourself) from blame or debt

redemption NOUN **1** the act of redeeming or state of being redeemed **2** *Christianity* the freeing of humanity from sin by Christ

red-handed ADVERB in the act of doing wrong: *caught red-handed*

red-letter ADJECTIVE of a day: especially important or happy for some reason

ⓘ From the custom of marking saints' days in red on calendars

red light NOUN **1** a danger signal **2** a signal to stop

redouble VERB to make twice as great: *redouble your efforts*

redress VERB to set right, make up for (a wrong etc) ▶NOUN something done or given to make up for a loss or wrong, compensation

red tape NOUN unnecessary and troublesome rules about how things are to be done

ⓘ After the red tape which was once used to tie up official documents

reduce VERB **1** to make smaller **2** to lessen **3** to bring to the point of by force of circumstances: *reduced to begging in the streets* **4** to bring to a lower rank or state **5** to change into other terms: *reduce pounds to pence*

reduction NOUN **1** an act or instance of reducing; the state of being reduced **2** the amount by which something is reduced **3** a reduced copy of a picture, document, etc **4** *chemistry* a reaction in which an atom or ion gains electrons

redundancy NOUN (*plural* **redundancies**) **1** being redundant, or an instance of this **2** a dismissal or a person dismissed because they are no longer needed

redundant ADJECTIVE **1** more than is needed **2** of a worker: no longer needed because of the lack of a suitable job

reed NOUN **1** a tall, stiff grass growing in moist or marshy places **2** a part (originally made of reed) of certain wind instruments which vibrates when the instrument is played

reedy ADJECTIVE (**reedier, reediest**) **1** full of reeds **2** like a reed **3** sounding like a reed instrument: *a reedy voice*

reef NOUN a chain of rocks lying at or near the surface of the sea

reef knot NOUN a square, very secure knot

reek NOUN **1** a strong, unpleasant smell **2** *Scottish* smoke ▶ VERB **1** *Scottish* to send out smoke **2** to smell strongly

reel NOUN **1** a cylinder of plastic, metal or wood on which thread, film, fishing lines, etc may be wound **2** a length of cinema film **3** a lively Scottish or Irish dance ▶ VERB **1** to wind on a reel **2** to stagger **reel in** to draw, pull in (a fish on a line) **reel off** to repeat or recite quickly, without pausing

ref ABBREVIATION **1** referee **2** reference

refectory NOUN (*plural* **refectories**) a communal dining hall for monks, students, etc

refer **refer to** **1** to mention **2** to turn to for information **3** to relate to, apply to **4** to direct to for information, consideration, etc: *I refer you to the managing director*

referee NOUN **1** someone to whom a matter is taken for settlement **2** a judge in a sports match **3** someone willing to provide a note about someone's character, work record, etc

reference NOUN **1** the act of referring **2** a mention **3** a note about a person's character, work, etc

reference book NOUN a book to be consulted for information, eg an encyclopedia

referendum NOUN (*plural* **referenda** *or* **referendums**) a vote about some important matter by the people of a country, rather than by their representatives in government

refine VERB **1** to purify **2** to improve, make more exact, etc

refined ADJECTIVE **1** purified **2** polite in manners, free of vulgarity

refinement NOUN **1** good manners, taste, learning **2** an improvement

refinery NOUN (*plural* **refineries**) a place where sugar, oil, etc is refined

refit VERB (**refitting, refitted**) to repair damages (especially to a ship) and re-equip

reflect VERB **1** to throw back (light

or heat): *reflecting the sun's heat* **2** to give an image of: *reflected in the mirror* (**reflect on**) **1** to throw blame on (someone): *Her behaviour reflects on her mother* **2** (**reflect on**) to think (something) over carefully

reflection NOUN **1** the change in direction of a wave, eg a ray of light, when it strikes a smooth surface **2** the act of throwing back **3** the image of someone etc reflected in a mirror **4** *maths* a transformation of a plane around an axis of symmetry in the plane, so that it produces a mirror image on the other side (*compare with*: **enlargement**, **rotation**, **translation**) **5** a reason for blame or unfavourable criticism: *Their appalling behaviour is a reflection on their parents*

reflective ADJECTIVE thoughtful

reflector NOUN something (eg a piece of shiny metal) which throws back light

reflex NOUN (*plural* **reflexes**) *physiology* an action which is automatic, not intended, *eg* jerking the leg when the kneecap is struck ▶ADJECTIVE **1** done as an automatic response, unthinking **2** *maths* of an angle: greater than 180° degrees (*compare with*: **acute**, **obtuse**)

reflexive pronoun NOUN, *grammar* a pronoun that turns the action of a verb back on the subject, eg: *himself* in: *He cut himself*

reflexive verb NOUN, *grammar* a verb which has a reflexive pronoun as its object, eg: *cut* in: *He cut himself*

reform VERB **1** to improve, remove faults from **2** to give up bad habits, evil, etc ▶NOUN an improvement, correction of a fault: *reforms to the voting system*

reformation (*pronounced* ref-*or*-**mei**-sh*o*n) NOUN a change for the better **the Reformation** the religious movement in the Christian Church in the 16th century from which Protestant churches arose

reformer NOUN someone who wishes to bring about improvements

refraction NOUN, *physics* a change in the direction of (a wave of light, sound *etc*)

refrain[1] NOUN a chorus coming at the end of each verse of a song

refrain[2] VERB to keep yourself back (from doing something): *Please refrain from smoking*

refresh VERB to give new strength, power or life to **refresh your memory** to go over facts again so that they are clear in your mind

refresher course NOUN a course of study intended to keep up or increase existing knowledge of a subject

refreshing ADJECTIVE **1** bringing back strength **2** cooling

refreshments PLURAL NOUN food and drink

refrigerate VERB to make or keep cold or frozen, especially food to prevent it from going bad

refrigeration NOUN the process whereby a cabinet or room and its contents are kept at a low temperature, especially in order to prevent food from going bad

a b c d e f g h i j k l m n o p q r s t u v w x y z

A B C D E F G H I J K L M N O P Q R S T U V W X Y Z

refrigerator NOUN a storage machine which keeps food cold and so prevents it from going bad

refuel VERB (**refuelling, refuelled**) to supply with, or take in, fresh fuel

refuge NOUN a place of safety (from attack, danger etc)

refugee NOUN someone who seeks shelter from persecution in another country

refund VERB (*pronounced* ri-**fund**) to pay back ▶ NOUN (*pronounced* **ree**-fund) a payment returned, eg for unsatisfactory goods

refusal NOUN **1** an act of refusing **2** the option of accepting or refusing something: *I promised to give him first refusal on my car* (= offered to sell it to him before advertising it generally)

refuse[1] (*pronounced* ri-**fyooz**) VERB **1** to say that you will not do something: *He refused to leave the room* **2** to withhold, not give (eg permission)

refuse[2] (*pronounced* **ref**-yoos) NOUN something which is thrown aside as worthless, rubbish

refute VERB to prove wrong (something that has been said or written)

reg- PREFIX forms words connected to the activity of ruling: *regent* (= a ruler)/*regular* (= governed by or according to rules)

ⓘ Comes from Latin *regere* meaning 'to rule'

regain VERB **1** to win back again **2** to get back to: *regain the shore*

regal ADJECTIVE kingly or queenly; royal

regale (*pronounced* ri-**geil**) VERB to entertain lavishly

regalia PLURAL NOUN symbols of royalty, eg a crown and sceptre

regard VERB **1** to look upon, consider: *I regard you as a nuisance* **2** to look at carefully **3** to pay attention to ▶ NOUN **1** concern **2** affection **3** respect **4** (**regards**) good wishes **with regard to** *or* **in regard to** concerning

regarding PREPOSITION concerning, to do with: *a reply regarding his application*

regardless ADVERB not thinking or caring about costs, problems, dangers, etc; in spite of everything: *carry on regardless* **regardless of** paying no care or attention to

regatta NOUN a meeting for yacht or boat races

ⓘ From the name of a gondola race held on the Grand Canal in Venice

regenerate VERB to make new or good again > **regeneration** NOUN

regent NOUN someone who governs in place of a king or queen

reggae NOUN a strongly rhythmic type of music, originally from the West Indies

regime *or* **régime** (*both pronounced* rei-**szeem**) NOUN a method or system of government or administration, or the government or administration itself

regiment NOUN (*pronounced* **rej**-i-ment) a body of soldiers, commanded by a colonel ▶ VERB (*pronounced* **rej**-i-ment) to organize or control too strictly

region NOUN an area, a district **in**

the region of somewhere near: *in the region of £100*

regional ADJECTIVE of a region

register NOUN **1** a written list (eg of attendances at school, of those eligible to vote, etc) **2** the distance between the highest and lowest notes of a voice or instrument ▶VERB **1** to write down in a register **2** to record, cast (a vote etc) **3** to show, record: *A thermometer registers temperature*

registrar NOUN a public official who keeps a register of births, deaths and marriages

registry office NOUN an office where records of births, deaths and marriages are kept and where marriages may be performed

regress VERB to go back to an earlier state > **regression** NOUN

regret VERB (**regretting, regretted**) **1** to be sorry about: *I regret any inconvenience you have suffered* **2** to be sorry (to have to say something): *we regret to inform you* ▶NOUN sorrow for anything

regretful ADJECTIVE feeling or showing regret > **regretfully** ADVERB

regrettable ADJECTIVE to be regretted, unwelcome > **regrettably** ADVERB

regular ADJECTIVE **1** done according to rule or habit; usual **2** arranged in order; even: *regular teeth* **3** happening at certain fixed times **4** *maths* of a polygon: with all its sides and angles equal ▶NOUN a soldier of the regular army

regularly ADVERB in a regular way or at a regular time

regulate VERB **1** to control or adjust (the amount of available heat, sound, etc) **2** to control or adjust (a machine) so that it functions correctly **3** to adjust to a certain order or rate

regulation NOUN a rule, an order

regulator NOUN someone or something that regulates

regurgitate (*pronounced* ri-**ger**-ji-teit) VERB to bring back into the mouth after swallowing > **regurgitation** NOUN

rehabilitate VERB **1** to give back rights, powers or health to **2** to train or accustom (a disabled person etc) to live a normal life > **rehabilitation** NOUN

rehash *informal*, VERB to express in different words, make or do again without any noticeable improvement

rehearsal NOUN **1** a private practice of a play, concert, etc before performance in public **2** a practice for a future event or action

rehearse VERB **1** to practise beforehand **2** to recount (facts, events, etc) in order

reign NOUN **1** rule **2** the time during which a king, queen, etc rules ▶VERB **1** to rule **2** to prevail: *Silence reigned at last*

reimburse VERB to pay (someone) an amount to cover expenses

rein NOUN **1** one of two straps attached to a bridle for guiding a horse **2** (**reins**) a simple device for controlling a very young child when walking ▶VERB to control with reins

reincarnation NOUN the rebirth of

A B C D E F G H I J K L M N O P Q R S T U V W X Y Z

the soul in another body after death

reindeer NOUN (*plural* **reindeer**) a type of deer found in the far North

reinforce VERB to strengthen (eg an army with men, concrete with iron)

reinforcement NOUN **1** the act of reinforcing **2** something which strengthens or assists **3** (**reinforcements**) additional troops

reinstate VERB to put back in a former position

reinstatement NOUN **1** reinstating **2** re-establishment

reiterate VERB to repeat several times > **reiteration** NOUN

reject VERB (*pronounced* ri-**jekt**) **1** to throw away, cast aside **2** to refuse to take: *She rejected his offer of help* **3** to turn down (eg an application, request) ▶ NOUN (*pronounced* **ree**-jekt) something discarded or refused

rejection NOUN **1** rejecting or being rejected **2** something that is rejected

rejig VERB (**rejigging, rejigged**) to rearrange, especially in an unexpected way

rejoice VERB to feel or show joy

rejuvenate VERB to make young again > **rejuvenation** NOUN

relapse VERB to fall back (eg into ill health, bad habits) ▶ NOUN a falling back

relate VERB **1** to show a connection between (two or more things) **2** to tell (a story)

related ADJECTIVE **1** (often **related to someone**) of the same family (as): *I'm related to him/We are not related* **2** connected

relation NOUN **1** someone who is of the same family, either by birth or marriage **2** a connection between two or more things

relationship NOUN **1** a connection between things or people **2** an emotional or sexual partnership or affair: *He isn't married, but he's in a steady relationship*

relative NOUN someone who is of the same family, either by birth or marriage ▶ ADJECTIVE comparative: *relative merits*

relatively ADVERB more or less: *relatively happy*

relativity NOUN **1** the state of being relative **2** (*also*: **special theory of relativity**) Einstein's theory that the mass of a body varies with its speed, based on the fundamental assumptions that all motion is relative and that the speed of light relative to an observer is constant **3** (*also*: **general theory of relativity**) this same theory extended to include gravitation and accelerated motion

relax VERB **1** to become or make less tense **2** to slacken (eg your grip or control) **3** to make (laws or rules) less severe

relaxation NOUN **1** a slackening **2** rest from work, leisure

relay VERB (**relaying, relayed**) to receive and pass on (eg a message, a television programme) ▶ NOUN **1** a fresh set of people to replace others at a job etc **2** a relay race **in relays** in groups which take over from one another in series

relay race NOUN a race in which members of each team take over from each other, each running a set distance

release VERB **1** to set free **2** to allow (news etc) to be made public ▸NOUN the act of releasing or state of being released, from captivity, duty, etc

relegate VERB **1** to put down (to a lower position, group etc) **2** to leave (a task etc) to someone else > **relegation** NOUN

relent VERB to treat someone less severely or strictly

relentless ADJECTIVE **1** without pity **2** refusing to be turned from a purpose > **relentlessly** ADVERB

relevant ADJECTIVE having to do with what is being spoken about > **relevance** NOUN

reliable ADJECTIVE able to be trusted or counted on > **reliability** NOUN

reliant ADJECTIVE relying on or having confidence in > **reliance** NOUN

relic NOUN something left over from a past time; an antiquity

relief NOUN **1** a lessening of pain or anxiety **2** release from a post or duty **3** people taking over someone's duty etc **4** help given to those in need: *famine relief* **5** the act of freeing (a town etc) from a siege **6** *art* a way of carving or moulding in which the design stands out from its background

relief map NOUN a map in which variations in the height of the land are shown by shading

relieve VERB **1** to lessen (pain or anxiety) **2** to take over a duty from (someone else) **3** to come to the help of (a town etc under attack)

religion NOUN belief in, or worship of, a god

religious ADJECTIVE **1** of or relating to religion: *religious beliefs* **2** following the rules of worship of a particular religion very closely

relinquish VERB to give up, abandon: *relinquish control*

relish VERB **1** to enjoy **2** to like the taste of ▸NOUN (*plural* **relishes**) **1** enjoyment **2** flavour **3** something which adds flavour

relocate VERB to move to another position, residence, etc

reluctance NOUN unwillingness; lack of enthusiasm

reluctant ADJECTIVE unwilling

rely VERB (**relies, relying, relied**) to have full trust in, depend (on)

remain VERB **1** to stay, not leave **2** to be left: *Only two tins of soup remained* **3** to be still the same: *The problem remains unsolved*

remainder NOUN **1** something which is left behind after removal of the rest **2** *maths* the number left after subtraction or division

remains PLURAL NOUN **1** that which is left **2** a dead body

remake NOUN (*pronounced* **ree**-meik) a second making of a film etc ▸VERB (*pronounced* ree-**meik**) (**remaking, remade**) to make again

remand VERB to put (someone) back in prison until more evidence is found **on remand** having been remanded

remark VERB **1** to say **2** to comment (on) **3** to notice ▸NOUN something said

remarkable ADJECTIVE deserving notice, unusual > **remarkably** ADVERB: *She prepared it remarkably quickly*

remedial (*pronounced* ri-**mee**-di-*a*l) ADJECTIVE **1** remedying **2** *formerly* relating to the teaching of children with learning difficulties

remedy NOUN (*plural* **remedies**) a cure for an illness, evil, etc ▸ VERB (**remedies, remedying, remedied**) **1** to cure **2** to put right

remember VERB **1** to keep in mind **2** to recall after having forgotten **3** to send your best wishes (to): *Remember me to your mother* **4** to reward, give a present to: *He remembered her in his will*

remembrance NOUN **1** the act of remembering **2** memory **3** something given to remind someone of a person or event, a keepsake **4** (**remembrances**) a friendly greeting

remind VERB **1** to bring (something) back to a person's mind: *Remind me to post that letter* **2** to cause (someone) to think about (someone or something) by resemblance: *She reminds me of her sister*

reminder NOUN something which reminds

reminisce (*pronounced* rem-i-**nis**) VERB to think and talk about things remembered from the past

reminiscent (*pronounced* rem-i-**nis**-*e*nt) ADJECTIVE **1** reminding (of): *reminiscent of Paris* **2** in a mood to remember and think about past events etc

remiss ADJECTIVE careless, unthinking

remission NOUN **1** a shortening of a prison sentence **2** a lessening of a disease or illness

remit VERB (*pronounced* ri-**mit**) (**remitting, remitted**) **1** to pardon, excuse (a crime etc) **2** to wipe out, cancel (a debt etc) **3** to lessen, become less intense **4** to send (money) **5** to hand over (eg a prisoner to a higher court)

remittance NOUN **1** the sending of money in payment **2** the money sent

remnant NOUN a small piece or number left over

remorse NOUN regret about something done in the past

remorseful ADJECTIVE full of remorse, sorrowful

remote ADJECTIVE **1** far away in time or place **2** isolated, far from other people **3** slight: *a remote chance*

remote control NOUN **1** the control of devices from a distance, using electrical signals or radio waves **2** a battery-operated device for transmitting such waves

removal NOUN the act of removing, especially of moving furniture to a new home

remove VERB **1** to take (something) from its place **2** to dismiss from a job **3** to take off (clothes etc) **4** to get rid of: *remove a stain* ▸ NOUN a stage away (from): *one remove from anarchy*

removed ADJECTIVE **1** distant (from) **2** of cousins: separated by a generation: *my first cousin once removed* (my cousin's child)

remuneration NOUN pay, salary

renaissance (*pronounced* ri-**nei**-s*a*ns) NOUN **1** a rebirth **2** a period of cultural revival and growth

renal (*pronounced* **ree**-nal) ADJECTIVE of the kidneys

rend VERB (**rending, rent**) *old* to tear (apart), divide

render VERB **1** to give (eg thanks) **2** to translate into another language **3** to perform (music etc) **4** to cause to be: *His words rendered me speechless*

rendezvous (*pronounced* **ron**-dei-voo) NOUN (*plural* **rendezvous** – *pronounced* **ron**-dei-vooz) **1** a meeting place fixed beforehand **2** an arranged meeting

renegade (*pronounced* **ren**-i-geid) NOUN someone who deserts their own side, religion, or beliefs

renew VERB **1** to make as if new again **2** to begin again: *renew your efforts* **3** to make valid for a further period (eg a driving licence) **4** to replace: *renew the water in the tank*
> **renewable** ADJECTIVE

renewal NOUN renewing or being renewed: *My contract is due for renewal*

rennet NOUN a substance used in curdling milk for making cheeses etc, especially an extract from the stomachs of calves containing rennin

renounce VERB to give up publicly or formally

renovate VERB to make (something) like new again, mend
> **renovation** NOUN

renown NOUN fame

renowned ADJECTIVE famous

rent NOUN payment made for the use of property or land ▸VERB **1** to pay rent for (a house etc) **2** (also **rent out**) to receive rent for (a house etc)

rental NOUN money paid as rent

renunciation NOUN an act of renouncing: *their renunciation of trade links with Japan*

reorganize *or* **reorganise** VERB to put in a different order
> **reorganization** NOUN

rep NOUN, *short for* **1** representative: *a sales rep* **2** repertory

repair[1] VERB **1** to mend **2** to make up for (a wrong) ▸NOUN **1** state, condition: *in bad repair* **2** mending: *in need of repair* **3** a mend, a patch

repair[2] VERB, *old* to go, move: *repair to the drawing room*

reparation NOUN compensation for a wrong

repatriate VERB to send (someone) back to their own country
> **repatriation** NOUN

repay VERB (**repaying, repaid**) **1** to pay back **2** to give or do something in return: *He repaid her kindness with a gift*

repayment NOUN repaying

repeal VERB to do away with, cancel (especially a law) ▸NOUN the cancellation of a law etc

repeat VERB **1** to say or do over again **2** to say from memory **3** to pass on (someone's words) ▸NOUN a musical passage, television programme etc played or shown for a second time

repeatedly ADVERB again and again

repel VERB (**repelling, repelled**) **1** to drive back or away **2** to disgust

repellent ADJECTIVE disgusting

a b c d e f g h i j k l m n o p q r s t u v w x y z

▶NOUN something that repels: *insect repellent*

repent VERB to be sorry for your actions **repent of something** to regret it

repentant ADJECTIVE feeling or showing sorrow and regret for your actions > **repentance** NOUN

repercussion NOUN an indirect or resultant effect of something which has happened

repertoire (*pronounced* **rep**-*er*-twah) NOUN the range of works performed by a musician, theatre company etc

repertory theatre NOUN a theatre with a permanent company which performs a series of plays

repetition NOUN **1** the act of repeating or being repeated **2** a thing which is repeated

repetitive ADJECTIVE repeating too often, predictable

replace VERB **1** to put (something) back where it was **2** to put in place of another > **replacement** NOUN

replay NOUN (*pronounced* **ree**-plei) **1** a repeat of a contest or game, because there was no winner the first time **2** the playing again of a recording, piece of film, etc ▶VERB (*pronounced* ree-**plei**) to play (a game, recording, etc) again

replenish VERB to refill (a stock, supply)

replica NOUN an exact copy of a work of art, etc

reply VERB (**replies, replying, replied**) to speak or act in answer to something ▶NOUN (*plural* **replies**) an answer

report VERB **1** to pass on news **2** to give a description of (an event) **3** to give information about events for a newspaper **4** to make a formal complaint against ▶NOUN **1** a statement of facts **2** an account, a description **3** a news article **4** a rumour **5** a written description of a school pupil's work **6** a loud, explosive noise

reported speech *see* **indirect speech**

reporter NOUN a news journalist

repose[1] *formal*, NOUN sleep, rest ▶VERB to rest

repose[2] VERB, *formal* to place (eg trust in a person)

repository NOUN (*plural* **repositories**) a storage place for safe keeping

repossess VERB to take back (goods, property), especially because of non-payment

represent VERB **1** to speak or act on behalf of others: *representing the tenants' association* **2** to stand for, be a symbol of: *Each letter represents a sound* **3** to claim to be **4** to explain, point out

representation NOUN **1** an image, a picture **2** (**representations**) a strong claim or appeal

representative ADJECTIVE **1** typical, characteristic: *a representative specimen* **2** standing or acting for others ▶NOUN **1** someone who acts or speaks on behalf of others **2** (*short form* **rep**) a travelling salesperson for a company

repress VERB **1** to keep down by force **2** to keep under control

repression NOUN **1** the strict controlling of people, not allowing them to do things such as vote in elections or attend religious worship **2** *psychology* the defence mechanism whereby an unpleasant or unacceptable thought, memory or wish is deliberately excluded from conscious thought

repressive ADJECTIVE severe; harsh

reprieve VERB **1** to pardon (a criminal) **2** to relieve from trouble or difficulty ▶NOUN a pardon, a relief

reprimand VERB to scold severely, censure ▶NOUN scolding, censure

reprint VERB (*pronounced* ree-**print**) to print more copies of (a book etc) ▶NOUN (*pronounced* **ree**-print) another printing of a book

reprisal NOUN a return of wrong for wrong, a repayment in kind

reproach VERB to scold, blame ▶NOUN (*plural* **reproaches**) **1** blame, discredit **2** a cause of blame or censure

reproachful ADJECTIVE expressing or full of reproach

reproduce VERB **1** to produce a copy of **2** to produce (children or young)

reproduction NOUN **1** a copy or imitation (especially of a work of art) **2** the act or process of producing (offspring)

reproductive system NOUN, *biology* the system of organs involved with reproduction, which includes the uterus in human females and the testes in human males

reptile NOUN a scaly, cold-blooded animal, such as a snake, lizard, etc

republic NOUN (a state with) a form of government without a monarch, in which power is in the hands of elected representatives

republican ADJECTIVE **1** of or favouring a republic **2** (**Republican**) *US* belonging to the Republican Party ▶NOUN **1** someone who believes in a republican form of government **2** (**Republican**) *US* a supporter of the Republican Party **3** (**Republican**) in Northern Ireland: someone who advocates union with the Republic of Ireland > **republicanism** NOUN (meaning 1)

Republican Party NOUN the more conservative of the two chief political parties in the USA (*compare with*: **Democratic Party**)

repugnance NOUN aversion, disgust

repugnant ADJECTIVE hateful, distasteful

repulse VERB **1** to drive back **2** to reject, snub

repulsion NOUN disgust

repulsive ADJECTIVE causing disgust, loathsome

reputable (*pronounced* **rep**-*yuw-ta*-bl) ADJECTIVE having a good reputation, well thought of

reputation NOUN **1** opinion held by people in general of a particular person **2** good name

repute NOUN reputation

reputed ADJECTIVE **1** considered, thought (to be something): *reputed to be dangerous* **2** supposed: *the reputed author of the book*

A B C D E F G H I J K L M N O P Q R S T U V W X Y Z

reputedly ADVERB in the opinion of most people

request VERB to ask for ▸NOUN **1** an asking for something **2** something asked for

requiem (*pronounced* **rek**-wi-em) NOUN a hymn or mass sung for the dead

[i] A Latin word meaning literally 'rest', the first word in former church services for the dead

require VERB **1** to need **2** to demand, order

requirement NOUN **1** something needed **2** a demand

requisite (*pronounced* **rek**-wi-zit) ADJECTIVE required; necessary ▸NOUN something needed or necessary

requisition NOUN a formal request for supplies, eg for a school or army ▸VERB to put in a formal request for

rerun VERB (*pronounced* ree-**run**) (**rerunning, reran, rerun**) to run again ▸NOUN (*pronounced* **ree**-run) a repeated television programme

rescue VERB **1** to save from danger **2** to free from capture ▸NOUN an act of saving from danger or capture
> **rescuer** NOUN

research NOUN (*plural* **researches**) close and careful scientific study to try to find out new facts: *cancer research* ▸VERB to study carefully
> **researcher** NOUN

resemblance NOUN likeness

resemble VERB to look like or be like: *He doesn't resemble his sister*

resent VERB to feel injured, annoyed, or insulted by

resentful ADJECTIVE full of or caused by resentment

resentment NOUN annoyance, bitterness

reservation NOUN **1** the act of reserving, booking **2** an exception or condition: *She agreed to the plan, but with certain reservations* **3** doubt, objection: *I had reservations about their friendship* **4** an area of land set aside by treaty for Native American people in the United States

reserve VERB **1** to set aside for future use **2** to book, have kept for you (eg a seat, a table) ▸NOUN **1** something reserved **2** (**reserves**) troops outside the regular army kept ready to help those already fighting **3** a piece of land set apart for some reason: *a nature reserve* **4** shyness, reluctance to speak or act openly

reserved ADJECTIVE **1** shy, reluctant to speak openly **2** kept back for a particular person or purpose

reservoir (*pronounced* **rez**-er-vwah) NOUN an artificial lake where water is kept in store

reshuffle *politics*, VERB (*pronounced* ree-**shuf**-l) to rearrange ministerial posts within (a government cabinet) ▸NOUN (*pronounced* **ree**-shuf-l) a rearrangement of a cabinet

reside VERB **1** *formal* to live, stay (in) **2** of authority etc: to be placed (in)

residence NOUN **1** *formal* the building where someone lives **2** living, or time of living, in a place

resident NOUN someone who lives in a particular place: *a resident of Dublin* ▸ADJECTIVE **1** living in (a place) **2** living in a place of work: *the resident caretaker*

residential ADJECTIVE **1** of an area: containing houses rather than shops, offices, etc **2** providing accommodation: *a residential course*

residual ADJECTIVE remaining; left over

residue NOUN something that is left over

resign VERB to give up (a job, position, etc) **resign yourself to** to accept (a situation) patiently and calmly

resignation NOUN **1** the act of resigning **2** a letter to say you are resigning **3** patient, calm acceptance of a situation

resigned ADJECTIVE patient, not actively complaining

resilient ADJECTIVE **1** able to recover easily from misfortune, hurt, etc **2** of an object: readily recovering its original shape after being bent, twisted, etc > **resilience** NOUN

resin (*pronounced* **rez**-in) NOUN a sticky substance produced by certain plants (eg firs, pines)

resist VERB **1** to struggle against, oppose **2** to stop yourself from (doing something)

resistance NOUN **1** the act of resisting **2** an organized opposition, especially to an occupying force **3** *electricity* ability to turn a passing electrical current into heat **4** *physics* a force that prevents or slows down motion

resistant ADJECTIVE able to resist or remain unaffected or undamaged by something

resistor NOUN a device that controls current in an electric circuit by providing resistance

resit VERB (*pronounced* ree-**sit**) (**resitting, resat**) to sit (an examination) again ▸NOUN (*pronounced* **ree**-sit) a retaking of an examination

resolute ADJECTIVE determined, with mind made up > **resolutely** ADVERB

resolution NOUN **1** determination of mind or purpose **2** a firm decision (to do something) **3** a proposal put before a meeting **4** a decision expressed by a public meeting

resolve VERB **1** to decide firmly (to do something) **2** to solve (a difficulty) **3** to break up into parts ▸NOUN a firm purpose

resonance NOUN a deep, echoing tone

resonant ADJECTIVE echoing, resounding

resonate VERB to echo

resort VERB: (**resort to**) **1** to begin to use **2** to turn to in a difficulty: *resorting to bribery* NOUN a popular holiday destination **in the last resort** when all else fails

resound (*pronounced* ri-**zound**) VERB **1** to sound loudly **2** to echo

resounding ADJECTIVE **1** echoing **2** thorough: *a resounding victory*

resourceful ADJECTIVE good at finding ways out of difficulties

resources PLURAL NOUN **1** a source of supplying what is required **2** the natural sources of wealth in a country etc **3** money or other property **4** an ability to handle situations skilfully and cleverly

respect VERB **1** to feel a high regard for **2** to treat with consideration: *respect his wishes* ▶ NOUN **1** high regard, esteem **2** consideration **3** a detail, a way: *alike in some respects* **4** (**respects**) good wishes **in respect of** *or* **with respect to** with reference to, concerning

respectable ADJECTIVE **1** worthy of respect **2** having a good reputation **3** considerable, fairly good: *a respectable score* > **respectability** NOUN

respectful ADJECTIVE showing respect > **respectfully** ADVERB

respective ADJECTIVE belonging to each (person or thing mentioned) separately: *My brother and his friends went to their respective homes* (that is, each went to their own home)

respectively ADVERB in the order given: *James, Andrew and Ian were first, second and third respectively*

respiration NOUN **1 2** *biology, chemistry* the process by which organisms exchange gases with the environment, *eg* breathing is a form of respiration **3** *biology, chemistry* the process by which food substances are broken down to supply energy cells

respirator NOUN **1** a mask worn over the mouth and nose to purify the air taken in **2** *medicine* a device to help people breathe when they are too ill to do so naturally

respiratory system (*pronounced* **res**-pir-*a*-to-ri) NOUN the system of organs in which gas exchange takes place, which includes the lungs and windpipe in humans

respire VERB to breathe

respite (*pronounced* **res**-pait) NOUN a pause, a rest: *no respite from work*

resplendent ADJECTIVE very bright or splendid in appearance

respond VERB **1** to answer **2** to react in response to: *I waved but he didn't respond* **3** to show a positive reaction to: *responding to treatment*

response NOUN **1** a reply **2** an action, feeling etc in answer to another **3** an answer made by the congregation during a church service

responsibility NOUN (*plural* **responsibilities**) something or someone for which one is responsible

responsible ADJECTIVE **1** involving making important decisions etc: *a responsible post* **2** trustworthy **responsible for 1** being the cause of: *responsible for this mess* **2** liable to be blamed for: *responsible for the conduct of his staff*

responsive ADJECTIVE quick to react, to show sympathy, etc

rest[1] NOUN **1** a break in work **2** a sleep **3** *music* a pause in playing or singing for a given number of beats **4** a support, a prop: *a book rest* ▶ VERB **1** to stop working for a time **2** to be still **3** to sleep **4** to depend (on), be based on: *The case rests on your evidence* **5** to stop, develop no further: *I can't let the matter rest there* **6** to lean or place on a support **rest with** to be the responsibility of:

The choice rests with you

rest² NOUN: **the rest 1** what is left, the remainder **2** the others, those not mentioned: *I went home but the rest went to the cinema*

restaurant NOUN a place where meals may be bought and eaten

restaurateur (*pronounced* res-*taw*-*ra*-**ter**) NOUN the owner or manager of a restaurant

restful ADJECTIVE **1** relaxing **2** relaxed

restive ADJECTIVE restless, impatient

restless ADJECTIVE **1** unable to keep still **2** agitated

restoration NOUN **1** the act of giving back something lost or stolen **2** a model or reconstruction (eg of a ruin)

restorative ADJECTIVE curing, giving strength

restore VERB **1** to put or give back **2** to repair (a building, a painting etc) so that it looks as it used to **3** to cure (a person)

restrain VERB **1** to hold back (from) **2** to keep under control

restraint NOUN **1** the act of restraining **2** self-control **3** a tie or bond used to restrain

restrict VERB **1** to limit, keep within certain bounds: *restricted space for parking* **2** to open only to certain people: *restricted area*

restriction NOUN **1** an act or instance of restricting **2** a regulation or rule which restricts or limits

restrictive ADJECTIVE restricting

result NOUN **1** a consequence of something already done or said **2** the answer to a sum **3** a score in a game **result from** to be the result or effect of **result in** to have as a result: *result in a draw*

resultant ADJECTIVE happening as a result

resume VERB **1** to begin again after an interruption: *resume a discussion* **2** to take again: *He resumed his seat*

résumé (*pronounced* **rez**-yoo-mei) NOUN **1** a summary **2** *US* a curriculum vitae

resumption NOUN the act of resuming

resurgence NOUN the act of returning to life, to a state of activity, etc after a period of decline

resurgent ADJECTIVE rising again, becoming prominent again

resurrect VERB to bring back to life or into use

resuscitate (*pronounced* ri-**sus**-i-teit) VERB to bring back to consciousness, revive

> **resuscitation** NOUN

retail VERB **1** (*pronounced* **ree**-teil) to sell goods to someone who is going to use them, rather than to another seller (*compare with*: **wholesale**) **2** (*pronounced* ree-**teil**) to tell (eg a story) fully and in detail ▸NOUN (*pronounced* **ree**-teil) the sale of goods to the actual user

retailer NOUN a shopkeeper, a trader

retain VERB **1** to keep possession of **2** to keep (something) in mind **3** to reserve (someone's services) by paying a fee in advance **4** to hold back, keep in place

retake VERB (*pronounced* ree-

a b c d e f g h i j k l m n o p q r s t u v w x y z

A B C D E F G H I J K L M N O P Q R S T U V W X Y Z

teik) (**retaking, retook, retaken**) to take or capture again ▸NOUN (*pronounced* **ree**-teik) the filming of part of a film again

retaliate VERB to return an insult, injury, etc with a similar one, hit back > **retaliation** NOUN

retarded ADJECTIVE slow in mental or physical growth

retch VERB to make the actions and sound of vomiting, without actually vomiting

retention NOUN **1** the act of holding in or keeping **2** the act of retaining the services of (eg a lawyer)

retentive ADJECTIVE able to hold or retain well: *a retentive memory*

reticent ADJECTIVE unwilling to speak openly and freely, reserved > **reticence** NOUN

retina (*pronounced* **ret**-i-n*a*) NOUN (*plural* **retinas** *or* **retinae** – *pronounced* **ret**-i-nee) the light-sensitive tissue at the back of the eye that relays nerve impulses to the brain, which interprets them as vision

retire VERB **1** to give up work permanently, usually because of age **2** *formal* to go to bed **3** to draw back, retreat

retired ADJECTIVE **1** having given up work **2** out-of-the-way, quiet

retirement NOUN **1** the act of retiring from work **2** someone's life after they have given up work

retiring ADJECTIVE shy, avoiding being noticed

retort VERB to make a quick and witty reply ▸NOUN a quick, witty reply

retrace VERB to go over again: *retrace your steps*

retract VERB **1** to take back (something said or given) **2** to draw back, pull in: *The cat retracted its claws*

retraction NOUN a retracting (especially of something one has said, agreed or promised)

retreat VERB **1** to draw back, withdraw **2** to go away ▸NOUN **1** a movement backwards corresponding to the advance of an enemy **2** a withdrawal **3** a quiet, peaceful place

retribution NOUN punishment

retrieve VERB **1** to get back, recover (something lost) **2** to search for and fetch

retriever NOUN a breed of dog trained to find and fetch shot birds

retro ADJECTIVE recreating a style of the past for effect

retro- PREFIX forms words containing the meaning 'backwards' or 'behind'

🄸 Comes from Latin *retro* meaning 'back' or 'behind'

retrospect NOUN: **in retrospect** considering or looking back on the past

retrospective ADJECTIVE **1** looking back on past events **2** of a law: applying to the past as well as the present and the future

return VERB **1** to go or come back **2** to give, send, pay etc back **3** to elect to parliament ▸NOUN **1** the act of returning **2** a profit: *the return on your investment* **3** a statement of income for calculating income tax

by return sent by the first post back

return ticket NOUN a ticket which covers a journey both to and from a place

reunion NOUN a meeting of people who have been apart for some time

reunite VERB to join after having been separated

Rev *or* **Revd** ABBREVIATION Reverend

rev *informal*, NOUN a revolution of an engine ▸VERB (often **rev up**) (**revving, revved**) to increase the speed of (an engine)

revamp VERB to renovate, renew the appearance of

reveal VERB **1** to make known **2** to show

revel VERB (**revelling, revelled**) **1** to take great delight (in) **2** to celebrate ▸NOUN (**revels**) festivities

revelation NOUN **1** the act of revealing **2** something unexpected which is made known

revelry NOUN (*plural* **revelries**) noisy lively enjoyment, festivities or merrymaking > **reveller** *or US* **reveler** NOUN

revenge NOUN **1** harm done to someone in return for harm they themselves have committed **2** the desire to do such harm ▸VERB to inflict punishment in return for harm done: *revenging his father's murder* **revenge yourself** to take revenge: *He revenged himself on his enemies*

revenue NOUN **1** money received as payment **2** a country's total income

reverberate VERB to echo and re-echo, resound > **reverberation** NOUN

revere VERB to look upon with great respect

reverence NOUN great respect

reverend ADJECTIVE **1** worthy of respect **2** (**Reverend**) a title given to a member of the clergy (*short form* **Rev** or **Revd**)

ℹ Comes from Latin *reverendus* meaning 'who must be respected'

reversal NOUN the act of reversing or being reversed

reverse VERB **1** to turn upside down or the other way round **2** to move backwards **3** to undo (a decision, policy, etc) ▸NOUN **1** the opposite (of) **2** the other side (of a coin etc) **3** a defeat

reversible ADJECTIVE of clothes: able to be worn with either side out

revert VERB **1** to go back to an earlier topic **2** to return to a previous owner

review VERB **1** to give an opinion or criticism of (an artistic work) **2** to consider again: *review the facts* **3** to inspect (eg troops) ▸NOUN **1** a critical opinion of a book etc **2** a magazine consisting of reviews **3** a second look, a reconsideration **4** an inspection of troops etc

> Do not confuse with: **revue**

reviewer NOUN someone who reviews, a critic

revile VERB to say harsh things about

revise VERB **1** to correct faults in and make improvements **2** to study notes etc in preparation for an examination **3** to change (eg an opinion)

revision NOUN **1** the act of revising **2** a revised version of a book etc

revival NOUN **1** a return to life, use, etc **2** a fresh show of interest: *a religious revival*

revive VERB to bring or come back to life, use or fame

revoke VERB **1** to cancel (a decision etc) **2** to fail to follow suit in a card game

revolt VERB **1** to rise up (against), rebel **2** to feel disgust (at) **3** to disgust ▸NOUN a rising, a rebellion

revolting ADJECTIVE causing disgust

revolution NOUN **1** a full turn round a centre **2** the act of turning round a centre **3** a general uprising against those in power **4** a complete change in ideas, way of doing things, etc

revolutionary ADJECTIVE **1** relating to a revolution **2** bringing about great changes **3** turning ▸NOUN (*plural* **revolutionaries**) someone who is involved in, or is in favour of, revolution

revolutionize *or* **revolutionise** VERB to bring about a complete change in

revolve VERB to roll or turn round

revolver NOUN a kind of pistol

revue NOUN a light theatre show, with short topical plays or sketches

> Do not confuse with: **review**

revulsion NOUN **1** disgust **2** a sudden change of feeling, especially from love to hate

reward NOUN **1** something given in return for work done or for good behaviour etc **2** a sum of money offered for helping to find a criminal, lost property, etc ▸VERB **1** to give a reward to **2** to give a reward for (a service)

rewarding ADJECTIVE giving pleasure or satisfaction

rewind VERB (**rewinding, rewound**) to wind back (a spool, tape, film, etc) to the beginning

rewrite VERB (*pronounced* ree-**rait**) (**rewriting, rewrote, rewritten**) to write again or in different words

rhapsodize *or* **rhapsodise** VERB to talk or write enthusiastically (about)

rhapsody NOUN (*plural* **rhapsodies**) music or poetry which expresses strong feeling **go into rhapsodies over** to show wild enthusiasm for

rhetoric (*pronounced* **ret**-*o*r-ik) NOUN **1** the art of good speaking or writing **2** language which is too showy, consisting of unnecessarily long or difficult words etc

rhetorical (*pronounced* ri-**tor**-i-k*a*l) ADJECTIVE **1** relating to or using rhetoric **2** of language: over-elaborate

rheumatic ADJECTIVE relating to or caused by rheumatism

rheumatism NOUN a disease which causes stiffness and pain in the joints

rhinestone NOUN an artificial paste diamond

rhino NOUN (*plural* **rhinos**) *short for* **rhinoceros**

rhino- *or* **rhin-** PREFIX of or relating to the nose

🛈 Comes from Greek *rhis* meaning 'nose'

rhinoceros NOUN (*plural* **rhinoceros** *or* **rhinoceroses**) a large, thick-skinned animal, with a horn (or two) on its nose (often shortened to **rhino**)

rhododendron NOUN a flowering shrub with thick evergreen leaves and large flowers

rhombus NOUN (*plural* **rhombuses** *or* **rhombi** – *pronounced* **rom**-bai), *maths* a geometrical figure with four equal straight sides

rhubarb NOUN a plant with long, red-skinned, edible stalks

rhyme NOUN **1** a similarity in sounds between words or their endings, eg *humble* and *crumble*, or *convention* and *prevention* **2** a word which sounds like another **3** a short poem ▶ VERB (sometimes **rhyme with**) to sound like, be rhymes: *'Harp' rhymes with 'carp'*

rhythm NOUN **1** a regular, repeated pattern of sounds or beats in music or poetry **2** a regularly repeated pattern of movements

rhythm and blues SINGULAR NOUN a type of music combining the styles of rock-and-roll and the blues

rib NOUN **1** *anatomy* any of the bones which curve round and forward from the backbone, enclosing the heart and lungs **2** a spar of wood in the framework of a boat, curving up from the keel **3** a ridged knitting pattern

ribbed ADJECTIVE arranged in ridges and furrows

ribbon NOUN a narrow strip of silk or other material, used for decoration, tying hair, etc

rice NOUN (the seeds of) a plant, grown for food in well-watered ground in tropical countries

rice paper NOUN a thin, edible, paper-like material often put under baking to prevent it sticking

rich ADJECTIVE **1** having a lot of money or valuables, wealthy **2** valuable: *a rich reward* **3** of food: containing a lot of fat, eggs, etc **4** of material: heavily decorated or textured, lavish **5** of a colour: deep in tone **rich in** having a lot of: *rich in natural resources*

riches PLURAL NOUN wealth

richly ADVERB **1** in a rich or elaborate way: *richly decorated* **2** fully and suitably: *richly deserved*

richness NOUN being rich

Richter scale (*pronounced* **rikh**-ter) NOUN a scale for measuring the intensity of earthquakes

rickety ADJECTIVE **1** suffering from rickets **2** unsteady: *a rickety table*

rickshaw NOUN a two-wheeled carriage pulled by a man, used in Japan etc

ricochet (*pronounced* **rik**-*o*-shei) VERB (**ricocheting, ricocheted**) of a bullet: to rebound at an angle from a surface

rid VERB (**ridding, rid**) to free from, clear of: *rid the city of rats* **get rid of** to free yourself of

riddance NOUN: **good riddance to** I am happy to have got rid of

riddle[1] NOUN **1** a puzzle in the form of a question which describes

A B C D E F G H I J K L M N O P Q R S T U V W X Y Z

something in a misleading way **2** something difficult to understand

riddle[2] VERB: **riddled with** covered with small holes made by: *riddled with woodworm*

ride VERB (**riding, rode, ridden**) **1** to travel on a horse or bicycle, or in a vehicle **2** to travel on and control (a horse) **3** of a ship: to float at anchor ▶NOUN **1** a journey on horseback, bicycle, etc **2** a path through a wood, for riding horses **ride up** of a skirt etc: to work itself up out of position

ridge NOUN **1** a raised part between furrows **2** a long crest on high ground

ridicule VERB to laugh at, mock ▶NOUN mockery

ridiculous ADJECTIVE deserving to be laughed at, very silly

rife ADJECTIVE very common: *Disease was rife in the country*

riff NOUN a short, repeated pattern in a piece of pop music

riff-raff NOUN worthless people

rifle[1] VERB **1** to search through and rob **2** to steal

rifle[2] NOUN a long gun fired from the shoulder

rift NOUN **1** a crack or gap left by splitting **2** a disagreement between friends

rift valley NOUN, *geography* a long valley formed when part of the earth's crust subsides between two faults

rig VERB (**rigging, rigged**) to fix (an election result) illegally or dishonestly **rig someone out** to clothe or dress them **rig up 1** to fit (a ship) with sails and ropes **2** to make or build hastily

rigging NOUN ship's spars, ropes, etc

right ADJECTIVE **1** on or belonging to the side of the body which in most people has the more skilful hand (*contrasted with*: **left**[1]) **2** correct, true **3** just, good **4** straight ▶ADVERB **1** to or on the right side **2** correctly **3** straight **4** all the way: *right along the pier and back* ▶NOUN **1** something good which ought to be done **2** something you are entitled to: *a right to a fair trial* **3** the right-hand side, direction, etc **4** the conservative side in politics ▶VERB to mend, set in order **by right** because you have the right **in your own right** not because of anyone else, independently

right angle NOUN, *maths* an angle of 90°

right-click VERB, *computing* to press and release the right-hand button on a computer mouse

righteous (*pronounced* **raich**-*us*) ADJECTIVE living a good life; just

rightful ADJECTIVE by right, proper: *the rightful owner*

right-handed ADJECTIVE using the right hand more easily than the left

right of way NOUN a road or path over private land along which people may go as a right

rigid ADJECTIVE **1** not easily bent, stiff **2** strict

rigidity NOUN a rigid state or quality

rigmarole NOUN a long, rambling speech

🛈 Originally *ragman roll*, a Scots term for a long list or catalogue

rigorous ADJECTIVE very strict

rigour *or US* **rigor** NOUN strictness; harshness

rim NOUN an edge or border, eg the top edge of a cup

rind (*pronounced* raind) NOUN a thick, firm covering, eg fruit peel, bacon skin, the outer covering of cheese

ring[1] NOUN **1** a small hoop worn on the finger, on the ear, etc **2** a hollow circle **3** an enclosed space for boxing, circus performances, etc **4** a small group of people formed for business or criminal purposes: *a drug ring* ▸VERB (**ringing, ringed**) **1** to encircle, go round **2** to mark (a bird etc) by putting on a ring

ring[2] VERB (**ringing, rang, rung**) **1** to make the sound of a bell **2** to strike (a bell etc) **3** to telephone ▸NOUN the sound of a bell being struck

ringleader NOUN someone who takes the lead in mischief etc

ringmaster NOUN someone who is in charge of the performance in a circus ring

ring road NOUN a road that circles a town etc, avoiding the centre

rink NOUN a sheet of ice, often artificial, for skating or curling

rinse VERB **1** to wash lightly to remove soap etc **2** to clean (a cup, your mouth, etc) by swilling with water ▸NOUN **1** the act of rinsing **2** liquid colour for the hair

riot NOUN **1** a noisy disturbance by a crowd **2** a striking display: *a riot of colour* **3** *informal* a hilarious event ▸VERB to take part in a riot > **rioter** NOUN

riotous ADJECTIVE noisy, uncontrolled

RIP ABBREVIATION may he or she rest in peace

rip VERB (**ripping, ripped**) **1** to tear apart or off **2** to come apart ▸NOUN a tear **let rip** to express yourself fully, without restraint

ripe ADJECTIVE **1** of fruit etc: ready to be picked or eaten **2** fully developed, mature > **ripeness** NOUN

ripen VERB to make or become ripe

rip-off NOUN, *slang* a cheat, a swindle

ripple NOUN **1** a little wave or movement on the surface of water **2** a soft sound etc that rises and falls quickly and gently: *a ripple of laughter*

rise VERB (**rising, rose, risen**) **1** to get up from bed **2** to stand up **3** to move upwards **4** of a river: to have its source (in): *The Rhone rises in the Alps* **5** to rebel (against) ▸NOUN **1** a slope upwards **2** an increase in wages, prices etc **give rise to** to cause

rising NOUN **1** an act of rising **2** a rebellion

risk NOUN a chance of loss or injury; a danger ▸VERB **1** to take the chance of: *risk death* **2** to take the chance of losing: *risk your life or health*

risky ADJECTIVE (**riskier, riskiest**) possibly resulting in loss or injury

rissole NOUN a fried cake or ball of minced meat, fish, etc

rite NOUN a solemn ceremony, especially a religious one

a b c d e f g h i j k l m n o p q r s t u v w x y z

A B C D E F G H I J K L M N O P Q R S T U V W X Y Z

ritual NOUN a traditional way of carrying out religious worship etc ▶ ADJECTIVE relating to a rite or ceremony

ritualistic ADJECTIVE done in a set, unchanging way

rival NOUN someone who tries to equal or beat another ▶ VERB (**rivalling, rivalled**) to try to equal

rivalry NOUN (*plural* **rivalries**) the state of being a rival or rivals

river NOUN a large stream of water flowing across land

rivet NOUN a bolt for fastening plates of metal together ▶ VERB (**riveting, riveted**) **1** to fasten with a rivet **2** to fix firmly (someone's attention etc): *riveted to the spot*

RNA ABBREVIATION, *biology* ribonucleic acid, a substance present in living cells, where it plays an important part in the production of proteins

roach NOUN (*plural* **roaches**) a type of freshwater fish

road NOUN **1** a hard, level surface for vehicles and people **2** a way of getting to (somewhere), a route **3** (**roads**) a place where ships may lie at anchor (*also called*: **roadstead**)

road hog NOUN, *informal* a reckless or selfish driver

road movie NOUN a film showing the travels of a character or characters

road rage NOUN anger directed at other road users by a driver

roadworthy ADJECTIVE (of a vehicle) fit to be used on the road

roam VERB to wander about

roar VERB **1** to give a loud, deep sound **2** to laugh loudly **3** to say (something) loudly ▶ NOUN a loud, deep sound or laugh

roast VERB to cook or be cooked in an oven or over a fire ▶ ADJECTIVE roasted: *roast beef* ▶ NOUN **1** meat roasted **2** meat for roasting

rob VERB (**robbing, robbed**) to steal from

robber NOUN a person who robs; a thief

robbery NOUN (*plural* **robberies**) the act of stealing

robe NOUN **1** a long, loose garment **2** *US* a dressing-gown **3** (**robes**) the official dress of a judge etc ▶ VERB, *formal* to dress

robin NOUN a type of small bird, known by its red breast

robot NOUN **1** a mechanical man or woman **2** a machine that can do the work of a person

ⓘ A word invented by Karl Capek, a Czech playwright, based on a Czech word meaning 'work'

robotic ADJECTIVE relating to or characteristic of robots

robust ADJECTIVE strong, healthy

rock[1] NOUN **1** a large lump of stone **2** a hard sweet made in sticks

rock[2] VERB to sway backwards and forwards or from side to side ▶ NOUN music with a heavy beat and simple melody (*also called*: **rock music**)

rock-and-roll *or* **rock'n'roll** NOUN a simpler, earlier form of rock music

rockery NOUN (*plural* **rockeries**) a collection of stones amongst which small plants are grown

rocket NOUN **1** a tube containing

inflammable materials, used for launching a spacecraft, for signalling, and as a firework **2** a spacecraft ▸ VERB (**rocketing, rocketed**) to move upwards rapidly: *Prices are rocketing*

rocking chair NOUN a chair which rocks backwards and forwards on rockers

rocking horse NOUN a toy horse which rocks backwards and forwards on rockers

rocky[1] ADJECTIVE (**rockier, rockiest**) full of rocks

rocky[2] ADJECTIVE (**rockier, rockiest**) inclined to rock, unsteady

rod NOUN **1** a long, thin stick **2** a fishing rod **3** an old measure of distance, about 5 metres

rode *past tense* of **ride**

rodent NOUN a gnawing animal, such as a rat, beaver etc

rodeo NOUN (*plural* **rodeos**) **1** a round-up of cattle for marking **2** a show of riding by cowboys

roe NOUN **1** the eggs of fishes **2** (*also called*: **roe deer**) a small kind of deer

rogue NOUN a dishonest or mischievous person, a rascal

roguery NOUN (*plural* **rogueries**) dishonesty; mischief

roguish ADJECTIVE characteristic of a rogue; mischievous, dishonest

role *or* **rôle** NOUN a part played by an actor

roll VERB **1** to move along by turning over like a wheel **2** of a ship: to rock from side to side **3** of thunder etc: to rumble **4** to wrap round and round: *roll up a carpet* **5** to flatten with a roller: *roll the lawn* ▸ NOUN **1** a sheet of paper, length of cloth etc rolled into a cylinder **2** a very small loaf of bread **3** a rocking movement **4** a list of names **5** a long, rumbling sound

roll-call NOUN the calling of names from a list

roller NOUN **1** a cylindrical tool for flattening **2** a tube over which hair is rolled and styled **3** a small, solid wheel **4** a long, heavy wave on the sea

Rollerblades PLURAL NOUN, *trademark* rollerskates with the wheels in a single line

rollerskates PLURAL NOUN skates with wheels at each corner of the shoe

rollicking ADJECTIVE noisy and full of fun

rolling pin NOUN a roller for flattening dough

ROM ABBREVIATION, *computing* read-only memory

Roman ADJECTIVE of Rome (especially ancient Rome) or its people

Roman Catholic Church NOUN the Church whose head is the Pope, the Bishop of Rome

romance NOUN **1** a story about heroic events not likely to happen in real life **2** a love story **3** a love affair ▸ VERB to write or tell imaginative stories

Roman numeral NOUN any of the figures in the number system developed by the ancient Romans, eg I, V, X, etc

romantic ADJECTIVE **1** of romance

A B C D E F G H I J K L M N O P Q R S T U V W X Y Z

2 full of feeling and imagination **3** relating to love

romanticism NOUN (often **Romanticism**) the late 18th- and early 19th-century movement in art, literature and music, characterized by an emphasis on feelings and emotions

Romany NOUN (*plural* **Romanies**) **1** a gypsy **2** the gypsy language

romp VERB **1** to play in a lively way **2** to move quickly and easily ▶NOUN a lively game

rompers PLURAL NOUN a short suit for a baby

rood NOUN, *old* **1** a measure of area, equal to a quarter of an acre **2** a cross carrying an image of Christ

roof NOUN (*plural* **roofs**) **1** the top covering of a building, car, etc **2** the upper part of the mouth ▶VERB to cover with a roof

rook NOUN **1** a kind of crow **2** *chess* a castle

rookery NOUN (*plural* **rookeries**) **1** a nesting place of rooks **2** a breeding place of penguins or seals

room NOUN **1** an inside compartment in a house **2** space: *room for everybody* **3** (**rooms**) lodgings

roomy ADJECTIVE (**roomier, roomiest**) having plenty of space

roost NOUN a perch on which a bird rests at night ▶VERB to sit or sleep on a roost

rooster NOUN a farmyard cock

root[1] NOUN **1** the underground part of a plant, which anchors the plant in the soil and absorbs water and nutrients **2** one of the branches of the larger root **3** the base of anything, eg a tooth or fingernail **4** a cause, a source **5** a word from which other words have developed **6** *maths* a factor of a quantity that, when multiplied by itself a specified number of times, produces that quantity, eg 2 is the square root of 4 and the cube root of 8 ▶VERB **1** to form roots and begin to grow **2** to be fixed **root out** *or* **root up** **1** to tear up by the roots **2** to get rid of completely **take root** **1** to form roots and grow firmly **2** to become firmly fixed

root[2] VERB **1** of an animal: to turn up ground in a search for food **2** to search (about)

rooted ADJECTIVE firmly planted

rope NOUN **1** a thick cord, made by twisting strands together **2** anything resembling a thick cord ▶VERB **1** to fasten or catch with a rope **2** to enclose, mark off with a rope

rose[1] *past tense* of **rise**

rose[2] NOUN **1** a type of flower, often scented, usually growing on a prickly bush **2** a deep pink colour

rosé (*pronounced* **roh**-zei) NOUN a pink-coloured wine produced by removing the skins of red grapes during fermentation

rosehip NOUN the fruit of the rose

rosemary NOUN an evergreen, sweet-smelling shrub, used as a cooking herb

rosette NOUN a badge shaped like a rose, made of ribbons

rosewood NOUN a dark Brazilian or Indian wood, which smells of roses when cut

roster NOUN a list showing a repeated order of duties etc

rosy ADJECTIVE (**rosier, rosiest**) **1** red, pink **2** (of the future etc) bright, hopeful

rot VERB (**rotting, rotted**) to go bad, decay ▸NOUN **1** decay **2** *informal* nonsense

rota NOUN a list of duties etc to be repeated in a set order

rotary ADJECTIVE turning round like a wheel

rotate VERB **1** to turn round like a wheel **2** to go through a repeating series of changes

rotation NOUN **1** an act of rotating or state of being rotated **2** one complete turn around an axis **3** *maths* a transformation of a plane with a rotating movement around an axis (*compare with*: **enlargement, reflection, translation**) **4** a regular and recurring sequence **5** (*also called*: **crop rotation**) the growing of different crops in a field, usually in an ordered sequence, to help keep the land fertile

rotor NOUN a turning part of a motor, dynamo, etc

rotten ADJECTIVE **1** decayed, bad **2** *informal* worthless, disgraceful

rotter NOUN, *informal* a very bad, worthless person

rotund ADJECTIVE round

rotundity NOUN roundness

rouble *or* **ruble** (*both pronounced* **roo**-bl) NOUN the standard unit of Russian coinage

rough ADJECTIVE **1** not smooth **2** uneven **3** coarse, harsh **4** boisterous, wild **5** not exact: *a rough guess* **6** stormy ▸NOUN **1** a hooligan, a bully **2** rough ground **rough and ready** not fine or carefully made, but effective **rough out** to sketch or shape roughly

roughage NOUN bran or fibre in food

roughen VERB to make rough

roulette NOUN a gambling game, played with a ball which is placed on a wheel

round ADJECTIVE **1** shaped like a circle **2** plump **3** even, exact: *a round dozen* ▸ADVERB & PREPOSITION **1** on all sides (of), around: *look round the room* **2** in a circle (about): *The earth moves round the sun* **3** from one (person, place, etc) to another: *The news went round* ▸NOUN **1** a circle, something round in shape **2** a single bullet or shell **3** a burst of firing, cheering etc **4** a song in which the singers take up the tune in turn **5** a usual route: *a postman's round* **6** a series of regular activities **7** each stage of a contest ▸VERB **1** to make or become round **2** of a ship: to go round (eg a headland) **round on** to make a sudden attack on **round up** to gather or drive together

roundabout NOUN **1** a revolving machine for children to ride on in a park etc **2** a meeting place of roads, where traffic must move in a circle ▸ADJECTIVE not straight or direct: *a roundabout route*

rounders SINGULAR NOUN a ball game played with a bat in which players run around a series of stations

a b c d e f g h i j k l m n o p q r s t u v w x y z

A B C D E F G H I J K L M N O P Q R S T U V W X Y Z

Roundhead NOUN a supporter of Parliament during the English Civil War (*compare with*: **Cavalier**) ℹ Because of the short-cut hair favoured by these soldiers

roundly ADVERB boldly, plainly: *He was roundly defeated*

round trip NOUN a journey to a place and back

rouse VERB **1** to awaken **2** to stir up, excite

rousing ADJECTIVE stirring, exciting

rout NOUN a complete defeat ▶ VERB to defeat utterly

route (*pronounced* root) NOUN the course to be followed, a way of getting to somewhere ▶ VERB to fix the route of

routine NOUN a fixed, unchanging order of doing things ▶ ADJECTIVE regular, usual: *routine enquiries*

rove VERB to wander or roam

rover NOUN **1** a wanderer; an unsettled person **2** *history* a pirate

Rover Scout NOUN an older member of the Scout Association

row[1] (*pronounced* roh) NOUN a line of people or things ▶ VERB to drive (a boat) by oars

row[2] (*pronounced* roh) NOUN a trip in a rowing boat

rowan (*pronounced* **roh**-*an or* **row**-*an*) NOUN a tree with clusters of bright red berries (*also called*: **mountain ash**)

rowdy ADJECTIVE (**rowdier, rowdiest**) noisy, disorderly

rower NOUN someone who rows a boat

rowing boat NOUN a boat rowed by oars

royal ADJECTIVE **1** relating to a king or queen **2** splendid, magnificent: *a royal welcome*

royal blue NOUN a deep, bright blue

royal jelly NOUN a jelly secreted by worker bees to feed developing larvae

royalty NOUN (*plural* **royalties**) **1** the state of being royal **2** royal people as a whole **3** a sum paid to the author of a book for each copy sold

RSA ABBREVIATION **1** Royal Society of Arts **2** Royal Scottish Academy

RSPB ABBREVIATION Royal Society for the Protection of Birds

RSPCA ABBREVIATION Royal Society for the Prevention of Cruelty to Animals

RSVP ABBREVIATION please reply

rub VERB (**rubbing, rubbed**) **1** to move one thing against the surface of another **2** to clean, polish (something) ▶ NOUN **1** the act of rubbing **2** a wipe **rub in 1** to work into (a surface) by rubbing **2** to keep reminding someone of (something unpleasant) **rub out** *or* **away** to remove (a mark)

rubber NOUN **1** a tough elastic substance made from plant juices **2** a piece of rubber used for erasing pencil marks

rubber bullet NOUN a hard rubber pellet fired by police in riot control

rubber stamp NOUN an instrument with rubber figures or letters for stamping dates etc on paper

rubber-stamp VERB to authorize, approve

rubbish NOUN **1** waste material, litter **2** nonsense

rubble NOUN small, rough stones, bricks etc left from a building

ruble *another spelling* of **rouble**

ruby NOUN (*plural* **rubies**) a type of red precious stone

ruck NOUN a wrinkle, a crease

rucksack NOUN a bag carried on the back by walkers, climbers, etc

rudder NOUN a device fixed to the stern of a boat, or tail of an aeroplane, for steering

ruddy ADJECTIVE (**ruddier, ruddiest**) **1** red **2** of the face: rosy, in good health

rude ADJECTIVE **1** showing bad manners, not polite **2** roughly made: *a rude shelter* **3** rough, not refined **4** startling and sudden: *a rude awakening* **5** coarse, vulgar, lewd
> **rudely** ADVERB

rudimentary ADJECTIVE in an early stage of development

rue[1] VERB (**ruing** *or* **rueing, rued**) to be sorry for, regret

rue[2] NOUN a shrub with bitter-tasting leaves

rueful ADJECTIVE sorrowful, regretful

ruff NOUN **1** in the past, a pleated frill worn round the neck **2** a band of feathers round a bird's neck

ruffle VERB **1** to make unsmooth, crumple (eg hair, a bird's feathers) **2** to annoy, offend

rug NOUN **1** a floor mat **2** a blanket

rugby *or* **Rugby** NOUN a form of football using an oval ball which can be handled

ⓘ Named after *Rugby* School in Warwickshire, where the game was supposedly invented

rugged (*pronounced* **rug**-id) ADJECTIVE **1** having a rough, uneven appearance **2** strong, robust **3** stern, harsh

ruin NOUN **1** complete loss of money etc **2** a downfall **3** (often **ruins**) the broken-down remains of a building ▸VERB **1** to destroy **2** to spoil completely: *ruin your chances* **3** to make very poor

ruination NOUN the act of ruining or state of being ruined

ruined ADJECTIVE in ruins, destroyed

ruinous ADJECTIVE **1** ruined **2** likely to cause ruin

rule NOUN **1** government: *under military rule* **2** a regulation: *school rules* **3** what usually happens **4** a guiding principle **5** *maths* a procedure **6** a measuring ruler ▸VERB **1** to govern, be in power **2** to decide (that) **3** to draw (a line) **4** to mark with lines **as a rule** usually **rule out** to leave out, not consider

ruler NOUN **1** someone who rules **2** a marked tool for measuring length and drawing straight lines

ruling ADJECTIVE governing; most important ▸NOUN a decision, a rule

rum NOUN an alcoholic spirit made from sugar cane

rumble VERB to make a low rolling noise like that of thunder etc ▸NOUN a low rolling noise

rummage VERB to turn things over in search ▸NOUN a thorough search

rumour *or US* **rumor** NOUN **1** general talk **2** a story passed from person to person which may not be true ▸ VERB **1** to spread a rumour of **2** to tell widely

rump NOUN **1** the hind part of an animal **2** the meat from this part

rumple VERB **1** to make untidy **2** to crease

rumpus NOUN, *informal* an uproar, a clamour

run VERB (**running, ran, run**) **1** to move swiftly, hurry **2** to race **3** to travel: *The train runs every day* **4** of water: to flow **5** to follow a certain route: *the main road running between Glasgow and Edinburgh* **6** of a machine: to work **7** to spread (rapidly): *This colour is running* **8** to continue, extend: *The programme runs for two hours* **9** to operate (machinery etc) **10** to organize, conduct (a business etc) **11** to compete with other candidates in an election ▸ NOUN **1** a trip **2** a distance run **3** a spell of running **4** a continuous period: *a run of good luck* **5** a ladder in a stocking etc **6** free use of: *the run of the house* **7** a single score in cricket **8** an enclosure for hens etc **run a risk** to take a chance of loss, failure, etc **run down 1** to knock (someone) down **2** to speak ill of **run into 1** to bump into, collide with **2** to meet accidentally **run out of** to become short of **run over** to knock down or pass over with a car

runaway NOUN a person that runs away ▸ ADJECTIVE of an animal or vehicle: out of control and moving very fast

run-down ADJECTIVE in poor health or condition

rung[1] NOUN a step of a ladder

rung[2] *past participle* of **ring**[2]

runner NOUN **1** someone who runs **2** a messenger **3** a plant stem that grows along the surface of the ground **4** a blade of a skate or sledge **do a runner** *slang* to leave without paying a bill

runner-up NOUN (*plural* **runners-up**) someone who comes second in a race or competition

running NOUN **1** the act of moving fast **2** management, control ▸ ADJECTIVE **1** for use in running: *running shoes* **2** giving out fluid: *a running sore* **3** carried on continuously: *a running commentary* ▸ ADVERB one after another: *three days running* **in** (or **out of**) **the running** having (or not having) a chance of success

runny ADJECTIVE (**runnier, runniest**) **1** running with liquid: *a runny egg* **2** too watery **3** of the nose: discharging mucus

run-of-the-mill ADJECTIVE ordinary

runway NOUN a path for aircraft to take off from or land on

rupee (*pronounced* roo-**pee**) NOUN the standard currency of India, Pakistan, and Sri Lanka

rupture NOUN **1** a breaking, eg of a friendship **2** a tear in a part of the body ▸ VERB to break, burst

rural ADJECTIVE of the country (*contrasted with*: **urban**)

ruse (*pronounced* rooz) NOUN a trick, a cunning plan

rush[1] VERB **1** to move quickly, hurry **2** to make (someone) hurry **3** to

A B C D E F G H I J K L M N O P Q R S T U V W X Y Z

take (a fort etc) by a sudden attack ▶NOUN (*plural* **rushes**) **1** a quick forward movement **2** a hurry

rush² NOUN (*plural* **rushes**) a tall grasslike plant growing near water

rusk NOUN a hard, dry biscuit like toast, especially as a baby food

russet ADJECTIVE reddish-brown ▶NOUN a type of apple of russet colour

rust NOUN a reddish-brown coating on metal, caused by air and moisture ▶VERB to form rust

rustic ADJECTIVE **1** relating to the country **2** roughly made **3** simple, unsophisticated ▶NOUN someone who lives in the country

rustle (*pronounced* **ru**-sl) VERB **1** of silk etc: to make a soft, whispering sound **2** to steal (cattle) ▶NOUN a soft, whispering sound **rustle up** *informal* to prepare quickly: *rustle up a meal*

rustler NOUN someone who steals cattle

rusty ADJECTIVE (**rustier, rustiest**) **1** covered with rust **2** *informal* showing lack of practice: *My French is rusty*

rut NOUN a deep track made by a wheel etc **in a rut** having a dull, routine way of life

ruthless (*pronounced* **rooth**-lis) ADJECTIVE without pity, cruel

rutted ADJECTIVE full of ruts

rye NOUN a kind of grain

Ss

S ABBREVIATION **1** south **2** southern

Sabbath NOUN the day of the week regularly set aside for religious services and rest (among Muslims, Friday; Jews, Saturday; and Christians, Sunday)

sabbatical NOUN a period of paid leave from work

sable NOUN a small weasel-like animal with dark brown or blackish fur ▸ADJECTIVE black or dark brown in colour

sabotage (*pronounced* **sab**-ot-ahsz) NOUN deliberate destruction of machinery, an organization, etc by enemies or dissatisfied workers ▸VERB to destroy or damage deliberately

From a French word meaning 'clog', popularly supposed to refer to a form of protest in which workers put their clogs into machines in order to stop them working

saboteur (*pronounced* sab-ot-**er**) NOUN someone who carries out sabotage: *hunt saboteurs*

sabre NOUN, *history* a curved sword used by cavalry

sac NOUN, *biology* any bag-like part in a plant or animal, especially containing liquid

saccharin *or* **saccharine** NOUN a very sweet substance used as a sugar substitute

sachet (*pronounced* **sash**-ei) NOUN **1** a small sealed packet containing powder or liquid, eg shampoo **2** a small bag containing pot pourri, used to perfume drawers etc

sack[1] NOUN **1** a large bag of coarse cloth for holding flour etc **2** (**the sack**) *informal* dismissal from your job ▸VERB, *informal* to dismiss from a job **get the sack** *informal* to be dismissed from your job

sack[2] NOUN the plundering of a captured town ▸VERB to plunder

sackcloth NOUN **1** coarse cloth for making sacks **2** a garment made of this, worn as a sign of repentance

sacking NOUN sackcloth

sacral (*pronounced* **seik**-ral) ADJECTIVE of the sacrum

Comes from Latin *sacrum* meaning 'a sacred object' + suffix *-al*

> Do not confuse with: **sacred**

sacrament NOUN a religious ceremony, *eg* baptism or communion

sacred ADJECTIVE **1** holy **2** dedicated to some purpose or person: *sacred to her memory* **3** religious: *sacred music*

ℹ Comes from Middle English *sacre* meaning 'make holy', combined with the suffix *-ed* to give the sense of 'made holy'

> Do not confuse with: **sacral**

sacrifice NOUN **1** the offering of an animal killed on an altar to a god **2** an animal etc offered to a god **3** the giving up of something for the benefit of another person or to gain something more important **4** something given up for this purpose ▶ VERB **1** to offer (an animal etc) as a sacrifice to a god **2** to give up (something) for someone or something else

sacrificial ADJECTIVE of or for sacrifice

sacrilege (*pronounced* **sak**-re-lij) NOUN the use of something holy in a blasphemous way > **sacrilegious** ADJECTIVE

sacrosanct ADJECTIVE **1** very sacred **2** not to be harmed or touched

sacrum (*pronounced* **seik**-rum) NOUN a triangular bone forming part of the human pelvis

sad ADJECTIVE (**sadder, saddest**) **1** sorrowful, unhappy **2** showing sorrow **3** causing sorrow: *sad story* **4** *informal* pitiful, feeble

sadden VERB to make or become sad

saddle NOUN **1** a seat for a rider on the back of a horse or bicycle **2** a cut or joint of meat from the back of an animal ▶ VERB to put a saddle on (an animal)

saddler NOUN a maker of saddles and harnesses

sadism (*pronounced* **seid**-i-zm) NOUN taking pleasure in cruelty to others

sadist (*pronounced* **seid**-ist) NOUN someone who gets pleasure from inflicting pain and suffering on others

sadistic (*pronounced* sa-**dis**-tik) ADJECTIVE getting, or seeming to get, pleasure from inflicting pain and suffering on others

SAE *or* **sae** ABBREVIATION stamped addressed envelope

safari NOUN an expedition for observing or hunting wild animals

safe ADJECTIVE **1** unharmed **2** free from harm or danger **3** reliable, trustworthy ▶ NOUN **1** a lockable box for keeping money and valuables **2** a storage place for meat etc **safe and sound** unharmed

safeguard NOUN anything that gives protection or security ▶ VERB to protect

safety NOUN freedom from harm or danger ▶ ADJECTIVE giving protection or safety: *safety harness*

saffron NOUN a type of crocus whose stigmas are dried and used to dye food yellow and flavour it

sag VERB (**sagging, sagged**) to droop or sink in the middle

saga NOUN **1** an ancient story about heroes etc **2** a novel or series of novels about several generations of a family **3** a long detailed story

sage NOUN **1** a type of herb with

A B C D E F G H I J K L M N O P Q R S T U V W X Y Z

grey-green leaves which are used for flavouring **2** a wise man ▸ADJECTIVE wise > **sagely** ADVERB

said ADJECTIVE mentioned before: *the said shopkeeper* ▸VERB *past form of* **say**

sail NOUN **1** a sheet of canvas spread out to catch the wind and drive forward a ship or boat **2** a journey in a ship or boat **3** an arm of a windmill ▸VERB **1** to travel in a ship or boat (with or without sails) **2** to navigate or steer a ship or boat **3** to begin a sea voyage **4** to glide along easily **set sail** to set out on a sea voyage

sailor NOUN **1** someone who sails **2** a member of a ship's crew

saint NOUN **1** a very good or holy person **2** (*abbrev* **St**) a title conferred after death on a holy person by the Roman Catholic Church

Saint Bernard *or* **St Bernard** NOUN a breed of large dog, famous for its use in mountain rescues

ⓘ From the use of such dogs by monks to rescue snowbound travellers in the *Saint Bernard* passes in the Alps

sainted ADJECTIVE very holy or very good

saintly ADJECTIVE (**saintlier, saintliest**) **1** relating to a saint or the saints **2** very good or holy

sake NOUN **1** cause, purpose: *for the sake of making money* **2** benefit, advantage: *for my sake*

salaam NOUN a low bow with the right palm on the forehead, a form of Eastern greeting ▸VERB to perform this greeting

salad NOUN a dish of raw vegetables, eg lettuce, tomatoes, etc

salamander NOUN a kind of small lizard-like animal

salami NOUN a type of highly seasoned sausage, usually eaten cold and thinly sliced

salary NOUN (*plural* **salaries**) fixed wages regularly paid for work

ⓘ Based on a Latin word for 'salt', from the money given to Roman soldiers to buy salt

salat NOUN the prayers said by Muslims five times daily

sale NOUN **1** the exchange of anything for money **2** a selling of goods at reduced prices **3** an auction

salesman, saleswoman *or* **salesperson** NOUN someone who sells or shows goods to customers

salient ADJECTIVE **1** pointing outwards: *salient angle* **2** outstanding, chief: *salient points of the speech*

saline ADJECTIVE containing salt, salty: *saline solution*

saliva NOUN the liquid that forms in the mouth to help digestion; spittle

salivate VERB **1** to produce saliva **2** to anticipate keenly

sallow ADJECTIVE (**sallower, sallowest**) of complexion: pale, yellowish

salmon (*pronounced* **sam**-*on*) NOUN a large fish with yellowish-pink flesh

salmonella (*pronounced* **sal**-*mon-el-a*) NOUN a bacterium which causes food poisoning

salon NOUN **1** a shop in which hairdressing etc is done **2** a large room for receiving important guests **3** a gathering of such people

saloon NOUN **1** a passengers' dining-room in a ship **2** any car with an enclosed compartment **3** a public house, a bar

salt NOUN **1** a substance used for seasoning, either mined from the earth or obtained from sea water **2** a chemical compound that is formed when an acid reacts with a base **3** *informal* a sailor ▶ADJECTIVE **1** containing salt: *salt water* **2** tasting of salt **3** preserved in salt: *salt herring* ▶VERB **1** to sprinkle with salt **2** to preserve with salt

salty ADJECTIVE (**saltier, saltiest**) **1** tasting of salt **2** piquant, racy

salubrious ADJECTIVE **1** health-giving **2** pleasant, respectable: *not a very salubrious neighbourhood*

salute VERB **1** to greet with words, an embrace, etc **2** *military* to raise the hand to the forehead to show respect to **3** to honour someone by a firing of guns etc ▶NOUN an act or way of saluting

salvage NOUN **1** goods saved from destruction or waste **2** the act of saving a ship's cargo, goods from a fire, etc **3** payment made for this act ▶VERB to save from loss or ruin

salvation NOUN **1** an act, means or cause of saving: *The arrival of the police was his salvation* **2** the saving of humanity from sin

salve NOUN an ointment for healing or soothing ▶VERB to soothe (pride, conscience, etc)

same ADJECTIVE **1** exactly alike, identical: *We both had the same feeling* **2** not different, unchanged: *He still looks the same* **3** mentioned before: *The same person came again* ▶PRONOUN the thing just mentioned **all the same** *or* **just the same** in spite of that **at the same time** still, nevertheless

[i] Comes from Old Norse *same*

samovar NOUN a Russian tea-urn

sample NOUN a small part extracted to represent the whole ▶VERB **1** to test a sample of: *sample a cake* **2** *music* to mix (a short extract) from one recording into a different backing track

sampler NOUN **1** someone who takes samples **2** a piece of needlework etc showing skill in different techniques

sanatorium NOUN (*plural* **sanatoriums** *or* **sanatoria**) **1** a hospital, especially for people suffering from respiratory diseases **2** a sick-room in a school etc

sanctify VERB (**sanctifies, sanctifying, sanctified**) to make holy or sacred > **sanctification** NOUN

sanctimonious ADJECTIVE self-righteous, priggish

sanction NOUN **1** permission, approval **2** a penalty for breaking a law or rule **3** (**sanctions**) measures applied to force another country etc to stop a course of action

sanctity NOUN holiness; sacredness

sanctuary NOUN (*plural* **sanctuaries**) **1** a sacred place **2** the most sacred part of a temple or church **3** a place of safety from arrest or violence **4** a protected reserve for birds or animals

sanctum NOUN: **inner sanctum** a very sacred or private room etc

sand NOUN **1** a mass of tiny particles of crushed rocks etc **2** (**sands**) a stretch of sand on the seashore ▶ VERB **1** to sprinkle with sand **2** to add sand to **3** to smooth or polish with sandpaper

sandal NOUN a shoe with straps to hold the sole onto the foot

sandalwood NOUN a fragrant E Indian wood

sand dune NOUN a ridge of sand blown up by the wind

sandpaper NOUN paper with a layer of sand glued to it for smoothing and polishing

sandshoe NOUN a light shoe with a canvas upper and rubber sole

sandstone NOUN a soft rock made of layers of sand pressed together

sandwich NOUN (*plural* **sandwiches**) two slices of bread, or a split roll, stuffed with a filling ▶ VERB to fit between two other objects

ⓘ After the 18th-century Earl of *Sandwich*, said to have invented it to allow him to gamble without interruption for meals

sandy ADJECTIVE (**sandier, sandiest**) **1** covered with sand **2** like sand **3** of hair: yellowish-red in colour

sane ADJECTIVE **1** of sound mind, not mad **2** sensible > **sanely** ADVERB

sang *past tense* of **sing**

sangui- PREFIX of or relating to blood

ⓘ Comes from Latin *sanguis* meaning 'blood'

sanguine ADJECTIVE **1** hopeful, cheerful **2** of a complexion: red, ruddy

ⓘ Comes from Latin *sanguineus* meaning 'blood-stained'

sanitary ADJECTIVE **1** promoting good health, especially by having good drainage and sewage disposal **2** free from dirt, infection, etc

sanitation NOUN arrangements for protecting health, especially drainage and sewage disposal

sanity NOUN **1** soundness of mind **2** mental health **3** good sense or judgement

sank *past tense* of **sink**

sanserif (*pronounced* san-**ser**-if) NOUN a printing font having characters without serifs

Sanskrit NOUN the ancient literary language of India

sap NOUN **1** the juice in plants, trees, etc that contains vital sugars and other nutrients **2** *informal* a weakling, a fool ▶ VERB (**sapping, sapped**) to weaken (someone's strength etc)

sapling NOUN a young tree

sapphire NOUN a precious stone of a deep blue colour

Saracen NOUN, *history* an Islamic opponent of the Crusaders; a Moor

sarcasm NOUN **1** scornful humour, characterized by the use of a mocking tone to say the exact opposite of what you really think **2** a hurtful remark made in scorn

sarcastic ADJECTIVE **1** of a remark: containing sarcasm **2** often using sarcasm, scornful > **sarcastically** ADVERB

sarcophagus NOUN a stone coffin

sardine NOUN a young pilchard, often tinned in oil **like sardines** crowded closely together

sardonic ADJECTIVE bitter, mocking, scornful

sari NOUN a long cloth wrapped round the waist and brought over the shoulder, traditionally worn by Indian women

sarong NOUN a skirt traditionally worn by Malay men and women

sartorial ADJECTIVE relating to dress or clothes: *sartorial elegance*

sash[1] NOUN (*plural* **sashes**) a decorative band worn round the waist or over the shoulder

sash[2] NOUN (*plural* **sashes**) a sliding frame for window panes

sat *past form* of **sit**

Satan NOUN the Devil

Satanic ADJECTIVE of Satan, devilish

satanism NOUN devil worship

satchel NOUN a small bag for carrying schoolbooks etc

satellite NOUN **1** a moon orbiting a larger planet **2** a man-made object launched into space to orbit a planet **3** a state controlled by a more powerful neighbour

satellite television NOUN the broadcasting of television programmes via satellite

satiate VERB to satisfy fully; to give more than enough to

satin NOUN a closely woven silk with a glossy surface

satire NOUN **1** a piece of writing etc which makes fun of particular people or events **2** ridicule, scorn

satirical ADJECTIVE containing or using satire to attack or criticize someone or something

satirist NOUN a writer of satire

satisfaction NOUN **1** the act of satisfying or being satisfied **2** a feeling of pleasure or comfort **3** something that satisfies **4** compensation for damage etc

satisfactory ADJECTIVE **1** satisfying **2** fulfilling the necessary requirements
> **satisfactorily** ADVERB: *He completed the test satisfactorily*

satisfy VERB (**satisfies, satisfying, satisfied**) **1** to give enough (of something) to **2** to please, make content **3** to give enough to lessen or quieten: *satisfied her curiosity* **4** to convince: *satisfied that he was innocent* **5** to fulfil: *satisfy all our requirements*

satsuma NOUN a small seedless orange

saturate VERB **1** to soak or immerse in water **2** to cover or fill completely (with): *saturated with information*

saturated ADJECTIVE **1** soaked in water **2** *chemistry* of a compound: unable to be combined with any other atoms **3** *chemistry* of a solution: unable to dissolve any more of a solute (*contrasted with*: **unsaturated**)

saturated fat NOUN a fat that can raise the amount of cholesterol in the blood

saturation NOUN saturating or being saturated: *The market has reached saturation point*

A B C D E F G H I J K L M N O P Q R S T U V W X Y Z

Saturday NOUN the seventh day of the week
[i] After *Saturn*, an old Roman god of the harvest

satyr (*pronounced* **sat**-er) NOUN a mythological creature, half man, half goat, living in the woods

sauce NOUN **1** a liquid seasoning added to food to improve flavour **2** *informal* cheek, impudence

saucepan NOUN a deep-sided cooking pan, usually with a long handle

saucer NOUN a small, shallow dish for placing under a cup

saucy ADJECTIVE (**saucier, sauciest**) impudent, cheeky

sauna NOUN a room filled with steam to induce sweating

saunter VERB to stroll about without hurrying ▶NOUN a leisurely stroll

sausage NOUN minced meat seasoned and stuffed into a tube of animal gut etc

savage ADJECTIVE **1** wild, untamed **2** fierce and cruel **3** uncivilized **4** very angry ▶NOUN **1** an uncivilized person **2** someone fierce or cruel ▶VERB to attack very fiercely
> **savagely** ADVERB

savagery NOUN extreme cruelty or fierceness

savanna *or* **savannah** NOUN, *geography* a grassy, treeless plain

save VERB **1** to bring out of danger, rescue **2** to protect from harm, damage or loss **3** to keep from spending or using: *saving money/saves time* **4** to put money aside for the future **5** *computing* to transfer (data etc) onto a disk or tape for storage ▶PREPOSITION except (for): *All the CDs were damaged save this one* **save up** to put money aside for future use

savings PLURAL NOUN money put aside for the future

saviour NOUN **1** someone who saves others from harm or evil **2** (**Saviour**) *Christianity* Jesus Christ

savour NOUN **1** characteristic taste or flavour **2** an interesting quality ▶VERB **1** to taste or smell of **2** to taste with enjoyment **3** to have a trace or suggestion (of): *His reaction savours of jealousy* **4** to experience

savoury ADJECTIVE **1** having a pleasant taste or smell **2** salt or sharp in flavour; not sweet ▶NOUN (*plural* **savouries**) a savoury dish or snack

saw[1] NOUN **1** a tool with a toothed edge for cutting wood etc **2** *old* a wise saying ▶VERB (**sawing, sawed, sawn**) to cut with a saw

saw[2] *past tense* of **see**

sawdust NOUN a dust of fine fragments of wood, made in sawing

Saxon NOUN, *history* one of a Germanic people who invaded southern Britain in the 5th and 6th centuries

saxophone NOUN a wind instrument with a curved metal tube and keys for the fingers
[i] After Belgian Adolfe *Sax*, who invented it in the 19th century

saxophonist NOUN a player of the saxophone

say VERB (**saying, said**) **1** to speak,

utter: *Why don't you say 'Yes'?* **2** to express in words, state: *They said they knew him* ▶ NOUN **1** the right to speak: *no say in the matter* **2** the opportunity to speak: *I've had my say* > **I say!** INTERJECTION **1** expressing surprise or protest **2** used to try to attract attention **that is to say** in other words

ⓘ Comes from Old English *secgan*

saying NOUN something often said; a proverb

scab NOUN **1** a crust formed over a sore **2** any of several diseases of animals or plants **3** *informal* a blackleg

scabby ADJECTIVE (**scabbier, scabbiest**) **1** covered in scabs **2** *informal* disgusting, revolting

scabies NOUN an itchy skin disease

scaffold NOUN a platform on which people are put to death by hanging

scaffolding NOUN a framework of poles and platforms used by people doing repairs on a building etc

scalar NOUN, *maths* a quantity, eg mass, length or speed, that has magnitude but not direction (*compare with*: **vector**)

scald VERB **1** to burn with hot liquid or steam **2** to heat (milk etc) to just below boiling point ▶ NOUN a burn caused by hot liquid or steam

scale[1] NOUN **1** a set of regularly spaced marks for measurement on a thermometer etc **2** a series or system of increasing values: *salary scale* **3** *music* a group of notes going up or down in order **4** the ratio of a representation of something to its actual size: *drawn to the scale 1:50,000* **5** the size of a business etc: *manufacture on a small scale* ▶ VERB to climb up

scale[2] NOUN a small thin flake on the skin of a fish or snake ▶ VERB **1** to remove the scales from (eg a fish) **2** to remove in thin layers

scale[3] NOUN (*usually* **scales**) a weighing machine

scalene ADJECTIVE of a triangle: having each side of a different length

scallop NOUN a shellfish with a pair of hinged fan-shaped shells

scalloped ADJECTIVE of an edge: cut into curves or notches

scalp NOUN **1** the outer covering of the skull **2** the skin and hair on top of the head ▶ VERB to cut the scalp from

scalpel NOUN a small, thin-bladed knife, used in surgery

scaly ADJECTIVE (**scalier, saliest**) having scales; flaky

scamper VERB **1** to run about playfully **2** to run off in haste

scampi PLURAL NOUN large prawns cooked for eating

scan VERB (**scanning, scanned**) **1** to examine carefully **2** *informal* to read quickly, skim over **3** to pass an X-ray, ultrasonic wave, etc over **4** of poetry: to have the correct number of beats: *This line doesn't scan* ▶ NOUN an act of scanning

scandal NOUN **1** something disgraceful or shocking **2** talk or gossip about people's (supposed) misdeeds

scandalize *or* **scandalise** VERB to shock, horrify

scandalous ADJECTIVE **1** shameful,

A B C D E F G H I J K L M N O P Q R S T U V W X Y Z

disgraceful **2** containing scandal **>** **scandalously** ADVERB

scanner NOUN a machine which scans, eg a device for scanning and recording graphic images so that they can be edited or viewed on a computer

scant ADJECTIVE not plentiful, hardly enough: *pay scant attention*

scanty ADJECTIVE (**scantier, scantiest**) little or not enough in amount: *scanty clothing* **> scantily** ADVERB

scapegoat NOUN someone who bears the blame for the wrongdoing of others

ⓘ Literally 'escape goat', after an ancient Jewish ritual of transferring the people's sins to a goat which was afterwards let free in the wilderness

scar NOUN **1** the mark left by a wound or sore **2** a mark, a blemish ▶ VERB (**scarring, scarred**) to mark with a scar

scarab NOUN a beetle regarded as sacred by the ancient Egyptians

scarce ADJECTIVE **1** not plentiful, not enough **2** rare, seldom found **make yourself scarce** to go, run away

scarcely ADVERB **1** only just, barely: *could scarcely hear* **2** surely not: *You can scarcely expect me to eat that*

scarcity NOUN (*plural* **scarcities**) want, shortage

scare VERB **1** to drive away with fear **2** to startle, frighten ▶ NOUN a sudden fright or alarm

scarecrow NOUN a figure set up to scare birds away from crops

scarey *another spelling of* **scary**

scarf NOUN (*plural* **scarves** *or* **scarfs**) a length of fabric worn round the neck, shoulders or head

scarlet NOUN a bright red colour ▶ ADJECTIVE bright red

scarlet fever NOUN an infectious illness, causing a rash, fever and a sore throat

scarper VERB, *slang* to run away

scary *or* **scarey** ADJECTIVE (**scarier, scariest**) frightening

scathing ADJECTIVE cruel, hurtful: *scathing remark*

scatter VERB **1** to throw loosely about; sprinkle **2** to spread widely **3** to run away in all directions

scattered ADJECTIVE thrown or spread about widely

scattering NOUN a small amount thinly spread or scattered

scavenge VERB to search among waste for usable items **> scavenger** NOUN

scenario (*pronounced* si-**nah**-ri-oh) NOUN a scene-by-scene outline of a play, film, etc

ⓘ Comes from Italian *scenario* meaning 'scenery'

> Do not confuse with: **scene**

scene NOUN **1** the place where something happens: *scene of the accident* **2** a view, a landscape **3** a division of a play or opera **4** an area of activity: *the music scene* **5** a show of bad temper: *Don't make a scene*

ⓘ Comes from Latin *scaena*

meaning 'the scene presented' or 'the stage'

> Do not confuse with: **scenario**

scenery NOUN **1** the painted background on a theatre stage **2** the general appearance of a stretch of country

scenic ADJECTIVE **1** of scenery **2** picturesque

scent VERB **1** to discover by the smell **2** to have a suspicion of, sense: *scent danger* **3** to give a pleasant smell to: *Roses scented the air* ▶ NOUN **1** perfume **2** an odour, a smell **3** the trail of smell used to track an animal etc

sceptic (*pronounced* **skep**-tik) NOUN someone who doubts what they are told

Comes from Greek *skeptikos* meaning 'thoughtful'

> Do not confuse with: **septic**

sceptical (*pronounced* **skep**-tik-*a*l) ADJECTIVE unwilling to believe, doubtful > **sceptically** ADVERB

scepticism (*pronounced* **skep**-ti-sizm) NOUN a doubting state or attitude

sceptre (*pronounced* **sep**-ter) NOUN an ornamental rod carried by a monarch on ceremonial occasions

schedule (*pronounced* **shed**-yool *or* **sked**-yool) NOUN **1** the time set for doing something: *I'm two weeks behind schedule* **2** a written statement of details **3** a form for filling in information ▶ VERB **1** to form into a schedule **2** to plan, arrange

scheme (*pronounced* skeem) NOUN **1** a plan, a systematic arrangement **2** a dishonest or crafty plan ▶ VERB to make schemes, plot

scheming ADJECTIVE crafty, cunning

scherzo (*pronounced* **sker**-tsoh) NOUN, *music* (*plural* **scherzos**) a lively movement in triple time

schism (*pronounced* **si**-zm *or* **ski**-zm) NOUN a breaking away from the main group

schizo- (*pronounced* **skit**-so) PREFIX forms words containing the idea of a split or division: *schizophrenia* (= literally, 'a split mind')

Comes from Greek *schizein* meaning 'to split'

schizophrenia (*pronounced* skit-s*o*f-**ree**-ni-*a*) NOUN a mental illness involving a distorted perception of reality > **schizophrenic** NOUN & ADJECTIVE

scholar NOUN **1** someone of great learning **2** someone who has been awarded a scholarship **3** a pupil, a student

scholarly ADJECTIVE showing or having knowledge, high intelligence and a love of accuracy > **scholarliness** NOUN

scholarship NOUN **1** learning **2** a sum of money given to help a clever student to carry on further studies

school NOUN **1** a place for teaching, especially children **2** a group of artists etc who share the same ideas **3** a large number of fish, whales, etc ▶ VERB **1** to educate in a school **2** to train by practice

schooling NOUN **1** education in a school **2** training

A B C D E F G H I J K L M N O P Q R **S** T U V W X Y Z

schoolmaster *or* **schoolmistress** NOUN a teacher at a school

sci- PREFIX forms words containing the concept of knowledge: *science/prescient* (= having foreknowledge)
[i] Comes from Latin *scire* meaning 'to know', and *scientia* meaning 'knowledge'

science NOUN **1** knowledge obtained by observation and experiment **2** a branch of this knowledge, eg chemistry, physics, biology, etc **3** these sciences considered together

science fiction NOUN stories dealing with future life on earth, space travel, other planets, etc

scientific ADJECTIVE **1** of or relating to science **2** done according to the methods of science > **scientifically** ADVERB

scientist NOUN someone who studies one or more branches of science

sci fi ABBREVIATION science fiction

scimitar NOUN a sword with a short curved blade

scintillate VERB **1** to sparkle **2** to show brilliant wit etc

scion (*pronounced* **sai**-on) NOUN **1** a young member of a family **2** a descendant **3** a cutting for grafting onto another plant

scissors PLURAL NOUN a cutting instrument with two hinged blades

scoff VERB to express scorn **scoff at someone** *or* **something** to make fun of, mock them

scold VERB to tell off; blame or rebuke with angry words ▶NOUN a bad-tempered person

scolding NOUN a telling-off

scone NOUN a small plain cake made with flour, milk and a little fat

scoop NOUN **1** a hollow instrument used for lifting loose material, water, etc **2** an exclusive news story ▶VERB to lift or dig out with a scoop

scooter NOUN **1** a two-wheeled toy vehicle pushed along by foot **2** a low-powered motorcycle

scope NOUN **1** opportunity or room to do something: *scope for improvement* **2** extent, range: *outside the scope of this dictionary*

-scope SUFFIX forms words describing devices which make things visible, or which allow examination of something which cannot be seen: *telescope/stethoscope*
[i] Comes from Greek *skopeein* meaning 'to view'

scorch VERB **1** to burn slightly, singe **2** to dry up with heat

scorching ADJECTIVE **1** burning, singeing **2** very hot **3** harsh, severe: *scorching criticism*

score NOUN **1** a gash, a notch **2** an account, a debt: *settle old scores* **3** the total number of points gained in a game **4** a written piece of music showing separate parts for voices and instruments **5** a set of twenty **6** (**scores**) a great many: *scores of people* **7** a reason, account: *Don't worry on that score* ▶VERB **1** to mark with lines or notches **2** to gain (points) **3** to keep a note of points gained in a game **score out** to cross out

scorn VERB **1** to look down on,

despise **2** to refuse (help etc) because of pride ▸NOUN mocking contempt

scornful ADJECTIVE full of scorn > **scornfully** ADVERB

scorpion NOUN a spider-like creature with a poisonous sting in its tail

scoundrel NOUN a rascal

scour VERB **1** to clean by hard rubbing; scrub **2** to search thoroughly: *Police are scouring the area*

scourge NOUN **1** a whip **2** a cause of great suffering ▸VERB **1** to whip, lash **2** to afflict, cause to suffer

scout NOUN **1** a guide or spy sent ahead to bring back information **2** (**Scout**) a member of the Scout Association

scowl VERB to wrinkle the brows in displeasure or anger ▸NOUN a frown

Scrabble NOUN, *trademark* a word-building game

scrabble VERB to scratch or grope about

scramble VERB **1** to struggle to seize something before others **2** to wriggle along on hands and knees **3** to mix or toss together: *scrambled eggs* **4** to jumble up (a message) to make it unintelligible without decoding: *a scrambled TV channel* ▸NOUN **1** a rush and struggle to get something **2** a motorcycle race over rough country

scrap NOUN **1** a small piece, a fragment **2** a picture for pasting in a scrapbook **3** *informal* a fight **4** parts of a car etc no longer required: *sold as scrap* **5** (**scraps**) small pieces, odds and ends ▸VERB (**scrapping, scrapped**) **1** to abandon as useless **2** *informal* to fight, quarrel

scrapbook NOUN a blank book in which to stick pictures etc

scrape VERB **1** to rub and mark with something sharp **2** to drag or rub against or across a surface with a harsh grating sound ▸NOUN **1** an act of scraping **2** a mark or sound made by scraping **3** *informal* a difficult situation **scrape through** to only just avoid failure **scrape something up** *or* **together** to collect (money etc) with difficulty

scrapheap NOUN a heap of old metal etc, a rubbish heap **on the scrapheap** no longer needed

scrappy ADJECTIVE (**scrappier, scrappiest**) made up of odd scraps, not well put together > **scrappily** ADVERB

scratch VERB **1** to draw a sharp point across the surface of **2** to mark by doing this **3** to tear or dig with claws, nails, etc **4** to rub with the nails to relieve or stop itching **5** to withdraw from a competition ▸NOUN (*plural* **scratches**) **1** a mark or sound made by scratching **2** a slight wound ▸ADJECTIVE **1** *golf* too good to be allowed a handicap **2** of a team: made up of players hastily got together **start from scratch** to start from nothing, right at the beginning **up to scratch** satisfactory

scrawl VERB to write or draw untidily or hastily ▸NOUN **1** untidy, hasty or bad writing **2** something scrawled

scrawny ADJECTIVE (**scrawnier, scrawniest**) thin, skinny

a b c d e f g h i j k l m n o p q r s t u v w x y z

A B C D E F G H I J K L M N O P Q R S T U V W X Y Z

scream VERB to utter a shrill, piercing cry as in fear etc; shriek ▶NOUN a shrill cry

screech VERB to utter a harsh, shrill and sudden cry ▶NOUN a harsh shrill cry

screen NOUN **1** a flat covered framework to shelter from view or protect from heat, cold, etc **2** something that shelters from wind, danger, difficulties, etc **3** the surface on which cinema films are projected **4** the surface on which a television picture, or computer data, appears ▶VERB **1** to shelter, hide **2** to make a film of **3** to show on a screen **4** to sift, sieve **5** to sort out (the good from the bad) by testing **6** to conduct examinations on someone to test for disease **screen off** to hide behind, or separate by, a screen

screenplay NOUN the written text for a film, with dialogue and descriptions of characters and setting

screen saver NOUN an animated image displayed on a computer screen when the computer is not in use

screw NOUN **1** a nail with a slotted head and a winding groove or ridge (called the **thread**) on its surface **2** a kind of propeller (a **screw-propeller**) with spiral blades, used in ships and aircraft **3** a turn or twist (of a screw etc) ▶VERB **1** to fasten or tighten with a screw **2** to fix (eg a lid) in place with a twisting movement **3** to twist, turn round (your head etc) **4** to twist up, crumple, pucker

scribble VERB **1** to write carelessly **2** to make untidy or meaningless marks with a pencil etc ▶NOUN **1** careless writing **2** meaningless marks, a doodle

scrimp VERB to be sparing or stingy with money: *scrimping and saving for a holiday*

script NOUN **1** the text of a play, talk, etc **2** a piece of handwriting

scripture NOUN **1** sacred writings **2** (**Scripture**) the Christian Bible

scroll NOUN **1** a piece of paper rolled up **2** an ornament shaped like this ▶VERB, *computing* to move text up or down on a screen to see more of a document

scroll bar NOUN a strip at the side of a computer screen, where you can click to scroll down or up

scrotum NOUN (*plural* **scrota** *or* **scrotums**) the bag of skin enclosing the testicles

scrounge VERB, *slang* **1** to cadge **2** to get by begging ▶NOUN an attempt to beg or cadge: *on the scrounge*

scrounger NOUN, *slang* a person who scrounges

scrub VERB (**scrubbing, scrubbed**) to rub hard in order to clean ▶NOUN countryside covered with low bushes

scruff NOUN the back of the neck

scruffy ADJECTIVE (**scruffier, scruffiest**) untidy

scrum NOUN, *rugby* a struggle for the ball by the forwards of the opposing sides bunched together

scrumptious ADJECTIVE, *informal* delicious

scrunch VERB to crumple

scrunchie NOUN a fabric band to tie back the hair

scruple NOUN doubt over what is right or wrong that makes someone reluctant to do something ▶VERB to hesitate because of a scruple

scrupulous ADJECTIVE careful over the smallest details

scrutiny NOUN (*plural* **scrutinies**) careful examination, a close look

scuba diving NOUN swimming underwater using a device consisting of a breathing tube attached to a cylinder of air

scud VERB (**scudding, scudded**) to move or sweep along quickly: *scudding clouds*

scuffle NOUN a confused fight

scull NOUN a short oar ▶VERB **1** to move (a boat) with a pair of these or with one oar worked at the back of the boat **2** to move in water by using the hands as paddles

scullery NOUN (*plural* **sculleries**) a room next to a kitchen for rough cleaning work

sculpt VERB to carve or model

sculptor *or* **sculptress** NOUN an artist who carves or models figures in wood, stone, clay, etc

sculpture NOUN **1** the art of the sculptor or sculptress **2** a piece of their work

scum NOUN **1** foam that rises to the surface of liquids **2** the most worthless part of anything: *the scum of the earth*

scurrilous ADJECTIVE insulting, abusive: *a scurrilous attack*

scurry VERB (**scurries, scurrying, scurried**) to hurry along, scamper

scurvy NOUN a type of disease caused by a lack of fresh fruit and vegetables

scuttle NOUN **1** a fireside container for coal **2** an opening with a lid in a ship's deck or side ▶VERB **1** to make a hole in (a ship) in order to sink it **2** to hurry along, scamper

scythe (*pronounced* saidh) NOUN a large curved blade, on a long handle, for cutting grass etc by hand ▶VERB to cut with a scythe

SE ABBREVIATION south-east; south-eastern

sea NOUN **1** the mass of salt water covering most of the earth's surface **2** a great stretch of water of less size than an ocean **3** a great expanse or number: *a sea of faces* **at sea 1** on the sea **2** completely puzzled

sea anemone NOUN a type of small plant-like animal found on rocks at the seashore

seabed NOUN the land at the bottom of the sea

seaboard NOUN land along the edge of the sea

seafront NOUN a promenade with its buildings facing the sea

seagull NOUN a type of web-footed sea bird

seahorse NOUN a type of small fish with a horse-like head and neck

seal[1] NOUN a four-flippered sea animal living partly on land

seal[2] NOUN **1** a piece of wax with a design pressed into it, attached to a document to show that it is legal or official **2** a piece of wax used to keep a parcel closed **3** anything that closes tightly or the state of being closed tightly: *an airtight seal* **4** a piece of sticky paper with a picture on it: *a Christmas seal* ▶ VERB **1** to mark or fasten with a seal **2** to close up completely **3** to make (legally) binding and definite: *seal a bargain*

sea level NOUN the level of the surface of the sea

sealing wax NOUN a quickly hardening, waxy substance for sealing letters, documents, etc

sea lion NOUN a large kind of seal, the male of which has a mane

seam NOUN **1** the line formed when you sew together two pieces of cloth **2** a line or layer of metal, coal, etc in the earth

seaman NOUN (*plural* **seamen**) a sailor, especially a member of a ship's crew who is not an officer

seamstress NOUN a woman who sews for a living

seamy ADJECTIVE (**seamier, seamiest**) sordid; disreputable **the seamy side** the more unpleasant side (eg of life)

séance (*pronounced* **sei**-ons) NOUN a meeting of people to receive messages from the spirits of the dead

seaplane NOUN an aeroplane which can take off from and land on the water

sear VERB **1** to scorch, burn **2** to hurt severely

search VERB **1** to look over in order to find something **2** (**search for something**) to look for it ▶ NOUN (*plural* **searches**) **1** an act of searching **2** an attempt to find

search engine NOUN on the Internet, a program that compares search requests against items in its index and returns search results to the user

searching ADJECTIVE examining closely and carefully: *searching question*

searchlight NOUN a strong beam of light used for picking out objects at night

seascape NOUN a picture of a scene at sea

seashore NOUN the land next to the sea

seasick ADJECTIVE made ill by the rocking movement of a ship

seaside NOUN the land beside the sea, especially a holiday resort

season NOUN **1** one of the four divisions of the year (spring, summer, autumn, winter) **2** the proper time for anything **3** a time associated with a particular activity: *football season* ▶ VERB **1** to add (salt etc) to improve the flavour of (food) **2** to dry (wood) till it is ready for use

seasonable ADJECTIVE **1** happening at the proper time **2** of weather: suitable for the season

seasonal ADJECTIVE **1** of the seasons or a season **2** of work etc: taking place in one particular season only

seasoned ADJECTIVE **1** of food: flavoured **2** of wood: ready to be used **3** trained, experienced: *a seasoned traveller*

seasoning NOUN something (eg salt, pepper) added to food to give it more taste

seat NOUN **1** a piece of furniture

for sitting on **2** the part of a chair on which you sit **3** the buttocks **4** a mansion **5** a place in parliament, on a council, etc **6** the centre of some activity: *the seat of government* ▸VERB **1** to make to sit down **2** to have seats for (a certain number): *The room seats forty*

seat belt NOUN a belt fixed to a seat in a car etc to prevent an occupant from being thrown violently forward in the event of a crash

sea urchin NOUN a type of small sea creature with a spiny shell

seaward ADJECTIVE & ADVERB towards the sea

seaweed NOUN any of many kinds of plants growing in the sea

seaworthy ADJECTIVE in a good enough condition to go to sea

seclude VERB to keep (yourself) apart from people's notice or company

secluded ADJECTIVE of a place: private and quiet

seclusion NOUN the state of being secluded; peacefulness and privacy

second ADJECTIVE **1** next after the first in time, place, etc **2** other, alternate: *every second week* **3** another of the same kind as: *They thought him a second Mozart* ▸NOUN **1** someone or something that is second **2** an attendant to someone who boxes or fights a duel **3** (symbol **s**) the standard unit of measure of time, the 60th part of a minute **4** the 60th part of a degree (in measuring angles) **5** an article not quite perfectly made: *These gloves are seconds* ▸VERB **1** to support, back up **2** (*pronounced* se-**kond**) to transfer temporarily to a special job > **secondly** ADVERB

ⓘ Comes from Latin *secundus* meaning 'following'

secondary ADJECTIVE second in position or importance

secondary school NOUN a school between primary school and university etc

second-hand ADJECTIVE not new; having been used by another: *second-hand clothes*

second nature NOUN a firmly fixed habit: *Organizing people is second nature to her*

second-rate ADJECTIVE not of the best quality, inferior

secrecy NOUN the state of being secret, mystery

secret ADJECTIVE **1** hidden from, or not known by, others **2** secretive ▸NOUN a fact, plan, etc that is not told or known

secretarial ADJECTIVE of a secretary or their work

secretary NOUN (*plural* **secretaries**) **1** someone employed to write letters, keep records, etc in an office **2** someone elected to deal with the written business of a club etc

Secretary of State NOUN **1** a government minister in charge of an administrative department **2** *US* the person in charge of foreign affairs

secretive ADJECTIVE inclined to hide or conceal your feelings, activities, etc

secret service NOUN a government

A B C D E F G H I J K L M N O P Q R S T U V W X Y Z

department dealing with spying

sect NOUN a group of people who hold certain views, especially in religious matters

sectarian ADJECTIVE **1** of a sect **2** loyal to a sect **3** narrow-minded **4** of a crime, especially a murder: committed as a result of hatred between rival religious groups

section NOUN **1** a part, a division: *a section of the community* **2** *biology* a thin slice of a specimen for examination under a microscope **3** the view of the inside of anything when it is cut right through or across: *a section of a plant* **4** *maths* the surface formed when a plane cuts through a solid

sector NOUN **1** a part, a section **2** *maths* a three-sided part of a circle whose sides are two radii and a part of the circumference

secular ADJECTIVE **1** of worldly, not spiritual or religious things **2** of music etc: not sacred or religious

secure ADJECTIVE **1** safe, free from danger or fear **2** confident: *secure in the knowledge that she had no rivals* **3** firmly fixed or fastened: *The lock is secure* ▶VERB **1** to make safe, firm or established: *secure your position* **2** to seize, get hold of: *secure the diamonds* **3** to fasten: *secure the lock*

security NOUN **1** safety **2** (**securities**) property or goods which a lender may keep until the loan is paid back

sedan NOUN **1** (*also called*: **sedan chair**) an enclosed chair for one person, carried on two poles by two bearers **2** *US* a saloon car

sedate ADJECTIVE calm, serious, dignified

sedation NOUN the use of sedatives to calm a patient

sedative ADJECTIVE calming, soothing ▶NOUN a medicine with this effect

sedentary ADJECTIVE of a job etc: involving a lot of sitting

sediment NOUN **1** the grains or solid parts which settle at the bottom of a liquid **2** sand, rocks, etc carried and deposited by wind, water or ice

sedimentary ADJECTIVE of rocks: formed when sediment becomes tightly compacted

sedition NOUN the stirring up of rebellion against the government
> **seditious** ADJECTIVE

seduce VERB **1** to tempt (someone) away from right or moral behaviour **2** to persuade (someone) to have sexual intercourse **3** to attract
> **seducer** NOUN > **seduction** NOUN

seductive ADJECTIVE attractive, tempting

see VERB (**seeing, saw, seen**) **1** to have sight **2** to be aware of, notice by means of the eye: *He can see us coming* **3** to form a picture of in the mind **4** to understand: *I see what you mean* **5** to find out: *I'll see what is happening* **6** to make sure: *See that he finishes his homework* **7** to accompany: *I'll see you home* **8** to meet: *I'll see you at the usual time* ▶NOUN the district over which a bishop or archbishop has authority **seeing that** since, because **see through 1** to take part in to the end **2** to not be deceived by (a person, trick, etc) **see to** to take charge of (the preparation of): *see to a meal*

[i] Comes from Old English *seon*

seed NOUN **1** the part of a tree, plant, etc from which a new plant may grow **2** a seed-like part of a grain or a nut **3** the beginning from which anything grows: *the seeds of rebellion* **4** a seeded player in a tournament **5** *old* children, descendants ▸VERB **1** of a plant: to produce seed **2** to sow **3** to remove the seeds from (eg a fruit) **4** to arrange (good players) in a tournament so that they do not compete against each other till the later rounds **go to seed** *or* **run to seed 1** of a plant: to develop seeds **2** of a person, area, etc: to deteriorate, become run down

seedling NOUN a young plant just sprung from a seed

seedy ADJECTIVE (**seedier, seediest**) **1** full of seeds **2** shabby **3** sickly, not very well

seek VERB (**seeking, sought**) **1** to look or search for **2** to try (to do something): *seek to establish proof* **3** to try to get (advice etc)

seem VERB **1** to appear to be: *He seems kind* **2** to appear: *She seems to like it*

seeming ADJECTIVE apparent but not actual or real: *a seeming success*
> **seemingly** ADVERB

seemly ADJECTIVE (**seemlier, seemliest**) suitable; decent

seen *past participle* of **see**

seep VERB to flow slowly through a small opening, leak

seersucker NOUN a lightweight ribbed cotton fabric

seesaw NOUN **1** a plank balanced across a stand so that one end of it goes up when the other goes down **2** an up-and-down movement like that of a seesaw ▸VERB **1** to go up and down on a seesaw **2** to move with a seesaw-like movement

seethe VERB **1** to boil **2** to be very angry

seething ADJECTIVE **1** boiling **2** furious

see-through ADJECTIVE able to be seen through

segment NOUN **1** a part cut off **2** *maths* a part of a circle or ellipse cut off by a straight line intersecting it

segregate VERB to separate (someone or a group) from others
> **segregation** NOUN

seismic (*pronounced* **saiz**-mik) ADJECTIVE of earthquakes

seize VERB **1** to take suddenly by force: *The army has seized the town* **2** to overcome: *seized by panic* **3** (**seize up**) of machinery: to become stuck, break down

seizure NOUN **1** sudden capture **2** a sudden attack of illness, rage, etc

seldom ADVERB not often, rarely: *You seldom see an owl during the day*

select VERB to pick out from several according to your preference, choose ▸ADJECTIVE **1** picked out, chosen **2** very good **3** exclusive, allowing only certain people in

selection NOUN **1** the act of choosing **2** things chosen **3** a number of things from which to choose

selective ADJECTIVE **1** selecting carefully **2** of weedkiller: harmless to garden plants

self NOUN (*plural* **selves**) **1** someone's own person **2** someone's personality, character

self-assured ADJECTIVE trusting in your own power or ability, confident

self-centred ADJECTIVE concerned with your own affairs, selfish

self-confident ADJECTIVE believing in your own powers or abilities

self-conscious ADJECTIVE too aware of your faults etc and therefore embarrassed in the company of others

self-contained ADJECTIVE **1** of a house: complete in itself, not sharing any part with other houses **2** of a person: self-reliant

self-control NOUN control over yourself, your feelings, etc

self-defence NOUN the defence of your own person, property, etc

self-effacing ADJECTIVE keeping yourself from being noticed, modest

self-esteem NOUN respect for yourself; conceit

self-evident ADJECTIVE clear enough to need no proof

self-expression NOUN expressing your own personality in your activities

self-important ADJECTIVE having a mistakenly high sense of your importance

self-indulgent ADJECTIVE too ready to satisfy your own inclinations and desires

self-interest NOUN a selfish desire to consider only your own interests or advantage

selfish ADJECTIVE caring only for your own pleasure or advantage > **selfishly** ADVERB

selfless ADJECTIVE thinking of others before yourself, unselfish

self-made ADJECTIVE owing success etc to your own efforts: *a self-made man*

self-raising flour NOUN flour already containing an ingredient to make it rise

self-reliant ADJECTIVE trusting in your own abilities etc > **self-reliance** NOUN

self-respect NOUN respect for yourself and concern for your own character and reputation

self-righteous ADJECTIVE thinking highly of your own goodness and virtue

self-sacrifice NOUN the act of giving up your own life, possessions, etc in order to do good to others

self-satisfied ADJECTIVE pleased, smug, satisfied with yourself

self-service ADJECTIVE of a restaurant: where customers serve themselves and pay at a checkout

self-sufficient ADJECTIVE needing no help or support from anyone else

sell VERB (**selling, sold**) **1** to give or hand over for money **2** to have or keep for sale: *He sells newspapers* **3** (**sell for**) to be sold for, cost: *This book sells for £20*

seller NOUN someone who sells

Sellotape NOUN, *trademark* transparent adhesive tape, especially for use on paper

semantic ADJECTIVE relating to the meaning of words etc

semantics SINGULAR NOUN the branch of linguistics that deals with meaning

semaphore NOUN a form of signalling using the arms to form different positions for each letter

semblance NOUN an outward, often false, appearance: *a semblance of listening*

semen NOUN the liquid that carries sperm

semester NOUN a term at a university etc that lasts for half a year

semi- PREFIX **1** half: *semicircle* **2** *informal* partly

🛈 Comes from Latin prefix *semi-* meaning 'half'

semibreve NOUN, *music* a whole-note (𝅝), equal to four crotchets in length

semicircle NOUN half of a circle

semicolon NOUN the punctuation mark (;) indicating a pause stronger than a pause marked by a comma

semiconductor NOUN a substance, eg silicon, which can conduct electricity less easily than a conductor

semi-detached ADJECTIVE of a house: joined to another house on one side but not on the other

semi-final NOUN the stage or match of a contest immediately before the final

seminal ADJECTIVE influential, important

seminar NOUN a group of students working on, or meeting to discuss, a particular subject

seminary NOUN (*plural* **seminaries**) a school or college

semi-precious ADJECTIVE of a stone: having some value, but not considered a gem

Semitic ADJECTIVE Jewish

semitone NOUN, *music* **1** half a tone **2** the interval between notes on a keyboard instrument

senate NOUN **1** the upper house of parliament in the USA, Australia, etc **2** the governing council of some universities **3** *history* the law-making body in ancient Rome

senator NOUN a member of a senate

send VERB (**sending, sent**) **1** to make (someone) go **2** to have (something) carried or delivered to a place **send for** to order to be brought

sender NOUN a person who sends something, especially by post

senile ADJECTIVE **1** of old age **2** showing the mental feebleness of old age

senility NOUN **1** old age **2** mental deterioration in old age

senior ADJECTIVE older in age or higher in rank ▸NOUN someone older or in a senior position

senior citizen NOUN an elderly person

seniority NOUN the state of being senior

sensation NOUN **1** a feeling through any of the five senses **2** a

A B C D E F G H I J K L M N O P Q R S T U V W X Y Z

vague effect: *a floating sensation* **3** a state of excitement: *causing a sensation*

sensational ADJECTIVE causing great excitement, horror, etc

sense NOUN **1** one of the five powers by which humans feel or notice (hearing, taste, sight, smell, touch) **2** a feeling: *a sense of loss* **3** an ability to understand or appreciate: *a sense of humour* **4** (**senses**) right mind, common sense: *to take leave of your senses* **5** wisdom, ability to act in a reasonable way **6** ability to be understood: *Your sentence does not make sense* **7** meaning: *To what sense of this word are your referring?* ▶ VERB to feel, realize: *sense disapproval*

senseless ADJECTIVE stunned, unconscious; foolish

sense organ NOUN an organ, eg the eye, nose or mouth, that is sensitive to a stimulus such as sound or touch

sensibility NOUN (*plural* **sensibilities**) ability to feel, sensitivity

sensible ADJECTIVE **1** wise **2** able to be felt or noticed **3** (**sensible of**) aware of

sensitive ADJECTIVE **1** feeling, especially strongly or painfully **2** strongly affected by light, movements, etc **3** of a person: easily upset or offended

sensitivity NOUN the quality or condition of being sensitive

sensitize *or* **sensitise** VERB to make sensitive (especially to light)

sensor NOUN a device that detects a physical change and turns it into an electrical signal

sensory ADJECTIVE of the senses

sensual ADJECTIVE **1** driven by, or affecting, the senses rather than the mind: *Discover the sensual pleasures of aromatherapy* **2** indulging too much in bodily pleasures

> Do not confuse: **sensual** and **sensuous**

sensuality NOUN **1** the quality of being sensual **2** indulgence in physical pleasures

sensuous ADJECTIVE pleasing to the senses, particularly by being beautiful or luxurious: *car designs favouring smooth edges and sensuous curves*

sent *past form of* **send**

sentence NOUN **1** a number of words which together make a grammatically complete statement, usually containing a verb **2** a judgement announced by a judge or court ▶ VERB to condemn to a particular punishment

sentiment NOUN **1** a thought expressed in words **2** a show of feeling or emotion, often excessive

sentimental ADJECTIVE having or showing too much feeling or emotion > **sentimentality** NOUN

sentry NOUN (*plural* **sentries**) a soldier posted to guard an entrance

sepal NOUN one of the green leaves beneath the petals of a flower

separable ADJECTIVE able to be separated

separate VERB (*pronounced* **sep**-*a*-reit) **1** to set or keep apart **2** to divide into parts **3** to disconnect **4** to go different ways: *They separated at the station* **5** of a couple: to live apart by choice ▶ ADJECTIVE (*pronounced* **sep**-*a*-rat) **1** placed, kept, etc apart **2** divided **3** not connected **4** different > **separation** NOUN

separatism NOUN **1** a tendency to separate or to be separate **2** support for separation **3** the practices and principles of separatists

separatist NOUN someone who withdraws or urges separation from an established church, state, etc

sepia (*pronounced* **see**-pi-*a*) NOUN a brown colour

sept- PREFIX seven: *septet/ September* (which was the seventh month in the Roman calendar)

ⓘ Comes from Latin *septem* meaning 'seven'

September NOUN the ninth month of the year

ⓘ From a Latin word meaning 'seventh', because September was originally the seventh month of the year, before January and February were added

septet NOUN a group of seven musicians etc

septic ADJECTIVE of a wound: full of germs that are poisoning the blood

ⓘ Comes from Greek *sepein* meaning 'to putrefy'

Do not confuse with: **sceptic**

septuagenarian (*pronounced* sep-tyoo-*a*-ji-**neir**-ri-*a*n) NOUN someone from seventy to seventy-nine years old

sequel NOUN **1** a result, a consequence **2** a story that is a continuation of an earlier story

sequence NOUN **1** the order (of events) in time **2** a number of things following in order, a connected series

sequin NOUN a small round sparkling ornament sewn on a dress etc

seraph NOUN (*plural* **seraphs** *or* **seraphim**) an angel of the highest rank

serenade NOUN music played or sung in the open air at night, especially under a woman's window ▶ VERB to sing or play a serenade (to)

serendipitous ADJECTIVE discovered by luck or chance

serendipity NOUN happy chance, luck

ⓘ After a fairy story called *The Princess of Serendip*, in which the heroes were always making lucky discoveries. *Serendip* was an old name for Sri Lanka

serene ADJECTIVE **1** calm **2** not worried, happy, peaceful

serenity NOUN calmness, peacefulness

serf NOUN, *history* a slave bought and sold with the land on which he worked > **serfdom** NOUN

sergeant NOUN **1** an army rank above corporal **2** a rank in the police force above a constable

sergeant-major NOUN an army rank above sergeant

serial NOUN a story which is

A B C D E F G H I J K L M N O P Q R S T U V W X Y Z

published, broadcast or televised in instalments

series NOUN (*plural* **series**) **1** a number of things following each other in order **2** a set of things of the same kind: *a series of books on art* **3** a regularly broadcast TV or radio programme with the same characters or a similar subject

series circuit NOUN an electrical circuit where a power source is connected to two or more components one after the other (*compare with*: **parallel circuit**)

serif NOUN **1** a short line or stroke on the end of a printed character **2** a printing font having characters with serifs

serious ADJECTIVE **1** grave, thoughtful: *serious expression on her face* **2** not joking, in earnest: *serious remark* **3** important, needing careful thought: *a serious matter* **4** likely to have dangerous results: *serious accident* > **seriously** ADVERB

sermon NOUN a serious talk, especially one given in church

serpent NOUN, *old* a snake

serpentine ADJECTIVE like a serpent; winding, full of twists

serrated ADJECTIVE having notches or teeth like a saw: *a serrated edge*

serum NOUN a yellowish fluid in blood, which contains specific antibodies and can be used for vaccination

servant NOUN **1** someone paid to work for another, especially in helping to run a house **2** a government employee: *civil servant/public servant*

serve VERB **1** to work for and obey **2** to attend or wait upon at table **3** to give out food, goods, etc: *Are you being served?* **4** to be able to be used (as): *The cave will serve as a shelter* **5** to be suitable for: *serve a purpose* **6** to carry out duties as a member of the armed forces **7** to undergo (a sentence in prison etc) **8** *tennis* to throw up the ball and hit it with the racket to start play **serve someone right** to be deserved by them

server NOUN, *computing* a computer that stores and manages data from several other smaller computers on a network

service NOUN **1** an act of serving **2** the duty required of a servant or other employee **3** a performance of (public) worship **4** use: *bring the new machine into service* **5** time spent in the armed forces **6** (**services**) the armed forces **7** (**services**) help: *services to refugees* **8** a regular supply: *bus service* **9** (**services**) public supply of water, gas, electricity, etc **10** a set of dishes: *dinner service* ▸ VERB to keep (a car, machine, etc) in good working order by regular checks and repairs **active service** service in battle **at your service** ready to help or be of use

serviceable ADJECTIVE useful; lasting a long time: *serviceable clothes*

serviette NOUN a table napkin

servile ADJECTIVE slave-like; showing lack of spirit: *a servile attitude to his employer*

servility NOUN being servile

servitude NOUN slavery; the state of being under strict control

sesame (*pronounced* **ses**-*a*m-i) NOUN a SE Asian plant whose seeds produce an edible oil

session NOUN **1** a meeting of a court, council, etc **2** the period of the year when classes are held in a school etc **3** a period of time spent on a particular activity

sestet NOUN a group of six musicians etc

set VERB (**setting, set**) **1** to place or put **2** to fix in the proper place (eg broken bones) **3** to arrange (a table for a meal, jewels in a necklace, etc) **4** to fix (a date, a price, etc) **5** to fix hair (in waves or curls) **6** to give (a task etc): *set him three problems* **7** to put in a certain state or condition: *set free* **8** of a jelly etc: to become firm or solid **9** to compose music for: *He set the poem to music* **10** of the sun: to go out of sight below the horizon ▶ADJECTIVE **1** fixed or arranged beforehand; ready: *all set* **2** fixed, stiff: *a set expression on his face* ▶NOUN **1** a group of people **2** a number of things of a similar kind, or used together: *set of carving tools* **3** *maths* a group of objects or elements with something in common **4** an apparatus: *a television set* **5** scenery made ready for a play etc **6** pose, position: *the set of his head* **7** a series of six or more games in tennis **8** a fixing of hair in waves or curls **9** (*also called*: **sett**) a badger's burrow **10** (*also called*: **sett**) a street paving-block **set about** **1** to begin (doing something) **2** to attack **set in** to begin: *Winter has set in* **set off** *or* **out** *or* **forth** to start (on a journey etc) **set on** *or* **upon** to attack

🛈 Comes from Old English verb *settan* and noun *set* meaning 'a seat'

setback NOUN a movement in the wrong direction, a failure

set square NOUN a triangular drawing instrument, with one right angle

settee NOUN a sofa

setting NOUN **1** the act of someone or something that sets **2** an arrangement **3** a background: *against a setting of hills and lochs*

settle VERB **1** to place in a position or at rest **2** to come to rest: *A butterfly settled on his arm* **3** to agree over (a matter): *settle the price* **4** (sometimes **settle down**) to become calm or quiet **5** (sometimes **settle down**) to make your home in a place **6** to pay (a bill) **7** to fix, decide (on) **8** to bring (a quarrel etc) to an end **9** to sink to the bottom ▶NOUN a long high-backed bench

settlement NOUN **1** the act of settling **2** a decision, an agreement **3** payment of a bill **4** money given to a woman on her marriage **5** a number of people who have come to live in a country

settler NOUN someone who goes to live in a new area or country

seven NOUN the number 7 ▶ADJECTIVE 7 in number

seventeen NOUN the number 17 ▶ADJECTIVE 17 in number

seventeenth ADJECTIVE the last of a series of seventeen ▶NOUN one of seventeen equal parts

seventh ADJECTIVE the last of a series of seven ▶ NOUN one of seven equal parts

seventieth ADJECTIVE the last of a series of seventy ▶ NOUN one of seventy equal parts

seventy NOUN the number 70 ▶ ADJECTIVE 70 in number

sever VERB **1** to cut apart or away, break off **2** to separate, part

several ADJECTIVE **1** more than one or two, but not many **2** various **3** different: *going their several ways* ▶ PRONOUN more than one or two people, things, etc, but not a great many

severe ADJECTIVE **1** serious: *a severe illness* **2** harsh, strict **3** very plain and simple, not fancy: *a severe haircut*

severity NOUN strictness, harshness

sew VERB (**sewing, sewed, sewn**) **1** to join together with a needle and thread **2** to make or mend in this way

sewage NOUN water and waste matter

sewer NOUN an underground drain for carrying off water and waste matter

sex NOUN **1** either of the two classes (male or female) into which animals are divided according to the part they play in producing children or young **2** sexual intercourse

sex- PREFIX six

1 Comes from Latin *sex* meaning 'six'

sexagenarian NOUN someone from sixty to sixty-nine years old

sex chromosome NOUN an X- or Y-chromosome, that in combination determines the sex of an individual

sexism NOUN discrimination against someone on the grounds of their sex

sexist NOUN someone who treats the opposite sex unfairly or thinks that they are inferior ▶ ADJECTIVE relating to or characteristic of sexism: *a sexist attitude*

sextet NOUN a group of six musicians etc

sexual ADJECTIVE **1** of sex or gender **2** relating to sexual intercourse > **sexually** ADVERB

sexual intercourse NOUN physical union between a man and a woman involving the insertion of the penis into the vagina

sexuality NOUN the way in which a person expresses, or their ability to experience, sexual feelings

sexual reproduction NOUN reproduction by the union of male and female reproductive cells

sexy ADJECTIVE (**sexier, sexiest**) sexually attractive or sexually exciting

SF ABBREVIATION science fiction

shabby ADJECTIVE (**shabbier, shabbiest**) **1** worn-looking **2** poorly dressed **3** of behaviour: mean, unfair > **shabbily** ADVERB

shack NOUN a roughly built hut

shackle VERB **1** to fasten with a chain **2** to hold back, prevent, hinder

shackles PLURAL NOUN chains fastening a prisoner's legs or arms

shade NOUN **1** slight darkness

caused by cutting off some light **2** a place not in full sunlight **3** a screen from the heat or light **4** (**shades**) *informal* sunglasses **5** the deepness or a variation of a colour **6** the dark parts in a picture **7** a very small amount or difference: *a shade larger* **8** *literary* a ghost ▸VERB **1** to shelter from the sun or light **2** to make parts of a picture darker **3** to change gradually, eg from one colour into another

shading NOUN the marking of the darker places in a picture

shadow NOUN **1** shade caused by some object coming in the way of a light **2** the dark shape of that object on the ground **3** a dark part in a picture **4** a very small amount: *a shadow of doubt* ▸VERB **1** to shade, darken **2** to follow someone about, sometimes secretly, and watch them closely

shadow cabinet NOUN leading members of the opposition in parliament

shady ADJECTIVE (**shadier, shadiest**) **1** sheltered from light or heat **2** *informal* dishonest, underhand: *a shady character*

shaft NOUN **1** a long, straight handle or part of anything **2** the rod on which the head of an axe, arrow, etc is fixed **3** an arrow **4** a revolving rod which turns a machine or engine **5** the pole of a cart to which the horses are tied **6** the deep, narrow passageway leading to a mine **7** a deep vertical hole for a lift **8** a ray (of light)

shaggy ADJECTIVE (**shaggier, shaggiest**) rough, hairy or woolly

shake VERB (**shaking, shook, shaken**) **1** to move backwards and forwards or up and down with quick, jerky movements **2** to make or be made unsteady **3** to shock, disturb: *His parting words shook me* ▸NOUN **1** the act of shaking or trembling **2** a shock **3** a drink mixed by shaking or stirring quickly: *milk shake*

shaky ADJECTIVE (**shakier, shakiest**) unsteady; trembling > **shakily** ADVERB

shall VERB **1** used to form future tenses of other verbs when the subject is *I* or *we*: *I shall tell you later* **2** used for emphasis, or to express a promise, when the subject is *you, he, she, it* or *they*: *You shall go if I say you must/You shall go if you want to* (*see also*: **should**)

shallot NOUN a kind of small onion

shallow ADJECTIVE **1** not deep **2** not capable of thinking or feeling deeply ▸NOUN (often **shallows**) a place where the water is not deep

sham NOUN something which is not what it appears to be, a pretence ▸ADJECTIVE false, imitation, pretended: *a sham fight* ▸VERB (**shamming, shammed**) to pretend, feign: *shamming sleep*

shaman (*pronounced* **shah**-m*a*n *or* **shei**-m*a*n) NOUN a tribal healer or medicine man

shambles SINGULAR NOUN, *informal* a mess, confused disorder

ⓘ Originally meaning a place where animals were slaughtered

shambolic ADJECTIVE, *slang* chaotic, messy

shame NOUN **1** an uncomfortable

feeling caused by realization of guilt or failure **2** disgrace, dishonour **3** bad luck, a pity: *It's a shame that you can't go* ▸ VERB **1** to make to feel shame or ashamed **2** (**shame into**) to cause (someone to do something) by making them ashamed: *They shamed him into paying his share* **put to shame** to cause to feel ashamed

shameful ADJECTIVE disgraceful

shameless ADJECTIVE feeling or showing no shame

shampoo VERB to wash (the hair, carpet) ▸ NOUN **1** an act of shampooing **2** a soapy liquid used for cleaning the hair **3** a similar liquid used for cleaning carpets or upholstery

shamrock NOUN a plant like clover with leaves divided in three

shank NOUN **1** the part of the leg between the knee and the foot **2** a long straight part (of a tool etc)

shan't *short for* shall not

shanty NOUN (*plural* **shanties**) **1** a roughly made hut **2** a sailors' song

shantytown NOUN, *geography* a town or area where the people are poor and have built makeshift houses

shape NOUN **1** the form or outline of anything **2** a mould for a jelly etc **3** a jelly etc turned out of a mould **4** condition: *in good shape* **5** a geometric figure ▸ VERB **1** to make into a certain form **2** to model, mould **3** to develop (in a particular way): *Our plans are shaping well*

shapeless ADJECTIVE having no shape or regular form

shapely ADJECTIVE having an attractive shape

share NOUN **1** one part of something that is divided among several people **2** one of the parts into which the money of a business firm is divided ▸ VERB **1** to divide out among a number of people **2** to allow others to use (your possessions etc) **3** to have or use in common with someone else: *We share a liking for music*

shareholder NOUN someone who owns shares in a business company

shareware NOUN, *computing* software available to the public on a free trial, often for a limited time

shark NOUN **1** a large, flesh-eating fish **2** *informal* a swindler

sharp ADJECTIVE **1** cutting, piercing **2** having a thin edge or fine point **3** hurting, stinging, biting: *sharp wind/sharp words* **4** alert, quick-witted **5** sensitive, perceptive, able to pick up faint signals: *sharp eyes* **6** severe, inclined to scold **7** *music* of a note: raised half a tone in pitch **8** of a voice: shrill **9** of an outline: clear ▸ ADVERB punctually: *Come at ten o'clock sharp* ▸ NOUN, *music* a sign (♯) showing that a note is to be raised half a tone **look sharp** to hurry

sharpen VERB to make or grow sharp

sharpener NOUN an instrument for sharpening: *pencil sharpener*

shatter VERB to break in pieces; to upset, ruin (hopes, health, etc)

shave VERB **1** to cut away hair with a razor **2** to scrape away the surface of (wood etc) **3** to touch lightly, or just avoid touching, in passing ▶NOUN **1** the act of shaving **2** a narrow escape: *a close shave*

shaven ADJECTIVE shaved

shaver NOUN an electric device for shaving

shavings PLURAL NOUN very thin slices of wood etc

shawl NOUN a loose covering for the shoulders

she PRONOUN a woman, girl or female animal etc already spoken about (used only as the subject of a verb): *When the girl saw us, she waved*

sheaf NOUN (*plural* **sheaves**) a bundle (eg of corn, papers) tied together

shear VERB (**shearing, sheared, shorn**) **1** to clip, cut (especially wool from a sheep) **2** to cut through, cut off

🛈 Comes from Old English *sceran*, from a Germanic base meaning 'cut', 'divide', 'shear' or 'shave'

> Do not confuse with: **sheer**

shears PLURAL NOUN large scissors

sheath NOUN **1** a case for a sword or dagger **2** a long close-fitting covering **3** a condom

sheathe VERB to put into a sheath

shed NOUN **1** a building for storage or shelter: *coalshed/bicycle shed* **2** an outhouse ▶VERB (**shedding, shed**) **1** to throw or cast off (leaves, a skin, clothing) **2** to pour out (tears, blood) **3** to give out (light etc)

sheen NOUN brightness, gloss

sheep NOUN **1** an animal whose flesh is used as food and whose fleece is used for wool **2** a very meek person who lacks confidence

sheep-dip NOUN a liquid for disinfecting sheep

sheepdog NOUN a dog trained to look after sheep

sheepish ADJECTIVE shy; embarrassed, shamefaced

sheepskin NOUN **1** the skin of a sheep **2** a kind of leather made from this

sheer ADJECTIVE **1** very steep: *sheer drop from the cliff* **2** pure, not mixed: *sheer delight/sheer nonsense* **3** of cloth: very thin or fine ▶ADVERB straight up and down, very steeply: *rock face rising sheer* ▶VERB to turn aside from a straight line, swerve

🛈 Adjective and adverb: come perhaps from the Old English equivalent of Old Norse *skærr* meaning 'bright'; verb: formed from a combination of Late German or Dutch *scheren* meaning 'to cut', and an alternative spelling of English *shear*

> Do not confuse with: **shear**

sheet NOUN **1** a large piece of linen, cotton, nylon, etc used to cover the mattress of a bed **2** a large thin piece of metal, glass, ice, etc **3** a piece of paper **4** a sail **5** the rope fastened to the lower corner of a sail

sheikh (*pronounced* sheik *or* sheek) NOUN an Arab chief

shelf NOUN (*plural* **shelves**) **1** a board fixed on a wall, for laying things on **2** a flat layer of rock, a ledge **3** a sandbank

shell NOUN **1** a hard outer covering

A B C D E F G H I J K L M N O P Q R S T U V W X Y Z

(of a shellfish, egg, nut, etc) **2** a husk or pod (eg of peas) **3** a metal case filled with explosive fired from a gun **4** a framework, eg of a building not yet completed or burnt out: *Only the shell of the warehouse was left* ▸VERB **1** to take the shell from (a nut, egg, peas, etc) **2** to fire shells at

shellfish NOUN a water creature covered with a shell, eg an oyster, limpet or mussel

shelter NOUN **1** a building which acts as a protection from harm, rain, wind, etc **2** the state of being protected from any of these ▸VERB **1** to give protection to **2** to put in a place of safety or protection **3** to go to, or stay in, a place of safety **take shelter** to go to a place of safety

shelve VERB **1** to put up shelves in **2** to put aside (a problem etc) for later consideration **3** of land: to slope gently

shepherd NOUN a man who looks after sheep ▸VERB to watch over carefully, guide

shepherdess NOUN a woman who looks after sheep

sheriff NOUN **1** the chief representative of a monarch in a county, whose duties include keeping the peace **2** in Scotland, the chief judge of a county **3** *US* the chief law-enforcement officer of a county

sherry NOUN (*plural* **sherries**) a strong kind of wine, often drunk before a meal

shied *past form* of **shy**

shield NOUN **1** anything that protects from harm **2** a broad piece of metal carried by a soldier etc as a defence against weapons **3** a shield-shaped trophy won in a competition **4** a shield-shaped plaque bearing a coat-of-arms ▸VERB to protect, defend, shelter

shift VERB **1** to move, change the position of: *shift the furniture/trying to shift the blame* **2** to change position or direction: *The wind shifted* **3** to get rid of ▸NOUN **1** a change: *shift of emphasis* **2** a change of position, transfer **3** a group of workers on duty at the same time **4** a specified period of work or duty: *day shift/night shift* **5** a loose-fitting lightweight dress **shift for yourself** to manage to get on by your own efforts

shifty ADJECTIVE (**shiftier, shiftiest**) not to be trusted, looking dishonest

shilling NOUN a silver-coloured coin used before decimal currency, worth 1/20 of £1

shimmer VERB to shine with a quivering or unsteady light: *The lake shimmered in the moonlight* ▸NOUN a quivering light

shin NOUN the front part of the leg below the knee **shin up** to climb: *shin up a drainpipe*

shine VERB (**shining, shone**) **1** to give out or reflect light **2** to be bright **3** to polish (shoes etc) **4** to be very good at: *He shines at arithmetic* ▸NOUN **1** brightness **2** an act of polishing

shingle NOUN coarse gravel or rounded stones on the shores of rivers or of the sea

shingles SINGULAR NOUN, *medicine*

an infectious disease causing a painful rash
shining ADJECTIVE **1** very bright and clear **2** admired, distinguished: *a shining example*
shiny ADJECTIVE (**shinier, shiniest**) glossy, polished
ship NOUN a large vessel for journeys across water ▸ VERB (**shipping, shipped**) **1** to take onto a ship **2** to send by ship **3** to go by ship
-ship SUFFIX **1** a state or condition: *friendship* **2** a skill: *craftsmanship*
shipment NOUN **1** an act of putting on board ship **2** a load of goods sent by ship
shipping NOUN **1** ships as traffic: *a gale warning to shipping* **2** the commercial transport of goods and freight, especially by ship
shipshape ADJECTIVE in good order, neat, trim
shipwreck NOUN **1** the sinking or destruction of a ship (especially by accident) **2** a wrecked ship **3** ruin
shipyard NOUN the yard in which ships are built or repaired
shire NOUN a county
shirk VERB to avoid or evade (doing your duty etc)
shirker NOUN a person who avoids work or responsibilities
shirt NOUN **1** a garment worn by men on the upper part of the body, having a collar, sleeves and buttons down the front **2** a similar garment for a woman
shiver VERB to tremble with cold or fear ▸ NOUN **1** the act of shivering **2** a small broken piece: *shivers of glass*
shoal NOUN **1** a group of fishes, moving and feeding together **2** a shallow place, a sandbank
shock NOUN **1** a sudden forceful blow **2** a feeling of fright, horror, dismay, etc **3** *medicine* a state of extreme physical collapse occurring as a result of severe burns, drug overdose, etc **4** the effect on the body of an electric current passing through it **5** an earthquake **6** a bushy mass (of hair) ▸ VERB **1** to give a shock to **2** to upset or horrify
shock absorber NOUN a device in an aircraft, car, etc for lessening the impact or force of bumps
shocking ADJECTIVE causing horror or dismay; disgusting
shod ADJECTIVE wearing shoes ▸ VERB *past form of* **shoe**
shoddy ADJECTIVE (**shoddier, shoddiest**) **1** of poor material or quality: *shoddy goods* **2** mean, low: *a shoddy trick*
shoe NOUN **1** a stiff outer covering for the foot, not reaching above the ankle **2** a rim of iron nailed to the hoof of a horse ▸ VERB (**shoeing, shod**) to put shoes on (a horse)
shoelace NOUN a cord or string used for fastening a shoe
shoestring NOUN, *US* a shoelace
on a shoestring with very little money
shone *past form* of **shine**
shoo INTERJECTION used to scare away birds, animals, etc ▸ VERB (**shooing, shooed**) to drive or scare away
shook *past tense* of **shake**
shoot VERB (**shooting, shot**) **1** to

A B C D E F G H I J K L M N O P Q R S T U V W X Y Z

send a bullet from a gun, or an arrow from a bow **2** to hit or kill with an arrow, bullet, etc **3** to let fly swiftly and with force **4** to kick for a goal **5** of a plant: to grow new buds **6** to photograph, film **7** to move very swiftly or suddenly **8** to slide (a bolt) ▸NOUN **1** a new sprout on a plant **2** an expedition to shoot game **3** land where game is shot

shooting star NOUN, *informal* a meteor

shop NOUN **1** a place where goods are sold **2** a workshop ▸VERB (**shopping, shopped**) **1** to visit shops and buy goods **2** *slang* to betray (someone) to the police **talk shop** *informal* to talk about work when off duty

shopkeeper NOUN someone who owns and keeps a shop

shoplifter NOUN someone who steals goods from a shop > **shoplifting** NOUN

shopping NOUN **1** visiting shops to buy goods **2** goods bought

shop steward NOUN a worker elected by the other workers as their representative

shore NOUN the land bordering on a sea or lake ▸VERB to prop (up), support: *shoring up an unprofitable organization*

shorn *past participle* of **shear**

short ADJECTIVE **1** not long: *short skirt* **2** not tall **3** brief, not lasting long: *short talk* **4** not enough, less than it should be: *I'm £5 short* **5** rude, sharp, abrupt **6** of pastry: crisp and crumbling easily ▸ADVERB **1** suddenly, abruptly: *stop short* **2** not as far as intended: *The shot fell short* ▸NOUN **1** a short film **2** a short circuit **3** a drink of an alcoholic spirit **4** (**shorts**) short trousers ▸VERB to short-circuit **in short** in a few words **short of 1** not having enough of: *short of money* **2** less than, not as much or as far as: *5 miles short of Inverness/£5 short of the price* **3** without going as far as: *He didn't know how to get the money, short of stealing it*

shortage NOUN a lack

shortbread NOUN a thick biscuit made of butter and flour etc

short circuit NOUN the missing out of a major part of an intended electric circuit, sometimes causing blowing of fuses

shortcoming NOUN a fault, a defect

short cut NOUN a short way of going somewhere or doing something

shorten VERB to make less in length

shorthand NOUN a method of writing quickly using strokes and dots to show sounds

short list NOUN a list of candidates selected from the total number of applicants or contestants

shortly ADVERB **1** soon **2** curtly, abruptly **3** briefly

short-sighted ADJECTIVE **1** seeing clearly only things which are near **2** taking no account of what may happen in the future

short-term ADJECTIVE intended to last only a short time

short-wave ADJECTIVE of a radio wave: using wavelengths between

10 and 100 metres (*compare with*: **long-wave**)

shot NOUN **1** something which is shot or fired **2** small lead bullets, used in cartridges **3** a single act of shooting **4** the sound of a gun being fired **5** the distance covered by a bullet, arrow, etc **6** a marksman **7** a throw or turn in a game **8** an attempt at doing something, guessing, etc **9** a photograph **10** a scene in a motion picture ▶ADJECTIVE **1** of silk: showing changing colours **2** streaked or mixed with (a colour etc) ▶VERB *past form of* **shoot** **a shot in the dark** a guess

shotgun NOUN a light type of gun which fires shot

should VERB **1** the form of the verb **shall** used to express a condition: *I should go if I had time* **2** used to mean 'ought to': *You should know that already*

shoulder NOUN **1** the part of the body between the neck and upper arm **2** the upper part of an animal's foreleg **3** a hump, a ridge: *the shoulder of the hill* ▶VERB **1** to carry on the shoulders **2** to bear the full weight of (a burden etc) **3** to push with the shoulder

shoulderblade NOUN the broad flat bone of the shoulder

shout NOUN **1** a loud cry or call **2** a loud burst (of laughter etc) ▶VERB to make a loud cry

shove VERB to push roughly, thrust, push aside ▶NOUN a rough push

shovel NOUN a spade-like tool used for lifting coal, gravel, etc ▶VERB to lift or move with a shovel

show VERB (**showing, showed, shown**) **1** to allow, or cause, to be seen: *Show me your new dress* **2** to be able to be seen: *Your underskirt is showing* **3** to exhibit, display (an art collection etc) **4** to point out (the way etc) **5** to direct, guide: *Show her to a seat* **6** to make clear, demonstrate: *That shows that I was right* ▶NOUN **1** the act of showing **2** a display, an exhibition: *an art show* **3** a performance, an entertainment **show off 1** to show or display (something) **2** to try to impress others with your talents etc **show up 1** to make to stand out clearly **2** to expose, make obvious (especially someone's faults)

show business NOUN the entertainment industry, especially light entertainment in film, theatre and television

showdown NOUN, *informal* a confrontation to settle a long-running dispute

shower NOUN **1** a short fall of rain **2** a large quantity: *a shower of questions* **3** a room or cubicle fitted with an apparatus that sprays water for bathing under while standing up **4** the apparatus that sprays water for this **5** *US* a party at which gifts are given to someone about to be married, have a baby, etc ▶VERB **1** to pour (something) down on **2** to bathe under a shower

showery ADJECTIVE raining from time to time

shown *past participle* of **show**

showroom NOUN a room where goods are laid out for people to see

showy ADJECTIVE (**showier,**

A B C D E F G H I J K L M N O P Q R S T U V W X Y Z

showiest) bright, gaudy; (too) obvious, striking

shrank *past tense* of **shrink**

shrapnel NOUN **1** a shell containing bullets etc which scatter on explosion **2** splinters of metal, a bomb, etc

ⓘ After Henry *Shrapnel*, 18th-century British general who invented the shell

shred NOUN **1** a long narrow piece, cut or torn off **2** a scrap, a very small amount: *not a shred of evidence* ▸ VERB (**shredding, shredded**) to cut or tear into shreds

shrew NOUN **1** a small mouse-like type of animal with a long nose **2** a quarrelsome or scolding woman

shrewd ADJECTIVE clever, cunning

shriek VERB to make a shrill scream or laugh ▸ NOUN a shrill scream or laugh

shrill ADJECTIVE of a sound or voice: high in tone, piercing > **shrilly** ADVERB

shrimp NOUN **1** a small, long-tailed edible shellfish **2** *informal* a small person

shrine NOUN a holy or sacred place

shrink VERB (**shrinking, shrank, shrunk**) **1** to make or become smaller **2** to draw back in fear and disgust (from) ▸ NOUN, *informal* a psychiatrist

shrive VERB (**shriving, shrove, shriven**) *old* **1** to hear a confession **2** to confess

shrivel VERB (**shrivelling, shrivelled**) to dry up, wrinkle, wither

shroud NOUN **1** a cloth covering a dead body **2** something which covers: *a shroud of mist* ▸ VERB to wrap up, cover

Shrove Tuesday NOUN sometimes called Pancake Day: the day before Ash Wednesday

shrub NOUN a small bush or plant

shrubbery NOUN (*plural* **shrubberies**) a place where shrubs grow

shrug VERB (**shrugging, shrugged**) to show doubt, lack of interest, etc by drawing up the shoulders ▸ NOUN a movement of the shoulders to show doubt, lack of interest, etc

shrug off to dismiss, treat as being unimportant

shrunk *past participle* of **shrink**

shrunken ADJECTIVE shrunk

shudder VERB to tremble from fear, cold, disgust ▸ NOUN a trembling

shuffle VERB **1** to mix, rearrange (eg playing-cards) **2** to move by dragging or sliding the feet along the ground without lifting them **3** to move (the feet) in this way ▸ NOUN **1** a rearranging **2** a dragging movement of the feet

shun VERB (**shunning, shunned**) to avoid, keep clear of

shunt VERB to move (railway trains, engines, etc) onto a side track

shut VERB (**shutting, shut**) **1** to move (a door, window, lid, etc) so that it covers an opening **2** to close, lock (a building etc) **3** to become closed: *The door shut with a bang* **4** to confine, restrain in a building, etc: *Shut the dog in his kennel* **shut down** to close (a factory etc) **shut up 1** to close completely **2** *informal* to stop speaking or making other noise

shutter NOUN **1** a cover for a window **2** a cover which closes over a camera lens as it takes a picture

shuttle NOUN the part of a weaving loom which carries the cross thread from side to side ▶ADJECTIVE of a transport service: going to and fro between two places

shuttlecock NOUN a rounded cork stuck with feathers, used in the game of badminton

shy ADJECTIVE **1** of a wild animal: easily frightened, timid **2** lacking confidence in the presence of others **3** not wanting to attract attention ▶VERB (**shies, shying, shied**) **1** of a horse etc: to jump or turn suddenly aside in fear **2** (**shy away**) to shrink from or recoil, showing reluctance **3** to throw, toss ▶NOUN a try, an attempt > **shyly** ADVERB **fight shy of** to avoid, keep away from

Siamese cat NOUN a fawn-coloured domestic cat

Siamese twins PLURAL NOUN an old name for **conjoined twins**

sibilant ADJECTIVE of a sound: hissing

sibling NOUN a brother or sister

sibyl NOUN a prophetess

sick ADJECTIVE **1** wanting to vomit **2** vomiting **3** not well, ill **4** (**sick of**) tired of someone or something **be sick** to vomit

sick bed *or* **sick room** NOUN a bed or room for people to rest in when ill

sicken VERB to make or become sick

sickening ADJECTIVE **1** causing sickness **2** disgusting, revolting

sick leave NOUN time off work for illness

sickly ADJECTIVE (**sicklier, sickliest**) **1** unhealthy **2** feeble

sickness NOUN **1** an illness: *a mysterious sickness* **2** vomiting or nausea: *Have you been having any sickness or diarrhoea?*

side NOUN **1** an edge, border or boundary line **2** a surface that is not the top, bottom, front or back **3** either surface of a piece of paper, cloth, etc **4** the right or left part of the body **5** a division, a part: *the north side of the town* **6** an aspect, point of view: *all sides of the problem* **7** a slope (of a hill) **8** a team or party which is opposing another ▶ADJECTIVE **1** on or towards the side: *side door* **2** indirect, additional but less important: *side issue* ▶VERB (**side with**) to support (one person, group, etc against another) **take sides** to choose to support (a party, person) against another

sideboard NOUN a piece of furniture in a dining room for holding dishes etc

sidecar NOUN a small car for a passenger, attached to a motorcycle

side effect NOUN an additional (often bad) effect of a drug

sideline NOUN an extra bit of business outside regular work

sidelong ADJECTIVE & ADVERB from or to the side: *sidelong glance*

sideshow NOUN a less important show that is part of a larger one

sidestep VERB to avoid by stepping to one side

sidewalk NOUN, *US* a pavement

sideways ADVERB **1** with the side foremost **2** towards the side

siding NOUN a short line of rails on which trucks are shunted off the main line

sidle VERB **1** to go or move sideways **2** to move stealthily, sneak

siege (*pronounced* seej) NOUN **1** an attempt to capture a town etc by keeping it surrounded by an armed force **2** a constant attempt to gain control **lay siege to** to besiege

sienna NOUN a reddish-brown, or yellowish-brown, pigment used in paints

sierra NOUN a range of mountains with jagged peaks

siesta NOUN a short sleep or rest taken in the afternoon

sieve (*pronounced* siv) NOUN a container with a mesh used to separate liquids from solids, or fine pieces from coarse pieces, etc ▶ VERB to put through a sieve

sift VERB **1** to separate by passing through a sieve: *sift the flour* **2** to consider and examine closely: *sifting all the evidence*

sigh NOUN a long, deep-sounding breath, showing tiredness, longing, etc ▶ VERB to give out a sigh

sight NOUN **1** the act or power of seeing **2** a view, a glimpse: *catch sight of her* **3** (often **sights**) something worth seeing: *the sights of London* **4** something or someone unusual, ridiculous, shocking, etc: *She's quite a sight in that hat* **5** a guide on a gun for taking aim ▶ VERB **1** to get a view of, see suddenly **2** to look at through the sight of a gun

🛈 Comes from Old English *sihth* meaning 'vision' or 'appearance'

> Do not confuse with: **site** and **cite**

sightseeing NOUN visiting the chief buildings, monuments, etc of a place > **sightseer** NOUN

sign NOUN **1** a mark with a special meaning, a symbol **2** a gesture (eg a nod, wave of the hand) to show your meaning **3** an advertisement or notice giving information **4** something which shows what is happening or is going to happen: *signs of irritation/a sign of good weather* ▶ VERB **1** to write your name on (a document, cheque, etc) **2** to make a sign or gesture to **3** to show (your meaning) by a sign or gesture **sign off 1** to bring a broadcast to an end **2** to stop work etc **sign on** *or* **up** to enter your name on a list for work, the army, etc

signal NOUN **1** a gesture, light or sound giving a command, warning, etc: *air-raid signal* **2** something used for this purpose: *railway signals* **3** the wave of sound received or sent out by a radio etc set ▶ VERB (**signalling, signalled**) **1** to make signals (to) **2** to send (information) by signal ▶ ADJECTIVE remarkable: *a signal success*

signatory NOUN (*plural* **signatories**) someone who has signed an agreement etc

signature NOUN **1** a signed name

2 an act of signing 3 *music* the flats or sharps at the beginning of a piece which show its key, or figures showing its timing

signet NOUN a small seal, usually bearing someone's initials

ⓘ Comes from Medieval Latin *signetum* meaning 'a small seal'

> Do not confuse with: **cygnet**

significance NOUN 1 meaning 2 importance

significant ADJECTIVE meaning much; important: *no significant change* > **significantly** ADVERB

signify VERB (**signifies, signifying, signified**) 1 to mean, be a sign of 2 to show, make known by a gesture: *signifying disapproval* 3 to have meaning or importance

sign language NOUN communication, especially with deaf people, using gestures to represent words and ideas

signpost NOUN a post with a sign, especially one showing direction and distances to certain places

Sikhism NOUN a religion whose followers observe the teachings of its ten gurus > **Sikh** NOUN & ADJECTIVE

silence NOUN 1 absence of sound or speech 2 a time of quietness ▸ VERB to cause to be silent

silencer NOUN a device (on a car engine, gun, etc) for making it less noisy

silent ADJECTIVE 1 free from noise 2 not speaking > **silently** ADVERB

silhouette NOUN 1 an outline drawing of someone, often in profile, filled in with black 2 a dark outline seen against the light

ⓘ After the 18th-century French finance minister, Etienne de *Silhouette*, possibly because of his notorious stinginess

silk NOUN 1 very fine, soft fibres spun by silkworms 2 thread or cloth made from this ▸ ADJECTIVE 1 made of silk 2 soft, smooth

silken ADJECTIVE 1 made of silk 2 smooth like silk

silkworm NOUN the caterpillar of certain moths which spins silk

silky ADJECTIVE (**silkier, silkiest**) like silk

sill NOUN a ledge of wood, stone, etc below a window or a door

silly ADJECTIVE (**sillier, silliest**) foolish, not sensible

silt NOUN sand or mud left behind by flowing water **silt up** to become blocked by mud

silver NOUN 1 *chemistry* (symbol **Ag**) a white precious metal, able to take on a high polish 2 money made of silver or of a metal alloy resembling it 3 objects (especially cutlery) made of, or plated with, silver ▸ ADJECTIVE made of, or looking like, silver ▸ VERB 1 to cover with silver 2 to become like silver

silver medal NOUN a medal given to a competitor who comes second

silversmith NOUN someone who makes or sells articles of silver

silver wedding NOUN the 25th anniversary of a wedding

SIM card NOUN a removable electronic card inside a mobile

a b c d e f g h i j k l m n o p q r s t u v w x y z

A B C D E F G H I J K L M N O P Q R S T U V W X Y Z

phone that stores information about the user

simian ADJECTIVE ape-like

simil- *or* **simul-** PREFIX forms words containing the notion 'like': *simile/simulate*

ⓘ Comes from Latin *similis* meaning 'like'

similar ADJECTIVE alike, almost the same

similarity NOUN (*plural* **similarities**) **1** being similar, likeness **2** resemblance

similarly ADVERB **1** in the same, or a similar, way **2** likewise, also

simile NOUN an expression using 'like' or 'as', in which one thing is likened to another that is well-known for a particular quality (eg 'as black as night', 'to swim like a fish')

simmer VERB to cook gently just below boiling point

simper VERB **1** to smile in a silly manner **2** to say with a simper ▸NOUN a silly smile

simple ADJECTIVE **1** easy, not difficult or complicated **2** plain, not fancy: *simple hairstyle* **3** ordinary: *simple, everyday objects* **4** of humble rank: *a simple peasant* **5** mere, nothing but: *the simple truth* **6** too trusting, easily cheated **7** foolish, half-witted

simple fraction NOUN, *maths* a vulgar fraction

simple sentence NOUN, *grammar* a sentence that has only one verb and only one subject (*compare with*: **compound sentence, complex sentence**)

simplicity NOUN the state of being simple

simplification NOUN **1** an act of making simpler **2** a simple form of anything

simplify VERB (**simplifies, simplifying, simplified**) to make simpler

simply ADVERB **1** in a simple manner **2** only, merely: *I do it simply for the money* **3** completely, absolutely: *simply beautiful*

simulate VERB **1** to pretend, feign: *to simulate illness* **2** to have the appearance of, look like

simulated ADJECTIVE **1** pretended **2** having the appearance of: *simulated leather*

simulation NOUN **1** the act of simulating something or the methods used to simulate something **2** something that has been created artificially to reproduce a real event or real set of conditions

simultaneous ADJECTIVE happening, or done, at the same time > **simultaneously** ADVERB

sin NOUN **1** a wicked act, especially one which breaks religious laws **2** wrongdoing **3** *informal* a shame, pity ▸VERB (**sinning, sinned**) to commit a sin, do wrong **original sin** the supposed sinful nature of all human beings since the time of Adam

since ADVERB **1** (often **ever since**) from that time onwards: *I have avoided him ever since* **2** at a later time: *We have since become friends* **3** ago: *long since* ▸PREP from the time of: *since his arrival*

▶CONJUNCTION **1** after the time when: *I have been at home since I returned from Italy* **2** because: *Since you are going, I will go too*

sincere ADJECTIVE (**sincerer, sincerest**) **1** honest in word and deed, meaning what you say or do, true: *a sincere friend* **2** truly felt: *a sincere desire* > **sincerely** ADVERB

sincerity NOUN the state or quality of being truthful and genuine in what you believe and say

sinew NOUN **1** a tough cord that joins a muscle to a bone **2** (**sinews**) equipment and resources necessary for something: *sinews of war*

sinewy ADJECTIVE having strong sinews, tough

sinful ADJECTIVE wicked

sing VERB (**singing, sang, sung**) **1** to make musical sounds with your voice **2** to utter (words, a song, etc) by doing this

singe VERB to burn slightly on the surface, scorch ▶NOUN a surface burn

singer NOUN someone who sings or whose voice has been specially trained for singing

single ADJECTIVE **1** one only **2** not double **3** not married **4** for one person: *a single bed* **5** between two people: *single combat* **6** for one direction of a journey: *a single ticket* **single out** to pick out, treat differently in some way

single-handed ADJECTIVE working etc by yourself

single-minded ADJECTIVE having one aim only

singlet NOUN a vest, an undershirt

singly ADVERB one by one, separately

sing-song NOUN a gathering of people singing informally together ▶ADJECTIVE of a speaking voice etc: having a fluctuating rhythm

singular ADJECTIVE **1** *grammar* the opposite of **plural**, showing one person, thing, etc **2** exceptional: *singular success* **3** unusual, strange: *a singular sight*

singularly ADVERB strangely, exceptionally: *singularly ugly*

sinister ADJECTIVE suggesting evil, evil-looking

sink VERB (**sank, sunk**) **1** to go down below the surface of the water etc **2** to go down or become less: *My hopes sank* **3** of a very ill person: to become weaker **4** to lower yourself (into): *sink into a chair* **5** to make by digging (a well etc) **6** to push (your teeth etc) deep into (something) **7** to invest (money etc) in a business ▶NOUN a basin in a kitchen, bathroom, etc with a water supply connected to it and a drain for carrying off dirty water etc

sinner NOUN a person who has committed a sin or sins

Sino- PREFIX relating to China or the Chinese

🛈 Comes from Greek *Sinai* meaning 'Chinese'

sinuous ADJECTIVE bending in and out, winding

sinus (*pronounced* **sai**-*nus*) NOUN (*plural* **sinuses**) an air cavity in the head connected with the nose

sinusitis NOUN inflammation of (one of) the sinuses

sip VERB (**sipping, sipped**) to drink in very small quantities ▶NOUN a taste of a drink, a swallow

siphon *or* **syphon** NOUN **1** a bent tube for drawing off liquids from one container into another **2** a glass bottle, for soda water etc, containing such a tube ▶VERB to draw (off) through a siphon: *he siphoned off some of the club's funds*

sir NOUN **1** a polite form of address used to a man **2** (**Sir**) the title of a knight or baronet

sire NOUN **1** a male parent, especially of a horse **2** *old* a title used in speaking to a king ▶VERB of an animal: to be the male parent of

siren NOUN **1** an instrument that gives out a loud hooting noise as a warning or signal **2** (**Siren**) a mythical sea nymph whose singing enchanted sailors and tempted them into danger **3** an attractive but dangerous woman

sirloin NOUN the upper part of the loin of beef

sirocco NOUN a hot dry wind blowing from N Africa to the Mediterranean coast

sister NOUN **1** a female born of the same parents as yourself **2** a senior nurse, often in charge of a hospital ward **3** a nun ▶ADJECTIVE **1** closely related **2** of similar design or structure: *a sister ship*

sisterhood NOUN **1** the state of being a sister **2** a religious community of women

sister-in-law NOUN **1** the sister of your husband or wife **2** the wife of your brother or of your brother-in-law

sisterly ADJECTIVE like a sister

sit VERB (**sitting, sat**) **1** to rest on the buttocks, be seated **2** of a bird: to perch **3** to rest on eggs in order to hatch them **4** to be an official member: *sit in parliament/sit on a committee* **5** of a court etc: to meet officially **6** to pose for a photographer, painter, etc **7** to take (an examination etc) **sit tight** to be unwilling to move **sit up 1** to sit with your back straight **2** to stay up instead of going to bed

sitcom NOUN a television comedy series with the same characters and a running theme

site NOUN a place where a building, town, etc is or is to be placed ▶VERB to select a place for (a building etc)

[1] Comes from Latin *situs* meaning 'situation'

> Do not confuse with: **sight** and **cite**

sitter NOUN **1** someone who poses for a portrait etc **2** a babysitter **3** a bird sitting on eggs

sitting NOUN the state or time of sitting ▶ADJECTIVE **1** seated **2** for sitting in or on **3** in office: *sitting member of parliament* **4** in possession: *sitting tenant*

sitting-room NOUN a room chiefly for sitting in

situation NOUN **1** the place where anything stands: *a pleasant situation on the bank of the river* **2** a job, employment: *situations vacant* **3** a state of affairs, circumstances: *in an awkward situation*

six NOUN the number 6 ▸ADJECTIVE 6 in number **at sixes and sevens** in confusion

sixpence NOUN a silver-coloured coin used before decimal currency, worth 1/40 of £1

sixteen NOUN the number 16 ▸ADJECTIVE 16 in number

sixteenth ADJECTIVE the last of a series of sixteen ▸NOUN one of sixteen equal parts

sixth ADJECTIVE the last of a series of six ▸NOUN one of six equal parts

sixtieth ADJECTIVE the last of a series of sixty ▸NOUN one of sixty equal parts

sixty NOUN the number 60 ▸ADJECTIVE 60 in number

size NOUN **1** space taken up by anything **2** measurements, dimensions **3** largeness **4** a class into which shoes and clothes are grouped according to size: *She takes size 4 in shoes* **5** a weak kind of glue used, eg in wallpapering **size up** to form an opinion of a person, situation, etc

sizeable *or* **sizable** ADJECTIVE fairly large

sizzle VERB **1** to make a hissing sound **2** to fry, scorch

skate NOUN **1** a steel blade attached to a boot for gliding on ice **2** a boot with such a blade attached, for ice-skating **3** a rollerskate **4** a type of large flatfish ▸VERB to move on skates > **skater** NOUN

skateboard NOUN a narrow board on four rollerskate wheels > **skateboarding** NOUN

skeletal ADJECTIVE of or like a skeleton

skeleton NOUN **1** the bony framework of an animal or person, without the flesh **2** any framework or outline ▸ADJECTIVE of staff etc: reduced to a very small or minimum number

skeleton key NOUN a key from which the inner part has been cut away so that it can open many different locks

sketch NOUN (*plural* **sketches**) **1** a rough plan or drawing **2** a short or rough account **3** any of several short pieces of comedy presented as a programme ▸VERB **1** to draw roughly **2** to give the chief points of **3** to draw in pencil or ink

sketchy ADJECTIVE (**sketchier, sketchiest**) **1** roughly done **2** not thorough, incomplete: *My knowledge of geography is rather sketchy*

skew ADJECTIVE & ADVERB off the straight, slanting ▸VERB to set at a slant

skewer NOUN a long pin of wood or metal for holding meat, eg kebabs, together while grilling, roasting, etc ▸VERB to fix with a skewer or with something sharp

ski NOUN (*plural* **skis**) one of a pair of long narrow strips of wood or metal that are attached to boots for gliding over snow ▸VERB (**skiing, skied** *or* **ski'd**) to move or travel on skis

skid NOUN **1** a slide sideways: *The car went into a skid* **2** a wedge put under a wheel to check it on a steep slope **3** (**skids**) logs etc on which things can be moved by sliding ▸VERB (**skidding, skidded**) **1** of

A B C D E F G H I J K L M N O P Q R S T U V W X Y Z

a wheel: to slide along without turning **2** to slip sideways **on the skids** on the way down **put the skids under** to hurry along

ski-jump NOUN **1** a steep, snow-covered track ending in a platform from which a skier jumps **2** a jump made by a skier from such a platform > **ski-jumping** NOUN

skilful ADJECTIVE having or showing skill > **skilfully** ADVERB

skill NOUN cleverness at doing a thing, either from practice or as a natural gift

skilled ADJECTIVE **1** having skill, especially through training **2** of a job: requiring skill

skim VERB (**skimming, skimmed**) **1** to remove cream, scum, etc from the surface of (something) **2** to move lightly and quickly over (a surface) **3** to read quickly, missing parts

skimmed ADJECTIVE of milk: with some of the fat removed

skimp VERB **1** to give (someone) hardly enough **2** to do (a job) imperfectly **3** to spend too little money (on): *skimping on clothes*

skimpy ADJECTIVE (**skimpier, skimpiest**) **1** too small **2** of clothes: too short or tight

skin NOUN **1** the natural outer covering of an animal or person **2** a thin outer layer on a fruit **3** a thin film that forms on a liquid ▸ VERB (**skinning, skinned**) to strip the skin from **by the skin of your teeth** very narrowly

skin-deep ADJECTIVE as deep as the skin only, on the surface

skin-diver NOUN a diver who wears simple equipment

skinflint NOUN a very mean person

skinny ADJECTIVE (**skinnier, skinniest**) very thin

skint ADJECTIVE, *Brit informal* broke, without much money

skip VERB (**skipping, skipped**) **1** to go along with a rhythmic step and hop **2** to jump over a turning rope **3** to leap, especially lightly or joyfully **4** to leave out (parts of a book, a meal, etc) ▸ NOUN **1** an act of skipping **2** the captain of a side at bowls etc **3** a large metal container for collecting and transporting refuse

skipper NOUN the captain of a ship, aeroplane or team ▸ VERB to act as captain for (a ship, team, etc)

skipping rope NOUN a rope used in skipping

skirmish NOUN (*plural* **skirmishes**) **1** a fight between small parties of soldiers or planes **2** a short sharp contest or disagreement ▸ VERB to fight briefly or informally

skirt NOUN **1** a garment, worn by women, that hangs from the waist **2** the lower part of a dress **3** (**skirts**) the outer edge or border ▸ VERB to pass along, or lie along, the edge of

skittle NOUN **1** a bottle-shaped object used as a target in bowling, a ninepin **2** (**skittles**) a game in which skittles are knocked over by a ball

skive VERB, *informal* (often **skive off**) to avoid doing a duty > **skiver** NOUN

skivvy *informal*, NOUN (*plural*

skivvies) a domestic servant, a cleaner

skulduggery *or US* **skullduggery** NOUN trickery, underhand practices

skulk VERB **1** to wait about, stay hidden **2** to move stealthily away, sneak

skull NOUN **1** the bony case which encloses the brain **2** the head **skull and crossbones** the sign on a pirate's flag

skullcap NOUN a cap which fits closely to the head

skunk NOUN **1** a small American animal which defends itself by giving off a bad smell **2** *informal* a contemptible person

sky NOUN (*plural* **skies**) **1** the upper atmosphere, the heavens **2** the weather, the climate

skylark NOUN the common lark which sings while hovering far overhead

skylight NOUN a window in a roof or ceiling

skyline NOUN the horizon

skyscraper NOUN a high building of very many storeys

slab NOUN a thick flat slice or piece of anything: *stone slab/cut a slab of cake*

slack ADJECTIVE **1** not firmly stretched **2** not firmly in position **3** not strict **4** lazy and careless **5** not busy: *slack holiday season* ▶ NOUN **1** the loose part of a rope **2** small coal and coal-dust **3** (**slacks**) loose, casual trousers ▶ VERB **1** to do less work than you should, be lazy **2** to slacken

slacken VERB to make or become looser

slag NOUN waste left from metal-smelting ▶ VERB (**slagging, slagged**) *slang* to criticize, make fun of cruelly: *She's always slagging him off*

slalom NOUN **1** a downhill, zigzag ski run among posts or trees **2** an obstacle race in canoes

slam VERB (**slamming, slammed**) **1** to shut (a door, lid, etc) with a loud noise **2** to put down with a loud noise: *slammed the book on the table* ▶ NOUN **1** the act of slamming **2** (also **grand slam**) a winning of every trick in cards or every contest in a competition etc

slander NOUN an untrue statement (in England, a spoken one) aimed at harming someone's reputation ▶ VERB to speak slander against (someone)

slanderous ADJECTIVE of a statement: untrue and therefore unfairly damaging someone's reputation

slang NOUN **1** popular words and phrases that are used in informal, everyday speech or writing **2** the special language of a particular group: *Cockney rhyming slang*

slant VERB **1** to slope **2** to lie or move diagonally or in a sloping position **3** to give or present (facts or information) in a distorted way that suits your own purpose ▶ NOUN **1** a slope **2** a diagonal direction **3** a point of view

slap NOUN a blow with the palm of the hand or anything flat ▶ VERB (**slapping, slapped**) to give a slap to

A B C D E F G H I J K L M N O P Q R S T U V W X Y Z

slapdash ADJECTIVE hasty, careless

slapstick ADJECTIVE of comedy: boisterous, funny in a very obvious way ▸NOUN comedy in this style
ⓘ After the name of a theatrical device which made a loud noise when an actor was hit with it

slash VERB **1** to make long cuts in **2** to strike at violently ▸NOUN (*plural* **slashes**) **1** a long cut **2** a sweeping blow

slat NOUN a thin strip of wood, metal or other material > **slatted** ADJECTIVE

slate NOUN an easily split blue-grey rock, used for roofing, or at one time for writing upon ▸ADJECTIVE **1** made of slate **2** slate-coloured ▸VERB **1** to cover with slate **2** to say or write harsh things to or about: *The play was slated*

slaughter NOUN **1** the killing of animals, especially for food **2** cruel killing of large numbers of people ▸VERB **1** to kill (an animal) for food **2** to kill brutally

slaughterhouse NOUN a place where animals are killed in order to be sold for food

slave NOUN **1** someone forced to work for a master and owner **2** someone who serves another devotedly **3** someone who works very hard **4** someone who is addicted to something: *a slave to fashion* ▸VERB to work like a slave

slaver NOUN saliva running from the mouth ▸VERB to let saliva run out of the mouth

slavery NOUN **1** the state of being a slave **2** the system of owning slaves

Slavic ADJECTIVE relating to a group of E European people or their languages, including Russian, Polish, etc

slay VERB (**slaying, slew, slain**) *formal* to kill

sleaze NOUN, *informal* corrupt or illicit practices, especially in public life

sleazy ADJECTIVE (**sleazier, sleaziest**) squalid, disreputable > **sleaziness** NOUN

sled *or* **sledge** NOUN a vehicle with runners, made for sliding upon snow ▸VERB to ride on a sledge

sledgehammer NOUN a large, heavy hammer

sleek ADJECTIVE **1** smooth, glossy **2** of an animal: well-fed and well-cared for **3** elegant, well-groomed

sleep VERB (**sleeping, slept**) to rest with your eyes closed in a state of natural unconsciousness ▸NOUN **1** the state of sleeping **2** a spell of sleeping **go to sleep 1** to pass into the state of being asleep **2** of a limb: to become numb, tingle **put to sleep 1** to make to go to sleep, make unconscious **2** to put (an animal) to death painlessly, eg by an injection of a drug **sleep with** *informal* to have sexual intercourse with

sleeper NOUN **1** someone who sleeps **2** a beam of wood or metal supporting railway lines **3** a sleeping car or sleeping berth on a railway train

sleeping bag NOUN a large warm bag for sleeping in, used by campers etc

sleepless ADJECTIVE unable to sleep, without sleep

sleepwalker NOUN someone who walks etc while asleep

sleepy ADJECTIVE (**sleepier, sleepiest**) **1** drowsy, wanting to sleep **2** looking as if needing sleep **3** quiet, not bustling: *sleepy town*
> **sleepily** ADVERB

sleet NOUN rain mixed with snow or hail

sleeve NOUN **1** the part of a garment which covers the arm **2** a cover for a record or compact disc **3** a cover for an arm-like piece of machinery

sleeveless ADJECTIVE without sleeves

sleigh NOUN a large horse-drawn sledge

sleight of hand NOUN skill and quickness of hand movement in performing card tricks etc

slender ADJECTIVE **1** thin, narrow **2** slim **3** small in amount: *by a slender margin*

sleuth NOUN someone who tracks down criminals, a detective

slice NOUN **1** a thin, broad piece of something: *slice of toast* **2** a broad-bladed utensil for serving fish etc ▸VERB **1** to cut into slices **2** to cut through **3** to cut (off from etc) **4** *golf* to hit (a ball) in such a way that it curves away to the right

slick ADJECTIVE **1** smart, clever, often too much so **2** smooth ▸NOUN a thin layer of spilt oil

slide VERB (**sliding, slid**) **1** to move smoothly over a surface **2** to slip **3** to pass quietly or secretly ▸NOUN **1** an act of sliding **2** a smooth, slippery slope or track **3** a chute **4** a groove or rail on which a thing slides **5** a fastening for the hair **6** a picture for showing on a screen **7** a piece of glass on which to place objects to be examined under a microscope

slight ADJECTIVE **1** of little amount or importance: *slight breeze/slight quarrel* **2** small, slender ▸VERB to treat as unimportant, insult by ignoring ▸NOUN an insult, an offence

slightly ADVERB a little: *slightly annoyed*

slim ADJECTIVE (**slimmer, slimmest**) **1** slender, thin **2** small, slight: *slim chance* ▸VERB (**slimming, slimmed**) **1** to make slender **2** to use means (such as eating less) to become slender

slime NOUN sticky, half-liquid material, especially thin, slippery mud

slimy ADJECTIVE (**slimier, slimiest**) **1** covered with slime **2** *informal* of a person: too attentive or flattering

sling NOUN **1** a bandage hanging from the neck or shoulders to support an injured arm **2** a strap with a string attached to each end, for flinging stones **3** a net of ropes etc for hoisting and carrying heavy objects ▸VERB (**slinging, slung**) **1** to throw with a sling **2** to move or swing by means of a sling **3** *informal* to throw

slink VERB (**slinking, slunk**) to sneak away, move stealthily

slip VERB (**slipping, slipped**) **1** to slide accidentally and lose footing or balance: *slip on the ice* **2** to fall out of place, or out of your control: *The plate slipped from my grasp*

a b c d e f g h i j k l m n o p q r s t u v w x y z

3 to move quickly and easily **4** to move quietly, quickly and secretly **5** to escape from: *slip your mind* ▸NOUN **1** the act of slipping **2** an error, a slight mistake **3** a cutting from a plant **4** a strip or narrow piece of anything (eg paper) **5** a slim, slight person: *a slip of a girl* **6** a slipway **7** a thin undergarment worn under a dress, an underskirt **8** a cover for a pillow **9** *cricket* a fielding position near to the wicketkeeper on the offside **slip up** to make a mistake

slipknot NOUN a knot made with a loop so that it can slip

slipper NOUN a soft, loose indoor shoe

slippery ADJECTIVE **1** causing skidding or slipping **2** not trustworthy

slipstream NOUN the stream of air driven back by an aircraft propeller etc

slip-up NOUN a mistake

slipway NOUN a smooth slope on which a ship is built

slit VERB (**slitting, slit**) **1** to make a long narrow cut in **2** to cut into strips ▸NOUN a long narrow cut or opening

slither VERB **1** to slide or slip about (eg on mud) **2** to move with a gliding motion

sliver NOUN a thin strip or slice

slobber VERB to let saliva dribble from the mouth, slaver

slog VERB (**slogging, slogged**) to work or plod on steadily, especially against difficulty ▸NOUN a difficult spell of work

slogan NOUN an easily remembered and frequently repeated phrase, used in advertising etc

sloop NOUN a one-masted sailing ship

slop VERB (**slopping, slopped**) **1** to flow over, spill **2** to splash ▸NOUN **1** spilt liquid **2** (**slops**) dirty water **3** (**slops**) thin, tasteless food

slope NOUN **1** a position or direction that is neither level nor upright, a slant **2** a surface with one end higher than the other, eg a hillside ▸VERB to be in a slanting, sloping position

sloppy ADJECTIVE (**sloppier, sloppiest**) **1** wet, muddy **2** careless, untidy: *sloppy work* **3** silly, sentimental

slosh VERB **1** to splash **2** *informal* to hit

slot NOUN **1** a small, narrow opening, eg to insert coins **2** a position ▸VERB (**slotting, slotted**) **1** to make a slot in **2** (sometimes **slot into**) to find a position or place for

sloth NOUN **1** laziness **2** a slow-moving S American animal that lives in trees

slothful ADJECTIVE lazy

slouch NOUN a hunched-up body position ▸VERB to walk with shoulders rounded and head hanging

slough (*pronounced* slow) NOUN a bog, a marsh

slovenly ADJECTIVE untidy, careless, dirty

slow ADJECTIVE **1** not fast **2** not hasty or hurrying **3** of a clock: behind in time **4** not quick in learning, dull ▸VERB (often **slow down**) to make or become slower > **slowly** ADVERB

slowcoach NOUN someone who moves, works, etc slowly

slow motion NOUN **1** in film or television: a speed of movement that is much slower than real life **2** slower than normal real-life movement ▸ADJECTIVE (**slow-motion**) slower than actual motion: *a slow-motion clip*

sludge NOUN soft, slimy mud

slug NOUN **1** a snail-like animal with no shell **2** a small piece of metal used as a bullet **3** a heavy blow

sluggish ADJECTIVE moving slowly

sluice NOUN **1** (*also called*: **sluicegate**) a sliding gate for controlling a flow of water in an artificial channel **2** the stream which flows through this ▸VERB to clean out with a strong flow of water

slum NOUN **1** an overcrowded part of a town where the houses are dirty and unhealthy **2** a house in a slum

slumber VERB to sleep ▸NOUN sleep

slump VERB **1** to fall or sink suddenly and heavily **2** to lose value suddenly ▸NOUN a sudden fall in values, prices, etc

slung *past form* of **sling**

slunk *past form* of **slink**

slur VERB (**slurring, slurred**) **1** to pronounce indistinctly **2** to damage (a reputation etc), speak evil of ▸NOUN **1** a blot or stain (on someone's reputation) **2** a criticism, an insult

slurp VERB to drink or gulp noisily ▸NOUN a noisy gulp

slurry NOUN **1** thin, liquid cement **2** liquid waste

slush NOUN **1** watery mud **2** melting snow **3** something very sentimental **4** sentimentality

slushy ADJECTIVE **1** covered with, or like, slush **2** *informal* sentimental

slut NOUN, *derogatory* **1** a woman who regularly engages in casual sex **2** a prostitute **3** a dirty, untidy woman

sly ADJECTIVE cunning; wily; deceitful > **slyly** ADVERB **on the sly** secretly, surreptitiously

smack VERB **1** to strike smartly, slap **2** to have a trace or suggestion (of): *This smacks of treason* ▸NOUN **1** an act of smacking **2** the sound made by smacking **3** a boisterous kiss **4** a taste, a flavour **5** a trace, a suggestion **6** a small fishing vessel **7** *slang* the drug heroin ▸ADVERB with sudden violence: *run smack into the door*

small ADJECTIVE **1** little, not big or much **2** not important: *a small matter* **3** not having a large or successful business: *a small businessman* **4** of a voice: soft ▸NOUN the most slender or narrow part: *the small of the back* ▸ADVERB into small pieces: *cut up small*

smallholding NOUN a small farm

small hours PLURAL NOUN the hours just after midnight

small-minded ADJECTIVE having narrow opinions, ungenerous

smallpox NOUN a serious infectious illness, causing fever, vomiting and a rash of large pimples that often leave scars (**pocks**)

a b c d e f g h i j k l m n o p q r s t u v w x y z

small talk NOUN polite conversation about nothing very important

smarmy ADJECTIVE (**smarmier, smarmiest**) nauseatingly smooth or charming

smart ADJECTIVE **1** clever and quick in thought or action **2** well-dressed **3** brisk **4** sharp, stinging ▸NOUN a sharp, stinging pain ▸VERB **1** to feel a sharp, stinging pain **2** to feel annoyed, resentful, etc after being insulted

smash VERB **1** to break into pieces, shatter **2** to strike with force: *smash a ball with a racket* **3** to crash (into etc): *The car smashed into the wall* ▸NOUN (*plural* **smashes**) **1** an act of smashing **2** a crash, a collision (of vehicles) **3** the ruin of a business etc

smashing ADJECTIVE, *informal* excellent

smattering NOUN a very slight knowledge of a subject: *a smattering of Italian*

smear VERB **1** to spread (something sticky or oily): *smear paste on the wall* **2** to spread, smudge with (something sticky etc): *smear the wall with paste* **3** to become smeared **4** to slander, insult ▸NOUN a smudge of something sticky

smell NOUN **1** the sense or power of being aware of things through your nose **2** an act of using this sense **3** something sensed through the nose, a scent ▸VERB (**smelling, smelt** *or* **smelled**) **1** to notice by the sense of smell: *I smell gas* **2** to use your sense of smell on: *Smell this fish* **3** to give off a smell: *The dustbin smells* **smell out** to find out by prying or inquiring closely

smelling-salts PLURAL NOUN strong-smelling chemicals in a bottle, used to revive people who are fainting

smelly ADJECTIVE (**smellier, smelliest**) having a bad smell

smelt VERB **1** to melt (ore) in order to separate the metal from other material **2** *past form* of **smell**

smile VERB **1** to show pleasure by drawing up the corners of the lips **2** (sometimes **smile on**) to be favourable to: *Fortune smiled on him* ▸NOUN an act of smiling

smirch VERB to stain, soil ▸NOUN a stain

smirk VERB to smile in a self-satisfied or foolish manner ▸NOUN a self-satisfied smile

smith NOUN a worker in metals; a blacksmith

smithereens PLURAL NOUN fragments

smithy NOUN (*plural* **smithies**) the workshop of a smith

smitten ADJECTIVE affected (by); strongly attracted (by)

smock NOUN a loose shirt-like garment, sometimes worn over other clothes as a protection

smog NOUN thick, smoky fog

smoke NOUN **1** the cloud-like gases and particles of soot given off by anything burning **2** an act of smoking (a cigarette etc) ▸VERB **1** to give off smoke **2** to inhale and exhale tobacco smoke from a cigarette, pipe, etc **3** to cure or preserve (ham, fish, etc) by applying smoke **4** to darken (eg glass) by applying smoke

smokeless ADJECTIVE **1** burning without smoke **2** where the emission of smoke is prohibited: *a smokeless zone*

smoker NOUN **1** someone who smokes **2** a railway compartment in which smoking is allowed

smokescreen NOUN anything (originally smoke) meant to confuse or mislead

smoky ADJECTIVE (**smokier, smokiest**) **1** full of smoke **2** tasting of smoke

smooch VERB, *informal* to kiss, pet

smooth ADJECTIVE **1** not rough **2** having an even surface **3** without lumps: *a smooth sauce* **4** hairless **5** without breaks, stops or jolts: *smooth journey* **6** too agreeable in manner ▶ VERB **1** to make smooth **2** to calm, soothe **3** to free from difficulty

smoothie NOUN a thick drink made with puréed fruit

smother VERB **1** to kill by keeping air from, eg by covering over the nose and mouth **2** to die by this means **3** to cover up, conceal (feelings etc) **4** to put down, suppress (a rebellion etc)

smoulder VERB **1** to burn slowly without bursting into flame **2** to exist in a hidden state **3** to show otherwise hidden emotion, eg anger, hate: *Her eyes smouldered with hate*

SMS ABBREVIATION short message service, a service for sending text messages

smudge NOUN a smear ▶ VERB to make dirty with spots or smears

smug ADJECTIVE (**smugger, smuggest**) well-satisfied, too obviously pleased with yourself

smuggle VERB **1** to take (goods) into, or out of, a country without paying the required taxes **2** to send or take secretly

smuggler NOUN someone who smuggles goods

smut NOUN **1** a spot of dirt or soot **2** vulgar or indecent talk etc

smutty ADJECTIVE (**smuttier, smuttiest**) **1** dirty, grimy **2** indecent, vulgar

snack NOUN a light, hasty meal

snag NOUN a difficulty, an obstacle ▶ VERB (**snagging, snagged**) to catch or tear on something sharp

snail NOUN **1** a soft-bodied, small, crawling animal with a shell **2** someone who is very slow

snake NOUN **1** a legless reptile with a long body, which moves along the ground with a winding movement **2** anything snake-like in form or movement **3** a cunning, deceitful person

snap VERB (**snapping, snapped**) **1** to make a sudden bite **2** to break or shut suddenly with a sharp noise **3** to cause (the fingers) to make a sharp noise **4** to speak sharply **5** to take a photograph of ▶ NOUN **1** the noise made by snapping **2** a sudden spell (eg of cold weather) **3** a card game in which players try to match cards **4** a photograph **snap up** to eat up or grab something eagerly

snapdragon NOUN a garden plant

whose flower, when pinched, opens and shuts like a mouth

snappy ADJECTIVE (**snappier, snappiest**) irritable, inclined to speak sharply > **snappily** ADVERB

snapshot NOUN a quickly taken photograph

snare NOUN **1** a noose or loop that draws tight when pulled, for catching an animal **2** a trap **3** a hidden danger or temptation ▸VERB to catch in or with a snare

snarl VERB **1** to growl, showing the teeth **2** to speak in a furious, spiteful tone **3** to become tangled: *snarled up in the net* ▸NOUN **1** a growl, a furious noise **2** a tangle, a knot **3** a muddled or confused state

snatch VERB **1** to seize or grab suddenly **2** to take quickly when you have time: *snatch an hour's sleep* ▸NOUN (*plural* **snatches**) **1** an attempt to seize **2** a small piece or quantity: *a snatch of music*

sneak VERB **1** to creep or move in a stealthy, secretive way **2** to tell tales, tell on others ▸NOUN **1** someone who tells tales **2** a deceitful, underhand person

sneaky ADJECTIVE (**sneakier, sneakiest**) underhand, deceitful > **sneakily** ADVERB

sneer VERB to show contempt by a scornful expression, words, etc ▸NOUN a scornful expression or remark

sneeze VERB to make a sudden, unintentional and violent blowing noise through the nose and mouth ▸NOUN an involuntary blow through the nose

snicker VERB **1** to snigger **2** of a horse: to neigh

snide ADJECTIVE mean, malicious: *snide remark*

sniff VERB **1** to draw in air through the nose with a slight noise, eg when having a cold, or showing disapproval **2** to smell (a scent etc) **3** (**sniff at**) to treat something with scorn or suspicion ▸NOUN a quick drawing in of air through the nose

sniffle NOUN a light sniff, a snuffle ▸VERB to sniff lightly

snigger VERB to laugh in a quiet, sly manner ▸NOUN a quiet, sly laugh

snip VERB (**snipping, snipped**) to cut off sharply, especially with a single cut ▸NOUN **1** a cut with scissors **2** a small piece snipped off **3** *informal* a bargain: *a snip at the price*

snipe VERB **snipe at 1** to shoot at someone from a place of hiding **2** to attack someone with critical remarks

sniper NOUN someone who shoots at a single person from cover

snippet NOUN a little piece, especially of information or gossip

snitch NOUN (*plural* **snitches**), *informal* an informer, a tell-tale ▸VERB to inform (on)

snivel VERB (**snivelling, snivelled**) **1** to have a running nose, eg because of a cold **2** to whine or complain tearfully ▸NOUN **1** a running nose **2** a whine

snob NOUN someone who looks down on those in a lower social class

[i] Originally a slang term for

A B C D E F G H I J K L M N O P Q R S T U V W X Y Z

'shoemaker' which changed its meaning to someone of low social class, and later to someone who enjoys showing off their wealth and social standing

snobbery NOUN the behaviour that is typical of a snob or snobs

snobbish ADJECTIVE admiring things associated with the higher social classes and despising things associated with the lower classes

snooker NOUN a game like billiards, using 22 coloured balls

snoop VERB to spy or pry in a sneaking secretive way ▶ NOUN someone who pries

snooty ADJECTIVE (**snootier, snootiest**) haughty, snobbish

snooze VERB to sleep lightly, doze ▶ NOUN a light sleep

snore VERB to make a snorting noise in your sleep while breathing ▶ NOUN a snorting sound made in sleep

snorkel NOUN **1** a tube with one end above the water, to enable an underwater swimmer to breathe **2** a similar device for bringing air into a submarine

snort VERB **1** to force air noisily through the nostrils **2** to make such a noise to express disapproval, anger, laughter, etc ▶ NOUN a loud noise made through the nostrils

snot NOUN mucus of the nose

snotty ADJECTIVE (**snottier, snottiest**) *informal* haughty or standoffish

snout NOUN the projecting nose and mouth of an animal, eg of a pig

snow NOUN **1** frozen water vapour which falls in light white flakes **2** *slang* the drug cocaine ▶ VERB to fall down in, or like, flakes of snow

snowed under overwhelmed with work etc

snowball NOUN a ball made of snow pressed hard together ▶ VERB **1** to throw snowballs **2** to grow increasingly quickly: *Unemployment has snowballed recently*

snowboard NOUN a single board used as a ski on snow

snowdrift NOUN a bank of snow blown together by the wind

snowdrop NOUN a small white flower growing from a bulb in early spring

snowflake NOUN a flake of snow

snowman NOUN (*plural* **snowmen**) a figure shaped like a human being, made of snow

snowplough NOUN a large vehicle for clearing snow from roads etc

snowshoe NOUN a long broad frame with a mesh, one of a pair for walking on snow

snowy ADJECTIVE (**snowier, snowiest**) **1** covered with snow **2** white

snub VERB (**snubbing, snubbed**) to treat or speak to in an abrupt, scornful way; insult ▶ NOUN an act of snubbing ▶ ADJECTIVE of a nose: short and turned up at the end

snuff VERB to put out or trim the wick of (a candle)

snuffle VERB to make a sniffing noise through the nose, eg because of a cold ▶ NOUN a sniffling through the nose

A B C D E F G H I J K L M N O P Q R S T U V W X Y Z

snug ADJECTIVE (**snugger, snuggest**) **1** lying close and warm **2** cosy, comfortable **3** closely fitting; neat and trim

snuggle VERB **1** to curl up comfortably **2** to draw close to for warmth, affection, etc

so ADVERB **1** as shown, eg by a hand gesture: *so high* **2** to such an extent, to a great extent: *so heavy/you look so happy* **3** in this or that way: *Point your toes so* **4** correct: *Is that so?* **5** (used in contradicting) indeed: *It's not true. It is so* ▶CONJUNCTION therefore: *You don't need it, so don't buy it* **so as to** in order to **so far** up to this or that point **so forth** more of the same sort of thing: *pots, pans, and so forth* **so much for** that is the end of: *So much for that idea!* **so that** with the purpose or result that **so what?** what difference does it make? does it matter?

soak VERB **1** to let stand in a liquid until wet through **2** to drench (with) **soak something up** to suck it up, absorb it

soaking ADJECTIVE wet through ▶NOUN a wetting, drenching ▶ADVERB: **soaking wet** thoroughly wet, drenched

so-and-so NOUN (*plural* **so-and-sos**) *informal* **1** this or that person or thing **2** *euphemistic* used instead of a stronger insult: *She's a real so-and-so, saying that to you!*

soap NOUN **1** a mixture containing oils or fats and other substances, used in washing **2** *informal* a soap opera ▶VERB to use soap on

soapbox NOUN (*plural* **soapboxes**) **1** a small box for holding soap **2** a makeshift platform for standing on when speaking to a crowd out of doors

soap opera NOUN a television series about a group of characters and their daily lives
ⓘ So called because when these shows first started they were sponsored by soap companies and advertisements for soap were broadcast with them

soapy ADJECTIVE (**soapier, soapiest**) **1** like soap **2** full of soap

soar VERB **1** to fly high into the air **2** of prices: to rise high and quickly

sob VERB (**sobbing, sobbed**) to weep noisily ▶NOUN a noisy weeping

sober ADJECTIVE **1** not drunk **2** serious, staid **3** not florid, not elaborate ▶VERB (sometimes **sober up**) to make or become sober
> **soberly** ADVERB

soberness *or* **sobriety** (*pronounced* soh-**brai**-i-ti) NOUN the state of being sober

sob story NOUN (*plural* **sob stories**) a story told to arouse sympathy

so-called ADJECTIVE called by such a name, often mistakenly: *a so-called expert*

soccer NOUN football

sociable ADJECTIVE fond of the company of others, friendly
> **sociability** NOUN

social ADJECTIVE **1** relating to society, or to a community: *social history* **2** living in communities: *social insects* **3** of companionship: *social gathering* **4** of rank or level in society: *social class*

socialism NOUN the belief that a country's wealth should belong to the people as a whole, not to private owners

socialist NOUN someone who believes in socialism ▶ADJECTIVE relating to or characteristic of socialism

social security NOUN the system, paid for by taxes, of providing insurance against old age, illness, unemployment, etc

social work NOUN work which deals with the care of the people in a community, especially of the poor or underprivileged > **social worker** NOUN

society NOUN (*plural* **societies**) **1** humanity considered as a whole **2** a community of people **3** a social club, an association **4** the class of people who are wealthy, fashionable, etc **5** *formal* company, companionship: *I enjoy his society*

socio- PREFIX of or relating to society or social behaviour

ⓘ Comes from Latin *socius* meaning 'a companion'

sociological ADJECTIVE dealing or concerned with social questions and problems of human society

sociologist NOUN someone who studies the structure and organization of human societies and human behaviour in society

sociology NOUN the study of human society

sociopath NOUN someone who hates the company of others

sock[1] NOUN a stocking

sock[2] *informal*, VERB to hit with a powerful blow ▶NOUN a powerful blow

socket NOUN a hollow into which something is fitted: *an electric socket*

sod NOUN a piece of earth with grass growing on it, a turf

soda NOUN **1** the name of several substances formed from sodium, eg bicarbonate of soda **2** *informal* soda water

sodden ADJECTIVE soaked through and through

sodium NOUN, *chemistry* (symbol **Na**) a metallic element from which many substances are formed, including common salt

sofa NOUN a kind of long, stuffed seat with back and arms

sofa bed NOUN a sofa incorporating a fold-away bed

soft ADJECTIVE **1** easily put out of shape when pressed **2** not hard or firm **3** not loud **4** of a colour: not bright or glaring **5** not strict enough **6** lacking strength or courage **7** lacking common sense, weak in the mind **8** of a drink: not alcoholic **9** of water: containing little calcium etc

soften (*pronounced* **sof**-en) VERB to make or grow soft

softly ADVERB gently, quietly

software NOUN, *computing* programs etc as opposed to the machines (*contrasted with*: **hardware**)

soggy ADJECTIVE (**soggier, soggiest**) **1** soaked **2** soft and wet

soil[1] NOUN **1** the upper layer of the earth in which plants grow **2** loose earth; dirt

soil² VERB to make dirty

solace (*pronounced* **sol**-is) NOUN something which makes pain or sorrow easier to bear, comfort ▶ VERB to comfort

solar ADJECTIVE **1** relating to the sun **2** influenced by the sun **3** powered by energy from the sun's rays

solar cell NOUN an electric cell that converts light into electrical energy

solar energy NOUN **1** energy produced by the sun **2** energy derived from the sun's radiation, eg in a solar cell

solar system NOUN the sun with the planets (including the earth) going round it

sold *past form* of **sell**

solder NOUN melted metal used for joining metal surfaces ▶ VERB to join (with solder)

soldier NOUN someone in military service, especially someone who is not an officer

sole¹ NOUN **1** the underside of the foot **2** the underside of a shoe etc ▶ VERB to put a sole on (a shoe etc)

sole² ADJECTIVE **1** only: *the sole survivor* **2** belonging to one person or group only: *the sole right*

solely ADVERB only, alone

solemn (*pronounced* **sol**-em) ADJECTIVE **1** serious, earnest **2** of an occasion: celebrated with special ceremonies > **solemnity** (*pronounced* so-**lem**-ni-ti) NOUN

solenoid NOUN, *physics* a wire that is magnetized when an electric current passes through it

solicit VERB (**soliciting, solicited**) **1** *formal* to ask earnestly for: *solicit advice* **2** *formal* to ask (someone for something) **3** to offer yourself as a prostitute

solicitor NOUN a lawyer who advises people about legal matters

solicitous ADJECTIVE **1** anxious **2** considerate, careful > **solicitously** ADVERB

solicitude NOUN care or anxiety about someone or something

solid ADJECTIVE **1** fixed in shape, not in the form of gas or liquid **2** in three dimensions, with length, breadth, and height **3** not hollow **4** firm, strongly made **5** made or formed completely of one substance: *solid silver* **6** reliable, sound: *solid business* **7** *informal* without a break: *We waited for four solid hours* ▶ NOUN **1** a substance that is solid **2** a figure that has three dimensions

solidarity NOUN mutual support and unity of interests, aims, and actions

solidify VERB (**solidifies, solidifying, solidified**) to make or become firm or solid

solidity NOUN the state of being solid

soliloquize *or* **soliloquise** VERB to speak to yourself, especially on the stage

soliloquy NOUN (*plural* **soliloquies**) a speech made by an actor etc to themselves

solitaire NOUN a card game for one player (*also called*: **patience**)

solitary ADJECTIVE **1** lone, alone **2** single: *Not a solitary crumb remained*

solitude NOUN the state of being alone; lack of company

solo NOUN (*plural* **solos**) a musical piece for one singer or player ▸ADJECTIVE performed by one person alone: *solo flight*

soloist NOUN someone who plays or sings a solo

solstice NOUN the time of longest daylight (**summer solstice** about 21 June in the northern hemisphere, 21 December in the southern hemisphere) or longest dark (**winter solstice** about 21 December in the northern hemisphere, 21 June in the southern hemisphere)

soluble ADJECTIVE **1** able to be dissolved or made liquid **2** of a problem etc: able to be solved

solute NOUN, *chemistry* a substance that is dissolved in a liquid

solution NOUN **1** a mixture in which one substance is dissolved in another **2** the act of solving a problem etc **3** an answer to a problem, puzzle, etc

solve VERB **1** to clear up or explain (a mystery) **2** to discover the answer or solution to

solvency NOUN the state of being able to pay all debts

solvent ADJECTIVE able to pay all debts ▸NOUN, *chemistry* anything that dissolves another substance

sombre *or US* **somber** ADJECTIVE gloomy, dark, dismal

sombrero NOUN (*plural* **sombreros**) a broad-brimmed Mexican hat

some ADJECTIVE **1** several **2** a few: *some oranges, but not many* **3** a little: *some bread, but not much* **4** certain: *Some people are rich* ▸PRONOUN **1** a number or part out of a quantity: *Please try some* **2** certain people: *Some won't be happy*

somebody *or* **someone** PRONOUN an unknown or unnamed person: *somebody I'd never seen before* ▸NOUN an important person: *He really is somebody now*

somehow ADVERB in some way or other

somersault NOUN a forward or backward roll in which the heels go over the head ▸VERB to perform a somersault

something PRONOUN **1** a thing not known or not stated **2** a thing of importance **3** a slight amount, a degree: *He has something of his father's looks*

sometime ADVERB at a time not known or stated definitely

sometimes ADVERB at times, now and then

somewhat ADVERB rather: *somewhat boring*

somewhere ADVERB in some place

-somn- of or relating to sleep: *somnambulist/insomnia*

ⓘ Comes from Latin *somnus* meaning 'sleep'

son NOUN a male child

sonar NOUN a system using reflected sound waves to locate underwater objects

sonata NOUN a piece of classical music with three or more movements, usually for one instrument

song NOUN **1** a piece of music to be

sung **2** singing **going for a song** *informal* at a bargain price

songbird NOUN a bird that sings

songster *or* **songstress** NOUN (*plural* **songsters** *or* **songstresses**), *old* a talented singer

sonic ADJECTIVE of sound waves

son-in-law NOUN (*plural* **sons-in-law**) a daughter's husband

sonnet NOUN a type of poem in fourteen lines

soon ADVERB **1** in a short time from now or from the time mentioned: *He will come soon* **2** early: *too soon to tell* **3 as soon** as readily, as willingly: *I would as soon stand as sit*

sooner ADVERB more willingly, rather: *I would sooner stand than sit* **sooner or later** at some time in the future

soot NOUN the black powder left by smoke

soothe VERB **1** to calm or comfort (a person, feelings, etc) **2** to help or ease (a pain etc)

soothing ADJECTIVE **1** comforting, calming **2** helping to relieve pain

soothsayer NOUN someone who predicts the future

sooty ADJECTIVE (**sootier, sootiest**) like, or covered with, soot

soph- PREFIX forms words connected with the idea of wisdom

🄸 Comes from Greek *sophos* meaning 'wise', and *sophia* meaning 'wisdom'

sophism NOUN a convincing but false argument or explanation

sophist NOUN a person who uses clever arguments that are fundamentally unsound > **sophistic** ADJECTIVE > **sophistry** NOUN

sophisticated ADJECTIVE **1** of a person: full of experience, accustomed to an elegant, cultured way of life **2** of ways of thought, machinery, etc: highly developed, complicated, elaborate

sophomore NOUN, *US* a second-year college student

soporific ADJECTIVE causing sleep ▶ NOUN a drug which causes sleep

sopping ADJECTIVE wet through

soppy ADJECTIVE (**soppier, soppiest**) *informal* overly sentimental

soprano NOUN (*plural* **sopranos**), *music* **1** the female singing voice of the highest pitch **2** a singer with such a voice

sorcerer *or feminine* **sorceress** NOUN someone who works magic spells; a witch or wizard

sorcery NOUN magic, witchcraft

sordid ADJECTIVE **1** dirty, filthy **2** mean, selfish **3** contemptible

sore ADJECTIVE (**sorer, sorest**) painful ▶ NOUN a painful, inflamed spot on the skin

sorely ADVERB very greatly: *sorely in need*

sorority NOUN (*plural* **sororities**) in North America, a society of female college students (*compare with*: **fraternity**)

sorrow NOUN sadness caused by a loss, disappointment, etc ▶ VERB to be sad

sorrowful ADJECTIVE full of sadness

sorry ADJECTIVE (**sorrier, sorriest**)

1 feeling regret for something you have done: *I'm sorry I mentioned it* **2** feeling sympathy or pity (for): *sorry for you* **3** miserable: *in a sorry state*

sort NOUN a kind of (person or thing): *the sort of sweets I like* ▶ VERB to separate things, putting each in its place: *sort letters* **a sort of** used of something which is like something else, but not exactly: *He wore a sort of crown* **of a sort** *or* **of sorts** of a kind, usually inadequate: *a party of sorts* **out of sorts** *informal* not feeling very well

sortie (*pronounced* **saw**-ti) NOUN a sudden attack made by the defenders of a place on those who are trying to capture it

SOS NOUN **1** a code signal calling for help **2** *informal* any call for help

so-so ADJECTIVE, *informal* not particularly good

sotto voce (*pronounced* sot-oh **voh**-chi) ADVERB in a low voice, so as not to be overheard

sought *past form* of **seek**

sought after ADJECTIVE popular, much in demand

soul NOUN **1** the spirit, the part of someone which is not the body **2** *informal* a person: *a dear old soul* **3** a perfect example (of): *the soul of kindness*

soulful ADJECTIVE full of feeling

sound¹ NOUN **1** anything that can be heard, a noise **2** a distance from which something may be heard: *within the sound of Bow Bells* ▶ VERB **1** to strike you as being: *That sounds awful* **2** to make a noise with: *sound a horn* **3** to examine by listening carefully to: *sound a patient's chest* **sound like** to resemble in sound: *that sounds like Henry's voice*

sound² ADJECTIVE **1** healthy, strong **2** of sleep: deep **3** thorough: *a sound beating* **4** reliable: *sound opinions*

sound³ VERB **1** to measure (the depths of water) **2** to try to find out the opinion of: *I'll sound him out tomorrow*

sound⁴ NOUN a narrow passage of water

sound barrier NOUN a sudden increase in drag experienced by aircraft flying close to the speed of sound

soundproof ADJECTIVE built or made so that sound cannot pass in or out ▶ VERB to make soundproof

soundtrack NOUN the strip on a film where the speech and music are recorded

soup NOUN a liquid food made from meat, vegetables, etc

sour ADJECTIVE **1** having an acid or bitter taste, often as a stage in going bad: *sour milk* **2** bad-tempered ▶ VERB to make sour

source NOUN **1** the place, thing, or person that something begins or develops from **2** a spring, especially one from which a river flows

south NOUN one of the four chief directions, that to the left of someone facing the setting sun ▶ ADJECTIVE **1** in or to the south **2** of the wind: from the south ▶ ADVERB in, to or towards the south: *We headed south*

A B C D E F G H I J K L M N O P Q R S T U V W X Y Z

south-east NOUN the point of the compass midway between south and east

southerly ADJECTIVE **1** of the wind: coming from or facing the south **2** in or towards the south

southern ADJECTIVE of the south

southern lights PLURAL NOUN (**the southern lights**) the **aurora australis**

South Pole NOUN the point on the Earth's surface that represents the southern end of its axis

southward *or* **southwards** ADJECTIVE & ADVERB towards the south

south-west NOUN the point of the compass midway between south and west

souvenir NOUN something bought or given as a reminder of a person, place, or occasion

sovereign NOUN **1** a king or queen **2** an old British gold coin worth £1 ▸ADJECTIVE **1** supreme, highest: *sovereign lord* **2** having its own government: *sovereign state*

sovereignty NOUN highest power

sow[1] (*pronounced* sow) NOUN a female pig

sow[2] (*pronounced* soh) VERB (**sowing, sowed, sown**) **1** to scatter (seeds) so that they may grow **2** to cover (an area) with seeds > **sower** NOUN

soya bean *or* **soy bean** NOUN a kind of bean, rich in protein, used as a substitute for meat

soya sauce *or* **soy sauce** NOUN a sauce made from soya beans, used in Chinese cooking

spa NOUN a place where people go to drink or bathe in the water from a natural spring

[i] After the town of *Spa* in Belgium, which was famous for its healthy spring water

space NOUN **1** a gap, an empty place **2** the distance between objects **3** an uncovered part on a sheet of paper **4** length of time: *in the space of a day* **5** the empty region in which all stars, planets, etc are situated ▸VERB to put things apart from each other, leaving room between them

spacecraft NOUN a machine for travelling in space

spaceman *or* **spacewoman** NOUN (*plural* **spacemen** *or* **spacewomen**) a traveller in space

spaceship NOUN a manned spacecraft

space suit NOUN a sealed suit designed for space travel

spacious ADJECTIVE having plenty of room

spade NOUN a tool with a broad blade for digging in the earth **call a spade a spade** to say plainly and clearly what you mean

spaghetti NOUN a type of pasta made into long sticks

span NOUN **1** the distance between the tips of the little finger and the thumb when the hand is spread out (about 23 centimetres, 9 inches) **2** the full time anything lasts **3** an arch of a bridge ▸VERB (**spanning, spanned**) to stretch across: *The bridge spans the river*

spangle NOUN a thin sparkling piece of metal used as an ornament

▸ VERB to sprinkle with spangles etc

spaniel NOUN a breed of dog with large, hanging ears

spank VERB to strike with the flat of the hand ▸ NOUN a slap with the hand, especially on the buttocks

spanking[1] NOUN a beating with the hand

spanking[2] ADJECTIVE, *informal* fast: *a spanking pace*

spanner NOUN a tool used to tighten or loosen nuts, screws, etc

spar VERB (**sparring, sparred**) **1** to fight with the fists **2** to engage in an argument

spare VERB **1** to do without: *I can't spare you today* **2** to afford, set aside: *I can't spare the time to do it* **3** to treat with mercy, hold back from injuring **4** to avoid causing (trouble etc) to ▸ ADJECTIVE **1** extra, not yet in use: *spare tyre* **2** thin, small: *spare but strong* ▸ NOUN another of the same kind (eg a tyre, part of a machine) kept for emergencies **to spare** over and above what is needed

sparing ADJECTIVE careful, economical

spark[1] NOUN **1** a small red-hot part thrown off from something burning **2** a trace: *a spark of humanity* ▸ VERB to make sparks

spark[2] NOUN, *often ironic* a lively or intelligent person: *What bright spark left the oven on?*

sparkle NOUN **1** a little spark **2** brightness, liveliness **3** bubbles as in wine ▸ VERB **1** to shine in a glittering way **2** to be lively or witty **3** to bubble

sparkling ADJECTIVE **1** glittering **2** witty **3** of a drink: bubbling, fizzy

spark plug *or* **sparking-plug** NOUN a device in a car engine that produces a spark to set on fire explosive gases

sparrow NOUN a type of small dull-coloured bird

sparse ADJECTIVE **1** thinly scattered **2** not much, not enough

spartan ADJECTIVE of conditions etc: hard, without luxury

spasm NOUN **1** a sudden involuntary jerk of the muscles **2** a strong, short burst (eg of anger, work)

spasmodic ADJECTIVE **1** occurring in spasms **2** coming now and again, not regularly > **spasmodically** ADVERB

spastic ADJECTIVE suffering from cerebral palsy

spat *past form* of **spit**[1]

spatial *or* **spacial** ADJECTIVE of or relating to space

spatter VERB to splash (eg with mud)

spatula (*pronounced* **spat**-uw-l*a*) NOUN a tool with a broad, blunt blade

spawn NOUN a mass of eggs of fish, frogs, etc ▸ VERB **1** of fish etc: to lay eggs **2** to cause, produce: *The film's success spawned several sequels*

speak VERB (**speaking, spoke, spoken**) **1** to say words, talk **2** to hold a conversation (with): *I spoke to Jack about the holidays* **3** to make a speech **4** to be able to talk (a certain language) **speak your mind** to give your opinion openly **speak up 1** to speak more loudly or clearly

2 to give your opinion openly

speaker NOUN **1** someone who speaks, especially giving formal speeches **2** (**the Speaker**) a person in charge of debates in a parliament **3** a device attached to a radio etc which converts audio signals into sound

spear[1] NOUN a long weapon, with an iron or steel point ▶ VERB to pierce with a spear

spear[2] NOUN a long, pointed shoot or leaf (especially of grass)

special ADJECTIVE **1** not ordinary, exceptional: *special occasion/ special friend* **2** put on for a particular purpose: *special train* **3** belonging to one person or thing and not to others: *special skills/ special tool for drilling holes*

specialist NOUN someone who studies one branch of a subject or field: *heart specialist*

speciality NOUN (*plural* **specialities**) something for which a person is well-known

specialize *or* **specialise** VERB to work in, or study, a particular job, subject, etc > **specialization** NOUN

specialized *or* **specialised** ADJECTIVE of knowledge: obtained by specializing

specially ADVERB for a special purpose: *specially written for younger children*

> Do not confuse with: **especially**

species NOUN (*plural* **species**) **1** a group of plants or animals which are alike in most ways **2** a kind (of anything)

specific ADJECTIVE giving all the details clearly; particular, exactly stated: *a specific purpose*

specifically ADVERB **1** particularly or for the purpose stated and no other: *designed specifically for the elderly* **2** exactly and clearly: *I specifically told you not to leave*

specification NOUN **1** the act of specifying **2** a full description of details (eg in a plan or contract)

specify VERB (**specifies, specifying, specified**) **1** to set down or say clearly (what is wanted) **2** to make particular mention of

specimen NOUN something used as a sample of a group or kind of anything, especially for study or for putting in a collection

speck NOUN **1** a small spot **2** a tiny piece (eg of dust)

speckle NOUN a spot on a different-coloured background

speckled ADJECTIVE dotted with speckles

-spect- *or* **-spec-** forms words connected with looking or seeing: *spectacle/inspect* (= to look into)
ⓘ Comes from Latin *specere* meaning 'to look at'

spectacle NOUN a striking or wonderful sight

spectacles PLURAL NOUN glasses which someone wears to improve eyesight

spectacular ADJECTIVE **1** very impressive to see or watch: *spectacular scenery* **2** remarkable or dramatic: *a spectacular success* > **spectacularly** ADVERB (meaning 2): *The value of the shares has* *increased spectacularly*

spectator NOUN someone who watches an event, eg a football match

spectral ADJECTIVE ghostly

spectre *or US* **specter** NOUN a ghost

spectrum NOUN (*plural* **spectra** *or* **spectrums**) **1** *physics* the band of colours as seen in a rainbow, formed when white light is dispersed through a prism **2** the range or extent of anything: *the whole spectrum of human emotions*

speculate VERB **1** to guess **2** to wonder (about) **3** to buy goods, shares, etc in order to sell them again at a profit > **speculation** NOUN

speculator NOUN a person who buys things in the hope of making a profit when they sell them, without knowing for sure what the future selling price will be: *a property speculator*

sped *past form* of **speed**

speech NOUN (*plural* **speeches**) **1** the power of making sounds which have meaning for other people **2** a way of speaking: *His speech is always clear* **3** (*plural* **speeches**) a formal talk given to an audience

speechless ADJECTIVE so surprised, shocked, etc that you cannot speak

speed NOUN **1** quickness of, or rate of, movement or action **2** *slang* the drug amphetamine ▶VERB (**speeding, sped** *or* **speeded**) **1** (*past form* **sped**) to (cause to) move along quickly, hurry **2** (*past form* **speeded**) to drive very fast in a car etc (especially faster than is allowed by law)

speeding NOUN driving at (an illegally) high speed

speed limit NOUN the greatest speed a vehicle may legally travel at on a particular road

speedometer NOUN an instrument that shows how fast you are travelling

speedway NOUN a motorcycle racing track

speedy ADJECTIVE (**speedier, speediest**) fast; prompt; without delay

speleology (*pronounced* spee-li-**ol**-*o*-ji) NOUN the study or exploration of caves

spell[1] VERB (**spelling, spelt** *or* **spelled**) **1** to give or write correctly the letters which make up (a word) **2** to mean, imply: *This defeat spells disaster for us all* **spell out** to say (something) very frankly or clearly

spell[2] NOUN **1** words which, when spoken, are supposed to have magic power **2** magic or other powerful influence: *Many men fell under the spell of her beauty*

spell[3] NOUN **1** a (short) space of time: *a spell of dry weather* **2** a turn (at work, rest, play)

spellbind VERB (**spellbinding, spellbound**) to captivate, enchant or fascinate > **spellbound** ADJECTIVE

spellcheck *or* **spellchecker** NOUN a computer program that checks the accuracy of spelling > **spell-check** VERB to run a spellcheck over (a document)

spelling NOUN the ability to spell words

spelt *past form of* **spell**[1]

spend VERB (**spending, spent**) **1** to use (money) for buying **2** to use (energy etc) **3** to pass (time): *I spent a week there* **4** to use up energy, force: *The storm spent itself and the sun shone*

spendthrift NOUN someone who spends money freely and carelessly

spent ADJECTIVE exhausted; having lost force or power: *a spent bullet*

sperm NOUN, *biology* the male sex cell that fertilizes the female egg; a spermatozoon

spermatozoon (*pronounced* sper-m*a*-toh-**zoh**-on) NOUN (*plural* **spermatozoa** – *pronounced* sper-m*a*-toh-**zoh**-*a*), *biology* a male sex cell contained in semen

sperm whale NOUN a kind of whale from the head of which **spermaceti**, a waxy substance, is obtained

spew VERB to vomit

sphere NOUN **1** a ball or similar perfectly round object **2** a position or level in society: *He moves in the highest spheres* **3** range (of influence or action)

spherical (*pronounced* **sfe**-ri-k*a*l) ADJECTIVE having the shape of a sphere

spheroid (*pronounced* **sfee**-roid) NOUN, *maths* a figure that is almost a sphere

Sphinx NOUN **1** a mythological monster with the head of a woman and the body of a lioness **2** the large stone model of the Sphinx in Egypt **3** (**sphinx**) someone whose real thoughts you cannot guess

spice NOUN **1** any substance used for flavouring, eg pepper, nutmeg **2** anything that adds liveliness, interest ▸ VERB to flavour with spice

spicy ADJECTIVE (**spicier, spiciest**) **1** full of spices **2** *informal* lively and sometimes slightly indecent: *a spicy tale* **>** **spiciness** NOUN

spider NOUN a kind of small, insect-like creature with eight legs, that spins a web

spidery ADJECTIVE **1** like a spider **2** of handwriting: having fine, sprawling strokes

spiel (*pronounced* speel *or* shpeel) NOUN, *informal* a (long or often repeated) story or speech

ⓘ Comes from German *spielen* meaning 'to play'

spike NOUN **1** a pointed piece of rod (of wood, metal, etc) **2** a type of large nail ▸ VERB **1** to pierce with a spike **2** to make useless **3** *informal* to add an alcoholic drink to (a soft drink)

spiky ADJECTIVE (**spikier, spikiest**) having spikes or a sharp point

spill VERB (**spilling, spilt** *or* **spilled**) to (allow liquid to) run out or overflow ▸ NOUN *informal* a fall **spill the beans** *informal* to give away a secret, especially unintentionally

spillage NOUN an act of spilling or what is spilt

spin VERB (**spinning, spun**) **1** to draw out (cotton, wood, silk, etc) and twist into threads **2** to (cause to) whirl round quickly **3** to travel quickly, especially on wheels **4** to produce a fine thread as a spider does ▸ NOUN **1** a whirling motion

2 *informal* a ride (especially on wheels) **spin a yarn** to tell a long story **spin out** to make to last a long or longer time

spina bifida (*pronounced* **spai-**n*a* **bif**-i-d*a*) NOUN a birth defect which leaves part of the spinal cord exposed

spinach NOUN a type of plant whose leaves are eaten as a vegetable

spinal *see* **spine**

spinal cord NOUN a cord of nerve cells in the spine

spindle NOUN 1 the pin from which the thread is twisted in spinning wool or cotton 2 a pin on which anything turns round

spindly ADJECTIVE (**spindlier, spindliest**) *informal* long and thin

spindrier NOUN a machine for taking water out of clothes by whirling them round

spindrift NOUN the spray blown from the tops of waves

spine NOUN 1 the line of linked bones running down the back in animals and humans, the backbone 2 a stiff, pointed spike which is part of an animal's body (eg a porcupine) 3 a ridge 4 a thorn
> **spinal** ADJECTIVE

spineless ADJECTIVE, *informal* having no spine; weak

spinney NOUN (*plural* **spinneys**) a small clump of trees

spinning wheel NOUN a machine for spinning thread, consisting of a wheel which drives spindles

spinster NOUN a woman who is not married

spiral ADJECTIVE 1 coiled round like a spring 2 winding round and round, getting further and further away from the centre ▸NOUN 1 anything with a spiral shape 2 a spiral movement 3 an increase which gets ever more rapid ▸VERB (**spiralling, spiralled**) 1 to move in a spiral 2 to increase ever more rapidly

spire NOUN a tall, sharp-pointed tower (especially on the roof of a church)

spirit NOUN 1 the soul 2 a being without a body, a ghost: *an evil spirit* 3 liveliness, boldness: *he acted with spirit* 4 a feeling or attitude: *a spirit of kindness* 5 the intended meaning: *the spirit of the laws* 6 a distilled liquid, especially alcohol 7 (**spirits**) strong alcoholic drinks in general (eg whisky) 8 (**spirits**) state of mind, mood: *in high spirits* ▸VERB (**spiriting, spirited**) (*especially* **spirit away**) to remove, as if by magic

spirited ADJECTIVE lively

spiritual ADJECTIVE having to do with the soul or with ghosts ▸NOUN an emotional, religious song of a kind originally developed by the African American slaves

spiritualism NOUN the belief that living people can communicate with the souls of dead people
> **spiritualist** NOUN

spit[1] NOUN the liquid which forms in a person's mouth ▸VERB (**spitting, spat**) 1 to throw liquid out from the mouth 2 to rain slightly

spit[2] NOUN 1 a metal bar on which meat is roasted 2 *geography* a long stretch of sand running into the sea from the mainland ▸VERB (**spitting,**

A B C D E F G H I J K L M N O P Q R S T U V W X Y Z

spitted) to pierce with something sharp

spite NOUN the wish to hurt (especially feelings) ▸ VERB to annoy out of spite **in spite of** **1** taking no notice of: *He left in spite of his father's command* **2** although something has happened or is a fact: *The ground was dry in spite of all the rain*

spiteful ADJECTIVE motivated by spite; malicious

spitting image NOUN, *informal* an exact likeness

spittle NOUN spit

splash VERB **1** to spatter with water, mud, etc **2** to move or fall with a splash or splashes ▸ NOUN (*plural* **splashes**) **1** the sound made by, or the scattering of liquid caused by, something hitting water etc **2** a mark made by splashing (eg on your clothes) **3** a bright patch: *a splash of colour* **make a splash** to attract a lot of attention

splay VERB to turn out at an angle

spleen NOUN **1** a spongy, blood-filled organ inside the body, near the stomach **2** bad temper

splendid ADJECTIVE **1** magnificent, brilliant **2** *informal* excellent
> **splendidly** ADVERB

splendour *or US* **splendor** NOUN the state or quality of being very grand and beautiful in appearance or style

splint NOUN a piece of wood etc tied to a broken limb to keep it in a fixed position

splinter NOUN a sharp, thin, broken piece of wood, glass, etc ▸ VERB to split into splinters

split VERB (**splitting, split**) **1** to cut or break lengthways **2** to crack, break **3** to divide into pieces or groups etc ▸ NOUN **1** a crack, a break **2** (**the splits**) the feat of going down on the floor with one leg stretched forward and the other back **split your sides** *informal* to laugh heartily

split second NOUN a fraction of a second

splitting ADJECTIVE of a headache: severe, intense

splutter VERB **1** to make spitting noises **2** to speak hastily and unclearly

spoil VERB (**spoiling, spoiled** *or* **spoilt**) **1** to make useless; damage, ruin **2** to give in to the wishes of (a child etc) and so ruin its character **3** of food: to become bad or useless **4** (*past form* **spoiled**) to rob, plunder ▸ NOUN (often **spoils**) plunder **spoiling for** eager for (especially a fight)

spoilsport NOUN, *informal* someone who refuses to join in other people's fun

spoke[1] *past tense* of **speak**

spoke[2] NOUN one of the ribs or bars from the centre to the rim of a wheel

spoken *past participle* of **speak**

spokesman *or* **spokeswoman** NOUN (*plural* **spokesmen** *or* **spokeswomen**) someone who speaks on behalf of others

sponge NOUN **1** a sea animal which consists of a large cluster of cells supported by a soft, elastic skeleton

2 its skeleton, which can soak up water and is used for washing 3 an artificial object like this used for washing 4 a light cake or pudding ▶ VERB 1 to wipe with a sponge 2 *informal* to live off money etc given by others

sponger NOUN, *informal* someone who lives at others' expense

spongy ADJECTIVE (**spongier, spongiest**) soft and springy, like a sponge

sponsor NOUN 1 someone who takes responsibility for introducing something, a promoter 2 someone who promises to pay a sum of money if another person completes a set task (eg a walk, swim, etc) 3 a business firm which pays for a radio or television programme and advertises its products during it ▶ VERB to act as a sponsor to

sponsorship NOUN the act of sponsoring

spontaneity (*pronounced* spon-*ta*-**nei**-i-ti) NOUN being spontaneous

spontaneous ADJECTIVE 1 not planned beforehand 2 natural, not forced

spoof *informal*, NOUN 1 a satirical imitation; a parody 2 a trick played as a joke, a hoax

spook *informal*, NOUN 1 a ghost 2 a spy or undercover agent

spooky ADJECTIVE (**spookier, spookiest**) *informal* frightening or uncanny

spool NOUN a reel for thread, film, etc

spoon NOUN a piece of metal etc with a hollow bowl at one end, used for lifting food to the mouth ▶ VERB to lift with a spoon

spoonfeed VERB (**spoonfeeding, spoonfed**) 1 to feed with a spoon 2 to teach without encouraging independent thought

sporadic ADJECTIVE happening here and there, or now and again > **sporadically** ADVERB: *Fighting broke out sporadically*

spore NOUN the seed of certain plants (eg ferns, fungi)

sporran NOUN a small pouch worn hanging in front of a kilt

sport NOUN 1 games such as football, tennis, skiing, etc in general 2 any one game of this type 3 *informal* a good-natured, obliging person ▶ VERB 1 to have fun, play 2 to wear: *sporting a pink tie*

sporting ADJECTIVE 1 fond of sport 2 believing in fair play, good-natured

sporting chance NOUN a reasonably good chance

sports car NOUN a small, fast car with only two seats

sportsman *or* **sportswoman** NOUN (*plural* **sportsmen** *or* **sportswomen**) 1 someone who plays sports 2 someone who shows fair play in sports

sportsmanlike ADJECTIVE fair, sporting

spot NOUN 1 a small mark or stain (of mud, paint, etc) 2 a round mark as part of a pattern on material etc 3 a pimple 4 a place ▶ VERB (**spotting, spotted**) 1 to mark with spots 2 to catch sight of **in a spot** *informal* in trouble **on the spot** 1 in the place where someone is most needed **2** right away, immediately **3** in an embarrassing or difficult position

spotless ADJECTIVE very clean

spotlight NOUN a bright light that is shone on an actor on the stage ▸VERB (**spotlighting, spotlit** *or* **spotlighted**) **1** to show up clearly **2** to draw attention to

spotted *or* **spotty** ADJECTIVE (**spottier, spottiest**) covered with spots

spouse NOUN a husband or wife

spout NOUN **1** the part of a kettle, teapot, etc through which liquid is poured out **2** a strong jet of liquid ▸VERB to pour or spurt out

sprain NOUN a painful twisting (eg of an ankle) ▸VERB to twist painfully

sprang *past tense* of **spring**

sprawl VERB **1** to sit, lie, or fall with the limbs spread out widely **2** of a town etc: to spread out in an untidy, irregular way

spray NOUN **1** a fine mist of liquid like that made by a waterfall **2** a device with many small holes (eg on a watering-can or shower) for producing spray **3** a liquid for spraying ▸VERB to cover with a mist or fine jets of liquid

spread VERB (**spreading, spread**) **1** to put more widely or thinly over an area: *Spread the butter on the bread* **2** to cover: *Spread the bread with jam* **3** to open out (eg your arms, a map) **4** to scatter or distribute over a wide area, length of time, etc ▸NOUN **1** the act of spreading **2** the extent or range (of something) **3** a food which is spread on bread: *sandwich spread* **4** *informal* a large meal laid out on a table

spreadsheet NOUN, *computing* a computer program with which data can be viewed on screen and manipulated to make calculations etc

spree NOUN a careless spell of some activity: *a spending spree*

sprig NOUN a small twig or shoot

sprightly ADJECTIVE (**sprightlier, sprightliest**) lively, brisk

spring VERB (**springing, sprang, sprung**) **1** to jump, leap **2** to move swiftly **3** to set off (a trap etc) **4** to give, reveal unexpectedly: *She sprang the news on me* **5** to come (from)▸NOUN **1** a leap **2** a coil of wire used in a mattress **3** the ability to stretch and spring back **4** bounce, energy **5** a small stream flowing out from the ground **6** the season of the year following winter, when plants begin to grow again **spring a leak** to begin to leak **spring back** to return suddenly to an earlier position when released **spring up** to appear suddenly

springboard NOUN a springy board from which swimmers may dive into a swimming pool

spring-cleaning NOUN a thorough cleaning of a house, especially in the spring

springy ADJECTIVE (**springier, springiest**) able to spring back into its former position etc, elastic

sprinkle VERB to scatter or cover in small drops or pieces

sprinkler NOUN something which sprinkles water

sprinkling NOUN a few, a small amount: *We had a sprinkling of snow in the night*

sprint VERB to run at full speed ▸NOUN *athletics* a race at high speed over a short distance > **sprinter** NOUN

sprite NOUN **1** a supernatural spirit **2** *computing* an icon which can be moved about a screen

sprout VERB **1** to begin to grow **2** to put out new shoots ▸NOUN **1** a young bud **2** (**sprouts**) Brussels sprouts

spruce[1] NOUN a kind of fir tree

spruce[2] ADJECTIVE (**sprucer, sprucest**) neat, smart

sprung *past participle* of **spring**

spry ADJECTIVE (**spryer, spryest**) lively, active

spud NOUN, *informal* a potato

spume NOUN froth, foam

spun *past form* of **spin**

spur NOUN **1** a sharp point worn by a horse-rider on the heel and used to urge on a horse **2** a claw-like point at the back of a bird's leg **3** anything that urges someone on **4** a small line of mountains running off from a larger range ▸VERB (**spurring, spurred**) **1** to use spurs on (a horse) **2** to urge (on) **on the spur of the moment** without thinking beforehand

spurious (*pronounced* **spyoo**-ri-*us*) ADJECTIVE not genuine, false

spurn VERB to cast aside, reject with scorn

spurt VERB to pour out in a sudden stream ▸NOUN **1** a sudden stream pouring or squirting out **2** a sudden increase of effort: *put a spurt on*

sputnik (*pronounced* **spuwt**-nik) NOUN a Russian artificial satellite

sputter VERB to make a noise as of spitting and throw out moisture in drops

spy NOUN (*plural* **spies**) someone who secretly collects (and reports) information about another person, country, firm, etc ▸VERB (**spies, spying, spied**) to catch sight of **spy on someone** to watch them secretly

squabble VERB to quarrel noisily ▸NOUN a noisy quarrel

squad NOUN **1** a group of soldiers, workmen, etc doing a particular job **2** a group of people

squaddie NOUN, *informal* a private, an ordinary soldier

squadron NOUN a division of a regiment, section of a fleet, or group of military aircraft

squalid ADJECTIVE **1** very dirty, filthy **2** contemptible

squall[1] NOUN a sudden violent storm

squall[2] NOUN a squeal, a scream

squalor NOUN dirty or squalid living conditions

squander VERB to waste (money, goods, strength, etc)

square NOUN **1** a figure with four equal sides and four right angles, of this shape: □ **2** an open space enclosed by buildings in a town **3** *maths* the answer when a number is multiplied by itself (eg the square of 3 is 9) ▸ADJECTIVE **1** shaped like a square **2** in area: *one metre square* **3** equal in scores in a game **4** of two or more people: not owing one another anything **5** straight, level ▸VERB **1** to make like a square

a b c d e f g h i j k l m n o p q r s t u v w x y z

A B C D E F G H I J K L M N O P Q R S T U V W X Y Z

2 to straighten (the shoulders) **3** to multiply a number by itself **4** to fit, agree: *That doesn't square with what you said earlier* ▶ ADVERB **1** in a straight or level position **2** directly; exactly: *hit square on the nose* **square metre** etc an area equal to that of a square each side of which is one metre etc long **square up** *or* **square something up** to settle a debt

square deal NOUN fair treatment

square meal NOUN a large, satisfying meal

square root NOUN, *maths* the number which, multiplied by itself, gives a certain other number (eg 3 is the square root of 9)

squash[1] VERB **1** to crush flat or to a pulp **2** to put down, defeat (rebellion etc) ▶ NOUN **1** a crushing or crowding **2** a mass of people crowded together **3** a drink made from the juice of crushed fruit **4** a game with rackets and a rubber ball played in a walled court

squash[2] NOUN any of various trailing plants with marrow-like gourds

squat VERB (**squatting, squatted**) **1** to sit down on the heels **2** to settle without permission in property which you do not pay rent for ▶ ADJECTIVE short and thick

squatter NOUN someone who squats in a building, on land, etc

squaw NOUN, *offensive* a Native American woman or wife

squawk VERB to give a harsh cry ▶ NOUN a harsh cry

squeak VERB to give a short, high-pitched sound ▶ NOUN a high-pitched sound

squeaky ADJECTIVE (**squeakier, squeakiest**) **1** high-pitched: *a squeaky voice* **2** tending to squeak: *a squeaky floorboard*

squeal VERB **1** to give a loud, shrill cry **2** *informal* to inform on

squeamish ADJECTIVE **1** easily sickened or shocked **2** feeling sick

squeeze VERB **1** to press together **2** to grasp tightly **3** to force out (liquid or juice from) by pressing **4** to force a way: *squeezed through the hole in the wall* ▶ NOUN **1** a squeezing or pressing **2** a few drops got by squeezing: *a squeeze of lemon juice* **3** a crowd of people crushed together

squelch NOUN (*plural* **squelches**) a sound made, eg by walking through marshy ground ▶ VERB to make this sound

squid NOUN a sea animal with tentacles, related to the cuttlefish

squiggle NOUN a curly or wavy mark

squint VERB **1** to screw up the eyes in looking at something **2** to have the eyes looking in different directions ▶ NOUN **1** a fault in eyesight which causes squinting **2** *informal* a quick, close glance

squire NOUN, *history* **1** a country landowner **2** a knight's servant

squirm VERB to wriggle or twist the body, especially in pain or embarrassment

squirrel NOUN a small gnawing animal, either reddish-brown or grey, with a bushy tail

squirt VERB to shoot out (a narrow jet of liquid) ▸NOUN a narrow jet of liquid

St ABBREVIATION **1** saint **2** street **3** strait

stab VERB (**stabbing, stabbed**) **1** to wound or pierce with a pointed weapon **2** to poke (at) ▸NOUN **1** the act of stabbing **2** a wound made by stabbing **3** a sharp pain **have a stab at** to make an attempt at

stabilize *or* **stabilise** VERB to make steady

stable[1] ADJECTIVE firm, steady

stable[2] NOUN a building for keeping horses ▸VERB to put or keep (horses) in a stable

staccato (*pronounced* sta-**kah**-toh) ADJECTIVE of sounds: sharp and separate, like the sound of tapping ▸ADVERB, *music* with each note sounded separately and clearly

stack NOUN a large pile (of straw, hay, wood, etc) ▸VERB to pile in a stack

stadium NOUN (*plural* **stadiums** *or* **stadia**) a large sports ground or racecourse with seats for spectators

staff NOUN **1** a stick or pole carried in the hand **2** *music* a stave **3** workers employed in a business, school, etc **4** a group of army officers who assist a commanding officer ▸VERB to supply (a school etc) with staff

stag NOUN a male deer

stage NOUN **1** a platform for performing or acting on **2** a step in development: *the first stage of the plan* **3** a landing place (eg for boats) **4** a part of a journey **5** a stopping place on a journey ▸VERB **1** to prepare and put on a performance of (a play etc) **2** to arrange (an event, eg an exhibition) **on the stage** in the theatre-world **the stage** the theatre; the job of working as an actor

stagecoach NOUN (*plural* **stagecoaches**) *history* a coach running every day with passengers

stage whisper NOUN a loud whisper

stagger VERB **1** to walk unsteadily, totter **2** to astonish **3** to arrange (people's hours of work etc) so that they do not begin or end together

staggered ADJECTIVE of two or more things: arranged to begin and end at different times

staggering ADJECTIVE astonishing

staging NOUN **1** scaffolding **2** putting on the stage

stagnant ADJECTIVE of water: standing still, not flowing and therefore not pure

stagnate VERB **1** of water: to remain still and so become impure **2** to remain for a long time in the same situation and so become bored, inactive, etc

stagnation NOUN **1** stagnating **2** being stagnant

stag night *or* **stag party** NOUN (*plural* **stag nights** *or* **stag parties**) a party for men only, held shortly before one of them gets married

staid ADJECTIVE set in your ways, sedate

stain VERB **1** to give a different colour to (wood etc) **2** to mark or make dirty by accident ▸NOUN

A B C D E F G H I J K L M N O P Q R S T U V W X Y Z

1 a liquid which dyes or colours something **2** a mark which is not easily removed **3** something shameful in someone's character or reputation

stained glass NOUN decorative coloured glass cut in shapes and leaded together

stainless steel NOUN a mixture of steel and chromium which does not rust

stair NOUN **1** one or all of a number of steps one after the other **2** (**stairs**) a series or flight of steps

staircase NOUN a stretch of stairs with rails on one or both sides (*also called*: **stairway**)

stake¹ NOUN **1** a strong stick pointed at one end **2** *history* a post to which people were tied to be burned ▸VERB to mark the limits or boundaries (of a field etc) with stakes **stake a claim** to establish ownership or right (to something)

stake² NOUN money put down as a bet ▸VERB **1** to bet (money) **2** to risk **at stake 1** to be won or lost **2** in great danger: *His life is at stake* **have a stake in** to be concerned in (because you have something to gain or lose)

stalactite NOUN a spike of limestone hanging from the roof of a cave, formed by the dripping of water containing lime

stalagmite NOUN a spike of limestone, like a stalactite, rising from the floor of a cave

stale ADJECTIVE (**staler, stalest**) **1** of food: no longer fresh **2** no longer interesting because heard, done, etc too often before **3** not able to do your best (because of overworking, boredom, etc)

stalemate NOUN **1** *chess* a position in which a player cannot move without putting their king in danger **2** a position in an argument in which neither side can win

stalk¹ NOUN the stem of a plant, or of a leaf or flower

stalk² VERB **1** to hunt, follow, or approach stealthily **2** to walk stiffly or proudly > **stalking** NOUN

stall¹ NOUN **1** a division for one animal in a cowshed etc **2** a table on which things are laid out for sale **3** an open-fronted shop **4** a seat in a church (especially for choir or clergy) **5** (**stalls**) theatre seats on the ground floor ▸VERB **1** of a car engine: to come to a halt without the driver intending it to do so **2** of an aircraft: to lose flying speed and so fall out of control

stall² VERB, *informal* to avoid action or decision for the time being

stallion NOUN a male horse, especially one kept for breeding purposes

stalwart ADJECTIVE brave, stout-hearted ▸NOUN a loyal supporter

stamen NOUN (*plural* **stamens** *or* **stamina**), *botany* one of the thread-like spikes in the middle of a flower which bear the pollen

stamina NOUN strength, power to keep going during physical or mental exertion

stammer VERB **1** to have difficulty in saying the first letter of words in speaking **2** to stumble over words

▸NOUN a speech difficulty of this kind

stamp VERB **1** to bring (the foot) down firmly on the ground **2** to stick a (postage stamp) on **3** to mark with a design cut into a mould and inked **4** to fix or mark deeply: *forever stamped in my memory* ▸NOUN **1** the act of stamping **2** a design etc made by stamping **3** a cut or moulded design for stamping **4** kind, sort: *of a different stamp* **5** a postage stamp **stamp out 1** to put out (a fire) by stamping **2** to suppress, crush

stampede NOUN **1** a wild rush of frightened animals **2** a sudden, wild rush of people ▸VERB to rush wildly

stance NOUN **1** point of view or attitude to something **2** someone's manner of standing

stand VERB (**standing, stood**) **1** to be on your feet (not lying or sitting down) **2** to rise to your feet **3** of an object: to (cause to) be in a particular place: *It stood by the door/stood the case in the corner* **4** to bear: *I cannot stand this heat* **5** *old* to treat (someone) to: *stand you tea* **6** to remain: *This law still stands* **7** to be a candidate (for): *She stood for parliament* **8** to be short (for): *PO stands for Post Office* ▸NOUN **1** something on which anything is placed **2** an object made to hold, or for hanging, things: *a hat-stand* **3** lines of raised seats from which people may watch games etc **4** an effort made to support, defend, resist, etc: *a stand against violence* **5** *US* a witness box in a law court **stand by** to be ready or available to be used or help in an emergency etc **stand down** to withdraw (from a contest) or resign (from a job) **stand fast** to refuse to give in **stand in (for)** to take another's place, job, etc for a time **stand out** to stick out, be noticeable **stand to reason** to be likely or reasonable **stand up for** to defend strongly **stand up to** to face or oppose bravely

stand-alone NOUN & ADJECTIVE, *computing* (of) a system, device, etc that can operate unconnected to any other

standard NOUN **1** a level against which things may be judged **2** a level of excellence aimed at: *artistic standards* **3** a large flag etc on a pole ▸ADJECTIVE **1** normal, usual: *standard charge* **2** ordinary, without extras: *standard model*

standardize *or* **standardise** VERB to make all of one kind or size > **standardization** NOUN

standby NOUN **1** something that is kept ready for use, especially in an emergency **2** (*usually* **standby ticket**) a ticket for a journey by air that is offered at a reduced price because you must wait until just before the flight takes off to see if there is a seat available

stand-in NOUN a deputy or substitute

standing NOUN social position or reputation ▸ADJECTIVE **1** on your feet **2** placed on end **3** not moving **4** lasting, permanent: *a standing joke*

standoffish ADJECTIVE unfriendly

standpoint NOUN the position from which you look at something (eg a question, problem), point of view

standstill NOUN a complete stop

stank *past tense* of **stink**

stanza NOUN a group of lines making up a part of a poem, a verse

staple[1] NOUN **1** a U-shaped iron nail **2** a piece of wire driven through sheets of paper to fasten them together ▸VERB to fasten with a staple

staple[2] ADJECTIVE chief, main: *staple foods* ▸NOUN **1** the main item in a country's production, a person's diet, etc **2** a fibre of wool, cotton, etc

stapler NOUN a hand-held device for attaching staples

star NOUN **1** any of the bodies in the sky appearing as points of light **2** any of the fixed bodies which are really distant suns, not the planets **3** an object, shape, or figure with a number of pointed rays (often five) **4** a leading actor or actress or other well-known performer ▸ADJECTIVE for or of a star (in a film etc) ▸VERB (**starring, starred**) to act the chief part (in a film or play)

starboard NOUN the right side of a ship, as you look towards the bow (or front)

starch NOUN (*plural* **starches**) **1** a white carbohydrate (found in flour, potatoes, bread, biscuits, etc) **2** a form of this used for stiffening clothes

starchy ADJECTIVE (**starchier, starchiest**) **1** of food: containing starch **2** stiff and unfriendly

stardom NOUN the state of being a leading performer

stare VERB to look with a fixed gaze ▸NOUN a fixed gaze

starfish NOUN (*plural* **starfish** *or* **starfishes**) a type of small sea creature with five points or arms

stark ADJECTIVE **1** barren, bare **2** harsh, severe **3** sheer: *stark idiocy* ▸ADVERB completely: *stark naked*

starling NOUN a common bird with dark, glossy feathers

Stars and Stripes SINGULAR NOUN the flag of the United States of America

start VERB **1** to begin (an action): *He started to walk home* **2** to get (a machine etc) working: *She started the car* **3** to jump or jerk (eg in surprise) ▸NOUN **1** the act of starting (eg on a task, journey) **2** a sudden movement of the body **3** a sudden shock: *You gave me a start* **4** in a race etc the advantage of beginning before, or farther forward than, others, or the amount of this: *a start of five metres*

startle VERB to give a shock or fright to

startling ADJECTIVE that startles, surprising

starvation NOUN a potentially fatal form of malnutrition caused by eating insufficient quantities of food over a long period, or by total lack of food

starve VERB **1** to die for want of food **2** to suffer greatly from hunger **3** *informal* to be very hungry **4** to deprive (of something needed or wanted badly): *starved of company here*

state NOUN **1** the condition (of something): *the bad state of the roads* **2** the people of a country under a government **3** *US* an area and its people with its own laws forming part of the whole country **4** a government and its officials **5** great show, pomp: *The queen drove by in state* ▸ADJECTIVE **1** of the government **2** national and ceremonial: *state occasions* **3** *US* of a certain state of America: *The state capital of Texas is Austin* ▸VERB to tell, say, or write (especially clearly and fully)

stately ADJECTIVE (**statelier, stateliest**) noble-looking; dignified > **stateliness** NOUN

stately home NOUN a large, grand old house

statement NOUN that which is said or written

state-of-the-art ADJECTIVE most up-to-date

statesman NOUN (*plural* **statesmen**) an experienced and distinguished politician

static ADJECTIVE not moving ▸NOUN **1** atmospheric disturbances causing poor reception of radio or television programmes **2** (*also called*: **static electricity**) electricity on the surface of objects which will not conduct it, eg hair, nylons, etc

station NOUN **1** a building with a ticket office, waiting rooms, etc where trains, buses, or coaches stop to pick up or set down passengers **2** a place which is the centre for work or duty of any kind: *fire station/police station* **3** rank, position: *lowly station* ▸VERB **1** to assign to a position or place **2** to take up a position: *stationed himself by the door*

stationary ADJECTIVE standing still, not moving

ⓘ Comes from Latin *stationarius* meaning 'belonging to a military station'

> Do not confuse: **stationary** and **stationery**. Remember that a stationER's shop sells **stationERy**.

stationer NOUN someone who sells writing paper, envelopes, pens, etc

ⓘ In Medieval Latin, a *stationarius* was a tradesman, usually a bookseller, who did not travel from place to place, but had a regular station or a permanent shop

stationery NOUN writing paper, envelopes, pens, etc

ⓘ For origin, see **stationer**

statistician NOUN someone who produces or studies statistics

statistics PLURAL NOUN numerical data, interpreted and set out in order: *statistics of road accidents for last year* ▸NOUN **1** *plural* figures and facts set out in order: *statistics of road accidents for last year* **2** *singular* the study of these: *statistics is not an easy subject*

statue NOUN a likeness of someone or an animal carved in stone, metal, etc

statuesque (*pronounced* stat-chuw-**esk**) ADJECTIVE like a statue in dignity etc

statuette NOUN a small statue

stature NOUN **1** height **2** importance, reputation

status NOUN position, rank (of a person) in the eyes of others

status quo NOUN the state of affairs now existing, or existing before a certain time or event

status symbol NOUN a possession which is thought to show the high status of the owner

statute NOUN an official law passed by the government of a country

statutory ADJECTIVE according to law

staunch ADJECTIVE firm, loyal; trustworthy

stave NOUN **1** *music* a set of spaced lines on which music is written **2** one of the strips making the side of a barrel ▶ VERB (**staving, stove** *or* **staved**): **stave something in** to crush it in **stave something off** to keep it away, delay it

stay[1] VERB **1** to continue to be: *stayed calm/stay here while I go for help* **2** to live (for a time): *staying in a hotel* **3** *old* to stop ▶ NOUN time spent in a place **stay put** to remain in the same place

stay[2] NOUN a rope running from the side of a ship to the masthead

St Bernard *see* **Saint Bernard**

stead NOUN place: *She went in my stead* **stand you in good stead** to turn out to be helpful to you: *His German stood him in good stead*

steadfast ADJECTIVE **1** steady, fixed **2** faithful, loyal

steading NOUN farm buildings

steady ADJECTIVE (**steadier, steadiest**) **1** firm, not moving or changing **2** not easily upset or put off **3** even, regular, unchanging: *moving at a steady pace* ▶ VERB (**steadies, steadying, steadied**) to make or become steady > **steadily** ADVERB

steak NOUN a thick slice of meat, especially fine-quality beef, or fish, for cooking

steal VERB (**stealing, stole, stolen**) **1** to take (something not belonging to you) without permission **2** to move quietly **3** to take quickly or secretly: *stole a look at him*

stealth NOUN a secret way of doing, acting, etc

stealthy ADJECTIVE (**stealthier, stealthiest**) of movement: slow, quiet and secretive > **stealthily** ADVERB

steam NOUN **1** vapour from hot liquid, especially from boiling water **2** power produced by steam: *in the days of steam* ▶ VERB **1** to give off steam **2** to cook by steam **3** to open or loosen by putting into steam: *steam open the envelope* **4** to move or travel by steam **steam up** of glass: to become covered with condensed steam in the form of small drops of water

steam engine NOUN an engine (especially a railway engine) worked by steam

steamer NOUN a ship driven by steam

steamroller NOUN a steam-driven engine with large and very heavy wheels, used for flattening the surfaces of roads

steamship NOUN a steamer

steamy ADJECTIVE (**steamier, steamiest**) **1** full of steam: *steamy atmosphere* **2** *informal* passionate, erotic

steed NOUN, *old* a horse

steel NOUN **1** a very hard mixture of iron and carbon **2** a bar of steel for sharpening knife blades **of steel** hard, strong: *a grip of steel* **steel yourself** to get up courage (to do something)

steely ADJECTIVE (**steelier, steeliest**) hard, cold, strong etc like steel: *a steely gaze*

steep[1] ADJECTIVE **1** of a slope: rising nearly straight up **2** *informal* of a price: too great

steep[2] VERB to soak in a liquid **be steeped in something** to be very familiar with something (eg a subject of knowledge): *steeped in French literature*

steeple NOUN a tower of a church etc rising to a point, a spire

steeplechase NOUN **1** a horse race round a course with hurdles, usually in the form of man-made hedges **2** a track running race where athletes have to jump hurdles and, usually, a water jump

steeplejack NOUN someone who climbs steeples or other high buildings to make repairs

steer VERB **1** to control the course of (a car, ship, discussion, etc) **2** to follow (a course) **steer clear of** to keep away from

steering NOUN the parts of a ship, car, etc which have to do with controlling its course

steering wheel NOUN the wheel in a car used by the driver to steer it

stellar ADJECTIVE of the stars

stem[1] NOUN **1** the part of a plant from which the leaves and flowers grow **2** the thin support of a wine glass ▸VERB (**stemming, stemmed**) to start, spring (from): *Hate stems from envy*

stem[2] VERB (**stemming, stemmed**) to stop, halt: *stem the bleeding*

stem cell NOUN an undifferentiated cell that can develop into a cell with a specific function

stench NOUN (*plural* **stenches**) a strong unpleasant smell

stencil NOUN **1** a sheet of metal, cardboard, etc with a pattern cut out **2** the drawing or design made by rubbing ink or brushing paint etc over a cut-out pattern ▸VERB (**stencilling, stencilled**) to make a design or copy in one of these ways

step- PREFIX related as the result of a second marriage: *stepfather/ stepdaughter*

🄸 Comes from Old English prefix *steop-* meaning 'orphan'

step NOUN **1** a movement of the leg in walking, running, etc **2** the distance covered by this **3** a particular movement of the feet, as in dancing **4** the sound made by the foot in walking etc: *heard a step outside* **5** a single stair or a rung on a ladder **6** one of a series of moves in a plan, career, etc: *Take the first step* **7** a way of walking: *springy step* **8** (**steps**) a flight of stairs **9** (**steps**) a stepladder ▸VERB (**stepping, stepped**) **1** to take a step **2** to walk, move: *Step this way, please* **in step 1** of two or more people walking: with the same foot going forward at the same time **2** acting etc in agreement (with) **out of step** not in step (with) **step up** to increase (eg production) **take steps** to begin to do something for a certain purpose

stepladder NOUN a ladder with a support on which it rests

steppe NOUN a dry, grassy treeless plain in SE Europe and Asia

stepping-stone NOUN **1** a stone rising above water or mud, used to cross on **2** anything that helps you to advance

stereo- PREFIX solid, three-dimensional: *stereophonic* (= with sounds coming from different directions in three-dimensional space)/*stereotype* (= a solid metal plate for printing)

ⓘ Comes from Greek *stereos* meaning 'solid'

stereo ADJECTIVE, *short for* **stereophonic** ▸ NOUN (*plural* **stereos**) stereophonic equipment, especially a record-player and/or tape recorder, with amplifier and loudspeakers

stereophonic ADJECTIVE of sound: giving a lifelike effect, with different instruments, voices, etc coming from different directions

stereotype NOUN **1** a fixed and generalized idea of what characterizes someone or something **2** a characteristic type of person

ⓘ Originally a printing term for a fixed block of type

stereotyped *or* **stereotypical** ADJECTIVE fixed, not changing: *stereotyped ideas*

sterile ADJECTIVE **1** unable to have children or reproduce **2** producing no ideas etc: *sterile imagination* **3** free from germs

sterility NOUN the state of being sterile

sterilization *or* **sterilisation** NOUN **1** a surgical operation that is performed on humans or animals so that offspring can no longer be produced **2** the treatment of food etc in order to destroy germs

sterilize *or* **sterilise** VERB **1** to make sterile **2** to free from germs by boiling etc

sterling NOUN British money, when used in international trading: *one pound sterling* ▸ ADJECTIVE **1** of silver: of a certain standard of purity **2** worthy, good: *sterling qualities*

ⓘ So called after the image of a small star that was impressed on medieval silver pennies

stern[1] ADJECTIVE **1** looking or sounding angry, or displeased **2** severe, strict, harsh: *stern prison sentence* > **sternly** ADVERB

stern[2] NOUN the back part of a ship

sternness NOUN the state or quality of being stern

steroid NOUN any of a number of substances, including certain hormones

stethoscope NOUN an instrument by means of which a doctor listens to someone's heartbeats, breathing, etc

stew VERB to cook by boiling slowly ▸ NOUN **1** a dish of stewed food, often containing meat and vegetables 2 *informal* a state of worry; a flap

steward NOUN 1 a flight attendant on an aircraft 2 someone who shows people to their seats at a meeting etc 3 an official at a race meeting etc 4 someone who manages an estate or farm for someone else

stewardess NOUN (*plural* **stewardesses**) a female flight attendant (*formerly called*: **air hostess**)

stick[1] NOUN 1 a long thin piece of wood; a branch or twig from a tree 2 a piece of wood shaped for a special purpose: *hockey-stick/ drumstick* 3 a long piece (eg of rhubarb)

stick[2] VERB (**sticking, stuck**) 1 to push or thrust (something): *Stick the knife in your belt* 2 to fix with glue etc: *I'll stick the pieces back together* 3 to be or become caught, fixed or held back: *stuck in the ditch* 4 to hold fast to, keep to (eg a decision) **stick up for** to speak in defence of

sticker NOUN a label, small poster, etc with an adhesive back

stick insect NOUN a long, thin, tropical insect with legs that look like twigs

stickleback NOUN a type of small river-fish with prickles on its back

stickler NOUN someone who attaches great importance to a particular (often small) matter: *stickler for punctuality*

sticky ADJECTIVE (**stickier, stickiest**) 1 clinging closely (like glue, treacle, etc) 2 covered with something sticky 3 *informal* difficult: *a sticky problem* > **stickiness** NOUN

stiff ADJECTIVE 1 not easily bent or moved 2 of a mixture, dough, etc: thick, not easily stirred 3 cold and distant in manner 4 hard, difficult: *stiff examination* 5 severe: *stiff penalty* 6 strong: *stiff drink*

stiffen VERB to make or become stiff

stifle VERB 1 to suffocate 2 to put out (flames) 3 to keep back (tears, a yawn, etc)

stifling ADJECTIVE very hot and stuffy

stigma NOUN 1 (*plural* **stigmata**) a mark of disgrace 2 (*plural* **stigmas**) in a flower: the sticky surface that receives pollen

stigmatize *or* **stigmatise** VERB to mark, describe as something bad: *stigmatized for life*

stiletto NOUN (*plural* **stilettos**) 1 a dagger, or a type of instrument, with a narrow blade 2 (a shoe with) a stiletto heel

still[1] ADJECTIVE 1 not moving 2 calm, without wind; quiet 3 of drinks: not fizzy ▸ VERB to make calm or quiet ▸ ADVERB 1 up to the present time or the time spoken of: *It was still there* 2 even so, nevertheless: *It's difficult but we must still try* 3 even: *still more people* > **stillness** NOUN

still[2] NOUN an apparatus for distilling spirits (eg whisky)

stillborn ADJECTIVE of a child: dead at birth

stilted ADJECTIVE stiff, not natural

stilts PLURAL NOUN 1 long poles with footrests on which someone

A B C D E F G H I J K L M N O P Q R S T U V W X Y Z

may walk clear of the ground **2** tall poles (eg to support a house built above water)

stimulant NOUN something which makes a part of the body more active or which makes you feel livelier

stimulate VERB **1** to make more active **2** to encourage **3** to excite

stimulus (*pronounced* **stim**-yuw-lus) NOUN (*plural* **stimuli** – *pronounced* **stim**-yuw-lai) **1** something that brings on a reaction in a living thing **2** something that rouses (someone etc) to action or greater effort

sting NOUN **1** the part of some animals and plants (eg the wasp, the nettle) which can prick the skin and cause pain or irritation **2** the act of piercing with a sting **3** the wound, swelling, or pain caused by a sting ▶VERB (**stinging, stung**) **1** to pierce with a sting or cause pain like that of a sting **2** to be painful, smart: *made his eyes sting* **3** to hurt the feelings of: *stung by his words*

stink NOUN a bad smell ▶VERB (**stinking, stank** *or* **stunk, stunk**) to give out a bad smell

stint VERB to allow (someone) very little: *Don't stint on the sauce* ▶NOUN **1** limit: *praise without stint* **2** a fixed amount of work: *my daily stint*

stipulate VERB to state as a condition (of doing something)

stipulation NOUN something stipulated, a condition

stir VERB (**stirring, stirred**) **1** to set (liquid) in motion, especially with a spoon etc moved circularly **2** to move slightly: *He stirred in his sleep* **3** to arouse (a person, a feeling, etc) ▶NOUN disturbance, fuss **stir up** to rouse, cause (eg trouble)

stirring ADJECTIVE exciting or lively

stirrup NOUN a metal loop hung from a horse's saddle as a support for the rider's foot

stitch NOUN (*plural* **stitches**) **1** the loop made in a thread, wool, etc by a needle in sewing or knitting **2** a sharp, sudden pain in your side ▶VERB to put stitches in, sew

stoat NOUN a type of small fierce animal similar to a weasel, sometimes called an ermine when its fur turns white in winter

stock NOUN **1** family, race: *of ancient stock* **2** goods in a shop, warehouse, etc **3** the capital of a business company divided into shares **4** livestock **5** liquid (used for soup) obtained by boiling meat, bones, etc **6** a type of scented garden flower of the wallflower family **7** the handle of a whip, rifle, etc **8** (**stocks**) *history* a wooden frame, with holes for the ankles and wrists, in which criminals etc were fastened as a punishment **9** (**stocks**) the wooden framework upon which a ship is supported when being built ▶VERB **1** to keep a supply of (for sale) **2** to supply (a farm with animals etc) ▶ADJECTIVE **1** usual, known by everyone: *a stock joke* **2** usually stocked (by a shop etc) **take stock of** to form an opinion or estimation about (a situation etc)

stockade NOUN a fence of strong

posts set up round an area or building for defence

stockbroker NOUN someone who buys and sells shares in business companies on behalf of others

stock exchange NOUN **1** a place where stocks and shares are bought and sold **2** an association of people who do this

stocking NOUN a close-fitting covering in a knitted fabric (wool, nylon, etc) for the leg and foot

stock market NOUN the stock exchange; dealings in stocks and shares

stockpile NOUN a store, a reserve supply ▸ VERB to build up a store of

stock-still ADJECTIVE perfectly still

stocktaking NOUN a regular check of the goods in a shop or warehouse

stocky ADJECTIVE (**stockier, stockiest**) short and stout > **stockiness** NOUN

stodgy ADJECTIVE (**stodgier, stodgiest**) **1** of food: heavy, not easily digested **2** of a person, book, etc: dull > **stodginess** NOUN

stoic (*pronounced* **stoh**-ik) NOUN someone who bears pain, hardship, etc without showing any sign of feeling it > **stoical** ADJECTIVE

stoicism (*pronounced* **stoh**-i-sizm) NOUN the bearing of pain etc patiently

stoke VERB to put coal, wood, or other fuel on (a fire)

stole[1] NOUN a length of silk, linen, or fur worn over the shoulders

stole[2] *and* **stolen** *see* **steal**

stomach NOUN **1** the bag-like part of the body into which the food passes when swallowed **2** desire or courage (for something): *no stomach for a fight* ▸ VERB, *informal* to put up with, bear: *can't stomach her rudeness*

stomp VERB to stamp the feet, especially noisily

stone NOUN **1** the material of which rocks are composed **2** a (small) loose piece of this **3** a piece of this shaped for a certain purpose: *tombstone* **4** a precious stone (eg a diamond) **5** the hard shell around the seed of some fruits (eg peach, cherry) **6** (*plural*) a measure of weight (14 pounds, 6.35 kilograms) **7** a piece of hard material that forms in the kidney, bladder, etc, causing pain ▸ VERB **1** to throw stones at **2** to take the stones out of fruit ▸ ADJECTIVE made of stone **a stone's throw** a very short distance **leave no stone unturned** to do everything possible

Stone Age NOUN human culture before the use of metal

stony ADJECTIVE (**stonier, stoniest**) **1** like stone **2** covered with stones **3** hard, cold in manner: *stony look*

stood *past form* of **stand**

stool NOUN a seat without a back

stoop VERB **1** to bend the body forwards and downwards **2** to be low or wicked enough (to do a certain thing): *I wouldn't stoop to stealing* ▸ NOUN **1** the act of stooping **2** a forward bend of the body

stop VERB (**stopping, stopped**) **1** to bring to a halt: *stop the car* **2** to prevent from doing: *stop him from working* **3** to put an end to: *Stop this nonsense* **4** to come to an end:

a b c d e f g h i j k l m n o p q r s t u v w x y z

A B C D E F G H I J K L M N O P Q R S T U V W X Y Z

The rain has stopped ▸NOUN **1** the state of being stopped **2** a place where something stops **3** a full stop **4** a knob on an organ which brings certain pipes into use **stop something up** to block (a hole etc)

stoppage NOUN **1** something which blocks up (eg a tube or a passage in the body) **2** a halt (eg in work in a factory)

stopper NOUN something that stops up an opening (especially in the neck of a bottle, jar, etc)

stop press NOUN a space in a newspaper for news put in at the last minute

stopwatch NOUN (*plural* **stopwatches**) a watch that can be stopped and started, used in timing races

storage NOUN **1** the act of storing **2** the state of being stored: *Our furniture is in storage*

store NOUN **1** a supply (eg of goods) from which things are taken when needed **2** a place where goods are kept **3** a shop **4** a collected amount or number ▸VERB to put aside for future use **in store for** awaiting: *trouble in store for us* **set (great) store by** to value highly

storey *or US* **story** NOUN (*plural* **storeys** *or US* **stories**) all that part of a building on the same floor

> Do not confuse with: **story**

stork NOUN a wading bird with a long bill, long neck, and long legs

storm NOUN **1** a sudden burst of bad weather (especially with heavy rain, lightning, thunder, high wind) **2** a violent outbreak (eg of anger) ▸VERB **1** to be in a fury **2** to rain, blow, etc violently **3** to attack (a stronghold etc) violently **go down a storm** to be popular or well received **storm in a teacup** *informal* a great fuss over nothing

story NOUN (*plural* **stories**) an account of an event or events, real or imaginary

> Do not confuse with: **storey**

stout ADJECTIVE **1** fat, stocky **2** brave, reliable: *stout resistance* **3** strong: *stout walking-stick* ▸NOUN a strong, dark-coloured beer > **stoutness** NOUN

stove[1] NOUN an apparatus using coal, gas, or electricity, etc, used for heating, cooking, etc

stove[2] *a past form* of **stave**

stow (*pronounced* stoh) VERB **1** to pack or put away **2** to fill, pack

stowaway NOUN someone who hides in a ship, aeroplane, etc, in order to travel without paying a fare

straddle VERB **1** to stand or walk with legs apart **2** to sit with one leg on each side of (eg a chair or horse)

straggle VERB **1** to wander from the line of a march etc **2** to lag behind **3** to grow or spread beyond the intended limits: *His long beard straggled over his chest*

straggler NOUN a person or animal that wanders or lags behind

straggly ADJECTIVE (**stragglier, straggliest**) spread out untidily

straight ADJECTIVE **1** not bent or curved: *a straight line* **2** direct, frank, honest: *a straight answer* **3** in the proper position or order:

Your tie isn't straight **4** of a hanging picture etc: placed level with ceiling or floor **5** of a drink: without anything added: *a straight vodka* **6** expressionless: *He kept a straight face* ▸ADVERB **1** by the shortest way, directly: *straight across the desert* **2** at once, without delay: *I came straight here after work* **3** fairly, frankly: *She's not playing straight with you* ▸NOUN: **straight away** immediately

🛈 Comes from Old English *streht*

> Do not confuse with: **strait**

straighten VERB to make straight

straightforward ADJECTIVE **1** without any difficulties **2** honest, frank

strain[1] VERB **1** to hurt (a muscle or other part of the body) by overworking or misusing it **2** to work or use to the fullest: *He strained his ears to hear the whisper* **3** to make a great effort: *She strained to reach the rope* **4** to stretch too far, to the point of breaking (a person's patience etc) **5** to separate liquid from a mixture of liquids and solids by passing it through a sieve ▸NOUN **1** the act of straining **2** a hurt to a muscle etc caused by straining it **3** (the effect of) too much work, worry, etc: *suffering from strain* **4** too great a demand: *a strain on my patience* **5** manner: *They grumbled on in the same strain for hours* **6** a tune

strain[2] NOUN **1** a kind, breed: *a strain of fowls* **2** a streak: *a strain of selfishness*

strained ADJECTIVE **1** not natural, done with effort: *a strained conversation* **2** unfriendly: *strained relations*

strainer NOUN a sieve

strait NOUN **1** a narrow strip of sea between two pieces of land **2** (**straits**) difficulties, hardships: *dire straits*

🛈 Comes from Latin *strictus* meaning 'straight' or 'narrow'

> Do not confuse with: **straight**

straitened ADJECTIVE poor and needy

straitjacket NOUN a jacket with long sleeves tied behind to prevent a violent or disturbed person from using their arms

straitlaced ADJECTIVE strict in attitude and behaviour

strand NOUN a length of something soft and fine (eg hair, thread)

stranded ADJECTIVE **1** of a ship: run aground on the shore **2** left helpless without money or friends

strange ADJECTIVE (**stranger, strangest**) **1** unusual, odd: *a strange look on his face* **2** not known, seen, heard, etc, before, unfamiliar: *The method was strange to me* **3** not accustomed (to) **4** foreign: *a strange country* > **strangely** ADVERB

stranger NOUN **1** someone who is unknown to you **2** a visitor **a stranger to** someone who is quite unfamiliar with: *a stranger to hard work*

strangle VERB **1** to kill by gripping or squeezing the throat tightly **2** to keep in, prevent oneself from

a b c d e f g h i j k l m n o p q r s t u v w x y z

A B C D E F G H I J K L M N O P Q R S T U V W X Y Z

giving (eg a scream, a sigh) **3** to stop the growth of > **strangulation** NOUN

stranglehold NOUN a tight control over something which prevents it from escaping, growing, etc

strap NOUN a narrow strip of leather, cloth, etc, used to hold things in place or together etc ▸ VERB (**strapping, strapped**) **1** to bind or fasten with a strap etc **2** to beat with a strap

strapping ADJECTIVE tall and strong: *strapping young man*

strategic (*pronounced* stra-**tee**-jik) ADJECTIVE **1** of strategy **2** done according to a strategy: *a strategic retreat* **3** giving an advantage: *a strategic position*

strategist (*pronounced* **strat**-i-jist) NOUN someone who plans military operations

strategy NOUN (*plural* **strategies**) the art of guiding, forming, or carrying out a plan

stratosphere NOUN the layer of the earth's atmosphere between 10 and 60 kilometres above the earth

stratum (*pronounced* **strah**-t*u*m) NOUN (*plural* **strata** – *pronounced* **strah**-t*a*) **1** a layer of rock or soil **2** a level of society

straw NOUN **1** the stalk on which corn grows **2** a paper or plastic tube for sucking up a drink

strawberry NOUN (*plural* **strawberries**) a type of small, juicy, red fruit or the low creeping plant which bears it

stray VERB **1** to wander **2** to lose your way, become separated (from companions etc) ▸ ADJECTIVE **1** wandering, lost **2** happening etc here and there: *a stray example* ▸ NOUN a wandering animal which has been abandoned or lost

streak NOUN **1** a line or stripe different in colour from that which surrounds it **2** a smear of dirt, polish, etc **3** a flash (eg of lightning) **4** a trace of some quality in one's character: *a streak of selfishness* ▸ VERB **1** to mark with streaks **2** *informal* to move very fast

streaked ADJECTIVE having streaks

streaky ADJECTIVE (**streakier, streakiest**) marked with streaks > **streakiness** NOUN

stream NOUN **1** a flow (of water, air, light, etc) **2** a small river, a brook **3** any steady flow of people or things: *a stream of traffic* ▸ VERB to flow or pour out

streamer NOUN **1** a long strip, usually of paper, used for decorating rooms etc (especially at Christmas) **2** a narrow flag blowing in the wind

streamline VERB **1** to shape (a vehicle etc) so that it may cut through the air or water as easily as possible **2** to make more efficient: *We've streamlined our methods of paying*

street NOUN a road lined with houses etc **streets ahead of** *informal* much better etc than

strength NOUN **1** the state of being strong **2** an available number or force (of soldiers, volunteers, etc) **3** an area of high performance or particular ability: *Her greatest strength is her ability to listen to people* **on the strength of** encouraged by or counting on

strengthen VERB to make, or become, strong or stronger

strenuous ADJECTIVE performed with or needing great effort: *The plans met strenuous resistance/ Squash is a strenuous game*

stress NOUN (*plural* **stresses**) **1** force, pressure, pull, etc of one thing on another **2** physical or nervous pressure or strain: *the stress of modern life* **3** emphasis, importance **4** extra weight laid on a part of a word (as in **but**ter) ▶VERB to put stress, pressure, emphasis, or strain on

stretch VERB **1** to draw out to greater length, or too far, or from one point to another: *Don't stretch that elastic too far/Stretch a rope from post to post* **2** to be able to be drawn out to a greater length or width: *that material stretches* **3** to (cause to) exert (yourself): *The work stretched him to the full* **4** to hold (out) **5** to make (something, eg words, the law) appear to mean more than it does ▶NOUN (*plural* **stretches**) **1** the act of stretching **2** the state of being stretched **3** a length in distance or time: *a stretch of bad road* **at a stretch** continuously: *working three hours at a stretch* **at full stretch** at the limit, using all resources

stretcher NOUN a light folding bed with handles for carrying the sick or wounded

stricken ADJECTIVE **1** wounded **2** deeply affected (eg by illness) **3** struck

strict ADJECTIVE **1** insisting on exact obedience to rules **2** exact: *the strict meaning of a word* **3** allowing no exception: *strict orders* **4** rather severe **>** **strictly** ADVERB

stride VERB (**striding, strode, stridden**) **1** to walk with long steps **2** to take a long step **3** to walk over, along, etc ▶NOUN **1** a long step **2** the distance covered by a step **3** a step forward **take something in your stride** to manage to do it easily

strident ADJECTIVE **1** of a sound: harsh, grating **2** forceful; assertive: *Their demands for reform became more and more strident* **>** **stridency** NOUN

strife NOUN quarrelling; fighting

strike VERB (**striking, struck**) **1** to hit with force **2** to give, deliver (a blow) **3** to knock: *to strike your head on the beam* **4** to attack: *The enemy struck at dawn* **5** to light (a match) **6** to make (a musical note) sound **7** of a clock: to sound (eg at ten o'clock with ten chimes) **8** (often **strike something off** *or* **out**) to cross it out, cancel it **9** to hit or discover suddenly: *strike oil* **10** to take a course: *He struck out across the fields* **11** to stop working (in support of a claim for more pay etc) **12** to give (someone) the impression of being: *Did he strike you as lazy?* **13** to affect, impress: *I am struck by her beauty* **14** to make (an agreement etc) **strike camp** to take down tents **strike home 1** of a blow: to hit the point aimed at **2** of a remark: to have the intended effect

a b c d e f g h i j k l m n o p q r s t u v w x y z

A B C D E F G H I J K L M N O P Q R S T U V W X Y Z

strike up 1 to begin to play or sing (a tune) **2** to begin (a friendship, conversation, etc)

striker NOUN **1** someone participating in a strike **2** in football, a player whose main role is to score goals

striking ADJECTIVE **1** noticeable: *a striking resemblance* **2** impressive

string NOUN **1** a long narrow cord for binding, tying, etc, made of threads twisted together **2** a piece of wire or gut producing a note on a musical instrument **3** (**strings**) the stringed instruments in an orchestra **4** a line of objects threaded together: *string of pearls* **5** a number of things coming one after another: *string of abuse* ▶ VERB (**stringing, strung**) **1** to put on a string **2** to stretch out in a line **string along** to give false expectations to, deceive **string someone up** *informal* to hang them

stringent ADJECTIVE strictly enforced: *stringent rules*
> **stringency** NOUN

stringy ADJECTIVE (**stringier, stringiest**) **1** like string **2** of meat: tough and fibrous

strip NOUN a long narrow piece (eg of paper) ▶ VERB (**stripping, stripped**) **1** to pull (off) in strips **2** to remove (eg leaves, fruit) from **3** to remove the clothes from **4** to deprive: *stripped of his disguise* **5** to make bare or empty: *strip the bed*

stripe NOUN **1** a band of colour different from the background on which it lies **2** a blow with a whip or rod ▶ VERB to make stripes on

striptease NOUN an act in which a performer strips naked

stripy *or* **striped** ADJECTIVE (**stripier, stripiest**) patterned with stripes

strive VERB (**striving, strove, striven** – *pronounced* **striv**-*en*) **1** to try hard **2** to fight

strobe NOUN a light which produces a flickering beam

strode *past tense* of **stride**

stroke NOUN **1** the act of striking **2** a blow (eg with a sword, whip) **3** something unexpected: *a stroke of good luck* **4** one movement (of a pen, an oar) **5** one chime of a clock **6** one complete movement of the arms and legs in swimming **7** a particular style of swimming: *breast stroke* **8** a way of striking the ball (eg in tennis, cricket) **9** an achievement **10** *medicine* a sudden interruption of the blood supply to the brain, causing paralysis ▶ VERB to rub gently, especially as a sign of affection **at a stroke** in a single action or effort

stroll VERB to walk slowly in a leisurely way ▶ NOUN a leisurely walk; an amble

strong ADJECTIVE **1** not easily worn away: *strong cloth* **2** not easily defeated etc **3** forceful, not easily resisted: *strong wind* **4** very healthy and robust, with great muscular strength **5** forceful, commanding respect or obedience **6** of a smell, colour, etc: striking, very noticeable **7** of a feeling: intense: *strong dislike* **8** in number: *a workforce 500 strong*

stronghold NOUN a place built to

withstand attack, a fortress

strongly ADVERB **1** in a strong way **2** to a strong degree: *strongly flavoured*

strong point NOUN something in which a person excels

strop NOUN, *informal* a bad temper: *She went off in a strop*

stroppy ADJECTIVE (**stroppier, stroppiest**) *informal* quarrelsome, disobedient, rowdy

strove *past tense* of **strive**

struck *past form* of **strike**

structural ADJECTIVE of or relating to structure, or a basic structure or framework > **structurally** ADVERB

structure NOUN **1** a building; a framework **2** the way the parts of anything are arranged: *the structure of the story*

struggle VERB **1** to try hard (to do something) **2** to twist and fight to escape **3** to fight (with or against someone) **4** to move with difficulty: *struggling through the mud* ▸ NOUN **1** a great effort **2** a fight

strum VERB (**strumming, strummed**) to play (a guitar etc) in a relaxed way

strung *past form* of **string** **highly strung** easily excited or agitated

strut VERB (**strutting, strutted**) to walk in a proud manner ▸ NOUN **1** a proud way of walking **2** a bar etc which supports something

stub NOUN a small stump (eg of a pencil, cigarette) ▸ VERB (**stubbing, stubbed**) **1** to put out (eg a cigarette) by pressure against something **2** to knock (your toe) painfully against something

stubble NOUN **1** the short ends of the stalks of corn left after it is cut **2** a short growth of beard

stubborn ADJECTIVE **1** unwilling to give way, obstinate **2** of resistance etc: strong, determined **3** difficult to manage or deal with > **stubbornly** ADVERB > **stubbornness** NOUN

stubby ADJECTIVE (**stubbier, stubbiest**) short, thick, and strong: *stubby fingers*

stuck *past form* of **stick**[2]

stud[1] NOUN **1** a nail with a large head **2** a decorative knob on a surface **3** a button with two heads for fastening a collar ▸ VERB (**studding, studded**) **1** to cover or fit with studs **2** to sprinkle thickly (with): *The meadow is studded with flowers*

stud[2] NOUN a collection of horses kept for breeding

student NOUN someone who studies, especially at college, university, etc

studied ADJECTIVE **1** done on purpose, intentional: *a studied insult* **2** too careful, not natural: *a studied smile*

studio NOUN (*plural* **studios**) **1** the workshop of an artist or photographer **2** a building or place in which cinema films are made **3** a room from which television or radio programmes are broadcast

studious ADJECTIVE **1** studying carefully and much **2** careful: *his studious avoidance of quarrels* > **studiously** ADVERB

study VERB (**studies, studying, studied**) **1** to gain knowledge of (a subject) by reading, experiment, etc

2 to look carefully at **3** to consider carefully (eg a problem) ▸NOUN (*plural* **studies**) **1** the gaining of knowledge of a subject: *the study of history* **2** a room where someone reads and writes **3** a piece of music which is meant to develop the skill of the player **4** a work of art done as an exercise, or to try out ideas for a later work

stuff NOUN **1** the material of which anything is made **2** cloth, fabric **3** substance or material of any kind: *What is that stuff all over the wall?* ▸VERB **1** to pack full **2** to fill the skin of (a dead animal) to preserve it **3** to fill (a chicken, a pepper, etc) with stuffing before cooking **get stuffed** *slang* get lost, go away

stuffing NOUN **1** feathers, scraps of material, etc used to stuff a cushion, chair, etc **2** breadcrumbs, onions, etc packed inside a fowl or other meat and cooked with it

stuffy ADJECTIVE (**stuffier, stuffiest**) **1** full of stale air, badly ventilated **2** *informal* dull, having old-fashioned ideas > **stuffily** ADVERB

stumble VERB **1** to trip in walking **2** to walk unsteadily, as if blind **3** to make mistakes or hesitate in speaking ▸NOUN the act of stumbling **stumble on something** to find it by chance

stumbling block NOUN a difficulty in the way of a plan or of progress

stump NOUN **1** the part of a tree, leg, tooth, etc left after the main part has been cut away **2** *cricket* one of the three wooden stakes which make up a wicket ▸VERB **1** *cricket* to put out (a batsman) by touching the stumps with the ball **2** to puzzle completely **3** to walk stiffly or heavily **stump up** *informal* to pay up

stumpy ADJECTIVE (**stumpier, stumpiest**) short and thick

stun VERB (**stunning, stunned**) **1** to knock senseless (by a blow etc) **2** *informal* to surprise or shock very greatly: *stunned by the news*

stung *past form* of **sting**

stunk *past form* of **stink**

stunt[1] VERB to stop the growth of

stunt[2] NOUN **1** a daring trick **2** something done to attract attention: *a publicity stunt*

stunted ADJECTIVE small and badly shaped

stup- PREFIX forms words related to the idea of being knocked senseless

ⓘ Comes from Latin *stupere* meaning 'to be stunned'

stupefaction NOUN the state of being stupefied; numbness

stupefy VERB (**stupefies, stupefying, stupefied**) **1** to make stupid, deaden the feelings of **2** to astonish

stupendous ADJECTIVE wonderful, amazing (eg because of size and power)

stupid ADJECTIVE **1** foolish: *a stupid thing to do* **2** dull, slow at learning **3** stupefied (eg from lack of sleep) > **stupidity** NOUN

stupor NOUN the state of being only partly conscious

sturdy ADJECTIVE (**sturdier, sturdiest**) strong, well built; healthy > **sturdily** ADVERB

stutter VERB to speak in a halting, jerky way; stammer ▶NOUN a stammer

sty[1] NOUN (*plural* **sties**) a pen in which pigs are kept

sty[2] *or* **stye** NOUN (*plural* **sties** *or* **styes**) an inflamed swelling on the eyelid

style NOUN **1** manner of acting, writing, speaking, etc **2** fashion: *in the style of the late 19th century* **3** an air of elegance **4** *botany* the part of a flower that connects the stigma to the ovary **in style** with no expense or effort spared

stylesheet NOUN, *computing* a set of specifications used as a template for documents or web pages

stylish ADJECTIVE smart, elegant, fashionable

stylized *or* **stylised** ADJECTIVE elaborate, especially creating an impression of unnaturalness

stylus NOUN (*plural* **styluses**) a needle for a record-player

suave (*pronounced* swahv) ADJECTIVE (**suaver, suavest**) of a person: superficially polite and sophisticated, smooth

sub- PREFIX **1** under, below **2** less than **3** lower in rank or importance

ⓘ Comes from Latin *sub* meaning 'under' or 'near'

subatomic particle NOUN, *physics* one of the units, eg protons, neutrons, and electrons, from which atoms are made

subconscious NOUN the contents of the mind of which someone is not themselves aware ▶ADJECTIVE of the subconscious, not conscious or aware: *a subconscious desire for fame*

subcontract VERB to give a contract for (work forming part of a larger contract) to another company

subculture NOUN an identifiable group within a larger culture or group

subdivide VERB to divide into smaller parts

subdivision NOUN a part made by subdividing

subdue VERB **1** to conquer (an enemy etc) **2** to keep under control (eg a desire) **3** to make less bright (eg a colour, a light) **4** to make quieter: *He seemed subdued after the fight* > **subdued** ADJECTIVE

subheading NOUN a heading below the main heading in a document

subject ADJECTIVE (*pronounced* **sub**-jikt) under the power of another: *a subject nation* ▶NOUN (*pronounced* **sub**-jikt) **1** someone under the power of another: *the king's subjects* **2** a member of a nation with a monarchy: *a British subject* **3** something or someone spoken about, studied, etc **4** *grammar* the word in a sentence or clause which stands for the person or thing doing the action of the verb (eg *cat* is the subject in 'the *cat* drank the milk') ▶VERB (*pronounced* sub-**jekt**) (*often* **subject someone to something**) to force them to submit to it **subject to something 1** liable to suffer from it (eg colds) **2** depending on it: *subject to your approval*

subjection NOUN the act of

subjecting or the state of being subjected

subjective ADJECTIVE based on personal feelings, thoughts, etc, not impartial (*contrasted with*: **objective**) > **subjectivity** NOUN

subjugate VERB to bring under your power; make obedient

subjunctive *grammar*, ADJECTIVE of the mood a verb: indicating possibility etc, eg 'were' in: *If I were you* ▶NOUN a subjunctive form of a verb

sublimation NOUN changing from a solid to a gas, or a gas to a solid, without becoming a liquid

sublime ADJECTIVE very noble, great, or grand

subliminal ADJECTIVE working below the level of consciousness: *subliminal messages*

submachine-gun NOUN a light machine-gun fired from the hip or shoulder

submarine NOUN a type of ship which can travel under water ▶ADJECTIVE under the surface of the sea

submerge VERB to cover with water; sink

submersible NOUN a boat that can operate under water

submersion *or* **submergence** NOUN submerging or being submerged

submission NOUN **1** the act of submitting **2** readiness to yield, meekness **3** an idea, statement, etc offered for consideration

submissive ADJECTIVE meek, yielding easily

submit VERB (**submitting, submitted**) **1** to give in, yield **2** to place (a matter) before someone for making a judgement

subordinate ADJECTIVE (*pronounced* su-**baw**-di-nit) (often **subordinate to someone**) lower in rank or importance ▶NOUN (*pronounced* su-**baw**-di-nit) someone who is subordinate ▶VERB (*pronounced* su-**baw**-di-neit): **subordinate one person** *or* **subordinate something to another** to consider them as being of less importance > **subordination** NOUN

subordinate clause NOUN, *grammar* (*also called*: **dependent clause**) a clause in a sentence that adds information to a main clause and depends on it to make sense, eg 'I liked the book *that you gave me for my birthday*' (*compare with*: **main clause**)

subscribe VERB **1** to make a contribution (especially of money) towards a charity **2** to promise to take and pay for a number of issues of a magazine etc **subscribe to something** to agree with (an idea, statement, etc)

subscription NOUN a payment for eg a club membership fee or a number of issues of a magazine for a given period

subsequent ADJECTIVE following, coming after

subservient ADJECTIVE weak-willed, ready to do as you are told > **subservience** NOUN

subside VERB **1** to settle down, sink lower **2** of noise etc: to get less and less

subsidence (*pronounced* **sub-**si-dens) NOUN the sinking of land, buildings, etc to a lower level

subsidiarity NOUN **1** the state of being subsidiary **2** the concept of a central governing body permitting its member states or branches to make their own decisions on certain local issues

subsidiary ADJECTIVE **1** acting as a help **2** of less importance **3** of a company: controlled by another company

subsidize *or* **subsidise** VERB to give money as a help

subsidy NOUN (*plural* **subsidies**) money paid by a government or organization etc to help an industry

subsist VERB **1** to live (on a kind of food etc) **2** to exist

subsistence NOUN **1** existence **2** means or necessities for survival

subsoil NOUN the layer of the earth just below the surface soil

substance NOUN **1** a material that can be seen and felt: *Glue is a sticky substance* **2** general meaning (of a talk, essay, etc) **3** thickness, solidity **4** wealth, property: *a woman of substance*

substantial ADJECTIVE **1** solid, strong **2** large: *a substantial building* **3** able to be seen and felt **4** in the main, but not in detail: *substantial agreement*

substantially ADVERB for the most part: *substantially the same*

substantiate VERB to give proof of, or evidence for

substitute VERB: **substitute something** *or* **substitute one thing for another** to put one thing in place or instead of another NOUN someone or thing used instead of another

substitution NOUN **1** the process of substituting or being substituted **2** something which is substituted

subterfuge NOUN a cunning trick to get out of difficulty etc

subterranean ADJECTIVE found under the ground

subtitle NOUN **1** a second additional title of a book etc **2** a translation of a foreign-language film, appearing at the bottom of the screen

subtle (*pronounced* **sut**-l) ADJECTIVE **1** not straightforwardly or obviously stated or displayed: *by subtle means* **2** difficult to describe or explain: *a subtle difference* > **subtlety** NOUN (*plural* **subtleties**) > **subtly** ADVERB

subtotal NOUN a total of one set of figures within a larger group

subtract VERB **1** to take away (a part from) **2** to take away (one number from another) > **subtraction** NOUN

suburb NOUN a residential area on the outskirts of a town > **suburban** ADJECTIVE

suburbia NOUN the suburbs

subversive ADJECTIVE likely to overthrow (government, discipline, etc)

subway NOUN **1** an underground crossing for pedestrians etc **2** *Scot & US* an underground railway

succeed VERB **1** to manage to do what you have been trying to do:

A B C D E F G H I J K L M N O P Q R S T U V W X Y Z

She succeeded in getting the grades she needed **2** to get on well **3** to take the place of, follow **4** (often **succeed to**) to follow in order (to the throne etc)

success NOUN (*plural* **successes**) **1** the achievement of something you have been trying to do **2** someone who succeeds **3** something that turns out well

successful ADJECTIVE **1** having achieved what was aimed at **2** having achieved wealth, importance, etc **3** turning out as planned

succession NOUN **1** the act of following after **2** the right of becoming the next holder of a throne etc **3** a number of things coming one after the other: *a succession of failures* **in succession** one after another

successive ADJECTIVE following one after the other

successor NOUN someone who comes after, follows in a post, etc

succinct ADJECTIVE in a few words, brief, concise: *a succinct reply*

succulent ADJECTIVE **1** juicy **2** *botany* of a plant: having thick, juicy leaves or stems

succumb (*pronounced* su-**kum**) VERB to yield (to): *succumbed to temptation*

such ADJECTIVE **1** of a kind previously mentioned: *Such things are difficult to find* **2** similar: *doctors, nurses, and such people* **3** so great: *His excitement was such that he shouted out loud* **4** used for emphasis: *It's such a disappointment!* ▶ PRONOUN thing, people, etc of a kind already mentioned: *Such as these are not to be trusted* **as such** by itself **such as** of the same kind as

such-and-such ADJECTIVE & PRONOUN any given (person or thing): *such-and-such a book*

suck VERB **1** to draw into the mouth **2** to draw milk from with the mouth **3** to hold in the mouth and lick hard (eg a sweet) **4** (often **suck up** or **in**) to draw in, absorb ▶ NOUN **1** a sucking action **2** the act of sucking

sucker NOUN **1** *informal* someone easily fooled **2** a pad (of rubber etc) which can stick to a surface **3** *zoology* a part of an animal's body by which it sticks to objects **4** *botany* a side shoot rising from the stem or root of a plant

suckle VERB of a woman or female animal: to give milk from the breast or teat

suckling NOUN a baby or young animal which still sucks its mother's milk

suction NOUN **1** the act of sucking **2** the process of reducing the air pressure, and so producing a vacuum, on the surface or between surfaces

sudden ADJECTIVE happening all at once without being expected: *a sudden attack* > **suddenly** ADVERB > **suddenness** NOUN

suds PLURAL NOUN frothy, soapy water

sue VERB (**suing, sued**) to start a law case against

suede (*pronounced* sweid) NOUN

a soft leather, where the flesh side is brushed so that it has a velvety finish

suet NOUN a kind of hard animal fat used for making pastry etc

suffer VERB **1** to feel pain or punishment **2** to bear, endure **3** *old* to allow **4** to go through, undergo (a change etc)

sufferance NOUN: **on sufferance** allowed or tolerated but not really wanted

suffering NOUN pain or distress

suffice VERB to be enough, or good enough

sufficient ADJECTIVE enough > **sufficiency** NOUN > **sufficiently** ADVERB

suffix NOUN (*plural* **suffixes**) a small part added to the end of a word to make another word, such as *-ness* to *good* to make *goodness, -ly* to *quick* to make *quickly*, etc

suffocate VERB **1** to kill by preventing the breathing of **2** to die from lack of air **3** to feel unable to breathe freely: *suffocating in this heat* > **suffocation** NOUN

suffrage NOUN **1** a vote **2** the right to vote

suffuse VERB to spread over: *The sky was suffused with red*

sugar NOUN a sweet substance obtained mostly from sugar cane and sugar beet ▸ VERB to mix or sprinkle with sugar

sugar daddy NOUN (*plural* **sugar daddies**) an older man who lavishes money on a younger woman in exchange for companionship and, often, sex

sugary ADJECTIVE **1** tasting of sugar **2** too sweet

suggest VERB **1** to put forward, propose (an idea etc) **2** to put into the mind, hint

suggestible ADJECTIVE easily influenced by suggestions

suggestion NOUN **1** an act of suggesting **2** an idea put forward **3** a slight trace: *a suggestion of anger in her voice*

suggestive ADJECTIVE **1** that suggests something particular, especially sexually improper: *suggestive remarks* **2** giving the idea (of): *suggestive of mental illness*

suicidal ADJECTIVE **1** of or considering suicide **2** likely to cause your death or ruin: *suicidal action*

suicide NOUN **1** the taking of your own life **2** someone who kills themselves

suit NOUN **1** a set of clothes to be worn together **2** a case in a law court **3** *old* a request for permission to court a woman **4** one of the four divisions (spades, hearts, diamonds, clubs) of playing-cards ▸ VERB **1** to be convenient or suitable for: *The climate suits me* **2** to look well on: *That dress suits you* **suit to** to make fitting or suitable for: *suited his words to the occasion*

suitable ADJECTIVE **1** fitting the purpose **2** just what is wanted, convenient > **suitability** NOUN

suitcase NOUN a travelling case for carrying clothes etc

suite (*pronounced* sweet) NOUN **1** a number of things in a set, eg rooms,

A B C D E F G H I J K L M N O P Q R S T U V W X Y Z

furniture, pieces of music **2** a group of attendants for an important person

suitor NOUN, *old* a man who tries to gain the love of a woman

sulk VERB to keep silent because of being displeased ▸NOUN (*also*: **the sulks**) a fit of sulking

sulky ADJECTIVE (**sulkier, sulkiest**) sulking; inclined to sulk

sullen ADJECTIVE angry and silent, sulky > **sullenness** NOUN

sully VERB (**sullies, sullying, sullied**) to make less pure, dirty

sulphate *or US* **sulfate** NOUN a compound made from sulphuric acid which contains the group SO_4

sulphur *or US* **sulfur** NOUN, *chemistry* a yellow substance found in the ground which gives off a choking smell when burnt, used in matches, gunpowder, etc

sulphuric acid *or US* **sulfuric acid** NOUN, *chemistry* a powerful acid much used in industry

sultan NOUN **1** *history* the head of the Turkish Ottoman empire **2** an Islamic ruler

sultana NOUN **1** a sultan's wife **2** a light-coloured raisin

sultry ADJECTIVE (**sultrier, sultriest**) **1** of weather: very hot and close **2** passionate, steamy

sum NOUN **1** the amount made by two or more things added together **2** a quantity of money **3** a problem in arithmetic **4** the general meaning (of something said or written) ▸VERB (**summing, summed**): **sum up** to give the main points of (a discussion, evidence in a trial, etc)

summarize *or* **summarise** VERB to state briefly, make a summary of

summary NOUN (*plural* **summaries**) a shortened form (of a story, statement, etc) giving only the main points ▸ADJECTIVE **1** short, brief **2** done without wasting time or words > **summarily** ADVERB: *He was summarily dismissed*

summer NOUN the warmest season of the year, following spring ▸ADJECTIVE relating to summer

summit NOUN **1** the highest point of a hill etc **2** a summit conference

summon VERB to order (someone) to come to you, appear in a court of law, etc **summon up** to gather up (courage, strength, etc)

summons NOUN (*plural* **summonses**) an order to appear in court

sumo NOUN a Japanese form of wrestling

sump NOUN **1** part of a motor-engine which contains the oil **2** a small drainage pit

sumptuous ADJECTIVE costly, splendid

sun NOUN **1** the round body in the sky which gives light and heat to the earth **2** sunshine ▸VERB (**sunning, sunned**): **sun yourself** to lie in the sunshine, sunbathe

sunbathe VERB to lie or sit in the sun to acquire a suntan

sunbeam NOUN a ray of light from the sun

sunburn NOUN a burning or redness caused by over-exposure to the sun

sunburned *or* **sunburnt**

ADJECTIVE affected by sunburn

sundae (*pronounced* **sun**-dei) NOUN a sweet dish of ice-cream served with fruit, syrup, etc

Sunday NOUN the first day of the week

🛈 From an Old English word meaning 'day of the sun'

sundial NOUN an instrument for telling the time from the shadow of a rod on its surface cast by the sun

sundries PLURAL NOUN odds and ends

sundry ADJECTIVE several, various: *sundry articles for sale*

sunflower NOUN a large yellow flower with petals like rays of the sun

sung *past participle* of **sing**

sunglasses PLURAL NOUN spectacles with tinted lenses that shield the eyes from sunlight

sunken ADJECTIVE **1** that has been sunk **2** of cheeks etc: hollow

sunlight NOUN the light from the sun

sunlit ADJECTIVE lighted up by the sun

sunny ADJECTIVE (**sunnier, sunniest**) **1** full of sunshine **2** cheerful: *sunny nature*

sunrise NOUN the rising of the sun in the morning

sunset NOUN the setting of the sun in the evening

sunshine NOUN **1** bright sunlight **2** cheerfulness

sunstroke NOUN an illness caused by over-exposure to hot sunshine

suntan NOUN a browning of the skin caused by exposure to the sun

sup VERB (**supping, supped**) to eat or drink in small mouthfuls

super- PREFIX above, beyond, very, too: *superannuate* (= make someone retire because they are 'beyond the years')/*superhuman* (= beyond what a normal person is capable of)

🛈 Comes from Latin *super* meaning 'above'

super ADJECTIVE, *informal* extremely good

superb ADJECTIVE magnificent, very fine, excellent: *a superb view*

supercilious ADJECTIVE looking down on others, haughty

🛈 Based on a Latin word meaning 'eyebrow', from the habit of raising the eyebrows to show scorn or superiority

superficial ADJECTIVE **1** of a wound: affecting the surface of the skin only, not deep **2** not thorough or detailed: *superficial interest* **3** apparent at first glance, not actual: *superficial likeness* **4** of a person: not capable of deep thoughts or feelings > **superficiality** NOUN > **superficially** ADVERB

🛈 Comes from Latin *superficies* meaning 'surface'

> Do not confuse: **superficial** and **superfluous**

superfluous (*pronounced* soo-**per**-floo-*us*) ADJECTIVE beyond what is enough or necessary

🛈 Comes from Latin *superfluus* meaning 'overflowing'

> Do not confuse: **superficial** and **superfluous**

A B C D E F G H I J K L M N O P Q R S T U V W X Y Z

superhuman ADJECTIVE **1** divine, godly **2** greater than would be expected of an ordinary person: *superhuman effort*

superimpose VERB to lay or place (one thing on another)

superintend VERB to be in charge or control, manage

superintendent NOUN **1** someone who is in charge of an institution, building, etc **2** a police officer above a chief inspector

superior ADJECTIVE **1** higher in place or rank **2** better or greater than others: *superior forces/superior goods* **3** having an air of being better than others ▸NOUN someone better than, or higher in rank than, others

superiority NOUN **1** a superior state **2** pre-eminence **3** advantage

superlative ADJECTIVE **1** better than, or going beyond, all others: *superlative skill* **2** *grammar* an adjective or adverb of the highest degree of comparison, not positive or comparative, eg kind*est*, *worst*, *most* quickly

supermarket NOUN a large self-service store selling food etc

supernatural ADJECTIVE not happening in the ordinary course of nature, miraculous

supernova (*pronounced* soo-per-**noh**-v*a*) NOUN (*plural* **supernovas** *or* **supernovae** – *pronounced* soo-per-**noh**-vee) an exploding star surrounded by a bright cloud of gas

supersede VERB **1** to take the place of: *She superseded her brother as head teacher* **2** to replace (something with something else)

supersonic ADJECTIVE faster than the speed of sound: *supersonic flight*

superstition NOUN **1** belief in magic and in things which cannot be explained by reason **2** an example of such belief (eg not walking under ladders)

superstitious ADJECTIVE having superstitions

supervise VERB to be in charge of work and see that it is properly done

supervision NOUN the act of supervising; control, inspection

supervisor NOUN a person who is responsible for making sure that other people's work is done correctly

supper NOUN a meal taken in the evening

supplant VERB to take the place of: *The baby supplanted the dog in her affections*

supple ADJECTIVE **1** bending easily, flexible **2** of an object: bending easily without breaking > **supply** (*pronounced* **sup**-li) ADVERB

supplement NOUN (*pronounced* **sup**-li-m*e*nt) **1** something added to supply a need or lack **2** a special section added to the main part of a newspaper or magazine ▸VERB (*pronounced* **sup**-li-ment) to make or be an addition to: *Her earnings supplemented his income*

supplementary ADJECTIVE added to supply a need; additional

supply VERB (**supplies, supplying, supplied**) **1** to provide (what is wanted or needed) **2** to provide (someone with something) ▶NOUN (*plural* **supplies**) **1** an act of supplying **2** something supplied **3** a stock or store **4** (**supplies**) a stock of essentials, eg food, equipment, money, etc ▶ADJECTIVE of a teacher: filling another's place or position for a time

support VERB **1** to hold up, take part of the weight of **2** to help, encourage **3** to supply with a means of living: *support a family* **4** to bear, put up with: *I can't support lies* ▶NOUN **1** an act of supporting **2** something that supports

supporter NOUN someone who supports (eg a football club)

suppose VERB **1** to take as true, assume for the sake of argument: *suppose that we have £100 to spend* **2** to believe, think probable: *I suppose you know* **3** used to give a polite order: *suppose you leave now* **be supposed to** to be required or expected to (do) **supposing** in the event that: *supposing it rains*

supposed ADJECTIVE believed (often mistakenly) to be so: *her supposed generosity*

supposedly (*pronounced* su-**poh**-zid-li) ADVERB according to what is supposed

supposition NOUN **1** the act of supposing **2** something supposed

suppress VERB **1** to crush, put down (a rebellion etc) **2** to keep back (a yawn, a piece of news, etc) > **suppression** NOUN

supra- PREFIX above

🛈 Comes from Latin *supra* meaning 'above'

supremacist (*pronounced* soo-**prem**-*a*-sist) NOUN someone who believes in the supremacy of their own race etc: *white supremacist*

supremacy (*pronounced* soo-**prem**-*a*-si) NOUN highest power or authority

supreme ADJECTIVE **1** highest, most powerful: *supreme ruler* **2** greatest: *supreme courage*

surcharge NOUN an extra charge or tax

surd NOUN, *maths* an irrational number, especially shown as the root of a natural number

sure ADJECTIVE (**surer, surest**) **1** having no doubt: *I'm sure that I can come* **2** certain (to do, happen, etc): *He is sure to be there* **3** reliable, dependable: *a sure method* **be sure** to see to it that: *Be sure that he does it* **make sure** to act so that, or check that, something is sure **sure of yourself** confident **to be sure 1** certainly! **2** undoubtedly: *To be sure, you are correct*

sure-footed ADJECTIVE, *informal* unlikely to slip or stumble

surely ADVERB **1** certainly, without doubt **2** sometimes expressing a little doubt: *Surely you won't tell him?* **3** without hesitation, etc

surf NOUN the foam made by the breaking of waves ▶VERB **1** to stand or lie on a surfboard, try to catch the crest of a wave, and ride it to the shore **2** *computing* to browse through (the Internet) looking at websites

surface NOUN the outside or top part of anything (eg of the earth, of a road, etc) ▶VERB **1** to come up to the surface of water etc **2** to put a (smooth) surface on ▶ADJECTIVE

1 on the surface 2 travelling on the surface of land or water: *surface mail*

surfboard NOUN a long, narrow board on which someone can ride over the surf

surfeit NOUN too much of anything

surfer NOUN someone who surfs

surfing NOUN the sport of riding on a surfboard

surge VERB 1 to move (forward) like waves 2 to rise suddenly or excessively ▸NOUN 1 the swelling of a large wave 2 a swelling or rising movement like this 3 a sudden rise or increase (of pain etc)

surgeon NOUN a doctor who performs operations, often cutting the body open to examine or remove a diseased part

surgery NOUN (*plural* **surgeries**) 1 treatment of diseases etc by operation 2 a doctor's or dentist's consulting room

surgical ADJECTIVE of, for use in, or by means of surgery: *a surgical operation/a surgical mask/surgical equipment* > **surgically** ADVERB: *The lump will have to be surgically removed*

surly ADJECTIVE (**surlier, surliest**) gruff, rude, ill-mannered > **surliness** NOUN

surmise VERB to suppose, guess ▸NOUN a supposition

surmount VERB 1 to overcome (a difficulty etc) 2 to climb over, get over

surmountable ADJECTIVE capable of being overcome or dealt with successfully

surname NOUN a person's last name or family name

surpass VERB to go beyond, be more or better than: *His work surpassed my expectations*

surplus (*pronounced* **ser**-plus) NOUN the amount left over after what is needed has been used up ▸ADJECTIVE left over, extra

[i] Comes from French prefix *sur-* meaning 'over', and *plus* meaning 'more'

surprise NOUN 1 the feeling caused by an unexpected happening 2 an unexpected happening ▸VERB 1 to cause someone to feel surprise 2 to come upon (someone) suddenly and without warning **take by surprise** to come upon, or capture, without warning

surprised ADJECTIVE experiencing feelings of surprise

surreal ADJECTIVE dreamlike, using images from the subconscious

surrealism NOUN the use of surreal images in art

surrealist NOUN an adherent of surrealism ▸ADJECTIVE relating to or characteristic of surrealism: *a surrealist painting*

surrender VERB 1 to give up, give in, yield: *surrender to the enemy* 2 to hand over: *She surrendered the note to the teacher* ▸NOUN an act of surrender, especially in a war

surreptitious ADJECTIVE done in a secret, underhand way

surrogate ADJECTIVE used or acting as a substitute for another person or thing: *a surrogate mother* ▸NOUN a substitute

surround VERB **1** to be all round (someone or something) **2** to enclose, put round ▸ NOUN a border

surroundings PLURAL NOUN **1** the country lying round a place **2** the people and places with which you have to deal in daily life

surveillance NOUN a close watch or constant guard

survey VERB (*pronounced* ser-**vei**) (**surveying, surveyed**) **1** to look over **2** to inspect, examine **3** to make careful measurements of (a piece of land etc) ▸ NOUN (*pronounced* **ser**-vei) (*plural* **surveys**) **1** a general view **2** a detailed examination or inspection **3** a piece of writing giving results of this **4** a careful measuring of land etc **5** a map made with the measurements obtained

surveyor NOUN someone who makes surveys of land, buildings, etc

survival NOUN **1** the state of surviving **2** a custom, relic, etc that remains from earlier times

survive VERB **1** to remain alive, continue to exist (after an event etc) **2** to live longer than: *He survived his wife*

survivor NOUN someone who remains alive: *the only survivor of the crash*

susceptibility NOUN (*plural* **susceptibilities**) **1** the state or degree of being susceptible to something **2** (**susceptibilities**) strong feelings or sensibilities

susceptible ADJECTIVE easily affected or moved **susceptible to something** liable to be affected by it: *susceptible to colds*

suspect VERB (*pronounced* sus-**pekt**) **1** to be inclined to think (someone) guilty: *I suspect her of the crime* **2** to distrust, have doubts about: *I suspected his air of frankness* **3** to guess: *I suspect that we're wrong* ▸ NOUN (*pronounced* **sus**-pekt) someone thought to be guilty of a crime etc ▸ ADJECTIVE (*pronounced* **sus**-pekt) arousing doubt, suspected

suspend VERB **1** to hang **2** to keep from falling or sinking: *particles suspended in a liquid* **3** to stop for a time: *suspend business* **4** to take away a job, privilege, etc from for a time: *They suspended the student from classes*

suspender NOUN **1** an elastic strap to keep up socks or stockings **2** (**suspenders**) *US* braces

suspense NOUN **1** a state of being undecided **2** a state of uncertainty or worry

suspension NOUN **1** the act of suspending **2** the state of being suspended **3** *chemistry* the state of a solid which is mixed with a liquid or gas and does not sink or dissolve in it

suspicion NOUN **1** a feeling of doubt or mistrust **2** an opinion, a guess

suspicious ADJECTIVE **1** inclined to suspect or distrust **2** arousing suspicion > **suspiciously** ADVERB

sustain VERB **1** to hold up, support **2** to bear (an attack etc) without giving way **3** to suffer (an injury etc) **4** to give strength to: *The food will sustain you* **5** to keep up, keep going: *sustain a conversation*

sustainable development

A B C D E F G H I J K L M N O P Q R S T U V W X Y Z

NOUN the development and use of resources over the long term, to prevent damage to the environment

sustenance NOUN food, nourishment

svelte ADJECTIVE slender, trim

SW ABBREVIATION south-west; south-western

swab NOUN **1** a mop for cleaning a ship's deck **2** a piece of cotton wool used for cleaning, absorbing blood, etc ▶VERB (**swabbing, swabbed**) to clean with a swab

swaddle VERB to wrap up (a young baby) tightly

swag NOUN **1** *slang* stolen goods **2** *Aust* a bundle of possessions

swagger VERB **1** to walk proudly, swinging the arms and body **2** to boast ▶NOUN a proud walk or attitude

swallow[1] VERB **1** to pass (food or drink) down the throat into the stomach **2** to receive (an insult etc) without objection **3** to keep back (tears, a laugh, etc) ▶NOUN an act of swallowing **swallow something up** to make it disappear

swallow[2] NOUN a bird with pointed wings and a forked tail

swam *past tense* of **swim**

swamp NOUN wet, marshy ground ▶VERB **1** to fill (a boat) with water **2** to overwhelm: *swamped with work*

swan NOUN a large, stately water bird, with white feathers and a long neck

swan song NOUN the last work of a musician, writer, etc

swap *or* **swop** VERB (**swapping** *or* **swopping, swapped** *or* **swopped**) to give one thing in exchange for another: *swap addresses*

swarm NOUN **1** a large number of insects flying or moving together **2** a dense moving crowd ▶VERB **1** of insects: to gather together in great numbers **2** to move in crowds **3** to be crowded (with): *swarming with tourists*

swarthy ADJECTIVE (**swarthier, swarthiest**) dark-skinned

swashbuckler NOUN a daring and flamboyant adventurer > **swashbuckling** ADJECTIVE

swastika (*pronounced* **swos**-ti-k*a*) NOUN **1** an ancient design of a cross with four bent arms **2** this design taken up as a symbol of Nazism

swat VERB (**swatting, swatted**) to squash (a fly etc) ▶NOUN an instrument for squashing insects

swath (*pronounced* swoth) *or* **swathe** (*pronounced* sweidh) NOUN **1** a line of corn or grass cut by a scythe **2** a strip

swathe VERB to wrap round with clothes or bandages

sway VERB **1** to swing or rock to and fro **2** to bend in one direction or to one side **3** to influence: *sway opinion* ▶NOUN **1** a swaying movement **2** rule, power: *hold sway over*

swear VERB (**swearing, swore, sworn**) **1** to promise or declare solemnly **2** to vow **3** to curse, using the name of God or other sacred things without respect **4** to make (someone) take an oath: *swear someone to secrecy* **swear by** to rely on, have complete faith in

swear-word NOUN a word used in swearing or cursing

sweat NOUN moisture secreted by

the skin, perspiration ▶ VERB **1** to give out sweat **2** *informal* to work hard

sweater NOUN a jersey, a pullover

sweatshirt NOUN a long-sleeved jersey of a thick soft cotton fabric, usually fleecy on the inside

sweaty ADJECTIVE (**sweatier, sweatiest**) wet, or stained, with sweat

swede NOUN a kind of large yellow turnip

sweep VERB (**sweeping, swept**) **1** to clean (a floor etc) with a brush or broom **2** (often **sweep up** or **sweep something up**) to gather up (dust etc) by sweeping **3** to carry (away, along, off) with a long brushing movement **4** to travel over quickly, move with speed: *a new fad which is sweeping the country* **5** to move quickly in a proud manner (eg from a room) **6** to clear (something) of something: *Sweep the sea of enemy mines* **7** to curve widely or stretch far ▶ NOUN **1** a sweeping movement **2** a curve, a stretch **3** *informal* a chimney-sweep **4** *informal* a sweepstake

sweeper NOUN **1** a device for sweeping **2** *football* a player positioned behind the defenders

sweeping ADJECTIVE **1** that sweeps **2** of a victory etc: great, overwhelming **3** of a statement etc: too general, allowing no exceptions, rash

sweet ADJECTIVE **1** having the taste of sugar, not salty, sour or bitter **2** pleasing to the taste **3** pleasant to hear or smell **4** kindly, agreeable, charming ▶ NOUN **1** a small piece of sweet substance, eg chocolate, toffee, etc **2** something sweet served towards the end of a meal, a pudding

sweetcorn NOUN maize

sweeten VERB to make or become sweet

sweetener NOUN **1** an artificial substance used to sweeten food or drinks **2** *informal* a bribe

sweetheart NOUN a lover

sweetly ADVERB in a sweet way: *singing sweetly*

sweetness NOUN a sweet quality

sweet pea NOUN a sweet-smelling climbing flower grown in gardens

sweet talk *informal*, NOUN flattery, persuasion

swell VERB (**swelling, swelled, swollen** *or* **swelled**) **1** to grow in size or volume **2** of the sea: to rise into waves ▶ NOUN **1** an increase in size or volume **2** large, heaving waves **3** a gradual rise in the height of the ground **4** *old* a dandy ▶ ADJECTIVE, *US informal* fine, splendid

swelling NOUN a swollen part of the body, a lump

swelter VERB to be too hot

sweltering ADJECTIVE very hot

swept *past form* of **sweep**

swerve VERB to turn quickly to one side ▶ NOUN a quick turn aside

swift ADJECTIVE moving quickly; rapid ▶ NOUN a bird rather like the swallow > **swiftly** ADVERB

swig *informal*, NOUN a mouthful of liquid, a large drink ▶ VERB (**swigging, swigged**) to gulp down

swill VERB **1** to wash out **2** *informal* to drink a great deal ▶ NOUN **1** partly liquid food given to pigs **2** *informal* a big drink

swim VERB (**swimming, swam, swum**) **1** to move on or in water, using arms, legs, fins, etc **2** to cross by swimming: *swim the Channel* **3** to move with a gliding motion **4** to be dizzy **5** to be covered (with liquid): *meat swimming in grease* ▸NOUN an act of swimming

swimmer NOUN someone or something that swims: *He's not a very strong swimmer*

swimming costume *or* **swimsuit** NOUN a brief close-fitting garment for swimming in

swimming pool NOUN a large water-filled tank for swimming, diving in, etc

swindle VERB **1** to cheat, defraud **2** to get (money etc from someone) by cheating ▸NOUN a fraud, a deception > **swindler** NOUN

swine NOUN **1** (*plural*) *old* a pig **2** (*plural*) *informal* a contemptible person

swing VERB (**swinging, swung**) **1** to move to and fro, sway **2** to turn or whirl round **3** to walk quickly, moving the arms to and fro ▸NOUN **1** a swinging movement **2** a seat for swinging, hung on ropes etc from a support **in full swing** going on busily

[i] Comes from Old English *swingan*

swipe VERB **1** to strike with a sweeping blow **2** to pass (a swipe card) through a device that electronically interprets the information encoded on the card ▸NOUN a sweeping blow

swirl VERB to sweep along with a whirling motion ▸NOUN a whirling movement

swish VERB **1** to strike or brush against with a rustling sound **2** to move making such a noise: *swishing out of the room in her long dress* ▸NOUN (*plural* **swishes**) a rustling sound or movement

switch NOUN (*plural* **switches**) **1** a small lever or handle, eg for turning an electric current on and off **2** an act of switching **3** a change: *a switch of loyalty* **4** a thin stick ▸VERB **1** to strike with a switch **2** to turn (off or on) by means of a switch **3** to change, turn: *switch jobs/hastily switching the conversation*

switchboard NOUN a board with equipment for making telephone connections

swivel NOUN a joint that turns on a pin or pivot ▸VERB (**swivelling, swivelled**) to turn on a swivel, pivot

swollen ADJECTIVE increased in size by swelling ▸VERB, *past participle of* **swell**

swoon *old*, VERB to faint ▸NOUN a fainting fit

swoop VERB to come down with a sweep, like a bird of prey ▸NOUN a sudden downward rush **at one fell swoop** all at one time, at astroke

sword NOUN a type of weapon with a long blade for cutting or piercing

swordfish NOUN (*plural* **swordfish** *or* **swordfishes**) a large type of fish with a long pointed upper jaw like a sword

swore *past tense* of **swear**

sworn *past participle* of **swear** ADJECTIVE holding steadily to an attitude etc: *The two rivals* *became sworn enemies*

swot *informal*, VERB (**swotting, swotted**) to study hard ▶NOUN someone who studies hard

sycamore NOUN a name given to several different types of tree, the maple, plane, and a kind of fig tree

sycophant (*pronounced* **sik** *o*-fant) NOUN someone who flatters others in order to gain favour or personal advantage > **sycophantic** ADJECTIVE

syl- *see* **syn-**

syllabic ADJECTIVE to do with syllables, or the division of words into syllables

syllable NOUN a word or part of a word spoken with one breath (*cheese* has one syllable, *but-ter* two, *mar-gar-ine* three)

syllabus NOUN (*plural* **syllabuses** *or* **syllabi** – *pronounced* **sil**-*a*-bai) a programme or list of lectures, classes, etc

sylph NOUN a type of fairy supposed to inhabit the air

sym- *see* **syn-**

symbiosis NOUN (*plural* **symbioses**) *biology* a close association between two organisms of different species, to the benefit of one or both > **symbiotic** ADJECTIVE

symbol NOUN **1** something that stands for or represents another thing, eg the red cross, which stands for first aid **2** a character used as a short form of something, eg the signs + meaning 'plus', and O meaning 'oxygen'

symbolic *or* **symbolical** ADJECTIVE standing as a symbol of

symbolism NOUN the use of symbols to express ideas in art and literature

symbolize *or* **symbolise** VERB to be a symbol of

symmetrical ADJECTIVE having symmetry; not lopsided in appearance > **symmetrically** ADVERB: *coloured squares arranged symmetrically*

symmetry NOUN (*contrasted with*: **asymmetry**) the equality in size, shape and position of two halves on either side of a dividing line: *spoiling the symmetry of the building*

sympathetic ADJECTIVE feeling or showing sympathy > **sympathetically** ADVERB **sympathetic to** *or* **towards** inclined to be in favour of: *sympathetic to the scheme*

sympathize *or* **sympathise** VERB: **sympathize with** to express or feel sympathy for

sympathy NOUN (*plural* **sympathies**) **1** a feeling of pity or sorrow for someone in trouble **2** agreement with, or understanding of, the feelings, attitudes, etc of others

symphony NOUN (*plural* **symphonies**) a long piece of music written for an orchestra of many different instruments

symptom NOUN an outward sign indicating the presence of a disease etc: *symptoms of measles*

symptomatic ADJECTIVE serving as a symptom

syn- also **sym-**, **syl-** PREFIX with, together: *synthesis/sympathize* (= have so much pity for someone that you feel sorrow with them)/*syllable* (= sounds pronounced together in one breath)

A B C D E F G H I J K L M N O P Q R S T U V W X Y Z

ⓘ Comes from Greek *syn* meaning 'with'

synagogue NOUN a Jewish place of worship

synchronize *or* **synchronise** VERB **1** to cause to happen at the same time **2** to set to the same time: *synchronize watches*

syncopate VERB, *music* to change (the beat) by accenting beats not usually accented

syncopation NOUN **1** syncopating **2** the beat produced by syncopating

syndicate NOUN a number of persons who join together to manage some piece of business

syndrome NOUN a pattern of behaviour, events, etc characteristic of some problem or condition

synod (*pronounced* **sin**-*o*d) NOUN a meeting of members of the clergy

synonym NOUN a word which has the same, or nearly the same, meaning as another, eg 'ass' and 'donkey', or 'brave' and 'courageous'

synonymous ADJECTIVE: **synonymous with** having the same meaning as

synopsis NOUN (*plural* **synopses**) a short summary of the main points of a book, speech, etc

syntactic *or* **syntactical** ADJECTIVE relating or belonging to syntax

syntax NOUN rules for the correct combination of words to form sentences

synthesis NOUN **1** the act of making a whole by putting together its separate parts **2** *chemistry* the making of a substance by combining chemical elements

synthesize *or* **synthesise** VERB to make (eg a drug) by synthesis

synthesizer *or* **synthesiser** NOUN, *music* a computerized instrument which creates electronic musical sounds

synthetic ADJECTIVE **1** made artificially to look like a natural product: *synthetic leather* **2** not natural, pretended: *synthetic charm*
> **synthetically** ADVERB

syringe NOUN a tubular instrument with a needle and plunger, used to extract blood, inject drugs, etc ▶ VERB to clean out with a syringe: *had his ears syringed*

syrup NOUN **1** a thick sticky liquid made by boiling water or fruit juice with sugar **2** a purified form of treacle

system NOUN **1** an arrangement of several parts which work together: *railway system/solar system* **2** a way of organizing: *democratic system of government* **3** a regular method of doing something **4** the body, or its parts, considered as a whole: *My system is run down*

ⓘ Comes from Greek *sy-* meaning 'together', and the root of *histanai* meaning 'to set'

systematic ADJECTIVE following a system; methodical
> **systematically** ADVERB

Tt

tab NOUN **1** a small tag or flap attached to something **2** a running total, a tally

tabby (*plural* **tabbies**) *or* **tabby-cat** NOUN (*plural* **tabby-cats**) a striped (usually female) cat

tabernacle NOUN a place of worship for some nonconformist Christian denominations

table NOUN **1** a flat-topped piece of furniture, supported by legs **2** (*also called*: **tableland**) an area of high land, a plateau **3** facts or figures set out in columns: *multiplication tables* ▶ VERB **1** to make into a list or table **2** to put forward for discussion: *table a motion*

tablecloth NOUN a cloth for covering a table

tablespoon NOUN a large size of spoon, used eg for serving food

tablet NOUN **1** a small flat plate on which to write, paint, etc **2** a small flat piece, eg of soap or chocolate **3** a pill **4** a brittle sweet made with sugar and condensed milk

table tennis NOUN a form of tennis played across a table with small bats and a light ball

tabloid NOUN a small-sized newspaper giving news in shortened, often simplified form and an informal sensationalist style (*compare with*: **broadsheet**)
[i] Originally a trademark for a medicine in tablet form, and then, by association, the name for a small-sized newspaper giving information in concentrated form

taboo ADJECTIVE forbidden by common consent; not approved by social custom ▶ NOUN a taboo subject or behaviour

tacit (*pronounced* **tas**-it) ADJECTIVE understood but not spoken aloud, silent: *tacit agreement*

taciturn (*pronounced* **tas**-it-ern) ADJECTIVE not inclined to talk

tackle VERB **1** to come to grips with, deal with **2** in football etc: to try to stop, or take the ball from, another player ▶ NOUN **1** the ropes and rigging of a ship **2** equipment, gear: *fishing tackle* **3** ropes and pulleys for raising heavy weights **4** an act of tackling

tacky[1] ADJECTIVE (**tackier, tackiest**) slightly sticky

tacky[2] ADJECTIVE (**tackier, tackiest**) *informal* shabby; vulgar, in bad taste

tact NOUN skill in dealing with people so as to avoid giving offence

A B C D E F G H I J K L M N O P Q R S T U V W X Y Z

tactical ADJECTIVE **1** involving clever and successful planning **2** diplomatic, politic: *tactical withdrawal*

tactics PLURAL NOUN **1** a way of acting in order to gain an advantage or achieve something **2** the art of coordinating military forces in action

tactile ADJECTIVE of or perceived through touch

tadpole NOUN a young frog or toad in its first stage of life

taffeta NOUN a stiff glossy fabric made mainly of silk

tag NOUN **1** a label: *price tag* **2** a familiar saying or quotation **3** (*also called*: **tig**) a chasing game played by children ▸VERB (**tagging, tagged**) to put a tag or tags on

tail NOUN **1** an appendage sticking out from the end of the spine on an animal, bird or fish **2** an appendage on the rear of a machine etc: *tail of an aeroplane* **3** the stalk on a piece of fruit **4** (**tails**) the side of a coin opposite to the head ▸VERB **1** to follow closely **2** to remove the tails from (fruit etc) **tail off** to become less, fewer or worse **turn tail** to run away

tail-end NOUN the very end of a procession etc

tailor NOUN someone who cuts out and makes clothes ▸VERB **1** to make and fit (clothes) **2** to make to fit the circumstances, adapt: *tailored to your needs*

tailor-made ADJECTIVE exactly suited to requirements: *a tailor-made solution*

taint VERB **1** to spoil by contact with something bad or rotten **2** to corrupt ▸NOUN a trace of decay or evil

take VERB (**taking, took, taken**) **1** to lay hold of, grasp **2** to choose: *Take a card!* **3** to accept, agree to have: *Do you take credit cards?/ Please take a biscuit* **4** to have room for: *My car only takes four people* **5** to eat, swallow **6** to get or have regularly: *don't take sugar* **7** to capture (a fort etc) **8** (*also*: **take away**) to subtract: *Take two from eight* **9** to lead, carry, drive: *take the children to school* **10** to use, make use of: *Take care!* **11** to require: *It'll take too much time* **12** to travel by: *took the afternoon train* **13** to experience, feel: *takes great pride in his work* **14** to photograph: *took some shots inside the house* **15** to understand: *took what I said the wrong way* **16** of a plant: to root successfully **17** to become popular, please **take account of** to consider, remember **take advantage of 1** to make use of (an opportunity) **2** to treat or use unfairly **take after** to be like in appearance or behaviour **take care of** to look after **take down** to write, note down **take for** to believe (mistakenly) to be: *I took him for his brother* **take heed** to pay careful attention **take ill** to become ill **take in 1** to include **2** to receive **3** to understand: *didn't take in what you said* **4** to make smaller: *take in a dress* **5** to cheat, deceive **take leave of** to say goodbye to **taken with** attracted to **take off 1** to remove (clothes etc) **2** to imitate for comic effect **3** of an aircraft:

to leave the ground **take on 1** to undertake (work etc) **2** to accept (as an opponent): *take you on at tennis* **take over** to take control of **take part in** to share or help in **take place** to happen **take to 1** to like or be attracted by: *I took to him straightaway* **2** to begin to do or use regularly: *took to rising early* **take up 1** to lift, raise **2** to occupy (space, time, etc) **3** to begin to learn, show interest in: *take up playing the harp*
ⓘ Comes from Late Old English *tacan* meaning 'to touch' or 'to take'

takeaway NOUN **1** a meal prepared and bought in a restaurant or shop but taken away and eaten somewhere else **2** a restaurant or shop providing such meals

take-off NOUN **1** the act of an aircraft leaving the ground **2** an act of imitating or mimicking

taking ADJECTIVE pleasing, attractive ▶NOUN **1** an act of taking **2** (**takings**) money received from things sold

talc NOUN **1** a soft mineral, soapy to the touch **2** *informal* talcum powder

talcum NOUN a fine powder made from talc, used for sprinkling on the body (*also called*: **talcum powder**)

tale NOUN **1** a story **2** an untrue story, a lie

talent NOUN **1** a special ability or skill: *a talent for music* **2** an old measure of weight for gold or silver

talented ADJECTIVE skilled, gifted

talisman NOUN (*plural* **talismans**) an object believed to have magic powers; a charm

talk VERB **1** to speak **2** to gossip **3** to give information ▶NOUN **1** conversation **2** gossip **3** the subject of conversation: *The talk is of revolution* **4** a discussion or lecture: *gave a talk on stained glass* **talk over** to discuss **talk round 1** to discuss without coming to the main point **2** to persuade: *talked him round to her point of view*

talkative ADJECTIVE inclined to chatter

tall ADJECTIVE **1** high or higher than average **2** hard to believe: *tall story*

tall order NOUN a request to do something awkward or unreasonable

tally NOUN (*plural* **tallies**) **1** an account **2** a ticket, a label **3** *old* a notched stick for keeping a score ▶VERB (**tallies, tallying, tallied**) **1** to agree (with): *His story doesn't tally with yours* **2** to count by making a mark for each object

Talmud NOUN the fundamental body of Jewish law

talon NOUN a hooked claw

tambourine NOUN a small one-sided drum with tinkling metal discs set into the sides

tame ADJECTIVE **1** of an animal: not wild, used to living with humans **2** dull, not exciting ▶VERB to make tame, subdue

tamper VERB: **tamper with** to meddle with so as to damage or alter: *Someone had tampered with the brakes*

tampon NOUN a plug of cotton-wool inserted into the vagina to absorb blood during menstruation

tan VERB (**tanning, tanned**) **1** to

A B C D E F G H I J K L M N O P Q R S T U V W X Y Z

make (animal skin) into leather by treating with tannin **2** to make or become brown, eg by exposure to the sun ▸NOUN **1** a yellowish-brown colour **2** a suntan

tandem NOUN a long bicycle with two seats and two sets of pedals one behind the other ▸ADVERB one behind the other **in tandem** together, in conjunction

tang NOUN a strong taste, flavour or smell: *the tang of the sea air*

tangent NOUN *maths* a straight line which touches a circle or curve without crossing it **go off at a tangent** to go off suddenly in another direction or line of thought

tangerine NOUN a small type of orange

ℹ Originally meaning 'from Tangiers', from where the fruit was exported in the 19th century

tangible ADJECTIVE **1** able to be felt by touching **2** real, definite: *tangible profits* > **tangibly** ADVERB

tangle VERB **1** to twist together in knots **2** to make or become difficult or confusing ▸NOUN **1** a twisted mass of knots **2** a confused situation

tango NOUN (*plural* **tangos**) a ballroom dance with long steps and pauses, originally from South America

tank NOUN **1** a large container for water, petrol, etc **2** a heavy armoured vehicle which moves on caterpillar wheels

tankard NOUN a large drinking mug

tanker NOUN **1** a ship or large lorry for carrying liquids, eg oil **2** an aircraft carrying fuel

tannin NOUN a bitter-tasting substance found in tea, red wine, etc, also used in tanning and dyeing

tantalize *or* **tantalise** VERB to torment by offering something and keeping it out of reach

tantalizing *or* **tantalising** ADJECTIVE teasing; tormenting: *Tantalizing smells were coming from the kitchen*

tantamount ADJECTIVE: **tantamount to** coming to the same thing as, equivalent to: *tantamount to stealing*

tantrum NOUN a fit of rage or bad temper

tap NOUN **1** a light touch or knock **2** a device with a valve for controlling the flow of liquid, gas, etc ▸VERB (**tapping, tapped**) **1** to knock or strike lightly **2** to draw on, start using **3** to attach a listening device secretly to (a telephone) **on tap** ready, available for use

tapdance NOUN a dance done with special shoes that make a tapping sound ▸VERB to perform a tapdance

tape NOUN **1** a narrow band or strip used for tying **2** a piece of string over the finishing line on a racetrack **3** a tape measure **4** a strip of magnetic material for recording sound, pictures or data ▸VERB **1** to fasten with tape **2** to record on tape

tape measure NOUN a narrow strip of paper, plastic, etc used for measuring distance

taper NOUN **1** a long, thin kind of candle **2** a long waxed wick used for lighting oil lamps etc ▸VERB to make or become thinner at one end

tape recorder NOUN a kind of instrument for recording sound etc on magnetic tape

tapering ADJECTIVE becoming gradually thinner at one end

tapestry NOUN (*plural* **tapestries**) a cloth with designs or figures woven into it, used to decorate walls or cover furniture

tar NOUN **1** a thick, black, sticky substance derived from wood or coal, used in making roads etc **2** *informal* a sailor ▸ VERB (**tarring, tarred**) to smear with tar **tarred with the same brush (as)** having the same faults (as)

tarantula NOUN a type of large, poisonous spider

tardy ADJECTIVE (**tardier, tardiest**) slow; late

target NOUN **1** a mark to aim at in shooting, darts, etc **2** a result or sum that is aimed at: *a target of £3000* **3** someone at whom unfriendly remarks are aimed: *the target of her criticism*

tariff NOUN **1** a list of prices **2** a list of taxes payable on goods brought into a country

tarmac NOUN the surface of a road or airport runway, made of tarmacadam ▸ VERB to surface with tarmacadam

tarmacadam NOUN a mixture of small stones and tar used to make road surfaces etc

tarnish VERB **1** of metal: to (cause to) become dull or discoloured **2** to spoil (a reputation etc)

tarot (*pronounced* **ta**-roh) NOUN a system of fortune-telling using special cards divided into suits

tarpaulin NOUN **1** strong waterproof cloth **2** a sheet of this material

tarragon NOUN a herb used in cooking

tarry (*pronounced* **ta**-ri) VERB (**tarries, tarrying, tarried**) **1** to stay behind, linger **2** to be slow or late

tart NOUN a pie containing fruit, vegetables, etc ▸ ADJECTIVE sharp, sour

tartan NOUN **1** fabric patterned with squares of different colours, traditionally used by Scottish Highland clans **2** one of these patterns: *Macdonald tartan* ▸ ADJECTIVE with a pattern of tartan

tartar NOUN **1** a substance that gathers on the teeth **2** a difficult or demanding person **3** a substance that forms inside wine casks **cream of tartar** a white powder obtained from the tartar from wine casks, used in baking

task NOUN a set piece of work to be done **take to task** to scold, find fault with

tassel NOUN a hanging bunch of threads, used to decorate a hat, curtain, etc

taste VERB **1** to try by eating or drinking a sample **2** to eat or drink some of: *Taste this soup* **3** to recognize (a flavour): *Can you taste the chilli in it?* **4** to have a particular flavour: *tasting of garlic* **5** to experience: *taste success* ▸ NOUN **1** the act or sense of tasting **2** a flavour **3** a small quantity of something **4** a liking: *taste for*

a b c d e f g h i j k l m n o p q r s t u v w x y z

literature **5** ability to judge what is suitable in behaviour, dress, etc, or what is fine or beautiful

tasteful ADJECTIVE showing good taste and judgement > **tastefully** ADVERB > **tastefulness** NOUN

tasteless ADJECTIVE **1** without flavour **2** not tasteful; vulgar > **tastelessly** ADVERB

tasty ADJECTIVE (**tastier, tastiest**) having a good flavour

tattered ADJECTIVE ragged

tatters PLURAL NOUN torn, ragged pieces

tattie NOUN, *Scottish* a potato

tattoo NOUN **1** a coloured design on the skin, made by pricking with needles **2** a drumbeat **3** an outdoor military display with music etc ▶VERB (**tattooing, tattooed**) to prick coloured designs into the skin

🛈 From a Dutch term meaning to shut off beer taps at closing time, later applied to a military drumbeat at the end of the day

tattooed ADJECTIVE marked with tattoos

tatty ADJECTIVE (**tattier, tattiest**) shabby, tawdry

taught *past form* of **teach**

taut ADJECTIVE **1** pulled tight **2** tense, strained

tawdry ADJECTIVE (**tawdrier, tawdriest**) cheap-looking and gaudy

🛈 From *St Audrey's lace*, once used to make cheap lace neckties

tax NOUN (*plural* **taxes**) **1** a charge made by the government on income, certain types of goods, etc **2** a strain, a burden: *severe tax on my patience* ▶VERB **1** to make to pay a tax **2** to put a strain on: *taxing her strength* **tax with** to accuse of

taxation NOUN **1** the act or system of taxing **2** taxes

taxi NOUN (*plural* **taxis**) a vehicle which may be hired, with a driver (*also called*: **taxi-cab**) ▶VERB (**taxiing, taxied**) **1** to travel in a taxi **2** of an aeroplane: to travel on the runway before or after take-off

taxpayer NOUN someone who pays taxes

TB ABBREVIATION tuberculosis, an infectious disease of humans and animals, characterized by the formation of swellings, especially on the lungs

tea NOUN **1** a plant grown in India, China, etc, or its dried and prepared leaves **2** a drink made by infusing its dried leaves **3** a hot drink, an infusion: *beef tea/camomile tea* **4** an afternoon or early evening meal: *What's for tea?*

teabag NOUN a small sachet of tea to which boiling water is added

teach VERB (**teaching, taught**) **1** to give (someone) skill or knowledge **2** to give knowledge of, or training in (a subject): *She teaches French* **3** to be a teacher: *decide to teach*

teacher NOUN someone employed to teach others in a school, or in a particular subject: *guitar teacher*

tea chest NOUN a tall box of thin wood used to pack tea for export, often used as a packing case when empty

teaching NOUN **1** the work of a teacher **2** guidance, instruction

3 (**teachings**) beliefs or rules of conduct that are preached or taught

teacup NOUN a medium-sized cup for drinking tea

teak NOUN **1** a hardwood tree from the East Indies **2** its very hard wood **3** a type of African tree

teal NOUN **1** a small water bird like a duck **2** a dark greenish-blue colour

team NOUN **1** a group of people working together **2** a side in a game: *a football team* **3** two or more animals working together: *team of oxen* **team up with** to join together with, join forces with

[i] Comes from Old English *team* meaning 'child-bearing', 'brood' or 'team'

> Do not confuse with: **teem**

teapot NOUN a pot with a spout, for making and pouring tea

tear[1] (*pronounced* teer) NOUN **1** a drop of liquid from the eye **2** (**tears**) grief **in tears** weeping

tear[2] (*pronounced* teir) VERB (**tearing, tore, torn**) **1** to pull with force: *tear apart/tear down* **2** to make a hole or split in (material etc) **3** to hurt deeply **4** *informal* to rush: *tearing off down the road* ▶NOUN a hole or split made by tearing

tearful ADJECTIVE **1** inclined to weep **2** in tears, crying > **tearfully** ADVERB

tease VERB **1** to annoy, irritate on purpose **2** to pretend to upset or annoy for fun: *I'm only teasing* **3** to untangle (wool etc) with a comb **4** to sort out (a problem or puzzle) ▶NOUN someone who teases

teaser NOUN a problem, a puzzle

teaspoon NOUN a small spoon used for tea etc

teat NOUN **1** the part of an animal through which milk passes to its young **2** a rubber object shaped like this attached to a baby's feeding bottle

tea towel NOUN a cloth for drying dishes

techn- *see* **techno-**

technical ADJECTIVE **1** relating to a particular art or skill, especially a mechanical or industrial one: *What is the technical term for this?/a technical expert* **2** according to strict laws or rules: *technical defeat*

technicality NOUN (*plural* **technicalities**) a technical detail or point

technically ADVERB according to the rules, strictly speaking

technician NOUN someone trained in the practical side of an art, or who does the practical work in a laboratory etc

technique NOUN the way in which a process is carried out; a method

techno- *or* **techn-** PREFIX **1** forms words relating to the art or craft involved in doing something: *technical* **2** of or relating to technology

[i] Comes from Greek *techne* meaning 'skill'

technological ADJECTIVE relating to or involving technology > **technologically** ADVERB: *a technologically advanced country*

technologist NOUN a person skilled in technology and its applications

a b c d e f g h i j k l m n o p q r s **t** u v w x y z

technology NOUN **1** science applied to practical (especially industrial) purposes **2** the practical skills of a particular civilization, period, etc

teddy NOUN (*plural* **teddies**) a stuffed toy bear (*full form*: **teddy bear**)
ⓘ Named after the American President *Teddy* Roosevelt (1868–1919), who was well-known as a bear hunter

tedious ADJECTIVE long and tiresome > **tediously** ADVERB

tedium NOUN boredom: *the endless tedium of dinner with his family*

teem VERB **1** to be full: *teeming with people* **2** to rain heavily
ⓘ Meaning 1: comes from Old English *tieman*, related to the word *team*; meaning 2: comes from Old Norse *tema* meaning 'to empty'

> Do not confuse with: **team**

teenage ADJECTIVE suitable for, or typical of, those in their teens

teenager NOUN someone in their teens

teens PLURAL NOUN the years of age from thirteen to nineteen

teeny ADJECTIVE (**teenier, teeniest**) *informal* tiny, minute

tee-shirt *or* **T-shirt** NOUN a short-sleeved top pulled on over the head

teeter VERB **1** to wobble **2** to hesitate

teeth *plural* of **tooth**

teethe VERB of a baby: to grow its first teeth

teetotal ADJECTIVE never drinking alcohol

teetotaller NOUN a person who never drinks alcohol

tele- PREFIX at a distance: *television/ telegram* (= a message sent over a long distance)
ⓘ Comes from Greek *tele* meaning 'far'

telecommunications SINGULAR NOUN the sending of information over a distance by telephone, radio, television, etc

telegram NOUN a message sent by telegraph

telegraph NOUN an instrument for sending messages to a place at a distance using electrical impulses ▸ VERB to send (a message) by telegraph

telekinesis NOUN the supposed ability to move objects from a distance using willpower and no physical contact

telepathic ADJECTIVE relating to or involving telepathy

telepathy NOUN the supposed ability of people to communicate without using sight, hearing, etc

telephone NOUN (*short form* **phone**) an instrument for speaking over distances, which uses an electric current travelling along a wire, or radio waves ▸ VERB to send (a message) by telephone

telephonist NOUN an operator on a telephone switchboard

telephoto ADJECTIVE of a lens: used to photograph enlarged images of distant objects

telescope NOUN a tubular instrument fitted with lenses which magnify distant objects ▸ VERB **1** to push or fit together so that one thing slides inside another **2** to force together, compress > **telescopic** ADJECTIVE: *a telescopic umbrella*

teletext NOUN news and general information transmitted by television companies, viewable only on special television sets

televise VERB to broadcast on television: *Are they televising the football match?*

television NOUN **1** the reproduction on a small screen of pictures sent from a distance **2** an apparatus for receiving these pictures

tell VERB (**telling, told**) **1** to say or express in words: *She's telling the truth* **2** to give the facts of (a story) **3** to inform, give information: *Can you tell me when it's 9 o'clock?* **4** to order, command: *Tell him to go away!* **5** to make out, distinguish: *I can't tell one wine from the other* **6** to give away a secret: *promise not to tell* **7** to be effective, produce results: *Training will tell in the end* **all told** altogether, counting all **tell off** *informal* to scold **tell on 1** to have an effect on **2** to give information about: *Your sister told on you*

teller NOUN **1** a bank clerk who receives and pays out money **2** someone who counts votes at an election

telling ADJECTIVE having a marked effect: *telling remark*

tell-tale NOUN someone who spreads gossip about others ▶ADJECTIVE revealing: *tell-tale signs of illness*

telly NOUN (*plural* **tellies**), *informal* (a) television

temp ABBREVIATION **1** temperature **2** temporary ▶NOUN, *informal* a temporarily employed worker ▶VERB, *informal* to work as a temp

temper NOUN **1** habitual state of mind: *an even temper* **2** a passing mood: *in a good temper* **3** a tendency to get angry easily: *has a bit of a temper* **4** a fit of anger: *flew into a temper* **5** the amount of hardness in metal, glass, etc ▶VERB **1** to bring (metal) to the right degree of hardness by heating and cooling **2** to make less severe **lose your temper** to show anger

temperament NOUN someone's nature as it affects the way they feel and act; disposition

temperamental ADJECTIVE **1** of temperament **2** excitable, emotional

temperance NOUN the habit of not drinking much (or any) alcohol

temperate ADJECTIVE **1** moderate in temper, eating or drinking, etc **2** of climate: neither very hot nor very cold

temperature NOUN **1** degree of heat or cold: *today's temperature* **2** a body heat higher than normal: *has got a temperature*

tempest NOUN a storm, with strong winds

tempestuous ADJECTIVE **1** very stormy and windy **2** passionate, violently emotional

template NOUN a thin plate cut in a design for drawing round

temple[1] NOUN a building used for public worship; a church

temple[2] NOUN a small flat area on each side of the forehead

A B C D E F G H I J K L M N O P Q R S T U V W X Y Z

LANGUAGE workshop — Tense

All verbs have a **tense**. The tense indicates the time when an action happens – either in the present, the past or the future. A verb can be in one of a number of tenses.

The present tense

The present tense is used for actions or situations that are happening now.

She plays.
She is playing.

The past tense

The past tense describes actions that have already happened.

She played.
She was playing.

The future tense

There is no specific future tense in English. Actions that will happen in future time are expressed in several ways, using auxiliary verbs:

tempo NOUN (*plural* **tempos** *or* **tempi**) **1** the speed at which music is played **2** the speed or rate of an activity

temporary ADJECTIVE lasting only for a time, not permanent

tempt VERB **1** to try to persuade or entice **2** to attract **3** to make inclined (to): *tempted to phone him*

temptation NOUN **1** the act of tempting **2** the feeling of being tempted **3** something which tempts

tempting ADJECTIVE attractive

ten NOUN the number 10 ▶ADJECTIVE 10 in number

tenable ADJECTIVE able to be defended; justifiable

tenacious ADJECTIVE **1** keeping a firm hold or grip **2** obstinate, persistent, determined

Tense

LANGUAGE workshop

She will play next week.
She will be playing next week.
She is going to play next week.
She is playing next week.

Using tense

The tense you use can have an effect on your writing. If you use the present tense, for example, what you write will be more vivid and immediate. However, it is important to be consistent in the tense you use, and not change suddenly to another unless you have a reason to do so.

? There are various ways to change the tenses in this sentence so that it makes sense. What would you do?
I will be shopping and I buy lots of new clothes, which I wore at Melissa's party.

> **tenaciously** ADVERB

tenacity NOUN persistence, determination

tenancy NOUN (*plural* **tenancies**) **1** the holding of a house, farm, etc by a tenant **2** the period of this holding

tenant NOUN someone who pays rent for the use of a house, land, etc

tend VERB **1** to be likely or inclined to do something: *These flowers tend to wilt* **2** to move or slope in a certain direction **3** to take care of, look after

tendency NOUN (*plural* **tendencies**) a leaning or inclination (towards): *tendency to daydream*

tender ADJECTIVE **1** soft, not hard or tough **2** easily hurt or damaged **3** hurting when touched **4** loving, gentle ▸ VERB **1** to offer (a

A B C D E F G H I J K L M N O P Q R S T U V W X Y Z

resignation etc) formally **2** to make a formal offer for a job ▶NOUN **1** an offer to take on work, supply goods, etc for a fixed price **2** a small boat that carries stores for a large one **3** a truck for coal and water attached to a steam engine **legal tender** coins or notes which must be accepted when offered **of tender years** very young

tendon NOUN a tough cord joining a muscle to a bone

tendril NOUN **1** a thin curling stem of a climbing plant which attaches itself to a support **2** a curling strand of hair etc

tenement NOUN a large block of flats

tenner NOUN, *informal* a ten-pound note; ten pounds

tennis NOUN a game for two or four players using rackets to hit a ball to each other over a net

tennis court NOUN a place made level and prepared for tennis

tenor NOUN **1** *music* a male singing voice between baritone and alto **2** *music* a singer with such a voice **3** the general course: *the even tenor of country life* **4** general meaning: *the tenor of the speech*

tense[1] NOUN, *grammar* the form of a verb that shows time of action, eg '*I was*' (**past tense**), '*I am*' (**present tense**), '*I shall be*' (**future tense**) **future tense**) →See also **Language Workshop** panel

tense[2] ADJECTIVE **1** tightly stretched **2** nervous, strained: *feeling tense/ tense with excitement*

tension NOUN **1** the state of being stretched **2** strain, anxiety

tent NOUN a movable shelter of canvas or other material, supported by poles and pegged to the ground

tentacle NOUN a long thin flexible part of an animal used to feel or grasp, eg the arm of an octopus

tentative ADJECTIVE **1** experimental, initial: *a tentative offer* **2** uncertain, hesitating: *tentative smile* > **tentatively** ADVERB

tenterhooks PLURAL NOUN: **on tenterhooks** uncertain and very anxious about what will happen

tenth ADJECTIVE the last of ten items ▶NOUN one of ten equal parts

tenuous ADJECTIVE slight, weak: *tenuous connection*

tenure NOUN **1** the holding of property or a position of employment **2** the period, or terms or conditions, of this

tepee NOUN a traditional Native American tent made of animal skins

tepid ADJECTIVE lukewarm

term NOUN **1** a length of time: *term of imprisonment* **2** a division of an academic or school year: *autumn term* **3** a word, an expression: *dictionary of computing terms* **4** (**terms**) the rules or conditions of an agreement: *What are their terms?* **5** (**terms**) fixed charges **6** (**terms**) footing, relationship: *on good terms with his neighbours* ▶VERB to name, call **come to terms** to reach an agreement or understanding **come to terms with** to accept, be able to live with **in terms of** from the point of view of

terminal ADJECTIVE **1** of or growing

at the end: *terminal bud* **2** of an illness: fatal, incurable ▶NOUN **1** an end **2** a point of connection in an electric circuit **3** a computer monitor connected to a network **4** a terminus **5** an airport building containing arrival and departure areas **6** a bus station in a town centre running a service to a nearby airport

terminate VERB to bring or come to an end

termination NOUN an act of ending or the state of being brought to an end

terminology NOUN the special words or expressions used in a particular art, science, etc

terminus NOUN (*plural* **termini** *or* **terminuses**) **1** the end **2** an end point on a railway, bus route, etc

termite NOUN a pale-coloured wood-eating insect, like an ant

tern NOUN a type of sea bird like a small gull

terrace NOUN **1** a raised level bank of earth **2** a raised flat place **3** a connected row of houses ▶VERB to form into a terrace or terraces

terracotta NOUN a brownish-red mixture of clay and sand used for tiles, pottery, etc

terrain NOUN an area of land considered in terms of its physical features: *The terrain is a bit rocky*

terrapin NOUN a small turtle living in ponds or rivers

terrazzo NOUN a hard, shiny covering for concrete floors, consisting of marble chips set in cement and then polished

terrestrial ADJECTIVE of or living on the earth

terrible ADJECTIVE **1** causing great fear: *terrible sight* **2** causing great hardship or distress: *terrible disaster* **3** *informal* very bad: *a terrible writer*

terribly ADVERB, *informal* **1** badly: *sang terribly* **2** extremely: *terribly tired*

terrier NOUN a breed of small dog

terrific ADJECTIVE **1** powerful, dreadful **2** huge, amazing **3** *informal* marvellous, enjoyable, etc: *a terrific party*

terrify VERB (**terrifies, terrifying, terrified**) to frighten greatly

territorial ADJECTIVE of, belonging to a territory

territory NOUN (*plural* **territories**) **1** an area of land, a region **2** land under the control of a ruler or state **3** an area allocated to a salesman etc **4** a field of activity or interest

terror NOUN **1** very great fear **2** something which causes great fear **3** *informal* an uncontrollable child

terrorism NOUN the organized use of violence or intimidation for political or other ends

terrorist NOUN someone who practises terrorism

terrorize *or* **terrorise** VERB to frighten very greatly

terse ADJECTIVE using few words; curt, brusque > **tersely** ADVERB

tertiary ADJECTIVE third in position or order

tertiary education NOUN education at university or college level

a b c d e f g h i j k l m n o p q r s t u v w x y z

test NOUN **1** a short examination **2** something done to check soundness, reliability, etc: *ran tests on the new model* **3** a means of finding the presence of: *test for radioactivity* **4** an event that shows up a good or bad quality: *a test of courage* ▶ VERB to carry out tests on

testament NOUN **1** a written statement of someone's wishes **2** a will **Old Testament** *and* **New Testament** the two main divisions of the Christian Bible

testicle NOUN one of two sperm-producing glands enclosed in the male scrotum

testify VERB (**testifies, testifying, testified**) **1** to give evidence in a law court **2** to make a solemn declaration of **3** (**testify to**) to show, give evidence of: *testifies to his ignorance*

testimonial NOUN **1** a personal statement about someone's character, abilities, etc **2** a gift given in thanks for services given

testimony NOUN (*plural* **testimonies**) **1** the statement made by someone who testifies **2** evidence

testis NOUN (*plural* **testes**) a testicle

test match NOUN *cricket* one of a series of five-day matches between two countries

testosterone NOUN the chief male sex hormone, secreted by the testicles

test tube NOUN a glass tube closed at one end, used in chemical tests

testy ADJECTIVE (**testier, testiest**) easily angered, irritable > **testily** ADVERB > **testiness** NOUN

tetanus NOUN a disease, caused especially by an infected wound, that can cause stiffening and spasms in the jaw muscles

tetchy ADJECTIVE (**tetchier, tetchiest**) irritable, testy > **tetchily** ADVERB

tether NOUN a rope or chain for tying an animal to restrict its movement ▶ VERB **1** to tie with a tether **2** to limit the freedom of

tetrahedron NOUN a solid body with four faces, all of which are polygons

text NOUN **1** the main written part of a book, not the pictures, notes, etc **2** a printed or written version of a speech, play, etc **3** a Biblical passage used as the basis for a sermon **4** the subject matter of a speech, essay, etc ▶ VERB to send a text message

textbook NOUN a book used for teaching, giving the main facts about a subject

textile ADJECTIVE of weaving; woven ▶ NOUN a woven cloth or fabric

text message NOUN a short message typed into and sent by a mobile phone > **text messaging** NOUN

textual ADJECTIVE of or in a text

texture NOUN **1** the quality of cloth resulting from weaving: *loose texture* **2** the quality of a substance in terms of how it looks or feels: *rough texture/lumpy texture* **3** the effect of the number of different sounds in a piece of music

than CONJUNCTION & PREPOSITION used in comparisons: *easier than I expected/better than usual*

thank VERB to express gratitude to (someone) for a favour, gift, etc **thank you** *or* **thanks** a polite expression used to thank someone (*see also* **thanks**)

thankful ADJECTIVE grateful; relieved and glad > **thankfully** ADVERB: *Thankfully, no-one was badly injured in the crash*

thankless ADJECTIVE neither worthwhile nor appreciated: *thankless task*

thanks PLURAL NOUN gratitude; appreciation: *You'll get no thanks for it* **thanks to** **1** with the help of: *We arrived on time, thanks to our friends* **2** owing to: *We were late, thanks to our car breaking down*

thanksgiving NOUN **1** a church service giving thanks to God **2** (**Thanksgiving**) *US* the fourth Thursday of November, a national holiday commemorating the first harvest of the Puritan settlers

that ADJECTIVE & PRONOUN (*plural* **those**) used to point out a thing or person etc: (*contrasted with*: **this**) *that woman over there/Don't say that* ▸RELATIVE PRONOUN: *the colours that he chose/the man that I spoke to* ▸ADVERB to such an extent or degree: *Why were you that late?* ▸CONJUNCTION **1** used in reporting speech: *She said that she was there* **2** used to connect clauses: *I heard that you were ill*

thatch NOUN straw etc used to make the roof of a house ▸VERB to cover with thatch

thaw VERB **1** to melt **2** of frozen food: to defrost, become unfrozen **3** to become friendly ▸NOUN **1** the melting of ice and snow by heat **2** a change in the weather that causes this

the ADJECTIVE **1** referring to a particular person or thing: *the boy in the park/I like the jacket you're wearing* **2** referring to all or any of a general group: *The horse is of great use to man*

theatre *or US* **theater** NOUN **1** a place for the public performance of plays etc **2** a room in a hospital for surgical operations **3** the acting profession

theatrical ADJECTIVE **1** of theatres or acting **2** over-dramatic, overdone

theatricality NOUN a theatrical quality

thee PRONOUN, *old* you as the object of a sentence

theft NOUN stealing

their ADJECTIVE belonging to them: *their car*

> Do not confuse with: **there**. Remember that the 'y' in the pronoun 'they' turns into an 'i' in **their** and that **there** is spelt the same as 'here' except for the first letter.

theirs PRONOUN belonging to them: *The red car is theirs*

them PRONOUN PLURAL **1** people or things already spoken about (as the object of a verb): *we've seen them* **2** those: *one of them over in the corner* ▸PRONOUN SINGULAR used to avoid giving the gender of the person being referred to: *if anyone*

a b c d e f g h i j k l m n o p q r s t u v w x y z

A B C D E F G H I J K L M N O P Q R S T U V W X Y Z

phones, ask them to leave their number

theme NOUN **1** the subject of a discussion, essay, story, etc **2** *music* a main melody which is often repeated

themselves PRONOUN **1** used reflexively: *They tired themselves out walking* **2** used for emphasis: *They'll have to do it by themselves*

then ADVERB **1** at that time: *I didn't know you then* **2** after that: *And then where did you go?* ▶ CONJUNCTION in that case, therefore: *If you're busy, then don't come*

thence ADVERB, *old* from that time or place

thenceforth ADVERB from that time onwards

theo- PREFIX forms words relating to God or gods: *theology*
ⓘ Comes from Greek *theos* meaning 'God' or 'a god'

theocracy NOUN government of a state according to religious laws

theocratic ADJECTIVE relating to or involving theocracy

theologian NOUN someone who studies theology

theological ADJECTIVE relating to or involving theology

theology NOUN the study of God and religion

theoretical ADJECTIVE of theory, not experience or practice
> **theoretically** ADVERB: *It is theoretically possible to travel from Glasgow to Edinburgh in under one hour*

theorize *or* **theorise** VERB to form theories

theory NOUN (*plural* **theories**) **1** an explanation that has not been proved or tested **2** the underlying ideas in an art, science, etc, compared to practice or performance

therapeutic ADJECTIVE **1** of therapy **2** healing, curing

therapist NOUN someone who gives therapeutic treatment: *speech therapist*

therapy NOUN (*plural* **therapies**) treatment of disease or disorders

there ADVERB at, in or to that place: *What did you do there?* ▶ PRONOUN used (with *be*) as a subject of a sentence or clause when the real subject follows the verb: *There is nobody at home*

> Do not confuse with: **their**. Remember that **there** is spelt the same as 'here' except for the first letter and that the 'y' in the pronoun 'they' turns into an 'i' in **their**.

thereabouts ADVERB approximately

thereafter ADVERB after that

thereby ADVERB by that means

therefore ADVERB for this or that reason

thereupon ADVERB **1** because of this or that **2** immediately

therm NOUN a unit of heat used in measuring gas

thermal ADJECTIVE **1** of heat **2** of hot springs

thermo- *or* **therm-** PREFIX forms words relating to heat or temperature

🄸 Comes from Greek *therme* meaning 'heat', and *thermos* meaning 'hot'

thermodynamics SINGULAR NOUN the science of the relation between heat and other forms of energy, especially mechanical energy

thermometer NOUN an instrument for measuring temperature

thermonuclear ADJECTIVE relating to the fusion of nuclei at high temperatures

Thermos NOUN, *trademark* a kind of vacuum flask

thermostat NOUN a device for automatically controlling temperature in a room

thesaurus (*pronounced* the-**sor**-*us*) NOUN (*plural* **thesauri** *or* **thesauruses**) **1** a reference book listing words and their synonyms **2** a dictionary or encyclopedia

these *see* **this**

thesis NOUN (*plural* **theses**) **1** a long piece of written work on a topic, often part of a university degree **2** a statement of a point of view

thespian NOUN, *formal* an actor

🄸 Named after *Thespis*, founder of ancient Greek tragedy

they PRONOUN PLURAL some people or things already mentioned (used only as the subject of a verb): *they followed the others* ▶PRONOUN SINGULAR used to avoid giving the gender of the person being referred to: *anyone can come if they like*

thick ADJECTIVE **1** not thin, of reasonable width: *a thick slice/two metres thick* **2** of a mixture: containing solid matter, stiff: *a thick soup* **3** dense, difficult to see or pass through: *thick fog/thick woods* **4** of speech: not clear **5** *informal* stupid **6** *informal* very friendly ▶NOUN the thickest, most crowded or active part: *in the thick of the fight*

thicken VERB to make or become thick

thicket NOUN a group of close-set trees and bushes

thickness NOUN **1** the quality of being thick **2** the distance between opposite sides **3** a layer

thickset ADJECTIVE **1** closely set or planted **2** having a thick sturdy body

thick-skinned ADJECTIVE not sensitive or easily hurt

thief NOUN (*plural* **thieves**) someone who steals

thieve VERB to steal

thieving NOUN stealing ▶ADJECTIVE that thieves

thievish ADJECTIVE inclined to stealing

thigh NOUN the thick, fleshy part of the leg between the knee and the hip

thimble NOUN a small cap worn over a fingertip, used to push a needle while sewing

thin ADJECTIVE (**thinner, thinnest**) **1** not very wide between its two sides: *thin paper/thin slice* **2** slim, not fat **3** not dense or crowded: *thin population* **4** poor in quality: *thin wine* **5** of a voice: weak, not resonating **6** of a mixture: not stiff, watery: *a thin soup* ▶VERB (**thinning, thinned**) to make or become thin or thinner > **thinness** NOUN

A B C D E F G H I J K L M N O P Q R S T U V W X Y Z

thine ADJECTIVE, *old* belonging to you (used before words beginning with a vowel or a vowel sound): *thine enemies* ▶PRONOUN, *old* something belonging to you: *My heart is thine*

thing NOUN **1** an object that is not living **2** *informal* a person: *a nice old thing* **3** (**things**) belongings **4** an individual object, quality, idea, etc that may be referred to: *Several things must be taken into consideration*

ⓘ Comes from Old English and Old Norse *thing* meaning 'parliament' or 'object'

think VERB (**thinking, thought**) **1** to work things out, reason **2** to form ideas in the mind **3** to believe, judge or consider: *I think that we should go* **4** (**think of doing something**) to intend to do it: *She is thinking of resigning* **think better of** to change your mind about **think highly of** *or* **think much of** to have a good opinion of **think nothing of 1** to have a poor opinion of **2** to consider as easy **think out** to work out in the mind

ⓘ Comes from Old English *thencan*

think tank NOUN a group of people who give expert advice and come up with ideas

third ADJECTIVE the last of a series of three ▶NOUN one of three equal parts

Third World *see* **Developing World**

thirst NOUN **1** a dry feeling in the mouth caused by lack of fluid **2** an eager desire (for): *thirst for knowledge* ▶VERB **1** to feel thirsty **2** (**thirst for something**) to desire it eagerly

thirsty ADJECTIVE (**thirstier, thirstiest**) **1** needing or wanting to drink **2** of earth: parched, dry **3** eager (for)

thirteen NOUN the number 13 ▶ADJECTIVE 13 in number

thirteenth ADJECTIVE the last of a series of thirteen ▶NOUN one of thirteen equal parts

thirtieth ADJECTIVE the last of a series of thirty ▶NOUN one of thirty equal parts

thirty NOUN the number 30 ▶ADJECTIVE 30 in number

this ADJECTIVE & PRONOUN (*plural* **these**) **1** used to point out someone or something, especially one nearby: (*contrasted with*: **that**): *Look at this letter/Take this instead* **2** to such an extent or degree: *this early*

thistle NOUN a prickly plant with purple flowers

thither ADVERB to that place

-thon *see* **-athon**

thong NOUN **1** a thin strap of leather to fasten anything **2** the lash of a whip

thorax NOUN (*plural* **thoraxes** *or* **thoraces**) **1** the chest in the human or animal body **2** the middle section of an insect's body

thorn NOUN **1** a sharp prickle sticking out from the stem of a plant **2** a bush with thorns, especially the hawthorn **thorn in the flesh** a cause of constant irritation

thorny ADJECTIVE (**thornier,**

thorniest) **1** full of thorns; prickly **2** difficult, causing arguments: *a thorny problem*

thorough ADJECTIVE **1** complete, absolute: *a thorough muddle* **2** very careful, attending to every detail: *a thorough search*

thoroughbred NOUN an animal of pure breed

thoroughfare NOUN **1** a public street **2** a passage or way through: *no thoroughfare*

thoroughly ADVERB **1** completely, absolutely: *I thoroughly agree* **2** very carefully: *The product has been tested thoroughly*

those *see* **that**

thou PRONOUN, *old* you (as the subject of a sentence)

though CONJUNCTION although: *Though he disliked it, he ate it all* ▶ADVERB, *informal* however: *I wish I'd never said it, though*

thought NOUN **1** the act of thinking **2** something which you think, an idea **3** an opinion **4** consideration: *after much thought* ▶VERB *past form of* **think**

🛈 Noun: comes from Old English *thoht/gethoht*, past participle of *thencan* meaning 'to think'; verb past form: comes from Old English *thohte*, past tense of *thencan* meaning 'to think'

thoughtful ADJECTIVE **1** full of thought **2** thinking of others, considerate

thoughtless ADJECTIVE showing lack of thought; inconsiderate

thousand NOUN the number 1000 ▶ADJECTIVE 1000 in number

thousandth ADJECTIVE the last of a series of a thousand ▶NOUN one of a thousand equal parts

thrash VERB **1** to beat severely **2** to move or toss violently (about) **3** to thresh (grain) **thrash out** to discuss (a problem etc) thoroughly

thrashing NOUN a flogging, a beating

thread NOUN **1** a very thin strand of cotton, wool, silk, etc, often twisted and drawn out **2** the ridge which goes in a spiral round a screw **3** a connected series of details in correct order in a story ▶VERB **1** to put a thread through a needle etc **2** to make (your way) in a narrow space

threadbare ADJECTIVE of clothes: worn thin

threat NOUN **1** a warning that you intend to hurt or punish someone **2** a warning of something bad that may come: *a threat of war* **3** something likely to cause harm: *a threat to our plans*

threaten VERB **1** to make a threat: *threatened to kill himself* **2** to suggest the approach of something unpleasant **3** to be a danger to

three NOUN the number 3 ▶ADJECTIVE 3 in number

🛈 Comes from Old English *threo*

3-D short for **three-dimensional**

three-dimensional ADJECTIVE having height, width and depth (*short form* **3-D**)

thresh VERB to beat out (grain) from straw

threshold NOUN **1** a piece of wood or stone under the door of a building **2** a doorway **3** an entry or beginning: *on the threshold of a new era*

threw *past tense* of **throw**

thrice ADVERB three times

thrift NOUN careful management of money in order to save

thrifty ADJECTIVE (**thriftier, thriftiest**) careful about spending

thrill NOUN **1** an excited feeling **2** quivering, vibration ▶ VERB **1** to feel excitement **2** to make excited

thriller NOUN an exciting story, often about crime and detection

thrilling ADJECTIVE very exciting

thrive VERB **1** to grow strong and healthy **2** to get on well, be successful

throat NOUN **1** the back part of the mouth **2** the front part of the neck

throb VERB (**throbbing, throbbed**) **1** of a pulse etc: to beat, especially more strongly than normal **2** to beat or vibrate rhythmically and regularly

throes PLURAL NOUN great suffering or struggle **in the throes of** in the middle of (a struggle, doing a task, etc)

thrombosis NOUN, *medicine* the forming of a clot in a blood vessel

throne NOUN **1** the seat of a monarch or bishop **2** a monarch or their power

throng NOUN a crowd ▶ VERB **1** to move in a crowd **2** to crowd, fill (a place): *Revellers thronged the streets*

throttle NOUN the part of an engine through which steam or petrol can be turned on or off ▶ VERB to choke by gripping the throat

through PREPOSITION **1** entering from one direction and going out in the other: *through the tunnel* **2** from end to end, or side to side, of: *all through the performance* **3** by way of: *related through his grandmother* **4** as a result of: *through his expertise* **5** *US* from (one date) to (another) inclusive: *Monday through Friday is five days* ▶ ADVERB into and out, from beginning to end: *all the way through the tunnel* ▶ ADJECTIVE **1** without break or change: *through train* **2** *informal* finished: *Are you through with the newspaper?* **3** of a telephone call: connected: *I couldn't get through this morning*

through-and-through ADVERB completely, entirely: *a gentleman through-and-through*

throughout PREPOSITION **1** in all parts of: *throughout Europe* **2** from start to finish of: *throughout the journey*

throw VERB (**throwing, threw, thrown**) **1** to send through the air with force **2** of a horse: to make (a rider) fall to the ground **3** to shape (pottery) on a wheel **4** to give (a party) ▶ NOUN **1** the act of throwing **2** the distance a thing is thrown: *within a stone's throw of the house* **throw away** to get rid of

throwback NOUN a reversion to an earlier form

thrush NOUN **1** (*plural* **thrushes**) a type of singing bird with a speckled breast **2** an infection which can affect the mouth, throat or vagina

thrust VERB (**thrusting, thrust**)

A B C D E F G H I J K L M N O P Q R S T U V W X Y Z

1 to push with force 2 to make a sudden push forward with a pointed weapon ▶NOUN 1 a stab 2 the force produced by an engine that propels an aircraft or rocket forward

thud NOUN a dull, hollow sound like that made by a heavy body falling ▶VERB (**thudding, thudded**) to move or fall with such a sound

thug NOUN a violent, brutal person

thumb NOUN the short, thick finger on the side of the hand ▶VERB to turn over (the pages of a book) with the thumb or fingers **rule of thumb** a rough-and-ready practical method **thumbs down** *or* **thumbs up** a sign showing disapproval, or approval, of something

thumbscrew NOUN, *history* an instrument of torture which worked by squashing the thumbs

thump NOUN a heavy blow ▶VERB 1 to beat heavily 2 to move or fall with a dull, heavy noise

thunder NOUN 1 the deep, rumbling sound heard after a flash of lightning 2 any loud, rumbling noise ▶VERB 1 to produce the sound of, or a sound like, thunder 2 to shout out angrily > **thundery** ADJECTIVE

thunderbolt NOUN 1 a flash of lightning followed by thunder 2 a very great and sudden surprise

thunderclap NOUN a sudden roar of thunder

thunderous ADJECTIVE like thunder, very loud: *thunderous applause*

thunderstruck ADJECTIVE overcome by surprise

Thursday NOUN the fifth day of the week

ⓘ After *Thor*, the Norse god of thunder

thus ADVERB 1 in this or that manner: *Thread the shuttle thus* 2 to this degree or extent: *thus far* 3 because of this, therefore: *Thus, we must go on*

thwart VERB 1 to hinder (someone) from carrying out a plan, intention, etc 2 to prevent (an attempt etc) ▶NOUN a seat for a rower that lies across a boat

thy ADJECTIVE, *old* belonging to you: *thy wife and children*

thyme NOUN a small sweet-smelling herb used for seasoning food

thyroid gland a large gland in the neck which influences the rate at which energy is used by the body

ⓘ Based on a Greek word meaning 'door-shaped', because of the shape of the cartilage in the front of the throat

tiara NOUN a jewelled ornament for the head like a crown

tic NOUN a twitching motion of certain muscles, especially of the face

tick[1] NOUN 1 a mark (✓) used to show something is correct or to mark off items on a list 2 a small quick noise, made regularly by a clock or watch 3 *informal* a moment: *I'll just be a tick* ▶VERB 1 to mark with a tick 2 of a clock etc: to produce regular ticks > **ticking** NOUN

tick² NOUN a tiny blood-sucking animal

ticket NOUN **1** a card entitling the holder to admittance to a show, travel on public transport, etc **2** a notice that a traffic offence has been committed **3** a label on an item showing price, size, etc **just the ticket** exactly what is required

tickle VERB **1** to excite the surface nerves of a part of the body by touching lightly **2** to please or amuse

ticklish ADJECTIVE **1** sensitive to tickling **2** not easy to deal with: *ticklish problem*

tickly ADJECTIVE (**ticklier, tickliest**) ticklish

tidal ADJECTIVE of the tide

tidal wave NOUN an enormous wave in the sea often caused by an earthquake etc

tiddler NOUN, *informal* **1** a small fish **2** a small person or thing

tiddlywinks SINGULAR NOUN a game in which small plastic discs (**tiddlywinks**) are flipped into a cup

tide NOUN **1** the rise and fall of the sea which happens regularly twice each day **2** *old* time, season: *Christmastide* **tide over** to help to get over a difficulty for a time: *He lent me £50 to tide me over till pay day*

tidings PLURAL NOUN news

tidy ADJECTIVE (**tidier, tidiest**) **1** in good order, neat **2** *informal* fairly big: *a tidy sum of money* ▶ VERB (**tidies, tidying, tidied**) to make neat > **tidily** ADVERB

tie VERB (**ties, tying, tied**) **1** to fasten with a cord, string, etc **2** to knot or put a bow in (string, shoelaces, etc) **3** to join, unite **4** to limit, restrict: *tied to a tight schedule* **5** to score the same number of points (in a game etc), draw ▶ NOUN **1** a band of fabric worn round the neck, especially by men, tied with a knot or bow at the front **2** something that connects: *ties of friendship* **3** something that restricts or limits **4** an equal score in a competition **5** a game or match to be played

tie-break *or* **tie-breaker** NOUN an extra question or part of a tied contest to decide a winner

tier (*pronounced* teer) NOUN a row of seats in a theatre etc, with others above or below it

tiff NOUN a slight quarrel

tiger NOUN a large animal of the cat family with a tawny coat striped with black

tight ADJECTIVE **1** packed closely **2** firmly stretched, not loose **3** fitting too closely: *These jeans are a bit tight* **4** *informal* mean with money **5** *informal* drunk

tighten VERB to make or become tight or tighter

tight-fisted ADJECTIVE stingy

tight-lipped ADJECTIVE uncommunicative

tightrope NOUN a tightly stretched rope on which acrobats perform

tights PLURAL NOUN a close-fitting garment covering the feet, legs and body as far as the waist

tigress NOUN a female tiger

tile NOUN a piece of baked clay, linoleum, etc used in covering floors or roofs ▶ VERB to cover with tiles

till[1] NOUN a container or drawer for money in a shop ▶ VERB to cultivate (land); plough

till[2] *see* **until**

tilt VERB **1** to fall into, or place in, a sloping position **2** to joust (**tilt at**) to attack someone on horseback, using a lance NOUN **1** a slant **2** a thrust, a jab **at full tilt** with full speed and force

timber NOUN **1** wood for building etc **2** trees suitable for this **3** a wooden beam in a house or ship

timbre (*pronounced* **tim**-ber *or* **tam**-ber) NOUN the quality of a musical sound or voice

time NOUN **1** the hour of the day **2** the period at which something happens **3** (often **times**) a particular period: *in modern times* **4** opportunity: *no time to listen* **5** a suitable or right moment: *Now is the time to ask* **6** one of a number of occasions: *He won four times* **7** (**times**) multiplied by: *two times four* **8** the rhythm or rate of performance of a piece of music ▶ ADJECTIVE **1** of or to do with time **2** arranged to go off at a particular time: *a time bomb* ▶ VERB **1** to measure the minutes, seconds, etc taken to do anything **2** to choose the time for (well, badly, etc): *time your entrance well* **at times** occasionally **do time** *slang* to serve a prison sentence **in time** early enough **on time** punctual **the time being** the present time: *You'll have to use your old football boots for the time being*
[1] Comes from Old English *tima*

time-honoured ADJECTIVE respected because it has lasted a long time

timeless ADJECTIVE **1** not belonging to any particular time **2** never ending: *timeless beauty*

timely ADJECTIVE (**timelier, timeliest**) coming at the right moment: *a timely reminder*

timescale NOUN the time envisaged for the completion of a project

time-sharing NOUN **1** a system of using a computer so that it can deal with several programs at the same time **2** a scheme by which someone buys the right to use a holiday home for a specified period each year

timetable NOUN a list showing times of classes, arrivals or departures of trains, etc

timid ADJECTIVE easily frightened; shy > **timidity** NOUN

timidly ADVERB shyly

timing NOUN the coordination of when actions or events happen to achieve the best possible effect

timpani *or* **tympani** PLURAL NOUN kettledrums

tin NOUN a box or can made of **tinplate**, thin steel covered with tin or other metal ▶ VERB (**tinning, tinned**) **1** to cover with tin **2** to pack (food etc) in tins

tincture NOUN **1** a slight tinge of colour **2** a characteristic quality **3** a medicine mixed in alcohol

tinder NOUN dry material easily set alight by a spark

tinfoil NOUN a very thin sheet of tin, aluminium, etc used for wrapping food

tinge VERB to tint, colour slightly **tinge with** to add a trace or hint of (a quality, feeling, etc) to NOUN a slight amount; a hint: *tinge of pink/ tinge of sadness*

tingle VERB **1** to feel a sharp prickling sensation **2** to feel a thrill of excitement ▶ NOUN a sharp prickle

tinker a mender kettles, pans, etc NOUN ▶ VERB **1** to work clumsily or unskilfully **2** to meddle (with)

tinkle VERB to (cause to) make a light, ringing sound; clink, jingle ▶ NOUN a light, ringing sound

tinny ADJECTIVE (**tinnier, tinniest**) **1** like tin **2** of a sound: thin, high-pitched

tinsel NOUN a sparkling, glittering material used for decoration

tint NOUN a variety or shade of a colour ▶ VERB to give slight colour to

tiny ADJECTIVE (**tinier, tiniest**) very small

tip NOUN **1** the top or point of something thin or tapering **2** a piece of useful information **3** a small gift of money to a waiter etc **4** a rubbish dump **5** a light stroke, a tap ▶ VERB (**tipping, tipped**) **1** to slant **2** (also **tip off**) to give a hint to **3** to give a small gift of money **4** to strike lightly **tip out** *or* **into** to empty out or into **tip over** to overturn

Tipp-Ex NOUN, *trademark* correcting fluid for covering over mistakes in typing or writing

tipple VERB, *informal* to drink small amounts of alcohol regularly ▶ NOUN an alcoholic drink

tippler NOUN someone who regularly drinks alcohol

tipsiness NOUN being slightly drunk

tipsy ADJECTIVE (**tipsier, tipsiest**) rather drunk

tiptoe VERB to walk on your toes in order to go very quietly **on tiptoe** standing or walking on your toes

tirade NOUN a long, bitter, scolding speech

tire[1] VERB **1** to make or become weary **2** (**tire of**) to lose patience with or interest in

tire[2] *US spelling* of **tyre**

tired ADJECTIVE **1** weary **2** (**tired of**) bored with

tireless ADJECTIVE **1** never becoming weary **2** never resting

tiresome ADJECTIVE **1** making weary **2** long and dull **3** annoying: *a tiresome child*

tiring ADJECTIVE causing tiredness or weariness: *a tiring journey*

tissue NOUN **1** the substance of which body organs are made: *muscle tissue* **2** a mass, a network (of lies, nonsense, etc) **3** a paper handkerchief **4** finely woven cloth

tissue paper NOUN thin, soft paper used for wrapping

tit NOUN **1** a type of small bird: *blue tit/great tit* **2** a teat **tit for tat** blow for blow, the repayment of an injury with another injury

titanic ADJECTIVE huge, enormous

titbit NOUN a tasty piece of food etc

tithe (*pronounced* taidh) NOUN, *history* a tax paid to the church, a tenth part of someone's income or produce

titillate VERB to gently stimulate or

arouse (often sexually)
[i] Comes from Latin *titillare* meaning 'to tickle'

> Do not confuse: **titillate** and **titivate**

titivate VERB to make smarter; improve in appearance
[i] It is thought that **titivate** was created by taking 'tidy' and reforming it on the model of the verb 'cultivate'

title NOUN **1** the name of a book, poem, etc **2** a word in front of a name to show rank or office (eg *Sir, Lady, Major*), or in addressing anyone formally (eg *Mr, Mrs, Ms*) **3** right or claim to money, etc

titled ADJECTIVE having a title which shows noble rank

title deed NOUN a document that proves a right to ownership (of a house etc)

title role NOUN the part in a play which is the same as the title eg *Hamlet*

titter VERB to giggle ▶NOUN a giggle

TNT ABBREVIATION trinitrotoluene, a high explosive

to PREPOSITION **1** showing the place or direction aimed for: *going to the cinema/emigrating to New Zealand* **2** showing the indirect object in a phrase, sentence, etc: *show it to me* **3** used before a verb to indicate the infinitive: *To err is human* **4** showing that one thing belongs with another in some way: *key to the door* **5** compared with: *nothing to what happened before* **6** about, concerning: *What did he say to that?* **7** showing a ratio, proportion, etc: *odds are six to one against* **8** showing the purpose or result of an action: *Tear it to pieces* ▶ADVERB almost closed: *pull the door to* **to and fro** backwards and forwards

toad NOUN a type of amphibian like a frog

toadstool NOUN a mushroom-like fungus, often poisonous

toady VERB (**toadies, toadying, toadied**) to give way to someone's wishes, or flatter them, to gain favour ▶NOUN (*plural* **toadies**) someone who acts in this way

toast VERB **1** to brown (bread) by heating at a fire or grill **2** to drink to the success or health of (someone) **3** to warm (your feet etc) at a fire ▶NOUN **1** bread toasted **2** the person to whom a toast is drunk **3** the drinking of a toast

toaster NOUN an electric machine for toasting bread

toast rack NOUN a stand with partitions for slices of toast

tobacco NOUN a type of plant whose dried leaves are used for smoking

tobacconist NOUN someone who sells tobacco, cigarettes, etc

toboggan NOUN a long, light sledge ▶VERB to go in a toboggan

today ADVERB & NOUN **1** (on) this day **2** (at) the present time

toddle VERB to walk unsteadily, with short steps

toddler NOUN a young child just able to walk

toddy NOUN (*plural* **toddies**) a hot drink of whisky and honey

to-do NOUN (*plural* **to-dos**) a bustle, commotion

A B C D E F G H I J K L M N O P Q R S T U V W X Y Z

toe NOUN **1** one of the five finger-like parts of the foot **2** the front part of an animal's foot **3** the front part of a shoe, golf club, etc **on your toes** alert, ready for action **toe the line** to do as you are told

toffee NOUN a kind of sweet made of sugar and butter

toffee-nosed ADJECTIVE, *informal* snobbish, conceited

toga NOUN, *history* the loose outer garment worn by a citizen of ancient Rome

together ADVERB **1** with each other, in place or time: *We must stay together/Three buses arrived together* **2** so as to be in contact, joined or united: *Glue the pages together* **3** by joint action: *Together we can afford it*

toggle NOUN **1 2** *computing* a keyboard command which allows the user to switch between one mode and another ▶VERB, *computing* to switch quickly between two positions, states *etc* (especially between being on and off)

toil VERB **1** to work hard and for a long time **2** to walk, move, etc with effort ▶NOUN hard work

toilet NOUN **1** a receptacle for waste matter from the body, with a water-supply for flushing this away **2** a room containing this **3** *old* the act of washing yourself, doing your hair, etc

toiletries PLURAL NOUN soaps, cosmetics, etc

toilet water NOUN a lightly perfumed, spirit-based liquid for the skin

token NOUN **1** a mark, a sign: *a token of my friendship* **2** a stamped piece of plastic etc, or a voucher, for use in place of money: *bus token/book token* ▶ADJECTIVE done for show only, insincere: *token gesture*

told *past form* of **tell**

tolerable ADJECTIVE **1** bearable, endurable **2** fairly good: *tolerable player* > **tolerably** ADVERB

tolerance NOUN **1** accepting and being fair to people with different beliefs, manners, etc from your own **2** ability to resist the effects of a drug etc

tolerant ADJECTIVE **1** fair towards other people and accepting their right to have different political and religious beliefs **2** able to resist the effects of a drug etc

tolerate VERB **1** to bear, endure; put up with **2** to allow

toleration NOUN **1** the act of tolerating **2** the practice of allowing people to practise religions which are different from the established religion of the country

toll[1] NOUN **1** a tax charged for crossing a bridge, using a road, etc **2** loss, damage **take toll** to cause damage or loss

toll[2] VERB **1** to sound (a large bell) slowly, as for a funeral **2** of a bell: to be sounded slowly

tomahawk NOUN, *history* a Native American light axe used as a weapon and tool

tomato NOUN (*plural* **tomatoes**) a juicy red-skinned fruit, used in salads, sauces, etc

tomb NOUN **1** a grave **2** a burial vault or chamber

tomboy NOUN a high-spirited active girl who enjoys the rough, boisterous activities which people tend to associate with boys

tombstone NOUN a stone placed over a grave in memory of the dead person

tomcat NOUN a male cat

tome NOUN a large heavy book

tomorrow ADVERB & NOUN **1** (on) the day after today **2** (in) the future: *the children of tomorrow*

tomtom NOUN a type of drum beaten with the hands

-tomy also **-ectomy**, **-otomy** SUFFIX forms words relating to the surgical operation of cutting into an organ of the body: *vasectomy/ lobotomy*

[i] Comes from Greek *tome* meaning 'a cutting'

ton NOUN **1** a measure of weight equal to 2240 pounds, about 1016 kilograms **2** a unit (100 cubic feet) of space in a ship **metric ton** *or* **metric tonne** 1000 kilograms

tone NOUN **1** sound **2** quality of sound: *harsh tone* **3** *music* one of the larger intervals in a scale, eg between C and D **4** the quality of a voice expressing the mood of the speaker: *a gentle tone* **5** a shade of colour **6** muscle firmness or strength ▸VERB **1** to give tone to **2** (sometimes **tone in**) to blend, fit in well **tone down** to make or become softer

tongs PLURAL NOUN an instrument for lifting and grasping coals, sugar lumps, etc

tongue NOUN **1** the fleshy organ inside the mouth, used in tasting, speaking, and swallowing **2** a flap in a shoe **3** a long, thin strip of land **4** the tongue of an animal served as food **5** a language: *his mother tongue*

tongue-tied ADJECTIVE not able to speak freely

tongue-twister NOUN a phrase, sentence, etc not easy to say quickly, eg 'she sells sea shells'

tonic NOUN **1** a medicine which gives strength and energy **2** *music* the keynote of a scale **3** tonic water ▸ADJECTIVE **1** of tones or sounds **2** of a tonic

tonight ADVERB & NOUN (on) the night of the present day

tonnage NOUN the space available in a ship, measured in tons

tonne NOUN a metric ton

tonsil NOUN one of a pair of soft, fleshy lumps at the back of the throat that produce lymphocytes

tonsillitis NOUN inflammation and painfulness of the tonsils

too ADVERB **1** to a greater extent, in a greater quantity, etc than is wanted: *too hot to go outside/too many people in the room* **2** (with a negative) very, particularly: *not feeling too well* (ie not feeling very well) **3** also, as well: *I'm feeling quite cold, too*

took *past tense* of **take**

tool NOUN an instrument for doing work, especially by hand

toolbar NOUN, *computing* a bar with a list of features and functions which appears at the top of a computer screen

a b c d e f g h i j k l m n o p q r s t u v w x y z

A B C D E F G H I J K L M N O P Q R S T U V W X Y Z

toot NOUN the sound of a car horn etc

tooth NOUN (*plural* **teeth**) **1** any of the hard, bony objects projecting from the gums, arranged in two rows in the mouth **2** any of the points on a saw, cogwheel, etc **fight tooth and nail** to fight fiercely, determinedly

toothache NOUN pain in a tooth

toothpaste NOUN paste for cleaning the teeth

toothpick NOUN a small sharp instrument for picking out food from between the teeth

top NOUN **1** the highest part of anything **2** the upper surface **3** the highest place or rank **4** a lid **5** a circus tent **6** a kind of spinning toy ▶ ADJECTIVE highest, chief ▶ VERB (**topping, topped**) **1** to cover on the top **2** to rise above **3** to do better than **4** to reach the top of **5** to take off the top of

topaz NOUN a type of precious stone, of various colours

top hat NOUN a man's tall silk hat

top-heavy ADJECTIVE having the upper part too heavy for the lower

topiary NOUN the art of trimming bushes, hedges, etc into decorative shapes

topic NOUN a subject spoken or written about

topical ADJECTIVE of current interest, concerned with present events

topmost ADJECTIVE highest, uppermost

topographical ADJECTIVE relating to or involving topography

topography NOUN the description of the features of the land in a certain region

topple VERB to become unsteady and fall

top-secret ADJECTIVE (of information etc) very secret

topsyturvy ADJECTIVE & ADVERB turned upside down

Torah NOUN, *Judaism* the book of Jewish law

torch NOUN (*plural* **torches**) **1** a small hand-held light with a switch and electric battery **2** a flaming piece of wood or coarse rope carried as a light in processions ▶ VERB, *slang* to set fire to deliberately

tore *past tense* of **tear**[2]

toreador NOUN a bullfighter mounted on horseback

torment VERB **1** to treat cruelly and make suffer **2** to worry greatly **3** to tease ▶ NOUN **1** great pain, suffering **2** a cause of these

tormentor NOUN a person who torments

torn *past participle* of **tear**[2]

tornado NOUN (*plural* **tornadoes**) a violent whirling windstorm characterized by a long, funnel-shaped column of air

torpedo NOUN (*plural* **torpedoes**) a large cigar-shaped type of missile fired by ships, planes, etc ▶ VERB (**torpedoing, torpedoed**) to hit or sink (a ship) with a torpedo

torrent NOUN **1** a rushing stream **2** a heavy downpour of rain **3** a violent flow of words etc: *torrent of abuse*

torrential ADJECTIVE like a torrent; rushing violently

torrid ADJECTIVE **1** parched by heat; very hot **2** very passionate: *torrid love affair*

torso NOUN (*plural* **torsos**) the body, excluding the head and limbs

tortilla NOUN **1** a type of flat Mexican bread **2** a Spanish omelette

tortoise NOUN a four-footed, slow-moving kind of reptile, covered with a hard shell

tortoiseshell NOUN the shell of a kind of sea turtle, used in making ornamental articles ▸ADJECTIVE **1** made of this shell **2** mottled brown, yellow and black: *a tortoiseshell cat*

tortuous ADJECTIVE winding, roundabout, not straightforward

torture VERB **1** to treat someone cruelly as a punishment or to force them to confess something **2** to cause to suffer ▸NOUN **1** the act of torturing **2** great suffering

Tory NOUN (*plural* **Tories**) a member of the British Conservative Party

ⓘ Originally one of a group of Irish Catholics thrown off their land who waged guerrilla war on British settlers, later applied to any royalist supporter

toss VERB **1** to throw up in the air **2** to throw up (a coin) to see which side falls uppermost **3** to turn restlessly from side to side **4** of a ship: to be thrown about by rough water **toss off** to produce quickly **toss up** to toss a coin

toss-up NOUN an equal choice or chance

tot[1] NOUN **1** a little child **2** a small amount of alcoholic spirits

tot[2] VERB: **tot up** to add up

total ADJECTIVE **1** whole: *total number* **2** complete: *total wreck* ▸NOUN **1** the entire amount **2** the sum of amounts added together ▸VERB (**totalling, totalled**) **1** to add up **2** to amount to **3** *informal* to damage irreparably; wreck: *She totalled her dad's car*

totalitarianism NOUN government by a single party that demands obedience and allows no rivals > **totalitarian** NOUN & ADJECTIVE

totally ADVERB completely

totem NOUN an image of an animal or plant used as the badge or sign of a Native American tribe

totem pole NOUN a pole on which totems are carved and painted

totter VERB **1** to shake as if about to fall **2** to stagger

toucan NOUN a type of S American bird with a heavy curved beak

touch VERB **1** to feel (with the hand) **2** to come or be in contact (with): *A leaf touched his cheek* **3** to move, affect the feelings of: *The story touched those who heard it* **4** to mark slightly with colour: *touched with gold* **5** to reach the standard of: *I can't touch him at chess* **6** to have anything to do with: *I wouldn't touch a job like that* **7** to eat or drink: *He won't touch meat* **8** to concern (someone) **9** *informal* to persuade (someone) to lend you money: *I touched him for £10* ▸NOUN **1** the act of touching **2** the physical sense of touch **3** a small quantity or degree: *a touch of salt* **4** of an artist, pianist, etc: skill or style **5** *football* the ground beyond

a b c d e f g h i j k l m n o p q r s t u v w x y z

the edges of the pitch marked off by **touchlines** **in (*or* out of) touch with** **1** in (or not in) communication or contact with **2** aware (or unaware) of **touch down** of an aircraft: to land **touch off** to cause to happen **touch on** to mention briefly **touch up** to improve (a drawing, photograph, etc) by making details clearer or correcting faults

touch-and-go ADJECTIVE very uncertain: *It's touch-and-go whether we'll get it done on time*

touché (*pronounced* too-**shei**) INTERJECTION acknowledging a point scored in a game or argument

touching PREPOSITION about, concerning ▶ ADJECTIVE causing feelings of sympathy or pity, moving

touchstone NOUN a test or standard of measurement of quality etc

touchy ADJECTIVE (**touchier, touchiest**) **1** easily offended **2** needing to be handled with care and tact: *a touchy subject* > **touchily** ADVERB (meaning 1)

tough ADJECTIVE **1** strong, not easily broken **2** of meat etc: hard to chew **3** of strong character, able to stand hardship or strain **4** difficult to cope with or overcome: *tough opposition*

toughen VERB to (cause to) become tough

tour NOUN a journey in which you visit various places; a pleasure trip ▶ VERB to make a tour (of)

tourism NOUN **1** the practice of travelling to and visiting places for pleasure **2** the industry that is involved in offering services for tourists

tourist NOUN someone who travels for pleasure and visits places of interest

tournament NOUN **1** a competition involving many contests and players **2** *history* a meeting at which knights fought together on horseback

tourniquet (*pronounced* **toorn**-ik-ei) NOUN a bandage tied tightly round a limb to prevent loss of blood from a wound

tousled ADJECTIVE of hair: untidy, tangled

tout VERB to go about looking for support, votes, buyers, etc ▶ NOUN **1** someone who does this **2** someone who gives tips to people who bet on horse races

tow (*pronounced* toh) VERB to pull (a car etc) with a rope attached to another vehicle ▶ NOUN **1** the act of towing **2** the rope used for towing **in tow** accompanying as a companion or escort **on tow** being towed

towards *or* **toward** PREPOSITION **1** moving in the direction of (a place, person, etc): *walking towards the house* **2** to (a person, thing, etc): *his attitude towards his son* **3** as a help or contribution to: *I gave £5 towards the cost* **4** near, about (a time etc): *towards four o'clock*

towel NOUN a cloth for drying or wiping (eg the skin after washing) ▶ VERB (**towelling, towelled**) to rub dry with a towel **throw in the towel** to give up a fight or struggle

towelling NOUN a cotton cloth often used for making towels

tower NOUN **1** a high narrow building **2** a high narrow part of a castle etc ▸VERB to rise high (over, above)

towering ADJECTIVE **1** rising high **2** violent: *a towering rage*

town NOUN a place, larger than a village, which includes many buildings, houses, shops, etc

town hall NOUN the building where the official business of a town is done

towpath NOUN a path alongside a canal originally used by horses which tow barges

-tox- also **-toxi-**, **-toxico-** of or relating to poison: *toxaemia* (= blood poisoning)/*intoxication*

ⓘ Comes from Greek *toxikon pharmacon* meaning 'poison for the bow', from *toxon* meaning 'bow'

toxic ADJECTIVE **1** poisonous **2** caused by poison

toxicology NOUN the scientific study of poisons

toxin NOUN a naturally occurring poison

toy NOUN **1** an object for a child to play with **2** an object for amusement only **toy with** to play or trifle with

trace NOUN **1** a mark or sign left behind **2** a footprint **3** a small amount **4** a line drawn by an instrument recording a change (eg in temperature) **5** (**traces**) the straps by which a horse pulls a cart etc along ▸VERB **1** to follow the tracks or course of **2** to copy (a drawing etc) on transparent paper placed over it

traceable ADJECTIVE able to be traced (to)

tracery NOUN decorated stonework holding the glass in some church windows

tracing NOUN a traced copy

tracing paper NOUN semi-transparent paper used for tracing drawings etc

track NOUN **1** a mark left **2** (**tracks**) footprints **3** a path or rough road **4** a racecourse for runners, cyclists, etc **5** a railway line **6** an endless band on which wheels of a tank etc travel ▸VERB to follow (an animal) by its footprints and other marks left **keep** *or* **lose track of** to keep or fail to keep aware of the whereabouts or progress of **make tracks for** to set off towards **track down** to search for (someone or something) until caught or found

tracksuit NOUN a loose suit worn while jogging, before and after an athletic performance, etc

-tract- forms words related to the action of pulling or drawing: *tractable* (= easily pulled along)/*subtract* (= to draw away)

ⓘ Comes from Latin *trahere* meaning 'to draw', and *tractare* meaning 'to drag about' or 'to deal with'

tract NOUN **1** a stretch of land **2** a short pamphlet, especially on a religious subject **3** a system made up of connected parts of the body: *the digestive tract*

tractable ADJECTIVE easily made to do what is wanted

traction NOUN **1** the act of pulling

A B C D E F G H I J K L M N O P Q R S T U V W X Y Z

or dragging **2** the state of being pulled

tractor NOUN a motor vehicle for pulling loads, ploughs, etc

trade NOUN **1** the buying and selling of goods **2** someone's occupation, craft, job: *a carpenter by trade* ▶ VERB **1** to buy and sell **2** to have business dealings (with) **3** to deal (in) **4** to exchange, swap **trade in** to give as part-payment for something else (eg an old car for a new one) **trade on** to take advantage of, often unfairly

trademark NOUN a registered mark or name put on goods to show that they are made by a certain company

trader NOUN someone who buys and sells

tradesman NOUN **1** a shopkeeper **2** a workman in a skilled trade

trade union NOUN a group of workers of the same trade who join together to bargain with employers for fair wages etc

tradition NOUN **1** the handing-down of customs, beliefs, stories, etc from generation to generation **2** a custom, belief, etc handed down in this way

traditional ADJECTIVE of customs: having existed for a long time without changing: *the traditional English breakfast*

traditionalist NOUN someone who believes in maintaining traditions

traffic NOUN **1** the cars, buses, boats, etc which use roads or waterways **2** trade **3** dishonest dealings (eg in drugs) ▶ VERB (**trafficking, trafficked**) **1** to trade **2** to deal (in)

traffic lights PLURAL NOUN a system of red, amber and green lights for controlling traffic at road junctions or street crossings

tragedian NOUN **1** an actor who specializes in tragic roles **2** a person who writes tragedies

tragedy NOUN (*plural* **tragedies**) **1** a very sad event **2** a play about unhappy events and with a sad ending (*contrasted with*: **comedy**)

tragic ADJECTIVE very sad
> **tragically** ADVERB: *He was tragically killed in an accident*

trail VERB **1** to draw along, in or through: *trailing his foot through the water* **2** to hang down (from) or be dragged loosely behind **3** to hunt (animals) by following footprints etc **4** to walk wearily **5** of a plant: to grow over the ground or a wall ▶ NOUN **1** an animal's track **2** a pathway through a wild region: *a nature trail* **3** something left stretching behind: *a trail of dust*

trailer NOUN **1** a vehicle pulled behind a car **2** a short film advertising a longer film or TV programme to be shown at a later date

train NOUN **1** a railway engine with carriages or trucks **2** a part of a dress which trails behind the wearer **3** the attendants who follow an important person **4** a line (of thought, events, etc) **5** a line of animals carrying people or baggage ▶ VERB **1** to prepare yourself by practice or exercise for a sporting event, job, etc **2** to educate **3** to exercise (animals or people) in preparation for a race etc **4** to tame and teach (an animal) **5** (**train on** or **at**) to aim, point (a gun, telescope, etc) at (something) **6** to make (a tree or plant) grow in a certain direction

trainee NOUN someone who is being trained

trainer NOUN someone who trains people or animals for a sport, circus, etc

training NOUN **1** preparation for a sport **2** experience or learning of the practical side of a job

trait NOUN a point that stands out in a person's character: *Patience is one of his good traits*

traitor NOUN **1** someone who goes over to the enemy's side, or gives away secrets to the enemy **2** someone who betrays trust
> **traitorous** ADJECTIVE

trajectory NOUN (*plural* **trajectories**) *physics* the curved path of an object moving through the air or through space

tram NOUN a long vehicle running on rails and driven by electric power for carrying passengers (*also called*: **tramcar**)

tramline NOUN **1** a rail of a tramway **2** (**tramlines**) *tennis* the parallel lines marked at the sides of the court

tramp VERB **1** to walk with heavy footsteps **2** to walk along, over, etc: *tramping the streets in search of a job* ▸NOUN **1** someone with no fixed home and no job, who lives by begging **2** a journey made on foot **3** the sound of marching feet **4** a small cargo-boat with no fixed route

trample VERB **1** to tread under foot, stamp on **2** (*usually* **trample on**) to treat roughly or unfeelingly **3** to tread heavily

trampoline NOUN a bed-like framework holding a sheet of elastic material for bouncing on, used by gymnasts etc

tramway NOUN a system of tracks on which trams run

trance NOUN a sleep-like or half-conscious state

tranquil ADJECTIVE quiet, peaceful

tranquillity NOUN the state of being quiet, calm and peaceful: *She loved the tranquillity of the valley*

tranquillize, **tranquillise** *or US* **tranquilize** VERB to make calm, especially by administering a drug

tranquillizer, **tranquilliser** *or US* **tranquilizer** NOUN a drug to calm the nerves or make you sleep

trans- PREFIX across, through: *transatlantic/translate* (= to carry across into a different language)
[i] Comes from Latin *trans* meaning 'across' or 'beyond'

transact VERB to do (a piece of business)

transaction NOUN a piece of business, a deal

transatlantic ADJECTIVE **1** crossing the Atlantic Ocean: *transatlantic yacht race* **2** across or over the Atlantic: *transatlantic friends*

transcend VERB **1** to be, or rise, above **2** to be, or do, better than

transcribe VERB **1** to copy from one book into another or from one form of writing (eg shorthand) into another **2** to adapt (a piece of music) for a particular instrument

a b c d e f g h i j k l m n o p q r s t u v w x y z

transcript NOUN a written copy

transcription NOUN **1** the act of transcribing **2** a written copy

transect VERB to cut across (something)

transfer VERB (**transferring, transferred**) **1** to remove to another place **2** to hand over to another person ▶NOUN **1** the act of transferring **2** a design or picture which can be transferred from one surface to another

transferable ADJECTIVE able to be transferred

transference NOUN the act of moving or transferring something from one person, place or group to another: *the transference of power from central to local government*

transfiguration NOUN a change in appearance, especially to something more beautiful, glorious, or exalted

transfigure VERB to change (greatly and for the better) the form or appearance of

transfix VERB **1** to make unable to move or act (eg because of surprise): *transfixed by the sight* **2** to pierce through (as with a sword)

transform VERB to change in shape or appearance completely and often dramatically > **transformation** NOUN

transformer NOUN an apparatus for changing electrical energy from one voltage to another

transfuse VERB **1** to pass (liquid) from one thing to another **2** to transfer (blood of one person) to the body of another

transfusion NOUN (*in full* **blood transfusion**) the introduction of blood into a person's body by allowing it to drip through a needle inserted in a vein

transgress VERB to break a rule, law, etc

transgression NOUN the act of breaking a rule, law, etc; a sin

transience NOUN a transient quality

transient ADJECTIVE not lasting, passing

transistor NOUN **1** a small semiconductor device, made up of a crystal enclosed in plastic or metal, which controls the flow of an electrical current **2** a portable radio set using these

transit NOUN **1** the carrying or movement of goods, passengers, etc from place to place **2** the passing of a planet between the sun and the earth

transition NOUN a change from one form, place, appearance, etc to another

transitional ADJECTIVE involving transition; temporary: *The country will pass through a transitional period between constitutions*

transitive ADJECTIVE, *grammar* of a verb: having an object, eg the verb '*hit*' in 'he *hit* the ball'

transitory ADJECTIVE lasting only for a short time

translate VERB to turn (something said or written) into another language

translation NOUN **1** the act of translating **2** something translated

3 *maths* a transformation with a sliding movement but no turning (*compare with*: **enlargement, reflection, rotation**)

translator NOUN someone who translates

translucence NOUN a translucent quality

transmission NOUN **1** the act of transmitting **2** a radio or television broadcast

transmit VERB (**transmitting, transmitted**) **1** to pass on (a message, news, heat) **2** to send out signals which are received as programmes

transmitter NOUN an instrument for transmitting (especially radio signals)

transparency NOUN (*plural* **transparencies**) **1** the state of being transparent **2** a photograph printed on transparent material and viewed by shining light through it

transparent ADJECTIVE **1** able to be seen through **2** easily seen to be true or false: *a transparent excuse*

transpire VERB **1** of a secret: to become known **2** to happen: *Tell me what transpired* **3** of a plant: to absorb moisture through the roots and let out water vapour through the surface of leaves > **transpiration** NOUN

transplant VERB **1** to lift and plant (a growing plant) in another place **2** to remove (skin) and graft it on another part of the same body **3** to remove (an organ) and graft it in another person or animal ▶NOUN **1** the act of transplanting **2** a transplanted organ, plant, etc

transplantation NOUN the transfer of an organ or tissue from one person to another, or from one part of the body to another

transport VERB **1** to carry from one place to another **2** to overcome with strong feeling: *transported with delight* **3** *history* to send (a prisoner) to a prison in a different country ▶NOUN **1** the act of transporting **2** any means of carrying persons or goods: *rail transport* **3** strong feeling: *transports of joy*

transportation NOUN **1** the act of transporting **2** means of transport **3** *history* punishment of prisoners by sending them to a prison in a different country

transporter NOUN a vehicle that carries other vehicles, heavy objects, etc

transvestite NOUN someone who likes to wear clothes intended for the opposite sex

trap NOUN **1** a device for catching animals etc **2** a plan or trick for taking someone by surprise **3** a bend in a pipe which is kept full of water, for preventing the escape of air or gas **4** a carriage with two wheels ▶VERB (**trapping, trapped**) to catch in a trap, or in such a way that escape is not possible

trapdoor NOUN a door in a floor or ceiling

trapeze NOUN a swing used in performing gymnastic exercises or feats

trapezium NOUN a figure with four sides, two of which are parallel

trapezoid NOUN a figure with four sides, none of which are parallel

trapper NOUN someone who makes a living by catching animals for their skins and fur

trappings PLURAL NOUN **1** clothes or ornaments suitable for a particular person or occasion **2** ornaments put on horses

trash NOUN something of little worth, rubbish

trashy ADJECTIVE (**trashier, trashiest**) worthless

trauma NOUN **1** injury to the body **2** a very violent or distressing experience which has a lasting effect **3** a condition (of a person) caused by such an experience

traumatic ADJECTIVE very upsetting, unpleasant or frightening: *Moving to a new house can be traumatic*

travel VERB (**travelling, travelled**) **1** to go on a journey **2** to move **3** to go along, across **4** to visit foreign countries ▸ NOUN the act of travelling

traveller NOUN **1** someone who travels **2** a travelling representative of a business firm who tries to obtain orders for his or her firm's products

traverse VERB to go across, pass through ▸ NOUN **1** something that crosses or lies across **2** a movement across a rock face etc by a climber **3** a zigzag track of a ship

travesty NOUN (*plural* **travesties**) a poor or ridiculous imitation: *a travesty of justice*

trawl VERB to fish by dragging a trawl along the bottom of the sea ▸ NOUN a wide-mouthed, bag-shaped net

trawler NOUN a boat used for trawling

tray NOUN a flat piece of wood, metal, etc with a low edge, for carrying dishes

treacherous ADJECTIVE **1** likely to betray **2** dangerous: *treacherous road conditions* > **treacherously** ADVERB

treachery NOUN (*plural* **treacheries**) the act of betraying those who have trusted you

treacle NOUN a thick, dark syrup produced from sugar when it is being refined

tread VERB (**treading, trod, trodden**) **1** to walk on or along **2** (**tread on**) to put your foot on (something) **3** to crush, trample under foot: *treading mud into the carpet* ▸ NOUN **1** a step **2** a way of walking **3** the part of a tyre which touches the ground **tread on someone's toes** to offend or upset them **tread water** to keep yourself afloat in an upright position by moving your arms and legs

treadmill NOUN **1** *history* a mill turned by the weight of people who were made to walk on steps fixed round a big wheel **2** any tiring, routine work

treason NOUN disloyalty to your own country or its government, eg by giving away its secrets to an enemy

treasonable ADJECTIVE consisting of, or involving, treason

treasure NOUN **1** a store of money, gold, jewels, etc **2** anything of great value or highly prized ▸ VERB **1** to value greatly **2** to keep carefully because of its personal value: *She treasures the mirror her mother left her*

treasurer NOUN someone who has charge of the money of a club

treasure-trove NOUN treasure or money found hidden, the owner of which is unknown

treasury NOUN (*plural* **treasuries**) **1** (**Treasury**) the part of a government which has charge of the country's money **2** a store of valued items, eg a book containing popular poems

treat VERB **1** to deal with, handle, act towards: *I was treated very well in prison* **2** to try to cure (someone) of a disease **3** to try to cure (a disease) **4** to write or speak about **5** to buy (someone) a meal, drink, etc **6** to try to arrange (a peace treaty etc) with ▶ NOUN something special (eg an outing) that gives much pleasure: *They went to the theatre as a treat*

treatment NOUN **1** the act of treating (eg a disease) **2** remedy, medicine: *a new treatment for cancer* **3** the way in which someone or something is dealt with: *rough treatment*

treaty NOUN (*plural* **treaties**) an agreement made between countries

treble ADJECTIVE **1** three times or three times normal: *wood of treble thickness* **2** high in pitch: *treble note* ▶ VERB to become three times as great ▶ NOUN **1** the highest part in singing **2** a child who sings the treble part of a song

treble clef NOUN, *music* a sign (𝄞) at the beginning of a written piece of music placing the note G on the second line of the stave

tree NOUN **1** the largest kind of plant with a thick, firm wooden stem, and branches some distance from the ground **2** anything like a tree in shape

trek NOUN **1** a long or wearisome journey **2** *old* a journey by wagon ▶ VERB (**trekking, trekked**) **1** to make a long hard journey **2** *old* to make a journey by wagon

tremble VERB **1** to shake with cold, fear, weakness **2** to feel fear (for another person's safety etc) ▶ NOUN **1** the act of trembling **2** a fit of trembling

tremendous ADJECTIVE **1** very great or strong **2** *informal* very good, excellent

tremor NOUN a shaking or quivering: *a tremor in his voice*

tremulous ADJECTIVE **1** shaking **2** showing fear: *a tremulous voice*

trench NOUN (*plural* **trenches**) a long narrow ditch dug in the ground (eg by soldiers as a protection against enemy fire) ▶ VERB to dig a trench in

trenchcoat NOUN a kind of waterproof overcoat with a belt

trend NOUN a general direction: *the trend of events*

trendy ADJECTIVE (**trendier, trendiest**) *informal* of clothes, clubs, music, etc: fashionable

trepidation NOUN fear, nervousness

trespass VERB **1** to go illegally on private land etc **2** (**trespass on**) to intrude upon (someone's time,

A B C D E F G H I J K L M N O P Q R S T U V W X Y Z

privacy, etc) **3** to sin ▸NOUN (*plural* **trespasses**) the act of trespassing

trespasser NOUN someone who trespasses

tress NOUN (*plural* **tresses**) **1** a lock of hair **2** (**tresses**) hair, especially long

trestle NOUN a wooden support with legs, used for holding up a table, platform, etc

tri- PREFIX three: *triangle/tricycle*

ⓘ Comes from Latin *tres* and Greek *treis*, both meaning 'three'

triad NOUN *music* a chord of three notes played together

trial NOUN **1** the act of testing or trying (eg something new) **2** a test **3** the judging (of a prisoner) in a court of law **4** suffering **on trial 1** being tried (especially in a court of law) **2** for the purpose of trying out: *goods sent on trial* **3** being tested: *I'm still on trial with the company* **trial and error** the trying of various methods or choices until the right one is found

triangle NOUN **1** a figure with three sides and three angles: △ **2** a triangular metal musical instrument, played by striking with a small rod

triangular ADJECTIVE having the shape of a triangle

triangular number NOUN, *maths* **1** a number that can be shown as a triangular array of dots with the number of dots in each line decreasing by 1 **2** a number in the series 0, 1, 3, 6, 10, 15, etc, which is formed by adding 1 to the first number in the series, 2 to the second number in the series, and so on

triathlon NOUN a sporting contest consisting of three events, often swimming, running and cycling

tribal ADJECTIVE belonging to or done by a tribe or tribes: *tribal warfare*

tribe NOUN **1** a people who are all descended from the same ancestor **2** a group of families, especially of a wandering people ruled by a chief

tribesman *or* **tribeswoman** NOUN someone who belongs to a particular tribe

tribulation NOUN great hardship or sorrow

tribunal NOUN **1** a group of people appointed to give judgement, especially on an appeal **2** a court of justice

tribune NOUN, *history* a high official elected by the people in ancient Rome

tributary NOUN (*plural* **tributaries**) **1** a stream that flows into a river or other stream **2** someone who gives money as a tribute

tribute NOUN **1** an expression, in word or deed, of praise, thanks, admiration, etc: *a warm tribute to his courage* **2** money paid regularly by one nation or ruler to another in return for protection or peace

trice NOUN: **in a trice** in a very short time

triceps NOUN a muscle at the back of the arm that straightens the elbow

trick NOUN **1** a cunning or skilful action to puzzle, amuse, etc **2** in card games, the cards picked up by the winner when each player has played a card ▸ADJECTIVE meant to deceive: *trick photography* ▸VERB to cheat by some quick or cunning action

trickery NOUN cheating

trickle VERB **1** to flow in small amounts **2** to arrive or leave slowly and gradually: *Replies are trickling in* ▸NOUN a slow, gradual flow

trickster NOUN someone who deceives by tricks

tricky ADJECTIVE (**trickier, trickiest**) not easy to do

tricolour NOUN a three-coloured flag, especially that of France or of Ireland

tricycle NOUN a three-wheeled bicycle

tried *past form* of **try**

triennial ADJECTIVE **1** lasting for three years **2** happening every third year

tries *see* **try**

trifle NOUN **1** anything of little value **2** a small amount **3** a pudding of whipped cream, sponge cake, sherry, etc ▸VERB **trifle with 1** to treat (someone) without sufficient respect: *in no mood to be trifled with* **2** to amuse yourself in an idle way (with): *He trifled with her affections*

trifling ADJECTIVE very small in value or amount

trigger NOUN a small lever on a gun which, when pulled with the finger, causes the bullet to be fired ▸VERB (often **trigger off**) to start, be the cause of, an important event, chain of events, etc

trigonometry NOUN the branch of mathematics which has to do chiefly with the relationship between the sides and angles of triangles

trill VERB to sing, play or utter in a quivering or bird-like way ▸NOUN a trilled sound; in music, a rapid repeating of two notes several times

trillion NOUN **1** a million million millions **2** (originally *US*) a million millions

trilogy NOUN (*plural* **trilogies**) a group of three related plays, novels, etc by the same author, meant to be seen or read as a whole

trim VERB (**trimming, trimmed**) **1** to clip the edges or ends of: *trim the hedge* **2** to arrange (sails, cargo) so that a boat is ready for sailing **3** to decorate (eg a hat) ▸NOUN **1** the act of trimming **2** dress: *hunting trim* ▸ADJECTIVE (**trimmer, trimmest**) tidy, in good order, neat **in good trim 1** in good order **2** fit

trimming NOUN **1** a decoration added to a dress, cake, etc **2** a piece of cloth, hair, etc cut off while trimming

trinity NOUN **1** a group of three **2** *Christianity* **3** the union of Father, Son and Holy Ghost in one God

trinket NOUN a small ornament (especially one of little value)

trio NOUN (*plural* **trios**) **1** three people or things **2** *music* a piece of music for three singers or players

trip VERB (**tripping, tripped**) **1** (often **trip up**) to stumble, fall over **2** to move with short, light steps **3** (**trip up**) to make a mistake ▸NOUN **1** a journey for pleasure or business **2** a light short step

tripartite ADJECTIVE **1** in or having three parts **2** of an agreement: between three countries

tripe NOUN **1** part of the stomach of the cow or sheep used as food **2** *informal* rubbish, nonsense

triple ADJECTIVE **1** made up of three **2** three times as large (as something else) ▸ VERB to make or become three times as large

triplet NOUN **1** one of three children or animals born of the same mother at one time **2** three rhyming lines in a poem **3** *music* a group of three notes played in the time of two

triplicate NOUN: **in triplicate** in three copies

tripod NOUN a three-legged stand (especially for a camera)

triptych (*pronounced* **trip**-tik) NOUN three painted panels forming a whole work of art

trisect VERB to cut into three

trisection NOUN trisecting, dividing into three parts

trite ADJECTIVE of a remark: used so often that it has little force or meaning

triumph NOUN **1** a great success or victory **2** celebration after a success: *ride in triumph through the streets* ▸ VERB **1** to win a victory **2** to rejoice openly because of a victory

triumphant ADJECTIVE victorious; showing joy because of, or celebrating, triumph
> **triumphantly** ADVERB

trivia PLURAL NOUN unimportant matters or details

trivial ADJECTIVE of very little importance

triviality NOUN (*plural* **trivialities**) **1** something unimportant **2** trivialness

trivialness NOUN the state of being trivial

trod *past tense* of **tread**

troglodyte NOUN a cave-dweller

trojan NOUN, *computing* a type of computer virus

troll NOUN a mythological creature, giant or dwarf, who lives in a cave

trolley NOUN (*plural* **trolleys**) **1** a small cart (eg as used by porters at railway stations) **2** a supermarket basket on wheels **3** a hospital bed on wheels for transporting patients **4** a table on wheels, used for serving tea etc

trombone NOUN a brass wind instrument with a sliding tube which changes the notes

troop NOUN **1** a collection of people or animals **2** (**troops**) soldiers **3** a unit in cavalry etc ▸ VERB **1** to gather in numbers **2** to move as a group: *They all trooped out* **troop the colours** to carry a regiment's flag past the lined-up soldiers of the regiment

trooper NOUN a private soldier, especially one in a cavalry unit

trophy NOUN (*plural* **trophies**) **1** something taken from an enemy and kept in memory of the victory **2** a prize such as a silver cup won in a sports competition etc

tropic NOUN **1** either of two imaginary circles running round the earth at about 23° north (**tropic of Cancer**) or south (**tropic of Capricorn**) of the equator **2** (**tropics**) the hot regions between these circles ▶ADJECTIVE of the tropics

tropical ADJECTIVE **1** relating to or originating in the tropics: *tropical fish/tropical fruit* **2** of climate: very hot and wet

tropism NOUN, *biology* growth of a plant or movement of an animal towards or away from light, heat etc

trot VERB (**trotting, trotted**) **1** of a horse: to run with short, high steps **2** of a person: to run slowly with short steps **3** to make (a horse) trot ▶NOUN the pace of a horse or person when trotting

trotters PLURAL NOUN the feet of pigs or sheep, especially when used as food

trouble VERB **1** to cause worry or sorrow to **2** to cause inconvenience to **3** to make an effort, bother (to): *I didn't trouble to ring him* ▶NOUN **1** worry, uneasiness **2** difficulty; disturbance **3** something which causes worry, difficulty, etc **4** illness, weakness or mechanical failure: *heart trouble/engine trouble* **5** care and effort put into doing something

troubleshooter NOUN someone whose job is to solve difficulties (eg in a firm's business activities)

troublesome ADJECTIVE causing difficulty or inconvenience

trough NOUN **1** a long, open container for holding animals' food and water **2** an area of low atmospheric pressure **3** a dip between two sea waves

troupe (*pronounced* troop) NOUN a company of actors, dancers, etc

trouser ADJECTIVE of a pair of trousers: *trouser leg*

trousers PLURAL NOUN an outer garment for the lower part of the body which covers each leg separately

trousseau (*pronounced* **troos**-oh) NOUN (*plural* **trousseaux** *or* **trousseaus** – *both pronounced* **troos**-ohz) the clothes, linen, etc a bride used to collect for her married life

trout NOUN (*plural* **trout** *or* **trouts**) a freshwater or sea fish, used as food

trowel NOUN **1** a small hand-held spade used in gardening **2** a similar tool with a flat blade, used for spreading mortar

troy weight NOUN a system of weights for weighing gold, gems, etc

truancy NOUN the practice of being absent from school without permission

truant NOUN someone who stays away from school etc without permission **play truant** to stay away from school, work, etc without permission

truce NOUN a rest from fighting or quarrelling agreed to by both sides

truck NOUN **1** a wagon for carrying goods on a railway **2** a strong lorry for carrying heavy loads **have no truck with** to refuse to have dealings with

trucker NOUN, *US* a lorry driver

truculent ADJECTIVE fierce and threatening, aggressive

trudge VERB to walk with heavy steps, as if tired

true ADJECTIVE **1** of a story etc: telling of something which really happened **2** correct, not invented or wrong: *It's true that the earth is round* **3** accurate **4** faithful: *a true friend* **5** real, properly so called: *The spider is not a true insect* **6** rightful: *the true heir* **7** in the correct or intended position

truffle NOUN a round fungus found underground and much valued as a flavouring for food

truly ADVERB **1** really: *Is that truly what he said?* **2** genuinely; honestly: *I'm truly sorry* **3** completely, utterly: *a truly classless society*

trump NOUN **1** a suit having a higher value than cards of other suits **2** a card of this suit ▸ VERB to play a card which is a trump **trump up** to make up, invent **turn up trumps** to play your part well when things are difficult

trump card NOUN **1** a card which is a trump **2** something kept in reserve as a means of winning an argument etc

trumpet NOUN **1** a brass musical instrument with a clear, high-pitched tone **2** the cry of an elephant ▸ VERB **1** to announce (eg news) so that all may hear **2** to blow a trumpet **3** of elephants: to make a long, loud cry

truncate ADJECTIVE **1** to cut off at the top or end **2** to shorten
> **truncated** ADJECTIVE
> **truncation** NOUN

truncheon NOUN a short heavy staff or baton such as that used by police officers

trundle VERB to wheel or roll along

trunk NOUN **1** the main stem of a tree **2** the body (not counting the head, arms or legs) of a person or animal **3** the long nose of an elephant **4** a large box or chest for clothes etc **5** *US* the luggage compartment of a car **6** (**trunks**) short pants worn by boys and men for swimming

trunk road NOUN a main road

truss NOUN (*plural* **trusses**) **1** a bundle (eg of hay, straw) **2** a system of beams to support a bridge **3** a bandage or belt worn to support a hernia ▸ VERB **1** to bind, tie tightly (up) **2** (often **truss up**) to prepare (a bird ready for cooking) by tying up the legs and wings

trust NOUN **1** belief in the power, truth or goodness of a thing or person **2** something (eg a task or an item of value) handed over to someone in the belief that they will do it, guard it, etc **3** charge, keeping: *The child was put in my trust* **4** arrangement by which something (eg money) is given to someone for use in a particular way **5** a number of business firms working closely together ▸ VERB **1** to have faith or confidence (in) **2** to give (someone something) in the belief that they will use it well etc: *I can't trust your sister with my tennis racket* **3** to feel confident (that): *I trust that you can find your way here* **take on trust** to believe without checking or testing

trustee NOUN **1** someone who manages money or property for someone else **2** a member of a group of people managing the affairs of a company or institution

trustful *or* **trusting** ADJECTIVE ready to trust, not suspicious

trustworthy ADJECTIVE able to be trusted or depended on

trusty ADJECTIVE (**trustier, trustiest**) able to be trusted or depended on; loyal

truth NOUN **1** the state of being true **2** a true statement **3** the facts

truthful ADJECTIVE **1** telling the truth, not lying **2** of a statement: true > **truthfully** ADVERB

try VERB (**tries, trying, tried**) **1** to attempt, make an effort (to do something) **2** to test by using: *Try this new soap* **3** to test severely, strain: *You're trying my patience* **4** to attempt to use, open, etc: *I tried the door but it was locked* **5** to judge (a prisoner) in a court of law ▸ NOUN (*plural* **tries**) **1** an effort, an attempt **2** in rugby: an act of scoring by carrying the ball over the opponent's goal line and putting it down **try on** to put on (clothing) to see if it fits etc **try out** to test by using

trying ADJECTIVE hard to bear; testing

tsar *or* **tzar** *or* **czar** (*pronounced* zar) NOUN, *history* the emperor of Russia before the Revolution

tsarina *or* **tzarina** *or* **czarina** (*pronounced* za-**ree**-na) NOUN, *history* **1** the wife of a tsar **2** an empress of Russia before the Revolution

tsetse *or* **tsetse fly** (*pronounced* **tset**-si) NOUN an African biting fly which spreads dangerous diseases

T-shirt *another spelling* of **tee-shirt**

tsunami NOUN a very large wave caused by an underwater earthquake or volcanic eruption

tub NOUN **1** a round wooden container used for washing etc **2** a bath

tuba NOUN a large brass musical instrument giving a low note

tubby ADJECTIVE (**tubbier, tubbiest**) fat and round

tube NOUN **1** a hollow, cylindrical object through which liquid may pass **2** an organ of this kind in humans, animals, etc **3** a container from which something may be squeezed **4** an underground railway system, especially the one in London, or one of its trains **5** a cathode ray tube

tuber NOUN the swollen underground stem of a plant (eg a potato), where food is stored

tuberculosis NOUN an infectious disease affecting the lungs

tubing NOUN a length or lengths of tube

tubular ADJECTIVE shaped like a tube

TUC ABBREVIATION Trades Union Congress

tuck NOUN **1** a fold stitched in a piece of cloth **2** *informal* sweets, cakes, etc ▸ VERB **1** to gather (cloth) together into a fold **2** to fold or push (into or under a place): *tucked the envelope in her pocket* **tuck in** *informal* to eat with enjoyment or greedily **tuck someone in** *or* **up** to push bedclothes closely round (someone in bed)

Tuesday NOUN the third day of the week
🛈 After *Tiw*, the Norse god of war and the sky

tuft NOUN a bunch or clump of grass, hair, etc

tug VERB (**tugging, tugged**) **1** to pull hard **2** to pull along ▸NOUN **1** a strong pull **2** a tugboat

tugboat NOUN a small but powerful ship used for towing larger ones

tug-of-war NOUN a contest in which two teams, holding the ends of a strong rope, pull against each other

tuition NOUN **1** teaching **2** private coaching or teaching

tulip NOUN a type of plant with cup-shaped flowers grown from a bulb
🛈 Based on a Persian word for 'turban', because of the similarity in shape

tumble VERB **1** to fall or come down suddenly and violently **2** to roll, toss (about) **3** to do acrobatic tricks **4** to throw into disorder ▸NOUN **1** a fall **2** a confused state **tumble to something** to understand it suddenly

tumbledown ADJECTIVE falling to pieces

tumbler NOUN **1** a large drinking glass **2** an acrobat

tummy NOUN (*plural* **tummies**), *informal* the stomach

tumour NOUN an abnormal growth on or in the body

tumult NOUN **1** a great noise made by a crowd **2** excitement, agitation

tumultuous ADJECTIVE with great noise or confusion: *a tumultuous welcome*

tun NOUN a large cask, especially for wine

tuna NOUN (*plural* **tuna** *or* **tunas**) a large sea fish, used as food (*also called*: **tunny**)

tundra NOUN a level treeless plain in Arctic regions

tune NOUN **1** notes put together to form a melody **2** the music of a song ▸VERB **1** to put (a musical instrument) in tune **2** to adjust a radio set to a particular station **3** (sometimes **tune up**) to improve the working of an engine **change your tune** to change your opinions, attitudes, etc **in tune 1** of a musical instrument: having each note adjusted to agree with the others or with the notes of other instruments **2** of a voice: agreeing with the notes of other voices or instruments **3** in agreement (with): *in tune with public opinion* **to the tune of** to the sum of: *out of pocket to the tune of £300*

tuneful ADJECTIVE having a pleasant or recognizable tune
> **tunefully** ADVERB

tungsten NOUN, *chemistry* an element, a grey metal

tunic NOUN **1** a soldier's or police officer's jacket **2** *history* a loose garment reaching to the knees, worn in ancient Greece and Rome **3** a similar modern garment: *gym tunic*

tuning fork NOUN a steel fork which, when struck, gives a note of a certain pitch

tunnel NOUN an underground passage (eg for a railway train) ▸VERB (**tunnelling, tunnelled**) **1** to make a tunnel **2** of an animal: to burrow

turban NOUN **1** a long piece of cloth wound round the head, worn by some Muslim and Sikh men **2** a kind of hat resembling this

turbine NOUN an engine with curved blades, turned by the action of water, steam, hot air, etc

turbo- PREFIX using a turbine engine

ⓘ Comes from Latin *turbo* meaning 'a spinning-top'

turbot NOUN a type of large flat sea fish, used as food

turbulence NOUN irregular movement of air currents, especially when affecting the flight of aircraft

turbulent ADJECTIVE **1** disturbed, in a restless state **2** likely to cause a disturbance or riot

turd NOUN a lump of dung

tureen NOUN a large dish for holding soup at table

turf NOUN **1** grass and the soil below it **2** (**the turf**) the world of horse-racing ▸ VERB to cover with turf **turf out** *informal* to throw out

turgid ADJECTIVE **1** swollen **2** of language: sounding grand but meaning little, pompous

turkey NOUN (*plural* **turkeys**) a large farmyard bird, used as food

turmoil NOUN a state of wild, confused movement or disorder

turn VERB **1** to go round: *wheels turning* **2** to face or go in the opposite direction: *turned and walked away* **3** to change direction: *The road turns sharply to the left* **4** to direct (eg attention) **5** (**turn on**) to move, swing, etc on: *The door turns on its hinges* **6** of milk: to go sour **7** to become: *His hair turned white* **8** of leaves: to change colour **9** to shape in a lathe **10** to pass (the age of): *She must have turned 40* ▸ NOUN **1** the act of turning **2** a point where someone may change direction, eg a road junction: *Take the first turn on the left* **3** a bend (eg in a road) **4** a spell of duty: *your turn to wash the dishes* **5** an act (eg in a circus or show) **6** a short stroll: *a turn along the beach* **7** a fit of dizziness, shock, etc **8** requirement: *This will serve our turn* **by turns** *or* **in turn** one after another in a regular order **do someone a good (or bad) turn** to act helpfully (or unhelpfully) towards someone **to a turn** exactly, perfectly: *cooked to a turn* **turn against** to become hostile to **turn down 1** to say no to, refuse (eg an offer, a request) **2** to reduce, lessen (heat, volume of sound, etc) **turn in 1** to go to bed **2** to hand over to those in authority: *The bank robber turned himself in* **turn off 1** to stop the flow of (a tap) **2** to switch off the power for (a television etc) **turn on 1** to set running (eg water from a tap) **2** to switch on power for (a television etc) **3** to depend (on): *The whole argument turns on a single point* **4** to become angry with (someone) unexpectedly: *She suddenly turned on me* **5** *slang* to arouse sexually **turn out 1** to make to leave, drive out **2** to make, produce **3** to empty: *turn out your pockets* **4** of a crowd:

A B C D E F G H I J K L M N O P Q R S T U V W X Y Z

to come out, gather for a special purpose: *Thousands turned out to welcome him* **5** to switch off (a light) **6** to prove (to be): *He turned out to be right* **turn to 1** to set to work **2** to go to for help etc **turn up 1** to appear, arrive **2** to be found **3** to increase (eg heat, volume of sound, etc)

ⓘ Comes from Latin *tornare* meaning 'to turn in a lathe'

turncoat NOUN someone who betrays their party, principles, etc

turning NOUN **1** the act of turning **2** a point where one road etc joins another **3** the act of shaping in a lathe

turning-point NOUN a crucial point of change

turnip NOUN a plant with a large round root used as a vegetable

turnover NOUN **1** rate of change or replacement (eg of workers in a firm etc) **2** the total amount of sales made by a firm during a certain time

turnstile NOUN a gate which turns, allowing only one person to pass at a time

turntable NOUN **1** a revolving platform for turning a railway engine round **2** the revolving part of a record-player on which the record rests

turpentine NOUN an oil from certain trees used for mixing paints, cleaning paint brushes, etc

turquoise NOUN a greenish-blue precious stone

ⓘ Literally 'Turkish stone', because first found in Turkestan

turret NOUN **1** a small tower on a castle or other building **2** a structure for supporting guns on a warship

turtle NOUN a kind of large tortoise which lives in water **turn turtle** of a boat etc: to turn upside down, capsize

turtledove NOUN a type of dove noted for its sweet, soft song

tusk NOUN a large tooth (one of a pair) sticking out from the mouth of certain animals (eg an elephant, a walrus)

tussle NOUN a struggle ▶VERB to struggle, compete

tutor NOUN **1** a teacher of students in a university etc **2** a teacher employed privately to teach individual pupils ▶VERB to teach

tutorial ADJECTIVE relating to a tutor ▶NOUN a meeting for study or discussion between tutor and students

tutu NOUN a ballet dancer's short, stiff, spreading skirt

tuxedo NOUN (*plural* **tuxedos** *or* **tuxedoes**), *US* a dinner-jacket

TV ABBREVIATION television

twain NOUN, *old* two **in twain** *old* in two, apart

twang NOUN **1** a tone of voice in which the words seem to come through the nose **2** a sound like that of a tightly stretched string being plucked ▶VERB to make such a sound

tweak VERB to pull with a sudden jerk, twitch ▶NOUN a sudden jerk or pull

tweed NOUN **1** a woollen cloth with a rough surface **2** (**tweeds**) clothes made of this cloth ▶ADJECTIVE made of tweed

tweezers PLURAL NOUN small pincers for pulling out hairs, holding small things, etc

twelfth ADJECTIVE the last of a series of twelve ▶NOUN one of twelve equal parts

twelve NOUN the number 12 ▶ADJECTIVE 12 in number

twentieth ADJECTIVE the last of a series of twenty ▶NOUN one of twenty equal parts

twenty NOUN the number 20 ▶ADJECTIVE 20 in number

twice ADVERB two times

twiddle VERB to play with, twirl idly **twiddle your thumbs 1** to turn your thumbs around one another **2** to have nothing to do

twig NOUN a small branch of a tree

twilight NOUN **1** the faint light between sunset and night, or before sunrise **2** the time just before or after the peak of something: *the twilight of the dictatorship*

twill NOUN a kind of strong cloth with a ridged appearance

twin NOUN **1** one of two children or animals born of the same mother at the same birth **2** one of two things exactly the same ▶ADJECTIVE **1** born at the same birth **2** very like another **3** made up of two parts or things which are alike

twine NOUN a strong kind of string made of twisted threads ▶VERB **1** to wind or twist together **2** to wind (about or around something)

twinge NOUN a sudden, sharp pain

twinkle VERB **1** of a star etc: to shine with light which seems to vary in brightness **2** of eyes: to shine with amusement etc > **twinkle** *or* **twinkling** NOUN the act or state of twinkling **in a twinkling** in an instant

twirl VERB **1** to turn or spin round quickly and lightly **2** to turn round and round with the fingers: *twirling a baton* ▶NOUN a spin round and round

twist VERB **1** to wind (threads) together **2** to wind round or about something **3** to make (eg a rope) into a coil **4** to bend out of shape **5** to bend or wrench painfully (eg your ankle) **6** to make (eg facts) appear to have a meaning which is really false ▶NOUN **1** the act of twisting **2** a painful wrench **3** something twisted: *a twist of tissue paper*

twister NOUN, *informal Brit* a dishonest and unreliable person

twitch VERB **1** to pull with a sudden light jerk **2** to jerk slightly and suddenly: *A muscle in his face twitched* ▶NOUN **1** a sudden jerk **2** a muscle spasm

twitter NOUN **1** high, rapidly repeated sounds, as are made by small birds **2** slight nervous excitement ▶VERB **1** of a bird: to make a series of high quivering notes **2** of a person: to talk continuously

two NOUN the number 2 ▶ADJECTIVE 2 in number

ℹ Comes from Old English *twa* meaning 'two'

two-dimensional ADJECTIVE having height and width, but not depth (*short form* **2-D**)

two-faced ADJECTIVE deceitful, insincere

A B C D E F G H I J K L M N O P Q R S T U V W X Y Z

twofold ADJECTIVE & ADVERB (by) twice as much

two-time VERB to have a love affair with two people at the same time

tycoon NOUN a business man of great wealth and power
ⓘ Based on a Japanese title for a warlord

tympani *another spelling of* **timpani**

type NOUN **1** kind **2** an example which has all the usual characteristics of its kind **3** a small metal block with a raised letter or sign, used for printing **4** a set of these **5** printed lettering ▸ VERB **1** to print with a typewriter **2** to use a typewriter **3** to identify or classify as a particular type

typecast VERB to give (an actor) parts very similar in character

typeface NOUN a set of printed letters and characters in a particular style

typescript NOUN a typed script for a play etc

typewriter NOUN a machine with keys which, when struck, print letters on a sheet of paper

typhoid NOUN an infectious disease caused by germs in infected food or drinking water

typhoon NOUN a violent tropical windstorm originating in the Pacific

typhus NOUN a dangerous fever carried by lice and characterized by fever, severe headache and a rash

typical ADJECTIVE having or showing the usual characteristics: *a typical Irishman/typical of her to be late* > **typically** ADVERB

typify VERB (**typifies, typifying, typified**) to be a good example of: *typifying the English abroad*

typographical ADJECTIVE relating to or involving printing or typography

typography NOUN the use of type for printing

tyrannical *or* **tyrannous** ADJECTIVE like a tyrant, cruel

tyrannize *or* **tyrannise** VERB to act as a tyrant; rule over harshly

tyranny NOUN (*plural* **tyrannies**) the rule of a tyrant

tyrant NOUN a ruler who governs cruelly and unjustly

tyre *or US* **tire** NOUN a thick rubber cover round a motor or cycle wheel

Uu

ubiquitous (*pronounced* yoo-**bik**-wit-*us*) ADJECTIVE **1** being everywhere at once **2** found everywhere

ubiquity (*pronounced* yoo-**bik**-wit-i) NOUN existence everywhere

udder NOUN a bag-like part of a cow, goat, etc with teats which supply milk

UFO (*pronounced* yoo-ef-**oh** *or* **yoo**-foh) ABBREVIATION unidentified flying object

ugly ADJECTIVE (**uglier, ugliest**) **1** unpleasant to look at or hear: *ugly sound* **2** threatening, dangerous: *gave me an ugly look* **ugly duckling** an unattractive or unappreciated person who later turns into a beauty, success, etc

UHT ABBREVIATION **1** ultra-heat treated **2** ultra high temperature

ukulele *or* **ukelele** (*pronounced* yook-*e*-**lei**-li) NOUN a small, stringed musical instrument played like a banjo

[i] A Hawaiian word meaning literally 'jumping flea'

ulcer NOUN an open sore on the skin or the mucous membrane inside the body

ulterior ADJECTIVE beyond what is admitted or seen: *ulterior motive*

ultimate ADJECTIVE last, final

ultimately ADVERB finally, in the end

ultimatum NOUN a final demand sent with a threat to break off discussion, declare war, etc if it is not met

ultra- PREFIX **1** very: *ultra-careful* **2** beyond: *ultramicroscopic*

[i] Comes from Latin *ultra* meaning 'beyond'

ultramarine ADJECTIVE of a deep blue colour

ultrasound NOUN **1** a sound whose frequency is too high to be heard by humans **2** the use of ultrasound waves to produce images of the inside of the body, to detect flaws in metals and to clean industrial tools

> **ultrasonic** ADJECTIVE

ultraviolet ADJECTIVE having rays of slightly shorter wavelength than visible light

umbilical cord NOUN a tube connecting an unborn mammal to its mother through the placenta

umbrage NOUN a feeling of offence or hurt: *took umbrage at my suggestion*

umbrella NOUN an object made up of a folding covered framework on a stick which protects against rain
ⓘ Literally 'little shadow' and originally used to refer to a sunshade

umlaut (*pronounced* **oom**-lowt) NOUN a character (¨) placed over a letter to modify its pronunciation

umpire NOUN **1** a sports official who sees that a game is played according to the rules **2** a judge asked to settle a dispute ▸ VERB to act as an umpire

umpteen ADJECTIVE many, lots
ⓘ Originally *umpty*, a signaller's slang term for a dash in Morse code

UN ABBREVIATION United Nations

un- PREFIX **1** not: *unequal* **2** (with verbs) used to show the reversal of an action: *unfasten*
ⓘ Comes from Old English prefixes *un-* meaning 'not' and *on-* meaning 'against'

unabashed ADJECTIVE shameless, blatant

unable ADJECTIVE lacking enough strength, power, skill, etc

unaccountable ADJECTIVE not able to be explained > **unaccountably** ADVERB: *She was feeling unaccountably depressed*

unaccustomed ADJECTIVE not used (to)

unadulterated ADJECTIVE pure, not mixed with anything else

unanimity (*pronounced* yoo-na-**nim**-it-i) NOUN unanimous agreement

unanimous (*pronounced* yoo-**nan**-im-*us*) ADJECTIVE **1** all of the same opinion: *We were unanimous* **2** agreed to by all: *a unanimous decision* > **unanimously** ADVERB: *He was elected unanimously*

unapproachable ADJECTIVE unfriendly and stiff in manner

unarmed ADJECTIVE not armed

unassuming ADJECTIVE modest

unattached ADJECTIVE **1** not attached **2** single, not married or having a partner

unaware ADJECTIVE not knowing, ignorant (of): *unaware of the danger*

unawares ADVERB **1** unexpectedly or without warning: *He caught me unawares* **2** unintentionally

unbalanced ADJECTIVE mad; lacking balance: *unbalanced view*

unbearable ADJECTIVE too painful or bad to be endured

unbeliever NOUN someone who does not follow a certain religion

unbending ADJECTIVE severe

unbridled ADJECTIVE not kept under control: *unbridled fury*

unburden VERB: **unburden yourself** to tell your secrets or problems to someone else

uncalled ADJECTIVE: **uncalled for** quite unnecessary: *Your remarks were uncalled for*

uncanny ADJECTIVE strange, mysterious > **uncannily** ADVERB

uncared ADJECTIVE: **uncared for** not looked after properly

unceremonious ADJECTIVE informal, offhand

uncertain ADJECTIVE **1** not certain, doubtful **2** not definitely known **3** of weather: changeable

uncharted ADJECTIVE **1** not shown on a map or chart **2** little known

uncle NOUN **1** the brother of your father or mother **2** the husband of your father's or mother's sister

unclean ADJECTIVE dirty, impure

uncoil VERB to unwind

uncomfortable ADJECTIVE not comfortable

uncommon ADJECTIVE not common, strange

uncommonly ADVERB very: *uncommonly talented*

uncompromising ADJECTIVE not willing to give in or make concessions to others

unconditional ADJECTIVE with no conditions attached; absolute: *our unconditional support*

unconscious ADJECTIVE **1** senseless, stunned (eg by an accident) **2** not aware (of) **3** not recognized by the person concerned: *unconscious prejudice against women* ▶NOUN (**the unconscious**) the deepest level of the mind

uncouth ADJECTIVE **1** clumsy, awkward **2** rude

uncover VERB **1** to remove a cover from **2** to disclose: *uncover a plot*

undaunted ADJECTIVE fearless; not discouraged

undecided ADJECTIVE not yet decided

undeniable ADJECTIVE not able to be denied, clearly true

under PREPOSITION **1** directly below or beneath: *under the table* **2** less than: *costing under £5* **3** within the authority or command of: *under General Montgomery* **4** going through, suffering: *under attack* **5** having, using: *under a false name* **6** in accordance with: *under our agreement* ▶ADVERB in or to a lower position, condition, etc **go under 1** to sink beneath the surface of water **2** to go bankrupt, go out of business **under way** in motion, started

[1] **under** is an Old English word

under- PREFIX **1** below, beneath: *underachieve/underarm* **2** lower in position or rank: *underdog/underling* **3** too little: *underdeveloped/underrate*

underachieve VERB to achieve less than your potential

under-age ADJECTIVE of a person: below an age required by law, too young: *I can't serve you: you're under-age*

underarm ADVERB of bowling etc: with the arm kept below the shoulder (*compare with*: **overarm**)

undercarriage NOUN the wheels of an aeroplane and their supports

underclothes PLURAL NOUN clothes worn next to the skin under other clothes

undercover ADJECTIVE acting or done in secret: *an undercover agent* (= a spy)

undercurrent NOUN **1** a flow or movement under the surface **2** a half-hidden feeling or tendency: *an undercurrent of despair in her voice*

undercut VERB to sell at a lower price than someone else

underdeveloped ADJECTIVE **1** not fully grown **2** of a country: lacking modern agricultural and industrial

A B C D E F G H I J K L M N O P Q R S T U V W X Y Z

systems, and with a low standard of living

underdog NOUN the weaker side, or the loser in any conflict or fight

underdone ADJECTIVE of food: not quite cooked

underestimate VERB to estimate at less than the real worth, value, etc

underfoot ADJECTIVE under the feet

undergo VERB **1** to suffer, endure **2** to receive (eg as medical treatment)

undergraduate NOUN a university student who has not yet passed final examinations

underground ADJECTIVE **1** below the surface of the ground **2** secret, covert ▸NOUN a railway which runs in a tunnel beneath the surface of the ground

undergrowth NOUN shrubs or low plants growing amongst trees

underhand ADJECTIVE sly, deceitful

underlie VERB to be the hidden cause or source of

underline VERB **1** to draw a line under **2** to stress the importance of, emphasize

underling NOUN someone of lower rank

underlying ADJECTIVE **1** lying under or beneath **2** fundamental, basic: *the underlying causes*

undermine VERB to do damage to, weaken gradually (health, authority, etc)

underneath ADVERB & PREPOSITION in a lower position (than), beneath: *Look underneath the table/wearing a jacket underneath his coat*

undernourished ADJECTIVE not well nourished

underpants PLURAL NOUN underwear covering the buttocks and upper legs

underpass NOUN a road passing under another one

underpay VERB to pay too little

underpin VERB to support from beneath, prop up

underprivileged ADJECTIVE not having normal living standards or rights

undersell VERB **1** to sell for less than the true value **2** to sell for less than someone else

undersigned NOUN: (**the undersigned**) the people whose names are written at the end of a letter or statement

undersized ADJECTIVE smaller than the usual or required size

underskirt NOUN a thin skirt worn under another skirt

understand VERB **1** to see the meaning of **2** to appreciate the reasons for: *I don't understand your behaviour* **3** to have a thorough knowledge of: *Do you understand economics?* **4** to have the impression that: *I understood that you weren't coming* **5** to take for granted as part of an agreement

understandable ADJECTIVE **1** reasonable, natural or normal: *He reacted with understandable fury* **2** capable of being understood: *His speech was barely understandable*

understanding NOUN **1** the ability to see the full meaning of something **2** an agreement **3** condition: *on the* *understanding that we both pay half* **4** appreciation of other people's feelings, difficulties, etc ▶ ADJECTIVE able to understand other people's feelings, sympathetic

understate VERB to represent something as being less important or smaller than it really is

understatement NOUN a statement which does not give the whole truth, making less of certain details than is actually the case

understudy NOUN (*plural* **understudies**) an actor who learns the part of another actor and is able to take their place if necessary

undertake VERB **1** to promise (to do something) **2** to take upon yourself (a task, duty, etc)

undertaker NOUN someone whose job is to organize funerals

undertaking NOUN **1** something which is being attempted or done **2** a promise **3** the business of an undertaker

under-the-counter ADJECTIVE hidden from customers' sight; illegal

undertone NOUN **1** a soft voice **2** a partly hidden meaning, feeling, etc: *an undertone of discontent*

undertow NOUN a current below the surface of the water which moves in a direction opposite to the surface movement

undervalue VERB to value (something) below its real worth

underwater ADJECTIVE under the surface of the water

underwear NOUN underclothes

underweight ADJECTIVE under the usual or required weight

underworld NOUN **1** the criminal world or level of society **2** the place where spirits go after death

underwrite VERB **1** to accept for insurance **2** to accept responsibility or liability for

undesirable ADJECTIVE not wanted; objectionable in some way

undeveloped ADJECTIVE not developed

undivided ADJECTIVE not split, complete, total: *undivided attention*

undo VERB **1** to unfasten (a coat, parcel, etc) **2** to cancel the effect of, reverse: *undoing all the good I did* **3** *old* to ruin, dishonour (especially a reputation): *Alas, I am undone*

undoing NOUN ruin, dishonour

undoubted ADJECTIVE not to be doubted

undoubtedly ADVERB without doubt, certainly

undreamt-of ADJECTIVE more, better, etc than could have been imagined: *undreamt-of success*

undress VERB to take your clothes off

undue ADJECTIVE too much, more than is necessary: *undue expense*

undulate VERB **1** to move as waves do **2** to have a rolling, wavelike appearance > **undulating** ADJECTIVE > **undulation** NOUN

unduly ADVERB excessively; unreasonably: *unduly worried*

undying ADJECTIVE unending, never fading: *undying love*

unearth VERB to bring or dig out from the earth, or from a place of hiding

A B C D E F G H I J K L M N O P Q R S T U V W X Y Z

unearthly ADJECTIVE **1** strange, as if not of this world **2** *informal* absurd, especially absurdly early: *at this unearthly hour*

uneasy ADJECTIVE anxious, worried > **uneasiness** NOUN

unemployed ADJECTIVE **1** without a job **2** not in use ▶NOUN (**the unemployed**) unemployed people as a group

unemployment NOUN **1** the state of being unemployed **2** the total number of unemployed people in a country

unenviable ADJECTIVE not arousing envy: *unenviable task*

unequal ADJECTIVE **1** not equal; unfair: *unequal distribution* **2** lacking enough strength or skill: *unequal to the job*

unequalled ADJECTIVE without an equal, unique

unerring ADJECTIVE always right, never making a mistake: *unerring judgement*

uneven ADJECTIVE **1** not smooth or level **2** not all of the same quality etc: *This work is very uneven*

unexceptionable ADJECTIVE not causing objections or criticism

> Do not confuse: **unexceptionable** and **unexceptional**

unexceptional ADJECTIVE not exceptional, ordinary

unexpected ADJECTIVE not expected, sudden

unfailing ADJECTIVE never failing, never likely to fail: *unfailing accuracy*

unfair ADJECTIVE not just

unfaithful ADJECTIVE **1** not true to your marriage vows **2** failing to keep promises

unfasten VERB to loosen, undo (eg a buttoned coat)

unfavourable ADJECTIVE not helpful: *unfavourable conditions for sailing*

unfeeling ADJECTIVE harsh, hard-hearted

unfit ADJECTIVE **1** not suitable **2** not good enough, or not in a suitable state (to, for): *unfit for drinking/ unfit to travel* **3** not in good physical condition: *I'm so unfit*

unfold VERB **1** to spread out **2** to give details of (a story, plan) **3** of details of a plot etc: to become known: *as the story unfolds*

unforgettable ADJECTIVE unlikely to ever be forgotten; memorable

unfortunate ADJECTIVE **1** unlucky **2** regrettable: *unfortunate turn of phrase* > **unfortunately** ADVERB

unfounded ADJECTIVE not based on fact; untrue: *Her fears proved unfounded*

unfurl VERB to unfold (eg a flag)

ungainly ADJECTIVE clumsy, awkward

ungracious ADJECTIVE rude, not polite

ungrateful ADJECTIVE not showing thanks for kindness

unguarded ADJECTIVE **1** without protection **2** thoughtless, careless: *unguarded remark*

unhappy ADJECTIVE **1** miserable, sad **2** unfortunate > **unhappily** ADVERB

unhealthy ADJECTIVE **1** not well, ill **2** harmful to health: *unhealthy climate* **3** showing signs of not being well: *unhealthy complexion*

unheard-of ADJECTIVE very unusual, unprecedented

unhinged ADJECTIVE mad, crazy

unholy ADJECTIVE **1** evil **2** outrageous

uni- PREFIX one, a single: *unilateral/unit*

🛈 Comes from Latin *unus* meaning 'one'

unicorn NOUN a mythological animal like a horse, but with one straight horn on its forehead

unification NOUN the act of unifying or the state of being unified

uniform ADJECTIVE the same in all parts or times, never varying ▶NOUN the form of clothes worn by people in the armed forces, children at a particular school, etc

uniformity NOUN sameness: *the uniformity of modern architecture*

unify VERB (**unifies, unifying, unified**) to combine into one

unilateral ADJECTIVE (compare with: **multilateral**) **1** involving or affecting one person or group out of several: *unilateral disarmament* **2** one-sided

unilateralism NOUN unilateral policy, especially the abandoning of nuclear weapons by one country, without waiting for others to do likewise

uninhibited ADJECTIVE not inhibited, unrestrained

uninitiated ADJECTIVE not knowing, ignorant

uninterested ADJECTIVE not interested

> Do not confuse with: **disinterested**. It is generally a negative thing to be **uninterested** (= bored). It is generally a positive thing to be **disinterested** (= fair), especially if you are trying to make an unbiased decision.

uninterrupted ADJECTIVE **1** continuing without a break **2** of a view: not blocked by anything

union NOUN **1** the act of joining together **2** partnership; marriage **3** countries or states joined together **4** a trade union

unionist NOUN **1** a member of a trade union **2** (**Unionist**) someone who supports the union of the countries comprising the United Kingdom

Union Jack *or* **Union flag** NOUN the flag of the United Kingdom

unique ADJECTIVE without a like or equal: *a unique sense of timing*

> Do not confuse with: **rare**. You can talk about something being **rare**, quite **rare**, very **rare**, etc. It would be incorrect, however, to describe something as 'very **unique**', since things either are or are not **unique** – there are no levels of this quality.

unisex ADJECTIVE suitable for either men or women: *a unisex hair salon*

unison NOUN **1** agreement, accord **2** exact sameness of musical pitch **in unison** all together

unit NOUN **1** a single thing, person or

group, especially when considered as part of a larger whole: *army unit/storage unit/kitchen unit* **2** a fixed amount or length used as a standard by which others are measured (eg metres, litres, centimetres, etc) **3** the number one

unitary ADJECTIVE **1** forming a unit, not divided **2** using or based on units

unite VERB **1** to join together; become one **2** to act together

united ADJECTIVE **1** in agreement about something: *united in their opposition* **2** joined together: *a united Ireland*

United Nations SINGULAR NOUN OR PLURAL NOUN (*abbrev* **UN**) an association of states formed in 1945 to promote peace and international co-operation

unit fraction NOUN, *maths* a fraction whose numerator is 1 and whose denominator is an integer that is not 0, eg 1/5

unity NOUN **1** complete agreement **2** the state of being one or a whole **3** the number one or numeral 1

universal ADJECTIVE **1** relating to the universe **2** relating to, or coming from, all people: *universal criticism* > **universally** ADVERB (meaning 2): *universally acclaimed*

universe NOUN all known things, including the earth and planets

university NOUN (*plural* **universities**) a college which teaches a wide range of subjects to a high level, and which awards degrees to students who pass its examinations

unkempt ADJECTIVE untidy

unkind ADJECTIVE not kind; harsh, cruel

unknown ADJECTIVE **1** not known; unfamiliar **2** not at all famous ▸ NOUN **1** a person who is not famous **2** (**the unknown**) things that are unexplained, undiscovered, etc

unleaded ADJECTIVE of petrol: not containing lead compounds

unleash VERB **1** to set free (a dog etc) **2** to let loose (eg anger)

unleavened (*pronounced* un-**lev**-*end*) ADJECTIVE of bread: not made to rise with yeast

unless CONJUNCTION if not, except in a case where: *Unless he's here soon, I'm going* (= if he's not here soon)

unlike ADJECTIVE different, not similar ▸ PREPOSITION **1** different from **2** not characteristic of: *It was unlike her not to phone*

unlikely ADJECTIVE **1** not probable: *It's unlikely that it will rain today* **2** probably not true: *an unlikely tale*

unload VERB **1** to take (the load) from: *unloading the truck/unloaded the packages* **2** to remove the charge from a gun

unlucky ADJECTIVE **1** not lucky or fortunate **2** unsuccessful > **unluckily** ADVERB

unmanly ADJECTIVE weak, cowardly

unmask VERB **1** to take a covering off **2** to show the true character of **3** to bring to light (a plot etc)

unmentionable ADJECTIVE not fit to be spoken of, scandalous, indecent

unmistakable *or*

unmistakeable ADJECTIVE very clear; impossible to confuse with any other: *unmistakable handwriting*
unmoved ADJECTIVE not affected, unsympathetic: *unmoved by my pleas*
unnatural ADJECTIVE not natural, perverted
unnecessary ADJECTIVE not necessary; avoidable
unnerve VERB to disconcert, perturb
unobtrusive ADJECTIVE not obvious or conspicuous; modest
unpack VERB to open (a piece of luggage) and remove the contents
unparalleled ADJECTIVE not having an equal, unprecedented: *unparalleled success*
unpick VERB to take out sewing stitches from
unpleasant ADJECTIVE not pleasant, nasty
unprecedented ADJECTIVE never having happened before
unprincipled ADJECTIVE without (moral) principles
unprintable ADJECTIVE not suitable to be printed; obscene
unquestionable ADJECTIVE undoubted, certain
unravel VERB (**unravelling, unravelled**) **1** to unwind, take the knots out of **2** to solve (a problem or mystery)
unreal ADJECTIVE **1** not real, imaginary **2** *informal* amazing, incredible
unrequited ADJECTIVE of love: not given in return, one-sided
unrest NOUN a state of trouble or discontent, especially among a group of people
unrivalled ADJECTIVE without an equal
unruly ADJECTIVE **1** badly behaved **2** not obeying laws or rules
> **unruliness** NOUN
unsaturated ADJECTIVE, *chemistry* **1** of a compound: unable to combine with any other atoms (*contrasted with*: **saturated**) **2** of a solution: unable to dissolve any more of a solute
unsaturated fat NOUN a fat that can raise the amount of cholesterol in the blood
unsavoury ADJECTIVE very unpleasant, causing a feeling of disgust: *a rather unsavoury character*
unscathed ADJECTIVE not harmed
unscrew VERB to loosen (something screwed in)
unscrupulous ADJECTIVE having no scruples or principles
unseat VERB **1** to remove from a political seat **2** to throw from the saddle (of a horse)
unseen ADJECTIVE not seen **sight unseen** (bought etc) without having been seen, at the buyer's risk
unselfish ADJECTIVE **1** showing concern for others **2** generous
unsettle VERB to disturb, upset
unsettled ADJECTIVE **1** disturbed **2** of weather: changeable **3** of a bill: unpaid
unsettling ADJECTIVE disturbing, upsetting
unsightly ADJECTIVE ugly

a b c d e f g h i j k l m n o p q r s t u v w x y z

A B C D E F G H I J K L M N O P Q R S T U V W X Y Z

unsociable ADJECTIVE not willing to mix with other people

unsolicited ADJECTIVE not requested: *unsolicited advice*

unsophisticated ADJECTIVE **1** simple, uncomplicated **2** naive, inexperienced

unsound ADJECTIVE **1** incorrect, unfounded **2** not sane: *of unsound mind*

unspeakable ADJECTIVE too bad to describe in words: *unspeakable rudeness*

unsteady ADJECTIVE **1** not secure or firm **2** not regular or constant **3** of movement: unsure

unstoppable ADJECTIVE not able to be stopped

unsung ADJECTIVE not celebrated, neglected: *an unsung Scots poet*

unsuspecting ADJECTIVE not aware of coming danger

unthinkable ADJECTIVE **1** very unlikely **2** too bad to be thought of

untidy ADJECTIVE not neat or well-organized

untie VERB **1** to release from bonds **2** to loosen (a knot)

until PREPOSITION up to the time of: *Can you wait until Tuesday?* ▸CONJUNCTION up to the time that: *Keep walking until you come to the corner*

untimely ADJECTIVE **1** happening too soon: *untimely arrival* **2** not suitable to the occasion: *untimely remark*

unto PREPOSITION, *old* to

untold ADJECTIVE **1** not yet told: *the untold story* **2** too great to be counted or measured: *untold riches*

untoward ADJECTIVE **1** unlucky, unfortunate **2** inconvenient

untrue ADJECTIVE **1** not true, false **2** unfaithful

untruth NOUN a lie

untruthful ADJECTIVE lying or dishonest

unusual ADJECTIVE **1** not usual **2** rare, remarkable

unusually ADVERB to an unusual degree: *unusually cold for the time of year*

unvarnished ADJECTIVE **1** not varnished **2** plain, straightforward: *the unvarnished truth*

unveil VERB **1** to remove a veil from **2** to remove a cover from (a memorial, statue, etc)

unwarranted ADJECTIVE uncalled for, unnecessary

unwell ADJECTIVE not in good health

unwieldy ADJECTIVE not easily moved or handled > **unwieldiness** NOUN

unwind VERB **1** to wind off from a ball or reel **2** to relax

unworthy ADJECTIVE **1** not worthy **2** low, worthless, despicable **3** (**unworthy of something**) not deserving it: *unworthy of attention* **4** below someone's usual standard, out of character: *That remark is unworthy of you*

up ADVERB **1** towards or in a higher or more northerly position: *They live up in the Highlands* **2** completely, so as to finish: *Drink up your tea* **3** to a larger size: *blow up a balloon* **4** as far as: *He came up to me and shook hands* **5** towards a bigger city etc, not necessarily one further north: *going up to London from Manchester* ▶PREPOSITION **1** towards or in the higher part of: *climbed up the ladder* **2** along: *walking up the road* ▶ADJECTIVE **1** ascending, going up: *the up escalator* **2** ahead in score: *2 goals up* **3** better off, richer: *£50 up on the deal* **4** risen: *The sun is up* **5** of a given length of time: ended: *Your time is up* **6** *informal* wrong: *What's up with her today?* **on the up and up** progressing steadily, getting better all the time **up and about 1** awake **2** out of bed after an illness **up front 1** at the front **2** of money: paid in advance **3** candidly, openly **ups and downs** times of good and bad luck **up to 1** until: *up to the present* **2** capable of: *Are you up to the job?* **3** dependent on, falling as a duty to: *It's up to you to decide* **4** doing: *up to his tricks again* **up to date 1** to the present time **2** containing recent facts etc **3** aware of recent developments **up to scratch** of the required standard **up to speed** fully competent at a new job etc

up-and-coming ADJECTIVE likely to succeed

upbeat ADJECTIVE, *informal* cheerful, optimistic

upbraid VERB to scold

upbringing NOUN the rearing of, or the training given to, a child

update VERB to bring up to date ▶NOUN **1** the act of updating **2** new information: *an update on yesterday's report*

up-end VERB to turn upside down

upfront *or* **up-front** ADJECTIVE **1** candid, frank **2** foremost

upgrade VERB **1** to raise to a more important position **2** to improve the quality of ▶NOUN, *computing* a newer version of a software program

upheaval NOUN a violent disturbance or change

uphill ADJECTIVE **1** going upwards **2** difficult: *uphill struggle* ▶ADVERB upwards

uphold VERB **1** to defend, give support to **2** to maintain, keep going (eg a tradition)

upholster VERB to fit (furniture) with springs, stuffing, covers, etc

upholstery NOUN **1** covers, cushions, etc **2** the skill of upholstering

upkeep NOUN **1** the act of keeping (eg a house or car) in a good state of repair **2** the cost of this

upland NOUN **1** high ground **2** (**uplands**) a hilly or mountainous region

uplift VERB to raise the spirits of, cheer up

up-market ADJECTIVE of high quality or price, luxury

upon PREPOSITION **1** on the top of: *upon the table* **2** at or after the time of: *upon completion of the task*

upper ADJECTIVE higher, further up ▶NOUN **1** the part of a shoe etc above the sole **2** *slang* the drug amphetamine **upper hand** advantage; dominance, control

upper-case ADJECTIVE of a letter: capital, eg *A* not *a* (*contrasted with*: **lower-case**)

a b c d e f g h i j k l m n o p q r s t u v w x y z

A B C D E F G H I J K L M N O P Q R S T U V W X Y Z

upper-class ADJECTIVE belonging to the highest social class, aristocratic

uppermost ADJECTIVE highest, furthest up

upright ADJECTIVE **1** standing up, vertical **2** honest, moral ▸NOUN an upright post, piano, etc

uprising NOUN a revolt against a government etc

uproar NOUN a noisy disturbance

uproarious ADJECTIVE very noisy

uproot VERB **1** to tear up by the roots **2** to leave your home and go to live in another place

upset VERB (*pronounced* up-**set**) (**upsetting, upset**) **1** to make unhappy, angry, worried, etc **2** to overturn **3** to disturb, put out of order **4** to ruin (plans etc) ▸ADJECTIVE (*pronounced* up-**set**) distressed, unhappy, etc; ill ▸NOUN (*pronounced* **up**-set) **1** distress, unhappiness, worry, etc **2** something that causes distress

upshot (*pronounced* **up**-shot) NOUN the result or end of a matter: *What was the upshot of all this?*

upside-down ADJECTIVE & ADVERB **1** with the top part underneath **2** in confusion: *turned the room upside-down looking for his camera*

upstage ADVERB away from the footlights on a theatre stage ▸ADJECTIVE, *informal* haughty, proud ▸VERB to divert attention from (someone) to yourself

upstairs ADVERB in or to the upper storey of a house etc ▸NOUN the upper storey or storeys of a house ▸ADJECTIVE in the upper storey or storeys: *upstairs bedroom*

upstanding ADJECTIVE **1** honest, respectable **2** strong and healthy **3** *old* standing up

upstart (*pronounced* **up**-staht) NOUN someone who has risen quickly from a low to a high position in society, work, etc

upstream ADVERB higher up a river or stream, towards the source

upsurge (*pronounced* **up**-serj) NOUN a rising, a swelling up

uptake (*pronounced* **up**-teik) NOUN: **quick on the uptake** quick to understand

uptight ADJECTIVE nervous, tense

up-to-date ADJECTIVE **1** modern, in touch with recent ideas etc **2** belonging to the present time **3** containing all recent facts etc: *an up-to-date account*

upturn NOUN a positive change, an improvement

upward ADJECTIVE moving up, ascending > **upwards** ADVERB from lower to higher, up **upwards of** more than

upwardly mobile ADJECTIVE moving to a higher social status

uranium (*pronounced* yoo-**rei**-ni-*u*m) NOUN, *chemistry* a dense radioactive metallic element, chiefly used to produce nuclear energy

-urb- of or relating to a town or city: *urban/urbane* (= cultured and sophisticated like a city-dweller)/ *suburb*

ℹ Comes from Latin *urbs* meaning 'a city'

urban ADJECTIVE relating to a town or city (*contrasted with*: **rural**)

urbane ADJECTIVE polite in a smooth way

urbanity NOUN **1** smoothness of manner **2** (*plural* **urbanities**) urbane actions

urbanize *or* **urbanise** VERB to make (an area or areas) less rural and more like a town > **urbanization** NOUN

urchin NOUN a dirty, ragged child

ⓘ Originally meaning 'hedgehog', the prickly sense of which survives in *sea urchin*

urethra (*pronounced* yoo-**reeth**-r*a*) NOUN, *anatomy* the tube leading from the bladder down which urine travels on its way out of the body

urethritis (*pronounced* yoo-reeth-**rai**-t*i*s) NOUN, *medicine* inflammation of the urethra

urge VERB **1** to drive (on) **2** to try to persuade: *urging me to go home* **3** to advise, recommend: *urge caution* ▸NOUN a strong desire or impulse

urgency NOUN an urgent state or condition

urgent ADJECTIVE **1** requiring immediate attention **2** asking for immediate action > **urgently** ADVERB

urinary ADJECTIVE of or relating to urine or the passing of urine

urinate VERB to pass urine from the bladder

urine NOUN the waste liquid passed out of the body of animals and humans from the bladder

URL ABBREVIATION, *computing* Uniform Resource Locator, the system of addresses for the World Wide Web

urn NOUN **1** a vase for the ashes of the dead **2** a metal drum with a tap, used for heating water for tea or coffee

US *or* **USA** ABBREVIATION United States of America

us PRONOUN used by a speaker or writer in referring to themselves together with other people (as the object in a sentence): *When would you like us to come?*

usage NOUN **1** the act or manner of using: *a guide to correct usage of the product* **2** the established way of using a word etc **3** custom, habit **4** treatment: *rough usage*

use VERB **1** to put to some purpose: *use a knife to open it* **2** to bring into action: *use your common sense* **3** (often **use up**) to spend, exhaust (eg patience, energy) **4** to treat: *He used his wife cruelly* ▸NOUN **1** the act of using **2** value or suitability for a purpose: *no use to anybody* **3** the fact of being used: *It's in use at the moment* **4** custom **no use** useless **used to 1** accustomed to **2** was or were in the habit of (doing something): *We used to go there every year*

ⓘ Comes from Latin *uti* meaning 'to use', and *usus* meaning 'a using'

used ADJECTIVE **1** employed, put to a purpose **2** not new: *used cars*

useful ADJECTIVE serving a purpose; helpful > **usefully** ADVERB

useless ADJECTIVE having no use or effect

user NOUN someone who uses anything (especially a computer)

user-friendly ADJECTIVE easily

a b c d e f g h i j k l m n o p q r s t u v w x y z

understood, easy to use

username *or* **user ID** NOUN, *computing* in e-mail addresses, the name or alias of an individual, usually appearing before the @ sign

usher NOUN someone who shows people to their seats in a theatre, at a wedding, etc ▶ VERB: **usher in** *or* **out** to lead or convey (someone) into or out of a room, building, etc

usherette NOUN a woman who shows people to their seats in a theatre or cinema

USSR ABBREVIATION, *history* Union of Soviet Socialist Republics

usual ADJECTIVE **1** done or happening most often: *usual method* **2** customary: *with his usual cheerfulness* **3** ordinary ▶ NOUN a customary event, order, etc

usually ADVERB on most occasions

utensil NOUN an instrument or container used in the home (eg a ladle, knife, pan)

uterus NOUN (*plural* **uteri** – *pronounced* **yoo**-*te*-rai) the womb

utilitarian ADJECTIVE intended to be useful rather than beautiful ▶ NOUN

utility NOUN (*plural* **utilities**) **1** usefulness **2** a public service supplying water, gas, etc

utilize *or* **utilise** VERB to make use of > **utilization** NOUN

utmost ADJECTIVE **1** the greatest possible: *utmost care* **2** furthest **do your utmost** to make the greatest possible effort

utopia (*pronounced* yoo-**toh**-pi-*a*) NOUN a perfect place, a paradise

ⓘ Literally 'no place', coined by Thomas More for his fictional book *Utopia* (1516)

utopian (*pronounced* yoo-**toh**-pi-*a*n) ADJECTIVE unrealistically ideal

utter[1] VERB to produce with the voice (words, a scream, etc)

utter[2] ADJECTIVE complete, total: *utter darkness*

utterance NOUN something said

utterly ADVERB completely, absolutely

uttermost ADJECTIVE most complete, utmost

U-turn NOUN a complete change in direction, policy, etc

UVA ABBREVIATION ultraviolet A, a type of ultraviolet radiation

Vv

-vac- forms words containing the idea 'empty': *vacant/evacuate*
ⓘ Comes from Latin *vacare* meaning 'to be empty', and *vacuus* meaning 'empty'

vacancy NOUN (*plural* **vacancies**) **1** a job that has not been filled **2** a room not already booked in a hotel etc

vacant ADJECTIVE **1** empty, not occupied **2** of an expression: showing no interest or intelligence > **vacantly** ADVERB (meaning 2): *stare vacantly into space*

vacate VERB to leave empty, cease to occupy

vacation NOUN **1** the act of vacating **2** a holiday

vaccinate VERB to give a vaccine to, eg by injection into the skin

vaccination NOUN the act or process of injecting someone with a vaccine

vaccine NOUN a substance made from the germs that cause a disease, given to people and animals to try to prevent them catching that disease: *flu vaccine*

vacuous ADJECTIVE **1** empty **2** empty-headed, stupid > **vacuously** ADVERB

vacuum NOUN a space from which all, or almost all, the air has been removed

vacuum cleaner NOUN a machine which cleans carpets etc by sucking up dust

vagabond NOUN **1** someone with no permanent home; a wanderer **2** a rascal, a rogue

vagina NOUN, *anatomy* the passage connecting a woman's genitals to her womb

vaginal ADJECTIVE of or to do with the vagina

vagrancy NOUN the state of being a tramp

vagrant ADJECTIVE unsettled, wandering ▶NOUN a wanderer or tramp, with no settled home

vague ADJECTIVE **1** not clear; not definite: *vague idea/vague shape* **2** not practical or efficient; forgetful > **vaguely** ADVERB

vain ADJECTIVE **1** conceited, self-important **2** useless: *vain attempt* **3** empty, meaningless: *vain promises* **in vain** without success: *He tried in vain to start the engine* > **vainly** ADVERB

vale NOUN, *literary* a valley

valentine NOUN **1** a greetings

card sent on St Valentine's Day, 14 February **2** a sweetheart, a lover

valet (*pronounced* **val**-et *or* **val**-ei) NOUN a manservant ▸VERB **1** to work as a valet **2** (*pronounced* **val**-et) to clean out (a car) as a service

valiant ADJECTIVE brave > **valiantly** ADVERB

valid ADJECTIVE **1** sound, acceptable: *valid reason for not going* **2** legally in force: *valid passport*

validate VERB **1** to make (a document etc) valid with a mark, stamp, etc **2** to confirm that (something) is true or sound **3** *computing* to check (a file) has been input according to certain rules
> **validation** NOUN

validity NOUN **1** the state of being valid or acceptable for use **2** soundness of an argument or proposition

valley NOUN (*plural* **valleys**) low land between hills, often with a river flowing through it

valorous ADJECTIVE brave, courageous

valour NOUN courage, bravery

valuable ADJECTIVE of great value or usefulness

valuables PLURAL NOUN articles of worth

valuation NOUN **1** the act of valuing **2** an estimated price or value

value NOUN **1** worth; price **2** purchasing power (of a coin etc) **3** importance **4** usefulness **5** *maths* a number or quantity put as equal to an expression: *The value of x is 8* ▸VERB **1** to put a price on **2** to think highly of: *I'd value your opinion*

value-added tax NOUN a government tax raised on the selling-price of an article, or charged on certain services

valueless ADJECTIVE worthless

valuer *or* **valuator** NOUN someone trained to estimate the value of property

valve NOUN **1** a device allowing air, steam or liquid to flow in one direction only **2** *anatomy* a small flap of tissue controlling the flow of blood in the body **3** an electronic component found in older television sets, radios, etc

vamp NOUN the upper part of a boot or shoe

vampire NOUN a dead person supposed to rise at night and suck the blood of the living

vampire bat NOUN a South American bat that sucks blood

van[1] NOUN **1** a commercial road vehicle with a large space at the rear, lighter than a lorry **2** *Brit* a railway carriage in which luggage and parcels are transported

van[2] *short for* **vanguard**

vandal NOUN someone who pointlessly destroys or damages public buildings, private property, etc

ⓘ After the *Vandals*, a German tribe who invaded and destroyed Rome in the 5th century

vandalism NOUN the activity of a vandal

vandalize *or* **vandalise** VERB to damage by vandalism

vane NOUN **1** a weathervane **2** the blade of a windmill, propeller, etc

vanguard NOUN **1** the leading group in a movement etc **2** the part of an army going in front of the main body

vanilla NOUN a sweet-scented flavouring obtained from the pods of a type of orchid

vanish VERB **1** to go out of sight **2** to fade away to nothing

vanity NOUN (*plural* **vanities**) **1** conceit **2** worthlessness **3** something vain and worthless

vanquish VERB to defeat

vantage point NOUN a position giving an advantage or a clear view

vapid ADJECTIVE dull, uninteresting

vaporize *or* **vaporise** VERB to change into vapour

vaporizer *or* **vaporiser** NOUN a device which sprays liquid very finely

vapour NOUN **1** the air-like or gas-like state of a substance that is usually liquid or solid: *water vapour* **2** tiny drops of liquid forming mist or smoke in the air

variable ADJECTIVE changeable; that may be varied ▸ NOUN something that can vary eg in value

variance NOUN a state of differing or disagreement **at variance** in disagreement or conflict

variant NOUN a different form or version ▸ ADJECTIVE in a different form

variation NOUN **1** a varying, a change **2** the extent of a difference or change: *variations in temperature* **3** *music* a repetition, in a slightly different form, of a main theme

varied ADJECTIVE having variety, diverse

variety NOUN (*plural* **varieties**) **1** the quality of being of many kinds, or of being different **2** a mixed collection: *a variety of books* **3** a sort, a type: *a variety of potato* **4** mixed theatrical entertainment including songs, comedy, etc

various ADJECTIVE **1** of different kinds: *various shades of green* **2** several: *various attempts*

variously ADVERB in different ways or at different times: *variously described as fascinating and dull*

varnish NOUN a sticky liquid which gives a glossy surface to paper, wood, etc ▸ VERB **1** to cover with varnish **2** to cover up (faults)

vary VERB (**varies, varying, varied**) **1** to make, be or become different **2** to make changes in (a routine etc) **3** to differ, disagree

vase (*pronounced* vahz *or US* veiz) NOUN a jar of pottery, glass, etc used as an ornament or for holding cut flowers

Vaseline NOUN, *trademark* a type of ointment made from petroleum

vast ADJECTIVE of very great size or amount

vastly ADVERB greatly or to a considerable extent: *vastly different*

vastness NOUN immensity

VAT *or* **vat** ABBREVIATION value-added tax; a tax on goods and services

vat NOUN a large tub or tank, used eg for fermenting liquors and dyeing

vaudeville NOUN theatrical entertainment of dances and songs, usually comic

vault NOUN **1** an arched roof **2** an underground room, a cellar ▶ VERB to leap, supporting your weight on your hands, or on a pole

vaunt VERB to boast

VCR ABBREVIATION video cassette recorder

VD ABBREVIATION venereal disease

VDU ABBREVIATION visual display unit

veal NOUN the flesh of a calf, used as food

vector NOUN **1** *maths* a description of horizontal and vertical motion, shown in a pair of brackets with the horizontal value above the vertical value **2** *maths* a quantity, eg velocity or change of position, that has both magnitude and direction (*compare with*: **scalar**)

Veda NOUN one, or all, of four ancient books of the Hindus

veer VERB **1** to change direction or course **2** to change mood, etc

veg (*pronounced* vedj) **veg out** to relax, laze about

vegan (*pronounced* **vee**-gan) NOUN a vegetarian who does not eat or use any animal products

vegetable NOUN a plant, especially one grown for food ▶ ADJECTIVE **1** of plants **2** made from or consisting of plants: *vegetable dye/vegetable oil*

vegetarian NOUN someone who eats no meat, only vegetable or dairy foods ▶ ADJECTIVE consisting of, or eating, only vegetable or dairy foods

vegetate VERB **1** to grow as a plant does **2** to lead a dull, aimless life: *sitting at home vegetating*

vegetation NOUN **1** plants in general **2** the plants growing in a particular area

vehemence NOUN strong and forceful feeling

vehement ADJECTIVE emphatic and forceful in expressing opinions etc
> **vehemently** ADVERB

vehicle NOUN **1** a means of transport used on land, especially one with wheels: *motor vehicle* **2** a means of conveying information, eg television or newspapers

veil NOUN **1** a piece of cloth or netting worn to shade or hide the face **2** something that hides or covers up: *a veil of secrecy* ▶ VERB **1** to cover with a veil **2** to hide **take the veil** to become a nun

vein NOUN **1** a blood vessel that carries the blood back to the heart **2** a small rib of a leaf **3** a thin layer of mineral in a rock **4** a streak in wood, stone, etc **5** a mood or personal characteristic: *a vein of cheerfulness*

Velcro NOUN, *trademark* a fastening material consisting of one surface of tiny hooks, and another of tiny loops

vellum NOUN **1** a fine parchment used for bookbinding, made from the skins of calves, kids or lambs **2** paper made in imitation of this

velocity NOUN rate or speed of movement

velour (*pronounced* ve-**loor**) NOUN a fabric with a soft, velvet-like surface

velvet NOUN a fabric made from silk etc, with a thick, soft surface ▶ADJECTIVE **1** made of velvet **2** soft or smooth as velvet; silky

velvety ADJECTIVE soft, like velvet

venal (*pronounced* **vee**-n*a*l) ADJECTIVE **1** willing to be bribed: *The majority of the councillors are venal and corrupt* **2** done for a bribe; unworthy

Comes from Latin *venalis* meaning 'for sale'

> Do not confuse with: **venial**. **Venal** is related to the verb 'vend', since they both contain the concept of selling (from Latin *venum*). **Venial** comes from the Latin *venia* (= forgiveness) and means 'forgivable'.

vend VERB to sell

Comes from Latin *vendere* meaning 'to sell'

vendetta NOUN a bitter, long-lasting quarrel or feud

vending machine NOUN a machine with sweets, drinks, etc for sale, operated by putting coins in a slot

vendor NOUN someone who sells

veneer VERB **1** to cover a piece of wood with another thin piece of finer quality **2** to give a good appearance to what is really bad ▶NOUN **1** a thin surface layer of fine wood **2** a false outward show hiding some bad quality: *a veneer of good manners*

venerable ADJECTIVE worthy of respect because of age or wisdom

venerate VERB to respect or honour greatly

veneration NOUN **1** the act of venerating **2** great respect

venereal disease (*pronounced* vi-**neer**-ri-*a*l) NOUN a disease contracted through sexual intercourse

Venetian blind NOUN a window blind formed of horizontal slats of metal or plastic hung on tapes, that can be tilted to let in or shut out light

vengeance NOUN punishment given or harm done in return for wrong or injury, revenge **with a vengeance** with unexpected force or enthusiasm

vengeful ADJECTIVE seeking revenge > **vengefully** ADVERB

venial (*pronounced* **vee**-ni-*a*l) ADJECTIVE of a sin: not very bad, pardonable (*compare with*: **cardinal**)

Comes from Latin *venialis* meaning 'pardonable'

> Do not confuse with: **venal**. **Venial** comes from the Latin *venia* (= forgiveness). **Venal** literally means 'willing to be bought' and is related to the verb 'vend', since they both contain the concept of selling (from the Latin *venum*).

venison NOUN the flesh of a deer, used as food

Venn diagram NOUN, *maths* a diagram showing the relationship between sets using overlapping circles and other figures

venom NOUN **1** poison **2** hatred, spite

venomous ADJECTIVE **1** poisonous

a b c d e f g h i j k l m n o p q r s t u v w x y z

A
B
C
D
E
F
G
H
I
J
K
L
M
N
O
P
Q
R
S
T
U
V
W
X
Y
Z

LANGUAGE workshop — Verbs

A **verb** is often described as a 'doing' word, one that expresses an action or a happening, for example:

digs, *ran*, *is shouting*

A verb can also be a 'being' word, one that expresses a process or a state, such as:

is, *knew*, *becomes*

There is a verb in every sentence. A sentence cannot make sense without a verb.

Subjects and objects of verbs

Every verb has a subject. The subject is the person or thing doing the action.

The sun shone.

In some sentences, the verb has an object as well as a subject. The object tells you whom or what the verb affects.

The sun warmed *the earth*.

➲

2 spiteful > **venomously** ADVERB (meaning 2)

vent NOUN **1** a small opening **2** a hole to allow air or smoke to pass through **3** an outlet: *a vent for his feelings* **4** a slit in a garment, especially upwards from the hem at the back of a jacket, skirt, etc ▶ VERB to express (strong emotion) in some way: *vented his frustration on her* **give vent to** to express, let out

ventilate VERB **1** to allow fresh air to pass through (a room etc) **2** to talk about, discuss

ventilation NOUN circulation of fresh air: *This room has poor ventilation*

ventilator NOUN a device that circulates or draws in fresh air

ventriloquism NOUN the art of speaking in a way that makes the sound appear to come from elsewhere, especially a puppet's mouth

Verbs LANGUAGE workshop

Agreement of verbs

Each verb has a number of different forms, and the form of the verb you use depends on the subject of the verb. The verb 'agrees' with the subject. It is important not to get this wrong when you are using Standard English.

✗ They was very clever.
✓ They *were* very clever.

? Change the verb forms in these sentences so they are correct:

1. You was wrong to say that.
2. These apples looks bad.
3. They is going to a party.

ventriloquist NOUN someone who can speak without appearing to move their lips and can project their voice on to a puppet etc

1 Literally 'stomach speaker' and originally meaning someone possessed by a talking evil spirit

venture NOUN an undertaking which involves some risk: *business venture* ▶ VERB **1** to risk, dare **2** to do or say something at the risk of causing annoyance or opposition: *may I venture to suggest*

venue NOUN the scene of an event, eg a sports contest or conference

ver- *see* **veri-**

veracious ADJECTIVE truthful

1 Comes from Latin *verax* meaning 'truthful'

Do not confuse with: **voracious**

veracity NOUN truthfulness

veranda *or* **verandah** NOUN a kind of terrace with a roof supported by pillars, extending along the side of a house

verb NOUN a word that tells what someone or something does in a sentence, eg 'I *sing*'/'He *had* no idea'

-verb- forms words concerned with words: *verbose/proverb* (= well-known wise words)

ℹ Comes from Latin *verbum* meaning 'a word'

verbal ADJECTIVE **1** of words **2** spoken, not written: *verbal agreement* **3** of verbs

verbatim ADJECTIVE in the exact words, word for word: *a verbatim account*

verbose ADJECTIVE using more words than necessary

verdict NOUN **1** the judge's decision at the end of a trial **2** someone's personal opinion on a matter

verge NOUN **1** the grassy border along the edge of a road etc **2** edge, brink: *on the verge of a mental breakdown* **verge on** to be close to: *verging on the absurd*

verger NOUN a church caretaker, or church official

veri- *or* **ver-** PREFIX forms words containing the concept of truth: *verify/veracity*

ℹ Comes from Latin *verus* meaning 'true'

verifiable ADJECTIVE able to be verified

verify VERB (**verifies, verifying, verified**) to prove, show to be true, confirm > **verification** NOUN

veritable ADJECTIVE **1** true **2** real, genuine

verity NOUN truth

vermicelli NOUN a type of food like spaghetti but in much thinner strands

vermin PLURAL NOUN animals or insects that are considered pests, eg rats, mice, fleas, etc

verminous ADJECTIVE full of vermin

vernacular NOUN the ordinary spoken language of a country or district ▸ ADJECTIVE in the vernacular

vernal ADJECTIVE of the season of spring

verruca (*pronounced* ve-**roo**-ka) NOUN (*plural* **verrucas** *or* **verrucae** – *pronounced* ve-**roo**-see) a wart, especially on the foot

-vers- *see* **-vert-**

versatile ADJECTIVE **1** able to turn easily from one subject or task to another **2** useful in many different ways

versatility NOUN the ability to be adaptable

verse NOUN **1** a number of lines of poetry forming a planned unit **2** poetry as opposed to prose **3** a short division of a chapter of the Bible **versed in** skilled or experienced in: *well versed in the classics*

version NOUN **1** an account from one point of view **2** a form: *another version of the same tune* **3** a translation

verso NOUN the left-hand page of an open book (*compare with*: **recto**)

versus PREPOSITION against (*short form* **v**)

-vert- *or* **-vers-** forms words related to the action of turning: *vertigo* (= a turning or whirling around)/*aversion* (= a turning away from)
ⓘ Comes from Latin *vertere* meaning 'to turn'

vertebra NOUN (*plural* **vertebrae**) one of the segments that forms the spine

vertebrate NOUN an animal with a backbone

vertex NOUN (*plural* **vertices**) **1** the top or summit **2** the point of a cone, pyramid or angle **3** a point where two or more lines meet

vertical ADJECTIVE **1** standing upright **2** straight up and down
> **vertically** ADVERB

vertigo NOUN giddiness, dizziness

verve NOUN lively spirit, enthusiasm

very ADVERB **1** to a great extent or degree: *seem very happy/walk very quietly* **2** exactly: *the very same* ▶ ADJECTIVE **1** same, identical: *The very people who claimed to support him voted against him* **2** ideal, exactly what is wanted: *the very man for the job* **3** actual: *in the very act of stealing* **4** mere: *the very thought of blood*

vespers SINGULAR NOUN a church service in the evening

vessel NOUN **1** a ship **2** a container for liquid **3** a tube carrying fluids in the body: *blood vessels*

vest NOUN **1** an undergarment for the top half of the body **2** *US* a waistcoat

vestibule NOUN an entrance hall; a lobby

vestige NOUN a trace, an indication of something's existence

vestment NOUN a ceremonial garment, worn eg by a religious officer during a service

vestry NOUN (*plural* **vestries**) a room in a church in which vestments are kept

vet¹ NOUN, *informal* a veterinary surgeon

vet² VERB (**vetting, vetted**) to examine, check for suitability or reliability

veteran ADJECTIVE old, experienced ▶ NOUN **1** someone who has given long service **2** an old soldier **3** *US* anyone who has served in the armed forces

veterinary ADJECTIVE relating to the treatment of animal diseases

veterinary surgeon NOUN a doctor who treats animals

veto (*pronounced* **vee**-toh) NOUN (*plural* **vetoes**) **1** the power to forbid or block (a proposal) **2** an act of forbidding or blocking ▶ VERB (**vetoing, vetoed**) to forbid, block
ⓘ Latin for 'I forbid', a phrase originally used by people's tribunes in the Roman Senate when objecting to proposals

vex VERB to annoy; cause trouble to

vexation NOUN **1** the state of being vexed **2** something that vexes

vexatious ADJECTIVE causing trouble or annoyance

VHF ABBREVIATION very high frequency; a range of radio waves that produce good quality sound

via PREPOSITION by way of: *travelling to Paris via London*

A B C D E F G H I J K L M N O P Q R S T U V W X Y Z

viable ADJECTIVE of a plan etc: having a chance of success; practicable: *viable proposition*

viaduct NOUN a long bridge taking a railway or road over a river etc

vibrant ADJECTIVE full of energy; lively, sparkling

vibrate VERB **1** to shake, tremble **2** to swing to and fro rapidly **3** of sound: to resound, ring > **vibration** NOUN

vicar NOUN an Anglican member of the clergy who is in charge of a parish

vicarage NOUN the house of a vicar

vicarious ADJECTIVE **1** in place or on behalf of another person **2** not experienced personally but imagined through the experience of others: *vicarious thrill*

vice NOUN **1** a bad habit, a serious fault **2** wickedness, immorality **3** a tool with two jaws for gripping objects firmly

vice- PREFIX second in rank to: *vice-chancellor/vice-president*

ⓘ Comes from Latin *vicis* meaning 'a turn'

vice versa ADVERB the other way round: *I needed his help and vice versa* (= he needed mine)

vicinity NOUN (*plural* **vicinities**) **1** nearness **2** neighbourhood

vicious ADJECTIVE wicked; spiteful > **viciously** ADVERB

> ⓘ If you have trouble spelling the '-sh-' sound in **viCious**, remember the single 'c' in the related word 'vice'.

vicious circle NOUN a bad situation whose results cause it to get worse

victim NOUN **1** someone who is killed or harmed, intentionally or by accident: *victim of a brutal attack/ victim of the financial situation* **2** an animal for sacrifice

victimize *or* **victimise** VERB to single someone out for hostile, unfair or vindictive treatment; to make a victim of

victor NOUN a winner of a contest etc

victorious ADJECTIVE successful in a battle or other contest

victory NOUN (*plural* **victories**) success in any battle, struggle or contest

video ADJECTIVE **1** relating to the recording and broadcasting of TV pictures and sound **2** relating to recording by video ▸NOUN (*plural* **videos**) **1** a videocassette recorder **2** a recording on videotape **3** *US* television ▸VERB (**videoing, videoed**) to make a recording by video

video camera NOUN a portable camera that records images onto videotape

videocassette NOUN a cassette containing videotape

videotape NOUN magnetic tape for carrying pictures and sound

vie **vie with** to compete with, try to outdo

view NOUN **1** a range or field of sight *a good view* **2** a scene **3** an opinion ▸VERB **1** to look at **2** to watch (television) **3** to consider **in view 1** in sight **2** in your mind as an aim **in view of** taking into consideration **on view** on show; ready for inspecting **with a view to** with the purpose or intention of

viewpoint NOUN **1** a place from which a scene is viewed **2** (*also*: **point of view**) a personal opinion

vigil NOUN a time of watching or of keeping awake at night, often before a religious festival

vigilance NOUN watchfulness, alertness

vigilant ADJECTIVE watchful, alert

vigilante (*pronounced* vij-i-**lan**-tei) NOUN a private citizen who assumes the task of keeping order in a community

vigorous ADJECTIVE strong, healthy; forceful: *vigorous defence* > **vigorously** ADVERB: *vigorously denied the charge*

vigour NOUN strength of body or mind; energy

Viking NOUN, *history* a Norse invader of Western Europe between the 8th and 11th centuries

vile ADJECTIVE **1** very bad **2** disgusting, revolting > **vilely** ADVERB

vilify VERB (**vilifies, vilifying, vilified**) to say bad things about

villa NOUN a house in the country, at the sea, etc used for holidays

village NOUN a collection of houses, not big enough to be called a town

villager NOUN someone who lives in a village

villain NOUN a scoundrel, a rascal

villainous ADJECTIVE wicked

villainy NOUN (*plural* **villainies**) wickedness

villein NOUN, *history* a serf

vindicate VERB **1** to clear from blame **2** to justify

vindictive ADJECTIVE revengeful; spiteful

vine NOUN **1** a grapevine **2** any climbing or trailing plant

vinegar NOUN a sour-tasting liquid made from wine, beer, etc, used for seasoning or pickling

vineyard (*pronounced* **vin**-y*a*d) NOUN an area planted with grapevines

vintage NOUN **1** the gathering of ripe grapes **2** the grapes gathered **3** wine of a particular year, especially when of very high quality **4** time of origin or manufacture ▶ ADJECTIVE **1** of a vintage **2** of wine: of a particular year **3** very characteristic of an author, style, etc: *vintage Monty Python*

viola (*pronounced* vi-**oh**-l*a*) NOUN **1** a stringed instrument like a large violin **2** a member of the family of plants which include violets and pansies

violate VERB **1** to break (a law, a treaty, etc) **2** to harm sexually, especially rape **3** to treat with disrespect **4** to disturb, interrupt > **violator** NOUN

violation NOUN the act or process of violating

violence NOUN great roughness and force

violent ADJECTIVE **1** acting with great force: *violent storm* **2** caused or characterized by violence: *violent death/a violent film* **3** uncontrollable: *violent temper*

violently ADVERB **1** in a violent

A B C D E F G H I J K L M N O P Q R S T U V W X Y Z

or aggressive way **2** extremely; severely; ardently: *violently opposed to our involvement*

violet NOUN a kind of small bluish-purple flower

violin NOUN a musical instrument with four strings, held under the chin and played with a bow

violinist NOUN someone who plays the violin

violoncello *see* **cello**

VIP ABBREVIATION very important person

viper NOUN **1** an adder **2** a vicious or treacherous person

viral ADJECTIVE of or relating to a virus

virgin NOUN someone who has had no sexual intercourse **the Virgin Mary** the mother of Christ

virginal ADJECTIVE of or like a virgin; chaste

virile ADJECTIVE manly; strong, vigorous

virility NOUN manhood; manliness; strength, vigour

virtual ADJECTIVE **1** in effect, though not in strict fact: *Traffic is at a virtual standstill* **2** *computing* any system that behaves or functions in the same way as a real person or thing

virtually ADVERB almost, nearly: *The war is virtually over*

virtual reality NOUN a computer-created environment that the person operating the computer is able to be a part of

virtue NOUN **1** goodness of character and behaviour **2** a good quality, eg honesty, generosity, etc **3** a good point: *One virtue of plastic crockery is that it doesn't break* **by virtue of** because of

virtuosity NOUN brilliance of technique

virtuoso NOUN (*plural* **virtuosos**) a highly skilled artist, especially a musician

virtuous ADJECTIVE good, just, honest > **virtuously** ADVERB

virulence NOUN **1** causing extreme harm; poisonousness **2** bitter hostility

virulent ADJECTIVE **1** full of poison **2** bitter, spiteful **3** of a disease: dangerous

virus NOUN (*plural* **viruses**) **1** a germ that is smaller than any bacteria, and causes diseases such as mumps, chickenpox, etc **2** a self-replicating program that attaches to a computer system and spreads to other systems, and which can destroy data stored on the hard disk

visa NOUN a permit given by the authorities of a country to allow someone to stay for a time in that country

viscosity NOUN the resistance of a fluid to flow, eg treacle has a higher viscosity than water

viscount (*pronounced* **vai**-kownt) NOUN a title of nobility next below an earl

viscountess (*pronounced* **vai**-kownt-es) NOUN a title of nobility next below a countess

viscous (*pronounced* **vis**-kus) ADJECTIVE of a liquid: sticky, not flowing easily

visibility NOUN **1** the clearness with

which objects may be seen **2** the extent or range of vision as affected by fog, rain, etc

visible ADJECTIVE able to be seen > **visibly** ADVERB: *visibly upset*

vision NOUN **1** the act or power of seeing **2** something seen in the imagination **3** a strange, supernatural sight: *a vision of the Virgin Mary* **4** the ability to foresee likely future events: *a man of great vision*

visionary ADJECTIVE seen in imagination only, not real ▶NOUN (*plural* **visionaries**) someone who dreams up imaginative plans

visit VERB **1** to go to see; call on **2** to stay with as a guest ▶NOUN **1** a call at a person's house or at a place of interest etc **2** a short stay

visitation NOUN **1** a visit of an important official **2** a great misfortune, seen as a punishment from God

visitor NOUN someone who makes a visit

visor (*pronounced* **vai**-zor) NOUN **1** a part of a helmet covering the face **2** a movable shade on a car's windscreen **3** a peak on a cap for shading the eyes

vista NOUN a view, especially one seen through a long, narrow opening

visual ADJECTIVE relating to, or received through, sight: *visual aids*

visual display unit NOUN a device like a television set, on which data from a computer's memory can be displayed

visualize *or* **visualise** VERB to form a clear picture of in the mind > **visualization** NOUN

vital ADJECTIVE **1** of the greatest importance: *vital information* **2** necessary to life **3** of life: *vital signs* **4** vigorous, energetic: *a vital personality*

vitality NOUN life; liveliness, strength; ability to go on living

vitalize *or* **vitalise** VERB to give life or vigour to

vitally ADVERB essentially; urgently: *It is vitally important to keep copies of all documents*

vitamin NOUN one of a group of substances necessary for health, occurring in different natural foods

vitreous ADJECTIVE of or like glass

vitriol NOUN **1** sulphuric acid **2** bitter or hateful criticism

vitriolic ADJECTIVE biting, scathing

vivacious ADJECTIVE lively, sprightly > **vivaciously** ADVERB

vivacity NOUN liveliness, spark

-vivi- *or* **-viv-** forms words related to living, or to things which are alive: *vivisection/survive*

ⓘ Comes from Latin *vivere* meaning 'to live', and *vivus* meaning 'alive'

vivid ADJECTIVE **1** lifelike **2** brilliant, striking

vividly ADVERB brightly, clearly, intensely: *I remember my grandmother vividly*

vivisection NOUN the carrying out of experiments on living animals

vixen NOUN **1** a female fox **2** an ill-tempered woman

vizier NOUN, *history* a minister of state in some Muslim countries

a b c d e f g h i j k l m n o p q r s t u v w x y z

A B C D E F G H I J K L M N O P Q R S T U V W X Y Z

vocabulary NOUN (*plural* **vocabularies**) **1** the range of words used by an individual or group **2** the words of a particular language **3** a list of words in alphabetical order, with their meanings

vocal ADJECTIVE **1** of the voice **2** expressing your opinions loudly and fully

vocalist NOUN a singer

vocation NOUN **1** an occupation or profession to which someone feels called to dedicate themselves **2** a strong inclination or desire to follow a particular course of action or work

vodka NOUN an alcoholic spirit made from grain or potatoes

vogue NOUN the fashion of the moment; popularity **in vogue** in fashion

voice NOUN **1** the sound produced from the mouth in speech or song **2** ability to sing: *has a lovely voice* **3** an opinion ▶ VERB to express (an opinion)

voice mail *or* **voicemail** NOUN a telephone-answering system by which telephone messages can be stored to be picked up later

voice recognition NOUN the ability of a computer or other machine to receive and interpret spoken language and commands

void ADJECTIVE **1** empty, vacant **2** not valid ▶ NOUN an empty space **void of** lacking completely

volatile ADJECTIVE **1** of a liquid: quickly turning into vapour **2** of a person: changeable in mood or behaviour, fickle

volcanic ADJECTIVE **1** relating to volcanoes **2** caused or produced by heat within the earth

volcano NOUN (*plural* **volcanoes**) a mountain with an opening through which molten rock, ashes, etc are periodically thrown up from inside the earth

ⓘ Named after *Vulcan*, the Roman god of fire

vole NOUN any of a group of small rodents, including the water rat

volition NOUN an act of will or choice: *He did it of his own volition*

volley NOUN (*plural* **volleys**) **1** a number of shots fired or missiles thrown at the same time **2** an outburst of abuse or criticism **3** *tennis* a return of a ball before it bounces on the ground ▶ VERB **1** to shoot or throw in a volley **2** to return (a ball) before it bounces on the ground

volt NOUN the unit used in measuring the force of electricity

voltage NOUN electrical force measured in volts

voluble ADJECTIVE speaking with a great flow of words

volume NOUN **1** a book, often one of a series **2** the amount of space taken up by anything **3** amount: *volume of trade* **4** loudness or fullness of sound

voluminous ADJECTIVE bulky, of great volume

voluntary ADJECTIVE **1** done or acting by choice, not under compulsion **2** working without payment ▶ NOUN (*plural* **voluntaries**) a piece of organ music of the organist's choice played at a church service

volunteer NOUN someone who offers to do something of their own accord, often for no payment ▶VERB **1** to act as a volunteer **2** to give (information, an opinion, etc) unasked

vomit VERB to throw up the contents of the stomach through the mouth ▶NOUN the matter thrown up by vomiting

voracious ADJECTIVE very greedy, difficult to satisfy: *voracious appetite/voracious reader*
ⓘ Comes from Latin *vorax* meaning 'devouring'

> Do not confuse with: **veracious**

voracity NOUN extreme greed or eagerness

-vore also **-vorous** SUFFIX forms technical terms concerned with the eating habits of an animal or person: *carnivore* (= flesh-eating)/ *herbivore* (= grass-eating)
ⓘ Comes from Latin *vorare* meaning 'to devour'

vortex NOUN (*plural* **vortices** *or* **vortexes**) **1** a whirlpool **2** a whirlwind

vote VERB **1** to give your support to (a particular candidate, a proposal, etc) in a ballot or show of hands **2** to decide by voting ▶NOUN **1** an expression of opinion or support by voting **2** the right to vote

voter NOUN someone who votes

vouch VERB: **vouch for something** to say that you are sure of it or can guarantee it: *I can vouch for his courage*

voucher NOUN a paper which can be exchanged for money or goods

vow NOUN a solemn promise or declaration, especially one made to God ▶VERB **1** to make a vow **2** to threaten (revenge etc)

vowel NOUN **1** a sound made by the voice that does not require the use of the tongue, teeth or lips **2** the letters *a, e, i, o, u* (or various combinations of them), and sometimes *y*, which represent those sounds

voyage NOUN a journey, usually by sea ▶VERB to make a journey

vulgar ADJECTIVE **1** coarse, ill-mannered **2** indecent **3** of the common people

vulgar fraction NOUN, *maths* a fraction not written as a decimal, eg ⅓, ⅘ (*also called*: **common fraction, simple fraction**)

vulgarity NOUN coarseness in speech or behaviour

vulgarly ADVERB in a vulgar or coarse way

vulnerability NOUN a state of being vulnerable or easily harmed

vulnerable ADJECTIVE **1** exposed to, or in danger of, attack **2** liable to be hurt physically or emotionally

vulture NOUN a large bird that feeds mainly on the flesh of dead animals

a b c d e f g h i j k l m n o p q r s t u v w x y z

Ww

W[1] ABBREVIATION west; western

W[2] SYMBOL **1** *chemistry* **2** tungsten (formerly called wolfram) **3 4** watt(s)

wad NOUN **1** a lump of loose material (eg wool, cloth, paper) pressed together **2** a bunch of banknotes

wadding NOUN soft material (eg cotton wool) used for packing or padding

waddle VERB to walk with short, unsteady steps, moving from side to side as a duck does ▸ NOUN the act of waddling

wade VERB **1** to walk through deep water or mud **2** to get through with difficulty: *still wading through this book*

wader NOUN **1** a long-legged bird that wades in search of food **2** (**waders**) high waterproof boots worn by anglers for wading

wafer NOUN **1** a very thin, light type of biscuit **2** a very thin slice of anything

waffle[1] NOUN a light, crisp cake made from batter

waffle[2] NOUN pointless, long-drawn-out talk ▸ VERB to talk long and meaninglessly

waft VERB to carry or drift lightly through the air or over water

wag VERB (**wagging, wagged**) to move from side to side or up and down ▸ NOUN **1** an act of wagging **2** someone who is always joking

wage VERB to carry on (a war etc) ▸ NOUN (often **wages**) payment for work

wager NOUN a bet ▸ VERB to bet

waggle VERB to move from side to side in an unsteady manner ▸ NOUN an unsteady movement from side to side

wagon *or* **waggon** NOUN **1** a four-wheeled vehicle for carrying loads **2** an open railway carriage for goods

waif NOUN an uncared-for or homeless child or animal **waifs and strays** homeless children or animals

wail VERB to cry or moan in sorrow ▸ NOUN a sorrowful cry

waist NOUN the narrow part of the body, between the ribs and the hips

waistcoat NOUN a short, sleeveless jacket, often worn under an outer jacket

wait VERB **1** to put off or delay action **2 wait for** to remain in expectation or readiness for:

waiting for the bus to come **3** to be employed as a waiter or waitress ▶NOUN a delay **wait on 1** to serve (someone) at table **2** to act as a servant to

waiter NOUN a man whose job it is to serve people at table in a restaurant

waitress NOUN a woman whose job it is to serve people at table in a restaurant

waive VERB to give up (a claim or right)

🛈 Comes from Old French *guesver* meaning 'to abandon'

> Do not confuse with: **wave**

waiver NOUN **1** the act of waiving **2** a document indicating this

> Do not confuse with: **waver**

🛈 For origin, see **waive**

wake¹ VERB (often **wake up**) (**waking, woke** *or* **waked, woken**) to stop sleeping ▶NOUN a night of watching beside a dead body

wake² NOUN a streak of foamy water left in the track of a ship **in the wake of** immediately behind or after

wakeful ADJECTIVE not sleeping, unable to sleep

waken VERB to wake, arouse or be aroused

waking ADJECTIVE being or becoming awake

walk VERB **1** to move along on foot **2** to travel along (streets etc) on foot ▶NOUN **1** an act of walking **2** a manner of walking **3** a distance to be walked over: *a short walk from here* **4** a place for walking: *a covered walk* **walk of life** someone's rank or occupation **walk the plank** to be put to death by pirates by being made to walk off the end of a plank over a ship's side

walkie-talkie NOUN a portable radio set for sending and receiving messages

walking stick NOUN a stick used for support when walking

Walkman NOUN, *trademark* a personal stereo

walkover NOUN an easy victory

wall NOUN **1** a structure built of stone, brick, etc used to separate or enclose **2** the side of a building or room ▶VERB: **wall in** *or* **off** to enclose or separate with a wall **off the wall** unusual, eccentric

wallaby NOUN (*plural* **wallabies**) a small kind of kangaroo

wallet NOUN a small folding case for holding banknotes, credit cards, etc

wallflower NOUN **1** a sweet-smelling spring flower **2** someone who is continually without a partner at a dance etc

wallop *informal*, VERB to beat, hit ▶NOUN an act of hitting

wallow VERB to roll about with enjoyment in water, mud, etc

wallpaper NOUN **1** paper used in house decorating for covering walls **2** a background pattern on a computer screen ▶VERB to cover with wallpaper

walnut NOUN **1** a tree whose wood is used for making furniture **2** the nut it produces

a b c d e f g h i j k l m n o p q r s t u v w x y z

A B C D E F G H I J K L M N O P Q R S T U V W X Y Z

walrus NOUN (*plural* **walruses**) a large sea animal, like a seal, with two long tusks

ⓘ A Dutch word meaning literally 'whale horse'

waltz NOUN (*plural* **waltzes**) **1** a ballroom dance for couples, with a circling movement **2** music for this dance, with three beats to each bar ▶VERB to dance a waltz

WAN ABBREVIATION, *computing* wide area network, a computer network that operates over a wide area, not just in a single place

wan (*pronounced* won) ADJECTIVE pale and sickly looking

wand NOUN a long slender rod used by a conjuror, magician, etc

wander VERB **1** to roam about with no definite purpose; roam **2** to go astray **3** to be mentally confused because of illness etc

wanderer NOUN a person or animal that wanders

wanderlust NOUN a keen desire for travel

wane VERB **1** to become smaller (*contrasted with*: **wax**[2]) **2** to lose power, importance, etc **on the wane** becoming less

wangle VERB to get or achieve through craftiness, skilful planning, etc

want VERB **1** to wish for **2** to need, lack ▶NOUN **1** poverty **2** scarcity, lack

ⓘ Comes from Old Norse *vant* meaning 'lacking', and *vanta* meaning 'to lack'

wanted ADJECTIVE looked for, especially by the police

wanting ADJECTIVE **1** absent, missing; without **2** not good enough: *He tried, but was found wanting* **3** (**wanting in**) lacking: *wanting in good taste*

wanton (*pronounced* **won**-ton) ADJECTIVE thoughtless, pointless, without motive: *wanton cruelty*

WAP ABBREVIATION Wireless Application Protocol, technology which allows Internet access from a mobile phone (**WAP phone**)

war NOUN an armed struggle, especially between nations ▶VERB (**warring, warred**) to fight in a war, make war

warble VERB to sing like a bird, trill

warbler NOUN a type of songbird

ward VERB: **ward off** to keep off, defend yourself against (a blow etc) ▶NOUN **1** a hospital room containing a number of beds **2** one of the parts into which a town is divided for voting **3** someone who is in the care of a guardian

warden NOUN **1** someone who guards a game reserve **2** someone in charge of a hostel or college

warder NOUN a prison guard

wardrobe NOUN **1** a cupboard for clothes **2** someone's personal supply of clothes

-ware SUFFIX manufactured material: *earthenware/glassware*

warehouse NOUN a building where goods are stored

wares PLURAL NOUN goods for sale

ⓘ Comes from Old English *waru*

warfare NOUN the carrying on of war

warhead NOUN the part of a missile containing the explosive

warlike ADJECTIVE **1** fond of war **2** threatening war

warm ADJECTIVE **1** fairly hot **2** of clothes: keeping the wearer warm **3** of a person: friendly, loving ▸VERB to make or become warm

warm-blooded ADJECTIVE of an animal: having a body temperature that is relatively constant regardless of changes in the surrounding environment

warm-hearted ADJECTIVE kind, generous

warmth NOUN **1** pleasant or comfortable heat, or the condition or quality of being warm **2** affection, friendliness or enthusiasm: *We were immediately won over by her warmth and friendliness*

warn VERB **1** to tell (someone) beforehand about possible danger, misfortune, etc: *I warned him about the icy roads* **2** to advise against: *I warned him not to be late*

warning NOUN a remark, notice, etc that warns

warp VERB **1** to become twisted out of shape **2** to distort, make unsound: *His previous experiences had warped his judgement* ▸NOUN the threads stretched lengthwise on a loom, which are crossed by the weft

warpath NOUN: **on the warpath** in a fighting or angry mood

warrant (*pronounced* **wor**-*ant*) NOUN a certificate granting someone a right or authority: *search warrant* ▸VERB to justify, be a good enough reason for: *The crime does not warrant such punishment* **I warrant you** *or* **I'll warrant** you may be sure, I assure you

warren NOUN **1** a collection of rabbit burrows **2** a building with many rooms and passages; a maze

warrior NOUN a great fighter

warship NOUN a ship armed with guns etc

wart NOUN a small hard growth on the skin

wary ADJECTIVE cautious, on guard > **warily** ADVERB

was *a past form of* **be**

wash VERB **1** to clean with water, soap, etc **2** to clean yourself with water etc **3** of water: to flow over or against **4** to sweep (away, along, etc) by force of water ▸NOUN (*plural* **washes**) **1** a washing **2** a streak of foamy water left behind by a moving boat **3** a liquid with which anything is washed **4** a thin coat of paint etc **wash up** to wash the dishes **wash your hands of** to give up all responsibility for

washer NOUN **1** someone or something that washes **2** a flat ring of metal, rubber, etc for keeping joints tight

washing NOUN **1** the act of cleaning by water **2** clothes to be washed

washing machine NOUN an electric machine for washing clothes

washing-up NOUN dishes to be washed

wasp NOUN a stinging, winged insect, with a slender, yellow and black striped body

wastage NOUN **1** an amount wasted **2** loss through decay or squandering

waste ADJECTIVE **1** thrown away, rejected as useless: *waste paper* **2** of land: uncultivated, barren and desolate ▶VERB **1** to spend (money, time, energy) extravagantly, without result or profit **2** to decay or wear away gradually ▶NOUN **1** extravagant use, squandering **2** rubbish, waste material **3** a stretch of barren or devastated land

wasteful ADJECTIVE causing waste, extravagant

wasteland NOUN a desolate and barren place

wastepipe NOUN a pipe for carrying away dirty water or semi-liquid waste

waster *or* **wastrel** NOUN an idle, good-for-nothing person

watch VERB **1** to look at, observe closely **2** (often **watch over**) to look after, mind **3** *old* to keep awake ▶NOUN (*plural* **watches**) **1** the act of keeping guard **2** someone who keeps, or those who keep, guard **3** a sailor's period of duty on deck **4** a small clock worn on the wrist or kept in a pocket

watchdog NOUN **1** a dog which guards a building **2** an organization which monitors business practices etc

watchful ADJECTIVE alert, cautious > **watchfully** ADVERB

watchman NOUN a man who guards a building etc at night

watchword NOUN a motto, a slogan

water NOUN **1** a colourless odourless tasteless liquid that freezes to form ice at 0°C and boils to form steam at 100°C **2** an expanse of this liquid in a lake, river, etc **3** a fluid produced by the body, eg urine, sweat, etc ▶VERB **1** to supply with water **2** to dilute or mix with water **3** of the mouth: to fill with saliva **4** of the eyes: to fill with tears

ⓘ Comes from Old English *wæter*

water butt NOUN a large barrel for rain water

water closet NOUN a toilet, a lavatory (*abbreviation* **WC**)

watercolour NOUN **1** a paint which is mixed with water, not oil **2** a painting done with this paint

watercress NOUN a plant which grows beside streams, with hot-tasting leaves which are eaten in salads

water cycle NOUN the process by which water is distributed throughout the earth and its atmosphere

waterfall NOUN a place where a river falls from a height, often over a ledge of rock

waterlily NOUN (*plural* **waterlilies**) a plant which grows in ponds etc, with flat floating leaves and large flowers

waterlogged ADJECTIVE **1** filled with water **2** soaked with water

watermark NOUN a faint design on paper, visible only when it is held up to the light

watermelon NOUN a large melon with red juicy flesh and a thick, green rind

watermill NOUN a mill driven by water

water polo NOUN a ball game played in a pool between teams of swimmers

waterproof ADJECTIVE not allowing water to pass through ▶NOUN an overcoat made of waterproof material

water rat NOUN a kind of vole

watershed NOUN a high ridge separating two river valleys

water-skiing NOUN the sport of being towed very fast on skis behind a motorboat

watertight ADJECTIVE so closely fitted that water cannot leak through

waterway NOUN a channel along which ships can sail

waterwheel NOUN a wheel moved by water

waterworks PLURAL NOUN **1** a place which purifies and stores a town's water supply **2** *euphemistic* the urinary system **3** *informal* tears

watery ADJECTIVE **1** full of water **2** too liquid, textureless

watt (*pronounced* wot) NOUN (symbol **W**) the standard unit of electric power, equal to the power that produces energy at the rate of one joule per second

ⓘ After James *Watt*, who pioneered the steam engine

wattage NOUN (*pronounced* wot) electric power measured in watts

wattle NOUN (*pronounced* **wot-l**) **1** interwoven twigs and branches used for fences etc **2** an Australian acacia tree **3** a fleshy part hanging from the neck of a turkey

wave NOUN **1** a moving ridge on the surface of the water **2** a hand gesture for attracting attention, or saying hello or goodbye **3** *physics* a vibration travelling through the air carrying light, sound etc **4** a ridge or curve of hair **5** a rush of an emotion (eg despair, enthusiasm, etc) ▶VERB **1** to make a wave with the hand **2** to move to and fro, flutter: *flags waving in the wind* **3** to curl, curve

🛈 Comes from Old English *wafian* meaning 'to wave'

Do not confuse with: **waive**

wavelength NOUN the distance from the highest or lowest point on a wave or vibration to the next similar point

waver VERB **1** to be unsteady, wobble **2** to be uncertain or undecided

🛈 Comes from Old Norse *vafra* meaning 'to flicker'

Do not confuse with: **waiver**

wavy ADJECTIVE (**wavier, waviest**) having waves

wax¹ NOUN **1** a sticky solid or semi-solid substance, either natural or synthetic, that is easily moulded when warm **2** beeswax **3** sealing wax **4** a brown, fatty substance secreted in the ear ▶ADJECTIVE made of wax ▶VERB to rub with wax

wax² VERB to grow, increase (*contrasted with*: **wane**)

waxen ADJECTIVE **1** of or like wax **2** pale

waxwork NOUN **1** a lifelike model, especially of a famous person, made of wax **2** an object modelled from wax **3** (**waxworks**) a museum

A B C D E F G H I J K L M N O P Q R S T U V W X Y Z

displaying wax models of famous people

waxy ADJECTIVE (**waxier, waxiest**) of, or like, wax

way NOUN **1** an opening, a passage: *the way out* **2** a road, path **3** room to go forward or pass: *Block the way* **4** direction: *He went that way* **5** correct route: *do you know the way?* **6** distance: *a long way* **7** condition: *in a bad way* **8** means, method: *There must be a way to do this* **9** manner: *in a clumsy way/his way of doing things* **10** someone's own wishes or choice: *He always gets his own way* **by the way** incidentally, in passing **by way of** **1** travelling through **2** as if, with the purpose of: *by way of a favour* **in the way** blocking progress **make your way** to go

[i] Comes from Old English *weg*

waylay VERB (**waylaying, waylaid**) to wait for and stop (someone)

-ways SUFFIX in the direction of: *lengthways/sideways*

wayside NOUN the edge of a road or path ▸ ADJECTIVE located by the side of a road

wayward ADJECTIVE wilful, following your own way

WC ABBREVIATION water closet

we PRONOUN used by a speaker or writer in mentioning themselves together with other people (as the subject of a verb): *We are having a party this weekend*

weak ADJECTIVE **1** not strong, feeble **2** lacking determination, easily persuaded **3** not able to support a great weight: *weak bridge*

weaken VERB to make or become weak

weakling NOUN a person or animal that is lacking in strength

weakly ADJECTIVE (**weaklier, weakliest**) lacking strength, sickly

weakness NOUN (*plural* **weaknesses**) **1** lack of strength **2** a fault **3** a special fondness (for): *a weakness for chocolate*

wealth NOUN **1** riches **2** a large quantity: *wealth of information*

wealthy ADJECTIVE (**wealthier, wealthiest**) rich

wean[1] (*pronounced* ween) VERB **1** to make (a child or young animal) used to food other than the mother's milk **2** **wean from** *or* **off** to make (someone or something) gradually give up (a bad habit etc)

wean[2] (*pronounced* wein) NOUN, *Scottish* a child

weapon NOUN **1** an instrument used for fighting, eg a sword, gun, etc **2** any means of attack

wear VERB (**wearing, wore, worn**) **1** to be dressed in, have on the body **2** to arrange in a particular way: *She wears her hair long* **3** to have (a beard, moustache) on the face **4** to damage or weaken by use, rubbing etc **5** to be damaged in this way **6** to last: *wear well* ▸ NOUN **1** use by wearing: *for my own wear* **2** damage by use **3** ability to last **4** clothes etc: *school wear* **wear and tear** damage by ordinary use **wear off** to disappear gradually **wear on** to become later: *The afternoon wore on* **wear out** **1** to make or become unfit for further use **2** to exhaust

wearable ADJECTIVE fit to be worn

wearer NOUN a person who wears something: *wearers of contact lenses*

wearing ADJECTIVE tiring, exhausting

wearisome ADJECTIVE causing tiredness, boredom or impatience

weary ADJECTIVE (**wearier, weariest**) **1** tired, having used up your strength or patience **2** (**weary of**) tired of, bored with **3** tiring, boring ▸ VERB (**wearies, wearying, wearied**) to make or become tired, bored or impatient

weasel NOUN a small wild animal with a long and slender body, that lives on mice, birds, etc

weather NOUN the state of the atmosphere, eg heat, coldness, cloudiness, etc ▸ VERB **1** *geography* to dry or wear away (rock etc) through exposure to the air, water, etc **2** to come safely through (a storm, difficulty, etc)

weatherbeaten ADJECTIVE showing signs of having been out in all weathers

weathervane NOUN a flat piece of metal that swings in the wind to show its direction

weave[1] VERB (**weaving, wove, woven**) **1** to pass threads over and under each other on a loom etc to form cloth **2** to plait cane etc for basket-making **3** to put together (a story, plan, etc)

weave[2] VERB (**weaving, weaved**) to move in and out between objects, or move from side to side: *weaving through the traffic*

weaver NOUN someone who weaves

Web NOUN: **the Web** the World Wide Web

web NOUN **1** the net made by a spider, a cobweb **2** the skin between the toes of ducks, swans, frogs, etc **3** something woven

webbed ADJECTIVE of feet: having the toes joined by a web

webcam NOUN a small digital video camera attached to a computer that can be used to send images across the Internet

webcast NOUN a programme broadcast live over the Internet ▸ VERB to broadcast over the Internet

web-footed *or* **web-toed** ADJECTIVE having webbed feet or toes

weblog NOUN a document containing personal comments, often in the form of a journal, posted on the Internet (*short form*: **blog**)

web page NOUN one of the linked pages or files that make up a website

website *or* **web site** NOUN a linked collection of Web pages or files with a home page from which the other pages can be accessed

wed VERB (**wedding, wed**) to marry

we'd *short for* **1** we would; we should **2** we had

wedding NOUN **1** marriage **2** a marriage ceremony

wedge NOUN **1** a piece of wood, metal, etc thick at one end with a thin edge at the other, used in splitting wood, forcing two surfaces

a b c d e f g h i j k l m n o p q r s t u v w x y z

A B C D E F G H I J K L M N O P Q R S T U V W X Y Z

apart, etc **2** anything shaped like a wedge ▶VERB **1** to fix or become fixed with a wedge **2** to push or squeeze (in): *wedged in amongst the crowd*

wedlock NOUN the state of being married

Wednesday NOUN the fourth day of the week

ⓘ After *Woden*, the Germanic god of war and wisdom

wee ADJECTIVE, *Scot* small, tiny

weed NOUN **1** a useless, troublesome plant **2** a weak, worthless person **3** (**weeds**) a widow's mourning clothes ▶VERB to clear (a garden etc) of weeds

weedy ADJECTIVE (**weedier, weediest**) **1** full of weeds **2** like a weed **3** thin and puny

week NOUN **1** the space of seven days from Sunday to Saturday **2** the working days of the week, not Saturday and Sunday

ⓘ Comes from Old English *wice*

weekday NOUN any day except Saturday and Sunday

weekend NOUN Saturday and Sunday

weekly ADJECTIVE happening, or done, once a week ▶ADVERB once a week ▶NOUN (*plural* **weeklies**) a newspaper, magazine, etc coming out once a week

weep VERB (**weeping, wept**) **1** to shed tears **2** to ooze, drip: *a weeping wound*

weeping willow NOUN a willow tree with drooping branches

weevil NOUN a small beetle that destroys grain, flour, etc

weigh VERB **1** to find out how heavy (something) is by putting it on a scale etc **2** to have a certain heaviness: *weighing 10 kilograms* **3** to raise (a ship's anchor) **4** of burdens etc: to be heavy or troublesome **5** to consider (a matter, a point) carefully **6** to consider (something) important **weigh in** to test your weight before a boxing match **weigh out** to measure out a quantity by weighing it on a scale

weighbridge NOUN a large scale for weighing vehicles

weight NOUN **1** the amount that anything weighs **2** *physics* the force put on an object by the pull of gravity **3** a piece of metal weighing a certain amount: *a 100 gram weight* **4** a load, a burden **5** importance: *attach weight to the story* ▶VERB to make heavy by adding or attaching a weight

weightless ADJECTIVE **1** weighing nothing or almost nothing **2** not affected by gravity, so able to float about > **weightlessness** NOUN

weighty ADJECTIVE (**weightier, weightiest**) **1** heavy **2** important

weir NOUN a dam across a stream

weird ADJECTIVE **1** odd, strange **2** mysterious, supernatural

welcome VERB **1** to receive with warmth or pleasure **2** to accept gladly: *I welcome the challenge* ▶NOUN a welcoming, a warm reception ▶ADJECTIVE received with pleasure **welcome to** permitted to do or take: *You're welcome to those chocolates*

weld VERB **1** to join (pieces of metal) by pressure, with or without heating **2** to join closely ▶NOUN a joint made by welding

welfare NOUN comfort, good health

welfare state NOUN a country with a health service, insurance against unemployment, pensions for those who cannot work etc

we'll *short for* we will; we shall

well[1] ADJECTIVE in good health ▶ADVERB (**better, best**) **1** in a good and correct manner: *write well* **2** thoroughly: *well beaten* **3** successfully: *do well* **4** conveniently: *It fits in well with my plans* ▶INTERJECTION expressing surprise, or used in explaining, narrating, etc: *Well! What a shock!* **as well as** in addition to **it is as well** *or* **it is just as well** it is a good thing, it is lucky **well off** rich

well[2] NOUN **1** a spring of water **2** a shaft in the earth to extract water, oil, etc **3** an enclosed space round which a staircase winds ▶VERB (often **well up**) to rise up and gush: *Tears welled up in her eyes*

well-advised ADJECTIVE wise

well-behaved ADJECTIVE with good manners

wellbeing NOUN welfare; contentment

well-disposed ADJECTIVE: **well-disposed to** inclined to favour

well-informed ADJECTIVE having or showing knowledge

wellingtons PLURAL NOUN high rubber boots covering the lower part of the legs

> ⓘ After the Duke of *Wellington*, who wore boots like this

well-known ADJECTIVE **1** celebrated, famous **2** familiar

well-meaning ADJECTIVE having good intentions

well-meant ADJECTIVE rightly, kindly intended

well-off ADJECTIVE rich

well-read ADJECTIVE having read many good books

well-to-do ADJECTIVE rich

well-wisher NOUN someone who wishes someone success

welt NOUN **1** a firm edging or band, eg on the wrist or waist of a garment **2** a weal

wench NOUN (*plural* **wenches**), *old* a young woman, a girl

wend VERB: **wend your way** to make your way slowly

went *past tense* of **go**

wept *past form* of **weep**

were *a past form* of **be** (plural)

we're *short for* we are

werewolf NOUN a mythical creature which changes periodically from a human into a wolf

west NOUN the direction in which the sun sets, one of the four main points of the compass ▶ADJECTIVE in or to the west ▶ADVERB in, to or towards the west: *move out west*

westerly ADJECTIVE **1** of the wind: coming from or facing the west **2** in or towards the west

western ADJECTIVE of the west ▶NOUN a film or story about life among the early settlers in the western United States

westward ADJECTIVE & ADVERB towards the west

westwards ADVERB towards the west

wet ADJECTIVE **1** soaked or covered with water or other liquid **2** rainy: *a wet day* ▸ NOUN **1** water **2** rain ▸ VERB (**wetting, wet** *or* **wetted**) to make wet

wet suit NOUN a suit that allows water to pass through but retains body heat

whack NOUN a loud, violent slap or blow ▸ VERB to slap or hit violently

whale NOUN a very large mammal living in the sea ▸ VERB to catch whales

whaler NOUN a ship engaged in catching whales

wharf NOUN (*plural* **wharfs** *or* **wharves**) a landing stage for loading and unloading ships

what ADJECTIVE & PRONOUN used to indicate something about which a question is being asked: *What day is this?/What are you doing?* ▸ ADJECTIVE any that: *Give me what money you have* ▸ CONJUNCTION anything that: *I'll take what you can give me* ▸ ADJECTIVE, ADVERB & PRONOUN used for emphasis in exclamations: *What terrible ties he wears!/What rubbish!* **what about?** used in asking whether the listener would like something: *What about a glass of milk?* **what if?** what will or would happen if: *What if he comes back?* **what with** because of: *What with all this noise, I can't hear myself think*

whatever ADJECTIVE & PRONOUN **1** anything (that): *Show me whatever you have* **2** no matter what: *whatever happens*

whatsoever ADJECTIVE at all: *nothing whatsoever to do with me*

wheat NOUN a grain from which the flour used for bread etc is made

wheaten ADJECTIVE **1** made of wheat **2** wholemeal

wheatgerm NOUN the vitamin-rich embryo of wheat

wheedle VERB to beg or coax, often by flattery

wheel NOUN **1** a circular frame or disc turning on an axle, used for transporting things **2** a steering wheel of a car etc ▸ VERB **1** to move or push on wheels **2** to turn like a wheel or in a wide curve **3** to turn round suddenly: *wheeled round in surprise*

wheelbarrow NOUN a handcart with one wheel in front, two handles and legs behind

wheelchair NOUN a chair on wheels for an invalid

wheeze VERB to breathe with difficulty, making a whistling or croaking sound ▸ NOUN **1** the sound of difficult breathing **2** *informal* a joke

whelk NOUN a type of small shellfish, used as food

whelp NOUN **1** a puppy **2** *old* a young lion ▸ VERB of a lion, dog, etc: to give birth to young

when ADVERB at what time: *When did you arrive?* ▸ ADVERB & CONJUNCTION the time at which: *I know when you left/I fell when I was coming in* ▸ RELATIVE PRONOUN at which: *at the time when I saw him* ▸ CONJUNCTION seeing that, since: *Why walk when you have a car?*

whence *old*, ADVERB from what place: *Whence did you come?* ▸CONJUNCTION to the place from which: *He's gone back whence he came*

whenever ADVERB & CONJUNCTION **1** at any given time: *Come whenever you're ready* **2** at every time: *I go whenever I get the chance*

where ADVERB & CONJUNCTION to or in what place: *Where are you going?/I wonder where we are* ▸RELATIVE PRONOUN & CONJUNCTION (in the place) in which, (to the place) to which: *Go where he tells you to go/It's still where it was*

whereabouts ADVERB & CONJUNCTION near or in what place: *Whereabouts is it?/I don't know whereabouts it is* ▸NOUN the place where someone or something is: *I don't know her whereabouts*

whereas CONJUNCTION **1** when in fact: *They thought I was lying, whereas I was telling the truth* **2** but, on the other hand: *He's tall, whereas I'm short*

whereupon ADVERB & CONJUNCTION at or after which time, event, etc

wherever ADVERB to what place: *Wherever did you go?* ▸CONJUNCTION to any place: *Wherever you may go*

wherewithal NOUN **1** the means of doing something **2** money

whether CONJUNCTION **1** either if: *whether you come or not* **2** if: *I don't know whether it's possible*

which ADJECTIVE & PRONOUN **1** used to refer to a particular person or thing from a group: *Which colour do you like best?* **2** the one that: *Show me which dress you would like* ▸RELATIVE PRONOUN referring to the person or thing just named: *I bought the chair which you are sitting on* **which is which** which is one and which is the other: *They are twins and I can't tell which is which*

whichever ADJECTIVE & PRONOUN any (one), no matter which: *I'll take whichever you don't want/I saw trees whichever way I turned*

whiff NOUN a sudden puff or scent: *whiff of perfume*

while *or* **whilst** CONJUNCTION **1** during the time that: *while I'm at the office* **2** although: *While I sympathize, I can't really help* ▸NOUN a space of time ▸VERB: **while away** to pass (time) without boredom: *He whiled away the time by reading*

whim NOUN a sudden thought or desire

whimper VERB to cry with a low, whining voice ▸NOUN a low, whining cry

whimsical ADJECTIVE **1** full of whims, fanciful **2** humorous

whine VERB **1** to make a high-pitched, complaining cry **2** to complain unnecessarily ▸NOUN an unnecessary complaint

whinge VERB (**whingeing** *or* **whinging, whinged**) to whine, complain peevishly ▸NOUN a peevish complaint

whinny VERB (**whinnies, whinnying, whinnied**) of a horse: to neigh ▸NOUN (*plural* **whinnies**) a neighing sound

A B C D E F G H I J K L M N O P Q R S T U V W X Y Z

whip NOUN **1** a lash with a handle, for punishing, urging on animals, etc **2** a member of a party in parliament who sees that all the party's members attend to give their vote when needed ▶ VERB (**whipping, whipped**) **1** to hit or drive with a lash **2** to beat (eggs, cream, etc) into a froth **3** to snatch (away, off, out, up, etc): *whipped out a revolver* **4** to move fast, like a whip

whippet NOUN a breed of racing dog, like a small greyhound

whipping NOUN a beating with a whip

whir *or* **whirr** NOUN a sound of fast, continuous whirling ▶ VERB (**whirring, whirred**) to move or whirl with a buzzing noise

whirl VERB **1** to turn round quickly **2** to carry (off, away, etc) quickly ▶ NOUN **1** a fast circling movement **2** great excitement, confusion: *in a whirl over the wedding arrangements*

whirlpool NOUN a place in a river or sea where the current moves in a circle

whirlwind NOUN a violent current of wind with a whirling motion

whisk VERB **1** to move quickly and lightly, sweep: *Their car whisked past* **2** to beat or whip (a mixture) ▶ NOUN **1** a quick sweeping movement **2** a kitchen utensil for beating eggs or mixtures **3** a small bunch of twigs etc used as a brush

whisker NOUN **1** a long bristle on the upper lip of a cat etc **2** (**whiskers**) hair on the sides of a man's face, sideburns

whisky *or Irish & US* **whiskey** NOUN (*plural* **whiskies** *or* **whiskeys**) an alcoholic spirit made from grain

[i] Based on Scottish Gaelic *uisge beatha*, meaning 'water of life'

whisper VERB **1** to speak very softly, using the breath only, not the voice **2** to make a soft, rustling sound ▶ NOUN a soft sound made with the breath

whist NOUN a type of card game for four players

whistle VERB **1** to make a high-pitched sound by forcing breath through the lips or teeth **2** to make such a sound with an instrument **3** to move with such a sound, like a bullet ▶ NOUN **1** the sound made by whistling **2** any instrument for whistling

White ADJECTIVE **1** of people: belonging to one of the pale-skinned races **2** belonging to or relating to White people ▶ NOUN a white-skinned person

white ADJECTIVE **1** of the colour of pure snow **2** pale or light-coloured: *white wine* ▶ NOUN **1** the colour of pure snow **2** the light part of the eyeball **3** the part of an egg surrounding the yolk

white elephant NOUN something useless and costly or troublesome to maintain

[i] From a story that the King of Siam gave white elephants as gifts to rude courtiers. The elephants cost a lot of money to look after, but could not be disposed of or put to work because they were thought to be sacred

white-hot ADJECTIVE having

reached a degree of heat at which metals glow with a white light (hotter than **red-hot**)

whiten VERB to make or become white or whiter

whiteness NOUN a white state or quality

whitewash NOUN a mixture of ground chalk and water, or lime and water, for whitening walls etc ▶ VERB **1** to put whitewash on **2** to cover up the faults of, give a good appearance to

whither ADVERB & CONJUNCTION, *old* to what place?

whiting NOUN a small type of fish related to the cod

Whitsun NOUN the week beginning with the seventh Sunday after Easter

whittle VERB **1** to pare or cut (wood etc) with a knife **2** (often **whittle away** or **down**) to make gradually less: *whittled away his savings*

whizz *or* **whiz** VERB (**whizzing, whizzed**) **1** to move with a hissing sound, like an arrow **2** to move very fast ▶ NOUN someone remarkably good at something

whizz kid *or* **whiz kid** NOUN someone who achieves rapid success while relatively young

WHO ABBREVIATION World Health Organization, a United Nations agency monitoring people's health around the world

who PRONOUN used to refer to someone or some people unknown or unnamed (only as the subject of a verb): *Who is that woman in the green hat?* ▶ RELATIVE PRONOUN referring to the person or people just named: *Do you know who those people are?*

whoever PRONOUN any person or people

whole ADJECTIVE **1** complete **2** all, with nothing or no one missing **3** not broken **4** in good health ▶ NOUN the entire thing **on the whole** when everything is taken into account

wholefood NOUN unprocessed food produced without the aid of artificial fertilizers

wholehearted ADJECTIVE enthusiastic, generous

wholemeal NOUN flour made from the entire wheat grain

whole number NOUN, *maths* a number without fractions, ie positive integer or zero

wholesale NOUN the sale of goods in large quantities to a shop from which they can be bought in small quantities by ordinary buyers (*compare with*: **retail**) ▶ ADJECTIVE **1** buying or selling in large quantities **2** on a large scale: *wholesale killing*

wholesaler NOUN a person who buys goods on a large scale and sells them in smaller quantities to shopkeepers for sale to the public

wholesome ADJECTIVE giving health, healthy: *wholesome food*

who'll *short for* who will; who shall

wholly ADVERB entirely, altogether

whom PRONOUN **1** used to refer to someone or some people unknown or unnamed (only as the object of a sentence): *Whom did you see?/ To whom am I speaking?* **2** which

A B C D E F G H I J K L M N O P Q R S T U V **W** X Y Z

person: *Do you know to whom I gave it?* ▶RELATIVE PRONOUN referring to the person or people just named: *the person whom I liked best*

whoop NOUN a loud cry, rising in pitch ▶VERB to give a whoop

whooping cough NOUN an infectious disease in which violent bouts of coughing are followed by a whoop as the breath is drawn in

whose ADJECTIVE & PRONOUN belonging to whom?: *Whose handwriting is this?* ▶RELATIVE PRONOUN of whom: *the man whose wife I know*

why ADVERB & PRONOUN for which reason?: *Why did you not stay?* **the whys and wherefores** all the reasons, details

wick NOUN the twisted threads in a candle or lamp which draw up the oil or grease to the flame

wicked ADJECTIVE **1** evil, sinful **2** mischievous, spiteful > **wickedly** ADVERB

wicker ADJECTIVE of a chair: made of woven willow twigs

wicket NOUN **1** a small gate or door, especially in or beside a larger one **2** *cricket* the set of three stumps, or one of these, at which the ball is bowled **3** *cricket* the ground between the bowler and the batsman

wide ADJECTIVE **1** broad, not narrow **2** stretching far: *a wide grin* **3** general, big: *a wide selection* **4** measuring a certain amount from side to side: *5 centimetres wide* ▶ADVERB **1** off the target: *the shots went wide* **2** (often **wide apart**) far apart: *hold your arms wide* **wide of the mark** off the target, inaccurate

wide awake ADJECTIVE fully awake; alert

wide-eyed ADJECTIVE with eyes wide open in surprise etc

widely ADVERB **1** over a wide area; among many: *widely believed* **2** far apart: *widely set eyes/widely different ideas*

widen VERB to make or become wide

wideness NOUN a wide state or quality

wide open ADJECTIVE opened to the full extent

widespread ADJECTIVE spread over a large area or among many people: *a widespread belief*

widow NOUN a woman whose husband is dead

widower NOUN a man whose wife is dead

width NOUN **1** measurement across, from side to side **2** large extent

wield VERB **1** to swing or handle (a cricket bat, sword, etc) **2** to use (power, authority, etc)

wife NOUN (*plural* **wives**) **1** a married woman **2** the woman to whom a man is married

Wi-Fi (*pronounced* **wai**-fai) NOUN, *trademark* a method of transmitting data between computers without wires, using high-frequency radio waves

ⓘ A shortening of *wireless fidelity*, modelled on **hi-fi**

wig NOUN an artificial covering of hair for the head

wiggle VERB to move from side

to side with jerky or twisting movements ▶ NOUN a jerky movement from side to side

wiggly ADJECTIVE (**wigglier, wiggliest**) wriggly, wavy: *She drew a wiggly line*

wigwam NOUN, *history* a conical tent of skins made by some Native Americans

wild ADJECTIVE **1** of an animal: not tamed **2** of a plant: not cultivated in a garden **3** uncivilized **4** unruly, uncontrolled **5** of weather: stormy **6** frantic, mad: *wild with anxiety* **7** of a guess etc: rash, inaccurate ▶ NOUN (usually **wilds**) an uncultivated or uncivilized region

wild boar NOUN a wild type of pig

wildcat NOUN (often **wild cat**) a wild type of European cat ▶ ADJECTIVE **1** of an industrial strike: not called by a trade union **2** of a business scheme: financially unsound or risky

wilderness NOUN a wild, uncultivated or desolate region

wild-goose chase NOUN a troublesome and useless errand

wildlife NOUN wild animals, birds, etc in their natural habitats

wile NOUN a crafty trick

wilful ADJECTIVE **1** fond of having one's own way: *a wilful child* **2** intentional: *wilful damage*

will[1] VERB **1** (*past form* **would**) used to form future tenses of other verbs when the subject is **he, she, it, you** or **they**: *You will see me there* **2** *informal* often used for the same purpose when the subject is **I** or **we**: *I will tell you later* **3** used for emphasis, or to express a promise, when the subject is **I** or **we**: *I will do it if possible* (*see also* **shall, would**)

🛈 Comes from Old English *wyllan* meaning 'to wish' or 'to be willing'

will[2] NOUN **1** the power to choose or decide **2** wish or desire: *against my will* **3** determination: *the will to win* **4** feeling towards someone: *bore him ill will* **5** a written statement about what is to be done with your property after your death ▶ VERB **1** to try to influence someone by exercising your will: *He willed her to win* **2** to hand down (property etc) by will **at will** as or when you choose **with a will** eagerly

🛈 Comes from Old English *willa* meaning 'will' or 'determination'

willing ADJECTIVE ready to do what is asked; eager

will-o'-the-wisp NOUN a pale light sometimes seen by night over marshy places

willow NOUN **1** a tree with long slender branches **2** its wood, used in cricket bats

willy-nilly ADVERB **1** whether you wish or not **2** notwithstanding other people's feelings

🛈 From the phrase *will I, nill I,* meaning 'whether I want or don't want'

wilt VERB **1** of a flower or plant: to droop **2** to lose strength

wily ADJECTIVE (**wilier, wiliest**) cunning

wimp NOUN, *informal* an ineffectual person

win VERB (**winning, won**) **1** to come first in a contest **2** to gain by luck or

a b c d e f g h i j k l m n o p q r s t u v w x y z

A B C D E F G H I J K L M N O P Q R S T U V W X Y Z

in a contest: *I won a teddy bear* **3** to gain (the love of someone etc) by effort **4** (often **win over**) to gain the support or friendship of ▶NOUN an act of winning; a victory

wince VERB to shrink or start back in pain etc, flinch: *Her singing made me wince*

winch NOUN (*plural* **winches**) **1** a handle or crank for turning a wheel **2** a machine for lifting things, worked by winding a rope round a revolving cylinder **3** (usually **winch up**) to lift up with a winch

wind[1] (*pronounced* wind) NOUN **1** a current of air **2** breath **3** the scent of an animal, predator, etc carried by the wind **4** air or gas in the stomach **5** the wind instruments in an orchestra ▶VERB to put out of breath **get the wind up** *informal* to become afraid **get wind of** *informal* to hear about in an indirect way

wind[2] (*pronounced* waind) VERB (**winding, wound**) **1** to turn, twist or coil **2** (sometimes **wind up**) to screw up the spring of (a watch, clockwork toy, etc) **3** to wrap closely **wind up 1** to bring or come to an end: *wind up a meeting* **2** *informal* to annoy, tease **wind your way** to make your way circuitously

winder NOUN a key etc for winding a clock

windfall NOUN **1** a fruit blown from a tree **2** an unexpected gain, eg a sum of money

wind farm NOUN a group of wind-driven turbines generating electricity

winding ADJECTIVE curving, twisting

wind instrument NOUN a musical instrument sounded by blowing into it

windmill NOUN a mill driven by sails which are moved by the wind, used for pumping water, grinding grain, etc

window NOUN an opening in a wall, protected by glass, which lets in light and air

Windows SINGULAR NOUN, *trademark* a type of computer operating system

windpipe NOUN the air tube leading from the throat to the lungs (*also called*: **trachea**)

windscreen *or esp US* **windshield** NOUN a pane of glass in front of the driver of a car etc

windsurfer NOUN a board with a sail for riding the waves

windsurfing NOUN the sport of riding the waves on a sailboard or windsurfer

windswept ADJECTIVE exposed to strong winds and showing the effects of it: *windswept hair*

windy ADJECTIVE (**windier, windiest**) **1** of weather: with a strong wind blowing **2** of a place: exposed to strong winds

wine NOUN **1** an alcoholic drink made from the fermented juice of grapes or other fruit **2** a rich dark red colour

wing NOUN **1** one of the arm-like limbs of a bird, bat or insect by means of which it flies **2** one of the two projections on the sides of an aeroplane **3** a part of a house built out to the side **4** the side of a stage, where actors wait to enter **5** *football etc* a player positioned at the edge of the field **6** a section of a political party: *the left wing* ▶VERB **1** to wound (a bird) in the wing **2** to soar **on the wing** flying, in motion **under someone's wing** under the protection or care of someone

winged ADJECTIVE **1** having wings **2** swift

wink VERB **1** to open and close an eye quickly **2** to give a hint by winking **3** of lights etc: to flicker, twinkle ▶NOUN **1** an act of winking **2** a hint given by winking **forty winks** a short sleep

winkle NOUN a small edible shellfish (*also called*: **periwinkle**) **winkle out** to force out gradually

winning ADJECTIVE **1** victorious, successful **2** charming, attractive: *winning smile*

winnings PLURAL NOUN money etc that has been won

winsome ADJECTIVE charming

winter NOUN the coldest season of the year, following autumn ▶ADJECTIVE relating to winter ▶VERB **1** to pass the winter **2** to keep, feed (sheep etc) during the winter

winter sports PLURAL NOUN sports on snow or ice, eg skiing, tobogganing, etc

wintry ADJECTIVE **1** cold, frosty **2** cheerless, unfriendly: *a wintry look*

wipe VERB **1** to clean or dry by rubbing **2** (**wipe away, out, off** or **up**) to clear away by wiping ▶NOUN the act of cleaning by rubbing **wipe out** to destroy totally

wiper NOUN one of a pair of moving parts which wipe the windscreen of a car

wire NOUN **1** a thread-like length of metal **2** the metal thread connecting points by telephone etc **3** *informal* a telegram ▶ADJECTIVE made of wire ▶VERB **1** to bind or fasten with wire **2** *informal* to send a telegram **3** (sometimes **wire up**) to supply (a building, equipment, etc) with wires for carrying an electric current

wireless ADJECTIVE of communication: by radio waves ▶NOUN, *old* a radio set

wiry ADJECTIVE **1** made of wire **2** of a person: thin but strong

wisdom NOUN the quality of being wise

wisdom tooth PLURAL NOUN one of four large back teeth which appear after childhood

wise ADJECTIVE **1** very knowledgeable **2** judging rightly; sensible

-wise SUFFIX **1** in the manner or way of: *crabwise* **2** with reference or regard to: *careerwise*

wish VERB **1** to feel or express a desire: *I wish he'd leave* **2** (often **wish for**) to long for, desire: *She wished for peace and quiet* **3** to hope for on behalf of (someone): *wish someone luck* ▶NOUN (*plural* **wishes**) **1** desire, longing **2** a thing desired or wanted: *Her great wish was to live abroad* **3** an expression of desire: *Make a wish* **4** (**wishes**) expression of hope for another's happiness, good fortune, etc: *best wishes* **wish someone well** to feel goodwill towards them

wishbone NOUN a forked bone in the breast of fowls

a b c d e f g h i j k l m n o p q r s t u v w x y z

A B C D E F G H I J K L M N O P Q R S T U V W X Y Z

wishful ADJECTIVE wishing, eager **wishful thinking** basing your belief on (false) hopes rather than known facts

wishy-washy ADJECTIVE **1** of liquid: thin and weak **2** feeble, not energetic or lively **3** lacking colour

wisp NOUN a small tuft or strand: *a wisp of hair*

wispy ADJECTIVE (**wispier, wispiest**) wisp-like; light and fine in texture: *wispy white clouds*

wistful ADJECTIVE thoughtful and rather sad: *a wistful glance* > **wistfully** ADVERB

wit NOUN **1** (often **wits**) intelligence, common sense **2** the ability to express ideas neatly and funnily **3** someone who can do this **at your wits' end** unable to solve your difficulties, desperate **keep your wits about you** to keep alert **to wit** namely, that is to say

witch NOUN (*plural* **witches**) **1** a woman with magic power obtained through evil spirits **2** an ugly old woman

witchcraft NOUN magic performed by a witch

witch doctor NOUN someone believed to have magical powers to cure illnesses etc

with PREPOSITION **1** in the company of: *I was walking with my father* **2** by means of: *cut it with a knife* **3** in the same direction as: *drifting with the current* **4** against: *fighting with his brother* **5** on the same side as: *I'm with Tommy on this one* **6** having: *a man with a limp* **7** in the keeping of: *Leave the keys with me*

withdraw VERB (**withdrawing, withdrew, withdrawn**) **1** to go back or away **2** to take away, remove: *withdraw cash/withdraw troops* **3** to take back (an insult etc) > **withdrawal** NOUN

withdrawn ADJECTIVE **1** of a person: unwilling to communicate with others, unsociable **2** of a place: lonely, isolated

wither VERB **1** to fade, dry up or decay **2** to make to feel very unimportant or embarrassed: *She withered him with a look*

withering ADJECTIVE **1** drying up, dying **2** of a remark etc: scornful, sarcastic

withhold VERB (**withholding, withheld**) to keep back, refuse to give

within PREPOSITION inside the limits of: *keep within the law* ▸ ADVERB on the inside

without PREPOSITION **1** in the absence of: *We went without you* **2** not having: *without a penny* **3** *old* outside the limits of: *without the terms of the agreement* ▸ ADVERB, *old* **1** on the outside **2** out-of-doors

withstand VERB (**withstanding, withstood**) to oppose or resist successfully

witness NOUN (*plural* **witnesses**) **1** someone who sees or has direct knowledge of a thing **2** someone who gives evidence in a law court **3** proof, evidence ▸ VERB **1** to see, be present at **2** to sign your name to confirm the authenticity of (someone else's signature) **3** to give or be evidence **bear witness** to give or be evidence of: *bear witness to his character*

-witted ADJECTIVE (*added to another word*) having wits (of a certain kind): *slow-witted/quick-witted*

witticism NOUN a witty remark

wittingly ADVERB knowingly

witty ADJECTIVE (**wittier, wittiest**) clever and amusing

wizard NOUN a man believed to have the power of magic

wizardry NOUN magic

wizened ADJECTIVE dried up, shrivelled: *a wizened old man*

wobble VERB to rock unsteadily from side to side ▸NOUN an unsteady rocking

wobbly ADJECTIVE (**wobblier, wobbliest**) unsteady, rocking

woe NOUN **1** grief, misery **2** a cause of sorrow, a trouble

woebegone ADJECTIVE dismal, sad-looking

woeful ADJECTIVE sorrowful; pitiful > **woefully** ADVERB

wok NOUN an Asian cooking-pan shaped like a large bowl

wolf NOUN (*plural* **wolves**) a wild animal like a dog that hunts in packs ▸VERB (usually **wolf down**) to eat greedily: *wolfing down his food* **cry wolf** to give a false alarm **keep the wolf from the door** to keep away hunger or want

woman NOUN (*plural* **women**) **1** an adult human female **2** human females in general **3** a domestic help

ⓘ Comes from Old English *wif* meaning 'a woman', and *man* meaning 'man' or 'human being'

womanhood NOUN the state of being a woman

womankind *or* **womenkind** NOUN women generally

womanly ADJECTIVE like, or suitable for, a woman

womb NOUN the part of a female mammal's body in which the young develop and stay till birth

wombat NOUN a small, beaver-like Australian animal, with a pouch

women *plural* of **woman**

won *past form* of **win**

wonder NOUN **1** the feeling produced by something unexpected or extraordinary; surprise, awe **2** something strange, amazing or miraculous ▸VERB **1** to be curious or in doubt: *I wonder what will happen/I wonder whether to go or not* **2** to feel surprise or amazement (at, that): *I wonder at you sometimes!*

wonderful ADJECTIVE **1** excellent **2** arousing wonder; strange, marvellous

wondrous ADJECTIVE, *old* wonderful

won't *short for* will not

woo VERB (**wooing, wooed**) **1** to try to win the love of (someone) **2** to try to gain (eg success)

wood NOUN **1** a group of growing trees **2** the hard tissue beneath the bark of a tree, especially when cut for use

woodcut NOUN **1** a picture engraved on wood **2** a print made from this engraving

woodcutter NOUN someone who fells trees, cuts up wood, etc

wooded ADJECTIVE covered with trees

A B C D E F G H I J K L M N O P Q R S T U V W X Y Z

wooden ADJECTIVE **1** made of wood **2** dull, stiff, not lively: *a wooden speech* > **woodenly** ADVERB

woodland NOUN land covered with trees

woodlouse NOUN (*plural* **woodlice**) a small beetle-like creature with a jointed shell, found under stones etc

woodpecker NOUN a bird that pecks holes in the bark of trees with its beak, in search of insects

wood spirit *same as* **methanol**

woodwind NOUN a family of wind instruments made of wood or metal, eg the flute or clarinet

woodwork NOUN **1** the making of wooden articles **2** the wooden parts of a house, room, etc

woodworm NOUN the larva of a beetle that bores holes in wood and destroys it

woody ADJECTIVE (**woodier, woodiest**) **1** like wood **2** wooded

wooer NOUN someone who woos

wool NOUN **1** the soft hair of sheep and other animals **2** yarn or cloth made of wool

woollen ADJECTIVE made of wool ▸ NOUN a knitted garment made of wool

woolly ADJECTIVE (**woollier, woolliest**) **1** made of, or like, wool **2** vague, hazy: *a woolly argument* ▸ NOUN (*plural* **woollies**) a knitted woollen garment

word NOUN **1** a written or spoken sign representing a thing or an idea **2** (**words**) talk, remarks: *kind words* **3** news: *word of his death* **4** a promise: *break your word* ▸ VERB to choose words for: *He worded his refusal carefully* **have words** *informal* to quarrel **in a word** in short, to sum up **take someone at their word** to treat what they say as true **take someone's word for something** to trust that what they say is true **word for word** in the exact words

wording NOUN choice or arrangement of words

word processor NOUN an electronic machine or computer program which can store, edit and print out text

wordy ADJECTIVE (**wordier, wordiest**) using too many words

wore *past tense* of **wear**

work NOUN **1** a physical or mental effort to achieve or make something **2** a job, employment: *out of work* **3** a task: *I've got work to do* **4** anything made or done **5** something produced by art, eg a book, musical composition, painting, etc **6** manner of working, workmanship: *poor work* **7** (**works**) a factory **8** (**works**) a mechanism (eg of a watch) **9** (**works**) deeds: *good works* ▸ VERB **1** to be engaged in physical or mental work **2** to be employed **3** to run or operate smoothly and efficiently **4** of a plan etc: to be successful **5** to manage, control: *work the land/work a machine/work magic* **6** to get into a position slowly and gradually: *The screw worked loose* **work out 1** to solve **2** to discover as a result of deep thought **3** of a situation: to turn out all right in the end **work up** to arouse, excite: *working himself up into a fury*

[1] Comes from Old English *weorc*

workable ADJECTIVE able to be done, practical

worker NOUN someone who works at a job

working ADJECTIVE operating properly, not broken

working class NOUN the social class including manual workers

working day *or* **working hours** NOUN the hours each day that someone spends at work, on duty, etc

workman NOUN (*plural* **workmen**) someone who works with their hands

workmanship NOUN **1** the skill of a workman **2** the degree of expertise in making something: *satisfactory workmanship*

workshop NOUN a room or building where manufacturing, craftwork, etc is done

world NOUN **1** the earth and all things on it **2** the people of the world **3** any planet or star **4** the universe **5** a state of existence: *the next world* **6** a particular area of life or activity: *the insect world/the world of fashion* **7** a great deal: *a world of good*

[i] Comes from Old English *weorold* meaning 'age or life of man'

worldly ADJECTIVE (**worldlier, worldliest**) concerned with material things such as money, possessions, etc, not the soul or spirit

worldwide ADJECTIVE extending throughout the world ▶ ADVERB throughout the world

World Wide Web NOUN a vast collection of linked documents and stored information located on computers all around the world, which can be accessed via the Internet

worm NOUN **1** a small creeping animal without a backbone, often living in soil **2** *informal* a low, contemptible person **3** something spiral-shaped, eg the thread of a screw **4** (**worms**) the condition of having parasitic worms in the intestines **5** *computing* an unauthorized program designed to sabotage a system by reproducing itself throughout a network ▶ VERB **1** to move gradually and stealthily (in or into) **2** (also **worm out**) to draw out (information) bit by bit

wormwood NOUN a plant with a bitter taste

worn ADJECTIVE **1** damaged by use **2** tired, worn-out

worn-out ADJECTIVE tired, exhausted

worried ADJECTIVE in an unhappy and unrelaxed state, as a result of thinking about something bad which is happening, or which you fear may happen

worry VERB (**worries, worrying, worried**) **1** to annoy **2** to make troubled and anxious **3** to be troubled and anxious **4** of a dog: to shake or tear (something) with its teeth ▶ NOUN (*plural* **worries**) **1** uneasiness, anxiety **2** a cause of unease or anxiety

worse ADJECTIVE **1** bad or evil to a greater degree **2** more ill ▶ ADVERB badly to a greater degree, more severely: *It's snowing worse than* *ever* **worse off** in a worse position, less wealthy, etc

worsen VERB to make or become worse

worship NOUN **1** a religious ceremony or service **2** deep reverence, adoration **3** a title used in addressing a mayor, magistrate, etc ▸VERB (**worshipping, worshipped**) **1** to pay honour to (a god) **2** to adore or admire deeply

worst ADJECTIVE bad or evil to the greatest degree ▸ADVERB badly to the greatest degree ▸VERB (**worsting, worsted**) to beat, defeat **at worst** under the least favourable circumstances **if the worst comes to the worst** if the worst possible circumstances occur

worth NOUN **1** value; price **2** importance **3** excellence of character etc ▸ADJECTIVE **1** equal in value to: *jewellery worth a thousand pounds* **2** deserving of: *worth considering* **worth your while** worth the trouble spent

worthless ADJECTIVE of no merit or value

worthwhile ADJECTIVE deserving time and effort

worthy ADJECTIVE (**worthier, worthiest**) **1** (often **worthy of**) deserving, suitable **2** of good character ▸NOUN (*plural* **worthies**) a highly respected person: *local worthy*

would VERB **1** the form of the verb **will** used to express a condition: *He would go if he could* **2** used for emphasis: *I tell you I would do it if possible* **3** *old* expressing a wish: *I would that he were gone*
ⓘ Comes from Old English *wolde* which is the past tense of *wyllan* meaning 'to wish'

would-be ADJECTIVE trying to be or pretending to be: *would-be actor*

wound (*pronounced* woond) NOUN **1** a cut or injury caused by a weapon, in an accident, etc **2** a hurt to someone's feelings ▸VERB **1** to make a cut or injury in **2** to hurt the feelings of

wounded (*pronounced* **woond**-*ed*) ADJECTIVE having a wound, injured, hurt

WPC ABBREVIATION Woman Police Constable

wraith (*pronounced* reith) NOUN an apparition of a living person, often as a warning of death

wrap VERB (**wrapping, wrapped**) **1** to fold or roll round: *Wrap the foil around the turkey* **2** (also **wrap up**) to cover by folding or winding something round: *Wrap it in tissue paper* ▸NOUN **1** a cloak or shawl **2** a snack made from a tortilla rolled around a filling

wrapper NOUN a loose paper cover, eg round a book or sweet

wrath (*pronounced* roth *or* rawth *or* rath) NOUN violent anger

wrathful (*pronounced* **roth**-fuwl *or* **rawth**-fuwl *or* **rath**-fuwl) ADJECTIVE very angry

wreak (*pronounced* reek) VERB **1** to carry out: *wreak vengeance* **2** to cause: *wreak havoc*

wreath (*pronounced* reeth) NOUN **1** a ring of flowers or leaves **2** a curling wisp of smoke, mist, etc

wreck NOUN **1** destruction, especially of a ship by the sea **2** the remains of anything destroyed, especially a ship **3** someone whose health or nerves are in bad condition ▸ VERB to destroy

wreckage (*pronounced* **rek**-ij) NOUN the remains of something wrecked

wren NOUN a very small type of bird

wrench VERB **1** to pull with a violent, often twisting, motion **2** to sprain (your ankle etc) ▸ NOUN (*plural* **wrenches**) **1** a violent twist **2** a tool for gripping and turning nuts, bolts, etc **3** sadness caused by parting from someone or something

wrest VERB, *formal* to twist or take by force

wrestle (*pronounced* **re**-sl) VERB **1** to fight with someone, trying to bring them to the ground **2** (also **wrestle with**) to struggle with or think deeply about (a problem etc)

wrestler (*pronounced* **res**-ler) NOUN someone who wrestles as a sport

wrestling (*pronounced* **res**-ling) NOUN the sport in which two people fight to throw each other to the ground

wretch NOUN (*plural* **wretches**) **1** a miserable, pitiable person: *a poor wretch* **2** a worthless or contemptible person

wretched (*pronounced* **rech**-id) ADJECTIVE **1** very miserable **2** worthless, very bad > **wretchedly** ADVERB

wriggle VERB **1** to twist to and fro **2** to move by doing this, as a worm does **3** (**wriggle out of**) to escape or evade (a difficulty etc)

-wright (*pronounced* rait) SUFFIX a maker: *shipwright/playwright*

ⓘ Comes from Old English *wyrht* meaning 'a work'

wring VERB (**wringing, wrung**) **1** to twist or squeeze (especially water out of wet clothes) **2** to clasp and unclasp (your hands) in grief, anxiety, etc **3** to cause pain to: *the story wrung everybody's heart* **4** to force out (eg a promise)

wringer NOUN a machine for forcing water from wet clothes

wrinkle NOUN a small crease or fold on the skin or other surface ▸ VERB to make or become wrinkled

wrinkly ADJECTIVE (**wrinklier, wrinkliest**) having wrinkles

wrist NOUN the joint by which the hand is joined to the arm

write (*pronounced* rait) VERB (**writing, wrote, written**) **1** to form letters with a pen, pencil, etc **2** to put into writing: *write your name* **3** to compose (a letter, a book, etc) **4** to send a letter (to) **5** *computing* to copy (a data file) **write down** to record in writing **write off 1** to damage a vehicle beyond repair (in a crash) **2** to cancel (a debt) **3** to dismiss as unimportant etc: *wrote off our chances of winning* **write up** to make a written record or review of

writer (*pronounced* **rai**-ter) NOUN someone who writes, an author

writhe (*pronounced* raidh) VERB to twist or roll about, eg in pain

writing (*pronounced* **rai**-ting) NOUN a written text

wrong ADJECTIVE **1** not correct: *the*

wrong answer **2** mistaken: *You are wrong if you think that* **3** unsuitable: *the wrong weather for camping/ quite the wrong dress for the occasion* **4** not right or just: *It was wrong to punish him* **5** evil ▶NOUN **1** whatever is not right or just **2** an injury done to another ▶VERB to do wrong to, harm > **wrongly** ADVERB
go wrong 1 to fail to work properly **2** to make a mistake or mistakes
in the wrong guilty of injustice or error

wrongdoer (*pronounced* **rong**-doo-*er*) NOUN someone who does wrong

wrongdoing (*pronounced* **rong**-doo-ing) NOUN immoral or illegal behaviour or actions

wrongful ADJECTIVE not lawful or just: *wrongful criminal convictions*

wrote *past tense* of **write**

wrought (*pronounced* rawt) ADJECTIVE, *old* made, manufactured ▶VERB, *old past form* of **work**

wrought iron (*pronounced* rawt **ai**-r*o*n) NOUN iron hammered, rather than cast, into shape

wrung *past form* of **wring**

wry (*pronounced* rai) ADJECTIVE **1** slightly mocking or bitter: *wry remark* **2** twisted or turned to one side > **wryly** ADVERB

WWW *or* **www** ABBREVIATION World Wide Web

WYSIWYG ABBREVIATION, *computing* what *you* see (on the screen) *is* what *you* get (in the printout)

Xx

X-chromosome NOUN the sex chromosome when present and paired with another X-chromosome determines the female sex in most animals

xenophobia (*pronounced* zen-*o*-**foh**-bi-*a or* zeen-*o*-**foh**-bi-*a*) NOUN hatred of foreigners or strangers

xenotransplantation (*pronounced* zen-*o*- *or* zeen-*o*-) NOUN the transplantation of an animal organ into an animal of a different species

xerophyte (*pronounced* **zee**-ro-fait) NOUN a desert plant, eg a cactus, adapted to grow in conditions where water is scarce

Xerox (*pronounced* **zeer**-roks) NOUN, *trademark* **1** a photographic process used for copying documents **2** a copy made in this way ▶ VERB to copy by Xerox

Xmas (*pronounced* **eks**-m*a*s *or* **kris**-m*a*s) NOUN, *informal* Christmas

X-ray NOUN **1** an electromagnetic ray that can pass through material impenetrable by light, and produce a photographic image of the object through which it has passed **2** a shadow picture produced by X-rays on photographic film ▶ VERB to take a photographic image of with X-rays

xylem NOUN (*pronounced* **zai**-lem) a tissue in some plants that conducts water from the roots to the leaves

xylophone NOUN a musical instrument consisting of a series of graded wooden bars which are struck with hammers

A B C D E F G H I J K L M N O P Q R S T U V W X Y Z

Yy

yacht (*pronounced* yawt) NOUN a boat or small ship, with sails and sometimes with an engine, for racing or cruising

yachtsman *or* **yachtswoman** NOUN someone who sails a yacht

yak NOUN a Tibetan long-haired ox

yam NOUN a tropical root vegetable, similar to a potato

Yank *or* **Yankee** NOUN, *Brit informal* an American

ⓘ Originally a nickname for Dutch settlers in New England in the 18th century, possibly because of the Dutch forename *Jan*

yank *informal* VERB, to tug or pull with a violent jerk ▸ NOUN a violent tug

yap VERB (**yapping, yapped**) to bark sharply

yard NOUN **1** a measure of length (0.9144 metres, or 3 feet) **2** a long beam on a mast for spreading sails **3** an enclosed space used for a particular purpose: *railway yard/ shipbuilding yard* **4** *US* a garden

yardstick NOUN **1** a yard-long measuring stick **2** any standard for comparison

yarn NOUN **1** wool, cotton, etc spun into thread **2** one of several threads forming a rope **3** a long, often improbable, story

yarrow NOUN a strong-smelling plant with flat clusters of white flowers

yashmak NOUN a veil covering the lower half of the face, worn by Muslim women

yawl NOUN a small rowing boat or fishing boat

yawn VERB **1** to take a deep breath unintentionally with an open mouth, because of boredom or sleepiness **2** of a hole: to be wide open, gape ▸ NOUN an open-mouthed deep breath

Y-chromosome NOUN the sex chromosome which when present and paired with an X-chromosome determines the male sex in most animals

ye PRONOUN, *old* you

yea (*pronounced* yei) INTERJECTION, *old* yes

year NOUN **1** the time taken by the earth to go once round the sun, about 365 days **2** the period 1 January to 31 December **3** a period of twelve months starting at any point **4** (**years**) age: *wise for her years*

ⓘ Comes from Old English *gear*

yearling NOUN a year-old animal

yearly ADJECTIVE happening every year, or once a year

yearn (*pronounced* yern) VERB **1** to long (for, to do something etc) **2** to feel pity or tenderness (for)

yearning (*pronounced* **yern**-ing) NOUN an eager longing

yeast NOUN a substance which causes fermentation, used to make bread dough rise and in brewing

yell VERB to give a loud, shrill cry; scream ▶NOUN a loud, shrill cry

yellow NOUN the colour of gold, egg-yolks, etc ▶ADJECTIVE of this colour ▶VERB to become yellow, due to ageing

yelp VERB to give a sharp bark or cry ▶NOUN a sharp bark or cry

yen[1] NOUN the standard unit of Japanese currency

yen[2] NOUN, *informal* a strong desire, longing: *a yen to return to Scotland*

yeoman (*pronounced* **yoh**-m*a*n) NOUN, *history* a farmer with his own land **Yeomen of the Guard** the company acting as bodyguard to the British king or queen on certain occasions

yeomanry (*pronounced* **yoh**-m*a*n-ri) NOUN, *history* **1** farmers **2** a troop of cavalrymen serving voluntarily in the British army

yes INTERJECTION expressing agreement or consent ▶NOUN **1** an expression of agreement or consent **2** a vote in favour

yesterday NOUN **1** the day before today **2** the past ▶ADVERB on the day before today: *I bought it yesterday*

yet ADVERB **1** by now, by this time: *Have you seen that film yet?* **2** still, before the matter is finished: *We may win yet* ▶CONJUNCTION but, nevertheless: *I am defeated, yet I shall not surrender* **yet another** and another one still **yet more** still more

Yeti NOUN (**the yeti**) a large animal believed to exist in the Himalayas (*also called*: **the Abominable Snowman**)

yew NOUN **1** a tree with dark green leaves and red berries **2** its wood

YHA ABBREVIATION Youth Hostels Association

yield VERB **1** to give in, surrender **2** to give way to pressure or persuasion **3** to produce (a crop, results, etc) ▶NOUN an amount produced; a crop

yielding ADJECTIVE giving way easily

yob *or* **yobbo** NOUN (*plural* **yobboes** *or* **yobbos**) a lout, a hooligan

yodel VERB (**yodelling, yodelled**) to sing in a style involving frequent changes between an ordinary and a very high-pitched voice

yoga NOUN a Hindu system of philosophy and meditation, often involving special physical exercises

yogurt *or* **yoghurt** NOUN a semi-liquid food product made from fermented milk

yoke NOUN **1** a wooden frame joining oxen when pulling a plough or cart **2** a pair of oxen or horses **3** something that joins together **4** a frame placed across the shoulders for carrying pails etc ▶VERB **1** to put a yoke on **2** to join together

yokel (*pronounced* **yoh**-kel) NOUN, *derogatory* an unsophisticated country person; a rustic

yolk NOUN the yellow part of an egg

Yom Kippur NOUN the Day of Atonement, a Jewish fast day

yonder *old*, ADVERB in that place (at a distance but within sight) ▶ ADJECTIVE that (object) over there: *by yonder tree*

yore NOUN: **of yore** *old* formerly, in times past

you PRONOUN the person(s) spoken or written to, used as the singular or plural subject or object of a verb: *What did you say?/Are you both free tomorrow?*

you'd **1** *short for* you would; you should **2** you had

you'll *short for* you will; you shall

young ADJECTIVE **1** in the early part of life, mental or physical growth, etc **2** in the early stages: *The night is young* ▶ NOUN **1** the offspring of animals **2** (**the young**) young people

Comes from Old English *geong*

(adjective) juvenile, immature

youngster NOUN a young person

your ADJECTIVE belonging to you: *It's your life*

you're *short for* you are

yours PRONOUN belonging to you: *Is this pen yours?* **Yours**, **Yours faithfully**, **Yours sincerely**, **Yours truly** expressions used before a signature at the end of a letter

yourself PRONOUN (*plural* **yourselves**) **1** used reflexively: *Don't trouble yourself* **2** used for emphasis: *You yourself can't go*

youth NOUN **1** the state of being young **2** the early part of life **3** a young person **4** young people in general

youthful ADJECTIVE **1** young **2** fresh and vigorous

youth hostel NOUN a hostel where hikers etc may spend the night

you've *short for* you have

yo-yo NOUN a toy consisting of a reel which spins up and down on a string

Yule NOUN, *old* Christmas

Yuletide NOUN, *old* Christmas time

with a zip **2** to whiz, fly past at speed **3** *computing* to compress the data in a computer file, so that it takes up less memory

zip code NOUN in the US: a post code

zither NOUN a flat, stringed musical instrument, played with the fingers

zodiac NOUN an imaginary strip in space, divided into twelve equal parts **signs of the zodiac** the divisions of the zodiac used in astrology, each named after a group of stars

ⓘ From Greek, meaning literally 'circle of animals'

zombie NOUN **1** a corpse reanimated by witchcraft **2** a very slow or stupid person

ⓘ After the name of a voodoo snake god

zone NOUN **1** any of the five main bands into which the earth's surface is divided according to temperature: *temperate zone* **2** a section of a place marked off for a particular purpose: *no-parking zone/ smokeless zone* ▶ VERB to divide into zones

zoo NOUN a place where wild animals are kept and shown to the public

zoo- PREFIX of or relating to animals

ⓘ Comes from Greek *zoion* meaning 'animal'

zoological ADJECTIVE **1** relating to animals **2** relating to zoos; containing a zoo: *zoological gardens*

zoologist NOUN someone who studies animal life

zoology NOUN the science of animal life

zoom VERB **1** to move quickly with a loud, low buzzing noise **2** to make such a noise **3** of an aircraft: to climb sharply at high speed for a short time **4** to use a zoom lens on a camera

zoom lens NOUN a lens used in photography which makes a distant object appear gradually nearer without the camera being moved

zygote (*pronounced* **zai**-goht) NOUN, *biology* the cell formed when two gametes are joined, especially an egg cell fertilized by a male gamete

Zz

zany ADJECTIVE (**zanier, zaniest**), *informal* crazy, madcap
ⓘ After the name of a clownish character in Italian comic drama

zap VERB (**zapping, zapped**) **1** to strike, shoot, etc suddenly **2** to move rapidly; zip

zeal NOUN enthusiasm, keenness

zealot (*pronounced* **zel**-*o*t) NOUN a fanatical enthusiast

zealous (*pronounced* **zel**-*u*s) ADJECTIVE full of zeal > **zealously** ADVERB

zebra NOUN a striped African animal of the horse family

zebra crossing NOUN a pedestrian street crossing, painted in black and white stripes

zeitgeist (*pronounced* **zait**-gaist) NOUN the attitudes of a particular time period: *the zeitgeist of Britain today*

zenith NOUN **1** the point of the heavens exactly overhead **2** the highest point, the peak

zephyr (*pronounced* **zef**-*e*r) NOUN, *formal* a soft, gentle breeze

zero NOUN **1** nothing or the sign for it (0) **2** the point (marked 0) from which a scale (eg on a thermometer) begins

zero hour NOUN the exact time fixed for some action

zero option NOUN, *politics* a proposal to limit or abandon the deployment of nuclear missiles if the opposing side does likewise

zero-rated ADJECTIVE of goods: having no value-added tax

zest NOUN **1** relish, keen enjoyment **2** orange or lemon peel

zestful ADJECTIVE keen; full of enjoyment > **zestfully** ADVERB

zigzag ADJECTIVE having sharp bends or angles ▸ VERB (**zigzagging, zigzagged**) move in a zigzag direction

zimmer NOUN, *trademark* a hand-held metal frame used to give support in walking

zinc NOUN, *chemistry* a bluish-white metallic element used in dry batteries and as a coating to galvanize steel

zip NOUN **1** a fastening device for clothes, bags, etc, consisting of two rows of metal or nylon teeth which interlock when a sliding tab is pulled between them **2** a whizzing sound, eg made by a fast-flying object **3** *informal* energy, vigour ▸ VERB (**zipping, zipped**) **1** to fasten